NIV
Compact
Concordance

John R. Kohlenberger III

ZondervanPublishingHouse
Grand Rapids, Michigan

A Division of HarperCollins*Publishers*

The NIV Compact Concordance
Copyright © 1993 by John R. Kohlenberger III

Requests for information should be addressed to:
Zondervan Publishing House
Grand Rapids, Michigan 49530

Library of Congress Cataloging-in-Publication Data

The NIV Compact Concordance
by John R. Kohlenberger III>
   p.   cm.
Abridged ed. of: The NIV Complete Concordance. c1990.
ISBN 0-310-22872-7 (softcover)
1. Bible—Concordances. English—New International.   I. Goodrick,
Edward W., 1913-1992   II. Title.
BS425.K6448   1993
220.5'208   93–16721
                                                            CIP

Printed in the United States of America

00 01 02 /DC/ 20 19 18 17 16 15 14 13 12 11 10 9

Contents

Acknowledgments

Small though *The NIV Compact Concordance* may be, it is the product of the energies of many individuals in addition to the editor whose name is on the cover.

Stan Gundry, Vice President and Publisher/Academic Books and Electronic Publishing, initiated the project and allowed me a free hand in design and production. Acquisitions Editor Ed van der Maas was involved in all aspects of design, proofreading, and production and, as usual, was a source of great encouragement to me and my family. Rachel Berens was my regular point of contact at Zondervan and provided valuable editorial assistance.

Dennis Thomas once again applied his expertise to develop original software to analyze, sort, and set the contexts for the concordance.

The staff of Multnomah Graphics, particularly its president, Mike Petersen, permitted me 24-hour access to their offices and equipment. Art director Bruce DeRoos offered useful insights on the page design.

My wife Carolyn and our children, Sarah and Joshua, showed great patience and offered much-needed encouragement and affection.

This sixth product of The NIV Concordance Project was intended to be a collaboration with my mentor and colleague Dr. Edward W. Goodrick, as had all the previous concordances to the NIV. But before the project got underway, the Lord saw fit to take Ed home. Even in his absence, this book bears the imprint of his involvement, being based on the concordance-making skills we developed together over the past fifteen years.

During those fifteen years, Ed's daughter Janet endured (she would probably say welcomed) the chaos of concordance construction in the basement of her home. Ever tolerant and always encouraging, Janet was a gracious hostess to as many as a dozen editors and publishers at a time. It is to Janet Goodrick, with deep appreciation and repect, that *The NIV Compact Concordance* is dedicated.

Dedication

To Janet Goodrick
with deep appreciation and respect

Introduction:
How to Use This Book

A concordance is an index to a book. It is usually arranged in alphabetical order and shows the location of key words in the book. In addition, it often supplies several words of the context in which each word is found.

The NIV Complete Concordance (1981) was the first concordance to the New International Version. Based on the model of *Cruden's Complete Concordance*, it offered an exhaustive to 12,800 of the major words of the NIV. *The NIV Handy Concordance* followed in 1982, containing 35,000 key references selected from its predecessor. *The NIV Exhaustive Concordance* (1991) indexed every English word of the NIV and showed the relationship of the English to the original Hebrew, Aramaic, and Greek from which the NIV was translated.

The NIV Compact Concordance (*NIVCC*) is an abridgement of *The NIV Exhaustive*. All 363,965 occurrences of the 14,452 NIV words, numerals, and compound proper names from the main concordance of the *Exhaustive* were scanned to select those most significant for general biblical knowledge, theology, and spiritual development. More than half of the vocabulary of the NIV and 70,000 biblical references are represented in this contribution to The NIV Compact Reference Library.

FEATURES OF THE NIV COMPACT CONCORDANCE

The *NIVCC* has four major features: (1) concordance entries, (2) key phrase indexes, (3) capsule biographies, and (4) KJV "See" references.

Concordance Entries

The *NIVCC* indexes 7,629 of the 14,452 words in the NIV from Aaron to 603,550. 55,790 context lines represent 56,790 occurrences of these words. Below is a typical entry from the *NIVCC*:

> **AVENGES*** [VENGEANCE]
> 2Sa 22:48 He is the God who **a** me,
> Ps 9:12 For he who **a** blood remembers;
>   18:47 He is the God who **a** me,
>   94: 1 O LORD, the God who **a**, O God who **a**,

Entries are arranged in alphabetical order. Numerals follow the letter Z. Entries index words exactly as they are spelled in the NIV. The asterisk (*) marks entries that index every occurrence of the word in the NIV. 2,355 entries are exhaustive.

Related words, if any, follow in brackets []. Rather than listing all related words after each indexed word, the editor chose one indexed word to act as the "group heading." All related words are listed after the group heading, and each of the related word headings points back to the group heading. By looking up the related word, you can study additional texts containing other forms of the word and other members of the word's cognate "family." For example, VENGEANCE lists six additional terms you can study within the *NIVCC* to get a fuller biblical picture of revenge, both human and divine.

There are two entries for LORD and LORD'S. The proper name of God, "Yahweh," is represented in the NIV as Lᴏʀᴅ in small caps. The title Lord is capitalized when referring to God and in lower case when referring to a human being or false god. Lord and lord are indexed in the *NIVCC* under the heading *LORD; Lord's under the heading *LORD'S. Lᴏʀᴅ is indexed under the heading †LORD and Lᴏʀᴅ's under the heading †LORD'S.

Contexts are organized in biblical order. A key to the abbreviations of the books of the Bible follows the introduction. Only the first appearance of a book's abbreviation is listed, as in the case of Ps (Psalms) above. The purpose of context lines in a concordance is simply to help the reader recognize or locate a specific verse in the Bible. For word study—or any kind of Bible study—the context offered by a concordance is rarely enough to go on. Nevertheless, sometimes a short sentence or a whole verse fits on one line, as in the case of John 11:35, "Jesus began to weep."

Taken by themselves, context lines can and do misrepresent the teaching of Scripture by taking statements out of the larger context. "There is no God" is a context taken straight from Psalm 14:1. Of course the Bible does not teach this; it is what "Fools say in their hearts"! Similarly, a context for Leviticus 24:16 might read, "the Lᴏʀᴅ shall be put to death" while the text actually says, "One who blasphemes the name of the Lᴏʀᴅ shall be put to death."

Great care has been taken by the editor, programmer, and proofreaders of the *NIVCC* to create contexts that are informative and accurate. But the reader should always check word contexts by looking them up in the NRSV itself. "The Wicked Bible," a KJV edition of 1631, accidentally omitted the word "not" from the seventh commandment, for which the printers were fined 300 pounds sterling! Though there are no longer such fines for misleading contexts, the editor and publisher are still deeply concerned that the *NIVCC* be used discerningly.

Key Phrase Indexes

Following the entries for 188 highly frequent words are 459 key phrase indexes:

FEAR
...

FEAR OF THE †LORD 2Ch 17:10; 19:7, 9; Ps 19:9; 34:11; 111:10; Pr 1:7; 2:5; 9:10; 10:27; 14:27; 15:16, 33; 16:6; 19:23; 22:4; 23:17; Isa 11:2, 3; 33:6

†LORD
...
FEAR OF THE †LORD See FEAR

These list biblical references to all occurrences of significant phrases—11,608 total references—but without contexts. Thus even in this compact concordance, you can find every reference for such phrases as the FEAR OF THE LORD, HOLY SPIRIT, SON OF GOD and SON OF MAN. Phrases are indexed at only one location; other words in the phrase are cross-referenced to the index. In the example above, FEAR OF THE †LORD is indexed under FEAR with a cross-reference at †LORD.

Capsule Biographies

410 prominent personalities are given capsule biographies:

DEBORAH
1. Prophetess who led Israel to victory over Canaanites (Jdg 4-5).
2. Rebekah's nurse (Ge 35:8).

It is easier to represent and to locate key events in an individual's life in such an entry, rather than by using context lines, especially in the entry on Jesus. As in the example above, different individuals of the same name are distinguished by separately numbered biographies. These entries index 2,087 biblical texts.

KJV "See" References

The King James, or Authorized, Version has been the dominant English Bible translation from the early seventeenth century to the latter half of the twentieth century. Because of this, the KJV has had profound impact on the language of both the church and English-speaking society. To help users familiar with KJV vocabulary find the proper NIV terms, 196 KJV words appear in 177 KJV "See" references, pointing to 319 NIV words. These include such headings as:

COMFORTER (KJV)
See COUNSELOR

[HOLY] GHOST (KJV)
See [HOLY] SPIRIT

Note that multiple-word "See" references, such as HOLY SPIRIT, do *not* refer to a multiple-word heading. Rather, they direct the user to look for that *combination* of words under the heading for *any* of the words in the multiple-word reference.

ADDITIONAL RESOURCES

The *NIVCC* is a concise word index to the New International Version. Its two companion volumes in The NIV Compact Reference Library supplement the *NIVCC* as indispensable guides to inductive biblical study.

The NIV Compact Dictionary of the Bible is an illustrated guide to the people, places, events, customs and books of the Bible, conveniently arranged in alphabetical order. *The NIV Nave's Compact Topical Bible* supplements the *NIVCC* by indexing synonyms, phrases and additional biographies, allowing even more thorough concept-oriented biblical study. The forthcoming *NIV Compact Commentary of the Bible* will offer a section-by-section explanation of the Bible and round out this valuable compact series.

Abbreviations and Symbols

Other Abbreviations and Symbols

*	following entry heading
=	exhaustive entry
*LORD	Lord or lord
*LORD'S	Lord's
†LORD	Lord
†LORD'S	Lord's
KJV	King James Version
NIV	New International Version
T	Psalm title

The NIV
Compact Concordance

The NIV Compact Concordance

A

AARON

Genealogy of (Ex 6:16-20; Jos 21:4, 10; 1Ch 6:3-15).

Priesthood of (Ex 28:1; Nu 17; Heb 5:1-4; 7), garments (Ex 28; 39), consecration (Ex 29), ordination (Lev 8).

Spokesman for Moses (Ex 4:14-16, 27-31; 7:1-2). Supported Moses' hands in battle (Ex 17:8-13). Built golden calf (Ex 32; Dt 9:20). Talked against Moses (Nu 12). Priesthood opposed (Nu 16); staff budded (Nu 17). Forbidden to enter land (Nu 20:1-12). Death (Nu 20:22-29; 33:38-39).

AARON AND HIS SONS See SONS

SON OF AARON See SON

SONS OF AARON See SONS

AARON'S SONS See SONS

ABADDON*

Rev 9:11 whose name in Hebrew is **A,**

ABANDON [ABANDONED]

Dt	4:31	not **a** or destroy you
Jos	10: 6	"Do not **a** your servants.
1Ki	6:13	and will not **a** my people Israel."
2Ch	12: 5	I now **a** you to Shishak.' "
Ne	9:19	not **a** them in the desert.
	9:31	not put an end to them or **a** them,
Ps	16:10	you will not **a** me to the grave,
	138: 8	not **a** the works of your hands.
Jer	12: 7	forsake my house, **a** my inheritance;
Ac	2:27	you will not **a** me to the grave,
1Ti	4: 1	in later times some will **a** the faith

ABANDONED [ABANDON]

Ge	24:27	not **a** his kindness and faithfulness

Dt	29:25	people **a** the covenant of the LORD,
	32:15	He **a** the God who made him
Jdg	6:13	But now the LORD has **a** us
1Ki	18:18	You have **a** the LORD's commands
Isa	54: 7	"For a brief moment I **a** you,
Ac	2:31	that he was not **a** to the grave,
Ro	1:27	the men also **a** natural relations with women
2Co	4: 9	persecuted, but not **a;**

ABBA*

Mk	14:36	"**A,** Father," he said,
Ro	8:15	And by him we cry, "**A,** Father.
Gal	4: 6	the Spirit who calls out, "**A,** Father."

ABDON

A judge of Israel (Jdg 12:13-15).

ABEDNEGO

Deported to Babylon with Daniel (Da 1:1-6). Name changed from Azariah (Da 1:7). Refused defilement by food (Da 1:8-20). Refused idol worship (Da 3:1-12); saved from furnace (Da 3:13-30).

ABEL

Second son of Adam (Ge 4:2). Offered proper sacrifice (Ge 4:4; Heb 11:4). Murdered by Cain (Ge 4:8; Mt 23:35; Lk 11:51; 1Jn 3:12).

ABHOR* [ABHORS]

Lev	26:11	and I will not **a** you.
	26:15	and **a** my laws and fail
	26:30	and I will **a** you.
	26:44	I will not reject them or **a** them
Dt	7:26	Utterly **a** and detest it,
	23: 7	Do not **a** an Edomite,
	23: 7	Do not **a** an Egyptian,
Ps	26: 5	I **a** the assembly of evildoers
	119:163	and a falsehood but I love your law.
	139:21	and **a** those who rise up against you?
Am	6: 8	declares: "I **a** the pride of Jacob

Ro   2:22 You who **a** idols,

ABHORS* [ABHOR]

Ps   5: 6 and deceitful men the LORD **a**.
Pr 11: 1 The LORD **a** dishonest scales,

ABIATHAR

High priest in days of Saul and David (1Sa 22; 2Sa 15; 1Ki 1-2; Mk 2:26). Escaped Saul's slaughter of priests (1Sa 22:18-23). Supported David in Absalom's revolt (2Sa 15:24-29). Supported Adonijah (1Ki 1:7-42); deposed by Solomon (1Ki 2:22-35; cf. 1Sa 2:31-35).

ABIB*

The month of the Exodus and Passover (Ex 13:4; 23:15; 34:18; Dt: 16:1).

ABIDE, ABIDETH (KJV) See LIVE, REMAIN

ABIGAIL

1. Sister of David (1Ch 2:16-17).
2. Wife of Nabal (1Sa 25:30); pled for his life with David (1Sa 25:14-35). Became David's wife after Nabal's death (1Sa 25:36-42); bore him Kileab (2Sa 3:3) also known as Daniel (1Ch 3:1).

ABIHU

Son of Aaron (Ex 6:23; 24:1, 9); killed for offering unauthorized fire (Lev 10; Nu 3:2-4; 1Ch 24:1-2).

ABIJAH

1. Second son of Samuel (1Ch 6:28); a corrupt judge (1Sa 8:1-5).
2. An Aaronic priest (1Ch 24:10; Lk 1:5).
3. Son of Jeroboam I of Israel; died as prophesied by Ahijah (1Ki 14:1-18).
4. Son of Rehoboam; king of Judah who fought Jeroboam I attempting to reunite the kingdom (1Ki 14:31-15:8; 2Ch 12:16-14:1; Mt 1:7).

ABILITY* [ABLE]

Ge 47: 6 of any among them with special **a**,
Ex 31: 3 with skill, **a** and knowledge
     35:31 with skill, **a** and knowledge
     35:34 the **a** to teach others.
     36: 1 whom the LORD has given skill and **a**
     36: 2 the LORD had given **a**
Dt   8:18 for it is he who gives you the **a**
Ezr 2:69 to their **a** they gave to the treasury
Da   5:12 and also the **a** to interpret dreams,
Mt 25:15 each according to his **a**.
Ac   8:19 "Give me also this **a**
     11:29 each according to his **a**,
2Co 1: 8 far beyond our **a** to endure,
     8: 3 and even beyond their **a**.

ABIMELECH

1. King of Gerar who took Abraham's wife Sarah, believing her to be his sister (Ge 20). Later made a covenant with Abraham (Ge 21:22-33).
2. King of Gerar who took Isaac's wife Rebe-

kah, believing her to be his sister (Ge 26:1-11). Later made a covenant with Isaac (Ge 26:12-31).
3. Son of Gideon (Jdg 8:31). Attempted to make himself king (Jdg 9).

ABIRAM

Sided with Dathan in rebellion against Moses and Aaron (Nu 16; 26:9; Dt 11:6).

ABISHAG

Shunammite virgin; attendant of David in his old age (1Ki 1:1-15; 2:17-22).

ABISHAI

Son of Zeruiah, David's sister (1Sa 26:6; 1Ch 2:16). One of David's chief warriors (1Ch 11:15-21): against Edom (1Ch 18:12-13), Ammon (2Sa 10), Absalom (2Sa 18), Sheba (2Sa 20). Wanted to kill Saul (1Sa 26), killed Abner (2Sa 2:18-27; 3:22-39), wanted to kill Shimei (2Sa 16:5-13; 19:16-23).

ABLAZE

Dt   5:23 while the mountain was **a** with fire,
Da   7: 9 and its wheels were all **a**.
Rev 8: 8 like a huge mountain, all **a**,

ABLE [ABILITY, DISABLED, ENABLE, ENABLED, ENABLES, ENABLING]

Ge 13: 6 that they were not **a** to stay together.
Lev 26:37 be **a** to stand before your enemies.
Nu 14:16 not **a** to bring these people into the
Jos 24:19 "You are not **a** to serve the LORD.
1Sa 17:33 not **a** to go out against this Philistine
1Ki 3: 9 who is **a** to govern this great people
1Ch 29:14 be **a** to give as generously as this?
2Ch 2: 6 who is **a** to build a temple for him.
Job 41:10 Who then is **a** to stand against me?
Eze 7:19 and gold will not be **a** to save them
Da   2:26 "Are you **a** to tell me what I saw
     3:17 the God we serve is **a** to save us
     4:37 who walk in pride he is **a** to humble.
Hos 5:13 But he is not **a** to cure you,
Mt   9:28 "Do you believe that I am **a**
     26:61 'I am **a** to destroy the temple of God
Lk 13:24 will try to enter and will not be **a** to.
     14:30 to build and was not **a** to finish.'
     21:15 none of your adversaries will be **a** to
     21:36 pray that you may be **a** to escape
     21:36 that you may be **a** to stand before
Ac   5:39 you will not be **a** to stop these men;
     15:10 nor our fathers have been **a** to bear?
     22:13 that very moment I was **a** to see him.
Ro   8:39 will be **a** to separate us from the love of God
     11:23 for God is **a** to graft them in again.
     14: 4 for the Lord is **a** to make him stand.
     16:25 Now to him who is **a** to establish you
1Co 12:28 those **a** to help others,
2Co 8: 3 they gave as much as they were **a**,
     9: 8 God is **a** to make all grace abound to
Eph 3: 4 **a** to understand my insight into the mystery
     3:20 who is **a** to do immeasurably more

6:13 you may be **a** to stand your ground,
1Ti 3: 2 respectable, hospitable, **a** to teach,
2Ti 1:12 is **a** to guard what I have entrusted
      2:24 **a** to teach, not resentful.
      3: 7 but never **a** to acknowledge the truth.
      3:15 which are **a** to make you wise
Heb 2:18 he is **a** to help those who are being
          tempted.
      3:19 we see that they were not **a** to enter,
      5: 2 He is **a** to deal gently
      7:25 Therefore he is **a** to save completely
      9: 9 not **a** to clear the conscience
Jas 3: 2 to keep his whole body in check.
      4:12 the one who is **a** to save and destroy.
2Pe 1:15 always be **a** to remember these
Jude 1:24 To him who is **a** to keep you
Rev 5: 5 he is **a** to open the scroll

ABNER

Cousin of Saul and commander of his army (1Sa 14:50; 17:55-57; 26). Made Ish-Bosheth king after Saul (2Sa 2:8-10), but later defected to David (2Sa 3:6-21). Killed Asahel (2Sa 2:18-32), for which he was killed by Joab and Abishai (2Sa 3:22-39).

ABODE*

Job 38:19 "What is the way to the **a** of light?
Isa 33:20 a peaceful **a**, a tent that will not be

ABOLISH* [ABOLISHED, ABOLISHING]

Da 11:31 and will **a** the daily sacrifice.
Hos 2:18 and sword and battle I will **a** from
Mt 5:17 come to **a** the Law or the Prophets;
     5:17 not come to **a** them but to fulfill

ABOLISHED* [ABOLISH]

Da 12:11 the time that the daily sacrifice is **a**
Gal 5:11 the offense of the cross has been **a.**

ABOLISHING* [ABOLISH]

Eph 2:15 by **a** in his flesh the law

ABOMINATION* [ABOMINATIONS]

Da 9:27 set up an **a** that causes desolation,
     11:31 set up the **a** that causes desolation.
     12:11 the **a** that causes desolation is set up,
Mt 24:15 'the **a** that causes desolation,'
Mk 13:14 'the **a** that causes desolation'

ABOMINATIONS* [ABOMINATION]

Pr 26:25 for seven **a** fill his heart.
Isa 66: 3 and their souls delight in their **a;**
Rev 17: 5 AND OF THE **A** OF THE EARTH.

ABOUND [ABOUNDING]

Ps 72: 7 righteous will flourish; prosperity
          will **a**
     72:16 Let grain **a** throughout the land;
2Co 9: 8 And God is able to make all grace **a**
     9: 8 you will **a** in every good work.
Php 1: 9 that your love may **a** more and more

ABOUNDING* [ABOUND]

Ex 34: 6 **a** in love and faithfulness,
Nu 14:18 **a** in love and forgiving sin
Dt 33:23 Naphtali he said: "Naphtali is **a**
Ne 9:17 slow to anger and **a** in love.
Ps 86: 5 **a** in love to all who call to you.
     86:15 **a** in love and faithfulness.
   103: 8 slow to anger, **a** in love.
Pr 8:24 when there were no springs **a**
Joel 2:13 slow to anger and **a** in love,
Jnh 4: 2 slow to anger and **a** in love,

ABOVE

Ge 3:14 "Cursed are you **a** all the livestock
     28:13 There **a** it stood the LORD,
Lev 26:19 and make the sky **a** you like iron
Dt 4:39 the LORD is God in heaven **a**
Ps 8: 1 You have set your glory **a**
     18:48 You exalted me **a** my foes;
     57: 5 Be exalted, O God, **a** the heavens;
     68:33 to him who rides the ancient skies **a,**
     95: 3 the great King **a** all gods.
   103:11 high as the heavens are **a** the earth,
Da 11:36 and magnify himself **a** every god
Mt 10:24 "A student is not **a** his teacher,
Jn 3:31 one who comes from **a** is **a** all;
     8:23 I am from **a.**
Ro 12:10 Honor one another **a** yourselves.
Php 2: 9 him the name that is **a** every name,
Col 3: 2 Set your minds on things **a,**
1Ti 3: 2 the overseer must be **a** reproach,
Jas 1:17 and perfect gift is from **a,**
1Pe 4: 8 **A** all, love each other deeply,

ABRAHAM [ABRAM]

Abram, son of Terah (Ge 11:26-27), husband of Sarah (Ge 11:29).

Covenant relation with the LORD (Ge 12:1-3; 13:14-17; 15; 17; 22:15-18; Ex 2:24; Ne 9:8; Ps 105; Mic 7:20; Lk 1:68-75; Ro 4; Heb 6:13-15).

Called from Ur, via Haran, to Canaan (Ge 12:1; Ac 7:2-4; Heb 11:8-10). Moved to Egypt, nearly lost Sarah to Pharoah (Ge 12:10-20). Divided the land with Lot; settled in Hebron (Ge 13). Saved Lot from four kings (Ge 14:1-16); blessed by Melchizedek (Ge 14:17-20; Heb 7:1-20). Declared righteous by faith (Ge 15:6; Ro 4:3; Gal 3:6-9). Fathered Ishmael by Hagar (Ge 16).

Name changed from Abram (Ge 17:5; Ne 9:7). Circumcised (Ge 17; Ro 4:9-12). Entertained three visitors (Ge 18); promised a son by Sarah (Ge 18:9-15; 17:16). Questioned destruction of Sodom and Gomorrah (Ge 18:16-33). Moved to Gerar; nearly lost Sarah to Abimelech (Ge 20). Fathered Isaac by Sarah (Ge 21:1-7; Ac 7:8; Heb 11:11-12); sent away Hagar and Ishmael (Ge 21:8-21; Gal 4:22-30). Covenant with Abimelech (Ge 21:22-32). Tested by offering Isaac (Ge 22; Heb 11:17-19; Jas 2:21-24). Sarah died; bought field of Ephron for burial (Ge 23). Secured wife for Isaac (Ge 24). Fathered children by Keturah (Ge 25:1-6; 1Ch 1:32-33). Death (Ge 25:7-11).

Called servant of God (Ge 26:24), friend of God (2Ch 20:7; Isa 41:8; Jas 2:23), prophet (Ge 20:7), father of Israel (Ex 3:15; Isa 51:2; Mt 3:9; Jn 8:39-58).

FATHER ABRAHAM See FATHER

GOD OF ABRAHAM See GOD

ABRAM [ABRAHAM]

Ge 17: 5 No longer will you be called **A**;

ABSALOM

Son of David by Maacah (2Sa 3:3; 1Ch 3:2). Killed Amnon for rape of his sister Tamar; banished by David (2Sa 13). Returned to Jerusalem; received by David (2Sa 14). Rebelled against David (2Sa 15-17). Killed (2Sa 18).

ABSENT

Pr 10:19 When words are many, sin is not **a**,
Col 2: 5 For though I am **a** from you in body,

ABSOLUTE*

1Ti 5: 2 women as sisters, with **a** purity.

ABSTAIN* [ABSTAINED, ABSTAINS]

Ex 19:15 **A** from sexual relations."
Nu   6: 3 he must **a** from wine
Ac 15:20 to **a** from food polluted by idols,
    15:29 to **a** from food sacrificed to idols,
    21:25 should **a** from food sacrificed
1Ti 4: 3 order them to **a** from certain foods,
1Pe 2:11 to **a** from sinful desires,

ABSTAINED* [ABSTAIN]

Ex 31:17 on the seventh day he **a** from work

ABSTAINS* [ABSTAIN]

Ro 14: 6 and he who **a**,

ABSTINENCE (KJV) See FAST, FASTING

ABUNDANCE [ABUNDANT]

Ge 41:29 Seven years of great **a** are coming
Job 36:31 the nations and provides food in **a**.
Ps 36: 8 They feast on the **a** of your house;
    66:12 but you brought us to a place of **a**.
Ecc 5:12 **a** of a rich man permits him no sleep.
Isa 66:11 and delight in her overflowing **a**."
Jer 2:22 with soda and use an **a** of soap,
Mt 13:12 and he will have an **a**.
    25:29 and he will have an **a**.
Lk 12:15 a man's life does not consist in the **a**
1Pe 1: 2 Grace and peace be yours in **a**.
2Pe 1: 2 Grace and peace be yours in **a**.
Jude 1: 2 Mercy, peace and love be yours in **a**.

ABUNDANT [ABUNDANCE, ABUNDANTLY]

Dt 28:11 LORD will grant you **a** prosperity—
    32: 2 like a rain on tender plants.
Job 36:28 and **a** showers fall on mankind.
Ps 68: 9 You gave **a** showers, O God;
    78:15 and gave them water as **a** as the seas;
    132:15 I will bless her with **a** provisions;
    145: 7 They will celebrate your **a** goodness

Pr 12:11 who works his land will have **a** food,
    28:19 who works his land will have **a** food,
Jer 33: 9 the **a** prosperity and peace I provide
Eze 17: 5 like a willow by **a** water,
    31: 7 for its roots went down to **a** waters.
Joel 2:23 He sends you **a** showers,
Ro 5:17 receive God's **a** provision of grace

ABUNDANTLY [ABUNDANT]

Jos 17:14 and the LORD has blessed us **a**."
1Ti 1:14 of our Lord was poured out on me **a**,

ABUSE [ABUSIVE]

Pr 9: 7 rebukes a wicked man incurs **a**.
1Pe 4: 4 and they heap **a** on you.

ABUSIVE* [ABUSE]

Ac 18: 6 Jews opposed Paul and became **a**,
2Ti 3: 2 lovers of money, boastful, proud, **a**,

ABYSS*

Lk 8:31 not to order them to go into the **A**.
Rev 9: 1 the key to the shaft of the **A**.
    9: 2 When he opened the **A**,
    9: 2 by the smoke from the **A**.
    9:11 as king over them the angel of the **A**,
    11: 7 up from the **A** will attack them,
    17: 8 and will come up out of the **A** and go
    20: 1 having the key to the **A** and holding
    20: 3 He threw him into the **A**,

ACACIA

Ex 25:10 a chest of **a** wood—
    25:23 "Make a table of **a** wood—
    26:15 frames of **a** wood for the tabernacle.
    27: 1 "Build an altar of **a** wood,

ACCENT*

Mt 26:73 for your **a** gives you away."

ACCEPT [ACCEPTABLE, ACCEPTANCE, ACCEPTED, ACCEPTS]

Ge 14:23 I will **a** nothing belonging to you,
Ex 23: 8 "Do not **a** a bribe,
Lev 26:23 you do not **a** my correction
Dt 16:19 Do not **a** a bribe,
2Sa 24:23 "May the LORD your God **a** you."
Job 2:10 Shall we **a** good from God,
    42: 8 and I will **a** his prayer and not deal
Ps 119:108 **A**, O LORD, the willing praise of my
Pr 4:10 Listen, my son, **a** what I say,
    10: 8 The wise in heart **a** commands,
    19:20 Listen to advice and **a** instruction,
Eze 43:27 Then I will **a** you,
Zep 3: 7 you will fear me and **a** correction!'
Mal 1:10 I will **a** no offering from your hands.
Mt 11:14 And if you are willing to **a** it,
    19:11 "Not everyone can **a** this word,
Jn 3:11 you people do not **a** our testimony.
    5:41 "I do not **a** praise from men,
    14:17 The world cannot **a** him,
Ac 22:18 not **a** your testimony about me.'
Ro 14: 1 **A** him whose faith is weak,
    15: 7 **A** one another, then,

1Co 2:14 man without the Spirit does not **a**
Jas 1:21 that is so prevalent and humbly **a**
1Jn 5: 9 We a man's testimony,

ACCEPTABLE [ACCEPT]

Pr 21: 3 more **a** to the LORD than sacrifice.
Isa 58: 5 a day **a** to the LORD?
Php 4:18 an **a** sacrifice, pleasing to God.
1Pe 2: 5 offering spiritual sacrifices **a** to God

ACCEPTANCE* [ACCEPT]

Ro 11:15 will their **a** be but life from the dead?
1Ti 1:15 saying that deserves full **a:**
     4: 9 saying that deserves full **a**

ACCEPTED [ACCEPT]

Ge 4: 7 will you not be **a?**
Lev 1: 4 and it will be **a** on his behalf
     7:18 it will not be **a.**
1Sa 8: 3 and a bribes and perverted justice.
Job 42: 9 and the LORD **a** Job's prayer.
Lk 4:24 "no prophet is **a** in his hometown.
Ac 2:41 who **a** his message were baptized,
Ro 10:16 not all the Israelites **a** the good news.
     15: 7 then, just as Christ **a** you,
2Co 11: 4 different gospel from the one you **a,**
Gal 1: 9 a gospel other than what you **a,**
1Th 2:13 you **a** it not as the word of men,

ACCEPTS [ACCEPT]

Dt 27:25 "Cursed is the man who **a** a bribe
Ps 6: 9 the LORD **a** my prayer.
Zep 3: 2 she **a** no correction.
Jn 3:32 but no one **a** his testimony.
     13:20 whoever **a** anyone I send **a** me; and
             whoever **a** me **a** the one who sent me
Jas 1:27 Religion that God our Father **a**

ACCESS*

Est 1:14 who had special **a** to the king
Ro 5: 2 whom we have gained **a**
Eph 2:18 For through him we both have **a** to

ACCLAIM*

Ps 89:15 who have learned to **a** you,
Isa 24:14 the west they **a** the LORD's majesty.

ACCOMPANIED [ACCOMPANY]

1Co 10: 4 from the spiritual rock that **a** them,
Jas 2:17 faith by itself, if it is not **a** by action,

ACCOMPANIES* [ACCOMPANY]

Isa 40:10 and his recompense **a** him.
     62:11 and his recompense **a** him.' "
2Co 9:13 the obedience that **a** your confession

ACCOMPANY [ACCOMPANIED, ACCOMPANIES]

Dt 28: 2 upon you and **a** you if you obey
Ecc 8:15 Then joy will **a** him in his work
Mk 16:17 these signs will **a** those who believe:
Heb 6: 9 things that **a** salvation.

ACCOMPLICE*

Pr 29:24 The **a** of a thief is his own enemy;

ACCOMPLISH [ACCOMPLISHED]

Dt 9: 5 to **a** what he swore to your fathers,
2Ki 19:31 zeal of the LORD Almighty will **a** this
Ecc 2: 2 And what does pleasure **a?"**
Isa 9: 7 zeal of the LORD Almighty will **a** this
     44:28 'He is my shepherd and will **a** all
     55:11 but will **a** what I desire and achieve

ACCOMPLISHED [ACCOMPLISH]

Isa 26:12 all that we have **a** you have done
Mt 5:18 from the Law until everything is **a.**
Eph 3:11 eternal purpose which he **a** in Christ
Rev 10: 7 the mystery of God will be **a,**

ACCORD [ACCORDANCE, ACCORDING]

Nu 24:13 I could not do anything of my own **a,**
Jn 10:18 but I lay it down of my own **a.**
     12:49 For I did not speak of my own **a,**
Tit 2: 1 what is in **a** with sound doctrine.

ACCORDANCE [ACCORD]

Nu 14:19 In **a** with your great love,
2Ki 14:25 in **a** with the word of the LORD,
     23:25 in **a** with all the Law of Moses.
Ps 119:149 Hear my voice in **a** with your love;
Eze 35:11 I will treat you in **a** with the anger
Ro 8: 5 who live in **a** with the Spirit
Eph 1: 5 in **a** with his pleasure and will—
2Th 2: 9 in **a** with the work of Satan

ACCORDING [ACCORD]

Ge 1:11 **a** to their various kinds."
Ex 26:30 "Set up the tabernacle **a** to the plan
Dt 26:13 **a** to all you commanded.
2Ch 6:30 deal with each man **a** to all he does,
Ps 18:24 The LORD has rewarded me **a** to my
             righteousness, **a** to the cleanness of
     119: 9 By living **a** to your word.
Pr 12: 8 A man is praised **a** to his wisdom,
Hos 12: 2 and repay him **a** to his deeds.
Mt 9:29 **A** to your faith will it be done to you
Jn 19: 7 and **a** to that law he must die,
Ro 8: 4 who do not live **a** to the sinful
             nature but **a** to the Spirit.
Gal 3:29 and heirs **a** to the promise.
2Ti 2: 5 unless he competes **a** to the rules.
1Jn 5:14 that if we ask anything **a** to his will,
Rev 20:12 The dead were judged **a** to what

ACCOUNT [ACCOUNTABLE, ACCOUNTING]

Ge 2: 4 the **a** of the heavens and the earth
     5: 1 This is the written **a** of Adam's line.
     6: 9 This is the **a** of Noah.
     10: 1 This is the **a** of Shem,
     11:10 This is the **a** of Shem.
     11:27 This is the **a** of Terah.
     25:12 the **a** of Abraham's son Ishmael,
     25:19 This is the **a** of Abraham's son Isaac.

36: 1 This is the **a** of Esau (that is, Edom).
36: 9 This is the **a** of Esau the father of
37: 2 This is the **a** of Jacob.
Dt 18:19 I myself will call him to **a.**
Jos 22:23 may the LORD himself call us to **a.**
Mt 12:36 to give **a** on the day of judgment
26:31 you will all fall away on **a** of me,
Lk 16: 2 Give an **a** of your management,
Ro 14:12 each of us will give an **a** of himself
Heb 4:13 of him to whom we must give **a.**
1Jn 2:12 have been forgiven on **a** of his name.

ACCOUNTABLE* [ACCOUNT]

Eze 3:18 and I will hold you **a** for his blood.
3:20 and I will hold you **a** for his blood.
33: 6 but I will hold the watchman **a**
33: 8 and I will hold you **a** for his blood.
34:10 the shepherds and will hold them **a**
Da 6: 2 The satraps were made **a** to them so
Jnh 1:14 Do not hold us **a** for killing
Ro 3:19 and the whole world held **a** to God.

ACCOUNTING [ACCOUNT]

Ge 9: 5 I will surely demand an **a.**

ACCREDITED* [CREDIT]

Ac 2:22 Jesus of Nazareth was a man **a** by

ACCUMULATE* [ACCUMULATED]

Dt 17:17 must not **a** large amounts of silver

ACCUMULATED [ACCUMULATE]

2Ch 1:14 Solomon **a** chariots and horses;

ACCURATE [ACCURATELY]

Dt 25:15 You must have **a** and honest weights
Pr 11: 1 but **a** weights are his delight.
Eze 45:10 You are to use **a** scales, an **a** ephah
and an **a** bath.

ACCURATELY* [ACCURATE]

Ac 18:25 and taught about Jesus **a,**

ACCURSED [CURSE]

2Pe 2:14 experts in greed—an **a** brood!

ACCUSATION [ACCUSE]

Mic 6: 2 Hear, O mountains, the LORD's **a;**
Col 1:22 without blemish and free from **a—**
1Ti 5:19 Do not entertain an **a** against an elder

ACCUSATIONS [ACCUSE]

2Pe 2:11 do not bring slanderous **a** against

ACCUSE [ACCUSATION, ACCUSATIONS, ACCUSED, ACCUSER, ACCUSERS, ACCUSES, ACCUSING]

Ps 103: 9 He will not always **a,**
Pr 3:30 Do not **a** a man for no reason—
Zec 3: 1 Satan standing at his right side to **a**
Mt 12:10 Looking for a reason to **a** Jesus,
Lk 3:14 and don't **a** people falsely—
1Pe 2:12 though they **a** you of doing wrong,

ACCUSED [ACCUSE]

Mk 15: 3 The chief priests **a** him
Ac 22:30 why Paul was being **a** by the Jews,

ACCUSER [ACCUSE]

Job 31:35 let my **a** put his indictment
Isa 50: 8 Who is my **a?**
Jn 5:45 Your **a** is Moses,
Rev 12:10 For the **a** of our brothers,

ACCUSERS [ACCUSE]

Ps 109:20 this be the LORD's payment to my **a,**

ACCUSES* [ACCUSE]

Job 40: 2 Let him who **a** God answer him!"
Isa 54:17 refute every tongue that **a** you.
Rev 12:10 who **a** them before our God day and

ACCUSING [ACCUSE]

Ps 31:20 you keep them safe from **a** tongues.
Ro 2:15 and their thoughts now **a,**

ACHAN*

Sin at Jericho caused defeat at Ai; stoned (Jos 7; 22:20; 1Ch 2:7).

ACHE*

Pr 14:13 Even in laughter the heart may **a,**

ACHIEVE [ACHIEVEMENT]

Job 5:12 so that their hands **a** no success.
Isa 55:11 and **a** the purpose for which I sent it.

ACHIEVEMENT* [ACHIEVE]

Ecc 4: 4 and all **a** spring from man's envy

ACHISH

King of Gath before whom David feigned insanity (1Sa 21:10-15). Later "ally" of David (2Sa 27-29).

ACHOR

Jos 7:26 called the Valley of **A** ever since.
Hos 2:15 make the Valley of **A** a door of hope.

ACKNOWLEDGE [ACKNOWLEDGED, ACKNOWLEDGES, ACKNOWLEDGMENT]

1Ch 28: 9 **a** the God of your father,
Ps 79: 6 on the nations that do not **a** you,
Pr 3: 6 in all your ways **a** him,
Isa 59:12 and we **a** our iniquities:
Jer 3:13 Only **a** your guilt—
9: 3 do not **a** me," declares the LORD.
Da 4:25 **a** that the Most High is sovereign
Hos 6: 3 Let us **a** the LORD; let us press on to
a him.
Mt 10:32 I will also **a** him before my Father
Lk 12: 8 also **a** him before the angels of God.
2Ti 3: 7 learning but never able to **a** the truth.
1Jn 4: 3 not **a** Jesus is not from God.
2Jn 1: 7 who do not **a** Jesus Christ as coming
in the flesh,

ACKNOWLEDGED
[ACKNOWLEDGE]

Lk   7:29 **a** that God's way was right,

ACKNOWLEDGES*
[ACKNOWLEDGE]

Ps   91:14 for he **a** my name.
Mt   10:32 "Whoever **a** me before men,
Lk   12: 8 whoever **a** me before men,
1Jn   2:23 whoever **a** the Son has the Father
      4: 2 Every spirit that **a** that Jesus Christ
      4:15 If anyone **a** that Jesus is the Son of

ACKNOWLEDGMENT*
[ACKNOWLEDGE]

Hos   4: 1 no love, no **a** of God in the land.
      6: 6 **a** of God rather than burnt offerings.

ACQUIRED [ACQUIRES, ACQUIRING]

Ge   12:16 and Abram **a** sheep and cattle,
Ru   4:10 I have also **a** Ruth the Moabitess,
Jer 48:36 The wealth they **a** is gone.

ACQUIRES [ACQUIRED]

Pr   18:15 heart of the discerning **a** knowledge;

ACQUIRING* [ACQUIRED]

Pr   1: 3 for **a** a disciplined and prudent life,

ACQUIT [ACQUITTED, ACQUITTING]

Ex   23: 7 for I will not **a** the guilty.

ACQUITTED* [ACQUIT]

Mt   12:37 For by your words you will be **a**,

ACQUITTING* [ACQUIT]

Dt   25: 1 **a** the innocent and condemning the
Pr   17:15 **A** the guilty and condemning the

ACT [ACTED, ACTION, ACTIONS, ACTIVE, ACTIVITY, ACTS]

Nu   23:19 Does he speak and then not **a**?
1Ki   8:32 then hear from heaven and **a**.
      8:39 Forgive and **a**;
Ps 119:126 It is time for you to **a**, O LORD;
Isa 43:13 When I **a**, who can reverse it?"
     52:13 See, my servant will **a** wisely;
Jn   8: 4 was caught in the **a** of adultery.

ACTED [ACT]

Ac   3:17 I know that you **a** in ignorance,
1Ti   1:13 mercy because I **a** in ignorance

ACTION [ACT]

2Co   9: 2 stirred most of them to **a**.
Jas   2:17 if it is not accompanied by **a**,
1Pe   1:13 Therefore, prepare your minds for **a**;

ACTIONS [ACT]

Pr   20:11 Even a child is known by his **a**,
Mt   11:19 wisdom is proved right by her **a**."
Gal   6: 4 Each one should test his own **a**.
Tit   1:16 but by their **a** they deny him.

ACTIVE* [ACT]

Phm   1: 6 be **a** in sharing your faith,
Heb   4:12 For the word of God is living and **a**.

ACTIVITY [ACT]

Ecc   3: 1 a season for every **a** under heaven:
      3:17 for there will be a time for every **a**,

ACTS [ACT]

Ex   7: 4 and with mighty **a** of judgment
1Ch 16: 9 tell of all his wonderful **a**.
Ps   71:16 and proclaim your mighty **a**,
     71:24 tell of your righteous **a** all day long,
     105: 2 tell of all his wonderful **a**.
     106: 2 proclaim the mighty **a** of the LORD
     145: 4 tell of your mighty **a**.
     145:12 all men may know of your mighty **a**
     150: 2 Praise him for his **a** of power;
Pr   12:10 the kindest **a** of the wicked are cruel.
Isa 64: 6 and all our righteous **a** are
Mt   6: 1 not to do your '**a** of righteousness'
Ro   1:27 indecent **a** with other men,
Gal   5:19 **a** of the sinful nature are obvious:
Rev 15: 4 your righteous **a** have been revealed.
     19: 8 (Fine linen stands for the righteous **a**

ADAM

  1. First man (Ge 1:26-2:25; Ro 5:14; 1Ti 2:13).
Sin of (Ge 3; Hos 6:7; Ro 5:12-21). Children of
(Ge 4:1-5:5). Death of (Ge 5:5; Ro 5:12-21; 1Co
15:22).

  2. Town (Jos 3:16).

ADAMANT (KJV) See FLINT

ADAR

  Month in which temple was rebuilt (Ezr 6:15);
celebration of Purim (Est 3:7; 9:1-21).

ADD [ADDED, ADDS]

Dt   4: 2 Do not **a** to what I command you
     12:32 not **a** to it or take away from it.
Pr   1: 5 wise listen and **a** to their learning,
      9: 9 and he will **a** to his learning.
     30: 6 Do not **a** to his words,
Mt   6:27 by worrying can **a** a single hour
Lk   12:25 by worrying can **a** a single hour
2Pe   1: 5 to **a** to your faith goodness;
Rev 22:18 God will **a** to him

ADDED [ADD]

Pr   9:11 and years will be **a** to your life.
Ecc   3:14 nothing can be **a** to it
Ac   2:47 And the Lord **a** to their number daily
      5:14 and were **a** to their number.
Ro   5:20 The law was **a** so that the trespass
Gal   3:19 It was **a** because of transgressions

ADDICTED*

Tit   2: 3 slanderers or **a** to much wine,

ADDS [ADD]

Pr   10:27 fear of the LORD **a** length to life,

ADMAH
Dt 29:23 of Sodom and Gomorrah, **A**
Hos 11: 8 How can I treat you like **A?**

ADMINISTER [ADMINISTERING, ADMINISTRATION]
1Ki 3:28 wisdom from God to **a** justice.
Zec 7: 9 LORD Almighty says: '**A** true justice;
2Co 8:19 we **a** in order to honor the Lord

ADMINISTERING [ADMINISTER]
1Pe 4:10 faithfully **a** God's grace in its

ADMINISTRATION* [ADMINISTER]
1Co 12:28 those with gifts of **a,**
Eph 3: 2 the **a** of God's grace that was given
    3: 9 to everyone the **a** of this mystery,

ADMIRABLE*
Php 4: 8 whatever is lovely, whatever is **a—**

ADMIT
Job 27: 5 I will never **a** you are in the right;
Hos 5:15 to my place until they **a** their guilt.

ADMONISH* [ADMONISHED, ADMONISHING]
Col 3:16 and **a** one another with all wisdom,
1Th 5:12 over you in the Lord and who **a** you.

ADMONISHED [ADMONISH]
Ne 9:30 By your Spirit you **a** them

ADMONISHING* [ADMONISH]
Col 1:28 **a** and teaching everyone with all

ADONIJAH
1. Son of David by Haggith (2Sa 3:4; 1Ch 3:2). Attempted to be king after David; killed by Solomon's order (1Ki 1-2).
2. Levite; teacher of the Law (2Ch 17:8).

ADOPTED* [ADOPTION]
Est 2:15 for Esther (the girl Mordecai had **a,**
Ps 106:35 with the nations and **a** their customs.
Eph 1: 5 be **a** as his sons through Jesus Christ,

ADOPTION* [ADOPTED]
Ro 8:23 as we wait eagerly for our **a** as sons,
    9: 4 Theirs is the **a** as sons;

ADORE*
SS 1: 4 How right they are to **a** you!

ADORN [ADORNED, ADORNMENT, ADORNS]
Pr 1: 9 and a chain to **a** your neck.
Isa 60: 7 and I will **a** my glorious temple.
Jer 4:30 You **a** yourself in vain.

ADORNED [ADORN]
Eze 16:11 I **a** you with jewelry:
Lk 21: 5 temple was **a** with beautiful stones

ADORNMENT* [ADORN]
1Pe 3: 3 Your beauty should not come from outward **a,**

ADORNS* [ADORN]
Ps 93: 5 holiness **a** your house
Isa 61:10 bridegroom **a** his head like a priest, and as a bride **a** herself with her

ADULLAM
1Sa 22: 1 and escaped to the cave of **A.**
1Ch 11:15 to David to the rock at the cave of **A,**

ADULTERER* [ADULTERY]
Lev 20:10 the **a** and the adulteress must be put
Job 24:15 The eye of the **a** watches for dusk;
Heb 13: 4 for God will judge the **a** and all the

ADULTERERS [ADULTERY]
Jer 23:10 The land is full of **a;**
Hos 7: 4 They are all **a,**
Mal 3: 5 to testify against sorcerers, **a** and
1Co 6: 9 sexually immoral nor idolaters nor **a**
1Ti 1:10 for **a** and perverts, for slave traders

ADULTERESS [ADULTERY]
Pr 2:16 It will save you also from the **a,**
    5: 3 For the lips of an **a** drip honey,
    6:26 and the **a** preys upon your very life.
Hos 3: 1 she is loved by another and is an **a.**
Mt 5:32 causes her to become an **a,**

ADULTERIES [ADULTERY]
Jer 3: 8 sent her away because of all her **a.**
Rev 14: 8 the maddening wine of her **a."**
    19: 2 corrupted the earth by her **a.**

ADULTEROUS [ADULTERY]
Eze 6: 9 grieved by their **a** hearts,
Mt 16: 4 A wicked and a generation looks for
Mk 8:38 in this **a** and sinful generation,
Jas 4: 4 You **a** people, don't you know

ADULTERY [ADULTERER, ADULTERERS, ADULTERESS, ADULTERIES, ADULTEROUS]
Ex 20:14 "You shall not commit **a.**
Dt 5:18 "You shall not commit **a.**
Ps 51: T after David had committed **a**
Pr 6:32 man who commits **a** lacks judgment;
Eze 23:37 They committed **a** with their idols;
Hos 1: 2 vilest **a** in departing from the LORD."
Mt 5:27 'Do not commit **a.'**
    5:28 committed **a** with her in his heart.
    5:32 who marries the divorced woman commits **a.**
    15:19 murder, **a,** sexual immorality, theft,
    19: 9 marries another woman commits **a."**
    19:18 " 'Do not murder, do not commit **a,**
Mk 7:21 sexual immorality, theft, murder, **a,**
    10:11 marries another woman commits **a**
    10:12 marries another man, she commits **a.**
    10:19 do not commit **a,** do not steal,

Lk   16:18 marries another woman commits **a**,
     16:18 marries a divorced woman commits
            a.
     18:20 commandments: 'Do not commit **a**,
Jn   8: 3 brought in a woman caught in **a**.
Ro   2:22 You who say that people should not
            commit **a**, do you commit **a**?
Jas   2:11 For he who said, "Do not commit **a**,"
Rev 18: 3 The kings of the earth committed **a**

ADULTS*

1Co 14:20 but in your thinking be **a**.

ADVANCE [ADVANCED]

2Sa 22:30 your help I can **a** against a troop;
Ps   27: 2 When evil men **a** against me
Ro   9:23 whom he prepared in **a** for glory—
Gal   3: 8 the gospel in **a** to Abraham:
Eph   2:10 which God prepared in **a** for us
Php   1:12 has really served to the gospel.

ADVANCED [ADVANCE]

Job 32: 7 **a** years should teach wisdom.'

ADVANTAGE

Ex   22:22 not take **a** of a widow or an orphan.
Lev 25:14 do not take **a** of each other.
Dt   24:14 Do not take **a** of a hired man
Ecc   6: 8 What **a** has a wise man over a fool?
      7:12 but the **a** of knowledge is this:
Ro   3: 1 What **a**, then, is there in being a Jew,
2Co 11:20 or exploits you or takes **a** of you
1Th   4: 6 wrong his brother or take **a** of him.
Jude 1:16 and flatter others for their own **a**.

ADVERSARIES [ADVERSARY]

Dt   32:41 I will take vengeance on my **a**
Ps   44: 7 you put our **a** to shame.

ADVERSARY [ADVERSARIES, ADVERSITY]

Mt   5:25 "Settle matters quickly with your **a**
Lk   18: 3 'Grant me justice against my **a**.'

ADVERSITY* [ADVERSARY]

Pr   17:17 and a brother is born for **a**.
Isa 30:20 the Lord gives you the bread of **a**

ADVICE [ADVISERS]

Nu   31:16 the ones who followed Balaam's **a**
2Sa 20:22 to all the people with her wise **a**,
2Ch 10:13 Rejecting the **a** of the elders,
     10:14 he followed the **a** of the young men
Pr   1:25 since you ignored all my **a**
     12: 5 but the **a** of the wicked is deceitful.
     12:15 but a wise man listens to **a**.
     19:20 Listen to **a** and accept instruction,
     20:18 Make plans by seeking **a**;

ADVISERS [ADVICE]

Pr   11:14 but many **a** make victory sure.
     15:22 but with many **a** they succeed.
     24: 6 and for victory many **a**.

ADVOCATE*

Job 16:19 witness is in heaven; my **a** is on high

AENEAS*

Paralytic healed by Peter (Ac 9:33-34).

AFFAIRS

Ps 112: 5 who conducts his **a** with justice.
Pr   31:27 watches over the **a** of her household
1Co   7:32 concerned about the Lord's **a**—
      7:33 concerned about the **a** of this world

AFFECTION

Dt   10:15 Yet the Lord set his **a** on your
2Co   6:12 not withholding our **a** from you,

AFFLICTED [AFFLICTION]

Jos 24: 5 I **a** the Egyptians by what I did there,
Ru   1:21 The Lord has **a** me;
Job   2: 7 **a** Job with painful sores
     36: 6 but gives the **a** their rights.
Ps   9:12 not ignore the cry of the **a**.
      9:18 nor the hope of the **a** ever perish.
     34: 2 let the **a** hear and rejoice.
    119:67 Before I was **a** I went astray,
    119:71 It was good for me to be **a** so
    119:75 and in faithfulness you have **a** me.
Isa 49:13 compassion on his **a** ones.
     53: 4 smitten by him, and **a**.
     53: 7 He was oppressed and **a**,
Na   1:12 Although I have **a** you, [O Judah,]

AFFLICTION [AFFLICTED, AFFLICTIONS]

Dt   16: 3 the bread of **a**,
Ps 107:41 he lifted the needy out of their **a**
Isa 30:20 bread of adversity and the water of **a**,
     48:10 tested you in the furnace of **a**.
La   1: 9 "Look, O Lord, on my **a**,
      3:33 For he does not willingly bring **a**
Ro   12:12 Be joyful in hope, patient in **a**,

AFFLICTIONS [AFFLICT]

Lev 26:21 I will multiply your **a** seven times
Col   1:24 still lacking in regard to Christ's **a**,
Rev   2: 9 I know your **a** and your poverty—

AFRAID [FEAR]

Ge   3:10 and I was **a** because I was naked;
     26:24 Do not be **a**, for I am with you;
     50:19 Joseph said to them, "Don't be **a**.
Ex   2:14 Then Moses was **a** and thought,
      3: 6 because he was **a** to look at God.
     34:30 and they were **a** to come near him.
Lev 26: 6 and no one will make you **a**.
Dt   1:21 Do not be **a**;
      1:29 do not be **a** of them.
      2: 4 They will be **a** of you,
     20: 3 Do not be fainthearted or **a**;
Jos 10:25 Joshua said to them, "Do not be **a**;
Ru   3:11 And now, my daughter, don't be **a**.
1Sa 15:24 I was **a** of the people and so I gave in
     18:12 Saul was **a** of David,
1Ki 19: 3 Elijah was **a** and ran for his life.

2Ki 25:24 not be **a** of the Babylonian officials,"
1Ch 13:12 David was **a** of God that day
Ne 2: 2 I was very much **a**,
Ps 27: 1 of whom shall I be **a?**
56: 3 When I am **a**, I will trust in you.
56: 4 in God I trust; I will not be **a.**
Pr 3:24 you will not be **a**;
Isa 12: 2 I will trust and not be **a.**
44: 8 Do not tremble, do not be **a.**
Jer 1: 8 Do not be **a** of them,
Eze 39:26 with no one to make them **a.**
Da 4: 5 I had a dream that made me **a.**
Mt 8:26 why are you so **a?"**
10:28 not be **a** of those who kill the body
10:28 be **a** of the One who can destroy
10:31 So don't be **a;**
Mk 5:36 "Don't be **a;** just believe."
Lk 9:34 and they were **a** as they entered
12:32 "Do not be **a**, little flock,
Jn 14:27 hearts be troubled and do not be **a.**
Ac 27:24 'Do not be **a**, Paul.
Ro 11:20 Do not be arrogant, but be **a.**
Heb 13: 6 I will not be **a.**
2Pe 2:10 not **a** to slander celestial beings;
Rev 2:10 Do not be **a** of what you are about to suffer.

AGABUS*

A Christian prophet (Ac 11:28; 21:10).

AGAG [AGAGITE]

King of Amalekites not killed by Saul (1Sa 15).

AGAGITE [AGAG]

Est 8: 3 the evil plan of Haman the **A,**

AGAIN

Mk 8:31 be killed and after three days rise **a.**
Jn 2:19 and I will raise it **a** in three days."
3: 7 'You must be born **a.'**
Heb 6: 6 crucifying the Son of God all over **a**
Rev 7:16 Never **a** will they hunger; never **a** will they thirst.

AGE [AGED, AGES]

Mt 13:39 The harvest is the end of the **a,**
Lk 18:30 in the **a** to come, eternal life."
Tit 2:12 and godly lives in this present **a,**

AGED [AGE]

Job 12:12 Is not wisdom found among the **a?**
Pr 17: 6 children are a crown to the **a,**

AGES [AGE]

Ro 16:25 the mystery hidden for long **a** past,
Eph 2: 7 that in the coming **a** he might show
3: 9 for **a** past was kept hidden in God,
Col 1:26 that has been kept hidden for **a**
Heb 9:26 the end of the **a** to do away with sin
Rev 15: 3 King of the **a.**

AGONY

Jer 4:19 Oh, the **a** of my heart!
Lk 16:24 because I am in **a** in this fire.'
Ac 2:24 freeing him from the **a** of death,

Rev 16:10 Men gnawed their tongues in **a**

AGREE [AGREEMENT, AGREES, DISAGREE, DISAGREEMENT]

Mt 18:19 two of you on earth **a** about anything
Mk 14:59 even then their testimony did not **a.**
Ro 7:16 I **a** that the law is good.
Php 4: 2 with Syntyche to **a** with each other

AGREEMENT [AGREE]

Da 11:23 After coming to an **a** with him,
2Co 6:16 What **a** is there between the temple
1Jn 5: 8 and the three are in **a.**

AGREES* [AGREE]

Ac 7:42 **a** with what is written in the book
24:14 I believe everything that **a** with the Law
1Co 4:17 which **a** with what I teach

AGRIPPA*

Descendant of Herod; king before whom Paul pled his case in Caesarea (Ac 25:13-26:32).

AHAB

1. Son of Omri; king of Israel (1Ki 16:28-22:40), husband of Jezebel (1Ki 16:31). Promoted Baal worship (1Ki 16:31-33); opposed by Elijah (1Ki 17:1; 18; 21), a prophet (1Ki 20:35-43), Micaiah (1Ki 22:1-28). Defeated Ben-Hadad (1Ki 20). Killed for failing to kill Ben-Hadad and for murder of Naboth (1Ki 20:35-21:40).
2. A false prophet (Jer 29:21-22).

AHASUERUS (KJV) See XERXES

AHAZ

Son of Jotham; king of Judah, (2Ki 16; 2Ch 28; Mt 1:9). Idolatry of (2Ki 16:3-4, 10-18; 2Ch 28:1-4, 22-25). Defeated by Aram and Israel (2Ki 16:5-6; 2Ch 28:5-15). Sought help from Assyria rather than the LORD (2Ki 16:7-9; 2Ch 28:16-21; Isa 7).

AHAZIAH

1. Son of Ahab; king of Israel (1Ki 22:51-2Ki 1:18; 2Ch 20:35-37). Made an unsuccessful alliance with Jehoshaphat (2Ch 20:35-37). Died for seeking Baal rather than the LORD (2Ki 1).
2. Son of Jehoram; king of Judah (2Ki 8:25-29; 9:14-29), also called Jehoahaz (2Ch 21:17-22:9; 25:23). Killed by Jehu while visiting Joram (2Ki 9:14-29; 2Ch 22:1-9).

AHEAD [HEAD]

1Co 11:21 each of you goes **a** without waiting
Php 3:13 and straining toward what is **a,**
1Ti 5:24 reaching the place of judgment **a**
Heb 11:26 he was looking **a** to his reward.
2Jn 1: 9 Anyone who runs **a** and does not

AHIJAH

1. Priest during Sauls reign (1Sa 14:3,18).
2. Prophet of Shiloh (1Ki 11:29-39; 14:1-18).

AHIKAM

Father of Gedaliah (2Ki 25:22), protector of Jeremiah (Jer 26:24).

AHIMAAZ

1. Father-in-law of Saul (1Sa 14:50).
2. Son of Zadok, the high priest, loyal to David (2Sa 15:27,36; 17:17-20; 18:19-33).

AHIMELECH

1. Priest who helped David in his flight from Saul (1Sa 21-22).
2. One of David's warriors (1Sa 26:6).

AHINOAM

1. Wife of Saul (1Sa 14:50).
2. Wife of David (1Sa 25:43; 30:5; 1Ch 3:1).

AHITHOPHEL

One of David's counselors who sided with Absalom (2Sa 15:12, 31-37; 1Ch 27:33-34); committed suicide when his advice was ignored (2Sa 16:15-17:23).

AI

Jos 7: 4 routed by the men of **A**,
     8:26 he had destroyed all who lived in **A**.

AID

Ge 50:25 "God will surely come to your **a**,
Ex 13:19 "God will surely come to your **a**,
Ru 1: 6 the Lord had come to the **a** of his
Isa 38:14 come to my **a**!"
Php 4:16 you sent me **a** again and again

AIM* [AIMLESSLY]

Ps 21:12 when you **a** at them with drawn bow.
    64: 3 and **a** their words like dealy arrows.
1Co 7:34 Her **a** is to be devoted to the Lord
2Co 13:11 **A** for perfection, listen to my appeal,

AIMLESSLY* [AIM]

1Co 9:26 I do not run like a man running **a**;

AIR [MIDAIR]

Mt 8:20 and birds of the **a** have nests,
Mk 4:32 that the birds of the **a** can perch
1Co 9:26 not fight like a man beating the **a**.
    14: 9 You will just be speaking into the **a**.
Eph 2: 2 of the ruler of the kingdom of the **a**,
1Th 4:17 the clouds to meet the Lord in the **a**,
Rev 16:17 poured out his bowl into the **a**,

AKELDAMA* [FIELD, BLOOD]

Ac 1:19 **A**, that is, Field of Blood.)

ALABASTER*

Mt 26: 7 an **a** jar of very expensive perfume,
Mk 14: 3 an **a** jar of very expensive perfume,
Lk 7:37 she brought an **a** jar of perfume,

ALARM [ALARMED]

Joel 2: 1 sound the **a** on my holy hill.
2Co 7:11 what **a**, what longing, what concern,

ALARMED [ALARM]

Mk 13: 7 do not be **a**.
Ac 22:29 The commander himself was **a**
2Th 2: 2 or **a** by some prophecy,

ALERT*

Jos 8: 4 All of you be on the **a**.
Ps 17:11 they now surround me, with eyes **a**,
Isa 21: 7 let him be **a**, fully **a**."
Mk 13:33 Be on guard! Be **a**!
Eph 6:18 be **a** and always keep on praying
1Th 5: 6 but let us be **a** and self-controlled.
1Pe 5: 8 Be self-controlled and **a**.

ALEXANDER

Ac 19:33 The Jews pushed **A** to the front,
1Ti 1:20 Among them are Hymenaeus and **A**,
2Ti 4:14 **A** the metalworker did me a great deal of harm.

ALIEN [ALIENATED, ALIENS]

Ex 22:21 Do not mistreat an **a** or oppress him,
Lev 19:10 Leave them for the poor and the **a**.
    24:22 law for the **a** and the native-born.
Ps 146: 9 The Lord watches over the **a**

ALIENATED [ALIEN]

Gal 5: 4 by law have you been **a** from Christ;
Col 1:21 Once you were **a** from God

ALIENS [ALIEN]

Ex 23: 9 know how it feels to be **a**, because you were **a** in Egypt.
Eph 2:19 you are no longer foreigners and **a**,
Heb 11:13 they were **a** and strangers on earth.
1Pe 2:11 as **a** and strangers in the world,

ALIVE [LIVE]

Ge 7: 3 to keep their various kinds **a**
Dt 6:24 might always prosper and be kept **a**,
1Sa 2: 6 The Lord brings death and makes **a**;
Pr 1:12 let's swallow them **a**, like the grave,
Lk 24:23 who said he was **a**.
Ac 1: 3 convincing proofs that he was **a**.
Ro 6:11 dead to sin but **a** to God in Christ
    7: 9 Once I was **a** apart from law;
1Co 15:22 so in Christ all will be made **a**.
Col 2:13 God made you **a** with Christ.
1Th 4:17 we who are still **a** and are left
Rev 1:18 and behold I am **a** for ever and ever!

ALL ISRAEL See ISRAEL

ALL ... HEART See HEART

ALL PEOPLE See PEOPLE

ALL PEOPLES See PEOPLES

ALL THE PEOPLE See PEOPLE

ALL THE PEOPLES See PEOPLES

ALLELUIA (KJV) See HALLELUIA

ALLIANCE [ALLY]

1Ki 3: 1 Solomon made an **a** with Pharaoh
Isa 30: 1 forming an **a**, but not by my Spirit,

ALLOTMENT [ALLOTS, ALLOTTED]

Dt 14:29 the Levites who have no **a**
Eze 48:13 the Levites will have an **a**

ALLOTS [ALLOTMENT]

Job 27:13 the fate God **a** to the wicked,

ALLOTTED [ALLOTMENT]

Nu 34: 2 the land that will be **a** to you
Da 12:13 rise to receive your **a** inheritance."

ALLOW [ALLOWED]

Ps 132: 4 I will **a** no sleep to my eyes,
Pr 6: 4 **A** no sleep to your eyes,
Lk 4:41 and would not **a** them to speak,
Ac 16: 7 Spirit of Jesus would not **a** them to.

ALLOWED [ALLOW]

Ac 28:16 Paul was **a** to live by himself,
1Co 14:34 They are not **a** to speak,

ALLY [ALLIANCE]

Isa 48:14 The LORD's chosen **a** will carry out

ALMIGHTY [MIGHT]

Ge 17: 1 "I am God **A**;
Ex 6: 3 to Isaac and to Jacob as God **A**,
Nu 24: 4 who sees a vision from the **A**,
Ru 1:20 the **A** has made my life very bitter.
2Sa 7:26 'The LORD **A** is God over Israel!'
Job 6: 4 The arrows of the **A** are in me,
        11: 7 Can you probe the limits of the **A**?
        21:15 Who is the **A**,
        33: 4 the breath of the **A** gives me life.
Ps 84: 3 O LORD **A**, my King and my God.
        89: 8 O LORD God **A**, who is like you?
        91: 1 rest in the shadow of the **A**.
Isa 6: 3 holy, holy is the LORD **A**;
        47: 4 the LORD **A** is his name—
        48: 2 the LORD **A** is his name:
        51:15 the LORD **A** is his name.
        54: 5 the LORD **A** is his name—
Jer 11:17 The LORD **A**, who planted you,
Am 5:14 the LORD God **A** will be with you,
        5:15 the LORD God **A** will have mercy
Zec 8:22 to Jerusalem to seek the LORD **A**
Mal 3:10 Test me in this," says the LORD **A**,
Rev 4: 8 holy is the Lord God **A**, who was,
        19: 6 For our Lord God **A** reigns.

†LORD GOD ALMIGHTY See GOD

†LORD ALMIGHTY See †LORD

THE †LORD ALMIGHTY SAYS
See †LORD

ALMS (KJV) See ACTS OF
RIGHTEOUSNESS, GIVE, GIVING

ALONE [LONELY]

Ge 2:18 "It is not good for the man to be **a**.
Ex 18:18 heavy for you; you cannot handle it **a**
Dt 8: 3 man does not live on bread **a**
Ne 9: 6 You **a** are the LORD.
Ps 62: 1 My soul finds rest in God **a**;

        76: 7 You **a** are to be feared.
        148:13 for his name **a** is exalted;
Mt 4: 4 'Man does not live on bread **a**,
Mk 2: 7 Who can forgive sins but God **a**?"
        10:18 "No one is good—except God **a**.
Jas 2:24 by what he does and not by faith **a**.
Rev 15: 4 For you **a** are holy.

ALPHA*

Rev 1: 8 "I am the **A** and the Omega,"
        21: 6 I am the **A** and the Omega,
        22:13 I am the **A** and the Omega,

ALREADY [READY]

Php 3:12 Not that I have **a** obtained all this, or
        have **a** been made perfect,
2Th 2: 2 that the day of the Lord has **a** come.
        2: 7 power of lawlessness is **a** at work;
2Ti 2:18 the resurrection has **a** taken place,
1Jn 2: 8 and the true light is **a** shining.

ALTAR [ALTARS]

Ge 8:20 Noah built an **a** to the LORD and,
        12: 7 So he built an **a** there to the LORD.
        13:18 where he built an **a** to the LORD.
        22: 9 Abraham built an **a** there
        22: 9 son Isaac and laid him on the **a**,
        26:25 Isaac built an **a** there
        33:20 an **a** and called it El Elohe Israel.
        35: 1 and build an **a** there to God,
Ex 17:15 Moses built an **a** and called it
        20:24 " 'Make {an **a** of earth for me
        27: 1 "Build an **a** of acacia wood,
        30: 1 "Make an **a** of acacia wood
        37:25 the **a** of incense out of acacia wood.
Dt 27: 5 Build there an **a** to the LORD your
        God, an **a** of stones.
Jos 8:30 on Mount Ebal an **a** to the LORD,
        22:10 Manasseh built an imposing **a**
Jdg 6:24 Gideon built an **a** to the LORD there
        21: 4 an **a** and presented burnt offerings
1Sa 7:17 he built an **a** there to the LORD.
        14:35 Then Saul built an **a** to the LORD;
2Sa 24:25 David built an **a** to the LORD there
1Ki 12:33 on the **a** he had built at Bethel.
        12:33 for the Israelites and went up to the **a**
        13: 2 He cried out against the **a** by the
        word of the LORD: "O **a**, **a**!
        16:32 He set up an **a** for Baal in the temple
        18:30 and he repaired the **a** of the LORD,
2Ki 16:10 He saw an **a** in Damascus
1Ch 21:26 David built an **a** to the LORD there
        21:26 with fire from heaven on the **a**
2Ch 4: 1 a bronze **a** twenty cubits long,
        4:19 in God's temple: the golden **a**;
        15: 8 He repaired the **a** of the LORD
        32:12 'You must worship before one **a**
        33:16 Then he restored the **a** of the LORD
Ezr 3: 2 began to build the **a**
Isa 6: 6 taken with tongs from the **a**.
La 2: 7 The Lord has rejected his **a**
Eze 40:47 And the **a** was in front of the temple.
Am 9: 1 I saw the Lord standing by the **a**,
Mal 1: 7 "You place defiled food on my **a**.

Mt   5:24 leave your gift there in front of the **a.**
      23:18 'If anyone swears by the **a,**
Ac 17:23 even found an **a** with this inscription:
1Co 10:18 eat the sacrifices participate in the **a?**
Heb 13:10 We have an **a** from which
Jas   2:21 offered his son Isaac on the **a?**
Rev 6: 9 I saw under the **a** the souls

ALTARS [ALTAR]

Ex 34:13 Break down their **a,**
Nu 23: 1 "Build me seven **a** here,
2Ch 33: 3 also erected **a** to the Baals
      34: 4 the **a** of the Baals were torn down;

ALTER* [ALTERED]

Ps 89:34 or **a** what my lips have uttered.

ALTERED* [ALTER]

Da   6: 8 in writing so that it cannot be **a—**

ALWAYS

Dt 12:28 so that it may **a** go well with you
     15:11 There will **a** be poor people
1Ch 16:11 and his strength; seek his face **a.**
Ps 16: 8 I have set the LORD **a** before me.
     51: 3 and my sin is **a** before me.
  119:44 I will **a** obey your law,
Pr 28:14 the man who **a** fears the LORD,
Jer 12: 1 You are **a** righteous, O LORD,
Hos 12: 6 and wait for your God **a.**
Mt 26:11 The poor you will **a** have with you,
            but you will not **a** have me.
    28:20 And surely I am with you **a,**
Jn   5:17 "My Father is **a** at his work
Ac   2:25 " 'I saw the Lord **a** before me.
     7:51 You **a** resist the Holy Spirit!
1Co 13: 7 It **a** protects, **a** trusts, **a** hopes, **a**
             perseveres.
Eph 5:20 **a** giving thanks to God the Father
Php 4: 4 Rejoice in the Lord **a.**
Phm 1: 4 I **a** thank my God as I remember you
Heb 7:25 he **a** lives to intercede for them.
1Pe 3:15 **A** be prepared to give an answer

AMALEK [AMALEKITES]

Ex 17:14 completely blot out the memory of **A**

AMALEKITES [AMALEK]

Ex 17: 8 **A** came and attacked the Israelites
Dt 25:17 Remember what the **A** did to you
1Sa 15: 3 attack the **A** and totally destroy
     15: 8 He took Agag king of the **A** alive,

AMASA

Nephew of David (1Ch 2:17). Commander of Absalom's forces (2Sa 17:24-27). Returned to David (2Sa 19:13). Killed by Joab (2Sa 20:4-13).

AMASSES*

Pr 28: 8 by exorbitant interest **a** it for another,

AMAZED [AMAZEMENT]

Mk 1:22 The people were **a** at his teaching,
     6: 6 And he was **a** at their lack of faith.
  10:24 The disciples were **a** at his words.

Ac   2: 7 Utterly **a,** they asked:
  13:12 **a** at the teaching about the Lord.

AMAZEMENT [AMAZED, AMAZING]

Lk 24:41 not believe it because of joy and **a,**

AMAZIAH

1. Son of Joash; king of Judah (2Ki 14; 2Ch 25). Defeated Edom (2Ki 14:7; 2Ch 25:5-13); defeated by Israel for worshiping Edom's gods (2Ki 14:8-14; 2Ch 25:14-24).

2. Idolatrous priest who opposed Amos (Am 7:10-17).

AMAZING* [AMAZEMENT]

Jos   3: 5 the LORD will do **a** things
Jdg 13:19 And the LORD did an **a** thing
Pr 30:18 "There are three things that are too **a**

AMBASSADOR* [AMBASSADORS]

Eph 6:20 for which I am an **a** in chains.

AMBASSADORS [AMBASSADOR]

2Co 5:20 We are therefore Christ's **a,**

AMBITION*

Ro 15:20 It has always been my **a** to preach
Gal 5:20 fits of rage, selfish **a,** dissensions,
Php 1:17 former preach Christ out of selfish **a,**
     2: 3 Do nothing out of selfish **a** or vain
1Th 4:11 Make it your **a** to lead a quiet life,
Jas 3:14 and selfish **a** in your hearts,
     3:16 where you have envy and selfish **a,**

AMBUSH

Hos 6: 9 As marauders lie in **a** for a man,
Ac 23:21 of them are waiting in **a** for him.
    25: 3 an **a** to kill him along the way.

AMEN

Dt 27:15 Then all the people shall say, "**A!**"
1Co 14:16 who do not understand say "**A**"
2Co 1:20 so through him the "**A**" is spoken
Rev 3:14 the words of the **A,**
  22:20 I am coming soon." **A.**

AMENDS

Pr 14: 9 Fools mock at making **a** for sin,

AMMONITES

Ge 19:38 the father of the **A** of today.
Dt   2:19 When you come to the **A,**
Jdg 11: 4 when the **A** made war on Israel,
1Ki 11: 5 Molech the detestable god of the **A.**
Jer 49: 6 I will restore the fortunes of the **A,**"
Eze 25:10 the **A** will not be remembered among
Zep 2: 9 the **A** like Gomorrah—

AMNON [AMNON'S]

Firstborn of David (2Sa 3:2; 1Ch 3:1). Killed by Absalom for raping his sister Tamar (2Sa 13).

AMON

1. Son of Manasseh; king of Judah (2Ki 21:18-26; 1Ch 3:14; 2Ch 33:21-25).

2. Ruler of Samaria under Ahab (1Ki 22:26; 2Ch 18:25).

AMORITE [AMORITES]

Am   2: 9 "I destroyed the **A** before them,

AMORITES [AMORITE]

Ge 15:16 the sin of the **A** has not yet reached
Nu 21:31 So Israel settled in the land of the **A.**
Jdg 6:10 not worship the gods of the **A,**

AMOS

1. Prophet from Tekoa (Am 1:1; 7:10-17).
2. Ancestor of Jesus (Lk 3:25).

ANAK [ANAKITES]

Nu 13:28 We even saw descendants of **A** there.
Jos 15:13 (Arba was the forefather of **A.)**

ANAKITES [ANAK]

Dt   1:28 We even saw the **A** there.' "
     2:10 and as tall as the **A.**
     9: 2 The people are strong and tall— **A!**
Jos 11:22 No **A** were left in Israelite territory;

ANANIAS

1. Husband of Sapphira; died for lying to God (Ac 5:1-11).
2. Disciple who baptized Saul (Ac 9:10-19).
3. High priest at Paul's arrest (Ac 22:30-24:1).

ANATHEMA (KJV) See CURSE,
CURSED

ANCESTORS [ANCESTRY]

1Ki 19: 4 my life; I am no better than my **a."**
Am   2: 4 the gods their **a** followed,

ANCESTRY [ANCESTORS]

Ro   9: 5 them is traced the human **a** of Christ,

ANCHOR

Heb 6:19 this hope as an **a** for the soul,

ANCIENT

Ps   68:33 to him who rides the **a** skies above,
     119:52 I remember your **a** laws, O LORD,
Pr   22:28 Do not move an **a** boundary stone
Isa 43:13 Yes, and from **a** days I am he.
     44: 7 since I established my **a** people,
Da   7: 9 the **A** of Days took his seat.
     7:13 He approached the **A** of Days
     7:22 until the **A** of Days came
Rev 12: 9 that **a** serpent called the devil,
     20: 2 He seized the dragon, that **a** serpent,

ANDREW*

Apostle; brother of Simon Peter (Mt 4:18; 10:2; Mk 1:16-18, 29; 3:18; 13:3; Lk 6:14; Jn 1:35-44; 6:8-9; 12:22; Ac 1:13).

ANGEL [ANGELS, ARCHANGEL]

Ge   16: 7 The **a** of the LORD found Hagar
     21:17 and the **a** of God called to Hagar
     22:11 the **a** of the LORD called out to him

     24: 7 he will send his **a** before you
     31:11 The **a** of God said to me
     48:16 the **A** who has delivered me
Ex   3: 2 the **a** of the LORD appeared to him
     14:19 Then the **a** of God,
     23:20 an **a** ahead of you to guard you along
     32:34 and my **a** will go before you.
     33: 2 an **a** before you and drive out
Nu   20:16 an **a** and brought us out of Egypt.
     22:22 the **a** of the LORD stood in the road
Jdg   2: 1 The **a** of the LORD went up
      6:12 **a** of the LORD appeared to Gideon,
      6:22 I have seen the **a** of the LORD face
     13: 3 The **a** of the LORD appeared to her
1Sa 29: 9 as pleasing in my eyes as an **a**
2Sa 14:17 like an **a** of God in discerning good
     19:27 My lord the king is like an **a** of God;
     24:16 When the **a** stretched out his hand
1Ki 13:18 And an **a** said to me by the word of
     19: 7 The **a** of the LORD came back
2Ki   1: 3 the **a** of the LORD said to Elijah
     19:35 the **a** of the LORD went out and put
Job 33:23 "Yet if there is an **a** on his side as
Ps   34: 7 The **a** of the LORD encamps
Da   3:28 who has sent his **a** and rescued
      6:22 My God sent his **a,**
Hos 12: 4 struggled with the **a** and overcame
Zec   1:11 they reported to the **a** of the LORD,
      3: 1 the high priest standing before the **a**
Mt   1:20 an **a** of the Lord appeared to him
      2:13 an **a** of the Lord appeared to Joseph
     28: 2 for an **a** of the Lord came down
Lk   1:11 an **a** of the Lord appeared to him,
      1:26 God sent the **a** Gabriel to Nazareth,
      2: 9 An **a** of the Lord appeared to them,
     22:43 An **a** from heaven appeared to him
Jn   12:29 an **a** had spoken to him.
Ac   5:19 an **a** of the Lord opened the doors of
      6:15 like the face of an **a.**
      7:30 an **a** appeared to Moses in the flames
      8:26 Now an **a** of the Lord said to Philip,
     10: 3 He distinctly saw an **a** of God,
     12: 7 Suddenly an **a** of the Lord appeared
     27:23 an **a** of the God whose I am
1Co 10:10 and were killed by the destroying **a.**
2Co 11:14 masquerades as an **a** of light.
Gal   1: 8 an **a** from heaven should preach
      4:14 you welcomed me as if I were an **a**
Rev   1: 1 by sending his **a** to his servant John,
      2: 1 the **a** of the church in Ephesus write:
      5: 2 And I saw a mighty **a** proclaiming in
      7: 2 Then I saw another **a** coming up
      8: 3 Another **a,** who had a golden censer,
      9:11 as king over them the **a** of the Abyss,
     14: 6 I saw another **a** flying in midair,
     16: 2 The first **a** went and poured
     17: 3 the **a** carried me away in the Spirit
     19:17 And I saw an **a** standing in the sun,

ANGEL OF GOD Ge 21:17; 31:11; Ex 14:19; Jdg 6:20; 13:6, 9; 1Sa 29:9; 2Sa 14:17, 20; 19:27; Ac 10:3; Gal 4:14

ANGEL OF THE *LORD Mt 1:20, 24; 2:13, 19; 28:2; Lk 1:11; 2:9; Ac 5:19; 8:26; 12:7, 23

ANGEL OF THE †LORD Ge 16:7, 9, 11; 22:11, 15; Ex 3:2; Nu 22:22, 23, 24, 25, 26, 27, 31, 32, 34, 35; Jdg 2:1, 4; 5:23; 6:11, 12, 21, 21, 22, 22; 13:3, 13, 15, 16, 16, 17, 20, 21, 21; 2Sa 24:16; 1Ki 19:7; 2Ki 1:3, 15; 19:35; 1Ch 21:12, 15, 16, 18, 30; Ps 34:7; 35:5, 6; Isa 37:36; Zec 1:11, 12; 3:1, 5, 6; 12:8

ANGELS [ANGEL]

Ge	19: 1	The two **a** arrived at Sodom in
	28:12	and the **a** of God were ascending
	32: 1	and the **a** of God met him.
Job	1: 6	the **a** came to present themselves
Ps	78:25	Men ate the bread of **a;**
	91:11	For he will command his **a**
	103:20	Praise the LORD, you his **a,**
Mt	4: 6	written: " 'He will command his **a**
	13:39	and the harvesters are **a.**
	18:10	that their **a** in heaven always see
	25:41	for the devil and his **a.**
Mk	8:38	in his Father's glory with the holy **a.**
	12:25	be like the **a** in heaven.
	13:32	not even the **a** in heaven,
Lk	2:15	When the **a** had left them and gone
	4:10	is written: " 'He will command his **a**
	12: 9	be disowned before the **a** of God.
	16:22	the beggar died and the **a** carried him
	20:36	for they are like the **a.**
Jn	1:51	and the **a** of God ascending
Ac	7:53	law that was put into effect through **a**
	23: 8	that there are neither **a** nor spirits,
Ro	8:38	neither **a** nor demons,
1Co	4: 9	to **a** as well as to men.
	6: 3	not know that we will judge **a?**
	11:10	For this reason, and because of the **a,**
	13: 1	in the tongues of men and of **a,**
Gal	3:19	law was put into effect through **a**
Col	2:18	and the worship of **a** disqualify you
2Th	1: 7	in blazing fire with his powerful **a.**
1Ti	3:16	was seen by **a,**
	5:21	and Christ Jesus and the elect **a,**
Heb	1: 4	as much superior to the **a** as the
	1: 6	"Let all God's **a** worship him."
	1: 7	"He makes his **a** winds,
	1:14	Are not all **a** ministering spirits
	2: 2	message spoken by **a** was binding,
	2: 7	a little lower than the **a;**
	2: 9	a little lower than the **a,**
	12:22	to thousands upon thousands of **a**
	13: 2	some people have entertained **a**
1Pe	1:12	Even **a** long to look into these things.
	3:22	with **a,** authorities and powers
2Pe	2: 4	not spare **a** when they sinned,
Jude	1: 6	**a** who did not keep their positions of
Rev	1:20	the **a** of the seven churches,
	3: 5	before my Father and his **a.**
	5:11	and heard the voice of many **a,**
	7: 1	After this I saw four **a** standing at
	8: 2	the seven **a** who stand before God,
	9:14	"Release the four **a** who are bound at
	12: 7	and his **a** fought against the dragon,
	15: 1	great and marvelous sign: seven **a**
	21:12	and with twelve **a** at the gates.

ANGER [ANGERED, ANGRY]

Ex	4:14	Then the LORD's **a** burned
	15: 7	You unleashed your burning **a;**
	22:24	My **a** will be aroused,
	32:10	that my **a** may burn against them and
	32:11	"why should your **a** burn
	32:12	Turn from your fierce **a;**
	32:19	his **a** burned and he threw
	34: 6	gracious God, slow to **a,**
Lev	26:28	in my **a** I will be hostile toward you,
Nu	11: 1	he heard them his **a** was aroused.
	11:33	the **a** of the LORD burned against
	12: 9	The **a** of the LORD burned
	14:18	'The LORD is slow to **a,**
	25:11	has turned my **a** away from
	32:10	The LORD's **a** was aroused
Dt	6:15	is a jealous God and his **a** will burn
	9:19	the **a** and wrath of the LORD,
	29:28	In furious **a** and in great wrath
Jos	7: 1	LORD's **a** burned against Israel.
	7:26	the LORD turned from his fierce **a.**
Jdg	2:12	They provoked the LORD to **a**
	14:19	Burning with **a,**
1Sa	20:30	Saul's **a** flared up at Jonathan
2Sa	12: 5	David burned with **a** against the man
1Ki	16:13	to **a** by their worthless idols.
2Ki	22:13	the LORD's **a** that burns against us
	24:20	the LORD's **a** that all this happened
Ne	9:17	slow to **a** and abounding in love.
Ps	4: 4	In your **a** do not sin;
	30: 5	For his **a** lasts only a moment,
	37: 8	Refrain from **a** and turn from wrath;
	78:38	after time he restrained his **a** and did
	86:15	gracious God, slow to **a,**
	90: 7	We are consumed by your **a**
	103: 8	slow to **a,** abounding in love.
	103: 9	nor will he harbor his **a** forever;
	145: 8	slow to **a** and rich in love.
Pr	15: 1	but a harsh word stirs up **a.**
	29: 8	but wise men turn away **a.**
	29:11	A fool gives full vent to his **a,**
	30:33	so stirring up **a** produces strife."
Ecc	7: 9	for **a** resides in the lap of fools.
Isa	63: 6	I trampled the nations in my **a;**
Da	9:16	turn away your **a** and your wrath
Joel	2:13	slow to **a** and abounding in love,
Jnh	3: 9	compassion turn from his fierce **a**
	4: 2	slow to **a** and abounding in love,
Na	1: 3	The LORD is slow to **a** and great
Mk	3: 5	He looked around at them in **a** and,
2Co	12:20	jealousy, outbursts of **a,** factions,
Eph	4:26	"In your **a** do not sin":
Col	3: 8	of all such things as these: **a,**
Jas	1:20	for man's **a** does not bring about

ANGER OF THE †LORD Nu 11:33; 12:9; Jdg 3:8; 2Sa 24:1; 2Ch 25:15; 29:8; Jer 4:8; 23:20; 25:37; 30:24; 51:45; Zep 2:2

ANGERED [ANGER]

Ezr	5:12	our fathers **a** the God of heaven,
Ps	78:58	They **a** him with their high places;
Pr	22:24	do not associate with one easily, **a,**
1Co	13: 5	it is not easily **a,**

ANGRY [ANGER]

Ge	4: 5	So Cain was very **a,**
Dt	4:21	The LORD was **a** with me because
Ps	2:12	lest he be **a** and you be destroyed
	95:10	For forty years I was **a** with
Pr	25:23	so a sly tongue brings **a** looks.
	29:22	An **a** man stirs up dissension,
Isa	34: 2	The LORD is **a** with all nations;
Jer	3:12	'I will not be **a** forever.
Jnh	4: 4	"Have you any right to be **a?"**
Mic	7:18	You do not stay **a** forever but delight
Mt	5:22	But I tell you that anyone who is **a**
Lk	15:28	"The older brother became **a**
Jn	7:23	why are you **a** with me for healing
Heb	3:17	with whom was he **a** for forty years?
Jas	1:19	slow to speak and slow to become **a,**
Rev	11:18	The nations were **a;**

ANGUISH

Ps	6: 3	My soul is in **a.**
	118: 5	In my **a** I cried to the LORD,
Pr	31: 6	wine to those who are in **a;**
Jer	4:19	Oh, my **a,** my **a!**
La	1: 4	and she is in bitter **a.**
Zep	1:15	a day of distress and **a,**
Lk	21:25	nations will be in **a** and perplexity at
	22:44	And being in **a,**
Jn	16:21	forgets the **a** because of her joy
Ro	9: 2	I have great sorrow and unceasing **a**

ANIMAL [ANIMALS]

Lev	20:15	a man has sexual relations with an **a,**
Dt	14: 6	You may eat any **a** that has
Ps	50:10	for every **a** of the forest is mine,
Da	8: 4	No **a** could stand against him,

ANIMALS [ANIMAL]

Ge	1:24	and wild **a,**
	7:16	The **a** going in were male and female
Lev	11:46	the regulations concerning **a,**
Dt	14: 4	These are the **a** you may eat:
Job	12: 7	"But ask the **a,**
Ecc	3:19	Man's fate is like that of the **a;**
Isa	43:20	The wild **a** honor me,
Eze	34:28	nor will wild **a** devour them.
Hab	2:17	your destruction of **a** will terrify you.
Mal	1: 8	When you bring blind **a** for sacrifice,
Mk	1:13	He was with the wild **a,**
Ac	11: 6	and saw four-footed **a** of the earth,
	15:20	from the meat of strangled **a** and

ANNA*

Prophetess who spoke about the child Jesus (Lk 2:36-38).

ANNALS

BOOK OF THE ANNALS 1Ki 11:41; 14:19, 29; 15:7, 23, 31; 16:5, 14, 20, 27; 22:39, 45; 2Ki 1:18; 8:23; 10:34; 12:19; 13:8, 12; 14:15, 18, 28; 15:6, 11, 15, 21, 26, 31, 36; 16:19; 20:20; 21:17, 25; 23:28; 24:5; 1Ch 27:24; Ne 12:23; Est 2:23; 10:2

ANNAS

High priest A.D. 6-15 (Lk 3:2; Jn 18:13,24; Ac 4:6).

ANNIHILATE

Dt	9: 3	and **a** them quickly,
Est	3:13	kill and **a** all the Jews—
	8:11	kill and **a** any armed force
Da	11:44	a great rage to destroy and **a** many.

ANNOUNCE [ANNOUNCED]

Mt	6: 2	do not **a** it with trumpets,

ANNOUNCED [ANNOUNCE]

Ps	68:11	The Lord **a** the word,
Isa	48: 5	before they happened I **a** them
Gal	3: 8	**a** the gospel in advance to Abraham:
Heb	2: 3	which was first **a** by the Lord,
Rev	10: 7	as he **a** to his servants the prophets."

ANNOYANCE*

Pr	12:16	A fool shows his **a** at once,

ANNUAL*

Ex	30:10	This **a** atonement must be made with
Jdg	21:19	there is the festival of the LORD
1Sa	1:21	to offer the **a** sacrifice
	2:19	to offer the **a** sacrifice.
	20: 6	an **a** sacrifice is being made there
2Ch	8:13	New Moons and the three **a** feasts—
Heb	10: 3	sacrifices are an **a** reminder of sins,

ANOINT [ANOINTED, ANOINTING]

Ex	30:26	Then use it to **a** the Tent of Meeting,
	30:30	**"A** Aaron and his sons
Jdg	9:15	'If you really want to **a** me king
1Sa	9:16	A him leader over my people Israel;
	15: 1	to **a** you king over his people Israel;
1Ki	1:34	and Nathan the prophet **a** him king
	19:16	**a** Elisha son of Shaphat
2Ki	9: 3	the LORD says: I **a** you king
Ps	23: 5	You **a** my head with oil;
Ecc	9: 8	and always **a** your head with oil.
Da	9:24	and prophecy and to **a** the most holy.
Mk	16: 1	that they might go to **a** Jesus' body.
Jas	5:14	to pray over him and **a** him with oil

ANOINTED [ANOINT]

Ge	31:13	where you **a** a pillar and
Lev	7:36	On the day they were **a,**
1Sa	2:10	and exalt the horn of his **a."**
	10: 1	"Has not the LORD **a** you leader
	16:13	took the horn of oil and **a** him
	24: 6	for he is the **a** of the LORD."
2Sa	1:14	to destroy the LORD's **a?"**
	2: 4	and there they **a** David king over
	5: 3	and they **a** David king over Israel.
	19:21	He cursed the LORD's **a."**
1Ki	1:39	from the sacred tent and **a** Solomon.
1Ch	16:22	"Do not touch my **a** ones,
2Ch	6:42	do not reject your **a** one.
Ps	2: 2	the LORD and against his **A** One.
	105:15	"Do not touch my **a** ones;
Isa	61: 1	because the LORD has **a** me

Da   9:26   the **A** One will be cut off
Hab   3:13   to save your **a**.
Zec   4:14   the two who are **a** to serve the Lord
Lk   4:18   because he has **a** me
Ac   4:26   the Lord and against his **A** One.'
     10:38   how God **a** Jesus of Nazareth with
2Co   1:21   He **a** us,

ANOINTED ONE 1Sa 2:35; 2Ch 6:42; Ps 2:2; 28:8; 84:9; 89:38, 51; 132:10, 17; Da 9:25, 26; Hab 3:13; Ac 4:26

ANOINTING [ANOINT]

Ex   30:25   It will be the sacred **a** oil.
Lev   8:12   of the **a** oil on Aaron's head
1Ch   29:22   **a** him before the LORD to be ruler
Ps   45: 7   above your companions by **a** you
Heb   1: 9   above your companions by **a** you
1Jn   2:20   you have an **a** from the Holy One,
     2:27   the **a** you received from him remains
     2:27   as his **a** teaches you about all things
                and as that **a** is real,

ANOINTING OIL See OIL

ANOTHER

Lev   19:11   " 'Do not deceive one **a**.
Pr   27:17   so one man sharpens **a**.
Isa   48:11   I will not yield my glory to **a**.
Lk   19:44   They will not leave one stone on **a**,
Jn   1:16   all received one blessing after **a**.
     13:34   command I give you: Love one **a**.
Ro   12:10   Honor one **a** above yourselves.
1Co   16:20   Greet one **a** with a holy kiss.
Col   3:16   as you teach and admonish one **a**
Heb   3:13   But encourage one **a** daily,
1Jn   3:23   to love one **a** as he commanded us.

ONE ANOTHER See ONE

ANSWER [ANSWERED, ANSWERS]

1Ki   18:26   "O Baal, **a** us!"
     18:37   **A** me, O LORD, **a** me,
Job   30:20   O God, but you do not **a**;
     40: 2   Let him who accuses God **a** him!"
Ps   38:15   I wait for you, O LORD; you will **a**,
Pr   15: 1   A gentle **a** turns away wrath,
     24:26   An honest **a** is like a kiss on the lips.
     26: 5   **A** a fool according to his folly,
Ecc   10:19   but money is the **a** for everything.
Lk   23: 9   but Jesus gave him no **a**.
1Pe   3:15   Always be prepared to give an **a**

ANSWERED [ANSWER]

Ge   25:21   The LORD **a** his prayer,
1Ch   21:26   and the LORD **a** him with fire
Ps   118:21   I will give you thanks, for you **a** me;

ANSWERS [ANSWER]

1Ki   18:24   The god who **a** by fire— he is God."
Pr   18:13   He who **a** before listening—

ANT* [ANTS]

Pr   6: 6   Go to the **a**, you sluggard;

ANTICHRIST* [ANTICHRISTS]

1Jn   2:18   heard that the **a** is coming,

     2:22   Such a man is the **a**—
     4: 3   This is the spirit of the **a**,
2Jn   1: 7   the deceiver and the **a**.

ANTICHRISTS* [ANTICHRIST]

1Jn   2:18   even now many **a** have come.

ANTIOCH

Ac   11:26   were called Christians first at **A**.
     13: 1   the church at **A** there were prophets
Gal   2:11   When Peter came to **A**,

ANTIPAS* [HEROD]

Rev   2:13   even in the days of **A**,

ANTS* [ANT]

Pr   30:25   **A** are creatures of little strength,

ANXIETIES* [ANXIOUS]

Lk   21:34   drunkenness and the **a** of life,

ANXIETY [ANXIOUS]

Ecc   11:10   banish **a** from your heart and cast off
1Pe   5: 7   Cast all your **a** on him

ANXIOUS [ANXIETIES, ANXIETY]

Pr   12:25   An **a** heart weighs a man down,
Php   4: 6   Do not be **a** about anything,

ANYTHING

Ge   18:14   Is **a** too hard for the LORD?
Ru   1:17   if **a** but death separates you and me."
Pr   14:15   A simple man believes **a**,
Jer   32:27   Is **a** too hard for me?
Mk   2:12   "We have never seen **a** like this!"
1Jn   2:15   not love the world or **a** in the world.
     3:22   and receive from him **a** we ask,

APART [PART]

Lev   20:26   and I have set you **a** from the nations
Isa   45:21   And there is no God **a** from me,
Jn   15: 5   **a** from me you can do nothing.
Ro   1: 1   be an apostle and set **a** for the gospel
     3:21   righteousness from God, **a** from law,
Gal   1:15   who set me **a** from birth
1Pe   3:15   in your hearts set **a** Christ as Lord.

APOLLOS

Christian from Alexandria, learned in the Scriptures; instructed by Aquila and Priscilla (Ac 18:24-28). Ministered at Corinth (Ac 19:1; 1Co 1:12; 3; Tit 3:13).

APOLLYON*

Rev   9:11   Abaddon, and in Greek, **A**.

APOSTLE [APOSTLES, APOSTLES', APOSTLESHIP, SUPER-APOSTLES]

Ro   1: 1   be an **a** and set apart for the gospel
     11:13   as I am the **a** to the Gentiles,
1Co   1: 1   to be an **a** of Christ Jesus by the will
     9: 1   Am I not an **a**?
     15: 9   not even deserve to be called an **a**,
2Co   12:12   The things that mark an **a**—
Gal   2: 8   Peter as an **a** to the Jews,

2: 8 my ministry as an **a** to the Gentiles.
1Ti 1: 1 an **a** of Christ Jesus by the command
2: 7 appointed a herald and an **a—**
2Ti 1:11 a herald and an **a** and a teacher.
Heb 3: 1 and high priest whom we confess.
1Pe 1: 1 Peter, an **a** of Jesus Christ,

APOSTLES [APOSTLE]

See also Andrew, Bartholomew, James, John, Judas, Matthew, Matthias, Nathanael, Paul, Peter, Philip, Simon, Thaddaeus, Thomas.

Mt 10: 2 These are the names of the twelve **a:**
Mk 3:14 twelve—designating them **a—**
Lk 6:13 whom he also designated **a:**
11:49 'I will send them prophets and **a,**
Ac 1:26 so he was added to the eleven **a.**
2:43 miraculous signs were done by the **a.**
5:18 the **a** and put them in the public jail.
8: 1 and all except the **a** were scattered
14:14 **a** Barnabas and Paul heard of this,
Ro 16: 7 They are outstanding among the **a,**
1Co 12:28 God has appointed first of all **a,**
15: 9 For I am the least of the **a** and do not
2Co 11:13 For such men are false **a,**
11:13 masquerading as **a** of Christ.
Eph 2:20 the foundation of the **a** and prophets,
4:11 It was he who gave some to be **a,**
Rev 2: 2 who claim to be **a** but are not,
21:14 names of the twelve **a** of the Lamb.

APOSTLES' [APOSTLE]

Ac 2:42 devoted themselves to the **a** teaching
4:35 and put it at the **a** feet,
8:18 at the laying on of the **a** hands,

APOSTLESHIP* [APOSTLE]

Ro 1: 5 we received grace and **a**
1Co 9: 2 you are the seal of my **a** in the Lord.

APPALLED

Isa 52:14 Just as there were many who were **a**
Da 8:27 I was **a** by the vision;

APPEAL

Ac 25:11 I **a** to Caesar!"
2Co 5:20 God were making his **a** through us.
Phm 1: 9 yet I **a** to you on the basis of love.
1Pe 5: 1 I **a** as a fellow elder,

APPEAR [APPEARANCE, APPEARANCES, APPEARED, APPEARING, APPEARS]

Ge 1: 9 and let dry ground **a.**"
Ex 23:15 to **a** before me empty-handed.
Lev 16: 2 because I **a** in the cloud over
Da 11: 3 Then a mighty king will **a,**
Mt 24:30 the sign of the Son of Man will **a** in
Mk 13:22 and false prophets will **a**
Lk 19:11 the kingdom of God was going to **a**
2Co 5:10 **a** before the judgment seat of Christ,
Col 3: 4 you also will **a** with him in glory.
Heb 9:24 now to **a** for us in God's presence.
9:28 and he will **a** a second time,

APPEARANCE [APPEAR]

1Sa 16: 7 Man looks at the outward **a,**
2Sa 14:25 so highly praised for his handsome **a**
Isa 52:14 his **a** was so disfigured
53: 2 in his **a** that we should desire him.
Eze 1:28 the **a** of the likeness of the glory of
Mt 28: 3 His **a** was like lightning,
Gal 2: 6 God does not judge by external **a—**
Php 2: 8 And being found in **a** as a man,

APPEARANCES* [APPEAR]

Jn 7:24 Stop judging by mere **a,**

APPEARED [APPEAR]

Ge 12: 7 The LORD **a** to Abram and said,
26: 2 The LORD **a** to Isaac and said,
35: 9 God **a** to him again and blessed him.
Ex 3: 2 the LORD **a** to him in flames of fire
Nu 14:10 the glory of the LORD **a** at the Tent
Jdg 6:12 the angel of the LORD **a** to Gideon,
13: 3 The angel of the LORD **a** to her
1Ki 3: 5 At Gibeon the LORD **a** to Solomon
Mt 1:20 an angel of the Lord **a** to him in
Mk 9: 4 And there **a** before them Elijah
Lk 2: 9 An angel of the Lord **a** to them,
24:34 Lord has risen and **a** to Simon."
Jn 21:14 the third time Jesus **a** to his disciples
Ac 1: 3 He **a** to them over a period
12: 7 Suddenly an angel of the Lord **a** and
1Co 15: 5 and that he **a** to Peter,
Tit 2:11 that brings salvation has **a** to all men.
Heb 9:26 now he has **a** once for all at the end
1Jn 3: 8 The reason the Son of God **a** was

APPEARING [APPEAR]

1Ti 6:14 until the **a** of our Lord Jesus Christ,
2Ti 1:10 now been revealed through the **a**
4: 8 also to all who have longed for his **a.**
Tit 2:13 the glorious **a** of our great God

APPEARS [APPEAR]

SS 6:10 Who is this that **a** like the dawn,
Mal 3: 2 Who can stand when he **a?**
Col 3: 4 When Christ, who is your life, **a,**
Jas 4:14 You are a mist that **a** for a little
1Pe 5: 4 And when the Chief Shepherd **a,**
1Jn 2:28 when he **a** we may be confident
3: 2 But we know that when he **a,**

APPETITE

Pr 16:26 The laborer's **a** works for him;
Ecc 6: 7 yet his **a** is never satisfied.
Jer 50:19 his **a** will be satisfied

APPLE [APPLES]

Dt 32:10 as the **a** of his eye,
Ps 17: 8 Keep me as the **a** of your eye;
Zec 2: 8 touches the **a** of his eye—

APPLES* [APPLE]

Pr 25:11 A word aptly spoken is like **a** of gold
SS 2: 5 refresh me with **a,**
7: 8 the fragrance of your breath like **a,**

APPLIED [APPLY]

Ecc 1:17 Then I **a** myself to the understanding
1Co 4: 6 I have **a** these things to myself

APPLY [APPLIED, APPLYING]

Pr 22:17 **a** your heart to what I teach,
     23:12 **A** your heart to instruction

APPLYING [APPLY]

Pr 2: 2 and **a** your heart to understanding,

APPOINT [APPOINTED]

Nu 3:10 **A** Aaron and his sons to serve
Dt 17:15 be sure to **a** over you the king
1Sa 8: 5 now **a** a king to lead us,
Ps 61: 7 **a** your love and faithfulness
1Th 5: 9 For God did not **a** us to suffer wrath
Tit 1: 5 and **a** elders in every town,

APPOINTED [APPOINT]

Lev 23: 2 the **a** feasts of the LORD,
Dt 1:15 **a** them to have authority over you—
1Ki 1:35 **a** him ruler over Israel
Ezr 1: 2 he has **a** me to build a temple
Pr 8:23 I was **a** from eternity,
Da 11:27 an end will still come at the **a** time.
Mic 6: 9 the rod and the One who **a** it.
Hab 2: 3 For the revelation awaits an **a** time;
Mk 3:16 These are the twelve he **a:**
Lk 10: 1 the Lord **a** seventy-two others
Jn 15:16 and **a** you to go and bear fruit—
Ac 15: 2 So Paul and Barnabas were **a,**
Ro 9: 9 "At the **a** time I will return,
1Co 12:28 And in the church God has **a** first
Heb 1: 2 whom he **a** heir of all things,

APPOINTED FEASTS Lev 23:2, 2, 4, 37, 44;
Nu 10:10; 29:39; 1Ch 23:31; 2Ch 2:4; 31:3; Ezr
3:5; Ne 10:33; Isa 1:14; La 1:4; 2:6; Eze 36:38;
44:24; 45:17; 46:9, 11; Hos 2:11; 9:5; 12:9; Zep
3:18

APPOINTED TIME Ge 18:14; Ex 13:10;
23:15; 34:18; Nu 9:2, 3, 7, 13; 28:2; Ps 75:2;
102:13; Jer 33:20; Da 8:19; 11:27, 29, 35; Hab
2:3; Zep 2:2; Mt 8:29; 26:18; Ro 9:9; 1Co 4:5

APPROACH [APPROACHING]

Ex 24: 2 but Moses alone is to **a** the LORD;
Eph 3:12 in him we may **a** God with freedom
Heb 4:16 Let us then **a** the throne of grace

APPROACHING [APPROACH]

Heb 10:25 all the more as you see the Day **a.**
1Jn 5:14 the confidence we have in **a** God:

APPROPRIATE*

Ge 49:28 giving each the blessing **a** to him.
1Ti 2:10 **a** for women who profess

APPROVAL [APPROVE]

Jdg 18: 6 Your journey has the LORD's **a.**"
Jn 6:27 the Father has placed his seal of **a.**"
Ac 8: 1 Saul was there, giving **a** to his death.
1Co 11:19 to show which of you have God's **a.**

Gal 1:10 now trying to win the **a** of men,

APPROVE [APPROVAL, APPROVED, APPROVES]

Ro 1:32 also **a** of those who practice them.
     2:18 if you know his will and **a**
    12: 2 to test and **a** what God's will is—

APPROVED* [APPROVE]

Ro 14:18 in this way is pleasing to God and **a**
    16:10 Greet Apelles, tested and **a** in Christ.
2Co 10:18 who commends himself who is **a,**
1Th 2: 4 as men **a** by God to be entrusted with
2Ti 2:15 to present yourself to God as one **a,**

APPROVES* [APPROVE]

Ro 14:22 not condemn himself by what he **a.**

APT*

Pr 15:23 man finds joy in giving an **a** reply—

AQUILA*

Husband of Priscilla; co-worker with Paul, instructor of Apollos (Ac 18; Ro 16:3; 1Co 16:19;
2Ti 4:19).

ARABAH

Dt 4:49 as far as the Sea of the **A,**
Zec 14:10 will become like the **A.**

ARABIA [ARABS]

Isa 21:13 An oracle concerning **A:**
Gal 1:17 but I went immediately into **A**
    4:25 Hagar stands for Mount Sinai in **A**

ARABS [ARABIA]

Ne 4: 7 But when Sanballat, Tobiah, the **A,**
Ac 2:11 converts to Judaism); Cretans and **A**

ARAM [ARAMAIC, ARAMEAN, PADDAN ARAM]

Jdg 10: 6 and the gods of **A,** the gods of Sidon,
2Ki 13: 3 under the power of Hazael king of **A**
2Ch 16: 7 "Because you relied on the king of **A**

ARAMAIC [ARAM]

2Ki 18:26 "Please speak to your servants in **A,**
Ezr 4: 7 The letter was written in **A** script and
Da 2: 4 astrologers answered the king in **A,**
Jn 19:20 and the sign was written in **A,**
Ac 21:40 he said to them in **A:**
    26:14 I heard a voice saying to me in **A,**

ARAMEAN [ARAM]

Ge 31:20 Jacob deceived Laban the **A** by
Dt 26: 5 "My father was a wandering **A,**

ARARAT

Ge 8: 4 to rest on the mountains of **A.**

ARAUNAH

2Sa 24:16 the threshing floor of **A** the Jebusite.
1Ch 21:25 So David paid **A** six hundred shekels
2Ch 3: 1 the threshing floor of **A** the Jebusite,

ARBITER* [ARBITRATE]
Lk 12:14 who appointed me a judge or an **a**

ARBITRATE* [ARBITER]
Job 9:33 If only there were someone to **a**

ARCHANGEL* [ANGEL]
1Th 4:16 voice of the **a** and with the trumpet
Jude 1: 9 But even the **a** Michael,

ARCHELAUS*
Mt 2:22 that **A** was reigning in Judea in place

ARCHER [ARCHERS]
Ge 21:20 in the desert and became an **a.**
Pr 26:10 Like an **a** who wounds at random

ARCHERS [ARCHER]
Ge 49:23 With bitterness **a** attacked him;
Job 16:13 his **a** surround me.
Jer 50:29 "Summon **a** against Babylon,

ARCHIPPUS*
Co-worker of Paul (Col 4:17; Phm 2).

ARCHITECT*
Heb 11:10 whose **a** and builder is God.

ARENA*
1Co 4: 9 like men condemned to die in the **a.**

AREOPAGUS*
Ac 17:19 to a meeting of the **A,**
     17:22 then stood up in the meeting of the **A**
     17:34 Dionysius, a member of the **A,**

ARGUE [ARGUING, ARGUMENT, ARGUMENTS]
Job 13: 3 and to **a** my case with God.
     13: 8 Will you **a** the case for God?
Pr 25: 9 If you **a** your case with a neighbor,
Isa 43:26 let us **a** the matter together;
Ac 6: 3 These men began to **a** with Stephen,

ARGUING [ARGUE]
Ac 19: 8 **a** persuasively about the kingdom
Php 2:14 everything without complaining or **a,**

ARGUMENT [ARGUE]
Lk 9:46 An **a** started among the disciples as
Heb 6:16 and puts an end to all **a.**

ARGUMENTS [ARGUE]
Isa 41:21 "Set forth your **a,**" says Jacob's King
2Co 10: 5 We demolish **a** and every pretension
Col 2: 4 deceive you by fine-sounding **a.**
2Ti 2:23 to do with foolish and stupid **a,**
Tit 3: 9 controversies and genealogies and **a**

ARIMATHEA
Jn 19:38 Joseph of **A** asked Pilate for the body

ARISE [RISE]
2Ch 6:41 "Now **a,** O LORD God,

Pr 31:28 Her children **a** and call her blessed;
SS 2:10 My lover spoke and said to me, "**A,**
Isa 60: 1 "**A,** shine, for your light has come,

ARISTARCHUS*
Companion of Paul (Ac 19:29; 20:4; 27:2; Col 4:10; Phm 1:24).

ARK
Ge 6:14 make yourself an **a** of cypress wood;
Ex 25:16 Then put in the **a** the Testimony,
     37: 1 Bezalel made the **a** of acacia wood—
Nu 10:35 Whenever the **a** set out, Moses said,
Dt 10: 5 the tablets in the **a** I had made,
Jos 3: 3 "When you see the **a** of the covenant
1Sa 4:11 The **a** of God was captured,
     6: 3 you return the **a** of the god of Israel,
     7: 2 that the **a** remained at Kiriath Jearim,
2Sa 6:17 They brought the **a** of the LORD
1Ki 8: 9 in the **a** except the two stone tablets
1Ch 13: 9 his hand to steady the **a,**
2Ch 35: 3 the sacred **a** in the temple
Lk 17:27 up to the day Noah entered the **a.**
Heb 9: 4 This **a** contained the gold jar
     11: 7 built an **a** to save his family.
Rev 11:19 and within his temple was seen the **a**

ARK OF GOD 1Sa 3:3; 4:11, 13, 17, 18, 19, 21, 22; 5:1, 10, 10; 14:18; 2Sa 6:2, 3, 4, 6, 7, 12, 12; 7:2; 15:24, 25, 29; 1Ch 13:5, 6, 7, 12, 14; 15:1, 2, 15, 24; 16:1; 2Ch 1:4

ARK OF THE COVENANT Nu 10:33; Dt 10:8; 31:9, 25, 26; Jos 3:3, 6, 8, 11, 14, 17; 4:7, 9, 18; 6:6; 8:33; Jdg 20:27; 1Sa 4:4; 2Sa 15:24; 1Ki 6:19; 1Ch 15:25, 26, 28, 29; 16:6, 37; 17:1; 22:19; 28:2, 18; Jer 3:16; Heb 9:4

ARK OF THE †LORD Jos 3:13; 4:5, 11; 6:7, 11, 12, 13, 13; 7:6; 1Sa 4:6; 5:3, 4; 6:1, 2, 8, 11, 15, 18, 19, 21; 7:1, 1; 2Sa 6:9, 10, 11, 13, 15, 16, 17; 1Ki 8:4; 1Ch 15:2, 3, 12, 14; 16:4; 2Ch 8:11

ARK OF THE TESTIMONY Ex 25:22; 26:33, 34; 30:6, 26; 31:7; 39:35; 40:3, 5, 21; Nu 4:5; 7:89; Jos 4:16

ARM [ARMED, ARMIES, ARMOR, ARMOR-BEARER, ARMS, ARMY]
Ex 6: 6 redeem you with an outstretched **a**
Nu 11:23 "Is the LORD's **a** too short?
Dt 4:34 a mighty hand and an outstretched **a,**
     7:19 the mighty hand and outstretched **a,**
1Ki 8:42 mighty hand and your outstretched **a**
2Ch 32: 8 With him is only the **a** of flesh,
Job 40: 9 Do you have an **a** like God's,
Ps 44: 3 nor did their **a** bring them victory;
     44: 3 your **a,** and the light of your face,
     98: 1 and his holy **a** have worked salvation
SS 8: 3 His left **a** is under my head and his
           right **a** embraces me.
Isa 40:10 and his **a** rules for him.
Jer 27: 5 and outstretched **a** I made the earth
1Pe 4: 1 **a** yourselves also with the same

ARMAGEDDON*
Rev 16:16 the place that in Hebrew is called **A.**

ARMED [ARM]

2Sa 22:40 You **a** me with strength for battle;
Mk 14:43 With him was a crowd **a** with swords

ARMENIA (KJV) See ARARAT

ARMIES [ARM]

1Sa 17:36 he has defied the **a** of the living God.
Lk 21:20 Jerusalem being surrounded by **a,**
Rev 19:14 The **a** of heaven were following him,

ARMOR [ARM]

1Ki 20:11 'One who puts on his **a**
      22:34 between the sections of his **a.**
1Ch 10:10 They put his **a** in the temple
Jer 46: 4 Polish your spears, put on your **a!**
Ro 13:12 of darkness and put on the **a** of light.
Eph 6:11 Put on the full **a** of God so
      6:13 Therefore put on the full **a** of God,

ARMOR-BEARER [ARM]

1Sa 14: 6 Jonathan said to his young **a,**
      31: 4 Saul said to his **a,**

ARMS [ARM]

Ge 16: 5 I put my servant in your **a,**
Dt 33:27 and underneath are the everlasting **a.**
Jdg 16:12 But he snapped the ropes off his **a** as
Ps 18:32 It is God who **a** me with strength
Pr 31:17 her work vigorously; her **a** are strong
      31:20 She opens her **a** to the poor
SS 5:14 His **a** are rods of gold set
Isa 40:11 He gathers the lambs in his **a**
Mk 10:16 And he took the children in his **a,**
Heb 12:12 strengthen your feeble **a**

ARMY [ARM]

Ex 14:17 glory through Pharaoh and all his **a,**
Jos 5:14 as commander of the **a** of the LORD
Ps 33:16 saved by the size of his **a;**
Eze 37:10 stood up on their feet—a vast **a.**
Joel 2: 2 a large and mighty **a** comes,
      2: 5 like a mighty **a** drawn up for battle.
      2:25 the locust swarm— my great **a**
Rev 19:19 the rider on the horse and his **a.**

ARNON

Nu 21:13 The **A** is the border of Moab,
Jer 48:20 by the **A** that Moab is destroyed.

AROMA

Ge 8:21 The LORD smelled the pleasing **a**
Ex 29:18 to the LORD, a pleasing **a,**
Lev 1: 9 an **a** pleasing to the LORD.
Nu 15: 3 as an **a** pleasing to the LORD—
2Co 2:15 For we are to God the **a** of Christ

AROMA PLEASING See PLEASING

PLEASING AROMA See PLEASING

AROUND

Jos 6: 4 march **a** the city seven times,
Ezr 3: 3 Despite their fear of the peoples **a**
      9: 2 the holy race with the peoples **a**
Ps 3: 3 you are a shield **a** me, O LORD;

48:12 Walk about Zion, go **a** her,
Zec 2: 5 I myself will be a wall of fire **a** it,'
Lk 2: 9 the glory of the Lord shone **a** them,
1Pe 5: 8 Your enemy the devil prowls **a** like

AROUSE [ROUSE]

SS 2: 7 not **a** or awaken love until it
Ro 11:14 **a** my own people to envy
1Co 10:22 to **a** the Lord's jealousy?

AROUSED [ROUSE]

Ex 22:24 My anger will be **a,**
Nu 11: 1 when he heard them his anger was **a.**
Ps 78:58 they **a** his jealousy
Hos 11: 8 all my compassion is **a.**
Ro 7: 5 the sinful passions **a** by the law were

ARRANGED

1Co 12:18 But in fact God has **a** the parts in

ARRAYED*

Ps 110: 3 **A** in holy majesty,
Isa 61:10 **a** me in a robe of righteousness.

ARREST [ARRESTED]

Mt 10:19 But when they **a** you,
Mk 14: 1 looking for some sly way to **a** Jesus

ARRESTED [ARREST]

Mt 14: 3 Now Herod had **a** John
      26:50 seized Jesus and **a** him.
Ac 5:18 They **a** the apostles and put them in
      12: 1 King Herod **a** some who belonged
      28:17 I was **a** in Jerusalem and handed

ARROGANCE [ARROGANT]

1Sa 2: 3 or let your mouth speak such **a,**
      15:23 and **a** like the evil of idolatry.
Pr 8:13 I hate pride and **a,**
Jer 48:29 her pride and **a** and the haughtiness
Hos 7:10 Israel's **a** testifies against him,
Mk 7:22 lewdness, envy, slander, **a** and folly.
2Co 12:20 slander, gossip, **a** and disorder.

ARROGANT [ARROGANCE]

Ne 9:16 became **a** and stiff-necked,
Ps 5: 5 The **a** cannot stand in your presence;
      73: 3 For I envied the **a** when I saw
      119:78 May the **a** be put to shame
Pr 17: 7 **A** lips are unsuited to a fool—
      21:24 The proud and **a** man—
Hab 2: 5 indeed, wine betrays him; he is **a**
Zep 3: 4 Her prophets are **a;**
Mal 3:15 But now we call the **a** blessed.
Ro 1:30 God-haters, insolent, **a** and boastful;
      11:20 Do not be **a,** but be afraid.
1Co 4:18 Some of you have become **a,**
1Ti 6:17 rich in this present world not to be **a**
2Pe 2:10 Bold and **a,** these men are not afraid

ARROW [ARROWS]

1Sa 20:36 boy ran, he shot an **a** beyond him.
Ps 91: 5 nor the **a** that flies by day,
Pr 25:18 Like a club or a sword or a sharp **a** is
Jer 9: 8 Their tongue is a deadly **a;**

ARROWS [ARROW]

Dt 32:42 I will make my **a** drunk with blood,
2Ki 13:15 Elisha said, "Get a bow and some **a,**"
Job   6: 4 The **a** of the Almighty are in me,
Ps   38: 2 For your **a** have pierced me,
       64: 3 and aim their words like deadly **a.**
       64: 7 But God will shoot them with **a:**
    127: 4 Like **a** in the hands of a warrior
Pr 26:18 shooting firebrands or deadly **a**
La   3:13 He pierced my heart with **a**
Eph 6:16 the flaming **a** of the evil one.

ARTAXERXES

King of Persia; allowed rebuilding of temple under Ezra (Ezr 4; 7), and of walls of Jerusalem under his cupbearer Nehemiah (Ne 2; 5:14; 13:6).

ARTEMIS

Ac 19:27 temple of the great goddess **A**

ARTS

Ex   7:11 the same things by their secret **a:**
       8:18 to produce gnats by their secret **a,**
Rev 21: 8 those who practice magic **a,**
    22:15 those who practice magic **a,**

ASA

King of Judah (1Ki 15:8-24; 1Ch 3:10; 2Ch 14-16). Godly reformer (2Ch 15); in later years defeated Israel with help of Aram, not the LORD (1Ki 15:16-22; 2Ch 16).

ASAHEL

1. Nephew of David, one of his warriors (2Sa 23:24; 1Ch 2:16; 11:26; 27:7). Killed by Abner (2Sa 2); avenged by Joab (2Sa 3:22-39).

2. Levite; teacher (2Ch 17:8).

ASAPH

1. Recorder to Hezekiah (2Ki 18:18, 37; Isa 36:3, 22).

2. Levitical musician (1Ch 6:39; 15:17-19; 16:4-7, 37). Sons of (1Ch 25; 2Ch 5:12; 20:14; 29:13; 35:15; Ezr 2:41; 3:10; Ne 7:44; 11:17; 12:27-47). Psalms of (2Ch 29:30; Ps 50; 73-83).

ASCEND* [ASCENDED, ASCENDING, ASCENTS]

Dt 30:12 "Who will **a** into heaven to get it
Ps 24: 3 Who may **a** the hill of the LORD?
Isa 14:13 "I will **a** to heaven;
    14:14 I will **a** above the tops of the clouds;
Jn   6:62 What if you see the Son of Man **a** to
Ac   2:34 For David did not **a** to heaven,
Ro 10: 6 'Who will **a** into heaven?' "

ASCENDED [ASCEND]

Ps 47: 5 God has **a** amid shouts of joy,
    68:18 When you **a** on high,
Isa 37:24 'With my many chariots I have **a**
Eph 4: 8 it says: "When he **a** on high,

ASCENDING* [ASCEND]

Ge 28:12 of God were **a** and descending on it.

Eze 41: 7 the temple was built in **a** stages,
Jn   1:51 **a** and descending on the Son of Man.

ASCENTS* [ASCEND]

Songs of ascents (Ps 120-134).

ASCRIBE*

1Ch 16:28 **A** to the LORD,
    16:28 **a** to the LORD glory and strength,
    16:29 **a** to the LORD
Job 36: 3 I will **a** justice to my Maker.
Ps 29: 1 **A** to the LORD, O mighty ones,
    29: 1 **a** to the LORD glory and strength.
    29: 2 **A** to the LORD
    96: 7 **A** to the LORD,
    96: 7 **a** to the LORD glory and strength.
    96: 8 **A** to the LORD

ASH [ASHES]

1Sa 2: 8 and lifts the needy from the **a** heap;
La   4: 5 in purple now lie on **a** heaps.

ASHAMED [SHAME]

Isa 29:22 "No longer will Jacob be **a;**
Jer 48:13 Then Moab will be **a** of Chemosh,
Eze 43:10 that they may be **a** of their sins.
Mk 8:38 If anyone is **a** of me and my words
     8:38 the Son of Man will be **a** of him
Ro 1:16 I am not **a** of the gospel,
    6:21 from the things you are now **a** of?
Php 1:20 and hope that I will in no way be **a,**
2Ti 1: 8 do not be **a** to testify about our Lord,
    1: 8 or **a** of me his prisoner.
    2:15 workman who does not need to be **a**
Tit   2: 8 that those who oppose you may be **a**
Heb 2:11 Jesus is not **a** to call them brothers.
   11:16 God is not **a** to be called their God,

ASHDOD

Jos 13: 3 **A,** Ashkelon, Gath and Ekron—
1Sa 5: 1 they took it from Ebenezer to **A.**
Ne 13:23 of Judah who had married women from **A,**

ASHER

Son of Jacob by Zilpah (Ge 30:13; 35:26; 46:17; Ex 1:4; 1Ch 2:2). Tribe of blessed (Ge 49:20; Dt 33:24-25), numbered (Nu 1:40-41; 26:44-47), allotted land (Jos 10:24-31; Eze 48:2), failed to fully possess (Jdg 1:31-32), failed to support Deborah (Jdg 5:17), supported Gideon (Jdg 6:35; 7:23) and David (1Ch 12:36), 12,000 from (Rev 7:6).

ASHERAH [ASHERAHS]

Ex 34:13 and cut down their **A** poles.
Jdg 6:25 and cut down the **A** pole beside it.
1Ki 14:15 to anger by making **A** poles.
    18:19 and the four hundred prophets of **A,**
2Ch 34: 4 and smashed the **A** poles,

ASHERAHS* [ASHERAH]

Jdg 3: 7 and served the Baals and the **A.**

ASHES [ASH]

Ge 18:27 though I am nothing but dust and **a**,
Est   4: 1 put on sackcloth and **a**,
Job 42: 6 and repent in dust and **a**."
Ps 102: 9 For I eat **a** as my food
Isa 61: 3 a crown of beauty instead of **a**,
Mt 11:21 repented long ago in sackcloth and **a**.

ASHKELON

Jdg   1:18 men of Judah also took Gaza, **A**
2Sa   1:20 proclaim it not in the streets of **A**,

ASHTORETH [ASHTORETHS]

1Ki 11: 5 **A** the goddess of the Sidonians,

ASHTORETHS [ASHTORETH]

Jdg   2:13 and served Baal and the **A**.
1Sa   7: 4 put away their Baals and **A**,

ASIA

Ac   2: 9 and Cappadocia, Pontus and **A**,
     16: 6 the word in the province of **A**.
Rev   1: 4 seven churches in the province of **A**:

ASK [ASKED, ASKS]

Ex 12:26 And when your children **a** you,
Dt 32: 7 **A** your father and he will tell you,
Ps 27: 1 One thing I **a** of the LORD,
Pr 30: 7 "Two things I **a** of you, O LORD;
Isa   7:11 "**A** the LORD your God for a sign,
     65: 1 to those who did not **a** for me;
Mal   1: 2 you **a**, 'How have you loved us?'
Mt   6: 8 you need before you **a** him.
      7: 7 "**A** and it will be given to you;
Mk 11:24 whatever you **a** for in prayer,
Lk 11:13 the Holy Spirit to those who **a** him!"
Jn 14:14 You may **a** me for anything
Eph   3:20 do immeasurably more than all we **a**
Jas   4: 3 When you **a**, you do not receive,
            because you **a** with wrong motives,
1Jn   3:22 and receive from him anything we **a**,

ASKED [ASK]

Ps 106:15 So he gave them what they **a** for,
Lk 22:31 Satan has **a** to sift you as wheat.
Jn 16:24 now you have not **a** for anything

ASKS [ASK]

Lk   6:30 Give to everyone who **a** you,
     11:10 For everyone who **a** receives;
     11:29 It **a** for a miraculous sign,

ASLEEP [SLEEP]

Mk   5:39 The child is not dead but **a**."
     14:37 he said to Peter, "are you **a**?
Jn 11:11 "Our friend Lazarus has fallen **a**;
1Co 15:18 who have fallen **a** in Christ
1Th   4:13 be ignorant about those who fall **a**,

ASSASSINATE [ASSASSINATED]

Est   6: 2 who had conspired to **a** King Xerxes.

ASSASSINATED [ASSASSINATE]

2Ki 21:23 and **a** the king in his palace.

25:25 and **a** Gedaliah and also the men

ASSEMBLE [ASSEMBLED, ASSEMBLY]

Ps 102:22 the kingdoms **a** to worship the LORD.
Zep   3: 8 I have decided to **a** the nations,

ASSEMBLED [ASSEMBLE]

Ne   8: 1 all the people **a** as one man in
Est   9:16 **a** to protect themselves
1Co   5: 4 When you are **a** in the name

ASSEMBLY [ASSEMBLE]

Nu 14:10 whole **a** talked about stoning them.
     16:21 "Separate yourselves from this **a**
Dt 23: 1 may enter the **a** of the LORD.
2Ch 29:28 The whole **a** bowed in worship,
Ps   1: 1 nor sinners in the **a** of the righteous.
     35:18 I will give you thanks in the great **a**;
     82: 1 God presides in the great **a**;
    149: 1 his praise in the **a** of the saints.
Joel   1:14 Declare a holy fast; call a sacred **a**.
Heb 12:22 upon thousands of angels in joyful **a**,

ASSIGNED

1Ki   7:14 and did all the work **a** to him.
Ps 16: 5 you have **a** me my portion
Isa 53: 9 He was **a** a grave with the wicked,
Mk 13:34 each with his **a** task,
1Co   3: 5 as the Lord has **a** to each his task.
      7:17 place in life that the Lord **a** to him
2Co 10:13 to the field God has **a** to us,

ASSIST

Nu   8:26 They may **a** their brothers
Ro 15:24 have you **a** me on my journey

ASSOCIATE

Jos 23: 7 not **a** with these nations that remain
Pr 22:24 do not **a** with one easily angered,
Jn   4: 9 (For Jews do not **a** with Samaritans.)
Ac 10:28 against our law for a Jew to **a** with
Ro 12:16 to **a** with people of low position.
1Co   5: 9 not to **a** with sexually immoral
      5:11 not **a** with anyone who calls himself
2Th   3:14 Do not **a** with him,

ASSURANCE [ASSURED]

Job 24:22 they have no **a** of life.
1Ti   3:13 an excellent standing and great **a**
Heb 10:22 with a sincere heart in full **a** of faith,

ASSURED [ASSURANCE]

Jos   2:14 the men **a** her.
Col   4:12 mature and fully **a**.

ASSYRIA [ASSYRIANS]

Ge 10:11 From that land he went to **A**,
2Ki 15:29 and deported the people to **A**.
     18:11 The king of **A** deported Israel to **A**
     19:10 not be handed over to the king of **A**.'
Isa 30:31 of the LORD will shatter **A**;
Jer 50:18 as I punished the king of **A**.
Hos 14: 3 **A** cannot save us;

KING OF ASSYRIA See KING

ASSYRIANS [ASSYRIA]

Isa 10:24 do not be afraid of the **A,**
Eze 23: 5 she lusted after her lovers, the **A**—

ASTONISHED

Jn   7:21 "I did one miracle, and you are all **a.**
Rev 13: 3 The whole world was **a** and followed

ASTRAY [STRAY]

Nu   5:12 'If a man's wife goes **a**
Dt   17:17 or his heart will be led **a.**
1Ki 11: 3 and his wives led him **a.**
2Ki 21: 9 Manasseh led them **a,**
Ps   58: 3 Even from birth the wicked go **a;**
    119:67 Before I was afflicted I went **a,**
Pr   7:21 With persuasive words she led him **a**
     10:17 ignores correction leads others **a.**
     20: 1 Wine is a mocker and beer **a**
             brawler; whoever is led **a**
Isa 53: 6 We all, like sheep, have gone **a,**
Jer 50: 6 their shepherds have led them **a**
Am   2: 4 they have been led **a** by false gods,
Jn   16: 1 so that you will not go **a.**
Gal   2:13 even Barnabas was led **a.**
1Pe   2:25 For you were like sheep going **a,**
1Jn   3: 7 do not let anyone lead you **a.**
Rev 12: 9 who leads the whole world **a.**

ASTROLOGERS

Isa 47:13 Let your **a** come forward,
Da   2: 2 **a** to tell him what he had dreamed.

ATE [EAT]

Ge   3: 6 she took some and **a** it.
       3:13 "The serpent deceived me, and I **a.**"
      27:25 Jacob brought it to him and he **a;**
Ex   16:35 The Israelites **a** manna forty years,
Nu   25: 2 The people **a** and bowed down
Ru   2:14 She **a** all she wanted
2Sa   9:11 So Mephibosheth **a** at David's table
2Ki   6:29 So we cooked my son and **a** him.
Ezr 10: 6 he **a** no food and drank no water,
Ps   78:25 Men **a** the bread of angels;
Jer 15:16 When your words came, I **a** them;
Eze   3: 3 So I **a** it,
Mt   14:20 They all **a** and were satisfied,
      15:37 They all **a** and were satisfied.
Mk   6:42 They all **a** and were satisfied,
Lk   9:17 They all **a** and were satisfied,
Jn   6:58 Your forefathers **a** manna and died,
1Co 10: 3 They all **a** the same spiritual food
Rev 10:10 scroll from the angel's hand and **a** it.

ATHALIAH

Granddaughter of Omri; wife of Jehoram and
mother of Ahaziah; encouraged their evil ways
(2Ki 8:18, 27; 2Ch 22:2). At death of Ahaziah she
made herself queen, killing all his sons but Joash
(2Ki 11:1-3; 2Ch 22:10-12); killed six years later
when Joash revealed (2Ki 11:4-16; 2Ch 23:1-15).

ATHENS

Ac   17:16 Paul was waiting for them in **A,**

ATHLETE*

2Ti   2: 5 if anyone competes as an **a,**

ATONE* [ATONEMENT]

Ex   30:15 to the LORD to **a** for your lives.
2Ch 29:24 for a sin offering to **a** for all Israel,
Da   9:24 to **a** for wickedness,

ATONED* [ATONEMENT]

Dt   21: 8 And the bloodshed will be **a** for.
1Sa   3:14 guilt of Eli's house will never be **a**
Pr   16: 6 love and faithfulness sin is **a** for;
Isa   6: 7 and your sin **a** for."
     22:14 this sin will not be **a** for,"
     27: 9 then, will Jacob's guilt be **a** for,

ATONEMENT [ATONE, ATONED]

Ex   25:17 "Make an **a** cover of pure gold—
     29:36 Purify the altar by making **a** for it,
     30:10 Once a year Aaron shall make **a**
     32:30 perhaps I can make **a** for your sin."
Lev 17:11 to make **a** for yourselves on the altar;
     17:11 the blood that makes **a** for one's life.
     23:27 seventh month is the Day of **A.**
Nu   25:13 the honor of his God and made **a** for
1Ch   6:49 making **a** for Israel,
Ro   3:25 God presented him as a sacrifice of **a**
Heb   2:17 and that he might make **a** for the sins

ATTACK [ATTACKED, ATTACKS]

1Sa 17:48 the Philistine moved closer to **a** him,
     24: 7 and did not allow them to **a** Saul.
Ps 109: 3 they **a** me without cause.
Isa 54:15 If anyone does **a** you,
Ac   18:10 no one is going to **a** and harm you,
2Ti   4:18 will rescue me from every evil **a**
Rev 11: 7 up from the Abyss will **a** them,

ATTACKED [ATTACK]

Ge   4: 8 Cain **a** his brother Abel
Ex   17: 8 Amalekites came and **a** the Israelites
Est   8: 7 "Because Haman **a** the Jews,

ATTACKS [ATTACK]

Ex   21:15 "Anyone who **a** his father
Lk   11:22 But when someone stronger **a**
Jn   10:12 the wolf **a** the flock and scatters it.

ATTAIN* [ATTAINED, ATTAINING, ATTAINS]

Ps 139: 6 too lofty for me to **a.**
Pr   2:19 to her return or **a** the paths of life.
Gal   3: 3 to **a** your goal by human effort?
Php   3:11 to **a** to the resurrection from

ATTAINED* [ATTAIN]

Pr   16:31 it is **a** by a righteous life.
Ro   9:31 righteousness, has not **a** it.
Php   3:16 up to what we have already **a.**
Heb   7:11 If perfection could have been **a**

ATTAINING* [ATTAIN]

Pr   1: 2 for **a** wisdom and discipline;
Eph   4:13 **a** to the whole measure of

ATTAINS* [ATTAIN]
Pr 11:19 The truly righteous man **a** life,

ATTENDED
Da   7:10 Thousands upon thousands **a** him;
Mt   4:11 and angels came and **a** him.
Mk   1:13 and angels **a** him.

ATTENTION [ATTENTIVE]
Ex   4: 8 or pay **a** to the first miraculous sign,
    15:26 if you pay **a** to his commands
    16:20 some of them paid no **a** to Moses;
Dt 28:13 If you pay **a** to the commands of
1Ki 18:29 no one answered, no one paid **a**.
Ne   8:13 to give **a** to the words of the Law.
Pr   4: 1 to a father's instruction; pay **a**
     4:20 My son, pay **a** to what I say;
     5: 1 My son, pay **a** to my wisdom,
    17: 4 a liar pays **a** to a malicious tongue.
    22:17 Pay **a** and listen to the sayings of
Ecc 7:21 not pay **a** to every word people say,
Isa 42:20 but have paid no **a**;
Jer 44: 5 But they did not listen or pay **a**;
Tit 1:14 and will pay no **a** to Jewish myths or
Heb 2: 1 We must pay more careful **a**,
Jas 2: 3 If you show special **a** to
2Pe 1:19 and you will do well to pay **a** to it,
3Jn 1:10 I will call **a** to what he is doing,

ATTENTIVE [ATTENTION]
2Ch 6:40 your ears **a** to the prayers
Ne   1:11 let your ear be **a** to the prayer
1Pe 3:12 his ears are **a** to their prayer,

ATTITUDE [ATTITUDES]
Ge 31: 2 And Jacob noticed that Laban's **a**
1Ki 11:11 "Since this is your **a** and you have
Ezr 6:22 by changing the **a** of the king of
Da   3:19 and his **a** toward them changed.
Eph 4:23 be made new in the **a** of your minds;
Php 2: 5 Your **a** should be the same as that
1Pe 4: 1 arm yourselves also with the same **a**,

ATTITUDES* [ATTITUDE]
Heb 4:12 the thoughts and **a** of the heart.

ATTRACT* [ATTRACTED, ATTRACTIVE]
Isa 53: 2 He had no beauty or majesty to **a** us

ATTRACTED [ATTRACT]
Est 2:17 Now the king was **a** to Esther more

ATTRACTIVE [ATTRACT]
Tit 2:10 the teaching about God our Savior **a**.

AUDIENCE
2Ch 9:23 of the earth sought **a** with Solomon
Pr 29:26 Many seek an **a** with a ruler,

AUGUSTUS*
Lk   2: 1 In those days Caesar **A** issued

AUL (KJV) See AWL

AUTHOR*
Ac   3:15 You killed the **a** of life,
Heb 2:10 make the **a** of their salvation perfect
    12: 2 the **a** and perfecter of our faith,

AUTHORITIES* [AUTHORITY]
Lk 12:11 before synagogues, rulers and **a**,
Jn   7:26 Have the **a** really concluded that he
           is the Christ?
Ac 16:19 into the marketplace to face the **a**.
Ro 13: 1 submit himself to the governing **a**,
    13: 1 **a** that exist have been established by
    13: 5 it is necessary to submit to the **a**,
    13: 6 for the **a** are God's servants,
Eph 3:10 be made known to the rulers and **a** in
     6:12 but against the rulers, against the **a**,
Col 1:16 or powers or rulers or **a**;
     2:15 having disarmed the powers and **a**,
Tit 3: 1 to be subject to rulers and **a**,
1Pe 3:22 **a** and powers in submission to him.

AUTHORITY [AUTHORITIES]
Jer 5:31 the priests rule by their own **a**,
Da   7: 6 and it was given **a** to rule.
Mt   7:29 because he taught as one who had **a**,
     9: 6 that the Son of Man has **a** on earth
    28:18 "All **a** in heaven and
Mk   1:27 A new teaching— and with **a**!
    10:42 and their high officials exercise **a**
    11:28 what **a** are you doing these things?"
Lk   4:32 because his message had **a**.
     5:24 that the Son of Man has **a** on earth
     7: 8 For I myself am a man under **a**,
Jn 10:18 I have **a** to lay it down and **a** to take
           it up again.
Ac   1: 7 dates the Father has set by his own **a**.
Ro   7: 1 that the law has **a** over a man only
    13: 1 for there is no **a** except
    13: 2 he who rebels against the **a**
1Co 11:10 the woman ought to have a sign of **a**
    15:24 destroyed all dominion, **a** and power.
2Co 10: 8 the **a** the Lord gave us for building
Col 2:10 the head over every power and **a**.
1Ti 2: 2 for kings and all those in **a**,
     2:12 a woman to teach or to have **a** over
Tit 2:15 Encourage and rebuke with all **a**.
Heb 13:17 and submit to their **a**.
1Pe 2:13 the Lord's sake to every **a** instituted
2Pe 2:10 of the sinful nature and despise **a**.
Jude 1: 6 not keep their positions of **a**
Rev 2:27 as I have received **a** from my Father.
    12:10 and the **a** of his Christ.
    13: 4 the dragon because he had given **a** to

AUTUMN*
Dt 11:14 both **a** and spring rains,
Ps 84: 6 the **a** rains also cover it with pools.
Jer 5:24 who gives **a** and spring rains
Joel 2:23 for he has given you the **a** rains
     2:23 both **a** and spring rains, as before.
Jas 5: 7 and how patient he is for the **a**
Jude 1:12 **a** trees, without fruit and uprooted—

AVENGE [VENGEANCE]

Lev 26:25 to **a** the breaking of the covenant.
Dt 32:35 It is mine to **a**; I will repay.
    32:43 he will **a** the blood of his servants;
1Sa 24:12 And may the LORD **a**
2Ki 9: 7 and I will **a** the blood of my servants
Est 8:13 be ready on that day to **a** themselves
Ps 79:10 that you **a** the outpoured blood
Jer 5: 9 "Should I not **a** myself on such
Ro 12:19 "It is mine to **a**;
Heb 10:30 "It is mine to **a**;
Rev 6:10 of the earth and **a** our blood?"

AVENGED [VENGEANCE]

Ge 4:24 If Cain is **a** seven times,
Eze 5:13 and I will be **a**.
Rev 19: 2 He has **a** on her the blood

AVENGER [VENGEANCE]

Nu 35:12 be places of refuge from the **a**,
Jos 20: 3 find protection from the **a** of blood.
Ps 8: 2 to silence the foe and the **a**.

AVENGES* [VENGEANCE]

2Sa 22:48 He is the God who **a** me,
Ps 9:12 For he who **a** blood remembers;
   18:47 He is the God who **a** me,
   94: 1 O LORD, the God who **a**, O God
      who **a**,

AVENGING* [VENGEANCE]

1Sa 25:26 **a** yourself with your own hands,
   25:33 from **a** myself with my own hands.
Na 1: 2 The LORD is a jealous and **a** God;

AVOID [AVOIDS]

Pr 4:15 **A** it, do not travel on it;
   20: 3 It is to a man's honor to **a** strife,
   20:19 A gossip betrays a confidence; so **a**
Ecc 7:18 The man who fears God will **a** all
Ac 15:29 You will do well to **a** these things.
Gal 6:12 to **a** being persecuted for the cross
1Th 4: 3 that you should **a** sexual immorality;
   5:22 **A** every kind of evil.
2Ti 2:16 **A** godless chatter,
Tit 3: 9 But **a** foolish controversies

AVOIDS* [AVOID]

Pr 16: 6 the fear of the LORD a man **a** evil.
   16:17 The highway of the upright **a** evil;

AWAIT [WAIT]

Jer 48:43 Terror and pit and snare **a** you,
Gal 5: 5 But by faith we eagerly **a** through
Php 3:20 we eagerly **a** a Savior from there,

AWAITS [WAIT]

Ps 65: 1 Praise **a** you, O God, in Zion;
Pr 15:10 Stern discipline **a** him who leaves
   28:22 and is unaware that poverty **a** him.
Ecc 3:19 the same fate **a** them both:
Ob 1: 5 what a disaster **a** you—
Hab 2: 3 the revelation **a** an appointed time;

AWAKE [WAKE]

Ps 35:23 **A**, and rise to my defense!
   57: 8 **A**, harp and lyre!
Pr 6:22 when you **a**, they will speak
   20:13 or you will grow poor; stay **a**
Isa 51: 9 **A**, **a**! Clothe yourself with strength,
      O arm of the LORD; **a**, as in days
   52: 1 **A**, **a**, O Zion,
Da 12: 2 sleep in the dust of the earth will **a**:
1Th 5:10 whether we are **a** or asleep,
Rev 16:15 Blessed is he who stays **a**

AWAKEN [WAKE]

Ps 108: 2 I will **a** the dawn.
SS 8: 4 or **a** love until it so desires.

AWARD*

2Ti 4: 8 will **a** to me on that day—

AWARE

Ex 34:29 not **a** that his face was radiant
Nu 15:24 without the community being **a** of it,
Mt 24:50 and at an hour he is not **a** of.
Lk 12:46 and at an hour he is not **a** of.
Gal 4:21 are you not **a** of what the law says?

AWAY

Ge 5:24 because God took him **a**.
   30:23 "God has taken **a** my disgrace."
   31:49 between you and me when we are **a**
Dt 9:12 They have turned **a** quickly
1Sa 28:15 and God has turned **a** from me.
2Sa 12:13 "The LORD has taken **a** your sin.
Ezr 10:19 in pledge to put **a** their wives,
Job 1:21 and the LORD has taken **a**;
Ps 51: 2 Wash **a** all my iniquity
  148: 6 a decree that will never pass **a**.
Pr 14: 7 Stay **a** from a foolish man,
   15: 1 A gentle answer turns **a** wrath,
Ecc 3: 6 a time to keep and a time to throw **a**,
SS 8:14 Come **a**, my lover,
Eze 11:15 'They are far **a** from the LORD;
Jnh 1: 3 But Jonah ran **a** from the LORD
Na 1:12 they will be cut off and pass **a**.
Zep 1: 2 "I will sweep **a** everything from
   3:15 LORD has taken **a** your punishment,
Mk 4:17 they quickly fall **a**.
   13:31 Heaven and earth will pass **a**, but
      my words will never pass **a**.
Lk 24: 2 They found the stone rolled **a** from
Jn 1:29 who takes **a** the sin of the world!
   6:37 comes to me I will never drive **a**.
   14:28 'I am going **a** and I am coming back
1Co 7:31 world in its present form is passing **a**
2Co 3:16 the veil is taken **a**.
1Jn 2:17 The world and its desires pass **a**,
Rev 7:17 And God will wipe **a** every tear

AWE* [AWESOME, OVERAWED]

1Sa 12:18 the people stood in **a** of the LORD
1Ki 3:28 they held the king in **a**,
Job 25: 2 "Dominion and **a** belong to God;
Ps 119:120 I stand in **a** of your laws.
Ecc 5: 7 Therefore stand in **a** of God.

Isa   29:23 will stand in **a** of the God of Israel.
Jer   2:19 your God and have no **a** of me,"
      33: 9 be in **a** and will tremble at
Hab   3: 2 I stand in **a** of your deeds,
Mal   2: 5 and he revered me and stood in **a**
Mt   9: 8 they were filled with **a;**
Lk   1:65 The neighbors were all filled with **a,**
      5:26 They were filled with **a** and said,
      7:16 They were all filled with **a**
Ac   2:43 Everyone was filled with **a,**
Heb 12:28 acceptably with reverence and **a,**

AWESOME* [AWE]

Ge   28:17 "How **a** is this place!
Ex   15:11 **a** in glory, working wonders?
     34:10 how **a** is the work that I,
Dt   4:34 or by great and **a** deeds,
      7:21 is a great and **a** God.
     10:17 is the great God, mighty and **a,**
     10:21 and **a** wonders you saw
     28:58 revere this glorious and **a** name—
     34:12 or performed the **a** deeds
Jdg 13: 6 like an angel of God, very **a.**
2Sa   7:23 and **a** wonders by driving out nations
1Ch 17:21 and **a** wonders by driving out nations
Ne   1: 5 God of heaven, the great and **a** God,
      4:14 who is great and **a,**
      9:32 the great, mighty and **a** God,
Job 10:16 and again display your **a** power
     37:22 God comes in **a** majesty.
Ps   45: 4 right hand display **a** deeds.
     47: 2 How **a** is the LORD Most High,
     65: 5 with **a** deeds of righteousness,
     66: 3 Say to God, "How **a** are your deeds!
     66: 5 how **a** his works in man's behalf!
     68:35 You are **a,** O God, in your sanctuary;
     89: 7 more **a** than all who surround him.
     99: 3 praise your great and **a** name—
    106:22 and **a** deeds by the Red Sea.
    111: 9 holy and **a** is his name.
    145: 6 of the power of your **a** works,
Isa 64: 3 **a** things that we did not expect,
Eze   1:18 Their rims were high and **a,**
      1:22 sparkling like ice, and **a.**
Da   2:31 dazzling statue, **a** in appearance.
      9: 4 the great and **a** God,
Zep   2:11 be **a** to them when he destroys all

AWFUL

Jdg 20: 3 "Tell us how this **a** thing happened."
Ne   9:18 when they committed **a** blasphemies.
Jer 30: 7 How **a** that day will be!

AWL*

Ex   21: 6 and pierce his ear with an **a.**
Dt   15:17 an **a** and push it through his ear lobe

AWOKE [WAKE]

Ge   9:24 When Noah **a** from his wine
     28:16 When Jacob **a** from his sleep,
Jdg 16:20 He **a** from his sleep and thought,
1Ki   3:15 Then Solomon **a**—
Ps   78:65 Then the Lord **a** as from sleep,

AX [AXHEAD]

Ecc 10:10 **a** is dull and its edge unsharpened,
Isa 10:15 Does the **a** raise itself
Mt   3:10 The **a** is already at the root of

AXHEAD* [AX]

2Ki   6: 5 the iron **a** fell into the water.

AZARIAH

  1. King of Judah; see Uzziah (2Ki 15:1-7).
  2. Prophet (2Ch 15:1-8).
  3. Opponent of Jeremiah (Jer 43:2).
  4. Jewish exile; see Abednego (Da 1:6-19).

AZZAH (KJV) See GAZA

B

BAAL [BAAL-BERITH, BAAL-ZEBUB, BAALS]

Nu   25: 3 So Israel joined in worshiping the **B**
Jdg   2:13 and served **B** and the Ashtoreths.
      6:31 If **B** really is a god,
1Ki 16:32 up an altar for **B** in the temple of **B**
     18:25 Elijah said to the prophets of **B,**
     18:18 not bowed down to **B**
2Ki   3: 2 He got rid of the sacred stone of **B**
     10:28 Jehu destroyed **B** worship in Israel.
2Ch 23:17 to the temple of **B** and tore it down.
Jer 19: 5 the high places of **B** to burn their
             sons in the fire as offerings to **B**—
Hos 13: 1 But he became guilty of **B** worship
Ro   11: 4 not bowed the knee to **B.**"

BAAL-BERITH [BAAL]

Jdg   8:33 They set up **B** as their god

BAAL-ZEBUB [BAAL, BEELZEBUB]

2Ki   1: 2 saying to them, "Go and consult **B,**

BAALS [BAAL]

Jdg   3: 7 and served the **B** and the Asherahs.
     10:10 forsaking our God and serving the **B.**
1Sa   7: 4 Israelites put away their **B**
2Ch 17: 3 did not consult the **B**
     34: 4 the altars of the **B** were torn down;

BAASHA

   King of Israel (1Ki 15:16-16:7; 2Ch 16:1-6).

BABBLER* [BABBLING]

Ac   17:18 "What is this **b** trying to say?"

BABBLING* [BABBLER]

Mt   6: 7 do not keep on **b** like pagans,

BABBLINGS (KJV) See CHATTER

BABEL* [BABYLON]

Ge   11: 9 That is why it was called **B**—

BABE, BABES (KJV) See CHILDREN

BABIES* [BABY]

Ge 25:22 The **b** jostled each other within her,
Ex 2: 6 "This is one of the Hebrew **b**,"
Lk 18:15 People were also bringing **b** to Jesus
Ac 7:19 to throw out their newborn **b** so
1Pe 2: 2 newborn **b**, crave pure spiritual milk,

BABY [BABIES, BABY'S]

Ex 2: 6 She opened it and saw the **b**.
     2: 9 "Take this **b** and nurse him for me,
1Ki 3:26 my lord, give her the living **b**!
Isa 49:15 the **b** at her breast
Lk 1:41 the **b** leaped in her womb,
     1:44 the **b** in my womb leaped for joy.
     1:57 for Elizabeth to have her **b**,
     2: 6 the time came for the **b** to be born,
     2:12 You will find a **b** wrapped in cloths
     2:16 Mary and Joseph, and the **b**,
Jn 16:21 but when her **b** is born she forgets

BABY'S* [BABY]

Ex 2: 8 the girl went and got the **b** mother.

BABYLON [BABEL, BABYLONIANS]

Ge 10:10 first centers of his kingdom were **B**,
1Ch 9: 1 to **B** because of their unfaithfulness.
2Ch 36:18 to **B** all the articles from the temple
     36:20 into exile to **B** the remnant,
Ps 137: 1 By the rivers of **B** we sat and wept
Isa 14: 4 this taunt against the king of **B**:
     21: 9 gives back the answer: '**B** has fallen,
Jer 29:10 seventy years are completed for **B**,
     51:34 king of **B** has devoured us,
     51:37 **B** will be a heap of ruins,
Da 4:30 "Is not this the great **B** I have built as
1Pe 5:13 She who is in **B**,
Rev 14: 8 Fallen is **B** the Great,
     17: 5 written on her forehead: MYSTERY **B**
     18: 2 Fallen is **B** the Great!

KING OF BABYLON See KING

BABYLONIANS [BABYLON]

Jer 32: 5 If you fight against the **B**,
     38: 2 whoever goes over to the **B** will live.
Da 1: 4 the language and literature of the **B**.
Hab 1: 6 I am raising up the **B**,

BACK [BACKS, BACKSLIDING, BACKSLIDINGS]

Ge 3:24 a flaming sword flashing **b** and forth
    19:26 But Lot's wife looked **b**,
Ex 22: 7 if he is caught, must pay **b** double.
Ru 1:15 "your sister-in-law is going **b**
     2: 6 "She is the Moabitess who came **b**
1Sa 25:21 He has paid me **b** evil for good.
2Ki 20:11 the LORD made the shadow go **b**
Ps 31:23 but the proud he pays **b** in full.
    51:13 and sinners will turn **b** to you.
    90: 3 You turn men **b** to dust, saying,
Pr 14: 3 A fool's talk brings a rod to his **b**,

SS 6:13 Come **b**, come **b**, O Shulammite;
         come **b**, come **b**,
Isa 38:17 put all my sins behind your **b**.
Jer 29:14 "and will bring you **b** from captivity.
La 3:64 Pay them **b** what they deserve,
Mt 28: 2 rolled the stone and sat on it.
Ro 9:20 O man, to talk **b** to God?
Gal 4: 9 that you are turning **b** to those weak
Eph 4:14 tossed **b** and forth by the waves,
1Th 5:15 that nobody pays **b** wrong for wrong,
Heb 6: 6 to be brought **b** to repentance,
    10:39 But we are not of those who shrink **b**
2Pe 2:22 "A sow that is washed goes **b**

BACKBITING (KJV) See SLANDER

BACKS [BACK]

Ex 23:27 make all your enemies turn their **b**
Ne 9:29 Stubbornly they turned their **b**
Pr 19:29 and beatings for the **b** of fools.
Isa 59:13 turning our **b** on our God,
2Pe 2:21 turn their **b** on the sacred command

BACKSLIDERS, -ING (KJV)

See also FAITHLESS, STUBBORN,
UNFAITHFUL, WAYWARDNESS

BACKSLIDING* [BACK]

Jer 2:19 your **b** will rebuke you.
     3:22 I will cure you of **b**."
    14: 7 For our **b** is great;
    15: 6 "You keep on **b**.
Eze 37:23 save them from all their sinful **b**,

BACKSLIDINGS* [BACK]

Jer 5: 6 and their **b** many.

BAD

Ge 37: 2 and he brought their father a **b** report
Ex 7:21 and the river smelled so **b** that
Nu 13:32 among the Israelites a **b** report about
Ecc 7:14 but when times are **b**, consider:
Isa 5: 2 but it yielded only **b** fruit.
Jer 24: 2 so **b** they could not be eaten.
Mt 7:17 but a **b** tree bears **b** fruit.
    12:33 make a tree **b** and its fruit will be **b**,

BADGERS (KJV) See SEA COWS

BAG

Mic 6:11 with a **b** of false weights?
Lk 10: 4 Do not take a purse or **b** or sandals;
Jn 12: 6 as keeper of the money **b**,

BAKED [BAKER]

Ex 12:39 they **b** cakes of unleavened bread.
Lev 6:17 It must not be **b** with yeast;
Da 2:33 partly of iron and partly of **b** clay.

BAKER [BAKED]

Ge 40: 1 the cupbearer and the **b** of the king

BALAAM

Prophet who attempted to curse Israel (Nu 22-
24; Dt 23:4-5; 2Pe 2:15; Jude 11; Rev 2:14).

Killed in Israel's vengeance on Midianites (Nu 31:8; Jos 13:22).

BALAK

Moabite king who hired Balaam to curse Israel (Nu 22-24; Jos 24:9).

BALANCE

Ps   62: 9 if weighed on a **b,** they are nothing;
Isa 40:12 on the scales and the hills in a **b?**

BALD [BALDHEAD]

Isa   3:17 the LORD will make their scalps **b."**
Mic   1:16 as **b** as the vulture,

BALDHEAD [BALD]

2Ki   2:23 "Go on up, you **b!"**

BALM

Jer   8:22 Is there no **b** in Gilead?

BAN*

1Ch   2: 7 trouble on Israel by violating the **b**

BANDAGED*

Isa   1: 6 not cleansed or **b** or soothed with oil.
Lk 10:34 He went to him and **b** his wounds,

BANDIT [BANDITS]

Pr   6:11 poverty will come on you like a **b**
     23:28 Like a **b** she lies in wait,

BANDITS* [BANDIT]

Ezr   8:31 he protected us from enemies and **b**
Hos   7: 1 **b** rob in the streets;
2Co 11:26 in danger from **b,**

BANISH [BANISHED]

Ecc 11:10 **b** anxiety from your heart
Jer 25:10 I will **b** from them the sounds of joy
Zec 13: 2 I will **b** the names of the idols from

BANISHED [BANISH]

Ge   3:23 So the LORD God **b** him from
Dt   30: 4 Even if you have been **b** to
Jnh   2: 4 'I have been **b** from your sight;

BANK [BANKS]

Ge   41:17 on the **b** of the Nile,
Ex   2: 3 put it among the reeds along the **b**
      7:15 on the **b** of the Nile to meet him,
2Ki   2:13 and stood on the **b** of the Jordan.
Mk   5:13 rushed down the steep **b** into the lake

BANKS [BANK]

Eze 47:12 trees of all kinds will grow on both **b**

BANNER

Ex   17:15 and called it The LORD is my **B.**
SS   2: 4 and his **b** over me is love.
Isa 11:10 the Root of Jesse will stand as a **b** for

BANQUET [BANQUETS]

1Sa 25:36 he was in the house holding a **b**
Est   1: 3 the third year of his reign he gave a **b**

6:14 to the **b** Esther had prepared.
SS   2: 4 He has taken me to the **b** hall,
Isa 25: 6 a **b** of aged wine—
Da   5: 1 a great **b** for a thousand of his nobles
Mt   22: 4 Come to the wedding **b.'**
Lk   14:13 But when you give a **b,**

BANQUETS [BANQUET]

Mk   12:39 and the places of honor at **b.**

BAPTISM* [BAPTIZE]

Mt   21:25 John's **b**—where did it come from?
Mk   1: 4 a **b** of repentance for the forgiveness
     10:38 with the **b** I am baptized with?"
     10:39 be baptized with the **b** I am baptized
     11:30 John's **b**—was it from heaven,
Lk   3: 3 a **b** of repentance for the forgiveness
     12:50 But I have a **b** to undergo,
     20: 4 John's **b**—was it from heaven,
Ac   1:22 beginning from John's **b** to the time
     10:37 after the **b** that John preached—
     13:24 John preached repentance and **b**
     18:25 though he knew only the **b** of John.
     19: 3 "Then what **b** did you receive?"
     19: 3 "John's **b,**" they replied.
     19: 4 "John's **b** was a **b** of repentance.
Ro   6: 4 therefore buried with him through **b**
Eph   4: 5 one Lord, one faith, one **b;**
Col   2:12 with him in **b** and raised with him
1Pe   3:21 and this water symbolizes **b** that

BAPTISMS* [BAPTIZE]

Heb   6: 2 instruction about **b,**

BAPTIST [BAPTIZE]

Mt   3: 1 In those days John the **B** came,
     11:11 anyone greater than John the **B;**
     14: 8 on a platter the head of John the **B."**
     16:14 "Some say John the **B;**

BAPTIZE* [BAPTISM, BAPTISMS, BAPTIST, BAPTIZED, BAPTIZING]

Mt   3:11 "I **b** you with water for repentance.
      3:11 He will **b** you with the Holy Spirit
Mk   1: 8 I **b** you with water,
      1: 8 he will **b** you with the Holy Spirit."
Lk   3:16 "I **b** you with water.
      3:16 He will **b** you with the Holy Spirit
Jn   1:25 "Why then do you **b** if you are not
      1:26 "I **b** with water," John replied,
      1:33 except that the one who sent me to **b**
      1:33 down and remain is he who will **b**
1Co   1:14 I am thankful that I did not **b** any
      1:17 For Christ did not send me to **b,**

BAPTIZED* [BAPTIZE]

Mt   3: 6 they were **b** by him in the Jordan
      3:13 from Galilee to the Jordan to be **b**
      3:14 saying, "I need to be **b** by you,
      3:16 As soon as Jesus was **b,**
Mk   1: 5 they were **b** by him in the Jordan
      1: 9 from Nazareth in Galilee and was **b**
     10:38 the cup I drink or be **b** with the
            baptism I am **b** with?"

	10:39	be **b** with the baptism I am **b**
	16:16	Whoever believes and is **b** will
Lk	3: 7	to the crowds coming out to be **b**
	3:12	Tax collectors also came to be **b.**
	3:21	When all the people were being **b,**
	3:21	Jesus was **b** too.
	7:29	because they had been **b** by John.
	7:30	they had not been **b** by John.)
Jn	3:22	he spent some time with them, and **b.**
	3:23	were constantly coming to be **b.**
	4: 2	in fact it was not Jesus who **b,**
Ac	1: 5	For John **b** with water,
	1: 5	but in a few days you will be **b** with
	2:38	Peter replied, "Repent and be **b,**
	2:41	who accepted his message were **b,**
	8:12	they were **b,** both men and women.
	8:13	Simon himself believed and was **b.**
	8:16	they had simply been **b**
	8:36	Why shouldn't I be **b?"**
	8:38	into the water and Philip **b** him.
	9:18	He got up and was **b,**
	10:47	from being **b** with water?
	10:48	be **b** in the name of Jesus Christ.
	11:16	'John **b** with water, but you will be **b** with the Holy Spirit.'
	16:15	members of her household were **b,**
	16:33	he and all his family were **b.**
	18: 8	who heard him believed and were **b.**
	19: 5	**b** into the name of the Lord Jesus.
	22:16	be **b** and wash your sins away,
Ro	6: 3	that all of us who were **b** into Christ Jesus were **b** into his death?
1Co	1:13	Were you **b** into the name of Paul?
	1:15	so no one can say that you were **b**
	1:16	I also **b** the household of Stephanas,
	1:16	I don't remember if I **b** anyone else.)
	10: 2	They were all **b** into Moses in
	12:13	For we were all **b** by one Spirit
	15:29	who are **b** for the dead?
	15:29	why are people **b** for them?
Gal	3:27	for all of you who were **b**

BAPTIZING* [BAPTIZE]

Mt	3: 7	coming to where he was **b,**
	28:19	**b** them in the name of the Father and
Mk	1: 4	**b** in the desert region and preaching
Jn	1:28	where John was **b.**
	1:31	the reason I came **b** with water was
	3:23	John also was **b** at Aenon near Salim
	3:26	is **b,** and everyone is going to him."
	4: 1	that Jesus was gaining and **b** more
	10:40	the place where John had been **b** in

BAR [BARRED]

Jdg 16: 3 and tore them loose, **b** and all.

BAR-JESUS*

Ac 13: 6 sorcerer and false prophet named **B,**

BARABBAS*

Prisoner released by Pilate instead of Jesus (Mt 27:16-26; Mk 15:7-15; Lk 23:18-19; Jn 18:40).

BARAK*

Judge who fought with Deborah against Canaanites (Jdg 4-5; 1Sa 12:11; Heb 11:32).

BARBARIAN*

Col 3:11 circumcised or uncircumcised, **b,**

BARBARIANS (KJV) See FOREIGNER

BARBS*

Nu 33:55 to remain will become **b** in your eyes

BARE [BAREFOOT, BARELY, BARREN]

Jdg	14: 6	the lion apart with his **b** hands
Isa	52:10	The LORD will lay **b** his holy arm
Eze	16: 7	you who were naked and **b.**
	23:29	They will leave you naked and **b,**
1Co	14:25	the secrets of his heart will be laid **b.**
Heb	4:13	Everything is uncovered and laid **b**
2Pe	3:10	and everything in it will be laid **b.**

BAREFOOT [BARE, FOOT]

| Isa | 20: 3 | Isaiah has gone stripped and **b** |
| Mic | 1: 8 | I will go about **b** and naked. |

BARGAIN

Isa 36: 8 make a **b** with my master,

BARK

| Ge | 30:37 | stripes on them by peeling the **b** |
| Ex | 11: 7 | among the Israelites not a dog will **b** |

BARLEY

Ru	1:22	as the **b** harvest was beginning.
2Ki	7: 1	and two seahs of **b** for a shekel
Jn	6: 9	a boy with five small **b** loaves
Rev	6: 6	three quarts of **b** for a day's wages,

BARN [BARNS]

| Hag | 2:19 | Is there yet any seed left in the **b?** |
| Lk | 3:17 | and to gather the wheat into his **b,** |

BARNABAS

Disciple, originally Joseph (Ac 4:36), prophet (Ac 13:1), apostle (Ac 14:14). Brought Paul to apostles (Ac 9:27), Antioch (Ac 11:22-29; Gal 2:1-13), on the first missionary journey (Ac 13-14). Together at Jerusalem Council, they separated over John Mark (Ac 15). Later co-workers (1Co 9:6; Col 4:10).

BARNS* [BARN]

Dt	28: 8	a blessing on your **b** and
Ps	144:13	Our **b** will be filled with every kind
Pr	3:10	your **b** will be filled to overflowing,
Mt	6:26	not sow or reap or store away in **b,**
Lk	12:18	down my **b** and build bigger ones,

BARRED [BAR]

| Pr | 18:19 | and disputes are like the **b** gates of |
| Jnh | 2: 6 | the earth beneath **b** me in forever. |

BARREN [BARE]

| Ge | 11:30 | Sarai was **b;** she had no children. |
| | 25:21 | because she was **b.** |

29:31 but Rachel was **b.**
Ex   23:26 and none will miscarry or be **b**
1Sa   2: 5 who was **b** has borne seven children,
Ps 113: 9 He settles the **b** woman in her home
Isa 54: 1 "Sing, O **b** woman,
Lk   1: 7 because Elizabeth was **b;**
      23:29 'Blessed are the **b** women,
Gal   4:27 it is written: "Be glad, O **b** woman,
Heb 11:11 and Sarah herself was **b—**

BARRIER*

Jer   5:22 an everlasting **b** it cannot cross.
Eph   2:14 the two one and has destroyed the **b,**

BARSABBAS*

Ac   1:23 proposed two men: Joseph called **B**
     15:22 They chose Judas (called **B**)

BARTER*

Job   6:27 and **b** away your friend.
      41: 6 Will traders **b** for him?
La   1:11 they **b** their treasures for food

BARTHOLOMEW*

Apostle (Mt 10:3; Mk 3:18; Lk 6:14; Ac 1:13).
Possibly also called Nathanael (Jn 1:45-49; 21:2).

BARTIMAEUS*

Blind man healed by Jesus (Mk 10:46-52).

BARUCH

Jeremiah's secretary (Jer 32:12-16; 36; 43:1-6;
45:1-2).

BARZILLAI

1. Gileadite who aided David during Absalom's
revolt (2Sa 17:27; 19:31-39).
2. Son-in-law of 1. (Ezr 2:61; Ne 7:63).

BASE [BASIC, BASING, BASIS]

Ex   29:12 and pour out the rest of it at the **b** of
Job 30: 8 A **b** and nameless brood,

BASHAN

Nu   21:33 and Og king of **B**
Jos 13:30 the entire realm of Og king of **B—**
      22: 7 Moses had given land in **B,**
Ps   22:12 strong bulls of **B** encircle me.
Am   4: 1 you cows of **B** on Mount Samaria,

BASIC* [BASE]

Gal   4: 3 under the **b** principles of the world.
Col   2: 8 and the **b** principles of this world
      2:20 to the **b** principles of this world,

BASIN [WASHBASIN]

Ex   30:18 "Make a bronze **b,**
1Ki   7:30 had a **b** resting on four supports,
Jn   13: 5 he poured water into a **b** and began

BASING [BASE]

Isa 36: 4 On what are you **b** this confidence

BASIS [BASE]

Da   6: 5 "We will never find any **b**

Jn   18:38 "I find no **b** for a charge against him.
Phm   1: 9 yet I appeal to you on the **b** of love.

BASKET [BASKETFULS, BASKETS]

Ex   2: 3 a papyrus **b** for him and coated it
Dt   28: 5 Your **b** and your kneading trough
Isa 40:12 held the dust of the earth in a **b,**
Am   8: 1 a **b** of ripe fruit.
Zec   5: 6 He replied, "It is a measuring **b.**"
Ac   9:25 and lowered him in a **b**
2Co 11:33 in a **b** from a window in the wall

BASKETFULS [BASKET]

Mt   14:20 and the disciples picked up twelve **b**
     15:37 the disciples picked up seven **b**
     16: 9 and how many **b** you gathered?

BASKETS [BASKET]

Mt   13:48 and collected the good fish in **b,**

BATCH*

Ro   11:16 then the whole **b** is holy;
1Co   5: 6 through the whole **b** of dough?
      5: 7 be a new **b** without yeast—
Gal   5: 9 through the whole **b** of dough."

BATH [BATHE]

Eze 45:10 an accurate ephah and an accurate **b.**
Jn   13:10 a **b** needs only to wash his feet;

BATHE [BATH, BATHED, BATHING]

Ex   2: 5 went down to the Nile to **b,**
Dt   33:24 and let him **b** his feet in oil.
Ps   58:10 when they **b** their feet in the blood of

BATHED [BATHE]

Isa 34: 6 sword of the LORD is **b** in blood,
Eze 16: 9 " 'I **b** you with water and washed

BATHING [BATHE]

2Sa 11: 2 From the roof he saw a woman **b.**

BATHSHEBA

Wife of Uriah who committed adultery with and
became wife of David (2Sa 11; Ps 51), mother of
Solomon (2Sa 12:24; 1Ki 1-2; 1Ch 3:5).

BATTLE [BATTLEMENTS, BATTLES]

Ex   13:18 went up out of Egypt armed for **b.**
Jos   4:13 for **b** crossed over before the LORD
1Sa 17:47 for the **b** is the LORD's,
2Sa   1:25 "How the mighty have fallen in **b!**
     22:35 He trains my hands for **b;**
1Ki 22:30 "I will enter the **b** in disguise,
2Ch 20:15 For the **b** is not yours, but God's.
Ps   24: 8 the LORD mighty in **b.**
Ecc   9:11 or the **b** to the strong,
Isa 31: 4 down to do **b** on Mount Zion and
Eze 13: 5 so that it will stand firm in the **b**
Hos   1: 7 not by bow, sword or **b,**
      2:18 Bow and sword and **b** I will abolish
Ob   1: 1 "Rise, and let us go against her for **b**
Jas   4: 1 from your desires that **b** within you?
Rev 16:14 to gather them for the **b** on
     20: 8 to gather them for **b.**

BATTLEMENTS* [BATTLE]

Isa 54:12 I will make your **b** of rubies,

BATTLES* [BATTLE]

1Sa 8:20 to go out before us and fight our **b."**
18:17 and fight the **b** of
25:28 because he fights the LORD's **b.**
2Ch 32: 8 to help us and to fight our **b."**

BEAM* [BEAMS]

Ezr 6:11 a **b** is to be pulled from his house

BEAMS [BEAM]

1Ki 6: 9 roofing it with **b** and cedar planks.
Ne 3: 3 They laid its **b** and put its doors
Jer 22: 7 they will cut up your fine cedar **b**
Zep 2:14 the **b** of cedar will be exposed.

BEAR [AFTERBIRTH, BEARABLE,
BEARING, BEARS, BIRTH,
BIRTHRIGHT, BORE, BORN,
CHILDBEARING, CHILDBIRTH,
FIRSTBORN, NATIVE-BORN,
NEWBORN, REBIRTH]

Ge 4:13 My punishment is more than I can **b.**
17:19 but your wife Sarah will **b** you a son,
Ex 28:12 to **b** the names on his shoulders as
1Sa 17:36 killed both the lion and the **b;**
Job 9: 9 He is the Maker of the **B** and Orion,
Ps 38: 4 like a burden too heavy to **b.**
92:14 They will still **b** fruit in old age,
Pr 17:12 Better to meet a **b** robbed of her cubs
Isa 11: 1 from his roots a Branch will **b** fruit.
11: 7 The cow will feed with the **b,**
53:11 and he will **b** their iniquities.
Jer 14: 9 O LORD, and we **b** your name;
Eze 14:10 They will **b** their guilt—
Da 7: 5 which looked like a **b.**
Am 5:19 fled from a lion only to meet a **b,**
Mt 7:18 A good tree cannot **b** bad fruit, and a
bad tree cannot **b** good fruit.
Lk 1:13 Your wife Elizabeth will **b** you a son
1:42 and blessed is the child you will **b!**
Jn 15: 2 branch that does **b** fruit he prunes
15: 8 that you **b** much fruit,
15:16 to go and **b** fruit—
Ro 7: 4 in order that we might **b** fruit to God.
15: 1 to **b** with the failings of the weak
1Co 10:13 be tempted beyond what you can **b.**
15:49 so shall we **b** the likeness of the man
Gal 6:17 I **b** on my body the marks of Jesus.
Col 3:13 **B** with each other
1Pe 4:16 but praise God that you **b** that name.
Rev 13: 2 but had feet like those of a **b**

BEARABLE [BEAR]

Mt 10:15 be more **b** for Sodom and Gomorrah

BEARD

Lev 19:27 or clip off the edges of your **b.**
Isa 50: 6 to those who pulled out my **b;**
Jer 48:37 and every **b** cut off;

BEARING [BEAR]

Ge 1:12 produced vegetation: plants **b** seed
Nu 13:23 a branch **b** a single cluster of grapes.
Pr 30:29 four that move with stately **b:**
Joel 2:22 The trees are **b** their fruit;
Ro 2:15 their consciences also **b** witness,
Eph 4: 2 **b** with one another in love.
Col 1: 6 over the world this gospel is **b** fruit
1:10 **b** fruit in every good work,
Heb 13:13 **b** the disgrace he bore.
Rev 22: 2 **b** twelve crops of fruit,

BEARS [BEAR]

Ge 49:21 a doe set free that **b** beautiful fawns.
1Ki 8:43 this house I have built **b** your Name.
2Ki 2:24 Then two **b** came out of the woods
Ps 68:19 who daily **b** our burdens.
Jer 7:11 Has this house, which **b** my Name,
Da 9:18 of the city that **b** your Name.
Gal 4:24 and **b** children who are to be slaves:
1Pe 2:19 a man **b** up under the pain of unjust

BEAST [BEASTS]

Ps 36: 6 you preserve both man and **b.**
Isa 35: 9 nor will any ferocious **b** get up on it;
Da 7: 6 This **b** had four heads,
Jnh 3: 8 man and **b** be covered with sackcloth
Rev 11: 7 the **b** that comes up from
13: 1 And I saw a **b** coming out of the sea.
13: 2 The **b** I saw resembled a leopard,
13: 2 The dragon gave the **b** his power
13:11 Then I saw another **b,**
13:18 calculate the number of the **b,**
16: 2 the people who had the mark of the **b**
17: 3 a scarlet **b** that was covered
19:20 who had received the mark of the **b**
20: 4 not worshiped the **b** or his image

BEASTS [BEAST]

Ge 2:19 formed out of the ground all the **b**
Lev 26: 6 will remove savage **b** from the land,
Jer 12: 9 Go and gather all the wild **b;**
Eze 5:17 I will send famine and wild **b**
Da 7: 3 Four great **b,** each different
1Co 15:32 I fought wild **b** in Ephesus
2Pe 2:12 They are like brute **b,**
Rev 6: 8 and by the wild **b** of the earth.

BEAT [BEATEN, BEATING, BEATINGS,
BEATS]

Dt 24:20 you **b** the olives from your trees,
Ne 13:25 I **b** some of the men
Ps 78:66 He **b** back his enemies;
Pr 23:35 They **b** me, but I don't feel it!
SS 5: 7 They **b** me, they bruised me;
Isa 2: 4 They will **b** their swords
Joel 3:10 **B** your plowshares into swords
Mic 4: 3 They will **b** their swords
Mt 7:25 winds blew and **b** against that house;
Ac 22:19 to imprison and **b** those who believe
1Co 9:27 I **b** my body and make it my slave so

BEATEN [BEAT]

Ex	5:16	Your servants are being **b,**
Nu	22:32	you **b** your donkey these three times?
Jer	20: 2	he had Jeremiah the prophet **b**
Lk	12:48	be **b** with few blows.
Ac	16:22	to be stripped and **b.**
2Co	6: 9	**b,** and yet not killed;
	11:25	Three times I was **b** with rods,

BEATING [BEAT]

Ex	2:11	He saw an Egyptian **b** a Hebrew,
1Co	9:26	not fight like a man **b** the air.
1Pe	2:20	a **b** for doing wrong and endure it?

BEATINGS [BEAT]

Pr	19:29	and **b** for the backs of fools.

BEATS* [BEAT]

Ex	21:20	"If a man **b** his male or female slave

BEAUTIFUL* [BEAUTY]

Ge	6: 2	that the daughters of men were **b,**
	12:11	"I know what a **b** woman you are.
	12:14	that she was a very **b** woman.
	24:16	The girl was very **b,** a virgin;
	26: 7	because she is **b."**
	29:17	Rachel was lovely in form, and **b.**
	49:21	a doe set free that bears **b** fawns.
Nu	24: 5	"How **b** are your tents,
Dt	21:11	a **b** woman and are attracted to her,
Jos	7:21	the plunder a **b** robe from Babylonia,
1Sa	25: 3	She was an intelligent and **b** woman,
2Sa	11: 2	The woman was very **b,**
	13: 1	the **b** sister of Absalom son of David.
	14:27	and she became a **b** woman.
1Ki	1: 3	for a **b** girl and found Abishag.
	1: 4	The girl was very **b;**
Est	2: 2	a search be made for **b** young virgins
	2: 3	bring all these **b** girls into the harem
Job	38:31	"Can you bind the **b** Pleiades?
	42:15	women as **b** as Job's daughters.
Ps	48: 2	It is **b** in its loftiness,
Pr	11:22	a **b** woman who shows no discretion.
	24: 4	with rare and **b** treasures.
Ecc	3:11	He has made everything **b** in its time.
SS	1: 8	you do not know, most **b** of women,
	1:10	Your cheeks are **b** with earrings,
	1:15	How **b** you are, my darling! Oh, how **b!**
	2:10	"Arise, my darling, my **b** one,
	2:13	Arise, come, my darling; my **b** one,
	4: 1	How **b** you are, my darling! Oh, how **b!**
	4: 7	All **b** you are, my darling;
	5: 9	most **b** of women?
	6: 1	most **b** of women?
	6: 4	You are **b,** my darling, as Tirzah,
	7: 1	How **b** your sandaled feet,
	7: 6	How **b** you are and how pleasing,
Isa	4: 2	the Branch of the LORD will be **b**
	28: 5	a **b** wreath for the remnant
	52: 7	How **b** on the mountains are the feet
Jer	3:19	the most **b** inheritance of any nation.
	6: 2	so **b** and delicate.
	11:16	a thriving olive tree with fruit **b**
	46:20	"Egypt is a **b** heifer,
Eze	7:20	proud of their **b** jewelry
	16: 7	and became the most **b** of jewels.
	16:12	earrings on your ears and a **b** crown
	16:13	You became very **b** and rose to be
	20: 6	the most **b** of all lands.
	20:15	most **b** of all lands—
	23:42	and **b** crowns on their heads.
	27:24	with you **b** garments,
	31: 3	with **b** branches overshadowing
	31: 9	I made it **b** with abundant branches,
	33:32	with a **b** voice and plays
Da	4:12	Its leaves were **b,** its fruit abundant,
	4:21	with **b** leaves and abundant fruit,
	8: 9	to the east and toward the **B** Land.
	11:16	establish himself in the **B** Land
	11:41	He will also invade the **B** Land.
	11:45	the seas at the **b** holy mountain.
Zec	9:17	How attractive and **b** they will be!
Mt	23:27	which look **b** on the outside but on
	26:10	She has done a **b** thing to me.
Mk	14: 6	She has done a **b** thing to me.
Lk	21: 5	temple was adorned with **b** stones
Ac	3: 2	to the temple gate called **B,**
	3:10	at the temple gate called **B,**
Ro	10:15	"How **b** are the feet
1Pe	3: 5	in God used to make themselves **b.**

BEAUTIFULLY* [BEAUTY]

Rev	21: 2	as a bride **b** dressed for her husband.

BEAUTY* [BEAUTIFUL, BEAUTIFULLY]

Est	1:11	to display her **b** to the people
	2: 3	and let **b** treatments be given
	2: 9	with her **b** treatments
	2:12	of **b** treatments prescribed for
Ps	27: 4	to gaze upon the **b** of the LORD and
	37:20	be like the **b** of the fields,
	45:11	The king is enthralled by your **b;**
	50: 2	From Zion, perfect in **b,**
Pr	6:25	Do not lust in your heart after her **b**
	31:30	Charm is deceptive, and **b** is fleeting;
Isa	3:24	sackcloth; instead of **b,**
	28: 1	to the fading flower, his glorious **b,**
	28: 4	That fading flower, his glorious **b,**
	33:17	Your eyes will see the king in his **b**
	53: 2	He had no **b** or majesty to attract us
	61: 3	a crown of **b** instead of ashes,
La	2:15	that was called the perfection of **b,**
Eze	16:14	the nations on account of your **b,**
	16:14	I had given you made your **b** perfect,
	16:15	" 'But you trusted in your **b**
	16:15	and your **b** became his.
	16:25	and degraded your **b,**
	27: 3	O Tyre, "I am perfect in **b."**
	27: 4	your builders brought your **b**
	27:11	they brought your **b**
	28: 7	against your **b** and wisdom
	28:12	full of wisdom and perfect in **b.**
	28:17	proud on account of your **b,**
	31: 7	It was majestic in **b,**
	31: 8	the garden of God could match its **b.**
Jas	1:11	and its **b** is destroyed.

1Pe 3: 3 Your **b** should not come
     3: 4 the unfading **b** of a gentle

BECAME [BECOME]

Ge   2: 7 and the man **b** a living being.
Ex   7:10 and it **b** a snake.
     15:25 and the water **b** sweet.
Lev 18:27 and the land **b** defiled.
Jdg 8:27 it **b** a snare to Gideon and his family.
2Ki 17:15 and themselves **b** worthless.
1Ch 11: 9 David **b** more and more powerful,
2Ch 17:12 Jehoshaphat **b** more and more
     26:16 But after Uzziah **b** powerful,
Jn   1:14 The Word **b** flesh
1Co 9:20 To the Jews I **b** like a Jew,
2Co 8: 9 yet for your sakes he **b** poor,

BECOME [BECAME]

Ge   2:24 and they will **b** one flesh.
     9:15 Never again will the waters **b** a flood
Dt   8:14 then your heart will **b** proud
Jdg 16: 7 I'll **b** as weak as any other man."
Ps   2: 7 today I have **b** your Father.
Lk   4: 3 tell this stone to **b** bread."
Jn   1:12 the right to **b** children of God—
     3:30 He must **b** greater; I must **b** less.
Ac   4:11 which has **b** the capstone.'
Rev 11:15 "The kingdom of the world has **b**

BED [BEDS, SICKBED]

Ge   39: 7 "Come to **b** with me!"
     48: 2 and sat up on the **b**.
2Sa 13:11 "Come to **b** with me, my sister."
1Ki 1:47 the king bowed in worship on his **b**
Ps   36: 4 Even on his **b** he plots evil;
     41: 3 and restore him from his **b**
Pr   26:14 so a sluggard turns on his **b**.
SS   1:16 And our **b** is verdant.
Isa 28:20 The **b** is too short to stretch out on,
Mt   8:14 in **b** with a fever.
Lk   11: 7 and my children are with me in **b**.
     17:34 two people will be in one **b**;
Heb 13: 4 and the marriage **b** kept pure,
Rev 2:22 So I will cast her on a **b** of suffering,

BEDS [BED]

Mic 2: 1 to those who plot evil on their **b**!
Ac   5:15 and laid them on **b** and mats so that

BEELZEBUB* [BAAL-ZEBUB]

Mt   10:25 head of the house has been called **B**,
     12:24 they said, "It is only by **B**,
     12:27 And if I drive out demons by **B**,
Mk   3:22 "He is possessed by **B**!
Lk   11:15 But some of them said, "By **B**,
     11:18 that I drive out demons by **B**.
     11:19 Now if I drive out demons by **B**,

BEER

1Sa 1:15 I have not been drinking wine or **b**;
Pr   20: 1 Wine is a mocker and **b** a brawler;
     31: 4 not for rulers to crave **b**,
     31: 6 Give **b** to those who are perishing,
Isa 24: 9 the **b** is bitter to its drinkers.

28: 7 from wine and reel from **b**:
28: 7 and prophets stagger from **b**
29: 9 stagger, but not from **b**.
56:12 Let us drink our fill of **b**!
Mic 2:11 for you plenty of wine and **b**,"

BEERSHEBA

Ge   21:14 and wandered in the desert of **B**.
     21:33 planted a tamarisk tree in **B**,
     22:19 And Abraham stayed in **B**.
     46: 1 and when he reached **B**,
Jdg 20: 1 Then all the Israelites from Dan to **B**
1Sa 3:20 from Dan to **B** recognized
2Sa 3:10 over Israel and Judah from Dan to **B**.
     17:11 from Dan to **B**—
     24: 2 of Israel from Dan to **B** and enroll
     24:15 of the people from Dan to **B** died.
1Ki 4:25 from Dan to **B**, lived in safety,
1Ch 21: 2 count the Israelites from **B** to Dan.
2Ch 30: 5 from **B** to Dan,
Am   8:14 'As surely as the god of **B** lives'—

BEES*

Dt   1:44 like a swarm of **b** and beat you down
Jdg 14: 8 a swarm of **b** and some honey,
Ps   118:12 They swarmed around me like **b**,
Isa 7:18 and for **b** from the land of Assyria.

BEFALL* [BEFALLS]

Job 5:19 in seven no harm will **b** you.
Ps   91:10 then no harm will **b** you,

BEFALLS* [BEFALL]

Pr   12:21 No harm **b** the righteous,

BEFORE [BEFOREHAND]

Ge   10: 9 a mighty hunter **b** the LORD;
     18:22 but Abraham remained standing **b**
     24:15 **B** he had finished praying,
     27: 4 I may give you my blessing **b** I die."
Ex   4:21 that you perform **b** Pharaoh all
     9:11 The magicians could not stand **b**
     20: 3 "You shall have no other gods **b** me.
     32: 1 make us gods who will go **b** us.
     33: 2 I will send an angel **b** you
Lev 10: 2 and they died **b** the LORD.
Nu   17: 7 Moses placed the staffs **b** the LORD
Dt   7:22 God will drive out those nations **b**
     11:26 I am setting **b** you today a blessing
     30:15 I set **b** you today life and prosperity,
1Sa 4: 7 Nothing like this has happened **b**.
Ps   139: 4 **B** a word is on my tongue
Pr   8:23 **b** the world began.
     16:18 Pride goes **b** destruction,
     18:12 but humility comes **b** honor.
     18:13 He who answers **b** listening—
Isa 43:10 **B** me no god was formed,
     48: 5 I told you these things long ago; **b**
     65:24 **B** they call I will answer;
Mt   6: 8 your Father knows what you need **b**
     11:10 who will prepare your way **b** you.'
     24:38 For in the days **b** the flood,
Lk   22:34 Peter, **b** the rooster crows today,
Jn   8:58 "**b** Abraham was born, I am!"

13:19 "I am telling you now **b** it happens,
17: 5 with the glory I had with you **b**
Col   1:17 He is **b** all things,
Tit   1: 2 promised **b** the beginning of time,
1Pe   1:20 He was chosen **b** the creation of

BEFOREHAND [BEFORE]

Mk   13:11 do not worry **b** about what to say.
Ac   4:28 will had decided **b** should happen.
Ro   1: 2 the gospel he promised **b**

BEG [BEGGAR, BEGGARS, BEGGED, BEGGING]

La   4: 4 the children **b** for bread,
Lk   16: 3 and I'm ashamed to **b**—
Ac   3: 2 where he was put every day to **b**

BEGGAR [BEG]

Lk   16:20 a **b** named Lazarus,
Ac   3:11 the **b** held on to Peter and John,

BEGGED [BEG]

Mt   8:31 The demons **b** Jesus,
Mk   6:56 They **b** him to let them touch even

BEGGING [BEG]

Ps   37:25 or their children **b** bread.
Ac   16: 9 of Macedonia standing and **b** him,

BEGINNING

Ge   1: 1 In the **b** God created the heavens and
Ps   102:25 In the **b** you laid the foundations of
     111:10 fear of the LORD is the **b** of wisdom;
Pr   1: 7 fear of the LORD is the **b** of knowledge,
      9:10 fear of the LORD is the **b** of wisdom,
Ecc   3:11 what God has done from **b** to end.
      7: 8 end of a matter is better than its **b**,
Isa 40:21 Has it not been told you from the **b**?
     46:10 I make known the end from the **b**,
Da   12: 1 not happened from the **b** of nations
Mt   19: 8 But it was not this way from the **b**.
     24: 8 All these are the **b** of birth pains.
     24:21 distress, unequaled from the **b** of the
Mk   1: 1 **b** of the gospel about Jesus Christ,
Lk   1: 3 investigated everything from the **b**,
Jn   1: 1 In the **b** was the Word,
      8:44 He was a murderer from the **b**,
     15:27 you have been with me from the **b**.
Ac   1:22 **b** from John's baptism to the time
Gal   3: 3 After **b** with the Spirit,
Heb   7: 3 without **b** of days or end of life,
2Pe   2:20 at the end than they were at the **b**.
1Jn   1: 1 That which was from the **b**,
      3: 8 devil has been sinning from the **b**.
2Jn   1: 6 As you have heard from the **b**,
Rev 21: 6 the **B** and the End.
     22:13 the **B** and the End.

BEHALF

Ge   25:21 Isaac prayed to the LORD on **b**
Lev 22:19 that it may be accepted on your **b**.
     22:20 it will not be accepted on your **b**.
1Sa 14: 6 Perhaps the LORD will act in our **b**.

2Sa 24:25 the LORD answered prayer in **b** of
Ps   66: 5 how awesome his works in man's **b**!
Jn   8:14 "Even if I testify on my own **b**,
     16:26 that I will ask the Father on your **b**.

BEHAVE [BEHAVIOR]

Ro   13:13 Let us **b** decently, as in the daytime,

BEHAVIOR [BEHAVE]

Col   1:21 in your minds because of your evil **b**.
1Pe   3: 1 be won over without words by the **b**
      3:16 against your good **b** in Christ

BEHEADED

Lk   9: 9 But Herod said, "I **b** John.
Rev 20: 4 the souls of those who had been **b**

BEHEMOTH*

Job 40:15 "Look at the **b**,

BEHIND

Mt   16:23 "Get **b** me, Satan!
Mk   14:52 he fled naked, leaving his garment **b**.
Lk   2:43 the boy Jesus stayed **b** in Jerusalem,
1Co 13:11 I put childish ways **b** me.
Php   3:13 one thing I do: Forgetting what is **b**
1Ti   5:24 the sins of others trail **b** them.

BEHOLD*

Nu   24:17 "I see him, but not now; I **b** him,
Isa 65:17 "**B**, I will create new heavens and
Rev   1:18 and **b** I am alive for ever and ever!
     16:15 "**B**, I come like a thief!
     22: 7 "**B**, I am coming soon!
     22:12 "**B**, I am coming soon!

BEING [BE, BEINGS]

Ge   2: 7 and the man became a living **b**.
Job 10:19 If only I had never come into **b**,
Ps 103: 1 O my soul, all my inmost **b**,
    139:13 For you created my inmost **b**;
Pr   23:16 my inmost **b** will rejoice
1Co 15:45 Adam became a living **b**";
Eph   3:16 through his Spirit in your inner **b**,
Php   2: 6 **b** in very nature God,
Rev   4:11 created and have their **b**."

BEINGS* [BEING]

Ps   8: 5 a little lower than the heavenly **b**
     89: 6 the LORD among the heavenly **b**?
2Pe   2:10 not afraid to slander celestial **b**;
      2:11 accusations against such **b**
Jude 1: 8 and slander celestial **b**.

BEL

Isa 46: 1 **B** bows down, Nebo stoops low;

BELIAL*

2Co   6:15 is there between Christ and **B**?

BELIEVE [BELIEVED, BELIEVER, BELIEVERS, BELIEVES, BELIEVING]

Ex   4: 1 "What if they do not **b** me or listen
      4: 5 so that they may **b** that the LORD,
Nu   14:11 How long will they refuse to **b** in me

1Ki 10: 7 not **b** these things until I came
2Ch 32:15 Do not **b** him,
Ps 78:32 they did not **b.**
119:66 for I **b** in your commands.
Isa 43:10 so that you may know and **b** me
Hab 1: 5 in your days that you would not **b,**
Mt 9:28 "Do you **b** that I am able to do this?"
18: 6 of these little ones who **b** in me
21:22 If you **b,** you will receive
24:23 do not **b** it.
27:42 and we will **b** in him.
Mk 1:15 Repent and **b** the good news!"
5:36 "Don't be afraid; just **b."**
9:24 "I do **b.**
9:42 of these little ones who **b** in me
11:24 **b** that you have received it,
15:32 that we may see and **b."**
16:16 but whoever does not **b** will
16:17 signs will accompany those who **b:**
Lk 8:12 so that they may not **b** and be saved.
8:13 They **b** for a while,
8:50 to Jairus, "Don't be afraid; just **b,**
22:67 "If I tell you, you will not **b** me,
24:11 But they did not **b** the women,
24:25 and how slow of heart to **b** all that
Jn 1: 7 so that through him all men might **b.**
3:12 of earthly things and you do not **b;**
3:18 not **b** stands condemned already
4:21 Jesus declared, **"B** me, woman,
4:42 "We no longer **b** just because
5:38 for you do not **b** the one he sent.
5:47 since you do not **b** what he wrote,
6:29 to **b** in the one he has sent."
6:69 We **b** and know that you are
7: 5 his own brothers did not **b** in him.
8:24 if you do not **b** that I am
9:35 "Do you **b** in the Son of Man?"
9:38 Then the man said, "Lord, I **b,"**
10:26 not **b** because you are not my sheep.
10:37 Do not **b** me unless I do
10:38 I do it, even though you do not **b** me,
10:38 not believe me, **b** the miracles,
11:27 "I **b** that you are the Christ,
12:37 they still would not **b** in him.
12:39 For this reason they could not **b,**
12:44 he does not **b** in me only,
13:19 that when it does happen you will **b**
14:10 Don't you **b** that I am in the Father,
14:11 **B** me when I say that I am in
14:29 that when it does happen you will **b.**
16:30 This makes us **b** that you came
16:31 "You **b** at last!" Jesus answered.
17:20 I pray also for those who will **b**
19:35 he testifies so that you also may **b.**
20:27 Stop doubting and **b."**
20:31 But these are written that you may **b**
Ac 13:41 in your days that you would never **b,**
15: 7 the message of the gospel and **b.**
16:31 They replied, **"B** in the Lord Jesus,
19: 4 the people to **b** in the one coming
22:19 to imprison and beat those who **b**
24:14 I **b** everything that agrees with
26:27 do you **b** the prophets?
28:24 but others would not **b.**

Ro 3:22 in Jesus Christ to all who **b.**
4:11 he is the father of all who **b** but have
6: 8 we **b** that we will also live with him.
10:10 For it is with your heart that you **b**
10:14 And how can they **b** in the one
16:26 all nations might **b** and obey him—
1Co 1:21 to save those who **b.**
2Co 4:13 that same spirit of faith we also **b**
Gal 3: 5 or because you **b** what you heard?
3:22 might be given to those who **b.**
Eph 1:19 great power for us who **b.**
Php 1:29 on behalf of Christ not only to **b**
1Th 2:13 which is at work in you who **b.**
4:14 We **b** that Jesus died and rose again
4:14 and so we **b** that God will bring
2Th 2:11 so that they will **b**
1Ti 1:16 as an example for those who would **b**
4: 3 with thanksgiving by those who **b**
4:10 and especially of those who **b.**
Tit 1: 6 a man whose children **b** and are
Heb 10:39 but of those who **b** and are saved.
11: 6 comes to him must **b** that he exists
Jas 1: 6 he asks, he must **b** and not doubt,
2:19 You **b** that there is one God.
2:19 Even the demons **b** that—
1Pe 1: 8 you **b** in him and are filled with
2: 7 to you who **b,** this stone is precious.
3: 1 if any of them do not **b** the word,
1Jn 3:23 And this is his command: to **b** in
4: 1 Dear friends, do not **b** every spirit,
5:13 to you who **b** in the name of the Son
Jude 1: 5 later destroyed those who did not **b.**

BELIEVED [BELIEVE]

Ge 15: 6 Abram **b** the LORD,
Ex 4:31 and they **b.**
Ps 106:12 Then they **b** his promises
Isa 53: 1 Who has **b** our message and
Jnh 3: 5 The Ninevites **b** God.
Lk 1:45 Blessed is she who has **b** that what
Jn 1:12 to those who **b** in his name,
2:22 Then they **b** the Scripture and
3:18 because he has not **b** in the name
4:53 So he and all his household **b.**
5:46 If you **b** Moses,
7:39 whom those who **b** in him were later
7:48 of the rulers or of the Pharisees **b**
8:31 To the Jews who had **b** him,
10:42 And in that place many **b** in Jesus.
11:40 "Did I not tell you that if you **b,**
12:38 who has **b** our message and
17: 8 and they **b** that you sent me.
20: 8 He saw and **b.**
20:29 you have seen me, you have **b;**
20:29 not seen and yet have **b."**
Ac 4: 4 But many who heard the message **b,**
5:14 and more men and women **b** in
8:12 when they **b** Philip as he preached
9:42 and many people **b** in the Lord.
11:17 who **b** in the Lord Jesus Christ,
13:12 saw what had happened, he **b,**
13:48 were appointed for eternal life **b.**
14: 1 great number of Jews and Gentiles **b.**
17:12 Many of the Jews **b,**

	18: 8	his entire household **b** in the Lord;
	19: 2	receive the Holy Spirit when you **b?**
	21:20	how many thousands of Jews have **b,**
Ro	4: 3	"Abraham **b** God,
	10:14	on the one they have not **b** in?
	10:16	"Lord, who has **b** our message?"
1Co	15: 2	Otherwise, you have **b** in vain.
Gal	3: 6	Consider Abraham: "He **b** God,
Eph	1:13	Having **b,** you were marked in him
2Th	1:10	because you **b** our testimony to you.
	2:12	not **b** the truth but have delighted
1Ti	3:16	was **b** on in the world,
2Ti	1:12	because I know whom I have **b,**
Heb	4: 3	Now we who have **b** enter that rest,
Jas	2:23	"Abraham **b** God,
1Jn	5:10	not **b** the testimony God has given

BELIEVER* [BELIEVE]

1Ki	18: 3	(Obadiah was a devout **b** in
Ac	16: 1	whose mother was a Jewess and a **b,**
	16:15	"If you consider me a **b** in the Lord,"
1Co	7:12	brother has a wife who is not a **b**
	7:13	woman has a husband who is not a **b**
2Co	6:15	What does a **b** have in common with
1Ti	5:16	If any woman who is a **b** has widows

BELIEVERS* [BELIEVE]

Jn	4:41	of his words many more became **b.**
Ac	1:15	Peter stood up among the **b**
	2:44	All the **b** were together
	4:32	All the **b** were one in heart and mind.
	5:12	And all the **b** used to meet together
	9:41	Then he called the **b** and the widows
	10:45	The circumcised **b** who had come
	11: 2	the circumcised **b** criticized him
	15: 2	along with some other **b,**
	15: 5	**b** who belonged to the party of the
	15:23	To the Gentile **b** in Antioch,
	21:25	As for the Gentile **b,**
1Co	6: 5	to judge a dispute between **b?**
	14:22	not for **b** but for unbelievers;
	14:22	is for **b,** not for unbelievers.
Gal	6:10	who belong to the family of **b.**
1Th	1: 7	a model to all the **b** in Macedonia
1Ti	4:12	set an example for the **b** in speech,
	6: 2	benefit from their service are **b,**
Jas	2: 1	**b** in our glorious Lord Jesus Christ,
1Pe	2:17	Love the brotherhood of **b,**

BELIEVES* [BELIEVE]

Pr	14:15	A simple man **b** anything,
Mk	9:23	Everything is possible for him who **b**
	11:23	and does not doubt in his heart but **b**
	16:16	Whoever **b** and is baptized will
Jn	3:15	that everyone who **b**
	3:16	that whoever **b** in him shall
	3:18	Whoever **b** in him is not condemned,
	3:36	Whoever **b** in the Son has eternal life
	5:24	**b** him who sent me has eternal life
	6:35	he who **b** in me will never be thirsty.
	6:40	and **b** in him shall have eternal life,
	6:47	he who **b** has everlasting life.
	7:38	Whoever **b** in me,
	11:25	He who **b** in me will live,

	11:26	and **b** in me will never die.
	12:44	"When a man **b** in me,
	12:46	that no one who **b** in me should stay
Ac	10:43	who **b** in him receives forgiveness
	13:39	everyone who **b** is justified
Ro	1:16	for the salvation of everyone who **b:**
	10: 4	be righteousness for everyone who **b.**
1Jn	5: 1	Everyone who **b** that Jesus is
	5: 5	Only he who **b** that Jesus is the Son
	5:10	Anyone who **b** in the Son

BELIEVING* [BELIEVE]

Jn	20:31	by **b** you may have life in his name.
Ac	9:26	not **b** that he really was a disciple.
1Co	7:14	sanctified through her **b** husband.
	7:15	A **b** man or woman is not bound
	9: 5	the right to take a **b** wife along
Gal	3: 2	or by **b** what you heard?
1Ti	6: 2	Those who have **b** masters are not

BELLY

Ge	3:14	You will crawl on your **b**
Jdg	3:21	and plunged it into the king's **b.**
2Sa	20:10	and Joab plunged it into his **b,**
Job	15: 2	or fill his **b** with the hot east wind?
Da	2:32	its **b** and thighs of bronze,
Mt	12:40	three nights in the **b** of a huge fish,

BELONG [BELONGED, BELONGING, BELONGINGS, BELONGS]

Ge	40: 8	"Do not interpretations **b** to God?
Ex	13:12	of your livestock **b** to the LORD.
Lev	25:55	for the Israelites **b** to me as servants.
Dt	10:14	To the LORD your God **b** the heavens
	29:29	The secret things **b** to the LORD
	29:29	but the things revealed **b** to us and
Job	12:13	"To God **b** wisdom and power;
	12:16	To him **b** strength and victory;
	25: 2	"Dominion and awe **b** to God;
Ps	47: 9	for the kings of the earth **b** to God;
	95: 4	and the mountain peaks **b** to him.
	115:16	The highest heavens **b** to the LORD,
Pr	16: 1	To man **b** the plans of the heart,
SS	7:10	I **b** to my lover.
Isa	44: 5	One will say, 'I **b** to the LORD';
Jer	5:10	these people do not **b** to the LORD.
Jn	8:44	You **b** to your father, the devil,
	8:47	not hear is that you do not **b** to God."
	15:19	As it is, you do not **b** to the world,
Ro	1: 6	called to **b** to Jesus Christ.
	7: 4	that you might **b** to another,
	8: 9	he does not **b** to Christ.
	14: 8	we **b** to the Lord,
1Co	7: 4	The wife's body does not **b**
	7: 4	the husband's body does not **b**
	7:39	but he must **b** to the Lord.
	9:19	Though I am free and **b** to no man,
	12:15	I do not **b** to the body,"
	15:23	when he comes, those who **b** to him.
Gal	3:29	If you **b** to Christ,
	5:24	Those who **b** to Christ Jesus
	6:10	to those who **b** to the family
1Th	5: 5	not **b** to the night or to the darkness.
	5: 8	But since we **b** to the day,

1Jn 2:19 but they did not really **b** to us.
3:19 This then is how we know that we **b**

BELONGED [BELONG]

Jn 15:19 If you **b** to the world,
Ac 9: 2 any there who **b** to the Way,
12: 1 arrested some who **b** to the church,
1Jn 2:19 that none of them **b** to us.
3:12 Cain, who **b** to the evil one

BELONGING [BELONG]

Ge 14:23 that I will accept nothing **b** to you,
Nu 16:26 Do not touch anything **b** to them,
Ru 2: 3 in a field **b** to Boaz,
1Pe 2: 9 a holy nation, a people **b** to God,
Rev 13: 8 the book of life **b** to the Lamb

BELONGINGS [BELONG]

Jer 46:19 Pack your **b** for exile,
Eze 12: 4 bring out your **b** packed for exile.

BELONGS [BELONG]

Ex 34:19 first offspring of every womb **b** to
Lev 27:30 **b** to the LORD; it is holy
Dt 1:17 for judgment **b** to God.
Job 41:11 Everything under heaven **b** to me.
Ps 22:28 for dominion **b** to the LORD
89:18 Indeed, our shield **b** to the LORD,
111:10 To him **b** eternal praise.
Jer 46:10 But that day **b** to the Lord,
Eze 18: 4 For every living soul **b** to me,
Mt 19:14 for the kingdom of heaven **b** to such
Jn 8:47 He who **b** to God hears
16:15 All that **b** to the Father is mine.
Ro 12: 5 and each member **b** to all the others.
2Co 10: 7 If anyone is confident that he **b**
Col 3: 5 whatever **b** to your earthly nature:
Rev 7:10 "Salvation **b** to our God,

BELOVED* [LOVE]

Dt 33:12 About Benjamin he said: "Let the **b**
SS 5: 9 How is your **b** better than others,
5: 9 How is your **b** better than others,
Jer 11:15 "What is my **b** doing in my temple

BELOW

Dt 4:39 in heaven above and on the earth **b**.
Isa 37:31 of the house of Judah will take root **b**
Jn 8:23 But he continued, "You are from **b**;
Ac 2:19 above and signs on the earth **b**,

BELSHAZZAR

King of Babylon in days of Daniel (Da 5).

BELT

Ex 12:11 with your cloak tucked into your **b**,
1Sa 18: 4 his bow and his **b**.
1Ki 18:46 tucking his cloak into his **b**,
2Ki 1: 8 garment of hair and with a leather **b**
4:29 "Tuck your cloak into your **b**,
9: 1 "Tuck your cloak into your **b**,
Isa 11: 5 Righteousness will be his **b**
Jer 13: 1 "Go and buy a linen **b**
Da 10: 5 with a **b** of the finest gold
Mk 1: 6 with a leather **b** around his waist,

Eph 6:14 with the **b** of truth buckled

BELTESHAZZAR [DANIEL]

Da 1: 7 new names: to Daniel, the name **B**;

BEN HINNOM

2Ki 23:10 which was in the Valley of **B**
Jer 7:31 Valley of **B** to burn their sons

BEN-HADAD [HADAD]

1. King of Syria in time of Asa (1Ki 15:18-20; 2Ch 16:2-4).
2. King of Syria in time of Ahab (1Ki 20; 2Ki 5-7; 8:7-15).
3. King of Syria in time of Jehoahaz (2Ki 13:3, 24-25; Am 1:4).

BEN-ONI* [BENJAMIN]

Ge 35:18 she named her son **B**.

BENAIAH

A commander of Davids army (2Sa 8:18; 20:23; 23:20-30); loyal to Solomon (1Ki 1:8-2:46; 4:4).

BEND [BENT]

2Sa 22:35 my arms can **b** a bow of bronze.
Isa 65:12 you will all **b** down for the slaughter;
Zec 9:13 I will **b** Judah as I **b** my bow

BENEFICIAL* [BENEFIT]

1Co 6:12 but not everything is **b**.
10:23 but not everything is **b**.

BENEFIT [BENEFICIAL, BENEFITS]

Job 22: 2 "Can a man be of **b** to God? Can even a wise man **b** him?
Isa 38:17 my **b** that I suffered such anguish.
Jn 11:42 for the **b** of the people standing here,
Ro 6:22 the **b** you reap leads to holiness,
2Co 1:15 so that you might **b** twice.
4:15 All this is for your **b**,
Phm 1:20 that I may have some **b** from you in

BENEFITS* [BENEFIT]

Dt 18: 8 He is to share equally in their **b**,
Ps 103: 2 O my soul, and forget not all his **b**—
Pr 11:17 A kind man **b** himself,
Ecc 7:11 and **b** those who see the sun.
Jn 4:38 you have reaped the **b** of their labor."

BENJAMIN [BEN-ONI]

Twelfth son of Jacob by Rachel (Ge 35:16-24; 46:19-21; 1Ch 2:2). Jacob refused to send him to Egypt, but relented (Ge 42-45). Tribe of blessed (Ge 49:27; Dt 33:12), numbered (Nu 1:37; 26:41), allotted land (Jos 18:11-28; Eze 48:23), failed to fully possess (Jdg 1:21), nearly obliterated (Jdg 20-21), sided with Ish-Bosheth (2Sa 2), but turned to David (1Ch 12:2, 29). 12,000 from (Rev 7:8).

BENT [BEND]

1Sa 24: 9 'David is **b** on harming you'?
Ps 44:16 who is **b** on revenge.
69:23 and their backs be **b** forever.
Pr 17:11 An evil man is **b** only on rebellion;

Hos 11: 4 and **b** down to feed them.
Lk 13:11 She was **b** over and could
Jn 20: 5 He **b** over and looked in at the strips
Ro 11:10 and their backs be **b** forever."
Rev 6: 2 as a conqueror **b** on conquest.

BERACAH
2Ch 20:26 called the Valley of **B** to this day.

BEREA [BEREANS]
Ac 17:10 sent Paul and Silas away to **B**.

BEREANS* [BEREA]
Ac 17:11 the **B** were of more noble character

BEREAVE* [BEREAVED, BEREAVEMENT, BEREAVES]
Hos 9:12 I will **b** them of every one.

BEREAVED* [BEREAVE]
Ge 43:14 As for me, if I am **b**, I am **b**."
Isa 49:21 I was **b** and barren;

BEREAVEMENT* [BEREAVE]
Isa 49:20 The children born during your **b** will
Jer 15: 7 I will bring **b** and destruction

BEREAVES* [BEREAVE]
La 1:20 Outside, the sword **b**;

BESIDES
Dt 32:39 There is no god **b** me.
1Sa 2: 2 there is no one **b** you;
2Sa 22:32 For who is God **b** the LORD?
Ps 18:31 For who is God **b** the LORD?
73:25 And earth has nothing I desire **b** you.
Isa 47: 8 'I am, and there is none **b** me.
64: 4 no eye has seen any God **b** you,
Zep 2:15 "I am, and there is none **b** me."

BESIEGED [SIEGE]
Ps 31:21 to me when I was in a **b** city.
La 3: 5 He has **b** me and surrounded me
Da 1: 1 to Jerusalem and **b** it.
Zec 12: 2 Judah will be **b** as well as Jerusalem.

BEST [GOOD]
Ge 45:18 I will give you the **b** of the land
47: 6 your brothers in the **b** part of
Ex 15: 4 **b** of Pharaoh's officers are drowned
Nu 18:29 as the LORD's portion the **b**
Dt 33:16 with the **b** gifts of the earth
SS 7: 9 and your mouth like the **b** wine.
Isa 1:19 you will eat the **b** from the land;
48:17 who teaches you what is **b** for you,
Eze 44:30 The **b** of all the firstfruits and
Mic 7: 4 The **b** of them is like a brier,
Jn 2:10 but you have saved the **b** till now."
Php 1:10 to discern what is **b** and may be pure
2Ti 2:15 Do your **b** to present yourself to God

BESTOW* [BESTOWED, BESTOWER, BESTOWING, BESTOWS]
Ps 3: 3 you **b** glory on me and lift up my

31:19 which you **b** in the sight of men
Isa 45: 4 I summon you by name and **b** on you
61: 3 to **b** on them a crown
62: 2 that the mouth of the LORD will **b**.
Jer 23: 2 I will **b** punishment on you for

BESTOWED [BESTOW]
1Ch 29:25 and **b** on him royal splendor such

BESTOWER* [BESTOW]
Isa 23: 8 the **b** of crowns,

BESTOWING* [BESTOW]
Pr 8:21 **b** wealth on those who love me

BESTOWS* [BESTOW]
Job 5:10 He **b** rain on the earth;
Ps 84:11 the LORD **b** favor and honor;
133: 3 For there the LORD **b** his blessing,

BETH AVEN [AVEN]
Hos 4:15 do not go up to **B**
10: 5 fear for the calf-idol of **B**

BETH SHAN
Jdg 1:27 not drive out the people of **B**
1Sa 31:10 fastened his body to the wall of **B**

BETH SHEMESH
1Sa 6:14 came to the field of Joshua of **B**

BETHANY
Mt 26: 6 While Jesus was in **B** in the home of
Mk 11:12 The next day as they were leaving **B**,
Jn 1:28 at **B** on the other side of the Jordan,

BETHEL [EL BETHEL, LUZ]
Ge 12: 8 on toward the hills east of **B**
28:19 He called that place **B**,
31:13 I am the God of **B**,
35: 8 buried under the oak below **B**.
Jos 8: 9 of ambush and lay in wait between **B**
Jdg 20:18 up to **B** and inquired of God.
1Sa 7:16 a circuit from **B** to Gilgal to Mizpah,
1Ki 12:29 One he set up in **B**,
13:11 a certain old prophet living in **B**,
2Ki 2: 2 the LORD has sent me to **B**."
10:29 the worship of the golden calves at **B**
23:15 Even the altar at **B**,
Am 4: 4 "Go to **B** and sin;
7:10 Then Amaziah the priest of **B** sent

BETHESDA*
Jn 5: 2 which in Aramaic is called **B**

BETHLEHEM [EPHRATH]
Ge 35:19 on the way to Ephrath (that is, **B**).
Ru 1: 1 and a man from **B** in Judah,
1:19 When they arrived in **B**,
4:11 in Ephrathah and be famous in **B**.
1Sa 16: 1 I am sending you to Jesse of **B**.
2Sa 23:15 from the well near the gate of **B**!"
Mic 5: 2 "But you, **B** Ephrathah,
Mt 2: 1 After Jesus was born in **B** in Judea,
2: 6 **B**, in the land of Judah,

2:16 to kill all the boys in **B**
Lk   2:15 "Let's go to **B** and see this thing
Jn   7:42 from David's family and from **B,**

BETHPHAGE
Mt   21: 1 to **B** on the Mount of Olives,

BETHSAIDA
Mt 11:21 Woe to you, **B!**
Jn 12:21 who was from **B** in Galilee,

BETRAY [BETRAYED, BETRAYER, BETRAYING, BETRAYS]
Ps 89:33 nor will I ever **b** my faithfulness.
Pr 16:10 and his mouth should not **b** justice.
    25: 9 do not **b** another man's confidence,
Isa 24:16 With treachery the treacherous **b!"**
Mt 10:21 "Brother will **b** brother to death,
  24:10 and will **b** and hate each other,
  26:21 one of you will **b** me."
Jn 13:11 he knew who was going to **b** him,

BETRAYED [BETRAY]
La   1: 2 All her friends have **b** her;
Mt 27: 4 "for I have **b** innocent blood."
Lk 21:16 You will be **b** even by parents,
Jn 18: 2 Now Judas, who **b** him,

BETRAYER [BETRAY]
Mk 14:42 Rise! Let us go! Here comes my **b!"**

BETRAYING [BETRAY]
Lk 22:48 **b** the Son of Man with a kiss?"

BETRAYS [BETRAY]
Pr 11:13 A gossip **b** a confidence,
  20:19 A gossip **b** a confidence;
Hab 2: 5 wine **b** him;
Mk 14:21 But woe to that man who **b** the Son

BETROTH
Hos 2:19 I will **b** you to me forever;

BETTER [GOOD]
Nu 11:18 We were **b** off in Egypt!"
1Sa 15:22 To obey is **b** than sacrifice,
Ps 37:16 **B** the little that the righteous have
  63: 3 Because your love is **b** than life,
 118: 8 It is **b** to take refuge in
Pr   8:19 My fruit is **b** than fine gold;
  12: 9 **B** to be a nobody and yet have
  15:16 **B** a little with the fear of the LORD
  15:17 **B** a meal of vegetables where there
  16: 8 **B** a little with righteousness
  16:16 much **b** to get wisdom than gold,
  16:19 **B** to be lowly in spirit and among
  16:32 **B** a patient man than a warrior,
  17: 1 **B** a dry crust with peace and quiet
  17:12 **B** to meet a bear robbed of her cubs
  19: 1 **B** a poor man whose walk is
  19:22 **b** to be poor than a liar.
  21: 9 **B** to live on a corner of
  21:19 **B** to live in a desert than with
  22: 1 be esteemed is **b** than silver or gold.
  27: 5 **B** is open rebuke than hidden love.

  28: 6 **B** a poor man whose walk is
Ecc   2:13 I saw that wisdom is **b** than folly,
  2:24 A man can do nothing **b** than to eat
  3:12 know that there is nothing **b** for men
  3:22 that there is nothing **b** for a man than
  4: 3 But **b** than both is he who has not
  4: 6 **B** one handful with tranquillity
  4: 9 Two are **b** than one,
  4:13 **B** a poor but wise youth than an old
  5: 5 It is **b** not to vow than to make a vow
  6: 3 that a stillborn child is **b** off than he.
  6: 9 **B** what the eye sees than the roving
  7: 1 A good name is **b** than fine perfume,
  7: 1 day of death **b** than the day of birth.
  7: 2 It is **b** to go to a house of mourning
  7: 3 Sorrow is **b** than laughter,
  7: 5 It is **b** to heed a wise man's rebuke
  7: 8 of a matter is **b** than its beginning,
  7: 8 and patience is **b** than pride.
  8:12 I know that it will go **b**
  8:15 nothing is **b** for a man under
  9: 4 even a live dog is **b** off than
  9:16 I said, "Wisdom is **b** than strength."
  9:18 Wisdom is **b** than weapons of war,
SS   5: 9 How is your beloved **b** than others,
Jnh 4: 3 for it is **b** for me to die than to live."
Mt   5:29 It is **b** for you to lose one part
  18: 6 it would be **b** for him to have
  26:24 It would be **b** for him if he had
Lk   5:39 for he says, 'The old is **b.'** "
  10:42 Mary has chosen what is **b,**
1Co 7: 9 for it is **b** to marry than to burn
Eph 1:17 so that you may know him **b.**
Heb 6: 9 we are confident of **b** things
  7:19 and a **b** hope is introduced,
  7:22 the guarantee of a **b** covenant.
  8: 6 and it is founded on **b** promises.
  9:23 with **b** sacrifices than these.
  10:34 that you yourselves had **b**
  11: 4 Abel offered God a **b** sacrifice
  11:16 they were longing for a **b** country—
  11:35 that they might gain a **b** resurrection.
  11:40 God had planned something **b** for us
  12:24 that speaks a **b** word than the blood
1Pe 3:17 It is **b,** if it is God's will,
2Pe 2:21 It would have been **b** for them not

BETWEEN
Ge   3:15 And I will put enmity **b** you and
  16: 5 the LORD judge **b** you and me."
  31:44 and let it serve as a witness **b** us."
Lev 10:10 You must distinguish **b** the holy and
1Sa   4: 4 who is enthroned **b** the cherubim.
Ro 10:12 For there is no difference **b** Jew
1Ti   2: 5 and one mediator **b** God and men,

BEULAH*
Isa 62: 4 and your land **B;**

BEWARE*
2Ki   6: 9 "**B** of passing that place,
Job 36:21 **B** of turning to evil,
Isa 22:17 "**B,** the LORD is about to take
Jer   7:32 So **b,** the days are coming,

9: 4   **"B** of your friends;
19: 6   So **b,** the days are coming,
Lk 20:46   **"B** of the teachers of the law.

BEWITCHED* [WITCHCRAFT]

Gal 3: 1   Who has **b** you?

BEYOND

Dt 30:11   not too difficult for you or **b**
Jos 24: 2   lived **b** the River
Jdg 13:18   It is **b** understanding."
Job 36:26   great is God—**b** our understanding!
     37:23   The Almighty is **b** our reach
Ecc 7:23   but this was **b** me.
Jer 17: 9   deceitful above all things and **b** cure.
     30:12   your injury **b** healing.
Ro 11:11   so as to fall **b** recovery?
1Co 4: 6   "Do not go **b** what is written."
     10:13   be tempted **b** what you can bear.
2Co 1: 8   far **b** our ability to endure,
     10:16   the gospel in the regions **b** you.

BEZALEL

Judahite craftsman in charge of building the tabernacle (Ex 31:1-11; 35:30-39:31).

BIDDING*

Ps 103:20   you mighty ones who do his **b,**
    148: 8   stormy winds that do his **b,**

BILDAD

One of Job's friends (Job 2:11; 8; 18; 25).

BILHAH

Servant of Rachel, mother of Jacob's sons Dan and Naphtali (Ge 30:1-7; 35:25; 46:23-25).

BIND [BINDING, BINDS, BOUND]

Dt 6: 8   and **b** them on your foreheads.
Ne 10:29   and **b** themselves with a curse and
Pr 3: 3   faithfulness never leave you; **b** them
    6:21   **B** them upon your heart forever;
    7: 3   **B** them on your fingers;
Isa 8:16   **B** up the testimony and seal up
   56: 6   And foreigners who **b** themselves to
   61: 1   to **b** up the brokenhearted,
Eze 34:16   I will **b** up the injured and strengthen
Mt 16:19   whatever you **b** on earth will
   18:18   whatever you **b** on earth will

BINDING [BIND]

Heb 2: 2   the message spoken by angels was **b,**

BINDS [BIND]

Job 5:18   For he wounds, but he also **b** up;
Isa 30:26   when the LORD **b** up the bruises
Col 3:14   which **b** them all together

BIRD [BIRDS]

Ge 1:21   every winged **b** according to its kind.
   6:20   Two of every kind of **b,**
Dt 14:11   You may eat any clean **b.**
Ps 50:11   I know every **b** in the mountains,
Pr 6: 5   like a **b** from the snare of the fowler.
   7:23   like a **b** darting into a snare,

27: 8   Like a **b** that strays from its nest is
Ecc 10:20   a **b** of the air may carry your words,
Isa 46:11   From the east I summon a **b** of prey:

BIRDS [BIRD]

Jer 7:33   food for the **b** of the air
Da 4:12   the **b** of the air lived in its branches;
Hos 11:11   They will come trembling like **b**
Mt 6:26   Look at the **b** of the air;
   8:20   and **b** of the air have nests,
   13: 4   and the **b** came and ate it up.
Rev 19:21   and all the **b** gorged themselves

BIRTH [BEAR]

Ge 3:16   with pain you will give **b** to children.
Lev 12: 7   for the woman who gives **b**
Dt 32:18   the God who gave you **b.**
Jdg 13: 5   set apart to God from **b,**
Job 3: 1   and cursed the day of his **b.**
Ps 51: 5   Surely I was sinful at **b,**
   58: 3   Even from **b** the wicked go astray;
   71: 6   From **b** I have relied on you;
Pr 8:24   there were no oceans, I was given **b,**
Ecc 7: 1   day of death better than the day of **b.**
Isa 7:14   with child and will give **b** to a son,
   8: 3   she conceived and gave **b** to a son.
   26:18   but we gave **b** to wind.
Jer 2:27   and to stone, 'You gave me **b.'**
Mt 1:18   the **b** of Jesus Christ came about:
   1:21   She will give **b** to a son,
   24: 8   the beginning of **b** pains.
Lk 1:57   she gave **b** to a son.
Jn 3: 6   Flesh gives **b** to flesh, but the Spirit gives **b** to spirit.
   9: 1   he saw a man blind from **b.**
Gal 1:15   who set me apart from **b**
Jas 1:15   it gives **b** to sin;
1Pe 1: 3   great mercy he has given us new **b**
Rev 12: 5   She gave **b** to a son, a male child,

BIRTHRIGHT [BEAR]

Ge 25:34   So Esau despised his **b.**

BIT [BITES, BIT]

Nu 21: 6   snakes among them; they **b**
2Ki 19:28   and my **b** in your mouth,

BITE [BIT, BITES, BITTEN]

Am 5:19   the wall only to have a snake **b** him.

BITES [BITE]

Pr 23:32   In the end it **b** like a snake

BITS [BIT]

Jas 3: 3   When we put **b** into the mouths

BITTEN [BITE]

Nu 21: 8   anyone who is **b** can look

BITTER [BITTERNESS, EMBITTER]

Ex 1:14   made their lives **b** with hard labor
   12: 8   along with **b** herbs,
Nu 5:19   may this **b** water that brings a curse
Ru 1:20   Almighty has made my life very **b.**

Pr   5: 4 but in the end she is **b** as gall,
      27: 7 even what is **b** tastes sweet.
Rev   8:11 A third of the waters turned **b,**

BITTERNESS [BITTER]

1Sa   1:10 In **b** of soul Hannah wept much
Pr   14:10 Each heart knows its own **b,**
     17:25 and **b** to the one who bore him.
Ro   3:14 mouths are full of cursing and **b.**"
Eph   4:31 Get rid of all **b,** rage and anger,

BLACK

Zec   6: 6 The one with the **b** horses is going
Mt   5:36 even one hair white or **b.**
Rev   6: 5 and there before me was a **b** horse!
      6:12 The sun turned **b** like sackcloth made

BLAME [BLAMELESS, BLAMELESSLY]

Ro   9:19 "Then why does God still **b** us?
1Ti   5: 7 too, so that no one may be open to **b.**
      6:14 without spot or **b** until the appearing

BLAMELESS* [BLAME]

Ge   6: 9 **b** among the people of his time,
     17: 1 walk before me and be **b.**
Dt   18:13 be **b** before the LORD your God.
2Sa 22:24 I have been **b** before him
     22:26 to the **b** you show yourself **b,**
Job   1: 1 This man was **b** and upright;
      1: 8 is no one on earth like him; he is **b**
      2: 3 is no one on earth like him; he is **b**
      4: 6 and your **b** ways your hope?
      8:20 "Surely God does not reject a **b** man
      9:20 if I were **b,**
      9:21 I am **b,** I have no concern for myself;
      9:22 'He destroys both the **b** and
     12: 4 though righteous and **b!**
     22: 3 if your ways were **b?**
     31: 6 and he will know that I am **b**—
Ps   15: 2 He whose walk is **b**
     18:23 I have been **b** before him
     18:25 to the **b** you show yourself **b,**
     19:13 Then will I be **b,**
     26: 1 O LORD, for I have led a **b** life;
     26:11 But I lead a **b** life;
     37:18 of the **b** are known to the LORD,
     37:37 Consider the **b,** observe the upright;
     84:11 from those whose walk is **b.**
    101: 2 I will be careful to lead a **b** life—
    101: 2 I will walk in my house with **b** heart.
    101: 6 he whose walk is **b** will minister
    119: 1 Blessed are they whose ways are **b,**
    119:80 heart be **b** toward your decrees,
Pr   2: 7 a shield to those whose walk is **b,**
      2:21 and the **b** will remain in it;
     11: 5 the **b** makes a straight way for them,
     11:20 in those whose ways are **b.**
     19: 1 a poor man whose walk is **b** than
     20: 7 The righteous man leads a **b** life;
     28: 6 a poor man whose walk is **b** than
     28:10 the **b** will receive a good inheritance.
     28:18 He whose walk is **b** is kept safe,
Eze 28:15 You were **b** in your ways from
1Co   1: 8 so that you will be **b** on the day

Eph   1: 4 of the world to be holy and **b**
      5:27 but holy and **b.**
Php   1:10 be pure and **b** until
      2:15 so that you may become **b** and pure,
1Th   2:10 righteous and **b** we were
      3:13 so that you will be **b** and holy in
      5:23 and body be kept **b** at the coming
Tit   1: 6 An elder must be **b,**
      1: 7 he must be **b**—
Heb   7:26 **b,** pure, set apart from sinners,
2Pe   3:14 **b** and at peace with him.
Rev 14: 5 found in their mouths; they are **b.**

BLAMELESSLY* [BLAME]

Lk   1: 6 commandments and regulations **b.**

BLASPHEME* [BLASPHEMED, BLASPHEMER, BLASPHEMES, BLASPHEMIES, BLASPHEMING, BLASPHEMOUS, BLASPHEMY]

Ex   22:28 "Do not **b** God or curse the ruler
Ac   26:11 and I tried to force them to **b.**
1Ti   1:20 over to Satan to be taught not to **b.**
2Pe   2:12 But these men **b** in matters they do
Rev 13: 6 He opened his mouth to **b** God,

BLASPHEMED* [BLASPHEME]

Lev 24:11 son of the Israelite woman **b** the
2Ki 19: 6 of the king of Assyria have **b** me.
     19:22 Who is it you have insulted and **b?**
Isa 37: 6 of the king of Assyria have **b** me.
     37:23 Who is it you have insulted and **b?**
     52: 5 all day long my name is constantly **b.**
Eze 20:27 In this also your fathers **b** me
Ac   19:37 nor **b** our goddess.
Ro   2:24 As it is written: "God's name is **b**

BLASPHEMER* [BLASPHEME]

Lev 24:14 "Take the **b** outside the camp.
     24:23 and they took the **b** outside the camp
1Ti   1:13 Even though I was once a **b** and

BLASPHEMES* [BLASPHEME]

Lev 24:16 anyone who **b** the name of
     24:16 when he **b** the Name,
Nu   15:30 **b** the LORD,
Mk   3:29 But whoever **b** against
Lk   12:10 but anyone who **b** against

BLASPHEMIES* [BLASPHEME]

Ne   9:18 or when they committed awful **b.**
      9:26 they committed awful **b.**
Mk   3:28 and **b** of men will be forgiven them.
Rev 13: 5 a mouth to utter proud words and **b**

BLASPHEMING* [BLASPHEME]

Mt   9: 3 "This fellow is **b!**"
Mk   2: 7 He's **b!**

BLASPHEMOUS* [BLASPHEME]

Rev 13: 1 and on each head a **b** name.
     17: 3 beast that was covered with **b** names

BLASPHEMY* [BLASPHEME]

Mt 12:31 every sin and **b** will be forgiven men,
       12:31 but the **b** against the Spirit will not
      26:65 "He has spoken **b**!
      26:65 Look, now you have heard the **b**.
Mk 14:64 "You have heard the **b**.
Lk   5:21 "Who is this fellow who speaks **b**?
Jn 10:33 "but for **b**, because you, a mere man,
      10:36 Why then do you accuse me of **b**
Ac   6:11 heard Stephen speak words of **b**

BLAST* [BLASTS]

Ex 15: 8 By the **b** of your nostrils
     19:13 a long **b** may they go up to
     19:16 and a very loud trumpet **b**.
Nu 10: 5 When a trumpet **b** is sounded,
     10: 6 At the sounding of a second **b**,
     10: 6 **b** will be the signal for setting out.
     10: 9 sound a **b** on the trumpets.
Jos   6: 5 When you hear them sound a long **b**
      6:16 the priests sounded the trumpet **b**,
2Sa 22:16 at the **b** of breath from his nostrils.
Job   4: 9 at the **b** of his anger they perish.
     39:25 At the **b** of the trumpet he snorts,
Ps 18:15 at the **b** of breath from your nostrils.
     98: 6 and the **b** of the ram's horn—
  147:17 Who can withstand his icy **b**?
Isa 27: 8 with his fierce **b** he drives her out,
Eze 22:20 a furnace to melt it with a fiery **b**,
Am   2: 2 and the **b** of
Heb 12:19 to a trumpet **b** or to such

BLASTS* [BLAST]

Lev 23:24 commemorated with trumpet **b**.
Rev 8:13 the trumpet **b** about to be sounded by

BLAZED [BLAZING]

Dt   4:11 at the foot of the mountain while it **b**
2Sa 22: 9 burning coals **b** out of it.
Jnh   4: 8 and the sun **b** on Jonah's head so

BLAZING [BLAZED]

Ge 15:17 with a **b** torch appeared and passed
SS   8: 6 It burns like **b** fire,
Isa 62: 1 her salvation like a **b** torch.
Eze 20:47 The **b** flame will not be quenched,
Da   3: 6 be thrown into a **b** furnace."
      7:11 and thrown into the **b** fire.
2Th   1: 7 in **b** fire with his powerful angels.
Rev 1:14 and his eyes were like **b** fire.
      8:10 and a great star, **b** like a torch,
    19:12 His eyes are like **b** fire,

BLEATING*

1Sa 15:14 then is this **b** of sheep in my ears?

BLEEDING [BLOOD]

Lev 12: 4 to be purified from her **b**.
Lk   8:43 subject to **b** for twelve years,

BLEMISH* [BLEMISHED, BLEMISHES]

Lev 22:21 without defect or **b** to be acceptable.
Nu 19: 2 a red heifer without defect or **b** and
2Sa 14:25 to the sole of his foot there was no **b**

Eph   5:27 or wrinkle or any other **b**,
Col   1:22 without **b** and free from accusation
1Pe   1:19 a lamb without **b** or defect.

BLEMISHED* [BLEMISH]

Mal 1:14 sacrifices a **b** animal to the Lord.

BLEMISHES* [BLEMISH]

2Pe 2:13 They are blots and **b**,
Jude 1:12 These men are **b** at your love feasts,

BLESS [BLESSED, BLESSES, BLESSING, BLESSINGS]

Ge 12: 3 I will **b** those who **b** you,
    17:16 I will **b** her and will surely give you
    22:17 I will surely **b** you
    26: 3 I will be with you and will **b** you.
    26:24 for I am with you; I will **b** you
    27:29 and those who **b** you be blessed."
    27:34 "**B** me—me too, my father!"
    28: 3 May God Almighty **b** you
    32:26 not let you go unless you **b** me."
    48: 9 "Bring them to me so I may **b** them."
Ex 12:32 And also **b** me."
    20:24 I will come to you and **b** you.
Nu   6:24 " ' "The LORD **b** you and keep you;
    22: 6 I know that those you **b** are blessed,
    23:20 I have received a command to **b**;
Dt   1:11 and **b** you as he has promised!
     7:13 He will love you and **b** you
    14:29 that the LORD your God may **b** you
    15: 4 he will richly **b** you,
    16:15 For the LORD your God will **b** you
    23:20 that the LORD your God may **b** you
    24:19 that the LORD your God may **b** you
    26:15 and **b** your people Israel and
    27:12 on Mount Gerizim to **b** the people:
    33:11 **B** all his skills, O LORD,
Jos   8:33 when he gave instructions to **b**
Jdg 17: 2 his mother said, "The LORD **b** you,
Ru   2: 4 "The LORD **b** you!"
     3:10 "The LORD **b** you, my daughter,"
1Sa 2:20 Eli would **b** Elkanah and his wife,
2Sa 2: 5 "The LORD **b** you
    21: 3 you will **b** the LORD's inheritance?"
1Ch 4:10 that you would **b** me
Ps   5:12 O LORD, you **b** the righteous;
    28: 9 and **b** your inheritance;
    67: 1 May God be gracious to us and **b** us
    72:15 for him and **b** him all day long.
  109:28 They may curse, but you will **b**;
  115:12 LORD remembers us and will **b** us:
  118:26 the house of the LORD we **b** you.
Pr 30:11 and do not **b** their mothers;
Isa 19:25 The LORD Almighty will **b** them,
Jer 31:23 'The LORD **b** you,
Eze 34:26 I will **b** them and
Hag 2:19 " 'From this day on I will **b** you.' "
Zec 4: 7 God **b** it!' "
Lk   6:28 **b** those who curse you,
Ro 12:14 **B** those who persecute you; **b**
1Co 4:12 When we are cursed, we **b**;
Heb 6:14 "I will surely **b** you

BLESSED [BLESS]

Ge	1:22	God **b** them and said,
	2: 3	And God **b** the seventh day
	9: 1	Then God **b** Noah and his sons,
	9:26	He also said, **"B** be the LORD,
	14:19	**"B** be Abram by God Most High,
	22:18	all nations on earth will be **b,**
	28:14	All peoples on earth will be **b**
	39: 5	the LORD **b** the household of
	47: 7	After Jacob **b** Pharaoh,
Ex	20:11	toward the people and **b** them.
	39:43	So Moses **b** them.
Lev	9:22	toward the people and **b** them.
Nu	24: 9	"May those who bless you be **b**
Dt	12: 7	the LORD your God has **b** you.
	28: 3	be **b** in the city and **b** in the country.
Jos	22: 6	Joshua **b** them and sent them away,
Jdg	5:24	"Most **b** of women be Jael,
	13:24	He grew and the LORD **b** him,
1Ch	17:27	have **b** it, and it will be **b** forever."
Ne	9: 5	**"B** be your glorious Name,
Job	5:17	**"B** is the man whom God corrects;
Ps	1: 1	**B** is the man who does not walk in
	2:12	**B** are all who take refuge in him.
	32: 1	**B** is he whose transgressions are
	33:12	**B** is the nation whose God is
	40: 4	**B** is the man who makes
	41: 1	**B** is he who has regard for the weak;
	84: 5	**B** are those whose strength is in you,
	89:15	**B** are those who have learned
	94:12	**B** is the man you discipline,
	106: 3	**B** are they who maintain justice,
	112: 1	**B** is the man who fears the LORD,
	118:26	**B** is he who comes in the name of
	119: 1	**B** are they whose ways are
	119: 2	**B** are they who keep his statutes
	127: 5	**B** is the man whose quiver is full
	128: 1	**B** are all who fear the LORD,
	144:15	**B** are the people of whom this is
Pr	3:13	**B** is the man who finds wisdom,
	8:34	**B** is the man who listens to me,
	22: 9	A generous man will himself be **b,**
	28:20	A faithful man will be richly **b,**
	29:18	but **b** is he who keeps the law.
	31:28	Her children arise and call her **b;**
SS	6: 9	maidens saw her and called her **b;**
Isa	30:18	**B** are all who wait for him!
Mal	3:12	"Then all the nations will call you **b,**
	3:15	But now we call the arrogant **b.**
Mt	5: 3	**"B** are the poor in spirit,
	5: 4	**B** are those who mourn,
	5: 5	**B** are the meek,
	5: 6	**B** are those who hunger and thirst
	5: 7	**B** are the merciful,
	5: 8	**B** are the pure in heart,
	5: 9	**B** are the peacemakers,
	5:10	**B** are those who are persecuted
	5:11	**"B** are you when people insult you,
	11: 6	**B** is the man who does not fall away
Mk	11: 9	**"B** is he who comes in the name of
Lk	1:42	**"B** are you among women,
	1:48	on all generations will call me **b,**
	6:20	**"B** are you who are poor,
	6:21	**B** are you who hunger now,
	6:21	**B** are you who weep now,
	6:22	**B** are you when men hate you,
Jn	12:13	**"B** is the King of Israel!"
	13:17	you will be **b** if you do them.
Ac	20:35	'It is more **b** to give than
Ro	4: 7	**"B** are they whose transgressions
Gal	3: 8	nations will be **b** through you."
Eph	1: 3	who has **b** us in the heavenly realms
1Ti	6:15	the **b** and only Ruler,
Tit	2:13	while we wait for the **b** hope—
Heb	7: 7	the lesser person is **b** by the greater.
Jas	1:12	**B** is the man who perseveres
	5:11	we consider **b** those who have
1Pe	3:14	suffer for what is right, you are **b.**
Rev	1: 3	**B** is the one who reads the words
	1: 3	and **b** are those who hear it and take
	14:13	**B** are the dead who die in
	16:15	**B** is he who stays awake
	19: 9	'**B** are those who are invited
	20: 6	**B** and holy are those who have part
	22: 7	**B** is he who keeps the words of
	22:14	**"B** are those who wash their robes,

BLESSES [BLESS]

Ps	29:11	the LORD **b** his people with peace.
Ro	10:12	and richly **b** all who call on him,

BLESSING [BLESS]

Ge	12: 2	and you will be a **b.**
	27: 4	I may give you my **b** before I die."
	48:20	name will Israel pronounce this **b:**
	49:28	giving each the **b** appropriate to him.
Dt	11:26	I am setting before you today a **b** and
	23: 5	but turned the curse into a **b** for you,
	33: 1	This is the **b** that Moses the man
Ne	13: 2	however, turned the curse into a **b.**)
Pr	10:22	The **b** of the LORD brings wealth,
Eze	34:26	be showers of **b.**
Joel	2:14	and have pity and leave behind a **b**—
Zec	8:13	and you will be a **b.**
Mal	3:10	and pour out so much **b**
Lk	24:51	While he was **b** them,
Jn	1:16	his grace we have all received one **b**
Ro	15:29	in the full measure of the **b** of Christ.
Gal	3:14	the **b** given to Abraham might come
Heb	12:17	when he wanted to inherit this **b,**
1Pe	3: 9	with insult, but with **b,**

BLESSINGS [BLESS]

Ge	49:26	Your father's **b** are greater than the **b**
Dt	11:29	to proclaim on Mount Gerizim the **b,**
Jos	8:34	the **b** and the curses—
1Ch	23:13	to pronounce **b** in his name forever.
Pr	10: 6	**B** crown the head of the righteous,
Mal	2: 2	and I will curse your **b.**
Ac	13:34	and sure **b** promised to David.'
Ro	15:27	shared in the Jews' spiritual **b,**
	15:27	to share with them their material **b.**

BLEW [BLOW]

Ex	15:10	But you **b** with your breath,
Jos	6: 9	of the priests who **b** the trumpets,
Hag	1: 9	What you brought home, I **b** away.

Mt   7:25   winds **b** and beat against that house;

BLIND [BLINDED, BLINDNESS, BLINDS]

Ex   4:11   sight or makes him **b?**
Dt   27:18   the man who leads the **b** astray on
2Sa   5: 8   "The **'b** and lame' will not enter
Job   29:15   I was eyes to the **b** and feet to
Ps   146: 8   the LORD gives sight to the **b,**
Isa   42:19   Who is **b** but my servant,
     56:10   Israel's watchmen are **b,**
Mt   9:27   two **b** men followed him, calling out,
     11: 5   The **b** receive sight,
     15:14   If a **b** man leads a **b** man,
     23:16   "Woe to you, **b** guides!
Mk   10:46   were leaving the city, a **b** man,
Lk   6:39   "Can a **b** man lead a **b** man?
Jn   9: 1   he saw a man **b** from birth.
     9:25   I was **b** but now I see!"
Ac   9: 9   For three days he was **b,**
Ro   2:19   that you are a guide for the **b,**
2Pe   1: 9   he is nearsighted and **b,**
Rev   3:17   pitiful, poor, **b** and naked.

BLINDED* [BLIND]

Zec   11:17   his right eye totally **b!"**
Jn   12:40   "He has **b** their eyes
Ac   22:11   the brilliance of the light had **b** me.
2Co   4: 4   The god of this age has **b** the minds
1Jn   2:11   because the darkness has **b** him.

BLINDFOLDED

Mk   14:65   began to spit at him; they **b** him,

BLINDNESS [BLIND]

Ge   19:11   with **b** so that they could not find
2Ki   6:18   "Strike these people with **b."**

BLINDS [BLIND]

Dt   16:19   for a bribe **b** the eyes of the wise

BLOCK

Isa   44:19   Shall I bow down to a **b** of wood?"
Eze   14: 7   a wicked stumbling **b** before his face
Mt   16:23   You are a stumbling **b** to me;
Ro   11: 9   a stumbling **b** and a retribution
     14:13   to put any stumbling **b** or obstacle
1Co   1:23   a stumbling **b** to Jews
2Co   6: 3   We put no stumbling **b**

BLOOD [AKELDAMA, BLEEDING, BLOODSHED, BLOODSHOT, BLOODTHIRSTY, LIFEBLOOD]

Ge   4:10   Your brother's **b** cries out to me
     9: 6   "Whoever sheds the **b** of man, by man shall his **b** be shed;
Ex   4:25   "Surely you are a bridegroom of **b**
     7:17   and it will be changed into **b.**
     12:13   The **b** will be a sign for you on
     24: 8   Moses then took the **b,**
Lev   7:27   If anyone eats **b,**
     16:15   for the people and take its **b** behind
     16:15   with it as he did with the bull's **b:**
     17:11   the **b** that makes atonement

     17:14   the life of every creature is its **b;**
Dt   12:23   because the **b** is the life,
Ps   50:13   of bulls or drink the **b** of goats?
     72:14   for precious is their **b** in his sight.
     106:38   They shed innocent **b,**
Pr   6:17   hands that shed innocent **b,**
Isa   1:11   in the **b** of bulls and lambs and goats.
     9: 5   and every garment rolled in **b** will
     34: 6   sword of the LORD is bathed in **b,**
Eze   3:18   I will hold you accountable for his **b.**
Joel   2:31   to darkness and the moon to **b** before
Na   3: 1   Woe to the city of **b,** full of lies,
Hab   2: 8   For you have shed man's **b;**
Mt   23:30   in shedding the **b** of the prophets.'
     26:28   This is my **b** of the covenant,
     27: 6   since it is **b** money."
     27: 8   is the Field of **B** to this day.
     27:24   "I am innocent of this man's **b,"**
Mk   14:24   "This is my **b** of the covenant,
Lk   22:44   like drops of **b** falling to the ground.
Jn   6:53   of the Son of Man and drink his **b,**
     19:34   a sudden flow of **b** and water.
Ac   2:20   to darkness and the moon to **b** before
     15:20   of strangled animals and from **b.**
     20:26   that I am innocent of the **b**
Ro   3:25   through faith in his **b.**
     5: 9   now been justified by his **b,**
1Co   11:25   the new covenant in my **b;**
Eph   1: 7   redemption through his **b,**
     2:13   near through the **b** of Christ.
     6:12   not against flesh and **b,**
Col   1:20   by making peace through his **b,**
Heb   9: 7   and never without **b,**
     9:12   not enter by means of the **b** of goats
     9:20   "This is the **b** of the covenant,
     9:22   shedding of **b** there is no forgiveness
     12:24   and to the sprinkled **b** that speaks
1Pe   1:19   but with the precious **b** of Christ,
1Jn   1: 7   and the **b** of Jesus, his Son,
     5: 6   the one who came by water and **b—**
Rev   1: 5   from our sins by his **b,**
     5: 9   with your **b** you purchased men
     6:10   of the earth and avenge our **b?"**
     6:12   the whole moon turned **b** red,
     7:14   and made them white in the **b** of
     8: 8   A third of the sea turned into **b,**
     12:11   overcame him by the **b** of the Lamb
     19:13   He is dressed in a robe dipped in **b,**

FLESH AND BLOOD See FLESH

BLOODGUILT* [GUILT]

Ps   51:14   Save me from **b,** O God,
Joel   3:21   Their **b,** which I have not pardoned,

BLOODSHED [BLOOD]

Nu   35:33   **B** pollutes the land,
Isa   5: 7   he looked for justice, but saw **b;**
Jer   48:10   on him who keeps his sword from **b!**
Eze   35: 6   Since you did not hate **b, b** will pursue you.
Hab   2:12   Woe to him who builds a city with **b**

BLOODSHOT* [BLOOD]

Pr   23:29   Who has **b** eyes?

BLOODTHIRSTY* [BLOOD]

Ps   5: 6 **b** and deceitful men the LORD abhors
      26: 9 my life with **b** men,
      55:23 **b** and deceitful men will not live
      59: 2 and save me from **b** men.
    139:19 Away from me, you **b** men!
Pr 29:10 **B** men hate a man of integrity

BLOOM

SS   2:15 our vineyards that are in **b.**
Isa 35: 2 it will burst into **b;**

BLOSSOM

Isa 35: 1 the wilderness will rejoice and **b.**
Hos 14: 5 be like the dew to Israel; he will **b**

BLOT [BLOTS, BLOTTED]

Ex 17:14 I will completely **b** out
      32:32 then **b** me out of the book
Dt   9:14 and **b** out their name from
Ne   4: 5 or **b** out their sins from your sight,
Ps 51: 1 compassion **b** out my transgressions,
Jer 18:23 or **b** out their sins from your sight.
Rev 3: 5 I will never **b** out his name from

BLOTS [BLOT]

Isa 43:25 am he who **b** out your transgressions,

BLOTTED [BLOT]

Dt 25: 6 so that his name will not be **b** out

BLOW [BLEW, BLOWN, BLOWS]

Jer 14:17 grievous wound, a crushing **b.**
Eze 33: 6 not **b** the trumpet to warn
Joel 2: 1 **B** the trumpet in Zion;

BLOWN [BLOW]

Eph 4:14 and **b** here and there by every wind
Jas   1: 6 **b** and tossed by the wind.
Jude 1:12 **b** along by the wind;

BLOWS [BLOW]

Pr   6:33 **B** and disgrace are his lot,
    20:30 **B** and wounds cleanse away evil,
Isa 40: 7 the breath of the LORD **b** on them.
Jn   3: 8 The wind **b** wherever it pleases.

BLUE

Ex 26:31 "Make a curtain of **b,**
    28:31 of the ephod entirely of **b** cloth,
Rev 9:17 dark **b,** and yellow as sulfur.

BLUSH*

Jer   3: 3 you refuse to **b** with shame.
     6:15 not even know how to **b.**
     8:12 not even know how to **b.**

BOANERGES*

Mk 3:17 **B,** which means Sons of Thunder);

BOARDS

Ex 27: 8 Make the altar hollow, out of **b.**
1Ki 6:15 lined its interior walls with cedar **b,**

BOAST [BOASTED, BOASTERS, BOASTFUL, BOASTING, BOASTS]

1Ki 20:11 not **b** like one who takes it off.' "
Ps 34: 2 My soul will **b** in the LORD;
    44: 8 In God we make our **b** all day long,
    52: 1 Why do you **b** of evil,
    75: 4 '**B** no more,' and to the wicked,
    97: 7 those who **b** in idols—
Pr 27: 1 Do not **b** about tomorrow,
Jer 9:23 not the wise man **b** of his wisdom or
              the strong man **b** of his strength
Ro 11:18 do not **b** over those branches.
1Co 1:31 it is written: "Let him who boasts **b**
    13: 4 It does not envy, it does not **b,**
2Co 10: 8 even if I **b** somewhat freely about
    10:17 "Let him who boasts **b** in the Lord."
    11:30 If I must **b,** I will **b** of the things that
              show my weakness.
Gal 6:14 May I never **b** except in the cross
Eph 2: 9 not by works, so that no one can **b.**
Php 2:16 that I may **b** on the day of Christ
Heb 3: 6 and the hope of which we **b.**
Jas   3:14 do not **b** about it or deny the truth.

BOASTED [BOAST]

Est 5:11 Haman **b** to them
Ac   8: 9 He **b** that he was someone great,

BOASTERS* [BOAST]

Jer 48:45 the skulls of the noisy **b.**

BOASTFUL* [BOAST]

Ps 12: 3 and every **b** tongue
Da   7:11 the **b** words the horn was speaking.
Ro 1:30 God-haters, insolent, arrogant and **b;**
2Ti   3: 2 lovers of money, **b,** proud, abusive,
2Pe 2:18 For they mouth empty, **b** words and,

BOASTING [BOAST]

1Co 5: 6 Your **b** is not good.
2Co 10:13 but will confine our **b** to
Jas   4:16 All such **b** is evil.
1Jn   2:16 and the **b** of what he has and does—

BOASTS [BOAST]

Pr 20:14 and **b** about his purchase.
Jer 9:24 but let him who **b** boast about this:
1Co 1:31 as it is written: "Let him who **b** boast
2Co 10:17 "Let him who **b** boast in the Lord."
Rev 18: 7 In her heart she **b,** 'I sit as queen;

BOAT [BOATS]

Mt   4:21 in a **b** with their father Zebedee,
     8:23 the **b** and his disciples followed him.
    13: 2 that he got into a **b** and sat in it,
    14:13 by **b** privately to a solitary place.
    14:29 Then Peter got down out of the **b,**
Jn 21: 6 net on the right side of the **b**

BOATS [BOAT]

Lk   5: 7 both **b** so full that they began to sink.

BOAZ

Wealthy Bethlehemite who showed favor to

Ruth (Ru 2), married her (Ru 4). Ancestor of David (Ru 4:18-22; 1Ch 2:12-15), Jesus (Mt 1:5-16; Lk 3:23-32).

BODIES [BODY]

Lev	19:28	" 'Do not cut your **b** for the dead
Nu	14:29	In this desert your **b** will fall—
1Ch	10:12	and took the **b** of Saul and his sons
Isa	26:19	your dead will live; their **b** will rise.
Da	3:27	that the fire had not harmed their **b**,
Lk	21:26	for the heavenly **b** will be shaken.
Ac	7:42	to the worship of the heavenly **b**.
Ro	1:24	degrading of their **b** with one another
	12: 1	to offer your **b** as living sacrifices,
1Co	6:15	not know that your **b** are members
Eph	5:28	to love their wives as their own **b**.
Php	3:21	will transform our lowly **b** so
Heb	10:22	and having our **b** washed
Jude	1: 8	these dreamers pollute their own **b**,
Rev	18:13	and **b** and souls of men.

BODILY [BODY]

Col	2: 9	fullness of the Deity lives in **b** form,

BODY [BODIES, BODILY, EMBODIMENT]

Ge	15: 4	from your own **b** will be your heir."
2Sa	7:12	who will come from your own **b**,
Ps	139:16	your eyes saw my unformed **b**.
Pr	14:30	A heart at peace gives life to the **b**,
Ecc	12:12	and much study wearies the **b**.
Zec	13: 6	'What are these wounds on your **b**?'
Mt	10:28	destroy both soul and **b** in hell.
	26:26	"Take and eat; this is my **b**."
	26:41	but the **b** is weak."
	27:58	he asked for Jesus' **b**,
Mk	14:22	"Take it; this is my **b**."
Lk	11:34	Your eye is the lamp of your **b**.
	12: 4	not be afraid of those who kill the **b**
	22:19	saying, "This is my **b** given for you;
Jn	13:10	his whole **b** is clean.
Ac	2:31	nor did his **b** see decay.
Ro	6:13	not offer the parts of your **b** to sin,
	8:10	your **b** is dead because of sin,
	12: 4	of us has one **b** with many members,
1Co	6:13	The **b** is not meant
	6:18	sins against his own **b**.
	6:19	your **b** is a temple of the Holy Spirit,
	6:20	Therefore honor God with your **b**.
	7: 4	the husband's **b** does not belong
	9:27	I beat my **b** and make it my slave so
	11:24	he broke it and said, "This is my **b**,
	12:12	The **b** is a unit,
	12:13	baptized by one Spirit into one **b**—
	15:44	it is sown a natural **b**, it is raised a spiritual **b**.
2Co	5: 8	away from the **b** and at home with the Lord.
Gal	6:17	I bear on my **b** the marks of Jesus.
Eph	1:23	which is his **b**, the fullness
	4:25	for we are all members of one **b**.
	5:30	for we are members of his **b**.
Php	1:20	be exalted in my **b**,
Col	1:24	for the sake of his **b**,

1Th	4: 4	to control his own **b** in a way
Heb	10: 5	but a **b** you prepared for me;
Jas	2:26	As the **b** without the spirit is dead,
1Pe	2:24	He himself bore our sins in his **b** on
Jude	1: 9	with the devil about the **b** of Moses,

BOILS

Ex	9: 9	festering **b** will break out on men
Dt	28:27	with the **b** of Egypt and with tumors,

BOLD [BOLDLY, BOLDNESS]

Ps	138: 3	you answered me; you made me **b**
Pr	21:29	A wicked man puts up a **b** front,
	28: 1	but the righteous are as **b** as a lion.
2Co	3:12	we have such a hope, we are very **b**.
	10: 1	but **"b"** when away!
Phm	1: 8	in Christ I could be **b** and order you

BOLDLY [BOLD]

Ex	14: 8	who were marching out **b**.
Ac	4:31	and spoke the word of God **b**.
	9:28	speaking **b** in the name of the Lord.
	14: 3	speaking **b** for the Lord,

BOLDNESS* [BOLD]

Lk	11: 8	because of the man's **b** he will get up
Ac	4:29	to speak your word with great **b**.

BOLTS

Job	38:35	the lightning **b** on their way?
Ps	18:14	great **b** of lightning and routed them.

BONDAGE

Ex	6: 9	of their discouragement and cruel **b**.
Ezr	9: 9	our God has not deserted us in our **b**.
Ro	8:21	liberated from its **b** to decay

BONE [BACKBONE, BONES]

Ge	2:23	"This is now **b** of my bones and flesh
Pr	25:15	and a gentle tongue can break a **b**.
Eze	37: 7	the bones came together, **b** to **b**.

BONES [BONE]

Ge	50:25	and then you must carry my **b** up
Ex	12:46	Do not break any of the **b**.
Jos	24:32	And Joseph's **b**,
2Ki	13:21	When the body touched Elisha's **b**,
Ps	22:14	and all my **b** are out of joint.
	22:17	I can count all my **b**;
	34:20	he protects all his **b**,
Pr	14:30	but envy rots the **b**.
	15:30	and good news gives health to the **b**.
Jer	20: 9	a fire shut up in my **b**.
Eze	37: 4	'Dry **b**, hear the word of the LORD!
Mt	23:27	on the inside are full of dead men's **b**
Jn	19:36	"Not one of his **b** will be broken,"
Heb	11:22	and gave instructions about his **b**.

BOOK [BOOKS]

Ex	24: 7	Then he took the **B** of the Covenant
	32:33	against me I will blot out of my **b**.
Dt	31:24	After Moses finished writing in a **b**
Jos	1: 8	Do not let this **B** of the Law depart
	23: 6	to obey all that is written in the **B** of
2Ki	22: 8	"I have found the **B** of the Law in

2Ch 34:15 "I have found the **B** of the Law in
Ne 8: 8 They read from the **B** of the Law
Ps 69:28 be blotted out of the **b** of life and not
Da 12: 1 name is found written in the **b—**
Jn 20:30 which are not recorded in this **b.**
Ac 1: 1 In my former **b,** Theophilus,
8:28 in his chariot reading the **b** of Isaiah
Php 4: 3 whose names are in the **b** of life.
Rev 3: 5 from the **b** of life,
13: 8 the **b** of life belonging to the Lamb
17: 8 not been written in the **b**
20:12 Another **b** was opened, which is the **b** of life.
20:15 not found written in the **b** of life,
21:27 written in the Lamb's **b** of life.
22:18 the words of the prophecy of this **b:**
22:18 the plagues described in this **b.**

BOOK OF THE LAW See LAW
THE BOOK OF THE ANNALS
See ANNALS
WRITTEN IN THE BOOK See WRITTEN

BOOKS* [BOOK]
Ecc 12:12 Of making many **b** there is no end,
Da 7:10 and the **b** were opened.
Jn 21:25 world would not have room for the **b**
Rev 20:12 and **b** were opened.
20:12 as recorded in the **b.**

BOOTH [BOOTHS]
Lk 5:27 the name of Levi sitting at his tax **b.**

BOOTHS [BOOTH]
Lev 23:42 Live in **b** for seven days:
Ne 8:14 the Israelites were to live in **b** during

BORDER [BORDERS]
2Ch 9:26 as far as the **b** of Egypt.
Ps 78:54 Thus he brought them to the **b**

BORDERS [BORDER]
Ex 23:31 "I will establish your **b** from
Mal 1: 5 even beyond the **b** of Israel!'

BORE [BEAR]
Isa 53:12 For he **b** the sin of many,
Ro 7: 5 so that we **b** fruit for death.
Heb 13:13 bearing the disgrace he **b.**
1Pe 2:24 He himself **b** our sins in his body on
Rev 17: 6 the blood of those who **b** testimony

BORN [BEAR]
Ge 17:17 be **b** to a man a hundred years old?
Job 14: 1 "Man **b** of woman is of few days
Ps 90: 2 Before the mountains were **b**
Pr 17:17 and a brother is **b** for adversity.
Ecc 3: 2 a time to be **b** and a time to die,
Isa 9: 6 For to us a child is **b,**
66: 8 Can a country be **b** in a day
Jer 1: 5 before you were **b** I set you apart;
Mt 1:16 of whom was **b** Jesus,
2: 1 After Jesus was **b** in Bethlehem
Lk 1:35 to be **b** will be called the Son of God.
2:11 of David a Savior has been **b** to you;

7:28 among those **b** of women
Jn 1:13 but **b** of God.
3: 3 of God unless he is **b** again."
3: 5 unless he is **b** of water and
3: 7 'You must be **b** again.'
3: 8 it is with everyone **b** of the Spirit."
8:58 "before Abraham was **b,** I am!"
1Co 15: 8 as to one abnormally **b.**
Gal 4: 4 God sent his Son, **b** of a woman,
1Pe 1:23 For you have been **b** again,
1Jn 3: 9 No one who is **b** of God
4: 7 Everyone who loves has been **b**
5: 1 that Jesus is the Christ is **b** of God,
5: 4 for everyone **b** of God overcomes
5:18 We know that anyone **b** of God does
Rev 12: 4 the moment it was **b.**

BORROW [BORROWER]
Dt 15: 6 (but will **b** from none.
Ps 37:21 The wicked **b** and do not repay,
Mt 5:42 the one who wants to **b** from you.

BORROWER* [BORROW]
Ex 22:15 the **b** will not have to pay.
Pr 22: 7 and the **b** is servant to the lender.
Isa 24: 2 for **b** as for lender,

BOTHER [BOTHERING]
Lk 8:49 "Don't **b** the teacher any more."
11: 7 one inside answers, 'Don't **b** me.

BOTHERING [BOTHER]
Lk 18: 5 yet because this widow keeps **b** me,

BOTTOM
Am 9: 3 Though they hide from me at the **b**
Mk 15:38 was torn in two from top to **b.**

BOTTOMLESS (KJV) See ABYSS

BOUGHS
Ps 118:27 With **b** in hand,
Eze 31: 6 All the birds of the air nested in its **b,**

BOUGHT [BUY]
Ge 25:10 the field Abraham had **b** from
Ex 15:16 until the people you **b** pass by.
2Sa 24:24 So David **b** the threshing floor and
Ne 5: 8 we have **b** back our Jewish brothers
Job 28:15 It cannot be **b** with the finest gold,
Mt 13:46 and sold everything he had and **b** it.
Ac 1:18 Judas **b** a field;
20:28 which he **b** with his own blood.
1Co 6:20 you were **b** at a price.
7:23 You were **b** at a price;
2Pe 2: 1 the sovereign Lord who **b** them—

BOUND [BIND]
Ge 22: 9 He **b** his son Isaac and laid him on
Pr 22:15 Folly is **b** up in the heart of a child,
Jer 39: 7 and **b** him with bronze shackles
40: 1 He had found Jeremiah **b** in chains
Mt 16:19 on earth will be **b** in heaven,
18:18 whatever you bind on earth will be **b**
Lk 13:16 whom Satan has kept **b**

Ro   7: 2 a married woman is **b** to her husband
1Co   7:15 A believing man or woman is not **b**
      7:39 A woman is **b** to her husband as long
Jude 1: 6 **b** with everlasting chains
Rev   9:14 "Release the four angels who are **b** at
      20: 2 and **b** him for a thousand years.

BOUNDARIES [BOUNDARY]

Ps   74:17 It was you who set all the **b** of
Pr   15:25 but he keeps the widow's **b** intact.

BOUNDARY [BOUNDARIES, BOUNDS]

Nu   34: 3 your southern **b** will start from
Dt   19:14 Do not move your neighbor's **b** stone
Job 24: 2 Men move **b** stones;
Ps   16: 6 The **b** lines have fallen for me
     104: 9 You set a **b** they cannot cross;
Pr   22:28 Do not move an ancient **b** stone set
Eze 47:15 "This is to be the **b** of the land:
Hos   5:10 like those who move **b** stones.

BOUNDS* [BOUNDARY]

Hos   4: 2 they break all **b**,
2Co   7: 4 all our troubles my joy knows no **b**.

BOUNTY*

Ge   49:26 than the **b** of the age-old hills.
Dt   28:12 the storehouse of his **b**,
1Ki 10:13 given her out of his royal **b**.
Ps   65:11 You crown the year with your **b**,
     68:10 and from your **b**, O God,
Jer 31:12 in the **b** of the LORD—
     31:14 my people will be filled with my **b**,"

BOX   (KJV) See CHEST, HORN, FLASK

BOW [BOWED, BOWS]

Ge   27:29 May nations serve you and peoples **b**
Dt   5: 9 not **b** down to them or worship them;
Jos 23: 7 You must not serve them or **b** down
2Sa   1:18 be taught this lament of the **b**
     22:35 my arms can bend a **b** of bronze.
1Ki 22:34 But someone drew his **b** at random
Ps   5: 7 in reverence will I **b** down
     44: 6 I do not trust in my **b**,
     95: 6 Come, let us **b** down in worship,
     138: 2 I will **b** down
Isa 44:19 Shall I **b** down to a block of wood?"
     45:23 Before me every knee will **b**;
Mt   4: 9 if you will **b** down and worship me.
Ro   14:11 'every knee will **b** before me;
Php   2:10 of Jesus every knee should **b**,
Rev   6: 2 Its rider held a **b**,

BOWED [BOW]

Ge   18: 2 and **b** low to the ground.
     37: 7 around mine and **b** down to it."
     42: 6 they **b** down to him with their faces
Ex   34: 8 Moses **b** to the ground at once
2Ch 33: 3 He **b** down to all the starry hosts
Ps   35:14 I am **b** down in grief as
     38: 6 I am **b** down and brought very low;
     145:14 and lifts up all who are **b** down.

146: 8 the LORD lifts up those who are **b**
Mt   2:11 and they **b** down and worshiped him.
Jn   19:30 he **b** his head and gave up his spirit.

BOWELS

2Ch 21:15 with a lingering disease of the **b**,

BOWL [BOWLS]

Mk   4:21 a lamp to put it under a **b** or a bed?
Rev 16: 2 and poured out his **b** on the land,

BOWLS [BOWL]

Rev   5: 8 and they were holding golden **b** full
     16: 1 pour out the seven **b** of God's wrath

BOWS [BOW]

Ps   66: 4 All the earth **b** down to you;
Isa 44:15 he makes an idol and **b** down to it.
     46: 1 Bel **b** down, Nebo stoops low;

BOY [BOY'S, BOYS]

Ge   21:17 God heard the **b** crying,
     22:12 "Do not lay a hand on the **b**,"
Lev 12: 3 On the eighth day the **b** is to
Jdg 13: 5 because the **b** is to be a Nazirite,
1Sa   2:11 the **b** ministered before the LORD
      3: 8 that the LORD was calling the **b**.
Isa   7:16 before the **b** knows enough to reject
      8: 4 the **b** knows how to say 'My father'
Mt   17:18 and it came out of the **b**,
Lk   2:43 **b** Jesus stayed behind in Jerusalem,

BOY'S [BOY]

1Ki 17:22 and the **b** life returned to him,
2Ki   4:34 the **b** body grew warm.

BOYS [BOY]

Ge   25:24 there were twin **b** in her womb.
     38:27 there were twin **b** in her womb.
Ex   1:18 Why have you let the **b** live?"
Mt   2:16 to kill all the **b** in Bethlehem

BRACE*

Job 38: 3 **B** yourself like a man;
     40: 7 "**B** yourself like a man;
Na   2: 1 watch the road, **b** yourselves,

BRACELETS

Ge   24:22 and two gold **b** weighing ten shekels.
Eze 16:11 I adorned you with jewelry: I put **b**

BRAG*

Am   4: 5 and **b** about your freewill offerings
Ro   2:17 and **b** about your relationship to God
      2:23 You who **b** about the law,
Jas   4:16 As it is, you boast and **b**.

BRAIDED [BRAIDS]

1Ti   2: 9 not with **b** hair or gold or pearls
1Pe   3: 3 such as **b** hair and the wearing

BRAIDS [BRAIDED]

Jdg 16:13 Delilah took the seven **b** of his head,

BRAMBLE   (KJV) See THORNBUSH

BRANCH [BRANCHES]

Nu 13:23 a **b** bearing a single cluster of grapes.
Isa 4: 2 the **B** of the Lord will be beautiful
14:19 of your tomb like a rejected **b**;
Jer 23: 5 raise up to David a righteous **B,**
33:15 righteous **B** sprout from David's line
Zec 3: 8 to bring my servant, the **B.**
6:12 the man whose name is the **B,**
6:12 and he will **b** out from his place
Jn 15: 2 He cuts off every **b** in me
15: 4 No **b** can bear fruit by itself;

BRANCHES [BRANCH]

Ge 30:38 Then he placed the peeled **b** in all
Ex 25:32 Six **b** are to extend from the sides of
Dt 24:20 do not go over the **b** a second time.
Eze 17: 6 Its **b** turned toward him,
Zec 4:12 "What are these two olive **b** beside
Lk 13:19 the birds of the air perched in its **b.**"
Jn 12:13 They took palm **b** and went out
15: 5 "I am the vine; you are the **b.**
Ro 11:21 if God did not spare the natural **b,**
Rev 7: 9 and were holding palm **b**

BRASEN, BRASS (KJV)

See BRONZE

BRAVE [BRAVEST]

2Sa 2: 7 Now then, be strong and **b,**
13:28 Be strong and **b.**"
1Ch 12: 8 They were **b** warriors,

BRAVEST* [BRAVE]

2Sa 17:10 Then even the **b** soldier,
Am 2:16 Even the **b** warriors will flee naked

BRAWLER*

Pr 20: 1 Wine is a mocker and beer a **b;**

BRAZEN*

Pr 7:13 and with a **b** face she said:
Jer 3: 3 you have the **b** look of a prostitute;
Eze 16:30 acting like a **b** prostitute!

BREACH [BREAK]

Ps 106:23 stood in the **b** before him to keep

BREACHING [BREAK]

Pr 17:14 Starting a quarrel is like **b** a dam;

BREAD

Ex 12: 8 and **b** made without yeast.
12:17 the Feast of Unleavened **B,**
16: 4 "I will rain down **b** from heaven
23:15 Celebrate the Feast of Unleavened **B**
25:30 the **b** of the Presence on this table to
Dt 8: 3 man does not live on **b** alone
16: 3 the **b** of affliction.
1Ki 17: 6 The ravens brought him **b** and meat
22:27 give him nothing but **b** and water
2Ch 4:19 on which was the **b** of the Presence;
Ne 9:15 In their hunger you gave them **b**
Ps 37:25 or their children begging **b.**

41: 9 whom I trusted, he who shared my **b,**
78:25 Men ate the **b** of angels;
Pr 30: 8 but give me only my daily **b.**
Ecc 11: 1 Cast your **b** upon the waters,
Isa 55: 2 Why spend money on what is not **b,**
Mt 4: 3 tell these stones to become **b.**"
4: 4 'Man does not live on **b** alone,
6:11 Give us today our daily **b.**
15:33 "Where could we get enough **b**
16: 5 the disciples forgot to take **b.**
26:26 Jesus took **b,** gave thanks
Lk 11: 3 Give us each day our daily **b.**
22:19 And he took **b,**
24:35 by them when he broke the **b.**
Jn 6:33 **b** of God is he who comes down
6:35 Jesus declared, "I am the **b** of life.
6:41 the **b** that came down from heaven."
6:48 I am the **b** of life.
6:51 I am the living **b** that came down
6:51 This **b** is my flesh,
13:27 As soon as Judas took the **b,**
21:13 took the **b** and gave it to them,
Ac 2:42 to the breaking of **b** and to prayer.
1Co 10:16 the **b** that we break a participation in
11:23 on the night he was betrayed, took **b,**
11:26 For whenever you eat this **b**
2Th 3:12 and earn the **b** they eat.

THE FEAST OF UNLEAVENED BREAD

See FEAST

BREAK [BREACH, BREACHING, BREAKERS, BREAKING, BREAKS, BROKE, BROKEN, BROKENNESS, LAWBREAKER, LAWBREAKERS]

Ex 12:46 Do not **b** any of the bones.
Nu 30: 2 he must not **b** his word
Jos 22:16 'How could you **b** faith with
Jdg 2: 1 'I will never **b** my covenant
Pr 25:15 and a gentle tongue can **b** a bone.
Isa 42: 3 A bruised reed he will not **b,**
Mal 2:15 and do not **b** faith with the wife
Mt 12:20 A bruised reed he will not **b,**
15: 3 "And why do you **b** the command
Jn 19:33 they did not **b** his legs.
Ac 20: 7 came together to **b** bread.
Ro 2:25 but if you **b** the law,
1Co 10:16 the bread that we **b** a participation in
Rev 5: 2 to **b** the seals and open the scroll?"

BREAKERS* [BREAK]

Ps 42: 7 and **b** have swept over me.
93: 4 mightier than the **b** of the sea—
Jnh 2: 3 and **b** swept over me.

BREAKING [BREAK]

Ex 32:19 **b** them to pieces at the foot of
Lev 26:44 **b** my covenant with them.
Dt 31:20 rejecting me and **b** my covenant.
Jos 9:20 not fall on us for **b** the oath we swore
Eze 16:59 my oath by **b** the covenant.
17:18 the oath by **b** the covenant.
Zec 11:14 **b** the brotherhood between Judah
Ac 2:42 to the **b** of bread and to prayer.

Ro   2:23 do you dishonor God by **b** the law?
Jas 2:10 at just one point is guilty of **b** all

BREAKS [BREAK]

Ex   1:10 if war **b** out, will join our enemies,
Ps 29: 5 voice of the LORD **b** the cedars;
    76:12 He **b** the spirit of rulers;
Jer 23:29 a hammer that **b** a rock in pieces?
Da   2:40 and as iron **b** things to pieces,
Mt   5:19 Anyone who **b** one of the least
1Jn 3: 4 Everyone who sins **b** the law;

BREAST [BREASTPIECE, BREASTPLATE, BREASTPLATES, BREASTS]

Ps 22: 9 in you even at my mother's **b.**
Eze 21:12 Therefore beat your **b.**
Lk 18:13 but beat his **b** and said, 'God,

BREASTPIECE [BREAST]

Ex 28:15 "Fashion a **b** for making decisions—
    28:30 the Urim and the Thummim in the **b,**

BREASTPLATE* [BREAST]

Isa 59:17 He put on righteousness as his **b,**
Eph 6:14 with the **b** of righteousness in place,
1Th 5: 8 putting on faith and love as a **b,**

BREASTPLATES [BREAST]

Rev 9: 9 They had **b** like breastplates of iron,

BREASTS [BREAST]

Pr   5:19 may her **b** satisfy you always,
SS   4: 5 Your two **b** are like two fawns,
La   4: 3 Even jackals offer their **b**
Na   2: 7 like doves and beat upon their **b.**

BREATH [BREATHED, BREATHING, GOD-BREATHED]

Ge   1:30 that has the **b** of life in it—
     2: 7 and breathed into his nostrils the **b**
     6:17 every creature that has the **b** of life
Ex 15:10 But you blew with your **b,**
2Sa 22:16 at the blast of **b** from his nostrils.
Job 27: 3 the **b** of God in my nostrils,
Ps 39: 5 Each man's life is but a **b.**
    150: 6 Let everything that has **b** praise
Ecc 3:19 All have the same **b;**
La   4:20 LORD's anointed, our very life **b,**
Eze 37: 8 but there was no **b** in them.
Ac 17:25 he himself gives all men life and **b**
Rev 11:11 after the three and a half days a **b**
    13:15 He was given power to give **b** to

BREATHED [BREATH]

Ge   2: 7 **b** into his nostrils the breath of life,
Mk 15:37 With a loud cry, Jesus **b** his last.
Jn 20:22 And with that he **b** on them and said,

BREATHING [BREATH]

Ac   9: 1 Saul was still **b** out murderous

BREEDS*

Pr 13:10 Pride only **b** quarrels,

BRIBE [BRIBERY, BRIBES]

Ex 23: 8 for a **b** blinds those who see
Dt 16:19 for a **b** blinds the eyes of the wise
    27:25 "Cursed is the man who accepts a **b**
1Sa 12: 3 a **b** to make me shut my eyes?
Pr   6:35 he will refuse the **b,**
Ecc 7: 7 and a **b** corrupts the heart.
Isa 5:23 who acquit the guilty for a **b,**
Mic 3:11 Her leaders judge for a **b,**
Ac 24:26 that Paul would offer him a **b,**

BRIBERY* [BRIBE]

2Ch 19: 7 no injustice or partiality or **b."**

BRIBES [BRIBE]

Dt 10:17 no partiality and accepts no **b.**
1Sa 8: 3 and accepted **b** and perverted justice.

BRICK [BRICKS]

Ge 11: 3 They used **b** instead of stone,
Ex   1:14 with hard labor in **b** and mortar and

BRICKS [BRICK]

Ge 11: 3 "Come, let's make **b**

BRIDE [BRIDE-PRICE]

Ge 34:12 Make the price for the **b** and the gift
1Sa 18:25 wants no other price for the **b**
Ps 45: 9 at your right hand is the royal **b**
SS   4: 8 Come with me from Lebanon, my **b,**
Isa 49:18 you will put them on, like a **b.**
    62: 5 as a bridegroom rejoices over his **b,**
Jer 2:32 a **b** her wedding ornaments?
Jn   3:29 The **b** belongs to the bridegroom.
Rev 19: 7 and his **b** has made herself ready.
    21: 2 prepared as a **b** beautifully dressed
    21: 9 "Come, I will show you the **b,**
    22:17 The Spirit and the **b** say, "Come!"

BRIDE-PRICE [BRIDE]*

Ex 22:16 he must pay the **b,**
    22:17 he must still pay the **b** for virgins.

BRIDEGROOM

Ex   4:25 "Surely you are a **b** of blood to me,"
Ps 19: 5 a **b** coming forth from his pavilion,
Jer 25:10 the voices of bride and **b,**
Mt 25: 1 and went out to meet the **b.**
    25: 5 The **b** was a long time in coming,
Mk   2:20 when the **b** will be taken from them,
Rev 18:23 The voice of **b** and bride will never

BRIEF*

Ezr 9: 8 "But now, for a **b** moment,
Job 20: 5 that the mirth of the wicked is **b,**
Isa 54: 7 "For a **b** moment I abandoned you,

BRIER* [BRIERS]

Mic 7: 4 The best of them is like a **b,**

BRIERS [BRIER]

Isa 55:13 instead of **b** the myrtle will grow.
Lk 6:44 or grapes from **b.**

BRIGHT [BRIGHTENS, BRIGHTER, BRIGHTNESS]

SS 6:10 fair as the moon, **b** as the sun,
Lk 9:29 and his clothes became as **b** as
Ac 22: 6 a **b** light from heaven flashed
Rev 19: 8 Fine linen, **b** and clean,
22:16 and the **b** Morning Star."

BRIGHTENS* [BRIGHT]

Pr 16:15 When a king's face **b,** it means life;
Ecc 8: 1 Wisdom **b** a man's face

BRIGHTER [BRIGHT]

Pr 4:18 shining ever **b** till the full light
Ac 26:13 **b** than the sun,

BRIGHTNESS* [BRIGHT]

2Sa 22:13 Out of the **b** of his presence bolts
23: 4 the **b** after rain that brings the grass
Ps 18:12 Out of the **b**
Isa 59: 9 for **b,** but we walk in deep shadows.
60: 3 and kings to the **b** of your dawn.
60:19 nor will the **b** of the moon shine
Da 12: 3 like the **b** of the heavens,
Am 5:20 without a ray of **b?**

BRILLIANCE* [BRILLIANT]

Ac 22:11 the **b** of the light had blinded me.
Rev 1:16 like the sun shining in all its **b.**
21:11 and its **b** was like that of

BRILLIANT* [BRILLIANCE]

Ecc 9:11 or wealth to the **b** or favor to the
Eze 1: 4 and surrounded by **b** light.
1:27 and **b** light surrounded him.

BRIM*

Pr 3:10 your vats will **b** over with new wine.
Jn 2: 7 so they filled them to the **b.**

BRIMSTONE (KJV) See SULFUR

BRING [BRINGING, BRINGS, BROUGHT]

Ge 6:17 to **b** floodwaters on the earth
6:19 You are to **b** into the ark two
28:15 and I will **b** you back to this land.
Ex 3: 8 to **b** them up out of that land into
6:26 "**B** the Israelites out of Egypt
18:22 but have them **b** every difficult case
25: 2 the Israelites to **b** me an offering.
32:12 and do not **b** disaster on your people.
Nu 20: 5 Why did you **b** us up out of Egypt
Dt 24: 4 Do not **b** sin upon the land
26:10 I **b** the firstfruits of the soil that you,
1Ki 21:21 'I am going to **b** disaster on you.
2Ki 22:16 to **b** disaster on this place
Pr 3: 8 This will **b** health to your body
10: 4 but diligent hands **b** wealth.

13: 5 the wicked **b** shame and disgrace.
18: 6 A fool's lips **b** him strife,
Isa 40: 9 You who **b** good tidings to Zion,
52: 7 the feet of those who **b** good news,
54: 7 deep compassion I will **b** you back.
Jer 24: 6 and I will **b** them back to this land.
26: 3 Then I will relent and not **b** on them
Eze 5:17 and I will **b** the sword against you.
Da 9:24 to **b** in everlasting righteousness,
Hos 4: 1 because the LORD has a charge to **b**
Lk 12:51 Do you think I came to **b** peace
Jn 10:16 I must **b** them also.
14:13 the Son may **b** glory to the Father.
Ro 10:15 the feet of those who **b** good news!"
1Co 8: 8 But food does not **b** us near to God;
2Jn 10 to you and does not **b** this teaching,
Rev 15: 4 O Lord, and **b** glory to your name?

BRINGING [BRING]

Ex 36: 5 "The people are **b** more than enough
Isa 1:13 Stop **b** meaningless offerings!
Mt 27:13 the testimony they are **b** against you?
Lk 18:15 People were also **b** babies to Jesus
Heb 2:10 In **b** many sons to glory,

BRINGS [BRING]

Dt 6:10 When the LORD your God **b** you
1Sa 2: 6 LORD **b** death and makes alive;
Pr 11:17 but a cruel man **b** trouble on himself.
12:18 but the tongue of the wise **b** healing.
15:20 A wise son **b** joy to his father,
Lk 6:45 The good man **b** good things out of
Ro 4:15 because law **b** wrath.
2Co 7:10 Godly sorrow **b** repentance that leads
Tit 2:11 the grace of God that **b** salvation has
Heb 1: 6 God **b** his firstborn into the world,

BRINK*

Pr 5:14 I have come to the **b** of utter ruin in

BRITTLE*

Da 2:42 be partly strong and partly **b.**

BROAD

2Sa 12:11 with your wives in **b** daylight.
Isa 33:21 like a place of **b** rivers and streams.
Mt 7:13 For wide is the gate and **b** is the road
2Pe 2:13 to carouse in **b** daylight.

BROKE [BREAK]

Ex 9:10 and festering boils **b** out on men
34: 1 the first tablets, which you **b.**
2Ch 34: 4 These he **b** to pieces and scattered
36:19 and **b** down the wall of Jerusalem;
Jer 31:32 because they **b** my covenant,
Eze 44: 7 and you **b** my covenant.
Zec 11:10 I took my staff called Favor and **b** it,
Mt 26:26 gave thanks and **b** it,
27:52 The tombs **b** open and the bodies
Mk 14:22 gave thanks and **b** it,
Ac 2:46 They **b** bread in their homes
20:11 and **b** bread and ate.
1Co 11:24 he **b** it and said, "This is my body,
Rev 16: 2 and painful sores **b** out on

BROKEN [BREAK]

1Sa	4:18	His neck was **b** and he died,
	5: 4	His head and hands had been **b** off
Ne	1: 3	The wall of Jerusalem is **b** down,
Ps	34:20	not one of them will be **b**.
	51:17	The sacrifices of God are a **b** spirit;
Ecc	4:12	cord of three strands is not quickly **b**.
	12: 6	or the golden bowl is **b;**
Jer	2:13	**b** cisterns that cannot hold water.
Da	8: 8	his power his large horn was **b** off,
Hos	6: 7	they have **b** the covenant—
Mal	2:11	Judah has **b** faith.
Lk	20:18	on that stone will be **b** to pieces,
Jn	7:23	that the law of Moses may not be **b,**
	10:35	and the Scripture cannot be **b—**
	19:36	"Not one of his bones will be **b,"**
Ro	11:20	they were **b** off because of unbelief,

BROKENHEARTED* [HEART]

Ps	34:18	The LORD is close to the **b**
	109:16	the poor and the needy and the **b.**
	147: 3	He heals the **b** and binds up their
Isa	61: 1	He has sent me to bind up the **b,**

BROKENNESS* [BREAK]

Isa	65:14	and wail in **b** of spirit.

BRONZE

Ge	4:22	who forged all kinds of tools out of **b**
Ex	27: 2	and overlay the altar with **b.**
	30:18	"Make a **b** basin,
Lev	26:19	and the ground beneath you like **b.**
Nu	21: 9	So Moses made a **b** snake and put it
Dt	28:23	The sky over your head will be **b,**
1Ki	7:15	He cast two **b** pillars,
	7:27	also made ten movable stands of **b;**
2Ki	16:14	The **b** altar that stood before
	25:13	Babylonians broke up the **b** pillars,
Ps	18:34	my arms can bend a bow of **b.**
Isa	48: 4	your forehead was **b.**
Da	2:32	its belly and thighs of **b,**
	10: 6	like the gleam of burnished **b,**
Zec	6: 1	two mountains—mountains of **b!**
Rev	1:15	His feet were like **b** glowing in
	2:18	and whose feet are like burnished **b.**

BROOD

Nu	32:14	"And here you are, a **b** of sinners,
Job	30: 8	A base and nameless **b,**
Isa	57: 4	Are you not a **b** of rebels,
Lk	3: 7	"You **b** of vipers!
2Pe	2:14	are experts in greed—an accursed **b!**

BROOK

1Ki	17: 4	You will drink from the **b,**
Ps	110: 7	He will drink from a **b** beside

BROOM

1Ki	19: 4	He came to a **b** tree,

BROTHER [BROTHER-IN-LAW,
BROTHER'S, BROTHERHOOD,
BROTHERLY, BROTHERS]

Ge	4: 8	Now Cain said to his **b** Abel,

	20:13	say of me, "He is my **b." ""**
	27:41	then I will kill my **b** Jacob."
	42:20	But you must bring your youngest **b**
	43:30	Deeply moved at the sight of his **b,**
	45: 4	he said, "I am your **b** Joseph,
Ex	7: 1	your **b** Aaron will be your prophet.
Lev	19:17	" 'Do not hate your **b** in your heart.
Dt	15: 7	or tightfisted toward your poor **b.**
	19:18	giving false testimony against his **b,**
	23:19	Do not charge your **b** interest,
	25: 5	Her husband's **b** shall take her
2Sa	13:12	"Don't, my **b!"**
Pr	17:17	and a **b** is born for adversity.
	18:24	a friend who sticks closer than a **b.**
	27:10	a neighbor nearby than a **b** far away.
SS	8: 1	If only you were to me like a **b,**
Isa	19: 2	**b** will fight against **b,**
Jer	9: 4	For every **b** is a deceiver,
Ob	1:10	of the violence against your **b** Jacob,
Mt	5:22	Again, anyone who says to his **b,**
	5:24	First go and be reconciled to your **b;**
	10:21	"**B** will betray to death,
	18:15	"If your **b** sins against you,
Mk	3:35	Whoever does God's will is my **b**
Lk	15:28	"The older **b** became angry
	17: 3	"If your **b** sins, rebuke him,
Ro	14:15	Do not by your eating destroy your **b**
	14:21	that will cause your **b** to fall.
1Co	5:11	with anyone who calls himself a **b**
	6: 6	one **b** goes to law against another—
	8:13	if what I eat causes my **b** to fall
2Th	3: 6	keep away from every **b** who is idle
	3:15	but warn him as a **b.**
Phm	1:16	but better than a slave, as a dear **b.**
Jas	2:15	a **b** or sister is without clothes
	4:11	against his **b** or judges him speaks
1Jn	2:10	Whoever loves his **b** lives in
	2:11	whoever hates his **b** is in
	3:10	not love his **b.**
	3:15	Anyone who hates his **b** is
	3:17	and sees his **b** in need but has no pity
	4:20	"I love God," yet hates his **b,**
	4:21	also love his **b.**
	5:16	If anyone sees his **b** commit a sin

BROTHER'S [BROTHER]

Ge	4: 9	"Am I my **b** keeper?"
Dt	25: 7	not want to marry his **b** wife,
Mt	7: 5	to remove the speck from your **b** eye.
Mk	6:18	for you to have your **b** wife."
Ro	14:13	or obstacle in your **b** way.

BROTHER-IN-LAW [BROTHER]

Ge	38: 8	to her as a **b** to produce offspring
Dt	25: 5	and fulfill the duty of a **b** to her.

BROTHERHOOD* [BROTHER]

Am	1: 9	disregarding a treaty of **b,**
Zec	11:14	the **b** between Judah and Israel.
1Pe	2:17	Love the **b** of believers,

BROTHERLY* [BROTHER]

Ro	12:10	Be devoted to one another in **b** love.
1Th	4: 9	about **b** love we do not need to write

2Pe 1: 7 and to godliness, **b** kindness;
　　 1: 7 and to **b** kindness,

BROTHERS [BROTHER]

Ge 9:25 lowest of slaves will he be to his **b**."
　　 27:29 Be lord over your **b**,
　　 37:11 His **b** were jealous of him,
Dt 10: 9 or inheritance among their **b**;
　　 18:18 like you from among their **b**;
Jos 1:14 must cross over ahead of your **b**.
　　 1:14 are to help your **b**
Jdg 9: 5 on one stone murdered his seventy **b**,
2Ch 21:13 You have also murdered your own **b**,
Ne 4:14 and fight for your **b**,
Ps 22:22 I will declare your name to my **b**;
　　 133: 1 when **b** live together in unity!
Pr 6:19 stirs up dissension among **b**.
Hos 2: 1 "Say of your **b**, 'My people,'
Mt 5:47 And if you greet only your **b**,
　　 12:49 "Here are my mother and my **b**.
　　 19:29 who has left houses or **b** or sisters
　　 25:40 of the least of these **b** of mine,
Mk 3:33 "Who are my mother and my **b**?"
　　 12:20 Now there were seven **b**.
Lk 21:16 **b**, relatives and friends,
　　 22:32 strengthen your **b**."
Jn 7: 5 his own **b** did not believe in him.
Ac 15:32 to encourage and strengthen the **b**.
Ro 8:29 be the firstborn among many **b**,
　　 9: 3 from Christ for the sake of my **b**,
1Co 8:12 you sin against your **b**
2Co 11:26 and in danger from false **b**.
Gal 2: 4 some false **b** had infiltrated our ranks
Eph 6:23 Peace to the **b**,
Col 1: 2 To the holy and faithful **b** in Christ
1Th 4:10 you do love all the **b** throughout
　　 5:26 Greet all the **b** with a holy kiss.
1Ti 5: 1 Treat younger men as **b**,
　　 6: 2 for them because they are **b**.
Heb 2:11 Jesus is not ashamed to call them **b**.
　　 2:17 to be made like his **b** in every way,
　　 13: 1 Keep on loving each other as **b**.
1Pe 1:22 sincere love for your **b**,
　　 3: 8 love as **b**,
1Jn 3:14 because we love our **b**.
　　 3:16 to lay down our lives for our **b**.
3Jn 1:10 he refuses to welcome the **b**.
Rev 12:10 For the accuser of our **b**,
　　 22: 9 and with your **b** the prophets and

BROUGHT [BRING]

Ge 2:19 He **b** them to the man
　　 2:22 and he **b** her to the man.
　　 15: 7 who **b** you out of Ur of
　　 21: 6 Sarah said, "God has **b** me laughter,
Ex 13: 9 For the LORD **b** you out of Egypt
　　 18:26 The difficult cases they **b** to Moses,
　　 32: 1 As for this fellow Moses who **b** us
Nu 11:11 "Why have you **b** this trouble
　　 21: 5 "Why have you **b** us up out of Egypt
Dt 8:15 He **b** you water out of hard rock.
Jdg 2: 1 "I **b** you up out of Egypt and led you
1Ch 11:14 the LORD **b** about a great victory.
Ne 9:15 in their thirst you **b** them water from

Ps 18:19 He **b** me out into a spacious place;
　　 30: 3 you **b** me up from the grave;
Pr 8:22 "The LORD **b** me forth as the first
La 1: 5 The LORD has **b** her grief because
Eze 11: 1 the Spirit lifted me up and **b** me
　　 37: 1 and he **b** me out by the Spirit of
Da 5:13 one of the exiles my father the king **b**
Jnh 2: 6 But you **b** my life up from the pit,
Mk 6:28 and **b** back his head on a platter.
　　 8:22 and some people **b** a blind man
　　 12:16 They **b** the coin, and he asked them,
　　 15:22 They **b** Jesus to
Ro 6:13 who have been **b** from death to life;
2Co 7: 7 Now if the ministry that **b** death,
Eph 2:13 once were far away have been **b** near
1Ti 6: 7 For we **b** nothing into the world,
Heb 6: 6 to be **b** back to repentance,

BROW

Ge 3:19 the sweat of your **b** you will eat

BROWN*

Zec 1: 8 **b** and white horses.

BRUISE* [BRUISED, BRUISES]

Ex 21:25 wound for wound, **b** for **b**.

BRUISED [BRUISE]

Isa 42: 3 A **b** reed he will not break,
Mt 12:20 A **b** reed he will not break,

BRUISES* [BRUISE]

Pr 23:29 Who has needless **b**?
Isa 30:26 the LORD binds up the **b**

BRUTAL* [BRUTE]

Eze 21:31 hand you over to **b** men,
2Ti 3: 3 slanderous, without self-control, **b**,

BRUTE* [BRUTAL, BRUTES]

Ps 73:22 I was a **b** beast before you.
2Pe 2:12 They are like **b** beasts,

BRUTES* [BRUTE]

Tit 1:12 "Cretans are always liars, evil **b**,

BUBBLING*

Pr 18: 4 the fountain of wisdom is a **b** brook.
Isa 35: 7 the thirsty ground **b** springs.

BUCKET*

Isa 40:15 the nations are like a drop in a **b**;

BUCKLED* [BUCKLER]

Eph 6:14 the belt of truth **b** around your waist,

BUCKLER* [BUCKLED]

Ps 35: 2 Take up shield and **b**;

BUCKLERS (KJV) See SHIELDS

BUD [BUDDED]

Isa 27: 6 Israel will **b** and blossom and fill all
Hab 3:17 Though the fig tree does not **b**

BUDDED [BUD]

Nu 17: 8 had not only sprouted but had **b**,
Eze 7:10 Doom has burst forth, the rod has **b**,
Heb 9: 4 Aaron's staff that had **b**,

BUILD [BUILDER, BUILDERS, BUILDING, BUILDINGS, BUILDS, BUILT, REBUILD, REBUILT]

Ge   6:15 This is how you are to **b** it:
      11: 4 "Come, let us **b** ourselves a city,
Ex 27: 1 "**B** an altar of acacia wood,
Nu 23: 1 "**B** me seven altars here,
Dt   6:10 flourishing cities you did not **b**,
2Sa 7: 5 the one to **b** me a house to dwell in?
1Ki 6: 1 to **b** the temple of the LORD.
Ezr 1: 3 and **b** the temple of the LORD,
Ps 51:18 **b** up the walls of Jerusalem.
Ecc 3: 3 a time to tear down and a time to **b**,
Isa 57:14 And it will be said: "**B** up, b up,
     62:10 **B** up, b up the highway!
Mic 3:10 who **b** Zion with bloodshed,
Zep 1:13 They will **b** houses but not live
Hag 1: 8 down timber and **b** the house,
Mt 16:18 and on this rock I will **b** my church,
     23:29 You **b** tombs for the prophets
     27:40 the temple and **b** it in three days,
Jn   2:20 forty-six years to **b** this temple,
Ac 20:32 which can **b** you up and give you
Ro 15: 2 to **b** him up.
1Co 14:12 to excel in gifts that **b** up the church.
1Th 5:11 and **b** each other up,
Jude 1:20 **b** yourselves up in your most holy

BUILDER* [BUILD]

1Co 3:10 I laid a foundation as an expert **b**,
Heb 3: 3 just as the **b** of
      3: 4 but God is the **b** of everything.
    11:10 whose architect and **b** is God.

BUILDERS [BUILD]

Ps 118:22 The stone the **b** rejected has become
    127: 1 its **b** labor in vain.
Mt 21:42 The stone the **b** rejected has become
Mk 12:10 The stone the **b** rejected has become
Lk 20:17 The stone the **b** rejected has become
Ac   4:11 He is " 'the stone you **b** rejected,
1Pe 2: 7 "The stone the **b** rejected has become

BUILDING [BUILD]

Ge 11: 5 and the tower that the men were **b**.
1Ki 9: 1 When Solomon had finished **b**
2Ki 25: 9 Every important **b** he burned down.
Ezr 4: 1 that the exiles were **b** a temple
Ne   4:17 who were **b** the wall.
Mic 7:11 The day for **b** your walls will come,
Lk   6:48 He is like a man **b** a house,
Ro 15:20 be **b** on someone else's foundation.
1Co 3: 9 you are God's field, God's **b**.
2Co 5: 1 we have a **b** from God,
     10: 8 for **b** you up rather than pulling you
    13:10 the Lord gave me for **b** you up,
Eph 2:21 In him the whole **b** is joined together
     4:29 but only what is helpful for **b** others

BUILDINGS [BUILD]

Mk 13: 1 What magnificent **b**!"

BUILDS [BUILD]

Ps 127: 1 Unless the LORD **b** the house,
    147: 2 The LORD **b** up Jerusalem;
Pr 14: 1 The wise woman **b** her house,
Jer 22:13 "Woe to him who **b** his palace
Hab 2: 9 "Woe to him who **b** his realm
     2:12 to him who **b** a city with bloodshed
1Co 3:10 each one should be careful how he **b.**
     3:12 If any man **b**
     8: 1 Knowledge puffs up, but love **b** up.
Eph 4:16 grows and **b** itself up in love,

BUILT [BUILD]

Ge   8:20 Noah **b** an altar to the LORD and,
    12: 7 So he **b** an altar there to the LORD,
    22: 9 Abraham **b** an altar there
    26:25 Isaac **b** an altar there and called on
    35: 7 There he **b** an altar,
Ex 17:15 Moses **b** an altar and called it
    24: 4 the next morning and **b** an altar at
    32: 5 he **b** an altar in front of the calf
Jos   8:30 Then Joshua **b** an altar on Mount Ebal
    22:11 they had **b** the altar on the border
Jdg   6:24 Gideon **b** an altar to the LORD
1Sa 7:17 he **b** an altar there to the LORD.
    14:35 Then Saul **b** an altar to the LORD;
2Sa 24:25 David **b** an altar to the LORD there
1Ki 6:14 So Solomon **b** the temple
    12:31 Jeroboam **b** shrines on high places
2Ki 23:12 the altars Manasseh had **b** in
Ezr 3: 3 they **b** the altar on its foundation
Ps 122: 3 Jerusalem is **b** like a city
Pr   9: 1 Wisdom has **b** her house;
    24: 3 By wisdom a house is **b**,
Hos 10: 1 his fruit increased, he **b** more altars;
Hag 1: 2 for the LORD's house to be **b.** "
Zec 8: 9 so that the temple may be **b**.
Mt   7:24 like a wise man who **b** his house on
Lk   6:49 a man who **b** a house on the ground
Ac 17:24 not live in temples **b** by hands.
1Co 3:14 If what he has **b** survives,
2Co 5: 1 not **b** by human hands.
Eph 2:20 **b** on the foundation of the apostles
    4:12 that the body of Christ may be **b** up
Col 2: 7 rooted and **b** up in him,
Heb 11: 7 in holy fear **b** an ark
1Pe 2: 5 are being **b** into a spiritual house to
    3:20 of Noah while the ark was being **b.**

BULL [BULLS]

Ex 21:28 a **b** gores a man or a woman to death,
Lev 1: 5 He is to slaughter the young **b** before
    4: 3 to the LORD a young **b** without defect
    16: 6 to offer the **b** for his own sin offering
Ps 50: 9 I have no need of a **b** from your stall
  106:20 for an image of a **b**,
Isa 66: 3 a **b** is like one who kills a man,

BULLS [BULL]

Ex 24: 5 and sacrificed young **b**
Nu 23: 1 and prepare seven **b** and seven rams

29:13 a burnt offering of thirteen young **b**,
1Ki 7:25 The Sea stood on twelve **b**,
1Ch 29:21 a thousand **b**, a thousand rams
Ezr 6:17 of God they offered a hundred **b**,
Ps 22:12 Many **b** surround me; strong **b** of
Bashan encircle me.
50:13 Do I eat the flesh of **b**
Jer 52:20 Sea and the twelve bronze **b** under it,
Heb 10: 4 it is impossible for the blood of **b**

BURDEN [BURDENED, BURDENS, BURDENSOME]

Nu 11:14 the **b** is too heavy for me.
Ps 38: 4 like a **b** too heavy to bear.
Ecc 1:13 a heavy **b** God has laid on men!
3:10 I have seen the **b** God has laid
Isa 1:14 They have become a **b** to me;
10:27 In that day their **b** will be lifted
Mal 1:13 And you say, 'What a **b!**'
Mt 11:30 my yoke is easy and my **b** is light."
Ac 15:28 and to us not to **b** you
2Co 11: 9 I was not a **b** to anyone,
12:14 and I will not be a **b** to you,
1Th 2: 6 we could have been a **b** to you,
2Th 3: 8 so that we would not be a **b** to any
Heb 13:17 a joy, not a **b**,
Rev 2:24 (I will not impose any other **b**

BURDENED* [BURDEN]

Isa 43:23 not **b** you with grain offerings
43:24 But you have **b** me with your sins
Mic 6: 3 How have I **b** you?
Mt 11:28 all you who are weary and **b**,
2Co 5: 4 we groan and are **b**,
Gal 5: 1 and do not let yourselves be **b** again
1Ti 5:16 not let the church be **b** with them,

BURDENS [BURDEN]

Ps 68:19 who daily bears our **b**.
Lk 11:46 down with **b** they can hardly carry,
Gal 6: 2 Carry each other's **b**,

BURDENSOME* [BURDEN]

Isa 46: 1 that are carried about are **b**,
1Jn 5: 3 And his commands are not **b**,

BURIAL [BURY]

Ge 23: 4 a **b** site here so I can bury my dead."
49:30 which Abraham bought as a **b** place
Mt 26:12 she did it to prepare me for **b**.
27: 7 to buy the potter's field as a **b** place

BURIED [BURY]

Ge 15:15 in peace and be **b** at a good old age.
Ru 1:17 and there I will be **b**.
Ecc 8:10 Then too, I saw the wicked **b**—
Ro 6: 4 **b** with him through baptism
1Co 15: 4 that he was **b**, that he was raised
Col 2:12 having been **b** with him in baptism

BURIES [BURY]

Pr 19:24 The sluggard **b** his hand in the dish;

BURN [BURNED, BURNING, BURNT]

Ex 3: 2 the bush was on fire it did not **b** up.
21:25 **b** for **b**, wound for wound,
Dt 6:15 is a jealous God and his anger will **b**
7: 5 and **b** their idols in the fire.
29:20 his wrath and zeal will **b**
Ps 79: 5 How long will your jealousy **b**
89:46 long will your wrath **b** like fire?
Jer 7:31 to **b** their sons and daughters in
Lk 3:17 but he will **b** up the chaff
1Co 7: 9 for it is better to marry than to **b**
2Co 11:29 and I do not inwardly **b?**

BURNED [BURN]

Ex 4:15 the LORD's anger **b** against Moses
32:19 his anger **b** and he threw
Nu 11: 3 fire from the LORD had **b** among
Pr 6:27 without his clothes being **b?**
Jer 36:23 the entire scroll was **b** in the fire.
1Co 3:15 If it is **b** up, he will suffer loss;
Heb 6: 8 In the end it will be **b.**
Rev 8: 7 A third of the earth was **b** up,

BURNING [BURN]

Ex 27:20 so that the lamps may be kept **b.**
Lev 6: 9 the fire must be kept **b** on the altar.
Ps 18:28 You, O LORD, keep my lamp **b;**
118:12 they died out as quickly as **b** thorns;
Pr 25:22 you will heap **b** coals on his head,
Am 4:11 like a **b** stick snatched from the fire,
Zec 3: 2 not this man a **b** stick snatched from
Ac 7:30 the flames of a **b** bush in the desert
Ro 12:20 you will heap **b** coals on his head."
Rev 19:20 into the fiery lake of **b** sulfur.
20:10 was thrown into the lake of **b** sulfur,
21: 8 be in the fiery lake of **b** sulfur.

BURNISHED*

1Ki 7:45 temple of the LORD were of **b** bronze
Eze 1: 7 of a calf and gleamed like **b** bronze.
Da 10: 6 and legs like the gleam of **b** bronze,
Rev 2:18 and whose feet are like **b** bronze.

BURNT [BURN]

Ge 8:20 he sacrificed **b** offerings on it.
22: 2 Sacrifice him there as a **b** offering
Ex 10:25 to have sacrifices and **b** offerings
18:12 a **b** offering and other sacrifices
40: 6 "Place the altar of **b** offering in front
Lev 1: 3 is a **b** offering from the herd,
6: 9 the regulations for the **b** offering:
Jos 8:31 to the LORD **b** offerings
22:26 but not for **b** offerings or sacrifices.'
Jdg 6:26 offer the second bull as a **b** offering."
13:16 But if you prepare a **b** offering,
1Ki 3: 4 a thousand **b** offerings on that altar.
9:25 year Solomon sacrificed **b** offerings
10: 5 the **b** offerings he made at the temple
Ezr 3: 2 of Israel to sacrifice **b** offerings on it,
8:35 a **b** offering to the LORD.
Job 1: 5 a **b** offering for each of them,
Ps 51:16 not take pleasure in **b** offerings,
Isa 1:11 more than enough of **b** offerings,
40:16 animals enough for **b** offerings.

Eze 43:18 for sacrificing **b** offerings
Hos 6: 6 of God rather than **b** offerings.
Mic 6: 6 before him with **b** offerings,
Mk 12:33 is more important than all **b** offerings
Heb 10: 6 with **b** offerings and sin offerings

BURNT OFFERING Ge 22:2, 3, 6, 7, 8, 13; Ex
18:12; 29:18, 25, 42; 30:9, 28; 31:9; 35:16; 38:1;
40:6, 10, 29; Lev 1:3, 4, 6, 9, 10, 13, 14, 17; 3:5;
4:7, 10, 18, 24, 25, 29, 30, 33, 34; 5:7, 10; 6:9, 9,
10, 12, 25; 7:2, 8, 37; 8:18, 21, 28; 9:2, 3, 7, 12,
13, 14, 16, 17, 22, 24; 10:19; 12:6, 8; 14:13, 19,
22, 31; 15:15, 30; 16:3, 5, 24, 24; 17:8; 22:18;
23:12, 18; Nu 6:11, 14, 16; 7:15, 21, 27, 33, 39,
45, 51, 57, 63, 69, 75, 81, 87; 8:12; 15:5, 8, 24;
28:3, 6, 10, 11, 13, 14, 15, 19, 23, 24, 27, 31;
29:2, 8, 11, 13, 16, 19, 22, 25, 28, 31, 34, 36, 38;
Dt 13:16; Jdg 6:26; 11:31; 13:16, 23; 1Sa 6:14;
7:9, 10; 13:9, 9, 12; 2Sa 24:22; 2Ki 10:25; 16:13,
15, 15, 15; 1Ch 6:49; 16:40; 21:24, 26, 29; 22:1;
2Ch 7:1; 29:18, 24, 27, 28; Ezr 8:35; Job 1:5;
42:8; Eze 43:24; 45:23; 46:2, 4, 12, 12, 13, 15

BURNT OFFERINGS Ge 8:20; Ex 10:25;
20:24; 24:5; 32:6; 40:29; Lev 23:37; Nu 10:10;
15:3; 29:6, 39; Dt 12:6, 11, 13, 27; 27:6; 33:10;
Jos 8:31; 22:23, 26, 27, 28, 29; Jdg 20:26; 21:4;
1Sa 6:15; 10:8; 15:22; 2Sa 6:17, 18; 24:24, 25;
1Ki 3:4, 15; 8:64, 64; 9:25; 10:5; 2Ki 5:17;
10:24; 16:15; 1Ch 16:1, 2, 40; 21:23, 26; 23:31;
29:21; 2Ch 1:6; 2:4; 4:6; 7:7, 7; 8:12; 9:4; 13:11;
23:18; 24:14, 14; 29:7, 31, 32, 32, 34, 35, 35;
30:15; 31:2, 3, 3; 35:12, 14, 16; Ezr 3:2, 3, 4, 5,
6; 6:9; 8:35; Ne 10:33; Ps 20:3; 40:6; 50:8;
51:16, 19; 66:13, 19; Isa 1:11; 40:16; 43:23; 56:7; Jer
6:20; 7:21, 22; 14:12; 17:26; 33:18; Eze 40:38,
39, 42, 42; 43:18, 24, 27; 44:11; 45:15, 17, 25; Hos
6:6; Am 5:22; Mic 6:6; Mk 12:33; Heb 10:6, 8

BURST
Ge 7:11 the springs of the great deep **b** forth,
Job 32:19 like new wineskins ready to **b**.
Ps 60: 1 O God, and **b** forth upon us;
      98: 4 **b** into jubilant song with music;
Isa 35: 2 it will **b** into bloom;
     44:23 **B** into song, you mountains,
     49:13 **b** into song, O mountains!
     52: 9 **B** into songs of joy together,
     54: 1 **b** into song, shout for joy,
     55:12 and hills will **b** into song before you,
Jer 23:19 the storm of the LORD will **b** out
Eze 7:10 Doom has **b** forth,
Lk 5:37 the new wine will **b** the skins,
Ac 1:18 his body **b** open

BURY [BURIAL, BURIED, BURIES]
Ge 23: 4 so I can **b** my dead."
     47:29 Do not **b** me in Egypt,
     50: 7 So Joseph went up to **b** his father.
Mt 8:22 and let the dead **b** their own dead."
Lk 9:60 "Let the dead **b** their own dead,

BUTLER (KJV) See CUPBEARER

BUSH
Ex 3: 2 in flames of fire from within a **b**.

Dt 33:16 of him who dwelt in the burning **b**.
Mk 12:26 in the account of the **b**,
Lk 20:37 in the account of the **b**,
Ac 7:35 angel who appeared to him in the **b**.

BUSINESS
Ecc 4: 8 too is meaningless—a miserable **b**!
Da 8:27 I got up and went about the king's **b**.
Ac 19:24 in no little **b** for the craftsmen.
1Co 5:12 What **b** is it of mine
1Th 4:11 to mind your own **b** and to work
Jas 1:11 even while he goes about his **b**.
     4:13 carry on **b** and make money."

BUSY*
1Ki 18:27 Perhaps he is deep in thought, or **b**,
     20:40 your servant was **b** here and there,
Isa 32: 6 his mind is **b** with evil:
Hag 1: 9 each of you is **b** with his own house.
2Th 3:11 They are not **b**; they are busybodies.
Tit 2: 5 to be **b** at home, to be kind,

BUSYBODIES*
2Th 3:11 They are not busy; they are **b**.
1Ti 5:13 but also gossips and **b**,

BUY [BOUGHT, BUYS]
Ge 41:57 to Egypt to **b** grain from Joseph,
Ex 21: 2 "If you **b** a Hebrew servant,
Dt 28:68 but no one will **b** you.
Ru 4: 5 the day you **b** the land from Naomi
2Sa 24:21 "To **b** your threshing floor,"
Pr 23:23 **B** the truth and do not sell it;
Isa 55: 1 come, **b** and eat!
     55: 1 **b** wine and milk without money and
Jer 32: 7 '**B** my field at Anathoth,
Mt 27: 7 the money to **b** the potter's field as
Rev 3:18 to **b** from me gold refined in the fire,
     13:17 so that no one could **b** or sell

BUYS* [BUY]
Lev 22:11 But if a priest **b** a slave with money,
Pr 31:16 She considers a field and **b** it;
Rev 18:11 no one **b** their cargoes any more—

BYWORD [WORD]
1Ki 9: 7 Israel will then become a **b** and
Job 17: 6 "God has made me a **b** to everyone,
Ps 44:14 You have made us a **b** among
Eze 23:10 She became a **b** among women,
Joel 2:17 a **b** among the nations.

C

CAESAR
Mt 22:21 "Give to **C** what is Caesar's,
Lk 2: 1 **C** Augustus issued a decree that a
     3: 1 of the reign of Tiberius **C**—
Jn 19:12 you are no friend of **C**.
Ac 25:11 I appeal to **C**!"
     26:32 if he had not appealed to **C**."

CAESAREA
Mt 16:13 to the region of **C** Philippi,
Ac 10: 1 **C** there was a man named Cornelius,
    12:19 Then Herod went from Judea to **C**
    25: 4 "Paul is being held at **C,**

CAIAPHAS*
High priest at trial of Jesus (Mt 26:3, 57; Lk 3:2; Jn 11:49; 18:13-28); at trial of disciples (Ac 4:6).

CAIN*
Firstborn of Adam (Ge 4:1), murdered brother Abel (Ge 4:1-25; Heb 11:4; 1Jn 3:12; Jude 11).

CAKE [CAKES]
1Ki 17:13 But first make a small **c** of bread
Hos   7: 8 Ephraim is a flat **c** not turned over.

CAKES [CAKE]
Ex   12:39 they baked **c** of unleavened bread.
Nu   11: 8 in a pot or made it into **c.**
Jer   7:18 **c** of bread for the Queen of Heaven.
    44:19 making **c** like her image
Hos   3: 1 and love the sacred raisin **c.**"

CALAMITIES [CALAMITY]
Dt   32:23 "I will heap **c** upon them
1Sa 10:19 who saves you out of all your **c**
La   3:38 that both **c** and good things come?

CALAMITY [CALAMITIES]
Ne   13:18 so that our God brought all this **c**
Pr   21:23 and his tongue keeps himself from **c.**
    24:16 the wicked are brought down by **c.**
Eze   7:26 **C** upon **c** will come,
Joel 2:13 and he relents from sending **c.**
Jnh   2:13 a God who relents from sending **c.**

CALCULATE*
Rev 13:18 let him **c** the number of the beast,

CALEB
Judahite who spied out Canaan (Nu 13:6); allowed to enter land because of faith (Nu 13:30-14:38; Dt 1:36). Given Hebron (Jos 14:6-15:19).

CALF [CALF-IDOL, CALVES]
Ex   32: 4 into an idol cast in the shape of a **c,**
Dt   9:16 an idol cast in the shape of a **c.**
Pr   15:17 than a fattened **c** with hatred.
Isa 11: 6 the **c** and the lion and
Jer 31:18 'You disciplined me like an unruly **c,**
Lk   15:23 Bring the fattened **c** and kill it.
Ac   7:41 an idol in the form of a **c.**

CALF-IDOL [CALF, IDOL]
Hos   8: 5 Throw out your **c,** O Samaria!

CALL [CALLED, CALLING, CALLS, SO-CALLED]
Ge   4:26 to **c** on the name of the LORD.
    30:13 The women will **c** me happy."
Dt   4:26 I **c** heaven and earth as witnesses
Ru   1:20 "Don't **c** me Naomi," she told them.

1Ki 18:24 you **c** on the name of your god, and I will **c** on the name of the LORD.
1Ch 16: 8 **c** on his name;
Ps   4: 1 Answer me when I **c** to you,
    10:13 "He won't **c** me to account"?
    50:15 and **c** upon me in the day of trouble;
    61: 2 From the ends of the earth I **c** to you,
    86: 3 O Lord, for I **c** to you all day long.
   105: 1 **c** on his name;
   116:13 and **c** on the name of the LORD.
   145:18 LORD is near to all who **c** on him,
Pr   1:28 "Then they will **c** to me but I will
     8: 1 Does not wisdom **c** out?
    31:28 Her children arise and **c** her blessed;
Ecc   3:15 and God will **c** the past to account.
Isa   5:20 Woe to those who **c** evil good
     7:14 and will **c** him Immanuel.
    12: 4 **c** on his name;
    55: 6 **c** on him while he is near.
    65:24 Before they **c** I will answer;
Jer 33: 3 '**C** to me and I will answer you
La   3:21 Yet this I **c** to mind and
Hos   1: 4 to Hosea, "**C** him Jezreel,
     2:16 "you will **c** me 'my husband';
Jnh   1: 6 Get up and **c** on your god!
     3: 8 Let everyone **c** urgently on God.
Zep   3: 9 that all of them may **c** on the name
Zec   3: 9 They will **c** on my name
Mal   3:12 all the nations will **c** you blessed,
Mt   1:23 and they will **c** him Immanuel"—
     9:13 I have not come to **c** the righteous,
Mk   10:18 "Why do you **c** me good?"
Lk   6:46 "Why do you **c** me, 'Lord, Lord,'
Jn   13:13 "You **c** me 'Teacher' and 'Lord,'
    15:15 I no longer **c** you servants,
Ac   2:39 all whom the LORD our God will **c.**"
     9:14 arrest all who **c** on your name."
    10:15 "Do not **c** anything impure
Ro   10:12 and richly blesses all who **c** on him,
    11:29 God's gifts and his **c** are irrevocable.
1Co   1: 2 with all those everywhere who **c** on
1Th   4: 7 For God did not **c** us to be impure,
2Ti   2:22 with those who **c** on the Lord out of
Heb   2:11 not ashamed to **c** them brothers.
Jas   5:14 He should **c** the elders of the church

CALLED [CALL]
Ge   1: 5 God **c** the light "day,"
     1: 8 God **c** the expanse "sky."
     1:10 God **c** the dry ground "land,"
     1:10 and the gathered waters he **c** "seas."
     2:19 the man **c** each living creature,
     2:23 she shall be **c** 'woman,'
     5: 2 they were created, he **c** them "man."
    12: 8 and **c** on the name of the LORD.
    17: 5 No longer will you be **c** Abram;
    21:33 and there he **c** on the name of
    26:25 an altar there and **c** on the name of
Ex   3: 4 God **c** to him from within the bush,
    16:31 of Israel the house of Israel **c** it manna.
    19: 3 and the LORD **c** to him from
1Sa   3: 4 Then the LORD **c** Samuel.
2Ch   7:14 who are **c** by my name,
Ne   13:25 I rebuked them and **c** curses down

Ps   34: 6 This poor man **c**,
    116: 4 Then I **c** on the name of the LORD:
SS   6: 9 maidens saw her and **c** her blessed;
Isa   9: 6 he will be **c** Wonderful Counselor,
     49: 1 Before I was born the LORD **c** me;
     56: 7 for my house will be a house
La   3:55 I **c** on your name, O LORD,
Hos 11: 1 and out of Egypt I **c** my son.
Mt   1:16 who is **c** Christ.
      2:15 of Egypt I **c** my son."
      5: 9 for they will be **c** sons of God.
     21:13 " 'My house will be **c** a house
     23: 8 "But you are not to be **c** 'Rabbi,'
Lk   1:32 will be **c** the Son of the Most High.
      1:35 to be born will be **c** the Son of God.
      1:76 will be **c** a prophet of the Most High;
     23:46 Jesus **c** out with a loud voice,
Jn   10:35 If he **c** them 'gods,'
     15:15 Instead, I have **c** you friends,
Ro   1: 1 **c** to be an apostle and set apart for
      1: 6 among those who are **c** to belong
      1: 7 by God and **c** to be saints:
      8:28 who have been **c** according
      8:30 And those he predestined, he also **c**;
            those he **c**, he also justified:
1Co   1: 1 **c** to be an apostle of Christ Jesus by
      1: 2 in Christ Jesus and to be holy,
      1: 9 who has **c** you into fellowship
      1:24 but to those whom God has **c**,
      1:26 of what you were when you were **c**.
      7:15 God has **c** us to live in peace.
      7:17 to him and to which God has **c** him.
Gal   1: 6 the one who **c** you by the grace
      1:15 from birth and **c** me by his grace,
      5:13 You, my brothers, were **c** to be free.
Eph   1:18 the hope to which he has **c** you,
      4: 4 as you were **c** to one hope when you
            were **c**—
Php   3:14 for which God has **c** me heavenward
Col   3:15 as members of one body you were **c**
2Th   2:14 He **c** you to this through our gospel.
1Ti   6:12 to which you were **c**
2Ti   1: 9 who has saved us and **c** us to
Heb   9:15 that those who are **c** may receive
     11:16 not ashamed to be **c** their God,
Jas   2:23 and he was **c** God's friend.
1Pe   1:15 But just as he who **c** you is holy,
      2: 9 of him who **c** you out of darkness
      3: 9 because to this you were **c** so
      5:10 who **c** you to his eternal glory
2Pe   1: 3 of him who **c** us by his own glory
1Jn   3: 1 that we should be **c** children of God!
Jude 1: 1 To those who have been **c**,
Rev 12: 9 that ancient serpent **c** the devil,
     16:16 that in Hebrew is **c** Armageddon.
     17:14 and with him will be his **c**,
     19:11 whose rider is **c** Faithful and True.

CALLING [CALL]

1Sa   3: 8 that the LORD was **c** the boy.
Isa   6: 3 And they were **c** to one another:
     40: 3 A voice of one **c**
     41: 2 **c** him in righteousness
Mt   3: 3 "A voice of one **c** in the desert,

Mk   1: 3 "a voice of one **c** in the desert,
     10:49 He's **c** you."
Lk   3: 4 "A voice of one **c** in the desert,
Jn   1:23 the voice of one **c** in the desert,
Ac   22:16 **c** on his name.'
Eph   4: 1 worthy of the **c** you have received.
2Th   1:11 may count you worthy of his **c**,
Heb   3: 1 who share in the heavenly **c**,
2Pe   1:10 to make your **c** and election sure.

CALLOUS* [CALLOUSED]

Ps   17:10 They close up their **c** hearts,
     73: 7 From their **c** hearts comes iniquity;
    119:70 Their hearts are **c** and unfeeling,

CALLOUSED* [CALLOUS]

Isa   6:10 Make the heart of this people **c**;
Mt   13:15 this people's heart has become **c**;
Ac   28:27 this people's heart has become **c**;

CALLS [CALL]

Ps 147: 4 the stars and **c** them each by name.
Pr   1:20 Wisdom **c** aloud in the street,
Isa 40:26 and **c** them each by name.
Hos   7: 7 and none of them **c** on me.
Joel 2:32 And everyone who **c** on the name of
Mt   22:43 speaking by the Spirit, **c** him 'Lord'?
Jn   10: 3 He **c** his own sheep by name
Ac   2:21 And everyone who **c** on the name of
Ro   9:12 not by works but by him who **c**—
     10:13 "Everyone who **c** on the name of
1Th   2:12 who **c** you into his kingdom
      5:24 The one who **c** you is faithful
Rev   2:20 who **c** herself a prophetess.
     13:10 This **c** for patient endurance
     13:18 This **c** for wisdom.
     14:12 This **c** for patient endurance on
     17: 9 "This **c** for a mind with wisdom.

CALM [CALMS]

Ps 107:30 They were glad when it grew **c**,
Isa   7: 4 keep **c** and don't be afraid.
Eze 16:42 be **c** and no longer angry.
Jnh   1:11 to make the sea **c** down for us?"
Mk   4:39 down and it was completely **c**.

CALMS* [CALM]

Pr   15:18 but a patient man **c** a quarrel.

CALVARY (KJV) See SKULL

CALVES [CALF]

2Ki 10:29 the worship of the golden **c** at Bethel
Mal   4: 2 like **c** released from the stall.
Heb   9:12 by means of the blood of goats and **c**

CAME [COME]

Ge   7: 6 when the floodwaters **c** on the earth.
     11: 5 LORD **c** down to see the city
Ex   13: 3 the day you **c** out of Egypt,
     34: 5 the LORD **c** down in the cloud
Lev   9:24 Fire **c** out from the presence of
Nu   12: 5 LORD **c** down in a pillar of cloud;
     24: 2 the Spirit of God **c** upon him
Jdg   3:10 The Spirit of the LORD **c** upon him,

6:34 Spirit of the LORD c upon Gideon,
11:29 Spirit of the LORD c upon Jephthah.
14: 6 Spirit of the LORD c upon him
14:19 the Spirit of the LORD c upon him
15:14 The Spirit of the LORD c upon him
1Sa 10:10 the Spirit of God c upon him
11: 6 Spirit of God c upon him in power,
16:13 Spirit of the LORD c upon David
16:23 the spirit from God c upon Saul,
18:10 an evil spirit from God c forcefully
19: 9 an evil spirit from the LORD c
19:20 the Spirit of God c upon Saul's men
19:23 the Spirit of God c even upon him,
1Ch 12:18 Then the Spirit c upon Amasai,
2Ch 15: 1 The Spirit of God c upon Azariah
20:14 Spirit of the LORD c upon Jahaziel
24:20 the Spirit of God c upon Zechariah
Eze 2: 2 the Spirit c into me and raised me
3:24 the Spirit c into me and raised me
11: 5 the Spirit of the LORD c upon me,
Ac 10:44 the Holy Spirit c on all who heard
11:15 the Holy Spirit c on them
19: 6 the Holy Spirit c on them,

WORD OF THE †LORD CAME
See WORD

CAMEL [CAMEL'S]

Lev 11: 4 The c, though it chews the cud,
Mt 19:24 it is easier for a c to go through
23:24 a gnat but swallow a c.
Mk 10:25 It is easier for a c to go through
Lk 18:25 it is easier for a c to go through

CAMEL'S [CAMEL]

Mk 1: 6 John wore clothing made of c hair,

CAMP [CAMPED, ENCAMP, ENCAMPED, ENCAMPS]

Ge 32: 2 he said, "This is the c of God!"
Ex 16:13 quail came and covered the c,
33: 7 to the tent of meeting outside the c.
Nu 11:26 and they prophesied in the c.
Dt 23:14 Your c must be holy,
1Sa 4: 7 "A god has come into the c,"
26: 5 Saul was lying inside the c,
Heb 13:13 Let us, then, go to him outside the c,

OUTSIDE THE CAMP Ex 29:14; 33:7, 7; Lev 4:12, 21; 6:11; 8:17; 9:11; 10:4, 5; 13:46; 14:3; 16:27; 24:14, 23; Nu 5:3, 4; 12:14, 15; 15:35, 36; 19:3, 9; 31:13, 19; Dt 23:10, 12; Jos 6:23; Heb 13:11, 13

CAMPED [CAMP]

Ex 19: 2 and Israel c there in the desert
Nu 33:49 There on the plains of Moab they c
Jos 3: 1 where they c before crossing over.

CAN [CAN'T, CANNOT]

Ge 4:13 My punishment is more than I c bear.
15: 5 if indeed you c count them."
19: 5 so that we c have sex with them."
41:15 and no one c interpret it.
Nu 23: 8 How c I curse those whom God has

Dt 32:39 and no one c deliver out of my hand.
Job 25: 4 c a man be righteous before God?
40: 4 "I am unworthy—how c I reply
Ps 22:17 I c count all my bones;
49: 7 No man c redeem the life of another
56: 4 What c mortal man do to me?
139: 7 Where c I go from your Spirit?
Pr 20: 6 but a faithful man who c find?
31:10 wife of noble character who c find?
Ecc 2:24 A man c do nothing better than to eat
7:13 Who c straighten what he has made crooked?
Isa 22:22 and what he shuts no one c open.
64: 5 How then c we be saved?
Jer 33:20 'If you c break my covenant with
Eze 37: 3 "Son of man, c these bones live?"
Da 2: 9 that you c interpret it for me."
Hos 11: 8 "How c I give you up, Ephraim?
Joel 2:11 Who c endure it?
Mt 6:24 "No one c serve two masters.
Mk 2: 7 Who c forgive sins but God alone?"
Lk 3: 8 that out of these stones God c raise
18:26 "Who then c be saved?"
Jn 3: 4 c a man be born when he is old?"
6:44 "No one c come to me unless
10:28 no one c snatch them out
15: 5 apart from me you c do nothing.
Ro 8:31 If God is for us, who c be against us?
10:14 And how c they believe in the one
1Co 13: 2 I have a faith that c move mountains,
Php 4:13 I c do everything through him
Heb 13: 6 What c man do to me?"
Jas 2:14 C such faith save him?
3: 8 but no man c tame the tongue.
1Jn 4: 2 how you c recognize the Spirit
Rev 3: 7 What he opens no one c shut,
13: 4 Who c make war against him?"

CAN'T [CAN]

Mt 27:42 they said, "but he c save himself!
Jn 13:37 "Lord, why c I follow you now?

CANA

Jn 2: 1 a wedding took place at C in Galilee.

CANAAN [CANAANITE, CANAANITES]

Ge 9:25 he said, "Cursed be C!
13:12 Abram lived in the land of C,
42: 5 the famine was in the land of C also.
Ex 6: 4 to give them the land of C,
Lev 14:34 "When you enter the land of C,
25:38 of Egypt to give you the land of C
Nu 13: 2 to explore the land of C,
33:51 'When you cross the Jordan into C,
Dt 32:49 across from Jericho, and view C,
Jdg 4: 2 a king of C, who reigned in Hazor.
1Ch 16:18 "To you I will give the land of C
Ps 106:38 sacrificed to the idols of C,
Zep 2: 5 O C, land of the Philistines.
Ac 13:19 he overthrew seven nations in C

CANAANITE [CANAAN]

Ge 10:18 Later the C clans scattered
28: 1 "Do not marry a C woman.

Jos 5: 1 and all the **C** kings along
Jdg 1:32 among the **C** inhabitants of the land.
Zec 14:21 that day there will no longer be a **C**
Mt 15:22 A **C** woman from that vicinity came

CANAANITES [CANAAN]

Ge 12: 6 At that time the **C** were in the land.
Ex 33: 2 before you and drive out the **C**,
Jdg 1: 1 up and fight for us against the **C?"**
     3: 5 The Israelites lived among the **C**,

CANCEL [CANCELED, CANCELING]

Dt 15: 1 every seven years you must **c** debts.
Ne 10:31 the land and will **c** all debts.

CANCELED [CANCEL]

Mt 18:27 **c** the debt and let him go.
Lk   7:42 so he **c** the debts of both.
Col 2:14 having **c** the written code,

CANCELING [CANCEL]

Dt 15: 2 for **c** debts has been proclaimed.
    31:10 in the year for **c** debts,

CANDLE (KJV) See LAMP

CANDLESTICK(S) (KJV)
See LAMPSTAND(S)

CANNOT [CAN]

Ex 19:23 "The people **c** come up Mount Sinai,
    33:20 But," he said, "you **c** see my face,
Nu 11:14 I **c** carry all these people by myself;
2Sa 5: 6 They thought, "David **c** get in here."
1Ki 8:27 highest heaven, **c** contain you.
Job 12:14 What he tears down **c** be rebuilt.
Ps 5: 5 arrogant **c** stand in your presence;
  115: 5 They have mouths, but **c** speak,
Ecc 1:15 What is twisted **c** be straightened;
SS 8: 7 Many waters **c** quench love; rivers **c**
         wash it away.
Isa 45:20 who pray to gods that **c** save.
Da 6: 8 in writing so that it **c** be altered—
Mt 5:14 A city on a hill **c** be hidden.
  16: 3 you **c** interpret the signs of the times.
Mk 3:24 that kingdom **c** stand.
Lk 16:13 You **c** serve both God and Money."
Ro 8: 8 by the sinful nature **c** please God.
Jas 1:13 For God **c** be tempted by evil,
1Jn 5:18 and the evil one **c** harm him.

CANOPY*

2Sa 22:12 He made darkness his **c**
2Ki 16:18 the Sabbath **c** that had been built at
Ps 18:11 his **c** around him—
Isa 4: 5 over all the glory will be a **c**.
  40:22 He stretches out the heavens like a **c**,
Jer 43:10 he will spread his royal **c**

CAPERNAUM

Mt 4:13 he went and lived in **C**,
  11:23 **C**, will you be lifted up to the skies?
Jn 6:59 teaching in the synagogue in **C**.

CAPITAL

Dt 21:22 a man guilty of a **c** offense is put

CAPSTONE* [STONE]

Ps 118:22 The stone the builders rejected has
         become the **c**;
Zec 4: 7 the **c** to shouts of 'God bless it!
Mt 21:42 builders rejected has become the **c**;
Mk 12:10 builders rejected has become the **c**;
Lk 20:17 builders rejected has become the **c**'?
Ac 4:11 which has become the **c**.'
1Pe 2: 7 builders rejected has become the **c**,"

CAPTAIN

2Ki 1: 9 The **c** went up to Elijah,
Jnh 1: 6 The **c** went to him and said,
Rev 18:17 "Every sea **c**, and all who travel

CAPTIVATE* [CAPTURE]

Pr 6:25 or let her **c** you with her eyes,

CAPTIVATED* [CAPTURE]

Pr 5:19 may you ever be **c** by her love.
  5:20 Why be **c**, my son, by an adulteress?

CAPTIVE [CAPTURE]

Ge 14:14 that his relative had been taken **c**,
Ps 69:33 and does not despise his **c** people.
SS 7: 5 the king is held **c** by its tresses.
Isa 52: 2 O **c** Daughter of Zion.
Jer 13:17 the LORD's flock will be taken **c**.
Eze 21:24 you will be taken **c**.
Ac 8:23 full of bitterness and **c** to sin."
2Co 10: 5 and we take **c** every thought
Col 2: 8 See to it that no one takes you **c**
2Ti 2:26 who has taken them **c** to do his will.

CAPTIVES [CAPTURE]

Ps 68:18 you led **c** in your train;
  126: 1 LORD brought back the **c** to Zion,
Isa 14: 2 They will make **c** of their captors
  61: 1 to proclaim freedom for the **c**
Eph 4: 8 he led **c** in his train and gave gifts

CAPTIVITY [CAPTURE]

Dt 28:41 because they will go into **c**.
2Ki 25:21 So Judah went into **c**,
Ps 144:14 no going into **c**,
Jer 15: 2 those for **c**, to **c**.'
  30: 3 and Judah back from **c** and restore
  52:27 So Judah went into **c**,
Eze 29:14 I will bring them back from **c**
Rev 13:10 If anyone is to go into **c**,

CAPTORS [CAPTURE]

Ps 137: 3 for there our **c** asked us for songs,

CAPTURE [CAPTIVATE,
CAPTIVATED, CAPTIVE, CAPTIVES,
CAPTIVITY, CAPTORS, CAPTURED]

1Sa 4:21 because of the **c** of the ark of God
  19:14 When Saul sent the men to **c** David,
  23:26 in on David and his men to **c** them,
Mt 26:55 with swords and clubs to **c** me?

CAPTURED [CAPTURE]

1Sa 4:11 The ark of God was **c**,
2Sa 5: 7 David **c** the fortress of Zion,
2Ki 17: 6 the king of Assyria **c** Samaria
Rev 19:20 But the beast was **c**,

CARAVAN

2Ch 9: 1 Arriving with a very great **c**—

CARCASS [CARCASSES]

Jdg 14: 9 the honey from the lion's **c**.
Mt 24:28 Wherever there is a **c**,

CARCASSES [CARCASS]

Dt 28:26 Your **c** will be food for all the birds
1Sa 17:46 the **c** of the Philistine army to
Jer 7:33 the **c** of this people will become food

CARE [CARED, CAREFREE,
CAREFUL, CAREFULLY, CARELESS,
CARES, CARING]

Ge   2:15 Garden of Eden to work it and take **c**
Nu   3:25 for the **c** of the tabernacle
Dt   7:11 take **c** to follow the commands,
1Ki 1: 2 to attend the king and take **c** of him.
Ps   8: 4 the son of man that you **c** for him?
    65: 9 You **c** for the land and water it;
    95: 7 the flock under his **c**.
   144: 3 what is man that you **c** for him,
Pr 29: 7 The righteous **c** about justice for
Jer 15:15 remember me and **c** for me.
Eze 34: 2 not shepherds take **c** of the flock?
Zec 10: 3 for the LORD Almighty will **c**
Mk   5:26 under the **c** of many doctors
Lk 10:34 took him to an inn and took **c** of him.
    18: 1 I don't fear God or **c** about men,
Jn 21:16 Jesus said, "Take **c** of my sheep."
1Co 4: 3 I **c** very little if I am judged by you
1Ti 3: 5 how can he take **c** of God's church?)
     6:20 to your **c**.
Heb 2: 6 the son of man that you **c** for him?
1Pe 5: 2 under your **c**, serving as overseers—
Rev 12: 6 she might be taken **c** of for 1,260

CARED [CARE]

Hos 12:13 by a prophet he **c** for him.
Mk 15:41 and **c** for his needs.

CAREFREE* [CARE]

Ps 73:12 what the wicked are like—always **c**,
Eze 23:42 of a **c** crowd was around her;
Zep 2:15 This is the **c** city that lived in safety.

CAREFUL* [CARE]

Ge 31:24 "Be **c** not to say anything to Jacob,
    31:29 'Be **c** not to say anything to Jacob,
Ex 19:12 'Be **c** that you do not go up
    23:13 "Be **c** to do everything I have said
    34:12 Be **c** not to make a treaty
    34:15 "Be **c** not to make a treaty
Lev 18: 4 You must obey my laws and be **c**
    25:18 " 'Follow my decrees and be **c**
    26: 3 and are **c** to obey my commands,

Dt   2: 4 but be very **c**.
     4: 9 Only be **c**, and watch yourselves
     4:23 Be **c** not to forget the covenant of
     5:32 So be **c** to do what
     6: 3 be **c** to obey so that it may go well
     6:12 be **c** that you do not forget
     6:25 if we are **c** to obey all this law before
     7:12 and are **c** to follow them,
     8: 1 Be **c** to follow every command
     8:11 Be **c** that you do not forget
    11:16 Be **c**, or you will be enticed
    12: 1 and laws you must be **c** to follow in
    12:13 Be **c** not to sacrifice
    12:19 Be **c** not to neglect the Levites
    12:28 Be **c** to obey
    12:30 be **c** not to be ensnared by inquiring
    15: 5 and are **c** to follow all
    15: 9 Be **c** not to harbor this
    17:10 Be **c** to do everything they direct you
    24: 8 be very **c** to do exactly as the priests,
Jos 1: 7 Be **c** to obey all the law
     1: 8 be **c** to do everything written in it.
    22: 5 be very **c** to keep the commandment
    23: 6 "Be very strong; be **c** to obey all
    23:11 So be very **c** to love
1Ki 8:25 if only your sons are **c** in all they do
2Ki 10:31 not **c** to keep the law of the LORD,
    17:37 You must always be **c** to keep
    21: 8 if only they will be **c**
1Ch 22:13 if you are **c** to observe the decrees
    28: 8 Be **c** to follow all the commands of
2Ch 6:16 only your sons are **c** in all they do
    33: 8 if only they will be **c**
Ezr 4:22 Be **c** not to neglect this matter.
Job 36:18 Be **c** that no one entices you
Ps 101: 2 I will be **c** to lead a blameless life—
Pr 13:24 but he who loves him is **c**
    27:23 give **c** attention to your herds;
Isa 7: 4 Say to him, 'Be **c**,
Jer 17:21 This is what the LORD says: Be **c**
    17:24 But if you are **c** to obey me,
    22: 4 For if you are **c**
Eze 11:20 and be **c** to keep my laws.
    18:19 and right and has been **c**
    20:19 and be **c** to keep my laws.
    20:21 they were not **c** to keep my laws—
    36:27 to follow my decrees and be **c**
    37:24 They will follow my laws and be **c**
Mic 7: 5 in your embrace be **c** of your words.
Hag 1: 5 "Give **c** thought to your ways.
     1: 7 "Give **c** thought to your ways.
     2:15 " 'Now give **c** thought to this
     2:18 give **c** thought to the day when
     2:18 Give **c** thought:
Mt   2: 8 and make a **c** search for the child.
     6: 1 "Be **c** not to do your 'acts
    16: 6 "Be **c**," Jesus said to them.
Mk   8:15 "Be **c**," Jesus warned them.
Lk 17:20 not come with your **c** observation,
    21:34 "Be **c**, or your hearts will
Ro 12:17 Be **c** to do what is right in the eyes
1Co 3:10 each one should be **c** how he builds.
     8: 9 Be **c**, however, that the exercise
    10:12 be **c** that you don't fall!

Eph	5:15	Be very **c**, then, how you live—
2Ti	4: 2	with great patience and **c** instruction.
Tit	3: 8	be **c** to devote themselves
Heb	2: 1	We must pay more **c** attention,
	4: 1	let us be **c** that none of you be found

CAREFULLY [CARE]

Ex	15:26	"If you listen **c** to the voice of
Dt	28:58	If you do not **c** follow all the words
Da	10:11	consider **c** the words I am about

CARELESS* [CARE]

Mt	12:36	for every **c** word they have spoken.

CARES* [CARE]

Dt	11:12	a land the LORD your God **c** for;
Job	39:16	she **c** not that her labor was in vain,
Ps	55:22	Cast your **c** on the LORD
	142: 4	I have no refuge; no one **c**
Pr	12:10	A righteous man **c** for the needs
Ecc	5: 3	when there are many **c**,
Jer	12:11	because there is no one who **c**.
	30:17	Zion for whom no one **c**.'
Na	1: 7	He **c** for those who trust in him,
Jn	10:13	a hired hand and **c** nothing for
Eph	5:29	but he feeds and **c** for it,
1Pe	5: 7	on him because he **c** for you.

CARGO

Eze	27:25	with heavy **c** in the heart of the sea.
Jnh	1: 5	the **c** into the sea to lighten the ship.
Ac	27:18	to throw the **c** overboard.

CARING* [CARE]

1Th	2: 7	like a mother **c** for her little children.
1Ti	5: 4	by **c** for their own family and

CARMEL

1Sa	25: 5	"Go up to Nabal at **C** and greet him
1Ki	18:20	assembled the prophets on Mount **C**.

CARNAL, CARNALLY (KJV)
See UNSPIRITUAL, SINFUL, SINFUL
NATURE, MATERIAL, WORLDLY

CAROUSE* [CAROUSING]

2Pe	2:13	of pleasure is to **c** in broad daylight.

CAROUSING* [CAROUSE]

1Pe	4: 3	orgies, **c** and detestable idolatry.

CARPENTER* [CARPENTER'S, CARPENTERS]

Isa	44:13	The **c** measures with a line
Mk	6: 3	Isn't this the **c**?

CARPENTER'S* [CARPENTER]

Mt	13:55	"Isn't this the **c** son?

CARPENTERS [CARPENTER]

1Ch	14: 1	stonemasons and **c** to build a palace
2Ch	24:12	They hired masons and **c** to restore
Ezr	3: 7	to the masons and **c**,

CARRIED [CARRY]

Ge	14:12	They also **c** off Abram's nephew Lot
	40:15	For I was forcibly **c** off from
Ex	19: 4	and how I **c** you on eagles' wings
Dt	1:31	how the LORD your God **c** you,
	31: 9	who **c** the ark of the covenant of
	33:21	he **c** out the LORD's righteous will,
Jos	3:15	as the priests who **c** the ark reached
1Sa	5: 2	Then they **c** the ark into Dagon's
	17:34	When a lion or a bear came and **c** off
2Ki	24:14	He **c** into exile all Jerusalem:
Ezr	6:12	Let it be **c** out with diligence.
Est	2: 6	who had been **c** into exile
Ecc	8:11	for a crime is not quickly **c** out,
Isa	53: 4	up our infirmities and **c** our sorrows,
	63: 9	he lifted them up and **c** them
Jer	52:28	Nebuchadnezzar **c** into exile:
Mt	8:17	our infirmities and **c** our diseases."
Jn	20:15	"Sir, if you have **c** him away,
Heb	13: 9	Do not be **c** away by all kinds
2Pe	1:21	they were **c** along by the Holy Spirit.
	3:17	not be **c** away by the error
Rev	17: 3	the angel **c** me away in the Spirit
	21:10	And he **c** me away in the Spirit to

CARRIES [CARRY]

Nu	11:12	as a nurse **c** an infant,
Dt	1:31	as a father **c** his son,
	32:11	and **c** them on its pinions.
Isa	40:11	and **c** them close to his heart;
	44:26	who **c** out the words of his servants

CARRY [CARRIED, CARRIES, CARRYING]

Ge	47:30	**c** me out of Egypt and bury me
	50:25	and then you must **c** my bones up
Ex	13:19	and then you must **c** my bones up
Lev	16:22	The goat will **c** on itself all their sins
	26:15	and fail to **c** out all my commands
Dt	10: 8	of Levi to **c** the ark of the covenant
1Ch	15: 2	the Levites may **c** the ark of God,
Isa	45:20	Ignorant are those who **c** about idols
	46: 4	I have made you and I will **c** you;
Jer	51:12	The LORD will **c** out his purpose,
Hos	11: 9	I will not **c** out my fierce anger,
Mt	3:11	whose sandals I am not fit to **c**.
	27:32	and they forced him to **c** the cross.
Lk	14:27	anyone who does not **c** his cross
2Co	4:10	We always **c** around in our body
Gal	6: 2	**C** each other's burdens,
	6: 5	for each one should **c** his own load.

CARRYING [CARRY]

Lk	5:18	Some men came **c** a paralytic on
	22:10	a man **c** a jar of water will meet you.
Jn	19:17	**C** his own cross,
1Jn	5: 2	and **c** out his commands.

CART

1Sa	6: 7	"Now then, get a new **c** ready,
1Ch	13: 7	from Abinadab's house on a new **c**,

CARVED [CARVES]
Nu 33:52 Destroy all their **c** images
Jdg 18:14 a **c** image and a cast idol?
1Ki   6:32 two olive wood doors he **c** cherubim,
Ps   74: 6 They smashed all the **c** paneling
    144:12 be like pillars **c** to adorn a palace.
Eze 41:18 were **c** cherubim and palm trees.
Mic   5:13 I will destroy your **c** images
Hab   2:18 since a man has **c** it?

CARVES* [CARVED]
Dt 27:15 "Cursed is the man who **c** an image

CASE [CASES]
Ex 18:22 but have them bring every difficult **c**
Jos 20: 4 of the city gate and state his **c** before
2Sa 15: 4 a complaint or **c** could come to me
1Ki 15: 5 in the **c** of Uriah the Hittite.
2Ki   8: 6 Then he assigned an official to her **c**
Job 13: 8 Will you argue the **c** for God?
Pr 18:17 The first to present his **c** seems right,
    22:23 the LORD will take up their **c**
    23:11 he will take up their **c** against you.
    25: 9 If you argue your **c** with a neighbor,
Isa   1:17 plead the **c** of the widow.
    41:21 "Present your **c,**" says the LORD.
Jer 12: 1 when I bring a **c** before you.
La   3:58 O Lord, you took up my **c;**
Mic   6: 1 plead your **c** before the mountains;
Ac 23:35 "I will hear your **c**
    25:14 Festus discussed Paul's **c** with

CASES [CASE]
Ex 18:26 difficult **c** they brought to Moses,
1Co   6: 2 not competent to judge trivial **c?**

CAST [CASTING, CASTS]
Ex 32: 4 an idol **c** in the shape of a calf,
    34:17 "Do not make **c** idols.
Lev 16: 8 He is to **c** lots for the two goats—
Jos 18: 8 and I will **c** lots for you here
1Ki   7:15 He **c** two bronze pillars,
Est   3: 7 they **c** the pur (that is, the lot)
    9:24 the Jews to destroy them and had **c**
Ps 22:18 and **c** lots for my clothing.
    55:22 **C** your cares on the LORD
    71: 9 Do not **c** me away when I am old;
Pr 16:33 The lot is **c** into the lap,
Ecc 11: 1 **C** your bread upon the waters,
Isa 14:12 You have been **c** down to the earth,
La   3:31 not **c** off by the Lord forever.
Joel   3: 3 They **c** lots for my people
Ob 1:11 and **c** lots for Jerusalem.
Jnh   1: 7 They **c** lots and the lot fell on Jonah.
Jn 19:24 and **c** lots for my clothing."
Ac   1:26 Then they **c** lots,
1Pe   5: 7 **C** all your anxiety on him

CASTING* [CAST]
Pr 18:18 **C** the lot settles disputes
Eze 24: 6 by piece without **c** lots for them.
    26: 3 like the sea **c** up its waves.
Mt   4:18 They were **c** a net into the lake,
    27:35 they divided up his clothes by **c** lots.

Mk   1:16 and his brother Andrew **c** a net into
Lk 23:34 they divided up his clothes by **c** lots.

CASTS [CAST]
Dt 18:11 or **c** spells, or who is a medium
Isa 40:19 As for an idol, a craftsman **c** it,
    44:10 Who shapes a god and **c** an idol,

CATASTROPHE*
Ge 19:29 out of the **c** that overthrew the cities
Isa 47:11 **c** you cannot foresee will suddenly

CATCH [CATCHES, CAUGHT]
Mt 17:27 Take the first fish you **c;**
Lk   5: 4 and let down the nets for a **c."**
    5:10 from now on you will **c** men."
    11:54 to **c** him in something he might say.
    20:20 to **c** Jesus in something he said so

CATCHES [CATCH]
Job   5:13 He **c** the wise in their craftiness,
1Co   3:19 As it is written: "He **c** the wise

CATTLE
Ge 12:16 and Abram acquired sheep and **c,**
1Sa 15:14 What is this lowing of **c** that I hear?"
2Sa 12: 2 a very large number of sheep and **c,**
Ps 50:10 and the **c** on a thousand hills.
   104:14 He makes grass grow for the **c,**
Hab   3:17 in the pen and no **c** in the stalls,
Jn   2:14 temple courts he found men selling **c**

CAUGHT [CATCH]
Ge 22:13 a thicket he saw a ram **c** by its horns.
    39:12 She **c** him by his cloak and said,
Ex 22: 7 if he is **c,** must pay back double.
Dt 24: 7 If a man is **c** kidnapping one
2Sa 18: 9 Absalom's head got **c** in the tree.
Lk   5: 5 and haven't **c** anything.
Jn   8: 4 woman was **c** in the act of adultery.
2Co 12: 2 was **c** up to the third heaven.
Gal   6: 1 Brothers, if someone is **c** in a sin,
1Th   4:17 and are left will be **c** up together

CAUSE [CAUSED, CAUSES]
Ex 23:33 or they will **c** you to sin against me,
Dt 10:18 He defends the **c** of the fatherless
Jdg   6:31 "Are you going to plead Baal's **c?**
Ps   9: 4 you have upheld my right and my **c;**
    109: 3 they attack me without **c.**
   119:86 for men persecute me without **c.**
  119:154 Defend my **c** and redeem me;
Pr 24:28 against your neighbor without **c,**
Ecc   8: 3 Do not stand up for a bad **c,**
Isa   1:23 not defend the **c** of the fatherless;
Jer 51:36 I will defend your **c** and avenge you;
La   3:59 Uphold my **c!**
Mt 18: 7 the things that **c** people to sin!
Lk 17: 2 for him to **c** one of these little ones
Ro 14:21 that will **c** your brother to fall.
    16:17 for those who **c** divisions
1Co   8:13 so that I will not **c** him to fall.
    10:32 Do not **c** anyone to stumble,
Rev 13:15 and **c** all who refused to worship

CAUSED [CAUSE]

1Ki 14:16 and has **c** Israel to commit."
2Ki 23:15 who had **c** Israel to sin—

CAUSES [CAUSE]

Ps   7:16 The trouble he **c** recoils on himself;
Isa   8:14 be a stone that **c** men to stumble and
Mt   5:29 If your right eye **c** you to sin,
      5:30 And if your right hand **c** you to sin,
      5:32 **c** her to become an adulteress,
    18: 6 But if anyone **c** one
    18: 8 If your hand or your foot **c** you
Ro 14:20 that **c** someone else to stumble.
1Co 8:13 if what I eat **c** my brother to fall
Jas   4: 1 What **c** fights and quarrels
1Pe   2: 8 "A stone that **c** men to stumble and

CAUTIOUS*

Pr 12:26 A righteous man is **c** in friendship,

CAVE [CAVERNS, CAVES]

Ge 19:30 and his two daughters lived in a **c.**
    23: 9 he will sell me the **c** of Machpelah,
    25: 9 in the **c** of Machpelah near Mamre,
    49:29 Bury me with my fathers in the **c** in
Jos 10:16 and hidden in the **c** at Makkedah.
1Sa 22: 1 David left Gath and escaped to the **c**
    24: 3 and his men were far back in the **c.**
1Ki 19: 9 There he went into a **c** and spent
Ps   57: T he had fled from Saul into the **c.**
  142: T When he was in the **c.**

CAVERNS* [CAVE]

Isa   2:21 They will flee to **c** in the rocks and

CAVES [CAVE]

1Ki 18: 4 and hidden them in two **c,**
Isa   2:19 Men will flee to **c** in the rocks and
Heb 11:38 and in **c** and holes in the ground.
Rev   6:15 and every free man hid in **c** and

CEASE

Ge   8:22 day and night will never **c.**"
Ne   9:19 By day the pillar of cloud did not **c**
Ps 46: 9 He makes wars **c** to the ends of
1Co 13: 8 there are prophecies, they will **c;**

CEDAR [CEDARS]

2Sa   7: 2 "Here I am, living in a palace of **c,**
1Ki   5:10 kept Solomon supplied with all the **c**
2Ch 25:18 sent a message to a **c** in Lebanon.
Ezr   3: 7 that they would bring **c** logs by sea
Job 40:17 His tail sways like a **c;**
Ps   92:12 they will grow like a **c** of Lebanon;
SS   8: 9 we will enclose her with panels of **c.**
Eze 31: 3 once a **c** in Lebanon,
Hos 14: 5 Like a **c** of Lebanon he will send

CEDARS [CEDAR]

Nu 24: 6 like **c** beside the waters.
Ps   29: 5 voice of the LORD breaks the **c;**

CELEBRATE* [CELEBRATED,

CELEBRATING, CELEBRATION,
CELEBRATIONS]

Ex 10: 9 because we are to **c** a festival to
    12:14 to come you shall **c** it as a festival to
    12:17 "**C** the Feast of Unleavened Bread,
    12:17 **C** this day as a lasting ordinance for
    12:47 whole community of Israel must **c** it.
    12:48 among you who wants to **c**
    23:14 a year you are to **c** a festival to me.
    23:15 "**C** the Feast of Unleavened Bread;
    23:16 "**C** the Feast of Harvest with
    23:16 "**C** the Feast of Ingathering at
    34:18 "**C** the Feast of Unleavened Bread.
    34:22 "**C** the Feast of Weeks with
Lev 23:39 **c** the festival to the LORD
    23:41 **C** this as a festival to the LORD
    23:41 **c** it in the seventh month.
Nu   9: 2 "Have the Israelites **c** the Passover at
    9: 3 **C** it at the appointed time,
    9: 4 So Moses told the Israelites to **c**
    9: 6 not **c** the Passover on
    9:10 they may still **c**
    9:11 They are to **c** it on the fourteenth day
    9:12 When they **c** the Passover,
    9:13 on a journey fails to **c**
    9:14 to **c** the LORD's Passover must do
   29:12 **C** a festival to the LORD
Dt 16: 1 **c** the Passover of the LORD your God
    16:10 Then **c** the Feast of Weeks to
    16:13 **C** the Feast of Tabernacles
    16:15 For seven days **c** the Feast to
Jdg 16:23 to Dagon their god and to **c,**
2Sa   6:21 I will **c** before the LORD.
2Ki 23:21 gave this order to all the people: "**C**
2Ch 30: 1 in Jerusalem and **c** the Passover to
    30: 2 in Jerusalem decided to **c**
    30: 3 to **c** it at the regular time because
    30: 5 to Jerusalem and **c** the Passover to
    30:13 to **c** the Feast of Unleavened Bread
    30:23 The whole assembly then agreed to **c**
Ne   8:12 to send portions of food and to **c**
    12:27 to **c** joyfully the dedication
Est   9:21 to have them **c** annually
Ps 145: 7 They will **c** your abundant goodness
Isa 30:29 as on the night you **c** a holy festival;
Na   1:15 **C** your festivals, O Judah,
Zec 14:16 and to **c** the Feast of Tabernacles.
    14:18 on the nations that do not go up to **c**
    14:19 the nations that do not go up to **c**
Mt 26:18 to **c** the Passover with my disciples
Lk 15:23 Let's have a feast and **c.**
    15:24 So they began to **c.**
    15:29 even a young goat so I could **c**
    15:32 But we had to **c** and be glad,
Rev 11:10 gloat over them and will **c**

CELEBRATED [CELEBRATE]

Jos   5:10 the Israelites **c** the Passover.
1Ki   8:65 They **c** it before the LORD our God
2Ki 23:23 this Passover was **c** to the LORD
2Ch 30: 5 It had not been **c** in large numbers
   35: 1 Josiah **c** the Passover to the LORD
Ezr   3: 4 they **c** the Feast of Tabernacles with

6:19 the exiles **c** the Passover.
Ne 8:17 the Israelites had not **c** it like this.
Est 9:28 of Purim should never cease to be **c**

CELEBRATING [CELEBRATE]

1Ch 15:29 she saw King David dancing and **c,**
Est 8:17 with feasting and **c.**

CELEBRATION [CELEBRATE]

Est 9:22 and their mourning into a day of **c.**
Col 2:16 a New Moon **c** or a Sabbath day.

CELEBRATIONS* [CELEBRATE]

Hos 2:11 I will stop all her **c:**

CELESTIAL*

2Pe 2:10 not afraid to slander **c** beings;
Jude 1: 8 reject authority and slander **c** beings.

CELL*

Jer 37:16 Jeremiah was put into a vaulted **c** in
Ac 12: 7 and a light shone in the **c.**
16:24 the inner **c** and fastened their feet in

CENSER [CENSERS]

Lev 16:12 He is to take a **c** full of burning coals
Nu 16:18 So each man took his **c,**
2Ch 26:19 a **c** in his hand ready to burn incense,
Eze 8:11 Each had a **c** in his hand,
Rev 8: 3 Another angel, who had a golden **c,**

CENSERS [CENSER]

Lev 10: 1 Nadab and Abihu took their **c,**
Nu 16:38 the **c** of the men who sinned at

CENSUS

Ex 30:12 "When you take a **c** of the Israelites
Nu 1: 2 a **c** of the whole Israelite community
26: 2 a **c** of the whole Israelite community
2Sa 24: 1 and take a **c** of Israel and Judah."
1Ch 21: 1 and incited David to take a **c**
Lk 2: 1 Augustus issued a decree that a **c**

CENTER

Eze 48: 8 the sanctuary will be in the **c** of it.
48:15 The city will be in the **c** of it
Rev 4: 6 In the **c,** around the throne,
5: 6 standing in the **c** of the throne,
7:17 the Lamb at the **c** of the throne will

CENTURION

Mt 8: 5 a **c** came to him, asking for help.
27:54 the **c** and those with him
Mk 15:39 And when the **c,**
Lk 7: 3 the **c** heard of Jesus
23:47 The **c,** seeing what had happened,
Ac 10: 1 a man named Cornelius, a **c**
22:25 Paul said to the **c** standing there,
27: 1 over to a **c** named Julius,

CEPHAS* [PETER]

Jn 1:42 You will be called **C"** (which,
1Co 1:12 "I follow **C";**
3:22 whether Paul or Apollos or **C**
9: 5 and the Lord's brothers and **C?**

CEREMONIAL* [CEREMONY]

Lev 14: 2 at the time of his **c** cleansing,
15:13 for his **c** cleansing;
Mk 7: 3 give their hands a **c** washing,
Jn 2: 6 kind used by the Jews for **c** washing,
3:25 over the matter of **c** washing.
11:55 to Jerusalem for their **c** cleansing
18:28 to avoid **c** uncleanness the Jews did
Heb 9:10 and drink and various **c** washings—
13: 9 not by **c** foods,

CEREMONIALLY* [CEREMONY]

Lev 4:12 the camp to a place **c** clean,
5: 2 person touches anything **c** unclean—
6:11 the camp to a place that is **c** clean.
7:19 that touches anything **c** unclean must
7:19 anyone **c** clean may eat it.
10:14 Eat them in a **c** clean place;
11: 4 not have a split hoof; it is **c** unclean
12: 2 be **c** unclean for seven days,
12: 7 be **c** clean from her flow of blood.
13: 3 he shall pronounce him **c** unclean.
14: 8 then he will be **c** clean.
15:28 and after that she will be **c** clean.
15:33 with a woman who is **c** unclean.
17:15 and he will be **c** unclean till evening;
21: 1 not make himself **c** unclean for any
22: 3 of your descendants is **c** unclean and
27:11 a **c** unclean animal—
Nu 5: 2 or who is **c** unclean because of
6: 7 he must not make himself **c** unclean
8: 6 and make them **c** clean.
9: 6 that day because they were **c** unclean
9:13 a man who is **c** clean and not
18:11 household who is **c** clean may eat it.
18:13 household who is **c** clean may eat it.
19: 7 but he will be **c** unclean till evening.
19: 9 in a **c** clean place outside the camp.
19:18 Then a man who is **c** clean is
Dt 12:15 **c** unclean and the clean may eat it.
12:22 the **c** unclean and the clean may eat.
14: 7 have a split hoof; they are **c** unclean
15:22 **c** unclean and the clean may eat it,
1Sa 20:26 to David to make him **c** unclean—
2Ch 13:11 the **c** clean table and light the lamps
30:17 for all those who were not **c** clean
Ezr 6:20 and were all **c** clean.
Ne 12:30 Levites had purified themselves **c,**
Isa 66:20 of the LORD in **c** clean vessels.
Eze 22:10 when they are **c** unclean.
Ac 24:18 I was **c** clean when they found me in
Heb 9:13 who are **c** unclean sanctify them

CEREMONIES* [CEREMONY]

Heb 9:21 and everything used in its **c.**

CEREMONY* [CEREMONIAL,
CEREMONIALLY, CEREMONIES]

Ge 50:11 holding a solemn **c** of mourning."
Ex 12:25 observe this **c.**
12:26 'What does this **c** mean to you?'
13: 5 to observe this **c** in this month:

CERTAIN [CERTAINTY]

Heb 11: 1 and **c** of what we do not see.
2Pe 1:19 of the prophets made more **c**,

CERTAINTY* [CERTAIN]

Lk 1: 4 so that you may know the **c** of
Jn 17: 8 They knew with **c** that I came

CERTIFICATE* [CERTIFIED]

Dt 24: 1 and he writes her a **c** of divorce.
24: 3 and writes her a **c** of divorce,
Isa 50: 1 "Where is your mother's **c**
Jer 3: 8 I gave faithless Israel her **c**
Mt 5:31 must give her a **c** of divorce.'
19: 7 give his wife a **c** of divorce
Mk 10: 4 "Moses permitted a man to write a **c**

CERTIFIED* [CERTIFICATE]

Jn 3:33 The man who has accepted it has **c**

CHAFF

Ps 1: 4 like **c** that the wind blows away.
35: 5 May they be like **c** before the wind,
Isa 33:11 You conceive **c**, you give birth
Da 2:35 and became like **c** on
Hos 13: 3 like **c** swirling from a threshing floor
Zep 2: 2 and that day sweeps on like **c**,
Mt 3:12 the **c** with unquenchable fire."

CHAIN [CHAINED, CHAINS]

Ge 41:42 and put a gold **c** around his neck.
Pr 1: 9 and a **c** to adorn your neck.
Da 5: 7 in purple and have a gold **c** placed
Mk 5: 3 not even with a **c**.
Ac 28:20 that I am bound with this **c**."
Rev 20: 1 and holding in his hand a great **c**.

CHAINED [CHAIN]

Mk 5: 4 he had often been **c** hand and foot,
2Ti 2: 9 But God's word is not **c**.
Heb 11:36 while still others were **c** and put

CHAINS [CHAIN]

Ex 28:14 and two braided **c** of pure gold,
Ps 2: 3 "Let us break their **c**," they say,
Ecc 7:26 a trap and whose hands are **c**.
La 3: 7 he has weighed me down with **c**.
Mk 5: 4 but he tore the **c** apart and broke
Ac 12: 7 and the **c** fell off Peter's wrists.
16:26 and everybody's **c** came loose.
Eph 6:20 for which I am an ambassador in **c**.
Php 1: 7 for whether I am in **c** or defending
Col 4:18 Remember my **c**.
2Ti 1:16 and was not ashamed of my **c**.
Phm 1:10 became my son while I was in **c**
Jude 1: 6 with everlasting for judgment

CHAIR

1Sa 4:18 Eli fell backward off his **c** by

CHALDAEANS (KJV) See BABYLON, BABYLONIANS

CHALDEA [CHALDEAN, CHALDEANS]

Eze 23:16 and sent messengers to them in **C**.

CHALDEAN* [CHALDEA]

Ezr 5:12 over to Nebuchadnezzar the **C**,

CHALDEANS [CHALDEA]

Ge 11:31 from Ur of the **C** to go to Canaan.
Ne 9: 7 and brought him out of Ur of the **C**

CHALDEES (KJV) See CHALDEANS

CHALLENGE [CHALLENGED]

Jer 49:19 Who is like me and who can **c** me?
Mal 3:15 and even those who **c** God escape.' "

CHALLENGED* [CHALLENGE]

Jn 8:13 The Pharisees **c** him, "Here you are,
18:26 **c** him, "Didn't I see you

CHAMBER [CHAMBERS]

Job 37: 9 The tempest comes out from its **c**,

CHAMBERLAIN (KJV) See EUNUCH, OFFICERS

CHAMBERS [CHAMBER]

Ps 104:13 the mountains from his upper **c**;
SS 1: 4 Let the king bring me into his **c**.

CHAMPION* [CHAMPIONS]

1Sa 17: 4 A **c** named Goliath,
17:23 Goliath, the Philistine **c** from Gath,
Ps 19: 5 like a **c** rejoicing to run his course.

CHAMPIONS* [CHAMPION]

Isa 5:22 and **c** at mixing drinks,

CHANCE

1Sa 6: 9 and that it happened to us by **c**."
Ecc 9:11 but time and **c** happen to them all.

CHANGE [CHANGED, CHANGERS]

Nu 23:19 that he should **c** his mind.
1Sa 15:29 of Israel does not lie or **c** his mind;
15:29 that he should **c** his mind."
1Ki 8:47 if they have a **c** of heart in the land
Ps 110: 4 and will not **c** his mind:
Jer 7: 5 If you really **c** your ways
13:23 Can the Ethiopian **c** his skin or
Mal 3: 6 "I the LORD do not **c**.
Mt 18: 3 you **c** and become like little children,
Heb 7:12 there must also be a **c** of the law.
7:21 and will not **c** his mind:
Jas 1:17 not **c** like shifting shadows.
Jude 1: 4 who **c** the grace of our God into

CHANGED [CHANGE]

1Sa 10: 9 God **c** Saul's heart,
Jer 2:11 Has a nation ever **c** its gods?
Da 3:19 and his attitude toward them **c**.
6:15 or edict that the king issues can be **c**.
Hos 11: 8 My heart is **c** within me;
Lk 9:29 the appearance of his face **c**,
1Co 15:51 but we will all be **c**—

Heb 1:12 like a garment they will be **c.**

CHANGERS* [CHANGE]

Mt	21:12	the tables of the money **c**
Mk	11:15	the tables of the money **c**
Jn	2:15	the coins of the money **c**

CHAPEL (KJV) See SANCTUARY

CHARACTER*

Ru	3:11	that you are a woman of noble **c.**
Pr	12: 4	A wife of noble **c** is her husband's crown,
	31:10	A wife of noble **c** who can find?
Ac	17:11	of more noble **c** than
Ro	5: 4	perseverance, **c;** and **c,** hope.
1Co	15:33	"Bad company corrupts good **c.**"

CHARGE [CHARGES, CHARGING]

Ge	39: 4	in **c** of his household,
	39:22	in **c** of all those held in the prison,
	41:40	You shall be in **c** of my palace,
Nu	4:16	to be in **c** of the entire tabernacle
Dt	23:19	Do not **c** your brother interest,
Job	34:13	put him in **c** of the whole world?
Ps	69:27	**C** them with crime upon crime;
SS	5: 8	O daughters of Jerusalem, I **c** you—
Hos	12: 2	The LORD has a **c** to bring
Mt	24:47	in **c** of all his possessions.
Jn	13:29	Since Judas had **c** of the money,
	18:38	"I find no basis for a **c** against him.
Ro	8:33	Who will bring any **c**
1Co	9:18	the gospel I may offer it free of **c,**
2Co	11: 7	the gospel of God to you free of **c?**
2Ti	4: 1	I give you this **c:**
Phm	1:18	owes you anything, **c** it to me.
Rev	14:18	who had **c** of the fire,
	16: 5	the angel in **c** of the waters say:

CHARGES [CHARGE]

Job	4:18	if he **c** his angels with error,
Isa	50: 8	Who then will bring **c** against me?
Jer	25:31	for the LORD will bring **c** against
Lk	23:14	and have found no basis for your **c**
Ac	24: 1	and they brought their **c** against Paul

CHARGING [CHARGE]

| Job | 1:22 | not sin by **c** God with wrongdoing. |

CHARIOT [CHARIOTS]

Ge	41:43	in a **c** as his second-in-command,
1Ki	22:34	The king told his **c** driver,
2Ki	2:11	suddenly a **c** of fire and horses
2Ch	1:17	They imported a **c** from Egypt
Ps	104: 3	He makes the clouds his **c** and rides
Zec	6: 2	The first **c** had red horses,
Ac	8:28	in his **c** reading the book of Isaiah

CHARIOTS [CHARIOT]

Ex	14: 7	He took six hundred of the best **c,**
	15:19	**c** and horsemen went into the sea,
Jos	11: 4	and a large number of horses and **c—**
	17:18	though the Canaanites have iron **c**
Jdg	4: 3	Because he had nine hundred iron **c**
2Sa	8: 4	David captured a thousand of his **c,**

2Ki	6:17	and saw the hills full of horses and **c**
2Ch	1:14	Solomon accumulated **c** and horses;
Ps	20: 7	Some trust in **c** and some in horses,
	68:17	The **c** of God are tens of thousands
Na	2: 3	The metal on the **c** flashes on
Hag	2:22	I will overthrow **c** and their drivers;
Rev	9: 9	thundering of many horses and **c**

CHARM* [CHARMING, CHARMS]

| Pr | 17: 8 | bribe is a **c** to the one who gives it; |
| | 31:30 | **C** is deceptive, and beauty is fleeting |

CHARMING* [CHARM]

| Pr | 26:25 | Though his speech is **c,** |
| SS | 1:16 | Oh, how **c!** |

CHARMS* [CHARM]

Isa	3:20	the perfume bottles and **c,**
Eze	13:18	to the women who sew magic **c**
	13:20	against your magic **c**

CHASE [CHASED, CHASES, CHASING]

Lev	26: 8	a hundred of you will **c** ten thousand,
Dt	32:30	How could one man **c** a thousand,
Hos	2: 7	She will **c** after her lovers but

CHASED [CHASE]

| Dt | 1:44 | came out against you; they **c** you |
| Jos | 7: 5 | They **c** the Israelites from the city |

CHASES* [CHASE]

| Pr | 12:11 | he who **c** fantasies lacks judgment. |
| | 28:19 | but the one who **c** fantasies will have |

CHASING [CHASE]

| Ecc | 1:14 | a **c** after the wind. |

CHASM*

| Lk | 16:26 | and you a great **c** has been fixed, |

CHASTE (KJV) See PURE

CHASTENED*

| Job | 33:19 | Or a man may be **c** on a bed of pain |
| Ps | 118:18 | The LORD has **c** me severely, |

CHATTER* [CHATTERING]

| 1Ti | 6:20 | Turn away from godless **c** and |
| 2Ti | 2:16 | Avoid godless **c,** |

CHATTERING* [CHATTER]

| Pr | 10: 8 | but a **c** fool comes to ruin. |
| | 10:10 | and a **c** fool comes to ruin. |

CHEAPER*

| Jn | 2:10 | and then the **c** wine after |

CHEAT* [CHEATED, CHEATING, CHEATS]

| Mal | 1:14 | the **c** who has an acceptable male |
| 1Co | 6: 8 | you yourselves **c** and do wrong, |

CHEATED* [CHEAT]

| Ge | 31: 7 | yet your father has **c** me |
| 1Sa | 12: 3 | Whom have I **c?** |

12: 4 "You have not **c** or oppressed us,"
Lk 19: 8 if I have **c** anybody out of anything,
1Co 6: 7 Why not rather be **c?**

CHEATING* [CHEAT]

Am 8: 5 the price and **c** with dishonest scales,

CHEATS* [CHEAT]

Lev 6: 2 or if he **c** him,

CHEEK* [CHEEKS]

Job 16:10 they strike my **c** in scorn
La 3:30 Let him offer his **c**
Mic 5: 1 on the **c** with a rod.
Mt 5:39 someone strikes you on the right **c,**
Lk 6:29 If someone strikes you on one **c,**

CHEEKS* [CHEEK]

SS 1:10 Your **c** are beautiful with earrings,
 5:13 His **c** are like beds
Isa 50: 6 my **c** to those who pulled out my
La 1: 2 tears are upon her **c.**

CHEER* [CHEERFUL, CHEERFULLY, CHEERING, CHEERS]

1Ki 21: 7 Get up and eat! **C** up.
Mk 10:49 they called to the blind man, "**C** up!

CHEERFUL* [CHEER]

Pr 15:13 A happy heart makes the face **c,**
 15:15 but the **c** heart has a continual feast.
 15:30 A **c** look brings joy to the heart,
 17:22 A **c** heart is good medicine,
2Co 9: 7 for God loves a **c** giver.

CHEERFULLY* [CHEER]

Ro 12: 8 let him do it **c.**

CHEERING* [CHEER]

1Ki 1:45 From there they have gone up **c,**
2Ch 23:12 the noise of the people running and **c**
Ecc 2: 3 I tried **c** myself with wine,

CHEERS* [CHEER]

Jdg 9:13 which **c** both gods and men,
Pr 12:25 but a kind word **c** him up.

CHEMOSH

Nu 21:29 You are destroyed, O people of **C!**
1Ki 11: 7 for **C** the detestable god
2Ki 23:13 for **C** the vile god of Moab,
Jer 48: 7 and **C** will go into exile,

CHERISH* [CHERISHED, CHERISHES]

Ps 17:14 You still the hunger of those you **c;**
 83: 3 they plot against those you **c.**

CHERISHED* [CHERISH]

Ps 66:18 If I had **c** sin in my heart,
Hos 9:16 I will slay their **c** offspring."

CHERISHES* [CHERISH]

Pr 19: 8 he who **c** understanding prospers.

CHERUB [CHERUBIM]

Ex 25:19 Make one **c** on one end and the second **c** on the other;
1Ki 6:26 The height of each **c** was ten cubits.
2Ch 3:11 touched the wing of the other **c.**
Eze 10:14 One face was that of a **c,**
 28:14 You were anointed as a guardian **c,**
 41:18 Each **c** had two faces:

CHERUBIM [CHERUB]

Ge 3:24 of the Garden of Eden **c**
Ex 25:18 And make two **c** out
 26: 1 with **c** worked into them by
Nu 7:89 the two **c** above the atonement cover
1Sa 4: 4 who is enthroned between the **c.**
2Sa 6: 2 between the **c** that are on the ark.
 22:11 He mounted the **c** and flew;
1Ki 6:23 a pair of **c** of olive wood,
2Ki 19:15 enthroned between the **c,**
1Ch 13: 6 who is enthroned between the **c—**
2Ch 3: 7 and he carved **c** on the walls.
Ps 18:10 He mounted the **c** and flew;
 80: 1 between the **c,**
 99: 1 between the **c,**
Isa 37:16 enthroned between the **c,**
Eze 9: 3 of Israel went up from above the **c,**
 10: 1 that was over the heads of the **c.**
 41:18 were carved **c** and palm trees.
Heb 9: 5 the ark were the **c** of the Glory,

CHEST [CHESTS]

Ex 25:10 "Have them make a **c**
Dt 10: 2 Then you are to put them in the **c.**"
2Ki 12: 9 the **c** all the money that was brought
Da 2:32 its **c** and arms of silver,
Rev 1:13 and with a golden sash around his **c.**

CHESTS* [CHEST]

Rev 15: 6 golden sashes around their **c.**

CHEW [CHEWS]

Lev 11: 4 " 'There are some that only **c** the cud
Dt 14: 7 that **c** the cud or that have

CHEWS [CHEW]

Lev 11: 3 and that **c** the cud.

CHICKS*

Mt 23:37 a hen gathers her **c** under her wings,
Lk 13:34 a hen gathers her **c** under her wings,

CHIEF [CHIEFS]

2Sa 23:13 the thirty **c** men came down to David
Ezr 7: 5 the son of Aaron the **c** priest—
Isa 2: 2 as **c** among the mountains;
Da 10:13 Then Michael, one of the **c** princes,
Mt 20:18 to the **c** priests and the teachers of
 27: 6 The **c** priests picked up the coins
Mk 15: 3 The **c** priests accused him
Eph 2:20 Jesus himself as the **c** cornerstone.
1Pe 5: 4 And when the **C** Shepherd appears,

CHIEF PRIESTS Mt 2:4; 16:21; 20:18; 21:15, 23, 45; 26:3, 14, 47, 59; 27:1, 3, 6, 12, 20, 41, 62; 28:11, 12; Mk 8:31; 10:33; 11:18, 27; 14:1, 10,

43, 53, 55; 15:1, 3, 10, 11, 31; Lk 9:22; 19:47; 20:1, 19; 22:2, 4, 52, 66; 23:4, 10, 13; 24:20; Jn 7:32, 45; 11:47, 57; 12:10; 18:3, 35; 19:6, 15, 21; Ac 4:23; 5:24; 9:14, 21; 22:30; 23:14; 25:2, 15; 26:10, 12

CHIEFS [CHIEF]

1Ch 11:10 the **c** of David's mighty men—

CHILD [CHILDHOOD, CHILDISH, CHILDLESS, CHILDREN, CHILDREN'S, GRANDCHILDREN]

Ge	4:25	"God has granted me another **c**
	17:17	Will Sarah bear a **c** at the age
Ex	2: 2	When she saw that he was a fine **c,**
Jdg	11:34	She was an only **c.**
Ru	4:16	Then Naomi took the **c,**
1Sa	1:27	I prayed for this **c,**
2Sa	12:16	David pleaded with God for the **c.**
1Ki	3: 7	a little **c** and do not know how
2Ch	22:11	she hid the **c** from Athaliah
Job	3:16	in the ground like a stillborn **c,**
Ps	131: 2	a weaned **c** is my soul within me.
Pr	20: 3	and an only **c** of my mother,
	20:11	Even a **c** is known by his actions,
	22: 6	Train a **c** in the way he should go,
	22:15	Folly is bound up in the heart of a **c,**
	23:13	Do not withhold discipline from a **c;**
	29:15	but a **c** left to himself disgraces his
Ecc	6: 3	that a stillborn **c** is better off than he.
Isa	7:14	The virgin will be with **c**
	9: 6	For to us a **c** is born,
	11: 6	and a little **c** will lead them.
	54: 1	you who never bore a **c;**
	66:13	As a mother comforts her **c,**
Jer	1: 6	I am only a **c."**
Hos	11: 1	"When Israel was a **c,** I loved him,
Zec	12:10	for him as one mourns for an only **c,**
Mt	1:23	be with **c** and will give birth to a son,
	2:11	they saw the **c** with his mother Mary,
	18: 2	He called a little **c** and had him stand
Mk	5:39	The **c** is not dead but asleep."
	10:15	like a little **c** will never enter it."
Lk	1:42	and blessed is the **c** you will bear!
	1:80	**c** grew and became strong in spirit;
Ac	13:10	a **c** of the devil and an enemy
1Co	13:11	When I was a **c,** I talked like a **c,** I thought like a **c,** reasoned like a **c.**
Gal	4: 1	that as long as the heir is a **c,**
Heb	11:23	they saw he was no ordinary **c,**
1Jn	5: 1	the father loves his **c** as well.
Rev	12: 4	so that he might devour her **c**

CHILDBEARING* [BEAR]

Ge	3:16	I will greatly increase your pains in **c**
	18:11	and Sarah was past the age of **c.**
1Ti	2:15	But women will be saved through **c**

CHILDBIRTH [BEAR]

Ro	8:22	groaning as in the pains of **c**
Gal	4:19	the pains of **c** until Christ is formed

CHILDHOOD [CHILD]

Ge 8:21 of his heart is evil from **c.**

CHILDISH* [CHILD]

1Co 13:11 I put **c** ways behind me.

CHILDLESS [CHILD]

Ge	15: 2	since I remain **c** and
1Sa	15:33	"As your sword has made women **c,**

CHILDREN [CHILD]

Ge	3:16	with pain you will give birth to **c.**
	21: 7	that Sarah would nurse **c?**
Ex	20: 5	the **c** for the sin of the fathers
Lev	20: 3	for by giving his **c** to Molech,
Dt	4: 9	Teach them to your **c** and to their **c** after them.
	6: 7	Impress them on your **c.**
	11:19	Teach them to your **c,**
	14: 1	the **c** of the LORD your God.
	24:16	nor **c** put to death for their fathers;
	29:29	to us and to our **c** forever,
	30:19	so that you and your **c** may live
	32:46	that you may command your **c**
Jos	4: 6	In the future, when your **c** ask you,
1Sa	2: 5	who was barren has borne seven **c,**
Ezr	10:44	some of them had **c** by these wives.
Ne	13:24	Half of their **c** spoke the language
Job	1: 5	"Perhaps my **c** have sinned
Ps	8: 2	From the lips of **c** and infants
	37:25	or their **c** begging bread.
	78: 5	forefathers to teach their **c,**
	103:13	As a father has compassion on his **c,**
	112: 2	His **c** will be mighty in the land;
Pr	14:26	and for his **c** it will be a refuge.
	17: 6	Children's **c** are a crown to the aged,
	17: 6	and parents are the pride of their **c.**
	20: 7	a blameless life; blessed are his **c**
	31:28	Her **c** arise and call her blessed;
Isa	1: 4	given to corruption!
	49:25	and your **c** I will save.
Jer	4:22	They are senseless **c;**
	31:15	Rachel weeping for her **c**
La	4: 4	the **c** beg for bread,
Eze	5:10	in your midst fathers will eat their **c,**
	23:37	even sacrificed their **c,**
Hos	2: 4	because they are the **c** of adultery.
Joel	1: 3	Tell it to your **c,**
Zec	10: 7	Their **c** will see it and be joyful;
Mal	4: 6	the hearts of the **c** to their fathers;
Mt	2:18	Rachel weeping for her **c**
	3: 9	of these stones God can raise up **c**
	7:11	how to give good gifts to your **c,**
	11:25	and revealed them to little **c.**
	18: 3	you change and become like little **c,**
	19:14	"Let the little **c** come to me,
	21:16	" ' From the lips of **c**
Mk	9:37	welcomes one of these little **c**
	10:14	"Let the little **c** come to me,
	10:16	And he took the **c** in his arms,
	10:30	sisters, mothers, **c** and fields—
	13:12	**C** will rebel against their parents
Lk	10:21	and revealed them to little **c.**
	18:16	Jesus called the **c** to him and said,

	18:16	"Let the little **c** come to me,
Jn	1:12	the right to become **c** of God—
	8:39	"If you were Abraham's **c,**"
Ac	2:39	The promise is for you and your **c**
Ro	8:16	with our spirit that we are God's **c.**
	9: 8	not the natural **c** who are God's **c,**
1Co	14:20	Brothers, stop thinking like **c.**
2Co	12:14	**c** should not have to save up for
		their parents, but parents for their **c.**
Gal	3: 7	those who believe are **c** of Abraham.
	4:24	and bears **c** who are to be slaves:
Eph	5: 8	Live as **c** of light
	6: 1	**C**, obey your parents in the Lord,
	6: 4	Fathers, do not exasperate your **c;**
Php	2:15	**c** of God without fault in a crooked
Col	3:20	**C**, obey your parents in everything,
	3:21	Fathers, do not embitter your **c,**
1Th	2: 7	like a mother caring for her little **c.**
1Ti	3: 4	and see that his **c** obey him
	3:12	but one wife and must manage his **c**
	5:10	such as bringing up **c,**
	5:14	younger widows to marry, to have **c,**
Tit	1: 6	a man whose **c** believe and are
	2: 4	to love their husbands and **c,**
Heb	2:13	and the **c** God has given me."
	12: 8	then you are illegitimate **c** and
1Pe	1:14	As obedient **c,**
1Jn	3: 1	that we should be called **c** of God!
	3:10	how we know who the **c** of God are
	5:19	We know that we are **c** of God,
2Jn	1: 1	elder, To the chosen lady and her **c,**
3Jn	1: 4	that my **c** are walking in the truth.

CHILDREN'S [CHILD]

Pr	13:22	an inheritance for his **c** children,
	17: 6	**C** children are a crown to the aged,
Isa	54:13	and great will be your **c** peace.
Jer	31:29	and the **c** teeth are set on edge.'
Eze	18: 2	and the **c** teeth are set on edge'?
Mt	15:26	the **c** bread and toss it to their dogs."

CHISEL [CHISELED]

Ex	34: 1	"**C** out two stone tablets like

CHISELED [CHISEL]

Dt	10: 3	and **c** out two stone tablets like

CHOICE [CHOICEST, CHOOSE, CHOOSES, CHOSE, CHOSEN]

1Ch	21:11	the LORD says: 'Take your **c:**
Pr	8:10	knowledge rather than **c** gold,
	10:20	tongue of the righteous is **c** silver,
	18: 8	words of a gossip are like **c** morsels;
SS	4:13	of pomegranates with **c** fruits,
	4:16	into his garden and taste its **c** fruits.
Jer	2:21	a **c** vine of sound and reliable stock.
Da	1:16	the guard took away their **c** food and
	10: 3	I ate no **c** food;
Ro	8:20	not by its own **c,**

CHOICEST [CHOICE]

Dt	33:15	the **c** gifts of the ancient mountains
Isa	5: 2	and planted it with the **c** vines.
	16: 8	trampled down the **c** vines,

CHOIR* [CHOIRS]

Ne	12:38	The second **c** proceeded in

CHOIRS [CHOIR]

1Ch	15:27	in charge of the singing of the **c.**
Ne	12:31	I also assigned two large **c**

CHOKE [CHOKED]

Mt	18:28	He grabbed him and began to **c** him.

CHOKED* [CHOKE]

Mt	13: 7	which grew up and **c** the plants,
Mk	4: 7	which grew up and **c** the plants,
Lk	8: 7	which grew up with it and **c**
	8:14	as they go on their way they are **c**

CHOOSE [CHOICE]

Nu	14: 4	"We should **c** a leader and go back
	17: 5	to the man I **c** will sprout,
Dt	12:14	at the place the LORD will **c** in one
	30:19	Now **c** life, so that you
Jos	24:15	then **c** for yourselves this day whom
		you will serve,
2Ki	18:32	**c** life and not death!
Ps	65: 4	Blessed are those you **c** and bring
Pr	1:29	and did not to fear the LORD,
	3:31	Do not envy a violent man or **c** any
	8:10	**C** my instruction instead of silver,
	16:16	to **c** understanding rather than silver!
Isa	7:15	to reject the wrong and **c** the right.
	14: 1	once again he will **c** Israel
Zec	2:12	and will again **c** Jerusalem.
Jn	15:16	You did not **c** me,
Ac	1:21	Therefore it is necessary to **c** one of
	6: 3	**c** seven men from
2Co	12: 6	Even if I should **c** to boast,
Php	1:22	Yet what shall I **c?**
1Pe	4: 3	the past doing what pagans **c** to do—

CHOOSES [CHOICE]

Nu	16: 7	The man the LORD **c** will be
Ps	68:16	the mountain where God **c** to reign,
Mt	11:27	the Son and those to whom the Son **c**
Lk	10:22	the Son and those to whom the Son **c**
Jn	7:17	If anyone **c** to do God's will,
Jas	4: 4	Anyone who **c** to be a friend of

CHOSE [CHOICE]

Ge	13:11	Lot **c** for himself the whole plain
Dt	4:37	and **c** their descendants after them,
	10:15	and he **c** you, their descendants,
Jdg	5: 8	When they **c** new gods,
1Sa	2:28	I **c** your father out of all the tribes
	17:40	**c** five smooth stones from the stream
Ne	9: 7	who **c** Abram and brought him out
Ps	33:12	the people he **c** for his inheritance.
	78:70	He **c** David his servant and took him
Isa	65:12	and **c** what displeases me."
Eze	20: 5	On the day I **c** Israel,
Lk	6:13	and **c** twelve of them,
Jn	15:16	but I **c** you and appointed you to go
Ac	6: 5	They **c** Stephen, a man full of faith
	15:22	They **c** Judas (called Barsabbas)
	15:40	but Paul **c** Silas and left,

1Co	1:27	But God **c** the foolish things of
Eph	1: 4	For he **c** us in him before
2Th	2:13	the beginning God **c** you to be saved
Heb	11:25	He **c** to be mistreated along with
Jas	1:18	He **c** to give us birth through

CHOSEN [CHOICE]

Ge	18:19	For I have **c** him,
Ex	31: 2	I have **c** Bezalel son of Uri,
Lev	16:10	But the goat **c** by lot as
Dt	7: 6	The LORD your God has **c** you out
Jdg	10:14	and cry out to the gods you have **c**
1Sa	8:18	for relief from the king you have **c,**
	10:21	Finally Saul son of Kish was **c.**
	16: 1	I have **c** one of his sons to be king."
1Ki	8:44	toward the city you have **c** and
Ne	1: 9	and bring them to the place I have **c**
Ps	89: 3	a covenant with my **c** one,
	105: 6	O sons of Jacob, his **c** ones.
	119:30	I have **c** the way of truth;
Isa	41: 8	my servant, Jacob, whom I have **c,**
Am	3: 2	"You only have I **c** of all the families
Hag	2:23	for I have **c** you,'
Zec	3: 2	The LORD, who has **c** Jerusalem,
Mt	12:18	"Here is my servant whom I have **c,**
	22:14	For many are invited, but few are **c."**
Mk	13:20	the sake of the elect, whom he has **c,**
Lk	9:35	"This is my Son, whom I have **c;**
	10:42	Mary has **c** what is better,
	23:35	Christ of God, the **c** One."
Jn	6:70	Jesus replied, "Have I not **c** you,
	15:19	but I have **c** you out of the world.
Ac	9:15	This man is my **c** instrument
Ro	8:33	against those whom God has **c?**
	11: 5	the present time there is a remnant **c**
Eph	1:11	In him we were also **c,**
Col	3:12	Therefore, as God's **c** people,
1Th	1: 4	that he has **c** you,
Jas	2: 5	God **c** those who are poor in
1Pe	1:20	He was **c** before the creation of
	2: 4	rejected by men but **c** by God
	2: 9	But you are a **c** people,
2Jn	1: 1	elder, To the **c** lady and her children,
Rev	17:14	**c** and faithful followers."

CHRIST [CHRIST'S, CHRISTIAN, CHRISTIANS, CHRISTS, MESSIAH]

Mt	1: 1	record of the genealogy of Jesus **C**
	1:16	who is called **C.**
	16:16	"You are the **C,**
	22:42	"What do you think about the **C?**
	23:10	for you have one Teacher, the **C.**
	24: 5	'I am the **C,**' and will deceive many.
Mk	1: 1	of the gospel about Jesus **C,**
	8:29	Peter answered, "You are the **C."**
	14:61	"Are you the **C,**
Lk	2:11	he is **C** the Lord.
	9:20	Peter answered, "The **C** of God."
	23:39	"Aren't you the **C?**
Jn	1:17	and truth came through Jesus **C.**
	1:20	"I am not the **C.**"
	1:41	the Messiah" (that is, the **C**).
	4:25	that Messiah" (called **C**) "is coming.
	7:41	"How can the **C** come from Galilee?

	20:31	believe that Jesus is the **C,**
Ac	2:36	both Lord and **C.**"
	3: 6	In the name of Jesus **C** of Nazareth,
	4:10	by the name of Jesus **C** of Nazareth,
	5:42	the good news that Jesus is the **C.**
	8: 5	and proclaimed the **C** there.
	9:22	by proving that Jesus is the **C.**
	9:34	"Jesus **C** heals you.
	17: 3	that the **C** had to suffer and rise from
	18:28	the Scriptures that Jesus was the **C.**
	26:23	that the **C** would suffer and,
Ro	1: 4	Jesus **C** our Lord.
	3:22	comes through faith in Jesus **C**
	5: 1	with God through our Lord Jesus **C,**
	5: 6	**C** died for the ungodly.
	5: 8	**C** died for us.
	5:11	in God through our Lord Jesus **C,**
	5:17	in life through the one man, Jesus **C.**
	6: 4	just as **C** was raised from the dead
	6:23	eternal life in **C** Jesus our Lord.
	7: 4	to the law through the body of **C,**
	8: 1	for those who are in **C** Jesus,
	8: 9	does not have the Spirit of **C,** he does not belong to **C.**
	8:17	heirs of God and co-heirs with **C,**
	8:35	separate us from the love of **C?**
	9: 5	the human ancestry of **C,**
	10: 4	**C** is the end of the law so
	12: 5	in **C** we who are many form one
	13:14	clothe yourselves with the Lord Jesus **C,**
	14: 9	**C** died and returned to life so
	15: 3	even **C** did not please himself but,
	15: 5	as you follow **C** Jesus,
	15: 7	then, just as **C** accepted you,
	16:18	not serving our Lord **C,**
1Co	1: 2	in **C** Jesus and called to be holy,
	1: 7	eagerly wait for our Lord Jesus **C**
	1:13	Is **C** divided?
	1:17	For **C** did not send me to baptize,
	1:23	but we preach **C** crucified:
	1:30	of him that you are in **C** Jesus,
	2: 2	except Jesus **C** and him crucified.
	2:16	But we have the mind of **C.**
	3:11	which is Jesus **C.**
	5: 7	For **C,** our Passover lamb,
	6:15	Shall I then take the members of **C**
	8: 6	**C,** through whom all things came
	8:12	you sin against **C.**
	10: 4	and that rock was **C.**
	11: 1	as I follow the example of **C.**
	11: 3	that the head of every man is **C,**
	11: 3	and the head of **C** is God.
	12:27	Now you are the body of **C,**
	15: 3	that **C** died for our sins
	15:14	And if **C** has not been raised,
	15:22	so in **C** all will be made alive.
	15:57	victory through our Lord Jesus **C.**
2Co	1: 5	For just as the sufferings of **C** flow
	2:14	in triumphal procession in **C**
	3: 3	that you are a letter from **C,**
	3:14	because only in **C** is it taken away.
	4: 4	of the gospel of the glory of **C,**
	4: 5	but Jesus **C** as Lord,

4: 6 of the glory of God in the face of **C.**
5:10 before the judgment seat of **C,**
5:17 anyone is in **C,** he is a new creation;
6:15 What harmony is there between **C**
10: 1 the meekness and gentleness of **C,**
11: 2 I promised you to one husband, to **C,**
11:13 masquerading as apostles of **C.**
Gal 1: 7 to pervert the gospel of **C.**
2: 4 the freedom we have in **C** Jesus and
2:16 but by faith in Jesus **C.**
2:16 that we may be justified by faith in **C**
2:17 does that mean that **C** promotes sin?
2:20 I have been crucified with **C**
2:21 **C** died for nothing!"
3:13 **C** redeemed us from the curse of
3:16 meaning one person, who is **C.**
3:26 of God through faith in **C** Jesus,
4:19 of childbirth until **C** is formed
5: 1 for freedom that **C** has set us free.
5: 4 by law have been alienated from **C;**
5:24 to **C** Jesus have crucified
6:14 in the cross of our Lord Jesus **C,**
Eph 1: 3 with every spiritual blessing in **C.**
1:10 under one head, even **C.**
1:20 in **C** when he raised him from
2: 5 with **C** even when we were dead
2:10 created in **C** Jesus to do good works,
2:12 that time you were separate from **C,**
2:20 with **C** Jesus himself as the chief
cornerstone.
3: 8 the unsearchable riches of **C,**
3:17 so that **C** may dwell in your hearts
4: 7 given as **C** apportioned it.
4:13 of the fullness of **C.**
4:15 into him who is the Head, that is, **C.**
4:32 just as in **C** God forgave you.
5: 2 just as **C** loved us and gave himself
5:21 out of reverence for **C.**
5:23 as **C** is the head of the church,
5:25 just as **C** loved the church
Php 1: 6 until the day of **C** Jesus.
1:18 false motives or true, **C** is preached.
1:21 to me, to live is **C** and to die is gain.
1:23 to depart and be with **C,**
1:27 a manner worthy of the gospel of **C.**
1:29 on behalf of **C** not only to believe
2: 5 be the same as that of **C** Jesus:
2:11 confess that Jesus **C** is Lord,
3: 7 now consider loss for the sake of **C.**
3:10 to know **C** and the power
3:18 as enemies of the cross of **C.**
4:19 to his glorious riches in **C** Jesus.
Col 1: 4 heard of your faith in **C** Jesus
1:27 which is **C** in you, the hope of glory.
1:28 may present everyone perfect in **C.**
2: 2 the mystery of God, namely, **C,**
2: 6 just as you received **C** Jesus as Lord,
2: 9 For in **C** all the fullness of
2:13 God made you alive with **C.**
2:17 the reality, however, is found in **C.**
3: 1 **C** is seated at the right hand of God.
3: 3 and your life is now hidden with **C**
3:15 the peace of **C** rule in your hearts,
3:16 the word of **C** dwell in you richly

1Th 4:16 and the dead in **C** will rise first.
5: 9 salvation through our Lord Jesus **C.**
5:18 this is God's will for you in **C** Jesus.
2Th 2: 1 the coming of our Lord Jesus **C**
2:14 in the glory of our Lord Jesus **C.**
1Ti 1:12 I thank **C** Jesus our Lord,
1:15 **C** Jesus came into the world to save
1:16 **C** Jesus might display his unlimited
2: 5 the man **C** Jesus,
4: 6 be a good minister of **C** Jesus,
6:14 the appearing of our Lord Jesus **C,**
2Ti 1: 9 This grace was given us in **C** Jesus
1:10 the appearing of our Savior, **C** Jesus,
2: 1 in the grace that is in **C** Jesus.
2: 3 like a good soldier of **C** Jesus.
2: 8 Remember Jesus **C,**
2:10 the salvation that is in **C** Jesus,
3:12 to live a godly life in **C** Jesus will
3:15 salvation through faith in **C** Jesus.
4: 1 of **C** Jesus, who will judge the living
Tit 2:13 our great God and Savior, Jesus **C,**
Phm 1: 6 of every good thing we have in **C.**
1:20 refresh my heart in **C.**
Heb 3: 6 But **C** is faithful as a son
3:14 to share in **C** if we hold firmly till
5: 5 So **C** also did not take upon himself
6: 1 the elementary teachings about **C**
9:11 When **C** came as high priest of
9:15 For this reason **C** is the mediator of
9:24 For **C** did not enter a man-made
9:26 **C** would have had to suffer
9:28 so **C** was sacrificed once
10:10 of the body of Jesus **C** once
11:26 disgrace for the sake of **C** as
13: 8 Jesus **C** is the same yesterday
1Pe 1: 2 for obedience to Jesus **C**
1: 3 through the resurrection of Jesus **C**
1:11 the Spirit of **C** in them was pointing
1:11 he predicted the sufferings of **C**
1:19 but with the precious blood of **C,**
2:21 because **C** suffered for you,
3:15 in your hearts set apart **C** as Lord.
3:18 For **C** died for sins once for all,
3:21 by the resurrection of Jesus **C,**
4: 1 since **C** suffered in his body,
4:13 participate in the sufferings of **C,**
4:14 because of the name of **C,**
2Pe 1: 1 a servant and apostle of Jesus **C,**
1: 1 our God and Savior Jesus **C**
1:16 and coming of our Lord Jesus **C,**
3:18 of our Lord and Savior Jesus **C.**
1Jn 2: 1 the Father in our defense—Jesus **C,**
2:22 who denies that Jesus is the **C.**
3:16 Jesus **C** laid down his life for us.
3:23 in the name of his Son, Jesus **C,**
4: 2 that Jesus **C** has come in the flesh is
5: 1 that Jesus is the **C** is born of God,
5: 6 came by water and blood—Jesus **C.**
5:20 even in his Son Jesus **C.**
2Jn 1: 7 not acknowledge Jesus **C** as coming
1: 9 not continue in the teaching of **C.**
Jude 1: 1 the Father and kept by Jesus **C:**
1: 4 and deny Jesus **C** our only Sovereign
1:17 apostles of our Lord Jesus **C** foretold

Rev 1: 1 The revelation of Jesus C,
     1: 5 and from Jesus C,
 11:15 kingdom of our Lord and of his C,
 20: 4 and reigned with C a thousand years.
 20: 6 they will be priests of God and of C

CHRIST JESUS See JESUS

JESUS CHRIST See JESUS

LORD JESUS CHRIST See JESUS

CHRIST'S* [CHRIST]

1Co 7:22 when he was called is C slave.
   9:21 but am under C law),
2Co 5:14 For C love compels us,
   5:20 We are therefore C ambassadors,
   5:20 We implore you on C behalf:
  12: 9 so that C power may rest on me.
  12:10 That is why, for C sake,
Col 1:22 by C physical body through death
   1:24 lacking in regard to C afflictions,
2Th 3: 5 into God's love and C perseverance.
1Pe 5: 1 a witness of C sufferings

CHRISTIAN* [CHRIST]

Ac 26:28 persuade me to be a C?"
1Pe 4:16 However, if you suffer as a C,

CHRISTIANS* [CHRIST]

Ac 11:26 The disciples were called C first

CHRISTS* [CHRIST]

Mt 24:24 For false C and false prophets
Mk 13:22 For false C and false prophets

CHRONICLES*

Est   6: 1 so he ordered the book of the c,

CHURCH [CHURCHES]

Mt 16:18 and on this rock I will build my c,
  18:17 if he refuses to listen even to the c,
Ac   5:11 Great fear seized the whole c
   8: 1 persecution broke out against the c
   8: 3 But Saul began to destroy the c.
  12: 1 arrested some who belonged to the c,
  14:23 elders for them in each c and,
  15: 4 by the c and the apostles and elders,
  20:28 Be shepherds of the c of God,
Ro 16: 5 also the c that meets at their house.
1Co 4:17 I teach everywhere in every c.
   5:12 to judge those outside the c?
   6: 4 even men of little account in the c!
  10:32 Greeks or the c of God—
  11:18 that when you come together as a c,
  12:28 And in the c God has appointed first
  14: 4 but he who prophesies edifies the c.
  14:12 to excel in gifts that build up the c.
  14:26 for the strengthening of the c.
  14:35 for a woman to speak in the c.
  15: 9 because I persecuted the c of God.
Gal 1:13 the c of God and tried to destroy it.
Eph 1:22 to be head over everything for the c,
   3:10 intent was that now, through the c,
   5:23 as Christ is the head of the c,
   5:25 just as Christ loved the c
Php 3: 6 as for zeal, persecuting the c;

Col 1:18 he is the head of the body, the c;
   1:24 which is the c.
1Ti   3: 5 how can he take care of God's c?)
   5:16 c can help those widows who are
Heb 12:23 to the c of the firstborn,
Jas   5:14 the elders of the c to pray over him
3Jn   1: 9 I wrote to the c, but Diotrephes,

CHURCHES [CHURCH]

Ac 15:41 strengthening the c.
  16: 5 the c were strengthened in the faith
1Co 7:17 the rule I lay down in all the c.
  11:16 nor do the c of God.
  14:34 women should remain silent in the c.
2Co 11: 8 I robbed other c by receiving support
1Th   2:14 the same things those c suffered
2Th   1: 4 among God's c we boast
Rev 1: 4 the seven c in the province of Asia:
   1:20 seven lampstands are the seven c.
   2: 7 the Spirit says to the c.
  22:16 to give you this testimony for the c.

CHURNING

Pr 30:33 For as c the milk produces butter,
Da   7: 2 the four winds of heaven c up

CILICIA

Ac 21:39 "I am a Jew, from Tarsus in C,

CIRCLE [CIRCLED, CIRCLING, CIRCUIT, CIRCULAR, ENCIRCLE, ENCIRCLED]

Isa 40:22 He sits enthroned above the c of
Mk   3:34 Then he looked at those seated in a c

CIRCLED* [CIRCLE]

Jos   6:15 that day they c the city seven times.

CIRCLING* [CIRCLE]

Jos   6:11 around the city, c it once.

CIRCUIT* [CIRCLE]

1Sa   7:16 a c from Bethel to Gilgal to Mizpah,
Ps   19: 6 and makes its c to the other;

CIRCULAR [CIRCLE]

2Ch   4: 2 Sea of cast metal, c in shape,

CIRCULATED*

Mt 28:15 And this story has been widely c

CIRCUMCISE* [CIRCUMCISED, CIRCUMCISION]

Dt 10:16 C your hearts, therefore,
   30: 6 LORD your God will c your hearts
Jos   5: 2 and c the Israelites again."
Jer   4: 4 C yourselves to the LORD, c your
        hearts,
Lk   1:59 On the eighth day they came to c
   2:21 when it was time to c him,
Jn   7:22 you c a child on the Sabbath.
Ac 21:21 telling them not to c their children

CIRCUMCISED [CIRCUMCISE]

Ge 17:10 Every male among you shall be **c.**
      17:26 and his son Ishmael were both **c**
      21: 4 eight days old, Abraham **c** him,
Lev 12: 3 On the eighth day the boy is to be **c.**
Jos   5: 3 So Joshua made flint knives and **c**
Ac 10:45 The **c** believers who had come
      11: 2 the **c** believers criticized him
      15: 1 "Unless you are **c,**
      16: 3 so he **c** him because of the Jews
Ro   2:26 not **c** keep the law's requirements,
      4: 9 Is this blessedness only for the **c,**
1Co 7:18 He should not be **c.**
Gal   5: 2 that if you let yourselves be **c,**
      6:13 to be **c** that they may boast
Col   2:11 In him you were also **c,**
      3:11 **c** or uncircumcised, barbarian,

CIRCUMCISION [CIRCUMCISE]

Ro   2:25 **C** has value if you observe the law,
      2:29 and **c** is **c** of the heart,
1Co 7:19 **C** is nothing and uncircumcision is
Gal   2:12 who belonged to the **c** group.
      5: 6 For in Christ Jesus neither **c**
Php   3: 3 For it is we who are the **c,**
Col   2:11 but with the **c** done by Christ,
Tit   1:10 especially those of the **c** group.

CIRCUMSTANCES

1Co 7:15 or woman is not bound in such **c;**
Php   4:11 to be content whatever the **c.**
1Th   5:18 give thanks in all **c,**
Jas   1: 9 in humble **c** ought to take pride

CISTERN [CISTERNS]

Ge 37:22 Throw him into this **c** here in
2Ki 18:31 and drink water from his own **c,**
Pr   5:15 Drink water from your own **c,**
Jer 38: 6 took Jeremiah and put him into the **c**

CITADEL [CITADELS]

2Sa 12:26 and captured the royal **c.**
Ne   1: 1 while I was in the **c** of Susa,

CITADELS* [CITADEL]

Ps 48: 3 God is in her **c;**
      48:13 her ramparts, view her **c,**
  122: 7 and security within your **c."**
Isa 34:13 Thorns will overrun her **c,**

CITIES [CITY]

Ge 13:12 Lot lived among the **c** of the plain
      19:25 Thus he overthrew those **c** and
Nu 13:28 and the **c** are fortified and very large.
      21: 2 we will totally destroy their **c."**
      35:11 to be your **c** of refuge,
Dt   6:10 flourishing **c** you did not build,
Jos 24:13 not toil and **c** you did not build;
Ps 69:35 and rebuild the **c** of Judah.
Isa 64:10 Your sacred **c** have become a desert;
Jer   4:16 a war cry against the **c** of Judah.
Mt 10:23 not finish going through the **c**
Lk 19:17 take charge of ten **c.'**
      19:19 'You take charge of five **c.'**

2Pe   2: 6 if he condemned the **c** of Sodom
Rev 16:19 and the **c** of the nations collapsed.

CITIZEN [CITIZENS, CITIZENSHIP]

Ac 21:39 a **c** of no ordinary city.
      22:25 "Is it legal for you to flog a Roman **c**

CITIZENS [CITIZEN]

Ac 16:38 that Paul and Silas were Roman **c,**
Eph   2:19 but fellow **c** with God's people

CITIZENSHIP* [CITIZEN]

Ac 22:28 "I had to pay a big price for my **c."**
Eph   2:12 excluded from **c** in Israel
Php   3:20 But our **c** is in heaven.

CITY [CITIES]

Ge   4:17 Cain was then building a **c,**
      11: 4 "Come, let us build ourselves a **c,**
      18:24 righteous people in the **c?**
      19:14 the LORD is about to destroy the **c!"**
Dt 28: 3 You will be blessed in the **c**
      28:16 You will be cursed in the **c**
Jos   6:16 For the LORD has given you the **c!**
      18:28 the Jebusite **c** (that is, Jerusalem),
Jdg 16: 3 took hold of the doors of the **c** gate,
2Sa   5: 9 and called it the **C** of David.
1Ki   8:44 toward the **c** you have chosen and
1Ch 11: 7 and so it was called the **C** of David.
Ne 11: 1 in Jerusalem, the holy **c,**
Ps 46: 4 streams make glad the **c** of God,
    48: 1 in the **c** of our God,
  122: 3 Jerusalem is built like a **c**
  127: 1 the LORD watches over the **c,**
Pr   8: 3 beside the gates leading into the **c,** at
    11:10 the righteous prosper, the **c** rejoices;
    31:23 respected at the **c** gate,
    31:31 bring her praise at the **c** gate.
Isa   1:21 See how the faithful **c** has become
     1:26 Afterward you will be called the **C**
        of Righteousness, the Faithful **C."**
Jer 34: 2 about to hand this **c** over to the king
    34:22 and I will bring them back to this **c.**
La   1: 1 How deserted lies the **c,**
Eze   4: 1 put it in front of you and draw the **c**
    11: 3 This **c** is a cooking pot,
Da   9:24 for your people and your holy **c**
Jnh   1: 2 "Go to the great **c** of Nineveh
     4:11 be concerned about that great **c?**
Hab   2:12 who builds a **c** with bloodshed
Zep   2:15 the carefree **c** that lived in safety.
Zec 14: 2 Half of the **c** will go into exile,
Mt   4: 5 the devil took him to the holy **c**
     5:14 A **c** on a hill cannot be hidden.
Ac 18:10 I have many people in this **c."**
Heb 11:10 For he was looking forward to the **c**
    12:22 the **c** of the living God.
    13:14 but we are looking for the **c** that is
Rev   2:13 who was put to death in your **c—**
     3:12 and the name of the **c** of my God,
    11: 2 They will trample on the holy **c**
    16:19 The great **c** split into three parts,
    17:18 the great **c** that rules over the kings
    18:10 O great **c,** O Babylon, **c** of power!

20: 9 the **c** he loves.
21: 2 I saw the Holy **C**,
22: 3 and of the Lamb will be in the **c**,

CITY OF DAVID 2Sa 5:7, 9; 6:10, 12, 16; 1Ki
2:10; 3:1; 8:1; 9:24; 11:27, 43; 14:31; 15:8;
22:50; 2Ki 8:24; 9:28; 12:21; 14:20; 15:7, 38;
16:20; 1Ch 11:5, 7; 13:13; 15:1, 29; 2Ch 5:2;
8:11; 9:31; 12:16; 14:1; 16:14; 21:1, 20; 24:16,
25; 27:9; 32:5, 30; 33:14; Ne 3:15; 12:37; Isa
22:9

HOLY CITY See HOLY

CIVILIAN*

2Ti 2: 4 a soldier gets involved in **c** affairs—

CLAIM [CLAIMED, CLAIMING, CLAIMS, RECLAIM]

Job 41:11 a **c** against me that I must pay?
Pr 25: 6 do not **c** a place among great men;
Jn 9:41 but now that you **c** you can see,
 10:33 a mere man, **c** to be God."
Tit 1:16 They **c** to know God,
1Jn 1: 6 If we **c** to have fellowship with him
 1: 8 If we **c** to be without sin,
 1:10 If we **c** we have not sinned,
Rev 2: 2 who **c** to be apostles but are not,
 3: 9 who **c** to be Jews though they are not

CLAIMED [CLAIM]

Jn 19: 7 because he **c** to be the Son of God."
 19:21 this man **c** to be king of the Jews."
Ro 1:22 Although they **c** to be wise,

CLAIMING [CLAIM]

Mk 13: 6 Many will come in my name, **c**,

CLAIMS [CLAIM]

Jas 2:14 if a man **c** to have faith
1Jn 2: 6 Whoever **c** to live in him must walk
 2: 9 Anyone who **c** to be in the light

CLAN [CLANS]

Ge 24:40 a wife for my son from my own **c**
Lev 25:10 and each to his own **c**.
 25:49 relative in his **c** may redeem him.
Nu 27: 4 father's name disappear from his **c**
1Sa 18:18 or my father's **c** in Israel,

CLANGING*

1Co 13: 1 a resounding gong or a **c** cymbal.

CLANS [CLAN]

Nu 1: 2 by their **c** and families,
Jos 14: 1 the tribal **c** of Israel allotted to them.
Jer 31: 1 be the God of all the **c** of Israel,
Mic 5: 2 you are small among the **c** of Judah,

CLAP* [CLAPPED, CLAPS]

Job 21: 5 **c** your hand over your mouth.
Ps 47: 1 **C** your hands, all you nations;
 98: 8 Let the rivers **c** their hands,
Pr 30:32 **c** your hand over your mouth!
Isa 55:12 trees of the field will **c** their hands.
La 2:15 All who pass your way **c** their hands

CLAPPED* [CLAP]

2Ki 11:12 the people **c** their hands and shouted,
Eze 25: 6 Because you have **c** your hands

CLAPS* [CLAP]

Job 27:23 It **c** its hands in derision
 34:37 scornfully he **c** his hands among us
Na 3:19 about you **c** his hands at your fall,

CLASPED* [CLASPS]

Mt 28: 9 **c** his feet and worshiped him.

CLASPS [CLASPED]

Ex 26: 6 Then make fifty gold **c** and use them

CLASSIFY*

2Co 10:12 not dare to **c** or compare ourselves

CLAUDIUS*

Ac 11:28 during the reign of **C**.)
 18: 2 because **C** had ordered all the Jews
 23:26 **C** Lysias, To His Excellency,

CLAWS*

Da 4:33 and his nails like the **c** of a bird.
 7:19 with its iron teeth and bronze **c**—

CLAY

Job 10: 9 that you molded me like **c**.
 33: 6 I too have been taken from **c**.
Isa 29:16 potter were thought to be like the **c**!
 41:25 as if he were a potter treading the **c**.
 45: 9 Does the **c** say to the potter,
 64: 8 We are the **c**, you are the potter;
Jer 18: 6 "Like **c** in the hand of the potter,
 19: 1 and buy a **c** jar from a potter.
La 4: 2 are now considered as pots of **c**,
Eze 4: 1 "Now, son of man, take a **c** tablet,
Da 2:33 of iron and partly of baked **c**.
Ro 9:21 same lump of **c** some pottery
2Co 4: 7 this treasure in jars of **c**
2Ti 2:20 but also of wood and **c**;

CLEAN [CLEANNESS, CLEANSE, CLEANSED, CLEANSES, CLEANSING]

Ge 7: 2 seven of every kind of **c** animal,
Lev 4:12 the camp to a place ceremonially **c**,
 10:10 between the unclean and the **c**,
 16:30 you will be **c** from all your sins.
Dt 14:11 You may eat any **c** bird.
Ps 24: 4 He who has **c** hands and
 51: 7 and I will be **c**;
Pr 20: 9 I am **c** and without sin"?
Ecc 9: 2 the **c** and the unclean,
Eze 36:25 I will sprinkle **c** water on you, and
 you will be **c**;
Zec 3: 5 I said, "Put a **c** turban on his head."
Mt 8: 2 you can make me **c**."
 12:44 swept and put in order.
 23:25 You **c** the outside of the cup
 27:59 wrapped it in a **c** linen cloth,
Mk 7:19 Jesus declared all foods "**c**.")
Jn 13:10 And you are **c**,
 15: 3 You are already **c** because of

Ac 10:15 that God has made **c.**"
Ro 14:20 All food is **c,**
Rev 15: 6 They were dressed in **c,**
19: 8 Fine linen, bright and **c,**
19:14 fine linen, white and **c.**

CLEANNESS [CLEAN]

2Sa 22:25 according to my **c** in his sight.
Ps 18:20 according to the **c** of my hands

CLEANSE [CLEAN]

Ps 51: 2 and **c** me from my sin.
51: 7 **C** me with hyssop,
Pr 20:30 Blows and wounds **c** away evil,
Zec 13: 1 to **c** them from sin and impurity.
Mt 10: 8 **c** those who have leprosy,
Heb 9:14 **c** our consciences from acts that lead
10:22 **c** us from a guilty conscience

CLEANSED [CLEAN]

Jos 22:17 not **c** ourselves from that sin,
2Ki 5:10 be restored and you will be **c.**"
Pr 30:12 and yet are not **c** of their filth;
Isa 1: 6 **c** or bandaged or soothed with oil.
Lk 4:27 yet none of them was **c**—
17:14 And as they went, they were **c.**
Heb 9:22 that nearly everything be **c**
10: 2 worshipers would have been **c** once
2Pe 1: 9 that he has been **c** from his past sins.

CLEANSES* [CLEAN]

2Ti 2:21 If a man **c** himself from the latter,

CLEANSING [CLEAN]

Mk 1:44 that Moses commanded for your **c,**
Eph 5:26 **c** her by the washing with water

CLEAR [CLEARED, CLEARLY]

Ex 24:10 **c** as the sky itself.
Lev 24: 2 to bring you **c** oil of pressed olives
Ne 8: 8 making it **c** and giving the meaning
Mt 3:12 and he will **c** his threshing floor,
Ac 18: 6 I am **c** of my responsibility.
1Co 4: 4 My conscience is **c,**
1Ti 3: 9 of the faith with a **c** conscience.
2Ti 1: 3 with a **c** conscience,
Heb 13:18 that we have a **c** conscience
1Pe 3:16 keeping a **c** conscience,
4: 7 be **c** minded and self-controlled so
Rev 4: 6 a sea of glass, **c** as crystal.
21:11 like a jasper, **c** as crystal.
22: 1 as **c** as crystal,

CLEARED [CLEAR]

Ps 80: 9 You **c** the ground for it,
Isa 5: 2 and **c** it of stones and planted it with

CLEARLY [CLEAR]

Mk 8:25 and he saw everything **c.**
Lk 6:42 and then you will see **c** to remove
Ro 1:20 and divine nature—have been seen,

CLEAVE, CLEAVED (KJV) CLING, CLUNG, DIVIDED, HELD, HOLD, REMAIN TRUE, STICK, STUCK, UNITED

CLEFT* [CLEFTS]

Ex 33:22 in a **c** in the rock and cover you

CLEFTS [CLEFT]

SS 2:14 My dove in the **c** of the rock,
Ob 1: 3 you who live in the **c** of the rocks

CLEVER*

Isa 3: 3 skilled craftsman and **c** enchanter.
5:21 and **c** in their own sight.

CLIMAX*

Eze 21:25 of punishment has reached its **c,**
21:29 of punishment has reached its **c.**
35: 5 time their punishment reached its **c,**

CLIMB [CLIMBED]

1Sa 14:10 'Come up to us,' we will **c** up,
SS 7: 8 I said, "I will **c** the palm tree;
Am 9: 2 Though they **c** up to the heavens,

CLIMBED [CLIMB]

Lk 19: 4 and **c** a sycamore-fig tree to see him,

CLING [CLINGS, CLUNG]

Ps 31: 6 I hate those who **c** to worthless idols;
137: 6 May my tongue **c** to the roof
Jnh 2: 8 "Those who **c** to worthless idols
Ro 12: 9 Hate what is evil; **c** to what is good.

CLINGS [CLING]

Ps 63: 8 My soul **c** to you;

CLOAK [CLOAKS]

Ge 39:12 She caught him by his **c** and said,
Ex 4: 6 "Put your hand inside your **c.**"
12:11 with your **c** tucked into your belt,
22:26 If you take your neighbor's **c** as
Dt 22:12 the four corners of the **c** you wear.
1Ki 11:30 the new **c** he was wearing and tore it
18:46 tucking his **c** into his belt,
2Ki 2: 8 Elijah took his **c,**
2:13 up the **c** that had fallen from Elijah
4:29 "Tuck your **c** into your belt,
9: 1 "Tuck your **c** into your belt,
Mt 5:40 let him have your **c** as well.
Mk 13:16 in the field go back to get his **c.**
Lk 8:44 and touched the edge of his **c,**

CLOAKS [CLOAK]

Mk 11: 8 Many people spread their **c** on

CLOSE [CLOSED, CLOSER, CLOSES, ENCLOSE, ENCLOSED]

2Ki 11: 8 Stay **c** to the king wherever he goes."
Ps 34:18 The LORD is **c** to the brokenhearted
41: 9 Even my **c** friend, whom I trusted,
55:13 my companion, my **c** friend,
148:14 of Israel, the people **c** to his heart.
Pr 16:28 and a gossip separates **c** friends.
Isa 40:11 and carries them **c** to his heart;
Jer 30:21 near and he will come **c** to me,
30:21 will devote himself to be **c** to me?'
Da 12: 4 **c** up and seal the words of the scroll

Joel 2: 1 It is c at hand—
Zec 13: 7 against the man who is c to me!"
Mt   6: 6 c the door and pray to your Father,
Rev 6: 8 Hades was following c behind him.

CLOSED [CLOSE]

Ge   2:21 the man's ribs and c up the place
     20:18 for the LORD had c up every womb
1Sa   1: 5 and the LORD had c her womb.
Jer   6:10 Their ears are c so they cannot hear.
Da   12: 9 the words are c up and sealed until
Mt   13:15 and they have c their eyes.
Ac   28:27 and they have c their eyes.

CLOSER [CLOSE]

Ex   3: 5 "Do not come any c," God said.
Pr   18:24 a friend who sticks c than a brother.

CLOSES [CLOSE]

Pr   28:27 but he who c his eyes to them

CLOTH [CLOTHS]

Ex   28:31 of the ephod entirely of blue c,
Dt   22:17 Then her parents shall display the c
2Ki   8:15 But the next day he took a thick c,
Mt   9:16 "No one sews a patch of unshrunk c
     27:59 wrapped it in a clean linen c,

CLOTHE [CLOTHED, CLOTHES, CLOTHING]

Ps   45: 3 c yourself with splendor
    132:16 I will c her priests with salvation,
    132:18 I will c his enemies with shame,
Isa 52: 1 O Zion, c yourself with strength.
Mt   25:43 and you did not c me,
Lk   12:28 how much more will he c you,
Ro   13:14 c yourselves with the Lord
1Co 15:53 For the perishable must c itself with
Col   3:12 c yourselves with compassion,
1Pe   5: 5 c yourselves with humility

CLOTHED [CLOTHE]

Ge   3:21 for Adam and his wife and c them.
2Ch   6:41 O LORD God, be c with salvation,
Ps   30:11 and c me with joy,
    104: 1 you are c with splendor
Pr   31:22 she is c in fine linen and purple.
     31:25 She is c with strength and dignity;
Isa 61:10 For he has c me with garments
Zec   3: 5 a clean turban on his head and c him,
Mt   25:36 I needed clothes and you c me,
Lk   24:49 until you have been c with power
Jn   19: 2 They c him in a purple robe
2Co   5: 2 to be c with our heavenly dwelling,
Gal   3:27 have c yourselves with Christ.
Rev 12: 1 a woman c with the sun,

CLOTHES [CLOTHE]

Dt   8: 4 Your c did not wear out
     29: 5 your c did not wear out,
Pr   6:27 without his c being burned?
Jer 52:33 So Jehoiachin put aside his prison c
Hag   1: 6 You put on c, but are not warm.
Zec   3: 3 Now Joshua was dressed in filthy c

Mt   6:25 the body more important than c?
      6:28 "And why do you worry about c?
     17: 2 his c became as white as the light.
     22:12 in here without wedding c?'
     25:36 I needed c and you clothed me,
     27:35 they divided up his c by casting lots.
Jn   11:44 Take off the grave c and let him go."
Ac   10:30 a man in shining c stood before me
1Ti   2: 9 or gold or pearls or expensive c,
Jas   2: 2 poor man in shabby c also comes in.
1Pe   3: 3 wearing of gold jewelry and fine c.
Rev 16:15 and keeps his c with him,

CLOTHING [CLOTHE]

Ex   3:22 of silver and gold and for c,
     12:35 of silver and gold and for c.
Dt   22: 5 A woman must not wear men's c,
                 nor a man wear women's c.
Job 29:14 I put on righteousness as my c;
Ps   22:18 among them and cast lots for my c.
    102:26 Like c you will change them
Da   7: 9 His c was as white as snow;
Mt   7:15 They come to you in sheep's c,
Mk   1: 6 John wore c made of camel's hair,
1Ti   6: 8 But if we have food and c,
Jude 1:23 the c stained by corrupted flesh.

CLOTHS* [CLOTH]

Eze 16: 4 with salt or wrapped in c.
Lk   2: 7 in c and placed him in a manger,
      2:12 You will find a baby wrapped in c

CLOUD [CLOUDS, THUNDERCLOUD]

Ex   13:21 of them in a pillar of c to guide them
     19: 9 to come to you in a dense c,
     24:18 Then Moses entered the c as he went
     40:34 the c covered the Tent of Meeting,
Nu   9:15 was set up, the c covered it.
1Ki   8:10 the c filled the temple of the LORD.
     18:44 "A c as small as a man's hand
Ne   9:19 By day the pillar of c did not cease
Ps 105:39 He spread out a c as a covering,
Pr   16:15 his favor is like a rain c in spring.
Isa 19: 1 the LORD rides on a swift c
Eze   1: 4 an immense c with flashing lightning
Mk   9: 7 a c appeared and enveloped them,
Lk   21:27 Son of Man coming in a c
Ac   1: 9 and a c hid him from their sight.
1Co 10: 2 all baptized into Moses in the c
Heb 12: 1 by such a great c of witnesses,
Rev 10: 1 He was robed in a c,
     11:12 And they went up to heaven in a c,
     14:14 on the c was one "like a son of man"

CLOUDS [CLOUD]

Ge   9:13 I have set my rainbow in the c,
Dt   33:26 and on the c in his majesty.
1Ki 18:45 the sky grew black with c,
Ps   68: 4 extol him who rides on the c—
    104: 3 He makes the c his chariot and rides
Pr   8:28 he established the c above
     25:14 Like c and wind without rain is
Isa 14:14 ascend above the tops of the c;
Eze   1:28 the appearance of a rainbow in the c

Da	7:13	coming with the **c** of heaven.
Joel	2: 2	a day of **c** and blackness.
Na	1: 3	and **c** are the dust of his feet.
Zep	1:15	a day of **c** and blackness,
Mt	24:30	Son of Man coming on the **c** of the
	26:64	the Mighty One and coming on the **c**
1Th	4:17	with them in the **c** to meet the Lord
Jude	1:12	They are **c** without rain,
Rev	1: 7	Look, he is coming with the **c,**

CLUB [CLUBS]

Pr	25:18	Like a **c** or a sword or a sharp arrow
Isa	10: 5	in whose hand is the **c** of my wrath!
Jer	51:20	"You are my war **c,**

CLUBS [CLUB]

| Mk | 14:43 | a crowd armed with swords and **c,** |

CLUNG* [CLING]

Ru	1:14	but Ruth **c** to her.
2Ki	3: 3	Nevertheless he **c** to the sins
La	1: 9	Her filthiness **c** to her skirts;

CLUSTER

| Nu | 13:23 | a branch bearing a single **c** of grapes. |

CO-HEIRS* [INHERIT]

| Ro | 8:17 | heirs of God and **c** with Christ, |

COAL* [COALS]

| 2Sa | 14: 7 | the only burning **c** I have left, |
| Isa | 6: 6 | the seraphs flew to me with a live **c** |

COALS [COAL]

Nu	16:37	scatter the **c** some distance away,
Ps	11: 6	On the wicked he will rain fiery **c**
	18: 8	burning **c** blazed out of it.
Pr	6:28	Can a man walk on hot **c**
	25:22	you will heap burning **c** on his head,
Eze	1:13	like burning **c** of fire
	10: 2	Fill your hands with burning **c** from
Ro	12:20	you will heap burning **c** on his head."

COARSE*

| Eph | 5: 4 | foolish talk or **c** joking, |

COAST

| Nu | 34: 6 | will be the **c** of the Great Sea. |

COAT [COATED]

Ge	6:14	and **c** it with pitch.
Dt	27: 4	and **c** them with plaster.
1Sa	17: 5	and wore a **c** of scale armor

COAT OF MANY COLOURS

(KJV) See RICHLY ORNAMENTED ROBE

COATED* [COAT]

| Ex | 2: 3 | for him and **c** it with tar and pitch. |

COBRA*

Ps	58: 4	that of a **c** that has stopped its ears,
	91:13	tread upon the lion and the **c;**
Isa	11: 8	play near the hole of the **c,**

CODE*

Ro	2:27	even though you have the written **c**
	2:29	by the Spirit, not by the written **c.**
	7: 6	not in the old way of the written **c.**
Col	2:14	having canceled the written **c,**

COFFIN*

| Ge | 50:26 | he was placed in a **c** in Egypt. |
| Lk | 7:14 | Then he went up and touched the **c,** |

COILED* [COILING]

| 2Sa | 22: 6 | The cords of the grave **c** around me; |
| Ps | 18: 5 | The cords of the grave **c** around me; |

COILING* [COILED]

| Isa | 27: 1 | Leviathan the **c** serpent; |

COIN* [COINS]

Mt	17:27	and you will find a four-drachma **c.**
	22:19	Show me the **c** used for paying
Mk	12:16	They brought the **c,**
Lk	15: 9	I have found my lost **c.'**

COINS [COIN]

Mt	26:15	for him thirty silver **c.**
Lk	15: 8	a woman has ten silver **c**
Jn	2:15	the **c** of the money changers

COLD

Ge	8:22	seedtime and harvest, **c** and heat,
Pr	25:25	Like **c** water to a weary soul
Zec	14: 6	no **c** or frost.
Mt	10:42	even a cup of **c** water
	24:12	the love of most will grow **c,**
Rev	3:16	lukewarm—neither hot nor **c—**

COLLAPSE [COLLAPSED]

| Jos | 6: 5 | then the wall of the city will **c** |
| Mt | 15:32 | or they may **c** on the way." |

COLLAPSED [COLLAPSE]

| Rev | 11:13 | and a tenth of the city **c.** |
| | 16:19 | and the cities of the nations **c.** |

COLLECT [COLLECTED, COLLECTION, COLLECTOR, COLLECTORS]

| Ne | 10:37 | for it is the Levites who **c** the tithes |
| Mk | 12: 2 | servant to the tenants to **c** from them |

COLLECTED [COLLECT]

| Mt | 13:48 | down and **c** the good fish in baskets, |
| Heb | 7: 6 | yet he **c** a tenth from Abraham |

COLLECTION* [COLLECT]

| Isa | 57:13 | let your **c** [of idols] save you! |
| 1Co | 16: 1 | Now about the **c** for God's people: |

COLLECTOR [COLLECT]

Da	11:20	"His successor will send out a tax **c**
Mt	10: 3	and Matthew the tax **c;**
Lk	5:27	a tax **c** by the name of Levi sitting
	18:10	one a Pharisee and the other a tax **c.**
	19: 2	Zacchaeus; he was a chief tax **c**

COLLECTORS [COLLECT]

Mt	5:46	Are not even the tax **c** doing that?
	9:10	many tax **c** and "sinners" came
	11:19	a friend of tax **c** and "sinners." '
	17:24	the **c** of the two-drachma tax came
	21:32	but the tax **c** and the prostitutes did.

COLONNADE*

1Ki	7: 6	a **c** fifty cubits long and thirty wide.
Jn	10:23	temple area walking in Solomon's **C.**
Ac	3:11	in the place called Solomon's **C.**
	5:12	to meet together in Solomon's **C.**

COLONY*

Ac	16:12	a Roman **c** and the leading city of

COLT

Ge	49:11	his **c** to the choicest branch;
Zec	9: 9	on a **c,** the foal of a donkey.
Mt	21: 5	on a **c,** the foal of a donkey.' "
Jn	12:15	seated on a donkey's **c.**"

COMB*

Ps	19:10	than honey from the **c.**
Pr	24:13	honey from the **c** is sweet to your

COMBINE* [COMBINED]

Heb	4: 2	who heard did not **c** it with faith.

COMBINED* [COMBINE]

1Co	12:24	God has **c** the members of the body

COME [CAME, COMES, COMING]

Ge	8:16	"**C** out of the ark,
	15:16	your descendants will **c** back here,
	38:16	"**C** now, let me sleep with you."
	39: 7	"**C** to bed with me!"
	50:24	But God will surely **c** to your aid
Ex	3: 5	"Do not **c** any closer," God said.
	19:11	on that day the LORD will **c** down
	24: 1	"**C** up to the LORD, you and Aaron,
Nu	24:17	A star will **c** out of Jacob;
Dt	28: 2	All these blessings will **c** upon you
	28:45	All these curses will **c** upon you.
Ru	1: 6	that the LORD had **c** to the aid
1Sa	4: 7	"A god has **c** into the camp,"
2Sa	7:12	who will **c** from your own body,
Ps	14: 7	that salvation for Israel would **c** out
	17: 2	May my vindication **c** from you;
	24: 7	that the King of glory may **c** in.
	31: 2	**c** quickly to my rescue;
	40:13	**c** quickly to help me.
	88: 2	May my prayer **c** before you;
	91:10	no disaster will **c** near your tent.
	119:41	May your unfailing love **c** to me,
	121: 1	where does my help **c** from?
	132: 8	and **c** to your resting place,
	144: 5	O LORD, and **c** down;
Pr	2: 6	and from his mouth **c** knowledge
	9: 4	"Let all who are simple **c** in here!"
	10:28	the hopes of the wicked **c** to nothing.
	24:34	and poverty will **c** on you like
Ecc	1: 4	Generations **c** and generations go,
	9:12	no man knows when his hour will **c:**

	11: 8	Everything to **c** is meaningless.
SS	2:13	Arise, **c,** my darling; my beautiful one, **c** with me."
Isa	1:18	"**C** now, let us reason together,"
	37:32	out of Jerusalem will **c** a remnant,
	41:22	Or declare to us the things to **c,**
	59:20	"The Redeemer will **c** to Zion,
Jer	51:45	"**C** out of her, my people!
Eze	7: 6	The end has **c!**
	36: 8	for they will soon **c** home.
	37: 5	and you will **c** to life.
Hos	3: 5	They will **c** trembling to the LORD
Hab	2: 3	it linger, wait for it; it will certainly **c**
Mal	3: 1	I will **c** near to you for judgment.
Mt	2: 2	the east and have **c** to worship him."
	4:19	"**C,** follow me," Jesus said,
	6:10	your kingdom **c,** your will be done
	10:34	I did not **c** to bring peace,
	12:28	the kingdom of God has **c** upon you.
	15:19	For out of the heart **c** evil thoughts,
	16:24	"If anyone would **c** after me,
	17:12	But I tell you, Elijah has already **c,**
	18:20	two or three **c** together in my name,
	19:14	"Let the little children **c** to me,
	20:28	Son of Man did not **c** to be served,
	24: 5	For many will **c** in my name,
	27:40	**C** down from the cross,
Jn	2: 4	"My time has not yet **c.**"
	6:37	that the Father gives me will **c** to me,
	12:23	"The hour has **c** for the Son of Man
	14: 3	I will **c** back and take you to be
Ac	1:11	will **c** back in the same way
1Co	16:22	**C,** O Lord!
Gal	4: 4	But when the time had fully **c,**
2Th	2: 2	the day of the Lord has already **c.**
Heb	10: 9	I have **c** to do your will."
	12:22	But you have **c** to Mount Zion,
Jas	4: 8	**C** near to God and he will **c** near to
1Pe	2: 4	As you **c** to him, the living Stone—
2Pe	3: 9	but everyone to **c** to repentance.
1Jn	2:18	even now many antichrists have **c.**
	4: 2	that Jesus Christ has **c** in the flesh is
Rev	1: 4	and who was, and who is to **c,**
	4: 8	who was, and is, and is to **c.**"
	22:17	Whoever is thirsty, let him **c;**
	22:20	**C,** Lord Jesus.

DAYS TO COME See DAYS

COMES [COME]

1Ch	16:33	for he **c** to judge the earth.
	29:14	Everything **c** from you,
Ps	3: 8	From the LORD **c** deliverance.
	96:13	for he **c,** he **c** to judge the earth.
	118:26	Blessed is he who **c** in the name of
	121: 2	My help **c** from the LORD,
Pr	10: 2	but a chattering fool **c** to ruin.
	11: 2	When pride **c,** then **c** disgrace,
	11:27	but evil **c** to him who searches for it.
	15:33	and humility **c** before honor.
Ecc	5:15	Naked a man **c** from his mother's womb, and as he **c,** so he departs.
Isa	40:10	the Sovereign LORD **c** with power,
Jnh	2: 9	Salvation **c** from the LORD."
Zec	14: 7	When evening **c,** there will be light.

Mt	12:43	"When an evil spirit **c** out of a man,
	21: 5	'See, your king **c** to you,
Mk	11: 9	"Blessed is he who **c** in the name of
Lk	18: 8	However, when the Son of Man **c,**
Jn	3:31	one who **c** from above is above all;
	6:33	bread of God is he who **c** down
	10:10	The thief **c** only to steal and kill
	14: 6	No one **c** to the Father except
	15:26	"When the Counselor **c,**
	16:13	But when he, the Spirit of truth, **c,**
Ac	1: 8	when the Holy Spirit **c** on you;
Ro	4:13	the righteousness that **c** by faith.
1Co	11:12	But everything **c** from God.
2Co	3: 5	but our competence **c** from God.
Php	3: 9	the righteousness that **c** from God
1Jn	2:21	and because no lie **c** from the truth.
	4: 7	for love **c** from God.
2Jn	1:10	If anyone **c** to you and does not
Rev	11: 5	fire **c** from their mouths
	11: 7	the beast that **c** up from
	19:15	Out of his mouth **c** a sharp sword

COMFORT* [COMFORTED, COMFORTER, COMFORTERS, COMFORTING, COMFORTS]

Ge	5:29	"He will **c** us in the labor
	37:35	and daughters came to **c** him,
Ru	2:13	"You have given me **c**
1Ch	7:22	and his relatives came to **c** him.
Job	2:11	and sympathize with him and **c** him.
	7:13	When I think my bed will **c** me
	16: 5	my mouth would encourage you; **c**
	36:16	to the **c** of your table laden
Ps	23: 4	they **c** me.
	71:21	and **c** me once again.
	119:50	My **c** in my suffering is this:
	119:52	O LORD, and I find **c** in them.
	119:76	May your unfailing love be my **c,**
	119:82	"When will you **c** me?"
Isa	40: 1	**C, c** my people,
	51: 3	The LORD will surely **c** Zion
	51:19	who can **c** you?—
	57:18	and restore **c**
	61: 2	to **c** all who mourn,
	66:13	so will I **c** you;
Jer	16: 7	to those who mourn for the dead—
	31:13	I will give them **c** and joy
La	1: 2	there is none to **c** her.
	1: 9	was none to **c** her.
	1:16	No one is near to **c** me,
	1:17	but there is no one to **c** her.
	1:21	but there is no one to **c** me.
	2:13	that I may **c** you,
Eze	16:54	in giving them **c.**
Na	3: 7	Where can I find anyone to **c** you?"
Zec	1:17	and the LORD will again **c** Zion
	10: 2	they give **c** in vain.
Lk	6:24	you have already received your **c.**
Jn	11:19	to **c** them in the loss
1Co	14: 3	encouragement and **c.**
2Co	1: 3	of compassion and the God of all **c,**
	1: 4	we can **c** those in any trouble with the **c** we ourselves have received

	1: 5	also through Christ our **c** overflows.
	1: 6	it is for your **c** and salvation;
	1: 6	it is for your **c,**
	1: 7	so also you share in our **c.**
	2: 7	you ought to forgive and **c** him,
	7: 7	but also by the **c** you had given him.
Php	2: 1	if any **c** from his love,
Col	4:11	and they have proved a **c** to me.

COMFORTED* [COMFORT]

Ge	24:67	Isaac was **c** after his mother's death.
	37:35	but he refused to be **c.**
2Sa	12:24	Then David **c** his wife Bathsheba.
Job	42:11	They **c** and consoled him over all
Ps	77: 2	and my soul refused to be **c.**
	86:17	have helped me and **c** me.
Isa	12: 1	and you have **c** me.
	52: 9	for the LORD has **c** his people,
	54:11	lashed by storms and not **c,**
	66:13	I comfort you; and you will be **c**
Jer	31:15	for her children and refusing to be **c,**
Mt	2:18	for her children and refusing to be **c,**
	5: 4	for they will be **c.**
Lk	16:25	he is here and you are in agony.
Ac	20:12	and were greatly **c.**
2Co	1: 6	if we are **c,**
	7: 6	**c** us by the coming of Titus,

COMFORTER* [COMFORT]

Ecc	4: 1	and they have no **c;**
	4: 1	and they have no **c.**
Jer	8:18	O my **C** in sorrow,

COMFORTER (KJV) See COUNSELOR

COMFORTERS* [COMFORT]

Job	16: 2	miserable **c** are you all!
Ps	69:20	but there was none, for **c,**

COMFORTING* [COMFORT]

Isa	66:11	and be satisfied at her **c** breasts;
Zec	1:13	So the LORD spoke kind and **c** words
Jn	11:31	with Mary in the house, **c** her,
1Th	2:12	**c** and urging you to live lives worthy

COMFORTS* [COMFORT]

Job	29:25	like one who **c** mourners.
Isa	49:13	the LORD **c** his people
	51:12	"I, even I, am he who **c** you.
	66:13	As a mother **c** her child,
2Co	1: 4	who **c** us in all our troubles,
	7: 6	But God, who **c** the downcast,

COMING [COME]

Ex	32: 1	that Moses was so long in **c** down
Ecc	10:14	No one knows what is **c**—
Isa	13: 9	See, the day of the LORD is **c**—
Jer	7:32	So beware, the days are **c,**
Eze	43: 2	I saw the glory of the God of Israel **c**
Da	7:13	**c** with the clouds of heaven.
Joel	2: 1	for the day of the LORD is **c.**
Mic	1: 3	LORD is **c** from his dwelling place;
Zep	1:14	near and **c** quickly.
Mk	13:26	Son of Man **c** in clouds with great

1Th 1:10 who rescues us from the **c** wrath.
2Th 2: 1 the **c** of our Lord Jesus Christ
Heb 10:37 "He who is **c** will come and will
Jas 5: 8 because the Lord's **c** is near.
2Pe 1:16 power and **c** of our Lord Jesus Christ
3: 4 "Where is this '**c**' he promised?
Jude 1:14 the Lord is **c** with thousands
Rev 1: 7 Look, he is **c** with the clouds,
3:11 I am **c** soon.
13: 1 And I saw a beast **c** out of the sea.
21: 2 **c** down out of heaven from God,
21:10 **c** down out of heaven from God.
22: 7 "Behold, I am **c** soon!

DAYS ARE COMING See DAYS

COMMAND [COMMANDED, COMMANDER, COMMANDING, COMMANDMENT, COMMANDMENTS, COMMANDS]

Ex 7: 2 You are to say everything I **c** you,
34:11 Obey what I **c** you today.
Nu 14:41 you disobeying the LORD's **c?**
24:13 to go beyond the **c** of the LORD—
Dt 4: 2 Do not add to what I **c** you
8: 1 I follow every **c** I am giving you today
12:32 See that you do all I **c** you;
15:11 Therefore I **c** you to be openhanded
30:16 For I **c** you today to love the LORD
32:46 so that you may **c** your children
1Sa 13:14 you have not kept the LORD's **c.**"
1Ki 11:10 Solomon did not keep the LORD's **c.**
Ps 91:11 For he will **c** his angels
Pr 8:29 the waters should not overstep his **c,**
13:13 but he who respects a **c** is rewarded.
Ecc 8: 2 Obey the king's **c,** I say,
Jer 1: 7 to and say whatever I **c** you.
1:17 up and say to them whatever I **c** you.
7:23 Walk in all the ways I **c** you,
11: 4 'Obey me and do everything I **c** you,
26: 2 Tell them everything I **c** you;
La 1:18 yet I rebelled against his **c.**
Joel 2:11 and mighty are those who obey his **c.**
Mt 4: 6 it is written: " 'He will **c** his angels
15: 3 "And why do you break the **c** of God
Lk 4:10 it is written: " 'He will **c** his angels
Jn 10:18 This **c** I received from my Father."
12:50 I know that his **c** leads to eternal life.
13:34 new **c** I give you: Love one another.
14:15 you love me, you will obey what I **c.**
15:12 My **c** is this: Love each other
15:14 my friends if you do what I **c.**
15:17 This is my **c:** Love each other.
1Co 14:37 I am writing to you is the Lord's **c.**
Gal 5:14 up in a single **c:**
1Ti 1: 5 The goal of this **c** is love,
6:14 to keep this **c** without spot or blame
6:17 C those who are rich
Heb 11: 3 the universe was formed at God's **c,**
2Pe 2:21 on the sacred **c** that was passed on
3: 2 by the holy prophets and the **c** given
1Jn 2: 7 I am not writing you a new **c** but
3:23 And this is his **c:**
4:21 And he has given us this **c:**

2Jn 1: 6 his **c** is that you walk in love.
Rev 3:10 Since you have kept my **c**

COMMANDED [COMMAND]

Ge 2:16 And the LORD God **c** the man,
3:11 the tree that I **c** you not to eat from?"
7: 5 Noah did all that the LORD **c** him.
50:12 Jacob's sons did as he had **c** them:
Ex 7: 6 as the LORD **c** them.
19: 7 all the words the LORD had **c** him
Dt 4: 5 as the LORD my God **c** me,
6:24 The LORD **c** us to obey
18:20 anything I have not **c** him
Jos 1: 9 Have I not **c** you?
1:16 "Whatever you have **c** us we will do,
2Sa 5:25 So David did as the LORD **c** him,
2Ki 17:13 the entire Law that I **c** your fathers
21: 8 be careful to do everything I **c** them
2Ch 33: 8 be careful to do everything I **c** them
Ps 33: 9 he **c,** and it stood firm.
78: 5 which he **c** our forefathers to teach
148: 5 for he **c** and they were created.
Isa 13: 3 I have **c** my holy ones;
Am 2:12 and **c** the prophets not to prophesy.
Jnh 2:10 And the LORD **c** the fish,
Mt 28:20 to obey everything I have **c** you.
Lk 8:29 For Jesus had **c** the evil spirit
Jn 12:49 the Father who sent me **c** me what
14:31 I do exactly what my Father has **c** me
Ac 10:42 He **c** us to preach to the people and
1Co 9:14 the Lord has **c** that those who preach
1Jn 3:23 and to love one another as he **c** us.
2Jn 1: 4 just as the Father **c** us.

AS THE †LORD COMMANDED
See †LORD

COMMANDER [COMMAND]

Jos 5:15 The **c** of the LORD's army replied,
2Ki 18:17 king of Assyria sent his supreme **c,**

COMMANDING [COMMAND]

Dt 30:11 I am **c** you today is not too difficult
2Ti 2: 4 he wants to please his **c** officer.

COMMANDMENT* [COMMAND]

Jos 22: 5 to keep the **c** and the law
Mt 22:36 which is the greatest **c** in the Law?"
22:38 This is the first and greatest **c.**
Mk 12:31 There is no **c** greater than these."
Lk 23:56 on the Sabbath in obedience to the **c.**
Ro 7: 8 the opportunity afforded by the **c,**
7: 9 but when the **c** came,
7:10 that the very **c** that was intended
7:11 the opportunity afforded by the **c,**
7:11 and through the **c** put me to death.
7:12 the law is holy, and the **c** is holy,
7:13 **c** sin might become utterly sinful.
13: 9 and whatever other **c** there may be,
Eph 6: 2 the first **c** with a promise—
Heb 9:19 When Moses had proclaimed every **c**

COMMANDMENTS* [COMMAND]

Ex 20: 6 who love me and keep my **c.**
34:28 words of the covenant—the Ten **C.**

Dt　4:13　his covenant, the Ten **C,**
　　5:10　who love me and keep my **c.**
　　5:22　the **c** that the LORD proclaimed in
　　6: 1　These **c** that I give you today are to
　　9:10　the **c** the LORD proclaimed to you
　　10: 4　the Ten **C** he had proclaimed to you
Ecc　12:13　Fear God and keep his **c,**
Mt　5:19　of these **c** and teaches others to do
　　19:17　If you want to enter life, obey the **c."**
　　22:40　the Prophets hang on these two **c."**
Mk　10:19　You know the **c:**
　　12:28　he asked him, "Of all the **c,**
Lk　1: 6　observing all the Lord's **c**
　　18:20　You know the **c:**
Ro　13: 9　The **c,** "Do not commit adultery,"
Eph　2:15　the law with its **c** and regulations.
Rev　12:17　offspring—those who obey God's **c**
　　14:12　of the saints who obey God's **c**

COMMANDS [COMMAND]

Ge　26: 5　my **c,** my decrees and my laws."
Ex　24:12　with the law and **c** I have written
　　25:22　give you all my **c** for the Israelites.
　　34:32　the **c** the LORD had given him
Lev　4: 2　forbidden in any of the LORD's **c—**
　　22:31　"Keep my **c** and follow them.
　　26: 3　and are careful to obey my **c,**
　　26:15　and fail to carry out all my **c**
Nu　15:39　at and so you will remember all the **c**
Dt　5:29　to fear me and keep all my **c** always,
　　7: 9　who love him and keep his **c**
　　7:11　Therefore, take care to follow the **c,**
　　11: 1　his laws and his **c** always.
　　11:28　the curse if you disobey the **c** of
　　28: 1　carefully follow all his **c** I give you
　　30:10　and keep his **c** and decrees
Jos　22: 5　to walk in all his ways, to obey his **c,**
Jdg　3: 4　they would obey the LORD's **c,**
1Sa　12:14　and do not rebel against his **c,**
1Ki　2: 3　and keep his decrees and **c,**
　　8:58　in all his ways and to keep the **c,**
　　8:61　to live by his decrees and obey his **c,**
1Ch　28: 7　unswerving in carrying out my **c** and
　　29:19　devotion to keep your **c,**
2Ch　31:21　in obedience to the law and the **c,**
Ezr　9:10　For we have disregarded the **c**
Ne　1: 5　who love him and keep his **c,**
Ps　19: 8　The **c** of the LORD are radiant,
　　78: 7　but would keep his **c.**
　　112: 1　who finds great delight in his **c.**
　　119:10　not let me stray from your **c.**
　　119:32　I run in the path of your **c,**
　　119:35　Direct me in the path of your **c,**
　　119:47　in your **c** because I love them.
　　119:48　I lift up my hands to your **c,**
　　119:73　understanding to learn your **c.**
　　119:86　All your **c** are trustworthy;
　　119:96　but your **c** are boundless.
　　119:98　**c** make me wiser than my enemies,
　　119:115　that I may keep the **c** of my God!
　　119:127　Because I love your **c** more than gold
　　119:131　longing for your **c.**
　　119:143　but your **c** are my delight.
　　119:151　O LORD, and all your **c** are true.

　　119:172　for all your **c** are righteous.
　　119:176　for I have not forgotten your **c.**
Pr　2: 1　and store up my **c** within you,
　　3: 1　but keep my **c** in your heart,
　　6:23　For these **c** are a lamp,
　　7: 2　Keep my **c** and you will live;
　　10: 8　The wise in heart accept **c,**
Isa　48:18　only you had paid attention to my **c,**
Jer　7:22　I did not just give them **c** about
Da　9: 4　who love him and obey his **c,**
Mt　5:19　and teaches these **c** will
Mk　7: 9　of setting aside the **c** of God
Jn　14:21　Whoever has my **c** and obeys them,
　　15:10　If you obey my **c,**
　　15:10　just as I have obeyed my Father's **c**
Ac　17:30　but now he **c** all people everywhere
1Co　7:19　Keeping God's **c** is what counts.
Col　2:22　because they are based on human **c**
1Jn　2: 3　to know him if we obey his **c.**
　　2: 4　but does not do what he **c** is a liar,
　　3:22　because we obey his **c**
　　3:24　Those who obey his **c** live in him,
　　5: 2　loving God and carrying out his **c.**
　　5: 3　This is love for God: to obey his **c.**
　　5: 3　And his **c** are not burdensome,
2Jn　1: 6　that we walk in obedience to his **c.**

COMMANDS OF THE †LORD　Lev　4:22;
　Nu 15:39; Dt 4:2; 6:17; 8:6; 11:27, 28; 28:9, 13;
　2Ki 17:16, 19; 1Ch 28:8; Ps 19:8

COMMEMORATE

Ex　12:14　"This is a day you are to **c;**

COMMEND* [COMMENDABLE, COMMENDED, COMMENDS]

Ps　145: 4　One generation will **c** your works
Ecc　8:15　So I **c** the enjoyment of life,
Ro　13: 3　do what is right and he will **c** you.
　　16: 1　I **c** to you our sister Phoebe,
2Co　3: 1　beginning to **c** ourselves again?
　　4: 2　the truth plainly we **c** ourselves
　　5:12　We are not trying to **c** ourselves
　　6: 4　of God we **c** ourselves in every way:
　　10:12　with some who **c** themselves.
1Pe　2:14　and to **c** those who do right.

COMMENDABLE* [COMMEND]

1Pe　2:19　For it is **c** if a man bears up under
　　2:20　this is **c** before God.

COMMENDED* [COMMEND]

Ne　11: 2　The people **c** all the men
Job　29:11　and those who saw me **c** me,
Lk　16: 8　"The master **c** the dishonest manager
Ac　15:40　**c** by the brothers to the grace of
2Co　12:11　I ought to have been **c** by you,
Heb　11: 2　This is what the ancients were **c** for.
　　11: 4　By faith he was **c** as
　　11: 5　he was **c** as one who pleased God.
　　11:39　These were all **c** for their faith,

COMMENDS* [COMMEND]

Pr　15: 2　The tongue of the wise **c** knowledge,
2Co　10:18　one who **c** himself who is approved,

10:18 but the one whom the Lord **c**.

COMMISSION

Dt   3:28 But **c** Joshua, and encourage
Col 1:25 the **c** God gave me to present to you

COMMIT [COMMITS, COMMITTED]

Ex 20:14 "You shall not **c** adultery.
Dt   5:18 "You shall not **c** adultery.
1Sa 7: 3 and **c** yourselves to the LORD
1Ki 14:16 and has caused Israel to **c**."
2Ki 21:16 the sin that he had caused Judah to **c**,
Ps 31: 5 Into your hands I **c** my spirit;
     37: 5 **C** your way to the LORD;
Pr 16: 3 **C** to the LORD whatever you do,
Mt   5:27 'Do not **c** adultery.'
   19:18 " 'Do not murder, do not **c** adultery,
Mk 10:19 do not **c** adultery, do not steal,
Lk 18:20 'Do not **c** adultery.
   23:46 into your hands I **c** my spirit."
Ac 20:32 "Now I **c** you to God and to
Ro   2:22 that people should not **c** adultery, do
        you **c** adultery?
    13: 9 "Do not **c** adultery,"
1Co 10: 8 We should not **c** sexual immorality,
Jas 2:11 he who said, "Do not **c** adultery,"
     2:11 do not **c** adultery but do **c** murder,
1Pe ·4:19 to God's will should **c** themselves
1Jn 5:16 If anyone sees his brother **c** a sin
Rev 2:22 and I will make those who **c** adultery

COMMITS [COMMIT]

Lev 20:10 " 'If a man **c** adultery with another
Pr   6:32 man who **c** adultery lacks judgment;
   29:22 and a hot-tempered one **c** many sins.
Ecc 8:12 a wicked man **c** a hundred crimes
Eze 18:14 sees all the sins his father **c**,
   18:24 from his righteousness and **c** sin
   22:11 In you one man **c** a detestable
Mt   5:32 marries the divorced woman **c**
        adultery.
   19: 9 marries another woman **c** adultery."
Mk 10:11 marries another woman **c** adultery
   10:12 she **c** adultery."
Lk 16:18 marries another woman **c** adultery,
   16:18 marries a divorced woman **c** adultery

COMMITTED [COMMIT]

Ge 50:17 and the wrongs they **c** in treating you
Ex 32:30 "You have **c** a great sin.
Nu   5: 7 and must confess the sin he has **c**.
Jdg 20: 6 because they **c** this lewd
1Ki 8:61 be fully **c** to the LORD our God,
   15:14 Asa's heart was fully **c** to
2Ch 16: 9 those whose hearts are fully **c**
Isa 42:19 Who is blind like the one **c** to me,
Jer 2:13 "My people have **c** two sins:
    3: 9 and **c** adultery with stone and wood.
Mt   5:28 lustfully has already **c** adultery
   11:27 "All things have been **c** to me
   27:23 What crime has he **c**?"
Lk 10:22 "All things have been **c** to me
Ac 14:23 **c** them to the Lord,
Ro   1:27 Men **c** indecent acts with other men,

3:25 left the sins **c** beforehand unpunished
1Co 9:17 I am simply discharging the trust **c**
2Co 5:19 And he has **c** to us the message
1Pe 2:22 "He **c** no sin,
Rev 17: 2 kings of the earth **c** adultery
   18: 3 The kings of the earth **c** adultery

COMMON

Ge 11: 1 one language and a **c** speech.
Lev 10:10 between the holy and the **c**,
Pr 22: 2 Rich and poor have this in **c**:
   29:13 and the oppressor have this in **c**:
Ecc 9: 2 All share a **c** destiny—
Eze 22:26 between the holy and the **c**;
Ac   2:44 and had everything in **c**.
Ro   9:21 and some for **c** use?
1Co 10:13 No temptation has seized you except
        what is **c** to man.
   12: 7 of the Spirit is given for the **c** good.
2Co 6:14 and wickedness have in **c**?
    6:15 What does a believer have in **c** with

COMMUNION (KJV)
See PARTICIPATION, FELLOWSHIP

COMMUNITY

Ge 28: 3 until you become a **c** of peoples.
   35:11 a **c** of nations will come from you,
   48: 4 I will make you a **c** of peoples,
Ex 16: 2 the whole **c** grumbled against Moses
Lev 4:13 whole Israelite **c** sins unintentionally
Nu 14:27 How long will this wicked **c** grumble

COMPANION* [COMPANIONS]

1Ki 20:35 the sons of the prophets said to his **c**,
Job 30:29 a **c** of owls.
Ps 55:13 it is you, a man like myself, my **c**,
   55:20 My **c** attacks his friends;
Pr 13:20 but a **c** of fools suffers harm.
    28: 7 a **c** of gluttons disgraces his father.
    29: 3 **c** of prostitutes squanders his wealth.
Rev 1: 9 and **c** in the suffering and kingdom

COMPANIONS [COMPANION]

Ps 38:11 My friends and **c** avoid me because
    45: 7 above your **c** by anointing you with
Pr 18:24 A man of many **c** may come to ruin,
Heb 1: 9 has set you above your **c**

COMPANY

2Ki 2: 7 Fifty men of the **c** of the prophets
    4:38 the **c** of the prophets was meeting
Ps 14: 5 for God is present in the **c** of
Pr 21:16 to rest in the **c** of the dead.
    24: 1 do not desire their **c**;
Jer 15:17 I never sat in the **c** of revelers,
Lk   2:13 great **c** of the heavenly host
1Co 15:33 "Bad **c** corrupts good character."

COMPARE* [COMPARED, COMPARING, COMPARISON]

Job 28:17 Neither gold nor crystal can **c**
   28:19 The topaz of Cush cannot **c** with it;
   39:13 but they cannot **c** with the pinions
Ps 86: 8 no deeds can **c** with yours.

	89: 6	can **c** with the LORD?
Pr	3:15	nothing you desire can **c** with her.
	8:11	nothing you desire can **c** with her.
Isa	40:18	To whom, then, will you **c** God?
	40:18	What image will you liken him to?
	40:25	"To whom will you **c** me?
	46: 5	"To whom will you **c** me
La	2:13	With what can I **c** you,
Eze	31: 8	the plane trees **c** with its branches—
Da	1:13	Then **c** our appearance with that of
Mt	11:16	"To what can I **c** this generation?
Lk	7:31	can I **c** the people of this generation?
	13:18	What shall I **c** it to?
	13:20	"What shall I **c** the kingdom
2Co	10:12	not dare to classify or **c** ourselves
	10:12	and **c** themselves with themselves.

COMPARED* [COMPARE]

Jdg	8: 2	"What have I accomplished **c** to you?
	8: 3	What was I able to do **c** to you?"
Isa	46: 5	liken me that we may be **c**?
Eze	31: 2	be **c** with you in majesty?
	31:18	the trees of Eden can be **c** with you
Php	3: 8	a loss **c** to the surpassing greatness

COMPARING* [COMPARE]

Ro	8:18	not worth **c** with the glory
2Co	8: 8	the sincerity of your love by **c** it with
Gal	6: 4	without **c** himself to somebody else,

COMPARISON* [COMPARE]

2Co	3:10	now in **c** with the surpassing glory.

COMPASSION* [COMPASSIONATE, COMPASSIONS]

Ex	33:19	I will have **c** on whom I will have **c**.
Dt	13:17	show you mercy, have **c** on you,
	28:54	among you will have no **c**
	30: 3	and have **c** on you
	32:36	and have **c** on his servants
Jdg	2:18	for the LORD had **c** on them
1Ki	3:26	was filled with **c** for her son
2Ki	13:23	and had **c** and showed concern
2Ch	30: 9	and your children will be shown **c**
Ne	9:19	"Because of your great **c** you did
	9:27	great **c** you gave them deliverers,
	9:28	in your **c** you delivered them time
Ps	51: 1	great **c** blot out my transgressions.
	77: 9	Has he in anger withheld his **c**?"
	90:13	Have **c** on your servants.
	102:13	You will arise and have **c** on Zion;
	103: 4	and crowns you with love and **c**,
	103:13	As a father has **c** on his children,
	103:13	LORD has **c** on those who fear him;
	116: 5	our God is full of **c**.
	119:77	Let your **c** come to me
	119:156	Your **c** is great, O LORD;
	135:14	and have **c** on his servants.
	145: 8	The LORD is good to all; he has **c**
Isa	13:18	nor will they look with **c** on children.
	14: 1	The LORD will have **c** on Jacob;
	27:11	so their Maker has no **c** on them,
	30:18	to show you **c**.
	49:10	He who has **c** on them will guide

	49:13	and will have **c** on his afflicted ones.
	49:15	and have no **c** on the child she
	51: 3	and will look with **c** on all her ruins!
	54: 7	with deep **c** I will bring you back.
	54: 8	everlasting kindness I will have **c**
	54:10	says the LORD, who has **c** on you.
	60:10	in favor I will show you **c**.
	63: 7	to his **c** and many kindnesses.
	63:15	Your tenderness and **c** are withheld
Jer	12:15	I will again have **c**
	13:14	I will allow no pity or mercy or **c**
	15: 6	I can no longer show **c**.
	21: 7	no mercy or pity or **c**.'
	30:18	and have **c** on his dwellings;
	31:20	I have great **c** for him,"
	33:26	and have **c** on them.' "
	42:12	I will show you **c** so
	42:12	so that he will have **c** on you
La	3:32	he brings grief, he will show **c**,
Eze	9: 5	without showing pity or **c**.
	16: 5	with pity or had **c** enough to do any
	39:25	and will have **c** on all the people
Hos	2:19	in love and **c**.
	11: 8	all my **c** is aroused.
	13:14	"I will have no **c**,
	14: 3	for in you the fatherless find **c**."
Am	1:11	with a sword, stifling all **c**,
Jnh	3: 9	and with **c** turn from his fierce anger
	3:10	he had **c** and did not bring
Mic	7:19	You will again have **c** on us;
Zec	7: 9	and **c** to one another.
	10: 6	I will restore them because I have **c**
Mal	3:17	just as in **c** a man spares
Mt	9:36	he had **c** on them,
	14:14	he had **c** on them
	15:32	"I have **c** for these people;
	20:34	Jesus had **c** on them
Mk	1:41	Filled with **c**,
	6:34	he had **c** on them,
	8: 2	"I have **c** for these people;
Lk	15:20	and was filled with **c** for him;
Ro	9:15	and I will have **c** on whom I have **c**."
2Co	1: 3	the Father of **c** and the God of all
Php	2: 1	if any tenderness and **c**,
Col	3:12	clothe yourselves with **c**, kindness,
Jas	5:11	The Lord is full of **c** and mercy.

COMPASSIONATE* [COMPASSION]

Ex	22:27	I will hear, for I am **c**.
	34: 6	the LORD, the **c** and gracious God,
2Ch	30: 9	LORD your God is gracious and **c**.
Ne	9:17	a forgiving God, gracious and **c**,
Ps	86:15	O Lord, are a **c** and gracious God,
	103: 8	The LORD is **c** and gracious,
	111: 4	the LORD is gracious and **c**.
	112: 4	gracious and **c** and righteous man.
	145: 8	The LORD is gracious and **c**,
La	4:10	**c** women have cooked their own
Joel	2:13	for he is gracious and **c**,
Jnh	4: 2	that you are a gracious and **c** God,
Eph	4:32	Be kind and **c** to one another,
1Pe	3: 8	love as brothers, be **c** and humble.

COMPASSIONS* [COMPASSION]

La   3:22 for his **c** never fail.

COMPELLED [COMPELS]

Ac   20:22 "And now, **c** by the Spirit,
1Co   9:16 I cannot boast, for I am **c** to preach.

COMPELS* [COMPELLED]

Ex   3:19 unless a mighty hand **c** him.
Job 32:18 and the spirit within me **c** me;
2Co   5:14 For Christ's love **c** us,

COMPETENCE* [COMPETENT]

2Co   3: 5 but our **c** comes from God.

COMPETENT* [COMPETENCE]

Ro   15:14 and **c** to instruct one another.
1Co   6: 2 are you not **c** to judge trivial cases?
2Co   3: 5 Not that we are **c** in ourselves
      3: 6 He has made us **c** as ministers of

COMPETES*

1Co   9:25 Everyone who **c** in the games goes
2Ti   2: 5 Similarly, if anyone **c** as an athlete,
      2: 5 unless he **c** according to the rules.

COMPLACENCY* [COMPLACENT]

Pr   1:32 and the **c** of fools will destroy them;
Eze 30: 9 to frighten Cush out of her **c**.

COMPLACENT* [COMPLACENCY]

Isa 32: 9 You women who are so **c**,
     32:11 Tremble, you **c** women;
Am   6: 1 Woe to you who are **c** in Zion,
Zep   1:12 and punish those who are **c**,

COMPLAIN [COMPLAINED,
COMPLAINING, COMPLAINT,
COMPLAINTS]

Job   7:11 I will **c** in the bitterness of my soul.
Isa 29:24 those who **c** will accept instruction."
     40:27 Why do you say, O Jacob, and **c**,
La   3:39 man **c** when punished for his sins?

COMPLAINED [COMPLAIN]

Nu   11: 1 the people **c** about their hardships in

COMPLAINING* [COMPLAIN]

Php   2:14 Do everything without **c** or arguing,

COMPLAINT [COMPLAIN]

Job 10: 1 therefore I will give free rein to my **c**
Ps   64: 1 Hear me, O God, as I voice my **c**;
    142: 2 I pour out my **c** before him;
Hab   2: 1 what answer I am to give to this **c**.

COMPLAINTS* [COMPLAIN]

Nu   14:27 the **c** of these grumbling Israelites.
Pr   23:29 Who has **c**?

COMPLETE [COMPLETED,
COMPLETELY, COMPLETION]

Dt   16:15 and your joy will be **c**.

2Ki 12:15 because they acted with **c** honesty.
Jn   3:29 That joy is mine, and it is now **c**.
     15:11 in you and that your joy may be **c**.
     16:24 and your joy will be **c**.
     17:23 May they be brought to **c** unity to let
Ac   3:16 that has given this **c** healing to him,
     20:24 if only I may finish the race and **c**
Ro   15:14 **c** in knowledge and competent
2Co   7:16 I am glad I can have **c** confidence
     10: 6 once your obedience is **c**.
Php   2: 2 then make my joy **c**
Col   4:17 "See to it that you **c** the work
Jas   1: 4 so that you may be mature and **c**,
      2:22 his faith was made **c** by what he did.
1Jn   1: 4 We write this to make our joy **c**.
      2: 5 God's love is truly made **c** in him.
      4:12 in us and his love is made **c** in us.
      4:17 love is made **c** among us so
2Jn   1:12 so that our joy may be **c**.
Rev   3: 2 for I have not found your deeds **c** in

COMPLETED [COMPLETE]

Ge   2: 1 the heavens and the earth were **c**
Ex   39:32 the Tent of Meeting, was **c**.
1Ki   6:14 So Solomon built the temple and **c** it.
2Ch 36:21 the seventy years were **c**
Ezr   6:15 The temple was **c** on the third day of
Ne   6:15 So the wall was **c** on the twenty-fifth
Isa 40: 2 that her hard service has been **c**,
Jer 29:10 "When seventy years are **c**
Da   11:36 until the time of wrath is **c**,
     12: 7 all these things will be **c**."
Lk   12:50 and how distressed I am until it is **c**!
Jn   19:28 Later, knowing that all was now **c**,
Rev 15: 1 because with them God's wrath is **c**.

COMPLETELY [COMPLETE]

Ex   11: 1 he will drive you out **c**.
Nu   21: 3 They **c** destroyed them
Jos 17:13 but did not drive them out **c**.
Jdg   1:28 but never drove them out **c**.
1Sa 15: 9 they were unwilling to destroy **c**,
Jer 14:19 Have you rejected Judah **c**?
     30:11 I will not **c** destroy you.
Mk   3: 5 and his hand was **c** restored.
      4:39 wind died down and it was **c** calm.

COMPLETION [COMPLETE]

Php   1: 6 good work in you will carry it on to **c**

COMPLIMENTS*

Pr   23: 8 and will have wasted your **c**.

COMPREHEND*
[COMPREHENDED]

Job 28:13 Man does not **c** its worth;
Ecc   8:17 No one can **c** what goes on under
      8:17 he cannot really **c** it.

COMPREHENDED*
[COMPREHEND]

Job 38:18 Have you **c** the vast expanses of

COMPULSION* [COMPEL]

1Co 7:37 who is under no **c** but has control
2Co 9: 7 not reluctantly or under **c,**

CONCEAL [CONCEALED, CONCEALS]

Ps 40:10 I do not **c** your love and your truth
Pr 25: 2 It is the glory of God to **c** a matter;
Isa 26:21 she will **c** her slain no longer.

CONCEALED [CONCEAL]

Isa 49: 2 and **c** me in his quiver.
Jer 16:17 nor is their sin **c** from my eyes.
Mt 10:26 There is nothing **c** that will not
Mk 4:22 and whatever is **c** is meant to
Lk 8:17 and nothing **c** that will not be known
12: 2 There is nothing **c** that will not

CONCEALS* [CONCEAL]

Pr 10:18 He who **c** his hatred has lying lips,
28:13 He who **c** his sins does not prosper,

CONCEIT* [CONCEITED, CONCEITS]

Isa 16: 6 her overweening pride and **c,**
Jer 48:29 her overweening pride and **c,**
Php 2: 3 out of selfish ambition or vain **c.**

CONCEITED* [CONCEIT]

1Sa 17:28 I know how **c** you are and
Ro 11:25 brothers, so that you may not be **c:**
12:16 Do not be **c.**
2Co 12: 7 To keep me from becoming **c**
Gal 5:26 Let us not become **c,**
1Ti 3: 6 or he may become **c** and fall under
6: 4 he is **c** and understands nothing.
2Ti 3: 4 rash, **c,** lovers of pleasure

CONCEITS* [CONCEIT]

Ps 73: 7 evil **c** of their minds know no limits.

CONCEIVE [CONCEIVED, CONCEIVES]

Nu 11:12 Did I **c** all these people?
Job 15:35 They **c** trouble and give birth to evil;
Isa 33:11 You **c** chaff, you give birth to straw;

CONCEIVED [CONCEIVE]

1Sa 2:21 LORD was gracious to Hannah; she **c**
Ps 51: 5 sinful from the time my mother **c** me.
Isa 8: 3 and she **c** and gave birth to a son.
Mt 1:20 **c** in her is from the Holy Spirit.
1Co 2: 9 mind has **c** what God has prepared
Jas 1:15 desire has **c,** it gives birth to sin;

CONCEIVES* [CONCEIVE]

Ps 7:14 pregnant with evil and **c** trouble

CONCERN* [CONCERNED]

Ge 39: 6 not **c** himself with anything except
39: 8 "my master does not **c** himself
1Sa 23:21 "The LORD bless you for your **c**
2Ki 13:23 and had compassion and showed **c**
Job 9:21 I have no **c** for myself;

9: 4 my error remains my **c** alone.
Ps 131: 1 not **c** myself with great matters
Pr 29: 7 but the wicked have no such **c.**
Eze 36:21 I had **c** for my holy name,
Ac 15:14 at first showed his **c** by taking from
18:17 But Gallio showed no **c** whatever.
1Co 7:32 I would like you to be free from **c.**
12:25 but that its parts should have equal **c**
2Co 7: 7 your ardent **c** for me,
7:11 what alarm, what longing, what **c,**
8:16 the heart of Titus the same **c** I have
11:28 I face daily the pressure of my **c**
Php 4:10 that at last you have renewed your **c**

CONCERNED [CONCERN]

Ex 2:25 the Israelites and was **c** about them.
3: 7 and I am **c** about their suffering.
4:31 that the LORD was **c** about them
Ps 142: 4 Look to my right and see; no one is **c**
Eze 36: 9 I am **c** for you and will look on you
Jnh 4:10 "You have been **c** about this vine,
4:11 not be **c** about that great city?"
1Co 7:32 unmarried man is **c** about
9: 9 Is it about oxen that God is **c?**
Php 4:10 Indeed, you have been **c,**

CONCESSION*

1Co 7: 6 I say this as a **c,** not as a command.

CONCUBINE [CONCUBINES]

Ge 35:22 and slept with his father's **c** Bilhah,
Jdg 19: 9 the man, with his **c** and his servant,
2Sa 3: 7 sleep with my father's **c?**"

CONCUBINES [CONCUBINE]

Ge 25: 6 he gave gifts to the sons of his **c**
2Sa 5:13 David took more **c** and wives
1Ki 11: 3 of royal birth and three hundred **c,**
Da 5: 3 his wives and his **c** drank from them.

CONCUPISCENCE (KJV)

See DESIRE, LUST

CONDEMN* [CONDEMNATION, CONDEMNED, CONDEMNING, CONDEMNS, SELF-CONDEMNED]

Job 9:20 my mouth would **c** me;
10: 2 I will say to God: Do not **c** me,
34:17 Will you **c** the just and mighty One?
34:29 if he remains silent, who can **c** him?
40: 8 Would you **c** me to justify yourself?
Ps 94:21 and **c** the innocent to death.
109: 7 and may his prayers **c** him.
109:31 from those who **c** him.
Isa 50: 9 Who is he that will **c** me?
Mt 12:41 with this generation and **c** it;
12:42 with this generation and **c** it;
20:18 They will **c** him to death
Mk 10:33 They will **c** him to death
Lk 6:37 Do not **c,** and you will
11:31 of this generation and **c** them;
11:32 with this generation and **c** it;
Jn 3:17 not send his Son into the world to **c**
7:51 "Does our law **c** anyone

8:11 neither do I **c** you," Jesus declared.
12:48 very word which I spoke will **c** him
Ro 2:27 yet obeys the law will **c** you who,
14: 3 not eat everything must not **c**
14:22 not **c** himself by what he approves.
2Co 7: 3 I do not say this to **c** you;
1Jn 3:20 whenever our hearts **c** us.
3:21 if our hearts do not **c** us,

CONDEMNATION* [CONDEMN]

Jer 42:18 of **c** and reproach;
44:12 of **c** and reproach.
Ro 3: 8 Their **c** is deserved.
5:16 followed one sin and brought **c**,
5:18 as the result of one trespass was **c**
8: 1 no **c** for those who are in Christ Jesus
2Pe 2: 3 Their **c** has long been hanging
Jude 1: 4 For certain men whose **c** was written

CONDEMNED* [CONDEMN]

Dt 13:17 of those **c** things shall be found
Job 32: 3 and yet had **c** him.
Ps 34:21 the foes of the righteous will be **c**.
34:22 be **c** who takes refuge in him.
37:33 in their power or let them be **c**
79:11 of your arm preserve those **c** to die.
102:20 release those **c** to death."
Mt 12: 7 you would not have **c** the innocent.
12:37 and by your words you will be **c**."
23:33 How will you escape being **c** to hell?
27: 3 saw that Jesus was **c**,
Mk 14:64 They all **c** him as worthy of death.
16:16 whoever does not believe will be **c**.
Lk 6:37 and you will not be **c**.
Jn 3:18 Whoever believes in him is not **c**,
3:18 not believe stands **c** already
5:24 and will not be **c**;
5:29 have done evil will rise to be **c**.
8:10 Has no one **c** you?"
16:11 prince of this world now stands **c**.
Ac 25:15 against him and asked that he be **c**.
Ro 3: 7 why am I still **c** as a sinner?"
8: 3 And so he **c** sin in sinful man,
14:23 man who has doubts is **c** if he eats,
1Co 4: 9 like men **c** to die in the arena.
11:32 that we will not be **c** with the world.
Gal 1: 8 let him be eternally **c**!
1: 9 let him be eternally **c**!
2Th 2:12 be **c** who have not believed the truth
Tit 2: 8 of speech that cannot be **c**,
Heb 11: 7 By his faith he **c** the world
Jas 5: 6 You have **c** and murdered
5:12 and your "No," no, or you will be **c**.
2Pe 2: 6 if he **c** the cities of Sodom
Rev 19: 2 He has **c** the great prostitute

CONDEMNING* [CONDEMN]

Dt 25: 1 the innocent and **c** the guilty.
1Ki 8:32 **c** the guilty and bringing down
Pr 17:15 the guilty and **c** the innocent—
Ac 13:27 yet in **c** him they fulfilled the words
Ro 2: 1 you are **c** yourself,

CONDEMNS* [CONDEMN]

Job 15: 6 Your own mouth **c** you, not mine;
Pr 12: 2 but the LORD **c** a crafty man.
Ro 8:34 Who is he that **c**?
2Co 3: 9 If the ministry that **c** men is glorious,

CONDITION

Mt 12:45 the final **c** of that man is worse than

CONDUCT [CONDUCTED, CONDUCTS, SAFE-CONDUCT]

Job 34:11 upon him what his **c** deserves.
Pr 10:23 A fool finds pleasure in evil **c**,
20:11 by whether his **c** is pure and right.
21: 8 but the **c** of the innocent is upright.
Ecc 6: 8 how to **c** himself before others?
Jer 4:18 "Your own **c** and actions
6:15 ashamed of their loathsome **c**?
17:10 to reward a man according to his **c**,
Eze 7: 3 judge you according to your **c**
Php 1:27 **c** yourselves in a manner worthy of
1Ti 3:15 to **c** themselves in God's household,

CONDUCTED* [CONDUCT]

2Co 1:12 that we have **c** ourselves in

CONDUCTS* [CONDUCT]

Ps 112: 5 who **c** his affairs with justice.

CONFESS* [CONFESSED, CONFESSES, CONFESSING, CONFESSION]

Lev 5: 5 he must **c** in what way he has sinned
16:21 and **c** over it all the wickedness
26:40 if they will **c** their sins and the sins
Nu 5: 7 and must **c** the sin he has committed.
1Ki 8:33 back to you and **c** your name,
8:35 toward this place and **c** your name
2Ch 6:24 back and **c** your name,
6:26 toward this place and **c** your name
Ne 1: 6 I **c** the sins we Israelites,
Ps 32: 5 "I will **c** my transgressions to
38:18 I **c** my iniquity;
Jn 1:20 He did not fail to **c**,
12:42 not **c** their faith for fear they would
Ro 10: 9 That if you **c** with your mouth,
10:10 and it is with your mouth that you **c**
14:11 bow before me; every tongue will **c**
Php 2:11 and every tongue **c**
Heb 3: 1 apostle and high priest whom we **c**.
13:15 the fruit of lips that **c** his name.
Jas 5:16 Therefore **c** your sins to each other
1Jn 1: 9 If we **c** our sins,

CONFESSED* [CONFESS]

1Sa 7: 6 that day they fasted and there they **c**,
Ne 9: 2 and **c** their sins and the wickedness
Da 9: 4 to the LORD my God and **c**:
Jn 1:20 but **c** freely, "I am not the Christ."
Ac 19:18 and openly **c** their evil deeds.

CONFESSES* [CONFESS]

Pr 28:13 but whoever **c** and renounces

2Ti 2:19 "Everyone who c the name of

CONFESSING* [CONFESS]

Ezr 10: 1 While Ezra was praying and c,
Da   9:20 c my sin and the sin
Mt   3: 6 C their sins, they were baptized
Mk   1: 5 C their sins, they were baptized

CONFESSION* [CONFESS]

Ezr 10:11 Now make c to the LORD,
Ne   9: 3 and spent another quarter in c and
2Co 9:13 obedience that accompanies your c
1Ti 6:12 when you made your good c in
     6:13 made the good c,

CONFIDE* [CONFIDES]

Jdg 16:15 when you won't c in me?

CONFIDENCE* [CONFIDENT]

Jdg 9:26 and its citizens put their c in him.
2Ki 18:19 On what are you basing this c
2Ch 32: 8 And the people gained c
    32:10 On what are you basing your c,
Job 4: 6 Should not your piety be your c
Ps 71: 5 my c since my youth.
Pr   3:26 for the LORD will be your c
     3:32 but takes the upright into his c.
    11:13 A gossip betrays a c,
    20:19 A gossip betrays a c;
    25: 9 do not betray another man's c,
    31:11 Her husband has full c in her
Isa 32:17 be quietness and c forever.
    36: 4 On what are you basing this c
Jer 17: 7 whose c is in him.
    49:31 which lives in c,"
Eze 29:16 no longer be a source of c
Mic 7: 5 put no c in a friend.
2Co 2: 3 I had c in all of you,
     3: 4 Such c as this is ours through Christ
     7: 4 I have great c in you;
     7:16 I am glad I can have complete c
     8:22 even more so because of his great c
Eph 3:12 approach God with freedom and c.
Php 3: 3 and who put no c in the flesh—
     3: 4 I myself have reasons for such c.
     3: 4 to put c in the flesh, I have more:
2Th 3: 4 We have c in the Lord
Heb 3:14 till the end the c we had at first.
     4:16 approach the throne of grace with c,
    10:19 since we have c to enter
    10:35 So do not throw away your c;
    13: 6 So we say with c,
1Jn 3:21 we have c before God
     4:17 that we will have c on the day
     5:14 the c we have in approaching God:

CONFIDENT* [CONFIDENCE]

Job 6:20 because they had been c;
Ps 27: 3 even then will I be c.
    27:13 I am still c of this:
Lk 18: 9 To some who were c of their own
2Co 1:15 Because I was c of this,
     5: 6 Therefore we are always c and know
     5: 8 We are c, I say,

      9: 4 be ashamed of having been so c.
     10: 7 anyone is c that he belongs to Christ,
Gal 5:10 I am c in the Lord
Php 1: 6 being c of this,
     2:24 And I am c in the Lord
Phm 1:21 C of your obedience, I write to you,
Heb 6: 9 we are c of better things
1Jn 2:28 when he appears we may be c

CONFIDES* [CONFIDE]

Ps 25:14 The LORD c in those who fear him;

CONFINED [CONFINE]

Ge 40: 3 the same prison where Joseph was c.
Ps 88: 8 I am c and cannot escape;
Jer 32: 2 the prophet was c in the courtyard of
    33: 1 While Jeremiah was still c in
    39:15 While Jeremiah had been c in

CONFIRM [CONFIRMED, CONFIRMING]

Ge 17: 2 I will c my covenant between me
    26: 3 and will c the oath I swore
Dt 29:13 to c you this day as his people,
Da   9:27 He will c a covenant with many
Ro 15: 8 to c the promises made to

CONFIRMED [CONFIRM]

Dt   4:31 which he c to them by oath.
Ps 105:10 He c it to Jacob as a decree,
Ac 14: 3 who c the message of his grace
Heb 2: 3 was c to us by those who heard him.

CONFIRMING* [CONFIRM]

2Ki 23: 3 thus c the words of the covenant
Php 1: 7 or defending and c the gospel,

CONFORM* [CONFORMED, CONFORMITY, CONFORMS]

Ro 12: 2 Do not c any longer to the pattern
1Pe 1:14 do not c to the evil desires you had

CONFORMED* [CONFORM]

Eze 5: 7 even to the standards of the nations
    11:12 or kept my laws but have c to
Ro   8:29 to be c to the likeness of his Son,

CONFORMITY* [CONFORM]

Eph 1:11 in c with the purpose of his will,

CONFORMS* [CONFORM]

1Ti 1:11 that c to the glorious gospel of

CONFRONT [CONFRONTED, CONFRONTS]

Ex   9:13 c Pharaoh and say to him,
Job 9:32 that we might c each other in court.
Ps 17:13 Rise up, O LORD, c them,
Eze 23:36 c her with all her detestable practices

CONFRONTED [CONFRONT]

2Sa 22: 6 the snares of death c me.
Ps 18:18 They c me in the day of my disaster,

CONFRONTS* [CONFRONT]

Job 31:14 what will I do when God **c** me?

CONFUSE* [CONFUSION]

Ge 11: 7 go down and **c** their language
Ps 55: 9 **C** the wicked, O Lord,

CONFUSION [CONFUSE]

Ex 14:24 Egyptian army and threw it into **c**.
     23:27 into **c** every nation you encounter.
Dt   7:23 into great **c** until they are destroyed.
     28:28 blindness and **c** of mind.
Jos 10:10 The LORD threw them into **c**
1Sa 14:20 They found the Philistines in total **c**,
Ps   70: 2 be put to shame and **c**;
Jer 51:34 he has thrown us into **c**,
Mic   7: 4 Now is the time of their **c**.
Gal   5:10 into **c** will pay the penalty,

CONGREGATION*

[CONGREGATIONS]

Ps 22:22 in the **c** I will praise you.
     68:26 Praise God in the great **c**;
Ac 13:43 When the **c** was dismissed,
Heb 2:12 of the **c** I will sing your praises."

CONGREGATIONS*

[CONGREGATION]

1Co 14:33 As in all the **c** of the saints,

CONNECTION

Col   2:19 He has lost **c** with the Head,

CONQUER [CONQUERED,
CONQUEROR, CONQUERORS]

Rev 13: 7 against the saints and to **c** them.

CONQUERED [CONQUER]

Jos 10:42 kings and their lands Joshua **c**
Heb 11:33 who through faith **c** kingdoms,

CONQUEROR* [CONQUER]

Mic   1:15 I will bring a **c** against you who live
Rev   6: 2 he rode out as a **c** bent on conquest.

CONQUERORS* [CONQUER]

1Ki   8:47 plead with you in the land of their **c**
      8:50 cause their **c** to show them mercy;
Ro   8:37 in all these things we are more than **c**

CONSCIENCE* [CONSCIENCE',
CONSCIENCE-STRICKEN,
CONSCIENCES, CONSCIENTIOUS]

Ge 20: 5 with a clear **c** and clean hands."
     20: 6 I know you did this with a clear **c**,
1Sa 25:31 master will not have on his **c**
Job 27: 6 my **c** will not reproach me
Ac   23: 1 I fulfilled my duty to God in all good **c**
     24:16 So I strive always to keep my **c** clear
Ro   9: 1 my **c** confirms it in the Holy Spirit—
     13: 5 but also because of **c**.
1Co   4: 4 My **c** is clear,

      8: 7 and since their **c** is weak,
      8:10 with a weak **c** sees you who have this
      8:12 in this way and wound their weak **c**,
     10:25 without raising questions of **c**,
     10:27 without raising questions of **c**.
     10:29 the other man's **c**,
     10:29 be judged by another's **c**?
2Co   1:12 Now this is our boast: Our **c** testifies
      4: 2 commend ourselves to every man's **c**
      5:11 and I hope it is also plain to your **c**.
1Ti   1: 5 from a pure heart and a good **c** and
      1:19 holding on to faith and a good **c**.
      3: 9 truths of the faith with a clear **c**.
2Ti   1: 3 as my forefathers did, with a clear **c**,
Heb   9: 9 to clear the **c** of the worshiper.
     10:22 cleanse us from a guilty **c**
     13:18 a clear **c** and desire to live honorably
1Pe   3:16 keeping a clear **c**,
      3:21 the pledge of a good **c** toward God.

CONSCIENCE'* [CONSCIENCE]

1Co 10:28 and for **c** sake—

CONSCIENCE-STRICKEN*

[CONSCIENCE]

1Sa 24: 5 David was **c** for having cut off
2Sa 24:10 David was **c** after he had counted

CONSCIENCES* [CONSCIENCE]

Ro   2:15 their **c** also bearing witness,
1Ti   4: 2 whose **c** have been seared as with
Tit   1:15 both their minds and **c** are corrupted.
Heb   9:14 cleanse our **c** from acts that lead

CONSCIENTIOUS* [CONSCIENCE]

2Ch 29:34 for the Levites had been more **c**

CONSCIOUS*

Ro   3:20 through the law we become **c** of sin.
1Pe   2:19 because he is **c** of God.

CONSECRATE [CONSECRATED]

Ex 13: 2 "**C** to me every firstborn male.
     19:10 "Go to the people and **c** them today
     28:41 **C** them so they may serve me
     40: 9 **c** it and all its furnishings.
Lev 20: 7 " '**C** yourselves and be holy,
     25:10 **C** the fiftieth year
Jos   7:13 '**C** yourselves in preparation
1Ch 15:12 to **c** yourselves and bring up the ark
2Ch 29: 5 **C** yourselves now and **c** the temple

CONSECRATED [CONSECRATE]

Ex 29:43 and the place will be **c** by my glory.
Lev   8:30 So he **c** Aaron and his garments
Nu 15:40 and will be **c** to your God.
1Sa 21: 4 there is some **c** bread here—
2Ch   7:16 I have chosen and **c** this temple so
Ps   50: 5 "Gather to me my **c** ones,
Mk   2:26 the house of God and ate the **c** bread,
Lk   2:23 "Every firstborn male is to be **c** to
1Ti   4: 5 because it is **c** by the word of God

CONSENT

1Co 7: 5 by mutual **c** and for a time,
Phm 1:14 to do anything without your **c,**

CONSEQUENCES

Eze 16:58 You will bear the **c** of your lewdness

CONSIDER [CONSIDERATE, CONSIDERED, CONSIDERS]

Dt 17:20 not **c** himself better than his brothers
1Sa 12:24 **c** what great things he has done
      16: 7 not **c** his appearance or his height,
2Ch 19: 6 "C carefully what you do,
Job 37:14 stop and **c** God's wonders.
Ps   5: 1 O LORD, **c** my sighing.
      8: 3 When I **c** your heavens,
    50:22 "C this, you who forget God,
    77:12 and **c** all your mighty deeds.
  107:43 and **c** the great love of the LORD.
  143: 5 and **c** what your hands have done.
Pr   6: 6 to the ant, you sluggard; **c** its ways
    20:25 and only later to **c** his vows.
Ecc 2:12 I turned my thoughts to **c** wisdom,
    7:13 C what God has done:
Isa 47: 7 But you did not **c** these things
Jer 2:31 **c** the word of the LORD:
La   1:11 "Look, O LORD, and **c,**
Mk 4:24 "C carefully what you hear,"
Lk 12:24 C the ravens: They do not sow
    12:27 "C how the lilies grow.
Ac 20:24 I **c** my life worth nothing to me,
Ro 11:22 C therefore the kindness
Gal 3: 6 C Abraham: "He believed God,
Php 2: 3 in humility **c** others better than
    2: 6 not **c** equality with God something to
    3: 8 I **c** everything a loss compared to
Heb 10:24 us **c** how we may spur one another
    12: 3 C him who endured such opposition
Jas 1: 2 C it pure joy, my brothers,

CONSIDERATE* [CONSIDER]

Tit 3: 2 to be peaceable and **c,**
Jas 3:17 first of all pure; then peace-loving, **c,**
1Pe 2:18 only to those who are good and **c,**
    3: 7 be **c** as you live with your wives,

CONSIDERED [CONSIDER]

1Ki 16:31 He not only **c** it trivial to commit
Job 1: 8 "Have you **c** my servant Job?
    2: 3 "Have you **c** my servant Job?
    34: 6 Although I am right, I am **c** a liar;
Ps 44:22 we are **c** as sheep to be slaughtered.
Isa 53: 4 yet we **c** him stricken by God,
Hos 9: 7 the prophet is **c** a fool,
Mt 14: 5 because they **c** him a prophet.
Ro 8:36 we are **c** as sheep to be slaughtered."
1Ti 1:12 that he **c** me faithful,
Heb 11:11 he **c** him faithful who had made
Jas 2:21 our ancestor Abraham **c** righteous
    2:25 Rahab the prostitute **c** righteous

CONSIDERS [CONSIDER]

Pr 31:16 She **c** a field and buys it;
Ro 14: 5 One man **c** one day more sacred

Jas 1:26 If anyone **c** himself religious and

CONSIST [CONSISTS]

Lk 12:15 a man's life does not **c** in

CONSISTS [CONSIST]

Eph 5: 9 fruit of the light **c** in all goodness,

CONSOLATION* [CONSOLE]

Job 6:10 Then I would still have this **c—**
    21: 2 be the **c** you give me.
Ps 94:19 your **c** brought joy to my soul.
Lk 2:25 He was waiting for the **c** of Israel,

CONSOLATIONS* [CONSOLE]

Job 15:11 Are God's **c** not enough for you,

CONSOLE* [CONSOLATION, CONSOLATIONS]

Job 21:34 can you **c** me with your nonsense?
Isa 22: 4 not try to **c** me over the destruction
    51:19 who can **c** you?
Jer 16: 7 a drink to **c** them.

CONSORT*

Ps 26: 4 nor do I **c** with hypocrites;
Hos 4:14 the men themselves **c** with harlots

CONSPIRACY [CONSPIRE]

Ps 64: 2 Hide me from the **c** of the wicked,
Isa 8:12 "Do not call **c** everything that these
          people call **c;**

CONSPIRE [CONSPIRACY]

Ps 2: 1 the nations **c** and the peoples plot
  59: 3 Fierce men **c** against me
Mic 7: 3 they all **c** together.
Ac 4:27 to **c** against your holy servant Jesus,

CONSTANT

Dt 28:66 You will live in **c** suspense,
Pr 19:13 quarrelsome wife is like a **c** dripping.
    27:15 like a **c** dripping on a rainy day;
Ac 27:33 "you have been in **c** suspense
Heb 5:14 by **c** use have trained themselves

CONSTRUCTIVE*

1Co 10:23 but not everything is **c.**

CONSULT [CONSULTED, CONSULTS]

1Sa 28: 8 "C a spirit for me," he said,
2Ki 1: 2 "Go and **c** Baal-Zebub,
    8: 8 C the LORD through him;
2Ch 17: 3 He did not **c** the Baals
    25:15 "Why do you **c** this people's gods,
Pr 15:12 he will not **c** the wise.
Isa 8:19 When men tell you to **c** mediums
    40:14 Whom did the LORD **c** to enlighten
Eze 21:21 he will **c** his idols,
Hos 4:12 They **c** a wooden idol
Gal 1:16 I did not **c** any man,

CONSULTED [CONSULT]

1Ch 10:13 and even **c** a medium for guidance,

CONSULTS* [CONSULT]

Dt   18:11 or spiritist or who **c** the dead.
Eze 14:10 be as guilty as the one who **c** him.

CONSUME [CONSUMED, CONSUMES, CONSUMING]

Dt   5:25 This great fire will **c** us,
1Ki 21:21 I will **c** your descendants and cut off
Ps   21: 9 and his fire will **c** them.
      59:13 **c** them till they are no more.
Isa 26:11 fire reserved for your enemies **c** them
Jer 17:27 that will **c** her fortresses.' "
Eze 15: 7 the fire will yet **c** them.
Jn   2:17 "Zeal for your house will **c** me."
Heb 10:27 of raging fire that will **c** the enemies

CONSUMED [CONSUME]

Lev 10: 2 presence of the LORD and **c** them,
Nu   11: 1 and **c** some of the outskirts of
     16:35 and **c** the 250 men who were offering
2Ki   1:10 Then fire fell from heaven and **c**
2Ch   7: 1 from heaven and **c** the burnt offering
Ps   90: 7 We are **c** by your anger and terrified
Ecc 10:12 but a fool is **c** by his own lips.
La   3:22 the LORD's great love we are not **c**,
Zep   3: 8 The whole world will be **c** by the fire
Zec   9: 4 and she will be **c** by fire.
Rev 18: 8 She will be **c** by fire,

CONSUMES [CONSUME]

Ps   69: 9 for zeal for your house **c** me,

CONSUMING [CONSUME]

Ex   24:17 of the LORD looked like a **c** fire
Dt   4:24 For the LORD your God is a **c** fire,
2Sa 22: 9 **c** fire came from his mouth,
Heb 12:29 for our "God is a **c** fire."

CONTAIN* [CONTAINED, CONTAINS]

1Ki   8:27 the highest heaven, cannot **c** you.
2Ch   2: 6 the highest heavens, cannot **c** him?
      6:18 highest heavens, cannot **c** you.
Ecc   8: 8 power over the wind to **c** it;
2Pe   3:16 His letters **c** some things

CONTAINED* [CONTAIN]

Ac   10:12 It **c** all kinds of four-footed animals,
Heb   9: 4 This ark **c** the gold jar of manna,

CONTAINS [CONTAIN]

Pr   15: 6 of the righteous **c** great treasure,

CONTAMINATES*

2Co   7: 1 from everything that **c** body

CONTEMPT

Nu   14:11 will these people treat me with **c**?
Dt   17:12 The man who shows **c** for the judge
1Sa   2:17 treating the LORD's offering with **c**.
     25:39 against Nabal for treating me with **c**.
Ps 123: 3 for we have endured much **c**.
Pr   14:31 He who oppresses the poor shows **c**
      17: 5 who mocks the poor shows **c** for
      18: 3 When wickedness comes, so does **c**,

Da   12: 2 others to shame and everlasting **c**.
Mal   1: 6 O priests, who show **c** for my name.
Ro   2: 4 Or do you show **c** for the riches
Gal   4:14 you did not treat me with **c** or scorn.
1Th   5:20 do not treat prophecies with **c**.

CONTEND [CONTENDED, CONTENDING, CONTENDS]

Ge   6: 3 My Spirit will not **c** with man
Jdg   6:32 saying, "Let Baal **c** with him,"
Ps   35: 1 **C**, O LORD, with those who **c** with
Isa 49:25 I will **c** with those who **c** with you,
Jude 1: 3 and urge you to **c** for the faith

CONTENDED* [CONTEND]

Dt   33: 8 **c** with him at the waters of Meribah.
Php   4: 3 women who have **c** at my side

CONTENDING* [CONTEND]

Php   1:27 **c** as one man for the faith of

CONTENDS* [CONTEND]

Job 40: 2 who **c** with the Almighty correct him
Jer 15:10 the whole land strives and **c**!

CONTENT* [CONTENTMENT]

Jos   7: 7 If only we had been **c** to stay on
Pr   13:25 The righteous eat to their hearts' **c**,
     19:23 Then one rests **c**,
Ecc   4: 8 his eyes were not **c** with his wealth.
Lk   3:14 be **c** with your pay."
Php   4:11 to be **c** whatever the circumstances.
      4:12 of being **c** in any and every situation,
1Ti   6: 8 we will be **c** with that.
Heb 13: 5 and be **c** with what you have,

CONTENTIOUS* [CONTEND]

1Co 11:16 If anyone wants to be **c** about this,

CONTENTMENT* [CONTENT]

Job 36:11 in prosperity and their years in **c**.
SS   8:10 in his eyes like one bringing **c**.
1Ti   6: 6 But godliness with **c** is great gain.

CONTEST*

Heb 10:32 in a great **c** in the face of suffering.

CONTINUAL [CONTINUE]

Pr   15:15 but the cheerful heart has a **c** feast.
Eph   4:19 with a **c** lust for more.

CONTINUALLY [CONTINUE]

Lev 24: 2 the lamps may be kept burning **c**.
Nu   4: 7 the bread that is **c** there is to remain
Ps   26: 3 and I walk **c** in your truth.
Isa 27: 3 the LORD, watch over it; I water it **c**.
Lk   24:53 And they stayed **c** at the temple,
1Th   5:17 pray **c**;
Heb 13:15 **c** offer to God a sacrifice of praise—

CONTINUE [CONTINUAL, CONTINUALLY, CONTINUED, CONTINUES, CONTINUING]

1Ch 17:27 that it may **c** forever in your sight;

2Ch 6:14 your servants who **c** wholeheartedly
Ps 36:10 **C** your love to those who know you,
 89:36 that his line will **c** forever
Jer 3: 5 Will your wrath **c** forever?'
Ac 13:43 urged them to **c** in the grace of God.
Ro 11:22 provided that you **c** in his kindness.
2Co 1:10 that he will **c** to deliver us,
Gal 3:10 not **c** to do everything written in
Php 2:12 to work out your salvation with
Col 1:23 if you **c** in your faith,
 2: 6 **c** to live in him,
1Ti 2:15 if they **c** in faith,
2Ti 3:14 **c** in what you have learned
1Jn 2:28 And now, dear children, **c** in him,
 3: 9 No one who is born of God will **c**
 5:18 born of God does not **c** to sin;
2Jn 1: 9 does not **c** in the teaching of Christ
Rev 22:11 let him who does right **c** to

CONTINUED [CONTINUE]

Jdg 1:29 Canaanites **c** to live there among
Ps 78:17 But they **c** to sin against them,
Isa 64: 5 But when we **c** to sin against them,
Ac 14: 7 they **c** to preach the good news.

CONTINUES [CONTINUE]

Ps 100: 5 faithfulness **c** through all generations
 119:90 faithfulness **c** through all generations
2Co 10:15 as your faith **c** to grow,
1Jn 3: 6 No one who **c** to sin has

CONTINUING [CONTINUE]

Ro 13: 8 the **c** debt to love one another.

CONTRARY

Lev 10: 1 **c** to his command.
2Ch 30:18 **c** to what was written.
Ac 18:13 worship God in ways **c** to the law."
Ro 11:24 and **c** to nature were grafted into
Gal 5:17 the sinful nature desires what is **c** to

CONTRIBUTING* [CONTRIBUTION]

Ro 12: 8 if it is **c** to the needs of others,

CONTRIBUTION [CONTRIBUTING, CONTRIBUTIONS]

Ro 15:26 and Achaia were pleased to make a **c**

CONTRIBUTIONS
[CONTRIBUTION]

2Ch 24:10 the people brought their **c** gladly,
 31:12 Then they faithfully brought in the **c,**

CONTRITE*

Ps 51:17 a broken and **c** heart, O God,
Isa 57:15 but also with him who is **c** and lowly
 57:15 and to revive the heart of the **c.**
 66: 2 who is humble and **c** in spirit,

CONTROL [CONTROLLED, CONTROLS, SELF-CONTROL, SELF-CONTROLLED]

Ex 32:25 Aaron had let them get out of **c**

Jos 18: 1 country was brought under their **c,**
Pr 29:11 a wise man keeps himself under **c.**
Ecc 2:19 Yet he will have **c** over all the work
Ro 6:20 from the **c** of righteousness.
1Co 7: 9 But if they cannot **c** themselves,
 7:37 under no compulsion but has **c**
1Th 4: 4 to **c** his own body in a way
1Jn 5:19 world is under the **c** of the evil one.
Rev 16: 9 who had **c** over these plagues,

CONTROLLED [CONTROL]

Ps 32: 9 but must be **c** by bit and bridle
Ro 7: 5 when we were **c** by the sinful nature,
 8: 6 but the mind **c** by the Spirit is life

CONTROLS [CONTROL]

Job 37:15 Do you know how God **c** the clouds
Pr 16:32 a man who **c** his temper than one

CONTROVERSIES*

Ac 26: 3 with all the Jewish customs and **c.**
1Ti 1: 4 promote **c** rather than God's work—
 6: 4 an unhealthy interest in **c**
Tit 3: 9 avoid foolish **c** and genealogies

CONVERSATION

Col 4: 6 Let your **c** be always full of grace,

CONVERT* [CONVERTED, CONVERTS]

Mt 23:15 over land and sea to win a single **c,**
Ac 6: 5 Nicolas from Antioch, a **c** to Judaism
Ro 16: 5 the first **c** to Christ in the province
1Ti 3: 6 He must not be a recent **c,**

CONVERTED* [CONVERT]

Ac 15: 3 how the Gentiles had been **c.**

CONVERTS* [CONVERT]

Ac 2:11 (both Jews and **c** to Judaism);
 13:43 many of the Jews and devout **c**
1Co 16:15 of Stephanas were the first **c**

CONVICT* [CONVICTED, CONVICTION]

Dt 19:15 to **c** a man accused of any crime
2Sa 14:13 does he not **c** himself,
Pr 24:25 But it will go well with those who **c**
Jn 16: 8 he will **c** the world of guilt in regard
Jude 1:15 and to **c** all the ungodly of all

CONVICTED* [CONVICT]

Jas 2: 9 and are **c** by the law as lawbreakers.

CONVICTION* [CONVICT]

1Th 1: 5 with the Holy Spirit and with deep **c.**

CONVINCE* [CONVINCED, CONVINCING]

Ac 28:23 and tried to **c** them about Jesus from

CONVINCED* [CONVINCE]

Ge 45:28 And Israel said, "I'm **c!**
Lk 16:31 not be **c** even if someone rises from

Ac 19:26 how this fellow Paul has c
   26: 9 "I too was c that I ought to do all
   26:26 I am c that none of this
   28:24 Some were c by what he said,
Ro 2:19 if you are c that you are a guide for
   8:38 For I am c that neither death nor life,
   14: 5 be fully c in his own mind.
   14:14 I am fully c that no food is unclean
   15:14 I myself am c, my brothers,
1Co 14:24 he will be c by all that he is a sinner
2Co 5:14 we are c that one died for all,
Php 1:25 C of this, I know that I will remain,
2Ti 1:12 and am c that he is able
   3:14 and have become c of,

CONVINCING* [CONVINCE]

Ac 1: 3 gave many c proofs that he was alive

CONVULSION*

Mk 9:20 threw the boy into a c.
Lk 9:42 threw him to the ground in a c.

COOK [COOKED]

Ex 23:19 "Do not c a young goat
Eze 24:10 C the meat well,

COOKED [COOK]

2Ki 6:29 So we c my son and ate him.
La 4:10 women have c their own children,

COOL* [COOLNESS]

Ge 3: 8 in the garden in the c of the day,
Jer 18:14 Do its c waters
Lk 16:24 in water and c my tongue,

COOLNESS* [COOL]

Pr 25:13 Like the c of snow at harvest time is

COPIED* [COPY]

Jos 8:32 Joshua c on stones the law of Moses,
Pr 25: 1 c by the men of Hezekiah king
Eze 16:47 and c their detestable practices,

COPIES [COPY]

Heb 9:23 for the c of the heavenly things to

COPPER

Mt 10: 9 not take along any gold or silver or c
Mk 12:42 and put in two very small c coins,

COPY [COPIED, COPIES]

Dt 17:18 to write for himself on a scroll a c
2Ki 11:12 with a c of the covenant
Heb 8: 5 a c and shadow of what is in heaven.
   9:24 that was only a c of the true one;

CORBAN*

Mk 7:11 C' (that is, a gift devoted

CORD [CORDS]

Ge 38:18 "Your seal and its c,
Nu 15:38 with a blue c on each tassel.
Jos 2:18 you have tied this scarlet c in
Ecc 4:12 A c of three strands is

CORDS [CORD]

2Sa 22: 6 The c of the grave coiled around me;
Job 4:21 Are not the c of their tent pulled up,
Ps 129: 4 free from the c of the wicked.
Pr 5:22 the c of his sin hold him fast.
Isa 54: 2 lengthen your c,
Hos 11: 4 I led them with c of human kindness,
Jn 2:15 So he made a whip out of c,

CORINTH [CORINTHIANS]

Ac 18: 1 this, Paul left Athens and went to C.
1Co 1: 2 To the church of God in C,
2Co 1: 1 To the church of God in C,

CORINTHIANS* [CORINTH]

Ac 18: 8 of the C who heard him believed
2Co 6:11 We have spoken freely to you, C,

CORN [EARS OF] (KJV)

See GRAIN [HEADS OF], KERNEL

CORNELIUS*

Roman to whom Peter preached; first Gentile
Christian (Ac 10).

CORNER [CORNERS, CORNERSTONE]

Ru 3: 9 the c of your garment over me,
1Sa 24: 4 and cut off a c of Saul's robe.
Pr 7:12 at every c she lurks.)
   21: 9 on a c of the roof than share a house
Eze 16: 8 the c of my garment over you
Ac 26:26 because it was not done in a c.

CORNERS [CORNER]

Dt 22:12 on the four c of the cloak you wear.
Isa 41: 9 from its farthest c I called you.
Eze 7: 2 The end has come upon the four c of
Mt 6: 5 and on the street c to be seen by men.
   22: 9 Go to the street c and invite to
Ac 10:11 down to earth by its four c.
Rev 7: 1 at the four c of the earth,
   20: 8 in the four c of the earth—

CORNERSTONE* [CORNER, STONE]

Job 38: 6 or who laid its c—
Isa 28:16 a precious c for a sure foundation;
Jer 51:26 rock will be taken from you for a c,
Zec 10: 4 From Judah will come the c,
Eph 2:20 Christ Jesus himself as the chief c.
1Pe 2: 6 a chosen and precious c,

CORRECT* [CORRECTED, CORRECTING, CORRECTION, CORRECTIONS, CORRECTLY, CORRECTS]

Job 6:26 Do you mean to c what I say,
   40: 2 with the Almighty c him?
Jer 10:24 C me, LORD, but only with justice—
2Ti 4: 2 c, rebuke and encourage—with great

CORRECTED* [CORRECT]

Pr 29:19 servant cannot be **c** by mere words;

CORRECTING* [CORRECT]

2Ti 3:16 **c** and training in righteousness,

CORRECTION* [CORRECT]

Lev 26:23 not accept my **c** but continue to
Job 36:10 He makes them listen to **c**
Pr 5:12 How my heart spurned **c**!
10:17 whoever ignores **c** leads others astray
12: 1 but he who hates **c** is stupid.
13:18 but whoever heeds **c** is honored.
15: 5 whoever heeds **c** shows prudence.
15:10 He who hates **c** will die.
15:12 A mocker resents **c**;
15:32 whoever heeds **c** gains understanding
29:15 The rod of **c** imparts wisdom,
Jer 2:30 they did not respond to **c**.
5: 3 but they refused **c**,
7:28 or responded to **c**.
Zep 3: 2 She obeys no one, she accepts no **c**.
3: 7 you will fear me and accept **c**!'

CORRECTIONS* [CORRECT]

Pr 6:23 the **c** of discipline are the way to life,

CORRECTLY* [CORRECT]

Jdg 12: 6 he could not pronounce the word **c**,
Jer 1:12 "You have seen **c**,
Lk 7:43 "You have judged **c**," Jesus said.
10:28 "You have answered **c**,"
2Ti 2:15 and who **c** handles the word

CORRECTS* [CORRECT]

Job 5:17 "Blessed is the man whom God **c**;
Pr 9: 7 "Whoever **c** a mocker invites insult;

CORRODED*

Jas 5: 3 Your gold and silver are **c**.

CORRUPT [CORRUPTED, CORRUPTION, CORRUPTS]

Ge 6:11 Now the earth was **c** in God's sight
Ex 32: 7 have become **c**.
Dt 4:16 so that you do not become **c**
Jdg 2:19 to ways even more **c** than those
Ps 14: 1 They are **c**, their deeds are vile;
53: 3 they have together become **c**;
Pr 4:24 keep **c** talk far from your lips.
6:12 who goes about with a **c** mouth,
19:28 A **c** witness mocks at justice,
Da 6: 4 and neither **c** nor negligent.
Ac 2:40 yourselves from this **c** generation."

CORRUPTED [CORRUPT]

Eze 28:17 and you **c** your wisdom because
2Co 7: 2 we have **c** no one,
Tit 1:15 but to those who are **c** and do
1:15 their minds and consciences are **c**.
Jude 1:23 even the clothing stained by **c** flesh.
Rev 19: 2 the great prostitute who **c** the earth

CORRUPTION [CORRUPT]

Ezr 9:11 to possess is a land polluted by the **c**
Da 6: 4 They could find no **c** in him,
2Pe 1: 4 and escape the **c** in the world
2:20 If they have escaped the **c** of the

CORRUPTS* [CORRUPT]

Ecc 7: 7 and a bribe **c** the heart.
1Co 15:33 "Bad company **c** good character."
Jas 3: 6 It **c** the whole person,

COST [COSTLY, COSTS]

Nu 16:38 of the men who sinned at the **c**
Jos 6:26 "At the **c** of his firstborn
2Sa 24:24 burnt offerings that **c** me nothing."
1Ki 16:34 at the **c** of his firstborn son Abiram,
Pr 4: 7 it **c** all you have, get understanding.
7:23 little knowing it will **c** him his life.
Isa 55: 1 milk without money and without **c**.
Lk 14:28 estimate the **c** to see if he has
Rev 21: 6 I will give to drink without **c**

COSTLY [COST]

Ps 49: 8 the ransom for a life is **c**,
1Co 3:12 silver, **c** stones, wood, hay or straw,
Rev 18:12 **c** wood, bronze, iron and marble;

COSTS [COST]

Pr 6:31 it **c** him all the wealth of his house.

COULD*

Ge 13:16 if anyone **c** count the dust, then your
offspring **c** be counted
Ex 40:35 Moses **c** not enter the Tent
Nu 22:18 I **c** not do anything great or small
2Ch 7: 2 The priests **c** not enter the temple
25:15 gods, which **c** not save
Eze 14:14 they **c** save only themselves
Mt 22:46 No one **c** say a word in reply,
Mk 6: 5 He **c** not do any miracles there,
Jn 12:39 For this reason they **c** not believe,
Rev 15: 8 and no one **c** enter the temple

COUNCIL [COUNCILS]

Job 15: 8 Do you listen in on God's **c**?
Ps 89: 7 In the **c** of the holy ones
107:32 the people and praise him in the **c**
Mk 15:43 a prominent member of the **C**,
Jn 3: 1 a member of the Jewish ruling **c**.
Ac 17:33 At that, Paul left the **C**.

COUNCILS [COUNCIL]

Mk 13: 9 over to the local **c** and flogged

COUNSEL [COUNSELOR, COUNSELORS, COUNSELS]

2Ch 18: 4 "First seek the **c** of the Lord."
25:16 and have not listened to my **c**."
Job 12:13 **c** and understanding are his.
38: 2 "Who is this that darkens my **c**
42: 3 'Who is this that obscures my **c**
Ps 1: 1 the man who does not walk in the **c**
73:24 You guide me with your **c**,
107:11 and despised the **c** of the Most High.

Pr 8:14 **C** and sound judgment are mine;
15:22 Plans fail for lack of **c,**
27: 9 springs from his earnest **c.**
Isa 11: 2 the Spirit of **c** and of power,
28:29 wonderful in **c** and magnificent in
1Ti 5:14 So I **c** younger widows to marry,
Rev 3:18 I **c** you to buy from me gold refined

COUNSELOR [COUNSEL]

Isa 9: 6 And he will be called Wonderful **C,**
40:13 or instructed him as his **c?**
Jn 14:16 and he will give you another **C** to be
14:26 But the **C,** the Holy Spirit,
15:26 "When the **C** comes,
16: 7 the **C** will not come to you;
Ro 11:34 Or who has been his **c?"**

COUNSELORS [COUNSEL]

Ezr 4: 5 They hired **c** to work against them
Job 12:17 He leads **c** away stripped
Ps 119:24 are my delight; they are my **c.**

COUNSELS* [COUNSEL]

Ps 16: 7 I will praise the LORD, who **c** me;
Na 1: 1 against the LORD and **c** wickedness.

COUNT [COUNTED, COUNTING, COUNTLESS, COUNTS]

Ge 13:16 so that if anyone could **c** the dust,
15: 5 up at the heavens and **c** the stars—
16:10 that they will be too numerous to **c."**
Nu 23:10 Who can **c** the dust of Jacob
31:26 the community are to **c** all the people
Job 38:37 the wisdom to **c** the clouds?
Ps 22:17 I can **c** all my bones;
32: 2 the LORD does not **c** against him
48:12 go around her, **c** her towers,
139:18 Were I to **c** them,
Ro 4: 8 the Lord will never **c** against him."
6:11 **c** yourselves dead to sin but alive
2Th 1:11 that our God may **c** you worthy
Rev 7: 9 multitude that no one could **c,**
11: 1 and **c** the worshipers there.

COUNTED [COUNT]

Ge 13:16 then your offspring could be **c.**
Nu 1:19 so he **c** them in the Desert of Sinai:
2Sa 24:10 after he had **c** the fighting men,
Hos 1:10 which cannot be measured or **c.**
Mt 26:15 **c** out for him thirty silver coins.
Ac 5:41 because they had been **c** worthy
2Th 1: 5 be **c** worthy of the kingdom of God,

COUNTERFEIT*

2Th 2: 9 in all kinds of **c** miracles,
1Jn 2:27 that anointing is real, not **c—**

COUNTING [COUNT]

2Co 5:19 not **c** men's sins against them.

COUNTLESS [COUNT]

Nu 10:36 to the **c** thousands of Israel."
Heb 11:12 and as **c** as the sand

COUNTRIES [COUNTRY]

Ge 41:57 the **c** came to Egypt to buy grain
Dt 29:16 and how we passed through the **c** on
Isa 36:20 the gods of these **c** has been able
Eze 11:16 and scattered them among the **c,**
20:34 and gather you from the **c**
Da 9: 7 the **c** where you have scattered us
Zec 8: 7 "I will save my people from the **c**

COUNTRY [COUNTRIES, COUNTRYMEN]

Ge 12: 1 "Leave your **c,**
15:13 be strangers in a **c** not their own,
Ex 1:10 fight against us and leave the **c."**
6:11 to let the Israelites go out of his **c."**
Dt 28: 3 in the city and blessed in the **c.**
28:16 in the city and cursed in the **c.**
Jos 9: 6 "We have come from a distant **c;**
11:16 Joshua took this entire land: the hill **c**
Pr 28: 2 When a **c** is rebellious,
29: 4 By justice a king gives a **c** stability,
Isa 66: 8 Can a **c** be born in a day or a nation
Jer 17: 3 because of sin throughout your **c.**
Lk 15:13 set off for a distant **c**
Jn 4:44 prophet has no honor in his own **c.)**
2Co 11:26 in danger in the **c,** in danger at sea;
Heb 11:14 that they are looking for a **c**

THE HILL COUNTRY See HILL

COUNTRYMEN [COUNTRY, MAN]

2Co 11:26 in danger from my own **c,**
1Th 2:14 You suffered from your own **c**

COUNTS [COUNT]

Jn 6:63 The Spirit gives life; the flesh **c**
1Co 7:19 Keeping God's commands is what **c.**
Gal 5: 6 that **c** is faith expressing itself

COURAGE* [COURAGEOUS]

Jos 2:11 everyone's **c** failed because of you,
5: 1 and they no longer had the **c** to face
2Sa 4: 1 lost **c,** and all Israel became alarmed.
7:27 So your servant has found **c**
1Ch 17:25 So your servant has found **c** to pray
2Ch 15: 8 he took **c.**
19:11 Act with **c,**
Ezr 7:28 I took **c** and gathered leading men
10: 4 so take **c** and do it."
Ps 107:26 in their peril their **c** melted away.
Eze 22:14 Will your **c** endure or your hands
Da 11:25 he will stir up his strength and **c**
Mt 14:27 immediately said to them: "Take **c!**
Mk 6:50 to them and said, "Take **c!**
Ac 4:13 the **c** of Peter and John and realized
23:11 stood near Paul and said, "Take **c!**
27:22 now I urge you to keep up your **c,**
27:25 So keep up your **c,** men,
1Co 16:13 be men of **c;** be strong.
Php 1:20 but will have sufficient **c** so that now
Heb 3: 6 if we hold on to our **c** and the hope

COURAGEOUS* [COURAGE]

Dt 31: 6 Be strong and **c.**

	31: 7	"Be strong and **c**,
	31:23	"Be strong and **c**,
Jos	1: 6	"Be strong and **c**,
	1: 7	Be strong and very **c**.
	1: 9	Be strong and **c**.
	1:18	Only be strong and **c**!"
	10:25	Be strong and **c**.
1Ch	22:13	Be strong and **c**.
	28:20	"Be strong and **c**, and do the work.
2Ch	26:17	the priest with eighty other **c** priests
	32: 7	"Be strong and **c**. Do not be afraid

COURSE

Ps	19: 5	a champion rejoicing to run his **c**.
Pr	2: 8	for he guards the **c** of the just
	15:21	of understanding keeps a straight **c**.
	16: 9	In his heart a man plans his **c**,
	17:23	in secret to pervert the **c** of justice.
Ecc	1: 6	ever returning on its **c**.
Jas	3: 6	sets the whole **c** of his life on fire,

COURT [COURTS, COURTYARD]

Dt	25: 1	to **c** and the judges will decide
Jdg	4: 5	She held **c** under the Palm
Job	9:32	we might confront each other in **c**.
Pr	22:22	and do not crush the needy in **c**,
	25: 8	do not bring hastily to **c**,
	29: 9	If a wise man goes to **c** with a fool,
Isa	3:13	The LORD takes his place in **c**;
Mt	5:25	adversary who is taking you to **c**.
Ac	18:12	on Paul and brought him into **c**.
	25:10	now standing before Caesar's **c**,
1Co	4: 3	judged by you or by any human **c**;
Jas	2: 6	ones who are dragging you into **c**?

COURTS [COURT]

Dt	17: 8	before your **c** that are too difficult
1Ch	28: 6	who will build my house and my **c**,
Ps	65: 4	and bring near to live in your **c**!
	84:10	in your **c** than a thousand elsewhere;
	100: 4	and his **c** with praise;
Isa	1:12	this trampling of my **c**?
Am	5:15	maintain justice in the **c**.
Zec	8:16	true and sound judgment in your **c**;
Lk	2:46	found him in the temple **c**,
	20: 1	in the temple **c** and preaching
	22:53	I was with you in the temple **c**,
Jn	2:14	temple **c** he found men selling cattle,
Ac	5:42	in the temple **c** and from house

COURTYARD [COURT]

Ex	27: 9	"Make a **c** for the tabernacle.
1Ki	7: 9	from the outside to the great **c** and
Mk	14:66	While Peter was below in the **c**,

COUSIN

Lev	25:49	An uncle or a **c** or any blood relative
Est	2: 7	Mordecai had a **c** named Hadassah,
Col	4:10	as does Mark, the **c** of Barnabas.

COVENANT [COVENANTS]

Ge	6:18	But I will establish my **c** with you,
	9: 9	"I now establish my **c** with you and
	15:18	the LORD made a **c** with Abram
	17: 2	I will confirm my **c** between me

	31:44	Come now, let's make a **c**,
Ex	2:24	and he remembered his **c**
	6: 5	and I have remembered my **c**.
	19: 5	if you obey me fully and keep my **c**,
	24: 7	he took the Book of the **C** and read
	34:28	on the tablets the words of the **c**—
Lev	26: 9	and I will keep my **c** with you.
Dt	4:13	He declared to you his **c**,
	29: 1	the **c** the LORD commanded Moses
	29: 1	in addition to the **c** he had made
Jos	3: 6	"Take up the ark of the **c** and pass on
Jdg	2: 1	'I will never break my **c** with you,
1Sa	20:16	So Jonathan made a **c** with the house
	23:18	of them made a **c** before the LORD.
1Ki	8: 1	to bring up the ark of the LORD's **c**
	8:21	the **c** of the LORD that he made
	8:23	you who keep your **c**
2Ki	23: 2	all the words of the Book of the **C**,
1Ch	16:15	He remembers his **c** forever,
2Ch	34:30	the words of the Book of the **C**,
Ne	1: 5	who keeps his **c** of love
Job	31: 1	a **c** with my eyes not to look lustfully
Ps	78:37	they were not faithful to his **c**.
	105: 8	He remembers his **c** forever,
	132:12	if your sons keep my **c** and
Pr	2:17	ignored the **c** she made
Isa	42: 6	be a **c** for the people and a light for
	61: 8	and make an everlasting **c**
Jer	11: 3	to the terms of this **c** and tell them to
	31:31	a new **c** with the house of Israel
	32:40	I will make an everlasting **c**
Eze	16:60	and I will establish an everlasting **c**
	37:26	I will make a **c** of peace with them;
Da	9:27	He will confirm a **c** with many
	11:28	heart be set against the holy **c**.
Hos	6: 7	Like Adam, they have broken the **c**
Mal	2:14	the wife of your marriage **c**.
	3: 1	the messenger of the **c**,
Mt	26:28	This is my blood of the **c**,
Mk	14:24	"This is my blood of the **c**,
Lk	22:20	"This cup is the new **c** in my blood,
Ro	11:27	And this is my **c** with them
1Co	11:25	"This cup is the new **c** in my blood;
2Co	3: 6	as ministers of a new **c**—
Gal	3:17	the **c** previously established by God
	4:24	One **c** is from Mount Sinai
Heb	7:22	the guarantee of a better **c**.
	8: 8	a new **c** with the house of Israel and
	9:15	Christ is the mediator of a new **c**,
	12:24	to Jesus the mediator of a new **c**,
Rev	11:19	temple was seen the ark of his **c**.

ARK OF THE COVENANT See ARK

COVENANT OF THE †LORD Nu 10:33; Dt
4:23; 10:8; 29:25; 31:9, 25, 26; Jos 3:3, 17; 4:7,
18; 6:6; 7:15; 8:33; 23:16; 1Sa 4:4; 1Ki 6:19;
8:21; 1Ch 15:25, 26, 28, 29; 16:37; 17:1; 22:19;
28:2, 18; 2Ch 6:11; Jer 3:16; 22:9

EVERLASTING COVENANT
See EVERLASTING

COVENANTS* [COVENANT]

| Ro | 9: 4 | the **c**, the receiving of the law, |
| Gal | 4:24 | for the women represent two **c**. |

Eph 2:12 foreigners to the **c** of the promise,

COVER [COVER-UP, COVERED, COVERING, COVERINGS, COVERS, GOLD-COVERED]

Ex   25:17 an atonement **c** of pure gold—
      25:21 Place the **c** on top of the ark and put
      33:22 in the rock and **c** you with my hand
Lev 16: 2 of the atonement **c** on
      16: 2 in the cloud over the atonement **c.**
Nu   4: 6 Then they are to **c** this with hides
Ne   4: 5 Do not **c** up their guilt
Ps   32: 5 to you and did not **c** up my iniquity.
      91: 4 He will **c** you with his feathers,
Jer 51:42 Babylon; its roaring waves will **c** her
Eze 13:10 they **c** it with whitewash,
Hos 10: 8 to the mountains, **"C** us!"
Hab   2:14 as the waters **c** the sea.
Lk   23:30 and to the hills, **"C** us!"'
1Co 11: 6 If a woman does not **c** her head,
      11: 7 A man ought not to **c** his head,
Jas   5:20 and **c** over a multitude of sins.

COVER-UP* [COVER]

1Pe   2:16 not use your freedom as a **c** for evil;

COVERED [COVER]

Ge   7:20 The waters rose and **c** the mountains
      38:14 herself with a veil to disguise
Ex   10:22 and total darkness **c** all Egypt
      14:28 and **c** the chariots and horsemen—
      16:13 That evening quail came and **c**
      19:18 Mount Sinai was **c** with smoke,
      24:15 the cloud **c** it,
      40:34 the cloud **c** the Tent of Meeting,
Nu   9:15 was set up, the cloud **c** it.
Jdg   6:39 the fleece dry and the ground **c**
Ps   32: 1 whose sins are **c**,
      85: 2 of your people and **c** all their sins.
Isa   6: 2 With two wings they **c** their faces,
      51:16 **c** you with the shadow of my hand—
Da   9: 7 but this day we are **c** with shame—
Ob   1:10 you will be **c** with shame;
Jnh   3: 8 man and beast be **c** with sackcloth.
Ro   4: 7 whose sins are **c**.
1Co 11: 4 with his head **c** dishonors his head.
Rev   4: 6 and they were **c** with eyes,
      17: 3 that was **c** with blasphemous names

COVERING [COVER]

Ex   35:11 the tabernacle with its tent and its **c**,
Mal   2:16 a man's **c** himself with violence
1Co 11:15 For long hair is given to her as a **c**.

COVERINGS [COVER]

Ge   3: 7 and made **c** for themselves.
Pr   31:22 She makes **c** for her bed;

COVERS [COVER]

Ex   22:15 money paid for the hire **c** the loss.
Pr   10:12 but love **c** over all wrongs.
      17: 9 He who **c** over an offense
Isa 25: 7 the sheet that **c** all nations;
2Co   3:15 a veil **c** their hearts.

1Pe   4: 8 love **c** over a multitude of sins.

COVET* [COVETED, COVETING, COVETOUS]

Ex   20:17 not **c** your neighbor's house.
      20:17 not **c** your neighbor's wife,
      34:24 and no one will **c** your land
Dt   5:21 not **c** your neighbor's wife.
      7:25 Do not **c** the silver and gold on them,
Mic   2: 2 They **c** fields and seize them,
Ro   7: 7 had not said, "Do not **c."**
      13: 9 "Do not steal," "Do not **c,"**
Jas   4: 2 You kill and **c**,

COVETED* [COVET]

Jos   7:21 I **c** them and took them.
Ac   20:33 I have not **c** anyone's silver or gold

COVETING* [COVET]

Ro   7: 7 not have known what **c** really was if

COVETOUS* [COVET]

Ro   7: 8 in me every kind of **c** desire.

COW [COWS]

Isa 11: 7 The **c** will feed with the bear,

COWARDLY* [COWER]

Rev 21: 8 But the **c**, the unbelieving, the vile,

COWER* [COWARDLY]

Dt   33:29 Your enemies will **c** before you,

COWS [COW]

Ge   41: 2 of the river there came up seven **c**,
Ex   25: 5 and hides of sea **c**;
Nu   4: 6 to cover this with hides of sea **c**,
1Sa   6: 7 with two **c** that have calved
Job 21:10 bulls never fail to breed; their **c** calve
Am   4: 1 you **c** of Bashan on Mount Samaria,

CRAFT* [CRAFTINESS, CRAFTS, CRAFTSMAN, CRAFTSMEN, CRAFTY]

1Ch 28:21 man skilled in any **c** will help you

CRAFTINESS* [CRAFT]

Job   5:13 He catches the wise in their **c**,
1Co   3:19 the wise in their **c**";
Eph   4:14 of teaching and by the cunning and **c**

CRAFTS* [CRAFT]

Ex   31: 3 and knowledge in all kinds of **c**—
      35:31 and knowledge in all kinds of **c**—

CRAFTSMAN [CRAFT]

Ex   38:23 a **c** and designer,
1Ki   7:14 a man of Tyre and a **c** in bronze.
Pr   8:30 Then I was the **c** at his side.
Isa 40:19 As for an idol, a **c** casts it,
Jer 10: 3 and a **c** shapes it with his chisel.
Hos   8: 6 This calf—a **c** has made it;

CRAFTSMEN [CRAFT]

Ex   31: 6 I have given skill to all the **c**

1Ki 5:18 The **c** of Solomon and Hiram and
Zec 1:20 Then the LORD showed me four **c**.
Ac 19:24 in no little business for the **c**.

CRAFTY* [CRAFT]

Ge 3: 1 the serpent was more **c** than any of
1Sa 23:22 They tell me he is very **c**.
Job 5:12 He thwarts the plans of the **c**,
     15: 5 you adopt the tongue of the **c**.
Pr   7:10 like a prostitute and with **c** intent.
     12: 2 but the LORD condemns a **c** man.
     14:17 and a **c** man is hated.
2Co 12:16 Yet, **c** fellow that I am,

CRAG [CRAGS]

Ps 78:16 he brought streams out of a rocky **c**

CRAGS [CRAG]

1Sa 24: 2 for David and his men near the **C** of

CRASH*

Zep 1:10 and a loud **c** from the hills.
Mt   7:27 and it fell with a great **c**."

CRAVE* [CRAVED, CRAVES, CRAVING, CRAVINGS]

Nu 11: 4 with them began to **c** other food,
Dt 12:20 and you **c** meat and say,
Pr 23: 3 Do not **c** his delicacies,
    23: 6 do not **c** his delicacies;
    31: 4 not for rulers to **c** beer,
Mic 7: 1 none of the early figs that I **c**.
1Pe 2: 2 **c** pure spiritual milk,

CRAVED* [CRAVE]

Nu 11:34 the people who had **c** other food.
Ps 78:18 by demanding the food they **c**.
    78:29 for he had given them what they **c**.
    78:30 they turned from the food they **c**,

CRAVES* [CRAVE]

Pr 13: 4 The sluggard **c** and gets nothing,
    21:10 The wicked man **c** evil;
    21:26 All day long he **c** for more,

CRAVING* [CRAVE]

Job 20:20 he will have no respite from his **c**;
Ps 106:14 In the desert they gave in to their **c**;
Pr 10: 3 but he thwarts the **c** of
    13: 2 the unfaithful have a **c** for violence.
    21:25 sluggard's **c** will be the death of him,
Jer 2:24 sniffing the wind in her **c**—

CRAVINGS* [CRAVE]

Ps 10: 3 He boasts of the **c** of his heart;
Eph 2: 3 gratifying the **c** of our sinful nature
1Jn 2:16 For everything in the world—the **c**

CRAWL*

Ge 3:14 You will **c** on your belly
Mic 7:17 like creatures that **c** on the ground.

CREATE* [CREATED, CREATES, CREATING, CREATION, CREATOR]

Ps 51:10 **C** in me a pure heart, O God,
Isa 4: 5 Then the LORD will **c** over all
    45: 7 I form the light and **c** darkness,
    45: 7 I bring prosperity and **c** disaster;
    45:18 not **c** it to be empty, but formed it to
    65:17 I will **c** new heavens and
    65:18 and rejoice forever in what I will **c**,
    65:18 for I will **c** Jerusalem to be a delight
Jer 31:22 The LORD will **c** a new thing
Mal 2:10 Did not one God **c** us?
Eph 2:15 to **c** in himself one new man out of

CREATED* [CREATE]

Ge 1: 1 In the beginning God **c** the heavens
     1:21 So God **c** the great creatures of
     1:27 So God **c** man in his own image, in
           the image of God he **c** him; male
           and female he **c** them.
     2: 4 and the earth when they were **c**.
     5: 1 When God **c** man,
     5: 2 He **c** them male and female
     5: 2 they were **c**, he called them "man."
     6: 7 whom I have **c**,
Dt   4:32 the day God **c** man on the earth;
Ps 89:12 You **c** the north and the south;
    89:47 For what futility you have **c** all men!
   102:18 that a people not yet **c** may praise
   104:30 you send your Spirit, they are **c**,
   139:13 For you **c** my inmost being;
   148: 5 for he commanded and they were **c**.
Isa 40:26 look to the heavens: Who **c** all these?
    41:20 that the Holy One of Israel has **c** it.
    42: 5 what God the LORD says—he who **c**
    43: 1 what the LORD says—he who **c** you,
    43: 7 whom I **c** for my glory,
    45: 8 the LORD, have **c** it.
    45:12 the earth and **c** mankind upon it.
    45:18 what the LORD says—who **c**
    48: 7 They are **c** now, and not long ago;
    54:16 it is I who **c** the blacksmith who fans
    54:16 And it is I who have **c** the destroyer
    57:16 the breath of man that I have **c**.
Eze 21:30 In the place where you were **c**,
    28:13 day you were **c** they were prepared.
    28:15 from the day you were **c**
Mk 13:19 when God **c** the world, until now—
Ro   1:25 and served **c** things rather than
1Co 11: 9 neither was man **c** for woman,
Eph 2:10 **c** in Christ Jesus to do good works,
     3: 9 who **c** all things,
     4:24 **c** to be like God
Col 1:16 For by him all things were **c**:
     1:16 all things were **c** by him
1Ti 4: 3 which God **c** to be received
     4: 4 For everything God **c** is good,
Heb 12:27 that is, **c** things—
Jas 1:18 be a kind of firstfruits of all he **c**.
Rev 4:11 for you **c** all things,
     4:11 and by your will they were **c**
    10: 6 who **c** the heavens and all that is

CREATES* [CREATE]

Am   4:13 **c** the wind, and reveals his thoughts

CREATING* [CREATE]

Ge   2: 3 on it he rested from all the work of **c**
Isa 57:19 **c** praise on the lips of the mourners

CREATION* [CREATE]

Hab   2:18 he who makes it trusts in his own **c;**
Mt   13:35 I will utter things hidden since the **c**
     25:34 for you since the **c** of the world.
Mk   10: 6 beginning of **c** God 'made them male
     16:15 and preach the good news to all **c.**
Jn   17:24 because you loved me before the **c**
Ro   1:20 For since the **c** of the world
      8:19 The **c** waits in eager expectation for
      8:20 the **c** was subjected to frustration,
      8:21 the **c** itself will be liberated
      8:22 the whole **c** has been groaning as in
      8:39 nor anything else in all **c,**
2Co   5:17 if anyone is in Christ, he is a new **c;**
Gal   6:15 what counts is a new **c.**
Eph   1: 4 chose us in him before the **c** of the
Col   1:15 the firstborn over all **c.**
Heb   4: 3 since the **c** of the world.
      4:13 Nothing in all **c** is hidden
      9:11 that is to say, not a part of this **c.**
      9:26 to suffer many times since the **c** of
1Pe   1:20 He was chosen before the **c** of
2Pe   3: 4 as it has since the beginning of **c.''**
Rev   3:14 the ruler of God's **c.**
     13: 8 to the Lamb that was slain from the **c**
     17: 8 written in the book of life from the **c**

CREATOR* [CREATE]

Ge   14:19 **C** of heaven and earth.
     14:22 **C** of heaven and earth,
Dt   32: 6 Is he not your Father, your **C,**
Ecc 12: 1 Remember your **C** in the days
Isa 27:11 and their **C** shows them no favor.
     40:28 the **C** of the ends of the earth.
     43:15 your Holy One, Israel's **C,**
Mt   19: 4 the **C** 'made them male and female,'
Ro   1:25 created things rather than the **C—**
Col   3:10 in knowledge in the image of its **C.**
1Pe   4:19 themselves to their faithful **C**

CREATURE [CREATURES]

Ge   1:28 and over every living **c** that moves
      7: 4 the face of the earth every living **c**
Lev 11:42 not to eat any **c** that moves about on
     17:11 For the life of a **c** is in the blood,
     17:14 the life of every **c** is its blood.
Job 12:10 In his hand is the life of every **c** and
Ps 136:25 and who gives food to every **c.**
Eze   1:15 a wheel on the ground beside each **c**
Rev   4: 7 The first living **c** was like a lion,
      5:13 I heard every **c** in heaven and

CREATURES [CREATURE]

Ge   1:20 "Let the water teem with living **c,**
      1:24 "Let the land produce living **c**
      6:19 into the ark two of all living **c,**
      8:21 never again will I destroy all living **c,**

      9:16 everlasting covenant between God
             and all living **c** of every kind
Ps 104:24 the earth is full of your **c.**
Pr   30:25 Ants are **c** of little strength,
Eze   1: 5 what looked like four living **c.**
     10:15 These were the living **c** I had seen by
     47: 9 Swarms of living **c** will live
Rev   4: 6 around the throne, were four living **c,**
      5: 6 by the four living **c** and the elders.
      8: 9 a third of the living **c** in the sea died,
     19: 4 and the four living **c** fell down

CREDIT [ACCREDITED, CREDITED, CREDITOR, CREDITORS, CREDITS]

Lk   6:33 what **c** is that to you?
Ro   4:24 to whom God will **c** righteousness—
1Pe   2:20 how is it to your **c** if you receive

CREDITED [CREDIT]

Ge   15: 6 and he **c** it to him as righteousness.
Ps 106:31 This was **c** to him as righteousness
Eze 18:20 the righteous man will be **c** to him,
Ro   4: 3 it was **c** to him as righteousness."
      4: 4 his wages are not **c** to him as a gift,
      4: 9 it was **c** to him as righteousness."
Gal   3: 6 it was **c** to him as righteousness."
Php   4:17 but I am looking for what may be **c**
Jas   2:23 it was **c** to him as righteousness,"

CREDITOR [CREDIT]

Dt   15: 2 Every **c** shall cancel the loan he has
Ps 109:11 May a **c** seize all he has;

CREDITORS* [CREDIT]

Isa 50: 1 Or to which of my **c** did I sell you?

CREDITS* [CREDIT]

Ro   4: 6 man to whom God **c** righteousness

CRETANS* [CRETE]

Ac   2:11 Jews and converts to Judaism); **C**
Tit   1:12 "**C** are always liars, evil brutes,

CRETE [CRETANS]

Ac   27:12 This was a harbor in **C,**
Tit   1: 5 The reason I left you in **C** was

CRIB (KJV) See MANGER

CRIED [CRY]

Ex   2:23 in their slavery and **c** out,
     14:10 They were terrified and **c** out to
Nu   20:16 but when we **c** out to the LORD,
Jos 24: 7 But they **c** to the LORD for help,
Jdg   3: 9 But when they **c** out to the LORD,
      4: 3 they **c** to the LORD for help.
      6: 6 the Israelites **c** out to
     10:12 and you **c** to me for help,
1Sa   7: 9 He **c** out to the LORD
     12: 8 they **c** to the LORD for help,
     28:12 she **c** out at the top of her voice
Job 29:12 I rescued the poor who **c** for help,
Ps   18: 6 I **c** to my God for help,
     22: 5 They **c** to you and were saved;
    107:13 they **c** to the LORD in their trouble,

Jnh 1: 5 each **c** out to his own god.
     1:14 Then they **c** to the LORD,
Mt 14:30 beginning to sink, **c** out, "Lord,
    27:46 Jesus **c** out in a loud voice,
Rev 19: 4 And they **c:** "Amen, Hallelujah!"

CRIES [CRY]

Ge   4:10 Your brother's blood **c** out to me
Pr   8: 3 at the entrances, she **c** aloud:

CRIME [CRIMES, CRIMINAL, CRIMINALS]

1Sa 20: 1 What is my **c?**
Ps 69:27 Charge them with **c** upon **c;**
Hab 2:12 and establishes a town by **c!**
Mk 15:14 What **c** has he committed?"
Ac. 28:18 not guilty of any **c** deserving death.

CRIMES [CRIME]

Rev 18: 5 and God has remembered her **c.**

CRIMINAL* [CRIME]

Lk 23:40 But the other **c** rebuked him.
Jn 18:30 "If he were not a **c,**" they replied,
2Ti 2: 9 to the point of being chained like a **c.**
1Pe 4:15 or thief or any other kind of **c,**

CRIMINALS [CRIME]

Lk 23:32 Two other men, both **c,**

CRIMSON

Isa 1:18 though they are red as **c,**
    63: 1 with his garments stained **c?**

CRIPPLE* [CRIPPLED]

Ac   4: 9 for an act of kindness shown to a **c**

CRIPPLED [CRIPPLE]

2Sa 9: 3 a son of Jonathan; he is **c**
Mal 1: 8 you sacrifice **c** or diseased animals,
Mt 15:30 bringing the lame, the blind, the **c,**
Mk   9:45 It is better for you to enter life **c** than
Lk 14:13 invite the poor, the **c,** the lame,
Ac   3: 2 a man **c** from birth was being carried
    14: 8 In Lystra there sat a man **c**

CRISIS*

1Co 7:26 Because of the present **c,**

CRITICISM*

2Co 8:20 We want to avoid any **c** of the way

CROOKED*

Dt 32: 5 but a warped and **c** generation.
2Sa 22:27 to the **c** you show yourself shrewd.
Ps 18:26 to the **c** you show yourself shrewd.
   125: 5 But those who turn to **c** ways
Pr   2:15 whose paths are **c,**
     5: 6 her paths are **c,**
     8: 8 none of them is **c** or perverse.
    10: 9 but he who takes **c** paths will
Ecc 7:13 can straighten what he has made **c?**
Isa 59: 8 They have turned them into **c** roads;
La   3: 9 he has made my paths **c.**

Lk   3: 5 The **c** roads shall become straight,
Php 2:15 children of God without fault in a **c**

CROP [CROPS]

Isa 5: 2 Then he looked for a **c**
Mt 13: 8 where it produced a **c—**
    21:41 who will give him his share of the **c**
Jn   4:36 now he harvests the **c** for eternal life,

CROPS [CROP]

Ge   4:12 it will no longer yield its **c** for you.
Pr   3: 9 with the firstfruits of all your **c;**
    10: 5 He who gathers **c** in summer is
    28: 3 like a driving rain that leaves no **c.**
Eze 34:29 for them a land renowned for its **c,**
    36:30 of the trees and the **c** of the field,
Zec 8:12 the ground will produce its **c,**
2Ti 2: 6 the first to receive a share of the **c.**
Rev 22: 2 bearing twelve **c** of fruit,

CROSS [CROSSED, CROSSES, CROSSING]

Dt   4:21 that I would not **c** the Jordan
    12:10 But you will **c** the Jordan and settle
    30:13 "Who will **c** the sea to get it
    31: 3 The LORD your God himself will **c**
Jos 3:14 So when the people broke camp to **c**
Ps 104: 9 You set a boundary they cannot **c;**
Jer 5:22 an everlasting barrier it cannot **c.**
Mt 10:38 and anyone who does not take his **c**
    16:24 and take up his **c** and follow me.
Mk 15:21 and they forced him to carry the **c.**
    15:30 down from the **c** and save yourself!"
Jn 19:17 Carrying his own **c,**
    19:25 Near the **c** of Jesus stood his mother,
Ac   2:23 to death by nailing him to the **c.**
1Co 1:17 lest the **c** of Christ be emptied
     1:18 the message of the **c** is foolishness
Gal 5:11 of the **c** has been abolished.
     6:12 to avoid being persecuted for the **c**
     6:14 May I never boast except in the **c**
Eph 2:16 both of them to God through the **c,**
Php 2: 8 even death on a **c!**
     3:18 many live as enemies of the **c**
Col 1:20 through his blood, shed on the **c.**
     2:14 nailing it to the **c.**
     2:15 triumphing over them by the **c.**
Heb 12: 2 the joy set before him endured the **c,**

CROSSED [CROSS]

Jos 4: 7 When it **c** the Jordan,
2Ki 2: 8 two of them **c** over on dry ground.
Jn   5:24 (he has **c** over from death to life.

CROSSES [CROSS]

Jn 19:31 not want the bodies left on the **c**

CROSSING [CROSS]

Ge 48:14 and **c** his arms,
Dt   4:14 the land that you are **c** the Jordan to

CROSSROADS* [ROAD]

Jer 6:16 "Stand at the **c** and look;
Ob   1:14 at the **c** to cut down their fugitives,

CROUCHING
Ge 4: 7 sin is **c** at your door;

CROW* [CROWED, CROWS]
Jn 18:27 at that moment a rooster began to **c.**

CROWD [CROWDING, CROWDS]
Ex 23: 2 by siding with the **c,**
Eze 7:12 for wrath is upon the whole **c.**
Mt 21: 8 A very large **c** spread their cloaks on
Lk 9:13 and buy food for all this **c."**
Jn 7:31 many in the **c** put their faith in him.

CROWDING [CROWD]
Mk 3: 9 to keep the people from **c** him.
5:31 "You see the people **c** against you,"

CROWDS [CROWD]
Mt 9:36 When he saw the **c,**
Ac 8: 6 When the **c** heard Philip and saw
17:13 agitating the **c** and stirring them up.

CROWED [CROW]
Mt 26:74 Immediately a rooster **c.**

CROWN [CROWNED, CROWNS]
Job 19: 9 and removed the **c** from my head.
31:36 I would put it on like a **c.**
Pr 4: 9 present you with a **c** of splendor."
10: 6 Blessings **c** the head of
12: 4 of noble character is her husband's **c,**
14:24 The wealth of the wise is their **c,**
16:31 Gray hair is a **c** of splendor;
17: 6 Children's children are a **c** to
27:24 a **c** is not secure for all generations.
Isa 35:10 everlasting joy will **c** their heads.
51:11 everlasting joy will **c** their heads.
61: 3 to bestow on them a **c** of beauty
62: 3 You will be a **c** of splendor in
La 5:16 The **c** has fallen from our head.
Eze 16:12 and a beautiful **c** on your head.
Zec 9:16 in his land like jewels in a **c.**
Mt 27:29 a **c** of thorns and set it on his head.
Mk 15:17 then twisted together a **c** of thorns
Jn 19: 2 a **c** of thorns and put it on his head.
19: 5 When Jesus came out wearing the **c**
1Co 9:25 They do it to get a **c** that will
9:25 to get a **c** that will last forever.
Php 4: 1 my joy and **c,**
1Th 2:19 or the **c** in which we will glory in
2Ti 2: 5 the victor's **c** unless he competes
4: 8 in store for me the **c** of righteousness
Jas 1:12 the **c** of life that God has promised
1Pe 5: 4 you will receive the **c** of glory
Rev 2:10 and I will give you the **c** of life.
3:11 so that no one will take your **c.**
6: 2 and he was given a **c,**
12: 1 and a **c** of twelve stars on her head.
14:14 of man" with a **c** of gold on his head

CROWNED* [CROWN]
Ps 8: 5 and **c** him with glory and honor.
Pr 14:18 the prudent are **c** with knowledge.
SS 3:11 crown with which his mother **c** him

Heb 2: 7 than the angels; you **c** him with glory
2: 9 now **c** with glory and honor

CROWNS [CROWN]
Ps 103: 4 and **c** you with love and compassion,
149: 4 he **c** the humble with salvation.
Pr 11:26 but blessing **c** him who is willing
Isa 23: 8 the bestower of **c,**
Jer 13:18 for your glorious **c** will fall
Rev 4: 4 and had **c** of gold on their heads.
4:10 They lay their **c** before the throne
9: 7 they wore something like **c** of gold,
12: 3 heads and ten horns and seven **c**
13: 1 with ten **c** on his horns,
19:12 and on his head are many **c.**

CROWS [CROW]
Mt 26:34 "this very night, before the rooster **c,**

CRUCIFIED* [CRUCIFY]
Mt 20:19 to be mocked and flogged and **c.**
26: 2 of Man will be handed over to be **c."**
27:26 and handed him over to be **c.**
27:35 When they had **c** him,
27:38 Two robbers were **c** with him,
27:44 the robbers who were **c** with him
28: 5 Jesus, who was **c.**
Mk 15:15 and handed him over to be **c.**
15:24 And they **c** him.
15:25 the third hour when they **c** him.
15:27 They **c** two robbers with him,
15:32 Those **c** with him also heaped insults
16: 6 Jesus the Nazarene, who was **c.**
Lk 23:23 that he be **c,**
23:33 there they **c** him,
24: 7 be **c** and on the third day
24:20 and they **c** him;
Jn 19:16 over to them to be **c.**
19:18 Here they **c** him,
19:20 where Jesus was **c** was near the city,
19:23 When the soldiers **c** Jesus,
19:32 of the first man who had been **c**
19:41 At the place where Jesus was **c,**
Ac 2:36 whom you **c,** both Lord and Christ."
4:10 whom you **c** but whom God raised
Ro 6: 6 For we know that our old self was **c**
1Co 1:13 Was Paul **c** for you?
1:23 but we preach Christ **c:**
2: 2 except Jesus Christ and him **c.**
2: 8 they would not have **c** the Lord
2Co 13: 4 For to be sure, he was **c** in weakness,
Gal 2:20 I have been **c** with Christ
3: 1 Christ was clearly portrayed as **c.**
5:24 to Christ Jesus have **c**
6:14 which the world has been **c** to me,
Rev 11: 8 where also their Lord was **c.**

CRUCIFY* [CRUCIFIED, CRUCIFYING]
Mt 23:34 Some of them you will kill and **c;**
27:22 They all answered, "**C** him!"
27:23 the louder, "**C** him!"
27:31 Then they led him away to **c** him.
Mk 15:13 "**C** him!" they shouted.
15:14 the louder, "**C** him!"

	15:20	Then they led him out to **c** him.
Lk	23:21	they kept shouting, "**C** him! **C** him!"
Jn	19: 6	saw him, they shouted, "**C! C!**"
	19: 6	"You take him and **c** him.
	19:10	either to free you or to **c** you?"
	19:15	Take him away! **C** him!"
	19:15	"Shall I **c** your king?"

CRUCIFYING* [CRUCIFY]

Heb	6: 6	are **c** the Son of God all over again

CRUEL [CRUELTY]

Ex	6: 9	discouragement and **c** bondage.
Dt	28:33	but **c** oppression all your days.
Pr	11:17	a **c** man brings trouble on himself.
	12:10	the kindest acts of the wicked are **c**.
	27: 4	Anger is **c** and fury overwhelming,
Isa	13: 9	a **c** day, with wrath and fierce anger

CRUELTY* [CRUEL]

Na	3:19	for who has not felt your endless **c**?

CRUMBS*

Mt	15:27	"but even the dogs eat the **c** that fall
Mk	7:28	under the table eat the children's **c**."

CRUSH [CRUSHED]

Ge	3:15	He will **c** your head,
Nu	24:17	He will **c** the foreheads of Moab,
Ps	68:21	God will **c** the heads of his enemies,
Isa	53:10	Yet it was the LORD's will to **c** him
Da	2:40	so it will **c** and break all the others.
Ro	16:20	The God of peace will soon **c** Satan

CRUSHED [CRUSH]

Ps	34:18	and saves those who are **c** in spirit.
	51: 8	the bones you have **c** rejoice.
Pr	17:22	but a **c** spirit dries up the bones.
	18:14	but a **c** spirit who can bear?
Isa	53: 5	he was **c** for our iniquities;
Jer	8:21	Since my people are **c**, I am **c**;
Da	7: 7	It had large iron teeth; it **c**
Mt	21:44	but he on whom it falls will be **c**."
2Co	4: 8	hard pressed on every side, but not **c**;

CRY [CRIED, CRIES, CRYING]

Ex	2:23	and their **c** for help because
	3: 9	the **c** of the Israelites has reached me,
Nu	20:16	he heard our **c** and sent an angel
Jdg	10:14	**c** out to the gods you have chosen.
1Sa	9:16	for their **c** has reached me."
1Ki	17:22	The LORD heard Elijah's **c**,
Ps	5: 2	Listen to my **c** for help,
	6: 9	LORD has heard my **c** for mercy;
	29: 9	And in his temple all **c**, "Glory!"
	34:15	and his ears are attentive to their **c**;
	40: 1	he turned to me and heard my **c**.
	130: 1	Out of the depths I **c** to you,
Pr	2: 3	and **c** aloud for understanding,
	21:13	If a man shuts his ears to the **c** of
	21:13	he too will **c** out and not
Isa	3: 7	But in that day he will **c** out,
Jer	4:31	I hear a **c** as of a woman in labor,
	14:12	they fast, I will not listen to their **c**;

La	2:18	The hearts of the people **c** out to
Hos	7:14	not **c** out to me from their hearts
Hab	2:11	The stones of the wall will **c** out,
Mk	15:39	heard his **c** and saw how he died,
Lk	19:40	the stones will **c** out."
Ro	8:15	And by him we **c**, "Abba, Father."
Rev	18:10	they will stand far off and **c**: " 'Woe!

CRYING [CRY]

Ge	21:17	God heard the boy **c**,
Jn	20:11	but Mary stood outside the tomb **c**.
Rev	21: 4	be no more death or mourning or **c**

CRYSTAL*

Job	28:17	Neither gold nor **c** can compare
Rev	4: 6	like a sea of glass, clear as **c**.
	21:11	like a jasper, clear as **c**.
	22: 1	the water of life, as clear as **c**,

CUBS

2Sa	17: 8	fierce as a wild bear robbed of her **c**.
Pr	17:12	to meet a bear robbed of her **c** than
Hos	13: 8	Like a bear robbed of her **c**,

CUD

Lev	11: 3	divided and that chews the **c**.
Dt	14: 6	divided in two and that chews the **c**.

CULTIVATE* [CULTIVATED]

Dt	28:39	You will plant vineyards and **c** them
Ps	104:14	and plants for man to **c**—

CULTIVATED [CULTIVATE]

Ro	11:24	were grafted into a **c** olive tree,

CUMBERED (KJV) See DISTRACTED

CUNNING*

Ps	64: 6	the mind and heart of man are **c**.
	83: 3	With **c** they conspire
2Co	11: 3	Eve was deceived by the serpent's **c**,
Eph	4:14	and by the **c** and craftiness of men

CUP [CUPS]

Ge	40:11	Pharaoh's **c** was in my hand,
	44: 2	Then put my **c**, the silver one,
2Sa	12: 3	drank from his **c** and even slept
1Ki	7:26	and its rim was like the rim of a **c**,
Ps	23: 5	my head with oil; my **c** overflows.
	75: 8	In the hand of the LORD is a **c** full
Pr	23:31	when it sparkles in the **c**,
Isa	51:22	I have taken out of your hand the **c**
Jer	25:15	**c** filled with the wine of my wrath
Eze	23:31	so I will put her **c** into your hand.
Mt	10:42	gives even a **c** of cold water
	20:22	"Can you drink the **c** I am going
	23:25	You clean the outside of the **c**
	23:26	First clean the inside of the **c**
	26:27	Then he took the **c**,
	26:39	may this **c** be taken from me.
Mk	9:41	gives you a **c** of water in my name
	10:38	the **c** I drink or be baptized with
	14:23	Then he took the **c**,
	14:36	Take this **c** from me.
Lk	11:39	clean the outside of the **c** and dish,

22:17 After taking the **c,**
22:20 "This **c** is the new covenant
22:42 take this **c** from me;
Jn 18:11 the **c** the Father has given me?"
1Co 10:21 You cannot drink the **c** of the Lord
11:25 "This **c** is the new covenant
11:27 the **c** of the Lord in an unworthy
Rev 14:10 into the **c** of his wrath.
16:19 the **c** filled with the wine of the fury
17: 4 She held a golden **c** in her hand,
18: 6 a double portion from her own **c.**

CUPBEARER

Ge 40: 1 the **c** and the baker of the king
41: 9 Then the chief **c** said to Pharaoh,
Ne 1:11 I was **c** to the king.

CUPS [CUP]

Ex 25:33 Three **c** shaped like almond flowers
Mk 7: 4 such as the washing of **c,**

CURDS

Ge 18: 8 then brought some **c** and milk and
Dt 32:14 with **c** and milk from herd and flock
Isa 7:15 He will eat **c** and honey
Eze 34: 3 You eat the **c,**

CURE [CURED]

2Ki 5: 3 He would **c** him of his leprosy."
Jer 17: 9 above all things and beyond **c.**
30:15 your pain that has no **c?**
Hos 5:13 But he is not able to **c** you,
Lk 9: 1 and to **c** diseases,

CURED [CURE]

Mt 8: 3 Immediately he was **c** of his leprosy.
11: 5 those who have leprosy are **c,**
Lk 6:18 Those troubled by evil spirits were **c,**
Jn 5: 9 At once the man was **c;**
Ac 19:12 and their illnesses were **c** and
28: 9 sick on the island came and were **c.**

CURRENTS·

Jnh 2: 3 and the **c** swirled about me;

CURSE [ACCURSED, CURSED, CURSES, CURSING]

Ge 4:11 Now you are under a **c** and driven
8:21 "Never again will I **c** the ground
12: 3 and whoever curses you I will **c;**
27:13 "My son, let the **c** fall on me.
Ex 22:28 or **c** the ruler of your people.
Lev 19:14 " 'Do not **c** the deaf or put
24:11 blasphemed the Name with a **c;**
Nu 5:18 the bitter water that brings a **c.**
22: 6 and put a **c** on these people,
22:12 not put a **c** on those people,
Dt 11:26 before you today a blessing and a **c**
11:28 the **c** if you disobey the commands
21:23 hung on a tree is under God's **c.**
23: 5 not listen to Balaam but turned the **c**
Jos 9:23 You are now under a **c:**
24: 9 for Balaam son of Beor to put a **c**
2Sa 16: 9 "Why should this dead dog **c** my lord

2Ki 2:24 at them and called down a **c** on them
Ne 10:29 a **c** and an oath to follow the Law
13: 2 turned the **c** into a blessing.)
Job 1:11 he will surely **c** you to your face."
2: 5 surely **c** you to your face."
2: 9 **C** God and die!"
Ps 62: 4 but in their hearts they **c.**
109:28 They may **c,** but you will bless;
Pr 3:33 The LORD's **c** is on the house of
24:24 peoples will **c** him and nations
30:11 "There are those who **c** their fathers
Isa 24: 6 Therefore a **c** consumes the earth;
La 3:65 and may your **c** be on them!
Mal 2: 2 and I will **c** your blessings.
4: 6 and strike the land with a **c.**"
Lk 6:28 bless those who **c** you,
Jn 7:49 there is a **c** on them."
Ro 12:14 and do not **c.**
1Co 16:22 not love the Lord—a **c** be on him.
Gal 3:10 on observing the law are under a **c,**
3:13 the **c** of the law by becoming a curse
3:13 the curse of the law by becoming a **c**
Jas 3: 9 and with it we **c** men,
Rev 22: 3 No longer will there be any **c.**

CURSED [CURSE]

Ge 3:14 "**C** are you above all the livestock
3:17 "**C** is the ground because of you;
9:25 "**C** be Canaan!
27:29 May those who curse you be **c**
Lev 20: 9 He has **c** his father or his mother,
Nu 22: 6 and those you curse are **c.**"
23: 8 I curse those whom God has not **c?**
Dt 27:15 "**C** is the man who carves an image
27:16 "**C** is the man who dishonors his
27:17 "**C** is the man who moves his
27:18 "**C** is the man who leads
27:19 "**C** is the man who withholds justice
27:20 "**C** is the man who sleeps
27:21 "**C** is the man who has sexual
27:22 "**C** is the man who sleeps with
27:23 "**C** is the man who sleeps with
27:24 "**C** is the man who kills his neighbor
27:25 "**C** is the man who accepts a bribe
27:26 "**C** is the man who does not uphold
28:16 You will be **c** in the city and **c** in the
Jos 6:26 "**C** before the LORD is the man
1Sa 17:43 the Philistine **c** David by his gods.
2Sa 16: 7 As he **c,** Shimei said, "Get out,
19:21 He **c** the LORD's anointed."
2Ki 9:34 "Take care of that **c** woman,"
Job 1: 5 and **c** God in their hearts."
3: 1 Job opened his mouth and **c** the day
Jer 17: 5 This is what the LORD says: "**C** is
Mal 1:14 "**C** is the cheat who has
Mk 11:21 The fig tree you **c** has withered!"
Ro 9: 3 For I could wish that I myself were **c**
1Co 4:12 When we are **c,** we bless;
12: 3 "Jesus be **c,**" and no one can say,
Gal 3:10 is written: "**C** is everyone who does
3:13 written: "**C** is everyone who is hung
Heb 6: 8 and is in danger of being **c.**
Rev 16: 9 and they **c** the name of God,
16:11 and **c** the God of heaven because

16:21 **c** God on account of the plague of

CURSES [CURSE]

Ge 12: 3 and whoever **c** you I will curse;
Ex 21:17 "Anyone who **c** his father or mother
Lev 20: 9 " 'If anyone **c** his father or mother,
    24:15 'If anyone **c** his God, he will
Nu   5:23 to write these **c** on a scroll
Dt 11:29 and on Mount Ebal the **c.**
    27:13 on Mount Ebal to pronounce **c:**
    28:15 all these **c** will come upon you
Jos 8:34 the blessings and the **c—**
2Ch 34:24 the **c** written in the book
Ne 13:25 I rebuked them and called **c** down
Ps 10: 7 His mouth is full of **c** and lies
Pr 20:20 If a man **c** his father or mother,
    28:27 to them receives many **c.**
Mt 15: 4 and 'Anyone who **c** his father
Mk 14:71 He began to call down **c** on himself,

CURSING [CURSE]

2Sa 16:10 If he is **c** because the LORD said
Ps 109:18 He wore **c** as his garment;
Jer 24: 9 an object of ridicule and **c,**
Hos 4: 2 There is only **c,** lying and murder,
Ro   3:14 "Their mouths are full of **c**
Jas 3:10 the same mouth come praise and **c.**

CURTAIN [CURTAINS]

Ex 26:31 "Make a **c** of blue,
    26:36 to the tent make a **c** of blue,
Mt 27:51 the **c** of the temple was torn in two
Mk 15:38 The **c** of the temple was torn in two
Lk 23:45 the **c** of the temple was torn in two.
Heb 6:19 the inner sanctuary behind the **c,**
     9: 3 the second a room called
    10:20 opened for us through the **c,**

CURTAINS [CURTAIN]

Ex 26: 1 tabernacle with ten **c** of finely
              twisted linen
Nu   3:26 the **c** of the courtyard, the curtain at

CUSH [CUSHITE]

Ge   2:13 through the entire land of **C.**
    10: 6 The sons of Ham: **C,** Mizraim,
Ps   7: T he sang to the LORD concerning **C,**
Isa 20: T and portent against Egypt and **C,**

CUSHITE [CUSH]

Nu 12: 1 against Moses because of his **C** wife,
2Sa 18:21 Then Joab said to a **C,** "Go,
Jer 38: 7 But Ebed-Melech, a **C,** an official

CUSTOM [CUSTOMS]

Job 1: 5 This was Job's regular **c.**
Mk 10: 1 and as was his **c,** he taught them.
    15: 6 it was the **c** at the Feast
Lk   4:16 as was his **c.**
Ac 15: 1 according to the **c** taught by Moses,
    17: 2 As his **c** was,

CUSTOMS [CUSTOM]

Lev 18:30 the detestable **c** that were practiced

20:23 You must not live according to the **c**
Ps 106:35 with the nations and adopted their **c.**
Jer 10: 3 the **c** of the peoples are worthless;
Jn 19:40 in accordance with Jewish burial **c.**
Gal 2:14 force Gentiles to follow Jewish **c?**

CUT [CUTS, CUTTING]

Ge   9:11 Never again will all life be **c** off
    15:10 **c** them in two and arranged
    17:14 will be **c** off from his people;
Ex 34:13 and **c** down their Asherah poles.
Lev 19:27 not **c** the hair at the sides of your
    19:28 " 'Do not **c** your bodies for the dead
    21: 5 of their beards or **c** their bodies.
Dt 20:20 you may **c** down trees
Jos 4: 7 that the flow of the Jordan was **c** off
Jdg 21: 6 "Today one tribe is **c** off
1Sa 17:51 he **c** off his head with the sword.
    24: 4 and **c** off a corner of Saul's robe.
2Sa 14:26 Whenever he **c** the hair
1Ki 3:25 "**C** the living child in two
2Ch 15:16 Asa **c** the pole down,
    31: 1 smashed the sacred stones and **c**
    34: 7 and **c** to pieces all the incense altars
Ps 31:22 "I am **c** off from your sight!"
    37: 9 For evil men will be **c** off,
   118:10 the name of the LORD I **c** them off.
Pr   2:22 wicked will be **c** off from the land,
    10:31 but a perverse tongue will be **c** out.
    23:18 and your hope will not be **c** off
Isa 9:14 So the LORD will **c** off from Israel
    14:22 "I will **c** off from Babylon her name
    51: 1 rock from which you were **c**
    53: 8 For he was **c** off from the land of
Jer 34:18 I will treat like the calf they **c** in two
Eze 37:11 our hope is gone; we are **c** off.'
Da   2:45 the rock **c** out of a mountain,
     9:26 the Anointed One will be **c** off
Mt   3:10 be **c** down and thrown into the fire.
    24:22 If those days had not been **c** short,
Mk   9:43 hand causes you to sin, **c** it off.
    15:46 and placed it in a tomb **c** out of rock.
Jn 18:26 the man whose ear Peter had **c** off,
Ac   2:37 they were **c** to the heart and said
Ro 11:22 Otherwise, you also will be **c** off;
1Co 11: 6 she should have her hair **c** off;

MUST BE CUT OFF See MUST

CUTS [CUT]

Jn 15: 2 He **c** off every branch in me

CUTTING [CUT]

Pr 26: 6 Like **c** off one's feet
Jn 18:10 **c** off his right ear.

CYMBAL* [CYMBALS]

1Co 13: 1 a resounding gong or a clanging **c.**

CYMBALS [CYMBAL]

2Sa 6: 5 lyres, tambourines, sistrums and **c.**
1Ch 15:16 instruments: lyres, harps and **c.**
2Ch 5:12 dressed in fine linen and playing **c,**
    29:25 in the temple of the LORD with **c,**
Ezr 3:10 Levites (the sons of Asaph) with **c,**

Ne 12:27 and with the music of **c,**
Ps 150: 5 praise him with the clash of **c,**

CYPRESS
Ge 6:14 So make yourself an ark of **c** wood;

CYPRUS
Ac 4:36 Joseph, a Levite from **C,**
13: 4 and sailed from there to **C.**

CYRENE
Lk 23:26 they seized Simon from **C,**

CYRUS
Persian king who allowed exiles to return (2Ch 36:22-Ezr 1:8), to rebuild temple (Ezr 5:13-6:14), as appointed by the LORD (Isa 44:28-45:13).

D

DAGON [DAGON'S]
Jdg 16:23 offer a great sacrifice to **D** their god
1Ch 10:10 up his head in the temple of **D.**

DAGON'S [DAGON]
1Sa 5: 2 carried the ark into **D** temple

DAILY [DAY]
1Ki 4:22 Solomon's **d** provisions were thirty
2Ch 8:13 to the **d** requirement
Job 23:12 of his mouth more than my **d** bread.
Ps 68:19 who **d** bears our burdens.
Pr 30: 8 but give me only my **d** bread.
Da 8:13 the vision concerning the **d** sacrifice.
11:31 and will abolish the **d** sacrifice.
Mt 6:11 Give us today our **d** bread.
Lk 9:23 up his cross **d** and follow me.
11: 3 Give us each day our **d** bread.
Jas 2:15 without clothes and **d** food.

DAMASCUS
2Ki 8: 7 Elisha went to **D,**
16:10 He saw an altar in **D**
Isa 7: 8 for the head of Aram is **D,**
17: 1 An oracle concerning **D:**
Jer 49:23 Concerning **D:** "Hamath
Am 1: 3 "For three sins of **D,**
Ac 9: 3 As he neared **D** on his journey,
22: 6 "About noon as I came near **D,**
Gal 1:17 into Arabia and later returned to **D.**

DAMNATION (KJV) See CONDEMNED, CONDEMNATION, DESTRUCTION, JUDGMENT, PUNISHED, SIN

DAN
1. Son of Jacob by Bilhah (Ge 30:4-6; 35:25; 46:23). Tribe of blessed (Ge 49:16-17; Dt 33:22), numbered (Nu 1:39; 26:43), allotted land (Jos 19:40-48; Eze 48:1), failed to fully possess (Jdg 1:34-35), failed to support Deborah (Jdg 5:17), possessed Laish/Dan (Jdg 18).

2. Northernmost city in Israel (Ge 14:14; Jdg 18; 20:1).

DANCE [DANCED, DANCES, DANCING]
Ecc 3: 4 a time to mourn and a time to **d,**
Jer 31: 4 and go out to **d** with the joyful.
31:13 Then maidens will **d** and be glad,
Lk 7:32 and you did not **d;**

DANCED* [DANCE]
1Sa 18: 7 As they **d,** they sang:
2Sa 6:14 **d** before the LORD
1Ki 18:26 And they **d** around
Mt 14: 6 the daughter of Herodias **d** for them
Mk 6:22 of Herodias came in and **d,**

DANCES* [DANCE]
1Sa 21:11 the one they sing about in their **d:**
29: 5 the David they sang about in their **d:**

DANCING [DANCE]
Ex 15:20 with tambourines and **d.**
32:19 the camp and saw the calf and the **d,**
Jdg 11:34 **d** to the sound of tambourines!
21:23 While the girls were **d,**
2Sa 6:16 and **d** before the LORD,
1Ch 15:29 she saw King David **d**
Ps 30:11 You turned my wailing into **d;**
149: 3 Let them praise his name with **d**
La 5:15 our **d** has turned to mourning.

DANGER
Pr 22: 3 prudent man sees **d** and takes refuge,
27:12 The prudent see **d** and take refuge,
Mt 5:22 will be in **d** of the fire of hell.
Ac 19:40 in **d** of being charged with rioting
Ro 8:35 or nakedness or **d**
2Co 11:26 in **d** from my own countrymen, in **d**
Heb 8: 8 and is in **d** of being cursed.

DANIEL
1. Hebrew exile to Babylon, name changed to Belteshazzar (Da 1:6-7). Refused to eat unclean food (Da 1:8-21). Interpreted Nebuchadnezzar's dreams (Da 2; 4), writing on the wall (Da 5). Thrown into lion's den (Da 6). Visions of (Da 7-12).

2. Son of David (1Ch 3:1).

DARE [DARED]
Jn 2:16 How **d** you turn my Father's house
9:34 how **d** you lecture us!"
Ac 7:32 with fear and did not **d** to look.
Ro 5: 7 someone might possibly **d** to die.

DARED [DARE]
Mk 12:34 no one **d** ask him any more questions
Jn 21:12 None of the disciples **d** ask him,

DARIUS
1. King of Persia (Ezr 4:5), allowed rebuilding of temple (Ezr 5-6).
2. Mede who conquered Babylon (Da 5:31).

DARK [DARKENED, DARKENS, DARKNESS]

2Sa	22:10	**d** clouds were under his feet.
2Ch	6: 1	that he would dwell in a **d** cloud;
Job	34:22	There is no **d** place, no deep shadow,
Ps	35: 6	may their path be **d** and slippery,
	139:12	the darkness will not be **d** to you;
Pr	2:13	the straight paths to walk in **d** ways,
	31:15	She gets up while it is still **d**;
SS	1: 5	**D** am I, yet lovely,
Isa	50:10	Let him who walks in the **d**,
Jer	4:28	and the heavens above grow **d**,
Lk	12: 3	in the **d** will be heard in the daylight,
Jn	12:35	The man who walks in the **d** does
Ro	2:19	a light for those who are in the **d**,
Eph	6:12	against the powers of this **d** world
2Pe	1:19	as to a light shining in a **d** place,
Rev	8:12	so that a third of them turned **d**.

DARKENED [DARK]

SS	1: 6	because I am **d** by the sun.
Joel	2:10	the sun and moon are **d**,
Mt	24:29	of those days " 'the sun will be **d**,
Ro	1:21	and their foolish hearts were **d**.
Eph	4:18	They are **d** in their understanding
Rev	9: 2	and sky were **d** by the smoke from

DARKENS* [DARK]

Job	38: 2	"Who is this that **d** my counsel
Am	5: 8	and **d** day into night,

DARKNESS [DARK]

Ge	1: 2	**d** was over the surface of the deep,
	1: 4	and he separated the light from the **d**.
	15:12	and a thick and dreadful **d** came
Ex	10:22	and total **d** covered all Egypt
	14:20	the cloud brought **d** to the one side
	20:21	while Moses approached the thick **d**
Dt	5:23	you heard the voice out of the **d**,
Jos	24: 7	and he put **d** between you and
2Sa	22:29	the LORD turns my **d** into light.
Job	12:22	He reveals the deep things of **d**
Ps	18:11	He made **d** his covering,
	91: 6	nor the pestilence that stalks in the **d**,
	97: 2	Clouds and thick **d** surround him;
	112: 4	Even in **d** light dawns for the upright
	139:12	even the **d** will not be dark to you;
Pr	4:19	the way of the wicked is like deep **d**;
Ecc	2:13	just as light is better than **d**.
	5:17	All his days he eats in **d**,
Isa	5:20	who put **d** for light and light for **d**,
	9: 2	The people walking in **d** have seen
	42:16	the **d** into light before them
	45: 7	I form the light and create **d**,
	58:10	then your light will rise in the **d**,
	61: 1	and release from **d** for the prisoners,
Jer	13:16	before he brings the **d**,
Joel	2:31	The sun will be turned to **d**
Am	5:20	Will not the day of the LORD be **d**,
Na	1: 8	he will pursue his foes into **d**.
Zep	1:15	a day of **d** and gloom,
Mt	4:16	the people living in **d** have seen
	6:23	your whole body will be full of **d**.
	22:13	and throw him outside, into the **d**,
Lk	11:34	your body also is full of **d**.
	23:44	and **d** came over the whole land until
Jn	1: 5	The light shines in the **d**, but the **d** has not understood it.
	3:19	but men loved **d** instead of light
	8:12	in **d**, but will have the light
Ac	2:20	The sun will be turned to **d**
Ro	13:12	let us put aside the deeds of **d**
2Co	4: 6	who said, "Let light shine out of **d**,"
	6:14	fellowship can light have with **d**?
Eph	5: 8	For you were once **d**,
	5:11	to do with the fruitless deeds of **d**,
Col	1:13	rescued us from the dominion of **d**
1Th	5: 5	not belong to the night or to the **d**.
1Pe	2: 9	of him who called you out of **d**
2Pe	2:17	Blackest **d** is reserved for them.
1Jn	1: 5	in him there is no **d** at all.
	2: 8	because the **d** is passing and
	2: 9	but hates his brother is still in the **d**.
Jude	1: 6	in **d**, bound with everlasting chains
	1:13	blackest **d** has been reserved forever.
Rev	16:10	and his kingdom was plunged into **d**.

DARLING

SS	1:15	How beautiful you are, my **d**!
	2:10	"Arise, my **d**, my beautiful one,
	5: 2	my **d**, my dove, my flawless one.

DASH [DASHED]

2Ki	8:12	**d** their little children to the ground,
Ps	2: 9	you will **d** them to pieces
Lk	19:44	They will **d** you to the ground,
Rev	2:27	he will **d** them to pieces

DASHED [DASH]

Hos	10:14	when mothers were **d** to the ground
Na	3:10	Her infants were **d** to pieces at

DATES*

2Sa	6:19	a cake of **d** and a cake of raisins
1Ch	16: 3	a cake of **d** and a cake of raisins
Ac	1: 7	not for you to know the times or **d**
1Th	5: 1	and **d** we do not need to write to you,

DATHAN*

Involved in Korah's rebellion against Moses and Aaron (Nu 16:1-27; 26:9; Dt 11:6; Ps 106:17).

DAUGHTER [DAUGHTER-IN-LAW, DAUGHTERS, DAUGHTERS-IN-LAW, GRANDDAUGHTER, GRANDDAUGHTERS]

Ge	19:31	the older **d** said to the younger,
	24:24	"I am the **d** of Bethuel,
	29:10	When Jacob saw Rachel **d** of Laban,
	34: 3	His heart was drawn to Dinah **d**
	38: 2	There Judah met the **d** of
Ex	2: 5	Then Pharaoh's **d** went down to
	21: 7	"If a man sells his **d** as a servant,
Lev	12: 5	If she gives birth to a **d**
Nu	27: 8	turn his inheritance over to his **d**.
Jdg	11:34	come out to meet him but his **d**,

Ru 2: 2 Naomi said to her, "Go ahead, my **d.**
    3: 10 "The LORD bless you, my **d,"**
1Sa 18: 20 Now Saul's **d** Michal was in love
2Sa 6: 16 Michal **d** of Saul watched from
1Ki 11: 1 foreign women besides Pharaoh's **d**
Est 2: 7 Mordecai had taken her as his own **d**
Ps   9: 14 of the **D** of Zion and there rejoice
    137: 8 O **D** of Babylon,
Isa 47: 1 sit in the dust, Virgin **D** of Babylon;
    52: 2 O captive **D** of Zion.
    62: 11 "Say to the **D** of Zion,
Jer 6: 2 I will destroy the **D** of Zion,
    46: 11 O Virgin **D** of Egypt.
Eze 16: 45 You are a true **d** of your mother,
Mic 7: 6 a **d** rises up against her mother,
Zep 3: 14 Sing, O **D** of Zion;
Zec 9: 9 Rejoice greatly, O **D** of Zion!
     9: 9 Shout, **D** of Jerusalem!
Mal 2: 11 by marrying the **d** of a foreign god.
Mt 14: 6 the **d** of Herodias danced for them
    15: 28 her **d** was healed from that very hour
Mk   5: 35 "Your **d** is dead," they said.
     7: 29 the demon has left your **d."**
Lk 12: 53 mother against **d** and **d** against

DAUGHTER OF JERUSALEM 2Ki 19:21;
Isa 37:22; La 2:13, 15; Mic 4:8; Zep 3:14; Zec
9:9

DAUGHTER OF ZION 2Ki 19:21; Ps 9:14; Isa
1:8; 10:32; 16:1; 37:22; 52:2; 62:11; Jer 4:31;
6:2, 23; La 1:6; 2:1, 4, 8, 10, 13, 18; 4:22; Mic
1:13; 4:8, 10, 13; Zep 3:14; Zec 2:10; 9:9; Mt
21:5; Jn 12:15

DAUGHTER-IN-LAW [DAUGHTER]

Ge 11: 31 and his **d** Sarai,
    38: 16 Not realizing that she was his **d,**
Lev 20: 12 " 'If a man sleeps with his **d,**
Ru   1: 22 Ruth the Moabitess, her **d,**
1Ch 2: 4 Judah's **d,** bore him Perez and Zerah.
Mic 7: 6 a **d** against her mother-in-law—
Mt 10: 35 a **d** against her mother-in-law—

DAUGHTERS [DAUGHTER]

Ge   6: 4 the sons of God went to the **d** of men
    19: 36 So both of Lot's **d** became pregnant
    29: 16 Now Laban had two **d;**
Ex   2: 16 Now a priest of Midian had seven **d,**
Nu 27: 1 So Zelophehad son of Hepher,
    36: 36 So Zelophehad's **d** did as
Dt   7: 3 Do not give your **d** to their sons
    12: 31 even burn their sons and **d** in the fire
Ezr 9: 12 do not give your **d** in marriage
Job 42: 15 women as beautiful as Job's **d,**
Ps 144: 12 and our **d** will be like pillars carved
Pr 30: 15 "The leech has two **d.**
SS   1: 5 yet lovely, O **d** of Jerusalem,
Eze 23: 2 **d** of the same mother.
Joel 2: 28 Your sons and **d** will prophesy,
Lk 23: 28 **D** of Jerusalem, do not weep for me;
Ac   2: 17 Your sons and **d** will prophesy,
    21: 9 four unmarried **d** who prophesied.
2Co 6: 18 and you will be my sons and **d,**
1Pe 3: 6 You are her **d** if you do what is right

DAUGHTERS OF JERUSALEM SS 1:5;
2:7; 3:5, 10; 5:8, 16; 8:4; Lk 23:28

DAUGHTERS-IN-LAW
[DAUGHTER]

Ru   1: 8 Then Naomi said to her two **d,**

DAVID

Son of Jesse (Ru 4:17-22; 1Ch 2:13-15), ancestor of Jesus (Mt 1:1-17; Lk 3:31). Wives and
children (1Sa 18; 25:39-44; 2Sa 3:2-5; 5:13-16;
11:27; 1Ch 3:1-9).
    Anointed king by Samuel (1Sa 16:1-13).
Musician to Saul (1Sa 16:14-23; 18:10). Killed
Goliath (1Sa 17). Relation with Jonathan (1Sa
18:1-4; 19-20; 23:16-18; 2Sa 1). Disfavor of Saul
(1Sa 18:6-23:29). Spared Saul's life (1Sa 24; 26).
Among Philistines (1Sa 21:10-14; 27-30). Lament
for Saul and Jonathan (2Sa 1).
    Anointed king of Judah (2Sa 2:1-11). Conflict
with house of Saul (2Sa 2-4). Anointed king of
Israel (2Sa 5:1-4; 1Ch 11:1-3). Conquered Jerusalem (2Sa 5:6-10; 1Ch 11;4-9). Brought ark to Jerusalem (2Sa 6; 1Ch 13; 15-16). The LORD
promised eternal dynasty (2Sa 7; 1Ch 17; Ps 132).
Showed kindness to Mephibosheth (2Sa 9). Adultery with Bathsheba, murder of Uriah (2Sa 11-12).
Son Amnon raped daughter Tamar; killed by Absalom (2Sa 13). Absalom's revolt (2Sa 14-17);
death (2Sa 18). Sheba's revolt (2Sa 20). Victories:
Philistines (2Sa 5:17-25; 21:15-22; 1Ch 14:8-17;
20:4-8), Ammonites (2Sa 10; 1Ch 19), various
(2Sa 8; 1Ch 18). Mighty men (2Sa 23:8-39; 1Ch
11-12). Punished for numbering army (2Sa 24;
1Ch 21). Appointed Solomon king (1Ki 1:28-2:9).
Prepared for building of temple (1Ch 22-29). Last
words (2Sa 23:1-7). Death (1Ki 2:10-12; 1Ch
29:28).
    Psalmist (Mt 22:43-45), musician (Am 6:5),
prophet (2Sa 23:2-7; Ac 1:16; 2:30).
    Psalms of: 2 (Ac 4:25), 3-32, 34-41, 51-65,
68-70, 86, 95 (Heb 4:7), 101, 103, 108-110, 122,
124, 131, 133, 138-145.

CITY OF DAVID See CITY

HOUSE OF DAVID See HOUSE

SON OF DAVID See SON

DAWN [DAWNED, DAWNS]

Job 38: 12 or shown the **d** its place,
Ps 37: 6 righteousness shine like the **d,**
    57: 8 I will awaken the **d.**
    139: 9 If I rise on the wings of the **d,**
Pr   4: 18 like the first gleam of **d,**
SS   6: 10 Who is this that appears like the **d,**
Isa 14: 12 O morning star, son of the **d!**
    62: 1 righteousness shines out like the **d,**
Am   4: 13 he who turns **d** to darkness,
Mt 28: 1 at **d** on the first day of the week,

DAWNED [DAWN]

Isa 9: 2 of the shadow of death a light has **d.**
Mt   4: 16 of the shadow of death a light has **d.**

DAWNS* [DAWN]

Ps	65: 8	where morning **d** and evening fades
	112: 4	in darkness light **d** for the upright,
Hos	10:15	When that day **d,**
2Pe	1:19	the day **d** and the morning star rises

DAY [DAILY, DAY'S, DAYBREAK, DAYLIGHT, DAYS, MIDDAY]

Ge	1: 5	God called the light **"d,"**
	1: 5	the first **d.**
	1: 8	the second **d.**
	1:13	the third **d.**
	1:19	the fourth **d.**
	1:23	the fifth **d.**
	1:31	the sixth **d.**
	2: 2	By the seventh **d** God had finished
	2: 2	so on the seventh **d** he rested
	8:22	**d** and night will never cease."
Ex	12:17	Celebrate this **d** as a lasting
	13:21	By **d** the LORD went ahead of them
	16:30	the people rested on the seventh **d.**
	20: 8	the Sabbath **d** by keeping it holy.
	40: 2	on the first **d** of the first month.
Lev	12: 3	On the eighth **d** the boy is to
	16:30	on this **d** atonement will be made
	23:28	because it is the **D** of Atonement,
Nu	14:14	before them in a pillar of cloud by **d**
Dt	1:33	in fire by night and in a cloud by **d,**
	24:15	Pay him his wages each **d**
	30:19	This **d** I call heaven and earth
	34: 6	but to this **d** no one knows
Jos	1: 8	meditate on it **d** and night,
	10:14	There has never been a **d** like it
2Ki	7: 9	This is a **d** of good news
	25:30	**D** by **d** the king gave Jehoiachin
1Ch	16:23	all the earth; proclaim his salvation
	16:23	proclaim his salvation day after **d.**
Ne	8:10	This **d** is sacred to our Lord.
	8:18	**D** after **d,** from the first **d** to the last,
Ps	1: 2	on his law he meditates **d** and night.
	19: 2	**D** after **d** they pour forth speech;
	37:13	for he knows their **d** is coming.
	50:15	and call upon me in the **d** of trouble;
	84:10	Better is one **d** in your courts than
	96: 2	proclaim his salvation **d** after **d.**
	118:24	This is the **d** the LORD has made;
	119:97	I meditate on it all **d** long.
	119:164	Seven times a **d** I praise you
Pr	11: 4	Wealth is worthless in the **d** of wrath
	27: 1	not know what a **d** may bring forth.
Ecc	7: 1	and the **d** of death better than the **d**
Isa	2:12	The LORD Almighty has a **d**
	13: 9	See, the **d** of the LORD is coming—
	49: 8	in the **d** of salvation I will help you;
	60:19	sun will no more be your light by **d,**
	66: 8	Can a country be born in a **d**
Jer	17:22	but keep the Sabbath **d** holy,
	30: 7	How awful that **d** will be!
	46:10	But that **d** belongs to the Lord,
	50:31	"for your **d** has come,
Eze	4: 6	a **d** for each year.
	7: 7	The time has come, the **d** is near;
	30: 2	"Alas for that **d!**"

Da	6:13	He still prays three times a **d.**"
Joel	1:15	For the **d** of the LORD is near;
	2:31	great and dreadful **d** of the LORD.
Am	3:14	"On the **d** I punish Israel for her sins,
	5:20	not the **d** of the LORD be darkness,
Ob	1:15	"The **d** of the LORD is near
Mic	7: 4	the **d** God visits you.
Hab	3:16	Yet I will wait patiently for the **d**
Zep	1:14	"The great **d** of the LORD is near—
	3: 5	and every new **d** he does not fail,
Zec	2:11	joined with the LORD in that **d**
	14: 1	A **d** of the LORD is coming
	14: 7	It will be a unique **d,**
Mal	3: 2	who can endure the **d** of his coming?
	4: 5	and dreadful **d** of the LORD comes.
Mt	10:15	and Gomorrah on the **d** of judgment
	12:36	to give account on the **d** of judgment
	20:19	the third **d** he will be raised to life!"
	24:38	up to the **d** Noah entered the ark;
	25:13	you do not know the **d** or the hour.
	28: 1	at dawn on the first **d** of the week,
Lk	1:59	the eighth **d** they came to circumcise
	2:21	On the eighth **d,** when it was time
	11: 3	Give us each **d** our daily bread.
	17:24	the Son of Man in his **d** will be like
	24:46	and rise from the dead on the third **d,**
Jn	6:40	and I will raise him up at the last **d.**"
Ac	2: 1	When the **d** of Pentecost came,
	2:20	the great and glorious **d** of the Lord.
	2:46	Every **d** they continued to meet
	5:42	**D** after **d,** in the temple courts
	17:11	and examined the Scriptures every **d**
	17:31	a **d** when he will judge
Ro	2: 5	for the **d** of God's wrath,
	14: 5	considers one **d** more sacred than
1Co	5: 5	and his spirit saved on the **d** of
	15: 4	that he was raised on the third **d**
	15:31	I die every **d**—
2Co	4:16	we are being renewed **d** by **d.**
	6: 2	in the **d** of salvation I helped you."
	11:25	a night and a **d** in the open sea,
Eph	4:30	were sealed for the **d** of redemption.
	6:13	so that when the **d** of evil comes,
Php	1: 6	until the **d** of Christ Jesus.
1Th	5: 2	that the **d** of the Lord will come like
	5: 8	But since we belong to the **d,**
2Th	2: 2	the **d** of the Lord has already come.
Heb	7:27	not need to offer sacrifices **d** after **d,**
2Pe	3: 8	the Lord a **d** is like a thousand years, and a thousand years are like a **d.**
	3:10	**d** of the Lord will come like a thief.
1Jn	4:17	we will have confidence on the **d**
Jude	1: 6	for judgment on the great **D.**
Rev	1:10	On the Lord's **D** I was in the Spirit,
	6:17	the great **d** of their wrath has come,
	8:12	A third of the **d** was without light,
	16:14	on the great **d** of God Almighty.
	20:10	They will be tormented **d** and night
	21:25	On no **d** will its gates ever be shut.

DAY OF THE †LORD Isa 13:6, 9; Eze 13:5; 30:3; Joel 1:15; 2:1, 11, 31; 3:14; Am 5:18, 18, 20; Ob 1:15; Zep 1:7, 14, 14; Zec 14:1; Mal 4:5

THIRD DAY Ge 1:13; 22:4; 31:22; 40:20; 42:18;

Ex 19:11, 15, 16; Lev 7:17, 18; 19:6, 7; Nu 7:24;
19:12, 29:20; Jos 9:17; Jdg 20:30; 1Sa 30:1; 2Sa
1:2; 1Ki 3:18; 2Ki 20:5, 8; Ezr 6:15; Est 5:1; Hos
6:2; Mt 16:21; 17:23; 20:19; 27:64; Lk 9:22;
13:32; 18:33; 24:7, 21, 46; Jn 2:1; Ac 10:40;
27:19; 1Co 15:4

DAY'S [DAY]

1Ki 19: 4 while he himself went a **d** journey
Ac   1:12 a Sabbath **d** walk from the city.

DAYBREAK [DAY]

Ge 32:24 and a man wrestled with him till **d.**
Ex 14:27 at **d** the sea went back to its place.
Lk   4:42 At **d** Jesus went out to
     22:66 At **d** at the council of the elders of
Ac   5:21 At **d** they entered the temple courts,

DAYLIGHT [DAY, LIGHT]

2Sa 12:12 but I will do this thing in broad **d**
Mt 10:27 speak in the **d;**
Lk 12: 3 in the dark will be heard in the **d,**
2Pe 2:13 of pleasure is to carouse in broad **d.**

DAYS [DAY]

Ge 1:14 to mark seasons and **d** and years,
    3:14 and you will eat dust all the **d**
    3:17 eat of it all the **d** of your life.
    7: 4 will send rain on the earth for forty **d**
Ex 24:18 mountain forty **d** and forty nights.
    34:28 the LORD forty **d** and forty nights
Nu 13:25 At the end of forty **d** they returned
    14:34 for each of the forty **d** you explored
Dt 17:19 and he is to read it all the **d** of his life
    32: 7 Remember the **d** of old;
Jdg 17: 6 In those **d** Israel had no king;
    18: 1 In those **d** Israel had no king.
    21:25 In those **d** Israel had no king;
1Sa 17:16 For forty **d** the Philistine
1Ki 19: 8 he traveled forty **d** and forty nights
Ps 21: 4 you gave it to him—length of **d,**
    23: 6 and love will follow me all the **d**
    34:12 and desires to see many good **d,**
    39: 5 You have made my **d**
    90:10 length of our **d** is seventy years—
    90:12 Teach us to number our **d** aright,
   103:15 As for man, his **d** are like grass,
   128: 5 from Zion all the **d** of your life;
Pr 9:11 For through me your **d** will be many,
   31:11 not harm, all the **d** of her life.
Ecc 9: 9 all the **d** of this meaningless life
   12: 1 Creator in the **d** of your youth,
Isa 43:13 Yes, and from ancient **d** I am he.
   53:10 and prolong his **d,**
Da 7: 9 and the Ancient of **D** took his seat.
    7:13 He approached the Ancient of **D**
    7:22 Ancient of **D** came and pronounced
   12:11 there will be 1,290 **d.**
   12:12 and reaches the end of the 1,335 **d.**
Hos 3: 5 and to his blessings in the last **d.**
Joel 2:29 I will pour out my Spirit in those **d.**
Mt 4: 2 After fasting forty **d** and forty nights,
Mk 1:13 and he was in the desert forty **d,**
   10:34 Three **d** later he will rise."

Lk 4: 2 forty **d** he was tempted by the devil.
   19:43 The **d** will come upon you
Ac 1: 3 to them over a period of forty **d**
    2:17 " 'In the last **d,** God says,
Gal 4:10 You are observing special **d**
Eph 5:16 because the **d** are evil.
2Ti 3: 1 be terrible times in the last **d.**
Heb 1: 2 in these last **d** he has spoken to us
2Pe 3: 3 that in the last **d** scoffers will come,
Rev 11: 3 and they will prophesy for 1,260 **d,**
   11:11 the three and a half **d** a breath of life
   12: 6 be taken care of for 1,260 **d.**

DAYS ARE COMING Jer 7:32; 9:25; 16:14;
19:6; 23:5, 7; 30:3; 31:27, 38; 33:14; 48:12; 49:2;
51:52; Am 8:11; 9:13

DAYS TO COME Ge 49:1; Ex 13:14; Nu
24:14; Dt 31:29; Pr 31:25; Ecc 2:16; Isa 27:6;
30:8; Jer 23:20; 30:24; 48:47; 49:39; Eze 38:16;
Da 2:28

FORTY DAYS See FORTY

DAYSMAN (KJV) See ARBITRATE

DAYSPRING (KJV) See DAWN, RISING SUN

DAZZLING*

Da 2:31 **d** statue, awesome in appearance.
Mk 9: 3 His clothes became **d** white,

DEACON* [DEACONS]

1Ti 3:12 A **d** must be the husband of

DEACONS* [DEACON]

Php 1: 1 together with the overseers and **d:**
1Ti 3: 8 **D,** likewise, are to be men worthy
    3:10 let them serve as **d.**

DEAD [DIE]

Ex 12:30 not a house without someone **d.**
Lev 17:15 who eats anything found **d** or torn
   19:28 " 'Do not cut your bodies for the **d**
Nu 16:48 stood between the living and the **d,**
Dt 18:11 or spiritist or who consults the **d.**
Ru 4: 5 you acquire the **d** man's widow,
Ps 6: 5 No one remembers you when he is **d.**
   115:17 It is not the **d** who praise the LORD,
Pr 2:18 and her paths to the spirits of the **d.**
Ecc 9: 4 a live dog is better off than a **d** lion!
Isa 8:19 Why consult the **d** on behalf of
Mt 8:22 and let the **d** bury their own **d."**
    9:24 The girl is not **d** but asleep."
   10: 8 Heal the sick, raise the **d,**
   11: 5 the deaf hear, the **d** are raised,
   14: 2 he has risen from the **d!**
   28: 7 'He has risen from the **d**
Mk 12:27 He is not the God of the **d,**
Lk 15:24 of mine was **d** and is alive again;
   20:37 even Moses showed that the **d** rise,
   24: 5 look for the living among the **d?**
   24:46 and rise from the **d** on the third day,
Jn 5:21 For just as the Father raises the **d**
   11:44 The **d** man came out,
   20: 9 that Jesus had to rise from the **d.)**

| | 21:14 | after he was raised from the **d.** |

Ac   2:24 But God raised him from the **d,**
Ro   6:11 count yourselves **d** to sin but alive
1Co   15:12 Christ has been raised from the **d,**
      15:29 who are baptized for the **d?**
2Co   4:14 the **d** will also raise us with Jesus
Eph   2: 1 you were **d** in your transgressions
       5:14 O sleeper, rise from the **d,**
Php   3:11 attain to the resurrection from the **d.**
Col   2:13 When you were **d** in your sins and in
1Th   4:16 and the **d** in Christ will rise first.
2Ti   4: 1 who will judge the living and the **d,**
Heb   11:19 that God could raise the **d,**
Jas   2:26 so faith without deeds is **d.**
1Pe   4: 5 to judge the living and the **d.**
Rev   1: 5 the firstborn from the **d,**
       1:18 I am the Living One; I was **d,**
      11:18 The time has come for judging the **d,**
      14:13 Blessed are the **d** who die
      20:12 The **d** were judged according to what

DEADENED* [DIE]

Jn   12:40 and **d** their hearts,

DEAF

Ex   4:11 Who makes him **d** or mute?
Lev   19:14 " 'Do not curse the **d**
Pr   28: 9 If anyone turns a **d** ear to the law,
Isa   29:18 In that day the **d** will hear the words
      35: 5 and the ears of the **d** unstopped.
      42:19 and **d** like the messenger I send?
Lk   7:22 the **d** hear, the dead are raised,

DEAL [DEALING, DEALT]

Ex   8:22 " 'But on that day I will **d** differently
2Ch   6:30 and **d** with each man according
Heb   5: 2 He is able to **d** gently

DEALING [DEAL]

2Sa   7:19 Is this your usual way of **d** with man,

DEALT [DEAL]

Ps   18:20 The LORD has **d** with me according
1Th   2:11 that we **d** with each of you as

DEAR* [DEARER, DEARLY]

2Sa   1:26 my brother; you were very **d** to me.
Ps   102:14 For her stones are **d** to your servants;
Jer   31:20 Is not Ephraim my **d** son,
Jn   2: 4 "**D** woman, why do you involve me?
      19:26 he said to his mother, "**D** woman,
Ac   15:25 to you with our **d** friends Barnabas
Ro   16: 5 Greet my **d** friend Epenetus,
      16: 9 and my **d** friend Stachys,
      16:12 Greet my **d** friend Persis,
1Co   4:14 but to warn you, as my **d** children,
      10:14 my **d** friends, flee from idolatry.
      15:58 Therefore, my **d** brothers, stand firm.
2Co   7: 1 **d** friends, let us purify ourselves
      12:19 **d** friends, is for your strengthening.
Gal   4:19 My **d** children,
Eph   6:21 the **d** brother and faithful servant in
Php   2:12 Therefore, my **d** friends,
       4: 1 in the Lord, **d** friends!

Col   1: 7 our **d** fellow servant,
       4: 7 He is a **d** brother,
       4: 9 our faithful and **d** brother,
       4:14 Our **d** friend Luke, the doctor,
1Th   2: 8 because you had become so **d** to us.
1Ti   6: 2 and **d** to them.
2Ti   1: 2 To Timothy, my **d** son:
Phm   1: 1 To Philemon our **d** friend
       1:16 but better than a slave, as a **d** brother.
       1:16 He is very **d** to me but even dearer
Heb   6: 9 we speak like this, **d** friends,
Jas   1:16 Don't be deceived, my **d** brothers.
       1:19 My **d** brothers, take note of this:
       2: 5 Listen, my **d** brothers:
1Pe   2:11 **D** friends, I urge you,
       4:12 **D** friends, do not be surprised at
2Pe   3: 1 **D** friends, this is
       3: 8 not forget this one thing, **d** friends:
       3:14 So then, **d** friends,
       3:15 as our **d** brother Paul also wrote you
       3:17 Therefore, **d** friends,
1Jn   2: 1 My **d** children, I write this
       2: 7 **D** friends, I am not writing you
       2:12 I write to you, **d** children,
       2:13 I write to you, **d** children,
       2:18 **D** children, this is the last hour;
       2:28 And now, **d** children,
       3: 2 **D** friends, now we are children
       3: 7 **D** children, do not let
       3:18 **D** children, let us not love
       3:21 **D** friends, if our hearts do
       4: 1 **D** friends, do not believe every spirit,
       4: 4 **d** children, are from God
       4: 7 **D** friends, let us love one another,
       4:11 **D** friends, since God so loved us,
       5:21 **D** children, keep yourselves
2Jn   1: 5 And now, **d** lady,
3Jn   1: 1 The elder, To my **d** friend Gaius,
       1: 2 **D** friend, I pray that you may
       1: 5 **D** friend, you are faithful
       1:11 **D** friend, do not imitate what is evil
Jude   1: 3 **D** friends, although I was very eager
       1:17 **d** friends, remember what
       1:20 But you, **d** friends,

DEARER* [DEAR]

Phm   1:16 dear to me but even **d** to you,

DEARLY* [DEAR]

Hos   4:18 rulers **d** love shameful ways.
Eph   5: 1 as **d** loved children
Col   3:12 holy and **d** loved,

DEATH [DIE]

Ex   21:12 and kills him shall surely be put to **d.**
      21:15 or his mother must be put to **d.**
      21:16 when he is caught must be put to **d.**
      21:17 or mother must be put to **d.**
      22:19 with an animal must be put to **d,**
      23: 7 an innocent or honest person to **d,**
      31:14 must be put to **d;**
      31:15 on the Sabbath day must be put to **d.**
Nu   35:16 the murderer shall be put to **d.**
Dt   13: 5 or dreamer must be put to **d,**

17: 6 but no one shall be put to **d** on
30: 19 that I have set before you life and **d**,
32:39 I put to **d** and I bring to life,
Ru   1:17 if anything but **d** separates you
2Ki 4:40 there is **d** in the pot!"
     19:35 the LORD went out and put to **d**
2Ch 23:15 and there they put her to **d**.
      25: 4 nor children put to **d** for their fathers;
Job 26: 6 **D** is naked before God;
Ps 18: 4 The cords of **d** entangled me;
    23: 4 the valley of the shadow of **d**,
    44:22 for your sake we face **d** all day long;
    89:48 What man can live and not see **d**,
   116:15 of the LORD is the **d** of his saints.
Pr   5: 5 Her feet go down to **d**;
     8:36 all who hate me love **d**."
    10: 2 but righteousness delivers from **d**.
    11:19 he who pursues evil goes to his **d**.
    14:12 but in the end it leads to **d**.
    15:11 **D** and Destruction lie open before
    16:25 but in the end it leads to **d**.
    18:21 tongue has the power of life and **d**,
    19:18 not be a willing party to his **d**.
    21:25 sluggard's craving will be the **d**
    23:14 the rod and save his soul from **d**.
    27:20 **D** and Destruction are never satisfied
Ecc 7: 2 for **d** is the destiny of every man;
SS   8: 6 for love is as strong as **d**,
Isa 9: 2 the shadow of **d** a light has dawned.
    25: 8 he will swallow up **d** forever.
    53:12 he poured out his life unto **d**,
Jer 15: 2 " 'Those destined for **d**, to **d**;
    26:16 man should not be sentenced to **d**!
Eze 18:23 any pleasure in the **d** of the wicked?
    18:32 I take no pleasure in the **d** of anyone,
    33:11 I take no pleasure in the **d** of
Hos 13:14 Where, O **d**, are your plagues?
Mt 10:21 "Brother will betray brother to **d**,
    16:28 not taste **d** before they see the Son
    26:66 "He is worthy of **d**," they answered.
Jn   5:24 he has crossed over from **d** to life.
     8:51 he will never see **d**."
Ac   2:24 freeing him from the agony of **d**,
     8: 1 giving approval to his **d**.
Ro   4:25 over to **d** for our sins and was raised
     5:12 and in this way **d** came to all men,
     6: 3 were baptized into his **d**?
     6:23 For the wages of sin is **d**,
     7:24 will rescue me from this body of **d**?
     8:13 the Spirit you put to **d** the misdeeds
     8:36 your sake we face **d** all day long;
1Co 15:21 For since **d** came through a man,
    15:26 The last enemy to be destroyed is **d**.
    15:55 "Where, O **d**, is your victory?
2Co 4:10 around in our body the **d** of Jesus,
Php 2: 8 obedient to **d**—even **d** on a cross!
2Ti 1:10 who has destroyed **d**
Heb 2:14 by his **d** he might destroy him who
          holds the power of **d**—
Jas 5:20 will save him from **d**
1Jn 3:14 that we have passed from **d** to life,
          There is a sin that leads to **d**.
Rev 1:18 And I hold the keys of **d** and Hades.
     2:11 not be hurt at all by the second **d**.

6: 8 Its rider was named **D**,
9: 6 During those days men will seek **d**,
20: 6 second **d** has no power over them,
20:14 Then **d** and Hades were thrown into
20:14 The lake of fire is the second **d**.
21: 4 There will be no more **d** or mourning
21: 8 This is the second **d**."

MUST BE PUT TO DEATH See MUST

PUT ... TO DEATH See PUT

DEBATE* [DEBATED, DEBATING]
Ac 15: 2 into sharp dispute and **d** with them.
    18:28 refuted the Jews in public **d**,

DEBATED* [DEBATE]
Ac   9:29 and **d** with the Grecian Jews,

DEBATING* [DEBATE]
Mk 12:28 of the law came and heard them **d**.

DEBAUCHERY*
Ro 13:13 not in sexual immorality and **d**,
2Co 12:21 and **d** in which they have indulged.
Gal 5:19 impurity and **d**;
Eph 5:18 which leads to **d**.
1Pe 4: 3 living in **d**, lust, drunkenness,

DEBIR
Jos 12:13 king of **D** one the king of Geder one
Jdg 1:11 **D** (formerly called Kiriath Sepher).

DEBORAH
1. Prophetess who led Israel to victory over
Canaanites (Jdg 4-5).
2. Rebekah's nurse (Ge 35:8).

DEBT* [DEBTOR, DEBTORS, DEBTS]
Dt 15: 3 cancel any **d** your brother owes you.
    24: 6 as security for a **d**,
1Sa 22: 2 All those who were in distress or in **d**
Job 24: 9 of the poor is seized for a **d**.
Mt 18:25 that he had been sold to repay the **d**.
    18:27 canceled the **d** and let him go.
    18:30 into prison until he could pay the **d**.
    18:32 'I canceled all that **d** of yours
Lk   7:43 the bigger **d** canceled."
Ro 13: 8 Let no **d** remain outstanding,
    13: 8 the continuing **d** to love one another,

DEBTOR* [DEBT]
Isa 24: 2 for **d** as for creditor.

DEBTORS* [DEBT]
Hab 2: 7 Will not your **d** suddenly arise?
Mt   6:12 as we also have forgiven our **d**.
Lk 16: 5 called in each one of his master's **d**.

DEBTS* [DEBT]
Dt 15: 1 every seven years you must cancel **d**.
    15: 2 for canceling **d** has been proclaimed.
    15: 9 the year for canceling **d**, is near,"
    31:10 in the year for canceling **d**,
2Ki 4: 7 "Go, sell the oil and pay your **d**.
Ne 10:31 the land and will cancel all **d**.

Pr   22:26   in pledge or puts up security for **d**;
Mt   6:12   Forgive us our **d,**
Lk   7:42   so he canceled the **d** of both.

DECAPOLIS

Mt   4:25   Large crowds from Galilee, the **D,**

DECAY*

Ps   16:10   nor will you let your Holy One see **d.**
     49: 9   on forever and not see **d.**
     49:14   their forms will **d** in the grave.
Pr   12: 4   but a disgraceful wife is like **d**
Isa   5:24   so their roots will **d**
Hab   3:16   **d** crept into my bones,
Ac   2:27   nor will you let your Holy One see **d.**
      2:31   nor did his body see **d.**
     13:34   never to **d,** is stated in these words:
     13:35   not let your Holy One see **d.'**
     13:37   from the dead did not see **d.**
Ro   8:21   from its bondage to **d** and brought

DECEIT [DECEIVE]

Job 15:35   birth to evil; their womb fashions **d."**
     27: 4   and my tongue will utter no **d.**
Ps   5: 9   with their tongue they speak **d.**
     32: 2   and in whose spirit is no **d.**
    101: 7   No one who practices **d** will dwell
Pr   26:24   but in his heart he harbors **d.**
Isa 53: 9   nor was any **d** in his mouth.
Jer   5:27   their houses are full of **d;**
Da   8:25   He will cause **d** to prosper,
Zep   3:13   nor will **d** be found in their mouths.
Zec 10: 2   The idols speak **d,**
Mk   7:22   malice, **d,** lewdness, envy, slander,
Ac   13:10   of all kinds of **d** and trickery.
Ro   1:29   murder, strife, **d** and malice.
      3:13   their tongues practice **d."**
1Pe   2: 1   rid yourselves of all malice and all **d,**
      2:22   and no **d** was found in his mouth."

DECEITFUL [DECEIVE]

Ps   17: 1   does not rise from **d** lips.
    119:29   Keep me from **d** ways;
Pr   12: 5   but the advice of the wicked is **d.**
     14:25   but a false witness is **d.**
     15: 4   but a **d** tongue crushes the spirit.
Jer 17: 9   The heart is **d** above all things and
Hos 10: 2   Their heart is **d,**
2Co 11:13   false apostles, **d** workmen,
Eph   4:14   craftiness of men in their **d** scheming
      4:22   corrupted by its **d** desires;
1Pe   3:10   from evil and his lips from **d** speech.
Rev 21:27   who does what is shameful or **d,**

DECEITFULNESS* [DECEIVE]

Ps 119:118   for their **d** is in vain.
Mt   13:22   and the **d** of wealth choke it,
Mk   4:19   the **d** of wealth and the desires
Heb   3:13   may be hardened by sin's **d.**

DECEIVE [DECEIT, DECEITFUL,
   DECEITFULNESS, DECEIVED,

   DECEIVER, DECEIVERS, DECEIVES,
   DECEIVING, DECEPTION, DECEPTIVE]

Lev 19:11   " 'Do not **d** one another.
Jos   9:22   "Why did you **d** us by saying,
1Sa 19:17   "Why did you **d** me like this
Job 13: 9   you **d** him as you might **d** men?
Pr   14: 5   A truthful witness does not **d,**
     24:28   or use your lips to **d.**
Jer 29: 8   and diviners among you **d** you.
     37: 9   Do not **d** yourselves,
Zec 13: 4   garment of hair in order to **d.**
Mt   24: 5   'I am the Christ,' and will **d** many.
     24:11   will appear and **d** many people.
     24:24   great signs and miracles to **d**
Mk   13: 6   claiming, 'I am he,' and will **d** many.
     13:22   and perform signs and miracles to **d**
Ro   16:18   By smooth talk and flattery they **d**
1Co   3:18   Do not **d** yourselves.
Eph   5: 6   Let no one **d** you with empty words,
Col   2: 4   so that no one may **d** you
2Th   2: 3   Don't let anyone **d** you in any way,
Jas   1:22   and so **d** yourselves.
1Jn   1: 8   we **d** ourselves and the truth is not
Rev 20: 8   to **d** the nations in the four corners of

DECEIVED [DECEIVE]

Ge   3:13   The woman said, "The serpent **d** me,
     31:20   Jacob **d** Laban the Aramean by
Jer 20: 7   O Lord, you **d** me, and I was **d;**
Hos   7:11   easily **d** and senseless—
Ob   1: 3   The pride of your heart has **d** you,
Lk   21: 8   "Watch out that you are not **d.**
Jn   7:47   "You mean he has **d** you also?"
Ro   7:11   by the commandment, **d** me,
1Co   6: 9   Do not be **d:**
2Co 11: 3   Eve was **d** by the serpent's cunning,
Gal   6: 7   Do not be **d:** God cannot be mocked.
1Ti   2:14   And Adam was not the one **d;** it was
             the woman who was **d**
2Ti   3:13   deceiving and being **d.**
Tit   3: 3   **d** and enslaved by all kinds of
Jas   1:16   Don't be **d,** my dear brothers.
Rev 13:14   he **d** the inhabitants of the earth.
     20:10   And the devil, who **d** them,

DECEIVER* [DECEIVE]

Job 12:16   both deceived and **d** are his.
Jer   9: 4   For every brother is a **d,**
Mic   2:11   If a liar and **d** comes and says,
Mt   27:63   while he was still alive that **d** said,
2Jn   1: 7   Any such person is the **d** and

DECEIVERS* [DECEIVE]

Ps   49: 5   when wicked **d** surround me—
Tit   1:10   mere talkers and **d,**
2Jn   1: 7   Many **d,** who do not acknowledge

DECEIVES* [DECEIVE]

Pr   26:19   a man who **d** his neighbor and says,
Jer   9: 5   Friend **d** friend,
Mt   24: 4   "Watch out that no one **d** you.
Mk   13: 5   "Watch out that no one **d** you.
Jn   7:12   "No, he **d** the people."

Gal   6: 3 he **d** himself.
2Th   2:10 that **d** those who are perishing.
Jas   1:26 he **d** himself and his religion

DECEIVING* [DECEIVE]

Lev   6: 2 to the LORD by **d** his neighbor
1Ti   4: 1 abandon the faith and follow **d** spirits
2Ti   3:13 **d** and being deceived.
Rev 20: 3 from **d** the nations anymore until

DECENCY* [DECENTLY]

1Ti   2: 9 with **d** and propriety,

DECENTLY* [DECENCY]

Ro   13:13 Let us behave **d**, as in the daytime,

DECEPTION* [DECEIVE]

Ps   12: 2 their flattering lips speak with **d**.
       38:12 all day long they plot **d**.
Pr   14: 8 but the folly of fools is **d**.
       26:26 His malice may be concealed by **d**,
Jer   3:23 on the hills and mountains is a **d**;
         9: 6 You live in the midst of **d**;
Hos 10:13 you have eaten the fruit of **d**.
Mt   27:64 This last **d** will be worse than
2Co   4: 2 we do not use **d**,

DECEPTIVE* [DECEIVE]

Pr   11:18 The wicked man earns **d** wages,
       23: 3 for that food is **d**.
       31:30 Charm is **d**, and beauty is fleeting;
Jer   7: 4 Do not trust in **d** words and say,
         7: 8 trusting in **d** words that are worthless
       15:18 Will you be to me like a **d** brook,
Mic   1:14 The town of Aczib will prove **d** to
Col   2: 8 through hollow and **d** philosophy,

DECIDE [DECIDED, DECISION, DECISIONS]

Ex   18:16 and I **d** between the parties
1Sa 24:15 May the LORD be our judge and **d**
Isa   11: 3 or **d** by what he hears with his ears;
Eze 44:24 and **d** it according to my ordinances.
Jn   19:24 "Let's **d** by lot who will get it."
Ac   24:22 he said, "I will **d** your case."

DECIDED [DECIDE]

Ge   41:32 the matter has been firmly **d** by God,
Jdg   4: 5 to her to have their disputes **d**.
Jer   4:28 I have **d** and will not turn back."
Mt   27: 7 So they **d** to use the money to buy
Ac   4:28 had **d** beforehand should happen.
2Co   9: 7 Each man should give what he has **d**

DECISION [DECIDE]

Ex   28:29 the breastpiece of **d** as a continuing
Pr   16:33 but its every **d** is from the LORD.
Joel   3:14 multitudes in the valley of **d**!
Mk   1: 1 the whole Sanhedrin, reached a **d**.
Jn   1:13 nor of human **d** or a husband's will,

DECISIONS [DECIDE]

Ex   28:15 "Fashion a breastpiece for making **d**
Nu   27:21 who will obtain **d** for him

Isa   28: 7 they stumble when rendering **d**.
Jn   8:16 But if I do judge, my **d** are right,

DECLARE [DECLARED, DECLARING]

Ex   22: 9 judges **d** guilty must pay back double
Dt   5: 1 and laws I **d** in your hearing today.
1Ch 16:24 **D** his glory among the nations,
2Ch   6:23 **D** the innocent not guilty and
Ps   5:10 **D** them guilty, O God!
       19: 1 The heavens **d** the glory of God;
       40: 5 they would be too many to **d**.
       96: 3 **D** his glory among the nations,
Isa   42: 9 and new things I **d**;
Joel   1:14 **D** a holy fast; call a sacred assembly.
Heb   2:12 "I will **d** your name to my brothers;

DECLARED [DECLARE]

Dt   4:13 He **d** to you his covenant,
       26:17 You have **d** this day that
1Ki   8:53 as you **d** through your servant Moses
Mk   7:19 Jesus **d** all foods "clean.")
Ro   2:13 the law who will be **d** righteous.
         3:20 Therefore no one will be **d** righteous
Heb   3:11 So I **d** on oath in my anger,

DECLARES THE †LORD See †LORD

DECLARES THE SOVEREIGN †LORD
   See †LORD

DECLARING* [DECLARE]

Ps   71: 8 **d** your splendor all day long.
Jer 50:28 **d** in Zion how the LORD our God ha
Ac   2:11 we hear them **d** the wonders of God

DECREE [DECREED, DECREES]

Ex   15:25 There the LORD made a **d** and
1Ch 16:17 He confirmed it to Jacob as a **d**,
Ezr   5:13 King Cyrus issued a **d** to rebuild
Est   3: 9 let a **d** be issued to destroy them,
         8: 8 Now write another **d** in the king's
Ps   2: 7 I will proclaim the **d** of the LORD:
         7: 6 Awake, my God; **d** justice.
       81: 4 this is a **d** for Israel,
     148: 6 gave a **d** that will never pass away.
Jer 51:12 his **d** against the people of Babylon.
Da   2:13 the **d** was issued to put the wise men
         4:24 the **d** the Most High has issued
         6: 7 the **d** that anyone who prays
Lk   2: 1 Augustus issued a **d** that a census
Ro   1:32 they know God's righteous **d**

DECREED [DECREE]

1Ki 22:23 The LORD has **d** disaster for you."
2Ki   8: 1 because the LORD has **d** a famine
Est   9:31 and Queen Esther had **d** for them,
Ps   78: 5 He **d** statutes for Jacob
Isa 10:22 Destruction has been **d**,
Jer 13:25 the portion I have **d** for you,"
       40: 2 LORD your God **d** this disaster
La   3:37 if the Lord has not **d** it?
Da   9:24 "Seventy 'sevens' are **d**
Lk   22:22 Son of Man will go as it has been **d**,

DECREES [DECREE]

Ge   26: 5 my commands, my **d** and my laws."

Ex   15:26   to his commands and keep all his **d,**
      18:20   Teach them the **d** and laws,
Lev   10:11   all the **d** the LORD has given them
      18: 4   and be careful to follow my **d.**
      18:26   you must keep my **d** and my laws.
      26: 3   " 'If you follow my **d** and are careful
      26:15   if you reject my **d** and abhor my laws
Dt   4: 5   I have taught you **d** and laws as
Jos   24:25   at Shechem he drew up for them **d**
1Ki   6:12   if you follow my **d,**
Ps   119:12   O LORD; teach me your **d.**
     119:16   I delight in your **d;**
     119:48   and I meditate on your **d.**
     119:112 My heart is set on keeping your **d** to
Pr   31: 5   drink and forget what the law **d,**
Isa   10: 1   to those who issue oppressive **d,**
Jer   31:35   who the moon and stars to shine
Eze   5: 6   and has not followed my **d.**
Zec   1: 6   But did not my words and my **d,**
Mal   4: 4   the **d** and laws I gave him at Horeb
Ac   17: 7   They are all defying Caesar's **d,**

DEDICATE [DEDICATED, DEDICATION]

Lev   27: 2   a special vow to **d** persons to
Nu   6:12   He must **d** himself to the LORD for
Pr   20:25   to **d** something rashly and only later

DEDICATED [DEDICATE]

Lev   21:12   because he has been **d** by
Nu   6: 9   thus defiling the hair he has **d,**
      18: 6   **d** to the LORD to do the work at
2Sa   8:11   King David **d** these articles to
1Ki   7:51   in the things his father David had **d**
       8:63   and all the Israelites **d** the temple of
2Ch   29:31   now **d** yourselves to the LORD.
Ne   3: 1   They **d** it and set its doors in place,
Lk   21: 5   and with gifts **d** to God.

DEDICATION [DEDICATE]

Nu   6:19   shaved off the hair of his **d,**
2Ch   7: 9   they had celebrated the **d** of the altar
Ezr   6:16   the **d** of the house of God with joy.
Ne   12:27   At the **d** of the wall of Jerusalem,
Ps   30: T   For the **d** of the temple.
Da   3: 2   to the **d** of the image he had set up.
Jn   10:22   came the Feast of **D** at Jerusalem.
1Ti   5:11   sensual desires overcome their **d**

DEED [DEEDS]

Ecc   3:17   a time for every **d.**"
      12:14   For God will bring every **d**
Jer   32:10   I signed and sealed the **d,**
Lk   24:19   powerful in word and **d** before God
Col   3:17   whether in word or **d,**
2Th   2:17   and strengthen you in every good **d**

DEEDS [DEED]

Dt   3:24   the **d** and mighty works you do?
       4:34   or by great and awesome **d,**
      34:12   or performed the awesome **d**
1Sa   2: 3   and by him **d** are weighed.
      24:13   'From evildoers come evil **d,'**
1Ch   16:24   his marvelous **d** among all peoples.

Ezr   9:13   of our evil **d** and our great guilt,
Job   34:25   Because he takes note of their **d,**
Ps   26: 7   and telling of all your wonderful **d.**
      28: 4   Repay them for their **d**
      45: 4   your right hand display awesome **d.**
      65: 5   with awesome **d** of righteousness,
      66: 3   "How awesome are your **d!**
      71:17   this day I declare your marvelous **d.**
      72:18   who alone does marvelous **d.**
      73:28   I will tell of all your **d.**
      75: 1   men tell of your wonderful **d.**
      77:11   I will remember the **d** of the LORD;
      77:12   and consider all your mighty **d.**
      78: 4   the praiseworthy **d** of the LORD,
      78: 7   in God and would not forget his **d**
      86: 8   no **d** can compare
      86:10   you are great and do marvelous **d;**
      88:12   or your righteous **d** in the land
      90:16   May your **d** be shown
      92: 4   For you make me glad by your **d,**
      96: 3   his marvelous **d** among all peoples.
     107: 8   and his wonderful **d** for men,
     107:15   and his wonderful **d** for men,
     107:21   and his wonderful **d** for men.
     107:24   his wonderful **d** in the deep.
     107:31   and his wonderful **d** for men.
     111: 3   Glorious and majestic are his **d,**
     141: 4   to take part in wicked **d**
     145: 6   and I will proclaim your great **d.**
Pr   5:22   evil **d** of a wicked man ensnare him;
Isa   1:16   Take your evil **d** out of my sight!
Jer   32:19   and mighty are your **d.**
      32:19   to his conduct and as his **d** deserve.
Eze   22:28   Her prophets whitewash these **d**
Hos   5: 4   "Their **d** do not permit them to return
Ob   1:15   **d** will return upon your own head.
Hab   3: 2   I stand in awe of your **d,**
Mt   5:16   that they may see your good **d**
Lk   1:51   He has performed mighty **d**
      23:41   we are getting what our **d** deserve.
Jn   3:19   of light because their **d** were evil.
Ac   19:18   and openly confessed their evil **d.**
      26:20   prove their repentance by their **d.**
1Ti   2:10   but with good **d,**
       5:10   and is well known for her good **d,**
       6:18   to be rich in good **d,**
Heb   10:24   on toward love and good **d.**
Jas   2:14   to have faith but has no **d?**
       2:18   will say, "You have faith; I have **d."**
       2:26   so faith without **d** is dead.
1Pe   2:12   they may see your good **d**
Rev   2: 2   I know your **d,** your hard work
       2:19   I know your **d,** your love and faith,
       2:23   of you according to your **d.**
       3: 1   I know your **d;**
       3: 2   for I have not found your **d** complete
       3: 8   I know your **d.**
       3:15   I know your **d.**
      14:13   for their **d** will follow them."
      15: 3   "Great and marvelous are your **d,**

DEEP [DEPTH, DEPTHS]

Ge   1: 2   over the surface of the **d,**
       2:21   the man to fall into a **d** sleep;

7:11 the springs of the great **d** burst forth,
15:12 Abram fell into a **d** sleep.
Ex 15: 5 The **d** waters have covered them;
1Sa 26:12 LORD had put them into a **d** sleep.
2Sa 22:17 he drew me out of a **d** waters.
Ps 36: 6 your justice like the great **d.**
42: 7 **D** calls to **d** in the roar of your
Pr 4:19 way of the wicked is like **d** darkness;
22:14 The mouth of an adulteress is a **d** pit;
25: 3 heavens are high and the earth is **d,**
Isa 29:10 brought over you a **d** sleep:
La 2:13 Your wound is as **d** as the sea.
Eze 23:32 a cup large and **d;**
Da 2:22 He reveals deep and hidden things;
8:18 I was in a **d** sleep,
10: 9 I fell into a **d** sleep.
Jnh 1: 5 down and fell into a **d** sleep.
2: 3 You hurled me into the **d,**
Lk 5: 4 "Put out into **d** water,
Ac 20: 9 a **d** sleep as Paul talked on and on.
1Co 2:10 even the **d** things of God.
1Ti 3: 9 They must keep hold of the **d** truths
Rev 2:24 learned Satan's so-called **d** secrets

DEER

Ps 42: 1 As the **d** pants for streams of water,
Pr 5:19 A loving doe, a graceful **d**—
Hab 3:19 my feet like the feet of a **d,**

DEFAMED*

Isa 48:11 How can I let myself be **d?**

DEFEAT [DEFEATED]

Jdg 2:15 against them to **d** them,
1Sa 4: 3 the LORD bring **d** upon us today
Ps 92:11 My eyes have seen the **d**

DEFEATED [DEFEAT]

Nu 14:42 You will be **d** by your enemies,
Jos 12: 1 of the land whom the Israelites had **d**
1Co 6: 7 you have been completely **d** already.

DEFECT

Lev 22:20 Do not bring anything with a **d,**
1Pe 1:19 a lamb without blemish or **d.**

DEFEND [DEFENDED, DEFENDER, DEFENDING, DEFENDS, DEFENSE]

Jdg 6:31 he can **d** himself
Job 13:15 surely **d** my ways to his face.
Ps 72: 4 He will **d** the afflicted among
74:22 Rise up, O God, and **d** your cause;
82: 2 "How long will you **d** the unjust
119:154 **D** my cause and redeem me;
Pr 31: 9 **d** the rights of the poor and needy."
Isa 1:17 **D** the cause of the fatherless,
1:23 not **d** the cause of the fatherless;
Jer 5:28 they do not **d** the rights of the poor.
51:36 I will **d** your cause and avenge you;
Lk 12:11 about how you will **d** yourselves
21:14 how you will **d** yourselves.

DEFENDED [DEFEND]

Jer 22:16 He **d** the cause of the poor

DEFENDER [DEFEND]

Ex 22: 2 the **d** is not guilty of bloodshed;
Ps 68: 5 a **d** of widows,
Pr 23:11 for their **D** is strong;
Isa 19:20 he will send them a savior and **d,**

DEFENDING [DEFEND]

Ps 10:18 **d** the fatherless and the oppressed,
Ro 2:15 now even **d** them.)
Php 1: 7 or **d** and confirming the gospel,

DEFENDS* [DEFEND]

Dt 10:18 He **d** the cause of the fatherless and
33: 7 With his own hands he **d** his cause.
Isa 51:22 your God, who **d** his people:

DEFENSE [DEFEND]

Job 31:35 I sign now my **d**—
Ps 35:23 Awake, and rise to my **d!**
Ac 22: 1 listen now to my **d.**"
25: 8 Then Paul made his **d:**
26: 1 with his hand and began his **d:**
Php 1:16 knowing that I am put here for the **d**
1Jn 2: 1 to the Father in our **d**—

DEFERRED*

Pr 13:12 Hope **d** makes the heart sick,

DEFIED [DEFY]

1Sa 17:36 because he has **d** the armies of
1Ki 13:26 It is the man of God who **d** the word
Jer 48:26 for she has **d** the LORD.
Da 3:28 They trusted in him and **d** the king's

DEFILE [DEFILED]

Ex 20:25 you will **d** it if you use a tool on it.
Lev 11:43 Do not **d** yourselves by any
18:28 And if you **d** the land,
Eze 20: 7 not **d** yourselves with the idols
Da 1: 8 But Daniel resolved not to **d** himself
Rev 14: 4 not **d** themselves with women,

DEFILED [DEFILE]

Ge 34: 5 that his daughter Dinah had been **d,**
Lev 18:25 Even the land was **d;**
Jos 22:19 If the land you possess is **d,**
Isa 24: 5 The earth is **d** by its people;
Jer 16:18 because they have **d** my land with
Mal 1: 7 "You place **d** food on my altar.

DEFRAUD [FRAUD]

Lev 19:13 " 'Do not **d** your neighbor
Mk 10:19 do not give false testimony, do not **d,**

DEFY [DEFIED]

1Sa 17:10 "This day I **d** the ranks of Israel!

DEGENERATE (KJV) See CORRUPT

DEITY*

Col 2: 9 fullness of the **D** lives in bodily form

DELAY [DELAYED]

Ps 40:17 O my God, do not **d.**

Ecc   5: 4   do not **d** in fulfilling it.
Isa   48: 9   my own name's sake I **d** my wrath;
Da   9:19   For your sake, O my God, do not **d**,
Hab   2: 3   and will not **d**.
Heb 10:37   will come and will not **d**.
Rev 10: 6   and said, "There will be no more **d**!

DELAYED [DELAY]

Jos 10:13   in the middle of the sky and **d** going
Isa   46:13   and my salvation will not be **d**.

DELICACIES* [DELICACY]

Ge   49:20   he will provide **d** fit for a king.
Ps   141: 4   not eat of their **d**.
Pr   23: 3   Do not crave his **d**,
       23: 6   do not crave his **d**,
Jer   51:34   and filled his stomach with our **d**,
La   4: 5   Those who once ate **d** are destitute in

DELICACY* [DELICACIES]

SS   7:13   and at our door is every **d**,

DELICIOUS*

Pr   9:17   food eaten in secret is **d!**"

DELIGHT* [DELIGHTED, DELIGHTFUL, DELIGHTING, DELIGHTS]

Lev   26:31   and I will take no **d** in
Dt   30: 9   The LORD will again **d** in you
1Sa   2: 1   for I **d** in your deliverance.
      15:22   the LORD **d** in burnt offerings
Ne   1:11   to the prayer of your servants who **d**
Job   22:26   then you will find **d** in the Almighty
      27:10   Will he find **d** in the Almighty?
Ps   1: 2   But his **d** is in the law of the LORD,
      16: 3   in whom is all my **d**.
      35: 9   in the LORD and **d** in his salvation.
      35:27   May those who **d** in my vindication
      37: 4   **D** yourself in the LORD
      43: 4   to God, my joy and my **d**.
      51:16   You do not **d** in sacrifice,
      51:19   whole burnt offerings to **d** you;
      62: 4   they take **d** in lies.
      68:30   Scatter the nations who **d** in war.
     111: 2   they are pondered by all who **d**
     112: 1   who finds great **d** in his commands.
     119:16   I **d** in your decrees;
     119:24   Your statutes are my **d;**
     119:35   for there I find **d**.
     119:47   for I **d** in your commands
     119:70   but I **d** in your law.
     119:77   for your law is my **d**.
     119:92   If your law had not been my **d**,
     119:143 but your commands are my **d**.
     119:174 O LORD, and your law is my **d**.
     147:10   nor his **d** in the legs of a man;
     149: 4   For the LORD takes **d** in his people;
Pr   1:22   How long will mockers **d** in mockery
       2:14   who **d** in doing wrong and rejoice in
       8:30   I was filled with **d** day after day,
      11: 1   but accurate weights are his **d**.
      29:17   he will bring **d** to your soul.
Ecc   2:10   My heart took **d** in all my work,
SS   1: 4   We rejoice and **d** in you;

        2: 3   I **d** to sit in his shade,
Isa   5: 7   men of Judah are the garden of his **d**.
      11: 3   he will **d** in the fear of the LORD.
      13:17   not care for silver and have no **d**
      32:14   the **d** of donkeys,
      42: 1   my chosen one in whom I **d;**
      55: 2   your soul will **d** in the richest of fare.
      58:13   if you call the Sabbath a **d** and
      61:10   I **d** greatly in the LORD;
      62: 4   for the LORD will take **d** in you,
      65:18   for I will create Jerusalem to be a **d**
      65:19   over Jerusalem and take **d**
      66: 3   their souls **d** in their abominations;
      66:11   and **d** in her overflowing abundance.
Jer   9:24   for in these I **d**," declares the LORD.
      15:16   and my heart's **d**,
      31:20   the child in whom I **d?**
      49:25   the town in which I **d?**
Eze   24:16   about to take away from you the **d**
      24:21   the **d** of your eyes,
      24:25   the **d** of their eyes,
Hos   7: 3   "They **d** the king
Mic   1:16   for the children in whom you **d;**
       7:18   angry forever but **d** to show mercy.
Zep   3:17   He will take great **d** in you,
Mt   12:18   the one I love, in whom I **d;**
Mk   12:37   crowd listened to him with **d**.
Lk   1:14   He will be a joy and **d** to you,
Ro   7:22   in my inner being I **d** in God's law;
1Co   13: 6   Love does not **d** in evil but rejoices
2Co   12:10   for Christ's sake, I **d** in weaknesses,
Col   2: 5   and **d** to see how orderly you are and

DELIGHTED [DELIGHT]

Ex   18: 9   Jethro was **d** to hear about all
Dt   30: 9   just as he **d** in your fathers,
2Sa   22:20   he rescued me because he **d**
2Ch   9: 8   who has **d** in you and placed you
Lk   13:17   but the people were **d** with all
      22: 5   They were **d** and agreed
2Th   2:12   the truth but have **d** in wickedness.

DELIGHTFUL* [DELIGHT]

Ps   16: 6   surely I have a **d** inheritance.
SS   1: 2   for your love is more **d** than wine.
       4:10   **d** is your love, my sister, my bride!
Mal   3:12   for yours will be a **d** land,"

DELIGHTING* [DELIGHT]

Pr   8:31   in his whole world and **d** in mankind.

DELIGHTS [DELIGHT]

Est   6: 6   for the man the king **d** to honor?"
Ps   22: 8   since he **d** in him."
      35:27   who **d** in the well-being
      36: 8   from your river of **d**.
      37:23   If the LORD **d** in a man's way,
     147:11   the LORD **d** in those who fear him,
Pr   3:12   as a father the son he **d** in.
      10:23   a man of understanding **d** in wisdom.
      11:20   of perverse heart but he **d**
      12:22   but he **d** in men who are truthful.
      14:35   A king **d** in a wise servant,
      15:21   Folly **d** a man who lacks judgment,

18: 2 but **d** in airing his own opinions.
23:24 a wise son **d** in him.
SS 7: 6 O love, with your **d**!
Col 2:18 who **d** in false humility

DELILAH

Philistine woman who betrayed Samson (Jdg 16:4-22).

DELIVER [DELIVERANCE, DELIVERED, DELIVERER, DELIVERS]

Nu 21: 2 "If you will **d** these people
Dt 7:23 the LORD your God will **d** them
32:39 and no one can **d** out of my hand.
Jos 8:18 for into your hand I will **d** the city."
1Sa 17:37 **d** me from the hand of this Philistine.
2Ch 32:14 How then can your god **d** you
Ps 6: 4 Turn, O LORD, and **d** me;
22: 8 Let him **d** him,
50:15 in the day of trouble; I will **d** you,
72:12 For he will **d** the needy who cry out,
109:21 of the goodness of your love, **d** me.
Pr 20:22 and he will **d** you.
Mt 6:13 but **d** us from the evil one.'
2Co 1:10 and he will **d** us.

DELIVERANCE [DELIVER]

Ge 45: 7 and to save your lives by a great **d**.
Ex 14:13 Stand firm and you will see the **d**
1Sa 2: 1 for I delight in your **d**.
Est 4:14 relief and **d** for the Jews will arise
Ps 3: 8 From the LORD comes **d**.
32: 7 and surround me with songs of **d**.
33:17 A horse is a vain hope for **d**;
78:22 not believe in God or trust in his **d**.
Ob 1:17 But on Mount Zion will be **d**;
Php 1:19 to me will turn out for my **d**.

DELIVERED [DELIVER]

Ge 48:16 Angel who has **d** me from all harm
Jos 6: 2 I have **d** Jericho into your hands,
Jdg 16:23 "Our god has **d** Samson, our enemy,
1Sa 17:37 The LORD who **d** me from the paw
Ps 34: 4 he **d** me from all my fears.
60: 5 that those you love may be **d**.
107: 6 and he **d** them from their distress.
116: 8 have **d** my soul from death,
Da 12: 1 written in the book—will be **d**.
Ro 4:25 He was **d** over to death for our sins
2Th 3: 2 be **d** from wicked and evil men,

DELIVERER* [DELIVER]

Jdg 3: 9 he raised up for them a **d**,
3:15 and he gave them a **d**—
2Sa 22: 2 my fortress and my **d**;
2Ki 13: 5 The LORD provided a **d** for Israel,
Ps 18: 2 my fortress and my **d**;
40:17 You are my help and my **d**;
70: 5 You are my help and my **d**;
140: 7 O Sovereign LORD, my strong **d**,
144: 2 my stronghold and my **d**, my shield,
Ac 7:35 be their ruler and **d** by God himself,
Ro 11:26 "The **d** will come from Zion;

DELIVERS [DELIVER]

Ps 34:17 and the LORD hears them; he **d** them
34:19 but the LORD **d** him from them all;
37:40 The LORD helps them and **d** them;
Pr 10: 2 but righteousness **d** from death.

DELUDED* [DELUSION]

Isa 44:20 a **d** heart misleads him;
Rev 19:20 With these signs he had **d** those

DELUSION* [DELUDED, DELUSIONS]

2Th 2:11 a powerful **d** so that they will believe

DELUSIONS* [DELUSION]

Ps 4: 2 How long will you love **d**
Jer 14:14 and the **d** of their own minds.
23:26 the **d** of their own minds?

DEMAND [DEMANDED]

Ge 9: 5 And for your lifeblood I will surely **d**
Lk 6:30 do not **d** it back.
1Co 1:22 Jews **d** miraculous signs

DEMANDED [DEMAND]

Lk 12:20 This very night your life will be **d**
12:48 given much, much will be **d**;

DEMAS*

Associate of Paul (Col 4:14; 2Ti 4:10; Phm 24).

DEMETRIUS

Ac 19:24 A silversmith named **D**,
3Jn 1:12 **D** is well spoken of by everyone—

DEMOLISH [DEMOLISHED]

Nu 33:52 and **d** all their high places.
Hos 10: 2 The LORD will **d** their altars
2Co 10: 4 divine power to **d** strongholds.

DEMOLISHED [DEMOLISH]

Jdg 6:28 there was Baal's altar, **d**,
2Ch 33: 3 places his father Hezekiah had **d**

DEMON* [DEMONS, DEMON-POSSESSED, DEMON-POSSESSION]

Mt 9:33 And when the **d** was driven out,
11:18 and they say, 'He has a **d**.'
17:18 Jesus rebuked the **d**,
Mk 7:26 She begged Jesus to drive the **d** out
7:29 the **d** has left your daughter."
7:30 and the **d** gone.
Lk 4:33 a man possessed by a **d**,
4:35 **d** threw the man down
7:33 and you say, 'He has a **d**.'
8:29 driven by the **d** into solitary places.
9:42 the **d** threw him to the ground in
11:14 Jesus was driving out a **d**
11:14 When the **d** left,
Jn 8:49 "I am not possessed by a **d**,"
10:21 of a man possessed by a **d**.
10:21 Can a **d** open the eyes of the blind?"

DEMON-POSSESSED* [DEMON, POSSESS]

Mt	4:24	those suffering severe pain, the **d**,
	8:16	many who were **d** were brought
	8:28	two **d** men coming from
	8:33	what had happened to the **d** men.
	9:32	a man who was **d** and could
	12:22	a **d** man who was blind and mute,
Mk	1:32	brought to Jesus all the sick and **d**.
	5:16	what had happened to the **d** man—
	5:18	the man who had been **d** begged
Lk	8:27	he was met by a **d** man from
	8:36	how the **d** man had been cured.
Jn	7:20	"You are **d**," the crowd answered.
	8:48	that you are a Samaritan and **d**?"
	8:52	"Now we know that you are **d**!
	10:20	"He is **d** and raving mad.
Ac	19:13	over those who were **d**.

DEMON-POSSESSION* [DEMON, POSSESS]

Mt	15:22	daughter is suffering terribly from **d**.

DEMONS* [DEMON]

Dt	32:17	They sacrificed to **d**,
Ps	106:37	and their daughters to **d**.
Mt	7:22	and in your name drive out **d**
	8:31	The **d** begged Jesus,
	9:34	the prince of **d** that he drives out **d**."
	10: 8	drive out **d**.
	12:24	the prince of **d**, that this fellow drives out **d**."
	12:27	And if I drive out **d** by Beelzebub,
	12:28	if I drive out **d** by the Spirit of God,
Mk	1:34	He also drove out many **d**,
	1:34	but he would not let the **d** speak
	1:39	and driving out **d**.
	3:15	and to have authority to drive out **d**.
	3:22	By the prince of **d** he is driving out **d**
	5:12	The **d** begged Jesus,
	5:15	been possessed by the legion of **d**,
	6:13	They drove out many **d**
	9:38	a man driving out **d** in your name
	16: 9	out of whom he had driven seven **d**.
	16:17	In my name they will drive out **d**;
Lk	4:41	**d** came out of many people,
	8: 2	from whom seven **d** had come out;
	8:30	because many **d** had gone into him.
	8:32	The **d** begged Jesus to let them go
	8:33	When the **d** came out of the man,
	8:35	from whom the **d** had gone out,
	8:38	the **d** had gone out begged to go
	9: 1	and authority to drive out all **d** and
	9:49	a man driving out **d** in your name
	10:17	the **d** submit to us in your name."
	11:15	"By Beelzebub, the prince of **d**, he is driving out **d**."
	11:18	because you claim that I drive out **d**
	11:19	Now if I drive out **d** by Beelzebub,
	11:20	if I drive out **d** by the finger of God,
	13:32	'I will drive out **d** and heal
Ro	8:38	death nor life, neither angels nor **d**,
1Co	10:20	sacrifices of pagans are offered to **d**,

	10:20	to be participants with **d**.
	10:21	of the Lord and the cup of **d** too;
	10:21	the Lord's table and the table of **d**.
1Ti	4: 1	spirits and things taught by **d**.
Jas	2:19	Even the **d** believe that—
Rev	9:20	not stop worshiping **d**, and idols
	16:14	of **d** performing miraculous signs,
	18: 2	for **d** and a haunt for every evil spirit

DEMONSTRATE* [DEMONSTRATES, DEMONSTRATION]

Ro	3:25	He did this to **d** his justice,
	3:26	to **d** his justice at the present time,

DEMONSTRATES* [DEMONSTRATE]

Ro	5: 8	God **d** his own love for us in this:

DEMONSTRATION* [DEMONSTRATE]

1Co	2: 4	but with a **d** of the Spirit's power,

DEN

Jer	7:11	become a **d** of robbers to you?
Da	6: 7	shall be thrown into the lions' **d**.
Na	2:11	Where now is the lions' **d**,
Mt	21:13	you are making it a '**d** of robbers.' "
Mk	11:17	you have made it 'a **d** of robbers.' "
Lk	19:46	but you have made it 'a **d**

DENARII* [DENARIUS]

Mt	18:28	who owed him a hundred **d**.
Lk	7:41	One owed him five hundred **d**,

DENARIUS [DENARII]

Mt	20: 2	He agreed to pay them a **d** for
Mk	12:15	"Bring me a **d** and let me look at it."
Lk	20:24	"Show me a **d**.

DENIED [DENY]

Ecc	2:10	I **d** myself nothing my eyes desired;
Mt	26:70	But he **d** it before them all.
Jn	18:25	He **d** it, saying, "I am not."
1Ti	5: 8	he has **d** the faith and is worse than
Rev	3: 8	and have not **d** my name.

DENIES [DENY]

1Jn	2:22	who **d** that Jesus is the Christ.
	2:23	No one who **d** the Son has

DENOUNCE [DENOUNCED]

Nu	23: 7	for me; come, **d** Israel.'

DENOUNCED [DENOUNCE]

Nu	23: 8	those whom the LORD has not **d**?

DENY [DENIED, DENIES, DENYING]

Ex	23: 6	"Do not **d** justice to your poor people
Lev	16:29	month you must **d** yourselves
	23:27	a sacred assembly and **d** yourselves,
Job	27: 5	I will not **d** my integrity;
Isa	5:23	but **d** justice to the innocent.
La	3:35	to **d** a man his rights before
Am	2: 7	and **d** justice to the oppressed.

Mt	16:24	he must **d** himself and take
Mk	8:34	he must **d** himself and take
Lk	9:23	he must **d** himself and take
	22:34	you will **d** three times
Ac	4:16	and we cannot **d** it.
Tit	1:16	but by their actions they **d** him.
Jas	3:14	do not boast about it or **d** the truth.
Jude	1: 4	**d** Jesus Christ our only Sovereign

DENYING* [DENY]

Eze	22:29	**d** them justice.
2Ti	3: 5	a form of godliness but **d** its power.
2Pe	2: 1	even **d** the sovereign Lord who

DEPART [DEPARTED, DEPARTS, DEPARTURE]

Ge	49:10	The scepter will not **d** from Judah,
Jos	1: 8	Do not let this Book of the Law **d**
2Sa	12:10	sword will never **d** from your house,
Job	1:21	and naked I will **d.**
Isa	52:11	**D, d,** go out from there!
Mt	25:41	'**D** from me, you who are cursed,
Php	1:23	I desire to **d** and be with Christ,

DEPARTED [DEPART]

1Sa	4:21	"The glory has **d** from Israel"—
	16:14	Now the Spirit of the LORD had **d**
Ps	119:102	I have not **d** from your laws,
La	1: 6	All the splendor has **d** from
Eze	10:18	the glory of the LORD **d** from

DEPARTS [DEPART]

Ecc	5:15	and as he comes, so he **d.**

DEPARTURE [DEPART]

Lk	9:31	They spoke about his **d,**
2Ti	4: 6	and the time has come for my **d.**
2Pe	1:15	after my **d** you will always be able

DEPEND [DEPENDED, DEPENDING, DEPENDS]

Ps	62: 7	My salvation and my honor **d**
Ro	9:16	not, therefore, **d** on man's desire or

DEPENDED [DEPEND]

Hos	10:13	Because you have **d** on your own

DEPENDING [DEPEND]

2Ki	18:20	On whom are you **d,**

DEPENDS [DEPEND]

Jer	17: 5	who **d** on flesh for his strength
Gal	3:18	then it no longer **d** on a promise;
Col	2: 8	which **d** on human tradition and

DEPORTED

2Ki	15:29	and **d** the people to Assyria.
	24:16	also **d** to Babylon the entire force

DEPOSES*

Da	2:21	he sets up kings and **d** them.

DEPOSIT [DEPOSITED]

Mt	25:27	you should have put my money on **d**

Lk	19:23	then didn't you put my money on **d,**
2Co	1:22	and put his Spirit in our hearts as a **d,**
	5: 5	and has given us the Spirit as a **d,**
Eph	1:14	a **d** guaranteeing our inheritance
2Ti	1:14	Guard the good **d** that was entrusted

DEPOSITED* [DEPOSIT]

1Sa	10:25	a scroll and **d** it before the LORD.
Ezr	6: 5	to be **d** in the house of God.

DEPRAVED* [DEPRAVITY]

Eze	16:47	you soon became more **d** than they.
	23:11	she was more **d** than her sister.
Ro	1:28	he gave them over to a **d** mind,
Php	2:15	in a crooked and **d** generation,
2Ti	3: 8	men of **d** minds,

DEPRAVITY* [DEPRAVED]

Ro	1:29	evil, greed and **d.**
2Pe	2:19	while they themselves are slaves of **d**

DEPRIVE [DEPRIVED]

Dt	24:17	Do not **d** the alien or the fatherless
Pr	18: 5	or to **d** the innocent of justice.
	31: 5	and the oppressed of their rights.
Isa	10: 2	to **d** the poor of their rights
	29:21	with false testimony **d** the innocent
La	3:36	to **d** a man of justice—
Am	5:12	and you **d** the poor of justice
Mal	3: 5	and **d** aliens of justice,
1Co	7: 5	Do not **d** each other except

DEPRIVED [DEPRIVE]

Jer	5:25	your sins have **d** you of good.

DEPTH [DEEP]

Ro	8:39	nor **d,** nor anything else in all
	11:33	the **d** of the riches of the wisdom
Php	1: 9	in knowledge and **d** of insight,

DEPTHS [DEEP]

Ex	15: 5	sank to the **d** like a stone.
Ps	69: 2	I sink in the miry **d,**
	130: 1	Out of the **d** I cry to you, O LORD;
Pr	9:18	her guests are in the **d** of the grave.
Mt	18: 6	and to be drowned in the **d**

DERIDE* [DERIDES, DERISION]

Hab	1:10	They **d** kings and scoff at rulers.

DERIDES* [DERIDE]

Pr	11:12	who lacks judgment **d** his neighbor,

DERISION [DERIDE]

Eze	23:32	it will bring scorn and **d,**
Mic	6:16	over to ruin and your people to **d;**

DERIVES*

Eph	3:15	in heaven and on earth **d** its name.

DESCEND [DESCENDANT, DESCENDANTS, DESCENDED, DESCENDING, DESCENT]

Dt	32: 2	like rain and my words **d** like dew,

Ro 10: 7 "or 'Who will **d** into the deep?' "

DESCENDANT [DESCEND]

Ro 1: 3 human nature was a **d** of David,

DESCENDANTS [DESCEND]

Ge 9: 9 with you and with your **d** after you
15:18 "To your **d** I give this land,
Ex 12:24 ordinance for you and your **d.**
28:43 ordinance for Aaron and his **d.**
Dt 4:37 and chose their **d** after them,
2Sa 22:51 to David and his **d** forever."
Ps 132:11 **d** I will place on your throne—
Isa 53: 8 And who can speak of his **d?**
Ac 2:30 that he would place one of his **d**
8:33 Who can speak of his **d?**

DESCENDED [DESCEND]

Ex 19:18 because the LORD **d** on it in fire.
Lk 3:22 and the Holy Spirit **d** on him
Eph 4: 9 that he also **d** to the lower,
2Ti 2: 8 raised from the dead, **d** from David.
Heb 7:14 it is clear that our Lord **d** from Judah

DESCENDING [DESCEND]

Ge 28:12 angels of God were ascending and **d**
Mt 3:16 the Spirit of God **d** like a dove
Mk 1:10 and the Spirit **d** on him like a dove.
Jn 1:51 ascending and **d** on the Son of Man."

DESCENT [DESCEND]

Jn 1:13 children born not of natural **d,**

DESECRATE [DESECRATING]

Eze 7:22 and they will **d** my treasured place;
Mt 12: 5 the priests in the temple **d** the day
Ac 24: 6 and even tried to **d** the temple;

DESECRATING* [DESECRATE]

Ne 13:17 **d** the Sabbath day?
13:18 against Israel by **d** the Sabbath."
Isa 56: 2 who keeps the Sabbath without **d** it,
56: 6 all who keep the Sabbath without **d** it
Eze 44: 7 **d** my temple while you offered me

DESERT [DESERTED, DESERTING, DESERTS]

Ex 3: 1 led the flock to the far side of the **d**
4:27 "Go into the **d** to meet Moses."
16:32 the bread I gave you to eat in the **d**
Nu 14:29 In this **d** your bodies will fall—
32:13 wander in the **d** forty years,
Dt 8:16 He gave you manna to eat in the **d,**
29: 5 that I led you through the **d,**
Ne 9:21 you sustained them in the **d;**
Ps 78:15 in the **d** and gave them water
78:19 "Can God spread a table in the **d?**
78:52 like sheep through the **d.**
Pr 21:19 to live in a **d** than with a quarrelsome
Isa 32:15 and the **d** becomes a fertile field,
35: 6 the wilderness and streams in the **d.**
40: 3 A voice of one calling: "In the **d**
Eze 20:13 of Israel rebelled against me in the **d.**
Hos 2:14 I will lead her into the **d**

13: 5 I cared for you in the **d,**
Am 2:10 and I led you forty years in the **d**
Mk 1: 3 "a voice of one calling in the **d,**
1:13 and he was in the **d** forty days,
Jn 6:31 forefathers ate the manna in the **d;**
Heb 3: 8 during the time of testing in the **d,**
Rev 12: 6 The woman fled into the **d** to a place
17: 3 carried me away in the Spirit into a **d**

DESERTED [DESERT]

Dt 32:18 You **d** the Rock, who fathered you;
Ezr 9: 9 our God has not **d** us in our bondage.
Isa 62: 4 No longer will they call you **D,**
La 1: 1 **d** lies the city, once so full of people!
Mt 26:56 Then all the disciples **d** him and fled.
2Ti 4:10 has **d** me and has gone

DESERTING [DESERT]

Gal 1: 6 so quickly **d** the one who called you

DESERTS [DESERT]

Pr 19: 4 but a poor man's friend **d** him.
Zec 11:17 who **d** the flock!

DESERVE* [DESERVED, DESERVES, DESERVING]

Ge 40:15 to **d** being put in a dungeon."
Lev 26:21 as your sins **d.**
Jdg 20:10 it can give them what they **d**
1Sa 26:16 you and your men **d** to die,
1Ki 2:26 You **d** to die,
Ps 28: 4 upon them what they **d.**
94: 2 to the proud what they **d.**
103:10 not treat us as our sins **d** or repay us
Pr 3:27 good from those who **d** it,
Ecc 8:14 the righteous
Isa 66: 6 repaying his enemies all they **d.**
Jer 14:16 on them the calamity they **d.**
17:10 according to what his deeds **d.**"
21:14 I will punish you as your deeds **d,**
32:19 to his conduct and as his deeds **d.**
49:12 not **d** to drink the cup
La 3:64 Pay them back what they **d,**
Eze 16:59 deal with you as you **d,**
Zec 1: 6 to us what our ways and practices **d,**
Mt 7: 6 I do not **d** to have you come
22: 8 but those I invited did not **d** to come.
Lk 7: 6 for I do not **d** to have you come
23:15 he has done nothing to **d** death.
23:41 for we are getting what our deeds **d.**
Ro 1:32 those who do such things **d** death,
1Co 15: 9 do not even **d** to be called an apostle,
16:18 Such men **d** recognition.
2Co 11:15 be what their actions **d.**
Rev 16: 6 blood to drink as they **d.**"

DESERVED* [DESERVE]

2Sa 19:28 grandfather's descendants **d** nothing
Ezr 9:13 punished us less than our sins have **d**
Job 33:27 but I did not get what I **d.**
Ac 23:29 that **d** death or imprisonment.
Ro 3: 8 Their condemnation is **d.**

DESERVES* [DESERVE]

Nu	35:31	who **d** to die.
Dt	25: 2	If the guilty man **d** to be beaten,
	25: 2	the number of lashes his crime **d,**
Jdg	9:16	and if you have treated him as he **d**
2Sa	12: 5	the man who did this **d** to die!
Job	34:11	upon him what his conduct **d.**
Jer	51: 6	he will pay her what she **d.**
Lk	7: 4	"This man **d** to have you do this,
	10: 7	for the worker **d** his wages.
Ac	26:31	not doing anything that **d** death
1Ti	1:15	saying that **d** full acceptance:
	4: 9	saying that **d** full acceptance
	5:18	and "The worker **d** his wages."
Heb	10:29	a man **d** to be punished

DESERVING [DESERVE]

Mt	10:13	If the home is **d,**
Ac	28:18	not guilty of any crime **d** death.

DESIGNATE [DESIGNATED]

Ex	21:13	he is to flee to a place I will **d.**
Jos	20: 2	the Israelites to **d** the cities of refuge,

DESIGNATED [DESIGNATE]

Lk	6:13	whom he also **d** apostles:
Heb	5:10	and was **d** by God to be high priest

DESIRABLE* [DESIRE]

Ge	3: 6	and also **d** for gaining wisdom,
Pr	22: 1	name is more **d** than great riches;
Jer	3:19	like sons and give you a **d** land,

DESIRE* [DESIRABLE, DESIRED, DESIRES]

Ge	3:16	Your **d** will be for your husband,
Dt	5:21	You shall not set your **d**
1Sa	9:20	to whom is all the **d** of Israel turned,
2Sa	19:38	anything you **d** from me
	23: 5	and grant me my every **d?**
1Ch	29:18	keep this **d** in the hearts
2Ch	1:11	"Since this is your heart's **d**
	9: 8	and his **d** to uphold them forever,
Job	13: 3	But I **d** to speak to the Almighty and
	21:14	We have no **d** to know your ways.
Ps	10:17	O LORD, the **d** of the afflicted;
	20: 4	May he give you the **d** of your heart
	21: 2	You have granted him the **d**
	27:12	not turn me over to the **d** of my foes,
	40: 6	Sacrifice and offering you did not **d,**
	40: 8	I **d** to do your will, O my God;
	40:14	may all who **d** my ruin
	41: 2	and not surrender him to the **d**
	51: 6	Surely you **d** truth in the inner parts;
	70: 2	may all who **d** my ruin
	73:25	earth has nothing I **d** besides you.
Pr	3:15	nothing you **d** can compare
	8:11	nothing you **d** can compare with her.
	10:24	what the righteous **d** will be granted.
	11:23	**d** of the righteous ends only in good,
	12:12	wicked **d** the plunder of evil men,
	17:16	since he has no **d** to get wisdom?
	24: 1	do not **d** their company;

Ecc	12: 5	and **d** no longer is stirred.
SS	6:12	my **d** set me among
	7:10	and his **d** is for me.
Isa	26: 8	and renown are the **d** of our hearts.
	53: 2	that we should **d** him.
	55:11	but will accomplish what I **d**
Eze	24:25	delight of their eyes, their heart's **d,**
Hos	6: 6	For I **d** mercy, not sacrifice,
Mic	7: 3	the powerful dictate what they **d—**
Mal	3: 1	whom you **d,** will come,"
Mt	9:13	learn what this means: 'I **d** mercy,
	12: 7	'I **d** mercy, not sacrifice,'
Jn	8:44	you want to carry out your father's **d.**
Ro	7: 8	in me every kind of covetous **d.**
	7:18	For I have the **d** to do what is good,
	9:16	depend on man's **d** or effort,
	10: 1	my heart's **d** and prayer to God for
1Co	12:31	But eagerly **d** the greater gifts.
	14: 1	of love and eagerly **d** spiritual gifts,
2Co	8:10	but also to have the **d** to do so.
	8:13	Our **d** is not that others might
Php	1:23	I **d** to depart and be with Christ,
Heb	10: 5	and offering you did not **d,**
	10: 8	and sin offerings you did not **d,**
	13:18	and **d** to live honorably in every way.
Jas	1:14	by his own evil **d,**
	1:15	**d** has conceived, it gives birth to sin;
2Pe	2:10	of those who follow the corrupt **d** of

DESIRED [DESIRE]

1Ki	9: 1	and had achieved all he had **d** to do,
Ecc	2:10	I denied myself nothing my eyes **d;**
Da	11:37	or for the one **d** by women,
Hag	2: 7	and the **d** of all nations will come,
Lk	22:15	"I have eagerly **d** to eat this Passover

DESIRES* [DESIRE]

Ge	4: 7	sin is crouching at your door; it **d**
	41:16	Pharaoh the answer he **d."**
2Sa	3:21	over all that your heart **d."**
1Ki	11:37	over all that your heart **d;**
Job	17:11	and so are the **d** of my heart.
	31:16	I have denied the **d** of the poor
Ps	34:12	Whoever of you loves life and **d**
	37: 4	give you the **d** of your heart.
	103: 5	who satisfies your **d** with good
	140: 8	do not grant the wicked their **d,**
	145:16	satisfy the **d** of every living thing.
	145:19	the **d** of those who fear him;
Pr	11: 6	the unfaithful are trapped by evil **d.**
	13: 4	**d** of the diligent are fully satisfied
	19:22	What a man **d** is unfailing love;
Ecc	6: 2	so that he lacks nothing his heart **d,**
SS	2: 7	or awaken love until it so **d.**
	3: 5	or awaken love until it so **d.**
	8: 4	or awaken love until it so **d.**
Hab	2: 4	puffed up; his **d** are not upright—
Mk	4:19	**d** for other things come in and choke
Ro	1:24	over in the sinful **d** of their hearts
	6:12	so that you obey its evil **d.**
	8: 5	set on what that nature **d;**
	8: 5	minds set on what the Spirit **d.**
	13:14	not think about how to gratify the **d**
Gal	5:16	not gratify the **d** of the sinful nature.

5:17 the sinful nature **d** what is contrary
5:24 sinful nature with its passions and **d.**
Eph 2: 3 sinful nature and following its **d**
4:22 corrupted by its deceitful **d;**
Col 3: 5 evil **d** and greed, which is idolatry.
1Ti 3: 1 he **d** a noble task.
5:11 sensual **d** overcome their dedication
6: 9 into many foolish and harmful **d**
2Ti 2:22 Flee the evil **d** of youth,
3: 6 and are swayed by all kinds of evil **d,**
4: 3 Instead, to suit their own **d,**
Jas 1:20 about the righteous life that God **d.**
4: 1 from your **d** that battle within you?
1Pe 1:14 do not conform to the evil **d** you had
2:11 to abstain from sinful **d,**
4: 2 of his earthly life for evil human **d,**
2Pe 1: 4 in the world caused by evil **d.**
2:18 the lustful **d** of sinful human nature,
3: 3 and following their own evil **d.**
1Jn 2:17 The world and its **d** pass away,
Jude 1:16 they follow their own evil **d;**
1:18 will follow their own ungodly **d."**

DESOLATE [DESOLATION]

Lev 26:34 all the time that it lies **d**
Isa 1: 7 Your country is **d,**
54: 1 are the children of the **d** woman
Jer 50:23 **d** is Babylon among the nations!
Da   9:17 look with favor on your **d** sanctuary.
Lk 13:35 Look, your house is left to you **d.**
Gal 4:27 are the children of the **d** woman

DESOLATION [DESOLATE]

2Ch 36:21 all the time of its **d** it rested,
Da   9:27 an abomination that causes **d,**
11:31 the abomination that causes **d.**
12:11 the abomination that causes **d** is set
Mt 24:15 'the abomination that causes **d,'**
Mk 13:14 'the abomination that causes **d'**
Lk 21:20 you will know that its **d** is near.

DESPAIR [DESPAIRED, DESPAIRING]

Isa 61: 3 of praise instead of a spirit of **d.**
2Co 4: 8 but not in **d;**

DESPAIRED* [DESPAIR]

2Co 1: 8 so that we **d** even of life.

DESPAIRING [DESPAIR]

Job 6:14 "A **d** man should have the devotion

DESPERATE*

2Sa 12:18 He may do something **d."**
Ps 60: 3 You have shown your people **d** times
79: 6 for we are in **d** need.
142: 6 Listen to my cry, for I am in **d** need;

DESPISE [DESPISED, DESPISES]

Ge 16: 4 she began to **d** her mistress.
2Sa 12: 9 Why did you **d** the word of
Job 5:17 not **d** the discipline of the Almighty.
36: 5 "God is mighty, but does not **d** men;
42: 6 Therefore I **d** myself and repent
Ps 51:17 O God, you will not **d.**

102:17 he will not **d** their plea.
Pr   1: 7 but fools **d** wisdom and discipline.
3:11 do not **d** the LORD's discipline
6:30 Men do not **d** a thief if he steals
23:22 not **d** your mother when she is old.
Jer 14:21 the sake of your name do not **d** us;
Am   5:10 and **d** him who tells the truth.
Mic 3: 9 **d** justice and distort all that is right;
Mt   6:24 be devoted to the one and **d**
Lk 16:13 be devoted to the one and **d**
1Co 11:22 Or do you **d** the church of God
Tit 2:15 Do not let anyone **d** you.
2Pe 2:10 of the sinful nature and **d** authority.

DESPISED [DESPISE]

Ge 25:34 So Esau **d** his birthright.
1Sa 17:42 ruddy and handsome, and he **d** him.
2Sa 6:16 she **d** him in her heart.
Ps 22: 6 scorned by men and **d** by the people.
Pr   8: 2 but men with warped minds are **d.**
Ecc 9:16 But the poor man's wisdom is **d,**
Isa 53: 3 He was **d** and rejected by men,
1Co 1:28 of this world and the **d** things—

DESPISES [DESPISE]

Pr 14:21 He who **d** his neighbor sins,
15:20 but a foolish man **d** his mother.
15:32 He who ignores discipline **d** himself,
Zec 4:10 "Who **d** the day of small things?

DESTINE* [DESTINED, DESTINY, PREDESTINED]

Isa 65:12 I will **d** you for the sword,

DESTINED [DESTINE]

Ps 49:14 Like sheep they are **d** for the grave,
Jer 43:11 bringing death to those **d** for death,
Lk   2:34 "This child is **d** to cause
1Co 2: 7 that God **d** for our glory
Col 2:22 These are all **d** to perish with use,
1Th 3: 3 You know quite well that we were **d**
Heb 9:27 Just as man is **d** to die once,
1Pe 2: 8 also what they were **d** for.

DESTINY* [DESTINE]

Job 8:13 Such is the **d** of all who forget God;
Ps 73:17 then I understood their final **d.**
Ecc 7: 2 for death is the **d** of every man;
9: 2 All share a common **d—**
9: 3 The same **d** overtakes all.
Isa 65:11 and fill bowls of mixed wine for **D,**
Php 3:19 Their **d** is destruction,

DESTITUTE

Ps 102:17 to the prayer of the **d;**
Pr 31: 8 for the rights of all who are **d.**
Heb 11:37 **d,** persecuted and mistreated—

DESTROY [DESTROYED, DESTROYER, DESTROYING, DESTROYS, DESTRUCTION, DESTRUCTIVE]

Ge   6:13 I am surely going to **d** both them and

<table>
<tr><td></td><td>9:11</td><td>be a flood to **d** the earth."</td></tr>
<tr><td></td><td>18:28</td><td>Will you **d** the whole city because</td></tr>
<tr><td>Ex</td><td>33: 3</td><td>and I might **d** you on the way."</td></tr>
<tr><td>Dt</td><td>6:15</td><td>and he will **d** you from the face of</td></tr>
<tr><td></td><td>7: 2</td><td>then you must **d** them totally.</td></tr>
<tr><td>1Sa</td><td>15: 9</td><td>they were unwilling to **d** completely,</td></tr>
<tr><td>1Ch</td><td>21:15</td><td>God sent an angel to **d** Jerusalem.</td></tr>
<tr><td>Est</td><td>3: 6</td><td>for a way to **d** all Mordecai's people,</td></tr>
<tr><td>Ps</td><td>94:23</td><td>and **d** them for their wickedness;</td></tr>
<tr><td>Pr</td><td>1:32</td><td>complacency of fools will **d** them;</td></tr>
<tr><td>Isa</td><td>65: 8</td><td>'Don't **d** it, there is yet some good</td></tr>
<tr><td>Jer</td><td>4:27</td><td>though I will not **d** it completely.</td></tr>
<tr><td>Mt</td><td>10:28</td><td>afraid of the One who can **d** both</td></tr>
<tr><td>Mk</td><td>14:58</td><td>'I will **d** this man-made temple and</td></tr>
<tr><td>Lk</td><td>4:34</td><td>Have you come to **d** us?</td></tr>
<tr><td>Jn</td><td>10:10</td><td>to steal and kill and **d**;</td></tr>
<tr><td>Ac</td><td>8: 3</td><td>But Saul began to **d** the church.</td></tr>
<tr><td>Gal</td><td>1:13</td><td>the church of God and tried to **d** it.</td></tr>
<tr><td>Rev</td><td>11:18</td><td>destroying those who **d** the earth."</td></tr>
</table>

DESTROYED [DESTROY]

<table>
<tr><td>Ge</td><td>19:29</td><td>when God **d** the cities of the plain,</td></tr>
<tr><td>Dt</td><td>8:19</td><td>that you will surely be **d.**</td></tr>
<tr><td>Jos</td><td>24: 8</td><td>I **d** them from before you,</td></tr>
<tr><td>2Ki</td><td>10:28</td><td>So Jehu **d** Baal worship in Israel.</td></tr>
<tr><td>Job</td><td>19:26</td><td>And after my skin has been **d,**</td></tr>
<tr><td>Ps</td><td>37:38</td><td>But all sinners will be **d;**</td></tr>
<tr><td>Pr</td><td>6:15</td><td>he will suddenly be **d—**</td></tr>
<tr><td></td><td>11: 3</td><td>unfaithful are **d** by their duplicity.</td></tr>
<tr><td></td><td>21:28</td><td>listens to him will be **d** forever.</td></tr>
<tr><td></td><td>29: 1</td><td>many rebukes will suddenly be **d—**</td></tr>
<tr><td>Isa</td><td>55:13</td><td>which will not be **d.**"</td></tr>
<tr><td>Da</td><td>2:44</td><td>a kingdom that will never be **d,**</td></tr>
<tr><td></td><td>6:26</td><td>his kingdom will not be **d,**</td></tr>
<tr><td></td><td>7:11</td><td>the beast was slain and its body **d**</td></tr>
<tr><td>Hos</td><td>4: 6</td><td>my people are **d** from lack</td></tr>
<tr><td>Lk</td><td>17:27</td><td>Then the flood came and **d** them all.</td></tr>
<tr><td>1Co</td><td>5: 5</td><td>that the sinful nature may be **d**</td></tr>
<tr><td></td><td>8:11</td><td>is **d** by your knowledge.</td></tr>
<tr><td></td><td>15:24</td><td>after he has **d** all dominion,</td></tr>
<tr><td></td><td>15:26</td><td>The last enemy to be **d** is death.</td></tr>
<tr><td>2Co</td><td>4: 9</td><td>struck down, but not **d.**</td></tr>
<tr><td></td><td>5: 1</td><td>that if the earthly tent we live in is **d,**</td></tr>
<tr><td>Gal</td><td>5:15</td><td>or you will be **d** by each other.</td></tr>
<tr><td>Eph</td><td>2:14</td><td>the two one and has **d** the barrier,</td></tr>
<tr><td>2Ti</td><td>1:10</td><td>who has **d** death and has brought life</td></tr>
<tr><td>Heb</td><td>10:39</td><td>of those who shrink back and are **d,**</td></tr>
<tr><td>2Pe</td><td>2:12</td><td>born only to be caught and **d,**</td></tr>
<tr><td></td><td>3:10</td><td>the elements will be **d** by fire,</td></tr>
<tr><td>Jude</td><td>1: 5</td><td>but later **d** those who did not believe.</td></tr>
</table>

DESTROYER [DESTROY]

<table>
<tr><td>Ex</td><td>12:23</td><td>not permit the **d** to enter your houses</td></tr>
<tr><td>Jer</td><td>6:26</td><td>suddenly the **d** will come upon us.</td></tr>
<tr><td>Heb</td><td>11:28</td><td>**d** of the firstborn would not touch</td></tr>
</table>

DESTROYING [DESTROY]

<table>
<tr><td>Ps</td><td>106:23</td><td>to keep his wrath from **d** them.</td></tr>
<tr><td>Jer</td><td>23: 1</td><td>"Woe to the shepherds who are **d**</td></tr>
<tr><td>1Co</td><td>10:10</td><td>and were killed by the **d** angel.</td></tr>
<tr><td>Rev</td><td>11:18</td><td>for **d** those who destroy the earth."</td></tr>
</table>

DESTROYS [DESTROY]

<table>
<tr><td>Pr</td><td>6:32</td><td>whoever does so **d** himself.</td></tr>
</table>

<table>
<tr><td></td><td>11: 9</td><td>the godless **d** his neighbor,</td></tr>
<tr><td></td><td>18: 9</td><td>in his work is brother to one who **d.**</td></tr>
<tr><td></td><td>28:24</td><td>he is partner to him who **d.**</td></tr>
<tr><td>Ecc</td><td>9:18</td><td>but one sinner **d** much good.</td></tr>
<tr><td>Lk</td><td>12:33</td><td>no thief comes near and no moth **d.**</td></tr>
<tr><td>1Co</td><td>3:17</td><td>If anyone **d** God's temple,</td></tr>
</table>

DESTRUCTION [DESTROY]

<table>
<tr><td>Nu</td><td>32:15</td><td>and you will be the cause of their **d.**"</td></tr>
<tr><td>Dt</td><td>7:10</td><td>he will repay to their face by **d;**</td></tr>
<tr><td>Est</td><td>7: 4</td><td>my people have been sold for **d**</td></tr>
<tr><td>Pr</td><td>16:18</td><td>Pride goes before **d,**</td></tr>
<tr><td></td><td>17:19</td><td>who builds a high gate invites **d.**</td></tr>
<tr><td></td><td>24:22</td><td>for those two will send sudden **d**</td></tr>
<tr><td></td><td>27:20</td><td>Death and **D** are never satisfied,</td></tr>
<tr><td>Isa</td><td>10:22</td><td>**D** has been decreed,</td></tr>
<tr><td>Hos</td><td>13:14</td><td>Where, O grave, is your **d?**</td></tr>
<tr><td>Hab</td><td>2:17</td><td>your **d** of animals will terrify you.</td></tr>
<tr><td>Mt</td><td>7:13</td><td>and broad is the road that leads to **d,**</td></tr>
<tr><td>Lk</td><td>6:49</td><td>it collapsed and its **d** was complete."</td></tr>
<tr><td>Jn</td><td>17:12</td><td>lost except the one doomed to **d**</td></tr>
<tr><td>Ro</td><td>9:22</td><td>of his wrath—prepared for **d?**</td></tr>
<tr><td>Gal</td><td>6: 8</td><td>from that nature will reap **d;**</td></tr>
<tr><td>Php</td><td>3:19</td><td>Their destiny is **d,**</td></tr>
<tr><td>1Th</td><td>5: 3</td><td>**d** will come on them suddenly,</td></tr>
<tr><td>2Th</td><td>1: 9</td><td>be punished with everlasting **d**</td></tr>
<tr><td></td><td>2: 3</td><td>the man doomed to **d.**</td></tr>
<tr><td>1Ti</td><td>6: 9</td><td>that plunge men into ruin and **d.**</td></tr>
<tr><td>2Pe</td><td>2: 1</td><td>bringing swift **d** on themselves.</td></tr>
<tr><td></td><td>2: 3</td><td>and their **d** has not been sleeping.</td></tr>
<tr><td></td><td>3: 7</td><td>of judgment and **d** of ungodly men.</td></tr>
<tr><td></td><td>3:12</td><td>about the **d** of the heavens by fire,</td></tr>
<tr><td></td><td>3:16</td><td>to their own **d.**</td></tr>
<tr><td>Rev</td><td>17: 8</td><td>up out of the Abyss and go to his **d.**</td></tr>
<tr><td></td><td>17:11</td><td>to the seven and is going to his **d.**</td></tr>
</table>

DESTRUCTIVE [DESTROY]

<table>
<tr><td>Ex</td><td>12:13</td><td>No **d** plague will touch you</td></tr>
<tr><td>2Pe</td><td>2: 1</td><td>will secretly introduce **d** heresies,</td></tr>
</table>

DETERMINED [DETERMINES]

<table>
<tr><td>Jdg</td><td>1:27</td><td>for the Canaanites were **d** to live in</td></tr>
<tr><td></td><td>1:35</td><td>the Amorites were **d** also to hold out</td></tr>
<tr><td>Ru</td><td>1:18</td><td>that Ruth was **d** to go with her,</td></tr>
<tr><td>2Sa</td><td>17:14</td><td>For the LORD had **d** to frustrate</td></tr>
<tr><td>Job</td><td>14: 5</td><td>Man's days are **d;**</td></tr>
<tr><td>Isa</td><td>14:26</td><td>the plan **d** for the whole world;</td></tr>
<tr><td>Da</td><td>11:36</td><td>for what has been **d** must take place.</td></tr>
<tr><td>Ac</td><td>17:26</td><td>and he **d** the times set for them and</td></tr>
<tr><td>1Co</td><td>15:38</td><td>But God gives it a body as he has **d,**</td></tr>
</table>

DETERMINES* [DETERMINED]

<table>
<tr><td>Ps</td><td>147: 4</td><td>He **d** the number of the stars</td></tr>
<tr><td>Pr</td><td>16: 9</td><td>but the LORD **d** his steps.</td></tr>
<tr><td>1Co</td><td>12:11</td><td>to each one, just as he **d.**</td></tr>
</table>

DETEST [DETESTABLE, DETESTED, DETESTS]

<table>
<tr><td>Lev</td><td>11:11</td><td>And since you are to **d** them,</td></tr>
<tr><td>Job</td><td>19:19</td><td>All my intimate friends **d** me;</td></tr>
<tr><td>Pr</td><td>8: 7</td><td>for my lips **d** wickedness.</td></tr>
<tr><td></td><td>13:19</td><td>but fools **d** turning from evil.</td></tr>
<tr><td></td><td>16:12</td><td>Kings **d** wrongdoing,</td></tr>
<tr><td></td><td>24: 9</td><td>and men **d** a mocker.</td></tr>
</table>

29:27 The righteous **d** the dishonest; the
       wicked **d** the upright.
Am 6: 8 pride of Jacob and **d** his fortresses;

DETESTABLE [DETEST]

Ge 46:34 all shepherds are **d** to the Egyptians."
Dt 18: 9 do not learn to imitate the **d** ways of
Pr 6:16 seven that are **d** to him:
    21:27 The sacrifice of the wicked is **d**—
    28: 9 even his prayers are **d**.
Isa 1:13 Your incense is **d** to me.
    41:24 he who chooses you is **d**.
    44:19 a **d** thing from what is left?
Jer 44: 4 'Do not do this **d** thing that I hate!'
Eze 5: 9 Because of all your **d** idols,
     8:13 that are even more **d**."
Mal 2:11 A **d** thing has been committed
Lk 16:15 among men is **d** in God's sight.
Tit 1:16 They are **d**, disobedient and unfit
1Pe 4: 3 orgies, carousing and **d** idolatry.
Rev 18: 2 a haunt for every unclean and **d** bird.

DETESTED* [DETEST]

Zec 11: 8 The flock **d** me,

DETESTS* [DETEST]

Dt 22: 5 your God anyone who does this.
   23:18 the LORD your God **d** them both.
   25:16 God **d** anyone who does these things,
Pr 3:32 for the LORD **d** a perverse man
   11:20 The LORD **d** men of perverse heart
   12:22 The LORD **d** lying lips,
   15: 8 LORD **d** the sacrifice of the wicked,
   15: 9 The LORD **d** the way of the wicked
   15:26 LORD **d** the thoughts of the wicked,
   16: 5 The LORD **d** all the proud of heart.
   17:15 the LORD **d** them both.
   20:10 the LORD **d** them both.
   20:23 the LORD **d** differing weights,

DEVIATE*

2Ch 8:15 not **d** from the king's commands to

DEVICES* [DEVISE]

Ps 81:12 stubborn hearts to follow their own **d**

DEVIL* [DEVIL'S]

Mt 4: 1 the desert to be tempted by the **d**.
    4: 5 the **d** took him to the holy city
    4: 8 took him to a very high mountain
    4:11 Then the **d** left him,
   13:39 the enemy who sows them is the **d**.
   25:41 the eternal fire prepared for the **d**
Lk 4: 2 forty days he was tempted by the **d**.
    4: 3 The **d** said to him,
    4: 5 The **d** led him up to a high place
    4: 9 The **d** led him to Jerusalem
    4:13 the **d** had finished all this tempting,
    8:12 the **d** comes and takes away the word
Jn 6:70 Yet one of you is a **d**!"
    8:44 You belong to your father, the **d**,
   13: 2 **d** had already prompted Judas
Ac 10:38 under the power of the **d**,
   13:10 "You are a child of the **d**

Eph 4:27 and do not give the **d** a foothold.
1Ti 3: 6 under the same judgment as the **d**.
2Ti 2:26 and escape from the trap of the **d**,
Heb 2:14 power of death—that is, the **d**—
Jas 3:15 unspiritual, of the **d**.
     4: 7 Resist the **d**, and he will flee
1Pe 5: 8 Your enemy the **d** prowls around like
1Jn 3: 8 what is sinful is of the **d**,
     3: 8 because the **d** has been sinning from
     3:10 and who the children of the **d** are:
Jude 1: 9 with the **d** about the body of Moses,
Rev 2:10 the **d** will put some of you in prison
    12: 9 that ancient serpent called the **d**,
    12:12 because the **d** has gone down to you!
    20: 2 that ancient serpent, who is the **d**,
    20:10 And the **d**, who deceived them,

DEVIL'S* [DEVIL]

Eph 6:11 your stand against the **d** schemes,
1Ti 3: 7 fall into disgrace and into the **d** trap.
1Jn 3: 8 appeared was to destroy the **d** work.

DEVILS (KJV) See DEMONS,
GOAT IDOLS

DEVIOUS* [DEVISE]

Pr 2:15 and who are **d** in their ways.
   14: 2 he whose ways are **d** despises him.
   21: 8 The way of the guilty is **d**,

DEVISE [DEVICES, DEVISED,
DEVISES]

Isa 8:10 **D** your strategy, but it will

DEVISED [DEVISE]

Est 8: 5 **d** and wrote to destroy the Jews in all
Mt 28:12 met with the elders and **d** a plan,

DEVISES [DEVISE]

Pr 6:18 a heart that **d** wicked schemes,

DEVOTE* [DEVOTED, DEVOTING,
DEVOTION, DEVOUT]

1Ch 22:19 **d** your heart and soul to seeking
2Ch 31: 4 so they could **d** themselves
Job 11:13 "Yet if you **d** your heart to him
Jer 30:21 will **d** himself to be close to me?
Mic 4:13 You will **d** their ill-gotten gains to
1Co 7: 5 that you may **d** yourselves to prayer.
Col 4: 2 **D** yourselves to prayer,
1Ti 1: 4 nor to **d** themselves to myths
     4:13 **d** yourself to the public reading
Tit 3: 8 be careful to **d** themselves
     3:14 **d** themselves to doing what is good,

DEVOTED [DEVOTE]

Jos 6:18 But keep away from the **d** things,
     7: 1 unfaithfully in regard to the **d** things;
1Ki 11: 4 not fully **d** to the LORD his God,
2Ch 17: 6 His heart was **d** to the ways of
Ezr 7:10 Ezra had **d** himself to the study
Ne   5:16 I **d** myself to the work on this wall.
Ps 86: 2 Guard my life, for I am **d** to you.
Ecc 1:13 I **d** myself to study and to explore

Eze 20:16 For their hearts were **d** to their idols.
Mt 6:24 or he will be **d** to the one and despise
Mk 7:11 a gift **d** to God),
Ac 2:42 They **d** themselves to the apostles'
18: 5 Paul **d** himself exclusively to
Ro 12:10 Be **d** to one another in brotherly love
1Co 7:34 to be **d** to the Lord in both body
16:15 and they have **d** themselves to
2Co 7:12 how **d** to us you are.

DEVOTING* [DEVOTE]

1Ti 5:10 helping those in trouble and **d** herself

DEVOTION* [DEVOTE]

2Ki 20: 3 faithfully and with wholehearted **d**
1Ch 28: 9 and serve him with wholehearted **d**
29: 3 in my **d** to the temple of my God
29:19 Solomon the wholehearted **d** to keep
2Ch 32:32 Hezekiah's reign and his acts of **d**
35:26 Josiah's reign and his acts of **d,**
Job 6:14 "A despairing man should have the **d**
15: 4 undermine piety and hinder **d** to God
Isa 38: 3 faithfully and with wholehearted **d**
Jer 2: 2 " 'I remember the **d** of your youth,
Eze 33:31 With their mouths they express **d,**
1Co 7:35 right way in undivided **d** to the Lord.
2Co 11: 3 astray from your sincere and pure **d**

DEVOUR [DEVOURED, DEVOURING, DEVOURS]

Lev 26:38 the land of your enemies will **d** you.
Dt 28:38 because locusts will **d** it.
2Sa 2:26 "Must the sword **d** forever?
1Ki 21:23 the LORD says: 'Dogs will **d** Jezebel
2Ki 9:36 at Jezreel dogs will **d** Jezebel's flesh.
Jer 5:17 **d** your sons and daughters;
46:10 The sword will **d** till it is satisfied,
Mk 12:40 They **d** widows' houses and for
1Pe 5: 8 lion looking for someone to **d.**

DEVOURED [DEVOUR]

Isa 1:20 you will be **d** by the sword."
Jer 30:16 " 'But all who devour you will be **d;**
Rev 20: 9 down from heaven and **d** them.

DEVOURING [DEVOUR]

Mal 3:11 prevent pests from **d** your crops,
Gal 5:15 on biting and **d** each other,

DEVOURS [DEVOUR]

2Sa 11:25 the sword **d** one as well as another.
Ps 50: 3 a fire **d** before him,
Pr 21:20 but a foolish man **d** all he has.
Rev 11: 5 their mouths and **d** their enemies.

DEVOUT* [DEVOTE]

1Ki 18: 3 (Obadiah was a **d** believer in
Isa 57: 1 **d** men are taken away,
Lk 2:25 who was righteous and **d.**
Ac 10: 2 He and all his family were **d**
10: 7 two of his servants and a **d** soldier
13:43 many of the Jews and **d** converts
22:12 a **d** observer of the law

DEW

Ge 27:28 May God give you of heaven's **d** and
Ex 16:13 in the morning there was a layer of **d**
Dt 32: 2 and my words descend like **d,**
Jdg 6:37 If there is **d** only on the fleece and all
Job 38:28 Who fathers the drops of **d?**
Pr 19:12 but his favor is like **d** on the grass.
Hos 6: 4 like the early **d** that disappears.
14: 5 I will be like the **d** to Israel;
Hag 1:10 the heavens have withheld their **d**

DIADEM

Ex 39:30 They made the plate, the sacred **d,**
Isa 62: 3 a royal **d** in the hand of your God.

DIANA (KJV) See ARTEMIS

DICTATED [DICTATING]

Jer 36: 4 and while Jeremiah **d** all the words

DICTATING* [DICTATED]

Jer 45: 1 the words Jeremiah was then **d:**

DIDYMUS* [THOMAS]

Alternate name of the disciple Thomas (Jn 11:16; 20:24; 21:2).

DIE [DEAD, DEADENED, DEATH, DIED, DIES, DYING]

Ge 2:17 when you eat of it you will surely **d.**
3: 3 or you will **d.' "**
3: 4 "You will not surely **d,"**
Ex 11: 5 Every firstborn son in Egypt will **d,**
14:11 brought us to the desert to **d?**
Nu 23:10 Let me **d** the death of the righteous,
Dt 24:16 each is to **d** for his own sin.
Ru 1:17 Where you **d** I will **d,**
2Ki 14: 6 each is to **d** for his own sins."
Job 2: 9 Curse God and **d!"**
Ps 37: 2 like green plants they will soon **d**
118:17 I will not **d** but live,
Pr 5:23 He will **d** for lack of discipline,
10:21 but fools **d** for lack of judgment.
15:10 he who hates correction will **d.**
23:13 he will not **d.**
Ecc 2:16 the wise man too must **d!**
3: 2 a time to be born and a time to **d,**
Isa 22:13 you say, "for tomorrow we **d!"**
66:24 their worm will not **d,** nor will their
Jer 31:30 everyone will **d** for his own sin;
Eze 3:18 that wicked man will **d** for his sin,
18: 4 soul who sins is the one who will **d.**
18:31 Why will you **d,** O house of Israel?
33: 8 that wicked man will **d** for his sin,
Jnh 4: 8 He wanted to **d,** and said,
Hab 1:12 my Holy One, we will not **d.**
Mt 26:35 "Even if I have to **d** with you,
26:52 "for all who draw the sword will **d**
Mk 9:48 where " 'their worm does not **d,**
Jn 6:50 which a man may eat and not **d.**
8:21 and you will **d** in your sin.
11:26 and believes in me will never **d.**
21:23 that this disciple would not **d.**
Ro 5: 7 someone might possibly dare to **d.**

14: 8 and if we **d,** we **d** to the Lord.
1Co 15:22 For as in Adam all **d,**
15:31 I **d** every day—
15:32 for tomorrow we **d."**
Php 1:21 to live is Christ and to **d** is gain.
Heb 9:27 Just as man is destined to **d** once,
1Pe 2:24 so that we might **d** to sins and live
Rev 9: 6 they will long to **d,**
14:13 Blessed are the dead who **d** in the Lord

MUST DIE See MUST

DIED [DIE]

Lev 10: 2 and they **d** before the LORD.
Nu 14: 2 "If only we had **d** in Egypt!
16:49 But 14,700 people **d** from the plague,
Jdg 16:30 when he **d** than while he lived.
2Sa 24:15 the people from Dan to Beersheba **d.**
1Ki 3:19 During the night this woman's son **d**
1Ch 10:13 Saul **d** because he was unfaithful to
Lk 16:22 when the beggar **d** and the angels
Jn 6:58 that your forefathers ate manna and **d,**
Ro 5: 6 Christ **d** for the ungodly.
5: 8 Christ **d** for us.
6: 2 We **d** to sin;
6: 8 Now if we **d** with Christ,
6:10 death he **d,** he **d** to sin once for all;
14: 9 Christ died and returned to life so
1Co 8:11 for whom Christ **d,**
15: 3 that Christ **d** for our sins
2Co 5:14 we are convinced that one **d** for all,
5:15 And he **d** for all,
Gal 2:19 For through the law I **d** to the law so
Col 2:20 Since you **d** with Christ to
3: 3 For you **d,** and your life is now
1Th 4:14 that Jesus **d** and rose again and
5:10 He **d** for us so that,
2Ti 2:11 If we **d** with him, we will also live
Heb 9:15 that he has **d** as a ransom
11:13 still living by faith when they **d.**
1Pe 3:18 For Christ **d** for sins once for all,
Rev 2: 8 who **d** and came to life again.
8: 9 of the living creatures in the sea **d,**
8:11 and many people **d** from the waters
16:3 and every living thing in the sea **d.**

DIES [DIE]

Job 14:14 If a man **d,** will he live again?
Pr 11: 7 a wicked man **d,** his hope perishes;
Ecc 3:19 As one **d,** so **d** the other.
Jn 11:25 will live, even though he **d;**
12:24 of wheat falls to the ground and **d,**
Ro 7: 2 but if her husband **d,**
14: 7 and none of us **d** to himself alone.
1Co 7:39 But if her husband **d,**
15:36 not come to life unless it **d.**

DIFFERENCE* [DIFFERENT]

2Sa 19:35 Can I tell the **d** between what is good
2Ch 12: 8 the **d** between serving me and
Eze 22:26 no **d** between the unclean and the
44:23 the **d** between the holy
Ro 3:22 There is no **d,**
10:12 For there is no **d** between Jew

Gal 2: 6 they were makes no **d** to me;

DIFFERENCES* [DIFFERENT]

1Co 11:19 to be **d** among you to show which

DIFFERENT* [DIFFERENCE,
DIFFERENCES, DIFFERENTLY,
DIFFERING, DIFFERS]

Lev 19:19 " 'Do not mate **d** kinds of animals.
Nu 14:24 my servant Caleb has a **d** spirit
1Sa 10: 6 be changed into a **d** person.
Est 1: 7 each one **d** from the other,
3: 8 whose customs are **d** from those of
Da 7: 3 each **d** from the others,
7: 7 It was **d** from all the former beasts,
7:19 which was **d** from all the others
7:23 be **d** from all the other kingdoms
7:24 **d** from the earlier ones;
11:29 but this time the outcome will be **d**
Mk 16:12 appeared in a **d** form
Ro 12: 6 We have **d** gifts,
1Co 4: 7 who makes you **d** from anyone else?
12: 4 There are **d** kinds of gifts,
12: 5 There are **d** kinds of service,
12: 6 There are **d** kinds of working,
12:10 to another speaking in **d** kinds
12:28 those speaking in **d** kinds of tongues.
2Co 11: 4 a **d** spirit from the one you received,
11: 4 **d** gospel from the one you accepted,
Gal 1: 6 and are turning to a **d** gospel—
4: 1 he is no **d** from a slave,
Heb 7:13 belonged to a **d** tribe,
Jas 2:25 and sent them off in a **d** direction?

DIFFERENTLY* [DIFFERENT]

Ex 8:22 that day I will deal **d** with the land
Php 3:15 And if on some point you think **d,**

DIFFERING* [DIFFERENT]

Dt 25:13 Do not have two **d** weights
25:14 Do not have two **d** measures
Pr 20:10 **D** weights and **d** measures—
20:23 The LORD detests **d** weights,

DIFFERS* [DIFFERENT]

1Co 15:41 and star **d** from star in splendor.

DIFFICULT [DIFFICULTIES]

Ge 47: 9 My years have been few and **d,**
Ex 18:22 have them bring every **d** case to you;
Dt 30:11 commanding you today is not too **d**
2Ki 2:10 "You have asked a **d** thing,"
Eze 3: 5 of obscure speech and **d** language,
Da 2:11 What the king asks is too **d.**
4: 9 and no mystery is too **d** for you.
Ac 15:19 not make it **d** for the Gentiles

DIFFICULTIES* [DIFFICULT]

Dt 31:17 Many disasters and **d** will come
31:21 when many disasters and **d** come
2Co 12:10 in hardships, in persecutions, in **d.**

DIG [DIGS, DUG, GRAVEDIGGERS]

Dt 6:11 wells you did not **d,**

Eze 8: 8 "Son of man, now **d** into the wall."
Am 9: 2 Though they **d** down to the depths of

DIGNITY
Ex 28: 2 to give him **d** and honor.
Pr 31:25 She is clothed with strength and **d;**

DIGS [DIG]
Pr 26:27 If a man **d** a pit, he will fall into it;

DILIGENCE [DILIGENT]
Ezr 5: 8 The work is being carried on with **d**
Heb 6:11 to show this same **d** to the very end,

DILIGENT* [DILIGENCE, DILIGENTLY]
2Ch 24:13 men in charge of the work were **d,**
Pr 10: 4 but **d** hands bring wealth.
    12:24 **D** hands will rule,
    12:27 but the **d** man prizes his possessions.
    13: 4 the desires of the **d** are fully satisfied
    21: 5 The plans of the **d** lead to profit as
1Ti 4:15 Be **d** in these matters;

DILIGENTLY* [DILIGENT]
Zec 6:15 if you **d** obey the LORD your God."
Jn 5:39 You **d** study the Scriptures
Ro 12: 8 let him govern **d;**

DINAH*
Only daughter of Jacob, by Leah (Ge 30:21; 46:15). Raped by Shechem; avenged by Simeon and Levi (Ge 34).

DINE [DINNER]
Est 7: 1 So the king and Haman went to **d**
Pr 23: 1 When you sit to **d** with a ruler,

DINNER [DINE]
Mk 2:15 Jesus was having **d** at Levi's house,
Lk 14:12 "When you give a luncheon or **d,**

DIOTREPHES*
3Jn 1: 9 but **D,** who loves to be first,

DIPPED [DIPPING]
2Ki 5:14 So he went down and **d** himself in
Mt 26:23 "The one who has **d** his hand into
Rev 19:13 He is dressed in a robe **d** in blood,

DIPPING* [DIPPED, DIPS]
Jn 13:26 Then, **d** the piece of bread,

DIPS* [DIPPING]
Mk 14:20 "one who **d** bread into the bowl

DIRECT [DIRECTED, DIRECTIVES, DIRECTS]
Ge 18:19 so that he will **d** his children
Dt 17:10 to do everything they **d** you to do.
Ps 119:35 **D** me in the path of your commands,
    119:133 **D** my footsteps according to your
Jer 10:23 not for man to **d** his steps.
2Th 3: 5 May the Lord **d** your hearts
1Ti 5:17 elders who **d** the affairs of the church

DIRECTED [DIRECT]
Ge 24:51 as the LORD has **d.**"
Nu 16:40 as the LORD **d** him through Moses.
Dt 2: 1 as the LORD had **d** me.
    6: 1 and laws the LORD your God **d** me
Jos 11: 9 to them as the LORD had **d:**
Pr 20:24 A man's steps are **d** by the LORD.
Jer 13: 2 So I bought a belt, as the LORD **d,**
Mt 26:19 the disciples did as Jesus had **d** them
Ac 7:44 It had been made as God **d** Moses,
Tit 1: 5 as I **d** you.

DIRECTIVES* [DIRECT]
1Co 11:17 In the following **d** I have no praise
FOR THE DIRECTOR OF MUSIC
See MUSIC

DIRECTS* [DIRECT]
Jdg 20: 9 up against it as the lot **d.**
Ps 42: 8 By day the LORD **d** his love,
Pr 21: 1 he **d** it like a watercourse wherever
Isa 48:17 who **d** you in the way you should go.

DIRGE*
Mt 11:17 we sang a **d,** and you did not mourn.'
Lk 7:32 sang a **d,** and you did not cry.'

DISABLED* [ABLE]
Jn 5: 3 number of **d** people used to lie—
Heb 12:13 so that the lame may not be **d,**

DISAGREEMENT* [AGREE]
Ac 15:39 a sharp **d** that they parted company.

DISAPPEAR [DISAPPEARED, DISAPPEARS]
Nu 27: 4 Why should our father's name **d**
Ru 4:10 will not **d** from among his family
Mt 5:18 until heaven and earth **d,**
Lk 16:17 for heaven and earth to **d** than for
Heb 8:13 obsolete and aging will soon **d.**
2Pe 3:10 The heavens will **d** with a roar;

DISAPPEARED* [DISAPPEAR]
Jdg 6:21 And the angel of the LORD **d.**
1Ki 20:40 the man **d.**"
Lk 24:31 and he **d** from their sight.

DISAPPEARS [DISAPPEAR]
Hos 13: 3 like the early dew that **d,**
1Co 13:10 perfection comes, the imperfect **d.**

DISAPPOINT* [DISAPPOINTED]
Ro 5: 5 And hope does not **d** us,

DISAPPOINTED [DISAPPOINT]
Ps 22: 5 in you they trusted and were not **d.**
Isa 49:23 hope in me will not be **d.**"

DISAPPROVE*
Pr 24:18 and **d** and turn his wrath away

DISARMED* [DISARMS]
Col 2:15 having **d** the powers and authorities,

DISARMS* [DISARMED]

Job 12:21 on nobles and **d** the mighty.

DISASTER [DISASTERS]

Ex	32:12	and do not bring **d** on your people.
Dt	32:35	their day of **d** is near
Jos	24:20	and bring **d** on you and make an end
2Ch	7:22	that is why he brought all this **d**
Est	8: 6	I bear to see **d** fall on my people?
Ps	57: 1	of your wings until the **d** has passed.
Pr	1:26	I in turn will laugh at your **d;**
	3:25	Have no fear of sudden **d** or of
	6:15	Therefore **d** will overtake him in
	16: 4	even the wicked for a day of **d.**
	17: 5	whoever gloats over **d** will not
	27:10	when **d** strikes you—
Isa	3: 9	have brought **d** upon themselves.
	45: 7	I bring prosperity and create **d;**
Jer	4:20	**D** follows **d;** the whole land lies in
	17:17	my refuge in the day of **d.**
	18: 8	not inflict on it the **d** I had planned.
Eze	7: 5	An unheard-of **d** is coming.
Ob	1:13	of my people in the day of their **d,**

DISASTERS [DISASTER]

Dt 31:17 Many **d** and difficulties will come

DISCERN* [DISCERNED, DISCERNING, DISCERNMENT]

Dt	32:29	and **d** what their end will be!
Job	6:30	Can my mouth not **d** malice?
	34: 4	Let us **d** for ourselves what is right;
Ps	19:12	Who can **d** his errors?
	139: 3	You **d** my going out
Php	1:10	be able to **d** what is best

DISCERNED* [DISCERN]

1Co 2:14 because they are spiritually **d.**

DISCERNING* [DISCERN]

Ge	41:33	"And now let Pharaoh look for a **d**
	41:39	there is no one so **d** and wise as you.
2Sa	14:17	an angel of God in **d** good and evil.
1Ki	3: 9	a **d** heart to govern your people and
	3:12	I will give you a wise and **d** heart,
Pr	1: 5	and let the **d** get guidance—
	8: 9	To the **d** all of them are right;
	10:13	Wisdom is found on the lips of the **d,**
	14: 6	but knowledge comes easily to the **d.**
	14:33	Wisdom reposes in the heart of the **d**
	15:14	The **d** heart seeks knowledge.
	16:21	The wise in heart are called **d,**
	17:24	A **d** man keeps wisdom in view,
	17:28	and if he holds his tongue.
	18:15	heart of the **d** acquires knowledge;
	19:25	rebuke a **d** man,
	28: 7	He who keeps the law is a **d** son,
Da	2:21	to the wise and knowledge to the **d.**
Hos	14: 9	Who is **d?**

DISCERNMENT* [DISCERN]

Dt   32:28 there is no **d** in them.
1Ki   3:11 but for **d** in administering justice,

2Ch	2:12	endowed with intelligence and **d,**
Job	12:20	and takes away the **d** of elders.
Ps	119:125	I am your servant; give me **d**
Pr	3:21	preserve sound judgment and **d,**
	17:10	A rebuke impresses a man of **d**
	28:11	but a poor man who has **d** sees

DISCHARGE [DISCHARGED, DISCHARGING]

Lev 15: 2 'When any man has a bodily **d,**
2Ti   4: 5 **d** all the duties of your ministry.

DISCHARGED* [DISCHARGE]

Ecc   8: 8 As no one is **d** in time of war,

DISCHARGING* [DISCHARGE]

1Co   9:17 I am simply **d** the trust committed

DISCIPLE [DISCIPLES, DISCIPLES']

Mt	10:42	because he is my **d,**
Lk	14:26	he cannot be my **d.**
	14:27	and follow me cannot be my **d.**
	14:33	up everything he has cannot be my **d.**
Jn	9:28	"You are this fellow's **d!**
	13:23	the **d** whom Jesus loved,
	18:15	this **d** was known to the high priest,
	19:26	**d** whom he loved standing nearby,
	19:38	Now Joseph was a **d** of Jesus,
	20: 2	to Simon Peter and the other **d,**
	21: 7	the **d** whom Jesus loved said to Peter
	21:20	**d** whom Jesus loved was following
Ac	9:10	there was a **d** named Ananias.
	16: 1	where a **d** named Timothy lived,

DISCIPLES [DISCIPLE]

Mt	9:10	and ate with him and his **d.**
	10: 1	He called his twelve **d** to him
	26:56	Then all the **d** deserted him and fled.
	28:19	go and make **d** of all nations,
Mk	3: 7	Jesus withdrew with his **d** to the lake
	6:29	John's **d** came and took his body
Lk	7: 5	"Why don't your **d** live according to
	6:13	he called his **d** to him
	9:46	An argument started among the **d**
	11: 1	just as John taught his **d."**
Jn	2:11	and his **d** put their faith in him.
	6:66	of his **d** turned back
	8:31	you are really my **d.**
	12:16	At first his **d** did not understand
	13:35	know that you are my **d,**
	15: 8	showing yourselves to be my **d.**
	20:20	The **d** were overjoyed when they saw
Ac	6: 1	the number of **d** was increasing,
	11:26	The **d** were called Christians first
	14:22	the **d** and encouraging them
	18:23	strengthening all the **d.**

DISCIPLES'* [DISCIPLE]

Jn 13: 5 a basin and began to wash his **d** feet,

DISCIPLINE* [DISCIPLINED, DISCIPLINES, SELF-DISCIPLINE]

Dt   4:36 hear his voice to **d** you.
      11: 2 who saw and experienced the **d**

	21:18	not listen to them when they **d** him,
Job	5:17	so do not despise the **d**
Ps	6:1	or **d** me in your wrath.
	38:1	or **d** me in your wrath.
	39:11	You rebuke and **d** men for their sin;
	94:12	Blessed is the man you **d**, O LORD,
Pr	1:2	for attaining wisdom and **d;**
	1:7	but fools despise wisdom and **d.**
	3:11	do not despise the LORD's **d**
	5:12	You will say, "How I hated **d!**
	5:23	He will die for lack of **d,**
	6:23	corrections of **d** are the way to life,
	10:17	He who heeds **d** shows the way
	12:1	Whoever loves **d** loves knowledge,
	13:18	He who ignores **d** comes to poverty
	13:24	he who loves him is careful to **d** him.
	15:5	A fool spurns his father's **d,**
	15:10	Stern **d** awaits him who leaves
	15:32	He who ignores **d** despises himself,
	19:18	**D** your son, for in that there is hope;
	22:15	rod of **d** will drive it far from him.
	23:13	Do not withhold **d** from a child;
	23:23	**d** and understanding.
	29:17	**D** your son, and he will give
Jer	17:23	and would not listen or respond to **d.**
	30:11	I will **d** you but only with justice;
	32:33	they would not listen or respond to **d.**
	46:28	I will **d** you but only with justice;
Hos	5:2	I will **d** all of them.
Heb	12:5	do not make light of the Lord's **d,**
	12:7	Endure hardship as **d;**
	12:8	(and everyone undergoes **d),**
	12:11	No **d** seems pleasant at the time,
Rev	3:19	Those whom I love I rebuke and **d.**

DISCIPLINED* [DISCIPLINE]

Pr	1:3	for acquiring a **d** and prudent life,
Isa	26:16	when you **d** them,
Jer	31:18	'You **d** me like an unruly calf,
	31:18	and I have been **d.**
1Co	11:32	we are being **d** so that we will not
Tit	1:8	upright, holy and **d.**
Heb	12:7	For what son is not **d** by his father?
	12:8	If you are not **d**
	12:9	have all had human fathers who **d** us
	12:10	Our fathers **d** us for a little while

DISCIPLINES* [DISCIPLINE]

Dt	8:5	as a man **d** his son, so the LORD your God **d** you.
Ps	94:10	Does he who **d** nations not punish?
Pr	3:12	because the LORD **d** those he loves,
Heb	12:6	because the Lord **d** those he loves,
	12:10	but God **d** us for our good,

DISCLOSED

Mk	4:22	is hidden is meant to be **d,**
Lk	12:2	concealed that will not be **d,**
Col	1:26	but is now **d** to the saints.
Heb	9:8	not yet been **d** as long as

DISCORD*

| Est | 1:18 | be no end of disrespect and **d.** |
| Gal | 5:20 | **d,** jealousy, fits of rage, |

DISCOURAGE* [DISCOURAGED, DISCOURAGEMENT]

| Nu | 32:7 | Why do you **d** the Israelites |
| Ezr | 4:4 | set out to **d** the people of Judah |

DISCOURAGED* [DISCOURAGE]

Nu	32:9	they **d** the Israelites from entering
Dt	1:21	Do not be afraid; do not be **d."**
	31:8	Do not be afraid; do not be **d."**
Jos	1:9	Do not be terrified; do not be **d,**
	8:1	"Do not be afraid; do not be **d.**
	10:25	"Do not be afraid; do not be **d.**
1Ch	22:13	Do not be afraid or **d.**
	28:20	Do not be afraid or **d,**
2Ch	20:15	'Do not be afraid or **d** because
	20:17	Do not be afraid; do not be **d.**
	32:7	be afraid or **d** because of the king
Job	4:5	trouble comes to you, and you are **d;**
Isa	42:4	or be **d** till he establishes justice
Eph	3:13	not to be **d** because of my sufferings
Col	3:21	or they will become **d.**

DISCOURAGEMENT* [DISCOURAGE]

| Ex | 6:9 | because of their **d** and cruel bondage. |

DISCOVER [DISCOVERED]

| Ecc | 7:14 | cannot **d** anything about his future. |
| | 8:17 | man cannot **d** its meaning. |

DISCOVERED [DISCOVER]

Jdg	16:9	the secret of his strength was not **d.**
2Ki	23:24	the book that Hilkiah the priest had **d**
Ecc	7:27	"this is what I have **d:**

DISCREDIT* [DISCREDITED]

| Ne | 6:13 | a bad name to **d** me. |
| Job | 40:8 | "Would you **d** my justice? |

DISCREDITED* [DISCREDIT]

| Ac | 19:27 | the great goddess Artemis will be **d,** |
| 2Co | 6:3 | so that our ministry will not be **d.** |

DISCREETLY* [DISCRETION]

| Pr | 26:16 | than seven men who answer **d.** |

DISCRETION* [DISCREETLY]

1Ch	22:12	the LORD give you **d**
Pr	1:4	knowledge and **d** to the young—
	2:11	**D** will protect you,
	5:2	that you may maintain **d**
	8:12	I possess knowledge and **d.**
	11:22	a beautiful woman who shows no **d.**

DISCRIMINATED*

| Jas | 2:4 | have you not **d** among yourselves |

DISCUSSED [DISCUSSION]

| Mk | 8:16 | They **d** this with one another |
| | 11:31 | They **d** it among themselves |

DISCUSSING [DISCUSSION]

| Lk | 24:17 | "What are you **d** together |

DISCUSSION [DISCUSSED, DISCUSSING]

Mk 8:17 Aware of their **d**, Jesus asked them:

DISEASE [DISEASED, DISEASES]

Dt 7:15 will keep you free from every **d**.
　　28:22 LORD will strike you with wasting **d**,
1Ki 8:37 whatever disaster or **d** may come,
Ps 106:15 but sent a wasting **d** upon them.
Mt 4:23 and healing every **d** and sickness.
　　9:35 and healing every **d** and sickness.
　　10: 1 and to heal every **d**

DISEASED [DISEASE]

Mal 1: 8 you sacrifice crippled or **d** animals,

DISEASES [DISEASE]

Dt 7:15 the horrible **d** you knew in Egypt,
　　28:21 The LORD will plague you with **d**
Ps 103: 3 and heals all your **d**,
Mt 8:17 up our infirmities and carried our **d**."
Mk 3:10 with **d** were pushing forward
Lk 9: 1 to drive out all demons and to cure **d**,

DISFIGURE* [DISFIGURED]

Mt 6:16 for they **d** their faces to show

DISFIGURED* [DISFIGURE]

Lev 21:18 blind or lame, **d** or deformed;
Isa 52:14 so **d** beyond that of any man

DISGRACE [DISGRACED, DISGRACEFUL, DISGRACES]

Ge 30:23 "God has taken away my **d**."
1Sa 17:26 and removes this **d** from Israel?
Ps 44:15 My **d** is before me all day long,
　　52: 1 you who are a **d** in the eyes of God?
　　74:21 Do not let the oppressed retreat in **d**;
Pr 6:33 Blows and **d** are his lot,
　　11: 2 When pride comes, then comes **d**,
　　14:34 but sin is a **d** to any people.
　　19:26 a son who brings shame and **d**.
Isa 4: 1 Take away our **d**!"
Eze 16:52 then, be ashamed and bear your **d**,
　　36:30 so that you will no longer suffer **d**
Mt 1:19 not want to expose her to public **d**,
Lk 1:25 and taken away my **d** among
Ac 5:41 worthy of suffering **d** for the Name.
1Co 11: 6 a **d** for a woman to have her hair cut
　　11:14 it is a **d** to him,
1Ti 3: 7 so that he will not fall into **d** and into
Heb 6: 6 and subjecting him to public **d**.
　　11:26 He regarded **d** for the sake of Christ
　　13:13 bearing the **d** he bore.

DISGRACED [DISGRACE]

2Sa 13:22 because he had **d** his sister Tamar.
Ezr 9: 6 and to lift up my face to you,
Isa 45:17 never be put to shame or **d**,
Jer 2:26 so the house of Israel is **d**—

DISGRACEFUL [DISGRACE]

Jdg 19:23 don't do this **d** thing.

Pr 10: 5 sleeps during harvest is a **d** son.
　　12: 4 a **d** wife is like decay in his bones.
　　17: 2 A wise servant will rule over a **d** son,
Hos 4: 7 their Glory for something **d**.
1Co 14:35 for it is **d** for a woman to speak in

DISGRACES* [DISGRACE]

Lev 21: 9 she **d** her father;
Pr 28: 7 a companion of gluttons **d** his father.
　　29:15 a child left to himself **d** his mother.

DISGUISE [DISGUISED, DISGUISES]

Ge 38:14 with a veil to **d** herself,
2Ch 18:29 "I will enter the battle in **d**,

DISGUISED [DISGUISE]

2Ch 35:22 but **d** himself to engage him in battle.

DISGUISES* [DISGUISE]

Pr 26:24 malicious man **d** himself with his

DISH [DISHES]

Pr 19:24 sluggard buries his hand in the **d**;
Mt 23:25 clean the outside of the cup and **d**,

DISHES [DISH]

Ex 25:29 make its plates and **d** of pure gold,
Ezr 1: 9 This was the inventory: gold **d** 30

DISHONEST*

Ex 18:21 trustworthy men who hate **d** gain—
Lev 19:35 " 'Do not use **d** standards
1Sa 8: 3 after **d** gain and accepted bribes
Pr 11: 1 The LORD abhors **d** scales,
　　13:11 **D** money dwindles away,
　　20:23 and **d** scales do not please him.
　　29:27 The righteous detest the **d**;
Jer 22:17 and your heart are set only on **d** gain,
Eze 28:18 **d** trade you have desecrated your
Hos 12: 7 The merchant uses **d** scales;
Am 8: 5 the price and cheating with **d** scales,
Mic 6:11 Shall I acquit a man with **d** scales
Lk 16: 8 master commended the **d** manager
　　16:10 whoever is **d** with very little will
　　　　　also be **d** with much.
1Ti 3: 8 and not pursuing **d** gain.
Tit 1: 7 not violent, not pursuing **d** gain.
　　1:11 and that for the sake of **d** gain.

DISHONOR* [DISHONORED, DISHONORS]

Lev 18: 7 " 'Do not **d** your father.
　　18: 8 that would **d** your father.
　　18:10 that would **d** you.
　　18:14 " 'Do not **d** your father's brother.
　　18:16 that would **d** your brother.
　　20:19 for that would **d** a close relative;
Dt 22:30 he must not **d** his father's bed.
Pr 30: 9 and so **d** the name of my God.
Jer 14:21 do not **d** your glorious throne.
　　20:11 their **d** will never be forgotten.
La 2: 2 princes down to the ground in **d**.
Eze 22:10 are those who **d** their fathers' bed;
Jn 8:49 I honor my Father and you **d** me.

Ro 2:23 do you **d** God by breaking the law?
1Co 15:43 it is sown in **d,** it is raised in glory;
2Co 6: 8 and **d,** bad report and good report;

DISHONORED* [DISHONOR]

Lev 20:11 he has **d** his father.
     20:17 He has **d** his sister and will
     20:20 he has **d** his uncle.
     20:21 he has **d** his brother.
Dt 21:14 since you have **d** her.
Ezr 4:14 not proper for us to see the king **d,**
1Co 4:10 You are honored, we are **d!**

DISHONORS* [DISHONOR]

Dt 27:16 "Cursed is the man who **d** his father
     27:20 for he **d** his father's bed."
Job 20: 3 I hear a rebuke that **d** me,
Mic 7: 6 For a son **d** his father,
1Co 11: 4 with his head covered **d** his head.
     11: 5 with her head uncovered **d** her head

DISILLUSIONMENT*

Ps 7:14 conceives trouble gives birth to **d.**

DISMAYED

1Sa 17:11 the Israelites were **d** and terrified.
Isa 28:16 the one who trusts will never be **d.**
    41:10 not be **d,** for I am your God.

DISOBEDIENCE* [DISOBEY]

Jos 22:22 If this has been in rebellion or **d** to
Jer 43: 7 entered Egypt in **d** to the LORD
Ro   5:19 as through the **d** of the one man
    11:30 as a result of their **d,**
    11:32 God has bound all men over to **d**
2Co 10: 6 be ready to punish every act of **d,**
Heb 2: 2 and **d** received its just punishment,
     4: 6 because of their **d.**
     4:11 by following their example of **d.**

DISOBEDIENT* [DISOBEY]

Ne   9:26 they were **d** and rebelled against you;
Lk   1:17 and the **d** to the wisdom of
Ac 26:19 not **d** to the vision from heaven.
Ro 10:21 to a **d** and obstinate people."
    11:30 as you who were at one time **d**
    11:31 now become **d** in order that they
Eph 2: 2 now at work in those who are **d.**
     5: 6 wrath comes on those who are **d.**
     5:12 to mention what the **d** do in secret.
2Ti 3: 2 **d** to their parents, ungrateful, unholy,
Tit 1: 6 to the charge of being wild and **d.**
     1:16 **d** and unfit for doing anything good.
     3: 3 At one time we too were foolish, **d,**
Heb 11:31 not killed with those who were **d.**

DISOBEY* [DISOBEDIENCE, DISOBEYED, DISOBEYING, DISOBEYS]

Dt 11:28 the curse if you **d** the commands of
2Ch 24:20 do you **d** the LORD's commands?
Est 3: 3 "Why do you **d**
Jer 42:13 and so **d** the LORD your God,
Ro   1:30 of doing evil; they **d** their parents;

1Pe 2: 8 because they **d** the message—

DISOBEYED* [DISOBEY]

Nu 14:22 and in the desert but who **d** me
    27:14 **d** my command to honor me as holy
Jdg 2: 2 Yet you have **d** me.
Ne   9:29 and **d** your commands.
Isa 24: 5 they have **d** the laws,
Jer 43: 4 and all the people **d**
Lk 15:29 for you and never **d** your orders.
Heb 3:18 if not to those who **d?**
1Pe 3:20 who **d** long ago when God waited

DISOBEYING* [DISOBEY]

Nu 14:41 "Why are you **d** the LORD's

DISOBEYS* [DISOBEY]

Eze 33:12 will not save him when he **d,**

DISORDER*

Job 10:22 of deep shadow and **d,**
1Co 14:33 God is not a God of **d** but of peace.
2Co 12:20 slander, gossip, arrogance and **d.**
Jas 3:16 you find **d** and every evil practice.

DISOWN [DISOWNED, DISOWNS]

Pr 30: 9 I may have too much and **d** you
Mt 10:33 I will **d** him before my Father
    26:35 I will never **d** you."
Mk 14:30 you yourself will **d** me three times.
2Ti 2:12 If we **d** him, he will also **d** us;

DISOWNED [DISOWN]

Lk 12: 9 be **d** before the angels of God.
Ac   3:14 You **d** the Holy and Righteous One

DISOWNS [DISOWN]

Lk 12: 9 But he who **d** me before men will

DISPENSATION (KJV) See
ADMINISTRATION, COMMISSION, TRUST

DISPERSE [DISPERSES]

Eze 12:15 when I **d** them among the nations

DISPERSES* [DISPERSE]

Dt 30: 1 the LORD your God **d** you among
Job 12:23 he enlarges nations, and **d** them.

DISPLACES*

Pr 30:23 a maidservant who **d** her mistress.

DISPLAY [DISPLAYED, DISPLAYS]

Ps 19: 2 night after night they **d** knowledge.
    45: 4 your right hand **d** awesome deeds.
Isa 49: 3 in whom I will **d** my splendor."
Eze 39:21 "I will **d** my glory among
Ro   9:17 that I might **d** my power in you and
1Co 4: 9 that God has put us apostles on **d** at
1Ti 1:16 Jesus might **d** his unlimited patience

DISPLAYED [DISPLAY]

Ex 14:31 the great power the LORD **d** against
Jn   9: 3 so that the work of God might be **d**
2Th 2: 9 with the work of Satan in all kinds

DISPLAYS* [DISPLAY]
Pr   14:29 but a quick-tempered man **d** folly.
Isa 44:23 he **d** his glory in Israel.

DISPLEASE [DISPLEASED]
Nu   11:11 What have I done to **d** you
1Th   2:15 They **d** God and are hostile

DISPLEASED [DISPLEASE]
2Sa 11:27 thing David had done **d** the LORD.
Isa 59:15 The LORD looked and was **d**
Jnh   4: 1 But Jonah was greatly **d**

DISPUTABLE* [DISPUTE]
Ro   14: 1 passing judgment on **d** matters.

DISPUTE [DISPUTABLE, DISPUTES, DISPUTING]
Job   9: 3 Though one wished to **d** with him,
Pr   17:14 the matter before a **d** breaks out.
Lk   22:24 a **d** arose among them as to which
Ac   15: 2 Paul and Barnabas into sharp **d**
1Co   6: 1 If any of you has a **d** with another,

DISPUTES [DISPUTE]
Pr   18:18 Casting the lot settles **d**
Isa   2: 4 and will settle **d** for many peoples.
1Co   6: 4 if you have such matters,

DISPUTING* [DISPUTE]
1Ti   2: 8 without anger or **d**.
Jude 1: 9 when he was **d** with the devil about

DISQUALIFIED* [DISQUALIFY]
1Co   9:27 I myself will not be **d** for the prize.

DISQUALIFY* [DISQUALIFIED]
Col   2:18 worship of angels **d** you for the prize

DISREGARDED*
Ezr   9:10 For we have **d** the commands
Isa 40:27 my cause is **d** by my God"?

DISREPUTE*
2Pe   2: 2 bring the way of truth into **d**.

DISSENSION* [DISSENSIONS]
Pr   6:14 he always stirs up **d**.
      6:19 and a man who stirs up **d**
     10:12 Hatred stirs up **d**,
     15:18 A hot-tempered man stirs up **d**,
     16:28 A perverse man stirs up **d**,
     28:25 A greedy man stirs up **d**,
     29:22 An angry man stirs up **d**,
Ro   13:13 not in **d** and jealousy.

DISSENSIONS* [DISSENSION]
Gal   5:20 fits of rage, selfish ambition, **d**,

DISSIPATION*
Lk   21:34 be weighed down with **d**,
1Pe   4: 4 with them into the same flood of **d**,

DISSOLVED*
Isa 34: 4 All the stars of the heavens will be **d**

DISTANCE [DISTANT]
Ex   2: 4 His sister stood at a **d** to see
     33: 7 outside the camp some **d** away,
Dt   32:52 you will see the land only from a **d**;
Mk   14:54 Peter followed him at a **d**,
     15:40 women were watching from a **d**.
Heb 11:13 and welcomed them from a **d**.

DISTANT [DISTANCE]
Jos   9: 6 "We have come from a **d** country;
Isa 49: 1 hear this, you **d** nations:
     66:19 to the **d** islands that have not heard
Jer   5:15 "I am bringing a **d** nation

DISTINCTION
Ex   8:23 I will make a **d** between my people
Ac   15: 9 He made no **d** between us and them,

DISTINGUISH [DISTINGUISHING]
Lev 10:10 You must **d** between the holy and
1Ki   3: 9 and to **d** between right and wrong.
Heb   5:14 to **d** good from evil.

DISTINGUISHING [DISTINGUISH]
1Co 12:10 to another **d** between spirits,

DISTORT*
Jer 23:36 so you **d** the words
Mic   3: 9 despise justice and **d** all that is right;
Ac   20:30 and **d** the truth in order
2Co   4: 2 nor do we **d** the word of God.
2Pe   3:16 and unstable people **d**,

DISTRACTED*
Lk   10:40 Martha was **d** by all the preparations

DISTRESS [DISTRESSED, DISTRESSES]
Jdg   2:15 They were in great **d**.
2Sa 22: 7 In my **d** I called to the LORD;
2Ch 15: 4 in their **d** they turned to the LORD,
Ne   9:37 We are in great **d**.
Est   4: 3 she was in great **d**.
Ps   18: 6 In my **d** I called to the LORD;
     77: 2 When I was in **d**, I sought the Lord;
     81: 7 In your **d** you called
    107: 6 and he delivered them from their **d**.
    120: 1 I call on the LORD in my **d**,
Jnh   2: 2 "In my **d** I called to the LORD,
Mt   24:21 For then there will be great **d**,
Jas   1:27 orphans and widows in their **d**

DISTRESSED [DISTRESS]
Isa 63: 9 In all their distress he too was **d**,
Mk   14:33 he began to be deeply **d** and troubled
Lk   12:50 and how **d** I am until it is completed!
Ro   14:15 If your brother is **d** because

DISTRESSES* [DISTRESS]
1Sa 10:19 of all your calamities and **d**.
2Co   6: 4 in troubles, hardships and **d**;

DISTRIBUTE [DISTRIBUTED, DISTRIBUTION]

Nu 33:54 **D** the land by lot,
Eze 47:21 to **d** this land among yourselves

DISTRIBUTED [DISTRIBUTE]

Jos 18:10 he **d** the land to the Israelites
Heb   2: 4 gifts of the Holy Spirit **d** according

DISTRIBUTION* [DISTRIBUTE]

Ac   6: 1 overlooked in the daily **d** of food.

DISTURBANCE* [DISTURBED]

Ac 19:23 there arose a great **d** about the Way.
     24:18 nor was I involved in any **d.**

DISTURBED [DISTURBANCE]

1Sa 28:15 "Why have you **d** me
Ps   .42: 5 Why so **d** within me?
Da   7:15 that passed through my mind **d** me.
Ac   4: 2 were greatly **d** because the apostles
     15:24 without our authorization and **d** you,

DIVIDE [DIVIDED, DIVIDING, DIVISION, DIVISIONS, DIVISIVE]

Ex 14:16 to **d** the water so that the Israelites
Ps 22:18 They **d** my garments among them
Isa 53:12 he will **d** the spoils with the strong,
Lk 12:13 tell my brother to **d** the inheritance
Jude   1:19 These are the men who **d** you,

DIVIDED [DIVIDE]

Ex 14:21 The waters were **d,**
Lev 11: 3 that has a split hoof completely **d**
Jos 14: 5 So the Israelites **d** the land,
2Ki   2: 8 The water **d** to the right and to
Ne   9:11 You **d** the sea before them,
Isa 63:12 who **d** the waters before them,
Da   5:28 *Peres:* Your kingdom is **d** and given
Mt 12:25 "Every kingdom **d** against itself will
Lk 11:18 If Satan is **d** against himself,
     23:34 they **d** up his clothes by casting lots.
1Co   1:13 Is Christ **d?**

DIVIDING [DIVIDE]

Jos 19:51 And so they finished **d** the land.
Jn 19:23 **d** them into four shares,
Eph   2:14 the **d** wall of hostility,
Heb   4:12 it penetrates even to **d** soul and spirit,

DIVINATION [DIVINATIONS, DIVINE, DIVINER, DIVINERS]

Ge 44: 5 drinks from and also uses for **d?**
Lev 19:26 " 'Do not practice **d** or sorcery.
Nu 23:23 no **d** against Israel.
Dt 18:10 who practices **d** or sorcery,
1Sa 15:23 For rebellion is like the sin of **d,**
Eze 13:23 see false visions or practice **d.**

DIVINATIONS [DIVINATION]

Jer 14:14 prophesying to you false visions, **d,**
Eze 13: 6 visions are false and their **d** a lie.

DIVINE [DIVINATION]

Isa 35: 4 with **d** retribution he will come
Ac   8:10 "This man is the **d** power known as
Ro   1:20 his eternal power and **d** nature—
      9: 4 theirs the **d** glory, the covenants,
2Co 10: 4 they have **d** power
2Pe   1: 3 His **d** power has given us everything

DIVINER* [DIVINATION]

Da   2:27 magician or **d** can explain to the king

DIVINERS [DIVINATION]

Isa 44:25 and makes fools of **d,**
Jer 29: 8 and **d** among you deceive you.
Zec 10: 2 **d** see visions that lie;

DIVISION [DIVIDE]

Lk 12:51 No, I tell you, but **d.**
1Co 12:25 that there should be no **d** in the body,

DIVISIONS [DIVIDE]

Ex 12:41 all the LORD's **d** left Egypt.
Nu   1: 3 to number by their **d** all the men
Ro 16:17 to watch out for those who cause **d**
1Co   1:10 so that there may be no **d** among you
     11:18 there are **d** among you,

DIVISIVE* [DIVIDE]

Tit   3:10 Warn a **d** person once,

DIVORCE* [DIVORCED, DIVORCES]

Dt 22:19 not **d** her as long as he lives.
     22:29 He can never **d** her as long
     24: 1 and he writes her a certificate of **d,**
     24: 3 and writes her a certificate of **d,**
Isa 50: 1 is your mother's certificate of **d**
Jer   3: 8 faithless Israel her certificate of **d**
Mal   2:16 "I hate **d,**" says the LORD
Mt   1:19 he had in mind to **d** her quietly.
      5:31 must give her a certificate of **d.'**
     19: 3 "Is it lawful for a man to **d** his wife
     19: 7 a man give his wife a certificate of **d**
     19: 8 Moses permitted you to **d** your wives
Mk 10: 2 Is it lawful for a man to **d** his wife?"
     10: 4 a certificate of **d** and send her away."
1Co   7:10 And a husband must not **d** his wife.
      7:12 he must not **d** her.
      7:13 she must not **d** him.
      7:27 Do not seek a **d.**

DIVORCED* [DIVORCE]

Lev 21: 7 or **d** from their husbands,
     21:14 not marry a widow, a **d** woman,
     22:13 daughter becomes a widow or is **d,**
Nu 30: 9 obligation taken by a widow or **d**
Dt 24: 4 **d** her, is not allowed to marry her
1Ch   8: 8 after he had **d** his wives Hushim
Eze 44:22 not marry widows or **d** women;
Mt   5:32 marries the **d** woman commits adultery.
Lk 16:18 marries a **d** woman commits adultery

DIVORCES* [DIVORCE]

Jer   3: 1 "If a man **d** his wife

Mt	5:31	'Anyone who **d** his wife must give
	5:32	I tell you that anyone who **d** his wife,
	19: 9	I tell you that anyone who **d** his wife,
Mk	10:11	"Anyone who **d** his wife
	10:12	And if she **d** her husband
Lk	16:18	"Anyone who **d** his wife

DO [DOES, DOING, DONE]

Ge	4: 7	If you **d** what is right,
	18:25	the Judge of all the earth **d** right?"
Ex	19: 8	"We will **d** everything the LORD has
	20:10	On it you shall not **d** any work,
Lev	18: 3	You must not **d** as they **d** in Egypt,
Jos	1: 8	be careful to **d** everything written
2Ki	17:15	ordered them, "**D** not **d** as they **d**,"
Ps	37: 3	Trust in the LORD and **d** good;
	143:10	Teach me to **d** your will,
Pr	16: 3	Commit to the LORD whatever you **d**,
	31:29	"Many women **d** noble things,
Ecc	2:24	A man can **d** nothing better than
Jer	22: 3	what the LORD says: **D** what is just
Mt	23: 3	But **d** not **d** what they **d**,
Mk	3: 4	on the Sabbath: to **d** good or to **d** evil
	6: 5	He could not **d** any miracles there,
Lk	6:31	**D** to others as you would have them
		d to you.
Jn	6:28	"What must we **d** to **d** the works
		God requires?"
	7:17	If anyone chooses to **d** God's will,
Ac	16:30	"Sirs, what must I **d** to be saved?"
	22:10	" 'What shall I **d**, Lord?'
Ro	7:15	For what I want to **d** I **d** not **d**, but
		what I hate I **d**.
Gal	6:10	let us **d** good to all people,
Eph	3:20	able to **d** immeasurably more
Col	3:17	And whatever you **d**, whether in
		word or deed, **d** it all in the name of
1Pe	3:11	He must turn from evil and **d** good;

DO NOT FEAR See FEAR

DOCTOR

Mt	9:12	"It is not the healthy who need a **d**,
Col	4:14	Our dear friend Luke, the **d**,

DOCTRINE⁺ [DOCTRINES]

1Ti	1:10	else is contrary to the sound **d**
	4:16	Watch your life and **d** closely.
2Ti	4: 3	will not put up with sound **d**.
Tit	1: 9	encourage others by sound **d**.
	2: 1	what is in accord with sound **d**.

DOCTRINES⁺ [DOCTRINE]

1Ti	1: 3	not to teach false **d** any longer
	6: 3	If anyone teaches false **d** and does

DOE

Ge	49:21	"Naphtali is a **d** set free
Pr	5:19	A loving **d**, a graceful deer—

DOEG⁺

Edomite; Saul's head shepherd; murdered 85 priests at Nob (1Sa 21:7; 22:6-23; Ps 52).

DOES [DO]

Dt	32: 4	A faithful God who **d** no wrong,
Ps	15: 5	He who **d** these things will never
	135: 6	The LORD **d** whatever pleases him,
Ecc	3:14	everything God **d** will endure forever
Da	9:14	God is righteous in everything he **d**;
Zep	3: 5	is righteous; he **d** no wrong.
Mk	3:35	Whoever **d** God's will is my brother
Jn	5:19	whatever the Father the Son also **d**.
Ro	10: 5	man who **d** these things will live
Gal	3:12	man who **d** these things will live
Jas	1:25	he will be blessed in what he **d**.

DOG [DOGS]

Jdg	7: 5	the water with their tongues like a **d**
1Sa	17:43	He said to David, "Am I a **d**,
Pr	26:11	As a **d** returns to its vomit,
Ecc	9: 4	a live **d** is better off than a dead lion!
2Pe	2:22	"A **d** returns to its vomit,"

DOGS [DOG]

1Ki	21:19	**d** will lick up your blood—
2Ki	9:10	As for Jezebel, **d** will devour her
Ps	22:16	**D** have surrounded me;
Isa	56:11	They are **d** with mighty appetites;
Mt	7: 6	"Do not give **d** what is sacred;
	15:26	and toss it to their **d**."
Php	3: 2	Watch out for those **d**,
Rev	22:15	Outside are the **d**,

DOING [DO]

Mk	11:28	"By what authority are you **d** these
1Pe	3:17	to suffer for **d** good than for **d** evil.

DOMINION

Job	25: 2	"**D** and awe belong to God;
Ps	22:28	for **d** belongs to the LORD
Da	4: 3	is an eternal kingdom; his **d** endures
1Co	15:24	after he has destroyed all **d**,
Eph	1:21	all rule and authority, power and **d**,
Col	1:13	rescued us from the **d** of darkness

DOMINIONS (KJV) See RULERS

DONE [DO]

Ge	3:13	"What is this you have **d**?"
	4:10	"What have you **d**?
Ex	18: 9	the good things the LORD had **d**
Est	6: 6	be **d** for the man the king delights
Ps	71:19	O God, you who have **d** great things.
	98: 1	for he has **d** marvelous things;
	105: 5	Remember the wonders he has **d**,
Pr	19:17	will reward him for what he has **d**.
	24:12	according to what he has **d**?
Ecc	1: 9	what has been **d** will be **d** again;
	8:17	then I saw all that God has **d**.
Isa	25: 1	you have **d** marvelous things,
Jer	50:29	do to her as she has **d**.
Eze	11:21	on their own heads what they have **d**,
Joel	2:21	Surely the LORD has **d** great things.
Ob	1:15	you have **d**, it will be **d** to you;
Mic	6: 3	"My people, what have I **d** to you?
Mt	6:10	will be **d** on earth as it is in heaven.
	26:42	may your will be **d**."

Lk 19:17 " 'Well, **d**, my good servant!'
Rev 16:17 saying, "It is **d**!"
18: 6 her back double for what she has **d**.
20:12 judged according to what they had **d**
21: 6 He said to me: "It is **d**.

DONKEY [DONKEY'S]

Nu 22:30 The **d** said to Balaam, "Am I not your own **d**,
Zec 9: 9 on a **d**, on a colt, the foal of a **d**.
Mt 21: 5 on a **d**, on a colt, the foal of a **d**.' "
2Pe 2:16 rebuked for his wrongdoing by a **d**—

DONKEY'S [DONKEY]

Nu 22:28 the LORD opened the **d** mouth,
Jdg 15:16 With a **d** jawbone I have killed

DOOMED

Ps 137: 8 of Babylon, **d** to destruction,
Jn 17:12 lost except the one **d** to destruction
2Th 2: 3 the man **d** to destruction.

DOOR [DOORFRAME, DOORFRAMES, DOORKEEPER, DOORPOST, DOORS, DOORWAY]

Ge 4: 7 sin is crouching at your **d**;
19: 9 to break down the **d**.
Dt 15:17 through his ear lobe into the **d**,
Jdg 19:22 Pounding on the **d**,
Job 31:32 for my **d** was always open to
Ps 141: 3 keep watch over the **d** of my lips.
Pr 5: 8 do not go near the **d** of her house,
9:14 She sits at the **d** of her house,
26:14 As a **d** turns on its hinges,
Mt 6: 6 close the **d** and pray to your Father,
7: 7 and the **d** will be opened to you.
Lk 13:24 to enter through the narrow **d**,
Ac 12:14 "Peter is at the **d**!"
14:27 and how he had opened the **d** of faith
1Co 16: 9 because a great **d** for effective work
2Co 2:12 that the Lord had opened a **d**
Col 4: 3 God may open a **d** for our message,
Jas 5: 9 The Judge is standing at the **d**!
Rev 3: 8 I have placed before you an open **d**
3:20 I stand at the **d** and knock.
3:20 and opens the **d**,
4: 1 a **d** standing open in heaven.

DOORFRAME [DOOR, FRAME]

Ex 12:23 blood on the top and sides of the **d**

DOORFRAMES [DOOR, FRAME]

Dt 6: 9 Write them on the **d** of your houses

DOORKEEPER [DOOR, KEEP]

Ps 84:10 rather be a **d** in the house of my God

DOORPOST [DOOR, POST]

Ex 21: 6 He shall take him to the door or the **d**

DOORS [DOOR]

1Ki 6:31 of the inner sanctuary he made **d**
Ne 3: 1 They dedicated it and set its **d**
Ps 24: 7 be lifted up, you ancient **d**,

Mal 1:10 one of you would shut the temple **d**,
Jn 20:26 Though the **d** were locked,
Ac 5:19 an angel of the Lord opened the **d** of
16:26 At once all the prison **d** flew open,

DOORWAY [DOOR, WAY]

Ex 12:23 and will pass over that **d**,

DORCAS*

Disciple, also known as Tabitha, whom Peter raised from the dead (Ac 9:36-43).

DOUBLE [DOUBLE-EDGED, DOUBLE-MINDED]

Ex 22: 7 if he is caught, must pay back **d**.
1Sa 1: 5 But to Hannah he gave a **d** portion
2Ki 2: 9 "Let me inherit a **d** portion
Isa 40: 2 the LORD's hand **d** for all her sins.
61: 7 and so they will inherit a **d** portion
Hos 10:10 to put them in bonds for their **d** sin.
1Ti 5:17 well are worthy of **d** honor,
Rev 18: 6 as she has given; pay her back **d**

DOUBLE-EDGED* [DOUBLE, EDGE]

Jdg 3:16 Now Ehud had made a **d** sword
Ps 149: 6 and a **d** sword in their hands,
Pr 5: 4 sharp as a **d** sword.
Heb 4:12 Sharper than any **d** sword,
Rev 1:16 of his mouth came a sharp **d** sword.
2:12 of him who has the sharp, **d** sword.

DOUBLE-MINDED* [DOUBLE, MIND]

Ps 119:113 I hate **d** men, but I love your law.
Jas 1: 8 he is a **d** man, unstable in all he does.
4: 8 and purify your hearts, you **d**.

DOUBT [DOUBTED, DOUBTING, DOUBTS]

Mt 14:31 he said, "why did you **d**?"
21:21 if you have faith and do not **d**,
Mk 11:23 not **d** in his heart but believes
Jas 1: 6 he asks, he must believe and not **d**,
Jude 1:22 Be merciful to those who **d**;

DOUBTED* [DOUBT]

Mt 28:17 they worshiped him; but some **d**.

DOUBTING* [DOUBT]

Jn 20:27 Stop **d** and believe."

DOUBTS* [DOUBT]

Lk 24:38 and why do **d** rise in your minds?
Ro 14:23 the man who has **d** is condemned
Jas 1: 6 he who **d** is like a wave of the sea,

DOUGH

Ex 12:39 The **d** was without yeast
Lk 13:21 until it worked all through the **d**."
1Co 5: 6 works through the whole batch of **d**?
Gal 5: 9 works through the whole batch of **d**.

DOVE [DOVES]

Ge   8: 8   a **d** to see if the water had receded
Ps 55: 6   "Oh, that I had the wings of a **d!**
SS   5: 2   my darling, my **d,** my flawless one.
Hos 7:11   "Ephraim is like a **d,**
Mk   1:10   the Spirit descending on him like a **d.**

DOVES [DOVE]

Lev 12: 8   to bring two **d** or two young pigeons,
SS   4: 1   Your eyes behind your veil are **d.**
Isa 59:11   we moan mournfully like **d.**
Eze 7:16   moaning like **d** of the valleys,
Mt 10:16   as snakes and as innocent as **d.**
    21:12   and the benches of those selling **d.**
Lk   2:24   "a pair of **d** or two young pigeons."

DOWN [DOWNCAST, DOWNFALL]

Ge 11: 5   LORD came **d** to see the city
    18:21   that I will go **d** and see
    46: 3   "Do not be afraid to go **d** to Egypt,
Ex   3: 8   So I have come **d** to rescue them
    19:11   on that day the LORD will come **d**
    34: 5   Then the LORD came **d** in the cloud
Nu 11:25   Then the LORD came **d** in the cloud
2Sa 22:10   He parted the heavens and came **d;**
Ne   1: 3   The wall of Jerusalem is broken **d,**
     9:13   "You came **d** on Mount Sinai;
Ps 18:16   He reached **d** from on high
    23: 2   He makes me lie **d** in green pastures,
   113: 6   who stoops **d** to look on the heavens
Pr   5: 5   Her feet go **d** to death;
Ecc 3: 3   a time to tear **d** and a time to build,
Da   8:10   and it threw some of the starry host **d**
Mt   7:25   The rain came **d,** the streams rose,
Mk   6:40   So they sat **d** in groups of hundreds
    15:30   come **d** from the cross and save
Lk   4: 9   he said, "throw yourself **d** from here.
Jn   6:41   the bread that came **d** from heaven."
    The good shepherd lays **d** his life for
Heb 1: 3   he sat **d** at the right hand of
     8: 1   who sat **d** at the right hand of
    10:12   he sat **d** at the right hand of God.
    12: 2   and sat **d** at the right hand of
1Jn 3:16   Jesus Christ laid **d** his life for us.
Rev 3:12   which is coming **d** out of heaven
    12: 9   The great dragon was hurled **d—**
    21: 2   coming **d** out of heaven from God,
    21:10   coming **d** out of heaven from God.

DOWNCAST [DOWN, CAST]

1Sa 1:18   and her face was no longer **d.**
Ps 42: 5   Why are you **d,** O my soul?
La   3:20   and my soul is **d** within me.
Lk 24:17   They stood still, their faces **d.**
2Co 7: 6   But God, who comforts the **d,**

DOWNFALL [DOWN, FALL]

2Ch 28:23   were his **d** and the **d** of all Israel.
Pr 18:12   Before his **d** a man's heart is proud,
Hos 14: 1   Your sins have been your **d!**

DRAGON

Rev 12: 3   an enormous red **d** with seven heads
    13: 2   The **d** gave the beast his power

    16:13   they came out of the mouth of the **d,**
    20: 2   He seized the **d,** that ancient serpent,

DRAGONS (KJV) See JACKALS, SERPENT

DRANK [DRINK]

Ge   9:21   When he **d** some of its wine,
Ex 24:11   and they ate and **d.**
Dt   9: 9   I ate no bread and **d** no water.
Jer 51: 7   The nations **d** her wine;
Da   5: 4   As they **d** the wine,
Ob   1:16   Just as you **d** on my holy hill,
Mk 14:23   and they all **d** from it.
1Co 10: 4   and **d** the same spiritual drink;

DRAW [DRAWING, DRAWS]

Ge 24:11   the women go out to **d** water.
Ex   2:16   and they came to **d** water and fill
1Sa 31: 4   **"D**raw your sword and run me through,
Isa 12: 3   With joy you will **d** water from
Zep 3: 2   she does not **d** near to her God.
Mt 26:52   "for all who **d** the sword will die by
Jn   2: 8   "Now **d** some out and take it to
     4: 7   a Samaritan woman came to **d** water,
    12:32   will **d** all men to myself."
Heb 7:19   by which we **d** near to God.
    10:22   let us **d** near to God with

DRAWING [DRAW]

Lk 21:28   because your redemption is **d** near."

DRAWS [DRAW]

Isa 51: 5   My righteousness **d** near speedily,
Jn   6:44   unless the Father who sent me **d** him,

DREAD [DREADED, DREADFUL]

Ex   1:12   the Egyptians came to **d** the Israelites
Nu 22: 3   Moab was filled with **d** because of
Ps 53: 5   where there was nothing to **d.**
Isa 8:13   he is the one you are to **d,**

DREADED [DREAD]

Dt 28:60   the diseases of Egypt that you **d,**
Job 3:25   what I **d** has happened to me.

DREADFUL [DREAD]

Joel 2:11   The day of the LORD is great; it is **d.**
Mal 4: 5   great and **d** day of the LORD comes.
Mt 24:19   How **d** it will be in those days
Heb 10:31   It is a **d** thing to fall into the hands of

DREAM [DREAMED, DREAMER, DREAMS]

Ge 20: 3   But God came to Abimelech in a **d**
    28:12   He had a **d** in which he saw
    31:11   The angel of God said to me in the **d,**
    37: 5   Joseph had a **d,**
    40: 5   and each **d** had a meaning of its own.
    41: 1   Pharaoh had a **d:**
Jdg 7:13   as a man was telling a friend his **d.**
1Ki 3: 5   to Solomon during the night in a **d,**
Ecc 5: 3   **d** comes when there are many cares,
Jer 23:28   Let the prophet who has a **d** tell his **d**

Da   2: 3 "I have had a **d** that troubles me
      4: 5 I had a **d** that made me afraid.
      7: 1 Daniel had a **d**,
Joel   2:28 your old men will **d** dreams,
Mt   1:20 of the Lord appeared to him in a **d**
      2:12 And having been warned in a **d** not
      2:13 the Lord appeared to Joseph in a **d.**
      2:19 of the Lord appeared in a **d** to Joseph
      2:22 Having been warned in a **d**,
    27:19 suffered a great deal today in a **d**
Ac   2:17 your old men will **d** dreams.

DREAMED* [DREAM]

Ps 126: 1 we were like men who **d.**
Da   2: 2 to tell him what he had **d.**

DREAMER [DREAM]

Ge 37:19 "Here comes that **d!**"
Dt   13: 5 prophet or **d** must be put to death,

DREAMS [DREAM]

Nu 12: 6 I speak to him in **d.**
Dt   13: 1 a prophet, or one who foretells by **d,**
1Sa 28: 6 the LORD did not answer him by **d**

DREGS*

Ps   75: 8 the earth drink it down to its very **d.**
Isa 51:17 you who have drained to its **d**
Jer 48:11 like wine left on its **d,**
Zep   1:12 who are like wine left on its **d,**

DRESS [DRESSED]

Ex   40:13 **d** Aaron in the sacred garments,
1Ti   2: 9 I also want women to **d** modestly,

DRESSED [DRESS]

Ex   20:25 do not build it with **d** stones,
1Sa 17:38 Then Saul **d** David in his own tunic.
Zec   3: 3 Now Joshua was **d** in filthy clothes
Lk   7:25 A man **d** in fine clothes?
      8:35 **d** and in his right mind;
   12:27 Solomon in all his splendor was **d**
Rev   3: 4 They will walk with me, **d** in white,
      4: 4 They were **d** in white
   15: 6 They were **d** in clean,
   17: 4 The woman was **d** in purple
   19:13 He is **d** in a robe dipped in blood,
   21: 2 a bride beautifully **d** for her husband.

DRIED [DRY]

Ge   8:13 the water had **d** up from the earth.
Jos   5: 1 the LORD had **d** up the Jordan
Ps   22:15 My strength is **d** up like a potsherd,
   106: 9 He rebuked the Red Sea, and it **d** up;
Isa 51:10 Was it not you who **d** up the sea,
Rev 16:12 and its water was **d** up to prepare

DRIFT*

Heb   2: 1 so that we do not **d** away.

DRINK [DRANK, DRINKING, DRINKS, DRUNK, DRUNKARD, DRUNKARD'S, DRUNKARDS, DRUNKENNESS]

Ge   19:33 they got their father to **d** wine,

Ex   15:23 not **d** its water because it was bitter.
   17: 1 no water for the people to **d.**
Lev 10: 9 and your sons are not to **d** wine
Nu   4: 7 and the jars for **d** offerings;
      6: 3 from wine and other fermented **d**
   20: 5 And there is no water to **d!**"
Jdg   7: 5 from those who kneel down to **d.**"
   13: 4 Now see to it that you **d** no wine
2Sa 23:15 that someone would get me a **d**
Ps   50:13 of bulls or **d** the blood of goats?
Pr   5:15 **D** water from your own cistern,
      7:18 let's **d** deep of love till morning;
   23:20 not join those who **d** too much wine
Ecc   2:24 to eat and **d** and find satisfaction
      9: 7 and **d** your wine with a joyful heart,
Jer   8:14 and given us poisoned water to **d,**
   25:15 the nations to whom I send you **d** it.
Eze 23:32 "You will **d** your sister's cup.
Da   1:12 but vegetables to eat and water to **d.**
Ob   1:16 so all the nations will **d** continually;
Mt   20:22 "Can you **d** the cup I am going to **d?**
   26:27 saying, "**D** from it, all of you.
   27:34 There they offered Jesus wine to **d,**
Lk   12:19 eat, **d** and be merry." '
Jn   7:37 let him come to me and **d.**
   18:11 Shall I not **d** the cup the Father
1Co 10: 4 and drank the same spiritual **d;**
   10:21 You cannot **d** the cup of the Lord
   12:13 we were all given the one Spirit to **d.**
Php   2:17 like a **d** offering on the sacrifice
Col   2:16 judge you by what you eat or **d,**
2Ti   4: 6 poured out like a **d** offering,
Heb   9:10 They are only a matter of food and **d**
Rev 14: 8 the nations the maddening wine
   14:10 too, will **d** of the wine of God's fury,
   16: 6 and you have given them blood to **d**
   21: 6 To him who is thirsty I will give to **d**

DRINK OFFERING
Ge 35:14; Ex 29:40, 41; 30:9; Lev 23:13; Nu 6:17; 15:5, 7, 10, 24; 28:7, 7, 8, 9, 10, 14, 15, 24; 29:16, 22, 25, 28, 31, 34, 38; 2Ki 16:13, 15; Php 2:17; 2Ti 4:6

DRINK OFFERINGS
Ex 37:16; Lev 23:18, 37; Nu 4:7; 6:15; 28:31; 29:6, 11, 18, 19, 21, 24, 27, 30, 33, 37, 39; Dt 32:38; 1Ch 29:21; 2Ch 29:35; Ezr 7:17; Isa 57:6; Jer 7:18; 19:13; 32:29; 44:17, 18, 19, 25; 52:19; Eze 20:28; 45:17; Joel 1:9, 13; 2:14

DRINKING [DRINK]

1Sa   1:15 I have not been **d** wine or beer;
Mt   11:19 The Son of Man came eating and **d,**
Lk   17:27 People were eating, **d,**
Ro   14:17 not a matter of eating and **d,**
1Ti   5:23 Stop **d** only water,

DRINKS [DRINK]

Isa   5:22 and champions at mixing **d,**
Am   4: 1 "Bring us some **d!**"
Jn   4:13 "Everyone who **d** this water will
      6:54 and **d** my blood has eternal life,
1Co 11:27 or **d** the cup of the Lord in

DRIP* [DRIPPING]

Pr   5: 3 For the lips of an adulteress **d** honey,

Joel 3:18 the mountains will **d** new wine,
Am   9:13 New wine will **d** from the mountains

DRIPPING [DRIP]

Pr   19:13 like a constant **d.**
     27:15 like a constant **d** on a rainy day;

DRIVE [DRIVEN, DRIVES, DRIVING, DROVE]

Ex   6: 1 my mighty hand he will **d** them out
     23:30 by little I will **d** them out before you,
Nu   33:52 **d** out all the inhabitants of the land
Dt   7:17 How can we **d** them out?"
Jos 13:13 the Israelites did not **d** out the people
     23:13 will no longer **d** out these nations
Jdg   1:19 but they were unable to **d** the people
Pr   22:10 **D** out the mocker,
Isa 22:23 I will **d** him like a peg into
Jer 49: 2 Israel will **d** out those who drove her
Mt   10: 1 to **d** out evil spirits and
Lk   11:19 if I **d** out demons by Beelzebub,
Jn   6:37 comes to me I will never **d** away.

DRIVEN [DRIVE]

Ex   12:39 they had been **d** out of Egypt
Dt   12:29 But when you have **d** them out
Jn   12:31 the prince of this world will be **d** out.

DRIVES [DRIVE]

Mt   12:26 If Satan **d** out Satan,
1Jn   4:18 But perfect love **d** out fear,

DRIVING [DRIVE]

Ex   14:25 so that they had difficulty **d.**
Lk   19:45 began **d** out those who were selling.
Ac   26:24 Your great learning is **d** you insane.

DROP [DROPS]

Pr   17:14 so **d** the matter before
Isa 40:15 the nations are like a **d** in a bucket;
Zec   8:12 and the heavens will **d** their dew.

DROPS [DROP]

Lk   22:44 like **d** of blood falling to the ground.

DROSS

Ps 119:119 of the earth you discard like **d;**
Pr   25: 4 Remove the **d** from the silver,
Isa   1:22 Your silver has become **d,**
Eze 22:18 house of Israel has become **d** to me;

DROUGHT

Dt   28:22 with scorching heat and **d,**
Jer 17: 8 It has no worries in a year of **d**
Hag   1:11 I called for a **d** on the fields

DROVE [DRIVE]

Nu   11:31 out from the LORD and **d** quail in
Jos 24:18 And the LORD **d** out before us all
Ps   44: 2 With your hand you **d** out the nations
Jer 49: 2 Israel will drive out those who **d** her
Mt   8:16 and he **d** out the spirits with a word
     21:12 and **d** out all who were buying

DROWN [DROWNED]

Mk   4:38 "Teacher, don't you care if we **d?**"

DROWNED [DROWN]

Ex   15: 4 The best of Pharaoh's officers are **d**
Mt   18: 6 and to be **d** in the depths of the sea.
Lk   8:33 steep bank into the lake and was **d.**
Heb 11:29 Egyptians tried to do so, they were **d.**

DROWSINESS* [DROWSY]

Pr   23:21 and **d** clothes them in rags.

DROWSY* [DROWSINESS]

Mt   25: 5 they all became **d** and fell asleep.

DRUNK [DRINK]

Ge   9:21 he became **d** and lay uncovered
Dt   32:42 I will make my arrows **d** with blood,
1Sa   1:13 Eli thought she was **d**
     25:36 He was in high spirits and very **d.**
2Sa 11:13 and David made him **d.**
Isa 29: 9 be **d,** but not from wine,
Jer 51: 7 she made the whole earth **d.**
Na   3:11 You too will become **d;**
Ac   2:15 These men are not **d,** as you suppose.
1Co 11:21 One remains hungry, another gets **d.**
Eph   5:18 Do not get **d** on wine,
Rev 17: 6 was **d** with the blood of the saints,
     18: 3 nations have **d** the maddening wine

DRUNKARD [DRINK]

Isa 19:14 as a **d** staggers around in his vomit.
     24:20 The earth reels like a **d,**
Mt   11:19 'Here is a glutton and a **d,**
1Co   5:11 a **d** or a swindler.

DRUNKARD'S* [DRINK]

Pr   26: 9 Like a thornbush in a **d** hand

DRUNKARDS [DRINK]

Pr   23:21 for **d** and gluttons become poor,
Isa 28: 1 the pride of Ephraim's **d,**
1Co   6:10 nor the greedy nor **d** nor slanderers

DRUNKENNESS* [DRINK]

Ecc 10:17 for strength and not for **d.**
Jer 13:13 to fill with **d** all who live in this land,
Eze 23:33 You will be filled with **d** and sorrow,
Lk   21:34 **d** and the anxieties of life,
Ro   13:13 not in orgies and **d,**
Gal   5:21 and envy; **d,** orgies, and the like.
1Ti   3: 3 not given to **d,**
Tit   1: 7 not quick-tempered, not given to **d,**
1Pe   4: 3 living in debauchery, lust, **d,**

DRY [DRIED]

Ge   1: 9 and let **d** ground appear."
      7:22 Everything on **d** land that had the
Ex   14:16 go through the sea on **d** ground.
Jos   3:17 completed the crossing on **d** ground.
Jdg   6:37 on the fleece and all the ground is **d,**
2Ki   2: 8 of them crossed over on **d** ground.
Ps   66:10 He turned the sea into **d** land,
     95: 5 and his hands formed the **d** land.

Isa 53: 2 and like a root out of **d** ground.
Eze 17:24 I **d** up the green tree and make the **d**
               tree flourish.
       37: 4 **D** bones, hear the word of the LORD!
Jnh   2:10 and it vomited Jonah onto **d** land.
Heb 11:29 through the Red Sea as on **d** land;

DUE

Dt   32:35 In **d** time their foot will slip;
1Ch 16:29 to the LORD the glory **d** his name.
Ps   90:11 as great as the fear that is **d** you.
Pr   11:31 the righteous receive their **d** on earth,
Mal   1: 6 where is the honor **d** me?
Ro   1:27 the **d** penalty for their perversion.
1Pe   5: 6 that he may lift you up in **d** time.

DUG [DIG]

Ps   57: 6 They **d** a pit in my path—
Isa   5: 2 He **d** it up and cleared it of stones
Jer 18:20 Yet they have **d** a pit for me.

DULL

Isa   6:10 people calloused; make their ears **d**
      59: 1 nor his ear too **d** to hear.
Mk   7:18 "Are you so **d?**"
2Co   3:14 But their minds were made **d,**

DUMB (KJV) See CANNOT SPEAK,
COULD NOT TALK, LIFELESS, MUTE,
ROBBED OF SPEECH, SILENT,
SPEECHLESS, WITHOUT SPEECH

DUNGEON [DUNGEONS]

Ge   40:15 to deserve being put in a **d."**
Isa 42: 7 and to release from the **d**
Jer 37:16 put into a vaulted cell in a **d,**

DUNGEONS* [DUNGEON]

2Pe   2: 4 putting them into gloomy **d** to

DUNGHILL (KJV) See ASH HEAP, PILE

DUST

Ge   2: 7 the man from the **d** of the ground
       3:14 will eat **d** all the days of your life
       3:19 for **d** you are and to **d** you will return
      13:16 I will make your offspring like the **d**
      28:14 Your descendants will be like the **d**
Nu   23:10 Who can count the **d** of Jacob
1Sa   2: 8 He raises the poor from the **d**
Job 42: 6 and repent in **d** and ashes."
Ps   22:15 in the **d** of death.
     103:14 he remembers that we are **d.**
Ecc   3:20 all come from **d,** and to **d** all return.
Isa 65:25 but **d** will be the serpent's food.
Mt   10:14 the **d** off your feet when you leave
Ac   13:51 So they shook the **d** from their feet
1Co 15:47 first man was of the **d** of the earth,
Rev 19:19 They will throw **d** on their heads,

DUTIES [DUTY]

1Ki   3: 7 not know how to carry out my **d.**
2Ti   4: 5 discharge all the **d** of your ministry.

DUTY [DUTIES]

Ge   38: 8 and fulfill your **d** to her as
Ac   23: 1 I have fulfilled my **d** to God
1Co   7: 3 husband should fulfill his marital **d**

DWELL [DWELLING, DWELLINGS,
DWELLS, DWELT]

Ex   25: 8 and I will **d** among them.
2Sa   7: 5 the one to build me a house to **d** in?
1Ki   8:27 "But will God really **d** on earth?
Ezr   6:12 who has caused his Name to **d** there,
Ps   23: 6 and I will **d** in the house of
      37: 3 **d** in the land and enjoy safe pasture.
      61: 4 to **d** in your tent forever
Pr   8:12 wisdom, **d** together with prudence;
Isa 26: 5 He humbles those who **d** on high,
      33:14 of us can **d** with the consuming fire?
      43:14 former things; do not **d** on the past.
Jn   5:38 nor does his word **d** in you,
Eph   3:17 so that Christ may **d** in your hearts
Col   1:19 to have all his fullness **d** in him,
       3:16 the word of Christ **d** in you richly
Rev 12:12 you heavens and you who **d** in them!

DWELLING [DWELL]

Lev 26:11 I will put my **d** place among you,
Dt   26:15 from heaven, your holy **d** place,
1Ki   8:30 Hear from heaven, your **d** place,
Ps   90: 1 you have been our **d** place
Isa 26:21 the LORD is coming out of his **d**
La   2: 6 He has laid waste his **d** like a garden;
Eze 37:27 My **d** place will be with them;
Mic   1: 3 LORD is coming from his **d** place;
Jn   1:14 and made his **d** among us.
2Co   5: 2 to be clothed with our heavenly **d,**
Eph   2:22 to become a **d** in which God lives
Rev 21: 3 "Now the **d** of God is with men,

DWELLINGS [DWELL]

Lk   16: 9 you will be welcomed into eternal **d.**

DWELLS [DWELL]

Ps   46: 4 holy place where the Most High **d.**
      91: 1 **d** in the shelter of the Most High
Isa   8:18 who **d** on Mount Zion.
Joel 3:21 The LORD **d** in Zion!

DWELT [DWELL]

Dt   33:16 of him who **d** in the burning bush.
1Ch 17: 5 I have not **d** in a house from

DYING [DIE]

Jn   11:37 have kept this man from **d?"**
Ro   7: 6 now, by **d** to what once bound us,
2Co   6: 9 **d,** and yet we live on;

DYNASTY

1Sa 25:28 make a lasting **d** for my master,
1Ki   2:24 founded a **d** for me as he promised—

E

EACH
Ge   1:24 e according to its kind."
    49:28 giving e the blessing appropriate
Ex   12: 3 one for e household.
    25:20 The cherubim are to face e other.
Lev 25:14 do not take advantage of e other.
Nu 14:34 for e of the forty days you explored
1Sa 17:10 a man and let us fight e other."
1Ki   8:39 with e man according to all he does,
Ps   62:12 Surely you will reward e person
Eze 10:14 E of the cherubim had four faces:
Zec   7:10 not think evil of e other.'
Mt   6:34 E day has enough trouble of its own.
    16:27 and then he will reward e person
Mk   9:50 and be at peace with e other."
Lk   11: 3 Give us e day our daily bread.
Jn   15:17 This is my command: Love e other.
Ac   2: 6 because e one heard them speaking
Ro   12: 5 e member belongs to all the others.
    14:12 e of us will give an account
1Co   7: 7 e man has his own gift from God;
    12: 7 to e one the manifestation of
Gal   5:15 or you will be destroyed by e other.
    6: 2 Carry e other's burdens,
Col   3: 9 Do not lie to e other,
1Th   4:18 encourage e other with these words.
    5:13 Live in peace with e other."
Heb 13: 1 Keep on loving e other as brothers.
Jas   5:16 confess your sins to e another
1Pe   1:17 who judges e man's work impartially
Rev   4: 8 E of the four living creatures had six
           wings
    6:11 e of them was given a white robe,
    13: 1 and on e head a blasphemous name.
    20:13 and e person was judged according

EAGER [EAGERLY]
Pr   31:13 and flax and works with e hands.
Zep   3: 7 But they were still e to act corruptly
Ro   8:19 in e expectation for the sons of God
1Co 14:12 you are e to have spiritual gifts,
    14:39 my brothers, be e to prophesy,
1Ti   6:10 Some people, e for money,
Tit   2:14 e to do what is good.
1Pe   3:13 to harm you if you are e to do good?
    5: 2 but e to serve;
2Pe   1:10 the more e to make your calling

EAGERLY [EAGER]
Ro   8:23 as we wait e for our adoption as sons
1Co 12:31 But e desire the greater gifts.
    14: 1 of love and e desire spiritual gifts,
Php   3:20 And we e await a Savior from there,

EAGLE [EAGLE'S, EAGLES, EAGLES']
Dt   14:12 But these you may not eat: the e,
    32:11 an e that stirs up its nest and hovers
Pr   30:19 the way of an e in the sky,
Jer   48:40 An e is swooping down,

Eze   1:10 also had the face of an e.
    17: 3 A great e with powerful wings,
Da   7: 4 and it had the wings of an e.
Hos   8: 1 An e is over the house of the LORD
Ob   1: 4 Though you soar like the e
Rev   4: 7 the fourth was like a flying e.
    8:13 an e that was flying in midair call out
    12:14 the two wings of a great e,

EAGLE'S* [EAGLE]
Ps 103: 5 that your youth is renewed like the e.
Jer 49:16 you build your nest as high as the e,

EAGLES [EAGLE]
Isa 40:31 They will soar on wings like e;

EAGLES'* [EAGLE]
Ex   19: 4 and how I carried you on e wings

EAR [EARS]
Ex   21: 6 and pierce his e with an awl.
Lev   8:23 put it on the lobe of Aaron's right e,
2Ki 19:16 Give e, O LORD, and hear;
Ne   1:11 let your e be attentive to the prayer
Job 12:11 Does not the e test words as
Ps   5: 1 Give e to my words, O LORD,
    28: 1 not turn a deaf e to me.
  116: 2 Because he turned his e to me,
Pr   2: 2 turning your e to wisdom
    25:12 a wise man's rebuke to a listening e.
    28: 9 If anyone turns a deaf e to the law,
Ecc   1: 8 nor the e its fill of hearing.
Isa 59: 1 nor his e too dull to hear.
    64: 4 no e has perceived,
Da   9:18 Give e, O God, and hear;
Mk 14:47 cutting off his e.
Lk   22:51 touched the man's e and healed him.
1Co   2: 9 no e has heard,
    12:17 If the whole body were an e,
Rev   2: 7 He who has an e,

EARLIER [EARLY]
Zec   1: 4 to whom the e prophets proclaimed:
    7: 7 proclaimed through the e prophets
Heb 10:32 Remember those e days

EARLY [EARLIER]
Ps 127: 2 In vain you rise e and stay up late,
Pr   27:14 a man loudly blesses his neighbor e
Isa   5:11 Woe to those who rise e in the
Hos   6: 4 like the e dew that disappears.
    9:10 like seeing the e fruit on the fig tree.
Mic   7: 1 none of the e figs that I crave.
Mt   27: 1 E in the morning,
Lk   24:22 to the tomb e this morning

EARN [EARNED, EARNINGS, EARNS]
Hag 1: 6 You e wages, only to put them
2Th 3:12 settle down and e the bread they eat.

EARNED [EARN]
Pr   31:31 Give her the reward she has e,

EARNEST* [EARNESTNESS, EARNESTLY]

Pr 27: 9 springs from his **e** counsel.
Rev 3: 19 So be **e**, and repent.

EARNESTLY [EARNEST]

Ps 63: 1 you are my God, **e** I seek you;
Hos 5: 15 in their misery they will **e** seek me."
Ro 11: 7 What Israel sought so **e** it did
Heb 11: 6 he rewards those who **e** seek him.
Jas 5: 17 He prayed **e** that it would not rain,

EARNESTNESS [EARNEST]

2Co 7: 11 sorrow has produced in you: what **e**,
8: 7 in complete **e** and in your love

EARNINGS [EARN]

Pr 31: 16 out of her **e** she plants a vineyard.

EARNS* [EARN]

Pr 11: 18 The wicked man **e** deceptive wages,

EARRING [EARRINGS]

Pr 25: 12 Like an **e** of gold or an ornament

EARRINGS [EARRING]

Ex 32: 2 "Take off the gold **e** that your wives,
SS 1: 10 Your cheeks are beautiful with **e**,
Isa 3: 19 the **e** and bracelets and veils,
Eze 16: 12 **e** on your ears and a beautiful crown

EARS [EAR]

Dt 29: 4 or eyes that see or **e** that hear.
Job 42: 5 My **e** had heard of you but
Ps 34: 15 his **e** are attentive to their cry;
40: 6 but my **e** you have pierced;
115: 6 they have **e**, but cannot hear,
Pr 20: 12 **E** that hear and eyes that see—
21: 13 man shuts his **e** to the cry of the poor
26: 17 Like one who seizes a dog by the **e** is
Isa 6: 10 people calloused; make their **e** dull
35: 5 the **e** of the deaf unstopped.
Jer 6: 10 **e** are closed so they cannot hear.
Eze 40: 4 with your **e** and pay attention
Mt 11: 15 He who has **e**, let him hear.
Mk 8: 18 and **e** but fail to hear?
Ac 7: 51 with uncircumcised hearts and **e!**
28: 27 they hardly hear with their **e**,
2Ti 4: 3 teachers to say what their itching **e**
1Pe 3: 12 and his **e** are attentive to their prayer,

EARTH [EARTH'S, EARTHLY]

Ge 1: 1 the heavens and the **e**.
1: 2 Now the **e** was formless and empty,
4: 12 be a restless wanderer on the **e**."
6: 11 Now the **e** was corrupt in God's sight
6: 17 Everything on **e** will perish.
7: 24 the **e** for a hundred and fifty days.
9: 13 the covenant between me and the **e**.
12: 3 and all peoples on **e** will be blessed
14: 19 Creator of heaven and **e**.
24: 3 the God of heaven and the God of **e**,
28: 14 be like the dust of the **e**,
Ex 19: 5 Although the whole **e** is mine,

Nu 16: 30 and the **e** opens its mouth
Jos 3: 13 the Lord of all the **e**—
1Ki 8: 27 "But will God really dwell on **e**?
1Ch 16: 23 Sing to the LORD, all the **e;**
16: 30 Tremble before him, all the **e!**
Job 26: 7 he suspends the **e** over nothing.
Ps 8: 1 majestic is your name in all the **e!**
24: 1 The **e** is the LORD's,
46: 6 he lifts his voice, the **e** melts.
47: 2 the great King over all the **e!**
73: 25 **e** has nothing I desire besides you.
90: 2 or you brought forth the **e** and
97: 1 The LORD reigns, let the **e** be glad;
102: 25 the foundations of the **e**,
108: 5 and let your glory be over all the **e**.
Pr 8: 26 before he made the **e** or its fields
Isa 6: 3 the whole **e** is full of his glory."
24: 20 The **e** reels like a drunkard,
37: 16 You have made heaven and **e**.
40: 22 enthroned above the circle of the **e**,
51: 6 the **e** will wear out like a garment
55: 9 the heavens are higher than the **e**,
65: 17 new heavens and a new **e**.
66: 1 and the **e** is my footstool.
Jer 10: 10 When he is angry, the **e** trembles;
23: 24 "Do not I fill heaven and **e?"**
33: 25 and the fixed laws of heaven and **e**,
Da 2: 39 will rule over the whole **e**.
12: 2 in the dust of the **e** will awake:
Joel 2: 30 wonders in the heavens and on the **e**,
Am 9: 5 he who touches the **e** and it melts,
Hab 2: 20 the **e** be silent before him."
Hag 2: 21 I will shake the heavens and the **e**.
Zec 14: 9 LORD will be king over the whole **e**.
Mt 5: 5 for they will inherit the **e**.
5: 13 "You are the salt of the **e**.
5: 18 until heaven and **e** disappear,
5: 35 or by the **e**, for it is his footstool;
6: 10 will be done on **e** as it is in heaven.
16: 19 on **e** will be bound in heaven,
24: 35 Heaven and **e** will pass away,
28: 18 "All authority in heaven and on **e**
Lk 2: 14 and on **e** peace to men
5: 24 the Son of Man has authority on **e**
Jn 12: 32 But I, when I am lifted up from the **e**,
Ac 2: 19 Above and signs on the **e** below,
4: 24 "you made the heaven and the **e** and
7: 49 and the **e** is my footstool.
1Co 10: 26 "The **e** is the Lord's,
15: 47 first man was of the dust of the **e**,
Eph 3: 15 in heaven and on **e** derives its name.
Php 2: 10 in heaven and on **e** and under the **e**,
Heb 1: 10 you laid the foundations of the **e**,
2Pe 3: 13 to a new heaven and a new **e**,
Rev 5: 3 in heaven or on **e** or under the **e**
could open the scroll
8: 7 A third of the **e** was burned up,
12: 12 But woe to the **e** and the sea,
20: 11 **E** and sky fled from his presence,
21: 1 I saw a new heaven and a new **e**,

HEAVEN AND EARTH Ge 14:19, 22; Dt
4:26; 30:19; 31:28; 2Ki 19:15; 1Ch 21:16; 29:11;
2Ch 2:12; Ezr 5:11; Ps 69:34; 115:15; 121:2;
124:8; 134:3; 146:6; Isa 37:16; Jer 23:24; 33:25;

51:48; Zec 5:9; Mt 5:18; 11:25; 24:35; Mk 13:31; Lk 10:21; 16:17; 21:33; Ac 14:15; 17:24

ENDS OF THE EARTH Dt 28:49; 33:17; 1Sa 2:10; Job 28:24; 37:3; Ps 2:8; 22:27; 46:9; 48:10; 59:13; 61:2; 65:5; 67:7; 72:8; 98:3; 135:7; Pr 17:24; 30:4; Isa 5:26; 24:16; 40:28; 41:5, 9; 42:10; 43:6; 45:22; 48:20; 49:6; 52:10; 62:11; Jer 6:22; 10:13; 16:19; 25:31, 32; 31:8; 50:41; 51:16; Mic 5:4; Mic 5:4; Zec 9:10; Mt 12:42; Mk 13:27; Lk 11:31; Ac 1:8; 13:47

EARTH'S [EARTH]

Job 38: 4 when I laid the **e** foundation?
Pr   3:19 By wisdom the LORD laid the **e** foundations,

EARTHENWARE*

Pr   26:23 Like a coating of glaze over **e**

EARTHLY [EARTH]

Jn   3:12 of **e** things and you do not believe;
Eph   4: 9 descended to the lower, **e** regions?
Php   3:19 Their mind is on **e** things.
Col   3: 2 not on **e** things.
      3: 5 whatever belongs to your **e** nature:
Jas   3:15 not come down from heaven but is **e**,

EARTHQUAKE [QUAKE]

1Ki 19:11 but the LORD was not in the **e**.
Isa 29: 6 will come with thunder and **e**
Eze 38:19 at that time there shall be a great **e** in
Mt   28: 2 There was a violent **e**,
Ac   16:26 Suddenly there was such a violent **e**
Rev   6:12 There was a great **e**.
     11:13 that very hour there was a severe **e**
     16:18 No **e** like it has ever occurred

EARTHQUAKES [QUAKE]

Mt   24: 7 be famines and **e** in various places.

EASE [EASIER, EASILY, EASY]

Pr   1:33 will live in safety and be at **e**,

EASIER [EASE]

Mt   9: 5 Which is **e**: to say, 'Your sins
Lk   16:17 It is **e** for heaven and earth
     18:25 it is **e** for a camel to go through

EASILY [EASE]

Pr   22:24 do not associate with one **e** angered,
1Co 13: 5 it is not **e** angered,
Heb 12: 1 and the sin that so **e** entangles,

EAST

Ge   2: 8 a garden in the **e**, in Eden;
Ex   14:21 the sea back with a strong **e** wind
Ps 103:12 as far as the **e** is from the west,
Eze 43: 2 the God of Israel coming from the **e**.
Hos 13:15 **e** wind from the LORD will come,
Jnh   4: 8 God provided a scorching **e** wind,
Mt   2: 1 Magi from the **e** came to Jerusalem
      2: 2 We saw his star in the **e**
      8:11 that many will come from the **e** and
Rev   7: 2 another angel coming up from the **e**,

EASTER (KJV) PASSOVER

EASY [EASE]

2Ki   3:18 an **e** thing in the eyes of the LORD;
Mt   11:30 my yoke is **e** and my burden is light.
Lk   12:19 Take life **e**; eat, drink and be merry."

EAT [ATE, EATEN, EATER, EATING, EATS]

Ge   2:16 "You are free to **e** from any tree in
      2:17 not **e** from the tree of the knowledge
      3:19 the sweat of your brow you will **e**
Ex   12:11 **E** it in haste;
     12:20 **E** nothing made with yeast.
     16:12 'At twilight you will **e** meat,
     16:32 bread I gave you to **e** in the desert
     32: 6 to **e** and drink and got up to indulge
Lev 11: 2 these are the ones you may **e**:
     17:12 "None of you may **e** blood,
Nu   11:13 'Give us meat to **e**!'
Dt   8:16 He gave you manna to **e** in
     14: 4 These are the animals you may **e**:
Jdg 14:14 "Out of the eater, something to **e**;
2Sa   9: 7 and you will always **e** at my table."
Ps   22:26 The poor will **e** and be satisfied;
     50:13 Do I **e** the flesh of bulls or drink
Pr   31:27 and does not **e** the bread of idleness.
Ecc   2:24 to **e** and drink and find satisfaction
      5:18 and proper for a man to **e** and drink,
Isa   7:15 He will **e** curds and honey
     11: 7 and the lion will **e** straw like the ox.
     55: 1 come, buy and **e**!
     65:25 and the lion will **e** straw like the ox,
Jer 19: 9 I will make them **e** the flesh
La   2:20 Should women **e** their offspring,
Eze   3: 1 **e** what is before you, **e** this scroll;
Da   1:12 Give us nothing but vegetables to **e**
Hag   1: 6 You **e**, but never have enough."
Mt   14:16 You give them something to **e**."
     15: 2 don't wash their hands before they **e**!
     25:35 and you gave me something to **e**,
     26:26 "Take and **e**; this is my body."
Mk   2:26 which is lawful only for priests to **e**.
     14:14 where I may **e** the Passover
Lk   10: 8 **e** what is set before you.
     12:19 Take life easy; **e**, drink and be merry.
     12:29 not set your heart on what you will **e**
Jn   4:32 have food to **e** that you know nothing
      6:31 gave them bread from heaven to **e**.' "
      6:53 unless you **e** the flesh of the Son
Ac   10:13 Kill and **e**."
Ro   14: 2 faith allows him to **e** everything,
     14:15 is distressed because of what you **e**,
     14:20 it is wrong for a man to **e** anything
1Co   5:11 With such a man do not even **e**.
      8:13 if what I **e** causes my brother to fall
     10:25 **E** anything sold in the meat market
     10:31 whether you **e** or drink
     11:26 For whenever you **e** this bread
Col   2:16 judge you by what you **e** or drink,
2Th   3:10 will not work, he shall not **e**."
Heb 13: 9 of no value to those who **e** them.
Rev   2: 7 the right to **e** from the tree of life,

3:20 I will come in and **e** with him,
10: 9 He said to me, "Take it and **e** it.

EATEN [EAT]

Ge   3:11 Have you **e** from the tree
Jer 31:29 'The fathers have **e** sour grapes,
Eze   4:14 I have never **e** anything found dead
Ac   10:14 "I have never **e** anything impure
     12:23 and he was **e** by worms and died.
Rev 10:10 but when I had **e** it,

EATER* [EAT]

Jdg 14:14 He replied, "Out of the **e,**
Isa 55:10 for the sower and bread for the **e,**
Na   3:12 the figs fall into the mouth of the **e.**

EATING [EAT]

Ex   34:28 without **e** bread or drinking water.
Mt   15:20 but **e** with unwashed hands does
Lk   7:34 Son of Man came **e** and drinking,
Ro   14:15 not by your **e** destroy your brother
     14:17 not a matter of **e** and drinking,
     14:23 because his **e** is not from faith;
1Co   8: 4 then, about **e** food sacrificed to idols:
Jude 1:12 **e** with you without

EATS [EAT]

Lev   7:27 If anyone **e** blood,
1Sa 14:24 "Cursed be any man who **e** food
Lk   15: 2 "This man welcomes sinners and **e**
Jn   6:51 If anyone **e** of this bread,
      6:54 Whoever **e** my flesh
Ro   14: 2 faith is weak, **e** only vegetables.
     14: 6 He who **e** meat, **e** to the Lord,
     14:23 doubts is condemned if he **e,**
1Co 11:27 whoever **e** the bread or drinks

EBAL

Dt   11:29 and on Mount **E** the curses.
Jos   8:30 on Mount **E** an altar to the LORD,

EBED-MELECH*

A Cushite; saved Jeremiah from the cistern (Jer 38:1-13; 39:16).

EBENEZER*

1Sa   4: 1 The Israelites camped at **E,**
      5: 1 they took it from **E** to Ashdod.
      7:12 He named it **E,** saying,

EBER

Ancestor of Abraham (Ge 11:14-17), of Jesus (Lk 3:35).

EDEN

Ge   2: 8 a garden in the east, in **E;**
Eze 28:13 You were in **E,** the garden of God;

EDGE [DOUBLE-EDGED]

Jos   3:15 and their feet touched the water's **e,**
Jer 31:29 and the children's teeth are set on **e.'**
Mt   9:20 and touched the **e** of his cloak.
     14:36 the sick just touch the **e** of his cloak,

EDICT

Est   4: 8 the text of the **e** for their annihilation,
      8:11 The king's **e** granted the Jews
Da   6: 7 that the king should issue an **e**
Heb 11:23 they were not afraid of the king's **e.**

EDIFICATION* [EDIFIED, EDIFIES]

Ro   14:19 what leads to peace and to mutual **e.**

EDIFIED* [EDIFICATION]

1Co 14: 5 so that the church may be **e.**
     14:17 but the other man is not **e.**

EDIFIES* [EDIFICATION]

1Co 14: 4 who speaks in a tongue **e** himself,
          but he who prophesies **e** the church.

EDOM [EDOMITE, EDOMITES, ESAU]

Ge   25:30 (That is why he was also called **E.**)
     36: 1 the account of Esau (that is, **E**).
Nu   20:18 But **E** answered: "You may not pass
1Ki 11:16 destroyed all the men in **E.**
Ps   60: 8 upon **E** I toss my sandal;
Isa 63: 1 Who is this coming from **E,**
Jer 49: 7 Concerning **E:** This is what the
La   4:21 O Daughter of **E,**
Eze 25:12 'Because **E** took revenge on
Am   1:11 "For three sins of **E,**
Ob   1: 1 the Sovereign LORD says about **E—**

EDOMITE [EDOM]

Dt   23: 7 Do not abhor an **E,**
1Sa 22: 9 But Doeg the **E,**
Ps   52: T When Doeg the **E** had gone to Saul

EDOMITES [EDOM]

Ge   36:43 This was Esau the father of the **E.**
1Ch 18:13 all the **E** became subject to David.
Ps   60: T and struck down twelve thousand **E**
    137: 7 the **E** did on the day Jerusalem fell.

EDUCATED*

Ac   7:22 Moses was **e** in all the wisdom of

EFFECT* [EFFECTIVE]

Job 41:26 The sword that reaches him has no **e,**
Isa 32:17 the **e** of righteousness will
Ac   7:53 law that was put into **e** through
          angels
1Co 15:10 his grace to me was not without **e.**
Gal   3:19 law was put into **e** through angels by
Eph   1:10 to be put into **e** when
Heb   9:17 it never takes **e** while the one
      9:18 the first covenant was not put into **e**

EFFECTIVE* [EFFECT]

1Co 16: 9 a great door for **e** work has opened
Jas   5:16 of a righteous man is powerful and **e.**

EFFEMINATE (KJV)

See MALE PROSTITUTES

EFFORT* [EFFORTS]

Ecc   2:19 into which I have poured my **e**

Da   6:14 to rescue Daniel and made every **e**
Lk   13:24 "Make every **e** to enter through
Jn   5:44 yet make no **e** to obtain the praise
Ro   9:16 depend on man's desire or **e,**
     14:19 Let us therefore make every **e**
Gal   3: 3 to attain your goal by human **e?**
Eph   4: 3 Make every **e** to keep the unity of
1Th   2:16 in their **e** to keep us from speaking to
      2:17 we made every **e** to see you.
Heb   4:11 make every **e** to enter that rest,
     12:14 Make every **e** to live in peace
2Pe   1: 5 make every **e** to add to your faith
      1:15 And I will make every **e** to see that
      3:14 make every **e** to be found spotless.

EFFORTS [EFFORT]

Ecc   6: 7 All man's **e** are for his mouth,
Gal   4:11 somehow I have wasted my **e** on you
1Th   3: 5 and our **e** might have been useless.

EGG* [EGGS]

Job   6: 6 is there flavor in the white of an **e?**
Lk   11:12 Or if he asks for an **e,**

EGGS [EGG]

Dt   22: 6 sitting on the young or on the **e,**
Isa 59: 5 Whoever eats their **e** will die,
Jer 17:11 that hatches **e** it did not lay

EGLON

  1. King of Moab killed by Ehud (Jdg 3:12-30).
  2. City in Canaan (Jos 10).

EGYPT [EGYPTIAN, EGYPTIANS]

Ge   12:10 down to **E** to live there for a while
     26: 2 "Do not go down to **E;**
     37:28 who took him to **E.**
     41:41 in charge of the whole land of **E.**"
     42: 3 down to buy grain from **E.**
     45: 9 God has made me lord of all **E.**
     45:20 the best of all **E** will be yours.' "
     46: 6 Jacob and all his offspring went to **E.**
     47:27 Now the Israelites settled in **E** in
Ex   1: 8 came to power in **E.**
      3:11 and bring the Israelites out of **E?**"
      7: 3 miraculous signs and wonders in **E,**
     11: 5 Every firstborn son in **E** will die,
     12:12 judgment on all the gods of **E.**
     12:40 people lived in **E** was 430 years.
     12:41 all the LORD's divisions left **E.**
     32: 1 who brought us up out of **E,**
Nu   11:18 We were better off in **E!**"
     14: 4 a leader and go back to **E.**"
     24: 8 "God brought them out of **E;**
Dt   6:21 "We were slaves of Pharaoh in **E,**
     16:12 Remember that you were slaves in **E,**
Jos 15:47 as far as the Wadi of **E**
1Ki   4:30 and greater than all the wisdom of **E.**
     10:28 horses were imported from **E**
     11:40 but Jeroboam fled to **E,**
     14:25 king of **E** attacked Jerusalem.
2Ch 35:20 Neco king of **E** went up to fight at
     36: 3 The king of **E** dethroned him in
Ne   9:18 who brought you up out of **E,'**

Ps   80: 8 You brought a vine out of **E;**
Isa 19: 1 An oracle concerning **E:**
Jer 42:19 'Do not go to **E.'**
     44: 1 all the Jews living in Lower **E—**
     46: 2 Concerning **E:** This is the message
La   5: 6 We submitted to **E** and Assyria
Eze 29: 2 against Pharaoh king of **E**
     30: 4 A sword will come against **E,**
Hos 11: 1 and out of **E** I called my son.
Mt   2:15 "Out of **E** I called my son."
Heb 11:22 the exodus of the Israelites from **E**
     11:27 By faith he left **E,**
Rev 11: 8 is figuratively called Sodom and **E,**

OUT OF EGYPT Ge 45:25; 47:30; Ex 3:10, 11,
    12; 6:13, 26, 27; 12:17, 39, 42, 51; 13:3, 8, 9, 14,
    16, 18; 14:11; 16:1, 6, 32; 17:3; 18:1; 20:2;
    23:15; 29:46; 32:1, 4, 7, 8, 11, 23; 33:1; 34:18;
    Lev 11:45; 19:36; 22:33; 23:43; 25:38, 42, 55;
    26:13, 45; Nu 1:1; 9:1; 15:41; 20:5, 16; 21:5;
    22:5, 11; 23:22; 24:8; 26:4; 32:11; 33:1, 38; Dt
    1:27; 4:20, 37, 45, 46; 5:6; 6:12, 21; 8:14; 9:12,
    26; 13:5, 10; 16:1; 20:1; 23:4; 24:9; 25:17; 26:8;
    29:25; Jos 2:10; 5:4; 24:6, 17; Jdg 2:1, 12; 6:8,
    13; 11:13, 16; 19:30; 1Sa 8:8; 10:18; 12:6, 8;
    15:6; 2Sa 7:6; 1Ki 6:1; 8:9, 16, 21, 51, 53; 9:9;
    12:28; 2Ki 17:7, 36; 21:15; 1Ch 17:5; 2Ch 5:10;
    6:5; 7:22; Ne 9:18; Ps 80:8; 81:10; 114:1; Jer 2:6;
    7:22; 11:4; 16:14; 23:7; 26:23; 31:32; 32:21;
    34:13; 37:5; Eze 20:6, 9, 10; Da 9:15; Hos 2:15;
    11:1; 12:9; 13:4; Am 2:10; 3:1; Mic 6:4; 7:15;
    Hag 2:5; Mt 2:15; Ac 7:36, 40; Heb 3:16; 8:9;
    Jude 1:5

KING OF EGYPT See KING

EGYPTIAN [EGYPT]

Ge   16: 1 an **E** maidservant named Hagar;
Ex   1:19 "Hebrew women are not like **E**
      2:11 He saw an **E** beating a Hebrew,
Dt   11: 4 what he did to the **E** army,
     23: 7 Do not abhor an **E,**

EGYPTIANS [EGYPT]

Ex   1:12 so the **E** came to dread the Israelites
      3:22 And so you will plunder the **E."**
     12:36 so they plundered the **E.**
     14: 4 **E** will know that I am the LORD."
     15:26 of the diseases I brought on the **E,**
Nu   14:13 "Then the **E** will hear about it!

EHUD

  Left-handed judge who delivered Israel from
  Moabite king, Eglon (Jdg 3:12-30).

EIGHT [EIGHTH]

Ge   17:12 male among you who is **e** days old
     21: 1 When his son Isaac was **e** days old,
2Ki 22: 1 Josiah was **e** years old
1Pe   3:20 In it only a few people, **e** in all,

EIGHTEEN

Lk   13:11 crippled by a spirit for **e** years.

EIGHTH [EIGHT]

Lev 12: 3 On the **e** day the boy is to

	25:22	While you plant during the **e** year,
Lk	1:59	the **e** day they came to circumcise
	2:21	On the **e** day, when it was time to
Php	3: 5	circumcised on the **e** day,
Rev	17:11	and now is not, is an **e** king.

EIGHTY

Ex	7: 7	Moses was **e** years old
2Sa	19:35	I am now **e** years old.
Ps	90:10	or **e**, if we have the strength;

EIGHTY-FIVE

Jos	14:10	So here I am today, **e** years old!

EITHER

Lk	16:13	**E** he will hate the one and love
Ro	11:21	he will not spare you **e**.
Rev	3:15	I wish you were **e** one or the other!

EKRON

Jos	13: 3	Ashdod, Ashkelon, Gath and **E**—
1Sa	5:10	So they sent the ark of God to **E**.
	6:17	Gaza, Ashkelon, Gath and **E**.
2Ki	1: 2	consult Baal-Zebub, the god of **E**,

EL BETHEL* [BETHEL]

Ge	35: 7	and he called the place **E**

EL ELOHE ISRAEL* [ISRAEL]

Ge	33:20	set up an altar and called it **E**

ELAH

1. Son of Baasha; king of Israel (1Ki 16:6-14).
2. Valley in which David fought Goliath (1Sa 17:2, 19; 21:9).

ELAM

1Ch	1:17	The sons of Shem: **E**, Asshur,
Jer	49:34	Jeremiah the prophet concerning **E**,

ELATION*

Pr	28:12	righteous triumph, there is great **e**;

ELDER* [ELDERLY, ELDERS]

Isa	3: 2	the soothsayer and **e**,
1Ti	5:19	an accusation against an **e**
Tit	1: 6	An **e** must be blameless,
1Pe	5: 1	I appeal as a fellow **e**,
2Jn	1: 1	The **e**, To the chosen lady
3Jn	1: 1	The **e**, To my dear friend Gaius,

ELDERLY* [ELDER]

Lev	19:32	for the **e** and revere your God.

ELDERS [ELDER]

Ex	3:16	assemble the **e** of Israel and say
	24: 1	and seventy of the **e** of Israel.
Dt	25: 7	she shall go to the **e** at the town gate
Jos	24: 1	He summoned the **e**, leaders,
Jdg	2: 7	and of the **e** who outlived him
Ru	4: 2	Boaz took ten of the **e** of the town
2Ch	10:13	Rejecting the advice of the **e**,
Ps	105:22	and teach his **e** wisdom.
	119:100	I have more understanding than the **e**
Isa	3:14	enters into judgment against the **e**
La	5:14	The **e** are gone from the city gate;

Eze	8:11	stood seventy **e** of the house of Israel
Mt	15: 2	disciples break the tradition of the **e?**
Mk	7: 3	holding to the tradition of the **e**.
Lk	9:22	and be rejected by the **e**,
Ac	4: 5	**e** and teachers of the law met
	11:30	gift to the **e** by Barnabas and Saul.
	14:23	and Barnabas appointed **e** for them
	15: 2	to Jerusalem to see the apostles and **e**
	15: 6	and **e** met to consider this question.
	15:23	following letter: The apostles and **e**,
	16: 4	by the apostles and **e** in Jerusalem
	20:17	to Ephesus for the **e** of the church.
	21:18	and all the **e** were present.
	23:14	They went to the chief priests and **e**
	24: 1	down to Caesarea with some of the **e**
	25:15	and **e** of the Jews brought charges
1Ti	4:14	the body of **e** laid their hands on you.
	5:17	The **e** who direct the affairs of
Tit	1: 5	and appoint **e** in every town,
Jas	5:14	the **e** of the church to pray over him
1Pe	5: 1	To the **e** among you,
Rev	4: 4	seated on them were twenty-four **e**.
	4:10	twenty-four **e** fall down before him
	5: 6	by the four living creatures and the **e**.
	7:11	around the throne and around the **e**
	11:16	And the twenty-four **e**,
	14: 3	the four living creatures and the **e**.
	19: 4	The twenty-four **e** and

ELEAZAR

Third son of Aaron (Ex 6:23-25). Succeeded Aaron as high priest (Nu 20:26; Dt 10:6). Allotted land to tribes (Jos 14:1). Death (Jos 24:33).

ELECT* [ELECTION]

Mt	24:22	of the **e** those days will be shortened.
	24:24	and miracles to deceive even the **e**—
	24:31	and they will gather his **e** from
Mk	13:20	But for the sake of the **e**,
	13:22	and miracles to deceive the **e**—
	13:27	and gather his **e** from the four winds,
Ro	11: 7	but the **e** did.
1Ti	5:21	and Christ Jesus and the **e** angels,
2Ti	2:10	everything for the sake of the **e**,
Tit	1: 1	for the faith of God's **e**
1Pe	1: 1	To God's **e**, strangers in the world,

ELECTION* [ELECT]

Ro	9:11	that God's purpose in **e** might stand:
	11:28	but as far as **e** is concerned,
2Pe	1:10	to make your calling and **e** sure.

ELEMENTARY* [ELEMENTS]

Heb	5:12	teach you the **e** truths of God's word
	6: 1	Therefore let us leave the **e** teachings

ELEMENTS* [ELEMENTARY]

2Pe	3:10	the **e** will be destroyed by fire,
	3:12	and the **e** will melt in the heat.

ELEVATE* [ELEVATED]

2Co	11: 7	to lower myself in order to **e** you

ELEVATED* [ELEVATE]

Est   5:11   and how he had **e** him above

ELEVEN

Ge   32:22   and his **e** sons and crossed the ford of
       37: 9   and moon and **e** stars were bowing
Ex   26: 8   All **e** curtains are to be
Dt   1: 2   (It takes **e** days to go from Horeb
Mt   28:16   Then the **e** disciples went to Galilee,
Lk   24: 9   they told all these things to the **E** and
      24:33   There they found the **E** and those
Ac   1:26   so he was added to the **e** apostles.
       2:14   Then Peter stood up with the **E,**

ELI [ELI'S]

High priest in youth of Samuel (1Sa 1-4). Blessed Hannah (1Sa 1:12-18); raised Samuel (1Sa 2:11-26). Prophesied against because of wicked sons (1Sa 2:27-36). Death of Eli and sons (1Sa 4:11-22).

ELIAH (KJV) ELIJAH

ELIAKIM [JEHOIAKIM]

1. Original name of king Jehoiakim (2Ki 23:34; 2Ch 36:4).
2. Hezekiah's palace administrator (2Ki 18:17-37; 19:2; Isa 36:1-22; 37:2).

ELIAS (KJV) ELIJAH

ELIASHIB

Ne   3: 1   **E** the high priest and his fellow

ELIEZER

1. Servant of Abraham (Ge 15:2).
2. Son of Moses (Ex 18:4; 1Ch 23:15-17).

ELIHU

A friend of Job (Job 32-37).

ELIJAH

Prophet; predicted famine in Israel (1Ki 17:1; Jas 5:17). Fed by ravens (1Ki 17:2-6). Raised Sidonian widow's son (1Ki 17:7-24). Defeated prophets of Baal at Carmel (1Ki 18:16-46). Ran from Jezebel (1Ki 19:1-9). Prophesied death of Azariah (2Ki 1). Succeeded by Elishah (1Ki 19:19-21; 2Ki 2:1-18). Taken to heaven in whirlwind (2Ki 2:11-12).

Return prophesied (Mal 4:5-6); equated with John the Baptist (Mt 17:9-13; Mk 9:9-13; Lk 1:17). Appeared with Moses in transfiguration of Jesus (Mt 17:1-8; Mk 9:1-8).

ELIM

Ex   15:27   Then they came to **E,**
Nu   33: 9   They left Marah and went to **E,**

ELIMELECH

Ru   1: 3   Now **E,** Naomi's husband, died,
       4: 9   from Naomi all the property of **E,**

ELIMINATE* [ELIMINATED]

Dt   7:22   You will not be allowed to **e** them all

ELIMINATED* [ELIMINATE]

Dt   2:15   until he had completely **e** them from

ELIPHAZ

1. Firstborn of Esau (Ge 36).
2. A friend of Job (Job 4-5; 15; 22; 42:7, 9).

ELISHA

Prophet; successor of Elijah (1Ki 19:16-21); inherited his cloak (2Ki 2:1-18). Purified bad water (2Ki 2:19-22). Cursed young men (2Ki 2:23-25). Aided Israel's defeat of Moab (2Ki 3). Provided widow with oil (2Ki 4:1-7). Raised Shunammite woman's son (2Ki 4:8-37). Purified food (2Ki 4:38-41). Fed 100 men (2Ki 4:42-44). Healed Naaman's leprosy (2Ki 5). Made axhead float (2Ki 6:1-7). Captured Arameans (2Ki 6:8-23). Political adviser to Israel (2Ki 6:24-8:6; 9:1-3; 13:14-19); Aram (2Ki 8:7-15). Death (2Ki 13:20).

ELIZABETH*

Mother of John the Baptist (Lk 1:5-58).

ELKANAH

Husband of Hannah, father of Samuel (1Sa 1-2).

ELOI*

Mt   27:46   **"E, E,** lama sabachthani?"—
Mk   15:34   **"E, E,** lama sabachthani?"—

ELON

Judge of Israel (Jdg 12:11-12).

ELOQUENCE* [ELOQUENT]

1Co   2: 1   not come with **e** or superior wisdom

ELOQUENT* [ELOQUENCE]

Ex   4:10   "O Lord, I have never been **e,**

ELSE

Ex   4:13   please send someone **e** to do it."
Nu   12: 3   more humble than anyone **e** on
Pr   4:23   Above all **e,** guard your heart,
      27: 2   someone **e,,** and not your own lips.
Lk   7:19   or should we expect someone **e?"**
Jn   5:43   if someone **e** comes in his own name,
Ac   4:12   Salvation is found in no one **e,**
Ro   8:39   nor anything **e** in all creation,

ELYMAS

Ac   13: 8   But **E** the sorcerer (for that is what

EMASCULATE* [EMASCULATED]

Gal   5:12   the whole way and **e** themselves!

EMASCULATED* [EMASCULATE]

Dt   23: 1   No one who has been **e** by crushing

EMBALMED*

Ge   50: 2   So the physicians **e** him,
      50:26   And after they **e** him,

EMBEDDED*

Ecc   12:11   collected sayings like firmly **e** nails

EMBERS*

Ps 102: 3 my bones burn like glowing **e**.
Pr 26:21 As charcoal to **e** and as wood to fire,

EMBITTER* [BITTER]

Col 3:21 Fathers, do not **e** your children,

EMBODIMENT* [BODY]

Ro 2:20 in the law the **e** of knowledge and

EMBRACE [EMBRACED, EMBRACES, EMBRACING]

Pr 3:18 a tree of life to those who **e** her;
5:20 Why **e** the bosom of another
Ecc 3: 5 a time to **e** and a time to refrain,

EMBRACED [EMBRACE]

Ge 48:10 his father kissed them and **e** them.
2Ch 7:22 and have **e** other gods,
Ac 20:37 as they **e** him and kissed him.

EMBRACES* [EMBRACE]

SS 2: 6 and his right arm **e** me.
8: 3 and his right arm **e** me.

EMBRACING* [EMBRACE]

Ecc 2: 3 myself with wine, and **e** folly—

EMBROIDERED [EMBROIDERER]

Ps 45:14 In **e** garments she is led to the king;
Eze 16:10 I clothed you with an **e** dress

EMBROIDERER [EMBROIDERED]

Ex 26:36 the work of an **e**.

EMERALD

Ex 28:18 a sapphire and an **e**;
Rev 4: 3 A rainbow, resembling an **e**,
21:19 the third chalcedony, the fourth **e**,

EMMANUEL (KJV) IMMANUEL

EMMAUS*

Lk 24:13 going to a village called **E**,

EMPEROR*

Ac 25:25 because he made his appeal to the **E**

EMPTIED [EMPTY]

Ne 5:13 a man be shaken out and **e**!"
1Co 1:17 the cross of Christ be **e** of its power.

EMPTY [EMPTY-HANDED, EMPTIED]

Ge 1: 2 Now the earth was formless and **e**,
Ru 1:21 the LORD has brought me back **e**.
2Ki 4: 3 and ask all your neighbors for **e** jars.
Job 26: 7 the northern [skies] over **e** space;
35:16 So Job opens his mouth with **e** talk;
Isa 45:18 not create it to be **e**,
55:11 It will not return to me **e**,
Jer 4:23 and it was formless and **e**;
Lk 1:53 but has sent the rich away **e**.
Eph 5: 6 Let no one deceive you with **e** words,
1Pe 1:18 the **e** way of life handed down to you

2Pe 2:18 For they mouth **e**, boastful words

EMPTY-HANDED [EMPTY, HAND]

Ge 31:42 surely have sent me away **e**.
Ex 3:21 when you leave you will not go **e**.
23:15 "No one is to appear before me **e**.
Dt 15:13 do not send him away **e**.
Ru 3:17 go back to your mother-in-law **e**.
Mk 12: 3 beat him and sent him away **e**.

EN GEDI

1Sa 24: 1 "David is in the Desert of **E**

ENABLE* [ABLE]

Ecc 6: 2 God does not **e** him to enjoy them,
Lk 1:74 and to **e** us to serve him without fear
Ac 4:29 **e** your servants to speak your word

ENABLED* [ABLE]

Lev 26:13 **e** you to walk with heads held high.
Ru 4:13 and the LORD **e** her to conceive,
Jn 6:65 to me unless the Father has **e** him."
Ac 2: 4 in other tongues as the Spirit **e** them.
7:10 He gave Joseph wisdom and **e** him
Heb 11:11 was **e** to become a father

ENABLES* [ABLE]

2Sa 22:34 he **e** me to stand on the heights.
Ps 18:33 he **e** me to stand on the heights.
Ecc 5:19 and **e** him to enjoy them,
Hab 3:19 he **e** me to go on the heights.
Php 3:21 power that **e** him to bring everything

ENABLING* [ABLE]

Ac 14: 3 by **e** them to do miraculous signs

ENCAMP [CAMP]

Ex 14: 2 They are to **e** by the sea,

ENCAMPED [CAMP]

Nu 9:23 At the LORD's command they **e**,
24: 2 and saw Israel **e** tribe by tribe,

ENCAMPS* [CAMP]

Ps 34: 7 angel of the LORD **e** around those

ENCHANTER [ENCHANTERS]

Isa 3: 3 skilled craftsman and clever **e**.
Da 2:27 Daniel replied, "No wise man, **e**,

ENCHANTERS [ENCHANTER]

Da 1:20 better than all the magicians and **e**
5: 7 The king called out for the **e**,

ENCIRCLE [CIRCLE]

Ps 22:12 strong bulls of Bashan **e** me.

ENCIRCLED [CIRCLE]

Rev 4: 3 resembling an emerald, **e** the throne.
5: 6 **e** by the four living creatures and

ENCLOSE* [CLOSE]

SS 8: 9 we will **e** her with panels of cedar.

ENCLOSED [CLOSE]
SS   4:12 my bride; you are a spring **e,**

ENCOURAGE* [ENCOURAGED,
ENCOURAGEMENT, ENCOURAGES,
ENCOURAGING]
Dt   1:38 **E** him, because he will lead Israel
     3:28 and **e** and strengthen him,
2Sa 11:25 Say this to **e** Joab."
    19: 7 Now go out and **e** your men.
Job 16: 5 But my mouth would **e** you;
Ps 10:17 **e** them, and you listen to their cry,
    64: 5 They **e** each other in evil plans,
Isa 1:17 Seek justice, **e** the oppressed.
Jer 29: 8 not listen to the dreams you **e** them
Ac 15:32 to **e** and strengthen the brothers.
Ro 12: 8 if it is encouraging, let him **e;**
Eph 6:22 and that he may **e** you.
Col 4: 8 and that he may **e** your hearts.
1Th 3: 2 to strengthen and **e** you in your faith,
     4:18 each other with these words.
     5:11 **e** one another and build each other
     5:14 warn those who are idle, **e** the timid,
2Th 2:17 **e** your hearts and strengthen you
2Ti 4: 2 rebuke and **e**—with great patience
Tit 1: 9 that he can **e** others
     2: 6 **e** the young men to be self-controlled
     2:15 **E** and rebuke with all authority.
Heb 3:13 But **e** one another daily,
    10:25 but let us **e** one another—

ENCOURAGED* [ENCOURAGE]
Jdg 7:11 you will be **e** to attack the camp."
    20:22 But the men of Israel **e** one another
2Ch 22: 3 for his mother **e** him in doing wrong.
    32: 6 and **e** them with these words:
    35: 2 and **e** them in the service of
Eze 13:22 you **e** the wicked not to turn
Ac   9:31 and **e** by the Holy Spirit,
    11:23 and **e** them all to remain true to
    16:40 with the brothers and **e** them.
    18:27 the brothers **e** him and wrote to
    27:36 They were all **e**
    28:15 Paul thanked God and was **e.**
Ro   1:12 be mutually **e** by each other's faith.
1Co 14:31 everyone may be instructed and **e.**
2Co 7: 4 I am greatly **e;**
     7:13 By all this we are **e.**
Php 1:14 in the Lord have been **e** to speak
Col 2: 2 that they may be **e** in heart
1Th 3: 7 and persecution we were **e** about you
Heb 6:18 to us may be greatly **e.**

ENCOURAGEMENT*
[ENCOURAGE]
Ac   4:36 Barnabas (which means Son of **E),**
    13:15 if you have a message of **e** for
    20: 2 speaking many words of **e** to
Ro 15: 4 so that through endurance and the **e**
    15: 5 God who gives endurance and **e**
1Co 14: 3 for their strengthening, **e** and comfort
2Co 7:13 In addition to our own **e,**

Php 2: 1 If you have any **e** from being united
2Th 2:16 and by his grace gave us eternal **e**
Phm 1: 7 love has given me great joy and **e,**
Heb 12: 5 you have forgotten that word of **e**

ENCOURAGES* [ENCOURAGE]
Isa 41: 7 The craftsman **e** the goldsmith,

ENCOURAGING* [ENCOURAGE]
Ac 14:22 and **e** them to remain true to
    15:31 and were glad for its **e** message.
    20: 1 after **e** them, said good-by
Ro 12: 8 if it is **e,** let him encourage;
1Th 2:12 **e,** comforting and urging you
1Pe 5:12 **e** you and testifying that this is

ENCROACH
Pr 23:10 or **e** on the fields of the fatherless,

END [ENDED, ENDS, ENDLESS]
Ge   6:13 "I am going to put an **e** to all people,
Ex 12:41 At the **e** of the 430 years,
Nu 16:21 so I can put an **e** to them
    23:10 and may my **e** be like theirs!"
Dt   8:16 in the **e** it might go well with you.
    31:24 of this law from beginning to **e,**
Ne   9:31 you did not put an **e** to them or
Job 19:25 in the **e** he will stand upon the earth.
Ps 48:14 be our guide even to the **e.**
   119:33 then I will keep them to the **e.**
   119:112 keeping your decrees to the very **e.**
Pr   1:19 Such is the **e** of all who go
     5: 4 but in the **e** she is bitter as gall,
     5:11 At the **e** of your life you will groan,
    14:12 but in the **e** it leads to death.
    14:13 and joy may **e** in grief.
    16:25 but in the **e** it leads to death.
    19:20 and in the **e** you will be wise.
    20:21 not be blessed at the **e.**
    23:32 In the **e** it bites like a snake
    25: 8 in the **e** if your neighbor puts you
    28:23 **e** gain more favor than he who has
    29:21 he will bring grief in the **e.**
Ecc 3:11 God has done from beginning to **e.**
     7: 8 The **e** of a matter is better than its
    12:12 Of making many books there is no **e,**
Isa 9: 7 and peace there will be no **e.**
Eze 7: 2 The **e** has come upon
Da   4:34 At the **e** of that time, I,
     6:26 his dominion will never **e.**
     8:17 the vision concerns the time of the **e.**
     9:26 The **e** will come like a flood:
    12:13 then at the **e** of the days you will rise
Mt 10:22 stands firm to the **e** will be saved.
    24:13 stands firm to the **e** will be saved.
    24:14 and then the **e** will come.
Lk 21: 9 but the **e** will not come right away."
Ro 10: 4 Christ is the **e** of the law
1Co 15:24 Then the **e** will come,
Heb 3:14 hold firmly till the **e** the confidence
     6: 8 In the **e** it will be burned.
1Pe 4: 7 The **e** of all things is near.
2Pe 2:20 they are worse off at the **e** than
Rev 2:26 and does my will to the **e,**

21: 6 the Beginning and the **E.**
22:13 the Beginning and the **E.**

ENDED [END]

Pr 22:10 quarrels and insults are **e.**
Rev 20: 3 until the thousand years were **e.**

ENDLESS [END]

Ps 106:31 as righteousness for **e** generations
Na 3:19 for who has not felt your **e** cruelty?

ENDOR

1Sa 28: 7 "There is one in **E,**" they said.

ENDOW [ENDOWED]

Ps 72: 1 **E** the king with your justice, O God,

ENDOWED [ENDOW]

Isa 55: 5 for he has **e** you with splendor."

ENDS [END]

Ps 2: 8 the **e** of the earth your possession.
19: 4 their words to the **e** of the world.
67: 7 all the **e** of the earth will fear him.
Pr 20:17 he **e** up with a mouth full of gravel.
Isa 40:28 the Creator of the **e** of the earth.
49: 6 salvation to the **e** of the earth."
62:11 proclamation to the **e** of the earth:
Mic 5: 4 then his greatness will reach to the **e**
Lk 11:31 for she came from the **e** of the earth
Ac 13:47 salvation to the **e** of the earth.'
Ro 10:18 their words to the **e** of the world."

ENDS OF THE EARTH See EARTH

ENDURANCE* [ENDURE]

Ro 15: 4 through **e** and the encouragement of
15: 5 May the God who gives **e**
2Co 1: 6 which produces in you patient **e** of
6: 4 in every way: in great **e;**
Col 1:11 so that you may have great **e**
1Th 1: 3 and your **e** inspired by hope
1Ti 6:11 faith, love, **e** and gentleness.
2Ti 3:10 my purpose, faith, patience, love, **e,**
Tit 2: 2 and sound in faith, in love and in **e,**
Rev 1: 9 suffering and kingdom and patient **e**
13:10 calls for patient **e** and faithfulness
14:12 for patient **e** on the part of the saints

ENDURE [ENDURANCE, ENDURED, ENDURES, ENDURING]

1Sa 13:14 But now your kingdom will not **e;**
2Sa 7:16 and your kingdom will **e** forever
Job 20:21 his prosperity will not **e.**
Ps 37:18 and their inheritance will **e** forever.
49:12 man, despite his riches, does not **e;**
72:17 May his name **e** forever;
89:29 his throne as long as the heavens **e.**
104:31 the glory of the LORD **e** forever;
Pr 12:19 Truthful lips **e** forever,
27:24 for riches do not **e** forever,
Ecc 1: 4 everything God does will **e** forever;
Isa 66:22 and the new earth that I make will **e**
Jer 44:22 LORD could no longer **e** your wicked
Da 2:44 but it will itself **e** forever.

Joel 2:11 Who can **e** it?
Na 1: 6 Who can **e** his fierce anger?
Mal 3: 2 who can **e** the day of his coming?
1Co 4:12 when we are persecuted, we **e** it;
2Co 1: 8 far beyond our ability to **e,**
2Ti 2: 3 **E** hardship with us like a good
2:10 Therefore I **e** everything for the sake
2:12 if we **e,** we will also reign with him.
4: 5 in all situations, **e** hardship,
Heb 12: 7 **E** hardship as discipline;
1Pe 2:20 suffer for doing good and you **e** it,
Rev 3:10 kept my command to **e** patiently,

ENDURED* [ENDURE]

Ps 123: 3 for we have **e** much contempt.
123: 3 We have **e** much ridicule from
132: 1 David and all the hardships he **e.**
Ac 13:18 **e** their conduct for about forty years
2Ti 3:11 the persecutions I **e.**
Heb 12: 2 for the joy set before him **e** the cross,
12: 3 Consider him who **e** such opposition
Rev 2: 3 and have **e** hardships for my name,

ENDURES [ENDURE]

Ge 8:22 "As long as the earth **e,**
1Ch 16:41 "for his love **e** forever."
Ps 102:12 renown **e** through all generations.
112: 9 his righteousness **e** forever;
136: 1 His love **e** forever.
145:13 dominion **e** through all generations.
Da 9:15 for yourself a name that **e** to this day,
Jn 6:27 but for food that **e** to eternal life,
2Co 9: 9 his righteousness **e** forever."

HIS LOVE ENDURES FOREVER
See LOVE

ENDURING [ENDURE]

Ps 19: 9 fear of the LORD is pure, **e** forever.
2Th 1: 4 the persecutions and trials you are **e.**
Heb 13:14 For here we do not have an **e** city,
1Pe 1:23 the living and **e** word of God.

ENEMIES [ENEMY]

Ex 1:10 if war breaks out, will join our **e,**
23:22 I will be an enemy to your **e**
Lev 26:37 not be able to stand before your **e.**
Dt 6:19 thrusting out all your **e** before you,
Jos 5:13 "Are you for us or for our **e?**"
21:44 Not one of their **e** withstood them;
Jdg 2:14 He sold them to their **e** all around,
2Sa 7: 1 rest from all his **e** around him,
Est 9: 5 The Jews struck down all their **e** with
Job 19:11 he counts me among his **e.**
Ps 23: 5 before me in the presence of my **e.**
44: 7 but you give us victory over our **e,**
110: 1 until I make your **e** a footstool for
Pr 16: 7 even his **e** live at peace with him.
Isa 59:18 so will he repay wrath to his **e**
Jer 12: 7 the one I love into the hands of her **e.**
Da 4:19 if only the dream applied to your **e**
Mic 7: 6 a man's **e** are the members
Mt 5:44 But I tell you: Love your **e** and pray
10:36 a man's **e** will be the members
Lk 6:35 But love your **e,** do good to them,

	20:43	until I make your **e** a footstool
Ro	5:10	For if, when we were God's **e**,
1Co	15:25	until he has put all his **e**
Php	3:18	many live as **e** of the cross of Christ.
Col	1:21	from God and were **e** in your minds
Heb	1:13	until I make your **e** a footstool for
	10:13	Since that time he waits for his **e** to
	10:27	fire that will consume the **e** of God.
Rev	11:5	their mouths and devours their **e**.

ENEMY [ENEMIES, ENMITY]

Ex	15:9	"The **e** boasted, 'I will pursue,
	23:22	I will be an **e** to your enemies
Dt	33:27	He will drive out your **e** before you,
2Sa	22:18	He rescued me from my powerful **e**,
Est	3:10	the Agagite, the **e** of the Jews.
	9:24	the Agagite, the **e** of all the Jews,
Ps	9:6	Endless ruin has overtaken the **e**,
	74:10	How long will the **e** mock you,
Pr	24:17	Do not gloat when your **e** falls;
	25:21	If your **e** is hungry,
	27:6	but an **e** multiplies kisses.
	29:24	accomplice of a thief is his own **e**;
Jer	30:14	I have struck you as an **e** would
La	2:5	The Lord is like an **e**,
Mic	2:8	my people have risen up like an **e**.
Mt	13:39	and the **e** who sows them is the devil.
Lk	10:19	to overcome all the power of the **e**;
Ro	12:20	On the contrary: "If your **e** is hungry,
1Co	15:26	The last **e** to be destroyed is death.
1Ti	5:14	the **e** no opportunity for slander.
1Pe	5:8	Your **e** the devil prowls around like

ENERGY*

Col	1:29	struggling with all his **e**,

ENGRAVE [ENGRAVED]

Ex	28:11	**E** the names of the sons of Israel
Zec	3:9	and I will **e** an inscription on it,'

ENGRAVED [ENGRAVE]

Ex	32:16	**e** on the tablets.
Isa	49:16	I have **e** you on the palms
Jer	17:1	"Judah's sin is **e** with an iron tool,
2Co	3:7	which was **e** in letters on stone,

ENHANCES*

Ro	3:7	If my falsehood **e** God's truthfulness

ENJOY [JOY]

Lev	26:34	the land will rest and **e** its sabbaths.
Nu	14:31	in to **e** the land you have rejected.
Dt	6:2	and so that you may **e** long life.
Ps	37:3	in the land and **e** safe pasture.
Pr	28:16	hates ill-gotten gain will **e** a long life.
Ecc	3:12	better for a man than to **e** his work,
	5:19	and enables him to **e** them,
	6:2	God does not enable him to **e** them,
	9:9	**E** life with your wife.
Eph	6:3	that you may **e** long life on the earth.
Heb	11:25	rather than to **e** the pleasures
3Jn	1:2	I pray that you may **e** good health

ENJOYED [JOY]

2Ch	36:21	The land **e** its sabbath rests;

ENJOYMENT* [JOY]

Ecc	2:25	who can eat or find **e**?
	4:8	why am I depriving myself of **e**?"
	8:15	So I commend the **e** of life,
1Ti	6:17	provides us with everything for our **e**

ENLARGE* [LARGE]

Ex	34:24	before you and **e** your territory,
1Ch	4:10	bless me and **e** my territory!
Isa	54:2	"**E** the place of your tent,
2Co	9:10	**e** the harvest of your righteousness.

ENLARGED [LARGE]

Dt	12:20	LORD your God has **e** your territory
Isa	9:3	You have **e** the nation and increased
	26:15	You have **e** the nation, O LORD; you have **e** the nation.

ENLARGES [LARGE]

Dt	19:8	LORD your God **e** your territory,

ENLIGHTEN* [LIGHT]

Isa	40:14	Whom did the LORD consult to **e** him

ENLIGHTENED* [LIGHT]

Eph	1:18	that the eyes of your heart may be **e**
Heb	6:4	for those who have once been **e**,

ENMITY* [ENEMY]

Ge	3:15	And I will put **e** between you and

ENOCH

1. Son of Cain (Ge 4:17-18).
2. Descendant of Seth; walked with God and taken by him (Ge 5:18-24; Heb 11:5). Prophet (Jude 14).

ENOUGH

Dt	1:6	"You have stayed long **e**
	9:8	that he was angry **e** to destroy you,
Ezr	9:14	not be angry **e** with us to destroy us,
Pr	30:15	four that never say, '**E**!':
Ecc	1:8	The eye never has **e** of seeing,
	5:10	loves money never has money **e**;
Isa	7:13	Is it not **e** to try the patience of men?
Joel	2:19	**e** to satisfy you fully;
Hag	1:6	You eat, but never have **e**.

ENRICH* [RICH]

Ps	65:9	and water it; you **e** it abundantly.
Pr	5:10	and your toil **e** another man's house.

ENRICHED [RICH]

1Co	1:5	For in him you have been **e**

ENSLAVED [SLAVE]

Ge	15:13	**e** and mistreated four hundred years.
Gal	4:9	Do you wish to be **e** by them all
Tit	3:3	and **e** by all kinds of passions

ENSLAVES* [SLAVE]

2Co	11:20	even put up with anyone who **e** you

ENSLAVING* [SLAVE]

Ex 6: 5 whom the Egyptians are **e,**

ENSNARE [SNARE]

Pr 5:22 evil deeds of a wicked man **e** him;
Ecc 7:26 but the sinner she will **e.**

ENSNARED* [SNARE]

Dt 7:25 or you will be **e** by it,
12:30 to be **e** by inquiring about their gods,
Ps 9:16 the wicked are **e** by the work
Pr 6: 2 **e** by the words of your mouth,
22:25 learn his ways and get yourself **e.**

ENTANGLE* [ENTANGLED, ENTANGLES]

Ps 35: 8 may the net they hid **e** them,

ENTANGLED [ENTANGLE]

Ps 116: 3 The cords of death **e** me,
2Pe 2:20 and are again **e** in it and overcome,

ENTANGLES* [ENTANGLE]

Heb 12: 1 and the sin that so easily **e,**

ENTER [ENTERED, ENTERING, ENTERS, ENTRANCE]

Ge 6:18 and you will **e** the ark—
Ex 40:35 Moses could not **e** the Tent of
Nu 20:24 not **e** the land I give the Israelites,
Dt 1:37 "You shall not **e**, either.
Ps 95:11 "They shall never **e** my rest."
100: 4 **E** his gates with thanksgiving
118:20 through which the righteous may **e.**
Pr 2:10 For wisdom will **e** your heart,
Isa 26: 2 that the righteous nation may **e,**
35:10 They will **e** Zion with singing;
51:11 They will **e** Zion with singing;
Eze 37: 5 I will make breath **e** you,
Joel 3: 2 There I will **e** into judgment
Mt 5:20 you will certainly not **e** the kingdom
7:13 "**E** through the narrow gate.
7:21 Lord,' will **e** the kingdom of heaven,
18: 3 you will never **e** the kingdom
18: 8 better for you to **e** life maimed
19:17 If you want to **e** life,
Mk 10:15 like a little child will never **e** it."
10:23 for the rich to **e** the kingdom of God!
Lk 13:24 to **e** through the narrow door,
24:26 and then **e** his glory?"
Jn 3: 5 can **e** the kingdom of God unless
Heb 3:11 'They shall never **e** my rest.' "
4: 3 we who have believed **e** that rest,
4:11 make every effort to **e** that rest,
9:12 not **e** by means of the blood of goats
10:19 since we have confidence to **e**
Rev 15: 8 and no one could **e** the temple until
21:27 Nothing impure will ever **e** it,

ENTERED [ENTER]

Ge 7: 9 came to Noah and **e** the ark,
Ex 24:18 Then Moses **e** the cloud as he went
Nu 7:89 When Moses **e** the Tent of Meeting

Dt 26: 1 When you have **e** the land
2Ch 26:16 and **e** the temple of the LORD
Ps 73:17 till I **e** the sanctuary of God;
Isa 28:15 have **e** into a covenant with death,
Eze 4:14 No unclean meat has ever **e** my
37:10 and breath **e** them;
43: 4 The glory of the LORD **e** the temple
Lk 9:34 they were afraid as they **e** the cloud.
22: 3 Then Satan **e** Judas, called Iscariot,
Jn 13:27 Satan **e** into him.
Ac 11: 8 or unclean has ever **e** my mouth.'
Ro 5:12 as sin **e** the world through one man,
Heb 6:20 has **e** on our behalf
9:12 but he **e** the Most Holy Place
Rev 11:11 a breath of life from God **e** them,

ENTERING [ENTER]

Nu 32: 9 discouraged the Israelites from **e** the
Mt 21:31 and the prostitutes are **e** the kingdom
Lk 11:52 you have hindered those who were **e.**
Heb 4: 1 the promise of **e** his rest still stands,

ENTERS [ENTER]

Mk 7:18 nothing that **e** a man from
Jn 10: 2 The man who **e** by the gate is
Heb 4:10 for anyone who **e** God's rest

ENTERTAIN* [ENTERTAINED, ENTERTAINMENT]

Jdg 16:25 "Bring out Samson to **e** us."
Mt 9: 4 "Why do you **e** evil thoughts
1Ti 5:19 not **e** an accusation against an elder
Heb 13: 2 Do not forget to **e** strangers,

ENTERTAINED* [ENTERTAIN]

Ac 28: 7 and for three days **e** us hospitably.
Heb 13: 2 so doing some people have **e** angels

ENTERTAINMENT* [ENTERTAIN]

Da 6:18 without any **e** being brought to him.

ENTHRALLED*

Ps 45:11 The king is **e** by your beauty;

ENTHRONED* [THRONE]

1Sa 4: 4 who is **e** between the cherubim.
2Sa 6: 2 who is **e** between the cherubim
2Ki 19:15 **e** between the cherubim,
1Ch 13: 6 who is **e** between the cherubim—
Ps 2: 4 The One **e** in heaven laughs;
9:11 praises to the LORD, **e** in Zion;
22: 3 Yet you are **e** as the Holy One;
29:10 The LORD sits **e** over the flood; the LORD is **e** as King forever.
55:19 God, who is **e** forever,
61: 7 be **e** in God's presence forever;
80: 1 you who sit **e** between the cherubim,
99: 1 he sits **e** between the cherubim,
102:12 But you, O LORD, sit **e** forever;
113: 5 the One who sits **e** on high,
132:14 here I will sit **e,**
Isa 14:13 I will sit **e** on the mount of assembly,
37:16 **e** between the cherubim,
40:22 He sits **e** above the circle of

52: 2 Shake off your dust; rise up, sit **e**,

ENTHRONES* [THRONE]

Job 36: 7 he **e** them with kings

ENTHUSIASM*

2Co 8:17 but he is coming to you with much **e**
9: 2 and your **e** has stirred most of them

ENTICE [ENTICED, ENTICES]

2Ch 18:19 'Who will **e** Ahab king of Israel
Pr   1:10 My son, if sinners **e** you,
2Pe 2:18 they **e** people who are just escaping
Rev 2:14 who taught Balak to **e** the Israelites

ENTICED* [ENTICE]

Dt   4:19 not be **e** into bowing down to them
11:16 or you will be **e** to turn away
2Ki 17:21 Jeroboam **e** Israel away
Job 31: 9 "If my heart has been **e** by a woman,
31:27 that my heart was secretly **e**
Eze 14: 9 the prophet is **e** to utter a prophecy, I
the LORD have **e** that prophet,
Jas 1:14 he is dragged away and **e**.

ENTICES* [ENTICE]

Dt 13: 6 or your closest friend secretly **e** you,
Job 36:18 Be careful that no one **e** you
Pr 16:29 A violent man **e** his neighbor

ENTIRE

Ex 14:28 **e** army of Pharaoh that had followed
Dt   2:14 that **e** generation of fighting men
Jos 11:16 So Joshua took this **e** land:
Lk   2: 1 be taken of the **e** Roman world.
Ac 11:28 spread over the **e** Roman world.
18: 8 his **e** household believed in the Lord;
Gal 5:14 The law is summed up in

ENTRANCE [ENTER]

Ex 26:36 "For the **e** to the tent make a curtain
27:16 "For the **e** to the courtyard,
Mt 27:60 he rolled a big stone in front of the **e**
Mk 15:46 Then he rolled a stone against the **e**,
16: 3 the stone away from the **e** of
Jn 11:38 a cave with a stone laid across the **e**.
20: 1 had been removed from the **e**.
Ac 12: 6 and sentries stood guard at the **e**.

ENTREAT [ENTREATY]

Zec 8:21 'Let us go at once to **e** the LORD

ENTREATY [ENTREAT]

2Ch 33:19 and how God was moved by his **e**,

ENTRUST [TRUST]

Jn   2:24 Jesus would not **e** himself to them,
2Ti 2: 2 **e** to reliable men who will also

ENTRUSTED [TRUST]

Ge 39: 4 he **e** to his care everything he owned.
2Ki 22: 7 not account for the money **e** to them,
Jer 13:20 Where is the flock that was **e** to you,
Lk 12:48 the one who has been **e** with much,
Jn   5:22 but has **e** all judgment to the Son,

Ro   3: 2 they have been **e** with the very words
6:17 of teaching to which you were **e**.
1Co 1: 1 and as those **e** with the secret things
Gal 2: 7 **e** with the task of preaching the
1Th 2: 4 as men approved by God to be **e** with
1Ti 1:11 which he **e** to me.
6:20 guard what has been **e** to your care.
2Ti 1:12 that he is able to guard what I have **e**
1:14 the good deposit that was **e** to you—
Tit 1: 3 through the preaching **e** to me by
1: 7 an overseer is **e** with God's work,
1Pe 2:23 **e** himself to him who judges justly.
5: 3 not lording it over those **e** to you,
Jude 1: 3 the faith that was once for all **e** to

ENVELOPED

Mk   9: 7 Then a cloud appeared and **e** them,

ENVIED [ENVY]

Ps 73: 3 For I **e** the arrogant when I saw

ENVIES* [ENVY]

Jas 4: 5 caused to live in us **e** intensely?

ENVIOUS [ENVY]

Dt 32:21 I will make them **e** by those who are
Ps 37: 1 not fret because of evil men or be **e**
Pr 24:19 not fret because of evil men or be **e**
Ro 10:19 "I will make you **e** by those who are
11:11 to the Gentiles to make Israel **e**.

ENVOY

Pr 13:17 but a trustworthy **e** brings healing.

ENVY [ENVIED, ENVIES, ENVIOUS, ENVYING]

Pr   3:31 Do not **e** a violent man or choose any
14:30 but **e** rots the bones.
23:17 Do not let your heart **e** sinners,
24: 1 Do not **e** wicked men,
Ecc 4: 4 spring from man's **e** of his neighbor.
Mt 27:18 of **e** that they had handed Jesus over
Mk   7:22 malice, deceit, lewdness, **e**, slander,
Ro   1:29 They are full of **e**, murder, strife,
11:14 arouse my own people to **e** and save
1Co 13: 4 It does not **e**, it does not boast,
Gal 5:21 and **e**; drunkenness, orgies,
Php 1:15 that some preach Christ out of **e**
1Ti 6: 4 quarrels about words that result in **e**,
Tit 3: 3 We lived in malice and **e**,
Jas 3:14 But if you harbor bitter **e** and selfish
3:16 you have **e** and selfish ambition,
1Pe 2: 1 **e**, and slander of every kind.

ENVYING* [ENVY]

Gal 5:26 provoking and **e** each other.

EPAPHRAS*

Associate of Paul (Col 1:7; 4:12; Phm 23).

EPAPHRODITUS*

Associate of Paul (Php 2:25; 4:18).

EPHAH

Ex 16:36 (An omer is one tenth of an **e**.)

Eze 45:10 an accurate **e** and an accurate bath.
Mic 6:10 and the short **e**, which is accursed?

EPHESIANS [EPHESUS]

Ac 19:28 "Great is Artemis of the **E**!"

EPHESUS [EPHESIANS]

Ac 18:19 They arrived at **E**,
19: 1 through the interior and arrived at **E**.
20:17 Paul sent to **E** for the elders of the
1Co 15:32 If I fought wild beasts in **E**
Eph 1: 1 To the saints in **E**,
Rev 2: 1 the angel of the church in **E** write:

EPHOD

Ex 28: 6 "Make the **e** of gold, and of blue,
Jdg 8:27 Gideon made the gold into an **e**,
17: 5 and he made an **e** and some idols
1Sa 2:18 a boy wearing a linen **e**.
1Ch 15:27 David also wore a linen **e**.
Hos 3: 4 without **e** or idol.

EPHPHATHA*

Mk 7:34 "**E**!" (which means, "Be opened!").

EPHRAIM

1. Second son of Joseph (Ge 41:52; 46:20). Blessed as firstborn by Jacob (Ge 48). Tribe of numbered (Nu 1:33; 26:37), blessed (Dt 33:17), allotted land (Jos 16:4-9; Eze 48:5), failed to fully possess (Jos 16:10; Jdg 1:29).
2. A term for the Northern Kingdom of Israel (Isa 7:17; Hos 5).

EPHRATH [BETHLEHEM, EPHRATHAH]

Ge 35:19 on the way to **E** (that is, Bethlehem).

EPHRATHAH [EPHRATH]

Ru 4:11 in **E** and be famous in Bethlehem.
Mic 5: 2 "But you, Bethlehem **E**,

EPHRON

Hittite who sold Abraham a field (Ge 23).

EPICUREAN*

Ac 17:18 A group of **E** and Stoic philosophers

EPISTLE (KJV) LETTER

EQUAL [EQUALED, EQUALITY, EQUITY]

Ge 44:18 though you are **e** to Pharaoh himself.
Dt 33:25 and your strength will **e** your days.
1Sa 9: 2 an impressive young man without **e**
1Ki 3:13 in your lifetime you will have no **e**
Isa 40:25 Or who is my **e**?"
46: 5 compare me or count me **e**?
Da 1:19 and he found none **e** to Daniel,
Jn 5:18 making himself **e** with God.
1Co 12:25 that its parts should have **e** concern
2Co 2:16 And who is **e** to such a task?

EQUALED [EQUAL]

Mk 13:19 and never to be **e** again.

EQUALITY* [EQUAL]

2Co 8:13 but that there might be **e**.
8:14 Then there will be **e**,
Php 2: 6 not consider **e** with God something

EQUIP* [EQUIPMENT, EQUIPPED]

Heb 13:21 **e** you with everything good

EQUIPMENT [EQUIP]

Nu 3:36 its crossbars, posts, bases, all its **e**,
Zec 11:15 the **e** of a foolish shepherd.

EQUIPPED [EQUIP]

2Ti 3:17 be thoroughly **e** for every good work.

EQUITY* [EQUAL]

Ps 96:10 he will judge the peoples with **e**.
98: 9 and the peoples with **e**.
99: 4 loves justice—you have established **e**

ER

Ge 38: 6 Judah got a wife for **E**, his firstborn,

ERASTUS*

Associate(s) of Paul (Ac 19:22; Ro 16:23; 2Ti 4:20).

ERECT [ERECTED]

Dt 16:22 and do not **e** a sacred stone,

ERECTED [ERECT]

1Ki 7:21 He **e** the pillars at the portico of
2Ki 21: 3 also **e** altars to Baal and made

ERODES*

Job 14:18 "But as a mountain **e** and crumbles

ERRED* [ERROR]

Nu 15:28 before the LORD for the one who **e**
1Sa 26:21 like a fool and have **e** greatly."

ERROR [ERRED, ERRORS]

Job 4:18 if he charges his angels with **e**,
Isa 47:15 Each of them goes on in his **e**;
Mt 22:29 in **e** because you do not know
Jas 5:20 a sinner from the **e** of his way will
2Pe 2:18 escaping from those who live in **e**.
3:17 carried away by the **e** of lawless men
Jude 1:11 rushed for profit into Balaam's **e**;

ERRORS* [ERROR]

Ps 19:12 Who can discern his **e**?
Ecc 10: 4 calmness can lay great **e** to rest.

ESAIAS (KJV) ISAIAH

ESAU [EDOM]

Firstborn of Isaac, twin of Jacob (Ge 25:21-26). Also called Edom (Ge 25:30). Sold Jacob his birthright (Ge 25:29-34); lost blessing (Gen 27). Married Hittites (Ge 26:34), Ishmaelites (Ge 28:6-9). Reconciled to Jacob (Gen 33). Genealogy (Ge 36). The LORD chose Jacob over Esau (Mal 1:2-3), but gave Esau land (Dt 2:2-12). Descendants eventually obliterated (Ob 1-21; Jer 49:7-22).

ESCAPE [ESCAPED, ESCAPES, ESCAPING]

Ge 7: 7 the ark to **e** the waters of the flood.
1Sa 19:10 That night David made good his **e.**
2Sa 15:14 or none of us will **e** from Absalom.
Job 11:20 and **e** will elude them;
Ps 68:20 Sovereign LORD comes **e** from death.
Pr 11: 9 through knowledge the righteous **e.**
Ecc 7:26 The man who pleases God will **e** her,
Jer 11:11 on them a disaster they cannot **e.**
Eze 6: 9 those who **e** will remember me—
Mt 23:33 will you **e** being condemned to hell?
Ro 2: 3 think you will **e** God's judgment?
1Th 5: 3 and they will not **e.**
2Ti 2:26 and **e** from the trap of the devil,
Heb 2: 3 **e** if we ignore such a great salvation?
    12:25 If they did not **e** when they refused
2Pe 1: 4 **e** the corruption in the world caused

ESCAPED [ESCAPE]

1Sa 22: 1 David left Gath and **e** to the cave
Ps 124: 7 We have **e** like a bird out of
La 2:22 of the LORD's anger no one **e**
Jn 10:39 but he **e** their grasp.
Heb 11:34 and **e** the edge of the sword;
2Pe 2:20 have **e** the corruption of the world

ESCAPES* [ESCAPE]

Ps 33:16 no warrior **e** by his great strength.
Pr 12:13 but a righteous man **e** trouble.
Joel 2: 3 a desert waste—nothing **e** them.

ESCAPING [ESCAPE]

1Co 3:15 but only as one **e** through the flames.
2Pe 2:18 they entice people who are just **e**

ESHCOL

Nu 13:23 When they reached the Valley of **E,**

ESTABLISH [ESTABLISHED, ESTABLISHES]

Ge 6:18 But I will **e** my covenant with you,
    9: 9 "I now **e** my covenant with you and
    17:21 But my covenant I will **e** with Isaac,
Ex 23:31 "I will **e** your borders from
Dt 28: 9 LORD will **e** you as his holy people,
2Sa 7:11 the LORD himself will **e** a house
1Ki 9: 5 I will **e** your royal throne
1Ch 28: 7 I will **e** his kingdom forever
Ps 89: 4 'I will **e** your line forever
    90:17 **e** the work of our hands.
Isa 26:12 LORD, you **e** peace for us;
Eze 16:60 and I will **e** an everlasting covenant
Ro 10: 3 from God and sought to **e** their own,
    16:25 Now to him who is able to **e** you
Heb 10: 9 He sets aside the first to **e** the second

ESTABLISHED [ESTABLISH]

Ge 9:17 the sign of the covenant I have **e**
Ex 6: 4 I also **e** my covenant with them
Dt 19:15 A matter must be **e** by the testimony
2Sa 7:16 your throne will be **e** forever.' "
1Ki 2:46 now firmly **e** in Solomon's hands.

Ps 78:69 like the earth that he **e** forever.
    93: 2 Your throne was **e** long ago;
    96:10 The world is firmly **e,**
    103:19 LORD has **e** his throne in heaven,
Pr 16:12 a throne is **e** through righteousness.
Isa 2: 2 of the LORD's temple will be **e**
    54:14 In righteousness you will be **e:**
Jer 33: 2 the LORD who formed it and **e** it—
Ro 13: 1 except that which God has **e.**
2Co 13: 1 must be **e** by the testimony of two
Gal 3:17 the covenant previously **e** by God
Eph 3:17 being rooted and **e** in love,
Col 1:23 **e** and firm, not moved from the hope
2Pe 1:12 and are firmly **e** in the truth

ESTABLISHES [ESTABLISH]

Job 25: 2 he **e** order in the heights of heaven.
Isa 42: 4 or be discouraged till he **e** justice
    62: 7 give him no rest till he **e** Jerusalem

ESTATE

Ge 15: 2 one who will inherit my **e** is Eliezer
Ru 4: 6 because I might endanger my own **e.**
Est 8: 7 I have given his **e** to Esther,
Ps 136:23 who remembered us in our low **e**
Lk 15:12 'Father, give me my share of the **e.'**

ESTEEM* [ESTEEMED]

Est 10: 3 in high **e** by his many fellow Jews,
Pr 4: 8 **E** her, and she will exalt you;
Isa 66: 2 "This is the one I **e:**

ESTEEMED [ESTEEM]

Pr 22: 1 to be **e** is better than silver or gold.
Isa 53: 3 and we **e** him not.
Da 10:11 "Daniel, you who are highly **e,**

ESTHER [HADASSAH]

Jewess, originally named Hadassah, who lived in Persia; cousin of Mordecai (Est 2:7). Chosen queen of Xerxes (Est 2:8-18). Persuaded by Mordecai to foil Haman's plan to exterminate the Jews (Est 3-4). Revealed Haman's plans to Xerxes, resulting in Haman's death (Est 7), the Jews' preservation (Est 8-9), Mordecai's exaltation (Est 8:15; 9:4; 10). Decreed celebration of Purim (Est 9:18-32).

ETERNAL* [ETERNALLY, ETERNITY]

Ge 21:33 the LORD, the **E** God.
Dt 33:27 The **e** God is your refuge,
1Ki 10: 9 of the LORD's **e** love for Israel,
Ps 16:11 with **e** pleasures at your right hand.
    21: 6 you have granted him **e** blessings
    111:10 To him belongs **e** praise.
    119:89 Your word, O LORD, is **e;**
    119:160 all your righteous laws are **e.**
Ecc 12: 5 Then man goes to his **e** home
Isa 26: 4 the LORD, is the Rock **e.**
    47: 7 I will continue forever—the **e** queen!
Jer 10:10 he is the living God, the **e** King.
Da 4: 3 His kingdom is an **e** kingdom;
    4:34 His dominion is an **e** dominion;
Hab 3: 6 His ways are **e.**

Mt 18: 8 or two feet and be thrown into **e** fire.
19:16 good thing must I do to get **e** life?"
19:29 times as much and will inherit **e** life.
25:41 into the **e** fire prepared for the devil
25:46 they will go away to **e** punishment,
25:46 but the righteous to **e** life."
Mk 3:29 he is guilty of an **e** sin."
10:17 "what must I do to inherit **e** life?"
10:30 and in the age to come, **e** life.
Lk 10:25 "what must I do to inherit **e** life?"
16: 9 be welcomed into **e** dwellings.
18:18 what must I do to inherit **e** life?"
18:30 in the age to come, **e** life."
Jn 3:15 believes in him may have **e** life.
3:16 shall not perish but have **e** life.
3:36 believes in the Son has **e** life,
4:14 spring of water welling up to **e** life."
4:36 now he harvests the crop for **e** life,
5:24 believes him who sent me has **e** life
5:39 that by them you possess **e** life.
6:27 but for food that endures to **e** life,
6:40 and believes in him shall have **e** life,
6:54 and drinks my blood has **e** life,
6:68 You have the words of **e** life.
10:28 I give them **e** life,
12:25 in this world will keep it for **e** life.
12:50 that his command leads to **e** life.
17: 2 that he might give **e** life
17: 3 Now this is **e** life:
Ac 13:46 consider yourselves worthy of **e** life,
13:48 were appointed for **e** life believed.
Ro 1:20 invisible qualities—his **e** power
2: 7 he will give **e** life.
5:21 through righteousness to bring **e** life
6:22 and the result is **e** life.
6:23 but the gift of God is **e** life
16:26 by the command of the **e** God,
2Co 4:17 are achieving for us an **e** glory
4:18 but what is unseen is **e**.
5: 1 an **e** house in heaven,
Gal 6: 8 from the Spirit will reap **e** life.
Eph 3:11 his **e** purpose which he accomplished
2Th 2:16 his grace gave us **e** encouragement
1Ti 1:16 believe on him and receive **e** life.
1:17 Now to the King **e**, immortal,
6:12 the **e** life to which you were called
2Ti 2:10 that is in Christ Jesus, with **e** glory.
Tit 1: 2 resting on the hope of **e** life.
3: 7 having the hope of **e** life.
Heb 5: 9 he became the source of **e** salvation
6: 2 of the dead, and **e** judgment.
9:12 having obtained **e** redemption.
9:14 through the **e** Spirit offered himself
9:15 receive the promised **e** inheritance—
13:20 the blood of the **e** covenant
1Pe 5:10 who called you to his **e** glory
2Pe 1:11 a rich welcome into the **e** kingdom
1Jn 1: 2 and we proclaim to you the **e** life,
2:25 what he promised us—even **e** life,
3:15 that no murderer has **e** life in him.
5:11 testimony: God has given us **e** life,
5:13 you may know that you have **e** life.
5:20 He is the true God and **e** life.
Jude 1: 7 who suffer the punishment of **e** fire.

1:21 to bring you to **e** life.
Rev 14: 6 and he had the **e** gospel to proclaim

ETERNAL LIFE Mt 19:16, 29; 25:46; Mk
10:17, 30; Lk 10:25; 18:18, 30; Jn 3:15, 16, 36;
4:14, 36; 5:24, 39; 6:27, 40, 54, 68; 10:28; 12:25,
50; 17:2, 3; Ac 13:46, 48; Ro 2:7; 5:21; 6:22, 23;
Gal 6:8; 1Ti 1:16; 6:12; Tit 1:2; 3:7; 1Jn 1:2;
2:25; 3:15; 5:11, 13, 20; Jude 1:21

ETERNALLY* [ETERNAL]
Gal 1: 8 let him be **e** condemned!
1: 9 let him be **e** condemned!

ETERNITY* [ETERNAL]
Ps 93: 2 you are from all **e**.
Pr 8:23 I was appointed from **e**,
Ecc 3:11 also set **e** in the hearts of men;

ETHAN
1Ki 4:31 including **E** the Ezrahite—
1Ch 15:19 The musicians Heman, Asaph and **E**
Ps 89: T A maskil of **E** the Ezrahite.

ETHIOPIAN*
Jer 13:23 Can the **E** change his skin or
Ac 8:27 and on his way he met an **E** eunuch,

EUNICE*
2Ti 1: 5 Lois and in your mother **E**

EUNUCH [EUNUCHS]
Est 2:14 the king's **e** who was in charge of
Isa 56: 3 And let not any **e** complain,
Ac 8:27 on his way he met an Ethiopian **e**,

EUNUCHS [EUNUCH]
2Ki 20:18 and they will become **e** in the palace
Isa 56: 4 "To the **e** who keep my Sabbaths,
Mt 19:12 **e** because they were born that way;

EUODIA*
Php 4: 2 with **E** and I plead with Syntyche

EUPHRATES
Ge 2:14 And the fourth river is the **E**.
15:18 of Egypt to the great river, the **E**—
Dt 11:24 from the **E** River to the western sea.
2Ki 24: 7 the Wadi of Egypt to the **E** River.
Rev 9:14 who are bound at the great river **E**."
16:12 on the great river **E**,

EUTYCHUS*
Ac 20: 9 was a young man named **E**,

EVANGELIST* [EVANGELISTS]
Ac 21: 8 stayed at the house of Philip the **e**,
2Ti 4: 5 endure hardship, do the work of an **e**,

EVANGELISTS* [EVANGELIST]
Eph 4:11 some to be prophets, some to be **e**,

EVE*
Ge 3:20 Adam named his wife **E**,
4: 1 Adam lay with his wife **E**,
2Co 11: 3 that just as **E** was deceived by

1Ti   2:13 For Adam was formed first, then **E**.

EVEN-TEMPERED* [TEMPER]
Pr   17:27 and a man of understanding is **e**.

EVENING [EVENINGS]
Ge   1: 5 And there was **e**,
      8:11 the dove returned to him in the **e**,
     24:11 toward **e**, the time the women go out
Ps 102:11 My days are like the **e** shadow;
Ecc 11: 6 and at **e** let not your hands be idle,
Zec 14: 7 When **e** comes, there will be light.

EVENINGS* [EVENING]
Da   8:14 "It will take 2,300 **e** and mornings;
      8:26 "The vision of the **e** and mornings

EVENTS
2Ch 10:15 for this turn of **e** was from God,
Est   9:20 Mordecai recorded these **e**,
Lk   21:11 and fearful **e** and great signs
Ac   5:11 and all who heard about these **e**.

EVER [EVERLASTING, FOREVER, FOREVERMORE]
Ex   9:18 the worst hailstorm that has **e** fallen
     11: 6 worse than there has **e** been or **e** will be again.
     15:18 LORD will reign for **e** and **e**."
Dt   4:32 has anything like it **e** been heard of?
      8:19 If you **e** forget the LORD your God
1Ki   3:12 nor will there **e** be.
2Ch 32:13 Were the gods of those nations **e** able
Job   4: 7 Where were the upright **e** destroyed?
Ps   5:11 let them **e** sing for joy.
      9:18 nor the hope of the afflicted **e** perish.
     10:16 The LORD is King for **e** and **e**;
     25: 3 No one whose hope is in you will **e**
     25:15 My eyes are **e** on the LORD,
     26: 3 for your love is **e** before me,
     38:17 and my pain is **e** with me.
     45: 6 O God, will last for **e**and **e**;
     45:17 nations will praise you for **e** and **e**.
     48:14 this God is our God for **e** and **e**;
     49: 8 no payment is **e** enough—
     52: 8 in God's unfailing love for **e** and **e**.
     61: 8 Then will I **e** sing praise
     71: 6 I will **e** praise you.
     83:17 May they **e** be ashamed
     84: 4 they are **e** praising you.
     89:33 nor will I **e** betray my faithfulness.
    111: 8 They are steadfast for **e** and **e**,
    119:98 for they are **e** with me.
    132:12 sit on your throne for **e** and **e**."
    145: 1 I will praise your name for **e** and **e**.
    145: 2 and extol your name for **e** and **e**.
    145:21 praise his holy name for **e** and **e**.
    148: 6 He set them in place for **e** and **e**;
Pr   4:18 shining **e** brighter till the full light
      5:19 may you **e** be captivated by her love.
Ecc   1: 6 **e** returning on its course.
Isa   6: 9 **e** hearing, but never understanding;
     66: 8 Who has **e** seen such things?
Jer   2:11 Has a nation **e** changed its gods?

      7: 7 I gave your forefathers for **e** and **e**.
     25: 5 and your fathers for **e** and **e**.
     31:36 descendants of Israel **e** cease to be a
Da   2:20 "Praise be to the name of God for **e** and **e**;
      7:18 possess it forever—yes, for **e** and **e**.'
     12: 3 like the stars for **e** and **e**.
Joel 2: 2 of old nor **e** will be in ages to come.
Mic   4: 5 the LORD our God for **e** and **e**.
Mt   9:33 like this has **e** been seen in Israel."
     13:14 " 'You will be hearing
Mk   11: 2 which no one has **e** ridden.
Jn   1:18 No one has **e** seen God,
      3:13 has **e** gone into heaven except
      7:46 "No one **e** spoke the way
Ac   28:26 **e** hearing but never understanding;
Gal   1: 5 to whom be glory for **e** and **e**.
Eph   3:21 all generations, for **e** and **e**!
Php   4:20 and Father be glory for **e** and **e**.
1Ti   1:17 be honor and glory for **e** and **e**.
2Ti   4:18 To him be glory for **e** and **e**.
Heb   1: 8 O God, will last for **e** and **e**,
     13:21 to whom be glory for **e** and **e**.
1Pe   4:11 the glory and the power for **e** and **e**.
      5:11 To him be the power for **e** and **e**.
1Jn   4:12 No one has **e** seen God;
Rev   1: 6 be glory and power for **e** and **e**!
      1:18 and behold I am alive for **e** and **e**!
      4: 9 and who lives for **e** and **e**,
      7:12 strength be to our God for **e** and **e**.
     10: 6 swore by him who lives for **e** and **e**,
     11:15 and he will reign for **e** and **e**."
     14:11 of their torment rises for **e** and **e**.
     20:10 tormented day and night for **e** and **e**.
     21:27 Nothing impure will **e** enter it,
     22: 5 And they will reign for **e** and **e**.

FOR EVER AND EVER Ex 15:18; Ps 9:5; 10:16; 21:4; 45:6, 17; 48:14; 52:8; 111:8; 119:44; 132:12, 14; 145:1, 2, 21; 148:6; Jer 7:7; 25:5; Da 2:20; 7:18; 12:3; Mic 4:5; Gal 1:5; Eph 3:21; Php 4:20; 1Ti 1:17; 2Ti 4:18; Heb 1:8; 13:21; 1Pe 4:11; 5:11; Rev 1:6, 18; 4:9, 10; 5:13; 7:12; 10:6; 11:15; 14:11; 15:7; 19:3; 20:10; 22:5

EVER-INCREASING* [INCREASE]
Ro   6:19 to impurity and to **e** wickedness,
2Co   3:18 into his likeness with **e** glory,

EVER-PRESENT* [PRESENT]
Ps   46: 1 an **e** help in trouble.

EVERLASTING* [EVER]
Ge   9:16 the **e** covenant between God
     17: 7 an **e** covenant between me and you
     17: 8 I will give as an **e** possession to you
     17:13 in your flesh is to be an **e** covenant.
     17:19 as an **e** covenant for his descendants
     48: 4 land as an **e** possession to your
Nu   18:19 an **e** covenant of salt before the LORD
Dt   33:15 and the fruitfulness of the **e** hills;
     33:27 and underneath are the **e** arms.
2Sa 23: 5 not made with me an **e** covenant,
1Ch 16:17 to Israel as an **e** covenant:
     16:36 the God of Israel, from **e** to **e**.

	29:10	God of our father Israel, from **e** to **e**.
Ezr	9:12	to your children as an **e** inheritance.'
Ne	9: 5	who is from **e** to **e**."
Ps	41:13	the God of Israel, from **e** to **e**.
	52: 5	God will bring you down to **e** ruin:
	74: 3	Turn your steps toward these **e** ruins,
	78:66	he put them to **e** shame.
	90: 2	from **e** to **e** you are God.
	103:17	But from **e** to **e** the LORD's love is
	105:10	to Israel as an **e** covenant:
	106:48	from **e** to **e**.
	119:142	Your righteousness is **e**
	139:24	and lead me in the way **e**.
	145:13	Your kingdom is an **e** kingdom,
Isa	9: 6	**E** Father, Prince of Peace.
	24: 5	and broken the **e** covenant.
	30: 8	days to come it may be an **e** witness.
	33:14	of us can dwell with **e** burning?"
	35:10	**e** joy will crown their heads.
	40:28	The LORD is the **e** God,
	45:17	by the LORD with an **e** salvation;
	45:17	or disgraced, to ages **e**.
	51:11	**e** joy will crown their heads.
	54: 8	**e** kindness I will have compassion
	55: 3	I will make an **e** covenant with you,
	55:13	for an **e** sign,
	56: 5	an **e** name that will not be cut off.
	60:15	I will make you the **e** pride and
	60:19	for the LORD will be your **e** light,
	60:20	the LORD will be your **e** light,
	61: 7	and **e** joy will be theirs.
	61: 8	and make an **e** covenant with them.
	63:12	to gain for himself **e** renown,
Jer	5:22	an **e** barrier it cannot cross.
	23:40	bring upon you **e** disgrace—**e** shame
	25: 9	and an **e** ruin.
	31: 3	"I have loved you with an **e** love;
	32:40	I will make an **e** covenant with them:
	50: 5	to the LORD in an **e** covenant
Eze	16:60	and I will establish an **e** covenant
	37:26	it will be an **e** covenant.
Da	7:14	His dominion is an **e** dominion
	7:27	His kingdom will be an **e** kingdom,
	9:24	to bring in **e** righteousness,
	12: 2	some to **e** life, others to shame and **e** contempt.
Mic	6: 2	you **e** foundations of the earth.
Hab	1:12	O LORD, are you not from **e**?
Jn	6:47	he who believes has **e** life.
2Th	1: 9	will be punished with **e** destruction
Jude	1: 6	bound with **e** chains for judgment on

EVERLASTING COVENANT Ge 9:16; 17:7, 13, 19; Nu 18:19; 2Sa 23:5; 1Ch 16:17; Ps 105:10; Isa 24:5; 55:3; 61:8; Jer 32:40; 50:5; Eze 16:60; 37:26

EVERY [EVERYBODY, EVERYONE, EVERYONE'S, EVERYTHING, EVERYWHERE]

Ge	1:29	"I give you **e** seed-bearing plant on
	6: 5	**e** inclination of the thoughts of his
	7: 4	from the face of the earth **e** living
	7:23	**E** living thing on the face of

	24: 1	LORD had blessed him in **e** way.
Ex	11: 5	**E** firstborn son in Egypt will die,
	13: 2	"Consecrate to me **e** firstborn male.
Lev	17:14	the life of **e** creature is its blood;
Dt	7:15	will keep you free from **e** disease.
	8: 1	to follow **e** command I am giving
	8: 3	on bread alone but on **e** word
Jos	21:45	**e** one was fulfilled.
	23:14	**E** promise has been fulfilled;
1Ch	28: 9	for the LORD searches **e** heart and understands **e** motive
Ps	7:11	God who expresses his wrath **e** day.
	50:10	for **e** animal of the forest is mine,
	136:25	and who gives food to **e** creature.
	145: 2	**E** day I will praise you
	145:21	Let **e** creature praise his holy name
Pr	16:33	but its **e** decision is from the LORD.
	30: 5	"**E** word of God is flawless;
Ecc	3: 1	a season for **e** activity under heaven:
	7: 2	for death is the destiny of **e** man;
	12:14	God will bring **e** deed into judgment,
Isa	40: 4	**E** valley shall be raised up,
	45:23	Before me **e** knee will bow; by me **e** tongue will swear.
Jer	2:20	on **e** high hill and under **e** spreading tree you lay down as a prostitute.
La	3:23	They are new **e** morning;
Eze	21: 7	**E** heart will melt and **e** hand go limp;
Mt	4: 4	on bread alone, but on **e** word
	7:17	Likewise **e** good tree bears good fruit
	12:25	"**E** kingdom divided against itself
Jn	13:11	he said not **e** one was clean.
	15: 2	**e** branch that does bear fruit
Ro	14:11	'**e** knee will bow before me; **e** tongue will confess
Php	2:10	name of Jesus **e** knee should bow,
1Th	5:22	Avoid **e** kind of evil.
1Jn	4: 1	Dear friends, do not believe **e** spirit,
Rev	1: 7	and **e** eye will see him,
	7:17	And God will wipe away **e** tear
	21: 4	He will wipe **e** tear from their eyes.
	22: 2	yielding its fruit **e** month.

EVERYBODY [BODY, EVERY]

1Co 10:33 as I try to please **e** in every way.

EVERYONE [EVERY, ONE]

Dt	12: 8	**e** as he sees fit,
Jdg	17: 6	**e** did as he saw fit.
	21:25	**e** did as he saw fit.
Ps	32: 6	Therefore let **e** who is godly pray
	53: 3	**E** has turned away,
Jer	31:30	Instead, **e** will die for his own sin;
Joel	2:32	And **e** who calls on the name of
Jnh	3: 8	Let **e** call urgently on God.
Lk	11: 4	also forgive **e** who sins against us.
	11:10	For **e** who asks receives;
Jn	3:15	that **e** who believes in him
Ac	2:21	And **e** who calls on the name of
Ro	10:13	"**E** who calls on the name of
1Pe	2:17	Show proper respect to **e**:
2Pe	3: 9	but **e** to come to repentance.
1Jn	3: 4	**E** who sins breaks the law;
	4: 7	**E** who loves has been born of God

5: 4 **e** born of God overcomes the world.
Rev 22:12 to **e** according to what he has done.

EVERYONE'S [EVERY, ONE]

Ac 1:24 "Lord, you know **e** heart.

EVERYTHING [EVERY, THING]

Ge 6:17 **E** on earth will perish.
    39: 6 So he left in Joseph's care **e** he had;
Ex 7: 2 You are to say **e** I command you,
    19: 8 "We will do **e** the LORD has said."
    23:13 "Be careful to do **e** I have said
    24: 3 "**E** the LORD has said we will do."
Dt 15:18 God will bless you in **e** you do.
    18:18 he will tell them **e** I command him.
    28:29 be unsuccessful in **e** you do;
    29: 9 so that you may prosper in **e** you do.
1Ch 29:14 **E** comes from you,
Ne 9: 6 You give life to **e**,
Job 1:11 and strike **e** he has,
Ps 24: 1 earth is the LORD's, and **e** in it,
    150: 6 Let **e** that has breath praise
Ecc 1: 2 **E** is meaningless."
    3: 1 There is a time for **e**,
    3:11 He has made **e** beautiful in its time.
    3:14 that **e** God does will endure forever;
    10:19 but money is the answer for **e**.
Da 4:37 because **e** he does is right
Mt 5:18 the Law until **e** is accomplished.
    28:20 to obey **e** I have commanded you.
Mk 9:23 **E** is possible for him who believes.
Lk 18:22 Sell **e** you have and give to the poor,
Jn 14:26 and will remind you of **e** I have said
Ac 2:44 and had **e** in common.
    3:22 you must listen to **e** he tells you.
    4:32 but they shared **e** they had.
Ro 14: 2 One man's faith allows him to eat **e**,
1Co 6:12 "**E** is permissible for me"—but not
        e is beneficial.
    10:23 "**E** is permissible"—but not **e** is
    15:27 For he "has put **e** under his feet."
    16:14 Do **e** in love.
Php 4:13 I can do **e** through him who gives me
1Th 5:21 Test **e**. Hold on to the good.
1Ti 4: 4 For **e** God created is good;
2Pe 1: 3 divine power has given us **e** we need
Rev 21: 5 "I am making **e** new!"

EVERYWHERE [EVERY, WHERE]

1Ch 18: 6 LORD gave David victory **e** he went.
Pr 15: 3 The eyes of the LORD are **e**,

EVIDENCE

Mk 14:55 looking for **e** against Jesus
Jn 14:11 believe on the **e** of the miracles
Ac 11:23 and saw the **e** of the grace of God,
2Th 1: 5 this is **e** that God's judgment is right,
Jas 2:20 you want **e** that faith without deeds

EVIDENT [EVIDENCE, EVIDENTLY]

Php 4: 5 Let your gentleness be **e** to all.

EVIL [EVILDOER, EVILDOERS, EVILS]

Ge 2: 9 tree of the knowledge of good and **e**.

3: 5 knowing good and **e**."
6: 5 of his heart was only **e** all the time.
44: 4 'Why have you repaid good with **e**?
Ex 32:22 how prone these people are to **e**.
Nu 32:13 generation of those who had done **e**
Dt 1:35 "Not a man of this **e** generation
    13: 5 purge the **e** from among you.
    28:20 because of the **e** you have done
Jos 23:15 on you all the **e** he has threatened,
Jdg 2:11 Then the Israelites did **e** in the eyes
    3: 7 The Israelites did **e** in the eyes of
    3:12 Once again the Israelites did **e** in
    4: 1 the Israelites once again did **e** in
    6: 1 Again the Israelites did **e** in the eyes
    10: 6 Again the Israelites did **e** in the eyes
    13: 1 Again the Israelites did **e** in the eyes
1Sa 12:20 "You have done all this **e**;
    16:14 and an **e** spirit from the LORD
    18:10 an **e** spirit from God came forcefully
    19: 9 an **e** spirit from the LORD came
1Ki 11: 6 So Solomon did **e** in the eyes of
    16:25 But Omri did **e** in the eyes of
2Ki 15:24 Pekahiah did **e** in the eyes of
Job 1: 1 he feared God and shunned **e**.
    1: 8 a man who fears God and shuns **e**."
    2: 3 a man who fears God and shuns **e**.
    15:35 and give birth to **e**;
    28:28 and to shun **e** is understanding.' "
    34:10 Far be it from God to do **e**,
    36:21 Beware of turning to **e**,
Ps 5: 4 not a God who takes pleasure in **e**;
    23: 4 I will fear no **e**, for you are with me;
    28: 4 for their deeds and for their **e** work;
    34:13 keep your tongue from **e**
    34:14 Turn from **e** and do good;
    34:16 against those who do **e**,
    37: 1 Do not fret because of **e** men or
    37: 8 do not fret—it leads only to **e**.
    37:27 Turn from **e** and do good;
    49: 5 when **e** days come,
    51: 4 have I sinned and done what is **e**
    97:10 who love the LORD hate **e**,
    101: 4 I will have nothing to do with **e**.
    141: 4 not my heart be drawn to what is **e**,
Pr 3: 7 fear the LORD and shun **e**.
    4:27 keep your foot from **e**.
    8:13 To fear the LORD is to hate **e**;
    8:13 **e** behavior and perverse speech.
    10:23 A fool finds pleasure in **e** conduct,
    11:19 he who pursues **e** goes to his death.
    11:27 **e** comes to him who searches for it.
    14:16 fears the LORD and shuns **e**,
    14:22 Do not those who plot **e** go astray?
    16: 6 the fear of the LORD a man avoids **e**.
    17:13 If a man pays back **e** for good, **e** will
        never leave his house.
    20:30 Blows and wounds cleanse away **e**,
    24:19 Do not fret because of **e** men
    24:20 for the **e** man has no future hope,
    26:23 with an **e** heart.
    28: 5 **E** men do not understand justice,
    29: 6 An **e** man is snared by his own sin,
Ecc 4: 3 who has not seen the **e** that is done
    12:14 whether it is good or **e**.

Isa	5:20	Woe to those who call **e** good and good **e**,
	13:11	I will punish the world for its **e**,
	55: 7	and the **e** man his thoughts.
Jer	4:14	wash the **e** from your heart and be
	18: 8	if that nation I warned repents of its **e**
	18:10	and if it does **e** in my sight and does
Eze	3:18	to dissuade him from his **e** ways
	33:11	Turn from your **e** ways!
	33:13	he will die for the **e** he has done.
	33:15	and does no **e**, he will surely live;
Hos	10:13	you have reaped **e**,
Am	5:13	for the times are **e**.
	5:14	Seek good, not **e**, that you may live.
Jnh	3: 8	their **e** ways and their violence.
Mic	3: 2	you who hate good and love **e**;
Hab	1:13	Your eyes are too pure to look on **e**;
Zec	8:17	do not plot **e** against your neighbor,
Mal	2:17	"All who do **e** are good in the eyes of
Mt	5:45	He causes his sun to rise on the **e** and
	6:13	but deliver us from the **e** one.'
	7:11	If you, then, though you are **e**,
	12:35	and the **e** man brings **e** things out of the **e** stored up in him.
	12:43	"When an **e** spirit comes out of
	13:38	The weeds are the sons of the **e** one,
	15:19	For out of the heart come **e** thoughts,
Mk	7:21	out of men's hearts, come **e** thoughts,
Lk	6: 9	to do good or to do **e**,
	11:13	If you then, though you are **e**,
Jn	3:19	of light because their deeds were **e**.
	3:20	Everyone who does **e** hates the light,
	17:15	that you protect them from the **e** one.
Ro	1:30	they invent ways of doing **e**;
	2: 8	who reject the truth and follow **e**,
	2: 9	for every human being who does **e**:
	3: 8	claim that we say—"Let us do **e**
	6:12	so that you obey its **e** desires.
	7:19	the **e** I do not want to do—
	7:21	**e** is right there with me.
	12: 9	Hate what is **e**;
	12:17	Do not repay anyone **e** for **e**.
	12:21	Do not be overcome by **e**, but overcome **e** with good.
	14:16	good to be spoken of as **e**.
	16:19	and innocent about what is **e**.
1Co	10: 6	from setting our hearts on **e** things
	13: 6	not delight in **e** but rejoices with
	14:20	In regard to **e** be infants,
Gal	1: 4	to rescue us from the present **e** age,
Eph	5:16	because the days are **e**.
	6:12	and against the spiritual forces of **e**
	6:16	the flaming arrows of the **e** one.
Col	1:21	because of your **e** behavior.
	3: 5	impurity, lust, **e** desires and greed,
1Th	5:22	Avoid every kind of **e**.
2Th	3: 3	and protect you from the **e** one.
1Ti	6:10	love of money is a root of all kinds of **e**.
2Ti	2:22	Flee the **e** desires of youth,
	3: 6	by all kinds of **e** desires,
	3:13	while **e** men and impostors will go
Heb	5:14	to distinguish good from **e**.
Jas	1:13	For God cannot be tempted by **e**,

	1:21	and the **e** that is so prevalent
	2: 4	and become judges with **e** thoughts?
	3: 6	a world of **e** among the parts of the
	3: 8	It is a restless **e**,
	4:16	All such boasting is **e**.
1Pe	1:14	do not conform to the **e** desires you
	2:16	your freedom as a cover-up for **e**;
	3: 9	Do not repay **e** with **e** or insult
	3:10	must keep his tongue from **e**
	3:12	the Lord is against those who do **e**."
	3:17	for doing good than for doing **e**.
2Pe	1: 4	in the world caused by **e** desires.
	3: 3	and following their own **e** desires.
1Jn	2:13	you have overcome the **e** one.
	2:14	and you have overcome the **e** one.
	3:12	Cain, who belonged to the **e** one
	3:12	Because his own actions were **e**
	5:18	and the **e** one cannot harm him.
	5:19	under the control of the **e** one.
3Jn	1:11	do not imitate what is **e**
	1:11	Anyone who does what is **e** has
Jude	1:16	they follow their own **e** desires;
Rev	16:13	Then I saw three **e** spirits that looked
	18: 2	and a haunt for every **e** spirit,

EVIL SPIRIT Jdg 9:23; 1Sa 16:14, 15, 16, 23; 18:10; 19:9; Mt 12:43; Mk 1:23, 26; 3:30; 5:2, 8; 7:25; 9:25; Lk 4:33; 8:29; 9:42; 11:24; Ac 19:15, 16; Rev 18:2

EVIL SPIRITS Mt 10:1; Mk 1:27; 3:11; 5:13; 6:7; Lk 4:36; 6:18; 7:21; 8:2; Ac 5:16; 8:7; 19:12, 13; Rev 16:13

EVIL IN THE EYES OF THE †LORD
See EYES

EVILDOER* [EVIL]

2Sa	3:39	repay the **e** according to his evil
Ps	101: 8	I will cut off every **e**
Mal	4: 1	and every **e** will be stubble,

EVILDOERS* [EVIL]

1Sa	24:13	'From **e** come evil deeds,'
Job	8:20	or strengthen the hands of **e**.
	34: 8	He keeps company with **e**;
	34:22	no deep shadow, where **e** can hide.
Ps	14: 4	Will **e** never learn—
	14: 6	You **e** frustrate the plans of the poor,
	26: 5	I abhor the assembly of **e**
	36:12	See how the **e** lie fallen—
	53: 4	Will the **e** never learn—
	59: 2	Deliver me from **e** and save me
	64: 2	from that noisy crowd of **e**.
	92: 7	up like grass and all **e** flourish,
	92: 9	all **e** will be scattered.
	94: 4	the **e** are full of boasting.
	94:16	take a stand for me against **e**?
	119:115	Away from me, you **e**,
	125: 5	the LORD will banish with the **e**.
	141: 4	with men who are **e**;
	141: 5	ever against the deeds of **e**;
	141: 9	from the traps set by **e**.
Pr	21:15	joy to the righteous but terror to **e**.
Isa	1: 4	a brood of **e**,
	31: 2	against those who help **e**.

Jer 23:14 They strengthen the hands of **e**,
Hos 10: 9 not war overtake the **e** in Gibeah?
Mal   3:15 Certainly the **e** prosper,
Mt   7:23 Away from me, you **e**!'
Lk   13:27 Away from me, all you **e**!'
     18:11 not like other men—robbers, **e**,

EVILS* [EVIL]

Mk   7:23 All these **e** come from inside

EWE

2Sa 12: 3 had nothing except one little **e** lamb

EXACT*

Ge   43:21 found his silver—the **e** weight—
Est   4: 7 the **e** amount of money Haman had
Mt   2: 7 and found out from them the **e** time
Jn   4:53 the **e** time at which Jesus had said
Ac   17:26 the **e** places where they should live.
Heb   1: 3 and the **e** representation of his being,

EXALT* [EXALTED, EXALTS]

Ex   15: 2 my father's God, and I will **e** him.
Jos   3: 7 to **e** you in the eyes of all Israel,
1Sa   2:10 and **e** the horn of his anointed."
1Ch 25: 5 the promises of God to **e** him.
     29:12 and power to **e** and give strength
Job 19: 5 If indeed you would **e** yourselves
Ps   30: 1 I will **e** you, O LORD,
     34: 3 let us **e** his name together.
     35:26 may all who **e** themselves
     37:34 He will **e** you to inherit the land;
     38:16 not let them gloat or **e** themselves
     75: 6 or from the desert can **e** a man.
     89:17 and by your favor you **e** our horn.
     99: 5 **E** the LORD our God and worship
     99: 9 **E** the LORD our God and worship
    107:32 Let them **e** him in the assembly of
    118:28 and I will **e** you.
    145: 1 I will **e** you, my God the King;
Pr   4: 8 Esteem her, and she will **e** you;
     25: 6 not **e** yourself in the king's presence,
Isa 24:15 **e** the name of the LORD,
     25: 1 LORD, you are my God; I will **e** you
Eze 29:15 and will never again **e** itself above
Da   4:37 and **e** and glorify the King of heaven,
     11:36 He will **e** and magnify himself
     11:37 but will **e** himself above them all.
Hos 11: 7 he will by no means **e** them.
2Th   2: 4 and will **e** himself over everything

EXALTED* [EXALT]

Ex   15: 1 for he is highly **e**.
     15:21 for he is highly **e**.
Nu   24: 7 their kingdom will be **e**.
Jos   4:14 That day the LORD **e** Joshua in
2Sa   5:12 had **e** his kingdom for the sake of his
     22:47 **E** be God, the Rock, my Savior!
     22:49 You **e** me above my foes;
     23: 1 of the man **e** by the Most High,
1Ch 14: 2 that his kingdom had been highly **e**
     17:17 as though I were the most **e** of men,
     29:11 O LORD, is the kingdom; you are **e**
     29:25 The LORD highly **e** Solomon in

Ne   9: 5 be **e** above all blessing and praise.
Job 24:24 For a little while they are **e**,
     36:22 "God is **e** in his power.
     37:23 beyond our reach and **e** in power;
Ps   18:46 **E** be God my Savior!
     18:48 You **e** me above my foes;
     21:13 Be **e**, O LORD, in your strength;
     27: 6 Then my head will be **e** above
     35:27 "The LORD be **e**,
     40:16 "The LORD be **e**!"
     46:10 I will be **e** among the nations,
     46:10 I will be **e** in the earth."
     47: 9 belong to God; he is greatly **e**.
     57: 5 Be **e**, O God, above the heavens;
     57:11 Be **e**, O God, above the heavens;
     70: 4 "Let God be **e**!"
     89:13 hand is strong, your right hand **e**.
     89:19 I have **e** a young man from among
     89:24 through my name his horn will be **e**.
     89:27 the most **e** of the kings of the earth.
     89:42 You have **e** the right hand of his foes
     92: 8 But you, O LORD, are **e** forever.
     92:10 You have **e** my horn like that of
     97: 9 you are **e** far above all gods.
     99: 2 Great is the LORD in Zion; he is **e**
    108: 5 Be **e**, O God, above the heavens,
    113: 4 The LORD is **e** over all the nations,
    138: 2 for you have **e** above all things
    148:13 for his name alone is **e**;
Pr   11:11 the blessing of the upright a city is **e**,
     30:32 played the fool and **e** yourself,
Isa   2:11 the LORD alone will be **e** in
      2:12 that is **e** (and they will be humbled),
      2:17 the LORD alone will be **e** in
      5:16 But the LORD Almighty will be **e**
      6: 1 Lord seated on a throne, high and **e**,
     12: 4 and proclaim that his name is **e**.
     24: 4 the **e** of the earth languish.
     33: 5 LORD is **e**, for he dwells on high;
     33:10 will I be **e**; now will I be lifted up.
     52:13 be raised and lifted up and highly **e**.
Jer 17:12 **e** from the beginning,
La   2:17 he has **e** the horn of your foes.
Eze 21:26 The lowly will be **e** and the **e** will be
                brought low.
Hos 13: 1 he was **e** in Israel.
Mic   6: 6 and bow down before the **e** God?
Mt   23:12 whoever humbles himself will be **e**.
Lk   14:11 he who humbles himself will be **e**."
     18:14 he who humbles himself will be **e**."
Ac   2:33 **E** to the right hand of God,
      5:31 God **e** him to his own right hand
Php   1:20 that now as always Christ will be **e**
      2: 9 God **e** him to the highest place
Heb   7:26 **e** above the heavens.

EXALTS* [EXALT]

1Sa   2: 7 he humbles and he **e**.
Job 36: 7 with kings and **e** them forever.
Ps   75: 7 He brings one down, he **e** another.
Pr   14:34 Righteousness **e** a nation,
Mt   23:12 whoever **e** himself will be humbled,
Lk   14:11 For everyone who **e** himself will
     18:14 For everyone who **e** himself will

EXAMINE [EXAMINED, EXAMINES]

Job 34:23 God has no need to **e** men further,
Ps 11: 4 the sons of men; his eyes **e** them.
17: 3 you probe my heart and **e** me
26: 2 and try me, **e** my heart and my mind;
Jer 17:10 "I the LORD search the heart and **e**
20:12 you who **e** the righteous and probe
La 3:40 Let us **e** our ways and test them,
1Co 11:28 to **e** himself before he eats of
2Co 13: 5 **E** yourselves to see whether you are

EXAMINED* [EXAMINED]

Job 5:27 "We have **e** this, and it is true.
13: 9 Would it turn out well if he **e** you?
Lk 23:14 I have **e** him in your presence
Ac 17:11 and **e** the Scriptures every day to see
28:18 They **e** me and wanted to release me,

EXAMINES [EXAMINE]

Lev 13: 3 When the priest **e** him,
Ps 11: 5 The LORD **e** the righteous,
Pr 5:21 and he **e** all his paths.

EXAMPLE* [EXAMPLES]

2Ki 14: 3 In everything he followed the **e**
Ecc 9:13 under the sun this **e** of wisdom
Eze 14: 8 against that man and make him an **e**
Jn 13:15 an **e** that you should do as I
Ro 7: 2 For **e,** by law a married woman
1Co 11: 1 my **e,** as I follow the **e** of Christ.
Gal 3:15 let me take an **e** from everyday life.
Php 3:17 Join with others in following my **e,**
2Th 3: 7 how you ought to follow our **e.**
1Ti 1:16 as an **e** for those who would believe
4:12 set an **e** for the believers in speech,
Tit 2: 7 an **e** by doing what is good.
Heb 4:11 by following their **e** of disobedience.
Jas 3: 4 Or take ships as an **e.**
5:10 **e** of patience in the face of suffering,
1Pe 2:21 leaving you an **e,**
2Pe 2: 6 an **e** of what is going to happen to
Jude 1: 7 as an **e** of those who suffer

EXAMPLES* [EXAMPLE]

1Co 10: 6 Now these things occurred as **e**
10:11 These things happened to them as **e**
1Pe 5: 3 but being **e** to the flock.

EXASPERATE*

Eph 6: 4 Fathers, do not **e** your children;

EXCEEDED

1Ki 10: 7 in wisdom and wealth you have far **e**

EXCEL* [EXCELLENT]

Ge 49: 4 you will no longer **e,**
1Co 14:12 to **e** in gifts that build up the church.
2Co 8: 7 But just as you **e** in everything—
8: 7 also **e** in this grace of giving.

EXCELLENT [EXCEL]

Ps 45: 2 You are the most **e** of men
1Co 12:31 now I will show you the most **e** way.
Php 4: 8 if anything is **e** or praiseworthy—

1Ti 3:13 an **e** standing and great assurance
Tit 3: 8 These things are **e** and profitable

EXCEPT

Nu 14:30 **e** Caleb son of Jephunneh
Dt 16: 6 **e** in the place he will choose as
2Sa 22:32 And who is the Rock **e** our God?
1Ki 15: 5 **e** in the case of Uriah the Hittite.
Hos 13: 4 no Savior **e** me.
Mt 5:32 **e** for marital unfaithfulness,
11:27 No one knows the Son **e** the Father,
19: 9 **e** for marital unfaithfulness,
Mk 10:18 "No one is good—**e** God alone.
Lk 11:29 will be given it **e** the sign of Jonah.
Jn 3:13 No one has ever gone into heaven **e**
6:46 No one has seen the Father **e**
14: 6 No one comes to the Father **e**
17:12 None has been lost **e** the one doomed
1Co 10:13 No temptation has seized you **e** what

EXCESSIVE

Eze 18: 8 not lend at usury or take **e** interest.
2Co 2: 7 not be overwhelmed by **e** sorrow.

EXCHANGE [EXCHANGED, EXCHANGING]

Mt 16:26 a man give in **e** for his soul?
Mk 8:37 a man give in **e** for his soul?
2Co 6:13 As a fair **e**—I speak as to my

EXCHANGED [EXCHANGE]

Ps 106:20 They **e** their Glory for an image of
Jer 2:11 But my people have **e** their Glory
Hos 4: 7 they **e** their Glory
Ro 1:23 and **e** the glory of the immortal God
1:25 They **e** the truth of God for a lie,
1:26 Even their women **e** natural relations

EXCHANGING* [EXCHANGE]

Jn 2:14 and others sitting at tables **e** money.

EXCLAIM

Ps 35:10 My whole being will **e,**

EXCLUDE* [EXCLUDED]

Isa 56: 3 "The LORD will surely **e** me
66: 5 and **e** you because of my name,
Lk 6:22 when they **e** you and insult you
Rev 11: 2 But **e** the outer court;

EXCLUDED [EXCLUDE]

Eph 2:12 **e** from citizenship in Israel

EXCUSE* [EXCUSES]

Ps 25: 3 who are treacherous without **e.**
Lk 14:18 Please **e** me.'
14:19 Please **e** me.'
Jn 15:22 however, they have no **e** for their sin.
Ro 1:20 so that men are without **e,**
2: 1 You, therefore, have no **e,**

EXCUSES* [EXCUSE]

Lk 14:18 "But they all alike began to make **e.**

EXECUTE [EXECUTED]

Isa 66:16 LORD will e judgment upon all men,
Eze 20:35 I will e judgment upon you.
Da 2:24 "Do not e the wise men of Babylon.
Jn 18:31 "But we have no right to e anyone,"

EXECUTED [EXECUTE]

Mt 27:20 for Barabbas and to have Jesus e.

EXERTED*

Eph 1:20 which he e in Christ when he raised

EXHAUST* [EXHAUSTED]

Jer 51:58 the peoples e themselves for nothing,
Hab 2:13 the nations e themselves for nothing?

EXHAUSTED [EXHAUST]

Da 8:27 was e and lay ill for several days.
Lk 12:33 treasure in heaven that will not be e,
     22:45 he found them asleep, e from sorrow.

EXHORT* [EXHORTATION]

1Ti 5: 1 but e him as if he were your father.

EXHORTATION* [EXHORT]

Heb 13:22 I urge you to bear with my word of e,

EXILE [EXILED, EXILES]

2Ki 17:23 their homeland into e in Assyria
     25:11 into e the people who remained in
Ezr 6:21 who had returned from the e ate it,
Ne 1: 2 Jewish remnant that survived the e,
Est 2: 6 who had been carried into e
Isa 5:13 Therefore my people will go into e
Jer 13:19 All Judah will be carried into e,
     48: 7 and Chemosh will go into e,
     49: 3 for Molech will go into e,
La 1: 3 Judah has gone into e.

EXILED [EXILE]

Ne 1: 9 then even if your e people are at
Am 9:14 I will bring back my e people Israel;

EXILES [EXILE]

Ezr 6:19 the e celebrated the Passover.
Ps 147: 2 he gathers the e of Israel.
Isa 56: 8 he who gathers the e of Israel:
Jer 24: 5 I regard as good the e from Judah,
Eze 11:25 and I told the e everything

EXISTED* [EXISTS]

2Pe 3: 5 by God's word the heavens e and

EXISTS* [EXISTED]

Ecc 6:10 Whatever e has already been named,
Heb 2:10 and through whom everything e,
     11: 6 to him must believe that he e and

EXODUS*

Heb 11:22 the e of the Israelites from Egypt

EXPANSE [EXPANSES]

Ge 1: 6 Let there be an e between the waters
    1: 8 God called the e "sky."

1:14 "Let there be lights in the e
Eze 1:22 was what looked like an e,
     10: 1 a throne of sapphire above the e

EXPANSES* [EXPANSE]

Job 38:18 Have you comprehended the vast e

EXPECT [EXPECTATION, EXPECTED, EXPECTING]

Isa 64: 3 awesome things that we did not e,
Mt 11: 3 or should we e someone else?"
     24:44 at an hour when you do not e him.
Lk 12:40 at an hour when you do not e him."
Php 1:20 I eagerly e and hope that I will

EXPECTATION* [EXPECT]

Ps 5: 3 my requests before you and wait in e.
Eze 19: 5 hope unfulfilled, her e gone,
Ro 8:19 The creation waits in eager e for
Heb 10:27 a fearful e of judgment and

EXPECTED [EXPECT]

Ge 48:11 "I never e to see your face again,
Pr 11: 7 all he e from his power comes to
Hag 1: 9 "You e much, but see,

EXPECTING [EXPECT]

Lk 6:35 without e to get anything back.

EXPEL* [EXPELLED]

1Co 5:13 "E the wicked man from among

EXPELLED* [EXPEL]

1Sa 28: 3 Saul had e the mediums and spiritists
1Ki 15:12 He e the male shrine prostitutes from
Ezr 10: 8 be e from the assembly of the exiles.
Eze 28:16 and I e you, O guardian cherub,
Ac 13:50 and e them from their region.

EXPENSE* [EXPENSIVE]

Lk 10:35 for any extra e you may have.'
1Co 9: 7 serves as a soldier at his own e?

EXPENSIVE* [EXPENSE]

Mt 26: 7 an alabaster jar of very e perfume,
Mk 14: 3 an alabaster jar of very e perfume,
Lk 7:25 those who wear e clothes and indulge
Jn 12: 3 pure nard, an e perfume;
1Ti 2: 9 or gold or pearls or e clothes,

EXPERIENCE [EXPERIENCED]

Heb 11: 5 so that he did not e death;

EXPERIENCED [EXPERIENCE]

Dt 11: 2 not the ones who saw and e
Jos 24:31 and who had e everything

EXPERT* [EXPERTS]

Mt 22:35 One of them, an e in the law,
Lk 10:25 an e in the law stood up to test Jesus.
     10:37 The e in the law replied,
1Co 3:10 I laid a foundation as an e builder,

EXPERTS [EXPERT]

Lk   11:52 "Woe to you **e** in the law,

EXPLAIN [EXPLAINED, EXPLAINING, EXPLAINS, EXPLANATION]

Ge   41:24 but none could **e** it to me."
2Ch   9: 2 nothing was too hard for him to **e**
Job 15:17 "Listen to me and I will **e** to you;
Da   2: 6 But if you tell me the dream and **e** it,
Mt   13:36 "**E** to us the parable of the weeds in
     15:15 Peter said, "**E** the parable to us."
Jn   4:25 he will **e** everything to us."
Heb   5:11 it is hard to **e** because you are slow
Rev 17: 7 **e** to you the mystery of the woman

EXPLAINED [EXPLAIN]

Jdg 14:17 She in turn **e** the riddle to her people.
1Sa 10:25 Samuel **e** to the people the
Mk   4:34 his own disciples, he **e** everything.
Lk   24:27 he **e** to them what was said in all
Ac   11: 4 and **e** everything to them precisely
     18:26 **e** to him the way of God more
     28:23 till evening he **e** and declared to

EXPLAINING* [EXPLAIN]

Jdg 14:15 "Coax your husband into **e** the riddle
Isa 28: 9 To whom is he **e** his message?
Ac   17: 3 **e** and proving that the Christ had

EXPLAINS* [EXPLAIN]

Ac   8:31 he said, "unless someone **e** it to me?"

EXPLANATION* [EXPLAIN]

Ecc   8: 1 Who knows the **e** of things?
Da   7:23 "He gave me this **e:**

EXPLOIT* [EXPLOITED, EXPLOITING, EXPLOITS]

Pr   22:22 not **e** the poor because they are poor
Isa 58: 3 as you please and **e** all your workers.
2Co 12:17 Did I **e** you through any of
     12:18 Titus did not **e** you, did he?
2Pe   2: 3 In their greed these teachers will **e**

EXPLOITED* [EXPLOIT]

2Co   7: 2 we have **e** no one.

EXPLOITING* [EXPLOIT]

Jas   2: 6 Is it not the rich who are **e** you?

EXPLOITS [EXPLOIT]

1Ch 11:19 the **e** of the three mighty men.
2Co 11:20 or **e** you or takes advantage of you

EXPLORE [EXPLORED]

Nu   13: 2 "Send some men to **e** the land
Jos 14: 7 from Kadesh Barnea to **e** the land.
Ecc   1:13 and to **e** by wisdom all that is done

EXPLORED [EXPLORE]

Nu   13:21 So they went up and **e** the land

EXPOSE [EXPOSED, EXPOSES]

Job 20:27 The heavens will **e** his guilt;
Mt   1:19 not want to **e** her to public disgrace,
1Co   4: 5 will **e** the motives of men's hearts.
Eph   5:11 but rather **e** them.

EXPOSED [EXPOSE]

Ex   20:26 lest your nakedness be **e** on it.'
Pr   26:26 but his wickedness will be **e** in
Eze 23:29 shame of your prostitution will be **e.**
Hab   2:16 Drink and be **e!**
Jn   3:20 for fear that his deeds will be **e.**
2Co 11:23 and been **e** to death again and again.
Eph   5:13 **e** by the light becomes visible,
Heb 10:33 you were publicly **e** to insult
Rev 16:15 not go naked and be shamefully **e.**"

EXPOSES* [EXPOSE]

Pr   13:16 but a fool **e** his folly.

EXPOUND*

Dt   1: 5 Moses began to **e** this law, saying:
Ps   49: 4 with the harp I will **e** my riddle:

EXPRESS [EXPRESSES, EXPRESSING]

2Sa 10: 2 a delegation to **e** his sympathy
Ro   8:26 with groans that words cannot **e.**

EXPRESSES* [EXPRESS]

Ps   7:11 a God who **e** his wrath every day.

EXPRESSING* [EXPRESS]

1Co   2:13 **e** spiritual truths in spiritual words.
Gal   5: 6 that counts is faith **e** itself

EXTEND [EXTENDED, EXTENDS, EXTENT]

Ex   25:32 Six branches are to **e** from the sides
Dt   11:24 Your territory will **e** from the desert
Jos   1: 4 Your territory will **e** from the desert
Ps 110: 2 LORD will **e** your mighty scepter
Isa 66:12 "I will **e** peace to her like a river,
Zec   9:10 His rule will **e** from sea to sea and

EXTENDED [EXTEND]

Ezr   7:28 and who has **e** his good favor to me
Est   8: 4 the king **e** the gold scepter to Esther

EXTENDS [EXTEND]

Pr   31:20 and **e** her hands to the needy.
Lk   1:50 His mercy **e** to those who fear him,

EXTENT [EXTEND]

Jn   13: 1 he now showed them the full **e**

EXTERMINATE* [EXTERMINATING]

1Ki   9:21 whom the Israelites could not **e—**
Eze 25: 7 and **e** you from the countries.

EXTERMINATING* [EXTERMINATE]

Jos 11:20 **e** them without mercy,

EXTERNAL*

Gal 2: 6 not judge by **e** appearance—
Heb 9:10 **e** regulations applying until the time

EXTINGUISH* [EXTINGUISHED]

Eph 6:16 **e** all the flaming arrows of the evil

EXTINGUISHED* [EXTINGUISH]

2Sa 21:17 that the lamp of Israel will not be **e.**"
Isa 43:17 **e**, snuffed out like a wick:

EXTOL*

Job 36:24 Remember to **e** his work,
Ps   34: 1 I will **e** the LORD at all times;
     68: 4 **e** him who rides on the clouds—
     95: 2 and **e** him with music and song.
    109:30 I will greatly **e** the LORD;
    111: 1 I will **e** the LORD with all my heart
    115:18 it is we who **e** the LORD,
    117: 1 the LORD, all you nations;
    145: 2 and **e** your name for ever and ever.
    145:10 O LORD; your saints will **e** you.
    147:12 **E** the LORD, O Jerusalem;

EXTORT* [EXTORTION]

Lk   3:14 "Don't **e** money and don't accuse

EXTORTION [EXTORT]

Lev 6: 4 what he has stolen or taken by **e**,
Ps 62:10 Do not trust in **e** or take pride
Ecc 7: 7 **E** turns a wise man into a fool,
Isa 33:15 who rejects gain from **e**
Eze 22:29 The people of the land practice **e**
Hab 2: 6 and makes himself wealthy by **e**!

EXTRAORDINARY*

Ac 19:11 God did **e** miracles through Paul,

EXTREME

2Co 8: 2 and their **e** poverty welled up in rich

EXULT*

Ps 89:16 they **e** in your righteousness.
Isa 14: 8 the cedars of Lebanon **e** over you
    45:25 be found righteous and will **e.**

EYE [EYES]

Ge   2: 9 that were pleasing to the **e** and good
     3: 6 for food and pleasing to the **e**,
Ex 21:24 **e** for **e**, tooth for tooth,
Lev 24:20 **e** for **e**, tooth for tooth.
Dt 19:21 Show no pity: life for life, **e** for **e**,
Ezr 5: 5 the **e** of their God was watching over
Ps 17: 8 Keep me as the apple of your **e**;
    94: 9 Does he who formed the **e** not see?
Pr   7: 2 as the apple of your **e**.
    30:17 "The **e** that mocks a father,
Ecc 1: 8 The **e** never has enough of seeing,
Isa 64: 4 no **e** has seen any God besides you,
Zec 2: 8 touches the apple of his **e**—
    12: 1 a watchful **e** over the house of Judah,
Mt   5:29 If your right **e** causes you to sin,
     5:38 '**E** for **e**, and tooth for tooth.'
     6:22 "The **e** is the lamp of the body.

     7: 3 speck of sawdust in your brother's **e**
     7: 3 attention to the plank in your own **e**?
    18: 9 And if your **e** causes you to sin,
Mk 10:25 camel to go through the **e** of a needle
1Co 2: 9 as it is written: "No **e** has seen,
    12:16 "Because I am not an **e**,
    15:52 in the twinkling of an **e**,
Eph 6: 6 their favor when their **e** is on you
Col 3:22 not only when their **e** is on you and
Rev 1: 7 and every **e** will see him,

EYES [EYE]

Ge   3: 7 the **e** of both of them were opened,
     6: 8 But Noah found favor in the **e** of
    18: 3 "If I have found favor in your **e**,
Ex 15:26 and do what is right in his **e**,
    34: 9 if I have found favor in your **e**,"
Nu 11:15 if I have found favor in your **e**—
    15:39 the lusts of your own hearts and **e**.
    22:31 Then the LORD opened Balaam's **e**,
    33:55 in your **e** and thorns
Dt 11:12 the **e** of the LORD your God
    12:25 what is right in the **e** of the LORD.
    16:19 for a bribe blinds the **e** of the wise
    34: 4 I have let you see it with your **e**,
Jos 23:13 on your backs and thorns in your **e**,
Jdg 16:28 on the Philistines for my two **e**."
1Sa 15:17 you were once small in your own **e**,
1Ki 10: 7 until I came and saw with my own **e**.
2Ki 6:17 open his **e** so he may see."
     9:30 she painted her **e**,
2Ch 16: 9 the **e** of the LORD range throughout
Job 31: 1 "I made a covenant with my **e** not
    36: 7 not take his **e** off the righteous;
    42: 5 but now my **e** have seen you.
Ps 13: 3 Give light to my **e**,
    19: 8 giving light to the **e**,
    25:15 My **e** are ever on the LORD,
    36: 1 no fear of God before his **e**.
    36: 2 in his own **e** he flatters himself too
    66: 7 his **e** watch the nations—
   101: 6 My **e** will be on the faithful in
   115: 5 **e**, but they cannot see;
   118:23 and it is marvelous in our **e**.
   119:18 Open my **e** that I may see
   119:37 Turn my **e** away
   121: 1 I lift up my **e** to the hills—
   123: 1 I lift up my **e** to you,
   123: 2 so our **e** look to the LORD our God,
   139:16 your **e** saw my unformed body.
   141: 8 But my **e** are fixed on you,
Pr   3: 7 Do not be wise in your own **e**;
     4:25 Let your **e** look straight ahead,
     6:17 haughty **e**, a lying tongue, hands
    15: 3 The **e** of the LORD are everywhere,
    17:24 but a fool's **e** wander to the ends of
    20: 8 he winnows out all evil with his **e**.
    22:12 The **e** of the LORD keep watch
    23:29 Who has bloodshot **e**?
    26: 5 or he will be wise in his own **e**.
    26:16 The sluggard is wiser in his own **e**
    28:11 rich man may be wise in his own **e**,
Ecc 2:10 I denied myself nothing my **e** desired
SS   4: 1 Your **e** behind your veil are doves.

Isa	1:15	I will hide my **e** from you;
	6: 5	and my **e** have seen the King,
	6:10	make their ears dull and close their **e**.
	11: 3	not judge by what he sees with his **e**,
	33:17	Your **e** will see the king in his beauty
	42: 7	to open **e** that are blind,
Jer	9: 1	and my **e** a fountain of tears!
	24: 6	My **e** will watch over them
La	3:48	Streams of tears flow from my **e**
Eze	1:18	four rims were full of **e** all around.
	24:16	from you the delight of your **e**.
Da	7: 8	This horn had **e** like the **e** of a man
	10: 6	his **e** like flaming torches,
Am	9: 4	I will fix my **e** upon them for evil
Hab	1:13	Your **e** are too pure to look on evil;
Zec	3: 9	There are seven **e** on that one stone,
	4:10	seven are the **e** of the LORD,
Mt	6:22	If your **e** are good,
	13:15	and they have closed their **e**.
	21:42	and it is marvelous in our **e'**?
Mk	8:25	Then his **e** were opened,
Lk	10:23	"Blessed are the **e** that see
	16:15	justify yourselves in the **e** of men,
	24:31	Then their **e** were opened
Jn	4:35	open your **e** and look at the fields!
	9:10	"How then were your **e** opened?"
	12:40	"He has blinded their **e**
Ac	1: 9	he was taken up before their very **e**,
	9: 8	he opened his **e** he could see nothing.
	28:27	and they have closed their **e**.
Ro	11:10	May their **e** be darkened
2Co	4:18	So we fix our **e** not on what is seen,
	8:21	not only in the **e** of the Lord but also
		in the **e** of men.
Gal	4:15	you would have torn out your **e**
Eph	1:18	that the **e** of your heart may
Heb	4:13	and laid bare before the **e** of him
	12: 2	Let us fix our **e** on Jesus,
Jas	2: 5	the **e** of the world to be rich in faith
1Pe	3:12	**e** of the Lord are on the righteous
1Jn	1: 1	which we have seen with our **e**,
	2:16	the lust of his **e** and the boasting
Rev	1:14	and his **e** were like blazing fire.
	2:18	whose **e** are like blazing fire
	4: 6	and they were covered with **e**,
	5: 6	He had seven horns and seven **e**,
	7:17	wipe away every tear from their **e**."
	19:12	His **e** are like blazing fire,
	21: 4	He will wipe every tear from their **e**.

EVIL IN THE EYES OF THE †LORD

Dt 4:25; 17:2; Jdg 2:11; 3:7, 12; 4:1; 6:1; 10:6; 13:1; 1Sa 15:19; 1Ki 11:6; 14:22; 15:26, 34; 16:19, 25, 30; 21:20, 25; 22:52; 2Ki 3:2; 8:18, 27; 13:2, 11; 14:24; 15:9, 18, 24, 28; 17:2, 17; 21:2, 6, 16, 20; 23:32, 37; 24:9, 19; 2Ch 21:6; 22:4; 29:6; 33:2, 6, 22; 36:5, 9, 12; Jer 52:2

RIGHT IN THE EYES OF THE †LORD

Dt 12:25, 28; 21:9; 1Ki 15:5, 11; 22:43; 2Ki 12:2; 14:3; 15:3, 34; 16:2; 18:3; 22:2; 2Ch 14:2; 20:32; 24:2; 25:2; 26:4; 27:2; 28:1; 29:2; 34:2

FAVOR IN ... EYES

Ge 6:8; 18:3; 19:19; 30:27; 32:5; 33:8, 10, 15; 34:11; 39:4, 21; 47:25, 29; 50:4; Ex 34:9; Nu 11:15; 32:5; Jdg 6:17; Ru

2:10, 13; 1Sa 1:18; 20:3, 29; 27:5; 2Sa 14:22; 16:4

EYEWITNESSES* [WITNESS]

Lk	1: 2	were **e** and servants of the word.
2Pe	1:16	but we were **e** of his majesty.

EZEKIAS (KJV) HEZEKIAH

EZEKIEL

Priest called to be prophet to the exiles (Eze 1-3). Symbolically acted out destruction of Jerusalem (Eze 4-5; 12; 24).

EZION GEBER [GEBER]

1Ki	9:26	King Solomon also built ships at **E**
	22:48	they were wrecked at **E**

EZRA

Priest and teacher of the Law who led a return of exiles to Israel to reestablish temple and worship (Ezr 7-8). Corrected intermarriage of priests (Ezr 9-10). Read Law at celebration of Feast of Tabernacles (Ne 8). Participated in dedication of Jerusalem's walls (Ne 12).

F

FABLES (KJV) See MYTHS, STORIES

FACE [FACED, FACEDOWN, FACES]

Ge	4: 6	Why is your **f** downcast?
	7: 4	I will wipe from the **f** of the earth
	11: 9	the LORD scattered them over the **f**
	32:30	"It is because I saw God **f** to **f**,
Ex	3: 6	At this, Moses hid his **f**,
	33:11	LORD would speak to Moses **f** to **f**,
	33:20	But," he said,"you cannot see my **f**,
	34:29	not aware that his **f** was radiant
Nu	6:25	the LORD make his **f** shine upon you
	12: 8	With him I speak **f** to **f**,
	14:14	you, O LORD, have been seen **f** to **f**,
Dt	5: 4	The LORD spoke to you **f** to **f**
	31:17	I will hide my **f**
	34:10	whom the LORD knew **f** to **f**,
Jdg	6:22	the angel of the LORD **f** to **f**!"
2Sa	14:24	and did not see the **f** of the king.
2Ki	14: 8	"Come, meet me **f** to **f**."
1Ch	16:11	seek his **f** always.
2Ch	7:14	and pray and seek my **f** and turn
	25:17	"Come, meet me **f** to **f**."
	30: 9	He will not turn his **f** from you if
Ezr	9: 6	and disgraced to lift up my **f** to you,
Ne	2: 2	"Why does your **f** look so sad
Est	7: 8	they covered Haman's **f**.
Job	1:11	he will surely curse you to your **f**."
Ps	4: 6	Let the light of your **f** shine upon us,
	10:11	"God has forgotten; he covers his **f**
	13: 1	How long will you hide your **f**
	27: 8	My heart says of you,"Seek his **f**!"
	31:16	Let your **f** shine on your servant;

44: 3 your arm, and the light of your **f**,
44:22 your sake we **f** death all day long;
51: 9 Hide your **f** from my sins
67: 1 and make his **f** shine upon us,
80: 3 O God; make your **f** shine
104:29 you hide your **f**, they are terrified;
105: 4 seek his **f** always.
119:135 Make your **f** shine upon your servant
Pr 15:13 A happy heart makes the **f** cheerful,
Ecc 7: 3 because a sad **f** is good for the heart.
8: 1 Wisdom brightens a man's **f**
SS 2:14 show me your **f**,
2:14 and your **f** is lovely.
Isa 8:17 who is hiding his **f** from the house
50: 7 Therefore have I set my **f** like flint,
50: 8 Let us **f** each other!
54: 8 a surge of anger I hid my **f** from you
Jer 32: 4 and will speak with him **f** to **f**
34: 3 and he will speak with you **f** to **f**.
Eze 1:10 the four had the **f** of a man,
1:10 right side each had the **f** of a lion,
1:10 and on the left the **f** of an ox;
1:10 also had the **f** of an eagle.
10:14 **f** was that of a cherub, the second
the **f** of a man, the third the **f** of a
lion, and the fourth the **f** of an eagle.
39:23 So I hid my **f** from them
39:29 I will no longer hide my **f**
Da 10: 6 his **f** like lightning,
Hos 5:15 And they will seek my **f**;
Mt 17: 2 his **f** shone like the sun.
18:10 always see the **f** of my Father
26:67 Then they spit in his **f**
Lk 9:29 the appearance of his **f** changed,
Jn 19: 3 And they struck him in the **f**.
Ac 6:15 that his **f** was like the **f** of an angel.
Ro 8:36 your sake we **f** death all day long;
1Co 13:12 then we shall see **f** to **f**.
2Co 3: 7 the **f** of Moses because of its glory,
4: 6 the glory of God in the **f** of Christ.
10: 1 Paul, who am "timid" when **f** to **f**
Jas 1:23 a man who looks at his **f** in a mirror
1Pe 3:12 but the **f** of the Lord is against
2Jn 1:12 and talk with you **f** to **f**,
3Jn 1:14 and we will talk **f** to **f**.
Rev 1:16 His **f** was like the sun shining
4: 7 the third had a **f** like a man,
10: 1 his **f** was like the sun,
22: 4 They will see his **f**,

FACED [FACE]

Ex 37: 9 The cherubim **f** each other,
Eze 1:17 the four directions the creatures **f**;

FACEDOWN [FACE]

Ge 17: 3 Abram fell **f**, and God said to him,
Lev 9:24 they shouted for joy and fell **f**.
Nu 16: 4 When Moses heard this, he fell **f**.
Jos 5:14 Then Joshua fell **f** to the ground
7: 6 and fell **f** to the ground before
Mt 17: 6 they fell **f** to the ground, terrified.

FACES [FACE]

1Ch 12: 8 Their **f** were the **f** of lions,

Ps 34: 5 their **f** are never covered with shame.
83:16 Cover their **f** with shame so
Isa 6: 2 With two wings they covered their **f**,
Eze 1: 6 but each of them had four **f**
10:14 Each of the cherubim had four **f**:
41:18 Each cherub had two **f**:
Mt 6:16 for they disfigure their **f** to show
2Co 3:18 who with unveiled **f** all reflect
Rev 9: 7 and their **f** resembled human faces.
11:16 fell on their **f** and worshiped God,

FACT [FACTS]

Ac 13:34 **f** that God raised him from the dead,

FACTIONS*

1Ki 16:21 people of Israel were split into two **f**;
2Co 12:20 jealousy, outbursts of anger, **f**,
Gal 5:20 selfish ambition, dissensions, **f**

FACTS* [FACT]

Ac 19:36 since these **f** are undeniable,

FADE [FADING]

Ps 109:23 I **f** away like an evening shadow;
Jas 1:11 the rich man will **f** away even
1Pe 1: 4 can never perish, spoil or **f**—
5: 4 of glory that will never **f** away.

FADING [FADE]

Isa 1:30 be like an oak with **f** leaves,
2Co 3: 7 because of its glory, **f** though it was,
3:11 if what was **f** away came with glory,
3:13 at it while the radiance was **f** away.

FAIL [FAILED, FAILING, FAILINGS, FAILS, FAILURE]

Lev 26:15 and **f** to carry out all my commands
Nu 15:22 if you unintentionally **f** to keep any
1Ki 2: 4 never **f** to have a man on the throne
1Ch 28:20 not **f** you or forsake you until all
2Ch 34:33 they did not **f** to follow the LORD,
Ps 69: 3 My eyes **f**, looking for my God.
89:28 my covenant with him will never **f**.
Pr 15:22 Plans **f** for lack of counsel,
Isa 51: 6 my righteousness will never **f**.
58:11 like a spring whose waters never **f**.
Jer 33:17 'David will never **f** to have a man to
La 3:22 for his compassions never **f**.
Eze 2: 5 whether they listen or **f** to listen—
47:12 nor will their fruit **f**.
Zep 3: 5 and every new day he does not **f**,
Mk 8:18 Do you have eyes but **f** to see,
Lk 22:32 Simon, that your faith may not **f**.
Ac 5:38 of human origin, it will **f**.
2Co 13: 5 of course, you **f** the test?

FAILED [FAIL]

Jos 21:45 promises to the house of Israel **f**;
23:14 fulfilled; not one has **f**.
1Ki 8:56 Not one word has **f** of all
15: 5 and had not **f** to keep any
Ne 9:17 They refused to listen and **f**
Ps 77: 8 Has his promise **f** for all time?
Ro 9: 6 It is not as though God's word had **f**.

2Co 13: 6 that we have not **f** the test.

FAILING* [FAIL]

Ge 48:10 Now Israel's eyes were **f** because
Dt   8:11 **f** to observe his commands,
1Sa 12:23 against the LORD by **f** to pray for you

FAILINGS* [FAIL]

Ro   15: 1 ought to bear with the **f** of the weak

FAILS [FAIL]

Ps 143: 7 quickly, O LORD; my spirit **f.**
Pr   8:36 whoever **f** to find me harms himself;
Joel 1:10 the new wine is dried up, the oil **f.**
Hab   3:17 though the olive crop **f** and
1Co 13: 8 Love never **f.**

FAILURE* [FAIL]

1Th   2: 1 that our visit to you was not a **f.**

FAINT [FAINTHEARTED, FAINTS]

Job 26:14 how **f** the whisper we hear
Ps 142: 3 When my spirit grows **f** within me,
SS   2: 5 for I am **f** with love.
Isa 40:31 they will walk and not be **f.**
Jer 31:25 refresh the weary and satisfy the **f.**"
La   5:17 Because of this our hearts are **f,**

FAINTHEARTED* [FAINT, HEART]

Dt   20: 3 Do not be **f** or afraid;
     20: 8 "Is any man afraid or **f?**

FAINTS* [FAINT]

Ps   84: 2 My soul yearns, even **f,**
    119:81 My soul **f** with longing

FAIR [FAIRLY, FAIRNESS]

Job 26:13 By his breath the skies became **f;**
Pr   1: 3 doing what is right and just and **f;**
Hos 10:11 so I will put a yoke on her **f** neck.
Mt   16: 2 you say, 'It will be **f** weather,
Col   4: 1 slaves with what is right and **f,**

FAIRLY [FAIR]

Lev 19:15 but judge your neighbor **f.**
Pr   31: 9 Speak up and judge **f;**
Eze 18: 8 and judges **f** between man

FAIRNESS* [FAIR]

Pr   29:14 If a king judges the poor with **f,**

FAITH* [FAITHFUL, FAITHFULLY, FAITHFULNESS, FAITHLESS]

Ex   21: 8 because he has broken **f** with her.
Dt   32:51 both of you broke **f** with me
Jos 22:16 'How could you break **f** with
Jdg   9:16 acted honorably and in good **f**
      9:19 and in good **f** toward Jerub-Baal
1Sa 14:33 "You have broken **f,"** he said.
2Ch 20:20 have **f** in the LORD your God
     20:20 have **f** in his prophets and you will
Isa   7: 9 If you do not stand firm in your **f,**
     26: 2 the nation that keeps **f.**
Hab   2: 4 but the righteous will live by his **f—**

Mal   2:10 by breaking **f** with one another?
      2:11 Judah has broken **f.**
      2:14 because you have broken **f** with her,
      2:15 and do not break **f** with the wife
      2:16 and do not break **f.**
Mt   6:30 O you of little **f?**
      8:10 in Israel with such great **f.**
      8:26 He replied,"You of little **f,**
      9: 2 When Jesus saw their **f,**
      9:22 he said,"your **f** has healed you."
      9:29 "According to your **f** will it be done
     13:58 because of their lack of **f.**
     14:31 "You of little **f,"** he said,
     15:28 "Woman, you have great **f!**
     16: 8 Jesus asked,"You of little **f,**
     17:20 "Because you have so little **f.**
     17:20 **f** as small as a mustard seed,
     21:21 if you have **f** and do not doubt,
     24:10 many will turn away from the **f**
Mk   2: 5 When Jesus saw their **f,**
      4:40 Do you still have no **f?"**
      5:34 "Daughter, your **f** has healed you.
      6: 6 he was amazed at their lack of **f.**
     10:52 said Jesus,"your **f** has healed you."
     11:22 "Have **f** in God," Jesus answered.
     16:14 he rebuked them for their lack of **f**
Lk   5:20 When Jesus saw their **f,** he said,
      7: 9 I have not found such great **f** even
      7:50 "Your **f** has saved you; go in peace."
      8:25 "Where is your **f?"**
      8:48 "Daughter, your **f** has healed you.
     12:28 O you of little **f!**
     17: 5 to the Lord,"Increase our **f!"**
     17: 6 **f** as small as a mustard seed,
     17:19 your **f** has made you well."
     18: 8 will he find **f** on the earth?"
     18:42 your **f** has healed you."
     22:32 Simon, that your **f** may not fail.
Jn   2:11 and his disciples put their **f** in him.
      7:31 many in the crowd put their **f** in him.
      8:30 as he spoke, many put their **f** in him.
     11:45 put their **f** in him.
     12:11 and putting their **f** in him.
     12:42 not confess their **f** for fear
     14:12 anyone who has **f** in me
Ac   3:16 By **f** in the name of Jesus,
      3:16 the **f** that comes through him
      6: 5 man full of **f** and of the Holy Spirit;
      6: 7 of priests became obedient to the **f.**
     11:24 full of the Holy Spirit and **f,**
     13: 8 to turn the proconsul from the **f.**
     14: 9 saw that he had **f** to be healed
     14:22 to remain true to the **f**
     14:27 and how he had opened the door of **f**
     15: 9 for he purified their hearts by **f.**
     16: 5 churches were strengthened in the **f**
     20:21 to God in repentance and have **f**
     24:24 as he spoke about **f** in Christ Jesus.
     26:18 among those who are sanctified by **f**
     27:25 for I have **f** in God
Ro   1: 5 to the obedience that comes from **f.**
      1: 8 because your **f** is being reported all
      1:12 encouraged by each other's **f.**
      1:17 a righteousness that is by **f** from first

1:17 "The righteous will live by **f**."
3: 3 What if some did not have **f**?
3: 3 lack of **f** nullify God's faithfulness?
3:22 from God comes through **f**
3:25 through **f** in his blood.
3:26 one who justifies those who have **f**
3:27 No, but on that of **f**.
3:28 a man is justified by **f** apart
3:30 justify the circumcised by **f** and the
     uncircumcised through that same **f**.
3:31 then, nullify the law by this **f**?
4: 5 his **f** is credited as righteousness.
4: 9 that Abraham's **f** was credited to him
4:11 of the righteousness that he had by **f**
4:12 of the **f** that our father Abraham had
4:13 the righteousness that comes by **f**.
4:14 **f** has no value and the promise
4:16 Therefore, the promise comes by **f**,
4:16 but also to those who are of the **f**
4:19 Without weakening in his **f**,
4:20 but was strengthened in his **f**
5: 1 we have been justified through **f**,
5: 2 access by **f** into this grace
9:30 a righteousness that is by **f**;
9:32 Because they pursued it not by **f** but
10: 6 the righteousness that is by **f** says:
10: 8 the word of **f** we are proclaiming:
10:17 **f** comes from hearing the message,
11:20 and you stand by **f**.
12: 3 the measure of **f** God has given you.
12: 6 let him use it in proportion to his **f**.
14: 1 Accept him whose **f** is weak,
14: 2 One man's **f** allows him
14: 2 but another man, whose **f** is weak,
14:23 because his eating is not from **f**;
14:23 that does not come from **f** is sin.
1Co 2: 5 so that your **f** might not rest
12: 9 to another **f** by the same Spirit,
13: 2 I have a **f** that can move mountains,
13:13 these three remain: **f**, hope and love.
15:14 is useless and so is your **f**.
15:17 your **f** is futile;
16:13 stand firm in the **f**;
2Co 1:24 Not that we lord it over your **f**,
1:24 because it is by **f** you stand firm.
4:13 that same spirit of **f** we also believe
5: 7 We live by **f**, not by sight.
8: 7 in **f**, in speech, in knowledge,
10:15 as your **f** continues to grow,
13: 5 to see whether you are in the **f**;
Gal 1:23 now preaching the **f** he once tried
2:16 but by **f** in Jesus Christ.
2:16 have put our **f** in Christ Jesus that
     we may be justified by **f** in Christ
2:20 I live by **f** in the Son of God,
3: 8 God would justify the Gentiles by **f**,
3: 9 So those who have **f** are blessed
3: 9 with Abraham, the man of **f**.
3:11 "The righteous will live by **f**."
3:12 The law is not based on **f**;
3:14 by **f** we might receive the promise of
3:22 given through **f** in Jesus Christ,
3:23 Before this **f** came,
3:23 locked up until **f** should be revealed.

3:24 that we might be justified by **f**.
3:25 Now that **f** has come,
3:26 You are all sons of God through **f**
5: 5 But by **f** we eagerly await through
5: 6 **f** expressing itself through love.
Eph 1:15 ever since I heard about your **f** in
2: 8 you have been saved, through **f**—
3:12 and through **f** in him
3:17 dwell in your hearts through **f**.
4: 5 one Lord, one **f**, one baptism;
4:13 until we all reach unity in the **f** and
6:16 take up the shield of **f**,
6:23 and love with **f** from God the Father
Php 1:25 for your progress and joy in the **f**,
1:27 contending as one man for the **f** of
2:17 and service coming from your **f**,
3: 9 that which is through **f** in Christ—
3: 9 that comes from God and is by **f**.
Col 1: 4 because we have heard of your **f**
1: 5 the **f** and love that spring from
1:23 if you continue in your **f**,
2: 5 and how firm your **f** in Christ is.
2: 7 in the **f** as you were taught,
2:12 raised with him through your **f**
1Th 1: 3 and Father your work produced by **f**,
1: 8 your **f** in God has become known
3: 2 and encourage you in your **f**,
3: 5 I sent to find out about your **f**.
3: 6 good news about your **f**
3: 7 about you because of your **f**.
3:10 and supply what is lacking in your **f**.
5: 8 on **f** and love as a breastplate,
2Th 1: 3 because your **f** is growing more
1: 4 about your perseverance and **f** in all
1:11 and every act prompted by your **f**.
3: 2 for not everyone has **f**.
1Ti 1: 2 To Timothy my true son in the **f**:
1: 4 which is by **f**.
1: 5 a good conscience and a sincere **f**.
1:14 along with the **f** and love that are
1:19 on to **f** and a good conscience.
1:19 and so have shipwrecked their **f**.
2: 7 and a teacher of the true **f** to
2:15 if they continue in **f**,
3: 9 the deep truths of the **f**
3:13 and great assurance in their **f**
4: 1 some will abandon the **f**
4: 6 brought up in the truths of the **f**
4:12 in life, in love, in **f** and in purity.
5: 8 he has denied the **f** and is worse than
6:10 have wandered from the **f**
6:11 **f**, love, endurance and gentleness.
6:12 Fight the good fight of the **f**
6:21 so doing have wandered from the **f**.
2Ti 1: 5 reminded of your sincere **f**,
1:13 with **f** and love in Christ Jesus.
2:18 and they destroy the **f** of some.
2:22 and pursue righteousness, **f**,
3: 8 who, as far as the **f** is concerned,
3:10 my way of life, my purpose, **f**,
3:15 salvation through **f** in Christ Jesus.
4: 7 I have kept the **f**.
Tit 1: 1 an apostle of Jesus Christ for the **f**
1: 2 a **f** and knowledge resting on

1: 4   my true son in our common **f**:
1:13   so that they will be sound in the **f**
2: 2   self-controlled, and sound in **f,**
3:15   Greet those who love us in the **f.**
Phm   1: 5   about your **f** in the Lord Jesus
1: 6   be active in sharing your **f,**
Heb   4: 2   did not combine it with **f.**
4:14   hold firmly to the **f** we profess.
6: 1   and of **f** in God,
6:12   through **f** and patience inherit
10:22   a sincere heart in full assurance of **f,**
10:38   But my righteous one will live by **f.**
11: 1   **f** is being sure of what we hope
11: 3   By **f** we understand that
11: 4   By **f** Abel offered God
11: 4   By **f** he was commended as
11: 4   And by **f** he still speaks,
11: 5   By **f** Enoch was taken from this life,
11: 6   And without **f** it is impossible
11: 7   By **f** Noah, when warned
11: 7   By his **f** he condemned the world
11: 7   of the righteousness that comes by **f.**
11: 8   By **f** Abraham, when called
11: 9   By **f** he made his home in
11:11   By **f** Abraham, even though he was
11:13   still living by **f** when they died.
11:17   By **f** Abraham, when God tested
11:20   By **f** Isaac blessed Jacob and Esau
11:21   By **f** Jacob, when he was dying,
11:22   By **f** Joseph, when his end was near,
11:23   By **f** Moses' parents hid him
11:24   By **f** Moses, when he had grown up,
11:27   By **f** he left Egypt,
11:28   By **f** he kept the Passover and
11:29   By **f** the people passed through the
11:30   By **f** the walls of Jericho fell,
11:31   By **f** the prostitute Rahab,
11:33   who through **f** conquered kingdoms,
11:39   all commended for their **f,**
12: 2   the author and perfecter of our **f,**
13: 7   their way of life and imitate their **f.**
Jas   1: 3   of your **f** develops perseverance.
2: 5   the eyes of the world to be rich in **f**
2:14   to have **f** but has no deeds?
2:14   Can such **f** save him?
2:17   In the same way, **f** by itself,
2:18   But someone will say,"You have **f;**
2:18   Show me your **f** without deeds,
2:18   show you my **f** by what I do.
2:20   that **f** without deeds is useless?
2:22   You see that his **f** and his actions
2:22   and his **f** was made complete
2:24   by what he does and not by **f** alone.
2:26   so **f** without deeds is dead.
5:15   in **f** will make the sick person well;
1Pe   1: 5   through **f** are shielded by God's
1: 7   These have come so that your **f—**
1: 9   you are receiving the goal of your **f,**
1:21   and so your **f** and hope are in God.
5: 9   Resist him, standing firm in the **f,**
2Pe   1: 1   received a **f** as precious as ours:
1: 5   to add to your **f** goodness;
1Jn   5: 4   overcome the world, even our **f.**
Jude   1: 3   the **f** that was once for all entrusted

1:20   yourselves up in your most holy **f**
Rev   2:13   You did not renounce your **f** in me,
2:19   I know your deeds, your love and **f,**

FAITHFUL* [FAITH]

Nu   12: 7   not true of my servant Moses; he is **f**
Dt   7: 9   he is the **f** God,
32: 4   A **f** God who does no wrong,
1Sa   2:35   I will raise up for myself a **f** priest,
2Sa   20:19   We are the peaceful and **f** in Israel.
22:26   "To the **f** you show yourself **f,**
1Ki   3: 6   because he was **f** to you
2Ch   31:18   were **f** in consecrating themselves.
31:20   doing what was good and right and **f**
Ne   9: 8   You found his heart **f** to you,
Ps   12: 1   the **f** have vanished from among men
18:25   To the **f** you show yourself **f,**
25:10   ways of the LORD are loving and **f**
31:23   The LORD preserves the **f,**
33: 4   he is **f** in all he does.
37:28   and will not forsake his **f** ones.
78: 8   whose spirits were not **f** to him.
78:37   they were not **f** to his covenant.
89:19   to your **f** people you said:
89:24   My **f** love will be with him,
89:37   the **f** witness in the sky."
97:10   for he guards the lives of his **f** ones
101: 6   My eyes will be on the **f** in the land,
111: 7   works of his hands are **f** and just;
145:13   The LORD is **f** to all his promises
146: 6   who remains **f** forever.
Pr   2: 8   and protects the way of his **f** ones.
20: 6   but a **f** man who can find?
28:20   A **f** man will be richly blessed,
31:26   and **f** instruction is on her tongue.
Isa   1:21   how the **f** city has become a harlot!
1:26   City of Righteousness, the **F** City."
49: 7   because of the LORD, who is **f,**
55: 3   my **f** love promised to David.
Jer   42: 5   a **f** witness against us if
Eze   43:11   so that they may be **f** to its design
48:11   who were **f** in serving me and did
Hos   11:12   even against the **f** Holy One.
Zec   8: 8   and I will be **f** and righteous to them
Mt   24:45   "Who then is the **f** and wise servant,
25:21   'Well done, good and **f** servant!
25:21   You have been **f** with a few things;
25:23   'Well done, good and **f** servant!
25:23   You have been **f** with a few things;
Lk   12:42   then is the **f** and wise manager,
Ro   12:12   patient in affliction, **f** in prayer.
1Co   1: 9   his Son Jesus Christ our Lord, is **f.**
4: 2   a trust must prove **f.**
4:17   who is **f** in the Lord.
10:13   And God is **f;**
2Co   1:18   But as surely as God is **f,**
Eph   1: 1   the **f** in Christ Jesus:
6:21   the dear brother and **f** servant in
Col   1: 2   To the holy and **f** brothers
1: 7   a **f** minister of Christ on our behalf,
4: 7   a **f** minister and fellow servant in
4: 9   our **f** and dear brother,
1Th   5:24   The one who calls you is **f**
2Th   3: 3   But the Lord is **f,**

1Ti	1:12	that he considered me **f**,
	5: 9	has been **f** to her husband,
2Ti	2:13	he will remain **f**,
Heb	2:17	a merciful and **f** high priest
	3: 2	He was **f** to the one who
	3: 2	as Moses was **f** in all God's house.
	3: 5	Moses was **f** as a servant
	3: 6	But Christ is **f** as a son
	8: 9	because they did not remain **f**
	10:23	for he who promised is **f**.
	11:11	he considered him **f** who had made
1Pe	4:19	commit themselves to their **f** Creator
	5:12	whom I regard as a **f** brother,
1Jn	1: 9	he is **f** and just
3Jn	1: 5	you are **f** in what you are doing for
Rev	1: 5	who is the **f** witness,
	2:10	Be **f**, even to the point of death,
	2:13	my **f** witness, who was put to death
	3:14	the **f** and true witness,
	14:12	God's commandments and remain **f**
	17:14	chosen and **f** followers."
	19:11	whose rider is called **F** and True.

FAITHFULLY* [FAITH]

Dt	11:13	So if you **f** obey the commands
Jos	2:14	we will treat you kindly and **f** when
1Sa	12:24	and serve him **f** with all your heart;
1Ki	2: 4	and if they walk **f** before me
2Ki	20: 3	I have walked before you **f**
	22: 7	because they are acting **f**."
2Ch	19: 9	You must serve **f** and wholeheartedly
	31:12	they **f** brought in the contributions,
	31:15	and Shecaniah assisted him **f** in
	32: 1	all that Hezekiah had so **f** done,
	34:12	The men did the work **f**.
Ne	9:33	you have been just; you have acted **f**,
	13:14	do not blot out what I have so **f** done
Isa	38: 3	before you **f** and with wholehearted
Jer	23:28	the one who has my word speak it **f**.
Eze	18: 9	my decrees and **f** keeps my laws.
	44:15	and who **f** carried out
1Pe	4:10	**f** administering God's grace

FAITHFULNESS* [FAITH]

Ge	24:27	not abandoned his kindness and **f**
	24:49	Now if you will show kindness and **f**
	32:10	and **f** you have shown your servant.
	47:29	you will show me kindness and **f**.
Ex	34: 6	abounding in love and **f**,
Jos	24:14	the LORD and serve him with all **f**.
1Sa	26:23	every man for his righteousness and **f**
2Sa	2: 6	now show you kindness and **f**,
	15:20	May kindness and **f** be with you."
Ps	30: 9	Will it proclaim your **f**?
	36: 5	your **f** to the skies.
	40:10	I speak of your **f**
	54: 5	in your **f** destroy them.
	57: 3	God sends his love and his **f**.
	57:10	your **f** reaches to the skies.
	61: 7	appoint your love and **f**
	71:22	with the harp for your **f**, O my God;
	85:10	Love and **f** meet together;
	85:11	**F** springs forth from the earth,
	86:15	abounding in love and **f**.

	88:11	your **f** in Destruction?
	89: 1	my mouth I will make your **f** known
	89: 2	that you established your **f**
	89: 5	O LORD, your **f** too,
	89: 8	and your **f** surrounds you.
	89:14	love and **f** go before you.
	89:33	nor will I ever betray my **f**.
	89:49	which in your **f** you swore to David?
	91: 4	his **f** will be your shield and rampart.
	92: 2	in the morning and your **f** at night,
	98: 3	and his **f** to the house of Israel;
	100: 5	**f** continues through all generations.
	108: 4	your **f** reaches to the skies.
	111: 8	done in **f** and uprightness.
	115: 1	because of your love and **f**.
	117: 2	the **f** of the LORD endures forever.
	119:75	and in **f** you have afflicted me.
	119:90	**f** continues through all generations;
	138: 2	for your love and your **f**,
	143: 1	in your **f** and righteousness come to
Pr	3: 3	Let love and **f** never leave you;
	14:22	plan what is good find love and **f**.
	16: 6	Through love and **f** sin is atoned for;
	20:28	Love and **f** keep a king safe;
Isa	11: 5	and **f** the sash around his waist.
	16: 5	in **f** a man will sit on it—
	25: 1	in perfect **f** you have done marvelous
	38:18	to the pit cannot hope for your **f**
	38:19	tell their children about your **f**.
	42: 3	In **f** he will bring forth justice;
	61: 8	In my **f** I will reward them and make
La	3:23	new every morning; great is your **f**.
Hos	2:20	I will betroth you in **f**,
	4: 1	who live in the land: "There is no **f**,
Mt	23:23	of the law—justice, mercy and **f**.
Ro	3: 3	lack of faith nullify God's **f**?
Gal	5:22	patience, kindness, goodness, **f**,
3Jn	1: 3	come and tell about your **f**
Rev	13:10	This calls for patient endurance and **f**

FAITHLESS* [FAITH]

Ps	78:57	they were disloyal and **f**,
	101: 3	The deeds of **f** men I hate;
	119:158	I look on the **f** with loathing,
Pr	14:14	**f** will be fully repaid for their ways,
Jer	3: 6	you seen what **f** Israel has done?
	3: 8	**f** Israel her certificate of divorce
	3:11	"**F** Israel is more righteous than
	3:12	**f** Israel, ' declares the LORD,
	3:14	"Return, **f** people,"
	3:22	"Return, **f** people; I will cure you of
	12: 1	Why do all the **f** live at ease?
Ro	1:31	**f**, heartless, ruthless.
2Ti	2:13	if we are **f**, he will remain faithful,

FALL [FALLEN, FALLING, FALLS, FELL]

Ge	2:21	the man to **f** into a deep sleep;
	27:13	"My son, let the curse **f** on me.
Lev	26: 7	they will **f** by the sword before you.
Nu	14:29	In this desert your bodies will **f**—
Dt	32: 2	Let my teaching **f** like rain
1Sa	3:19	and he let none of his words **f** to
1Ch	21:13	Let me **f** into the hands of
Ps	13: 4	and my foes will rejoice when I **f**.

37:24 he will not **f,**
46: 5 God is within her, she will not **f;**
55:22 he will never let the righteous **f.**
69: 9 the insults of those who insult you **f**
91: 7 A thousand may **f** at your side,
145:14 The LORD upholds all those who **f**
Pr 11:28 Whoever trusts in his riches will **f,**
16:18 a haughty spirit before a **f.**
Ecc 10: 8 Whoever digs a pit may **f** into it;
Isa 8:14 and a rock that makes them **f.**
40: 7 The grass withers and the flowers **f,**
40:30 and young men stumble and **f;**
Jer 6:15 So they will **f** among the fallen;
34:17 to **f** by the sword, plague and famine.
La 1: 9 Her **f** was astounding;
Hos 10: 8 and to the hills, **"F** on us!"
Mt 7:25 yet it did not **f,** because it had
11: 6 not **f** away on account of me."
Mk 4:17 they quickly **f** away.
13:25 the stars will **f** from the sky,
14:27 "You will all **f** away,"
Lk 10:18 "I saw Satan **f** like lightning
11:17 a house divided against itself will **f.**
23:30 to the mountains, **"F** on us!"
Ro 3:23 for all have sinned and **f** short of
9:33 and a rock that makes them **f,**
11:11 so as to **f** beyond recovery?
14:21 that will cause your brother to **f.**
1Co 8:13 if what I eat causes my brother to **f**
10:12 be careful that you don't **f!**
Heb 6: 6 if they **f** away,
10:31 to **f** into the hands of the living God.
1Pe 2: 8 and a rock that makes them **f."**
2Pe 1:10 you will never **f,**
Rev 6:16 **"F** on us and hide us from the face

FALLEN [FALL]

1Sa 5: 3 **f** on his face on the ground before
2Sa 1:19 How the mighty have **f!**
Ps 36:12 See how the evildoers lie **f—**
Isa 14:12 How you have **f** from heaven,
21: 9 'Babylon has **f,** has **f!**
Am 9:11 that day I will restore David's **f** tent.
Jn 11:11 "Our friend Lazarus has **f** asleep;
Ac 15:16 and rebuild David's **f** tent.
1Co 11:30 and a number of you have **f** asleep.
15: 6 though some have **f** asleep.
15:18 Then those also who have **f** asleep
15:20 of those who have **f** asleep.
Gal 5: 4 you have **f** away from grace.
1Th 4:15 not precede those who have **f** asleep.
Heb 4: 1 of you to be found to have **f** short of it.
Rev 9: 1 that had **f** from the sky to the earth.
14: 8 **"F! F** is Babylon the Great,
17:10 Five have **f,** one is,
18: 2 **"F! F** is Babylon the Great!

FALLING [FALL]

Lk 22:44 like drops of blood **f** to the ground.
Jude 1:24 who is able to keep you from **f**

FALLS [FALL]

Pr 11:14 For lack of guidance a nation **f,**
24:16 though a righteous man **f** seven times

24:17 Do not gloat when your enemy **f;**
28:14 but he who hardens his heart **f**
Ecc 4:10 If one **f** down, his friend can help
Mt 13:21 he quickly **f** away.
Lk 20:18 Everyone who **f** on that stone will
Jn 12:24 of wheat **f** to the ground and dies,
Ro 14: 4 To his own master he stands or **f.**

FALSE [FALSEHOOD, FALSELY]

Ex 20:16 "You shall not give **f** testimony
23: 1 "Do not spread **f** reports.
23: 7 Have nothing to do with a **f** charge
Dt 5:20 "You shall not give **f** testimony
Job 36: 4 Be assured that my words are not **f;**
Ps 4: 2 love delusions and seek **f** gods?
Pr 12:17 but a **f** witness tells lies.
13: 5 The righteous hate what is **f,**
14: 5 but a **f** witness pours out lies.
14:25 but a **f** witness is deceitful.
19: 5 A **f** witness will not go unpunished,
21:28 A **f** witness will perish,
25:18 the man who gives **f** testimony
Isa 44:25 who foils the signs of **f** prophets
Jer 14:14 are prophesying to you **f** visions,
23:16 they fill you with **f** hopes.
50:36 A sword against her **f** prophets!
Eze 13: 6 Their visions are **f**
Am 2: 4 they have been led astray by **f** gods,
Mt 7:15 "Watch out for **f** prophets.
15:19 theft, **f** testimony, slander.
24:11 and many **f** prophets will appear
24:24 **f** Christs and **f** prophets will appear
Mk 10:19 do not steal, do not give **f** testimony,
13:22 **f** Christs and **f** prophets will appear
14:57 gave this **f** testimony against him:
Lk 6:26 their fathers treated the **f** prophets.
18:20 do not steal, do not give **f** testimony,
Jn 1:47 in whom there is nothing **f."**
Ac 6:13 They produced **f** witnesses,
13: 6 and **f** prophet named Bar-Jesus,
1Co 15:15 we are then found to be **f** witnesses
2Co 11:13 For such men are **f** apostles,
11:26 and in danger from **f** brothers.
Gal 2: 4 **f** brothers had infiltrated our ranks
Php 1:18 whether from **f** motives or true,
Col 2:18 **f** humility and the worship of angels
2:23 their **f** humility and their harsh
1Ti 1: 3 not to teach **f** doctrines any longer
6: 3 If anyone teaches **f** doctrines
2Pe 2: 1 also **f** prophets among the people,
2: 1 will be **f** teachers among you.
1Jn 4: 1 many **f** prophets have gone out
Rev 16:13 out of the mouth of the **f** prophet.
19:20 the **f** prophet who had performed
20:10 and the **f** prophet had been thrown.

FALSE PROPHETS Isa 44:25; Jer 50:36; Mt
7:15; 24:11, 24; Mk 13:22; Lk 6:26; 2Pe 2:1; 1Jn
4:1

FALSEHOOD* [FALSE]

Job 21:34 of your answers but **f!"**
31: 5 "If I have walked in **f**
Ps 52: 3 **f** rather than speaking the truth.
119:163 and abhor **f** but I love your law.

Pr   30: 8 Keep f and lies far from me;
Isa   28:15 and f our hiding place."
Ro   3: 7 "If my f enhances God's truthfulness
Eph   4:25 Therefore each of you must put off f
1Jn   4: 6 the Spirit of truth and the spirit of f.
Rev   22:15 who loves and practices f.

FALSELY [FALSE]

Lev   19:12 " 'Do not swear f by my name and
Da   6:24 the men who had f accused Daniel
Zec   5: 3 everyone who swears f will
Mt   5:11 f say all kinds of evil against you
Mk   14:56 Many testified f against him,
Lk   3:14 and don't accuse people f—
1Ti   6:20 ideas of what is f called knowledge,

FALTER* [FALTERED, FALTERING]

Pr   24:10 If you f in times of trouble,
Isa   42: 4 he will not f or be discouraged

FALTERED* [FALTER]

Ps   105:37 from among their tribes none f.

FALTERING* [FALTER]

Ex   6:12 since I speak with f lips?"
       6:30 "Since I speak with f lips,
Job   4: 4 you have strengthened f knees.

FAME [FAMOUS]

Dt   26:19 f and honor high above all the
Jos   9: 9 of the f of the LORD your God.
1Ch   14:17 So David's f spread
2Ch   9: 1 queen of Sheba heard of Solomon's f
Isa   66:19 not heard of my f or seen my glory.
Hab   3: 2 LORD, I have heard of your f;

FAMILIAR

Isa   53: 3 and f with suffering.

FAMILIES [FAMILY]

Ex   1:21 he gave them f of their own.
Nu   1: 2 community by their clans and f,
      26: 2 the whole Israelite community by f
Ps   68: 6 God sets the lonely in f,
     107:41 and increased their f like flocks.
Am   3: 2 "You only have I chosen of all the f

FAMILY [FAMILIES]

Ge   7: 1 you and your whole f,
      24:38 to my father's f and to my own clan,
Dt   25: 9 not build up his brother's f line."
Jos   6:23 They brought out her entire f
Ru   4:10 not disappear from among his f or
1Sa   18:18 "Who am I, and what is my f
2Ch   22:10 to destroy the whole royal f
Ezr   2:62 These searched for their f records,
Est   2:20 Esther had kept secret her f
Pr   15:27 greedy man brings trouble to his f,
      31:15 she provides food for her f
Mk   5:19 "Go home to your f
Lk   9:61 and say good-by to my f."
      12:52 there will be five in one f divided
Jn   7:42 Christ will come from David's f
Ac   10: 2 He and all his f were devout
      16:33 he and all his f were baptized.

Gal   6:10 who belong to the f of believers.
Eph   3:15 from whom his whole f in heaven
1Ti   3: 4 He must manage his own f well
       5: 4 by caring for their own f and
       5: 8 and especially for his immediate f,
Heb   11: 7 in holy fear built an ark to save his f.
1Pe   4:17 judgment to begin with the f of God;

FAMINE [FAMINES]

Ge   12:10 Now there was a f in the land,
      26: 1 Now there was a f in the land—
      41:27 They are seven years of f.
      42: 5 the f was in the land of Canaan also.
      43: 1 the f was still severe in the land.
Dt   32:24 I will send wasting f against them,
Ru   1: 1 there was a f in the land,
1Ki   18: 2 Now the f was severe in Samaria,
2Ki   4:38 and there was a f in that region.
       6:25 There was a great f in the city;
Ps   37:19 in days of f they will enjoy plenty.
Jer   14:15 prophets will perish by sword and f.
Eze   5:16 I will bring more and more f
Am   8:11 not a f of food or a thirst for water,
       8:11 a f of hearing the words of the LORD.
Lk   4:25 and there was a severe f
Ac   11:28 the Spirit predicted that a severe f
Ro   8:35 or persecution or f or nakedness
Rev   18: 8 overtake her: death, mourning and f.

FAMINES [FAMINE]

Lk   21:11 f and pestilences in various places,

FAMOUS [FAME]

Ru   4:11 in Ephrathah and be f in Bethlehem.
2Sa   8:13 And David became f
1Ki   1:47 Solomon's name more f than yours

FAN*

2Ti   1: 6 to f into flame the gift of God,

FANTASIES*

Ps   73:20 O Lord, you will despise them as f.
Pr   12:11 but he who chases f lacks judgment.
      28:19 one who chases f will have his fill of

FAR

Ge   18:25 F be it from you to do such
Nu   16: 3 "You have gone too f!
Jos   24:16 "F be it from us to forsake
1Sa   7:12 "Thus f has the LORD helped us."
      12:23 f be it from me that I should sin
Ps   22: 1 Why are you so f from saving me,
     103:12 as f as the east is from the west,
     119:155 Salvation is f from the wicked,
Pr   31:10 She is worth f more than rubies.
Isa   29:13 but their hearts are f from me.
      57:19 Peace, peace, to those f and near,"
Jer   23:23 "and not a God f away?
Mk   7: 6 but their hearts are f from me.

FARMER

Mk   4: 3 A f went out to sow his seed.
2Ti   2: 6 The hardworking f should be the first
Jas   5: 7 the f waits for the land

FARTHING (KJV) See PENNY

FASHIONED [FASHIONING]

Ex   39: 8 They **f** the breastpiece—
Isa   37:19 wood and stone, **f** by human hands.
      45:18 he who **f** and made the earth,

FASHIONING* [FASHIONED, FASHIONS]

Ex   32: 4 of a calf, **f** it with a tool.

FASHIONS [FASHIONING]

Isa   44:15 But he also **f** a god and worships it;

FAST [FASTED, FASTING]

Dt   10:20 Hold **f** to him and take your oaths
      11:22 to walk in all his ways and to hold **f**
      13: 4 and hold **f** to him.
      30:20 listen to his voice, and hold **f** to him.
Jos   22: 5 to hold **f** to him and to serve him
      23: 8 to hold **f** to the LORD your God,
1Ki   11: 2 Solomon held **f** to them in love.
2Ki   18: 6 He held **f** to the LORD and did
2Ch   20: 3 and he proclaimed a **f** for all Judah.
Ezr   8:21 I proclaimed a **f**,
Est   4:16 and **f** for me.
Ps   119:31 I hold **f** to your statutes, O LORD;
     139:10 your right hand will hold me **f**.
Isa   56: 4 and hold **f** to my covenant—
      58: 5 Is this the kind of **f** I have chosen,
Joel   1:14 Declare a holy **f;**
Jnh   3: 5 They declared a **f**, and all of them,
Mt   6:16 "When you **f**,
       9:14 that we and the Pharisees **f**,
1Pe   5:12 Stand **f** in it.

FASTED [FAST]

Isa   58: 3 'Why have we **f**, ' they say,
Zec   7: 5 was it really for me that you **f?**
Ac   13: 3 So after they had **f** and prayed,

FASTING [FAST]

Ps   35:13 and humbled myself with **f**.
Isa   58: 6 not this the kind of **f** I have chosen:
Da   9: 3 in **f**, and in sackcloth and ashes.
Mt   4: 2 After **f** forty days and forty nights,
       6:16 to show men they are **f**.
Ac   13: 2 they were worshiping the Lord and **f**,
      14:23 with prayer and **f**,

FAT [FATTENED]

Ge   4: 4 But Abel brought **f** portions
Lev   3:16 All the **f** is the LORD's.
Jdg   3:17 who was a very **f** man.
Ps   66:15 I will sacrifice **f** animals to you and
Eze   34:20 the **f** sheep and the lean sheep.

FATAL

Na   3:19 your wound; your injury is **f**.
Rev   13: 3 beast seemed to have had a **f** wound,

FATE

Job   20:29 Such is the **f** God allots the wicked,
Ps   49:13 This is the **f** of those who trust

Ecc   2:14 that the same **f** overtakes them both.

FATHER [FATHER-IN-LAW, FATHER'S,
FATHERED, FATHERLESS, FATHERS,
FOREFATHER, FOREFATHERS,
GRANDFATHER, GRANDFATHER'S]

Ge   2:24 this reason a man will leave his **f**
      17: 4 You will be the **f** of many nations.
      19:32 Let's get our **f** to drink wine and
      26:24 "I am the God of your **f** Abraham.
      27:38 you have only one blessing, my **f?**
      31: 5 the God of my **f** has been with me.
      46: 3 "I am God, the God of your **f,"**
Ex   20:12 "Honor your **f** and your mother,
      21:15 "Anyone who attacks his **f**
      21:17 "Anyone who curses his **f**
      22:17 If her **f** absolutely refuses to give her
Lev   18: 7 " 'Do not dishonor your **f**
      19: 3 of you must respect his mother and **f,**
      20: 9 " 'If anyone curses his **f** or mother,
      20: 9 He has cursed his **f** or his mother,
Dt   1:31 as a **f** carries his son,
       5:16 "Honor your **f** and your mother,
      21:18 who does not obey his **f** and mother
      32: 6 Is he not your **F,** your Creator,
Jdg   17:10 with me and be my **f** and priest,
      18:19 and be our **f** and priest.
Ru   4:22 and Jesse the **f** of David.
2Sa   7:14 I will be his **f,**
1Ki   2:12 on the throne of his **f** David,
1Ch   17:13 I will be his **f,**
      22:10 and I will be his **f.**
      28: 6 and I will be his **f.**
      29:10 O LORD, God of our **f** Israel,
Job   38:28 Does the rain have a **f?**
Ps   2: 7 today I have become your **F.**
      27:10 my **f** and mother forsake me,
      68: 5 A **f** to the fatherless,
      89:26 'You are my **F,** my God,
     103:13 a **f** has compassion on his children,
Pr   3:12 as a **f** the son he delights in.
      10: 1 A wise son brings joy to his **f,**
      15:20 A wise son brings joy to his **f,**
      17:21 no joy for the **f** of a fool.
      17:25 A foolish son brings grief to his **f**
      19:26 He who robs his **f**
      20:20 If a man curses his **f** or mother,
      23:22 Listen to your **f,** who gave you life,
      23:24 **f** of a righteous man has great joy;
      28: 7 companion of gluttons disgraces his **f**
      28:24 He who robs his **f** or mother
      29: 3 loves wisdom brings joy to his **f,**
Isa   8: 4 how to say 'My **f**' or 'My mother, '
       9: 6 Everlasting, Prince of Peace.
      43:27 Your first **f** sinned;
      45:10 Woe to him who says to his **f,**
      63:16 O LORD, are our **F,**
Jer   2:27 They say to wood, 'You are my **f,** '
       3:19 I thought you would call me '**F**' and
      31: 9 because I am Israel's **f,**
Eze   18:19 the son not share the guilt of his **f?'**
Mic   7: 6 For a son dishonors his **f,**
Mal   1: 6 "A son honors his **f,**

	2:10	Have we not all one **F**?
Mt	3: 9	'We have Abraham as our **f.**'
	5:16	and praise your **F** in heaven.
	6: 9	you should pray: " 'Our **F** in heaven,
	6:14	heavenly **F** will also forgive you.
	6:15	your **F** will not forgive your sins.
	6:26	and yet your heavenly **F** feeds them.
	10:37	"Anyone who loves his **f**
	11:27	No one knows the Son except the **F,**
	15: 4	'Honor your **f** and mother'
	18:10	always see the face of my **F**
	19: 5	a man will leave his **f** and mother
	19:19	honor your **f** and mother, '
	19:29	or sisters or **f** or mother
	23: 9	And do not call anyone on earth '**f,** '
	28:19	baptizing them in the name of the **F**
Mk	14:36	"Abba, **F,**" he said,
Lk	1:32	the throne of his **f** David,
	6:36	just as your **F** is merciful.
	9:59	Lord, first let me go and bury my **f.**"
	11: 2	" '**F,** hallowed be your name,
	12:30	your **F** knows that you need them.
	12:53	**f** against son and son against **f,**
	14:26	not hate his **f** and mother,
	15:12	'**F,** give me my share of the estate.'
	16:24	So he called to him, '**F** Abraham,
	18:20	honor your **f** and mother.' "
	23:34	Jesus said, "**F,** forgive them,
Jn	1:14	who came from the **F,**
	3:35	The **F** loves the Son
	4:23	worship the **F** in spirit and truth,
	5:17	"My **F** is always at his work
	5:18	he was even calling God his own **F,**
	5:20	For the **F** loves the Son
	6:44	unless the **F** who sent him draws him,
	6:46	No one has seen the **F** except
	8:19	"You do not know me or my **F,**"
	8:28	speak just what the **F** has taught me.
	8:41	The only **F** we have is God himself.'"
	8:44	You belong to your **f,** the devil,
	10:17	The reason my **F** loves me is
	10:30	I and the **F** are one."
	10:38	the **F** is in me, and I in the **F.**"
	12:27	'**F,** save me from this hour'?
	14: 6	No one comes to the **F** except
	14: 9	who has seen me has seen the **F.**
	14:11	that I am in the **F** and the **F** is in me;
	14:21	loves me will be loved by my **F,**
	14:28	be glad that I am going to the **F,**
	15: 9	**F** has loved me, so have I loved you.
	15:23	He who hates me hates my **F**
	20:17	for I have not yet returned to the **F.**
	20:21	**F** has sent me, I am sending you."
Ac	1: 4	but wait for the gift my **F** promised,
	13:33	today I have become your **F.**'
Ro	4:11	he is the **f** of all who believe
	4:16	He is the **f** of us all.
	8:15	And by him we cry, "Abba, **F.**"
1Co	4:15	for in Christ Jesus I became your **f**
2Co	1: 3	the **F** of compassion and the God
	6:18	"I will be a **F** to you,
Gal	4: 6	the Spirit who calls out, "Abba, **F.**"
Eph	5:31	a man will leave his **f** and mother
	6: 2	"Honor your **f** and mother"—

Php	2:11	to the glory of God the **F.**
1Th	2:11	as a **f** deals with his own children,
Heb	1: 5	today I have become your **F**"?
	1: 5	Or again,"I will be his **F,**
	12: 7	what son is not disciplined by his **f?**
	12: 9	we submit to the **F** of our spirits
Jas	1:17	from the **F** of the heavenly lights,
1Jn	1: 3	And our fellowship is with the **F** and
	2:15	the love of the **F** is not in him.
	2:22	he denies the **F** and the Son.
	3: 1	the love the **F** has lavished on us,
2Jn	1: 9	has both the **F** and the Son.
Rev	2:27	I have received authority from my **F.**
	3: 5	acknowledge his name before my **F**
	3:21	sat down with my **F** on his throne.

FATHER ABRAHAM Ge 22:7; 26:3, 15, 18, 24; 28:13; 32:9; Jos 24:2, 3; Lk 1:73; 16:24, 30; Jn 8:53, 56; Ac 7:2; Ro 4:12

FATHER IN HEAVEN Mt 5:16, 45; 6:1, 9; 7:11; 10:32, 33; 12:50; 16:17; 18:10, 14, 19; Mk 11:25; Lk 11:13

HEAVENLY FATHER Mt 5:48; 6:14, 26, 32; 15:13; 18:35

GOD AND FATHER See GOD

GOD OF ... FATHER See GOD

GOD THE FATHER See GOD

FATHER'S [FATHER]

Ge	12: 1	your people and your **f** household
	27:34	When Esau heard his **f** words,
	31:19	Rachel stole her **f** household gods.
	49: 4	for you went up onto your **f** bed,
Ex	15: 2	my **f** God, and I will exalt him.
	18: 4	"My **f** God was my helper;
2Sa	16:21	"Lie with your **f** concubines
Est	4:14	you and your **f** family will perish.
Pr	4: 1	Listen, my sons, to a **f** instruction;
	13: 1	A wise son heeds his **f** instruction,
	15: 5	A fool spurns his **f** discipline,
	19:13	A foolish son is his **f** ruin,
Eze	18:17	He will not die for his **f** sin;
Mt	16:27	in his **F** glory with his angels,
Lk	2:49	I had to be in my **F** house?"
Jn	1:18	who is at the **F** side,
	2:16	How dare you turn my **F** house into
	5:43	I have come in my **F** name,
	10:29	snatch them out of my **F** hand.
	14: 2	In my **F** house are many rooms;
	15: 8	This is to my **F** glory,
Rev	14: 1	his **F** name written on their foreheads

FATHER'S HOUSE See HOUSE

FATHER-IN-LAW [FATHER]

Ex	18: 8	Moses told his **f** about everything
Jn	18:13	who was the **f** of Caiaphas,

FATHERED* [FATHER]

Dt	32:18	You deserted the Rock, who **f** you;

FATHERLESS [FATHER]

Dt	10:18	He defends the cause of the **f** and
	14:29	the **f** and the widows who live
	24:17	Do not deprive the alien or the **f**

24:19 the **f** and the widow,
26:12 the alien, the **f** and the widow,
Ps 10:14 you are the helper of the **f.**
68: 5 A father to the **f,**
82: 3 Defend the cause of the weak and **f;**
Pr 23:10 or encroach on the fields of the **f,**
Isa 1:17 Defend the cause of the **f,**
Jer 5:28 not plead the case of the **f**
Hos 14: 3 for in you the **f** find compassion."
Mal 3: 5 who oppress the widows and the **f,**

FATHERS [FATHER]

Ex 3:15 'The LORD, the God of your **f**—
20: 5 for the sin of the **f** to
Dt 5: 3 It was not with our **f** that the LORD
24:16 nor children put to death for their **f;**
30: 9 just as he delighted in your **f,**
32:17 gods your **f** did not fear.
Jos 24: 6 When I brought your **f** out of Egypt,
1Ki 8:57 be with us as he was with our **f;**
Ezr 5:12 our **f** angered the God of heaven,
10:11 the God of your **f,** and do his will.
Ps 22: 4 In you our **f** put their trust;
Isa 49:23 Kings will be your foster **f,**
Jer 31:29 'The **f** have eaten sour grapes,
La 5: 7 Our **f** sinned and are no more,
Eze 18: 2 " 'The **f** eat sour grapes,
Mal 4: 6 the hearts of the **f** to their children,
4: 6 the hearts of the children to their **f;**
Lk 1:17 the hearts of the **f** to their children
11:11 "Which of you **f,**
Jn 4:20 Our **f** worshiped on this mountain,
1Co 4:15 you do not have many **f,**
Eph 6: 4 **F,** do not exasperate your children;
Col 3:21 **F,** do not embitter your children,
1Ti 1: 9 for those who kill their **f** or mothers,
Heb 12: 9 all had human **f** who disciplined us
2Pe 3: 4 Ever since our **f** died,
1Jn 2:13 I write to you, **f,**

GOD OF ... FATHERS See GOD

FATHOM* [FATHOMED]

Job 11: 7 "Can you **f** the mysteries of God?
Ps 145: 3 his greatness no one can **f.**
Ecc 3:11 yet they cannot **f** what God has done
Isa 40:28 and his understanding no one can **f.**
1Co 13: 2 of prophecy and can **f** all mysteries

FATHOMED* [FATHOM]

Job 5: 9 performs wonders that cannot be **f,**
9:10 performs wonders that cannot be **f,**

FATTENED [FAT]

2Sa 6:13 he sacrificed a bull and a **f** calf.
Pr 15:17 than a **f** calf with hatred.
Isa 1:11 of rams and the fat of **f** animals;
Lk 15:23 Bring the **f** calf and kill it.
Jas 5: 5 You have **f** yourselves in the day

FAULT [FAULTFINDERS, FAULTLESS, FAULTS, FAULTY]

1Sa 29: 3 I have found no **f** in him."
Job 33:10 Yet God has found **f** with me;
Jer 2: 5 "What **f** did your fathers find in me,

Jnh 1:12 I know that it is my **f**
Mt 18:15 go and show him his **f,**
Php 2:15 children of God without **f** in a
Jas 1: 5 generously to all without finding **f,**
3: 2 anyone is never at **f** in what he says,
Jude 1:24 without **f** and with great joy—

FAULTFINDERS* [FAULT, FIND]

Jude 1:16 These men are grumblers and **f;**

FAULTLESS* [FAULT]

Pr 8: 9 are **f** to those who have knowledge.
Php 3: 6 as for legalistic righteousness, **f.**
Jas 1:27 accepts as pure and **f** is this:

FAULTS* [FAULT]

Job 10: 6 that you must search out my **f**
Ps 19:12 Forgive my hidden **f.**

FAULTY* [FAULT]

Ps 78:57 as unreliable as a **f** bow.
Hos 7:16 they are like a **f** bow.

FAVOR [FAVORABLE, FAVORABLY, FAVORED, FAVORITISM, FAVORS]

Ge 4: 4 The LORD looked with **f** on Abel
6: 8 But Noah found **f** in the eyes of
Ex 33:12 and you have found **f** with me.'
34: 9 if I have found **f** in your eyes,"
Lev 26: 9 on you with **f** and make you fruitful
Nu 11:15 if I have found **f** in your eyes—
Jdg 6:17 "If now I have found **f** in your eyes,
1Sa 2:26 in stature and in **f** with the LORD
2Sa 2: 6 and I too will show you the same **f**
2Ki 13: 4 Jehoahaz sought the LORD's **f,**
2Ch 33:12 the **f** of the LORD his God
Ezr 7:28 and who has extended his good **f**
Ne 5:19 Remember me with **f,** O my God,
13:31 Remember me with **f,** O my God.
Est 2:15 And Esther won the **f** of everyone
7: 3 "If I have found **f** with you, O king,
Ps 30: 5 but his **f** lasts a lifetime;
77: 7 Will he never show his **f** again?
90:17 May the **f** of the Lord our God rest
Pr 8:35 and receives **f** from the LORD.
13:15 Good understanding wins **f,**
18:22 and receives **f** from the LORD.
19: 6 Many curry **f** with a ruler,
Isa 49: 8 In the time of my **f** I will answer you,
61: 2 the year of the LORD's **f** and
Eze 36: 9 for you and will look on you with **f;**
Zec 11: 7 two staffs and called one **F** and
Lk 1:30 Mary, you have found **f** with God.
2:14 peace to men on whom his **f** rests."
2:52 and in **f** with God and men.
4:19 to proclaim the year of the Lord's **f."**
Jn 5:32 There is another who testifies in my **f**
Ac 2:47 and enjoying the **f** of all the people.
2Co 6: 2 now is the time of God's **f,**

FAVOR IN ... EYES See EYES

FAVORABLE [FAVOR]

Jer 42: 6 Whether it is **f** or unfavorable,

FAVORABLY [FAVOR]

Ex   3:21 I will make the Egyptians **f** disposed
     11: 3 LORD made the Egyptians **f** disposed

FAVORED [FAVOR]

Ps   30: 7 O LORD, when you **f** me,
Lk   1:28 "Greetings, you who are highly **f!**
     1:43 But why am I so **f,**

FAVORITISM* [FAVOR]

Ex   23: 3 and do not show **f** to a poor man
Lev 19:15 not show partiality to the poor or **f** to
Ac 10:34 that God does not show **f**
Ro   2:11 For God does not show **f.**
Eph 6: 9 and there is no **f** with him.
Col 3:25 and there is no **f.**
1Ti 5:21 and to do nothing out of **f.**
Jas   2: 1 don't show **f.**
     2: 9 But if you show **f,**

FAVORS [FAVOR]

Ecc 9: 7 for it is now that God **f** what you do.

FAWNS

Ge 49:21 a doe set free that bears beautiful **f.**
SS   4: 5 Your two breasts are like two **f,**

FEAR [AFRAID, FEARED, FEARFUL, FEARFULLY, FEARLESSLY, FEARS, FRIGHTEN, FRIGHTENED, GOD-FEARING]

Ge   9: 2 The **f** and dread of you will fall
   22:12 Now I know that you **f** God,
   31:42 God of Abraham and the **F** of Isaac,
Ex   9:30 still do not **f** the LORD God."
   20:20 so that the **f** of God will be with you
Dt   2:25 and **f** of you on all the nations
   6:13 **F** the LORD your God,
  10:12 but to **f** the LORD your God,
  31:12 to **f** the LORD your God
Jos   2:24 the people are melting in **f** because
   4:24 and so that you might always **f**
  24:14 "Now **f** the LORD and serve him
1Sa 12:14 If you **f** the LORD and serve
  12:24 But be sure to **f** the LORD
2Sa 23: 3 when he rules in the **f** of God,
1Ki 8:43 may know your name and **f** you,
2Ch 19: 7 the **f** of the LORD be upon you.
   26: 5 who instructed him in the **f** of God.
Ezr 3: 3 Despite their **f** of the peoples
Est 8:17 because **f** of the Jews had seized
Job 1: 9 "Does Job **f** God for nothing?"
   6:14 he forsakes the **f** of the Almighty.
Ps   2:11 Serve the LORD with **f** and rejoice
   3: 6 I will not **f** the tens of thousands
  15: 4 but honors those who **f** the LORD,
  19: 9 The **f** of the LORD is pure,
  23: 4 I will **f** no evil, for you are with me;
  27: 1 and my salvation—whom shall I **f?**
  33: 8 Let all the earth **f** the LORD,
  34: 7 encamps around those who **f** him,
  34: 9 **F** the LORD, you his saints,
  34: 9 for those who **f** him lack nothing.

  34:11 I will teach you the **f** of the LORD.
  46: 2 Therefore we will not **f,**
  55:19 and have no **f** of God.
  67: 7 all the ends of the earth will **f** him.
  86:11 that I may **f** your name.
  90:11 For your wrath is as great as the **f**
  91: 5 You will not **f** the terror of night,
 111:10 The **f** of the LORD is the beginning
 118: 4 Let those who **f** the LORD say:
 119:63 I am a friend to all who **f** you,
 128: 1 Blessed are all who **f** the LORD,
 145:19 the desires of those who **f** him;
 147:11 LORD delights in those who **f** him,
Pr   1: 7 The **f** of the LORD is the beginning
  1:29 and did not choose to **f** the LORD,
  1:33 without **f** of harm."
  3: 7 **f** the LORD and shun evil.
  8:13 To **f** the LORD is to hate evil;
  9:10 "The **f** of the LORD is the beginning
 10:27 **f** of the LORD adds length to life,
 14:27 **f** of the LORD is a fountain of life,
 15:33 **f** of the LORD teaches a man wisdom,
 16: 6 the **f** of the LORD a man avoids evil.
 19:23 The **f** of the LORD leads to life:
 22: 4 and the **f** of the LORD bring wealth
 29:25 **F** of man will prove to be a snare,
 31:21 she has no **f** for her household;
Ecc 8:13 because the wicked do not **f** God,
  12:13 **F** God and keep his commandments,
Isa 8:12 do not **f** what they **f,**
  11: 3 he will delight in the **f** of the LORD.
  33: 6 the **f** of the LORD is the key
  35: 4 "Be strong, do not **f;**
  41:10 So do not **f,** for I am with you;
  41:13 Do not **f;** I will help you.
  43: 1 "**F** not, for I have redeemed you;
  51: 7 Do not **f** the reproach of men
  54:14 you will have nothing to **f.**
Jer   5:22 Should you not **f** me?"
  17: 8 It does not **f** when heat comes;
  30:10 " 'So do not **f,** O Jacob my servant;
Mic 6: 9 and to **f** your name is wisdom—
Zep 3:15 never again will you **f** any harm.
Lk 12: 5 I will show you whom you should **f:**
  18: 4 I don't **f** God or care about men,
Jn 12:42 not confess their faith for **f**
  20:19 the doors locked for **f** of the Jews,
Ac   5:11 Great **f** seized the whole church
Ro   8:15 that makes you a slave again to **f,**
  13: 3 Do you want to be free from **f** of
2Co 5:11 we know what it is to **f** the Lord,
Gal 4:11 I **f** for you,
Php 2:12 to work out your salvation with **f**
Heb 2:15 in slavery by their **f** of death.
1Pe 1:17 as strangers here in reverent **f.**
  3:14 "Do not **f** what they **f;**
1Jn 4:18 There is no **f** in love. But perfect love drives out **f,** because **f** has to do with punishment.
Jude 1:23 to others show mercy, mixed with **f**
Rev 14: 7 "**F** God and give him glory,
  15: 4 Who will not **f** you, O Lord,

DO NOT FEAR Ex 9:30; Ecc 8:13; Isa 8:12; 35:4; 41:10, 13; 51:7; 54:4; 57:11; Jer 10:5;

30:10; 46:27, 28; La 3:57; Zep 3:16; Hag 2:5;
Mal 3:5; 1Pe 3:14

FEAR GOD Ge 22:12; 42:18; Ex 18:21; Job 1:9;
Ps 66:16; Ecc 8:13; 12:13; Lk 18:4; 23:40; 1Pe
2:17; Rev 14:7

FEAR OF GOD Ge 20:11; Ex 20:20; Dt 25:18;
2Sa 23:3; 2Ch 20:29; 26:5; Ps 36:1; 55:19; Ro
3:18

FEAR OF THE †LORD 2Ch 17:10; 19:7, 9;
Ps 19:9; 34:11; 111:10; Pr 1:7; 2:5; 9:10; 10:27;
14:27; 15:16, 33; 16:6; 19:23; 22:4; 23:17; Isa
11:2, 3; 33:6

FEAR THE †LORD Ex 9:30; Dt 6:2, 13, 24;
10:12, 20; 31:12, 13; Jos 4:24; 24:14; 1Sa 12:14,
24; Ps 15:4; 22:23; 33:8; 34:9; 115:13; 118:4;
128:1; Pr 1:29; 3:7; 8:13; 24:21; Jer 5:24; 26:19

FEARED [FEAR]

Ex   1:21 And because the midwives f God,
       14:31 the people f the LORD
Job   1: 1 he f God and shunned evil.
Ps   76: 7 You alone are to be f.
      89: 7 of the holy ones God is greatly f;
Jnh   1:16 the men greatly f the LORD,
Hag   1:12 And the people f the LORD.
Mal   1:14 "and my name is to be f among
       3:16 Then those who f the LORD talked
Mk   6:20 Herod f John and protected him,
Jn   19:38 but secretly because he f the Jews.

FEARFUL [FEAR]

Heb   10:27 but only a f expectation of judgment

FEARFULLY* [FEAR]

Ps   139:14 I am f and wonderfully made;

FEARLESSLY* [FEAR]

Ac   9:27 how in Damascus he had preached f
Eph   6:19 so that I will f make known
       6:20 Pray that I may declare it f,
Php   1:14 of God more courageously and f.

FEARS [FEAR]

Job   1: 8 a man who f God and shuns evil."
       2: 3 a man who f God and shuns evil.
Ps   34: 4 delivered me from all my f.
      112: 1 the man who f the LORD,
Pr   14:16 A wise man f the LORD
      14:26 He who f the LORD has
      31:30 but a woman who f the LORD
Ecc   7:18 The man who f God will avoid all
2Co   7: 5 on the outside, f within.
1Jn   4:18 The one who f is not made perfect

FEAST [FEASTING, FEASTS]

Ex   12:17 the F of Unleavened Bread,
      23:16 the F of Harvest with the firstfruits
      23:16 "Celebrate the F of Ingathering at
      34:18 the F of Unleavened Bread.
      34:22 "Celebrate the F of Weeks
Lev   23:34 the LORD's F of Tabernacles begins,
Dt   16:14 Be joyful at your F—

2Ch   8:13 the F of Unleavened Bread, the F of
                Weeks and the F of Tabernacles.
Ezr   3: 4 they celebrated the F of Tabernacles
Ne   8:18 They celebrated the f for seven days,
Pr   15:15 the cheerful heart has a continual f.
Ecc   10:19 A f is made for laughter,
Isa   25: 6 will prepare a f of rich food
Zec   14:16 to celebrate the F of Tabernacles.
Mt   8:11 their places at the f with Abraham,
Mk   14: 2 "But not during the F," they said,
      15: 6 custom at the F to release a prisoner
Lk   2:41 for the F of the Passover.
      14: 8 someone invites you to a wedding f,
Jn   2:23 in Jerusalem at the Passover F,
       7: 2 Jewish F of Tabernacles was near,
       7:37 On the last and greatest day of the F,
      10:22 the F of Dedication at Jerusalem.
      13: 1 It was just before the Passover F.
2Pe   2:13 in their pleasures while they f

FEAST OF TABERNACLES Lev 23:34; Dt
16:13, 16; 31:10; 2Ch 8:13; Ezr 3:4; Zec 14:16,
18, 19; Jn 7:2

FEAST OF UNLEAVENED BREAD   Ex
12:17; 23:15; 34:18; Lev 23:6; Dt 16:16; 2Ch
8:13; 30:13, 21; 35:17; Ezr 6:22; Mt 26:17; Mk
14:1, 12; Lk 22:1; Ac 12:3; 20:6

FEASTING [FEAST]

Est   9:17 and made it a day of f and joy.
Job   1:13 were f and drinking wine
Pr   17: 1 and quiet than a house full of f,
Zec   7: 6 were you not just f for yourselves?

FEASTS [FEAST]

Lev   23: 2 'These are my appointed f,
Nu   10:10 appointed f and New Moon festivals
Job   1: 4 His sons used to take turns holding f
La   1: 4 for no one comes to her appointed f.
Am   5:21 "I hate, I despise your religious f;
Zep   3:18 "The sorrows for the appointed f
Jude   1:12 are blemishes at your love f,

APPOINTED FEASTS See APPOINTED

FEATHERS

Ps   91: 4 He will cover you with his f,
Eze   17: 3 long f and full plumage
Da   4:33 his hair grew like the f of an eagle

FEATURES

1Sa   16:12 a fine appearance and handsome f.
Est   2: 7 was lovely in form and f,

FED [FEED]

Hos   13: 6 When I f them, they were satisfied;
Lk   6:25 Woe to you who are well f now,
Php   4:12 whether well f or hungry,
Jas   2:16 keep warm and well f,"

FEEBLE

Job   4: 3 how you have strengthened f hands.
Ps   38: 8 I am f and utterly crushed;
Isa   35: 3 Strengthen the f hands,
Heb   12:12 strengthen your f arms

FEED [FED, FEEDS]

1Ki	17: 4	the ravens to **f** you there."
Isa	9:20	Each will **f** on the flesh
	11: 7	The cow will **f** with the bear,
	65:25	wolf and the lamb will **f** together,
Eze	34:14	and there they will **f** in a rich pasture
Hos	11: 4	and bent down to **f** them.
Mt	25:37	did we see you hungry and **f** you,
Mk	8: 4	get enough bread to **f** them?"
Jn	21:15	Jesus said, **"F** my lambs."
	21:17	Jesus said, **"F** my sheep.
Ro	12:20	"If your enemy is hungry, **f** him;
Jude	1:12	shepherds who **f** only themselves.

FEEDS [FEED]

Pr	15:14	but the mouth of a fool **f** on folly.
Isa	44:20	He **f** on ashes,
Hos	12: 1	Ephraim **f** on the wind;
Mic	3: 5	if one **f** them, they proclaim 'peace';
Mt	6:26	and yet your heavenly Father **f** them.
Jn	6:57	so the one who **f** on me will live

FEEL [FELT]

Jdg	16:26	where I can **f** the pillars that support
Ps	115: 7	they have hands, but cannot **f**,
2Co	11:29	Who is weak, and I do not **f** weak?

FEET [FOOT]

Ge	6:15	The ark is to be 450 **f** long,
	8: 9	dove could find no place to set its **f**
Ex	12:11	your sandals on your **f** and your staff
	24:10	his **f** was something like a pavement
	30:21	they shall wash their hands and **f** so
Dt	1:36	the land he set his **f** on,
	8: 4	not wear out and your **f** did not swell
Jos	3:15	and their **f** touched the water's edge,
Ru	3: 8	a woman lying at his **f**.
1Sa	2: 9	He will guard the **f** of his saints,
	17: 4	He was over nine **f** tall.
2Sa	22:34	He makes my **f** like the **f** of a deer;
Ps	8: 6	you put everything under his **f**:
	22:16	have pierced my hands and my **f**.
	40: 2	he set my **f** on a rock
	56:13	and my **f** from stumbling,
	66: 9	and kept our **f** from slipping.
	73: 2	as for me, my **f** had almost slipped;
	110: 1	your enemies a footstool for your **f**."
	115: 7	**f**, but they cannot walk;
	119:105	Your word is a lamp to my **f** and
Pr	4:26	Make level paths for your **f**
	5: 5	Her **f** go down to death;
	6:18	**f** that are quick to rush into evil,
Isa	6: 2	with two they covered their **f**,
	52: 7	the **f** of those who bring good news,
Eze	34:18	and muddy the rest with your **f**?
Da	2:33	its **f** partly of iron and partly
Na	1: 3	and clouds are the dust of his **f**.
	1:15	the **f** of one who brings good news,
Hab	3:19	he makes my **f** like the **f** of a deer,
Zec	14: 4	On that day his **f** will stand on
Mt	7: 6	they may trample them under their **f**,
	10:14	shake the dust off your **f**
	22:44	I put your enemies under your **f**." '
Lk	1:79	to guide our **f** into the path

	7:38	she began to wet his **f** with her tears.
	8:35	sitting at Jesus' **f**,
	24:39	Look at my hands and my **f**.
Jn	13: 5	and began to wash his disciples' **f**,
Ac	2:35	your enemies a footstool for your **f**."
	4:35	and put it at the apostles' **f**,
Ro	3:15	"Their **f** are swift to shed blood;
	10:15	"How beautiful are the **f**
	16:20	will soon crush Satan under your **f**.
1Co	12:21	And the head cannot say to the **f**,
	15:25	put all his enemies under his **f**.
Eph	1:22	God placed all things under his **f**
	6:15	with your **f** fitted with the readiness
1Ti	5:10	washing the **f** of the saints,
Heb	1:13	a footstool for your **f"**?
	2: 8	and put everything under his **f."**
	12:13	"Make level paths for your **f,"**
Rev	1:15	His **f** were like bronze glowing in

FELIX

Governor before whom Paul was tried (Ac 23:23-24:27).

FELL [FALL]

Ge	7:12	And rain **f** on the earth forty days
	15:12	Abram **f** into a deep sleep,
Nu	3: 4	**f** dead before the LORD
1Sa	4:18	Eli **f** backward off his chair by
	31: 4	so Saul took his own sword and **f**
1Ki	18:38	the fire of the LORD **f** and burned
2Ki	1:10	Then fire **f** from heaven
Job	1:16	"The fire of God **f** from the sky
Mt	25: 5	they all became drowsy and **f** asleep.
Mk	4: 8	Still other seed **f** on good soil.
Jn	18: 6	they drew back and **f** to the ground.
Ac	5: 5	he **f** down and died.
Heb	11:30	By faith the walls of Jericho **f**,
Rev	1:17	I **f** at his feet as though dead.
	5:14	the elders **f** down and worshiped.
	6:13	and the stars in the sky **f** to earth,

FELLOW [FELLOWMAN, FELLOWSHIP]

1Co	3: 9	For we are God's **f** workers;
2Co	6: 1	As God's **f** workers we urge you not
Eph	2:19	but **f** citizens with God's people
Heb	13: 3	as if you were their **f** prisoners,
1Pe	5: 1	I appeal as a **f** elder,
Rev	22: 9	I am a **f** servant with you and

FELLOWMAN [FELLOW, MAN]

Ps	15: 3	and casts no slur on his **f**,
Ro	13: 8	for he who loves his **f** has fulfilled

FELLOWSHIP [FELLOW]

Ex	20:24	your burnt offerings and **f** offerings,
Lev	3: 1	someone's offering is a **f** offering,
Ac	2:42	the apostles' teaching and to the **f**,
1Co	1: 9	who has called you into **f**
	5: 2	and have put out of your **f**
2Co	6:14	what **f** can light have with darkness?
	13:14	**f** of the Holy Spirit be with you all.
Gal	2: 9	and Barnabas the right hand of **f**
Php	2: 1	if any **f** with the Spirit,

3:10 and the **f** of sharing in his sufferings,
1Jn 1: 3 so that you also may have **f** with us.
1: 3 And our **f** is with the Father and
1: 6 If we claim to have **f** with him
1: 7 we have **f** with one another,

FELLOWSHIP OFFERING Lev 3:1, 3, 6, 9;
4:10, 26, 31, 35; 7:11, 13, 15, 18, 20, 21, 29, 33,
37; 9:4, 18, 22; 19:5; 22:21; 23:19; Nu 6:14, 17,
18; 7:17, 23, 29, 35, 41, 47, 53, 59, 65, 71, 77, 83,
88; 15:8

FELLOWSHIP OFFERINGS Ex 20:24; 24:5;
29:28; 32:6; Lev 6:12; 7:14, 32, 34; 10:14; 17:5;
Nu 10:10; 29:39; Dt 27:7; Jos 8:31; 22:23, 27;
Jdg 20:26; 21:4; 1Sa 10:8; 11:15; 13:9; 2Sa 6:17,
18; 24:25; 1Ki 3:15; 8:63, 64, 64; 9:25; 2Ki
16:13; 1Ch 16:1, 2; 21:26; 2Ch 7:7; 29:35;
30:22; 31:2; 33:16; Pr 7:14; Eze 43:27; 45:15,
17; 46:2, 12, 12; Am 5:22

FELT [FEEL]
Ex 10:21 darkness that can be **f."**
2Co 1: 9 our hearts we **f** the sentence of death.

FEMALE
Ge 1:27 male and **f** he created them.
5: 2 He created them male and **f**
6:19 two of all living creatures, male and **f**
Mt 19: 4 the Creator 'made them male and **f, '**
Mk 10: 6 God 'made them male and **f.'**
Gal 3:28 slave nor free, male nor **f,**

FERMENTED
Lev 10: 9 not to drink wine or other **f** drink
Nu 6: 3 from wine and other **f** drink
Dt 14:26 sheep, wine or other **f** drink,
Lk 1:15 to take wine or other **f** drink,

FEROCIOUS
Ge 37:33 Some **f** animal has devoured him.
Mt 7:15 but inwardly they are **f** wolves.

FERTILE [FERTILIZE]
Isa 5: 1 had a vineyard on a **f** hillside.
32:15 and the desert becomes a **f** field,
Jer 2: 7 I brought you into a **f** land

FERTILIZE* [FERTILE]
Lk 13: 8 and I'll dig around it and **f** it.

FERVENT* [FERVOR]
Pr 26:23 are **f** lips with an evil heart.

FERVOR* [FERVENT]
Ac 18:25 and he spoke with great **f** and taught
Ro 12:11 but keep your spiritual **f,**

FESTIVAL [FESTIVALS]
Ex 5: 1 so that they may hold a **f** to me in
23:14 times a year you are to celebrate a **f**
1Co 5: 8 Therefore let us keep the **F,**
Col 2:16 or with regard to a religious **f,**

FESTIVALS [FESTIVAL]
Hos 2:11 stop all her celebrations: her yearly **f,**
Na 1:15 Celebrate your **f,** O Judah,

FESTUS [PORCIUS]
Governor who sent Paul to Caesar (Ac 25-26).

FETTERS
Ps 2: 3 they say, "and throw off their **f."**

FEVER
Lev 26:16 and **f** that will destroy your sight
Job 30:30 my body burns with **f.**
Mk 1:30 mother-in-law was in bed with a **f,**
Lk 4:39 he bent over her and rebuked the **f,**
Jn 4:52 "The **f** left him yesterday at
Ac 28: 8 suffering from **f** and dysentery.

FEW [FEWEST]
Ge 47: 9 My years have been **f** and difficult,
Dt 26: 5 down into Egypt with a **f** people
1Ch 16:19 they were but **f** in number, **f** indeed,
Job 14: 1 "Man born of woman is of **f** days
Ecc 5: 2 so let your words be **f.**
Mt 7:14 and only a **f** find it.
22:14 many are invited, but **f** are chosen."
25:21 have been faithful with a **f** things;
Lk 10: 2 but the workers are **f.**

FEWEST* [FEW]
Dt 7: 7 for you were the **f** of all peoples.

FIELD [FIELDS, GRAINFIELD, GRAINFIELDS]
Ge 4: 8 "Let's go out to the **f."**
23:17 So Ephron's **f** in Machpelah
Lev 19: 9 not reap to the very edges of your **f**
19:19 not plant your **f** with two kinds
Ru 2: 3 in a **f** belonging to Boaz,
Ps 50:11 and the creatures of the **f** are mine.
103:15 he flourishes like a flower of the **f;**
Pr 24:30 I went past the **f** of the sluggard,
31:16 She considers a **f** and buys it;
Isa 1: 8 like a hut in a **f** of melons,
5: 8 and join **f** to **f** till no space is left
40: 6 glory is like the flowers of the **f.**
Jer 32: 7 'Buy my **f** at Anathoth,
Mt 6:28 See how the lilies of the **f** grow.
6:30 how God clothes the grass of the **f,**
13:38 The **f** is the world,
13:44 like treasure hidden in a **f.**
24:40 Two men will be in the **f;**
27: 8 called the **F** of Blood to this day.
Lk 14:18 first said, 'I have just bought a **f,**
Ac 1:18 Judas bought a **f;**
1Co 3: 9 fellow workers; you are God's **f,**
2Co 10:13 to the **f** God has assigned to us,
1Pe 1:24 glory is like the flowers of the **f;**

FIELDS [FIELD]
Ex 23:10 "For six years you are to sow your **f**
Ru 2: 2 "Let me go to the **f**
Ne 5: 3 "We are mortgaging our **f,**
Ps 96:12 let the **f** be jubilant,
144:13 by tens of thousands in our **f;**
Isa 32:12 Beat your breasts for the pleasant **f,**
Mic 2: 2 They covet **f** and seize them,
Lk 2: 8 shepherds living out in the **f** nearby,

Jn   4:35 open your eyes and look at the **f**!

FIERCE

Ge	49: 7	Cursed be their anger, so **f**,
Ex	32:12	Turn from your **f** anger;
Nu	25: 4	the LORD's **f** anger may turn away
Jos	7:26	the LORD turned from his **f** anger.
Ps	85: 3	and turned from your **f** anger.
Jer	30:24	The **f** anger of the LORD will not
Hos	11: 9	I will not carry out my **f** anger,
Jnh	3: 9	compassion turn from his **f** anger
Na	1: 6	Who can endure his **f** anger?

FIERY [FIRE]

Ps	11: 6	On the wicked he will rain **f** coals
Eze	21:31	upon you and breathe out my **f** anger
Mt	13:50	and throw them into the **f** furnace.
Rev	10: 1	and his legs were like **f** pillars.
	19:20	into the **f** lake of burning sulfur.
	21: 8	be in the **f** lake of burning sulfur.

FIFTIETH [FIFTY]

Lev 25:11 The **f** year shall be a jubilee for you;

FIFTY [FIFTIETH, 50]

Ge	18:24	What if there are **f** righteous people
Lev	23:16	Count off **f** days up to the day after
Jn	8:57	"You are not yet **f** years old,"

FIG [FIGS, SYCAMORE-FIG]

Ge	3: 7	so they sewed **f** leaves together
Jdg	9:10	"Next, the trees said to the **f** tree,
1Ki	4:25	under his own vine and **f** tree.
Pr	27:18	tends a **f** tree will eat its fruit,
Hos	9:10	seeing the early fruit on the **f** tree.
Mic	4: 4	under his own **f** tree,
Na	3:12	like **f** trees with their first ripe fruit;
Hab	3:17	Though the **f** tree does not bud
Zec	3:10	to sit under his vine and **f** tree, '
Mt	21:19	Seeing a **f** tree by the road,
	24:32	learn this lesson from the **f** tree:
Lk	13: 6	"A man had a **f** tree,
Jn	1:48	while you were still under the **f** tree
Jas	3:12	My brothers, can a **f** tree bear olives,
Rev	6:13	as late figs drop from a **f** tree

FIGHT [FIGHTING, FIGHTS, FOUGHT]

Ex	14:14	The LORD will **f** for you;
	17: 9	and go out to **f** the Amalekites.
Dt	1:30	will **f** for you, as he did for you
	3:22	the LORD your God himself will **f**
Jdg	1: 1	and **f** for us against the Canaanites?"
1Sa	17: 9	If he is able to **f** and kill me,
Ne	4:20	Our God will **f** for us!"
Ps	35: 1	**f** against those who **f** against me.
Jer	21: 5	I myself will **f** against you with
Zec	14: 3	Then the LORD will go out and **f**
Jn	18:36	If it were, my servants would **f**
1Co	9:26	I do not **f** like a man beating the air.
2Co	10: 4	The weapons we **f** with are not
1Ti	1:18	you may **f** the good **f**,
	6:12	**F** the good **f** of the faith.
2Ti	4: 7	I have fought the good **f**,
Rev	2:16	will **f** against them with the sword

FIGHTING [FIGHT]

Ex	2:13	and saw two Hebrews **f**.
	14:25	The LORD is **f** for them
Jos	10:14	Surely the LORD was **f** for Israel!
Ac	5:39	only find yourselves **f** against God."

FIGHTS [FIGHT]

Jos	23:10	the LORD your God **f** for you,
1Sa	25:28	because he **f** the LORD's battles.
Jas	4: 1	What causes **f** and quarrels

FIGS [FIG]

2Ki	20: 7	Isaiah said,"Prepare a poultice of **f**."
Jer	24: 1	LORD showed me two baskets of **f**
Mic	7: 1	none of the early **f** that I crave.
Na	3:12	the **f** fall into the mouth of the eater.
Mk	11:13	because it was not the season for **f**.
Lk	6:44	do not pick **f** from thornbushes,
Jas	3:12	or a grapevine bear **f?**
Rev	6:13	as late **f** drop from a fig tree

FIGURATIVELY* [FIGURE]

Jn	16:25	"Though I have been speaking **f**,
Gal	4:24	These things may be taken **f**,
Heb	11:19	raise the dead, and **f** speaking,
Rev	11: 8	which is **f** called Sodom and Egypt,

FIGURE* [FIGURATIVELY, FIGURES]

Eze	1:26	was a **f** like that of a man.
	8: 2	and I saw a **f** like that of a man.
Jn	7: 4	to become a public **f** acts in secret.
	10: 6	Jesus used this **f** of speech,

FIGURES* [FIGURE]

2Ch	4: 3	**f** of bulls encircled it—
Eze	23:14	**f** of Chaldeans portrayed in red,
Jn	16:29	and without **f** of speech.

FILL [FILLED, FILLING, FILLS, FULL, FULLNESS, FULLY]

Ge	1:28	in number; **f** the earth and subdue it.
Lev	25:19	and you will eat your **f** and thrive,
Dt	31:20	and when they eat their **f** and thrive,
Ps	16:11	you will **f** me with joy
	81:10	Open wide your mouth and I will **f** it.
Pr	12:21	the wicked have their **f** of trouble.
	28:19	fantasies will have his **f** of poverty.
Ecc	1: 8	nor the ear its **f** of hearing.
Isa	27: 6	and **f** all the world with fruit.
	33: 5	he will **f** Zion with justice
Jer	23:24	"Do not **f** heaven and earth?"
Eze	10: 2	**F** your hands with burning coals
Hag	1: 6	You drink, but never have your **f**.
	2: 7	and I will **f** this house with glory, '
Jn	2: 7	"**F** the jars with water";
	6:26	the loaves and had your **f**.
Ac	2:28	you will **f** me with joy
Ro	15:13	God of hope **f** you with all joy
Eph	4:10	in order to **f** the whole universe.)
Col	1: 9	God to **f** you with the knowledge
	1:24	I **f** up in my flesh what is still lacking

FILLED [FILL]

Ge	6:13	the earth is f with violence because
Ex	1: 7	so that the land was f with them.
	31: 3	and I have f him with the Spirit
	35:31	and he has f him with the Spirit
	40:34	glory of the LORD f the tabernacle.
Lev	19:29	and be f with wickedness.
Dt	6:11	houses f with all kinds of good
	34: 9	f with the spirit of wisdom
1Ki	8:11	the glory of the LORD f his temple.
2Ki	3:17	yet this valley will be f with water,
2Ch	5:14	the glory of the LORD f the temple
	7: 1	the glory of the LORD f the temple.
Ps	71: 8	My mouth is f with your praise,
	72:19	the whole earth be f with his glory.
	119:64	earth is f with your love, O LORD;
Pr	8:30	I was f with delight day after day,
Isa	6: 4	and the temple was f with smoke.
Jer	25:15	this cup f with the wine of my wrath
Eze	10: 4	The cloud f the temple,
	43: 5	the glory of the LORD f the temple.
Da	2:35	huge mountain and f the whole earth.
Hab	2:14	be f with the knowledge of the glory
	3: 3	and his praise f the earth.
Mt	5: 6	for they will be f.
Lk	1:15	and he will be f with the Holy Spirit
	1:41	Elizabeth was f with the Holy Spirit
	1:67	Zechariah was f with the Holy Spirit
	2:40	he was f with wisdom,
Jn	12: 3	the house was f with the fragrance
Ac	2: 4	of them were f with the Holy Spirit
	4: 8	Then Peter, f with the Holy Spirit,
	4:31	they were all f with the Holy Spirit
	5: 3	that Satan has so f your heart
	9:17	and be f with the Holy Spirit."
	13: 9	f with the Holy Spirit,
	13:52	And the disciples were f with joy
Eph	5:18	Instead, be f with the Spirit.
Php	1:11	f with the fruit of righteousness
Rev	8: 5	f it with fire from the altar,
	12:12	He is f with fury,
	15: 8	the temple was f with smoke from
	16:19	and gave her the cup f with the wine

FILLING [FILL]

Eze	44: 4	the glory of the LORD f the temple

FILLS [FILL]

Nu	14:21	surely as the glory of the LORD f
Ps	107: 9	and f the hungry with good things.
Eph	1:23	the fullness of him who f everything

FILTH [FILTHINESS, FILTHY]

2Ki	18:27	will have to eat their own f
Isa	4: 4	The Lord will wash away the f of
Jas	1:21	get rid of all moral f and the evil
Rev	17: 4	the f of her adulteries.

FILTHINESS* [FILTH]

La	1: 9	Her f clung to her skirts;

FILTHY* [FILTH]

Isa	64: 6	all our righteous acts are like f rags;
Zec	3: 3	Now Joshua was dressed in f clothes

	3: 4	"Take off his f clothes."
Col	3: 8	and f language from your lips.
2Pe	2: 7	who was distressed by the f lives

FINAL [FINALITY]

Ps	73:17	then I understood their f destiny.
Isa	41:22	and know their f outcome.
Lk	11:26	the f condition of that man is worse

FINALITY* [FINAL]

Ro	9:28	sentence on earth with speed and f."

FINANCIAL*

1Ti	6: 5	that godliness is a means to f gain.

FIND [FINDING, FINDS, FOUND]

Ge	18:26	"If I f fifty righteous people in
Ex	33:13	and continue to f favor with you.
Nu	32:23	be sure that your sin will f you out.
Dt	4:29	you will f him if you look for him
	13: 3	to f out whether you love him
1Sa	23:16	and helped him f strength in God.
	28: 7	"F me a woman who is a medium,
Job	23: 3	If only I knew where to f him;
Ps	36: 7	f refuge in the shadow of your wings.
	62: 5	F rest, O my soul, in God alone;
	91: 4	under his wings you will f refuge;
	119:35	for there I f delight.
	119:52	O LORD, and I f comfort in them.
	132: 5	till I f a place for the LORD,
Pr	2: 5	and f the knowledge of God.
	4:22	for they are life to those who f them
	8:17	and those who seek me f me.
	8:36	whoever fails to f me harms himself;
	14:22	those who plan what is good f love
	20: 6	but a faithful man who can f?
	24:14	if you f it, there is a future hope for
	31:10	wife of noble character who can f?
Ecc	2:24	to eat and drink and f satisfaction
	12:10	The Teacher searched to f just
SS	3: 2	I looked for him but did not f him.
Isa	58:14	you will f your joy in the LORD,
Jer	6:16	and you will f rest for your souls.
	29:13	and f me when you seek me
Da	6: 4	They could f no corruption in him,
Hos	14: 3	in you the fatherless f compassion."
Mt	7: 7	seek and you will f;
	11:29	and you will f rest for your souls.
	16:25	loses his life for me will f it.
	22: 9	invite to the banquet anyone you f.'
Lk	11: 9	seek and you will f;
	18: 8	will he f faith on the earth?"
	23: 4	"I f no basis for a charge
	24: 3	not f the body of the Lord Jesus.
Jn	10: 9	and go out, and f pasture.
Ac	23: 9	"We f nothing wrong with this man,"
Eph	5:10	and f out what pleases the Lord.

FINDING [FIND]

Ex	15:22	in the desert without f water.
Hos	9:10	it was like f grapes in the desert;

FINDS [FIND]

Ps	62: 1	My soul f rest in God alone;

	112:	1	who **f** great delight in his commands.
	119:162		like one who **f** great spoil.
Pr	3:13		Blessed is the man who **f** wisdom,
	8:35		For whoever **f** me **f** life
	10:23		A fool **f** pleasure in evil conduct,
	11:27		He who seeks good **f** goodwill,
	14: 6		mocker seeks wisdom and **f** none,
	18:22		He who **f** a wife **f** what is good
Ecc	9:10		Whatever your hand **f** to do,
Mt	7: 8		who asks receives; he who seeks **f;**
	10:39		Whoever **f** his life will lose it,
Lk	11:10		who asks receives; he who seeks **f;**
	12:37		whose master **f** them watching
	15: 4		go after the lost sheep until he **f** it?
	15: 8		and search carefully until she **f** it?

FINE [FINE-SOUNDING, FINEST]

Ex	2: 2	When she saw that he was a **f** child,
Pr	8:19	My fruit is better than **f** gold;
Ecc	7: 1	good name is better than **f** perfume,
Lk	7:25	A man dressed in **f** clothes?

FINE-SOUNDING* [FINE, SOUND]

Col	2: 4	may deceive you by **f** arguments.

FINEST [FINE]

Job	28:15	It cannot be bought with the **f** gold,
Ps	147:14	and satisfies you with the **f** of wheat.
Isa	25: 6	the best of meats and the **f** of wines.
Da	10: 5	a belt of the **f** gold around his waist.

FINGER [FINGERS]

Ex	8:19	"This is the **f** of God."
	31:18	the tablets of stone inscribed by the **f**
Lev	4: 6	He is to dip his **f** into the blood
Dt	9:10	tablets inscribed by the **f** of God.
2Ch	10:10	My little **f** is thicker than my father's
Mt	23: 4	not willing to lift a **f** to move them.
Lk	11:20	I drive out demons by the **f** of God,
	16:24	tip of his **f** in water and cool my
Jn	8: 6	to write on the ground with his **f**.
	20:25	and put my **f** where the nails were,

FINGERS [FINGER]

Ps	8: 3	the work of your **f**,
Pr	7: 3	Bind them on your **f;**
Da	5: 5	the **f** of a human hand appeared
Mk	7:33	Jesus put his **f** into the man's ears.

FINISH [FINISHED, FINISHING]

Ps	90: 9	we **f** our years with a moan.
Mt	10:23	not **f** going through the cities of
Jn	4:34	will of him who sent me and to **f** his
	5:36	that the Father has given me to **f**,
Ac	20:24	if only I may **f** the race and complete
2Co	8:11	Now **f** the work,
Jas	1: 4	Perseverance must **f** its work so

FINISHED [FINISH]

Ge	2: 2	the seventh day God had **f** the work
	24:15	Before he had **f** praying,
Ex	40:33	And so Moses **f** the work.
Dt	32:45	Moses **f** reciting all these words
Jos	19:51	And so they **f** dividing the land.

1Ki	8:54	Solomon had **f** all these prayers
Ezr	6:14	They **f** building the temple
Jn	19:30	Jesus said, "It is **f**."
2Ti	4: 7	I have **f** the race,
Heb	4: 3	And yet his work has been **f** since
Rev	11: 7	when they have **f** their testimony,

FINS

Lev	11: 9	you may eat any that have **f**

FIRE [FIERY, FIREPOT]

Ex	3: 2	the bush was on **f** it did not burn up.
	13:21	in a pillar of **f** to give them light,
	19:18	the LORD descended on it in **f**.
	40:38	and **f** was in the cloud by night,
Lev	6:12	**f** on the altar must be kept burning;
	9:24	**F** came out from the presence of
	10: 1	and they offered unauthorized **f**
Nu	11: 1	Then **f** from the LORD burned
	16:35	And **f** came out from the LORD
Dt	4:12	LORD spoke to you out of the **f**.
Jdg	6:21	**F** flared from the rock,
1Ki	18:38	the **f** of the LORD fell and burned
	19:12	but the LORD was not in the **f**.
2Ki	1:10	Then **f** fell from heaven
	2:11	a chariot of **f** and horses of **f**
	6:17	and chariots of **f** all around Elisha.
	16: 3	and even sacrificed his son in the **f**,
	25: 9	He set **f** to the temple of the LORD,
Ne	1: 3	its gates have been burned with **f**."
Ps	50: 3	a **f** devours before him,
	89:46	long will your wrath burn like **f?**
Pr	6:27	Can a man scoop **f** into his lap
Isa	5:24	as tongues of **f** lick up straw and,
	10:17	The Light of Israel will become a **f**,
	30:27	and his tongue is a consuming **f**.
	66:24	nor will their **f** be quenched,
Jer	23:29	"Is not my word like **f**,"
	36:23	the entire scroll was burned in the **f**.
Eze	1:13	**F** moved back and forth among
Da	3:25	four men walking around in the **f**,
	7: 9	His throne was flaming with **f**,
Am	4:11	a burning stick snatched from the **f**,
Zec	2: 5	And I myself will be a wall of **f**
	3: 2	burning stick snatched from the **f?**"
Mal	3: 2	For he will be like a refiner's **f**
Mt	3:11	you with the Holy Spirit and with **f**.
	5:22	will be in danger of the **f** of hell.
	18: 8	and be thrown into eternal **f**.
	25:41	the eternal **f** prepared for the devil
Mk	9:43	where the **f** never goes out.
	9:48	and the **f** is not quenched.'
	9:49	Everyone will be salted with **f**.
Lk	3:16	you with the Holy Spirit and with **f**.
	12:49	"I have come to bring **f** on the earth,
Jn	15: 6	thrown into the **f** and burned.
Ac	2: 3	saw what seemed to be tongues of **f**
1Co	3:13	and the **f** will test the quality
1Th	5:19	Do not put out the Spirit's **f;**
2Th	1: 7	revealed from heaven in blazing **f**
Heb	12:29	for our "God is a consuming **f**."
Jas	3: 6	The tongue also is a **f**,
1Pe	1: 7	perishes even though refined by **f—**

2Pe	3:10	the elements will be destroyed by **f**,
Jude	1: 7	the punishment of eternal **f**.
	1:23	snatch others from the **f** and save
Rev	1:14	and his eyes were like blazing **f**.
	8: 7	and there came hail and **f** mixed
	9:17	and out of their mouths came **f**,
	11: 5	**f** comes from their mouths
	15: 2	like a sea of glass mixed with **f** and,
	20:14	The lake of **f** is the second death.

FIREPOT [FIRE]

Ge	15:17	a smoking **f** with a blazing torch

FIRM* [FIRMLY]

Ex	14:13	Stand **f** and you will see
	15: 8	surging waters stood **f** like a wall;
Jos	3: 17	of the LORD stood **f** on dry ground
2Ch	20:17	Take up your positions; stand **f**
Ezr	9: 8	giving us a **f** place in his sanctuary,
Job	11:15	without shame; you will stand **f**
	36: 5	and **f** in his purpose.
	41:23	they are **f** and immovable.
Ps	20: 8	but we rise up and stand **f**.
	30: 7	you made my mountain stand **f**;
	33: 9	and it stood **f**.
	33:11	plans of the LORD stand **f** forever,
	37:23	he makes his steps **f**;
	40: 2	and gave me a **f** place to stand.
	75: 3	it is I who hold its pillars **f**.
	78:13	he made the water stand **f**
	89: 2	that your love stands **f** forever,
	89: 4	and make your throne **f**
	93: 5	Your statutes stand **f**;
	119:89	it stands **f** in the heavens.
Pr	4:26	and take only ways that are **f**.
	10:25	but the righteous stand **f** forever.
	12: 7	the house of the righteous stands **f**.
Isa	7: 9	If you do not stand **f** in your faith,
	22:17	the LORD is about to take **f** hold
	22:23	like a peg into a **f** place;
	22:25	into the **f** place will give way;
Eze	13: 5	so that it will stand **f** in the battle on
Zec	8:23	and nations will take **f** hold
Mt	10:22	stands **f** to the end will be saved.
	24:13	stands **f** to the end will be saved.
Mk	13:13	stands **f** to the end will be saved.
Lk	21:19	By standing **f** you will gain life.
1Co	10:12	So, if you think you are standing **f**,
	15:58	Therefore, my dear brothers, stand **f**.
	16:13	stand **f** in the faith;
2Co	1: 7	And our hope for you is **f**,
	1:21	both us and you stand **f** in Christ.
	1:24	because it is by faith you stand **f**.
Gal	5: 1	Stand **f**, then, and do not let
Eph	6:14	Stand **f** then, with the belt
Php	1:27	that you stand **f** in one spirit,
	4: 1	how you should stand **f** in the Lord,
Col	1:23	established and **f**, not moved
	2: 5	and how **f** your faith in Christ is.
	4:12	that you may stand **f** in all the will
1Th	3: 8	since you are standing **f** in the Lord.
2Th	2:15	stand **f** and hold to the teachings
1Ti	6:19	for themselves as a **f** foundation
2Ti	2:19	God's solid foundation stands **f**,

Heb	6:19	anchor for the soul, **f** and secure.
Jas	5: 8	You too, be patient and stand **f**,
1Pe	5: 9	Resist him, standing **f** in the faith,
	5:10	make you strong, **f** and steadfast.

FIRMLY [FIRM]

1Ch	16:30	The world is **f** established;
Ecc	12:11	sayings like **f** embedded nails—
1Co	15: 2	if you hold **f** to the word I preached
Heb	4:14	let us hold **f** to the faith we profess.

FIRST [FIRSTBORN, FIRSTFRUITS]

Ge	1: 5	and there was morning—the **f** day.
	13: 4	and where he had **f** built an altar.
Ex	12: 2	to be for you the **f** month,
	34: 1	the words that were on the **f** tablets,
	34:19	"The **f** offspring of every womb
	40:17	So the tabernacle was set up on the **f**
		day of the **f** month
Nu	18:15	The **f** offspring of every womb,
	28:11	" 'On the **f** of every month,
1Ki	22: 5	"**F** seek the counsel of the LORD."
Pr	8:22	LORD brought me forth as the **f** of his
	18:17	The **f** to present his case seems right,
Isa	44: 6	I am the **f** and I am the last;
	48:12	I am the **f** and I am the last.
Da	7: 4	"The **f** was like a lion,
Mt	5:24	**F** go and be reconciled
	6:33	But seek **f** his kingdom
	7: 5	**f** take the plank out of your own eye,
	8:21	**f** let me go and bury my father."
	19:30	But many who are **f** will be last, and
		many who are last will be **f**.
	22:38	the **f** and greatest commandment.
Mk	9:11	that Elijah must come **f**?"
	9:35	"If anyone wants to be **f**,
	10:31	who are **f** will be last, and the last **f**."
	10:44	and whoever wants to be **f** must
	13:10	And the gospel must **f** be preached
	16: 2	Very early on the **f** day of the week,
Lk	11:26	of that man is worse than the **f**."
Jn	8: 7	be the **f** to throw a stone at her."
Ac	11:26	disciples were called Christians **f** at
Ro	1:16	**f** for the Jew, then for the Gentile.
	1:17	that is by faith from **f** to last,
1Co	12:28	God has appointed **f** of all apostles,
	15:45	"The **f** man Adam became
2Co	8: 5	they gave themselves **f** to the Lord
Eph	1:12	who were the **f** to hope in Christ,
	6: 2	the **f** commandment with a promise
1Th	4:16	and the dead in Christ will rise **f**.
1Ti	2:13	For Adam was formed **f**, then Eve.
Heb	8:13	he has made the **f** one obsolete;
	10: 9	He sets aside the **f** to establish
Jas	3:17	from heaven is **f** of all pure;
1Jn	4:19	We love because he **f** loved us.
3Jn	1: 9	but Diotrephes, who loves to be **f**,
Rev	1:17	I am the **F** and the Last.
	2: 4	You have forsaken your **f** love.
	4: 7	The **f** living creature was like a lion,
	6: 1	I watched as the Lamb opened the **f**
	8: 7	The **f** angel sounded his trumpet,
	9:12	The **f** woe is past;
	13:12	its inhabitants worship the **f** beast,

20: 5 This is the **f** resurrection.
21: 1 for the **f** heaven and the **f** earth had
22:13 the **F** and the Last,

FIRSTBEGOTTEN (KJV)
See FIRSTBORN

FIRSTBORN [FIRST, BEAR]

Ge 27:19 "I am Esau your **f.**
48:18 "No, my father, this one is the **f;**
Ex   4:22 the LORD says: Israel is my **f** son,
11: 5 Every **f** son in Egypt will die,
12:29 the LORD struck down all the **f**
13: 2 "Consecrate to me every **f** male.
34:20 Redeem all your **f** sons.
Nu   3:41 Levites for me in place of all the **f**
Jos   6:26 "At the cost of his **f** son
1Ki 16:34 at the cost of his **f** son Abiram,
Ps 89:27 I will also appoint him my **f,**
Mic   6: 7 I offer my **f** for my transgression,
Zec 12:10 for him as one grieves for a **f** son.
Lk   2: 7 and she gave birth to her **f,**
Ro   8:29 be the **f** among many brothers.
Col   1:15 the **f** over all creation.
1:18 the **f** from among the dead,
Heb   1: 6 God brings his **f** into the world,
12:23 to the church of the **f,**
Rev   1: 5 the **f** from the dead,

FIRSTFRUITS [FIRST]

Ex 23:16 the Feast of Harvest with the **f** of
34:22 the Feast of Weeks with the **f** of
Pr   3: 9 with the **f** of all your crops;
Ro   8:23 who have the **f** of the Spirit,
1Co 15:23 each in his own turn: Christ, the **f;**
Jas   1:18 be a kind of **f** of all he created.
Rev 14: 4 among men and offered as **f** to God

FIRSTLING (KJV) See FIRSTBORN

FISH [FISHERMEN, FISHERS,
FISHHOOK]

Ge   1:26 and let them rule over the **f** of the sea
Ex   7:18 The **f** in the Nile will die,
Nu   11: 5 We remember the **f** we ate in Egypt
Eze 47: 9 There will be large numbers of **f,**
Jnh   1:17 But the LORD provided a great **f**
2: 1 From inside the **f** Jonah prayed to
Mt   7:10 Or if he asks for a **f,**
12:40 three nights in the belly of a huge **f,**
13:48 and collected the good **f** in baskets,
14:17 of bread and two **f,**"
Mk   8: 7 They had a few small **f** as well;
Lk   5: 6 they caught such a large number of **f**
Jn   6: 9 and two small **f,**
21: 5 "Friends, haven't you any **f?**"
21:11 It was full of large **f,** 153,

FISHERMEN [FISH]

Mk   1:16 for they were **f.**

FISHERS* [FISH]

Mt   4:19 "and I will make you **f** of men."
Mk   1:17 "and I will make you **f** of men."

FISHHOOK* [FISH, HOOK]

Job 41: 1 Can you pull in the leviathan with a **f**

FISTS

Isa 58: 4 in striking each other with wicked **f.**
Mt 26:67 and struck him with their **f.**

FIT [FITTING]

Dt   12: 8 everyone as he sees **f,**
Jdg 17: 6 everyone did as he saw **f.**
21:25 everyone did as he saw **f.**
Mt   3:11 whose sandals I am not **f** to carry.
Lk   9:62 and looks back is **f** for service in

FITTING* [FIT]

Ps 33: 1 it is **f** for the upright to praise him.
147: 1 how pleasant and **f** to praise him!
Pr 10:32 lips of the righteous know what is **f,**
19:10 not **f** for a fool to live in luxury—
26: 1 honor is not **f** for a fool.
1Co 14:40 But everything should be done in a **f**
Col   3:18 as is **f** in the Lord.
Heb   2:10 it was **f** that God,

FIVE

Lev 26: 8 **F** of you will chase a hundred,
1Sa   6: 4 "**F** gold tumors and **f** gold rats,
6:16 The **f** rulers of the Philistines
17:40 **f** smooth stones from the stream,
Isa 30:17 at the threat of **f** you will all flee
Mt   14:19 Taking the **f** loaves and the two fish
16: 9 the **f** loaves for the **f** thousand,
25: 2 **F** of them were foolish and **f** were
wise.
25:15 To one he gave **f** talents of money,
Jn   4:18 fact is, you have had **f** husbands,
1Co 14:19 rather speak **f** intelligible words
Rev   9: 5 only to torture them for **f** months.
17:10 **F** have fallen, one is,

FIX* [FIXED]

Dt   11:18 **F** these words of mine in your hearts
Job 14: 3 Do you **f** your eye on such a one?
Pr   4:25 **f** your gaze directly before you.
Isa 46: 8 "Remember this, **f** it in mind,
Am   9: 4 I will **f** my eyes upon them for evil
2Co   4:18 we **f** our eyes not on what is seen,
Heb   3: 1 **f** your thoughts on Jesus,
12: 2 Let us **f** our eyes on Jesus,

FIXED* [FIX]

2Ki   8:11 He stared at him with a **f** gaze
Job 38:10 when I **f** limits for it
Ps 141: 8 But my eyes are **f** on you,
Pr   8:28 **f** securely the fountains of the deep,
Jer 33:25 and the **f** laws of heaven
Lk   16:26 and you a great chasm has been **f,**

FLAME [FLAMES, FLAMING]

Jdg 13:20 angel of the LORD ascended in the **f.**
Isa 10:17 their Holy One a **f;**
2Ti   1: 6 to fan into **f** the gift of God,

FLAMES [FLAME]

Ex   3: 2 of the LORD appeared to him in **f**
Da   3:22 and the furnace so hot that the **f** of
1Co 3:15 only as one escaping through the **f.**
      13: 3 and surrender my body to the **f,**
Heb 11:34 quenched the fury of the **f,**

FLAMING [FLAME]

Ge   3:24 a **f** sword flashing back and forth
Da   7: 9 His throne was **f** with fire,
      10: 6 his eyes like **f** torches,
Eph 6:16 all the **f** arrows of the evil one.

FLANK

Eze 34:21 you shove with **f** and shoulder,

FLASH [FLASHED, FLASHES, FLASHING]

Eze 21:10 polished to **f** like lightning!
Lk   9:29 as bright as a **f** of lightning.
1Co 15:52 in a **f,** in the twinkling of an eye,

FLASHED [FLASH]

Eze 1:13 and lightning **f** out of it.
Ac   9: 3 a light from heaven **f** around him.

FLASHES [FLASH]

Eze 1:14 back and forth like **f** of lightning.
Lk 17:24 which **f** and lights up the sky
Rev 4: 5 From the throne came **f** of lightning,
      8: 5 **f** of lightning and an earthquake.
     11:19 And there came **f** of lightning,
     16:18 Then there came **f** of lightning,

FLASHING [FLASH]

Ge   3:24 a flaming sword **f** back and forth
Dt 32:41 when I sharpen my **f** sword

FLASK*

1Sa 10: 1 Then Samuel took a **f** of oil
2Ki 9: 1 take this **f** of oil with you and go
      9: 3 the **f** and pour the oil on his head

FLATTER* [FLATTERING, FLATTERS, FLATTERY]

Job 32:21 nor will I **f** any man;
Ps 78:36 they would **f** him with their mouths,
Jude 1:16 and **f** others for their own advantage.

FLATTERING* [FLATTER]

Ps 12: 2 their **f** lips speak with deception.
     12: 3 May the LORD cut off all **f** lips
Pr 26:28 and a **f** mouth works ruin.
     28:23 than he who has a **f** tongue.
Eze 12:24 or **f** divinations among the people

FLATTERS* [FLATTER]

Ps 36: 2 his own eyes he **f** himself too much
Pr 29: 5 Whoever **f** his neighbor is spreading

FLATTERY* [FLATTER]

Job 32:22 for if I were skilled in **f,**
Da 11:32 With **f** he will corrupt those who
Ro 16:18 By smooth talk and **f** they deceive

1Th 2: 5 You know we never used **f,**

FLAW* [FLAWLESS]

Dt 15:21 or has any serious **f,**
     17: 1 a sheep that has any defect or **f** in it,
SS   4: 7 my darling; there is no **f** in you.

FLAWLESS* [FLAW]

2Sa 22:31 the word of the LORD is **f.**
Job 11: 4 'My beliefs are **f** and I am pure
Ps 12: 6 And the words of the LORD are **f,**
     18:30 the word of the LORD is **f.**
Pr 30: 5 "Every word of God is **f;**
SS   5: 2 my darling, my dove, my **f** one.

FLAX

Jos 2: 6 hidden them under the stalks of **f**

FLED [FLEE]

Ex   2:15 but Moses **f** from Pharaoh and went
1Sa 19:18 David had **f** and made his escape,
2Sa 4: 4 His nurse picked him up and **f,**
     19: 9 **f** the country because of Absalom;
Ps   3: T When he **f** from his son Absalom.
     57: T he had **f** from Saul into the cave.
    114: 3 The sea looked and **f,**
Mk 14:50 Then everyone deserted him and **f.**
Rev 20:11 Earth and sky **f** from his presence,

FLEE [FLED, FLEES]

Ge 19:17 one of them said, **"F** for your lives!
Nu 35:11 killed someone accidentally may **f.**
Ps 68: 1 may his foes **f** before him.
    139: 7 Where can I **f** from your presence?
Isa 30:17 thousand will **f** at the threat of one;
Jer 46: 6 swift cannot **f** nor the strong escape.
     51: 6 **"F** from Babylon!
Jnh 1: 3 for Tarshish to **f** from the LORD.
Zec 2: 6 **F** from the land of the north,"
Lk   3: 7 you to **f** from the coming wrath?
1Co 6:18 **F** from sexual immorality.
     10:14 my dear friends, **f** from idolatry.
1Ti 6:11 But you, man of God, **f** from all this,
2Ti 2:22 **F** the evil desires of youth,
Jas 4: 7 and he will **f** from you.

FLEECE

Jdg 6:37 a wool **f** on the threshing floor.

FLEES [FLEE]

Dt 19: 4 and **f** there to save his life—
Pr 28: 1 The wicked man **f**

FLEETING* [FLEE]

Job 14: 2 withers away; like a **f** shadow,
Ps 39: 4 let me know how **f** is my life.
     89:47 Remember how **f** is my life.
    144: 4 like a **f** shadow.
Pr 21: 6 by a lying tongue is a **f** vapor and
     31:30 Charm is deceptive, and beauty is **f;**

FLESH

Ge   2:23 bone of my bones and **f** of my **f;**
      2:24 and they will become one **f.**
     17:13 My covenant in your **f** is to be

Lev 26:29 You will eat the **f** of your sons and
1Sa 17:44 "and I'll give your **f** to the birds of
2Ch 32: 8 With him is only the arm of **f,**
Job 19:26 yet in my **f** I will see God;
Ps 50:13 Do I eat the **f** of bulls or drink the
Jer 9:25 who are circumcised only in the **f—**
Eze 11:19 of stone and give them a heart of **f.**
36:26 of stone and give you a heart of **f.**
37: 6 make **f** come upon you and cover
Mal 2:15 In **f** and spirit they are his.
Mt 19: 5 and the two will become one **f?**
Lk 24:39 a ghost does not have **f** and bones,
Jn 1:14 The Word became **f**
3: 6 **F** gives birth to **f,**
6:51 This bread is my **f,**
1Co 6:16 "The two will become one **f.**"
15:39 All **f** is not the same:
2Co 12: 7 there was given me a thorn in my **f,**
Eph 2:15 by abolishing in his **f** the law
5:31 and the two will become one **f.**"
6:12 For our struggle is not against **f**
Php 3: 2 those mutilators of the **f.**
Col 1:24 I fill up in my **f** what is still lacking
1Jn 4: 2 that Jesus Christ has come in the **f** is
2Jn 1: 7 Jesus Christ as coming in the **f,**
Jude 1:23 the clothing stained by corrupted **f.**
Rev 19:18 so that you may eat the **f** of kings,

FLESH AND BLOOD Ge 29:14; 37:27; Jdg
9:2; 2Sa 5:1; 19:12, 13; 1Ki 8:19; 2Ki 20:18; 1Ch
11:1; 2Ch 6:9; Ne 5:5; Isa 39:7; 58:7; 1Co 15:50;
Eph 6:12; Heb 2:14

FLESH (KJV) See BODY, CREATURES,
EARTHLY, HUMAN, HUMAN NATURE,
HUMAN STANDARDS, MAN, MANKIND,
MEAT, MORTAL, OUTWARDLY, NATURAL,
PEOPLE, PHYSICAL, SINFUL NATURE,
SENSUAL, WORLD, WORLDLY

FLEW [FLY]
Ps 18:10 He mounted the cherubim and **f;**
Isa 6: 6 Then one of the seraphs **f** to me with

FLIES [FLY]
Ex 8:21 I will send swarms of **f** on you
Ps 91: 5 nor the arrow that **f** by day,
Isa 7:18 the LORD will whistle for **f** from

FLIGHT [FLY]
Dt 32:30 or two put ten thousand to **f,**
Mt 24:20 Pray that your **f** will not take place

FLINT
Ex 4:25 But Zipporah took a **f** knife,
Jos 5: 2 "Make **f** knives and circumcise
Isa 50: 7 Therefore have I set my face like **f,**
Zec 7:12 They made their hearts as hard as **f**

FLIRTING*
Isa 3:16 **f** with their eyes,

FLOAT* [FLOATED]
1Ki 5: 9 and I will **f** them in rafts by sea to
2Ki 6: 6 and made the iron **f.**

2Ch 2:16 and will **f** them in rafts by sea
Hos 10: 7 Samaria and its king will **f** away like

FLOATED* [FLOAT]
Ge 7:18 the ark **f** on the surface of the water.

FLOCK [FLOCKS]
Ex 2:17 to their rescue and watered their **f.**
3: 1 Moses was tending the **f** of Jethro
2Sa 7: 8 and from following the **f** to be ruler
Ps 77:20 You led your people like a **f**
78:52 he brought his people out like a **f;**
95: 7 the **f** under his care.
Isa 40:11 He tends his **f** like a shepherd:
Jer 10:21 and all their **f** is scattered.
23: 2 "Because you have scattered my **f**
31:10 and will watch over his **f** like
Eze 34: 2 not shepherds take care of the **f?**
Am 7:15 the LORD took me from tending the **f**
Zec 11: 7 I pastured the **f** marked for slaughter.
Mt 26:31 the sheep of the **f** will be scattered.'
Lk 12:32 "Do not be afraid, little **f,**
Jn 10:16 be one **f** and one shepherd.
Ac 20:28 and all the **f** of which the Holy Spirit
1Co 9: 7 Who tends a **f** and does not drink of
1Pe 5: 2 Be shepherds of God's **f**
5: 3 but being examples to the **f.**

FLOCKS [FLOCK]
Ge 4: 2 Now Abel kept **f,**
Nu 32: 1 who had very large herds and **f,**
Lk 2: 8 keeping watch over their **f** at night.

FLOG [FLOGGED, FLOGGING]
Pr 19:25 **F** a mocker, and the simple
Mt 10:17 and **f** you in their synagogues.
Lk 18:32 spit on him, **f** him and kill him.
Ac 22:25 As they stretched him out to **f** him,

FLOGGED [FLOG]
Dt 25: 3 If he is **f** more than that,
Jn 19: 1 Pilate took Jesus and had him **f.**
Ac 5:40 the apostles in and had them **f.**
16:23 After they had been severely **f,**
22:24 that he be **f** and questioned
2Co 11:23 been **f** more severely,

FLOGGING* [FLOG]
Ps 89:32 their iniquity with **f;**
Heb 11:36 Some faced jeers and **f,**

FLOOD [FLOODGATES,
FLOODWATERS]
Ge 7: 7 the ark to escape the waters of the **f.**
9:15 will the waters become a **f**
Ps 29:10 LORD sits enthroned over the **f;**
Da 9:26 The end will come like a **f:**
Mal 2:13 You **f** the LORD's altar with tears.
Mt 24:38 For in the days before the **f,**
Lk 6:48 When a **f** came,
2Pe 2: 5 brought the **f** on its ungodly people,

FLOODGATES [FLOOD]
Ge 7:11 the **f** of the heavens were opened.

Isa 24:18 The **f** of the heavens are opened,
Mal 3:10 not throw open the **f** of heaven

FLOODWATERS [FLOOD]

Ge 6:17 I am going to bring **f** on the earth
Isa 8: 7 to bring against them the mighty **f** of

FLOOR

Jdg 6:37 a wool fleece on the threshing **f.**
Ru 3: 3 Then go down to the threshing **f,**
1Ch 21:15 at the threshing **f** of Araunah
2Ch 3: 1 It was on the threshing **f** of Araunah
Hos 9: 1 of a prostitute at every threshing **f**
Mt 3:12 and he will clear his threshing **f,**
Jas 2: 3 or "Sit on the **f** by my feet,"

FLOUR

Lev 2: 1 his offering is to be of fine **f.**
Nu 7:13 each filled with fine **f** mixed with oil
1Ki 17:12 a handful of **f** in a jar and a little oil
2Ki 4:41 Elisha said, "Get some **f.**"
Lk 13:21 and mixed into a large amount of **f**

FLOURISH [FLOURISHES, FLOURISHING]

Ps 72: 7 In his days the righteous will **f;**
92: 7 up like grass and all evildoers **f,**
92:12 The righteous will **f** like a palm tree,
Pr 14:11 but the tent of the upright will **f.**
Isa 55:10 the earth and making it bud and **f,**
Eze 17:24 and make the dry tree **f.**

FLOURISHES* [FLOURISH]

Ps 103:15 he **f** like a flower of the field;
Pr 12:12 but the root of the righteous **f.**

FLOURISHING [FLOURISH]

Ps 37:35 and ruthless man **f** like a green tree
52: 8 an olive tree **f** in the house of God;

FLOW [FLOWED, FLOWING, FLOWS]

Ex 14:26 may **f** back over the Egyptians
Nu 13:27 and it does **f** with milk and honey!
Ps 78:16 made water **f** down like rivers.
119:136 Streams of tears **f** from my eyes,
Ecc 1: 7 All streams **f** into the sea,
Joel 3:18 and the hills will **f** with milk;
Am 9:13 and **f** from all the hills.
Zec 14: 8 On that day living water will **f** out
Jn 7:38 streams of living water will **f** from
19:34 a sudden **f** of blood and water.

FLOWED [FLOW]

Ge 2:10 A river watering the garden **f**
Rev 14:20 and blood **f** out of the press,

FLOWER [FLOWERS]

Job 14: 2 up like a **f** and withers away;
Ps 103:15 he flourishes like a **f** of the field;
Jas 1:10 he will pass away like a wild **f.**

FLOWERS [FLOWER]

Ex 25:33 Three cups shaped like almond **f**
1Ki 6:18 carved with gourds and open **f.**

Isa 40: 6 and all their glory is like the **f**
40: 7 The grass withers and the **f** fall,
1Pe 1:24 the grass withers and the **f** fall,

FLOWING [FLOW]

Ex 3: 8 a land **f** with milk and honey—
33: 3 to the land **f** with milk and honey.
Nu 16:14 you haven't brought us into a land **f**
Jos 5: 6 a land **f** with milk and honey.
2Ki 4: 6 Then the oil stopped **f.**
Ps 107:33 **f** springs into thirsty ground,
Jer 32:22 a land **f** with milk and honey.
Eze 20: 6 a land **f** with milk and honey,
32: 6 drench the land with your **f** blood
Da 7:10 A river of fire was **f,**
Rev 22: 1 **f** from the throne of God and of

FLOWING WITH MILK AND HONEY

Ex 3:8, 17; 13:5; 33:3; Lev 20:24; Nu 14:8;
16:13, 14; Dt 6:3; 11:9; 26:9, 15; 27:3; 31:20; Jos
5:6; Jer 11:5; 32:22; Eze 20:6, 15

FLOWS [FLOW]

Eze 47: 9 where the river **f** everything will live.

FLUTE

Ge 4:21 father of all who play the harp and **f.**
Ps 150: 4 praise him with the strings and **f,**
Da 3: 5 **f,** zither, lyre, harp,
Mt 11:17 the **f** for you, and you did not dance;
1Co 14: 7 such as the **f** or harp,
Rev 18:22 **f** players and trumpeters,

FLY [FLEW, FLIES, FLIGHT, FLYING]

Ge 1:20 and let birds **f** above the earth across
Pr 23: 5 and **f** off to the sky like an eagle.

FLYING [FLY]

Ge 8: 7 and it kept **f** back and forth until
Dt 14:19 All **f** insects that swarm are unclean
Isa 6: 2 and with two they were **f.**
Zec 5: 1 and there before me was a **f** scroll!
Rev 4: 7 the fourth was like a **f** eagle.
8:13 an eagle that was **f** in midair call out
14: 6 I saw another angel **f** in midair,

FOAL*

Zec 9: 9 on a colt, the **f** of a donkey.
Mt 21: 5 on a colt, the **f** of a donkey.' "

FOAM* [FOAMING]

Job 24:18 "Yet they are **f** on the surface of
Ps 46: 3 though its waters roar and **f** and

FOAMING* [FOAM]

Dt 32:14 You drank the **f** blood of the grape.
Ps 75: 8 full of **f** wine mixed with spices;
Mk 9:20 **f** at the mouth.
Jude 1:13 **f** up their shame;

FOE [FOES]

Ps 8: 2 to silence the **f** and the avenger.
61: 3 a strong tower against the **f.**

FOES [FOE]

2Sa	22:49	You exalted me above my **f**;
Ps	44: 5	through your name we trample our **f**.
	97: 3	and consumes his **f** on every side.
	106:41	and their **f** ruled over them.
Na	1: 2	The LORD takes vengeance on his **f**

FOILS*

Ps	33:10	LORD **f** the plans of the nations;
Isa	44:25	who **f** the signs of false prophets

FOLDED [FOLDING]

Jn	20: 7	The cloth was **f** up by itself,

FOLDING* [FOLDED, FOLDS]

Pr	6:10	a little **f** of the hands to rest—
	24:33	a little **f** of the hands to rest—

FOLDS [FOLDING]

Ecc	4: 5	fool **f** his hands and ruins himself.

FOLLOW [FOLLOWED, FOLLOWERS, FOLLOWING, FOLLOWS]

Ex	16: 4	whether they will **f** my instructions.
	23: 2	"Do not **f** the crowd in doing wrong.
Lev	18: 4	and be careful to **f** my decrees.
Dt	4: 1	**f** them so that you may live
	5: 1	Learn them and be sure to **f** them.
	6:14	Do not **f** other gods,
	17:19	and **f** carefully all the words
1Ki	11:10	forbidden Solomon to **f** other gods,
	18:21	If the LORD is God, **f** him;
2Ch	34:33	they did not fail to **f** the LORD.
Ps	23: 6	and love will **f** me all the days
	119:166	O LORD, and I **f** your commands.
Jer	25: 6	Do not **f** other gods to serve
Eze	13: 3	foolish prophets who **f** their own
Hos	11:10	They will **f** the LORD;
Mt	4:19	"Come, **f** me," Jesus said,
	8:19	I will **f** you wherever you go."
	8:22	But Jesus told him, **"F** me,
	16:24	and take up his cross and **f** me.
	19:27	"We have left everything to **f** you!
Lk	9:23	and take up his cross daily and **f** me.
	9:61	Still another said,"I will **f** you,
Jn	10: 4	and his sheep **f** him
	10: 5	But they will never **f** a stranger;
	10:27	I know them, and they **f** me.
	12:26	Whoever serves me must **f** me;
	13:36	you cannot **f** now,
	21:19	Then he said to him, **"F** me!"
1Co	1:12	One of you says,"I **f** Paul";
	11: 1	**F** my example, as I **f** the example of Christ.
	14: 1	**F** the way of love
Gal	2:14	force Gentiles to **f** Jewish customs?
2Th	3: 9	make ourselves a model for you to **f**.
1Ti	5:15	already turned away to **f** Satan.
1Pe	2:21	that you should **f** in his steps.
2Pe	1:16	We did not **f** cleverly invented stories
	2:15	to **f** the way of Balaam son of Beor,
Jude	1:18	scoffers who will **f** their own

Rev	14: 4	They **f** the Lamb wherever he goes.

FOLLOWED [FOLLOW]

Ex	14:23	and horsemen **f** them into the sea.
Nu	31:16	the ones who **f** Balaam's advice
	32:11	they have not **f** me wholeheartedly,
Dt	1:36	he **f** the LORD wholeheartedly."
Jos	14:14	because he **f** the LORD,
Jdg	2:12	They **f** and worshiped various gods
2Ki	17: 8	and **f** the practices of the nations
2Ch	10:14	he **f** the advice of the young men
Pr	7:22	**f** her like an ox going to the slaughter
Jer	9:14	they have **f** the stubbornness
Mt	9: 9	and Matthew got up and **f** him.
	26:58	But Peter **f** him at a distance,
Mk	1:18	they left their nets and **f** him.
Lk	18:43	he received his sight and **f** Jesus,
Jn	6:66	turned back and no longer **f** him.
Eph	2: 2	when you **f** the ways of this world
Rev	13: 3	world was astonished and **f** the beast.

FOLLOWERS [FOLLOW]

Nu	16: 5	Then he said to Korah and all his **f**:
Ps	106:18	Fire blazed among their **f**;
Ac	17:34	A few men became **f** of Paul
Rev	17:14	chosen and faithful **f**."

FOLLOWING [FOLLOW]

Nu	32:15	If you turn away from **f** him,
2Sa	15:12	and Absalom's **f** kept on increasing.
Ps	119:14	I rejoice in **f** your statutes
Php	3:17	Join with others in **f** my example,
1Ti	1:18	so that by **f** them you may fight
Heb	4:11	by **f** their example of disobedience.

FOLLOWS [FOLLOW]

Nu	14:24	and **f** me wholeheartedly,
Jer	4:20	Disaster **f** disaster;
Eze	18: 9	He **f** my decrees
Jn	8:12	Whoever **f** me will never walk

FOLLY [FOOL]

1Sa	25:25	and **f** goes with him.
Pr	9:13	The woman **F** is loud;
	13:16	but a fool exposes his **f**.
	14:18	The simple inherit **f**,
	14:24	but the **f** of fools yields **f**.
	14:29	a quick-tempered man displays **f**.
	16:22	but **f** brings punishment to fools.
	19: 3	A man's own **f** ruins his life,
	22:15	**F** is bound up in the heart of a child,
	26: 4	not answer a fool according to his **f**,
	26: 5	Answer a fool according to his **f**,
Ecc	2:13	I saw that wisdom is better than **f**,
	10: 1	so a little **f** outweighs wisdom
Mk	7:22	envy, slander, arrogance and **f**.
2Ti	3: 9	their **f** will be clear to everyone.

FOOD [FOODS]

Ge	1:30	I give every green plant for **f**."
	3: 6	the tree was good for **f** and pleasing
	3:19	of your brow you will eat your **f**
	9: 3	that lives and moves is **f**
Lev	3:11	burn them on the altar as **f**,

	21: 8	they offer up the **f** of your God.
Nu	21: 5	And we detest this miserable **f!**"
Jos	5:12	after they ate this **f** from the land;
Ps	42: 3	My tears have been my **f** day
	78:18	by demanding the **f** they craved.
	104:27	all look to you to give them their **f**
Pr	12: 9	to be somebody and have no **f**.
	12:11	works his land will have abundant **f**,
	20:13	stay awake and you will have **f**
	20:17	**F** gained by fraud tastes sweet to
	21:20	of the wise are stores of choice **f**
	22: 9	for he shares his **f** with the poor.
	23: 3	for that **f** is deceptive.
	23: 6	Do not eat the **f** of a stingy man,
	25:21	give him **f** to eat;
	31:14	bringing her **f** from afar.
	31:15	she provides **f** for her family
Isa	58: 7	to share your **f** with the hungry and
	65:25	but dust will be the serpent's **f**.
Eze	18: 7	but gives his **f** to the hungry
Da	1: 8	not to defile himself with the royal **f**
Mt	3: 4	His **f** was locusts and wild honey.
	6:25	Is not life more important than **f**,
Jn	4:32	"I have **f** to eat
	4:34	"My **f**," said Jesus,
	6:27	Do not work for **f** that spoils,
	6:55	For my flesh is real **f**
Ac	15:20	to abstain from **f** polluted by idols,
Ro	14:14	that no **f** is unclean in itself.
1Co	3: 2	I gave you milk, not solid **f**,
	6:13	"**F** for the stomach and the stomach for **f**"—
	8: 1	Now about **f** sacrificed to idols:
	8: 8	But **f** does not bring us near to God;
2Co	11:27	and have often gone without **f**;
1Ti	6: 8	But if we have **f** and clothing,
Heb	5:14	But solid **f** is for the mature,
Jas	2:15	without clothes and daily **f**.

FOODS [FOOD]

| Mk | 7:19 | Jesus declared all **f** "clean.") |
| 1Ti | 4: 3 | order them to abstain from certain **f**, |

FOOL [FOLLY, FOOL'S, FOOLISH, FOOLISHNESS, FOOLS]

1Sa	25:25	just like his name—his name is **F**,
Ps	14: 1	The **f** says in his heart,
Pr	10:10	and a chattering **f** comes to ruin.
	10:18	and whoever spreads slander is a **f**.
	12:15	The way of a **f** seems right to him,
	12:16	A **f** shows his annoyance at once,
	14:16	but a **f** is hotheaded and reckless.
	15: 5	A **f** spurns his father's discipline,
	17:12	a bear robbed of her cubs than a **f**
	17:16	money in the hand of a **f**,
	17:21	To have a **f** for a son brings grief;
	17:28	a **f** is thought wise if he keeps silent,
	18: 2	A **f** finds no pleasure
	19:10	not fitting for a **f** to live in luxury—
	20: 3	but every **f** is quick to quarrel.
	23: 9	Do not speak to a **f**,
	24: 7	Wisdom is too high for a **f**;
	26: 4	not answer a **f** according to his folly,
	26: 5	Answer a **f** according to his folly,

26: 7	a proverb in the mouth of a **f**.
26:11	so a **f** repeats his folly.
26:12	There is more hope for a **f** than
27:22	Though you grind a **f** in a mortar,
28:26	He who trusts in himself is a **f**,
29:11	A **f** gives full vent to his anger,
29:20	There is more hope for a **f** than
Ecc	2:16	For the wise man, like the **f**,
	4: 5	**f** folds his hands and ruins himself.
	7: 7	Extortion turns a wise man into a **f**,
Hos	9: 7	the prophet is considered a **f**,
Mt	5:22	But anyone who says, 'You **f!**'
Lk	12:20	"But God said to him, 'You **f!**'
1Co	3:18	a "**f**" so that he may become wise.
2Co	11: 1	I am speaking as a **f**—

FOOL'S [FOOL]

| Pr | 14: 3 | A **f** talk brings a rod to his back, |
| | 18: 7 | A **f** mouth is his undoing, |

FOOLISH [FOOL]

Pr	8: 5	you who are **f**, gain understanding.
	10: 1	but a **f** son grief to his mother.
	14: 1	the **f** one tears hers down.
	15:20	but a **f** man despises his mother.
	17:25	A **f** son brings grief to his father
	19:13	A **f** son is his father's ruin,
	21:20	but a **f** man devours all he has.
Jer	5:21	you **f** and senseless people,
Eze	13: 3	**f** prophets who follow their own
Mt	7:26	a **f** man who built his house
	25: 2	of them were **f** and five were wise.
Lk	11:40	You **f** people!
	24:25	He said to them, "How **f** you are,
1Co	1:20	Has not God made **f** the wisdom of
	1:27	the **f** things of the world to shame
Gal	3: 1	You **f** Galatians!
Eph	5: 4	**f** talk or coarse joking,
	5:17	Therefore do not be **f**,
2Ti	2:23	to do with **f** and stupid arguments,
Tit	3: 3	At one time we too were **f**,
	3: 9	But avoid **f** controversies

FOOLISHNESS* [FOOL]

2Sa	15:31	turn Ahithophel's counsel into **f**."
1Co	1:18	For the message of the cross is **f**
	1:21	through the **f** of what was preached
	1:23	block to Jews and **f** to Gentiles,
	1:25	For the **f** of God is wiser than
	2:14	for they are **f** to him,
	3:19	For the wisdom of this world is **f**
2Co	11: 1	put up with a little of my **f**;

FOOLS [FOOL]

Pr	1: 7	but **f** despise wisdom and discipline.
	1:32	complacency of **f** will destroy them;
	3:35	but **f** he holds up to shame.
	10:21	but **f** die for lack of judgment.
	12:23	but the heart of **f** blurts out folly.
	13:19	but **f** detest turning from evil.
	13:20	but a companion of **f** suffers harm.
	14: 9	**F** mock at making amends for sin,
	14:24	but the folly of **f** yields folly.
	16:22	but folly brings punishment to **f**.

Ecc 5: 4 He has no pleasure in f;
    7: 4 heart of f is in the house of pleasure.
    7: 5 to listen to the song of f.
    7: 6 so is the laughter of f.
    10: 6 F are put in many high positions,
Mt 23:17 You blind f!
Ro 1:22 claimed to be wise, they became f
1Co 4:10 We are f for Christ,
2Co 11:19 put up with f since you are so wise!

FOOT [BAREFOOT, FEET, FOOTHOLD]
Ex 21:24 hand for hand, f for f,
    32:19 breaking them to pieces at the f of
Dt 11:24 where you set your f will be yours:
Jos 1: 3 every place where you set your f,
Ps 91:12 not strike your f against a stone.
    121: 3 He will not let your f slip—
Pr 1:15 do not set f on their paths;
    3:23 and your f will not stumble;
    4:27 keep your f from evil.
    25:17 Seldom set f in your neighbor's
Isa 1: 6 From the sole of your f to the top
Mt 4: 6 not strike your f against a stone.' "
    18: 8 If your hand or your f causes you
Lk 4:11 not strike your f against a stone.' "
1Co 12:15 If the f should say,
Heb 10:29 trampled the Son of God under f,
Rev 10: 2 He planted his right f on the sea

FOOTHOLD* [FOOT]
Ps 69: 2 where there is no f.
    73: 2 I had nearly lost my f.
Eph 4:27 and do not give the devil a f.

FOOTSTEPS [STEP]
Ps 119:133 Direct my f according to your word;
Ro 4:12 who also walk in the f of the faith

FOOTSTOOL
1Ch 28: 2 for the f of our God,
Ps 99: 5 and worship at his f;
    110: 1 until I make your enemies a f
Isa 66: 1 and the earth is my f.
La 2: 1 he has not remembered his f
Mt 5:35 or by the earth, for it is his f;
Ac 7:49 and the earth is my f.
Heb 1:13 until I make your enemies a f
    10:13 for his enemies to be made his f,

FORBEARANCE*
Ro 3:25 because in his f he had left the sins

FORBID [FORBIDDEN, FORBIDS]
1Co 14:39 and do not f speaking in tongues.
1Ti 4: 3 They f people to marry

FORBIDDEN [FORBID]
1Ki 11:10 Although he had f Solomon
2Ki 17:15 the things the LORD had f them

FORBIDS* [FORBID]
Nu 30: 5 But if her father f her when he hears
    30: 8 if her husband f her when he hears
Jn 5:10 the law f you to carry your mat."

FORCE [FORCED, FORCEFUL,
   FORCEFULLY, FORCES, FORCING]
Ex 19:24 and the people must not f their way
Jn 6:15 to come and make him king by f,
Ac 26:11 and I tried to f them to blaspheme.
Gal 2:14 that you f Gentiles to follow

FORCED [FORCE]
Ex 1:11 to oppress them with f labor,
Jdg 1:28 the Canaanites into f labor
1Ki 9:15 f labor King Solomon conscripted
Mt 27:32 and they f him to carry the cross.
Phm 1:14 be spontaneous and not f.
Rev 13:16 He also f everyone, small and great,

FORCEFUL* [FORCE]
Mt 11:12 and f men lay hold of it.
2Co 10:10 "His letters are weighty and f,

FORCEFULLY* [FORCE]
1Sa 18:10 an evil spirit from God came f
Isa 28: 2 he will throw it f to the ground.
Mt 11:12 of heaven has been f advancing,

FORCES [FORCE]
Mt 5:41 If someone f you to go one mile,
Eph 6:12 and against the spiritual f of evil in

FORCING* [FORCE]
Lk 16:16 and everyone is f his way into it.
Ac 7:19 by f them to throw out their newborn

FORDED* [FORDS]
Jos 2:23 f the river and came to Joshua

FORDS [FORDED]
Jos 2: 7 that leads to the f of the Jordan,

FOREFATHER [FATHER]
1Ki 15: 3 as the heart of David his f had been.
Ro 4: 1 Abraham, our f, discovered in this

FOREFATHERS [FATHER]
Ex 13: 5 land he swore to your f to give you,
Dt 4:31 or forget the covenant with your f,
    10:15 the LORD set his affection on your f
Jos 24:14 the gods your f worshiped beyond
Ne 9: 9 "You saw the suffering of our f
Jer 7: 7 in the land I gave your f for ever
Zec 1: 4 Do not be like your f,
Lk 11:47 and it was your f who killed them.
Jn 6:58 Your f ate manna and died,
Heb 1: 1 the past God spoke to our f through
    8: 9 like the covenant I made with their f
1Pe 1:18 down to you from your f,

FOREHEAD [FOREHEADS]
Ex 13: 9 a reminder on your f that the law of
    28:38 It will be on Aaron's f,
1Sa 17:49 and struck the Philistine on the f.
Rev 13:16 a mark on his right hand or on his f,
    14: 9 and receives his mark on the f or on
    17: 5 This title was written on her f:

FOREHEADS [FOREHEAD]

Dt	6: 8	and bind them on your **f**.
Rev	7: 3	on the **f** of the servants of our God."
	9: 4	not have the seal of God on their **f**.
	14: 1	his Father's name written on their **f**.
	20: 4	not received his mark on their **f**
	22: 4	and his name will be on their **f**.

FOREIGN [FOREIGNER, FOREIGNERS]

Ge	35: 2	"Get rid of the **f** gods you have with
Dt	32:12	LORD alone led him; no **f** god was
Jos	24:23	"throw away the **f** gods that are
1Ki	11: 1	loved many **f** women besides
2Ch	14: 3	the **f** altars and the high places,
	33:15	the **f** gods and removed
Ps	81: 9	You shall have no **f** god among you;
Isa	28:11	with **f** lips and strange tongues
Jer	2:25	I love **f** gods,
Ac	17:18	"He seems to be advocating **f** gods."

FOREIGNER [FOREIGN]

Dt	23:20	You may charge a **f** interest,
1Ki	8:41	for the **f** who does not belong
Lk	17:18	give praise to God except this **f**?"
1Co	14:11	a **f** to the speaker, and he is a **f** to me.

FOREIGNERS [FOREIGN]

Ge	31:15	Does he not regard us as **f**?
Ex	21: 8	He has no right to sell her to **f**,
Jer	5:19	so now you will serve **f** in a land
1Co	14:21	and through the lips of **f** I will speak
Eph	2:12	and **f** to the covenants of the promise
	2:19	you are no longer **f** and aliens,

FOREKNEW* [KNOW]

Ro	8:29	For those God **f** he also predestined
	11: 2	not reject his people, whom he **f**.

FOREKNOWLEDGE* [KNOW]

Ac	2:23	to you by God's set purpose and **f**;
1Pe	1: 2	according to the **f** of God the Father,

FOREORDAINED (KJV)

See CHOSEN

FORESAW* [FORESEE]

Gal	3: 8	Scripture **f** that God would justify

FORESEE* [FORESAW]

Isa	47:11	a catastrophe you cannot **f** will

FORESKIN* [FORESKINS]

Ex	4:25	cut off her son's **f**

FORESKINS [FORESKIN]

1Sa	18:25	the bride than a hundred Philistine **f**,

FOREST

2Sa	18: 8	and the **f** claimed more lives
1Ki	7: 2	the Palace of the **F** of Lebanon
1Ch	16:33	Then the trees of the **f** will sing,
Ps	50:10	for every animal of the **f** is mine,
Jas	3: 5	Consider what a great **f** is set on fire

FORETELL* [FORETELLS, FORETOLD]

Isa	44: 7	let him **f** what will come.
	44: 8	Did I not proclaim this and **f** it

FORETELLS* [FORETELL]

Dt	13: 1	a prophet, or one who **f** by dreams,

FORETOLD [FORETELL]

Ps	105:19	till what he **f** came to pass,
Isa	48: 3	I **f** the former things long ago,
Jude	1:17	apostles of our Lord Jesus Christ **f**.

FOREVER [EVER]

Ge	3:22	and eat, and live **f**."
	6: 3	Spirit will not contend with man **f**,
Ex	3:15	This is my name **f**,
	31:17	sign between me and the Israelites **f**,
Dt	29:29	belong to us and to our children **f**,
2Sa	7:13	establish the throne of his kingdom **f**.
	7:26	so that your name will be great **f**.
1Ki	2:33	may there be the LORD's peace **f**."
	9: 3	by putting my Name there **f**.
1Ch	16:15	He remembers his covenant **f**,
	16:41	"for his love endures **f**."
	17:24	and that your name will be great **f**.
2Ch	5:13	"He is good; his love endures **f**."
	33: 7	I will put my Name **f**.
Ezr	3:11	his love to Israel endures **f**."
Ps	9: 7	The LORD reigns **f**;
	19: 9	fear of the LORD is pure, enduring **f**.
	23: 6	dwell in the house of the LORD **f**.
	28: 9	be their shepherd and carry them **f**.
	29:10	the LORD is enthroned as King **f**.
	33:11	the plans of the LORD stand firm **f**,
	37:28	They will be protected **f**,
	44: 8	and we will praise your name **f**.
	44:23	Do not reject us **f**.
	61: 4	I long to dwell in your tent **f**
	72:19	Praise be to his glorious name **f**;
	73:26	of my heart and my portion **f**.
	74:10	Will the foe revile your name **f**?
	77: 8	Has his unfailing love vanished **f**?
	79:13	will praise you **f**;
	81:15	and their punishment would last **f**.
	86:12	I will glorify your name **f**.
	89: 1	I will sing of the LORD's great love **f**;
	92: 8	But you, O LORD, are exalted **f**.
	100: 5	and his love endures **f**;
	102:12	But you, O LORD, sit enthroned **f**;
	104:31	the glory of the LORD endure **f**;
	107: 1	he is good; his love endures **f**.
	110: 4	"You are a priest **f**,
	111: 3	and his righteousness endures **f**.
	112: 6	righteous man will be remembered **f**.
	117: 2	faithfulness of the LORD endures **f**.
	118: 1	for he is good; his love endures **f**.
	119:111	Your statutes are my heritage **f**;
	119:152	that you established them to last **f**.
	136: 1	His love endures **f**.
	146: 6	who remains faithful **f**.
Pr	6:21	Bind them upon your heart **f**;
	10:25	but the righteous stand firm **f**.

	27:24	for riches do not endure f,
Ecc	3:14	everything God does will endure f;
Isa	25: 8	he will swallow up death f.
	26: 4	Trust in the LORD f,
	32:17	be quietness and confidence f.
	40: 8	but the word of our God stands f."
	51: 6	But my salvation will last f,
	51: 8	But my righteousness will last f,
	57:15	and lofty One says—he who lives f,
	59:21	from this time on and f,"
Jer	3:12	'I will not be angry f.
	33:11	the LORD is good; his love endures f.
La	5:19	You, O LORD, reign f;
Eze	37:26	will put my sanctuary among them f.
Da	2:44	but it will itself endure f.
	6:26	the living God and he endures f;
Hos	2:19	I will betroth you to me f;
Jn	6:51	he will live f.
	14:16	another Counselor to be with you f—
Ro	9: 5	who is God over all, f praised!
	16:27	be glory f through Jesus Christ!
1Co	9:25	to get a crown that will last f.
1Th	4:17	And so we will be with the Lord f.
Heb	5: 6	"You are a priest f,
	7:17	it is declared: "You are a priest f,
	7:24	but because Jesus lives f,
	13: 8	Jesus Christ is the same yesterday
		and today and f.
1Pe	1:25	but the word of the Lord stands f."
1Jn	2:17	who does the will of God lives f.
2Jn	1: 2	lives in us and will be with us f:

HIS LOVE ENDURES FOREVER
See LOVE

FOREVERMORE [EVER]

Ps	125: 2	surrounds his people both now and f.
	131: 1	hope in the LORD both now and f.

FORFEIT

Mk	8:36	yet f his soul?
Lk	9:25	and yet lose or f his very self?

FORGAVE* [FORGIVE]

Ps	32: 5	and you f the guilt of my sin.
	65: 3	you f our transgressions.
	78:38	he was merciful; he f their iniquities
	85: 2	You f the iniquity of your people
Eph	4:32	just as in Christ God f you.
Col	2:13	He f us all our sins,
	3:13	Forgive as the Lord f you.

FORGET [FORGETS, FORGETTING, FORGOT, FORGOTTEN]

Dt	4:23	Be careful not to f the covenant of
	6:12	that you do not f the LORD,
2Ki	17:38	Do not f the covenant I have made
Job	8:13	Such is the destiny of all who f God;
Ps	9:17	all the nations that f God.
	10:12	Do not f the helpless.
	50:22	"Consider this, you who f God,
	78: 7	in God and would not f his deeds
	103: 2	and f not all his benefits—
	119:93	I will never f your precepts,
	137: 5	If I f you, O Jerusalem,

Pr	3: 1	My son, do not f my teaching,
	4: 5	do not f my words or
	31: 5	drink and f what the law decrees,
Isa	49:15	a mother f the baby at her breast
	49:15	she may f, I will not f you!
	51:13	that you f the LORD your Maker,
Jer	2:32	Does a maiden f her jewelry,
	23:39	surely f you and cast you out
Heb	6:10	not f your work and
	13: 2	Do not f to entertain strangers,
	13:16	And do not f to do good and to share
2Pe	3: 8	do not f this one thing, dear friends:

FORGETS [FORGET]

Jn	16:21	but when her baby is born she f
Jas	1:24	immediately f what he looks like.

FORGETTING* [FORGET]

Php	3:13	But one thing I do: F what is behind
Jas	1:25	not f what he has heard,

FORGIVE* [FORGAVE, FORGIVEN, FORGIVENESS, FORGIVES, FORGIVING]

Ge	50:17	to f your brothers the sins and
	50:17	Now please f the sins of the servants
Ex	10:17	Now f my sin once more and pray to
	23:21	he will not f your rebellion,
	32:32	But now, please f their sin—
	34: 9	f our wickedness and our sin,
Nu	14:19	f the sin of these people,
Dt	29:20	will never be willing to f him;
Jos	24:19	not f your rebellion and your sins.
1Sa	15:25	f my sin and come back with me,
	25:28	Please f your servant's offense,
1Ki	8:30	and when you hear, f.
	8:34	and f the sin of your people Israel
	8:36	then hear from heaven and f the sin
	8:39	F and act;
	8:50	f all the offenses
2Ki	5:18	But may the LORD f your servant
	5:18	the LORD f your servant for this."
	24: 4	and the LORD was not willing to f.
2Ch	6:21	and when you hear, f.
	6:25	and f the sin of your people Israel
	6:27	and f the sin of your servants,
	6:30	F, and deal with each man according
	6:39	And f your people,
	7:14	and will f their sin and will heal
Job	7:21	and f my sins?
Ps	19:12	F my hidden faults.
	25:11	f my iniquity, though it is great.
	79: 9	and f our sins for your name's sake.
Isa	2: 9	do not f them.
Jer	5: 1	I will f this city.
	5: 7	"Why should I f you?
	18:23	Do not f their crimes
	31:34	"For I will f their wickedness
	33: 8	and will f all their sins
	36: 3	then I will f their wickedness
	50:20	for I will f the remnant I spare.
Da	9:19	O Lord, f!
Hos	1: 6	that I should at all f them.

14: 2 Say to him: **"F** all our sins
Am 7: 2 I cried out,"Sovereign LORD, **f!**
Mt 6:12 **F** us our debts,
6:14 For if you **f** men when they sin
6:14 your heavenly Father will also **f** you.
6:15 But if you do not **f** men their sins,
your Father will not **f** your sins.
9: 6 authority on earth to **f** sins...."
18:21 how many times shall I **f** my brother
18:35 each of you unless you **f** your brother
Mk 2: 7 Who can **f** sins but God alone?"
2:10 authority on earth to **f** sins...."
11:25 anything against anyone, **f** him,
11:25 Father in heaven may **f** you your sins
Lk 5:21 Who can **f** sins but God alone?"
5:24 authority on earth to **f** sins...."
6:37 **F,** and you will be forgiven.
11: 4 **F** us our sins, for we also **f** everyone
17: 3 rebuke him, and if he repents, **f** him.
17: 4 'I repent, ' **f** him."
23:34 Jesus said,"Father, **f** them,
Jn 20:23 If you **f** anyone his sins,
20:23 if you do not **f** them,
Ac 8:22 Perhaps he will **f** you
2Co 2: 7 you ought to **f** and comfort him,
2:10 If you **f** anyone, I also **f** him.
2:10 if there was anything to **f**—
12:13 **F** me this wrong!
Col 3:13 **f** whatever grievances you may have
3:13 **F** as the Lord forgave you.
Heb 8:12 For I will **f** their wickedness
1Jn 1: 9 and just and will **f** us our sins

FORGIVEN [FORGIVE]

Lev 4:20 and they will be **f.**
Nu 14:20 The LORD replied,"I have **f** them,
Ps 32: 1 he whose transgressions are **f,**
Mk 2: 9 'Your sins are **f,** ' or to say, 'Get up,
3:29 blasphemes against the Holy Spirit
will never be **f**
Lk 7:47 he who has been **f** little loves little."
Ro 4: 7 they whose transgressions are **f,**
Jas 5:15 If he has sinned, he will be **f.**

FORGIVENESS [FORGIVE]

Ps 130: 4 But with you there is **f;**
Mt 26:28 for many for the **f** of sins.
Mk 1: 4 a baptism of repentance for the **f**
Lk 1:77 salvation through the **f** of their sins,
3: 3 baptism of repentance for the **f** of
24:47 and repentance and **f** of sins will
Ac 5:31 that he might give repentance and **f**
10:43 believes in him receives **f** of sins
13:38 the **f** of sins is proclaimed to you.
26:18 that they may receive **f** of sins and
Eph 1: 7 through his blood, the **f** of sins,
Col 1:14 we have redemption, the **f** of sins.
Heb 9:22 the shedding of blood there is no **f.**

FORGIVES* [FORGIVE]

Ps 103: 3 who **f** all your sins
Mic 7:18 pardons sin and **f** the transgression
Lk 7:49 "Who is this who even **f** sins?"

FORGIVING* [FORGIVE]

Ex 34: 7 and **f** wickedness, rebellion and sin.
Nu 14:18 in love and **f** sin and rebellion.
Ne 9:17 But you are a **f** God,
Ps 86: 5 You are **f** and good, O Lord,
99: 8 you were to Israel a **f** God,
Da 9: 9 The Lord our God is merciful and **f,**
Eph 4:32 to one another, **f** each other,

FORGOT [FORGET]

Dt 32:18 you **f** the God who gave you birth.
1Sa 12: 9 "But they **f** the LORD their God;
Ps 78:11 They **f** what he had done,
106:21 They **f** the God who saved them,
Jer 23:27 just as their fathers **f** my name

FORGOTTEN [FORGET]

Job 11: 6 God has even **f** some of your sin.
Ps 10:11 He says to himself,"God has **f;**
44:20 If we had **f** the name of our God
77: 9 Has God **f** to be merciful?
Isa 17:10 You have **f** God your Savior;
49:14 the Lord has **f** me."
Jer 2:32 Yet my people have **f** me,
Hos 8:14 Israel has **f** his Maker
Lk 12: 6 Yet not one of them is **f** by God.
Heb 12: 5 have **f** that word of encouragement
2Pe 1: 9 and has **f** that he has been cleansed

FORM [FORMED, FORMS]

Ex 20: 4 an idol in the **f** of anything in heaven
Dt 4:15 You saw no **f** of any kind the day
Isa 52:14 his **f** marred beyond human likeness
Col 2: 9 fullness of the Deity lives in bodily **f,**
2Ti 3: 5 having a **f** of godliness but denying

FORMED [FORM]

Ge 2: 7 LORD God **f** the man from the dust
Dt 32: 6 who made you and **f** you?
Ps 94: 9 Does he who **f** the eye not see?
103:14 for he knows how we are **f,**
Ecc 11: 5 the body is **f** in a mother's womb,
Isa 29:16 Shall what is **f** say to him who **f** it,
43:10 Before me no god was **f,**
45:18 but **f** it to be inhabited—
49: 5 now the LORD says—he who **f** me
Jer 1: 5 "Before I **f** you in the womb
18: 4 so the potter **f** it into another pot,
Ro 9:20 "Shall what is **f** say to him who **f** it,
Gal 4:19 of childbirth until Christ is **f** in you,
1Ti 2:13 For Adam was **f** first, then Eve.
Heb 11: 3 universe was **f** at God's command,
2Pe 3: 5 heavens existed and the earth was **f**

FORMER

Dt 4:32 Ask now about the **f** days,
Ezr 3:12 who had seen the **f** temple,
Ps 77: 5 I thought about the **f** days,
Isa 46: 9 Remember the **f** things,
Lk 11:42 without leaving the **f** undone.

FORMLESS*

Ge 1: 2 Now the earth was **f** and empty,
Jer 4:23 and it was **f** and empty;

FORMS [FORM]

Ps   33:15 he who f the hearts of all,
Am   4:13 He who f the mountains,
Zec 12: 1 who f the spirit of man within him,

FORSAKE [FORSAKEN, FORSAKING]

Dt   31: 6 he will never leave you nor f you."
Jos   1: 5 I will never leave you nor f you.
     24:16 to f the LORD to serve other gods!
2Ch 15: 2 but if you f him, he will f you.
Ps   27:10 Though my father and mother f me,
    94:14 he will never f his inheritance.
Pr   4: 6 Do not f wisdom,
    27:10 Do not f your friend and the friend
Isa   1:28 those who f the LORD will perish.
    55: 7 Let the wicked f his way and
Jer 17:13 all who f you will be put to shame.
Heb 13: 5 leave you; never will I f you."

FORSAKEN [FORSAKE]

Ps   9:10 have never f those who seek you.
    22: 1 my God, why have you f me?
    37:25 yet I have never seen the righteous f
Isa 49:14 Zion said,"The LORD has f me,
Mt 27:46 my God, why have you f me?"
Rev 2: 4 You have f your first love.

FORSAKING [FORSAKE]

1Sa 8: 8 f me and serving other gods,
Eze 20:27 your fathers blasphemed me by f me:

FORTH

Ge   3:24 a flaming sword flashing back and f
Ps 19: 2 Day after day they pour f speech;
   50: 2 perfect in beauty, God shines f.
Eph 4:14 tossed back and f by the waves,

FORTIFIED [FORTRESS]

Nu 13:28 and the cities are f and very large.
Ne   9:25 They captured f cities

FORTRESS [FORTIFIED]

2Sa 5: 7 David captured the f of Zion,
   22: 2 my f and my deliverer;
Ps 28: 8 a f of salvation for his anointed one.
   31: 2 a strong f to save me.
   46: 7 the God of Jacob is our f.
   59:17 O God, are my f, my loving God.
   71: 3 for you are my rock and my f.
Pr 14:26 who fears the LORD has a secure f,
Isa 17:10 not remembered the Rock, your f.
Jer 16:19 O LORD, my strength and my f,

FORTUNE* [FORTUNE-TELLING, FORTUNES]

Ge 30:11 Then Leah said,"What good f!"
Job 31:25 the f my hands had gained,
Pr 21: 6 A f made by a lying tongue is
Isa 65:11 who spread a table for F

FORTUNE-TELLING* [FORTUNE]

Ac 16:16 deal of money for her owners by f.

FORTUNES [FORTUNE]

Dt 30: 3 LORD your God will restore your f
Ps 53: 6 God restores the f of his people,
Jer 32:44 because I will restore their f,
Hos 6:11 "Whenever I would restore the f
Mic 3:11 and her prophets tell f for money.

FORTY [40]

Ge   7: 4 on the earth for f days and f nights,
   18:29 "What if only f are found there?"
Ex 16:35 The Israelites ate manna f years,
   24:18 on the mountain f days and f nights.
Nu 14:34 For f years—one year for each of
      the f days you explored
Dt 25: 3 not give him more than f lashes.
Jos 14: 7 I was f years old when Moses
1Sa 4:18 He had led Israel f years.
2Sa 5: 4 and he reigned f years.
1Ki 19: 8 he traveled f days and f nights until
2Ch 9:30 in Jerusalem over all Israel f years.
Ne 9:21 For f years you sustained them in
Eze 29:12 her cities will lie desolate f years
Am 2:10 and I led you f years in the desert
Jnh 3: 4 "F more days and Nineveh will be
Mt 4: 2 After fasting f days and f nights,
Lk 4: 2 f days he was tempted by the devil.
2Co 11:24 from the Jews the f lashes minus one.
Heb 3:17 whom was he angry for f years?

FORTY DAYS Ge 7:4, 12, 17; 8:6; 50:3; Ex
24:18; 34:28; Nu 13:25; 14:34; Dt 9:9, 11, 18,
25; 10:10; 1Sa 17:16; 1Ki 19:8; Mt 4:2; Mk 1:13;
Lk 4:2; Ac 1:3

FORTY YEARS Ge 25:20; 26:34; Ex 16:35; Nu
14:33, 34; 32:13; Dt 2:7; 8:2, 4; 29:5; Jos 5:6;
14:7; Jdg 3:11; 5:31; 8:28; 13:1; 1Sa 4:18; 2Sa
2:10; 5:4; 1Ki 2:11; 11:42; 2Ki 12:1; 1Ch 29:27;
2Ch 9:30; 24:1; Ne 9:21; Job 42:16; Ps 95:10;
Eze 29:11, 12, 13; Am 2:10; 5:25; Ac 4:22; 7:23,
30, 36, 42; 13:18, 21; Heb 3:9, 17

FOUGHT [FIGHT]

Jos 10:42 the God of Israel, f for Israel.
1Co 15:32 I f wild beasts in Ephesus
2Ti 4: 7 I have f the good fight,
Rev 12: 7 and his angels f against the dragon,

FOUND [FIND]

Ge   6: 8 But Noah f favor in the eyes of
Ex 12:19 For seven days no yeast is to be f
   33:12 and you have f favor with me.'
2Ki 22: 8 "I have f the Book of the Law in
1Ch 28: 9 If you seek him, he will be f by you;
2Ch 15:15 and he was f by them.
Ps 37:10 they will not be f.
Pr 10:13 Wisdom is f on the lips of
   14: 9 but goodwill is f among the upright.
Isa 55: 6 Seek the LORD while he may be f;
   65: 1 I was f by those who did not seek me
Jer 29:14 I will be f by you,"
Da   1:19 and he f none equal to Daniel,
   5:27 weighed on the scales and f wanting,
   12: 1 everyone whose name is f written
Mt 1:18 she was f to be with child through

Lk	1:30	Mary, you have f favor with God.
	7: 9	not f such great faith even in Israel."
	15: 6	I have f my lost sheep.'
	15: 9	I have f my lost coin.'
	15:24	he was lost and is f.'
Ac	4:12	Salvation is f in no one else,
Ro	10:20	"I was f by those who did
Php	2: 8	And being f in appearance as a man,
Col	2:17	the reality, however, is f in Christ.
Heb	3: 3	Jesus has been f worthy
Jas	2: 8	If you really keep the royal law f
Rev	5: 4	no one was f who was worthy
	20:15	If anyone's name was not f written

FOUNDATION [FOUNDATIONS, FOUNDED]

1Ki	6:37	The f of the temple of the LORD
Ezr	3: 6	the f of the LORD's temple had not
Job	38: 4	were you when I laid the earth's f?
Ps	97: 2	and justice are the f of his throne.
Isa	28:16	a precious cornerstone for a sure f;
Mt	7:25	because it had its f on the rock.
Lk	14:29	For if he lays the f and is not able
Ro	15:20	not be building on someone else's f.
1Co	3:10	I laid a f as an expert builder,
	3:11	no one can lay any f other than
Eph	2:20	on the f of the apostles and prophets,
1Ti	3:15	the pillar and f of the truth.
2Ti	2:19	God's solid f stands firm,
Heb	6: 1	not laying again the f of repentance
Rev	21:19	The first f was jasper,

FOUNDATIONS [FOUNDATION]

1Sa	2: 8	the f of the earth are the LORD's;
Ps	102:25	In the beginning you laid the f of
	137: 7	they cried,"tear it down to its f!"
Pr	8:29	wisdom the LORD laid the earth's f,
Isa	48:13	My own hand laid the f of the earth,
Heb	1:10	O Lord, you laid the f of the earth,
Rev	21:14	The wall of the city had twelve f,

FOUNDED [FOUNDATION]

Jer	10:12	he f the world by his wisdom
Heb	8: 6	and it is f on better promises.

FOUNTAIN

Ps	36: 9	For with you is the f of life;
Pr	5:18	May your f be blessed,
	14:27	The fear of the LORD is a f of life,
	18: 4	the f of wisdom is a bubbling brook.
SS	4:12	you are a spring enclosed, a sealed f.
Jer	9: 1	and my eyes a f of tears!
Joel	3:18	A f will flow out of the LORD's
Zec	13: 1	a f will be opened to the house of

FOUR [FOURTH]

Ge	2:10	separated into f headwaters.
1Ki	18:19	f hundred and fifty prophets of Baal
Isa	11:12	from the f quarters of the earth.
Eze	1: 5	what looked like f living creatures.
	10: 9	I saw beside the cherubim f wheels,
	10:14	Each of the cherubim had f faces:
Da	1:17	f young men God gave knowledge
	7: 3	F great beasts, each different

	8: 8	in its place f prominent horns grew
Zec	1:20	the LORD showed me f craftsmen.
	6: 5	"These are the f spirits of heaven,
Mt	15:38	of those who ate was f thousand,
Mk	8:20	the seven loaves for the f thousand,
Rev	4: 6	were f living creatures,
	9:14	"Release the f angels who are bound

FOURTEEN

Mt	1:17	Thus there were f generations in all
2Co	12: 2	a man in Christ who f years ago was
Gal	2: 1	F years later I went up again to

FOURTH [FOUR]

Ge	15:16	f generation your descendants will
Ex	20: 5	to the third and f generation

FOWLER* [FOWLER'S]

Pr	6: 5	like a bird from the snare of the f.

FOWLER'S* [FOWLER]

Ps	91: 3	he will save you from the f snare
	124: 7	like a bird out of the f snare;

FOWLS (KJV) See BIRDS

FOX* [FOXES]

Ne	4: 3	if even a f climbed up on it,
Lk	13:32	He replied,"Go tell that f,

FOXES [FOX]

Jdg	15: 4	and caught three hundred f
SS	2:15	the little f that ruin the vineyards,
Lk	9:58	"F have holes and birds of

FRACTURE*

Lev	24:20	f for f, eye for eye,

FRAGRANCE [FRAGRANT]

Ex	30:38	makes any like it to enjoy its f
SS	4:10	f of your perfume than any spice!
Jn	12: 3	And the house was filled with the f
2Co	2:14	through us spreads everywhere the f
	2:16	to the other, the f of life.

FRAGRANT [FRAGRANCE]

Ex	25: 6	and for the f incense;
	30: 7	"Aaron must burn f incense on
Eph	5: 2	gave himself up for us as a f offering
Php	4:18	They are a f offering,

FRAME [FRAMES]

Ps	139:15	My f was not hidden from you

FRAMES [FRAME]

Ex	26:15	"Make upright f of acacia wood for
Nu	3:36	take care of the f of the tabernacle,

FRAUD* [DEFRAUD]

Pr	20:17	Food gained by f tastes sweet to
Jer	10:14	His images are a f;
	51:17	His images are a f;

FREE [FREED, FREEDMAN, FREEDOM, FREELY]

Ge   2:16 "You are f to eat from any tree in
  49:21 "Naphtali is a doe set f
Ex 21: 2 in the seventh year, he shall go f,
Ps 118: 5 and he answered by setting me f.
  119:32 for you have set my heart f.
  146: 7 The LORD sets prisoners f,
Pr   6: 3 my son, to f yourself,
Isa 42: 7 to f captives from prison and
Lk 13:12 you are set f from your infirmity."
Jn   8:32 and the truth will set you f."
  8:36 So if the Son sets you f, you will be f
  19:12 Pilate tried to set Jesus f,
Ro   6:18 You have been set f from sin
  8: 2 the law of the Spirit of life set me f
1Co 9:21 (though I am not f from God's law
  12:13 whether Jews or Greeks, slave or f—
Gal 3:28 slave nor f, male nor female,
  5: 1 for freedom that Christ has set us f.
1Pe 2:16 Live as f men,
Rev 20: 3 he must be set f for a short time.
  22:17 let him take the f gift of the water

FREED [FREE]

Ps 116:16 you have f me from my chains.
Mk 5:34 and be f from your suffering."
Ro   6: 7 anyone who has died has been f
Rev 1: 5 To him who loves us and has f us

FREEDMAN* [FREE]

1Co 7:22 by the Lord is the Lord's f;

FREEDOM [FREE]

Ps 119:45 I will walk about in f,
Isa 61: 1 to proclaim f for the captives
Lk   4:18 He has sent me to proclaim f for
Ro   8:21 the glorious f of the children
1Co 7:21 although if you can gain your f,
  10:29 For why should my f be judged
2Co 3:17 Spirit of the Lord is, there is f.
Gal 2: 4 to spy on the f we have in Christ
  5: 1 It is for f that Christ has set us free.
  5:13 But do not use your f to indulge
Jas 1:25 the perfect law that gives f,
1Pe 2:16 not use your f as a cover-up for evil;

FREELY [FREE]

Isa 55: 7 and to our God, for he will f pardon.
Mt 10: 8 F you have received, f give.
Ro   3:24 and are justified f by his grace
Eph 1: 6 which he has f given us in

FREEWILL [WILL]

Ex 35:29 brought to the LORD f offerings
Ezr 1: 4 and with f offerings for the temple
Ps 54: 6 I will sacrifice a f offering to you;

FRESH

Eze 47: 8 the water there becomes f.
Jas 3:11 Can both f water and salt water flow

FRET*

Ps 37: 1 Do not f because of evil men or

37: 7 do not f when men succeed in their
37: 8 do not f—it leads only to evil.
Pr 24:19 Do not f because of evil men or

FRICTION*

1Ti   6: 5 and constant f between men

FRIEND [FRIENDS, FRIENDSHIP]

Ex 33:11 as a man speaks with his f.
Dt 13: 6 your closest f secretly entices you,
2Sa 16:17 "Is this the love you show your f?
2Ch 20: 7 the descendants of Abraham your f?
Ps 41: 9 Even my close f, whom I trusted,
Pr 17:17 A f loves at all times,
  18:24 a f who sticks closer than a brother.
  27: 6 Wounds from a f can be trusted,
  27:10 Do not forsake your f and the f of
Ecc 4:10 his f can help him up.
SS   5:16 This is my lover, this my f,
Isa 41: 8 you descendants of Abraham my f,
Jer   9: 5 F deceives f, and no one speaks the
Mt 11:19 a f of tax collectors and "sinners." '
Lk 11: 8 the bread because he is his f,
Jn 19:12 you are no f of Caesar.
Jas 2:23 and he was called God's f.
  4: 4 a f of the world becomes an enemy

FRIENDS [FRIEND]

Job 2:11 When Job's three f,
  42:10 After Job had prayed for his f,
Pr 16:28 and a gossip separates close f.
  17: 9 repeats the matter separates close f.
La   1: 2 All her f have betrayed her;
Zec 13: 6 I was given at the house of my f.'
Jn 15:13 that he lay down his life for his f.
  15:14 You are my f

FRIENDSHIP [FRIEND]

Dt 23: 6 Do not seek a treaty of f with them
Ezr 9:12 Do not seek a treaty of f with them
Jas 4: 4 f with the world is hatred toward

FRIGHTEN [FEAR]

Dt 28:26 there will be no one to f them away.
Ne 6: 9 They were all trying to f us,

FRIGHTENED [FEAR]

Php 1:28 without being f in any way
1Pe 3:14 do not be f."

FROGS

Ex   8: 2 plague your whole country with f.
Rev 16:13 three evil spirits that looked like f;

FRONT

Ex 14:19 of God, who had been traveling in f
  32:15 inscribed on both sides, f and back.
Lev 19:14 a stumbling block in f of the blind,
Mt   5:24 leave your gift there in f of the altar.

FROST

Ex 16:14 thin flakes like f on the ground
Zec 14: 6 no cold or f.

FRUIT [FIRSTFRUITS, FRUITFUL, FRUITLESS]

Ge	1:11	and trees on the land that bear **f**
	3: 3	'You must not eat **f** from the tree
Lev	19:23	regard its **f** as forbidden.
Dt	28: 4	The **f** of your womb will be blessed,
	28:53	you will eat the **f** of the womb,
Jdg	9:11	'Should I give up my **f,**
Ps	1: 3	which yields its **f** in season
Pr	8:19	My **f** is better than fine gold;
	11:30	**f** of the righteous is a tree of life,
	12:14	the **f** of his lips a man is filled
	27:18	He who tends a fig tree will eat its **f,**
Isa	11: 1	from his roots a Branch will bear **f.**
	27: 6	and fill all the world with **f.**
	32:17	The **f** of righteousness will be peace;
Jer	17: 8	and never fails to bear **f."**
Eze	47:12	**F** trees of all kinds will grow on
Hos	9:10	like seeing the early **f** on the fig tree.
	10:12	reap the **f** of unfailing love,
	14: 2	that we may offer the **f** of our lips.
Am	8: 1	a basket of ripe **f.**
Mt	3: 8	Produce **f** in keeping with repentance
	3:10	not produce good **f** will be cut down
	7:16	By their **f** you will recognize them.
	7:17	every good tree bears good **f,**
Lk	6:44	Each tree is recognized by its own **f.**
	13: 6	and he went to look for **f** on it,
Jn	15: 2	branch that does bear **f** he prunes
	15:16	and appointed you to go and bear **f—**
Ro	7: 4	in order that we might bear **f** to God.
Gal	5:22	But the **f** of the Spirit is love, joy,
Eph	5: 9	(for the **f** of the light consists
Php	1:11	the **f** of righteousness that comes
Col	1:10	bearing **f** in every good work,
Heb	13:15	the **f** of lips that confess his name.
Jas	3:17	full of mercy and good **f,**
Jude	1:12	without **f** and uprooted—
Rev	22: 2	yielding its **f** every month.

FRUITFUL [FRUIT]

Ge	1:22	"Be **f** and increase in number
	9: 1	"Be **f** and increase in number
	17: 6	I will make you very **f;**
	35:11	be **f** and increase in number.
Ex	1: 7	but the Israelites were **f**
Ps	105:24	The LORD made his people very **f;**
	128: 3	be like a **f** vine within your house;
Isa	27: 2	"Sing about a **f** vineyard:
Jn	15: 2	so that it will be even more **f.**
Php	1:22	this will mean **f** labor for me.

FRUITLESS* [FRUIT]

Eph	5:11	Have nothing to do with the **f** deeds

FRUSTRATE* [FRUSTRATES, FRUSTRATION]

2Sa	17:14	to **f** the good advice of Ahithophel
Ezr	4: 5	and **f** their plans during
Ps	14: 6	You evildoers **f** the plans of
1Co	1:19	of the intelligent I will **f."**

FRUSTRATES* [FRUSTRATE]

Ps	146: 9	but he **f** the ways of the wicked.
Pr	22:12	but he **f** the words of the unfaithful.

FRUSTRATION* [FRUSTRATE]

Ecc	5:17	with great **f,** affliction and anger.
Ro	8:20	For the creation was subjected to **f,**

FUEL

Isa	44:19	"Half of it I used for **f;**
Eze	21:32	You will be **f** for the fire,

FULFILL [FULFILLED, FULFILLMENT, FULFILLS]

Ge	38: 8	**f** your duty to her as a brother-in-law
Nu	23:19	Does he promise and not **f?**
Dt	25: 7	not **f** the duty of a brother-in-law
2Ch	10:15	to **f** the word the LORD had spoken
	36:22	to **f** the word of the LORD spoken
Ps	61: 8	and **f** my vows day after day.
	116:14	I will **f** my vows to the LORD in
	138: 8	LORD will **f** [his purpose] for me;
Ecc	5: 5	to make a vow and not **f** it.
Isa	46:11	a man to **f** my purpose.
Jer	11: 5	Then I will **f** the oath I swore
	33:14	'when I will **f** the gracious promise
Mt	1:22	to **f** what the Lord had said through
	3:15	to do this to **f** all righteousness."
	4:14	to **f** what was said through
	5:17	to abolish them but to **f** them.
	8:17	This was to **f** what was spoken
	12:17	This was to **f** what was spoken
	21: 4	to **f** what was spoken through
Jn	12:38	to **f** the word of Isaiah the prophet:
	13:18	But this is to **f** the scripture:
	15:25	to **f** what is written in their Law:
1Co	7: 3	husband should **f** his marital duty
Gal	6: 2	and in this way you will **f** the law
2Th	1:11	power he may **f** every good purpose

FULFILLED [FULFILL]

Jos	21:45	every one was **f.**
	23:14	Every promise has been **f;**
2Ch	6:15	and with your hand you have **f** it—
Pr	13:12	but a longing **f** is a tree of life.
	13:19	A longing **f** is sweet to the soul,
Jer	25:12	"But when the seventy years are **f,**
Da	12: 6	before these astonishing things are **f?**
Mt	2:15	And so was **f** what the Lord had said
	2:17	through the prophet Jeremiah was **f:**
	2:23	was **f** what was said through
	13:14	In them is **f** the prophecy of Isaiah:
	13:35	So was **f** what was spoken through
	26:54	how then would the Scriptures be **f**
	26:56	writings of the prophets might be **f."**
	27: 9	by Jeremiah the prophet was **f:**
Mk	13: 4	that they are all about to be **f?"**
	14:49	But the Scriptures must be **f."**
Lk	1: 1	account of the things that have been **f**
	4:21	"Today this scripture is **f**
	18:31	about the Son of Man will be **f.**
	24:44	be **f** that is written about me in
Jn	17:12	so that Scripture would be **f.**

18: 9 the words he had spoken would be **f:**
19:24 the scripture might be **f** which said,
19:28 and so that the Scripture would be **f,**
19:36 so that the scripture would be **f:**
Ac 1:16 to be **f** which the Holy Spirit spoke
3:18 how God **f** what he had foretold
Ro 13: 8 loves his fellowman has **f** the law.
Jas 2:23 And the scripture was **f** that says,
Rev 17:17 until God's words are **f.**

FULFILLMENT [FULFILL]

2Ch 36:21 seventy years were completed in **f**
Lk 22:16 I will not eat it again until it finds **f**
Ro 13:10 Therefore love is the **f** of the law.
1Co 10:11 on whom the **f** of the ages has come.
Eph 1:10 the times will have reached their **f—**

FULFILLS* [FULFILL]

Ps 57: 2 to God, who **f** [his purpose] for me.
145:19 He **f** the desires of those
Isa 44:26 **f** the predictions of his messengers,

FULL [FILL]

Ge 6:11 in God's sight and was **f** of violence.
15:16 not yet reached its **f** measure."
2Ki 4: 6 When all the jars were **f,**
2Ch 24:10 into the chest until it was **f.**
Job 14: 1 of few days and **f** of trouble.
Ps 31:23 but the proud he pays back in **f.**
116: 5 our God is **f** of compassion.
127: 5 Blessed is the man whose quiver is **f**
Pr 27: 7 He who is **f** loathes honey,
31:11 Her husband has **f** confidence in her
Isa 1:15 Your hands are **f** of blood;
6: 3 the whole earth is **f** of his glory."
11: 9 be **f** of the knowledge of the LORD
Jer 51:56 he will repay in **f.**
La 1: 1 once so **f** of people!
Eze 10:12 were completely **f** of eyes,
Lk 4: 1 Jesus, **f** of the Holy Spirit,
11:34 your whole body also is **f** of light.
Jn 10:10 and have it to the **f.**
13: 1 he now showed them the **f** extent
Ac 6: 3 among you who are known to be **f** of
6: 5 man **f** of faith and of the Holy Spirit;
7:55 But Stephen, **f** of the Holy Spirit,
11:24 **f** of the Holy Spirit and faith,
Eph 6:11 Put on the **f** armor of God so

FULL-GROWN* [GROW]

Jas 1:15 when it is **f,** gives birth to death.

FULLER (KJV) See SOAP

FULLNESS* [FILL]

Dt 33:16 the best gifts of the earth and its **f**
Jn 1:16 From the **f** of his grace we have all
Ro 11:12 greater riches will their **f** bring!
Eph 1:23 the **f** of him who fills everything
3:19 be filled to the measure of all the **f**
4:13 the whole measure of the **f** of Christ.
Col 1:19 to have all his **f** dwell in him,
1:25 to you the word of God in its **f—**
2: 9 in Christ all the **f** of the Deity lives

2:10 and you have been given **f** in Christ,

FULLY [FILL]

Ex 19: 5 Now if you obey me **f**
Dt 28: 1 If you **f** obey the LORD your God
1Ki 16: 9 But your hearts must be **f** committed
2Ch 16: 9 those whose hearts are **f** committed
Ps 119: 4 precepts that are to be **f** obeyed.
119:138 they are **f** trustworthy.
Pr 13: 4 desires of the diligent are **f** satisfied.
Lk 6:40 but everyone who is **f** trained will be
Ro 4:21 being **f** persuaded that God
8: 4 of the law might be **f** met in us,
14: 5 be **f** convinced in his own mind.
1Co 13:12 I shall know **f,** even as I am **f** known.
15:58 Always give yourselves **f** to
Gal 4: 4 But when the time had **f** come,
2Ti 4:17 the message might be **f** proclaimed
2Jn 1: 8 but that you may be rewarded **f.**

FURIOUS [FURY]

Dt 29:28 In **f** anger and in great wrath
Jer 32:37 where I banish them in my **f** anger

FURNACE

Dt 4:20 out of the iron-smelting **f,**
1Ki 8:51 out of that iron-smelting **f.**
Isa 48:10 I have tested you in the **f**
Jer 11: 4 out of the iron-smelting **f.'**
Da 3: 6 be thrown into a blazing **f."**
Mal 4: 1 it will burn like a **f.**
Mt 13:42 They will throw them into the fiery **f,**
Rev 1:15 like bronze glowing in a **f,**

FURNISHED [FURNISHINGS]

Mk 14:15 **f** and ready.

FURNISHINGS [FURNISHED]

Ex 25: 9 Make this tabernacle and all its **f**
1Ki 7:48 Solomon also made all the **f**

FURTHER

Job 34:23 God has no need to examine men **f,**
Hos 11: 2 the **f** they went from me.

FURY [FURIOUS]

Isa 14: 6 and in **f** subdued nations
Jer 21: 5 and a mighty arm in anger and **f**
Rev 12:12 He is filled with **f,**
14:10 will drink of the wine of God's **f,**
16:19 the cup filled with the wine of the **f**
19:15 the winepress of the **f** of the wrath

FUTILE [FUTILITY]

Mal 3:14 "You have said, 'It is **f** to serve God.
Ro 1:21 but their thinking became **f**
1Co 3:20 that the thoughts of the wise are **f."**

FUTILITY [FUTILE]

Ps 78:33 So he ended their days in **f**
Eph 4:17 in the **f** of their thinking.

FUTURE

Dt 6:20 In the **f,** when your son asks you,
1Ch 17:17 the **f** of the house of your servant.

Ps   37:37 a **f** for the man of peace.
Pr   23:18 There is surely a **f** hope for you,
      24:20 for the evil man has no **f** hope,
Ecc   7:14 cannot discover anything about his **f**.
       8: 7 Since no man knows the **f**,
Jer   29:11 plans to give you hope and a **f**.
      31:17 So there is hope for your **f**,"
Da   8:26 for it concerns the distant **f**."
Mt   26:64 In the **f** you will see the Son
Ro   8:38 neither the present nor the **f**,
1Co   3:22 life or death or the present or the **f**—

G

GABBATHA*

Jn   19:13 Pavement (which in Aramaic is **G**).

GABRIEL*

Angel who interpreted Daniel's visions (Da 8:16-26; 9:20-27); announced births of John (Lk 1:11-20), Jesus (Lk 1:26-38).

GAD

1. Son of Jacob by Zilpah (Ge 30:9-11; 35:26; 1Ch 2:2). Tribe of blessed (Ge 49:19; Dt 33:20-21), numbered (Nu 1:25; 26:18), allotted land east of the Jordan (Nu 32; 34:14; Jos 18:7; 22), west (Eze 48:27-28), 12,000 from (Rev 7:5).

2. Prophet; seer of David (1Sa 22:5; 2Sa 24:11-19; 1Ch 29:29).

GADARENES*

Mt   8:28 the other side in the region of the **G**,

GAIN [GAINED, GAINING, GAINS]

Ge   15: 8 that I will **g** possession of it?"
Ex   14:17 And I will **g** glory through Pharaoh
1Sa   8: 3 after dishonest **g** and accepted bribes
Ps   30: 9 "What **g** is there in my destruction,
      60:12 With God we will **g** the victory,
      90:12 that we may **g** a heart of wisdom.
Pr   1:19 end of all who go after ill-gotten **g**;
       4: 1 and **g** understanding.
       8: 5 You who are simple, **g** prudence;
       8: 5 who are foolish, **g** understanding.
      16: 8 than much **g** with injustice.
      28:16 he who hates ill-gotten **g** will enjoy
      28:23 end **g** more favor than he who has
Ecc   1: 3 What does man **g** from all his labor
Isa   63:12 to **g** for himself everlasting renown,
Eze   28:22 and I will **g** glory within you.
Da   2: 8 that you are trying to **g** time,
Mk   8:36 for a man to **g** the whole world,
Lk   9:25 for a man to **g** the whole world,
      21:19 By standing firm you will **g** life.
1Co   13: 3 but have not love, I **g** nothing.
Php   1:21 to live is Christ and to die is **g**.
       3: 8 that I may **g** Christ
1Ti   3: 8 and not pursuing dishonest **g**.
       3:13 served well **g** an excellent standing
       6: 5 godliness is a means to financial **g**.

       6: 6 godliness with contentment is great **g**
2Ti   3: 6 **g** control over weak-willed women,
Tit   1: 7 not violent, not pursuing dishonest **g**.

GAINED [GAIN]

Ecc   2:11 nothing was **g** under the sun.
Jer   32:20 have **g** the renown that is still yours.
Ro   5: 2 **g** access by faith into this grace
Gal   2:21 if righteousness could be **g** through
Heb   11:33 and **g** what was promised;

GAINING [GAIN]

Ge   3: 6 and also desirable for **g** wisdom,
Jn   4: 1 was **g** and baptizing more disciples

GAINS* [GAIN]

Pr   3:13 the man who **g** understanding,
      11:16 A kindhearted woman **g** respect,
      11:24 gives freely, yet **g** even more;
      15:32 heeds correction **g** understanding.
      29:23 but a man of lowly spirit **g** honor.
Jer   17:11 who **g** riches by unjust means.
Mic   4:13 You will devote their ill-gotten **g** to
Mt   16:26 be for a man if he **g** the whole world,

GAINSAY, GAINSAYERS (KJV)

See OPPOSE, RESIST

GAINSAYING (KJV) See OBJECTION, OBSTINATE, REBELLION

GAIUS

Ro   16:23 **G**, whose hospitality I and
3Jn   1: 1 The elder, To my dear friend **G**,

GALATIA [GALATIANS]

Ac   16: 6 the region of Phrygia and **G**,
Gal   1: 2 To the churches in **G**:

GALATIANS* [GALATIA]

Gal   3: 1 You foolish **G**!

GALILEAN* [GALILEE]

Mk   14:70 for you are a **G**."
Lk   22:59 for he is a **G**."
      23: 6 Pilate asked if the man was a **G**.
Ac   5:37 Judas the **G** appeared in the days of

GALILEANS [GALILEE]

Lk   13: 1 the **G** whose blood Pilate had mixed
Jn   4:45 the **G** welcomed him.
Ac   2: 7 all these men who are speaking **G**?

GALILEE [GALILEAN, GALILEANS, TIBERIAS]

Isa   9: 1 but in the future he will honor **G** of
Mt   3:13 Jesus came from **G** to the Jordan
       4:15 **G** of the Gentiles—
      21:11 the prophet from Nazareth in **G**."
      26:32 I will go ahead of you into **G**."
      28:10 Go and tell my brothers to go to **G**;
Lk   23:49 who had followed him from **G**,
Jn   2: 1 a wedding took place at Cana in **G**.
       7:41 "How can the Christ come from **G**?

GALL
Ps 69:21 They put **g** in my food
Mt 27:34 Jesus wine to drink, mixed with **g**;

GALLIO*
Proconsul of Achaia, who refused to hear complaints against Paul (Ac 18:12-17).

GALLOWS
Est 7:10 So they hanged Haman on the **g**
     9:13 Haman's ten sons be hanged on **g**."

GAMALIEL
Ac   5:34 But a Pharisee named **G**,
     22: 3 Under **G** I was thoroughly trained in

GAME [GAMES]
Ge 25:28 Isaac, who had a taste for wild **g**,
    27: 3 to hunt some wild **g** for me.

GAMES* [GAME]
1Co 9:25 in the **g** goes into strict training.

GANGRENE*
2Ti 2:17 Their teaching will spread like **g**.

GAP [GAPS]
Ne   6: 1 rebuilt the wall and not a **g** was left
Eze 22:30 stand before me in the **g**

GAPE*
Ps 35:21 They **g** at me and say, "Aha!

GAPS* [GAP]
Ne   4: 7 and that the **g** were being closed,

GARDEN [GARDENER, GARDENS]
Ge   2: 8 had planted a **g** in the east, in Eden;
     2:15 and put him in the **G** of Eden
     3:23 banished him from the **G** of Eden
    13:10 like the **g** of the LORD,
SS   4:12 You are a **g** locked up, my sister,
Isa 58:11 You will be like a well-watered **g**,
Jer 31:12 You will be like a well-watered **g**,
Eze 28:13 You were in Eden, the **g** of God;
    31: 9 the trees of Eden in the **g** of God.
Mk   4:32 becomes the largest of all **g** plants,
Jn 19:41 and in the **g** a new tomb,

GARDENER* [GARDEN]
Jn 15: 1 and my Father is the **g**.
    20:15 Thinking he was the **g**, she said,

GARDENS [GARDEN]
Am   4: 9 "Many times I struck your **g**

GARLAND*
Pr   1: 9 They will be a **g** to grace your head
     4: 9 a **g** of grace on your head

GARMENT [GARMENTS]
Ge   9:23 But Shem and Japheth took a **g**
    25:25 his whole body was like a hairy **g**;
Ru   3: 9 the corner of your **g** over me,
2Ki 1: 8 "He was a man with a **g** of hair and

Job 31:19 or a needy man without a **g**,
Ps 102:26 they will all wear out like a **g**.
Pr 25:20 Like one who takes away a **g** on
Isa 50: 9 They will all wear out like a **g**
    51: 6 the earth will wear out like a **g**
    61: 3 and a **g** of praise instead of a spirit
Mt   9:16 patch of unshrunk cloth on an old **g**,
Mk 14:52 he fled naked, leaving his **g** behind.
Jn 19:23 This **g** was seamless,
Heb 1:11 they will all wear out like a **g**.

GARMENTS [GARMENT]
Ge   3:21 The LORD God made **g** of skin
Ex 28: 2 sacred **g** for your brother Aaron,
Lev 8: 2 "Bring Aaron and his sons, their **g**,
    16: 4 These are sacred **g**;
Pr 31:24 She makes linen **g** and sells them,
Isa 52: 1 Put on your **g** of splendor,
    61:10 he has clothed me with **g** of salvation
    63: 1 with his **g** stained crimson?
Eze 16:10 and covered you with costly **g**.
Joel 2:13 Rend your heart and not your **g**.
Zec 3: 4 and I will put rich **g** on you."
Jn 19:24 "They divided my **g** among them

GARNER, GARNERS (KJV)
See BARN, BARNS, STOREHOUSES

GATE [GATES, GATEWAY]
Dt 21:19 and bring him to the elders at the **g**
Jos 2: 5 when it was time to close the city **g**,
Ru   4:11 The elders and all those at the **g** said,
Est 2:19 Mordecai was sitting at the king's **g**.
Job 29: 7 "When I went to the **g** of the city
Ps 69:12 Those who sit at the **g** mock me,
   118:20 This is the **g** of the LORD
Pr 31:23 Her husband is respected at the city **g**
    31:31 works bring her praise at the city **g**.
Mt   7:13 "Enter through the narrow **g**.
Jn 10: 2 who enters by the **g** is the shepherd
    10: 7 I am the **g** for the sheep.
    10: 9 I am the **g**;
Ac   3: 2 to the temple **g** called Beautiful,
Heb 13:12 Jesus also suffered outside the city **g**
Rev 21:21 each **g** made of a single pearl.

GATES [GATE]
Ge 24:60 possess the **g** of their enemies."
Dt   6: 9 of your houses and on your **g**.
Ne   1: 3 its **g** have been burned with fire."
Ps 24: 7 Lift up your heads, O you **g**;
    87: 2 the LORD loves the **g** of Zion
   100: 4 Enter his **g** with thanksgiving
   118:19 Open for me the **g** of righteousness;
Isa 60:11 Your **g** will always stand open,
    60:18 and your **g** Praise.
    62:10 Pass through, pass through the **g**!
La   4:12 and foes could enter the **g**
Eze 48:31 the **g** of the city will be named after
Mt 16:18 the **g** of Hades will not overcome it.
Rev 21:12 a great, high wall with twelve **g**,
    21:12 On the **g** were written the names of
    21:21 The twelve **g** were twelve pearls,
    21:25 On no day will its **g** ever be shut,

22:14 of life and may go through the **g**

GATEWAY [GATE, WAY]

Ge   19: 1 Lot was sitting in the **g** of the city.
1Sa   9:18 Saul approached Samuel in the **g**
2Sa 19: 8 "The king is sitting in the **g**,"

GATH [MORESHETH GATH]

1Sa   5: 8 ark of the god of Israel moved to **G.**"
     17: 4 Goliath, who was from **G,**
     21:10 and went to Achish king of **G.**
2Sa   1:20 "Tell it not in **G,**
Mic   1:10 Tell it not in **G**; weep not at all.

GATHER [GATHERED, GATHERS, INGATHERING]

Ex   16: 4 and **g** enough for that day.
Lev   19: 9 or **g** the gleanings of your harvest.
Dt   30: 4 the LORD your God will **g** you
Ru   2: 7 'Please let me glean and **g** among
Ne   1: 9 I will **g** them from there
Ps   2: 2 rulers **g** together against the LORD
     106:47 and **g** us from the nations,
Isa   11:12 the nations and **g** the exiles of Israel;
      34:16 and his Spirit will **g** them together.
Jer   3:17 and all nations will **g** in Jerusalem
      23: 3 "I myself will **g** the remnant
      31:10 'He who scattered Israel will **g** them
Eze   39:28 I will **g** them to their own land,
Zep   2: 1 **G** together, **g** together,
       3:20 At that time I will **g** you;
Zec   14: 2 I will **g** all the nations to Jerusalem
Mt   12:30 he who does not **g** with me scatters.
      13:30 then **g** the wheat and bring it
      23:37 longed to **g** your children together,
      25:26 **g** where I have not scattered seed?
Mk   13:27 and **g** his elect from the four winds,
Lk   3:17 and to **g** the wheat into his barn,
      11:23 and he who does not **g** with me,
      13:34 longed to **g** your children together,
      17:37 there the vultures will **g**."
Ac   4:26 the rulers **g** together against the Lord
Rev   14:18 and the clusters of grapes from
      19:17 **g** together for the great supper
      20: 8 and Magog—to **g** them for battle.

GATHERED [GATHER]

Ge   1: 9 "Let the water under the sky be **g**
Ex   16:18 Each one **g** as much as he needed.
Nu   11:32 the people went out and **g** quail.
      16:19 When Korah had **g** all his followers
Ru   2:18 saw how much she had **g.**
Pr   30: 4 Who has **g** up the wind in the hollow
Mt   16: 9 and how many basketfuls you **g?**
      25:32 All the nations will be **g** before him,
2Co   8:15 as it is written: "He who **g** much did
2Th   2: 1 and our being **g** to him,
Rev   14:19 **g** its grapes and threw them into
      16:16 Then they **g** the kings together to
      19:19 and their armies **g** together

GATHERS [GATHER]

Ps   147: 2 he **g** the exiles of Israel.
Pr   10: 5 He who **g** crops in summer is

13:11 he who **g** money little by little
Isa   40:11 He **g** the lambs in his arms
      56: 8 he who **g** the exiles of Israel:
Mt   23:37 a hen **g** her chicks under her wings,

GAUNT

Ge   41: 3 seven other cows, ugly and **g,**

GAVE [GIVE]

Ge   2:20 the man **g** names to all the livestock,
       3: 6 She also **g** some to her husband,
      14:20 Abram **g** him a tenth of everything.
      16:13 She **g** this name to the LORD
      28: 4 the land God **g** to Abraham."
      35:12 The land I **g** to Abraham and Isaac
      39:23 with Joseph and **g** him success
      47:11 and **g** them property
Ex   4:11 "Who **g** man his mouth?
      31:18 he **g** him the two tablets of
      34:32 he **g** them all the commands
Nu   22:18 "Even if Balak **g** me his palace filled
Dt   2:12 in the land the LORD **g** them
       2:36 LORD our God **g** us all of them.
       3:12 I **g** the Reubenites and the Gadites
       8:16 He **g** you manna to eat in the desert,
       9:10 The LORD **g** me two stone tablets
      26: 9 and **g** us this land,
      31: 9 down this law and **g** it to the priests,
      32: 8 When the Most High **g**
Jos   11:23 and he **g** it as an inheritance to Israel
      13:14 the tribe of Levi he **g** no inheritance,
      15:13 Joshua **g** to Caleb son of Jephunneh
      19:49 the Israelites **g** Joshua son of Nun
      21:44 The LORD **g** them rest
      24:13 So I **g** you a land on which you did
Jdg   3: 6 and **g** their own daughters
1Sa   1: 5 But to Hannah he **g** a double portion
      27: 6 So on that day Achish **g** him Ziklag,
2Sa   8: 6 The LORD **g** David victory wherever
      12: 8 I **g** you the house of Israel
1Ki   4:29 God **g** Solomon wisdom
       5:12 The LORD **g** Solomon wisdom,
Ezr   2:69 to their ability they **g** to the treasury
Ne   9:15 In their hunger you **g** them bread
       9:20 You **g** your good Spirit
       9:20 and you **g** them water for their thirst.
       9:22 "You **g** them kingdoms and nations,
       9:27 compassion you **g** them deliverers,
       9:34 or the warnings you **g** them.
Job   1:21 The LORD **g** and the LORD
      42:10 and **g** him twice as much
Ps   69:21 and **g** me vinegar for my thirst.
     135:12 and he **g** their land as an inheritance,
Pr   8:29 he **g** the sea its boundary so
Ecc   12: 7 the spirit returns to God who **g** it.
Jer   3: 8 I **g** faithless Israel her certificate
Eze   3: 2 and he **g** me the scroll to eat.
Da   1: 7 The chief official **g** them new names:
       1:17 four young men God **g** knowledge
Mt   1:25 And he **g** him the name Jesus.
       2:16 and he **g** orders to kill all the boys
      25:35 and you **g** me something to eat,
      25:42 and you **g** me nothing to eat,
      26:26 and **g** it to his disciples, saying,

	27:50	he **g** up his spirit.
Mk	6: 7	**g** them authority over evil spirits.
	11:28	who **g** you authority to do this?"
Jn	1:12	he **g** the right to become children
	3:16	God so loved the world that he **g**
	17: 4	by completing the work you **g** me
	17: 6	whom you **g** me out of the world.
	19:30	and **g** up his spirit.
Ac	1: 3	and **g** many convincing proofs
	2:45	they **g** to anyone as he had need.
	11:17	So if God **g** them the same gift as he **g** us,
Ro	1:24	Therefore God **g** them over in
	1:26	God **g** them over to shameful lusts.
	1:28	he **g** them over to a depraved mind,
	8:32	but **g** him up for us all—
1Co	3: 1	I **g** you milk, not solid food,
2Co	5:18	through Christ and **g** us the ministry
	8: 3	For I testify that they **g** as much
	8: 5	but they **g** themselves first to
Gal	1: 4	who **g** himself for our sins
	2:20	who loved me and **g** himself for me.
Eph	4: 8	he led captives in his train and **g** gifts
	4:11	It was he who **g** some to be apostles,
	5: 2	just as Christ loved us and **g** himself
	5:25	the church and **g** himself up for her
Php	2: 9	the highest place and **g** him the name
2Th	2:16	his grace **g** us eternal encouragement
1Ti	2: 6	who **g** himself as a ransom
Tit	2:14	who **g** himself for us to redeem us
Heb	7: 2	and Abraham **g** him a tenth
1Jn	3:24	We know it by the Spirit he **g** us.
Rev	11:13	and **g** glory to the God of heaven.
	13: 2	The dragon the beast his power
	16:19	and **g** her the cup filled with the wine
	20:13	and death and Hades **g** up the dead

GAVE THANKS See THANKS

GAZA

Jdg	16: 1	One day Samson went to **G,**
1Sa	6:17	**G,** Ashkelon, Gath and Ekron.
Am	1: 6	"For three sins of **G,**

GAZE [GAZING]

Ps	27: 4	to **g** upon the beauty of the LORD
Pr	4:25	fix your **g** directly before you.
	23:31	Do not **g** at wine when it is red,
Rev	11: 9	and nation will **g** on their bodies

GAZELLE

2Sa	2:18	as fleet-footed as a wild **g.**
SS	2: 9	My lover is like a **g** or a young stag.
	7: 3	twins of a **g.**

GAZING [GAZE]

2Co	3:13	to keep the Israelites from **g** at it

GAZINGSTOCK (KJV)

See PUBLICLY EXPOSED, SPECTACLE

GEDALIAH

Governor of Judah appointed by Nebuchadnezzar (2Ki 25:22-26; Jer 39-41).

GEHAZI*

Servant of Elisha (2Ki 4:12-5:27; 8:4-5).

GEMS

Ex	25: 7	other **g** to be mounted on the ephod

GENEALOGIES [GENEALOGY]

1Ch	9: 1	All Israel was listed in the **g** recorded
1Ti	1: 4	to myths and endless **g.**
Tit	3: 9	But avoid foolish controversies and **g**

GENEALOGY [GENEALOGIES]

Mt	1: 1	A record of the **g** of Jesus Christ
Heb	7: 3	Without father or mother, without **g,**

GENERATION [GENERATIONS]

Ge	7: 1	I have found you righteous in this **g.**
	15:16	fourth **g** your descendants will come
Ex	1: 6	and all that **g** died,
	3:15	I am to be remembered from **g** to **g.**
	20: 5	the fathers to the third and fourth **g**
	34: 7	the fathers to the third and fourth **g**
Nu	32:13	until the whole **g** of those who had
Dt	1:35	"Not a man of this evil **g** shall see
Jdg	2:10	another **g** grew up, who knew neither
Ps	24: 6	Such is the **g** of those who seek him,
	48:13	you may tell of them to the next **g.**
	71:18	I declare your power to the next **g,**
	78: 4	we will tell the next **g**
	102:18	Let this be written for a future **g,**
	112: 2	the **g** of the upright will be blessed.
	145: 4	One **g** will commend your works
Isa	34:17	and dwell there from **g** to **g.**
La	5:19	your throne endures from **g** to **g.**
Da	4: 3	his dominion endures from **g** to **g.**
	4:34	his kingdom endures from **g** to **g.**
Joel	1: 3	and their children to the next **g.**
Mt	12:39	"A wicked and adulterous **g** asks for
	17:17	"O unbelieving and perverse **g,**"
	23:36	all this will come upon this **g.**
	24:34	this **g** will certainly not pass away
Mk	9:19	"O unbelieving **g,**" Jesus replied,
	13:30	this **g** will certainly not pass away
Lk	1:50	from **g** to **g.**
	7:31	can I compare the people of this **g**?
	11:29	Jesus said, "This is a wicked **g.**
	11:50	this **g** will be held responsible
	21:32	this **g** will certainly not pass away
Ac	2:40	Save yourselves from this corrupt **g.**"
Php	2:15	in a crooked and depraved **g,**
Heb	3:10	That is why I was angry with that **g,**

GENERATIONS [GENERATION]

Ge	9:12	a covenant for all **g** to come:
	17: 7	descendants after you for the **g** to
Ex	12:17	a lasting ordinance for the **g** to come.
	30:21	and his descendants for the **g** to come.
	31:13	a sign between me and you for the **g**
	40:15	priesthood that will continue for all **g**
Dt	7: 9	a thousand **g** of those who love him
	32: 7	consider the **g** long past.
1Ch	16:15	he commanded, for a thousand **g,**
Job	8: 8	"Ask the former **g**
Ps	22:30	future **g** will be told about the Lord.

	33:11	purposes of his heart through all **g**.
	45:17	your memory through all **g;**
	89: 1	faithfulness known through all **g**.
	90: 1	dwelling place throughout all **g**.
	100: 5	faithfulness continues through all **g**.
	102:12	renown endures through all **g**.
	105: 8	for a thousand **g,**
	119:90	faithfulness continues through all **g;**
	135:13	O LORD, through all **g**.
	145:13	your dominion endures through all **g**.
	146:10	your God, O Zion, for all **g**.
Pr	27:24	and a crown is not secure for all **g**.
Ecc	1: 4	**G** come and **g** go,
Isa	41: 4	the **g** from the beginning?
	51: 8	my salvation through all **g**."
Mt	1:17	Thus there were fourteen **g** in all
Lk	1:48	now on all **g** will call me blessed,
Eph	3: 5	not made known to men in other **g**
	3:21	and in Christ Jesus throughout all **g,**
Col	1:26	kept hidden for ages and **g,**

GENEROSITY* [GENEROUS]

2Co	8: 2	extreme poverty welled up in rich **g**.
	9:11	**g** will result in thanksgiving to God.
	9:13	and for your **g** in sharing with them

GENEROUS* [GENEROSITY, GENEROUSLY]

Ps	37:26	They are always **g** and lend freely;
	112: 5	to him who is **g** and lends freely,
Pr	11:25	A **g** man will prosper;
	22: 9	A **g** man will himself be blessed,
Mt	20:15	are you envious because I am **g**?'
2Co	9: 5	for the **g** gift you had promised.
	9: 5	Then it will be ready as a **g** gift,
	9:11	that you can be **g** on every occasion,
1Ti	6:18	and to be **g** and willing to share.

GENEROUSLY [GENEROUS]

Dt	15:10	Give **g** to him and do so without
1Ch	29:14	that we should be able to give as **g**
Ps	37:21	but the righteous give **g;**
2Co	9: 6	whoever sows **g** will also reap **g**.
Jas	1: 5	ask God, who gives **g** to all

GENTILE [GENTILES]

Ezr	6:21	practices of their **G** neighbors
Ne	5: 9	the reproach of our **G** enemies?
Ac	21:25	As for the **G** believers,
Ro	1:16	first for the Jew, then for the **G**.
	2: 9	first for the Jew, then for the **G;**
	2:10	first for the Jew, then for the **G**.
	10:12	no difference between Jew and **G—**

GENTILES [GENTILE]

Isa	42: 6	for the people and a light for the **G,**
	49: 6	also make you a light for the **G,**
	49:22	I will beckon to the **G,**
Mt	4:15	along the Jordan, Galilee of the **G—**
Lk	2:32	a light for revelation to the **G**
	21:24	be trampled on by the **G** until the times of the **G** are fulfilled.
	22:25	kings of the **G** lord it over them;
Ac	9:15	to carry my name before the **G**

	10:45	poured out even on the **G**.
	11: 1	that the **G** also had received the word
	11:18	even the **G** repentance unto life."
	13:16	and you **G** who worship God,
	13:46	we now turn to the **G**.
	13:47	a light for the **G,**
	14: 1	great number of Jews and **G** believed
	14:27	opened the door of faith to the **G**.
	15: 5	"The **G** must be circumcised
	15:19	should not make it difficult for the **G**
	18: 6	From now on I will go to the **G**."
	22:21	send you far away to the **G**.' "
	26:20	and to the **G** also,
	28:28	salvation has been sent to the **G,**
Ro	2:14	when **G,** who do not have the law,
	3: 9	Jews and **G** alike are all under sin.
	3:29	Is he not the God of **G** too?
	9:24	from the Jews but also from the **G?**
	11:11	to the **G** to make Israel envious.
	11:12	their loss means riches for the **G,**
	11:13	as I am the apostle to the **G,**
	15: 9	the **G** may glorify God for his mercy,
	15:27	For if the **G** have shared in the Jews'
1Co	1:23	block to Jews and foolishness to **G,**
2Co	11:26	in danger from **G,**
Gal	1:16	might preach him among the **G,**
	2: 2	that I preach among the **G**.
	2: 8	as an apostle to the **G**.
	2:14	force **G** to follow Jewish customs?
	3: 8	God would justify the **G** by faith,
	3:14	come to the **G** through Christ Jesus,
Eph	3: 6	the **G** are heirs together
	3: 8	to the **G** the unsearchable riches
	4:17	you must no longer live as the **G** do,
Col	1:27	among the **G** the glorious riches
1Ti	2: 7	a teacher of the true faith to the **G**.
2Ti	4:17	and all the **G** might hear it.
Rev	11: 2	because it has been given to the **G**.

GENTLE* [GENTLENESS, GENTLY]

Dt	28:54	Even the most **g** and sensitive man
	28:56	The most **g** and sensitive woman among you—so sensitive and **g**
2Sa	18: 5	"Be **g** with the young man Absalom
1Ki	19:12	And after the fire came a **g** whisper.
Job	41: 3	Will he speak to you with **g** words?
Pr	15: 1	A **g** answer turns away wrath,
	25:15	and a **g** tongue can break a bone.
Jer	11:19	like a **g** lamb led to the slaughter;
Zec	9: 9	**g** and riding on a donkey, on a colt,
Mt	11:29	for I am **g** and humble in heart,
	21: 5	**g** and riding on a donkey, on a colt,
Ac	27:13	When a **g** south wind began to blow,
1Co	4:21	or in love and with a **g** spirit?
Eph	4: 2	Be completely humble and **g;**
1Th	2: 7	but we were **g** among you,
1Ti	3: 3	not violent but **g,** not quarrelsome,
1Pe	3: 4	the unfading beauty of a **g**

GENTLENESS* [GENTLE]

2Co	10: 1	By the meekness and **g** of Christ,
Gal	5:23	and self-control.
Php	4: 5	Let your **g** be evident to all.
Col	3:12	kindness, humility, **g** and patience.

1Ti   6:11 faith, love, endurance and **g.**
1Pe   3:15 But do this with **g** and respect,

GENTLY [GENTLE]

Isa   40:11 he **g** leads those that have young.
Gal   6: 1 are spiritual should restore him **g.**
2Ti   2:25 who oppose him he must **g** instruct,
Heb   5: 2 to deal **g** with those who are ignorant

GENUINE*

2Co   6: 8 **g,** yet regarded as impostors;
Php   2:20 a **g** interest in your welfare.
1Pe   1: 7 be proved **g** and may result in praise,

GERAHS

Eze   45:12 The shekel is to consist of twenty **g.**

GERAR

Ge   20: 2 Abimelech king of **G** sent for Sarah
      26: 6 So Isaac stayed in **G.**

GERASENES

Lk   8:26 They sailed to the region of the **G,**

GERIZIM

Dt   27:12 stand on Mount **G** to bless the people
Jos   8:33 the people stood in front of Mount **G**

GERSHOM

Ex   2:22 and Moses named him **G,** saying,
1Ch   23:15 The sons of Moses: **G** and Eliezer.

GERSHON [GERSHONITE, GERSHONITES]

Ge   46:11 The sons of Levi: **G,**

GERSHONITE [GERSHON]

Nu   4:24 "This is the service of the **G** clans

GERSHONITES [GERSHON]

Nu   3:25 the **G** were responsible for the care
1Ch   6:71 the **G** received the following:

GESHEM

Ne   6: 1 **G** the Arab and the rest of our

GESHUR

2Sa   13:38 After Absalom fled and went to **G,**

GET [GETS, GOT, ILL-GOTTEN]

Ge   24: 4 and **g** a wife for my son Isaac."
      29:20 Jacob served seven years to **g** Rachel
Nu   16:10 you are trying to **g** the priesthood too
Dt   30:12 "Who will ascend into heaven to **g** it
Jdg   16:28 and let me with one blow **g** revenge
Pr   1: 5 and let the discerning **g** guidance—
       4: 5 **G** wisdom, **g** understanding;
      16:16 much better to **g** wisdom than gold,
      23: 4 Do not wear yourself out to **g** rich;
Eze   18:31 and **g** a new heart and a new spirit.
Mt   16:23 "**G** behind me, Satan!
Mk   6: 2 "Where did this man **g** these things?"
      13:16 in the field go back to **g** his cloak.
Jn   19:24 "Let's decide by lot who will **g** it."
1Co   9:24 Run in such a way as to **g** the prize.

GETHSEMANE*

Mt   26:36 with his disciples to a place called **G,**
Mk   14:32 They went to a place called **G,**

GETS [GET]

Pr   13: 4 The sluggard craves and **g** nothing,
      19: 8 who **g** wisdom loves his own soul;

GEZER

Jos   16:10 dislodge the Canaanites living in **G;**
1Ch   14:16 all the way from Gibeon to **G.**

GHOST

Mt   14:26 "It's a **g,**" they said,
Lk   24:39 a **g** does not have flesh and bones,

[GIVE UP THE] GHOST (KJV) See
BREATHED HIS LAST, DIE, DIED, DYING
GASP, GAVE UP HIS SPIRIT, PERISHED

[HOLY] GHOST (KJV)
See [HOLY] SPIRIT

GIBEAH

Jdg   19:12 We will go on to **G.**"
1Sa   10:26 Saul also went to his home in **G,**
2Sa   21: 6 and exposed before the LORD at **G**
Hos   10: 9 war overtake the evildoers in **G?**

GIBEON [GIBEONITES]

Jos   10:12 stand still over **G,** O moon,
2Sa   2:13 and met them at the pool of **G.**
1Ki   3: 5 At **G** the LORD appeared to Solomon

GIBEONITES [GIBEON]

Jos   9:16 they made the treaty with the **G,**
2Sa   21: 1 because he put the **G** to death."

GIDEON [JERUB-BAAL]

Judge, also called Jerub-Baal; freed Israel from
Midianites (Jdg 6-8; Heb 11:32). Given sign of
fleece (Jdg 8:36-40).

GIFT [GIFTED, GIFTS]

Ge   30:20 has presented me with a precious **g.**
Nu   18: 7 the service of the priesthood as a **g.**
Dt   16:17 a **g** in proportion to the way
2Ch   9:24 everyone who came brought a **g—**
Pr   18:16 A **g** opens the way for the giver
      21:14 A **g** given in secret soothes anger,
Ecc   3:13 this is the **g** of God.
       5:19 this is a **g** of God.
Mt   5:23 if you are offering your **g** at the altar
       8: 4 and offer the **g** Moses commanded,
Mk   7:11 a **g** devoted to God),
Jn   4:10 "If you knew the **g** of God
Ac   1: 4 wait for the **g** my Father promised,
       2:38 receive the **g** of the Holy Spirit.
       8:20 could buy the **g** of God with money!
      11:17 So if God gave them the same **g**
Ro   1:11 I may impart to you some spiritual **g**
       5:15 But the **g** is not like the trespass.
       6:23 but the **g** of God is eternal life
      12: 6 If a man's **g** is prophesying,
1Co   7: 7 each man has his own **g** from God;

14: 1 especially the **g** of prophecy.
2Co 8:12 the **g** is acceptable according
9:15 be to God for his indescribable **g!**
Eph 2: 8 it is the **g** of God—
Php 4:17 Not that I am looking for a **g,**
1Ti 4:14 Do not neglect your **g,**
2Ti 1: 6 to fan into flame the **g** of God,
Heb 6: 4 who have tasted the heavenly **g,**
Jas 1:17 Every good and perfect **g** is from
1Pe 3: 7 as heirs with you of the gracious **g**
4:10 Each one should use whatever **g** he
Rev 22:17 the free **g** of the water of life.

GIFTED* [GIFT]

1Co 14:37 thinks he is a prophet or spiritually **g,**

GIFTS [GIFT]

Nu 8:19 have given the Levites as **g** to Aaron
Dt 12: 6 your tithes and special **g,**
Ezr 1: 6 and with valuable **g,**
Ps 68:18 you received **g** from men,
76:11 the neighboring lands bring **g** to
112: 9 He has scattered abroad his **g** to
Pr 25:14 a man who boasts of **g** he does
Mt 2:11 and presented him with **g** of gold and
7:11 Father in heaven give good **g**
Lk 11:13 how to give good **g** to your children,
21: 1 Jesus saw the rich putting their **g** into
Ac 10: 4 "Your prayers and **g** to the poor
Ro 11:29 God's **g** and his call are irrevocable.
12: 6 We have different **g,**
1Co 12: 1 Now about spiritual **g,** brothers,
12: 4 There are different kinds of **g,**
12:28 also those having **g** of healing,
12:30 Do all have **g** of healing?
12:31 But eagerly desire the greater **g.**
14: 1 of love and eagerly desire spiritual **g,**
14:12 you are eager to have spiritual **g,** try
to excel in **g** that build up the church.
2Co 9: 9 "He has scattered abroad his **g**
Eph 4: 8 in his train and gave **g** to men."
Heb 2: 4 and **g** of the Holy Spirit distributed
9: 9 the **g** and sacrifices being offered

GIHON

Ge 2:13 name of the second river is the **G;**
2Ch 32:30 the **G** spring and channeled the water

GILBOA

1Ch 10: 8 Saul and his sons fallen on Mount **G.**

GILEAD [GILEADITE, JABESH GILEAD, RAMOTH GILEAD]

Nu 32:29 the land of **G** as their possession.
Dt 34: 1 the whole land—from **G** to Dan,
Jdg 11: 1 His father was **G;**
2Sa 2: 9 He made him king over **G,**
1Ch 27:21 over the half-tribe of Manasseh in **G:**
Jer 8:22 Is there no balm in **G?**
46:11 "Go up to **G** and get balm,
Hos 6: 8 **G** is a city of wicked men,
Mic 7:14 in Bashan and **G** as in days long ago.

GILEADITE [GILEAD]

Jdg 11: 1 Jephthah the **G** was a mighty warrior
2Sa 19:31 Barzillai the **G** also came down

GILGAL

Jos 4:20 And Joshua set up at **G**
5: 9 place has been called **G** to this day.
Jdg 2: 1 angel of the LORD went up from **G**
1Sa 7:16 a circuit from Bethel to **G** to Mizpah,

GIRD*

Ps 45: 3 **G** your sword upon your side,

GIRGASHITES

Dt 7: 1 **G,** Amorites, Canaanites, Perizzites,

GIRL [GIRLS]

Ge 24:16 The **g** was very beautiful, a virgin;
Ex 1:16 but if it is a **g,**
2Ki 5: 2 and had taken captive a young **g**
Job 31: 1 not to look lustfully at a **g.**
Mk 5:41 (which means, "Little **g,**
6:22 The king said to the **g,**
Ac 12:13 and a servant **g** named Rhoda came
16:16 we were met by a slave **g** who had

GIRLS [GIRL]

Jdg 21:21 the **g** of Shiloh come out to join in
Ru 2: 8 Stay here with my servant **g.**
Joel 3: 3 they sold **g** for wine
Zec 8: 5 filled with boys and **g** playing there."

GIVE [GAVE, GIVEN, GIVER, GIVES, GIVING, LIFE-GIVING]

Ge 1:29 "I **g** you every seed-bearing plant on
9: 3 I now **g** you everything.
12: 7 To your offspring I will **g** this land.
27: 4 that I may **g** you my blessing
28: 4 May he **g** you and your descendants
28:22 that you **g** me I will **g** you a tenth."
Ex 13: 5 to **g** you, a land flowing with milk
17: 2 "**G** us water to drink."
20:16 "You shall not **g** false testimony
30:15 not to **g** more than a half shekel and
Lev 18:21 " 'Do not **g** any of your children to
Nu 6:26 toward you and **g** you peace." '
11:13 '**G** us meat to eat!'
Dt 5:20 "You shall not **g** false testimony
15:10 **G** generously to him and do so
28: 1 all his commands I **g** you today,
Jos 1: 6 land I swore to their forefathers to **g**
Jdg 6:17 **g** me a sign that it is really you
1Sa 1:11 then I will **g** him to the LORD.
1:28 So now I **g** him to the LORD.
8: 6 they said, "**G** us a king to lead us,"
1Ki 3: 5 for whatever you want me to **g** you."
11:13 but will **g** him one tribe for the sake
2Ch 1:10 **G** me wisdom and knowledge,
15: 7 as for you, be strong and do not **g** up,
Ne 9: 6 You **g** life to everything,
Job 2: 4 "A man will **g** all he has
Ps 5: 1 **G** ear to my words, O LORD,
13: 3 **G** light to my eyes,
30:12 I will **g** you thanks forever.

Pr   21:26 but the righteous **g** without sparing.
      23:26 My son, **g** me your heart
      25:21 **g** him food to eat;
      25:21 **g** him water to drink.
      30: 8 but **g** me only my daily bread.
      30:15 leech has two daughters. **'G! G!'**
      31:31 **G** her the reward she has earned,
Ecc   3: 6 "a time to search and a time to **g** up,
SS   8: 7 **g** all the wealth of his house for love,
Isa   7:14 the Lord himself will **g** you a sign:
      42: 8 I will not **g** my glory to another
Eze   36:26 I will **g** you a new heart and put
Mt   6:11 **G** us today our daily bread.
       7: 6 "Do not **g** dogs what is sacred;
       7:11 how to **g** good gifts to your children,
      10: 8 Freely you have received, freely **g.**
      16:19 I will **g** you the keys of the kingdom
      22:21 **"G** to Caesar what is Caesar's,
Mk   6:23 "Whatever you ask I will **g** you,
       8:37 a man **g** in exchange for his soul?
      10:19 do not **g** false testimony,
      10:45 to **g** his life as a ransom for many."
Lk   6:38 **G,** and it will be given to you.
      11: 3 **G** us each day our daily bread.
      11:13 Father in heaven **g** the Holy Spirit
      14:33 not **g** up everything he has cannot
Jn   4:14 the water I **g** him will never thirst.
       6:52 "How can this man **g** us his flesh
      10:28 I **g** them eternal life,
      13:34 "A new command I **g** you:
      14:16 and he will **g** you another Counselor
      14:27 Peace I leave with you; my peace I **g**
      17: 2 that he might **g** eternal life
Ac   3: 6 but what I have I **g** you.
      20:35 more blessed to **g** than to receive.' "
Ro   6:13 he will **g** eternal life.
       8:32 graciously **g** us all things?
      12: 8 let him **g** generously;
      13: 7 **g** everyone what you owe him:
      14:12 will **g** an account of himself to God.
1Co   13: 3 If I **g** all I possess to the poor
2Co   9: 7 Each man should **g** what he has
              decided in his heart to **g,**
Gal   2: 5 not **g** in to them for a moment,
       6: 9 a harvest if we do not **g** up.
Eph   4:27 and do not **g** the devil a foothold.
Heb   10:25 Let us not **g** up meeting together,
      13:17 as men who must **g** an account.
1Pe   3:15 to **g** an answer to everyone who asks
              you to **g** the reason for the hope
Rev   2: 7 I will **g** the right to eat from the tree
       2:10 and I will **g** you the crown of life.
       2:17 I will **g** some of the hidden manna.
       2:17 I will also **g** him a white stone with
       2:26 I will **g** authority over the nations—
       2:28 I will also **g** him the morning star.
       3:21 I will **g** the right to sit with me
      14: 7 "Fear God and **g** him glory,
      18: 6 **G** back to her as she has given;
      22:12 I will **g** to everyone according to

GIVE THANKS See THANKS

GIVEN [GIVE]

Ex   4:21 the wonders I have **g** you the power

      16:15 "It is the bread the LORD has **g** you
Nu   8:16 the Israelites who are to be **g** wholly
Dt   1:21 LORD your God has **g** you the land.
      26:11 things the LORD your God has **g**
Job   3:23 Why is life **g** to a man
Ps   105:42 he remembered his holy promise **g**
     115:16 but the earth he has **g** to man.
     118:18 but he has not **g** me over to death.
Isa   9: 6 to us a child is born, to us a son is **g,**
Am   9:15 from the land I have **g** them,"
Mt   6:33 and all these things will be **g** to you
       7: 7 "Ask and it will be **g** to you;
      22:30 neither marry nor be **g** in marriage;
      25:29 everyone who has will be **g** more,
Mk   4:25 Whoever has will be **g** more;
       8:12 no sign will be **g** to it."
Lk   6:38 Give, and it will be **g** to you.
       8:10 kingdom of God has been **g** to you,
      11: 9 Ask and it will be **g** to you;
      22:19 saying, "This is my body **g** for you;
Jn   1:17 For the law was **g** through Moses;
       3:27 man can receive only what is **g** him
       6:39 lose none of all that he has **g** me,
      15: 7 and it will be **g** you.
      17:24 the glory you have **g** me
      18:11 the cup the Father has **g** me?"
Ac   5:32 Holy Spirit, whom God has **g**
      20:24 the task the Lord Jesus has **g** me—
Ro   5: 5 whom he has **g** us.
      11:35 "Who has ever **g** to God,
1Co   4: 2 that those who have been **g**
      11:24 he had **g** thanks, he broke it
      12:13 and we were all **g** the one Spirit
2Co   5: 5 and has **g** us the Spirit as a deposit,
      12: 7 there was **g** me a thorn in my flesh,
Gal   3:22 might be **g** to those who believe.
Eph   1: 6 which he has freely **g** us in
       4: 7 to each one of us grace has been **g**
Col   2:10 you have been **g** fullness in Christ,
1Ti   4:14 your gift, which was **g** you
1Pe   1: 3 his great mercy he has **g** us new birth
2Pe   1: 3 divine power has **g** us everything we
1Jn   4:13 because he has **g** us of his Spirit.
       5:20 and has **g** us understanding,
Rev   6: 2 and he was **g** a crown,
      15: 2 They held harps **g** them by God
      20: 4 those who had been **g** authority

GIVER* [GIVE]

Pr   18:16 gift opens the way for the **g**
2Co   9: 7 for God loves a cheerful **g.**

GIVES [GIVE]

Ex   4:11 Who **g** him sight
Job   33: 4 the breath of the Almighty **g** me life.
      35:10 who **g** songs in the night,
Ps   29:11 The LORD **g** strength to his people;
     119:130 The unfolding of your words **g** light;
     136:25 and who **g** food to every creature.
Pr   2: 6 For the LORD **g** wisdom,
       3:34 but **g** grace to the humble.
      11:24 One man gives freely,
      14:30 A heart at peace **g** life to the body,
      15:30 and good news **g** health to the bones.

19: 6 the friend of a man who **g** gifts.
25:26 a righteous man who **g** way to
28:27 who **g** to the poor will lack nothing,
29: 4 a king **g** a country stability,
Ecc 2:26 God **g** wisdom, knowledge and
Isa 40:29 He **g** strength to the weary
Hab 2:15 to him who **g** drink to his neighbors,
Mt 10:42 if anyone **g** even a cup of cold water
Jn 3:34 for God **g** the Spirit without limit.
5:21 the Son **g** life to whom he is pleased
6:37 All that the Father **g** me will come
6:63 The Spirit **g** life;
14:27 I do not give to you as the world **g**.
1Co 15:57 He **g** us the victory
2Co 3: 6 but the Spirit **g** life.
1Th 4: 8 who **g** you his Holy Spirit.
Jas 1:25 into the perfect law that **g** freedom,
4: 6 But he **g** us more grace.
4: 6 the proud but **g** grace to the humble."
1Pe 5: 5 the proud but **g** grace to the humble."
Rev 21:23 for the glory of God **g** it light,

GIVING [GIVE]

Ge 13:17 for I am **g** it to you."
Dt 11: 8 the commands I am **g** you today,
Jos 1:13 'The LORD your God is **g** you rest
Ne 8: 8 making it clear and **g** the meaning so
Est 9:19 a day for **g** presents to each other.
Ps 19: 8 **g** joy to the heart.
19: 8 **g** light to the eyes.
Pr 1: 4 for **g** prudence to the simple,
15:23 A man finds joy in **g** an apt reply—
Mt 6: 4 so that your **g** may be in secret.
24:38 marrying and **g** in marriage,
Ac 15: 8 accepted them by **g** the Holy Spirit
2Co 8: 7 that you also excel in this grace of **g**.
Php 4:15 in the matter of **g** and receiving,

GLAD* [GLADDENS, GLADNESS]

Ex 4:14 his heart will be **g** when he sees you.
Jos 22:33 They were **g** to hear the report
Jdg 8:25 "We'll be **g** to give them."
18:20 Then the priest was **g**.
1Sa 19: 5 and you saw it and were **g**.
2Sa 1:20 the daughters of the Philistines be **g**,
1Ki 8:66 and **g** in heart for all the good things
1Ch 16:31 let the earth be **g**;
2Ch 7:10 and be **g** for the good things
Ps 5:11 let all who take refuge in you be **g**;
9: 2 I will be **g** and rejoice in you;
14: 7 let Jacob rejoice and Israel be **g**!
16: 9 Therefore my heart is **g**
21: 6 and made him **g** with
31: 7 I will be **g** and rejoice in your love,
32:11 Rejoice in the LORD and be **g**,
40:16 rejoice and be **g** in you;
45: 8 the music of the strings makes you **g**.
46: 4 a river whose streams make **g**
48:11 are **g** because of your judgments.
53: 6 let Jacob rejoice and Israel be **g**!
58:10 be **g** when they are avenged,
67: 4 the nations be **g** and sing for joy,
68: 3 the righteous be **g** and rejoice
69:32 The poor will see and be **g**—

70: 4 and be **g** in you;
90:14 for joy and be **g** all our days.
90:15 Make us **g** for as many days
92: 4 For you make me **g** by your deeds,
96:11 let the earth be **g**;
97: 1 LORD reigns, let the earth be **g**;
97: 8 are **g** because of your judgments,
105:38 Egypt was **g** when they left,
107:30 They were **g** when it grew calm,
118:24 and be **g** in it.
149: 2 the people of Zion be **g** in their King.
Pr 23:15 then my heart will be **g**;
23:25 May your father and mother be **g**;
29: 6 a righteous one can sing and be **g**.
Ecc 8:15 to eat and drink and be **g**.
Isa 25: 9 let us rejoice and be **g**
35: 1 and the parched land will be **g**;
65:18 But be **g** and rejoice forever
66:10 be **g** for her, all you who love her;
Jer 20:15 who made him very **g**, saying,
31:13 Then maidens will dance and be **g**,
41:13 they were **g**.
50:11 "Because you rejoice and are **g**,
La 4:21 Rejoice and be **g**,
Joel 2:21 Be not afraid, O land; be **g**
2:23 Be **g**, O people of Zion,
Hab 1:15 and so he rejoices and is **g**.
Zep 3:14 Be **g** and rejoice with all your heart,
Zec 2:10 "Shout and be **g**,
8:19 and **g** occasions and happy festivals
10: 7 their hearts will be **g** as with wine.
Mt 5:12 Rejoice and be **g**,
Lk 15:32 But we had to celebrate and be **g**,
Jn 4:36 and the reaper may be **g** together.
8:56 he saw it and was **g**."
11:15 for your sake I am **g** I was not there,
14:28 be **g** that I am going to the Father,
Ac 2:26 Therefore my heart is **g**
2:46 and sincere hearts,
11:23 he was **g** and encouraged them all
13:48 they were **g** and honored the word of
15: 3 news made all the brothers very **g**.
15:31 The people read it and were **g**
1Co 16:17 I was **g** when Stephanas,
2Co 2: 2 who is left to make me **g**
7:16 am **g** I can have complete confidence
13: 9 We are **g** whenever we are weak
Gal 4:27 For it is written: "Be **g**,
Php 2:17 I am **g** and rejoice with all of you.
2:18 So you too should be **g** and rejoice
2:28 be **g** and I may have less anxiety.
Rev 19: 7 and be **g** and give him glory!

GLADDENS* [GLAD]

Ps 104:15 wine that **g** the heart of man,

GLADNESS* [GLAD]

2Ch 29:30 So they sang praises with **g**
Est 8:16 happiness and joy, **g** and honor.
8:17 there was joy and **g** among the Jews,
Job 3:22 who are filled with **g** and rejoice
Ps 35:27 shout for joy and **g**;
45:15 They are led in with joy and **g**;
51: 8 Let me hear joy and **g**;

	65:12	the hills are clothed with **g.**
	100: 2	Worship the LORD with **g;**
Ecc	5:20	occupied with **g** of heart.
	9: 7	Go, eat your food with **g,**
Isa	16:10	Joy and **g** are taken away from
	35:10	**G** and joy will overtake them,
	51: 3	Joy and **g** will be found in her,
	51:11	**G** and joy will overtake them.
	61: 3	the oil of **g** instead of mourning,
Jer	7:34	to the sounds of joy and **g** and
	16: 9	an end to the sounds of joy and **g** and
	25:10	from them the sounds of joy and **g,**
	31:13	I will turn their mourning into **g;**
	33:11	the sounds of joy and **g,** the voices
	48:33	Joy and **g** are gone from the orchards
Joel	1:16	and **g** from the house of our God?

GLASS*

Rev	4: 6	what looked like a sea of **g,**
	15: 2	like a sea of **g** mixed with fire and,
	21:18	of pure gold, as pure as **g.**
	21:21	of pure gold, as pure and transparent **g.**

GLASSES (KJV) See MIRROR

GLAZE*

Pr	26:23	Like a coating of **g** over earthenware

GLEAM* [GLEAMED]

Pr	4:18	of the righteous is like the first **g**
Da	10: 6	like the **g** of burnished bronze,

GLEAMED* [GLEAM]

Eze	1: 7	and **g** like burnished bronze.
Lk	24: 4	men in clothes that **g** like lightning

GLEAN [GLEANED, GLEANINGS]

Ru	2: 3	and began to **g** in the fields behind

GLEANED* [GLEAN]

Ru	2:17	So Ruth **g** in the field until evening.

GLEANINGS [GLEAN]

Lev	19: 9	or gather the **g** of your harvest.

GLIDE* [GLIDED, GLIDING]

Dt	32:24	the venom of vipers that **g** in

GLIDED* [GLIDE]

Job	4:15	A spirit **g** past my face,

GLIDING* [GLIDE]

Job	26:13	his hand pierced the **g** serpent.
Isa	27: 1	Leviathan the **g** serpent,

GLOAT [GLOATS]

Ps	22:17	people stare and **g** over me.
	30: 1	not let my enemies **g** over me.
Pr	24:17	Do not **g** when your enemy falls;
La	2:17	he has let the enemy **g** over you,
Rev	11:10	the earth will **g** over them

GLOATS* [GLOAT]

Pr	17: 5	whoever **g** over disaster will not go

GLOOM [GLOOMY]

Ps	107:10	in darkness and the deepest **g,**
Isa	9: 1	there will be no more **g** for those
Joel	2: 2	a day of darkness and **g,**
Zep	1:15	a day of darkness and **g,**
Heb	12:18	to darkness, **g** and storm;

GLOOMY* [GLOOM]

2Pe	2: 4	putting them into **g** dungeons to

GLORIES* [GLORY]

1Pe	1:11	and the **g** that would follow.

GLORIFIED* [GLORY]

Isa	66: 5	have said, 'Let the LORD be **g,**
Eze	39:13	and the day I am **g** will be
Da	4:34	honored and **g** him who lives forever
Jn	7:39	since Jesus had not yet been **g.**
	11: 4	that God's Son may be **g** through it."
	12:16	after Jesus was **g** did they realize
	12:23	for the Son of Man to be **g.**
	12:28	"I have **g** it,
	13:31	Son of Man **g** and God is **g** in him.
	13:32	If God is **g** in him,
Ac	3:13	has **g** his servant Jesus.
Ro	1:21	they neither **g** him as God
	8:30	those he justified, he also **g.**
2Th	1:10	he comes to be **g** in his holy people
	1:12	the name of our Lord Jesus may be **g**
1Pe	1:21	raised him from the dead and **g** him,

GLORIFIES* [GLORY]

Lk	1:46	And Mary said: "My soul **g** the Lord
Jn	8:54	is the one who **g** me.

GLORIFY* [GLORY]

Ps	34: 3	**G** the LORD with me;
	63: 3	my lips will **g** you.
	69:30	in song and **g** him with thanksgiving.
	86:12	I will **g** your name forever.
Isa	60:13	and I will **g** the place of my feet.
Da	4:37	and exalt and **g** the King of heaven,
Jn	8:54	Jesus replied, "If I **g** myself,
	12:28	Father, **g** your name!"
	12:28	and will **g** it again."
	13:32	God will **g** the Son in himself,
	13:32	and will **g** him at once.
	17: 1	**G** your Son, that your Son may **g** you
	17: 5	**g** me in your presence now
	21:19	death by which Peter would **g** God.
Ro	15: 6	and mouth you may **g** the God
	15: 9	so that the Gentiles may **g** God
1Pe	2:12	and **g** God on the day he visits us.
Rev	16: 9	but they refused to repent and **g** him.

GLORIFYING* [GLORY]

Lk	2:20	**g** and praising God for all the things

GLORIOUS* [GLORY]

Dt	28:58	and do not revere this **g**
	33:29	and helper and your **g** sword.
1Ch	29:13	and praise your **g** name.
Ne	9: 5	"Blessed be your **g** name,

Ps	16: 3	the **g** ones in whom is all my delight.
	45:13	All **g** is the princess
	66: 2	glory of his name; make his praise **g!**
	72:19	Praise be to his **g** name forever;
	87: 3	**G** things are said of you,
	111: 3	**G** and majestic are his deeds,
	145: 5	of the **g** splendor of your majesty,
	145:12	and the **g** splendor of your kingdom.
Isa	3: 8	defying his **g** presence.
	4: 2	Branch of the LORD will be beautiful and **g,**
	11:10	and his place of rest will be **g.**
	12: 5	for he has done **g** things;
	28: 1	to the fading flower, his **g** beauty,
	28: 4	That fading flower, his **g** beauty,
	28: 5	LORD Almighty will be a **g** crown,
	42:21	to make his law great and a **g.**
	60: 7	and I will adorn my **g** temple.
	63:12	who sent his **g** arm of power to be
	63:14	to make for yourself a **g** name.
	63:15	from your lofty throne, holy and **g.**
	64:11	Our holy and **g** temple,
Jer	13:18	for your **g** crowns will fall
	14:21	not dishonor your **g** throne.
	17:12	**g** throne, exalted from the beginning
	48:17	how broken the **g** staff!'
Mt	19:28	the Son of Man sits on his **g** throne,
Lk	9:31	appeared in **g** splendor.
Ac	2:20	of the great and **g** day of the Lord.
Ro	8:21	into the **g** freedom of the children
2Co	3: 8	ministry of the Spirit be even more **g**
	3: 9	the ministry that condemns men is **g,**
	3: 9	how much more **g** is the ministry
	3:10	For what was **g** has no glory now
Eph	1: 6	to the praise of his **g** grace,
	1:17	the **g** Father, may give you the Spirit
	1:18	of his **g** inheritance in the saints,
	3:16	of his **g** riches he may strengthen you
Php	3:21	so that they will be like his **g** body.
	4:19	according to his **g** riches in Christ
Col	1:11	according to his **g** might so
	1:27	among the Gentiles the **g** riches
1Ti	1:11	to the **g** gospel of the blessed God,
Tit	2:13	the **g** appearing of our great God
Jas	2: 1	believers in our **g** Lord Jesus Christ,
1Pe	1: 8	with an inexpressible and **g** joy,
Jude	1:24	to present you before his **g** presence

GLORIOUSLY* [GLORY]

Isa	24:23	and before its elders, **g.**

GLORY [GLORIES, GLORIFIED, GLORIFIES, GLORIFY, GLORIFYING, GLORIOUS, GLORIOUSLY]

Ex	14: 4	But I will gain **g** for myself
	14:17	And I will gain **g** through Pharaoh
	14:18	that I am the LORD when I gain **g**
	15:11	awesome in **g,** working wonders?
	16: 7	and in the morning you will see the **g**
	16:10	the **g** of the LORD appearing in
	24:16	and the **g** of the LORD settled
	24:17	the **g** of the LORD looked like
	29:43	place will be consecrated by my **g.**

	33:18	Moses said, "Now show me your **g.**"
	33:22	When my **g** passes by,
	40:34	**g** of the LORD filled the tabernacle.
	40:35	**g** of the LORD filled the tabernacle.
Lev	9: 6	**g** of the LORD may appear to you."
	9:23	the **g** of the LORD appeared to all
Nu	14:10	the **g** of the LORD appeared
	14:21	surely as I live and as surely as the **g**
	14:22	the men who saw my **g**
	16:19	the **g** of the LORD appeared to
	16:42	and the **g** of the LORD appeared.
	20: 6	and the **g** of the LORD appeared
Dt	5:24	LORD our God has shown us his **g**
Jos	7:19	"My son, give **g** to the LORD,
1Sa	4:21	"The **g** has departed from Israel"—
	15:29	He who is the **G** of Israel does not lie
2Sa	1:19	"Your **g,** O Israel, lies slain
1Ki	8:11	the **g** of the LORD filled his temple.
1Ch	16:10	**G** in his holy name;
	16:24	Declare his **g** among the nations,
	16:28	ascribe to the LORD **g** and strength,
	29:11	the power and the **g** and the majesty
2Ch	5:14	the **g** of the LORD filled the temple
	7: 1	the **g** of the LORD filled the temple.
Ps	4: 2	will you turn my **g** into shame?
	8: 1	You have set your **g** above
	8: 5	and crowned him with **g** and honor.
	19: 1	The heavens declare the **g** of God;
	24: 7	that the King of **g** may come in.
	26: 8	the place where your **g** dwells.
	29: 1	ascribe to the LORD **g** and strength.
	29: 3	the God of **g** thunders,
	29: 9	And in his temple all cry, **"G!"**
	57: 5	let your **g** be over all the earth.
	63: 2	and beheld your power and your **g.**
	66: 2	Sing the **g** of his name;
	72:19	the whole earth be filled with his **g.**
	73:24	afterward you will take me into **g.**
	85: 9	that his **g** may dwell in our land.
	89:17	For you are their **g** and strength,
	96: 3	Declare his **g** among the nations,
	96: 6	and **g** are in his sanctuary.
	96: 8	to the LORD the **g** due his name;
	97: 6	and all the peoples see his **g.**
	102:15	kings of the earth will revere your **g.**
	104:31	the **g** of the LORD endure forever;
	106:20	They exchanged their **G** for an image
	108: 5	and let your **g** be over all the earth.
	138: 5	for the **g** of the LORD is great.
	149: 9	This is the **g** of all his saints.
Pr	19:11	to his **g** to overlook an offense.
	20:29	The **g** of young men is their strength,
	25: 2	It is the **g** of God to conceal a matter;
Isa	4: 5	over all the **g** will be a canopy.
	6: 3	the whole earth is full of his **g.**"
	24:16	**"G** to the Righteous One."
	26:15	You have gained **g** for yourself;
	35: 2	they will see the **g** of the LORD,
	40: 5	the **g** of the LORD will be revealed,
	40: 6	and all their **g** is like the flowers of
	42: 8	I will not give my **g** to another
	42:12	Let them give **g** to the LORD
	43: 7	whom I created for my **g,**
	44:23	he displays his **g** in Israel.

	48:11	I will not yield my **g** to another.
	60:19	and your God will be your **g**.
	66:18	and they will come and see my **g**.
	66:19	They will proclaim my **g** among
Jer	2:11	my people have exchanged their **G**
Eze	1:28	the likeness of the **g** of the LORD.
	3:23	**g** of the LORD was standing there,
	8: 4	And there before me was the **g** of
	9: 3	Now the **g** of the God of Israel went
	10: 4	the **g** of the LORD rose from above
	10:18	Then the **g** of the LORD departed
	11:23	The **g** of the LORD went up from
	43: 2	and I saw the **g** of the God of Israel
	43: 5	the **g** of the LORD filled the temple.
	44: 4	and saw the **g** of the LORD filling
Hos	4: 7	they exchanged their **G**
Hab	2:14	be filled with the knowledge of the **g**
	3: 3	His **g** covered the heavens
Hag	2: 7	and I will fill this house with **g**,'
Zec	2: 5	'and I will be its **g** within.'
Mt	16:27	is going to come in his Father's **g**
	24:30	with power and great **g**.
	25:31	the Son of Man comes in his **g**,
	25:31	will sit on his throne in heavenly **g**.
Mk	8:38	when he comes in his Father's **g** with
	10:37	and the other at your left in your **g**."
	13:26	in clouds with great power and **g**.
Lk	2: 9	the **g** of the Lord shone around them,
	2:14	"**G** to God in the highest,
	2:32	and for **g** to your people Israel."
	9:26	in his **g** and in the **g** of the Father
	9:32	they saw his **g** and
	19:38	in heaven and **g** in the highest!"
	21:27	in a cloud with power and great **g**.
	24:26	and then enter his **g**?"
Jn	1:14	his **g**, the **g** of the One and Only,
	2:11	He thus revealed his **g**,
	8:50	I am not seeking **g** for myself;
	8:54	my **g** means nothing.
	11: 4	for God's **g** so that God's Son may
	11:40	you would see the **g** of God?"
	12:41	Isaiah said this because he saw Jesus' **g**
	14:13	the Son may bring **g** to the Father.
	15: 8	This is to my Father's **g**,
	16:14	He will bring **g** to me by taking
	17: 4	I have brought you **g** on earth
	17: 5	with the **g** I had with you before
	17:10	And **g** has come to me through them.
	17:22	I have given them the **g**
	17:24	and to see my **g**,
	17:24	the **g** you have given me
Ac	7: 2	The God of **g** appeared to our father
	7:55	to heaven and saw the **g** of God,
Ro	1:23	the **g** of the immortal God
	2: 7	by persistence in doing good seek **g**,
	2:10	but **g**, honor and peace
	3: 7	and so increases his **g**,
	3:23	and fall short of the **g** of God,
	4:20	in his faith and gave **g** to God,
	5: 2	And we rejoice in the hope of the **g**
	8:17	that we may also share in his **g**.
	8:18	not worth comparing with the **g**
	9: 4	the divine **g**,

	9:23	to make the riches of his **g** known to
	9:23	whom he prepared in advance for **g**
	11:36	To him be the **g** forever!
	15:17	Therefore I **g** in Christ Jesus
	16:27	be **g** forever through Jesus Christ!
1Co	2: 7	and that God destined for our **g**
	2: 8	not have crucified the Lord of **g**.
	10:31	do it all for the **g** of God.
	11: 7	since he is the image and **g** of God;
	11: 7	but the woman is the **g** of man.
	11:15	it is her **g**?
	15:43	it is raised in **g**;
2Co	1:20	the "Amen" is spoken by us to the **g**
	3: 7	in letters on stone, came with **g**,
	3: 7	at the face of Moses because of its **g**,
	3:10	what was glorious has no **g** now in
		comparison with the surpassing **g**,
	3:11	what was fading away came with **g**,
		how much greater is the **g** of
	3:18	unveiled faces all reflect the Lord's **g**,
	3:18	his likeness with ever-increasing **g**,
	4: 4	light of the gospel of the **g** of Christ,
	4: 6	of the **g** of God in the face of Christ.
	4:15	to overflow to the **g** of God.
	4:17	are achieving for us an eternal **g**
Gal	1: 5	to whom be **g** for ever and ever.
Eph	1:12	might be for the praise of his **g**.
	1:14	to the praise of his **g**.
	3:13	which are your **g**.
	3:21	be **g** in the church and in Christ Jesus
Php	1:11	to the **g** and praise of God.
	2:11	to the **g** of God the Father.
	3: 3	who **g** in Christ Jesus,
	3:19	and their **g** is in their shame.
	4:20	To our God and Father be **g** for ever
Col	1:27	which is Christ in you, the hope of **g**.
	3: 4	you also will appear with him in **g**.
1Th	2:12	calls you into his kingdom and **g**.
	2:19	the crown in which we will **g**
	2:20	Indeed, you are our **g** and joy.
2Th	2:14	share in the **g** of our Lord Jesus
1Ti	1:17	be honor and **g** for ever and ever.
	3:16	was taken up in **g**.
2Ti	2:10	that is in Christ Jesus, with eternal **g**.
	4:18	To him be **g** for ever and ever.
Heb	1: 3	Son is the radiance of God's **g**
	2: 7	you crowned him with **g** and honor
	2: 9	now crowned with **g** and honor
	2:10	In bringing many sons to **g**,
	5: 5	also did not take upon himself the **g**
	9: 5	the ark were the cherubim of the **G**,
	13:21	to whom be **g** for ever and ever.
1Pe	1: 7	**g** and honor when Jesus Christ is
	1:24	and all their **g** is like the flowers of
	4:11	be the **g** and the power for ever
	4:13	be overjoyed when his **g** is revealed.
	4:14	Spirit of **g** and of God rests on you.
	5: 1	and one who also will share in the **g**
	5: 4	you will receive the crown of **g**
	5:10	who called you to his eternal **g**
2Pe	1: 3	of him who called us by his own **g**
	1:17	he received honor and **g** from God
	1:17	came to him from the Majestic **G**,
	3:18	To him be **g** both now and forever!

Jude 1:25 to the only God our Savior be **g,**
Rev 1: 6 be **g** and power for ever and ever!
4: 9 the living creatures give **g,**
4:11 to receive **g** and honor and power,
5:12 and strength and honor and **g**
5:13 the Lamb be praise and honor and **g**
7:12 Praise and **g** and wisdom and thanks
11:13 and gave **g** to the God of heaven.
14: 7 "Fear God and give him **g,**
15: 4 O Lord, and bring **g** to your name?
15: 8 filled with smoke from the **g** of God
18: 7 as the **g** and luxury she gave herself.
19: 1 and **g** and power belong to our God,
19: 7 and be glad and give him **g!**
21:11 It shone with the **g** of God,
21:23 for the **g** of God gives it light,
21:26 The **g** and honor of the nations will

GLORY OF GOD Ps 19:1; Pr 25:2; Jn 11:40;
Ac 7:55; Ro 3:23; 5:2; 1Co 10:31; 11:7; 2Co
1:20; 4:6, 15; Php 2:11; Rev 15:8; 21:11, 23

GLORY OF THE †LORD Ex 16:7, 10; 24:16,
17; 40:34, 35; Lev 9:6, 23; Nu 14:10, 21; 16:19,
42; 20:6; 1Ki 8:11; 2Ch 5:14; 7:1, 2, 3; Ps
104:31; 138:5; Isa 35:2; 40:5; 58:8; 60:1; Eze
1:28; 3:12, 23; 10:4, 4, 18; 11:23; 43:4, 5; 44:4;
Hab 2:14

GLOWING

Eze 1:27 his waist up he looked like **g** metal,
8: 2 appearance was as bright as **g** metal.
Rev 1:15 His feet were like bronze **g** in

GLUTTON* [GLUTTONS, GLUTTONY]

Mt 11:19 'Here is a **g** and a drunkard,
Lk 7:34 'Here is a **g** and a drunkard,

GLUTTONS* [GLUTTON]

Pr 23:21 for drunkards and **g** become poor,
28: 7 companion of **g** disgraces his father.
Tit 1:12 evil brutes, lazy **g.**"

GLUTTONY* [GLUTTON]

Pr 23: 2 to your throat if you are given to **g.**

GNASH* [GNASHED, GNASHING]

Ps 37:12 and **g** their teeth at them;
112:10 he will **g** his teeth and waste away;
La 2:16 they scoff and **g** their teeth

GNASHED* [GNASH]

Ps 35:16 they **g** their teeth at me.
Ac 7:54 furious and **g** their teeth at him.

GNASHING* [GNASH]

Mt 8:12 there will be weeping and **g** of teeth.
13:42 there will be weeping and **g** of teeth.
13:50 there will be weeping and **g** of teeth.
22:13 there will be weeping and **g** of teeth.'
24:51 there will be weeping and **g** of teeth.
25:30 there will be weeping and **g** of teeth.'
Lk 13:28 weeping there, and **g** of teeth,

GNAT* [GNATS]

Mt 23:24 You strain out a **g** but swallow

GNATS [GNAT]

Ex 8:16 land of Egypt the dust will become **g.**
Ps 105:31 and **g** throughout their country.

GO [GOES, GOING, GONE]

Ge 4: 8 "Let's **g** out to the field."
7: 1 "**G** into the ark,
11: 7 let us **g** down and confuse
13:17 **G,** walk through the length
18:21 that I will **g** down and see
46: 4 I will **g** down to Egypt with you,
Ex 3:10 So now, **g**
3:19 the king of Egypt will not let you **g**
5: 1 God of Israel, says: 'Let my people **g**
12:31 **G,** worship the LORD
13:15 stubbornly refused to let us **g.**
32: 1 make us gods who will **g** before us.
33: 3 But I will not **g** with you,
34: 9 he said, "then let the Lord **g** with us.
Nu 13:30 "We should **g** up and take possession
14: 3 Wouldn't it be better for us to **g** back
Dt 1:26 But you were unwilling to **g** up;
4:40 so that it may **g** well with you
Jos 1: 9 God will be with you wherever you **g**
Ru 1:16 Where you **g** I will **g,**
Ps 122: 1 "Let us **g** to the house of the LORD."
139: 7 Where can I **g** from your Spirit?
Pr 6: 6 **G** to the ant, you sluggard;
22: 6 Train a child in the way he should **g,**
31:18 and her lamp does not **g** out at night.
Isa 2: 3 The law will **g** out from Zion,
55:12 You will **g** out in joy and be led forth
Jer 7:23 that it may **g** well with you.
Eze 1:12 Wherever the spirit would **g,**
Mic 4: 2 let us **g** up to the mountain of
Hab 3:19 he enables me to **g** on the heights.
Zec 14: 3 Then the LORD will **g** out and fight
Mal 4: 2 you will **g** out and leap like calves
Mt 5:41 If someone forces you to **g** one mile,
6: 6 when you pray, **g** into your room,
28:19 **g** and make disciples of all nations,
Mk 10:25 to **g** through the eye of a needle
Lk 9:57 "I will follow you wherever you **g.**"
Jn 6:68 "Lord, to whom shall we **g?**
8:21 Where I **g,** you cannot come."
14: 3 if I **g** and prepare a place for you,
16: 1 so that you will not **g** astray.
Rev 22:14 and may **g** through the gates

GOADS

Ecc 12:11 The words of the wise are like **g,**
Ac 26:14 hard for you to kick against the **g.**'

GOAL*

Lk 13:32 on the third day I will reach my **g.**'
2Co 5: 9 So we make it our **g** to please him,
Gal 3: 3 to attain your **g** by human effort?
Php 3:14 on toward the **g** to win the prize
1Ti 1: 5 The **g** of this command is love,
1Pe 1: 9 you are receiving the **g** of your faith,

GOAT [GOATS, SCAPEGOAT]

Ge 15: 9 a **g** and a ram, each three years old,
30:32 and every spotted or speckled **g.**

	37:31	a **g** and dipped the robe in the blood.
Ex	26: 7	"Make curtains of **g** hair for the tent
Lev	16: 9	the **g** whose lot falls to the LORD
	16:22	**g** will carry on itself all their sins
Nu	7:16	one male **g** for a sin offering;
Isa	11: 6	the leopard will lie down with the **g,**
Da	8: 5	suddenly a **g** with a prominent horn
	8:21	The shaggy **g** is the king of Greece,

GOATS [GOAT]

Lev	16: 5	to take two male **g** for a sin offering
Nu	7:17	five male **g** and five male lambs
Ps	50:13	of bulls or drink the blood of **g**?
Eze	34:17	and between rams and **g.**
Mt	25:32	separates the sheep from the **g.**
Heb	9:12	not enter by means of the blood of **g**
	10: 4	of bulls and **g** to take away sins.

GOBLET [GOBLETS]

Isa	51:22	the **g** of my wrath,

GOBLETS [GOBLET]

1Ki	10:21	All King Solomon's **g** were gold,
Da	5: 2	to bring in the gold and silver **g**

GOD [GOD'S, GOD-BREATHED, GOD-FEARING, GOD-HATERS, GODDESS, GODLESS, GODLESSNESS, GODLINESS, GODLY, GODS]

Ge	1: 1	In the beginning **G** created the
	1: 2	Spirit of **G** was hovering over the
	1: 3	And **G** said, "Let there be light,"
	1: 7	So **G** made the expanse
	1: 9	And **G** said, "Let the water
	1:11	Then **G** said, "Let the land
	1:21	So **G** created the great creatures of
	1:21	And **G** saw that it was good.
	1:22	**G** blessed them and said,
	1:25	**G** made the wild animals according
	1:25	And **G** saw that it was good.
	1:26	Then **G** said, "Let us make man
	1:27	So **G** created man in his own image,
	1:28	**G** blessed them and said to them,
	1:31	**G** saw all that he had made,
	2: 3	And **G** blessed the seventh day
	2: 4	When the LORD **G** made the earth
	2: 7	the LORD **G** formed the man from
	2: 8	the LORD **G** had planted a garden
	2:16	the LORD **G** commanded the man,
	2:22	the LORD **G** made a woman
	3: 1	"Did **G** really say,
	3: 5	and you will be like **G,**
	3: 8	hid from the LORD **G** among the
	3: 9	But the LORD **G** called to the man,
	3:13	the LORD **G** said to the woman,
	3:14	So the LORD **G** said to the serpent,
	3:21	The LORD **G** made garments
	3:23	the LORD **G** banished him from
	5: 1	When **G** created man,
	5:24	Enoch walked with **G;**
	6: 2	the sons of **G** saw that the daughters
	6: 9	and he walked with **G.**

	6:12	**G** saw how corrupt the earth
	8: 1	But **G** remembered Noah and all
	9: 1	Then **G** blessed Noah and his sons,
	9: 6	in the image of **G** has **G** made man.
	9:16	the everlasting covenant between **G**
	14:18	He was priest of **G** Most High,
	14:19	"Blessed be Abram by **G** Most High,
	16:13	the **G** who sees me,"
	17: 1	"I am **G** Almighty;
	17: 7	to be your **G** and the **G** of your descendants after you.
	19:29	So when **G** destroyed the cities of
	21: 2	at the very time **G** had promised him.
	21: 6	"**G** has brought me laughter,
	21:17	and the angel of **G** called to Hagar
	21:20	**G** was with the boy as he grew up.
	21:22	"**G** is with you in everything you do.
	21:33	the LORD, the Eternal **G.**
	22: 1	Some time later **G** tested Abraham.
	22: 8	"**G** himself will provide the lamb for
	22:12	Now I know that you fear **G,**
	25:11	**G** blessed his son Isaac,
	26:24	"I am the **G** of your father Abraham.
	28:12	angels of **G** were ascending and
	28:17	none other than the house of **G;**
	30: 2	"Am I in the place of **G,**
	31:13	I am the **G** of Bethel,
	31:42	But **G** has seen my hardship and
	31:50	that **G** is a witness between you
	32: 1	and the angels of **G** met him.
	32:28	because you have struggled with **G**
	32:30	"It is because I saw **G** face to face,
	33:11	for **G** has been gracious to me
	35: 1	and build an altar there to **G,**
	35: 5	the terror of **G** fell upon the towns
	35:10	**G** said to him, "Your name is Jacob,
	35:11	**G** said to him, "I am **G** Almighty;
	41:38	one in whom is the spirit of **G**?"
	41:51	**G** has made me forget all my trouble
	41:52	"It is because **G** has made me fruitful
	46: 2	And **G** spoke to Israel in a vision
	48:15	**G** who has been my shepherd all my
	50:19	Am I in the place of **G**?
	50:20	but **G** intended it for good
	50:24	But **G** will surely come to your aid
Ex	1:17	feared **G** and did not do what
	2:24	heard their groaning
	3: 4	**G** called to him from within the bush
	3: 5	"Do not come any closer," **G** said.
	3: 6	he said, "I am the **G** of your father, the **G** of Abraham, the **G** of Isaac and the **G** of Jacob."
	3:12	And **G** said, "I will be with you.
	3:14	**G** said to Moses, "I AM WHO I AM.
	3:18	'The LORD, the **G** of the Hebrews,
	4:27	he met Moses at the mountain of **G**
	6: 7	and I will be your **G.**
	6: 7	that I am the LORD your **G,**
	7: 1	I have made you like **G** to Pharaoh,
	8:10	no one like the LORD our **G.**
	8:19	"This is the finger of **G.**"
	10:16	have sinned against the LORD your **G**
	13:19	"**G** will surely come to your aid,
	14:19	Then the angel of **G,**

15: 2 He is my **G**, and I will praise him,
15: 2 and I will praise him, my father's **G**,
16:12 know that I am the LORD your **G**.' "
17: 9 on top of the hill with the staff of **G**
18: 4 "My father's **G** was my helper;
18: 5 near the mountain of **G**.
19: 3 Then Moses went up to **G**,
20: 1 And **G** spoke all these words:
20: 2 "I am the LORD your **G**,
20: 5 I, the LORD your **G**, am a jealous **G**,
20: 7 misuse the name of the LORD your **G**
20:10 a Sabbath to the LORD your **G**.
20:12 land the LORD your **G** is giving you.
20:19 But do not have **G** speak to us
20:20 **G** has come to test you,
20:20 so that the fear of **G** will be with you
22:20 to any **g** other than the LORD
22:28 not blaspheme **G** or curse the ruler
23:19 to the house of the LORD your **G**.
24:10 and saw the **G** of Israel.
31:18 of stone inscribed by the finger of **G**.
34: 6 the compassionate and gracious **G**,
34:14 Do not worship any other **g**,
34:14 is a jealous **G**.
Lev 2:13 the salt of the covenant of your **G**
11:44 I am the LORD your **G**;
18:21 not profane the name of your **G**.
19: 2 the LORD your **G**, am holy.
20: 7 because I am the LORD your **G**.
21: 6 They must be holy to their **G**
22:33 out of Egypt to be your **G**.
26:12 will walk among you and be your **G**,
Nu 15:40 and will be consecrated to your **G**.
16:22 **G** of the spirits of all mankind,
22: 9 **G** came to Balaam and asked,
22:18 the command of the LORD my **G**.
22:38 I must speak only what **G** puts
23:19 **G** is not a man, that he should lie,
25:13 he was zealous for the honor of his **G**
27:16 the **G** of the spirits of all mankind,
Dt 1:17 for judgment belongs to **G**.
1:21 LORD your **G** has given you the land.
1:32 not trust in the LORD your **G**,
3:22 the LORD your **G** himself will fight
3:24 For what **g** is there in heaven or
4: 7 the way the LORD our **G** is near
4:24 LORD your **G** is a consuming fire, a jealous **G**.
4:29 you seek the LORD your **G**,
4:31 LORD your **G** is a merciful **G**;
4:39 that the LORD is **G** in heaven
5: 9 I, the LORD your **G**, am a jealous **G**,
5:11 misuse the name of the LORD your **G**
5:12 LORD your **G** has commanded you.
5:14 a Sabbath to the LORD your **G**.
5:15 the LORD your **G** brought you out
5:15 LORD your **G** has commanded you
5:16 the LORD your **G** is giving you.
5:24 LORD our **G** has shown us his glory
5:24 that a man can live even if **G** speaks
5:26 heard the voice of the living **G**
6: 2 may fear the LORD your **G**
6: 4 Hear, O Israel: The LORD our **G**,
6: 5 Love the LORD your **G** with all

6:13 Fear the LORD your **G**,
6:16 Do not test the LORD your **G**
7: 6 a people holy to the LORD your **G**.
7: 9 Know therefore that the LORD your **G** is **G**; he is the faithful **G**,
7:12 LORD your **G** will keep his covenant
7:19 the LORD your **G** brought you out.
7:19 The LORD your **G** will do the same
7:21 is a great and awesome **G**.
8: 5 the LORD your **G** disciplines you.
8:11 do not forget the LORD your **G**,
8:18 But remember the LORD your **G**,
9:10 tablets inscribed by the finger of **G**.
10:12 but to fear the LORD your **G**,
10:12 to serve the LORD your **G**
10:14 the LORD your **G** belong the heavens,
10:17 For the LORD your **G** is **G** of gods
10:21 He is your praise; he is your **G**,
11: 1 Love the LORD your **G**
11:13 to love the LORD your **G**
12:12 rejoice before the LORD your **G**,
12:28 right in the eyes of the LORD your **G**.
13: 3 The LORD your **G** is testing you
13: 4 the LORD your **G** you must follow,
14: 1 the children of the LORD your **G**.
14: 2 a people holy to the LORD your **G**.
15: 6 the LORD your **G** will bless you
15:19 LORD your **G** every firstborn male
16:11 rejoice before the LORD your **G**
16:17 the LORD your **G** has blessed you.
16:22 for these the LORD your **G** hates.
18:13 blameless before the LORD your **G**.
18:15 The LORD your **G** will raise up
19: 9 to love the LORD your **G** and
22: 5 your **G** detests anyone who does this.
23: 5 your **G** would not listen to Balaam
23:14 For the LORD your **G** moves about
23:21 a vow to the LORD your **G**,
23:21 LORD your **G** will certainly demand
25:16 your **G** detests anyone who does
26: 5 declare before the LORD your **G**:
27: 5 an altar to the LORD your **G**,
28: 1 If you fully obey the LORD your **G**
28:15 if you do not obey the LORD your **G**
29:13 he may be your **G** as he promised
29:29 The secret things belong to the LORD our **G**,
30: 2 return to the LORD your **G** and obey
30: 4 the LORD your **G** will gather you
30: 6 your **G** will circumcise your hearts
30:16 to love the LORD your **G**, to walk
30:16 the LORD your **G** will bless you in
30:20 you may love the LORD your **G**,
31: 6 the LORD your **G** goes with you;
32: 3 Oh, praise the greatness of our **G**!
32: 4 A faithful **G** who does no wrong,
32:18 the **G** who gave you birth.
32:39 There is no **g** besides me.
33:27 The eternal **G** is your refuge,
Jos 1: 9 the LORD your **G** will be with you
1:13 the LORD your **G** is giving you rest
14: 8 the LORD my **G** wholeheartedly.
14:14 the **G** of Israel, wholeheartedly.
22: 5 to love the LORD your **G**,

22:22 "The Mighty One, G, the LORD! The
      Mighty One, G, the LORD!
22:34 Between Us that the LORD is G.
23: 3 LORD your G who fought for you.
23: 8 to hold fast to the LORD your G,
23:11 to love the LORD your G.
23:14 the good promises the LORD your G
23:15 of the LORD your G has come true,
24:19 He is a holy G; he is a jealous G.

Jdg 1: 7 Now G has paid me back
   5: 5 before the LORD, the G of Israel.
   6:20 The angel of G said to him,
   6:31 If Baal really is a g,
   8:33 They set up Baal-Berith as their g
  13: 6 He looked like an angel of G,
 16:23 "Our g has delivered Samson,
 16:28 O G, please strengthen me just once
 20:27 ark of the covenant of G was there,

Ru 1:16 be my people and your G my G.

1Sa 2: 2 there is no Rock like our G.
   2: 3 for the LORD is a G who knows,
   2:25 G may mediate for him;
   3: 3 where the ark of G was.
   4:11 The ark of G was captured,
   5:11 "Send the ark of the g of Israel away;
  10: 9 G changed Saul's heart,
 10:26 men whose hearts G had touched.
 11: 6 Spirit of G came upon him in power,
 12:12 the LORD your G was your king.
 14:15 It was a panic sent by G.
 16:15 evil spirit from G is tormenting you.
 17:36 has defied the armies of the living G.
 17:45 the G of the armies of Israel,
 17:46 that there is a G in Israel.
 19:23 the Spirit of G came even upon him,
 23:16 and helped him find strength in G.
 28:15 and G has turned away from me.
 30: 6 in the LORD his G.

2Sa 6: 7 therefore G struck him down
   7:22 and there is no G but you,
   7:23 on earth that G went out to redeem
   7:27 "O LORD Almighty, G of Israel,
 14:14 But G does not take away life;
 14:17 like an angel of G in discerning good
 21:14 G answered prayer in behalf of
 22: 3 my G is my rock,
 22:31 "As for G, his way is perfect;
 22:32 For who is G besides the LORD?
 22:33 It is G who arms me with strength
 22:47 Exalted be G, the Rock, my Savior!

1Ki 2: 3 what the LORD your G requires:
   4:29 G gave Solomon wisdom
   5: 5 for the Name of the LORD my G,
   8:23 G of Israel, there is no G like you in
   8:27 "But will G really dwell on earth?
   8:60 know that the LORD is G and
   8:61 fully committed to the LORD our G,
 10:24 the wisdom G had put in his heart.
 11: 4 not fully devoted to the LORD his G,
 11:33 Chemosh the g of the Moabites,
 11:33 and Molech the g of the Ammonites,
 15:30 the G of Israel, to anger.
 18:21 If the LORD is G, follow him;
 18:24 The g who answers by fire—he is G.

18:36 G of Abraham, Isaac and Israel,
18:39 The LORD—he is G!"
20:28 think the LORD is a g of the hills

2Ki 1: 2 Baal-Zebub, the g of Ekron,
   5:15 "Now I know that there is no G in all
 17: 7 sinned against the LORD their G,
 19: 4 has sent to ridicule the living G,
 19:15 you alone are G over all
 19:19 Now, O LORD our G,

1Ch 12:18 for your G will help you."
 13: 2 if it is the will of the LORD our G,
 16:35 Cry out, "Save us, O G our Savior;
 17:20 O LORD, and there is no G but you,
 17:24 the G over Israel, is Israel's G!"
 21: 8 Then David said to G,
 21:15 G sent an angel to destroy Jerusalem.
 22: 1 house of the LORD G is to be here,
 22:19 to seeking the LORD your G.
 28: 2 for the footstool of our G,
 28: 9 acknowledge the G of your father,
 28:20 for the LORD G, my G,
 29: 1 the one whom G has chosen,
 29: 2 for the temple of my G—
 29:10 O LORD, G of our father Israel,
 29:13 Now, our G, we give you thanks,
 29:18 G of our fathers Abraham,

2Ch 1: 7 That night G appeared to Solomon
   2: 4 the LORD my G and to dedicate it
   2: 5 our G is greater than all other gods.
   5:14 of the LORD filled the temple of G.
   6:14 there is no G like you in heaven or
   6:18 "But will G really dwell on earth
 10:15 for this turn of events was from G,
 13:12 G is with us; he is our leader.
 15: 3 time Israel was without the true G,
 15:12 the G of their fathers,
 15:15 They sought G eagerly,
 18:13 I can tell him only what my G says."
 19: 3 set your heart on seeking G."
 19: 7 LORD our G there is no injustice
 20: 6 are you not the G who is in heaven?
 20:20 Have faith in the LORD your G
 25: 8 for G has the power to help or
 26: 5 who instructed him in the fear of G;
 30: 9 for the LORD your G is gracious
 30:19 who sets his heart on seeking G—
 31:21 he sought his G and worked
 32:15 for no g of any nation
 32:17 so the g of Hezekiah will not rescue
 32:31 G left him to test him and
 33:12 himself greatly before the G
 33:19 how G was moved by his entreaty,
 34:33 in Israel serve the LORD their G.

Ezr 1: 3 the G who is in Jerusalem.
   2:68 the rebuilding of the house of G
   6:16 the dedication of the house of G
   7: 9 gracious hand of his G was on him.
   7:18 accordance with the will of your G.
   7:23 the G of heaven has prescribed,
   8:22 "The gracious hand of G is on
   8:31 The hand of our G was on us,
   9: 6 and prayed: "O my G,
   9: 9 our G has not deserted us
 10: 3 a covenant before our G

Ne 1: 5 I said: "O LORD, **G** of heaven,
    4:20 Our **G** will fight for us!"
    5:15 But out of reverence for **G** I did
    7: 2 feared **G** more than most men do.
    8: 8 from the Book of the Law of **G**,
    8:18 from the Book of the Law of **G**.
    9: 5 and praise the LORD your **G**,
    9:17 But you are a forgiving **G**,
    9:31 you are a gracious and merciful **G**.
    9:32 the great, mighty and awesome **G**,
    10:29 an oath to follow the Law of **G** given
    10:39 not neglect the house of our **G**."
    12:43 because **G** had given them great joy.
    13: 2 (Our **G**, however, turned the curse
    13:11 "Why is the house of **G** neglected?"
    13:26 He was loved by his **G**,
    13:31 Remember me with favor, O my **G**.
Job 1: 1 blameless and upright; he feared **G**
    1: 9 "Does Job fear **G** for nothing?"
    1:22 sin by charging **G** with wrongdoing.
    2:10 Shall we accept good from **G**,
    4:17 a mortal be more righteous than **G**?
    5:17 the man whom **G** corrects;
    8: 3 Does **G** pervert justice?
    8:20 **G** does not reject a blameless
    9: 2 can a mortal be righteous before **G**?
    11: 7 fathom the mysteries of **G**?
    12:13 "To **G** belong wisdom and power;
    16: 7 Surely, O **G**, you have worn me out;
    19:26 yet in my flesh I will see **G**;
    20:29 Such is the fate **G** allots the wicked,
    21:19 '**G** stores up a man's punishment
    21:22 "Can anyone teach knowledge to **G**,
    22:12 "Is not **G** in the heights of heaven?
    22:13 Yet you say, 'What does **G** know?
    22:21 to **G** and be at peace with him;
    25: 2 "Dominion and awe belong to **G**;
    25: 4 can a man be righteous before **G**?
    26: 6 Death is naked before **G**;
    30:20 "I cry out to you, O **G**,
    31: 6 let **G** weigh me in honest scales
    31:14 what will I do when **G** confronts me?
    32:13 found wisdom; let **G** refute him,
    33: 6 I am just like you before **G**;
    33:14 For **G** does speak—
    33:26 to **G** and finds favor with him,
    33:26 by **G** to his righteous state.
    34:10 Far be it from **G** to do evil,
    34:23 **G** has no need to examine
    34:33 Should **G** then reward you
    36: 5 "**G** is mighty, but does
    36:26 How great is **G**—
    40: 2 Let him who accuses **G** answer him!
Ps 5: 2 my King and my **G**,
    5: 4 You are not a **G** who takes pleasure
    7:10 My shield is **G** Most High,
    7:11 **G** is a righteous judge,
    7:11 a **G** who expresses his wrath every
    10:14 you, O **G**, do see trouble and grief;
    14: 5 for **G** is present in the company of
    18: 2 my **G** is my rock,
    18:21 not done evil by turning from my **G**.
    18:28 my **G** turns my darkness
    18:30 As for **G**, his way is perfect;

18:31 And who is the Rock except our **G**?
18:32 It is **G** who arms me with strength
18:46 Exalted be **G** my Savior!
19: 1 The heavens declare the glory of **G**;
22: 1 My **G**, my **G**, why have you
22:10 womb you have been my **G**.
27: 9 O **G** my Savior.
29: 3 the **G** of glory thunders,
31: 5 O LORD, the **G** of truth.
31:14 "You are my **G**."
33:12 the nation whose **G** is the LORD,
35:23 Contend for me, my **G** and Lord.
37:31 The law of his **G** is in his heart;
40: 3 a hymn of praise to our **G**.
40: 8 I desire to do your will, O my **G**;
42: 1 so my soul pants for you, O **G**.
42: 2 My soul thirsts for **G**,
42: 2 for the living **G**.
42: 5 Put your hope in **G**,
42: 8 a prayer to the **G** of my life.
42:11 Put your hope in **G**,
43: 4 Then will I go to the altar of **G**,
43: 4 praise you with the harp, O **G**, my **G**.
44: 8 In **G** we make our boast all day long,
45: 6 Your throne, O **G**, will last for ever
45: 7 therefore **G**, your **G**, has set you
46: 1 **G** is our refuge and strength,
46: 5 **G** is within her, she will not fall;
46:10 "Be still, and know that I am **G**;
47: 1 shout to **G** with cries of joy.
47: 6 Sing praises to **G**, sing praises;
47: 7 For **G** is the King of all the earth;
48: 9 your temple, O **G**, we meditate
48:14 this **G** is our **G** for ever and ever;
49: 7 or give to **G** a ransom for him—
50: 2 perfect in beauty, **G** shines forth.
50: 3 Our **G** comes and will not be silent;
51: 1 Have mercy on me, O **G**,
51:10 Create in me a pure heart, O **G**,
51:17 sacrifices of **G** are a broken spirit;
53: 2 **G** looks down from heaven on
54: 4 Surely **G** is my help;
55:19 **G**, who is enthroned forever,
56: 4 whose word I praise, in **G** I trust;
56:11 in **G** I trust; I will not be afraid.
56:13 that I may walk before **G** in the light
57: 3 **G** sends his love
57: 7 O **G**, my heart is steadfast;
59:17 O **G**, my fortress, my loving **G**.
62: 1 My soul finds rest in **G** alone;
62: 7 and my honor depend on **G**;
62: 8 for **G** is our refuge.
62:11 One thing **G** has spoken,
62:11 O **G**, are strong,
63: 1 O **G**, you are my **G**,
65: 5 O **G** our Savior,
66: 1 Shout with joy to **G**, all the earth!
66: 3 Say to **G**, "How awesome
66: 5 Come and see what **G** has done,
66:16 all you who fear **G**;
66:20 Praise be to **G**,
68: 4 Sing to **G**, sing praise to his name,
68: 6 **G** sets the lonely in families,
68:20 Our **G** is a **G** who saves;

68:26 Praise **G** in the great congregation;
68:35 You are awesome, O **G,**
68:35 Praise be to **G!**
69: 5 You know my folly, O **G;**
70: 1 Hasten, O **G,** to save me;
70: 4 "Let **G** be exalted!"
70: 5 come quickly to me, O **G.**
71:17 Since my youth, O **G,**
71:18 do not forsake me, O **G,**
71:19 Who, O **G,** is like you?
71:22 for your faithfulness, O my **G;**
73:17 till I entered the sanctuary of **G;**
73:26 but **G** is the strength of my heart
76:11 Make vows to the LORD your **G**
77:13 Your ways, O **G,** are holy.
77:13 What **g** is so great as our **G?**
77:14 the **G** who performs miracles;
78:19 They spoke against **G,** saying,
78:59 **G** heard them, he was very angry;
79: 9 Help us, O **G** our Savior,
81: 1 Sing for joy to **G** our strength;
82: 1 **G** presides in the great assembly;
84: 2 and my flesh cry out for the living **G.**
84:10 a doorkeeper in the house of my **G**
84:11 the LORD **G** is a sun and shield;
86:12 I will praise you, O Lord my **G,**
86:15 are a compassionate and gracious **G,**
87: 3 O city of **G:**
89: 7 of the holy ones **G** is greatly feared;
90: 2 to everlasting you are **G.**
91: 2 my **G,** in whom I trust."
94: 1 O LORD, the **G** who avenges,
94:22 and my **G** the rock
95: 3 For the LORD is the great **G,**
95: 7 for he is our **G** and we are the people
99: 8 O LORD our **G,** you answered them;
            you were to Israel a forgiving **G,**
99: 9 for the LORD our **G** is holy.
100: 3 Know that the LORD is **G.**
106:21 They forgot the **G** who saved them,
106:33 they rebelled against the Spirit of **G,**
108: 1 My heart is steadfast, O **G;**
108: 5 Be exalted, O **G,** above the heavens,
113: 5 Who is like the LORD our **G,**
115: 3 Our **G** is in heaven;
116: 5 our **G** is full of compassion.
123: 2 our eyes look to the LORD our **G,**
136: 2 Give thanks to the **G** of gods.
136:26 Give thanks to the **G** of heaven.
139:17 to me are your thoughts, O **G!**
139:23 Search me, O **G,** and know my heart;
143:10 for you are my **G;**
144: 2 He is my loving **G** and my fortress,
145: 1 I will exalt you, my **G** the King;
147: 1 good it is to sing praises to our **G,**
150: 1 Praise **G** in his sanctuary;
Pr   2: 5 and find the knowledge of **G.**
3: 4 and a good name in the sight of **G**
14:31 kind to the needy honors **G.**
25: 2 the glory of **G** to conceal a matter;
30: 5 "Every word of **G** is flawless;
Ecc 1:13 a heavy burden **G** has laid on men!
2:26 **G** gives wisdom, knowledge and
2:26 over to the one who pleases **G.**

3:11 they cannot fathom what **G** has done
3:13 this is the gift of **G.**
3:14 everything **G** does will endure
5: 2 **G** is in heaven and you are on earth,
5: 4 When you make a vow to **G,**
5:19 when **G** gives any man wealth
7:18 The man who fears **G** will avoid all
8:12 who are reverent before **G.**
11: 5 cannot understand the work of **G,**
12: 7 the spirit returns to **G** who gave it.
12:13 Fear **G** and keep his commandments,
Isa 5:16 the holy **G** will show himself holy
7:11 "Ask the LORD your **G** for a sign,
9: 6 Mighty **G,** Everlasting Father,
12: 2 Surely **G** is my salvation;
17:10 You have forgotten **G** your Savior;
25: 9 "Surely this is our **G;**
28:11 and strange tongues **G** will speak
29:23 will stand in awe of the **G** of Israel.
30:18 For the LORD is a **G** of justice.
35: 4 do not fear; your **G** will come,
37:16 you alone are **G** over all
40: 1 comfort my people, says your **G.**
40: 3 the wilderness a highway for our **G.**
40: 8 the word of our **G** stands forever."
40:18 then, will you compare **G?**
40:28 The LORD is the everlasting **G,**
41:10 for I am your **G.**
41:13 For I am the LORD, your **G,**
43:10 Before me no **g** was formed,
44: 6 apart from me there is no **G.**
44:15 he also fashions a **g** and worships it;
45:18 created the heavens, he is **G;**
48:17 the LORD your **G,** who teaches you
49: 4 and my reward is with my **G."**
52: 7 who say to Zion, "Your **G** reigns!"
52:12 the **G** of Israel will be
53: 4 yet we considered him stricken by **G,**
55: 7 and to our **G,**
57:21 "There is no peace," says my **G,**
59: 2 have separated you from your **G;**
60:19 and your **G** will be your glory.
61: 2 and the day of vengeance of our **G,**
61:10 my soul rejoices in my **G.**
62: 5 so will your **G** rejoice over you.
Jer 3:23 in the LORD our **G** is the salvation
7:23 and I will be your **G** and you will
10:10 But the LORD is the true **G;** he is the
            living **G,**
10:12 But **G** made the earth by his power;
23:23 "Am I only a **G** nearby,"
23:23 "and not a **G** far away?
23:36 you distort the words of the living **G,**
31:33 I will be their **G,**
32:27 the **G** of all mankind.
42: 6 we will obey the LORD our **G,**
42:13 and so disobey the LORD your **G,**
51:10 what the LORD our **G** has done.'
51:56 For the LORD is a **G** of retribution;
Eze 1: 1 and I saw visions of **G.**
11:20 and I will be their **G.**
28: 2 "I am a **g;**
28:13 You were in Eden, the garden of **G;**
34:31 are people, and I am your **G,**

43: 2 and I saw the glory of the **G** of Israel
Da 2:19 Then Daniel praised the **G** of heaven
2:28 a **G** in heaven who reveals mysteries.
3:17 the **G** we serve is able to save us
3:29 for no other **g** can save in this way."
6:12 who prays to any **g** or man except
6:16 "May your **G,** whom you serve
9: 4 to the Lord my **G** and confessed:
9: 4 the great and awesome **G,**
10:12 to humble yourself before your **G,**
11:32 who know their **G** will firmly resist
11:36 and magnify himself above every **g**
Hos 1: 9 and I am not your **G.**
1:10 be called 'sons of the living **G.**'
4: 6 you have ignored the law of your **G,**
6: 6 acknowledgment of **G** rather than
9: 8 The prophet, along with my **G,**
12: 6 But you must return to your **G;**
13: 4 You shall acknowledge no **G** but me,
Joel 2:13 Return to the Lord your **G,**
2:23 rejoice in the Lord your **G,**
Am 4:12 prepare to meet your **G,** O Israel."
4:13 the Lord **G** Almighty is his name.
5:26 the star of your **g—**
Jnh 1: 6 Get up and call on your **g!**
3: 5 The Ninevites believed **G,**
4: 2 a gracious and compassionate **G,**
Mic 6: 8 and to walk humbly with your **G.**
7: 7 I wait for **G** my Savior;
7:18 Who is a **G** like you,
Na 1: 2 Lord is a jealous and avenging **G;**
Hab 1:11 whose own strength is their **g."**
3:18 I will be joyful in **G** my Savior.
Zep 3:17 The Lord your **G** is with you,
Hag 1:14 house of the Lord Almighty, their **G**
Zec 4: 7 the capstone to shouts of '**G** bless it!'
12: 8 the house of David will be like **G,**
14: 5 Then the Lord my **G** will come,
Mal 2:10 Did not one **G** create us?
2:11 marrying the daughter of a foreign **g.**
3: 8 "Will a man rob **G?**
Mt 1:23 call him Immanuel"—which means,
"**G** with us."
4: 4 that comes from the mouth of **G.**'"
4: 7 'Do not put the Lord your **G**
4:10 'Worship the Lord your **G,**
5: 8 for they will see **G.**
5: 9 for they will be called sons of **G.**
6:24 cannot serve both **G** and Money.
12:28 kingdom of **G** has come upon you.
16:16 the Son of the living **G.**"
19: 6 Therefore what **G** has joined
19:26 but with **G** all things are possible."
22:21 and to **G** what is God's."
22:32 'I am the **G** of Abraham,
22:32 not the **G** of the dead but of the
22:37 replied: " 'Love the Lord your **G**
27:40 if you are the Son of **G!**"
27:46 "My **G,** my **G,** why have you
27:54 "Surely he was the Son of **G!**"
Mk 1: 1 the Son of **G.**
1:24 the Holy One of **G!**"
2: 7 Who can forgive sins but **G** alone?"
7:13 the word of **G** by your tradition

10: 6 of creation **G** 'made them male
10: 9 what **G** has joined together,
10:18 "No one is good—except **G** alone.
10:24 hard it is to enter the kingdom of **G!**
10:27 all things are possible with **G."**
11:22 "Have faith in **G,"** Jesus answered.
12:17 and to **G** what is God's."
12:29 the Lord our **G,** the Lord is one.
12:30 the Lord your **G** with all your heart
15:34 "My **G,** my **G,** why have you
15:39 "Surely this man was the Son of **G!**"
Lk 1:19 I stand in the presence of **G,**
1:30 Mary, you have found favor with **G.**
1:35 be born will be called the Son of **G.**
1:37 For nothing is impossible with **G.**"
1:47 my spirit rejoices in **G** my Savior,
2:14 "Glory to **G** in the highest,
2:40 and the grace of **G** was upon him.
2:52 and in favor with **G** and men.
3:38 the son of Adam, the son of **G.**
4: 3 "If you are the Son of **G,**
4: 8 'Worship the Lord your **G**
4:41 shouting, "You are the Son of **G!**"
5:21 Who can forgive sins but **G** alone?"
8:39 how much **G** has done for you."
9:20 Peter answered, "The Christ of **G.**"
10: 9 'The kingdom of **G** is near you.'
10:27 answered: " 'Love the Lord your **G**
11:42 you neglect justice and the love of **G.**
13:18 "What is the kingdom of **G** like?
18:13 '**G,** have mercy on me, a sinner.'
18:19 "No one is good—except **G** alone.
18:27 with men is possible with **G.**"
20:25 and to **G** what is God's."
20:37 he calls the Lord 'the **G** of Abraham,
22:69 at the right hand of the mighty **G.**"
22:70 "Are you then the Son of **G?**"
Jn 1: 1 and the Word was with **G,** and the
Word was **G.**
1:12 the right to become children of **G—**
1:18 No one has ever seen **G,**
1:18 but **G** the One and Only,
1:29 "Look, the Lamb of **G,**
1:49 "Rabbi, you are the Son of **G;**
3: 2 a teacher who has come from **G.**
3:16 "For **G** so loved the world
3:34 For the one whom **G** has sent speaks
the words of **G,**
4:24 **G** is spirit, and his worshipers
5:18 making himself equal with **G.**
5:44 that comes from the only **G?**
6:29 "The work of **G** is this:
6:33 For the bread of **G** is he who comes
6:69 that you are the Holy One of **G.**"
7:17 whether my teaching comes from **G**
8:42 "If **G** were your Father,
8:42 for I came from **G** and now am here.
8:47 who belongs to **G** hears what **G** says.
11:40 you would see the glory of **G?**"
13: 3 and that he had come from **G** and
was returning to **G;**
13:31 of Man glorified and **G** is glorified
14: 1 Trust in **G;** trust also in me.
17: 3 the only true **G,** and Jesus Christ,

	20:17	to my **G** and your **G.'** "
	20:28	"My Lord and my **G!**"
	20:31	Jesus is the Christ, the Son of **G,**
Ac	1: 3	and spoke about the kingdom of **G.**
	2:11	wonders of **G** in our own tongues!"
	2:22	was a man accredited by **G**
	2:24	But **G** raised him from the dead,
	2:33	Exalted to the right hand of **G,**
	2:36	**G** has made this Jesus,
	3:15	but **G** raised him from the dead.
	3:19	Repent, then, and turn to **G,**
	4:31	and spoke the word of **G** boldly.
	5: 4	You have not lied to men but to **G."**
	5:29	"We must obey **G** rather than men!"
	5:31	**G** exalted him to his own right hand
	5:32	Holy Spirit, whom **G** has given
	5:39	find yourselves fighting against **G."**
	6: 7	So the word of **G** spread.
	7:55	up to heaven and saw the glory of **G,**
	7:55	Jesus standing at the right hand of **G.**
	8:21	your heart is not right before **G.**
	10:46	speaking in tongues and praising **G.**
	11: 9	that **G** has made clean.'
	12:24	the word of **G** continued to increase
	13:32	What **G** promised our fathers
	14:22	hardships to enter the kingdom of **G,**
	15:10	why do you try to test **G** by putting
	17:23	this inscription: TO AN UNKNOWN **G.**
	17:30	past **G** overlooked such ignorance,
	20:27	to you the whole will of **G.**
	20:32	"Now I commit you to **G**
	24:16	conscience clear before **G** and man.
	28: 6	and said he was a **g.**
Ro	1: 4	be the Son of **G** by his resurrection
	1:16	the power of **G** for the salvation
	1:17	righteousness from **G** is revealed,
	1:18	The wrath of **G** is being revealed
	1:24	Therefore **G** gave them over in
	1:26	**G** gave them over to shameful lusts.
	2:11	For **G** does not show favoritism.
	2:16	when **G** will judge men's secrets
	3: 4	Let **G** be true, and every man a liar.
	3:19	whole world held accountable to **G.**
	3:23	and fall short of the glory of **G,**
	3:29	Is **G** the **G** of Jews only?
	4: 3	"Abraham believed **G,**
	4: 6	whom **G** credits righteousness apart
	4:17	the **G** who gives life to the dead
	4:24	whom **G** will credit righteousness—
	5: 1	we have peace with **G**
	5: 5	because **G** has poured out his love
	5: 8	But **G** demonstrates his own love
	6:22	and have become slaves to **G,**
	6:23	but the gift of **G** is eternal life
	7: 4	that we might bear fruit to **G.**
	8: 7	The sinful mind is hostile to **G,**
	8: 8	by the sinful nature cannot please **G.**
	8:17	heirs of **G** and co-heirs with Christ,
	8:28	in all things **G** works for the good
	8:31	If **G** is for us, who can be against us?
	9:14	Is **G** unjust? Not at all!
	9:18	Therefore **G** has mercy
	10: 9	in your heart that **G** raised him from
	11: 2	**G** did not reject his people,

	11:22	the kindness and sternness of **G:**
	11:32	For **G** has bound all men over
	13: 1	that which **G** has established.
	14:12	will give an account of himself to **G.**
	16:20	**G** of peace will soon crush Satan
1Co	1:18	it is the power of **G.**
	1:20	Has not **G** made foolish the wisdom
	1:24	Christ the power of **G** and the
		wisdom of **G.**
	1:25	For the foolishness of **G** is wiser
	1:25	and the weakness of **G** is stronger
	1:27	But **G** chose the foolish things of
	2: 9	no mind has conceived what **G** has
	2:11	the thoughts of **G** except the Spirit
	3: 6	but **G** made it grow.
	3:17	**G** will destroy him;
	6:20	Therefore honor **G** with your body.
	7: 7	each man has his own gift from **G;**
	7:15	**G** has called us to live in peace.
	7:20	he was in when **G** called him.
	7:24	in the situation **G** called him to.
	8: 3	the man who loves **G** is known by **G.**
	8: 8	food does not bring us near to **G;**
	10:13	And **G** is faithful;
	10:31	do it all for the glory of **G.**
	12:24	**G** has combined the members of the
	14:25	"**G** is really among you!"
	14:33	**G** is not a **G** of disorder but of peace.
	15:24	over the kingdom to **G** the Father
	15:28	so that **G** may be all in all.
	15:34	are some who are ignorant of **G**—
	15:57	But thanks be to **G!**
2Co	1: 9	not rely on ourselves but on **G,**
	2:14	But thanks be to **G,**
	2:15	For we are to **G** the aroma of Christ
	2:17	not peddle the word of **G** for profit.
	3: 5	but our competence comes from **G.**
	4: 2	nor do we distort the word of **G.**
	4: 4	The **g** of this age has blinded
	4: 7	power is from **G** and not from us.
	5: 5	Now it is **G** who has made us
	5:19	that **G** was reconciling the world
	5:20	Christ's behalf: Be reconciled to **G.**
	5:21	**G** made him who had no sin to be sin
	6:16	we are the temple of the living **G.**
	9: 7	for **G** loves a cheerful giver.
	9: 8	And **G** is able to make all grace
	10:13	to the field **G** has assigned to us,
Gal	2: 6	**G** does not judge by external
	3: 5	Does **G** give you his Spirit
	3: 6	Consider Abraham: "He believed **G,**
	3:11	is justified before **G** by the law,
	3:26	You are all sons of **G** through faith
	4: 4	time had fully come, **G** sent his Son,
	6: 7	be deceived: **G** cannot be mocked.
	6:16	even to the Israel of **G.**
Eph	1:22	And **G** placed all things
	2: 8	it is the gift of **G**—
	2:10	which **G** prepared in advance for us
	2:22	in which **G** lives by his Spirit.
	4: 6	one **G** and Father of all,
	4:24	to be like **G** in true righteousness
	5: 1	Be imitators of **G,** therefore,
	6: 6	doing the will of **G** from your heart.

Php	2: 6	being in very nature **G**, did not consider equality with **G** something
	2: 9	Therefore **G** exalted him to
	2:13	it is **G** who works in you to will
	3:14	which **G** has called me heavenward
	3:19	their **g** is their stomach,
	4: 7	And the peace of **G**,
	4:19	And my **G** will meet all your needs
Col	1:19	For **G** was pleased to have all
	2:13	**G** made you alive with Christ.
	3: 1	Christ is seated at the right hand of **G**
1Th	2: 4	by **G** to be entrusted with the gospel.
	2: 4	not trying to please men but **G**,
	2:13	we also thank **G** continually because,
	2:13	when you received the word of **G**,
	3: 9	How can we thank **G** enough for you
	4: 1	how to live in order to please **G**,
	4: 7	For **G** did not call us to be impure,
	4: 9	taught by **G** to love each other.
	5: 9	**G** did not appoint us to suffer wrath
2Th	1: 8	punish those who do not know **G**
1Ti	1:17	immortal, invisible, the only **G**,
	2: 5	For there is one **G** and one mediator between **G** and men,
	4: 4	For everything **G** created is good,
	5: 4	for this is pleasing to **G**.
2Ti	1: 6	to fan into flame the gift of **G**,
Tit	1: 2	which **G**, who does not lie,
	2:13	the glorious appearing of our great **G**
Heb	1: 1	In the past **G** spoke to our forefathers
	3: 4	but **G** is the builder of everything.
	4: 4	"And on the seventh day **G** rested
	4:12	the word of **G** is living and active.
	5: 5	But **G** said to him, "You are my Son;
	6:10	**G** is not unjust;
	6:18	**G** did this so that,
	6:18	in which it is impossible for **G** to lie,
	7:19	by which we draw near to **G**.
	7:25	who come to **G** through him,
	10: 7	I have come to do your will, O **G**.' "
	10:22	draw near to **G** with a sincere heart
	10:31	to fall into the hands of the living **G**.
	11: 5	because **G** had taken him away.
	11: 5	as one who pleased **G**.
	11: 6	without faith it is impossible to please **G**,
	11:16	Therefore **G** is not ashamed to be called their **G**,
	12: 7	**G** is treating you as sons.
	12:10	but **G** disciplines us for our good,
	12:29	for our "**G** is a consuming fire."
	13:15	let us continually offer to **G**
Jas	1:12	the crown of life that **G** has promised
	1:13	For **G** cannot be tempted by evil,
	1:27	Religion that **G** our Father accepts
	2:19	You believe that there is one **G**.
	2:23	"Abraham believed **G**,
	4: 4	with the world is hatred toward **G**?
	4: 6	**G** opposes the proud but gives grace
	4: 8	Come near to **G** and he will come
1Pe	1:21	Through him you believe in **G**,
	1:23	the living and enduring word of **G**.
	2: 4	rejected by men but chosen by **G**
	2:10	but now you are the people of **G**;

	2:20	this is commendable before **G**.
	3:18	to bring you to **G**.
	4: 2	but rather for the will of **G**.
	4:11	so that in all things **G** may be praised
	4:17	to begin with the family of **G**;
	5: 5	"**G** opposes the proud
2Pe	1:21	but men spoke from **G** as they
	2: 4	For if **G** did not spare angels
1Jn	1: 5	and declare to you: **G** is light;
	2:14	and the word of **G** lives in you,
	2:17	the will of **G** lives forever.
	3: 1	we should be called children of **G**!
	3: 9	who is born of **G** will continue to sin
	3:10	how we know who the children of **G**
	3:17	how can the love of **G** be in him?
	3:20	For **G** is greater than our hearts,
	4: 2	you can recognize the Spirit of **G**:
	4: 7	for love comes from **G**.
	4: 8	because **G** is love.
	4: 9	how **G** showed his love among us:
	4:11	Dear friends, since **G** so loved us,
	4:12	No one has ever seen **G**;
	4:15	lives in him and he in **G**.
	4:16	and rely on the love **G** has for us.
	4:16	Whoever lives in love lives in **G**,
	4:20	If anyone says, "I love **G**,"
	5: 2	that we love the children of **G**:
	5: 3	This is love for **G**:
	5: 4	born of **G** overcomes the world.
	5:10	Son of **G** has this testimony in his
	5:11	**G** has given us eternal life,
	5:14	we have in approaching **G**:
	5:18	born of **G** does not continue to sin;
2Jn	1: 9	does not have **G**;
3Jn	1:11	who does what is good is from **G**.
Jude	1: 4	who change the grace of our **G** into
Rev	2:18	the words of the Son of **G**,
	3: 1	the seven spirits of **G** and
	4: 5	These are the seven spirits of **G**.
	4: 8	holy, holy is the Lord **G** Almighty,
	6: 9	slain because of the word of **G**
	7: 2	having the seal of the living **G**.
	7:10	"Salvation belongs to our **G**,
	7:12	and power and strength be to our **G**
	7:17	And **G** will wipe away every tear
	11:16	seated on their thrones before **G**,
	12: 5	And her child was snatched up to **G**
	13: 6	opened his mouth to blaspheme **G**,
	14: 7	"Fear **G** and give him glory,
	15: 3	the song of Moses the servant of **G**
	15: 7	bowls filled with the wrath of **G**,
	16:14	on the great day of **G** Almighty.
	17:17	For **G** has put it into their hearts
	18:20	**G** has judged her for
	19: 1	glory and power belong to our **G**,
	19: 6	For our Lord **G** Almighty reigns.
	19: 9	"These are the true words of **G**."
	19:13	and his name is the Word of **G**.
	21: 3	"Now the dwelling of **G** is with men,
	21: 3	and **G** himself will be with them and be their **G**.
	21:11	It shone with the glory of **G**,
	21:23	for the glory of **G** gives it light,
	22: 5	for the Lord **G** will give them light.

ANGEL OF GOD See ANGEL

ARK OF GOD See ARK

FEAR GOD See FEAR

FEAR OF GOD See FEAR

GLORY OF GOD See GLORY

GOD AND FATHER Ro 15:6; 2Co 1:3; 11:31; Gal 1:4; Eph 1:3; 4:6; Php 4:20; 1Th 1:3; 3:11, 13; 1Pe 1:3; Rev 1:6

GOD OF ABRAHAM Ge 31:42, 53; Ex 3:6, 15, 16; 4:5; 1Ki 18:36; 2Ch 30:6; Ps 47:9; Mt 22:32; Mk 12:26; Lk 20:37; Ac 3:13; 7:32

GOD OF HEAVEN Ge 24:3, 7; 2Ch 36:23; Ezr 1:2; 5:11, 12; 6:9, 10; 7:12, 21, 23, 23; Ne 1:4, 5; 2:4, 20; Ps 136:26; Da 2:18, 19, 37, 44; Jnh 1:9; Rev 11:13; 16:11

GOD OF ISRAEL Ex 5:1; 24:10; 32:27; 34:23; Nu 16:9; Jos 7:13, 19, 20; 8:30; 9:18, 19; 10:40, 42; 13:14, 33; 14:14; 22:16, 24; 24:2, 23; Jdg 4:6; 5:3, 5; 6:8; 11:21, 23; 21:3; Ru 2:12; 1Sa 1:17; 2:30; 5:7, 8, 8, 8, 10, 11; 6:3; 10:18; 14:41; 20:12; 23:10, 11; 25:32, 34; 2Sa 7:27; 12:7; 23:3; 1Ki 1:30, 48; 8:15, 17, 20, 23, 25, 26; 11:9, 31; 14:7, 13; 15:30; 16:13, 26, 33; 17:1, 14; 22:53; 2Ki 9:6; 10:31; 14:25; 18:5; 19:15, 20; 21:12; 22:15, 18; 1Ch 4:10; 5:26; 15:12, 14; 16:4, 36; 22:6; 23:25; 24:19; 28:4; 2Ch 2:12; 6:4, 7, 10, 14, 16, 17; 11:16; 13:5; 15:4, 13; 20:19; 29:7, 10; 30:1, 5; 32:17; 33:16, 18; 34:23, 26; 36:13; Ezr 1:3; 3:2; 4:1, 3; 5:1; 6:14, 21, 22; 7:6, 15; 8:35; 9:4, 15; Ps 41:13; 59:5; 68:8, 35; 69:6; 72:18; 106:48; Isa 17:6; 21:10, 17; 24:15; 29:23; 37:16, 21; 41:17; 45:3; 48:1, 2; 52:12; Jer 7:3, 21; 9:15; 11:3; 13:12; 16:9; 19:3, 15; 21:4; 23:2; 24:5; 25:15, 27; 27:4, 21; 28:2, 14; 29:4, 8, 21, 25; 30:2; 31:23; 32:14, 15, 36; 33:4; 34:2, 13; 35:13, 17, 18, 19; 37:7; 38:17; 39:16; 42:9, 15, 18; 43:10; 44:2, 7, 11, 25; 45:2; 46:25; 48:1; 50:18; 51:33; Eze 8:4; 9:3; 10:19, 20; 11:22; 43:2; 44:2; Zep 2:9; Mal 2:16; Mt 15:31; Lk 1:68

GOD OF JACOB Ex 3:6, 15; 4:5; 2Sa 23:1; Ps 20:1; 24:6; 46:7, 11; 75:9; 76:6; 81:1, 4; 84:8; 94:7; 114:7; 146:5; Isa 2:3; Mic 4:2; Mk 12:26; Lk 20:37; Ac 7:46

GOD OF ... FATHER Ge 26:24; 28:13; 31:5, 29, 42, 53; 32:9, 9; 43:23; 46:1, 3; 50:17; Ex 3:6; 2Ki 20:5; 1Ch 28:9; 29:10; 2Ch 17:4; 21:12; 34:3; Isa 38:5

GOD OF ... FATHERS Ex 3:13, 15, 16; 4:5; Dt 1:11, 21; 4:1; 6:3; 12:1; 26:7; 27:3; 29:25; Jos 18:3; Jdg 2:12; 2Ki 21:22; 1Ch 5:25; 12:17; 29:18, 20; 2Ch 7:22; 11:16; 13:12, 18; 14:4; 15:12; 19:4; 20:6, 33; 21:10; 24:18, 24; 28:6, 9, 25; 29:5; 30:7, 19, 22; 33:12; 34:32, 33; 36:15; Ezr 7:27; 8:28; 10:11; Da 2:23; Ac 3:13; 5:30; 7:32; 22:14; 24:14

GOD THE FATHER Jn 6:27; 1Co 15:24; Gal 1:1; Eph 5:20; 6:23; Php 2:11; Col 3:17; 1Th 1:1; 2Th 1:2; 1Ti 1:2; 2Ti 1:2; Tit 1:4; 1Pe 1:2; 2Pe 1:17; 2Jn 1:3; Jude 1:1

GRACE OF GOD See GRACE

HAND OF GOD See HAND

HOUSE OF GOD See HOUSE

KINGDOM OF GOD See KINGDOM

LIVING GOD Dt 5:26; Jos 3:10; 1Sa 17:26, 36; 2Ki 19:4, 16; Ps 42:2; 84:2; Isa 37:4, 17; Jer 10:10; 23:36; Da 6:20, 26; Hos 1:10; Mt 16:16; 26:63; Ac 14:15; Ro 9:26; 2Co 3:3; 6:16; 1Ti 3:15; 4:10; Heb 3:12; 9:14; 10:31; 12:22; Rev 7:2

†**LORD GOD** Ge 2:4, 5, 7, 8, 9, 15, 16, 18, 19, 21, 22; 3:1, 8, 8, 9, 13, 14, 21, 22, 23; Ex 9:30; 2Sa 5:10; 7:25; 1Ki 19:10, 14; 1Ch 17:16, 17; 22:1, 19; 28:20; 29:1; 2Ch 1:9; 6:41, 41, 42; 26:18; 32:16; Ne 9:7; Ps 59:5; 68:18; 72:18; 80:4, 19; 84:8, 11; 89:8; Jer 5:14; 15:16; 35:17; 38:17; 44:7; Hos 12:5; Am 3:13; 4:13; 5:14, 15, 16; 6:8, 14; Jnh 4:6; Mal 2:16

*****LORD GOD** Da 9:3; Lk 1:32; Rev 1:8; 4:8; 11:17; 15:3; 16:7; 18:8; 19:6; 21:22; 22:5

†**LORD GOD ALMIGHTY** 2Sa 5:10; 1Ki 19:10, 14; Ps 59:5; 80:4, 19; 84:8; 89:8; Jer 5:14; 15:16; 35:17; 38:17; 44:7; Hos 12:5; Am 3:13; 4:13; 5:14, 15, 16; 6:8, 14

†**LORD HIS/MY/OUR/YOUR GOD** See †LORD .

MAN OF GOD See MAN

SON OF GOD See SON

SPIRIT OF GOD See SPIRIT

TEMPLE OF GOD See TEMPLE

WORD OF GOD See WORD

GOD'S [GOD]

Ge	6:11	Now the earth was corrupt in **G** sight
Dt	21:23	hung on a tree is under **G** curse.
2Ch	20:15	For the battle is not yours, but **G.**
	36:19	They set fire to **G** temple and broke
Job	15: 8	Do you listen in on **G** council?
	37:14	stop and consider **G** wonders.
Ps	52: 8	in **G** unfailing love for ever and ever.
	69:30	I will praise **G** name in song
Ecc	9: 1	and what they do are in **G** hands,
Mk	3:35	Whoever does **G** will is my brother
Lk	3: 6	all mankind will see **G** salvation.' "
	20:25	and to God what is **G."**
Jn	7:17	If anyone chooses to do **G** will,
	10:36	'I am **G** Son'?
Ro	2: 3	think you will escape **G** judgment?
	2: 4	**G** kindness leads you toward repentance?
	3: 3	lack of faith nullify **G** faithfulness?
	7:22	in my inner being I delight in **G** law;
	8:16	that we are **G** children.
	9: 6	It is not as though **G** word had failed.
	9:16	but on **G** mercy.
	11:29	**G** gifts and his call are irrevocable.
	12: 2	to test and approve what **G** will is—
	12:13	with **G** people who are in need.
	13: 6	for the authorities are **G** servants,
1Co	2: 7	No, we speak of **G** secret wisdom,
	3: 9	For we are **G** fellow workers; you are **G** field, **G** building.
	3:16	that you yourselves are **G** temple and that **G** Spirit lives in you?

7:19 Keeping **G** commands is what counts
9:21 (though I am not free from **G** law
2Co 6: 2 I tell you, now is the time of **G** favor,
Eph 1: 7 with the riches of **G** grace
2:10 For we are **G** workmanship,
1Th 4: 3 **G** will that you should be sanctified:
5:18 this is **G** will for you in Christ Jesus.
1Ti 6: 1 so that **G** name and our teaching may
2Ti 2: 9 But **G** word is not chained.
2:19 **G** solid foundation stands firm,
Tit 1: 7 overseer is entrusted with **G** work,
Heb 1: 3 Son is the radiance of **G** glory
3: 6 Christ is faithful as a son over **G**
9:24 now to appear for us in **G** presence.
11: 3 universe was formed at **G** command,
Jas 2:23 and he was called **G** friend.
1Pe 2:15 For it is **G** will that by doing good
3: 4 which is of great worth in **G** sight.
2Pe 3: 5 by **G** word the heavens existed and
1Jn 2: 5 **G** love is truly made complete
5: 9 but **G** testimony is greater
Rev 3:14 the ruler of **G** creation.
11:19 **G** temple in heaven was opened,
14:10 too, will drink of the wine of **G** fury,
14:19 into the great winepress of **G** wrath.
16: 1 pour out the seven bowls of **G** wrath
22:21 of the Lord Jesus be with **G** people.

GOD-BREATHED* [GOD, BREATH]

2Ti 3:16 All Scripture is **G** and is useful

GOD-FEARING* [GOD, FEAR]

Ecc 8:12 that it will go better with **G** men,
Ac 2: 5 **G** Jews from every nation under
10: 2 all his family were devout and **G;**
10:22 He is a righteous and **G** man,
13:26 and you **G** Gentiles,
13:50 Jews incited the **G** women of
17: 4 as did a large number of **G** Greeks
17:17 with the Jews and the **G** Greeks,

GOD-HATERS* [GOD, HATE]

Ro 1:30 **G,** insolent, arrogant and boastful;

GODDESS [GOD]

1Ki 11: 5 Ashtoreth the **g** of the Sidonians,
Ac 19:27 the temple of the great **g** Artemis

GODHEAD (KJV) See DEITY, DIVINE

GODLESS [GOD]

Job 20: 5 the joy of the **g** lasts but a moment.
Pr 11: 9 the **g** destroys his neighbor,
Jer 23:11 "Both prophet and priest are **g;**
1Ti 4: 7 with **g** myths and old wives' tales;
6:20 Turn away from **g** chatter
2Ti 2:16 Avoid **g** chatter
Heb 12:16 or is **g** like Esau,

GODLESSNESS* [GOD]

Ro 1:18 the **g** and wickedness of men
11:26 he will turn **g** away

GODLINESS* [GOD]

Ac 3:12 or **g** we had made this man walk?

1Ti 2: 2 and quiet lives in all **g** and holiness.
3:16 the mystery of **g** is great:
4: 8 but **g** has value for all things,
6: 5 that **g** is a means to financial gain.
6: 6 But **g** with contentment is great gain.
6:11 and pursue righteousness, **g,** faith,
2Ti 3: 5 a form of **g** but denying its power.
Tit 1: 1 knowledge of the truth that leads to **g**
2Pe 1: 3 and **g** through our knowledge of him
1: 6 and to perseverance, **g;**
1: 7 and to **g,** brotherly kindness;

GODLY* [GOD]

Ps 4: 3 that the LORD has set apart the **g**
12: 1 Help, LORD, for the **g** are no more;
32: 6 Therefore let everyone who is **g** pray
Mic 7: 2 **g** have been swept from the land;
Mal 2:15 Because he was seeking **g** offspring.
Jn 9:31 to the **g** man who does his will
Ac 8: 2 **G** men buried Stephen
2Co 7:10 **G** sorrow brings repentance
7:11 See what this **g** sorrow has produced
11: 2 jealous for you with a **g** jealousy.
1Ti 4: 7 train yourself to be **g.**
6: 3 Lord Jesus Christ and to **g** teaching,
2Ti 3:12 everyone who wants to live a **g** life
Tit 2:12 and **g** lives in this present age,
2Pe 2: 9 how to rescue **g** men from trials
3:11 You ought to live holy and **g** lives

GODS [GOD]

Ge 31:19 Rachel stole her father's household **g**
35: 4 So they gave Jacob all the foreign **g**
Ex 12:12 and I will bring judgment on all the **g**
15:11 "Who among the **g** is like you,
20: 3 "You shall have no other **g**
23:13 Do not invoke the names of other **g;**
32: 4 Then they said, "These are your **g,**
Dt 5: 7 "You shall have no other **g**
7:25 The images of their **g** you are to burn
13: 2 "Let us follow other **g**" (**g** you have
not known)
Jos 24:14 Throw away the **g** your forefathers
Jdg 2:17 but prostituted themselves to other **g**
1Sa 17:43 the Philistine cursed David by his **g.**
1Ki 20:23 "Their **g** are **g** of the hills.
1Ch 16:26 For all the **g** of the nations are idols,
2Ch 2: 5 our God is greater than all other **g.**
Ps 82: 6 "I said, 'You are **"g";**
135: 5 that our Lord is greater than all **g.**
Isa 45:20 who pray to **g** that cannot save.
Jer 2:11 (Yet they are not **g** at all.)
10:11 "Tell them this: 'These **g,**
16:20 Do men make their own **g?**
Da 5: 4 they praised the **g** of gold and silver,
Hos 14: 3 We will never again say 'Our **g**'
Jn 10:34 'I have said you are **g**'?
Ac 19:26 that man-made **g** are no **g** at all.
1Co 8: 5 For even if there are so-called **g,**

GOES [GO]

Ex 12:23 When the LORD **g** through the land
Nu 5:12 'If a man's wife **g** astray
Dt 31: 6 for the LORD your God **g** with you;

2Ch 23: 7 Stay close to the king wherever he **g.**
Pr 11:19 he who pursues evil **g** to his death.
16:18 Pride **g** before destruction,
Ecc 12: 5 Then man **g** to his eternal home
2Pe 2:22 "A sow that is washed **g** back
Rev 14: 4 follow the Lamb wherever he **g.**

GOG
Eze 38: 2 set your face against **G,**
38:18 When **G** attacks the land of Israel,
Rev 20: 8 **G** and Magog—to gather them for

GOING [GO]
Ge 6:17 I am **g** to bring floodwaters on
Ps 30: 9 in my **g** down into the pit?
144:14 no **g** into captivity,
Pr 7:22 like an ox **g** to the slaughter,
Jn 13:21 one of you is **g** to betray me."
13:36 Jesus replied, "Where I am **g,**
14: 2 I am **g** there to prepare a place
16:10 because I am **g** to the Father,
1Pe 2:25 For you were like sheep **g** astray,

GOLD [GOLD-COVERED, GOLDEN, GOLDSMITH]
Ex 3:22 for articles of silver and **g**
12:35 Egyptians for articles of silver and **g**
20:23 gods of silver or gods of **g.**
25:17 "Make an atonement cover of pure **g**
25:31 "Make a lampstand of pure **g**
28: 6 "Make the ephod of **g,** and of blue,
32:31 have made themselves gods of **g.**
Dt 17:17 large amounts of silver and **g.**
Jos 7:21 a wedge of **g** weighing fifty shekels,
Jdg 8:27 Gideon made the **g** into an ephod,
1Sa 6: 4 "Five **g** tumors and five **g** rats,
1Ki 6:21 the inside of the temple with pure **g,**
20: 3 'Your silver and **g** are mine,
2Ch 9:13 The weight of the **g** that Solomon
Ezr 1: 6 with articles of silver and **g**
Job 22:25 then the Almighty will be your **g,**
23:10 I will come forth as **g.**
28:15 It cannot be bought with the finest **g,**
31:24 "If I have put my trust in **g** or said
Ps 19:10 They are more precious than **g,**
115: 4 But their idols are silver and **g,**
119:127 I love your commands more than **g,**
Pr 3:14 and yields better returns than **g.**
8:19 My fruit is better than fine **g;**
22: 1 be esteemed is better than silver or **g.**
25:11 like apples of **g** in settings of silver.
Isa 60:17 Instead of bronze I will bring you **g,**
Da 2:32 of the statue was made of pure **g,**
3: 1 Nebuchadnezzar made an image of **g**
Hag 2: 8 silver is mine and the **g** is mine,'
Zec 4: 2 a solid **g** lampstand with a bowl at
6:11 the silver and **g** and make a crown,
Mt 2:11 and presented him with gifts of **g** and
Ac 3: 6 Peter said, "Silver or **g** I do not have,
1Pe 1: 7 your faith—of greater worth than **g,**
Rev 3:18 to buy from me **g** refined in the fire,
4: 4 and had crowns of **g** on their heads.
14:14 with a crown of **g** on his head
21:18 and the city of pure **g,**

21:21 great street of the city was of pure **g,**

GOLD-COVERED* [GOLD, COVER]
Heb 9: 4 and the **g** ark of the covenant.

GOLDEN [GOLD]
1Ki 12:28 the king made two **g** calves.
Rev 1:12 I turned I saw seven **g** lampstands,
1:13 and with a **g** sash around his chest.
5: 8 holding **g** bowls full of incense,
15: 7 seven **g** bowls filled with the wrath

GOLDSMITH [GOLD]
Isa 46: 6 a **g** to make it into a god,
Jer 10:14 every **g** is shamed by his idols.

GOLGOTHA*
Mt 27:33 They came to a place called **G**
Mk 15:22 brought Jesus to the place called **G**
Jn 19:17 Skull (which in Aramaic is called **G**)

GOLIATH
Philistine giant killed by David (1Sa 17; 21:9).

GOMER
Hos 1: 3 he married **G** daughter of Diblaim,

GOMORRAH
Ge 13:10 the LORD destroyed Sodom and **G.**)
18:20 "The outcry against Sodom and **G** is
19:24 burning sulfur on Sodom and **G—**
Dt 29:23 like the destruction of Sodom and **G,**
Isa 1: 9 we would have been like **G.**
Jer 23:14 the people of Jerusalem are like **G."**
Mt 10:15 be more bearable for Sodom and **G**
Ro 9:29 we would have been like **G."**
2Pe 2: 6 and **G** by burning them to ashes,
Jude 1: 7 Sodom and **G** and the surrounding

GONE [GO]
Dt 34: 7 were not weak nor his strength **g.**
Jdg 4:14 Has not the LORD **g** ahead of you?"
Job 19: 4 If it is true that I have **g** astray,
Ps 90: 4 like a day that has just **g** by,
Pr 30: 4 Who has **g** up to heaven
Isa 53: 6 We all, like sheep, have **g** astray,
La 1: 3 Judah has **g** into exile.
Mk 5:30 that power had **g** out from him.
Jn 2: 3 When the wine was **g,**
2Co 5:17 he is a new creation; the old has **g,**
Heb 4:14 a great high priest who has **g** through
1Pe 3:22 who has **g** into heaven and is
1Jn 4: 1 many false prophets have **g** out
2Jn 1: 7 have **g** out into the world.
Rev 12:12 because the devil has **g** down to you!

GONG*
1Co 13: 1 a resounding **g** or a clanging cymbal.

GOOD [BETTER, BEST, GOODNESS]
Ge 1: 4 God saw that the light was **g,**
1:10 And God saw that it was **g.**
1:12 And God saw that it was **g.**
1:18 And God saw that it was **g.**
1:21 And God saw that it was **g.**

1:25 And God saw that it was **g**.
1:31 and it was very **g**.
2: 9 pleasing to the eye and **g** for food.
2: 9 tree of the knowledge of **g** and evil.
2:17 from the tree of the knowledge of **g**
2:18 "It is not **g** for the man to be alone.
3: 6 the fruit of the tree was **g** for food
3:22 knowing **g** and evil.
41:26 The seven **g** cows are seven years,
50:20 God intended it for **g** to accomplish

Ex 3: 8 into a **g** and spacious land,
18: 9 the **g** things the LORD had done

Nu 10:29 the LORD has promised **g** things

Dt 6:18 and **g** in the LORD's sight,
10:13 giving you today for your own **g**?

Jos 21:45 of all the LORD's **g** promises to
23:15 just as every **g** promise of the LORD

1Sa 25:21 He has paid me back evil for **g**.

2Sa 14:17 like an angel of God in discerning **g**

1Ki 8:56 of all the **g** promises he gave

2Ch 7: 3 "He is **g**; his love endures forever."
31:20 doing what was **g** and right

Ne 2:18 So they began this **g** work.
9:20 You gave your **g** Spirit

Job 2:10 Shall we accept **g** from God,

Ps 14: 1 there is no one who does **g**.
25: 7 for you are **g**, O LORD.
34: 8 Taste and see that the LORD is **g**;
34:14 Turn from evil and do **g**;
37: 3 Trust in the LORD and do **g**;
37:27 Turn from evil and do **g**;
52: 9 for your name is **g**.
73: 1 Surely God is **g** to Israel,
84:11 no **g** thing does he withhold
86: 5 You are forgiving and **g**, O Lord,
100: 5 For the LORD is **g**
103: 5 with **g** things so
109: 5 They repay me evil for **g**,
112: 5 **G** will come to him who is generous
119:68 You are **g**, and what you do is **g**;
133: 1 How **g** and pleasant it is
145: 9 The LORD is **g** to all;
147: 1 **g** it is to sing praises to our God,

Pr 3: 4 and a **g** name in the sight of God
3:27 Do not withhold **g**
11:27 He who seeks **g** finds goodwill,
13:22 A **g** man leaves an inheritance
14:22 those who plan what is **g** find love
15: 3 watch on the wicked and the **g**.
15:23 and how **g** is a timely word!
15:30 and **g** news gives health to the bones.
17:22 A cheerful heart is **g** medicine,
18:22 He who finds a wife finds what is **g**
19: 2 not **g** to have zeal without knowledge
22: 1 **g** name is more desirable than great
31:12 She brings him **g**, not harm,

Ecc 3:12 than to be happy and do **g**
12:14 whether it is **g** or evil.

Isa 5: 4 When I looked for **g** grapes,
5:20 Woe to those who call evil **g**
40: 9 You who bring **g** tidings to Zion,
52: 7 the feet of those who bring **g** news,
61: 1 to preach **g** news to the poor.

Jer 6:16 ask where the **g** way is,

13:23 Neither can you do **g** who are
16:19 worthless idols that did them no **g**.
24: 2 One basket had very **g** figs,
32:39 fear me for their own **g** and the **g** of
their children

La 3:26 it is **g** to wait quietly for

Eze 34:14 I will tend them in a **g** pasture,

Hos 8: 3 But Israel has rejected what is **g**;

Am 5:14 Seek **g**, not evil, that you may live.

Mic 6: 8 O man, what is **g**.

Na 1:15 the feet of one who brings **g** news,

Zec 8:15 now I have determined to do **g** again

Mt 5:13 It is no longer **g** for anything,
5:45 sun to rise on the evil and the **g**,
7:11 how to give **g** gifts to your children,
7:17 Likewise every **g** tree bears **g** fruit,
12:35 The **g** man brings **g** things out of the
g stored up in him,
13: 8 Still other seed fell on **g** soil,
13:24 a man who sowed **g** seed in his field.
13:48 and collected the **g** fish in baskets,
25:21 'Well done, **g** and faithful servant!

Mk 1:15 Repent and believe the **g** news!"
3: 4 to do **g** or to do evil,
4: 8 Still other seed fell on **g** soil.
8:36 What **g** is it for a man to gain
10:18 "Why do you call me **g**?"
10:18 "No one is **g**—except God alone.

Lk 2:10 I bring you **g** news of great joy
3: 9 not produce **g** fruit will be cut down
6:27 do **g** to those who hate you,
6:35 But love your enemies, do **g** to them,
6:43 "No **g** tree bears bad fruit,
7:22 the **g** news is preached to the poor.
8: 8 Still other seed fell on **g** soil.
9:25 What **g** is it for a man to gain
14:34 "Salt is **g**, but if it loses its saltiness,
18:19 "No one is **g**—except God alone.
19:17 " 'Well done, my **g** servant!'

Jn 1:46 Can anything **g** come from there?"
10:11 "I am the **g** shepherd.
10:11 The **g** shepherd lays down his life for
10:14 "I am the **g** shepherd;

Ac 11:20 the **g** news about the Lord Jesus.

Ro 3:12 there is no one who does **g**,
7:12 is holy, righteous and **g**.
7:16 I agree that the law is **g**.
7:18 I know that nothing **g** lives in me,
7:18 For I have the desire to do what is **g**,
8:28 that in all things God works for the **g**
10:15 the feet of those who bring **g** news!"
12: 2 what God's will is—his **g**,
12: 9 Hate what is evil; cling to what is **g**.
12:21 but overcome evil with **g**.
13: 4 For he is God's servant to do you **g**.
16:19 to be wise about what is **g**,

1Co 7: 1 It is **g** for a man not to marry.
10:24 Nobody should seek his own **g**,
10:33 For I am not seeking my own **g** but
the **g** of many,
15:33 "Bad company corrupts **g** character."

2Co 9: 8 you will abound in every **g** work.

Gal 4:18 provided the purpose is **g**,
5: 7 You were running a **g** race.

	6: 9	Let us not become weary in doing **g**,
	6:10	let us do **g** to all people,
Eph	2:10	created in Christ Jesus to do **g** works,
	6: 8	reward everyone for whatever **g** he
Php	1: 6	a **g** work in you will carry it on
	2:13	and to act according to his **g** purpose.
Col	1:10	in every **g** work,
1Th	5:21	Test everything. Hold on to the **g**.
2Th	2:17	and strengthen you in every **g** deed
1Ti	1: 5	from a pure heart and a **g** conscience
	1: 8	the law is **g** if one uses it properly.
	1:18	you may fight the **g** fight,
	3: 7	He must also have a **g** reputation
	4: 4	For everything God created is **g**,
	6:12	Fight the **g** fight of the faith.
	6:12	when you made your **g** confession in
	6:18	Command them to do **g**, to be rich in
		g deeds.
2Ti	2: 3	like a soldier of Christ Jesus.
	3:17	equipped for every **g** work.
	4: 7	I have fought the **g** fight,
Tit	1: 8	one who loves what is **g**,
	2: 3	but to teach what is **g**.
	2: 7	an example by doing what is **g**.
	2:14	eager to do what is **g**.
Heb	5:14	trained themselves to distinguish **g**
	10: 1	shadow of the **g** things that are
	10:24	on toward love and **g** deeds,
	12:10	but God disciplines us for our **g**,
	13:16	to do **g** and to share with others,
Jas	1:17	**g** and perfect gift is from above,
	4:17	who knows the **g** he ought to do
1Pe	2: 3	you have tasted that the Lord is **g**.
	2:12	Live such **g** lives among the pagans
	2:12	they may see your **g** deeds
	2:18	to those who are **g** and considerate,
	3:17	suffer for doing **g** than for doing evil.
3Jn	1: 2	I pray that you may enjoy **g** health
	1:11	who does what is **g** is from God.

GOOD NEWS 2Sa 4:10; 18:25, 26, 27, 31; 1Ki
1:42; 2Ki 7:9; Pr 15:30; 25:25; Isa 52:7; 61:1; Na
1:15; Mt 4:23; 9:35; 11:5; Mk 1:14, 15; 16:15;
Lk 1:19; 2:10; 3:18; 4:18, 43; 7:22; 8:1; 16:16;
Ac 5:42; 8:12, 35; 10:36; 11:20; 13:32; 14:7, 15,
21; 17:18; Ro 10:15, 16; 1Th 3:6

GOODNESS [GOOD]

Ex	33:19	"I will cause all my **g** to pass in front
2Ch	6:41	may your saints rejoice in your **g**.
Ps	23: 6	Surely **g** and love will follow me all
	116:12	repay the LORD for all his **g** to me?
Eph	5: 9	the fruit of the light consists in all **g**,
Heb	6: 5	who have tasted the **g** of the word
2Pe	1: 5	every effort to add to your faith **g**;

GOODS

Ps	62:10	or take pride in stolen **g**;
Ecc	5:11	As **g** increase, so do those who
Hab	2: 6	to him who piles up stolen **g**

GOODWILL*

Est	9:30	words of **g** and assurance—
Pr	11:27	He who seeks good finds **g**,
	14: 9	but **g** is found among the upright.

Ac	7:10	enabled him to gain the **g** of Pharaoh
Php	1:15	but others out of **g**.

GOPHER [WOOD] (KJV)

See CYPRESS

GORGE [GORGED]

Pr	23:20	much wine or **g** themselves on meat,
Eze	32: 4	the beasts of the earth **g** themselves

GORGED* [GORGE]

Rev	19:21	the birds **g** themselves on their flesh.

GOSHEN

Ge	45:10	You shall live in the region of **G** and
Ex	8:22	deal differently with the land of **G**,

GOSPEL

Mt	24:14	**g** of the kingdom will be preached
Mk	1: 1	The beginning of the **g** about Jesus
	13:10	And the **g** must first be preached
Lk	9: 6	preaching the **g** and healing people
Ro	1:16	I am not ashamed of the **g**,
	15:16	the priestly duty of proclaiming the **g**
	15:20	the **g** where Christ was not known,
1Co	1:17	but to preach the **g**—
	9:12	rather than hinder the **g** of Christ.
	9:14	who preach the **g** should receive
		their living from the **g**.
	9:16	Woe to me if I do not preach the **g**!
	15: 1	to remind you of the **g** I preached
	15: 2	By this **g** you are saved,
2Co	4: 3	And even if our **g** is veiled,
	4: 4	that they cannot see the light of the **g**
	9:13	your confession of the **g** of Christ,
	11: 4	or a different **g** from the one
Gal	1: 6	and are turning to a different **g**—
	1: 7	which is really no **g** at all.
	1: 7	and are trying to pervert the **g**
	3: 8	and announced the **g** in advance
Eph	3: 6	through the **g** the Gentiles are heirs
	6:15	the readiness that comes from the **g**
Php	1: 7	or defending and confirming the **g**,
	1:27	a manner worthy of the **g** of Christ.
Col	1: 6	over the world this **g** is bearing fruit
	1:23	from the hope held out in the **g**.
1Th	2: 4	by God to be entrusted with the **g**.
2Th	1: 8	not know God and do not obey the **g**
2Ti	1: 8	join with me in suffering for the **g**,
Phm	1:13	while I am in chains for the **g**.
Rev	14: 6	and he had the eternal **g** to proclaim

GOSSIP* [GOSSIPING, GOSSIPS]

Pr	11:13	A **g** betrays a confidence,
	16:28	and a **g** separates close friends.
	18: 8	words of a **g** are like choice morsels;
	20:19	A **g** betrays a confidence;
	26:20	without a **g** a quarrel dies down.
	26:22	words of a **g** are like choice morsels;
2Co	12:20	slander, **g**, arrogance and disorder.

GOSSIPING* [GOSSIP]

3Jn	1:10	**g** maliciously about us.

GOSSIPS* [GOSSIP]

Ro 1:29 They are **g,**
1Ti 5:13 but also **g** and busybodies,

GOT [GET]

Ex 32: 6 and **g** up to indulge in revelry.
1Co 10: 7 and **g** up to indulge in pagan revelry.

GOUGE

Mt 5:29 **g** it out and throw it away.

GOURDS

1Ki 6:18 carved with **g** and open flowers.
2Ki 4:39 He gathered some of its **g** and filled

GOVERN [GOVERNING, GOVERNMENT, GOVERNOR, GOVERNORS]

Ge 1:16 the greater light to **g** the day and
1Sa 9:17 he will **g** my people."
1Ki 3: 9 a discerning heart to **g** your people
2Ch 1:11 and knowledge to **g** my people
Job 34:17 Can he who hates justice **g?**
Ps 136: 8 the sun to **g** the day,
Ro 12: 8 let him **g** diligently;

GOVERNING [GOVERN]

Ro 13: 1 submit himself to the **g** authorities.

GOVERNMENT [GOVERN]

Isa 9: 6 and the **g** will be on his shoulders.

GOVERNOR [GOVERN]

Ge 42: 6 Now Joseph was the **g** of the land,
Ne 5:14 when I was appointed to be their **g** in
12:26 and in the days of Nehemiah the **g**
Isa 60:17 I will make peace your **g**
Hag 2:21 "Tell Zerubbabel **g** of Judah
Mal 1: 8 Try offering them to your **g!**
Lk 3: 1 when Pontius Pilate was **g** of Judea,

GOVERNORS [GOVERN]

Mk 13: 9 of me you will stand before **g**

GRACE* [GRACIOUS, GRACIOUSLY]

Ps 45: 2 your lips have been anointed with **g,**
Pr 1: 9 They will be a garland to **g** your head
3:22 an ornament to **g** your neck.
3:34 but gives **g** to the humble.
4: 9 a garland of **g** on your head
Isa 26:10 Though **g** is shown to the wicked,
Jnh 2: 8 cling to worthless idols forfeit the **g**
Zec 12:10 a spirit of **g** and supplication.
Lk 2:40 and the **g** of God was upon him.
Jn 1:14 full of **g** and truth.
1:16 From the fullness of his **g** we have
1:17 **g** and truth came through Jesus
Ac 4:33 and much **g** was upon them all.
6: 8 a man full of God's **g** and power,
11:23 saw the evidence of the **g** of God,
13:43 and urged them to continue in the **g**
14: 3 who confirmed the message of his **g**
14:26 committed to the **g** of God for the
15:11 through the **g** of our Lord Jesus

15:40 commended by the brothers to the **g**
18:27 to those who by **g** had believed.
20:24 testifying to the gospel of God's **g.**
20:32 to God and to the word of his **g,**
Ro 1: 5 we received **g** and apostleship
1: 7 **G** and peace to you from God
3:24 and are justified freely by his **g**
4:16 be by **g** and may be guaranteed
5: 2 into this **g** in which we now stand.
5:15 how much more did God's **g** and the gift that came by the **g**
5:17 God's abundant provision of **g**
5:20 **g** increased all the more,
5:21 **g** might reign through righteousness
6: 1 go on sinning so that **g** may increase?
6:14 not under law, but under **g.**
6:15 not under law but under **g?**
11: 5 there is a remnant chosen by **g.**
11: 6 if by **g,** then it is no longer by works;
11: 6 **g** would no longer be **g.**
12: 3 by the **g** given me I say to every one
12: 6 according to the **g** given us.
15:15 because of the **g** God gave me
16:20 The **g** of our Lord Jesus be with you.
1Co 1: 3 **G** and peace to you from God
1: 4 for you because of his **g** given you
3:10 By the **g** God has given me,
15:10 But by the **g** of God I am what I am,
15:10 his **g** to me was not without effect.
15:10 but the **g** of God that was with me.
16:23 The **g** of the Lord Jesus be with you.
2Co 1: 2 **G** and peace to you from God
1:12 but according to God's **g.**
4:15 that the **g** that is reaching more
6: 1 not to receive God's **g** in vain.
8: 1 to know about the **g** that God
8: 6 also to completion this act of **g**
8: 7 also excel in this **g** of giving.
8: 9 know the **g** of our Lord Jesus Christ,
9: 8 able to make all **g** abound to you,
9:14 the surpassing **g** God has given you.
12: 9 "My **g** is sufficient for you,
13:14 May the **g** of the Lord Jesus Christ,
Gal 1: 3 **G** and peace to you from God
1: 6 who called you by the **g** of Christ
1:15 and called you by his **g,**
2: 9 they recognized the **g** given to me.
2:21 I do not set aside the **g** of God,
3:18 but God in his **g** gave it to Abraham
5: 4 you have fallen away from **g.**
6:18 The **g** of our Lord Jesus Christ be
Eph 1: 2 **G** and peace to you from God
1: 6 to the praise of his glorious **g,**
1: 7 with the riches of God's **g**
2: 5 by **g** you have been saved.
2: 7 the incomparable riches of his **g,**
2: 8 For it is by **g** you have been saved,
3: 2 about the administration of God's **g**
3: 7 by the gift of God's **g** given me
3: 8 this **g** was given me:
4: 7 to each one of us **g** has been given
6:24 **G** to all who love our Lord Jesus
Php 1: 2 **G** and peace to you from God

1: 7 all of you share in God's **g** with me.
4:23 The **g** of the Lord Jesus Christ be
Col 1: 2 **G** and peace to you
1: 6 understood God's **g** in all its truth.
4: 6 conversation be always full of **g,**
4:18 **G** be with you.
1Th 1: 1 **G** and peace to you.
5:28 The **g** of our Lord Jesus Christ be
2Th 1: 2 **G** and peace to you from God
1:12 according to the **g** of our God
2:16 his **g** gave us eternal encouragement
3:18 The **g** of our Lord Jesus Christ be
1Ti 1: 2 Timothy my true son in the faith: **G,**
1:14 the **g** of our Lord was poured out
6:21 **G** be with you.
2Ti 1: 2 To Timothy, my dear son: **G,**
1: 9 because of his own purpose and **g.**
1: 9 This **g** was given us in Christ Jesus
2: 1 strong in the **g** that is in Christ Jesus.
4:22 **G** be with you.
Tit 1: 4 my true son in our common faith: **G**
2:11 the **g** of God that brings salvation
3: 7 having been justified by his **g,**
3:15 **G** be with you all.
Phm 1: 3 **G** to you and peace from God
1:25 The **g** of the Lord Jesus Christ be
Heb 2: 9 by the **g** of God he might taste death
4:16 Let us then approach the throne of **g**
4:16 find **g** to help us in our time of need.
10:29 who has insulted the Spirit of **g?**
12:15 that no one misses the **g** of God
13: 9 to be strengthened by **g,**
13:25 **G** be with you all.
Jas 4: 6 But he gives us more **g.**
4: 6 but gives **g** to the humble."
1Pe 1: 2 **G** and peace be yours in abundance.
1:10 who spoke of the **g** that was to come
1:13 on the **g** to be given you
4:10 faithfully administering God's **g**
5: 5 but gives **g** to the humble."
5:10 And the God of all **g,**
5:12 and testifying that this is the true **g**
2Pe 1: 2 **G** and peace be yours in abundance
3:18 grow in the **g** and knowledge of our
2Jn 1: 3 **G,** mercy and peace from God
Jude 1: 4 who change the **g** of our God into
Rev 1: 4 **G** and peace to you
22:21 The **g** of the Lord Jesus be

GRACE AND PEACE Ro 1:7; 1Co 1:3; 2Co
1:2; Gal 1:3; Eph 1:2; Php 1:2; Col 1:2; 1Th 1:1;
2Th 1:2; Tit 1:4; 1Pe 1:2; 2Pe 1:2; Rev 1:4

GRACE OF GOD Lk 2:40; Ac 11:23; 13:43;
14:26; 1Co 15:10, 10; Gal 2:21; 2Th 1:12; Tit
2:11; Heb 2:9; 12:15; 1Pe 5:12; Jude 1:4

GRACIOUS [GRACE]

Ge 21: 1 Now the LORD was **g** to Sarah
Ex 34: 6 the compassionate and **g** God,
Nu 6:25 shine upon you and be **g** to you;
1Sa 2:21 And the LORD was **g** to Hannah;
2Ki 13:23 But the LORD was **g** to them
2Ch 30: 9 for the LORD your God is **g**
Ezr 7: 9 the **g** hand of his God was on him.

8:22 "The **g** hand of our God is on
Ne 2: 8 the **g** hand of my God was upon me,
9:17 **g** and compassionate,
9:31 for you are a **g** and merciful God.
Ps 67: 1 May God be **g** to us and bless us
86:15 are a compassionate and **g** God,
103: 8 The LORD is compassionate and **g,**
145: 8 The LORD is **g** and compassionate,
Pr 22:11 and whose speech is **g** will have
Isa 30:18 Yet the LORD longs to be **g** to you;
Jer 33:14 the **g** promise I made to the house
Joel 2:13 for he is **g** and compassionate,
Jnh 4: 2 a **g** and compassionate God,
1Pe 3: 7 as heirs with you of the **g** gift

GRACIOUSLY [GRACE]

Hos 14: 2 Forgive all our sins and receive us **g,**

GRAFT* [GRAFTED]

Ro 11:23 for God is able to **g** them in again.

GRAFTED [GRAFT]

Ro 11:17 a wild olive shoot, have been **g** in

GRAIN [GRAINS]

Ge 41: 5 second dream: Seven heads of **g,**
Lev 2: 1 " 'When someone brings a **g** offering
2:13 Season all your **g** offerings with salt.
Dt 25: 4 an ox while it is treading out the **g.**
Ru 2: 2 and pick up the leftover **g**
Ps 78:24 he gave them the **g** of heaven.
Hos 14: 7 He will flourish like the **g.**
Joel 2:19 am sending you **g,** new wine and oil,
Mk 2:23 they began to pick some heads of **g.**
Lk 17:35 Two women will be grinding **g**
1Co 9: 9 an ox while it is treading out the **g."**
1Ti 5:18 the ox while it is treading out the **g,"**

GRAIN OFFERING Ex 29:41; 30:9; Lev 2:1,
3, 4, 5, 6, 7, 8, 9, 10, 11, 14, 15; 5:13; 6:14, 15,
20, 21, 23; 7:9, 10, 37; 9:4, 17; 10:12; 14:10, 20,
21, 31; 23:13; Nu 4:16; 5:15, 18, 25, 26; 6:17;
7:13, 19, 25, 31, 37, 43, 49, 55, 61, 67, 73, 79, 87;
8:8; 15:4, 6, 9, 24; 28:5, 8, 9, 12, 12, 13, 20, 28,
31; 29:3, 9, 11, 14, 16, 19, 22, 25, 28, 31, 34, 38;
Jdg 13:19, 23; 2Ki 16:13, 15, 15, 15; 1Ch 21:23;
2Ch 7:7; Ezr 7:17; Ne 10:33; 13:5, 9; Isa 19:21;
43:23; 57:6; 66:20; Jer 14:12; 17:26; 33:18; 41:5;
Eze 42:13; 44:29; 45:15, 17, 17, 25; Joel 1:9, 13;
2:14; Am 5:22

GRAIN OFFERINGS Ex 40:29; Lev 2:13, 13;
23:18, 37; Nu 6:15; 29:6, 18, 21, 24, 27, 30, 33,
37, 39; Jos 22:23, 29; 1Ki 8:64, 64; 1Ch 23:29;
2Ch 7:7; Ezr 7:17; Ne 10:33; 13:5, 9; Isa 19:21;
43:23; 57:6; 66:20; Jer 14:12; 17:26; 33:18; 41:5;
Eze 42:13; 44:29; 45:15, 17, 17, 25; Joel 1:9, 13;
2:14; Am 5:22

GRAINFIELDS [FIELD]

Lk 6: 1 Jesus was going through the **g,**

GRAINS* [GRAIN]

Job 29:18 days as numerous as the **g** of sand.
Ps 139:18 they would outnumber the **g** of sand.
Isa 48:19 your children like its numberless **g;**

GRANDCHILDREN [CHILD]

Ex 10: 2 that you may tell your children and **g**

1Ti 5: 4 But if a widow has children or **g,**

GRANDMOTHER [MOTHER]
2Ti 1: 5 faith, which first lived in your **g** Lois

GRANT [GRANTED, GRANTS]
Lev 26: 6 " 'I will **g** peace in the land,
Dt 28:11 LORD will **g** you abundant prosperity
Est 7: 3 **g** me my life—this is my petition.
Ps 20: 5 May the LORD **g** all your requests.
     51:12 and **g** me a willing spirit,
     85: 7 O LORD, and **g** us your salvation.
    140: 8 do not **g** the wicked their desires,
Isa 46:13 I will **g** salvation to Zion,
Hag 2: 9 'And in this place I will **g** peace,'
Mk 10:40 at my right or left is not for me to **g.**

GRANTED [GRANT]
Jos 1:13 and has **g** you this land.'
1Sa 1:27 the LORD has **g** me what I asked
Est 7: 2 up to half the kingdom, it will be **g."**
Ps 21: 6 you have **g** him eternal blessings
Pr 10:24 the righteous desire will be **g.**
Mt 15:28 Your request is **g."**
Ac 11:18 has **g** even the Gentiles repentance
Php 1:29 For it has been **g** to you on behalf

GRANTS* [GRANT]
Ps 127: 2 for he **g** sleep to those he loves.
    147:14 He **g** peace to your borders

GRAPE [GRAPES]
Nu 6: 3 not drink **g** juice or eat grapes
Ob 1: 5 If **g** pickers came to you,

GRAPES [GRAPE]
Lev 19:10 or pick up the **g** that have fallen.
Nu 13:23 a branch bearing a single cluster of **g.**
Dt 32:32 Their **g** are filled with poison,
Isa 5: 2 Then he looked for a crop of good **g,**
Jer 31:29 'The fathers have eaten sour **g,**
Eze 18: 2 " 'The fathers eat sour **g,**
Mic 6:15 you will crush **g** but not drink
Hab 3:17 and there are no **g** on the vines,
Mt 7:16 Do people pick **g** from thornbushes,
Rev 14:18 and gather the clusters of **g** from

GRASP [GRASPED, GRASPING]
Ecc 7:18 It is good to **g** the one and not let go
Jn 10:39 but he escaped their **g.**

GRASPED [GRASP]
Hos 12: 3 In the womb he **g** his brother's heel;
Php 2: 6 equality with God something to be **g,**

GRASPING [GRASP]
Ge 25:26 with his hand **g** Esau's heel;

GRASS
Ps 37: 2 for like the **g** they will soon wither,
    103:15 As for man, his days are like **g,**
    104:14 He makes **g** grow for the cattle,
Pr 19:12 but his favor is like dew on the **g.**
Isa 40: 6 "All men are like **g,**
Mt 6:30 how God clothes the **g** of the field,

1Pe 1:24 For, "All men are like **g,**
     1:24 the **g** withers and the flowers fall,
Rev 8: 7 and all the green **g** was burned up.

GRASSHOPPERS
Nu 13:33 We seemed like **g** in our own eyes,
Isa 40:22 and its people are like **g.**

GRATIFY* [GRATIFYING]
Ro 13:14 not think about how to **g** the desires
Gal 5:16 not **g** the desires of the sinful nature.

GRATIFYING* [GRATIFY]
Eph 2: 3 **g** the cravings of our sinful nature

GRATITUDE
Col 3:16 with **g** in your hearts to God.

GRAVE [GRAVES]
Nu 16:30 and they go down alive into the **g,**
     19:16 who touches a human bone or a **g,**
Dt 34: 6 no one knows where his **g** is.
Ps 5: 9 Their throat is an open **g;**
     6: 5 Who praises you from the **g?**
     9:17 The wicked return to the **g,**
     16:10 you will not abandon me to the **g,**
     49:15 God will redeem my life from the **g;**
Pr 7:27 Her house is a highway to the **g,**
SS 8: 6 its jealousy unyielding as the **g.**
Isa 14:15 But you are brought down to the **g,**
Hos 13:14 Where, O **g,** is your destruction?
Jn 11:44 Take off the **g** clothes and let him go.
Ac 2:27 you will not abandon me to the **g,**

GRAVES [GRAVE]
Ex 14:11 because there were no **g** in Egypt
Eze 37:12 to open your **g** and bring you up
Mt 23:29 and decorate the **g** of the righteous.
Lk 11:44 because you are like unmarked **g,**
Jn 5:28 in their **g** will hear his voice
Ro 3:13 "Their throats are open **g;**

GRAY
Ps 71:18 Even when I am old and **g,**
Pr 16:31 **G** hair is a crown of splendor;
     20:29 **g** hair the splendor of the old.

GREAT [GREATER, GREATEST, GREATLY, GREATNESS]
Ge 1:16 God made two **g** lights—
     6: 5 LORD saw how **g** man's wickedness
     12: 2 "I will make you into a **g** nation
     12: 2 I will make your name **g,**
     15: 1 your very **g** reward."
     15:18 from the river of Egypt to the **g** river,
     46: 3 I will make you into a **g** nation there.
Ex 32:10 I will make you into a **g** nation."
     32:11 with **g** power and a mighty hand?
Nu 14:19 In accordance with your **g** love,
Dt 4:32 anything so **g** as this ever happened,
     7:21 is a **g** and awesome God.
     10:17 the **g** God, mighty and awesome,
     29:28 in **g** wrath the LORD uprooted them
Jos 7: 9 do for your own **g** name?"

Jdg	16: 5	the secret of his **g** strength and
1Sa	18:14	everything he did he had **g** success,
2Sa	7: 9	Now I will make your name **g**,
	7:22	"How **g** you are,
	22:36	down to make me **g**.
	24:14	for his mercy is **g**;
1Ch	16:25	For **g** is the LORD and most worthy
	17:19	made known all these **g** promises.
Ne	1: 5	the **g** and awesome God,
	8: 6	Ezra praised the LORD, the **g** God;
Ps	18:35	you stoop down to make me **g**.
	19:11	in keeping them there is **g** reward.
	25:11	forgive my iniquity, though it is **g**.
	36: 6	your justice like the **g** deep.
	47: 2	the **g** King over all the earth!
	48: 2	the city of the **G** King.
	57:10	For **g** is your love,
	68:11	and **g** was the company
	89: 1	of the LORD's **g** love forever;
	95: 3	For the LORD is the **g** God,
	103:11	**g** is his love for those who fear him;
	107:43	consider the **g** love of the LORD.
	108: 4	For **g** is your love,
	117: 2	For **g** is his love toward us,
	119:165	**G** peace have they who love your
	145: 3	**G** is the LORD and most worthy
Pr	22: 1	name is more desirable than **g** riches;
	23:24	father of a righteous man has **g** joy;
Isa	42:21	to make his law and glorious.
Jer	10: 6	is like you, O LORD; you are **g**,
	27: 5	my **g** power and outstretched arm
	32:19	**g** are your purposes
La	3:23	every morning; **g** is your faithfulness
Eze	17: 3	A **g** eagle with powerful wings,
Da	2:45	"The **g** God has shown the king
	7: 3	Four **g** beasts, each different
	9: 4	the **g** and awesome God,
Joel	2:11	The day of the LORD is **g**;
	2:20	Surely he has done **g** things.
Jnh	1:17	But the LORD provided a **g** fish
Na	1: 3	The LORD is slow to anger and **g** in power;
Zep	1:14	"The **g** day of the LORD is near—
Mal	1:11	My name will be **g** among
	4: 5	that **g** and dreadful day of the LORD
Mt	4:16	in darkness have seen a **g** light;
	13:46	When he found one of **g** value,
	20:26	wants to become **g** among you
Mk	13:26	coming in clouds with **g** power
Lk	2:10	I bring you good news of **g** joy
	6:23	because **g** is your reward in heaven.
	6:35	Then your reward will be **g**,
	21:23	There will be **g** distress in the land
	21:27	in a cloud with power and **g** glory.
Eph	1:19	and his incomparably **g** power
	2: 4	But because of his **g** love for us,
1Ti	3:16	the mystery of godliness is **g**:
	6: 6	godliness with contentment is **g** gain.
Tit	2:13	the glorious appearing of our **g** God
Heb	2: 3	if we ignore such a **g** salvation?
	10:21	and since we have a **g** priest over
	12: 1	by such a **g** cloud of witnesses,
	13:20	that **g** Shepherd of the sheep,
1Pe	1: 3	**g** mercy he has given us new birth

1Jn	3: 1	How **g** is the love the Father
Jude	1: 6	for judgment on the **g** Day.
Rev	6:17	the **g** day of their wrath has come,
	7:14	have come out of the **g** tribulation;
	12: 9	The **g** dragon was hurled down—
	14: 8	Fallen is Babylon the **G**,
	16:14	on the **g** day of God Almighty.
	17: 1	the punishment of the **g** prostitute,
	18:10	Woe, O **g** city, O Babylon,
	20:11	Then I saw a **g** white throne
	21:21	**g** street of the city was of pure gold,

GREAT KING 2Ki 18:19, 28; Ezr 5:11; Ps 47:2; 48:2; 95:3; Isa 36:4, 13; Hos 5:13; 10:6; Mal 1:14; Mt 5:35

GREATER [GREAT]

Ge	1:16	the **g** light to govern the day and
Ex	18:11	the LORD is **g** than all other gods,
2Ch	2: 5	our God is **g** than all other gods.
Mt	11:11	not risen anyone **g** than John
	11:11	least in the kingdom of heaven is **g**
	12: 6	that one **g** than the temple is here.
Mk	12:31	no commandment **g** than these."
Lk	11:31	and now one **g** than Solomon is here.
	11:32	and now one **g** than Jonah is here.
Jn	1:50	You shall see **g** things than that."
	3:30	He must become **g**;
	14:12	He will do even **g** things than these,
	15:13	**G** love has no one than this,
1Co	12:31	But eagerly desire the **g** gifts.
2Co	3:11	how much **g** is the glory of
Heb	3: 3	worthy of **g** honor than Moses,
	7: 7	the lesser person is blessed by the **g**.
	11:26	for the sake of Christ as of **g** value
1Pe	1: 7	your faith—of **g** worth than gold,
1Jn	3:20	For God is **g** than our hearts,
	4: 4	in you is **g** than the one who is in

GREATEST [GREAT]

2Sa	3:16	the names of the **g** men of the earth.
Mt	18: 4	like this child is the **g** in the kingdom
	22:38	This is the first and **g** commandment.
	23:11	**g** among you will be your servant.
Lk	9:48	he is the **g**."
	22:24	of them was considered to be **g**.
Jn	7:37	On the last and **g** day of the Feast,
1Co	13:13	But the **g** of these is love.

GREATLY [GREAT]

Ge	3:16	"I will **g** increase your pains
2Ch	33:12	humbled himself **g** before the God
Ezr	10:13	we have sinned **g** in this thing.
Ps	47: 9	he is **g** exalted.
Isa	61:10	I delight **g** in the LORD;
Jnh	1:16	At this the men **g** feared the LORD,

GREATNESS* [GREAT]

Ex	15: 7	In the **g** of your majesty you threw
Dt	3:24	to show to your servant your **g**
	32: 3	Oh, praise the **g** of our God!
1Ch	29:11	Yours, O LORD, is the **g** and the
2Ch	9: 6	half the **g** of your wisdom was told
Est	10: 2	a full account of the **g** of Mordecai
Ps	145: 3	his **g** no one can fathom.

150: 2 praise him for his surpassing **g**.
Isa 63: 1 forward in the **g** of his strength?
Eze 38:30 so I will show my **g** and my holiness,
Da 4:22 your **g** has grown until it reaches
5:18 Nebuchadnezzar sovereignty and **g**
7:27 power and **g** of the kingdoms under
Mic 5: 4 for then his **g** will reach to the ends
Lk 9:43 all amazed at the **g** of God.
Php 3: 8 a loss compared to the surpassing **g**

GRECIAN* [GREECE]

Ac 6: 1 the **G** Jews among them complained
9:29 and debated with the **G** Jews,

GREECE [GRECIAN, GREEK, GREEKS]

Da 8:21 The shaggy goat is the king of **G**,
10:20 the prince of **G** will come;

GREED [GREEDY]

Mk 7:22 **g**, malice, deceit, lewdness,
Lk 12:15 on your guard against all kinds of **g**;
Ro 1:29 evil, **g** and depravity.
Eph 5: 3 or of any kind of impurity, or of **g**,
Col 3: 5 evil desires and **g**, which is idolatry.
2Pe 2: 3 In their **g** these teachers will exploit
2:14 they are experts in **g**—

GREEDY [GREED]

Pr 15:27 A **g** man brings trouble to his family,
28:25 A **g** man stirs up dissension,
Eze 33:31 but their hearts are **g** for unjust gain.
1Co 5:11 but is sexually immoral or **g**,
6:10 the **g** nor drunkards nor slanderers
Eph 5: 5 impure or **g** person—
1Pe 5: 2 not **g** for money, but eager to serve;

GREEK [GREECE]

Jn 19:20 written in Aramaic, Latin and **G**.
Ac 16: 1 but whose father was a **G**.
17:12 a number of prominent **G** women
21:37 "Do you speak **G**?"
Gal 3:28 There is neither Jew nor **G**,
Col 3:11 Here there is no **G** or Jew,

GREEKS [GREECE]

Jn 12:20 some **G** among those who went up
Ac 18: 4 trying to persuade Jews and **G**
20:21 both Jews and **G** that they must turn
1Co 1:22 and **G** look for wisdom,
12:13 whether Jews or **G**,

GREEN

Ge 1:30 I give every **g** plant
9: 3 Just as I gave you the **g** plants,
Ps 23: 2 He makes me lie down in **g** pastures,
Jer 17: 8 its leaves are always **g**,
Hos 14: 8 I am like a **g** pine tree;
Mk 6:39 sit down in groups on the **g** grass.

GREET [GREETED, GREETING, GREETINGS]

Mt 5:47 And if you **g** only your brothers,
1Co 16:20 **G** one another with a holy kiss.

GREETED [GREET]

Mt 23: 7 they love to be **g** in the marketplaces

GREETING [GREET]

Lk 1:29 what kind of **g** this might be.
1Co 16:21 I, Paul, write this **g** in my own hand.
Col 4:18 I, Paul, write this **g** in my own hand.
2Th 3:17 I, Paul, write this **g** in my own hand,

GREETINGS [GREET]

Mt 26:49 Judas said, "**G**, Rabbi!"
Lk 1:28 The angel went to her and said, "**G**,

GREW [GROW]

Ge 21:20 God was with the boy as he **g** up.
Jdg 13:24 He **g** and the LORD blessed him,
1Sa 2:21 Samuel **g** up in the presence of the
3:19 The LORD was with Samuel as he **g**
2Sa 3: 1 David **g** stronger and stronger,
Isa 53: 2 He **g** up before him like a tender
Lk 1:80 child **g** and became strong in spirit;
2:40 And the child **g** and became strong;
2:52 And Jesus **g** in wisdom and stature,
13:19 It **g** and became a tree,
Ac 9:31 it **g** in numbers,
16: 5 in the faith and **g** daily in numbers.

GRIEF [GRIEFS, GRIEVANCES, GRIEVE, GRIEVED, GRIEVES, GRIEVOUS]

Ps 10:14 you, O God, do see trouble and **g**;
Pr 10: 1 but a foolish son **g** to his mother.
14:13 and joy may end in **g**.
17:21 To have a fool for a son brings **g**;
Ecc 1:18 the more knowledge, the more **g**.
La 3:32 Though he brings **g**,
Jn 16:20 but your **g** will turn to joy.
1Pe 1: 6 while you may have had to suffer **g**

GRIEFS* [GRIEF]

1Ti 6:10 and pierced themselves with many **g**.

GRIEVANCES* [GRIEF]

Col 3:13 forgive whatever **g** you may have

GRIEVE [GRIEF]

2Sa 1:26 I **g** for you, Jonathan my brother;
Eph 4:30 And do not **g** the Holy Spirit of God,
1Th 4:13 or to **g** like the rest of men,

GRIEVED [GRIEF]

Ge 6: 6 LORD was **g** that he had made man
1Sa 15:11 "I am **g** that I have made Saul king,
2Sa 24:16 LORD was **g** because of the calamity
Isa 63:10 they rebelled and **g** his Holy Spirit.

GRIEVES* [GRIEF]

Zec 12:10 for him as one **g** for a firstborn son.

GRIEVOUS [GRIEF]

Ge 18:20 so great and their sin so **g**
Ecc 5:13 I have seen a **g** evil under the sun:
Jer 15:18 and my wound **g** and incurable?

GRIND [GRINDING]
Job 31:10 may my wife **g** another man's grain,

GRINDING [GRIND]
Jdg 16:21 they set him to **g** in the prison.
Lk 17:35 Two women will be **g** grain together;

GROAN [GROANED, GROANING, GROANS]
Pr 29: 2 when the wicked rule, the people **g**.
Ro 8:23 **g** inwardly as we wait eagerly
2Co 5: 2 we **g**, longing to be clothed
5: 4 we **g** and are burdened,

GROANED* [GROAN]
Ex 2:23 The Israelites **g** in their slavery
Jdg 2:18 as they **g** under those who oppressed
Ps 77: 3 I remembered you, O God, and I **g**;

GROANING [GROAN]
Ex 2:24 God heard their **g**
6: 5 I have heard the **g** of the Israelites,
Ps 22: 1 so far from the words of my **g**?
Eze 21: 7 'Why are you **g**?'
Ro 8:22 that the whole creation has been **g** as

GROANS [GROAN]
Ro 8:26 with **g** that words cannot express.

GROPE
Dt 28:29 At midday you will **g** about like
La 4:14 Now they **g** through the streets like

GROUND [GROUNDS]
Ge 1:10 God called the dry **g** "land,"
2: 7 the man from the dust of the **g**
3:17 "Cursed is the **g** because of you;
4:10 blood cries out to me from the **g**.
Ex 3: 5 where you are standing is holy **g**."
15:19 walked through the sea on dry **g**.
Jos 3:17 completed the crossing on dry **g**.
Jdg 6:37 on the fleece and all the **g** is dry,
1Sa 5: 3 Dagon, fallen on his face on the **g**
2Ki 2: 8 two of them crossed over on dry **g**.
Job 3:16 Or why was I not hidden in the **g** like
Ps 26:12 My feet stand on level **g**;
73:18 you place them on slippery **g**;
143:10 your good Spirit lead me on level **g**.
147: 6 but casts the wicked to the **g**.
Ecc 12: 7 dust returns to the **g** it came from,
Isa 53: 2 and like a root out of dry **g**.
Ob 1: 3 'Who can bring me down to the **g**?'
Mt 10:29 of them will fall to the **g** apart from
25:25 and hid your talent in the **g**.
Mk 4:31 the smallest seed you plant in the **g**.
Lk 22:44 like drops of blood falling to the **g**.
Jn 8: 6 down and started to write on the **g**
12:24 unless a kernel of wheat falls to the **g**
Eph 6:13 you may be able to stand your **g**,
Heb 10:32 when you stood your **g** in

GROUNDS [GROUND]
Da 6: 4 to find **g** for charges against Daniel
Lk 23:22 in him no **g** for the death penalty.

GROUP [GROUPS]
Nu 16: 3 They came as a **g** to oppose Moses

GROUPS [GROUP]
1Ch 23: 6 David divided the Levites into **g**
Mk 6:39 to have all the people sit down in **g**

GROVE [GROVES]
Jn 18: 3 So Judas came to the **g**,

GROVES [GROVE]
Dt 6:11 and olive **g** you did not plant—

GROW [FULL-GROWN, GREW, GROWING, GROWN, GROWS]
Ge 2: 9 all kinds of trees **g** out of the ground
Nu 6: 5 the hair of his head **g** long.
Jdg 16:22 the hair on his head began to **g** again
1Sa 2:26 the boy Samuel continued to **g**.
Ps 92:12 they will **g** like a cedar of Lebanon;
Pr 13:11 money little by little makes it **g**.
20:13 Do not love sleep or you will **g** poor;
Isa 40:31 they will run and not **g** weary,
45: 8 let righteousness **g** with it;
Eze 47:12 Fruit trees of all kinds will **g**
Jnh 4:10 you did not tend it or make it **g**.
Mt 6:28 See how the lilies of the field **g**.
1Co 3: 6 but God made it **g**.
2Co 10:15 as your faith continues to **g**,
1Pe 2: 2 by it you may **g** up in your salvation,
2Pe 3:18 But **g** in the grace and knowledge

GROWING [GROW]
Col 1: 6 this gospel is bearing fruit and **g**,
1:10 **g** in the knowledge of God,
2Th 1: 3 your faith is **g** more and more,

GROWN [GROW]
Ex 2:11 One day, after Moses had **g** up,
2Ch 10:10 young men who had **g** up with him
Heb 11:24 By faith Moses, when he had **g** up,

GROWS [GROW]
Ps 142: 3 When my spirit **g** faint within me,
Pr 13:20 He who walks with the wise **g** wise,
Mk 4:32 it **g** and becomes the largest
Eph 4:16 **g** and builds itself up in love,
Col 2:19 **g** as God causes it to grow.
Heb 12:15 and that no bitter root **g** up

GRUDGE* [GRUDGING, GRUDGINGLY]
Ge 27:41 Esau held a **g** against Jacob
50:15 if Joseph holds a **g** against us
Lev 19:18 " 'Do not seek revenge or bear a **g**
Mk 6:19 So Herodias nursed a **g** against John

GRUDGING* [GRUDGE]
Dt 15:10 to him and do so without a **g** heart;

GRUDGINGLY* [GRUDGE]
2Co 9: 5 not as one **g** given.

GRUMBLE [GRUMBLED, GRUMBLERS, GRUMBLING]

Ex 16: 7 that you should **g** against us?"
Nu 14:27 long will this wicked community **g**
16:11 Who is Aaron that you should **g**
1Co 10:10 And do not **g**, as some of them did—
Jas 5: 9 Don't **g** against each other, brothers,

GRUMBLED [GRUMBLE]

Ex 15:24 So the people **g** against Moses,
16: 2 In the desert the whole community **g**
17: 3 and they **g** against Moses.
Nu 14: 2 All the Israelites **g** against Moses
16:41 the whole Israelite community **g**
Ps 106:25 They **g** in their tents and did not obey

GRUMBLERS* [GRUMBLE]

Jude 1:16 These men are **g** and faultfinders;

GRUMBLING [GRUMBLE]

Ex 16: 7 he has heard your **g** against him.
Nu 14:27 the complaints of these **g** Israelites.
17: 5 I will rid myself of this constant **g**
Jn 6:43 "Stop **g** among yourselves,"
1Pe 4: 9 to one another without **g**.

GUARANTEE* [GUARANTEED, GUARANTEEING]

Ge 43: 9 I myself will **g** his safety;
Heb 7:22 Jesus has become the **g** of a better covenant.

GUARANTEED* [GUARANTEE]

Ge 44:32 Your servant the boy's safety
Ro 4:16 may be **g** to all Abraham's offspring

GUARANTEEING* [GUARANTEE]

2Co 1:22 **g** what is to come.
5: 5 **g** what is to come.
Eph 1:14 who is a deposit **g** our inheritance

GUARD [GUARDED, GUARDIAN, GUARDIANS, GUARDING, GUARDS, SAFEGUARD]

Ge 3:24 to **g** the way to the tree of life.
1Sa 2: 9 He will **g** the feet of his saints,
26:15 Why didn't you **g** your lord
Ne 4: 9 a **g** day and night to meet this threat.
Ps 25:20 **G** my life and rescue me;
91:11 to **g** you in all your ways;
141: 3 Set a **g** over my mouth, O LORD;
Pr 2:11 and understanding will **g** you.
4:13 do not let it go; **g** it well,
4:23 Above all else, **g** your heart,
7: 2 **g** my teachings as the apple
Isa 52:12 the God of Israel will be your rear **g**.
Mal 2:15 So **g** yourself in your spirit,
Mt 27:66 a seal on the stone and posting the **g**.
Mk 13:33 Be on **g**! Be alert!
Lk 4:10 concerning you to **g** you carefully;
12: 1 "Be on your **g** against the yeast of
12:15 on your **g** against all kinds of greed;

Ac 20:31 So be on your **g**!
1Co 16:13 Be on your **g**;
Php 4: 7 will **g** your hearts and your minds
1Ti 6:20 **g** what has been entrusted
2Ti 1:12 to **g** what I have entrusted to him for
1:14 **G** the good deposit that was
2Pe 3:17 be on your **g** so that you may not

GUARDED [GUARD]

Dt 32:10 he **g** him as the apple of his eye,
33: 9 over your word and **g** your covenant.

GUARDIAN [GUARD]

Eze 28:14 You were anointed as a **g** cherub,

GUARDIANS [GUARD]

1Co 4:15 you have ten thousand **g** in Christ,
Gal 4: 2 He is subject to **g** and trustees until

GUARDING [GUARD]

Lk 22:63 who were **g** Jesus began mocking

GUARDS [GUARD]

Ne 4:22 as **g** by night and workmen by day."
Ps 97:10 for he **g** the lives of his faithful ones
Pr 13: 3 He who **g** his lips **g** his life,
19:16 He who obeys instructions **g** his life,
21:23 He who **g** his mouth
22: 5 but he who **g** his soul stays far
Mt 28: 4 The **g** were so afraid of him

GUEST [GUESTS]

Mk 14:14 Where is my **g** room,
Lk 19: 7 to be the **g** of a 'sinner.' "

GUESTS [GUEST]

Pr 9:18 her **g** are in the depths of the grave.
Mt 9:15 the **g** of the bridegroom mourn
Lk 14: 7 how they picked the places of honor

GUIDANCE [GUIDE]

1Ch 10:13 and even consulted a medium for **g**,
Pr 1: 5 and let the discerning get **g**—
11:14 For lack of **g** a nation falls,
Hab 2:19 Can it give **g**?

GUIDE [GUIDANCE, GUIDED, GUIDES]

Ex 13:21 of them in a pillar of cloud to **g** them
15:13 In your strength you will **g** them
Ne 9:19 not cease to **g** them on their path,
Ps 25: 5 **g** me in your truth and teach me,
43: 3 let them **g** me;
48:14 be our **g** even to the end.
67: 4 and **g** the nations of the earth.
73:24 You **g** me with your counsel,
139:10 even there your hand will **g** me,
Pr 4:11 I **g** you in the way of wisdom
6:22 When you walk, they will **g** you;
Isa 9:16 who **g** this people mislead them,
58:11 The LORD will **g** you always;
Lk 1:79 to **g** our feet into the path of peace."
Jn 16:13 comes, he will **g** you into all truth.

GUIDED [GUIDE]

Job 31:18 and from my birth I **g** the widow—

Ps 107:30 and he **g** them to their desired haven.

GUIDES* [GUIDE]

Ps   23: 3 He **g** me in paths of righteousness
     25: 9 He **g** the humble in what is right
Pr   11: 3 The integrity of the upright **g** them,
     16:23 A wise man's heart **g** his mouth,
Isa   3:12 O my people, your **g** lead you astray;
Mt   15:14 Leave them; they are blind **g.**
     23:16 "Woe to you, blind **g!**
     23:24 You blind **g!**

GUILE (KJV) See DECEIT, FALSE, TRICKERY

GUILT [BLOODGUILT, GUILTLESS, GUILTY]

Ge   44:16 God has uncovered your servants' **g.**
Lev   5:15 It is a **g** offering.
1Sa   6: 4 "What **g** offering should we send
Ezr   9: 6 and our **g** has reached to the heavens.
Ps   32: 5 and you forgave the **g** of my sin.
     38: 4 My **g** has overwhelmed me like
Isa   1: 4 sinful nation, a people loaded with **g,**
      6: 7 your **g** is taken away
     53:10 LORD makes his life a **g** offering,
Jer   2:22 the stain of your **g** is still before me,"
Eze 18:19 the son not share the **g** of his father?'
Hos   5:15 to my place until they admit their **g.**
Jn   9:41 claim you can see, your **g** remains.
     16: 8 the world of **g** in regard to sin

GUILT OFFERING Lev 5:15, 16, 18, 19; 6:5, 6, 17; 7:1, 2, 5, 7, 37; 14:12, 13, 14, 17, 21, 24, 25, 28; 19:21, 22; Nu 6:12; 1Sa 6:3, 4, 8, 17; Ezr 10:19; Isa 53:10; Eze 46:20

GUILT OFFERINGS Nu 18:9; 2Ki 12:16; Eze 40:39; 42:13; 44:29

GUILTLESS [GUILT]

Ex   20: 7 not hold anyone **g** who misuses his name.

GUILTY [GUILT]

Ex   23: 7 for I will not acquit the **g.**
     34: 7 he does not leave the **g** unpunished;
Nu   14:18 he does not leave the **g** unpunished;
Pr   21: 8 The way of the **g** is devious,
Isa   5:23 who acquit the **g** for a bribe,
Na   1: 3 not leave the **g** unpunished.
Mk   3:29 he is **g** of an eternal sin."
Jn   8:46 Can any of you prove me **g** of sin?
     19:11 over to you is **g** of a greater sin."
1Co 11:27 in an unworthy manner will be **g**
Heb 10: 2 and would no longer have felt a
     10:22 to cleanse us from a **g** conscience
Jas   2:10 at just one point is **g** of breaking all

GUSH* [GUSHED, GUSHES]

Isa 35: 6 Water will **g** forth in the wilderness

GUSHED* [GUSH]

Nu   20:11 Water **g** out, and the community
Ps   78:20 he struck the rock, water **g** out,
     105:41 He opened the rock, and water **g** out;

Isa 48:21 split the rock and water **g** out.

GUSHES* [GUSH]

Pr   15: 2 but the mouth of the fool **g** folly.
     15:28 but the mouth of the wicked **g** evil.

H

HABAKKUK*

Prophet to Judah (Hab 1:1; 3:1).

HABIT

Nu   22:30 Have I been in the **h** of doing this
1Ti   5:13 the **h** of being idle and going about
Heb 10:25 as some are in the **h** of doing,

HAD [HAVE]

Ge   11: 1 the whole world **h** one language
Ex   36: 7 they already **h** was more than enough
Nu   11: 4 "If only we **h** meat to eat!
Jdg   1:19 because they **h** iron chariots.
1Sa   2:12 they **h** no regard for the LORD.
2Sa 12: 3 poor man **h** nothing except one little
2Ch 26:21 King Uzziah **h** leprosy until
Job 28:17 nor can it be **h** for jewels of gold.
     42:10 twice as much as he **h** before.
Ps   55: 6 "Oh, that I **h** the wings of a dove!
Isa   5: 1 My loved one **h** a vineyard on
     53: 2 He **h** no beauty or majesty to attract
Eze   1: 6 of them **h** four faces and four wings
     10:14 Each of the cherubim **h** four faces:
     41:18 Each cherub **h** two faces:
Mt   7:29 he taught as one who **h** authority,
     13:44 in his joy went and sold all he **h** and
     13:46 sold everything he **h** and bought it.
Mk   4: 6 withered because they **h** no root.
     10:22 because he **h** great wealth.
Jn   20: 9 that Jesus **h** to rise from the dead.)
Ac   1:16 the Scripture **h** to be fulfilled which
      2:13 "They have **h** too much wine."
      2:45 they gave to anyone as he **h** need.
     13:46 "We **h** to speak the word of God
     14: 9 saw that he **h** faith to be healed
     17: 3 Christ **h** to suffer and rise from the
Ro   4:21 fully persuaded that God **h** power
2Co   5:21 made him who **h** no sin to be sin
Rev   4: 8 the four living creatures **h** six wings
      5: 6 He **h** seven horns and seven eyes,
     13: 1 He **h** ten horns and seven heads,
     13: 3 beast seemed to have **h** a fatal wound
     14: 1 144,000 who **h** his name and his

HADAD [BEN-HADAD]

Edomite adversary of Solomon (1Ki 11:14-25).

HADADEZER

2Sa   8: 3 David fought **H** son of Rehob,

HADASSAH* [ESTHER]

Est   2: 7 Mordecai had a cousin named **H,**

HADES*

Mt	16:18	the gates of **H** will not overcome it.
Rev	1:18	And I hold the keys of death and **H.**
	6: 8	**H** was following close behind him.
	20:13	and death and **H** gave up the dead
	20:14	Then death and **H** were thrown into

HAGAR*

Servant of Sarah, wife of Abraham, mother of Ishmael (Ge 16:1-6; 25:12). Driven away by Sarah while pregnant (Ge 16:5-16); after birth of Isaac (Ge 21:9-21; Gal 4:21-31).

HAGGAI*

Post-exilic prophet who encouraged rebuilding of the temple (Ezr 5:1; 6:14; Hag 1-2).

HAGGITH

1Ki	1: 5	Now Adonijah, whose mother was **H**

HAIL [HAILSTONES]

Ex	9:19	because the **h** will fall on every man
	9:26	it did not **h** was the land of Goshen,
Ps	78:47	He destroyed their vines with **h**
	147:17	He hurls down his **h** like pebbles.
Jn	19: 3	saying, "**H,** king of the Jews!"
Rev	8: 7	and there came **h** and fire mixed
	16:21	on account of the plague of **h,**

HAILSTONES [HAIL]

Jos	10:11	the LORD hurled large **h** down
Eze	13:11	and I will send **h** hurtling down,
Rev	16:21	huge **h** of about a hundred pounds

HAIR [HAIRS, HAIRY]

Ex	26: 7	"Make curtains of goat **h** for the tent
Lev	19:27	not cut the **h** at the sides of your
Nu	6: 5	the **h** of his head grow long.
Jdg	16:19	to shave off the seven braids of his **h,**
	16:22	**h** on his head began to grow again
	20:16	of whom could sling a stone at a **h**
2Sa	14:26	Whenever he cut the **h** of his head—
2Ki	1: 8	a garment of **h** with a leather belt
Pr	16:31	Gray **h** is a crown of splendor;
	20:29	gray **h** the splendor of the old.
SS	7: 5	Your **h** is like royal tapestry;
Isa	3:24	instead of well-dressed **h,** baldness;
Eze	8: 3	and took me by the **h** of my head.
Da	4:33	until his **h** grew like the feathers of
	7: 9	**h** of his head was white like wool.
Mt	3: 4	clothes were made of camel's **h,**
Lk	7:44	and wiped them with her **h.**
	21:18	But not a **h** of your head will perish.
Jn	11: 2	and wiped his feet with her **h.**
	12: 3	and wiped his feet with her **h.**
1Co	11: 6	she should have her **h** cut off;
	11:14	that if a man has long **h**
	11:15	but that if a woman has long **h,**
1Ti	2: 9	not with braided **h** or gold or pearls
1Pe	3: 3	such as braided **h** and the wearing
Rev	1:14	His head and **h** were white like wool,

HAIRS [HAIR]

Ps	40:12	They are more than the **h** of my head
Mt	10:30	very **h** of your head are all numbered
Lk	12: 7	very **h** of your head are all numbered

HAIRY [HAIR]

Ge	27:11	"But my brother Esau is a **h** man,

HALAH

2Ki	18:11	to Assyria and settled them in **H,**

HALF [HALF-TRIBE, HALVES]

Ge	15:10	however, he did not cut in **h.**
Ex	24: 6	Moses took **h** of the blood and put it
	30:13	**h** shekel is an offering to the LORD.
Nu	34:13	be given to the nine and a **h** tribes,
Jos	8:33	**H** of the people stood in front of
2Sa	10: 4	shaved off **h** of each man's beard,
1Ki	3:25	Cut the living child in two and give **h**
	10: 7	Indeed, not even **h** was told me;
Ne	4:16	**h** of my men did the work,
	13:24	**H** of their children spoke the
Est	5: 3	Even up to **h** the kingdom,
Isa	44:19	"**H** of it I used for fuel;
Eze	16:51	not commit **h** the sins you did.
Da	7:25	a time, times and **h** a time.
	12: 7	a time, times and **h** a time.
Mk	6:23	up to **h** my kingdom."
Lk	19: 8	and now I give **h** of my possessions
Rev	8: 1	silence in heaven for about **h** an hour
	11:11	the three and a **h** days a breath of life
	12:14	a time, times and **h** a time,

HALF-TRIBE [HALF, TRIBE]

Nu	32:33	and the **h** of Manasseh son of Joseph
Jos	4:12	and the **h** of Manasseh crossed over,

HALL

1Ki	7: 7	the **H** of Justice,
SS	2: 4	He has taken me to the banquet **h,**
Da	5:10	came into the banquet **h.**
Mt	22:10	the wedding **h** was filled with guests.
Ac	19: 9	discussions daily in the lecture **h**

HALLELUJAH*

Rev	19: 1	multitude in heaven shouting: "**H!**
	19: 3	And again they shouted: "**H!**
	19: 4	And they cried: "Amen, **H!**"
	19: 6	loud peals of thunder, shouting: "**H!**

HALLOWED* [HOLY]

Mt	6: 9	Father in heaven, **h** be your name,
Lk	11: 2	**h** be your name, your kingdom come

HALLOW, HALLOWED (KJV)

See CONSECRATE, CONSECRATED, HOLY, SACRED, SET APART

HALT

Job	38:11	where your proud waves **h'**?

HALTER*

Pr	26: 3	a **h** for the donkey,

HALVES [HALF]

Ge	15:10	arranged the **h** opposite each other;

HAM

Son of Noah (Ge 5:32; 1Ch 1:4), father of Canaan (Ge 9:18; 10:6-20; 1Ch 1:8-16). Saw Noah's nakedness (Ge 9:20-27).

HAMAN

Agagite nobleman honored by Xerxes (Est 3:1-2). Plotted to exterminate the Jews because of Mordecai (Est 3:3-15). Forced to honor Mordecai (Est 5-6). Plot exposed by Esther (Est 5:1-8; 7:1-8). Hanged (Est 7:9-10).

HAMATH [HAMATHITES, LEBO HAMATH]

2Sa	8: 9	Tou king of **H** heard that David
2Ki	14:28	for Israel both Damascus and **H,**
	18:34	Where are the gods of **H** and Arpad?

HAMMER [HAMMERED]

Ex	25:31	a lampstand of pure gold and **h** it out
Nu	16:38	**H** the censers into sheets to overlay
Jdg	4:21	a tent peg and a **h** and went quietly
Jer	10: 4	they fasten it with **h** and nails

HAMMERED [HAMMER]

Ex	25:18	make two cherubim out of **h** gold
2Ch	9:15	large shields of **h** gold;
	9:16	small shields of **h** gold,

HAMOR

Ge	34: 2	When Shechem son of **H** the Hivite,

HAMPERED*

Pr	4:12	you walk, your steps will not be **h;**

HAMSTRING* [HAMSTRUNG]

Jos	11: 6	You are to **h** their horses

HAMSTRUNG [HAMSTRING]

Jos	11: 9	He **h** their horses
1Ch	18: 4	**h** all but a hundred of the chariot

HANAMEL

Jer	32: 7	**H** son of Shallum your uncle is

HANANEL

Ne	3: 1	and as far as the Tower of **H.**
Jer	31:38	rebuilt for me from the Tower of **H**

HANANI

Ne	7: 2	in charge of Jerusalem my brother **H,**

HANANIAH [SHADRACH]

1. False prophet; adversary of Jeremiah (Jer 28).
2. Original name of Shadrach (Da 1:6-19; 2:17).

HAND [HANDED, HANDFUL, HANDS, LEFT-HANDED, OPENHANDED, RIGHT-HANDED]

Ge	3:22	not be allowed to reach out his **h**
	4:11	brother's blood from your **h.**
	14:22	"I have raised my **h** to the LORD,
	16:12	his **h** will be against everyone
	22:12	"Do not lay a **h** on the boy," he said.
	24: 2	"Put your **h** under my thigh.
	25:26	with his **h** grasping Esau's heel;
	37:22	but don't lay a **h** on him."
	47:29	put your **h** under my thigh
	48:14	But Israel reached out his right **h**
Ex	3:19	unless a mighty **h** compels him.
	4: 6	"Put your **h** inside your cloak."
	6: 1	of my mighty **h** he will let them go;
	13: 3	brought you out of it with a mighty **h**
	15: 6	"Your right **h,** O LORD,
	21:24	tooth for tooth, **h** for **h,**
	33:22	in the rock and cover you with my **h**
Lev	1: 4	He is to lay his **h** on the head
	3: 2	He is to lay his **h** on the head
	4: 4	He is to lay his **h** on its head
Nu	14:30	with uplifted **h** to make your home,
Dt	3:24	your greatness and your strong **h.**
	4:34	a mighty **h** and an outstretched arm,
	12: 7	in everything you have put your **h** to,
	19:21	tooth for tooth, **h** for **h,**
	32:39	and no one can deliver out of my **h.**
Jos	8: 7	God will give it into your **h.**
Jdg	2:15	the **h** of the LORD was against them
1Sa	17:50	without a sword in his **h** he struck
	24:10	not lift my **h** against my master,
	26: 9	can lay a **h** on the LORD's anointed
2Sa	1:14	not afraid to lift your **h** to destroy
	18:12	not lift my **h** against the king's son.
1Ki	8:24	with your **h** you have fulfilled it—
	8:42	your mighty **h** and your outstretched
	13: 4	But the **h** he stretched out toward
	18:44	"A cloud as small as a man's **h**
1Ch	21:17	let your **h** fall upon me and my
	29:14	only what comes from your **h.**
	29:16	it comes from your **h,**
2Ch	6:15	with your **h** you have fulfilled it—
	32:15	your god deliver you from my **h!**
	32:22	from the **h** of Sennacherib king of
Ezr	7: 9	gracious **h** of his God was on him.
Ne	2: 8	the gracious **h** of my God was
	4:17	with one **h** and held a weapon
Job	40: 4	I put my **h** over my mouth.
Ps	10:12	Lift up your **h,** O God.
	16: 8	Because he is at my right **h,**
	32: 4	night your **h** was heavy upon me;
	37:24	the LORD upholds him with his **h.**
	44: 3	it was your right **h,**
	45: 9	at your right **h** is the royal bride
	63: 8	your right **h** upholds me.
	74:11	you hold back your **h,** your right **h?**
	75:11	In the **h** of the LORD is a cup full
	80:17	Let your **h** rest on the man at your right **h,**
	91: 7	ten thousand at your right **h,**
	95: 4	In his **h** are the depths of the earth,
	98: 1	his right **h** and his holy arm
	109:31	at the right **h** of the needy one,
	110: 1	"Sit at my right **h**
	137: 5	may my right **h** forget [its skill].
	139:10	even there your **h** will guide me,
	145:16	You open your **h** and satisfy
Pr	3:16	Long life is in her right **h;** in her left **h** are riches and honor.
	19:24	The sluggard buries his **h** in the dish;

21: 1 king's heart is in the **h** of the LORD;
27:16 the wind or grasping oil with the **h**.

Ecc   2:24 This too, I see, is from the **h** of God,
5:15 that he can carry in his **h**.
9:10 Whatever your **h** finds to do,

Isa   1:25 I will turn my **h** against you;
5:25 his **h** is still upraised.
11: 8 child put his **h** into the viper's nest.
40:12 the waters in the hollow of his **h**,
41:13 who takes hold of your right **h**
44: 5 another will write on his **h**,
48:13 My own **h** laid the foundations of
53:10 will of the LORD will prosper in his **h**
64: 8 we are all the work of your **h**.

Jer 22:24 were a signet ring on my right **h**,
31:32 by the **h** to lead them out of Egypt,
51: 7 a gold cup in the LORD's **h**;

La   3: 3 he has turned his **h** against me again

Eze   1: 3 the **h** of the LORD was upon him.
2: 9 and I saw a **h** stretched out to me.
20: 5 With uplifted **h** I said to them,

Da   3:17 and he will rescue us from your **h**,
5: 5 the fingers of a human **h** appeared
10:10 **h** touched me and set me trembling

Am   7: 7 with a plumb line in his **h**.

Jnh   4:11 people who cannot tell their right **h**

Hab   2:16 The cup from the LORD's right **h**
3: 4 rays flashed from his **h**,

Mt   3:12 His winnowing fork is in his **h**,
5:30 And if your right **h** causes you to sin,
6: 3 left **h** know what your right **h** is
12:10 a man with a shriveled **h** was there.
18: 8 If your **h** or your foot causes you
22:44 "Sit at my right **h** until
26:64 Son of Man sitting at the right **h**

Mk   1:31 took her **h** and helped her up.
3: 1 a man with a shriveled **h** was there.
5:41 He took her by the **h** and said to her,
9:43 If your **h** causes you to sin, cut it off.
12:36 "Sit at my right **h** until I put your
14:62 the Son of Man sitting at the right **h**

Lk   5:13 Jesus reached out his **h** and touched
9:62 "No one who puts his **h** to the plow
20:42 "Sit at my right **h**
22:69 will be seated at the right **h**

Jn   7:30 but no one laid a **h** on him,
10:28 no one can snatch them out of my **h**.
20:27 Reach out your **h** and put it

Ac   2:34 Lord: "Sit at my right **h**
7:55 Jesus standing at the right **h** of God.

Ro   8:34 is at the right **h** of God and is

1Co 12:15 "Because I am not a **h**,

Eph   1:20 and seated him at his right **h**

Col   3: 1 Christ is seated at the right **h** of God.

Heb   1:13 "Sit at my right **h**
1: 3 who sat down at the right **h**
10:12 he sat down at the right **h** of God.

1Pe   3:22 into heaven and is at God's right **h**—

Rev   1:16 In his right **h** he held seven stars,
5: 1 Then I saw in the right **h** of him
13:16 to receive a mark on his right **h** or

HAND OF GOD 2Ch 30:12; Job 19:21; Ecc
2:24; Mk 16:19; Ac 2:33; 7:55, 56; Ro 8:34; Col
3:1; Heb 10:12

HAND OF THE †LORD Ex 9:3; Jos 4:24; Jdg
2:15; 1Sa 7:13; 2Ki 3:15; 1Ch 28:19; Ezr 7:6, 28;
Job 12:9; Ps 75:8; Pr 21:1; Isa 25:10; 41:20;
51:17; 66:14; Eze 1:3; 3:14, 22; 33:22; 37:1; 40:1

MIGHTY HAND Ex 3:19; 6:1, 1; 13:3, 9, 14, 16;
32:11; Dt 4:34; 5:15; 6:21; 7:8, 19; 9:26; 11:2;
26:8; 1Ki 8:42; 2Ch 6:32; Ne 1:10; Ps 136:12;
Jer 32:21; Eze 20:33, 34; Da 9:15; 1Pe 5:6

RIGHT HAND Ge 48:13, 14, 17, 18; Ex 15:6, 6,
12; Lev 8:23; 14:14, 17, 25, 28; Jdg 5:26; 16:29;
2Sa 20:9; 1Ki 2:19; 1Ch 6:39; Job 40:14; Ps
16:8, 11; 17:7; 18:35; 20:6; 21:8; 44:3; 45:4, 9;
48:10; 60:5; 63:8; 73:23; 74:11; 77:10; 78:54;
80:15, 17; 89:13, 25, 42; 91:7; 98:1; 108:6;
109:6, 31; 110:1, 5; 118:15, 16, 16; 121:5; 137:5;
138:7; 139:10; Pr 3:16; Isa 41:10, 13; 44:20;
45:1; 48:13; 62:8; 63:12; Jer 22:24; La 2:3, 4;
Eze 21:22; 39:3; Da 12:7; Jnh 4:11; Hab 2:16; Mt
5:30; 6:3; 22:44; 26:64; 27:29; Mk 12:36; 14:62;
16:19; Lk 6:6; 20:42; 22:69; Ac 2:25, 33, 34; 3:7;
5:31; 7:55, 56; Ro 8:34; 2Co 6:7; Gal 2:9; Eph
1:20; Col 3:1; Heb 1:3, 13; 8:1; 10:12; 12:2; 1Pe
3:22; Rev 1:16, 17, 20; 2:1; 5:1, 7; 10:5; 13:16

HANDED [HAND]

Jos 21:44 the LORD **h** all their enemies
Jdg   2:14 the LORD **h** them over to raiders
2Ch 36:17 God **h** all of them over to
Ps   31: 8 not **h** me over to the enemy
106:41 He **h** them over to the nations,
La   2: 7 He has **h** over to the enemy the walls
Da   7:25 The saints will be **h** over to him for
Mt   26: 2 and the Son of Man will be **h** over to
Mk   15:15 and **h** him over to be crucified.
Ac   3:13 You **h** him over to be killed,
1Ti   1:20 whom I have **h** over to Satan to

HANDFUL [HAND]

Ecc   4: 6 Better one **h** with tranquillity than

HANDKERCHIEFS*

Ac   19:12 even **h** and aprons that had touched

HANDLE [HANDLES]

Ex   18:18 you cannot **h** it alone.
Col   2:21 "Do not **h**! Do not taste!"

HANDLES [HANDLE]

2Ti   2:15 who correctly **h** the word of truth.

HANDS [HAND]

Ge   5:29 and painful toil of our **h** caused by
27:22 but the **h** are the **h** of Esau."

Ex   17:11 As long as Moses held up his **h**,
29:10 shall lay their **h** on its head.
32:15 two tablets of the Testimony in his **h**.
34: 4 the two stone tablets in his **h**.

Dt   6: 8 Tie them as symbols on your **h**
11:18 tie them as symbols on your **h**
23:25 you may pick kernels with your **h**,

Jos 24:11 but I gave them into your **h**.

Jdg   2:16 who saved them out of the **h**
7: 6 lapped with their **h** to their mouths.
14: 6 tore the lion apart with his bare **h**

1Sa 5: 4 His head and **h** had been broken off
2Sa 24:14 Let us fall into the **h** of the LORD,
2Ki 11:12 people clapped their **h** and shouted,
    22:17 by all the idols their **h** have made,
2Ch 6: 4 his **h** has fulfilled what he promised
Job 1:12 then, everything he has is in your **h**,
    2: 6 "Very well, then, he is in your **h**;
Ps 22:16 they have pierced my **h** and my feet.
    24: 4 He who has clean **h** and a pure heart,
    31: 5 Into your **h** I commit my spirit;
    31:15 My times are in your **h**;
    47: 1 Clap your **h**, all you nations;
    63: 4 and in your name I will lift up my **h**.
    90:17 establish the work of our **h**.
    115: 7 they have **h**, but cannot feel,
    138: 8 not abandon the works of your **h**.
Pr 10: 4 Lazy **h** make a man poor, but
             diligent **h** bring wealth.
    12:24 Diligent **h** will rule,
    21:25 because his **h** refuse to work.
    24:33 a little folding of the **h** to rest—
    31:13 and flax and works with eager **h**.
    31:20 and extends her **h** to the needy.
Ecc 4: 5 fool folds his **h** and ruins himself.
    10:18 if his **h** are idle, the house leaks.
    11: 6 and at evening let not your **h** be idle,
Isa 5:12 no respect for the work of his **h**.
    35: 3 Strengthen the feeble **h**,
    37:19 fashioned by human **h**.
    45:12 My own **h** stretched out the heavens;
    49:16 engraved you on the palms of my **h**;
    55:12 the trees of the field will clap their **h**.
    65: 2 All day long I have held out my **h** to
Jer 1: 1 worshiping what their **h** have made.
    20:13 the needy from the **h** of the wicked.
    26:14 As for me, I am in your **h**;
La 3:41 and our **h** to God in heaven, and say:
Eze 1: 8 they had the **h** of a man.
    10: 8 what looked like the **h** of a man.)
Da 2:45 but not by human **h**—
Hos 14: 3 to what our own **h** have made,
Mic 7: 3 Both **h** are skilled in doing evil;
Zec 8:13 but let your **h** be strong."
Mal 1:10 I will accept no offering from your **h**.
Mk 7: 5 eating their food with 'unclean' **h**?"
    10:16 put his **h** on them and blessed them.
    14:41 the Son of Man is betrayed into the **h**
Lk 23:46 into your **h** I commit my spirit."
    24:40 he showed them his **h** and feet.
Jn 20:27 "Put your finger here; see my **h**.
Ac 6: 6 who prayed and laid their **h** on them.
    8:18 at the laying on of the apostles' **h**,
    13: 3 they placed their **h** on them
    19: 6 When Paul placed his **h** on them,
    28: 8 placed his **h** on him and healed him.
Ro 10:21 "All day long I have held out my **h**
1Co 15:24 when he **h** over the kingdom to God
1Th 4:11 and to work with your **h**,
1Ti 2: 8 to lift up holy **h** in prayer,
    4:14 body of elders laid their **h** on you.
    5:22 Do not be hasty in the laying on of **h**,
2Ti 1: 6 you through the laying on of my **h**.
Heb 6: 2 the laying on of **h**,
    10:31 to fall into the **h** of the living God.

1Jn 1: 1 and our **h** have touched—
Rev 20: 4 his mark on their foreheads or their **h**

HANDSOME*

Ge 39: 6 Now Joseph was well-built and **h**,
1Sa 16:12 with a fine appearance and **h** features
    17:42 ruddy and **h**, and he despised him.
2Sa 14:25 highly praised for his **h** appearance
1Ki 1: 6 He was also very **h** and was born
SS 1:16 How **h** you are, my lover!
Eze 23: 6 all of them **h** young men,
    23:12 mounted horsemen, all **h** young men.
    23:23 **h** young men, all of them governors
Da 1: 4 **h**, showing aptitude for every kind
Zec 11:13 the **h** price at which they priced me!

HANG [HANGED, HANGING, HUNG]

Ge 40:19 and **h** you on a tree.
Est 7: 9 The king said, "**H** him on it!"
Mt 22:40 Law and the Prophets **h** on these two

HANGED [HANG]

Ge 40:22 but he **h** the chief baker,
2Sa 17:23 house in order and then **h** himself.
Est 2:23 two officials were **h** on a gallows.
    7:10 So they **h** Haman on the gallows
Mt 27: 5 Then he went away and **h** himself.

HANGING [HANG]

2Sa 18: 9 He was left **h** in midair,
Ac 10:39 They killed him by **h** him on a tree,

HANNAH

Wife of Elkanah, mother of Samuel (1Sa 1).
Prayer at dedication of Samuel (1Sa 2:1-10).
Blessed (1Sa 2:18-21).

HANUN

1Ch 19: 2 thought, "I will show kindness to **H**

HAPPEN [HAPPENED, HAPPENING, HAPPENS]

Ge 49: 1 so I can tell you what will **h** to you
Ecc 6:12 Who can tell him what will **h** under
Da 8:19 what will **h** later in the time of wrath,
    10:14 will **h** to your people in the future,
Jnh 4: 5 to see what would **h** to the city.
Mk 10:32 told them what was going to **h** to him
Jn 13:19 that when it does **h** you will believe
    14:29 that when it does **h** you will believe.
    18: 4 knowing all that was going to **h**
Ac 4:28 had decided beforehand should **h**.

HAPPENED [HAPPEN]

Dt 4:32 Has anything so great as this ever **h**,
1Sa 4: 7 Nothing like this has **h** before.
2Ki 24:20 that all this **h** to Jerusalem and Judah
Ezr 9:13 "What has **h** to us is a result
Ne 9:33 In all that has **h** to us,
Jer 40: 3 All this **h** because you people sinned

HAPPENING [HAPPEN]

Lk 21:31 so, when you see these things **h**,
1Pe 4:12 as though something strange were **h**

HAPPENS [HAPPEN]

Jn   13:19 "I am telling you now before it **h**,
       14:29 I have told you now before it **h**,

HAPPIER* [HAPPY]

Ecc   4: 2 already died, are **h** than the living,
Mt   18:13 he is **h** about that one sheep than
1Co 7:40 she is **h** if she stays as she is—

HAPPINESS* [HAPPY]

Dt   24: 5 bring **h** to the wife he has married.
Est   8:16 the Jews it was a time of **h** and joy,
Job   7: 7 my eyes will never see **h** again.
Ecc 2:26 God gives wisdom, knowledge and **h**
Mt   25:21 Come and share your master's **h**.'
       25:23 Come and share your master's **h**.'

HAPPY* [HAPPIER, HAPPINESS]

Ge   30:13 Then Leah said, "How **h** I am!
       30:13 The women will call me **h**."
1Ki   4:20 they drank and they were **h**.
       10: 8 How **h** your men must be!
       10: 8 How **h** your officials,
2Ch   9: 7 How **h** your men must be!
       9: 7 How **h** your officials,
Est   5: 9 Haman went out that day **h** and
       5:14 with the king to the dinner and be **h**.
Ps   10: 6 I'll always be **h**
       68: 3 may they be **h** and joyful.
     113: 9 as a **h** mother of children.
     137: 8 **h** is he who repays you
Pr   15:13 A **h** heart makes the face cheerful,
Ecc   3:12 than to be **h** and do good
       5:19 to accept his lot and be **h** in his work
       7:14 When times are good, be **h**;
      11: 9 Be **h**, young man,
Jnh   4: 6 and Jonah was very **h** about the vine.
Zec   8:19 and glad occasions and **h** festivals
1Co 7:30 those who are **h**, as if they were not;
2Co   7: 9 yet now I am **h**,
       7:13 to see how **h** Titus was,
Jas   5:13 Is anyone **h**?

HARAN

Ge   11:26 the father of Abram, Nahor and **H**.
       11:27 And **H** became the father of Lot.

HARASS* [HARASSED]

Dt   2: 9 "Do not **h** the Moabites or provoke
       2:19 to the Ammonites, do not **h** them

HARASSED* [HARASS]

Mt   9:36 because they were **h** and helpless,
2Co   7: 5 but we were **h** at every turn—

HARBOR [HARBORS]

Dt   15: 9 not to **h** this wicked thought:
Job 36:13 "The godless in heart **h** resentment;
Ps 103: 9 nor will he **h** his anger forever;
Jas   3:14 But if you **h** bitter envy

HARBORS* [HARBOR]

Pr   26:24 but in his heart he **h** deceit.

HARD [HARDEN, HARDENED, HARDENING, HARDENS, HARDER, HARDSHIP, HARDSHIPS]

Ge   18:14 Is anything too **h** for the LORD?
Ex   1:14 with **h** labor in brick and mortar and
       7:13 Yet Pharaoh's heart became **h**
1Ki 10: 1 to test him with **h** questions.
Pr   14:23 All **h** work brings a profit,
Isa 40: 2 her **h** service has been completed,
Jer 32:17 Nothing is too **h** for you.
Zec   7:12 They made their hearts as **h** as flint
Mt   19:23 it is **h** for a rich man to enter
Mk 10: 5 "It was because your hearts were **h**
Jn   6:60 "This is a **h** teaching.
Ac 20:35 by this kind of **h** work we must help
      26:14 It is **h** for you to kick against
Ro   16:12 those women who work **h** in
      16:12 woman who has worked very **h**
1Co 4:12 We work **h** with our own hands.
2Co   4: 8 We are **h** pressed on every side,
       6: 5 in **h** work, sleepless nights
1Th   5:12 to respect those who work **h**
1Pe   4:18 If it is **h** for the righteous to be saved
2Pe   3:16 some things that are **h** to understand,
Rev   2: 2 your **h** work and your perseverance.

HARDEN [HARD]

Ex   4:21 But I will **h** his heart so that he will
      14:17 I will **h** the hearts of the Egyptians so
1Sa   6: 6 Why do you **h** your hearts as
Ps 95: 8 do not **h** your hearts as you did
Ro   9:18 and he hardens whom he wants to **h**.
Heb   3: 8 do not **h** your hearts as you did in
       4: 7 do not **h** your hearts."

HARDENED [HARD]

Ex   8:32 this time also Pharaoh **h** his heart
      10:20 But the LORD **h** Pharaoh's heart,
Jos 11:20 LORD himself who **h** their hearts
Mk   8:17 Are your hearts **h**?
Ro   11: 7 The others were **h**,
Heb   3:13 so that none of you may be **h**

HARDENING* [HARD]

Ro   11:25 Israel has experienced a **h** in part
Eph   4:18 due to the **h** of their hearts.

HARDENS* [HARD]

Pr   28:14 he who **h** his heart falls into trouble.
Ro   9:18 and he **h** whom he wants to harden.

HARDER [HARD]

Jer   5: 3 They made their faces **h** than stone
1Co 15:10 No, I worked **h** than all of them—
2Co 11:23 I have worked much **h**,

HARDHEARTED* [HEART]

Dt   15: 7 do not be **h** or tightfisted

HARDSHIP [HARD]

Dt   15:18 a **h** to set your servant free,
Ne   9:32 do not let all this **h** seem trifling
Ro   8:35 Shall trouble or **h** or persecution

2Ti   2: 3 Endure **h** with us like a good soldier
       4: 5 in all situations, endure **h,**
Heb 12: 7 Endure **h** as discipline;

HARDSHIPS [HARD]

Nu   11: 1 the people complained about their **h**
Ac   14:22 We must go through many **h** to enter
2Co   6: 4 in troubles, **h** and distresses;
      12:10 in **h,** in persecutions, in difficulties.
Rev   2: 3 and have endured **h** for my name,

HARDWORKING* [WORK]

2Ti   2: 6 The **h** farmer should be the first

HAREM

Est   2: 9 into the best place in the **h.**

HARLOT* [HARLOTS]

Isa   1:21 how the faithful city has become a **h!**
Na   3: 4 all because of the wanton lust of a **h,**

HARLOT (KJV) See also PROSTITUTE

HARLOTS* [HARLOT]

Hos   4:14 the men themselves consort with **h**

HARM [HARMED, HARMING, HARMS]

Ge   31: 7 God has not allowed him to **h** me.
     31:52 past this heap to your side to **h** you
     48:16 who has delivered me from all **h**
     50:20 You intended to **h** me,
1Sa 26:21 I will not try to **h** you again.
1Ch 16:22 do my prophets no **h."**
Ne   6: 2 But they were scheming to **h** me;
Ps   71:13 may those who want to **h** me
     121: 6 the sun will not **h** you by day,
Pr   3:29 Do not plot **h** against your neighbor,
     12:21 No **h** befalls the righteous,
     13:20 but a companion of fools suffers **h.**
     31:12 She brings him good, not **h,**
Isa 11: 9 They will neither **h** nor destroy
Jer   7: 6 not follow other gods to your own **h,**
     10: 5 Do not fear them; they can do no **h**
     29:11 to prosper you and not to **h** you,
Zep   3:15 never again will you fear any **h.**
Ac   9:13 the **h** he has done to your saints
Ro   13:10 Love does no **h** to its neighbor.
1Co 11:17 your meetings do more **h** than good.
1Pe   3:13 to **h** you if you are eager to do good?
2Pe   2:13 paid back with **h** for the **h** they have
1Jn   5:18 and the evil one cannot **h** him.
Rev 11: 5 If anyone tries to **h** them,

HARMED [HARM]

Da   3:27 that the fire had not **h** their bodies,

HARMING [HARM]

1Sa 25:34 who has kept me from **h** you,

HARMONY*

Zec   6:13 And there will be **h** between the two.
Ro   12:16 Live in **h** with one another.
2Co   6:15 What **h** is there between Christ
1Pe   3: 8 all of you, live in **h** with one another;

HARMS* [HARM]

Pr   8:36 whoever fails to find me **h** himself;

HARP [HARPIST, HARPISTS, HARPS]

Ge   4:21 the father of all who play the **h**
1Sa 16:23 David would take his **h** and play.
     18:10 while David was playing the **h,**
     19: 9 While David was playing the **h,**
1Ch 25: 3 using the **h** in thanking and praising
Job 30:31 My **h** is tuned to mourning,
Ps   33: 2 Praise the LORD with the **h;**
     98: 5 make music to the LORD with the **h,**
     108: 2 Awake, **h** and lyre!
     150: 3 praise him with the **h** and lyre,
Da   3: 5 lyre, **h,** pipes and all kinds of music,
Rev   5: 8 Each one had a **h**

HARPIST [HARP]

2Ki   3:15 But now bring me a **h."**

HARPISTS* [HARP]

Rev 14: 2 like that of **h** playing their harps.
     18:22 The music of **h** and musicians,

HARPS [HARP]

1Sa 10: 5 and **h** being played before them,
1Ch 15:16 instruments: lyres, **h** and cymbals.
     25: 1 of prophesying, accompanied by **h,**
Ps   137: 2 There on the poplars we hung our **h,**
Rev 15: 2 They held **h** given them by God

HARSH [HARSHLY]

2Ch 10: 4 but now lighten the **h** labor
Pr   15: 1 but a **h** word stirs up anger.
Mal   3:13 "You have said **h** things against me,"
2Co 13:10 when I come I may not have to be **h**
Col   2:23 and their **h** treatment of the body,
      3:19 love your wives and do not be **h**
1Pe   2:18 but also to those who are **h.**
Jude 1:15 **h** words ungodly sinners have

HARSHLY [HARSH]

Ge   42: 7 to be a stranger and spoke **h** to them.
2Ch 10:13 The king answered them **h.**
1Ti   5: 1 Do not rebuke an older man **h,**

HARVEST [HARVESTED, HARVESTERS, HARVESTS]

Ge   8:22 seedtime and **h,** cold and heat,
Ex   23:16 the Feast of **H** with the firstfruits of
Lev 19: 9 " 'When you reap the **h** of your land,
Dt   16:15 God will bless you in all your **h**
Pr   10: 5 but he who sleeps during **h** is
     20: 4 at **h** time he looks but finds nothing.
Jer   8:20 "The **h** is past,
Joel 3:13 Swing the sickle, for the **h** is ripe,
Mic   6:15 You will plant but not **h;**
Mt   9:37 "The **h** is plentiful but
     13:39 The **h** is the end of the age,
Lk   10: 2 Ask the Lord of the **h,** therefore,
Jn   4:35 They are ripe for **h.**
1Co   9:11 is it too much if we reap a material **h**
2Co   9:10 store of seed and will enlarge the **h**

Gal 6: 9 at the proper time we will reap a **h**
Heb 12:11 it produces a **h** of righteousness
Jas 3:18 in peace raise a **h** of righteousness.
Rev 14:15 for the **h** of the earth is ripe."

HARVESTED [HARVEST]

Hag 1: 6 but have **h** little.
Rev 14:16 and the earth was **h.**

HARVESTERS [HARVEST]

Ru 2: 3 to glean in the fields behind the **h.**
Mt 13:39 and the **h** are angels.

HARVESTS [HARVEST]

Jn 4:36 now he **h** the crop for eternal life,

HAS [HAVE]

Ge 31:32 if you find anyone who **h** your gods,
Nu 14:24 my servant Caleb **h** a different spirit
Dt 21:15 If a man **h** two wives,
2Ch 25: 8 God **h** the power to help or to
Job 1:12 everything he **h** is in your hands,
2: 4 will give all he **h** for his own life.
11: 6 for true wisdom **h** two sides.
42: 8 what is right, as my servant Job **h.**"
Ps 73:25 earth **h** nothing I desire besides you.
Pr 18:21 tongue **h** the power of life and death,
23:29 Who **h** needless bruises?
Ecc 5:10 loves money never **h** money enough;
6: 8 advantage **h** a wise man over a fool?
Isa 34: 8 For the LORD **h** a day of vengeance,
Jer 23:28 who **h** my word speak it faithfully.
Eze 9: 6 not touch anyone who **h** the mark.
Mk 2:10 Son of Man **h** authority on earth to
4: 9 Jesus said, "He who **h** ears to hear,
4:25 Whoever **h** will be given more;
Lk 9:58 Son of Man **h** no place to lay his
12: 5 **h** power to throw you into hell.
14:33 does not give up everything he **h**
Jn 3:36 believes in the Son **h** eternal life,
4:44 a prophet **h** no honor in his own
15:13 Greater love **h** no one than this,
Ro 6: 9 death no longer **h** mastery over him.
1Co 7: 7 each man **h** his own gift from God;
7:13 a woman **h** a husband who is not
11:14 that if a man **h** long hair,
1Ti 4: 8 but godliness **h** value for all things,
Jas 2:14 claims to have faith but **h** no deeds?
1Jn 2:23 whoever acknowledges the Son **h**
3: 3 Everyone who **h** this hope
5:12 He who **h** the Son **h** life;
Rev 20: 6 death **h** no power over them,

HASTE [HASTEN, HASTILY, HASTY]

Ex 12:11 Eat it in **h;**
Dt 16: 3 because you left Egypt in **h**—
Pr 21: 5 as surely as **h** leads to poverty.
29:20 Do you see a man who speaks in **h?**

HASTEN [HASTE]

Ps 70: 1 **H,** O God, to save me;
119:60 I will **h** and not delay
Isa 49:17 Your sons **h** back,

HASTILY* [HASTE]

Pr 25: 8 do not bring **h** to court,

HASTY* [HASTE]

Pr 19: 2 nor to be **h** and miss the way.
Ecc 5: 2 do not be **h** in your heart to utter
1Ti 5:22 Do not be **h** in the laying on of hands

HATE [GOD-HATERS, HATED, HATES, HATING, HATRED]

Ex 18:21 trustworthy men who **h** dishonest
20: 5 generation of those who **h** me,
Lev 19:17 not **h** your brother in your heart.
Dt 7:10 But those who **h** him he will repay
2Ch 18: 7 but I **h** him because he
Ps 5: 5 you **h** all who do wrong.
36: 2 to detect or **h** his sin.
45: 7 and **h** wickedness;
97:10 who love the LORD **h** evil,
119:104 therefore I **h** every wrong path.
119:163 I **h** and abhor falsehood
129: 5 May all who **h** Zion be turned back
139:21 Do I not **h** those who **h** you,
Pr 1:22 in mockery and fools **h** knowledge?
8:13 To fear the LORD is to **h** evil;
9: 8 not rebuke a mocker or he will **h** you
13: 5 The righteous **h** what is false,
25:17 and he will **h** you.
29:10 Bloodthirsty men **h** a man of
Ecc 3: 8 a time to love and a time to **h,**
Isa 61: 8 I, the LORD, love justice; I **h** robbery
Jer 44: 4 not do this detestable thing that I **h!'**
Eze 35: 6 Since you did not **h** bloodshed,
Am 5:15 **H** evil, love good;
Mal 2:16 "I **h** divorce," says the LORD
Mt 5:43 your neighbor and **h** your enemy.'
10:22 All men will **h** you because of me,
Lk 6:22 Blessed are you when men **h** you,
6:27 do good to those who **h** you,
14:26 and does not **h** his father and mother,
16:13 he will **h** the one and love the other,
Jn 7: 7 The world cannot **h** you,
Ro 7:15 but what I **h** I do.
12: 9 **H** what is evil; cling to what is good.

HATED [HATE]

Ge 37: 4 they **h** him and could not speak
Est 9: 1 upper hand over those who **h** them.
Ecc 2:17 So I **h** life,
Mal 1: 3 but Esau I have **h,**
Jn 15:18 keep in mind that it **h** me first.
Ro 9:13 "Jacob I loved, but Esau I **h.**"
Eph 5:29 no one ever **h** his own body,
Heb 1: 9 and **h** wickedness;

HATES [HATE]

Pr 6:16 There are six things the LORD **h,**
12: 1 but he who **h** correction is stupid.
13:24 He who spares the rod **h** his son,
15:27 but he who **h** bribes will live.
26:28 A lying tongue **h** those it hurts,
Jn 3:20 Everyone who does evil **h** the light,
12:25 while the man who **h** his life

15:19 That is why the world **h** you.
1Jn 2: 9 to be in the light but **h** his brother.
4:20 "I love God," yet **h** his brother.

HATING* [HATE]
Tit 3: 3 being hated and **h** one another.
Jude 1:23 **h** even the clothing stained by

HATRED [HATE]
Pr 10:12 **H** stirs up dissension,
15:17 than a fattened calf with **h.**
Gal 5:20 idolatry and witchcraft; **h,** discord,
Jas 4: 4 with the world is **h** toward God?

HAUGHTY
Job 41:34 He looks down on all that are **h;**
Ps 18:27 bring low those whose eyes are **h.**
131: 1 O LORD, my eyes are not **h;**
Pr 6:17 **h** eyes, a lying tongue, hands that
16:18 a **h** spirit before a fall.
Isa 13:11 an end to the arrogance of the **h**
Zep 3:11 Never again will you be **h**

HAUNT
Jer 10:22 a **h** of jackals.
51:37 a **h** of jackals,
Rev 18: 2 and a **h** for every evil spirit,

HAVE [HAD, HAS, HAVE, HAVING]
Ge 18:10 Sarah your wife will **h** a son."
27:38 "Do you **h** only one blessing,
Ex 16:18 gathered much did not **h** too much,
20: 3 You shall **h** no other gods before me.
33:19 **h** mercy on whom I will **h** mercy.
Dt 5: 7 You shall **h** no other gods before me.
Jos 22:25 You **h** no share in the LORD.'
Ezr 4: 3 **h** no part with us in building a
Job 40: 9 Do you **h** an arm like God's,
Ps 73:25 Whom **h** I in heaven but you?
115: 5 They **h** mouths, but cannot speak,
119:99 I **h** more insight than all my teachers,
Pr 4: 7 it cost all you **h,** get understanding.
Jer 2:28 you **h** as many gods as you **h** towns,
5:21 who **h** eyes but do not see,
Mal 2:10 **h** we not all one Father?
Mt 3: 9 'We **h** Abraham as our father.'
21:21 if you **h** faith and do not doubt,
Mk 10:21 you will **h** treasure in heaven.
14: 7 But you will not always **h** me.
Lk 17: 6 **h** faith as small as a mustard seed,
Jn 3:16 shall not perish but **h** eternal life.
4:32 "I **h** food to eat that you
8:12 but will **h** the light of life."
16:12 "I **h** much more to say to you,
16:33 In this world you will **h** trouble.
Ac 3: 6 Peter said, "Silver or gold I do not **h,**
Ro 2:14 though they do not **h** the law,
5: 1 we **h** peace with God through
8: 9 does not **h** the Spirit of Christ,
12: 6 We **h** different gifts,
1Co 2:16 the mind of Christ.
13: 2 but **h** not love, I am nothing.
2Co 4: 7 But we **h** this treasure in jars of clay
8:15 gathered much did not **h** too much,

Eph 1: 7 we **h** redemption through his blood,
2:18 we both **h** access to the Father
Heb 4:14 since we **h** a great high priest
6:19 We **h** this hope as an anchor
1Jn 2:20 But you **h** an anointing from
5:12 not **h** the Son of God does not **h** life.
Jude 1:19 and do not **h** the Spirit.
Rev 20: 6 who **h** part in the first resurrection.
22:14 may **h** the right to the tree of life

HAVEN
Ps 107:30 he guided them to their desired **h.**

HAVING [HAVE]
1Co 9:21 to win those not **h** the law.
2Co 6:10 **h** nothing, and yet possessing
2Ti 3: 5 **h** a form of godliness but denying its

HAVOC
Ac 9:21 the man who raised **h** in Jerusalem

HAY
1Co 3:12 costly stones, wood, **h** or straw,

HAZAEL
1Ki 19:15 anoint **H** king over Aram.
2Ki 8: 9 **H** went to meet Elisha,

HAZOR
Jos 11:11 and he burned up **H** itself.
Jer 49:33 "**H** will become a haunt of jackals,

HEAD [AHEAD, HEADS, HOTHEADED]
Ge 3:15 he will crush your **h,**
28:18 the stone he had placed under his **h**
48:18 put your right hand on his **h.**"
Lev 1: 4 He is to lay his hand on the **h** of
19:27 not cut the hair at the sides of your **h**
Nu 6: 5 the hair of his **h** grow long.
Dt 28:13 The LORD will make you the **h,**
Jdg 16:17 If my **h** were shaved,
1Sa 1:11 no razor will ever be used on his **h.**"
9: 2 a **h** taller than any of the others.
17:51 he cut off his **h** with the sword.
2Sa 18: 9 Absalom's **h** got caught in the tree.
Ps 7:16 violence comes down on his own **h.**
23: 5 You anoint my **h** with oil;
133: 2 is like precious oil poured on the **h,**
Pr 1: 9 will be a garland to grace your **h**
10: 6 Blessings crown the **h** of
25:22 you will heap burning coals on his **h,**
Isa 59:17 and the helmet of salvation on his **h;**
Jer 9: 1 that my **h** were a spring of water
Eze 8: 3 and took me by the hair of my **h.**
33: 4 his blood will be on his own **h.**
Da 2:32 The **h** of the statue was made
7: 9 the hair of his **h** was white like wool.
Mt 8:20 Son of Man has no place to lay his **h.**
Mk 6:28 and brought back his **h** on a platter.
Jn 19: 2 a crown of thorns and put it on his **h.**
Ro 12:20 you will heap burning coals on his **h.**
1Co 11: 3 the **h** of every man is Christ, and the **h** of the woman is man, and the **h** of Christ is God.

	11: 4	or prophesies with his **h** covered
		dishonors his **h.**
	11: 5	prophesies with her **h** uncovered
		dishonors her **h**—
	12:21	And the **h** cannot say to the feet,
Eph	1:22	be **h** over everything for the church,
	5:23	husband is the **h** of the wife as
		Christ is the **h** of the church,
Col	1:18	he is the **h** of the body, the church;
2Ti	4: 5	But you, keep your **h** in all situations
Rev	1:14	His **h** and hair were white like wool,
	10: 1	with a rainbow above his **h;**
	12: 1	and a crown of twelve stars on her **h.**
	13: 1	and on each **h** a blasphemous name.
	14:14	with a crown of gold on his **h**
	19:12	and on his **h** are many crowns.

HEADLONG

Ac	1:18	Judas bought a field; there he fell **h,**

HEADS [HEAD]

Ge	41: 5	a second dream: Seven **h**
Lev	26:13	to walk with **h** held high.
Ne	4: 4	insults back on their own **h.**
Ps	22: 7	they hurl insults, shaking their **h:**
	24: 7	Lift up your **h,** O you gates;
Isa	35:10	everlasting joy will crown their **h.**
	51:11	everlasting joy will crown their **h.**
Eze	11:21	on their own **h** what they have done,
Da	7: 6	This beast had four **h,**
Mt	27:39	insults at him, shaking their **h**
Mk	2:23	they began to pick some **h** of grain.
Lk	21:28	stand up and lift up your **h,**
Ac	18: 6	"Your blood be on your own **h!**
Rev	4: 4	and had crowns of gold on their **h.**
	12: 3	enormous red dragon with seven **h**
	17: 9	The seven **h** are seven hills on which

HEAL* [HEALED, HEALING, HEALS]

Nu	12:13	"O God, please **h** her!"
Dt	32:39	I have wounded and I will **h,**
2Ki	20: 5	I will **h** you.
	20: 8	that the LORD will **h** me
2Ch	7:14	and will **h** their land.
Job	5:18	but his hands also **h.**
Ps	6: 2	**h** me, for my bones are in agony.
	41: 4	"O LORD, have mercy on me; **h** me,
Ecc	3: 3	a time to kill and a time to **h,**
Isa	19:22	he will strike them and **h** them.
	19:22	to their pleas and **h** them.
	57:18	but I will **h** him;
	57:19	"And I will **h** them."
Jer	17:14	**H** me, O LORD.
	30:17	you to health and **h** your wounds,'
	33: 6	and healing to it; I will **h** my people
La	2:13	Who can **h** you?
Hos	5:13	not able to **h** your sores.
	6: 1	torn us to pieces but he will **h** us;
	7: 1	whenever I would **h** Israel,
	14: 4	"I will **h** their waywardness
Na	3:19	Nothing can **h** your wound;
Zec	11:16	or **h** the injured, or feed the healthy,
Mt	8: 7	"I will go and **h** him."
	10: 1	and to **h** every disease

	10: 8	**H** the sick, raise the dead,
	12:10	"Is it lawful to **h** on the Sabbath?"
	13:15	and I would **h** them.'
	17:16	but they could not **h** him."
Mk	3: 2	if he would **h** him on the Sabbath.
	6: 5	on a few sick people and **h** them.
Lk	4:23	to me: 'Physician, **h** yourself!
	5:17	was present for him to **h** the sick.
	6: 7	to see if he would **h** on the Sabbath.
	7: 3	asking him to come and **h** his servant
	8:43	but no one could **h** her.
	9: 2	kingdom of God and to **h** the sick.
	10: 9	**H** the sick who are there
	13:32	and **h** people today and tomorrow,
	14: 3	"Is it lawful to **h** on the Sabbath
Jn	4:47	to come and **h** his son,
	12:40	and I would **h** them."
Ac	4:30	to **h** and perform miraculous signs
	28:27	and I would **h** them.'

HEALED* [HEAL]

Ge	20:17	and God **h** Abimelech,
Ex	21:19	and see that he is completely **h.**
Lev	13:37	the itch is **h.**
	14: 3	If the person has been **h**
Jos	5: 8	they were in camp until they were **h.**
1Sa	6: 3	Then you will be **h,**
2Ki	2:21	the LORD says: 'I have **h** this water.
2Ch	30:20	heard Hezekiah and **h** the people.
Ps	30: 2	called to you for help and you **h** me.
	107:20	He sent forth his word and **h** them;
Isa	6:10	and turn and be **h.**"
	53: 5	and by his wounds we are **h.**
Jer	14:19	so that we cannot be **h?**
	17:14	Heal me, O LORD, and I will be **h;**
	51: 8	perhaps she can be **h.**
	51: 9	" 'We would have **h** Babylon,
	51: 9	but she cannot be **h;**
Eze	34: 4	or **h** the sick or bound up the injured,
Hos	11: 3	not realize it was I who **h** them.
Mt	4:24	and the paralyzed, and he **h** them.
	8: 8	and my servant will be **h.**
	8:13	his servant was **h** at that very hour.
	8:16	and **h** all the sick.
	9:21	If I only touch his cloak, I will be **h.**"
	9:22	he said, "your faith has **h** you."
	9:22	the woman was **h** from that moment.
	12:15	and he **h** all their sick,
	12:22	and Jesus **h** him,
	14:14	on them and **h** their sick.
	14:36	and all who touched him were **h.**
	15:28	And her daughter was **h** from
	15:30	and he **h** them.
	17:18	and he was **h** from that moment.
	19: 2	and he **h** them there.
	21:14	and he **h** them.
Mk	1:34	Jesus **h** many who had various
	3:10	For he had **h** many,
	5:23	on her so that she will be **h** and live."
	5:28	I will be **h.**"
	5:34	"Daughter, your faith has **h** you.
	6:13	sick people with oil and **h** them.
	6:56	and all who touched him were **h.**
	10:52	said Jesus, "your faith has **h** you."

Lk   4:40 hands on each one, he **h** them.
      5:15 and to be **h** of their sicknesses.
      6:18 and to be **h** of their diseases.
      7: 7 and my servant will be **h.**
      8:47 and how she had been instantly **h.**
      8:48 "Daughter, your faith has **h** you.
      8:50 and she will be **h."**
      9:11 and **h** those who needed healing.
      9:42 rebuked the evil spirit, **h** the boy
     13:14 because Jesus had **h** on the Sabbath,
     13:14 So come and be **h** on those days,
     14: 4 he **h** him and sent him away.
     17:15 One of them, when he saw he was **h,**
     18:42 your sight; your faith has **h** you."
     22:51 he touched the man's ear and **h** him.
Jn   5:10 said to the man who had been **h,**
      5:13 The man who was **h** had no idea
Ac   4: 9 and are asked how he was **h,**
      4:10 that this man stands before you **h.**
      4:14 man who had been **h** standing there
      4:22 the man who was miraculously **h**
      5:16 and all of them were **h.**
      8: 7 many paralytics and cripples were **h.**
     14: 9 saw that he had faith to be **h**
     28: 8 placed his hands on him and **h** him.
Heb 12:13 may not be disabled, but rather **h.**
Jas   5:16 for each other so that you may be **h.**
1Pe   2:24 by his wounds you have been **h.**
Rev 13: 3 but the fatal wound had been **h.**
     13:12 whose fatal wound had been **h.**

HEALING* [HEAL]

2Ch 28:15 food and drink, and **h** balm.
Pr   12:18 but the tongue of the wise brings **h.**
     13:17 but a trustworthy envoy brings **h.**
     15: 4 tongue that brings **h** is a tree of life,
     16:24 sweet to the soul and **h** to the bones.
Isa 58: 8 and your **h** will quickly appear;
Jer   8:15 a time of **h** but there was only terror.
      8:22 Why there is there no **h** for the wound
     14:19 a time of **h** but there is only terror.
     30:12 your injury beyond **h.**
     30:13 no **h** for you.
     33: 6 I will bring health and **h** to it;
     46:11 there is no **h** for you.
Eze 30:21 It has not been bound up for **h**
     47:12 for food and their leaves for **h."**
Mal   4: 2 will rise with **h** in its wings.
Mt   4:23 and **h** every disease and sickness
      9:35 and **h** every disease and sickness.
Lk   6:19 coming from him and **h** them all.
      9: 6 the gospel and **h** people everywhere.
      9:11 and healed those who needed **h.**
Jn   7:23 for **h** the whole man on the Sabbath?
Ac   3:16 that has given this complete **h** to him
     10:38 and **h** all who were under the power
1Co 12: 9 to another gifts of **h** by
     12:28 also those having gifts of **h,**
     12:30 Do all have gifts of **h?**
Rev 22: 2 the leaves of the tree are for the **h**

HEALS* [HEAL]

Ex   15:26 for I am the LORD, who **h** you."
Lev 13:18 a boil on his skin and it **h,**

Ps   103: 3 and **h** all your diseases,
     147: 3 He **h** the brokenhearted and binds
Isa   30:26 and **h** the wounds he inflicted.
Ac   9:34 "Jesus Christ **h** you.

HEALTH* [HEALTHIER, HEALTHY]

1Sa 25: 6 Good **h** to you and your household!
     25: 6 And good **h** to all that is yours!
Ps   38: 3 Because of your wrath there is no **h**
     38: 7 there is no **h** in my body.
Pr   3: 8 This will bring **h** to your body
      4:22 and **h** to a man's whole body.
     15:30 and good news gives **h** to the bones.
Isa 38:16 You restored me to **h** and let me live.
Jer 30:17 to **h** and heal your wounds,'
     33: 6 I will bring **h** and healing to it;
3Jn   1: 2 I pray that you may enjoy good **h**

HEALTHIER* [HEALTH]

Da   1:15 the end of the ten days they looked **h**

HEALTHY* [HEALTH]

Ge   41: 5 Seven heads of grain, **h** and good,
     41: 7 swallowed up the seven **h,** full heads.
Ps   73: 4 have no struggles; their bodies are **h**
Zec 11:16 or heal the injured, or feed the **h,**
Mt   9:12 "It is not the **h** who need a doctor,
Mk   2:17 "It is not the **h** who need a doctor,
Lk   5:31 "It is not the **h** who need a doctor,

HEAP [HEAPED, HEAPING]

Ge   31:48 "This **h** is a witness between you
Dt   32:23 "I will **h** calamities upon them
Jos   3:13 be cut off and stand up in a **h."**
1Sa   2: 8 and lifts the needy from the ash **h;**
Pr   25:22 you will **h** burning coals on his head,
Ro   12:20 you will **h** burning coals on his head.
1Th   2:16 always **h** up their sins to the limit.
1Pe   4: 4 and they **h** abuse on you.

HEAPED [HEAP]

Mt   27:44 crucified with him also **h** insults

HEAPING* [HEAP]

Ps   110: 6 **h** up the dead and crushing the rulers
Isa 30: 1 but not by my Spirit, **h** sin upon sin;

HEAR [HEARD, HEARERS, HEARING, HEARS]

Ex   15:14 The nations will **h** and tremble;
     18: 9 Jethro was delighted to **h** about all
     22:27 When he cries out to me, I will **h,**
Nu   14:13 "Then the Egyptians will **h** about it!
Dt   1:17 **h** both small and great alike.
      4:36 From heaven he made you **h** his
      5: 1 **H,** O Israel, the decrees and laws
      6: 3 **H,** O Israel, and be careful to obey so
      6: 4 **H,** O Israel: The LORD our God,
      9: 1 **H,** O Israel. You are now about to
     13:11 Then all Israel will **h** and be afraid,
     19:20 The rest of the people will **h** of this
     20: 3 **"H,** O Israel, today you are going
     31:13 must **h** it and learn to fear
Jos   7: 9 the other people of the country will **h**

1Ki	8:30	**H** from heaven, your dwelling place,
	10: 8	before you and **h** your wisdom!
2Ki	19:16	Give ear, O Lord, and **h;**
2Ch	7:14	then will I **h** from heaven
Job	5:27	So **h** it and apply it to yourself."
	20: 3	I **h** a rebuke that dishonors me,
	26:14	how faint the whisper we **h**
	31:35	that I had someone to **h** me!
Ps	30:10	**H,** O Lord, and be merciful to me;
	51: 8	Let me **h** joy and gladness;
	80: 1	**H** us, O Shepherd of Israel,
	94: 9	he who implanted the ear not **h?**
	95: 7	Today, if you **h** his voice,
	135:17	they have ears, but cannot **h,**
Ecc	7:21	you may **h** your servant cursing you
Isa	1:10	**H** the word of the Lord.
	21: 3	I am staggered by what I **h,**
	29:18	In that day the deaf will **h** the words
	30:21	your ears will **h** a voice behind you,
	51: 7	"**H** me, you who know what is right,
	59: 1	nor his ear too dull to **h.**
	65:24	while they are still speaking I will **h.**
Jer	5:21	**H** this, you foolish
	5:21	who have ears but do not **h:**
Eze	33: 7	so **h** the word I speak
	37: 4	**h** the word of the Lord!
Da	3: 5	soon as you **h** the sound of the horn,
Mic	6: 2	**H,** O mountains, the Lord's
Mt	11: 5	the deaf **h,** the dead are raised,
	11:15	He who has ears, let him **h.**
	13:17	to **h** what you **h** but did not **h** it.
Mk	12:29	'**H,** O Israel, the Lord our God,
Lk	7:22	the deaf **h,** the dead are raised,
Jn	5:25	the dead will **h** the voice of the Son
	8:47	not **h** is that you do not belong
Ac	13: 7	because he wanted to **h** the word
	13:44	the whole city gathered to **h** the word
	17:32	to **h** you again on this subject."
Ro	2:13	For it is not those who **h**
	10:14	And how can they **h** without
2Ti	4: 3	say what their itching ears want to **h.**
Heb	3: 7	if you **h** his voice,
Rev	1: 3	and blessed are those who **h** it

HEARD [HEAR]

Ge	3: 8	the man and his wife **h** the sound of
	21:17	God **h** the boy crying,
Ex	2:24	God **h** their groaning
	6: 5	I have **h** the groaning of the Israelites
	16: 7	he has **h** your grumbling against him.
Nu	12: 2	And the Lord **h** this.
	14:27	I have **h** the complaints
Dt	4:32	has anything like it ever been **h** of?
Jos	24:27	It has **h** all the words the Lord
2Sa	7:22	as we have **h** with our own ears.
1Ki	4:34	who had **h** of his wisdom.
	10: 1	the queen of Sheba **h** about the fame
Ne	9:27	From heaven you **h** them,
Job	42: 5	My ears had **h** of you but
Ps	18: 6	From his temple he **h** my voice;
	62:11	two things have I **h:**
	78:59	God **h** them, he was very angry;
	116: 1	I love the Lord, for he **h** my voice;
Isa	40:21	Have you not **h?**

	40:28	Have you not **h?**
	66: 8	Who has ever **h** of such a thing?
Jer	18:13	Who has ever **h** anything
La	3:56	You **h** my plea:
Eze	10: 5	the wings of the cherubim could be **h**
Da	10:12	your words were **h,**
	12: 8	I **h,** but I did not understand.
Hab	3:16	I **h** and my heart pounded,
Mt	2: 3	King Herod **h** this he was disturbed,
	5:21	"You have **h** that it was said to
	5:27	"You have **h** that it was said to
	5:33	you have **h** that it was said to
	5:38	"You have **h** that it was said,
	5:43	"You have **h** that it was said,
Mk	6: 2	and many who **h** him were amazed.
	14:64	"You have **h** the blasphemy.
	15:39	**h** his cry and saw how he died,
Lk	12: 3	in the dark will be **h** in the daylight,
Jn	8:26	and what I have **h** from him I tell
Ac	2: 6	because each one **h** them speaking
	10:44	the Holy Spirit came on all who **h**
Ro	10:14	in the one of whom they have not **h?**
1Co	2: 9	no ear has **h,**
2Co	12: 4	He **h** inexpressible things,
Gal	3: 2	or by believing what you **h?**
1Th	2:13	which you **h** from us,
2Ti	1:13	What you **h** from me,
Heb	4: 2	the message they **h** was of no value
Jas	1:25	not forgetting what he has **h,**
2Pe	1:18	We ourselves **h** this voice that came
1Jn	1: 3	to you what we have seen and **h,**
	3:11	This is the message you **h** from
2Jn	1: 6	As you have **h** from the beginning,
Rev	1:10	and I **h** behind me a loud voice like
	22: 8	the one who **h** and saw these things.

HEARERS* [HEAR]

1Ti	4:16	save both yourself and your **h.**

HEARING [HEAR]

Nu	11: 1	their hardships in the **h** of the Lord,
Dt	31:11	read this law before them in their **h.**
2Ch	34:30	in their **h** all the words of the Book
Isa	6: 9	Be ever **h,** but never understanding;
Am	8:11	famine of **h** the words of the Lord.
Mt	13:14	of Isaiah: " 'You will be ever **h**
Mk	4:12	and ever **h** but never understanding;
Lk	4:21	this scripture is fulfilled in your **h.''**
Jn	7:51	condemn anyone without first **h** him
Ac	28:26	be ever **h** but never understanding;
Ro	10:17	faith comes from **h** the message,
1Co	12:17	where would the sense of **h** be?

HEARS [HEAR]

Ps	69:33	The Lord **h** the needy and does
Pr	15:29	but he **h** the prayer of the righteous.
Isa	30:19	As soon as he **h,** he will answer you.
Mt	7:24	everyone who **h** these words of mine
Lk	6:47	**h** my words and puts them into
Jn	5:24	whoever **h** my word and believes
1Jn	5:14	according to his will, he **h** us.
Rev	3:20	If anyone **h** my voice and opens
	22:18	I warn everyone who **h** the words of

HEART [BROKENHEARTED;
    FAINTHEARTED, HARDHEARTED,
    HEART'S, HEARTACHE, HEARTLESS,
    HEARTS, HEARTS', KINDHEARTED,
    SIMPLEHEARTED, STOUTHEARTED,
    WHOLEHEARTED, WHOLEHEARTEDLY]

Ge   6: 5 of the thoughts of his **h** was only evil
      6: 6 and his **h** was filled with pain.
     24:45 "Before I finished praying in my **h,**
Ex   4:21 But I will harden his **h** so that he will
      7:13 Yet Pharaoh's **h** became hard
      7:22 and Pharaoh's **h** became hard;
      8:15 he hardened his **h** and would
      8:19 But Pharaoh's **h** was hard
      8:32 also Pharaoh hardened his **h**
      9: 7 Yet his **h** was unyielding
      9:12 But the LORD hardened Pharaoh's **h**
      9:35 So Pharaoh's **h** was hard
     10:20 the LORD hardened Pharaoh's **h,**
     10:27 the LORD hardened Pharaoh's **h,**
     11:10 the LORD hardened Pharaoh's **h,**
     14: 4 And I will harden Pharaoh's **h,**
     25: 2 from each man whose **h** prompts him
     28:30 over Aaron's **h** whenever he enters
     35:21 and whose **h** moved him came
Lev 19:17 Do not hate your brother in your **h.**
Dt   1:28 Our brothers have made us lose **h.**
      4: 9 or let them slip from your **h**
      4:29 all your **h** and with all your soul.
      6: 5 the LORD your God with all your **h**
      8:14 then your **h** will become proud
     10:12 the LORD your God with all your **h**
     11:13 and to serve him with all your **h** and
     13: 3 whether you love him with all your **h**
     15:10 and do so without a grudging **h;**
     26:16 with all your **h** and with all your soul
     29:18 today whose **h** turns away
     30: 2 with all your **h** and with all your soul
     30: 6 you may love him with all your **h**
     30:10 to the LORD your God with all your **h**
     30:14 it is in your mouth and in your **h**
Jos 22: 5 to serve him with all your **h**
     23:14 You know with all your **h** and soul
1Sa 10: 9 God changed Saul's **h,**
     12:20 but serve the LORD with all your **h.**
     12:24 serve him faithfully with all your **h;**
     13:14 a man after his own **h**
     14: 7 "Go ahead; I am with you **h**
     16: 7 but the LORD looks at the **h."**
     17:32 "Let no one lose **h** on account
2Sa   6:16 she despised him in her **h.**
1Ki   2: 4 faithfully before me with all their **h**
      3: 9 a discerning **h** to govern your people
      8:17 "My father David had it in his **h**
      8:48 they turn back to you with all their **h**
      9: 3 and my **h** will always be there.
      9: 4 in integrity of **h** and uprightness,
     10:24 the wisdom God had put in his **h.**
     11: 4 wives turned his **h** after other gods,
     14: 8 and followed me with all his **h,**
     15:14 Asa's **h** was fully committed to

2Ki 22:19 Because your **h** was responsive
     23: 3 regulations and decrees with all his **h**
1Ch 28: 9 for the LORD searches every **h**
2Ch   6:38 they turn back to you with all their **h**
      7:16 and my **h** will always be there.
     15:12 with all their **h** and soul.
     15:17 Asa's **h** was fully committed [to
     17: 6 His **h** was devoted to the ways of
     22: 9 sought the LORD with all his **h."**
     32:25 But Hezekiah's **h** was proud
     34:31 regulations and decrees with all his **h**
     36:13 and hardened his **h** and would
Ezr   1: 1 the LORD moved the **h** of Cyrus king
      1: 5 everyone whose **h** God had moved—
Ne   4: 6 the people worked with all their **h.**
Job 19:27 How my **h** yearns within me!
     22:22 and lay up his words in your **h.**
     31: 7 if my **h** has been led by my eyes,
     37: 1 "At this my **h** pounds and leaps
Ps   7:10 who saves the upright in **h.**
      9: 1 O LORD, with all my **h;**
     14: 1 fool says in his **h,** "There is no God."
     16: 9 Therefore my **h** is glad
     19:14 the meditation of my **h** be pleasing
     20: 4 May he give you the desire of your **h**
     24: 4 who has clean hands and a pure **h,**
     26: 2 examine my **h** and my mind;
     28: 7 My **h** leaps for joy
     37: 4 the desires of your **h.**
     37:31 The law of his God is in his **h;**
     44:21 since he knows the secrets of the **h?**
     45: 1 My **h** is stirred by a noble theme
     51:10 Create in me a pure **h,** O God,
     51:17 a broken and contrite **h,** O God,
     53: 1 fool says in his **h,** "There is no God."
     66:18 If I had cherished sin in my **h,**
     73: 1 to those who are pure in **h.**
     73:26 My flesh and my **h** may fail, but
              God is the strength of my **h**
     86:11 an undivided **h,**
     90:12 that we may gain a **h** of wisdom.
     97:11 and joy on the upright in **h.**
    104:15 wine that gladdens the **h** of man,
    108: 1 My **h** is steadfast, O God;
    109:22 and my **h** is wounded within me.
    111: 1 extol the LORD with all my **h**
    112: 7 **h** is steadfast, trusting in the LORD.
    112: 8 His **h** is secure, he will have no fear;
    119: 2 and seek him with all their **h.**
    119:10 I seek you with all my **h;**
    119:11 I have hidden your word in my **h**
    119:30 I have set my **h** on your laws.
    119:32 for you have set my **h** free.
    119:34 and obey it with all my **h.**
    119:36 Turn my **h** toward your statutes and
    119:58 sought your face with all my **h;**
    119:69 I keep your precepts with all my **h.**
    119:111 they are the joy of my **h.**
    119:112 My **h** is set on keeping your decrees
    119:145 I call with all my **h;**
    119:161 but my **h** trembles at your word.
    125: 4 to those who are upright in **h.**
    138: 1 O LORD, with all my **h;**
    139:23 Search me, O God, and know my **h;**

141: 4 not my **h** be drawn to what is evil,
148:14 of Israel, the people close to his **h.**
Pr   2: 2 applying your **h** to understanding,
    3: 1 but keep my commands in your **h,**
    3: 3 write them on the tablet of your **h.**
    3: 5 Trust in the LORD with all your **h**
    4: 4 of my words with all your **h;**
    4:21 keep them within your **h;**
    4:23 Above all else, guard your **h,**
    6:14 who plots evil with deceit in his **h—**
    6:21 Bind them upon your **h** forever;
    6:25 not lust in your **h** after her beauty
    7: 3 write them on the tablet of your **h.**
  10: 8 The wise in **h** accept commands,
  12:23 but the **h** of fools blurts out folly.
  12:25 An anxious **h** weighs a man down,
  13:12 Hope deferred makes the **h** sick,
  14:13 Even in laughter the **h** may ache,
  14:30 A **h** at peace gives life to the body,
  15:13 A happy **h** makes the face cheerful,
  15:15 the cheerful **h** has a continual feast.
  15:28 **h** of the righteous weighs its answers
  15:30 A cheerful look brings joy to the **h,**
  16: 5 LORD detests all the proud of **h.**
  16:23 A wise man's **h** guides his mouth,
  17: 3 but the LORD tests the **h.**
  17:20 man of perverse **h** does not prosper;
  17:22 A cheerful **h** is good medicine,
  19:21 Many are the plans in a man's **h,**
  20: 9 Who can say, "I have kept my **h** pure
  21: 1 king's **h** is in the hand of the LORD;
  21: 2 but the LORD weighs the **h.**
  22:11 He who loves a pure **h**
  22:15 Folly is bound up in the **h** of a child,
  22:17 the sayings of the wise; apply your **h**
  22:18 in your **h** and have all of them ready
  23:15 My son, if your **h** is wise,
  23:15 then my **h** will be glad;
  23:17 Do not let your **h** envy sinners,
  23:19 and keep your **h** on the right path.
  23:26 give me your **h**
  24:17 do not let your **h** rejoice,
  27:19 so a man's **h** reflects the man.
Ecc 2:10 My **h** took delight in all my work,
   5: 2 do not be hasty in your **h** to utter
   7: 7 and a bribe corrupts the **h.**
   8: 5 the wise **h** will know the proper time
   9: 7 and drink your wine with a joyful **h,**
  11:10 from your **h** and cast off the troubles
SS   3: 1 looked for the one my **h** loves;
   4: 9 You have stolen my **h,** my sister,
   5: 2 I slept but my **h** was awake.
   8: 6 Place me like a seal over your **h,**
Isa 6:10 Make the **h** of this people callused;
  40:11 and carries them close to his **h;**
  57:15 to revive the **h** of the contrite.
  66:14 your **h** will rejoice
Jer 3:10 not return to me with all her **h,**
   3:15 give you shepherds after my own **h,**
   4:14 the evil from your **h** and be saved.
   9:26 house of Israel is uncircumcised in **h.**
  17: 9 The **h** is deceitful above all things
  17:10 "I the LORD search the **h**
  20: 9 his word is in my **h** like a fire,

24: 7 I will give them a **h** to know me,
29:13 when you seek me with all your **h.**
32:39 I will give them singleness of **h**
32:41 in this land with all my **h**
51:46 Do not lose **h** or be afraid
Eze 11:19 from them their **h** of stone and give
         them a **h** of flesh.
  18:31 and get a new **h** and a new spirit.
  28: 2 of your **h** you say, "I am a god;
  36:26 I will give you a new **h** and put
  44: 7 uncircumcised in **h** and flesh
Da 7: 4 and the **h** of a man was given to it.
Hos 11: 8 My **h** is changed within me;
Joel 2:12 "return to me with all your **h,**
   2:13 Rend your **h** and not your garments.
Ob   1: 3 The pride of your **h** has deceived you
Zep 3:14 Be glad and rejoice with all your **h,**
Mal 2: 2 you have not set your **h** to honor me.
Mt 5: 8 Blessed are the pure in **h,**
   5:28 committed adultery with her in his **h.**
   6:21 there your **h** will be also.
  11:29 for I am gentle and humble in **h,**
  12:34 For out of the overflow of the **h**
  13:15 people's **h** has become calloused;
  15:18 out of the mouth come from the **h,**
  15:19 For out of the **h** come evil thoughts,
  18:35 forgive your brother from your **h."**
  22:37 with all your **h** and with all your soul
Mk 11:23 not doubt in his **h** but believes
  12:30 with all your **h** and with all your soul
  12:33 To love him with all your **h,**
Lk 2:19 and pondered them in her **h.**
   2:51 treasured all these things in her **h.**
   6:45 overflow of his **h** his mouth speaks.
   8:15 for those with a noble and good **h,**
  10:27 with all your **h** and with all your soul
  12:34 there your **h** will be also.
  24:25 and how slow of **h** to believe all that
Jn 12:27 "Now my **h** is troubled,
Ac 1:24 "Lord, you know everyone's **h.**
   2:37 they were cut to the **h** and said
   4:32 believers were one in **h** and mind.
   5: 3 so filled your **h** that you have lied to
   8:21 your **h** is not right before God.
  15: 8 God, who knows the **h,**
  16:14 The Lord opened her **h** to respond
  28:27 people's **h** has become calloused;
Ro 1: 9 whom I serve with my whole **h**
   2:29 is circumcision of the **h**
  10: 8 in your mouth and in your **h,"** that is,
  10: 9 believe in your **h** that God raised him
  15: 6 so that with one **h** and mouth
1Co 14:25 the secrets of his **h** will be laid bare.
2Co 2: 4 of great distress and anguish of **h** and
   4: 1 we do not lose **h.**
   4:16 Therefore we do not lose **h.**
   9: 7 decided in his **h** to give,
Eph 1:18 eyes of your **h** may be enlightened
   5:19 Sing and make music in your **h** to
   6: 5 and with sincerity of **h,**
   6: 6 doing the will of God from your **h.**
Php 1: 7 since I have you in my **h;**
Col 2: 2 that they may be encouraged in **h**
   3:22 but with sincerity of **h** and reverence

3:23 work at it with all your **h**,
1Ti 1: 5 from a pure **h** and a good conscience
3: 1 If anyone sets his **h** on being
2Ti 2:22 on the Lord out of a pure **h.**
Phm 1:12 sending him—who is my very **h—**
1:20 refresh my **h** in Christ.
Heb 3:12 unbelieving **h** that turns away from
4:12 the thoughts and attitudes of the **h.**
10:22 a sincere **h** in full assurance of faith,
12: 5 do not lose **h** when he rebukes you,
1Pe 1:22 love one another deeply, from the **h.**
Rev 18: 7 In her **h** she boasts, 'I sit as queen;

ALL ... HEART Dt 4:29; 6:5; 10:12; 11:13;
13:3; 26:16; 30:2, 6, 10; Jos 22:5; 23:14; 1Sa
12:20, 24; 2Sa 3:21; 22:46; 1Ki 2:4; 8:48; 11:37;
14:8; 2Ki 10:31; 23:3, 25; 2Ch 6:38; 15:12; 22:9;
34:31; Ne 4:6; Ps 9:1; 18:45; 86:12; 111:1; 119:2,
10, 34, 58, 69, 145; 138:1; Pr 3:5; 4:4; Jer 3:10;
24:7; 29:13; 32:41; Joel 2:12; Zep 3:14; Mt
22:37; Mk 12:30, 33; Lk 10:27; Col 3:23

HEART'S* [HEART]
2Ch 1:11 "Since this is your **h** desire
Jer 15:16 my joy and my **h** delight,
Eze 24:25 delight of their eyes, their **h** desire,
Ro 10: 1 my **h** desire and prayer to God for

HEARTACHE* [HEART]
Pr 15:13 but **h** crushes the spirit.

HEARTLESS* [HEART]
La 4: 3 but my people have become **h**
Ro 1:31 faithless, **h**, ruthless.

HEARTS [HEART]
Ex 9:34 He and his officials hardened their **h.**
14:17 I will harden the **h** of the Egyptians
Lev 26:36 I will make their **h** so fearful in
26:41 their uncircumcised **h** are humbled
Nu 15:39 going after the lusts of your own **h**
Dt 5:29 that their **h** would be inclined
6: 6 are to be upon your **h.**
10:16 Circumcise your **h**, therefore,
11:18 Fix these words of mine in your **h**
30: 6 will circumcise your **h** and the **h**
Jos 5: 1 their **h** melted and they no longer
7: 5 At this the **h** of the people melted
11:20 Lord himself who hardened their **h**
14: 8 the **h** of the people melt with fear.
24:23 and yield your **h** to the Lord.
1Sa 6: 6 Why do you harden your **h** as
7: 3 returning to the Lord with all your **h**
10:26 men whose **h** God had touched.
2Sa 15: 6 so he stole the **h** of the men of Israel.
1Ki 8:39 (for you alone know the **h** of all
8:61 But your **h** must be fully committed
18:37 you are turning their **h** back again."
1Ch 29:18 in the **h** of your people forever,
29:18 and keep their **h** loyal to you.
2Ch 6:30 (for you alone know the **h** of men),
11:16 of Israel who set their **h** on seeking
29:31 all whose **h** were willing brought
Job 1: 5 and cursed God in their **h.**"
Ps 4: 4 search your **h** and be silent.

7: 9 who searches minds and **h,**
33:15 he who forms the **h** of all,
33:21 In him our **h** rejoice,
62: 8 pour out your **h** to him,
78: 8 whose **h** were not loyal to God,
81:12 over to their stubborn **h**
95: 8 do not harden your **h** as you did
Ecc 3:11 also set eternity in the **h** of men;
9: 3 madness in their **h** while they live,
Isa 26: 8 and renown are the desire of our **h.**
29:13 but their **h** are far from me.
35: 4 to those with fearful **h**, "Be strong,
51: 7 who have my law in your **h:**
59:13 uttering lies our **h** have conceived.
63:17 harden our **h** so we do not revere
65:14 sing out of the joy of their **h,**
Jer 4: 4 to the Lord, circumcise your **h,**
12: 2 on their lips but far from their **h.**
17: 1 on the tablets of their **h**
31:33 in their minds and write it on their **h.**
La 5:15 Joy is gone from our **h;**
Eze 14: 3 these men have set up idols in their **h**
20:16 their **h** were devoted to their idols.
Mal 4: 6 the **h** of the fathers to their children,
Mt 15: 8 but their **h** are far from me.
19: 8 because your **h** were hard.
Mk 6:52 their **h** were hardened.
7: 6 but their **h** are far from me.
7:21 For from within, out of men's **h,**
Lk 1:17 the **h** of the fathers to their children
16:15 but God knows your **h.**
24:32 not our **h** burning within us
Jn 5:42 not have the love of God in your **h.**
12:40 and deadened their **h,**
14: 1 "Do not let your **h** be troubled.
14:27 Do not let your **h** be troubled
Ac 2:46 with glad and sincere **h,**
7:51 with uncircumcised **h** and ears!
11:23 true to the Lord with all their **h.**
15: 9 for he purified their **h** by faith.
28:27 understand with their **h** and turn,
Ro 1:21 and their foolish **h** were darkened.
2:15 of the law are written on their **h,**
5: 5 into our **h** by the Holy Spirit,
8:27 And he who searches our **h** knows
1Co 4: 5 expose the motives of men's **h.**
2Co 1:22 put his Spirit in our **h** as a deposit,
3: 2 written on our **h,**
3: 3 of stone but on tablets of human **h.**
3:15 a veil covers their **h.**
4: 6 made his light shine in our **h**
6:11 and opened wide our **h** to you.
6:13 open wide your **h** also.
7: 2 Make room for us in your **h.**
Gal 4: 6 the Spirit of his Son into our **h,**
Eph 3:17 so that Christ may dwell in your **h**
Php 4: 7 will guard your **h** and your minds
Col 3: 1 set your **h** on things above,
3:15 Let the peace of Christ rule in your **h**
3:16 with gratitude in your **h** to God.
1Th 2: 4 who tests our **h.**
3:13 May he strengthen your **h** so
2Th 2:17 encourage your **h** and strengthen you
Phm 1: 7 have refreshed the **h** of the saints.

Heb 3: 8 do not harden your **h** as you did in
     8:10 and write them on their **h.**
    10:16 I will put my laws in their **h,**
    10:22 having our **h** sprinkled to cleanse us
    13: 9 good for our **h** to be strengthened
Jas 4: 8 you sinners, and purify your **h,**
1Pe 3:15 But in your **h** set apart Christ as Lord
2Pe 1:19 and the morning star rises in your **h.**
1Jn 3:20 whenever our **h** condemn us.
     3:20 For God is greater than our **h,**
Rev 2:23 that I am he who searches **h**
    17:17 their **h** to accomplish his purpose

HEARTS'* [HEART]

Pr 13:25 The righteous eat to their **h** content,

HEAT

Ge   8:22 seedtime and harvest, cold and **h,**
Ps 19: 6 nothing is hidden from its **h.**
2Pe 3:12 and the elements will melt in the **h.**
Rev 16: 9 They were seared by the intense **h**

HEATHEN*

1Th 4: 5 not in passionate lust like the **h,**

HEAVE [OFFERING] (KJV)
See WAVE [OFFERING]

HEAVEN [HEAVENLY, HEAVENS, HEAVENWARD]

Ge 14:19 Creator of **h** and earth.
    21:17 angel of God called to Hagar from **h**
    22:11 the LORD called out to him from **h,**
    24: 3 the God of **h** and the God of earth,
    28:12 with its top reaching to **h,**
Ex 16: 4 "I will rain down bread from **h**
    20:22 that I have spoken to you from **h:**
Dt   3:24 in **h** or on earth who can do the
     4:26 I call **h** and earth as witnesses
    26:15 Look down from **h,**
    30:12 It is not up in **h,**
    31:28 and call **h** and earth to testify
Jos 2:11 for the LORD your God is God in **h**
1Ki 8:23 there is no God like you in **h** above
     8:27 The heavens, even the highest **h,**
     8:30 Hear from **h,** your dwelling place,
    22:19 with all the host of **h** standing
2Ki 1:10 Then fire fell from **h** and consumed
     2: 1 to take Elijah up to **h** in a whirlwind,
    19:15 You have made **h** and earth.
1Ch 29:11 for everything in **h** and earth is yours
2Ch 6:14 there is no God like you in **h** or
     7:14 from **h** and will forgive their sin
Ezr 7:12 a teacher of the Law of the God of **h:**
Job 16:19 Even now my witness is in **h;**
    41:11 Everything under **h** belongs to me.
Ps   2: 4 The One enthroned in **h** laughs;
    73:25 Whom have I in **h** but you?
    75: 5 Do not lift your horns against **h;**
   115: 3 Our God is in **h;**
   121: 2 the Maker of **h** and earth.
Pr 30: 4 Who has gone up to **h** and come
Ecc 3: 1 a season for every activity under **h:**
Isa 14:12 How you have fallen from **h,**

66: 1 the LORD says: "**H** is my throne,
Jer 23:24 "Do not I fill **h** and earth?"
Da   2:19 Then Daniel praised the God of **h**
     7:13 coming with the clouds of **h.**
Mt   3: 2 for the kingdom of **h** is near."
     3:16 At that moment **h** was opened,
     4:17 for the kingdom of **h** is near."
     5:12 because great is your reward in **h,**
     5:19 be called least in the kingdom of **h,**
     6: 9 " 'Our Father in **h,**
     6:10 will be done on earth as it is in **h.**
     6:20 store up for yourselves treasures in **h**
     7:21 Lord,' will enter the kingdom of **h,**
     7:21 the will of my Father who is in **h.**
    16:19 the keys of the kingdom of **h;**
    18: 3 never enter the kingdom of **h.**
    18:18 you bind on earth will be bound in **h,**
    19:14 for the kingdom of **h** belongs to such
    19:21 and you will have treasure in **h.**
    19:23 a rich man to enter the kingdom of **h.**
    23:13 shut the kingdom of **h** in men's faces
    24:35 **H** and earth will pass away,
    26:64 and coming on the clouds of **h.**"
    28:18 "All authority in **h** and on earth
Mk   1:10 he saw **h** being torn open and
     8:11 they asked him for a sign from **h.**
    10:21 and you will have treasure in **h.**
    11:30 John's baptism—was it from **h,**
    13:31 **H** and earth will pass away,
    14:62 and coming on the clouds of **h.**"
Lk   3:21 as he was praying, **h** was opened
     9:54 want us to call fire down from **h**
    10:18 Satan fall like lightning from **h.**
    10:20 that your names are written in **h.**"
    12:33 a treasure in **h** that will not
    15: 7 in **h** over one sinner who repents
    18:22 and you will have treasure in **h.**
    19:38 Peace in **h** and glory in the highest!
    21:33 **H** and earth will pass away,
    24:51 he left them and was taken up into **h.**
Jn   3:13 No one has ever gone into **h** except
                the one who came from **h**—
     6:31 'He gave them bread from **h** to eat.'
     6:38 down from **h** not to do my will but
    12:28 Then a voice came from **h,**
Ac   1:11 who has been taken from you into **h,**
     7:49 " '**H** is my throne,
     7:55 up to **h** and saw the glory of God,
     9: 3 a light from **h** flashed around him.
    11: 5 a large sheet being let down from **h**
    26:19 not disobedient to the vision from **h.**
Ro 10: 6 'Who will ascend into **h?**' "
1Co 15:47 the second man from **h.**
2Co 5: 1 an eternal house in **h,**
    12: 2 was caught up to the third **h.**
Gal 1: 8 or an angel from **h** should preach
Eph 1:10 to bring all things in **h** and
Php 2:10 in **h** and on earth and under the earth,
     3:20 But our citizenship is in **h.**
Col 1: 5 hope that is stored up for you in **h**
     1:16 things in **h** and on earth,
     4: 1 that you also have a Master in **h.**
1Th 1:10 and to wait for his Son from **h,**
     4:16 Lord himself will come down from **h**

Heb 1: 3 at the right hand of the Majesty in **h.**
8: 5 a copy and shadow of what is in **h.**
9:24 he entered **h** itself,
12:23 whose names are written in **h.**
Jas 3:17 the wisdom that comes from **h** is first
1Pe 1: 4 spoil or fade—kept in **h** for you,
3:22 into **h** and is at God's right hand—
2Pe 1:18 heard this voice that came from **h**
3:13 to a new **h** and a new earth,
Rev 4: 1 a door standing open in **h.**
5:13 I heard every creature in **h** and
11:19 Then God's temple in **h** was opened,
12: 1 and wondrous sign appeared in **h:**
12: 7 And there was war in **h.**
15: 5 After this I looked and in **h**
19: 1 of a great multitude in **h** shouting:
19:11 I saw **h** standing open and there
19:14 The armies of **h** were following him,
21: 1 Then I saw a new **h** and a new earth,
21: 2 coming down out of **h** from God,
21:10 coming down out of **h** from God.

GOD OF HEAVEN See GOD

HEAVEN AND EARTH See EARTH

KINGDOM OF HEAVEN See KINGDOM

HEAVENLY [HEAVEN]

Ps 8: 5 a little lower than the **h** beings
11: 4 the LORD is on his **h** throne.
89: 6 like the LORD among the **h** beings?
103:21 Praise the LORD, all his **h** hosts,
Mt 5:48 therefore, as your **h** Father is perfect.
Mk 13:25 and the **h** bodies will be shaken.'
Lk 2:13 the **h** host appeared with the angel,
2Co 5: 2 to be clothed with our **h** dwelling,
Eph 1: 3 who has blessed us in the **h** realms
1:20 at his right hand in the **h** realms,
6:12 forces of evil in the **h** realms.
2Ti 4:18 bring me safely to his **h** kingdom.
Heb 3: 1 who share in the **h** calling,
6: 4 who have tasted the **h** gift,
9:23 for the copies of the **h** things to
12:22 to the **h** Jerusalem,

HEAVENS [HEAVEN]

Ge 1: 1 In the beginning God created the **h**
2: 1 the **h** and the earth were completed
6:17 to destroy all life under the **h,**
7:11 the floodgates of the **h** were opened,
11: 4 with a tower that reaches to the **h,**
Ex 20:11 In six days the LORD made the **h**
Dt 10:14 To the LORD your God belong the **h,**
28:12 The LORD will open the **h,**
33:26 who rides on the **h** to help you and
2Sa 22:10 He parted the **h** and came down;
1Ki 8:27 The **h,** even the highest heaven,
2Ch 2: 6 since the **h,** even the highest **h,**
Ezr 9: 6 and our guilt has reached to the **h.**
Ne 9: 6 You made the **h,**
Job 11: 8 They are higher than the **h**—
38:33 Do you know the laws of the **h?**
Ps 8: 3 When I consider your **h,**
19: 1 The **h** declare the glory of God;
33: 6 word of the LORD were the **h** made,

57: 5 Be exalted, O God, above the **h;**
102:25 and the **h** are the work of your hands.
103:11 as high as the **h** are above the earth,
108: 4 great is your love, higher than the **h;**
115:16 The highest **h** belong to the LORD.
119:89 it stands firm in the **h.**
135: 6 in the **h** and on the earth,
136: 5 by his understanding made the **h,**
139: 8 If I go up to the **h,** you are there;
148: 1 Praise the LORD from the **h,**
Pr 3:19 by understanding he set the **h**
Isa 1: 2 Hear, O **h!**
24:18 The floodgates of the **h** are opened,
40:26 Lift your eyes and look to the **h:**
45: 8 "You **h** above, rain down
51: 6 the **h** will vanish like smoke,
55: 9 "As the **h** are higher than the earth,
65:17 I will create new **h** and a new earth.
Jer 10:11 who did not make the **h** and the earth
31:37 if the **h** above can be measured and
32:17 you have made the **h** and the earth
Eze 1: 1 the **h** were opened and I saw visions
Da 12: 3 will shine like the brightness of the **h**
Joel 2:30 I will show wonders in the **h** and on
Hab 3:11 Sun and moon stood still in the **h** at
Mt 24:31 from one end of the **h** to the other.
Mk 13:27 of the earth to the ends of the **h.**
Eph 4:10 who ascended higher than all the **h,**
Heb 4:14 priest who has gone through the **h,**
7:26 exalted above the **h.**
Jas 5:18 Again he prayed, and the **h** gave rain
2Pe 3: 5 by God's word the **h** existed and
3:10 The **h** will disappear with a roar;
Rev 14: 7 Worship him who made the **h,**

HEAVENWARD* [HEAVEN]

Php 3:14 prize for which God has called me **h**

HEAVIER [HEAVY]

2Ch 10:14 I will make it even **h.**
Pr 27: 3 provocation by a fool is **h** than both.

HEAVY [HEAVIER]

Ex 18:18 The work is too **h** for you;
Dt 25:13 in your bag—one **h,** one light.
1Ki 12: 4 "Your father put a **h** yoke on us,
Ecc 1:13 a **h** burden God has laid on men!
Isa 47: 6 on the aged you laid a very **h** yoke.
Mt 23: 4 They tie up **h** loads and put them

HEBREW [HEBREWS]

Ge 14:13 and reported this to Abram the **H.**
41:12 Now a young **H** was there with us,
Ex 1:19 "**H** women are not like Egyptian
2: 6 "This is one of the **H** babies,"
2:11 He saw an Egyptian beating a **H,**
21: 2 "If you buy a **H** servant,
2Ki 18:26 Don't speak to us in **H** in the hearing
Jer 34: 9 Everyone was to free his **H** slaves,
Jnh 1: 9 "I am a **H** and I worship the LORD,
Php 3: 5 a **H** of Hebrews;

HEBREWS [HEBREW]

Ex 3:18 the God of the **H,** has met with us.

9: 1 the God of the **H**, says:
2Co 11:22 Are they **H**?
Php 3: 5 a Hebrew of **H**;

HEBRON [KIRIATH ARBA]

Ge 13:18 near the great trees of Mamre at **H**,
23: 2 at Kiriath Arba (that is, **H**)
Jos 14:13 and gave him **H** as his inheritance.
20: 7 **H**) in the hill country of Judah.
21:13 of Aaron the priest they gave **H**
Jdg 16: 3 to the top of the hill that faces **H**.
2Sa 2:11 David was king in **H** over the house
3: 2 Sons were born to David in **H**:
1Ch 2:43 The sons of **H**:
11: 1 Israel came together to David at **H**

HEDGE* [HEDGED]

Job 1:10 "Have you not put a **h** around him
Isa 5: 5 I will take away its **h**,
Mic 7: 4 most upright worse than a thorn **h**.

HEDGED* [HEDGE]

Job 3:23 whom God has **h** in?

HEED [HEEDS]

1Sa 15:22 and to **h** is better than the fat of rams.
Pr 16:20 gives **h** to instruction prospers,
Ecc 7: 5 It is better to **h** a wise man's rebuke

HEEDS* [HEED]

Pr 10:17 **h** discipline shows the way to life,
13: 1 A wise son **h** his father's instruction,
13:18 but whoever **h** correction is honored.
15: 5 **h** correction shows prudence.
15:32 **h** correction gains understanding.

HEEL

Ge 3:15 and you will strike his **h**."
25:26 his hand grasping Esau's **h**;
Ps 41: 9 has lifted up his **h** against me.
Jn 13:18 lifted up his **h** against me.'

HEGAI

Est 2: 3 the care of **H**, the king's eunuch,

HEIFER

Ge 15: 9 LORD said to him, "Bring me a **h**,
Nu 19: 2 a red **h** without defect or blemish and
Jdg 14:18 "If you had not plowed with my **h**,
Heb 9:13 and the ashes of a **h** sprinkled

HEIGHT [HEIGHTS]

Nu 23: 3 Then he went off to a barren **h**.
1Sa 16: 7 not consider his appearance or his **h**,
Ro 8:39 neither **h** nor depth, nor anything
Rev 2: 5 the **h** from which you have fallen!

HEIGHTS [HEIGHT]

2Sa 1:19 O Israel, lies slain on your **h**.
Job 22:12 "Is not God in the **h** of heaven?
Ps 18:33 he enables me to stand on the **h**.
148: 1 praise him in the **h** above.
Ob 1: 3 and make your home on the **h**,
Hab 3:19 he enables me to go on the **h**.

HEIR [INHERIT]

Ge 15: 4 from your own body will be your **h**."
Lk 20:14 'This is the **h**,' they said.
Ro 4:13 the promise that he would be **h** of
Gal 4: 7 God has made you also an **h**.
Heb 1: 2 whom he appointed **h** of all things,
11: 7 and became **h** of the righteousness

HEIRS [INHERIT]

Ro 4:14 For if those who live by law are **h**,
8:17 **h** of God and co-heirs with Christ,
Gal 3:29 and **h** according to the promise.
Eph 3: 6 the gospel the Gentiles are **h** together
Tit 3: 7 we might become **h** having the hope
Heb 11: 9 **h** with him of the same promise.
1Pe 3: 7 and as **h** with you of the gracious gift

HELD [HOLD]

Ex 17:11 As long as Moses **h** up his hands,
Dt 4: 4 you who **h** fast to the LORD
1Ki 11: 2 Solomon **h** fast to them in love.
2Ki 18: 6 He **h** fast to the LORD and did
Ps 17: 5 My steps have **h** to your paths;
SS 3: 4 I **h** him and would not let him go
Isa 40:12 Who has **h** the dust of the earth in
65: 2 All day long I have **h** out my hands
Ro 10:21 "All day long I have **h** out my hands
Gal 3:23 we were **h** prisoners by the law,
Col 2:19 and **h** together by its ligaments
Rev 1:16 In his right hand he **h** seven stars,
6: 2 Its rider **h** a bow,
15: 2 They **h** harps given them by God
17: 4 She **h** a golden cup in her hand,

HELDAI

Zec 6:14 The crown will be given to **H**,

HELL*

Mt 5:22 will be in danger of the fire of **h**.
5:29 to be thrown into **h**.
5:30 for your whole body to go into **h**.
10:28 can destroy both soul and body in **h**.
18: 9 and be thrown into the fire of **h**.
23:15 twice as much a son of **h** as you are.
23:33 you escape being condemned to **h**?
Mk 9:43 than with two hands to go into **h**,
9:45 have two feet and be thrown into **h**.
9:47 have two eyes and be thrown into **h**,
Lk 12: 5 has power to throw you into **h**.
16:23 In **h**, where he was in torment,
Jas 3: 6 and is itself set on fire by **h**.
2Pe 2: 4 but sent them to **h**,

HELMET

Ps 108: 8 Ephraim is my **h**, Judah my scepter.
Isa 59:17 and the **h** of salvation on his head;
Eph 6:17 Take the **h** of salvation and the
1Th 5: 8 and the hope of salvation as a **h**.

HELP [HELPED, HELPER, HELPFUL, HELPING, HELPLESS, HELPS]

Ge 4: 1 "With the **h** of the LORD
Ex 2:23 cry for **h** because of their slavery
4:12 Now go; I will **h** you speak

23: 5 be sure you **h** him with it.
Lev 25:35 **h** him as you would an alien or
Dt 33:26 who rides on the heavens to **h** you
Jos 24: 7 But they cried to the LORD for **h,**
1Ch 12:22 Day after day men came to **h** David,
2Ch 16:12 he did not seek **h** from the LORD,
28:16 sent to the king of Assyria for **h.**
Ezr 4: 2 "Let us **h** you build because,
Ne 6:16 had been done with the **h** of our God.
Job 29:12 I rescued the poor who cried for **h,**
Ps 18: 6 to my God for **h.**
22:24 but has listened to his cry for **h.**
30: 2 to you for **h** and you healed me.
33:20 he is our **h** and our shield.
40:17 You are my **h** and my deliverer;
46: 1 an ever-present **h** in trouble.
72:12 the afflicted who have no one to **h.**
79: 9 **H** us, O God our Savior,
108:12 for the **h** of man is worthless.
115: 9 he is their **h** and shield.
121: 1 where does my **h** come from?
146: 5 Blessed is he whose **h** is the God
Ecc 4:10 his friend can **h** him up.
Isa 41:10 I will strengthen you and **h** you;
49: 8 in the day of salvation I will **h** you;
La 1: 7 there was no one to **h** her.
Jnh 2: 2 the depths of the grave I called for **h,**
Mk 7:11 'Whatever **h** you might otherwise
9:24 **h** me overcome my unbelief!'
Lk 11:46 will not lift one finger to **h** them.
Ac 16: 9 "Come over to Macedonia and **h** us."
18:27 he was a great **h** to those who
20:35 by this kind of hard work we must **h**
26:22 I have had God's **h** to this very day,
1Co 12:28 those able to **h** others,
2Co 9: 2 For I know your eagerness to **h,**
1Th 5:14 **h** the weak, be patient with everyone.
1Ti 5:16 church can **h** those widows who are
Heb 2:18 to **h** those who are being tempted.
4:16 find grace to **h** us in our time of need

HELPED [HELP]

1Sa 7:12 "Thus far has the LORD **h** us."
Ps 118:13 but the LORD **h** me.
Mk 1:31 took her hand and **h** her up.
Lk 1:54 He has **h** his servant Israel,
2Co 6: 2 and in the day of salvation I **h** you."

HELPER [HELP]

Ge 2:18 I will make a **h** suitable for him."
Ex 18: 4 "My father's God was my **h;**
Dt 33:29 He is your shield and **h**
Ps 10:14 you are the **h** of the fatherless.
118: 7 The LORD is with me; he is my **h.**
Heb 13: 6 "The Lord is my **h;**

HELPFUL [HELP]

Eph 4:29 but only what is **h** for building others

HELPING [HELP]

Ezr 5: 2 prophets of God were with them, **h**
Lk 8: 3 These women were **h** to support
Ac 9:36 who was always doing good and **h**
1Ti 5:10 **h** those in trouble

HELPLESS [HELP]

Ps 10:12 Do not forget the **h.**
Pr 28:15 a wicked man ruling over a **h** people.
Mt 9:36 because they were harassed and **h,**

HELPS [HELP]

Ps 37:40 The LORD **h** them
Isa 50: 7 Because the Sovereign LORD **h** me,
Ro 8:26 the Spirit **h** us in our weakness.
Heb 2:16 For surely it is not angels he **h,**

HEM

1Sa 15:27 Saul caught hold of the **h** of his robe,
Ps 139: 5 You **h** me in—
Hab 1: 4 The wicked **h** in the righteous,

HEMAN

1Ki 4:31 wiser than **H,** Calcol and Darda,
1Ch 15:19 The musicians **H,** Asaph and Ethan
Ps 88: T A maskil of **H** the Ezrahite.

HEN

Mt 23:37 as a **h** gathers her chicks
Lk 13:34 as a **h** gathers her chicks

HEPHZIBAH

Isa 62: 4 But you will be called **H,**

HERALD

Hab 2: 2 on tablets so that a **h** may run with it.
1Ti 2: 7 for this purpose I was appointed a **h**
2Ti 1:11 of this gospel I was appointed a **h**

HERBS

Ex 12: 8 along with bitter **h,**
Nu 9:11 with unleavened bread and bitter **h.**
La 3:15 with bitter **h** and sated me with gall.

HERD [HERDS, HERDSMEN]

Lev 27:32 The entire tithe of the **h** and flock—
Mt 8:31 send us into the **h** of pigs."

HERDS [HERD]

Nu 32: 1 who had very large **h** and flocks,
Dt 8:13 when your **h** and flocks grow large
12: 6 the firstborn of your **h** and flocks.

HERDSMEN [HERD]

Ge 13: 7 quarreling arose between Abram's **h**
26:20 **h** of Gerar quarreled with Isaac's **h**

HERE

Ge 3:12 "The woman you put **h** with me—
22: 1 "**H** I am," he replied.
Ex 3: 4 And Moses said, "**H** I am."
1Sa 3: 4 Samuel answered, "**H** I am."
Ps 40: 7 Then I said, "**H** I am, I have come—
Pr 9: 4 "Let all who are simple come in **h!**"
Isa 6: 8 And I said, "**H** am I.
40: 9 "**H** is your God!"
Eze 7:10 "The day is **h!**
Mt 12:42 now one greater than Solomon is **h.**
24:23 'Look, **h** is the Christ!'
Mk 14:42 **H** comes my betrayer!"
16: 6 He is not **h.**

Lk   24: 6 He is not **h**; he has risen!
Heb 10: 7 Then I said, '**H** I am—
Rev   3:20 **H** I am!
         4: 1 like a trumpet said, "Come up **h,**
       11:12 saying to them, "Come up **h."**

HERESIES*

2Pe   2: 1 will secretly introduce destructive **h,**

HERITAGE [INHERIT]

Ps   61: 5 you have given me the **h**
     119:111 Your statutes are my **h** forever;
       127: 3 Sons are a **h** from the LORD,
Isa   54:17 the **h** of the servants of the LORD,

HERMON

Dt   3: 8 the Arnon Gorge as far as Mount **H.**
Ps   133: 3 It is as if the dew of **H** were falling

HERO* [HEROES]

1Sa 17:51 Philistines saw that their **h** was dead,
Isa   3: 2 the **h** and warrior,

HEROD [HERODIANS]

1. King of Judea who tried to kill Jesus (Mt 2; Lk 1:5).

2. Son of 1. Tetrarch of Galilee who arrested and beheaded John the Baptist (Mt 14:1-12; Mk 6:14-29; Lk 3:1, 19-20; 9:7-9); tried Jesus (Lk 23:6-15).

3. Grandson of 1. King of Judea who killed James (Ac 12:2); arrested Peter (Ac 12:3-19). Death (Ac 12:19-23).

HERODIANS* [HEROD]

Mt   22:16 disciples to him along with the **H.**
Mk   3: 6 and began to plot with the **H**
       12:13 some of the Pharisees and **H** to Jesus

HERODIAS

Wife of Herod the Tetrarch who persuaded her daughter to ask for John the Baptist's head (Mt 14:1-12; Mk 6:14-29).

HEROES [HERO]

Isa   5:22 to those who are **h** at drinking wine

HESHBON

Nu   21:26 **H** was the city of Sihon king of
Dt   3: 6 we had done with Sihon king of **H,**

HESITATED

Ge   19:16 he **h,** the men grasped his hand
Ac   20:27 For I have not **h** to proclaim to you

HEWN*

Pr   9: 1 she has **h** out its seven pillars.
Isa   51: 1 the quarry from which you were **h;**

HEZEKIAH

King of Judah. Restored the temple and worship (2Ch 29-31). Sought the LORD for help against Assyria (2Ki 18-19; 2Ch 32:1-23; Isa 36-37). Illness healed (2Ki 20:1-11; 2Ch 32:24-26; Isa 38).

Judged for showing Babylonians his treasures (2Ki 20:12-21; 2Ch 32:31; Isa 39).

HEZRON

Ru   4:18 Perez was the father of **H,**
Mt   1: 3 Perez the father of **H,**

HID [HIDE]

Ge   3: 8 and they **h** from the LORD God
Ex   2: 2 she **h** him for three months.
         3: 6 At this, Moses **h** his face,
Jos   2: 4 because she **h** the spies we sent.
1Ki 18:13 I **h** a hundred of the LORD's prophets
2Ch 22:11 she **h** the child from Athaliah
Isa   49: 2 in the shadow of his hand he **h** me;
         54: 8 surge of anger I **h** my face from you
Eze   39:23 So I **h** my face from them
Mt   13:44 When a man found it, he **h** it again,
         25:25 and went out and **h** your talent in
Heb 11:23 By faith Moses' parents **h** him

HIDDEN [HIDE]

Ge   4:14 and I will be **h** from your presence;
Jos   2: 6 and **h** them under the stalks of flax
         7:22 and there it was, **h** in his tent,
1Sa 10:22 he has **h** himself among
2Ki 11: 3 He remained **h** with his nurse at
Job 38:11 and brings **h** things to light.
Ps   19:12 Forgive my **h** faults.
         69: 5 my guilt is not **h** from you.
         78: 2 I will utter **h** things,
     119:11 I have **h** your word in my heart
       142: 3 men have **h** a snare for me.
Pr   2: 4 and search for it as for **h** treasure,
         27: 5 Better is open rebuke than **h** love.
Ecc 12:14 including every **h** thing,
Isa   40:27 "My way is **h** from the LORD;
         59: 2 your sins have **h** his face
Da   2:22 He reveals deep and **h** things;
Mt   5:14 A city on a hill cannot be **h.**
       10:26 or **h** that will not be made known.
       13:35 I will utter things **h** since the creation
       13:44 of heaven is like treasure **h** in a field.
Mk   4:22 For whatever is **h** is meant to
Lk   10:21 because you have **h** these things
       18:34 Its meaning was **h** from them,
Ro   16:25 of the mystery **h** for long ages past,
1Co   2: 7 has been **h** and that God destined
         4: 5 to light what is **h** in darkness
Eph   3: 9 for ages past was kept **h** in God,
Col   1:26 the mystery that has been kept **h**
         2: 3 in whom are **h** all the treasures
         3: 3 your life is now **h** with Christ in God
Heb   4:13 in all creation is **h** from God's sight.
Rev   2:17 I will give some of the **h** manna.

HIDE [HID, HIDDEN, HIDES, HIDING]

Ge   18:17 "Shall I **h** from Abraham what I am
Ex   2: 3 But when she could **h** him no longer,
Lev   4:11 But the **h** of the bull and all its flesh,
Nu   19: 5 the heifer is to be burned—its **h,**
Dt   31:17 I will **h** my face
Ps   13: 1 How long will you **h** your face
       17: 8 **h** me in the shadow of your wings

27: 5 **h** me in the shelter of his tabernacle
51: 9 **H** your face from my sins
143: 9 O LORD, for I **h** myself in you.
Isa 53: 3 one from whom men **h** their faces
Eze 39:29 I will no longer **h** my face from them
Rev 6:16 "Fall on us and **h** us from the face

HIDES [HIDE]

Ex 26:14 over that a covering of **h** of sea cows
Nu   4: 6 Then they are to cover this with **h**
Isa 45:15 Truly you are a God who **h** himself,
Lk   8:16 No one lights a lamp and **h** it in a jar

HIDING [HIDE]

Ps 32: 7 You are my **h** place;
Pr 28:12 wicked rise to power, men go into **h.**

HIGH [HIGHER, HIGHEST, HIGHLY]

Ge 14:18 He was priest of God Most **H,**
14:22 to the LORD, God Most **H,**
Lev 16:32 to succeed his father as **h** priest is
26:30 I will destroy your **h** places,
1Sa 2: 1 in the LORD my horn is lifted **h.**
1Ki 3: 2 were still sacrificing at the **h** places,
11: 7 Solomon built a **h** place for Chemosh
12:31 Jeroboam built shrines on **h** places
Ps   7: 7 Rule over them from on **h;**
7:10 My shield is God Most **H,**
21: 7 the unfailing love of the Most **H**
46: 4 holy place where the Most **H** dwells.
82: 6 you are all sons of the Most **H.'**
103:11 **h** as the heavens are above the earth,
113: 5 the One who sits enthroned on **h,**
Pr 24: 7 Wisdom is too **h** for a fool;
Isa 14:14 I will make myself like the Most **H."**
Jer 2:20 on every **h** hill and under every
Eze 1:26 and **h** above on the throne was
Da   4:17 that the Most **H** is sovereign over
Mic 1: 3 and treads the **h** places of the earth.
Mt   4: 8 devil took him to a very **h** mountain
17: 1 up a **h** mountain by themselves.
Mk   5: 7 Jesus, Son of the Most **H** God?
14:53 They took Jesus to the **h** priest,
Jn 18:22 the way you answer the **h** priest?"
Ac 23: 4 "You dare to insult God's **h** priest?"
Eph 3:18 and **h** and deep is the love of Christ,
4: 8 "When he ascended on **h,**
Heb 2:17 a merciful and faithful **h** priest
7: 1 of Salem and priest of God Most **H.**
7:26 Such a **h** priest meets our need—

HIGH PLACE [1Sa 9:12, 13, 14, 19, 25; 10:5,

13; 1Ki 3:4; 11:7; 2Ki 17:11; 23:15, 15, 15; 1Ch
16:39; 21:29; 2Ch 1:3, 13; Isa 16:12; Eze 20:29;
Mic 1:5; Lk 4:5

HIGH PLACES Lev 26:30; Nu 33:52; Dt

33:29; 1Ki 3:2, 3; 12:31, 32; 13:2, 32, 33, 33;
14:23; 15:14; 22:43; 2Ki 12:3; 14:4; 15:4, 35;
16:4; 17:9, 11, 29, 32; 18:4, 22; 21:3; 23:5, 8, 9, 13,
19, 20; 2Ch 11:15; 14:3, 5; 15:17; 17:6; 20:33;
21:11; 28:4, 25; 31:1; 32:12; 33:3, 17, 19; 34:3;
Ps 78:58; Isa 15:2; 36:7; Jer 7:31; 17:3; 19:5;
32:35; 48:35; Eze 6:3, 6; 16:16; 43:7; Hos 10:8;
Am 4:13; 7:9; Mic 1:3

HIGH PRIEST Lev 16:32; 21:10; Nu 35:25, 28,

28, 32; Jos 20:6; 2Ki 12:10; 22:4, 8; 23:4; 2Ch
34:9; Ne 3:1, 20; 13:28; Hag 1:1, 12, 14; 2:2, 4;
Zec 3:1, 8; 6:11; Mt 26:3, 51, 57, 58, 62, 63, 65;
Mk 2:26; 14:47, 53, 54, 60, 61, 63, 66; Lk 22:50,
54; Jn 11:49, 51; 18:13, 15, 16, 19, 22, 24; Ac
4:6; 5:17, 21, 27; 7:1; 9:1; 22:5; 23:2, 4, 5; 24:1;
Heb 2:17; 3:1; 4:14, 15; 5:1, 5, 10; 6:20; 7:26;
8:1, 3; 9:7, 11, 25; 13:11

MOST HIGH Ge 14:18, 19, 20, 22; Nu 24:16; Dt

32:8; 2Sa 22:14; 23:1; Ps 7:8, 10, 17; 9:2; 18:13;
21:7; 46:4; 47:2; 50:14; 57:2; 73:11; 77:10;
78:17, 35, 56; 82:6; 83:18; 87:5; 91:1, 9; 92:1;
97:9; 107:11; Isa 14:14; La 3:35, 38; Da 3:26;
4:2, 17, 24, 25, 32, 34; 5:18, 21; 7:18, 22, 25, 27;
Hos 7:16; 11:7; Mk 5:7; Lk 1:32, 35, 76; 6:35;
8:28; Ac 7:48; 16:17; Heb 7:1

HIGHER [HIGH]

Dt 28:43 will rise above you **h** and **h,**
Ps 61: 2 to the rock that is **h** than I.
108: 4 great is your love, **h** than the heavens
Isa 55: 9 "As the heavens are **h** than the earth,

HIGHEST [HIGH]

1Ki 8:27 The heavens, even the **h** heaven,
Ps 115:16 The **h** heavens belong to the LORD,
Pr   9: 3 she calls from the **h** point of the city.
Mt   4: 5 and had him stand on the **h** point
21: 9 "Hosanna in the **h!"**
Lk   2:14 "Glory to God in the **h,**
19:38 Peace in heaven and glory in the **h!"**
Php 2: 9 God exalted him to the **h** place

HIGHLY [HIGH]

Ex 15: 1 for he is **h** exalted.
1Ch 29:25 The LORD **h** exalted Solomon in
Da 10:11 "Daniel, you who are **h** esteemed,
Lk   1:28 "Greetings, you who are **h** favored!
Ro 12: 3 of yourself more **h** than you ought,

HIGHWAY

Pr   7:27 Her house is a **h** to the grave,
16:17 The **h** of the upright avoids evil;
Isa 40: 3 in the wilderness a **h** for our God.

HILKIAH

2Ki 22:10 **"H** the priest has given me a book."
2Ch 34:14 **H** the priest found the Book of the

HILL [HILLS]

Ex 17: 9 I will stand on top of the **h**
1Sa 17: 3 The Philistines occupied one **h** and
1Ki 16:24 He bought the **h** of Samaria from
Ps 15: 1 Who may live on your holy **h?**
24: 3 Who may ascend the **h** of the LORD?
Isa 40: 4 every mountain and **h** made low;
Jer 26:18 the temple **h** a mound overgrown
Da   9:16 your city, your holy **h.**
Mic 3:12 the temple **h** a mound overgrown
Mt   5:14 A city on a **h** cannot be hidden.
Lk   3: 5 every mountain and **h** made low;

HILL COUNTRY Ge 10:30; 14:6; 31:21, 23, 25,

54; 36:8, 9; Nu 13:17, 29; 14:40, 44, 45; Dt 1:7,

19, 20, 24, 41, 43; 2:1, 3, 5; 3:12, 25; Jos 9:1;
10:6, 40; 11:3, 16, 21; 12:8; 14:12; 15:48; 16:1;
17:15-16, 18; 18:12; 19:50; 20:7; 21:11, 21; 24:4,
30, 33; Jdg 1:9, 19, 34; 2:9; 3:27; 4:5; 7:24; 10:1;
12:15; 17:1, 8; 18:2-13; 19:1, 16, 18; 1Sa 1:1;
9:4; 13:2; 14:22; 2Sa 20:21; 1Ki 4:8; 12:25; 2Ki
5:22; 1Ch 4:42; 6:67; 2Ch 13:4; 19:4; Ne 8:15;
Ps 78:54; Jer 17:26; 32:44; 33:13; Lk 1:39, 65

HOLY HILL See HOLY

HILLS [HILL]

1Ki 20:23 "Their gods are gods of the **h.**
2Ch 18:16 the **h** like sheep without a shepherd
Ps   50:10 and the cattle on a thousand **h.**
      114: 6 that you skipped like rams, you **h,**
     121: 1 I lift up my eyes to the **h—**
Pr   8:25 before the **h,** I was given birth,
Isa   2: 2 be raised above the **h,**
Hos 10: 8 and to the **h,** "Fall on us!"
Joel 3:18 and the **h** will flow with milk;
Am   9:13 and flow from all the **h.**
Lk 23:30 and to the **h,** "Cover us!" '
Rev 17: 9 The seven heads are seven **h**

HINDER [HINDERED, HINDERS, HINDRANCE]

1Sa 14: 6 Nothing can **h** the LORD from saving,
Mt 19:14 and do not **h** them,
1Co 9:12 anything rather than **h** the gospel
1Pe 3: 7 so that nothing will **h** your prayers.

HINDERED* [HINDER]

Lk 11:52 you have **h** those who were entering.
Ro 15:22 often been **h** from coming to you.

HINDERS* [HINDER]

Heb 12: 1 let us throw off everything that **h** and

HINDRANCE* [HINDER]

Ac 28:31 without **h** he preached the kingdom

HINGES*

Pr 26:14 As a door turns on its **h,**

HINT*

Eph 5: 3 not be even a **h** of sexual immorality,

HIP

Ge 32:25 he touched the socket of Jacob's **h**
            so that his **h** was wrenched

HIRAM

King of Tyre; helped David build his palace
(2Sa 5:11-12; 1Ch 14:1); helped Solomon build
the temple (1Ki 5; 2Ch 2) and his navy (1Ki
9:10-27; 2Ch 8).

HIRE [HIRED, HIRES]

1Sa 2: 5 Those who were full **h** themselves
Mt 20: 1 early in the morning to **h** men

HIRED [HIRE]

Lev 19:13 the wages of a **h** man overnight.
Dt 23: 4 and they **h** Balaam son of Beor

24:14 of a **h** man who is poor and needy,
Ezr 4: 5 They **h** counselors to work against
Ne 6:13 He had been **h** to intimidate me so
Lk 15:15 So he went and **h** himself out to
Jn 10:12 The **h** hand is not the shepherd

HIRES* [HIRE]

Pr 26:10 he who **h** a fool or any passer-by.

HISTORY*

Ezr 4:19 that this city has a long **h** of revolt

HIT [HITS]

Ex 21:22 are fighting **h** a pregnant woman
Dt 19: 5 and **h** his neighbor and kill him.
Pr 23:35 "They **h** me," you will say,
Lk 22:64 Who **h** you?"

HITS [HIT]

Ex 21:26 a man **h** a manservant or maidservant

HITTITE [HITTITES]

Ge 23:10 Ephron the **H** was sitting among his
     27:46 because of these **H** women.
Jos 1: 4 all the **H** country—
2Sa 11: 3 and the wife of Uriah the **H?"**
     11:17 Uriah the **H** died.

HITTITES [HITTITE]

Ge 25:10 Abraham had bought from the **H.**
Dt 20:17 Completely destroy them—the **H,**
Ezr 9: 1 **H,** Perizzites, Jebusites, Ammonites,

HIVITES

Ex 23:28 hornet ahead of you to drive the **H,**
Jos 9: 7 The men of Israel said to the **H,**

HOARDED [HOARDS]

Ecc 5:13 grievous evil under the sun: wealth **h**
Jas 5: 3 You have **h** wealth in the last days.

HOARDS* [HOARDED]

Pr 11:26 People curse the man who **h** grain,

HOBAB

Nu 10:29 Now Moses said to **H** son of Reuel

HOLD [HELD, HOLDING, HOLDS]

Ex 4: 4 So Moses reached out and took **h** of
     9: 2 and continue to **h** them back,
    20: 7 **h** anyone guiltless who misuses his
Lev 19:13 " 'Do not **h** back the wages of
Dt   5:11 **h** anyone guiltless who misuses his
    11:22 in all his ways and to **h** fast to him—
    13: 4 and **h** fast to him.
    30:20 listen to his voice, and **h** fast to him.
Jos 22: 5 to **h** fast to him and to serve him
2Sa 6: 6 and took **h** of the ark of God,
2Ki 4:16 "you will **h** a son in your arms."
Ps 18:16 down from on high and took **h** of me
  73:23 you **h** me by my right hand.
 119:31 I **h** fast to your statutes, O LORD;
Pr 4: 4 "Lay **h** of my words
    5:22 the cords of his sin **h** him fast.
Isa 22:17 the LORD is about to take firm **h**

41:13 who takes **h** of your right hand
54: 2 do not **h** back;
Jer 6:11 and I cannot **h** it in.
Eze 3:18 and I will **h** you accountable
3:20 and I will **h** you accountable
33: 6 I will **h** the watchman accountable
Zec 8:23 and nations will take firm **h**
Mk 11:25 if you **h** anything against anyone,
Jn 8:31 Jesus said, "If you **h** to my teaching,
20:17 Jesus said, "Do not **h** on to me,
Ac 2:24 for death to keep its **h** on him.
7:60 do not **h** this sin against them."
1Co 15: 2 you **h** firmly to the word I preached
Php 2:16 as you **h** out the word of life—
3:12 but I press on to take **h** of that for
which Christ Jesus took **h** of me.
Col 1:17 and in him all things **h** together.
1Th 5:21 Test everything. **H** on to the good.
2Th 2:15 and **h** to the teachings we passed on
1Ti 3: 9 They must keep **h** of the deep truths
6:12 Take **h** of the eternal life
6:19 so that they may take **h** of the life
Tit 1: 9 He must **h** firmly to the trustworthy
Heb 3:14 **h** firmly till the end the confidence
4:14 let us **h** firmly to the faith we profess
6:18 to take **h** of the hope offered
10:23 Let us **h** unswervingly to
Rev 1:18 And I **h** the keys of death and Hades.
12:17 and **h** to the testimony of Jesus.
19:10 who **h** to the testimony

HOLDING [HOLD]

Ne 4:21 the work with half the men **h** spears,
Mk 7: 3 **h** to the tradition of the elders.
1Co 11: 2 and for **h** to the teachings,

HOLDS [HOLD]

Pr 3:35 but fools he **h** up to shame.
10:19 but he who **h** his tongue is wise.
17:28 and discerning if he **h** his tongue.
2Th 2: 7 but the one who now **h** it back
Heb 2:14 who **h** the power of death—
Rev 2: 1 of him who **h** the seven stars
3: 1 him who **h** the seven spirits of God
3: 7 who **h** the key of David.

HOLE [HOLES]

Isa 11: 8 The infant will play near the **h** of

HOLES [HOLE]

Hag 1: 6 to put them in a purse with **h** in it."
Mt 8:20 Jesus replied, "Foxes have **h**

HOLIEST* [HOLY]

Nu 18:29 LORD's portion the best and **h** part

HOLINESS* [HOLY]

Ex 15:11 Who is like you—majestic in **h**,
Dt 32:51 not uphold my **h** among the Israelites
1Ch 16:29 the LORD in the splendor of his **h**.
2Ch 20:21 praise him for the splendor of his **h**
Ps 29: 2 the LORD in the splendor of his **h**.
89:35 Once for all, I have sworn by my **h**
93: 5 **h** adorns your house for endless days

96: 9 the LORD in the splendor of his **h**;
Isa 29:23 the **h** of the Holy One of Jacob,
35: 8 it will be called the Way of **H**.
Eze 36:23 I will show the **h** of my great name,
38:23 I will show my greatness and my **h**,
Am 4: 2 LORD has sworn by his **h**:
Lk 1:75 in **h** and righteousness
Ro 1: 4 through the Spirit of **h** was declared
6:19 slavery to righteousness leading to **h**.
6:22 the benefit you reap leads to **h**,
1Co 1:30 our righteousness, **h** and redemption.
2Co 1:12 the **h** and sincerity that are from God
7: 1 perfecting **h** out of reverence
Eph 4:24 like God in true righteousness and **h**.
1Ti 2: 2 and quiet lives in all godliness and **h**.
2:15 love and **h** with propriety.
Heb 12:10 that we may share in his **h**.
12:14 without **h** no one will see the Lord.

HOLLOW

Ex 27: 8 Make the altar **h**, out of boards.
Pr 30: 4 the wind in the **h** of his hands?
Isa 40:12 the waters in the **h** of his hand,
Col 2: 8 through **h** and deceptive philosophy,

HOLY [HALLOWED, HOLIEST, HOLINESS]

Ge 2: 3 the seventh day and made it **h**,
Ex 3: 5 where you are standing is **h** ground."
16:23 a **h** Sabbath to the LORD.
19: 6 a kingdom of priests and a **h** nation.'
20: 8 the Sabbath day by keeping it **h**.
26:33 The curtain will separate the **H**
Place from the Most **H** Place.
28:36 as on a seal: **H** TO THE LORD.
29:37 Then the altar will be most **h**,
30:10 It is most **h** to the LORD."
30:29 so they will be most **h**,
31:13 who makes you **h**.
40: 9 and it will be **h**.
Lev 10: 3 approach me I will show myself **h**;
10:10 You must distinguish between the **h**
10:13 Eat it in a **h** place,
11:44 and be **h**, because I am **h**.
11:45 therefore be **h**, because I am **h**.
19: 2 'Be **h** because I, the LORD your
God, am **h**.
19: 8 because he has desecrated what is **h**
19:24 the fourth year all its fruit will be **h**,
20: 3 and profaned my **h** name.
20: 7 " 'Consecrate yourselves and be **h**,
20: 8 I am the LORD, who makes you **h**.
20:26 **h** to me because I, the LORD, am **h**,
21: 6 They must be **h** to their God and
21: 8 Consider them **h**, because I the
LORD am **h**—I who make you **h**.
22: 9 I am the LORD, who makes them **h**.
22:32 Do not profane my **h** name.
22:32 I must be acknowledged as **h** by
25:12 it is a jubilee and is to be **h** for you;
27: 9 given to the LORD becomes **h**.
Nu 4:15 But they must not touch the **h** things
6: 5 be **h** until the period of his separation
16: 7 will be the one who is **h**.

	20:12	trust in me enough to honor me as **h**
	20:13	and where he showed himself **h**
Dt	5:12	the Sabbath day by keeping it **h,**
	23:14	Your camp must be **h,**
	26:15	your **h** dwelling place,
	33: 2	He came with myriads of **h** ones
Jos	5:15	place where you are standing is **h."**
	24:19	He is a **h** God; he is a jealous God.
1Sa	2: 2	"There is no one **h** like the LORD;
	6:20	the LORD, this **h** God?
	21: 5	The men's things are **h** even on
		missions that are not **h.**
2Ki	4: 9	comes our way is a **h** man of God.
1Ch	16:10	Glory in his **h** name;
	16:35	we may give thanks to your **h** name,
	29: 3	I have provided for this **h** temple:
2Ch	3: 8	He built the Most **H** Place,
	30:27	his **h** dwelling place.
Ezr	9: 2	and have mingled the **h** race with
Ne	11: 1	in Jerusalem, the **h** city,
Job	6:10	not denied the words of the **H** One.
Ps	2: 6	on Zion, my **h** hill."
	5: 7	I bow toward your **h** temple.
	11: 4	The LORD is in his **h** temple;
	16:10	will you let your **H** One see decay.
	22: 3	Yet you are enthroned as the **H** One;
	24: 3	Who may stand in his **h** place?
	30: 4	praise his **h** name.
	33:21	for we trust in his **h** name.
	47: 8	God is seated on his **h** throne.
	77:13	Your ways, O God, are **h.**
	78:54	to the border of his **h** land,
	89: 5	in the assembly of the **h** ones.
	89:18	our king to the **H** One of Israel.
	99: 3	great and awesome name—he is **h.**
	99: 9	and worship at his **h** mountain,
	105: 3	Glory in his **h** name;
	111: 9	**h** and awesome is his name.
Pr	9:10	of the **H** One is understanding.
Isa	1: 4	spurned the **H** One of Israel
	5:16	the **h** God will show himself **h**
	6: 3	"H, h, h is the LORD Almighty;
	6:13	**h** seed will be the stump in the land."
	8:13	the one you are to regard as **h,**
	29:23	the holiness of the **H** One of Jacob,
	40:25	says the **H** One.
	43: 3	the **H** One of Israel, your Savior;
	52:10	The LORD will lay bare his **h** arm in
	54: 5	**H** One of Israel is your Redeemer;
	57:15	whose name is **h:**
	58:13	doing as you please on my **h** day,
Jer	2: 3	Israel was **h** to the LORD,
	17:22	but keep the Sabbath day **h,**
Eze	20:41	and I will show myself **h** among you
	22:26	not distinguish between the **h** and
	28:22	on her and show myself **h** within her.
	28:25	I will show myself **h** among them in
	36:20	nations they profaned my **h** name,
	38:16	when I show myself **h** through you
	44:23	between the **h** and the common
Da	4:13	a **h** one, coming down from heaven.
	8:13	Then I heard a **h** one speaking,
	9:24	and to anoint the most **h.**
	11:28	be set against the **h** covenant.

Jnh	2: 4	look again toward your **h** temple.'
Hab	2:20	But the LORD is in his **h** temple;
Zec	8: 3	will be called the **H** Mountain."
	14: 5	and all the **h** ones with him.
	14:20	**H** TO THE LORD will be inscribed
Mt	1:18	to be with child through the **H** Spirit.
	3:11	He will baptize you with the **H** Spirit
	4: 5	the devil took him to the **h** city
	24:15	you see standing in the **h** place
	27:52	**h** people who had died were raised
	28:19	and of the Son and of the **H** Spirit,
Mk	1:24	who you are—the **H** One of God!"
	3:29	against the **H** Spirit will never be
Lk	1:15	and he will be filled with the **H** Spirit
	1:35	"The **H** Spirit will come upon you,
	1:35	So the **h** one to be born will be called
	1:49	**h** is his name.
	3:22	and the **H** Spirit descended on him
	4: 1	Jesus, full of the **H** Spirit,
	10:21	full of joy through the **H** Spirit, said,
	11:13	Father in heaven give the **H** Spirit
Jn	6:69	know that you are the **H** One of God.
	14:26	But the Counselor, the **H** Spirit,
	20:22	"Receive the **H** Spirit.
Ac	1: 5	be baptized with the **H** Spirit."
	2: 4	with the **H** Spirit and began to speak
	2:27	will you let your **H** One see decay.
	2:38	receive the gift of the **H** Spirit.
	4:27	conspire against your **h** servant Jesus
	5: 3	you have lied to the **H** Spirit
	8:15	that they might receive the **H** Spirit,
	10:44	the **H** Spirit came on all who heard
	13:35	not let your **H** One see decay.'
	15: 8	accepted them by giving the **H** Spirit
	19: 2	the **H** Spirit when you believed?"
Ro	1: 2	his prophets in the **H** Scriptures
	7:12	So then, the law is **h,**
	11:16	then the whole batch is **h;**
	12: 1	**h** and pleasing to God—
	15:16	sanctified by the **H** Spirit.
	16:16	Greet one another with a **h** kiss.
1Co	1: 2	in Christ Jesus and called to be **h,**
	7:14	but as it is, they are **h.**
Eph	1: 4	to be **h** and blameless in his sight.
	2:21	and rises to become a **h** temple
	3: 5	to God's **h** apostles and prophets.
	4:30	do not grieve the Spirit of God,
	5: 3	improper for God's **h** people.
	5:26	to make her **h,**
Col	1:22	to present you **h** in his sight,
1Th	2:10	of how **h,** righteous and blameless
	3:13	Lord Jesus comes with all his **h** ones.
	4: 7	but to live a **h** life.
2Th	1:10	comes to be glorified in his **h** people
1Ti	2: 8	to lift up **h** hands in prayer,
2Ti	1: 9	and called us to a **h** life—
	2:21	made **h,** useful to the Master
	3:15	you have known the **h** Scriptures,
Tit	1: 8	upright, **h** and disciplined.
	3: 5	rebirth and renewal by the **H** Spirit,
Heb	2: 4	and gifts of the **H** Spirit distributed
	2:11	Both the one who makes men **h**
	6: 4	who have shared in the **H** Spirit,
	7:26	priest meets our need—one who is **h,**

9:12 he entered the Most **H** Place once
10:10 we have been made **h** through
10:14 those who are being made **h.**
10:19 Most **H** Place by the blood of Jesus,
12:14 in peace with all men and to be **h;**
13:12 the city gate to make the people **h**
1Pe   1:15 But just as he who called you is **h,**
so be **h** in all you do;
1:16 "Be **h,** because I am **h.**"
2: 5 a spiritual house to be a **h** priesthood,
2: 9 a royal priesthood, a **h** nation,
3: 5 For this is the way the **h** women of
2Pe   1:21 were carried along by the **H** Spirit.
3:11 You ought to live **h** and godly lives
1Jn   2:20 an anointing from the **H** One,
Jude   1:14 upon thousands of his **h** ones
1:20 build yourselves up in your most **h**
faith and pray in the **H** Spirit.
Rev   3: 7 the words of him who is **h** and true,
4: 8 "**H, h, h** is the Lord God Almighty,
11: 2 They will trample on the **h** city
15: 4 For you alone are **h.**
20: 6 and **h** are those who have part in
21: 2 I saw the **H** City, the new Jerusalem,
21:10 and showed me the **H** City,
22:11 let him who is **h** continue to be **h.**"
22:19 in the tree of life and in the **h** city,

HOLY CITY Ne 11:1, 18; Isa 48:2; 52:1; Da
9:24; Mt 4:5; 27:53; Rev 11:2; 21:2, 10; 22:19

HOLY HILL Ps 2:6; 3:4; 15:1; Da 9:16, 20; Joel
2:1; 3:17; Ob 1:16; Zep 3:11

HOLY MOUNTAIN Ps 43:3; 48:1; 87:1; 99:9;
Isa 11:9; 27:13; 56:7; 57:13; 65:11, 25; 66:20;
Eze 20:40; Da 11:45; Zec 8:3

HOLY NAME Lev 20:3; 22:2, 32; 1Ch 16:10,
35; 29:16; Ps 30:4; 33:21; 97:12; 103:1; 105:3;
106:47; 145:21; Eze 20:39; 36:20, 21, 22; 39:7,
7, 25; 43:7, 8; Am 2:7

HOLY ONE 2Ki 19:22; Job 6:10; Ps 16:10; 22:3;
71:22; 78:41; 89:18; Pr 9:10; 30:3; Isa 1:4; 5:19,
24; 10:17, 20; 12:6; 17:7; 29:19, 23; 30:11, 12,
15; 31:1; 37:23; 40:25; 41:14, 16, 20; 43:3, 14,
15; 45:11; 47:4; 48:17; 49:7, 7; 54:5; 55:5; 60:9,
14; Jer 50:29; 51:5; Eze 39:7; Da 4:13, 23; 8:13,
13; Hos 11:9, 12; Hab 1:12; 3:3; Mk 1:24; Lk
1:35; 4:34; Jn 6:69; Ac 2:27; 13:35; 1Jn 2:20;
Rev 16:5

HOLY ONES Dt 33:2, 3; Job 5:1; 15:15; Ps
89:5, 7; Isa 13:3; Da 4:17; Zec 14:5; 1Th 3:13;
Jude 1:14

HOLY PLACE Ex 26:33, 33, 34; 28:29, 35, 43;
29:30; 31:11; Lev 6:16, 26, 27, 30; 7:6; 10:13,
18; 14:13; 16:2, 16, 17, 20, 23, 24, 27, 33; 24:9;
Jos 24:26; 1Ki 6:16; 7:50; 8:6, 8, 8, 10; 1Ch 6:49;
23:32; 2Ch 3:8, 10; 4:22; 5:7, 9, 11; 35:5; Ps
24:3; 28:2; 46:4; Ecc 8:10; Isa 57:15; 63:18; Eze
41:4, 21, 23; 45:3, 4; Mt 24:15; Ac 6:13; 21:28;
Heb 9:2, 3, 8, 12, 25; 10:19; 13:11

HOLY SPIRIT Ps 51:11; Isa 63:10, 11; Mt 1:18,
20; 3:11; 12:32; 28:19; Mk 1:8; 3:29; 12:36;
13:11; Lk 1:15, 35, 41, 67; 2:25, 26; 3:16, 22;
4:1; 10:21; 11:13; 12:10, 12; Jn 1:33; 14:26;

20:22; Ac 1:2, 5, 8, 16; 2:4, 33, 38; 4:8, 25, 31;
5:3, 32; 6:5; 7:51, 55; 8:15, 16, 17, 19; 9:17, 31;
10:38, 44, 45, 47; 11:15, 16, 24; 13:2, 4, 9, 52;
15:8, 28; 16:6; 19:2, 2, 6; 20:23, 28; 21:11;
28:25; Ro 5:5; 9:1; 14:17; 15:13, 16; 1Co 6:19;
12:3; 2Co 6:6; 13:14; Eph 1:13; 4:30; 1Th 1:5, 6;
4:8; 2Ti 1:14; Tit 3:5; Heb 2:4; 3:7; 6:4; 9:8;
10:15; 1Pe 1:12; 2Pe 1:21; Jude 1:20

HOLY TO THE †LORD Ex 28:36; 30:10, 37;
31:15; 39:30; Lev 19:8; 27:14, 23, 28, 30, 32; Dt
7:6; 14:2, 21; 26:19; Jer 2:3; 31:40; Eze 48:14;
Zec 14:20, 21

MOST HOLY Ex 26:33, 34; 29:37; 30:10, 29,
36; 40:10; Lev 2:3, 10; 6:17, 25, 29; 7:1, 6;
10:12, 17; 14:13; 16:2, 16, 17, 20, 23, 27, 33;
21:22; 24:9; 27:28; Nu 4:4, 19; 18:9, 9, 10; 1Ki
6:16; 7:50; 8:6; 1Ch 6:49; 23:13; 2Ch 3:8, 10;
4:22; 5:7; Ps 28:2; Eze 41:4, 21, 23; 42:13, 13;
43:12; 44:13; 45:3; 48:12; Da 9:24; Heb 9:3, 8,
12, 25; 10:19; 13:11; Jude 1:20

HOME [HOMELAND, HOMELESS,
HOMES]

Nu   14:30 with uplifted hand to make your **h,**
Dt   6: 7 Talk about them when you sit at **h**
11:19 talking about them when you sit at **h**
20: 5 Let him go **h,**
24: 5 to stay at **h** and bring happiness to
Jos   22: 7 When Joshua sent them **h,**
Jdg   19:15 but no one took them into his **h** for
Ru   1:11 But Naomi said, "Return **h,**
2Sa   7:10 so that they can have a **h**
1Ch 16:43 David returned **h** to bless his family.
2Ch 10:16 So all the Israelites went **h.**
Ps   84: 3 Even the sparrow has found a **h,**
113: 9 He settles the barren woman in her **h**
Pr   3:33 but he blesses the **h** of the righteous.
7:11 her feet never stay at **h;**
27: 8 a man who strays from his **h.**
Ecc   12: 5 Then man goes to his eternal **h**
Eze   36: 8 for they will soon come **h.**
Mic   2: 2 They defraud a man of his **h,**
Hag   1: 9 What you brought **h,** I blew away.
Mt   1:20 afraid to take Mary **h** as your wife,
Mk   2:11 get up, take your mat and go **h.**"
5:19 "Go **h** to your family and tell them
10:29 "no one who has left **h** or brothers
Lk   10:38 woman named Martha opened her **h**
Jn   9: 7 and came **h** seeing.
14:23 to him and make our **h** with him.
19:27 this disciple took her into his **h.**
Ac   10:32 a guest in the **h** of Simon the tanner,
16:15 she invited us to her **h.**
1Co 11:34 anyone is hungry, he should eat at **h,**
2Co   5: 8 from the body and at **h** with the Lord
Tit   2: 5 to be busy at **h,** to be kind,

HOMELAND [HOME]

Ge   30:25 so I can go back to my own **h.**
Ru   2:11 and your **h** and came to live with
2Ki   17:23 from their **h** into exile in Assyria,
Ps   79: 7 devoured Jacob and destroyed his **h.**

HOMELESS* [HOME]

1Co 4:11 we are brutally treated, we are **h.**

HOMES [HOME]

Nu 32:18 not return to our **h** until every
Jos 22: 6 and they went to their **h.**
Ne 4:14 your wives and your **h."**
Isa 32:18 peaceful dwelling places, in secure **h**
Hos 11:11 I will settle them in their **h,"**
Mk 10:30 times as much in this present age (**h,**
1Ti 5:14 to manage their **h** and to give
2Ti 3: 6 the kind who worm their way into **h**

HOMETOWN [TOWN]

Mt 13:57 "Only in his **h** and in his own house
Mk 6: 4 Jesus said to them, "Only in his **h,**
Lk 4:24 "no prophet is accepted in his **h.**

HOMOSEXUAL*

1Co 6: 9 nor male prostitutes nor **h** offenders

HONEST [HONESTLY, HONESTY]

Ex 23: 7 an innocent or **h** person to death,
Lev 19:36 Use **h** scales and **h** weights, an **h**
ephah and an **h** hin.
Dt 25:15 and **h** weights and measures,
Job 31: 6 let God weigh me in **h** scales
Pr 12:17 A truthful witness gives **h** testimony,
16:11 **H** scales and balances are from

HONESTLY* [HONEST]

Jer 5: 1 can find but one person who deals **h**

HONESTY* [HONEST]

Ge 30:33 my **h** will testify for me in the future,
2Ki 12:15 because they acted with complete **h.**
Isa 59:14 in the streets, **h** cannot enter.

HONEY [HONEYCOMB]

Ex 3: 8 a land flowing with milk and **h—**
16:31 and tasted like wafers made with **h.**
Lev 2:11 for you are not to burn any yeast or **h**
Jdg 14: 8 a swarm of bees and some **h,**
1Sa 14:26 they saw the **h** oozing out,
Ps 19:10 they are sweeter than **h,** than **h** from
119:103 sweeter than **h** to my mouth!
Pr 5: 3 For the lips of an adulteress drip **h,**
25:16 If you find **h,** eat just enough—
SS 4:11 milk and **h** are under your tongue.
Isa 7:15 He will eat curds and **h**
Eze 3: 3 it tasted as sweet as **h** in my mouth.
Mt 3: 4 His food was locusts and wild **h.**
Rev 10: 9 be as sweet as **h."**

HONEYCOMB* [HONEY]

1Sa 14:27 in his hand and dipped it into the **h.**
Pr 16:24 Pleasant words are a **h,**
SS 4:11 Your lips drop sweetness as the **h,**
5: 1 I have eaten my **h** and my honey;

HONOR [HONORABLE, HONORABLY, HONORED, HONORS]

Ge 43:28 And they bowed low to pay him **h.**
Ex 12:42 to **h** the LORD for the generations

20:12 "**H** your father and your mother,
Nu 20:12 trust in me enough to **h** me as holy
25:13 he was zealous for the **h** of his God
Dt 5:16 "**H** your father and your mother,
Jdg 4: 9 the **h** will not be yours,
1Sa 2: 8 and has them inherit a throne of **h.**
2:30 Those who **h** me I will **h,**
6: 5 and pay **h** to Israel's god.
2Ki 10:20 "Call an assembly in **h** of Baal."
1Ch 29:12 Wealth and **h** come from you;
2Ch 1:11 not asked for wealth, riches or **h,**
18: 1 Jehoshaphat had great wealth and **h,**
Est 6: 6 for the man the king delights to **h?"**
Ps 8: 5 and crowned him with glory and **h.**
45:11 **h** him, for he is your lord.
84:11 the LORD bestows favor and **h;**
112: 9 his horn will be lifted high in **h.**
Pr 3: 9 **H** the LORD with your wealth,
3:35 The wise inherit **h,**
15:33 and humility comes before **h.**
18:12 but humility comes before **h.**
20: 3 It is to a man's **h** to avoid strife,
22: 4 fear of the LORD bring wealth and **h**
25:27 is it honorable to seek one's own **h.**
29:23 but a man of lowly spirit gains **h.**
Ecc 10: 1 little folly outweighs wisdom and **h.**
Isa 9: 1 but in the future he will **h** Galilee of
29:13 to me with their mouth and **h** me
Jer 33: 9 and **h** before all nations on earth
Da 2:46 before Daniel and paid him **h**
5:23 you did not **h** the God who holds
Mal 1: 6 where is the **h** due me?
Mt 13:57 own house is a prophet without **h."**
15: 4 '**H** your father and mother'
15: 8 " 'These people **h** me with their lips,
19:19 **h** your father and mother,'
23: 6 the place of **h** at banquets
Mk 6: 4 own house is a prophet without **h."**
Lk 14: 8 do not take the place of **h,**
Jn 4:44 that a prophet has no **h**
5:23 that all may **h** the Son just as they **h**
the Father.
7:18 speaks on his own does so to gain **h**
8:49 I **h** my Father and you dishonor me.
12:26 My Father will **h** the one who serves
Ro 12:10 **H** one another above yourselves.
13: 7 if respect, then respect; if **h,** then **h.**
1Co 6:20 Therefore **h** God with your body,
12:23 honorable we treat with special **h.**
Eph 6: 2 "**H** your father and mother"—
1Ti 5:17 well are worthy of double **h,**
Heb 2: 7 crowned him with glory and **h**
3: 3 worthy of greater **h** than Moses,
1Pe 1: 7 and **h** when Jesus Christ is revealed.
2Pe 1:17 he received **h** and glory from God
Rev 4: 9 **h** and thanks to him who sits on
4:11 to receive glory and **h** and power,
5:12 and wisdom and strength and **h**
7:12 and **h** and power and strength be to
13:14 in **h** of the beast who was wounded
21:26 and **h** of the nations will be brought

HONORABLE [HONOR]

Pr 25:27 nor is it **h** to seek one's own honor.

1Th 4: 4 own body in a way that is holy and **h**

HONORABLY [HONOR]
Heb 13:18 clear conscience and desire to live **h**

HONORED [HONOR]
Ex 20:24 Wherever I cause my name to be **h,**
Ps 12: 8 when what is vile is **h** among men.
Pr 13:18 but whoever heeds correction is **h.**
    27:18 who looks after his master will be **h.**
Da 4:34 Then I praised the Most High; I **h**
Hag 1: 8 I may take pleasure in it and be **h,"**
Lk 14:10 Then you will be **h** in the presence
1Co 12:26 if one part is **h,** every part rejoices
Heb 13:   Marriage should be **h** by all,

HONORS* [HONOR]
Ps 15: 4 but **h** those who fear the LORD,
    50:23 who sacrifices thank offerings **h** me,
Pr 14:31 whoever is kind to the needy **h** God.
Mal 1: 6 "A son **h** his father,

HOOF
Ex 10:26 not a **h** is to be left behind.
Lev 11: 3 that has a split **h** completely divided

HOOK [FISHHOOK, HOOKS]
2Ch 33:11 prisoner, put a **h** in his nose,
Isa 37:29 I will put my **h** in your nose

HOOKS [HOOK]
Ex 26:37 Make gold **h** for this curtain
Isa 2: 4 and their spears into pruning **h.**
Joel 3:10 and your pruning **h** into spears.
Am 4: 2 when you will be taken away with **h,**
Mic 4: 3 and their spears into pruning **h.**

HOPE [HOPED, HOPELESS, HOPES]
Ru 1:12 if I thought there was still **h** for me—
Ezr 10: 2 there is still **h** for Israel.
Job 6: 8 that God would grant what I **h** for,
    13:15 he slay me, yet will I **h** in him;
    17:15 Who can see any **h** for me?
Ps 9:18 nor the **h** of the afflicted ever perish.
    25: 3 No one whose **h** is in you will ever
    31:24 all you who **h** in the LORD.
    33:17 A horse is a vain **h** for deliverance;
    33:18 whose **h** is in his unfailing love,
    39: 7 My **h** is in you.
    42: 5 Put your **h** in God,
    52: 9 in your name I will **h,**
    62: 5 my **h** comes from him.
    65: 5 the **h** of all the ends of the earth and
    71:14 But as for me, I will always have **h;**
    119:43 for I have put my **h** in your laws.
    119:74 for I have put my **h** in your word.
    130: 5 and in his word I put my **h.**
    130: 7 O Israel, put your **h** in the LORD,
    146: 5 whose **h** is in the LORD his God,
    147:11 who put their **h** in his unfailing love.
Pr 11: 7 a wicked man dies, his **h** perishes;
    13:12 **H** deferred makes the heart sick,
    23:18 There is surely a future **h** for you,
    24:14 and your **h** will not be cut off.

26:12 There is more **h** for a fool than
Ecc 9: 4 who is among the living has **h—**
Isa 40:31 who **h** in the LORD will renew their
    49:23 those who **h** in me will not
Jer 14: 8 O **H** of Israel,
    29:11 plans to give you **h** and a future.
La 3:21 call to mind and therefore I have **h:**
Eze 37:11 dried up and our **h** is gone;
Mic 7: 7 for me, I watch in **h** for the LORD,
Zec 9:12 O prisoners of **h;**
Mt 12:21 the nations will put their **h."**
Ac 2:26 my body also will live in **h,**
    23: 6 because of my **h** in the resurrection
Ro 4:18 Against all **h,** Abraham in **h** believed
    5: 4 character; and character, **h.**
    5: 5 And **h** does not disappoint us,
    8:20 of the one who subjected it, in **h**
    8:24 But **h** that is seen is no **h** at all.
    8:25 if we **h** for what we do not yet have,
    12:12 Be joyful in **h,** patient in affliction,
    15: 4 of the Scriptures we might have **h.**
    15:12 the Gentiles will **h** in him."
    15:13 May the God of **h** fill you with all
1Co 13:13 these three remain: faith, **h** and love.
    15:19 only for this life we have **h** in Christ,
2Co 1:10 On him we have set our **h**
Gal 5: 5 the righteousness for which we **h.**
Eph 1:12 who were the first to **h** in Christ,
    2:12 without **h** and without God in
    4: 4 just as you were called to one **h**
Col 1: 5 faith and love that spring from the **h**
    1:23 from the **h** held out in the gospel.
    1:27 Christ in you, the **h** of glory.
1Th 1: 3 and your endurance inspired by **h**
    4:13 who have no **h.**
    5: 8 and the **h** of salvation as a helmet.
1Ti 1: 1 and of Christ Jesus our **h,**
    4:10 we have put our **h** in the living God,
    6:17 arrogant nor to put their **h** in wealth,
Tit 1: 2 resting on the **h** of eternal life,
    2:13 while we wait for the blessed **h—**
Heb 3: 6 and the **h** of which we boast.
    6:11 in order to make your **h** sure.
    6:19 We have this **h** as an anchor for
    7:19 and a better **h** is introduced,
    10:23 unswervingly to the **h** we profess,
    11: 1 Now faith is being sure of what we **h**
1Pe 1: 3 a living **h** through the resurrection
    1:21 and so your faith and **h** are in God.
    3: 5 of the past who put their **h** in God
    3:15 to give the reason for the **h**
1Jn 3: 3 Everyone who has this **h** in him

HOPED [HOPE]
Job 30:26 Yet when I **h** for good, evil came;
Jer 8:15 **h** for peace but no good has come,
Lk 20:20 They **h** to catch Jesus in something

HOPELESS* [HOPE]
Isa 57:10 but you would not say, 'It is **h.'**

HOPES* [HOPE]
2Ki 4:28 'Don't raise my **h'?"**
Ps 119:116 do not let my **h** be dashed.

Pr 10:28 the **h** of the wicked come to nothing.
Jer 23:16 they fill you with false **h.**
Jn 5:45 on whom your **h** are set.
Ro 8:24 Who **h** for what he already has?
1Co 13: 7 always **h,** always perseveres.

HOPHNI*

A wicked priest (1Sa 1:3; 2:34; 4:4-17).

HOR

Nu 33:38 Aaron the priest went up Mount **H,**
Dt 32:50 your brother Aaron died on Mount **H**

HOREB

Ex 3: 1 and came to **H,** the mountain of God.
17: 6 before you by the rock at **H.**
Dt 5: 2 God made a covenant with us at **H.**
1Ki 19: 8 and forty nights until he reached **H,**
Ps 106:19 At **H** they made a calf and worshiped

HORIZON*

Ne 1: 9 exiled people are at the farthest **h,**
Job 26:10 the **h** on the face of the waters for
Pr 8:27 he marked out the **h** on the face

HORMAH

Nu 14:45 beat them down all the way to **H.**
21: 3 so the place was named **H.**

HORN [HORNS]

Ex 19:13 when the ram's **h** sounds
27: 2 Make a **h** at each of the four corners,
1Sa 2: 1 in the LORD my **h** is lifted high.
16: 1 Fill your **h** with oil and be
Ps 18: 2 and the **h** of my salvation,
92:10 You have exalted my **h** like that of
148:14 He has raised up for his people a **h,**
La 2: 3 he has cut off every **h** of Israel.
Da 3: 5 soon as you hear the sound of the **h,**
7: 8 This **h** had eyes like the eyes of
8: 5 suddenly a goat with a prominent **h**
Lk 1:69 He has raised up a **h** of salvation

HORNET*

Ex 23:28 I will send the **h** ahead of you
Dt 7:20 the LORD your God will send the **h**
Jos 24:12 I sent the **h** ahead of you,

HORNS [HORN]

Ge 22:13 a ram caught by its **h.**
Ex 27: 2 the altar are of one piece,
Lev 4: 7 the blood on the **h** of the altar of
Jos 6: 4 trumpets of rams' **h** in front of the
Ps 75: 5 Do not lift your **h** against heaven;
Da 7: 7 and it had ten **h.**
7:24 ten **h** are ten kings who will come
8: 3 before me was a ram with two **h.**
Rev 5: 6 He had seven **h** and seven eyes,
9:13 voice coming from the **h** of the
12: 3 and ten **h** and seven crowns
13: 1 He had ten **h** and seven heads, with
ten crowns on his **h,**
13:11 He had two **h** like a lamb,
17: 3 and had seven heads and ten **h.**

HORRIBLE [HORROR]

Dt 7:15 the **h** diseases you knew in Egypt,
Jer 5:30 **h** and shocking thing has happened
Hos 6:10 a **h** thing in the house of Israel.

HORROR [HORRIBLE]

Dt 28:25 a thing of **h** to all the kingdoms on
2Ch 29: 8 an object of dread and **h** and scorn,
Ps 55: 5 **h** has overwhelmed me.
Jer 2:12 O heavens, and shudder with great **h,**
25:18 an object of **h** and scorn and cursing,
Eze 20:26 with **h** so they would know that I am

HORSE [HORSEMAN, HORSEMEN, HORSES, HORSES']

Ex 15: 1 The **h** and its rider he has hurled into
Est 6: 8 and a **h** the king has ridden,
Ps 32: 9 Do not be like the **h** or the mule,
33:17 A **h** is a vain hope for deliverance;
147:10 is not in the strength of the **h,**
Pr 26: 3 A whip for the **h,**
Jer 51:21 with you I shatter **h** and rider,
Zec 1: 8 before me was a man riding a red **h!**
Rev 6: 2 and there before me was a white **h!**
6: 4 another **h** came out, a fiery red one.
6: 5 and there before me was a black **h!**
6: 8 and there before me was a pale **h!**
19:11 and there before me was a white **h,**

HORSEMAN [HORSE, MAN]

Am 2:15 and the **h** will not save his life.

HORSEMEN [HORSE, MAN]

Ex 14:28 and covered the chariots and **h—**
15:19 chariots and **h** went into the sea,
2Ki 2:12 The chariots and **h** of Israel!"
18:24 on Egypt for chariots and **h?**
Isa 31: 1 and in the great strength of their **h,**

HORSES [HORSE]

Ge 47:17 food in exchange for their **h,**
Ex 14:23 and all Pharaoh's **h** and chariots
Dt 17:16 must not acquire great numbers of **h**
Jos 11: 6 You are to hamstring their **h**
1Ki 4:26 four thousand stalls for chariot **h,**
10:26 Solomon accumulated chariots and **h**
2Ki 2:11 a chariot of fire and **h** of fire
6:17 full of **h** and chariots of fire
Ps 20: 7 Some trust in chariots and some in **h,**
Isa 31: 3 their **h** are flesh and not spirit.
Jer 12: 5 how can you compete with **h?**
Joel 2: 4 They have the appearance of **h;**
Zec 6: 2 The first chariot had red **h,**
Rev 9: 7 The locusts looked like **h** prepared
19:14 on white **h** and dressed in fine linen,

HORSES' [HORSE]

Rev 14:20 as high as the **h'** bridles for a

HOSANNA*

Mt 21: 9 "**H** to the Son of David!"
21: 9 "**H** in the highest!"
21:15 "**H** to the Son of David,"

Mk 11: 9 those who followed shouted, **"H!"**
    11:10 **"H** in the highest!"
Jn 12:13 out to meet him, shouting, **"H!"**

HOSEA
Prophet whose wife and family pictured the unfaithfulness of Israel (Hos 1-3).

HOSHEA [JOSHUA]
    1. Original name of Joshua (Nu 13:8, 16).
    2. Last king of Israel (2Ki 15:30; 17:1-6).

HOSPITABLE* [HOSPITALITY]
1Ti 3: 2 self-controlled, respectable, **h,**
Tit 1: 8 Rather he must be **h,**

HOSPITABLY* [HOSPITALITY]
Ac 28: 7 and for three days entertained us **h.**

HOSPITALITY* [HOSPITABLE, HOSPITABLY]
Ro 12:13 Practice **h.**
    16:23 Gaius, whose **h** I and the whole
1Ti 5:10 as bringing up children, showing **h,**
1Pe 4: 9 Offer **h** to one another without
3Jn 1: 8 therefore to show **h** to such men so

HOST [HOSTS]
1Ki 22:19 the **h** of heaven standing around him
Ne   9: 6 and all their starry **h,**
Isa 34: 4 the starry **h** will fall
    40:26 He who brings out the starry **h** one
Da   8:10 and it threw some of the starry **h**
Lk   2:13 a great company of the heavenly **h**

HOSTILE [HOSTILITY]
Lev 26:21 " 'If you remain **h** toward me
Ro   8: 7 the sinful mind is **h** to God.
1Th 2:15 They displease God and are **h**

HOSTILITY [HOSTILE]
Ge   16:12 in **h** toward all his brothers."
    25:18 in **h** toward all their brothers.
Hos   9: 8 and **h** in the house of his God.
Eph   2:14 the dividing wall of **h,**
     2:16 by which he put to death their **h.**

HOSTS [HOST]
2Ki 17:16 They bowed down to all the starry **h,**
2Ch 33: 5 he built altars to all the starry **h.**
Ps 103:21 Praise the LORD, all his heavenly **h,**
    148: 1 praise him, all his heavenly **h.**
Isa 45:12 I marshaled their starry **h.**

HOT [HOTLY, HOTTER]
Ex   11: 8 Moses, **h** with anger, left Pharaoh.
Ps   39: 3 My heart grew **h** within me,
Pr   6:28 Can a man walk on **h** coals
Eze 38:18 my **h** anger will be aroused,
Da   3:22 the furnace so **h** that the flames
1Ti   4: 2 seared as with a **h** iron.
Rev   3:15 that you are neither cold nor **h.**

HOT-TEMPERED* [TEMPER]
Jdg 18:25 or some **h** men will attack you,
Pr   15:18 A **h** man stirs up dissension,
    19:19 A **h** man must pay the penalty;
    22:24 Do not make friends with a **h** man,
    29:22 and a **h** one commits many sins.

HOTHEADED* [HEAD]
Pr   14:16 but a fool is **h** and reckless.

HOTTER* [HOT]
Da   3:19 furnace heated seven times **h** than

HOUNDED*
Ps 109:16 but **h** to death the poor and the needy
Eze 36: 3 and **h** you from every side

HOUR
Ecc   9:12 no man knows when his **h** will come:
Mt   6:27 you by worrying can add a single **h**
     8:13 his servant was healed at that very **h.**
    24:36 "No one knows about that day or **h,**
Mk   14:35 if possible the **h** might pass from him
    14:37 you not keep watch for one **h?**
Lk   12:40 at an **h** when you do not expect him.
Jn   12:23 "The **h** has come for the Son of Man
    12:27 for this very reason I came to this **h.**
1Jn   2:18 Dear children, this is the last **h;**
Rev   3:10 will also keep you from the **h** of trial
     8: 1 silence in heaven for about half an **h.**
    14: 7 the **h** of his judgment has come.
    17:12 for one **h** will receive authority
    18:10 In one **h** your doom has come!'

HOUSE [HOUSEHOLD, HOUSEHOLDS, HOUSES, STOREHOUSE, STOREHOUSES]
Ge   19: 2 please turn aside to your servant's **h.**
    24:23 there room in your father's **h** for us
    28:17 This is none other than the **h** of God;
Ex   12:22 of you shall go out the door of his **h**
    20:17 shall not covet your neighbor's **h.**
Lev 27:14 " 'If a man dedicates his **h**
Nu   12: 7 he is faithful in all my **h.**
Dt   5:21 your desire on your neighbor's **h**
Jos   2: 1 the **h** of a prostitute named Rahab
     6:22 the prostitute's **h** and bring her out
1Sa   1: 7 Whenever Hannah went up to the **h**
2Sa   2:10 **h** of Judah, however, followed David
     3: 1 **h** of Saul grew weaker and weaker.
     7: 5 the one to build me a **h** to dwell in?
     7:11 the LORD himself will establish a **h**
    23: 5 "Is not my **h** right with God?
1Ki   8:43 this **h** I have built bears your Name.
2Ki 15: 5 and he lived in a separate **h.**
1Ch   9:23 the **h** called the Tent.
    17:12 the one who will build a **h** for me,
    22: 1 **h** of the LORD God is to be here,
Ezr   1: 5 to build the **h** of the LORD in Jerusalem.
     3:11 foundation of the **h** of the LORD was
Ne   10:39 not neglect the **h** of our God."
Ps   23: 6 dwell in the **h** of the LORD forever.
    27: 4 that I may dwell in the **h**

52: 8 olive tree flourishing in the **h** of
God;
69: 9 for zeal for your **h** consumes me,
84:10 be a doorkeeper in the **h** of my God
112: 3 Wealth and riches are in his **h,**
122: 1 "Let us go to the **h** of the LORD."
127: 1 Unless the LORD builds the **h,**
Pr 7:27 Her **h** is a highway to the grave,
9: 1 Wisdom has built her **h;**
14: 1 The wise woman builds her **h,**
14:11 **h** of the wicked will be destroyed,
21: 9 than share a **h** with a quarrelsome
Ecc 10:18 if his hands are idle, the **h** leaks.
Isa 5: 8 Woe to you who add **h** to **h**
7:13 "Hear now, you **h** of David!
56: 7 for my **h** will be called a **h** of prayer
Jer 3:18 In those days the **h** of Judah will
join the **h** of Israel,
7:11 Has this **h,** which bears my Name,
18: 2 "Go down to the potter's **h,**
31:31 a new covenant with the **h** of Israel
32:34 abominable idols in the **h** that bears
Eze 2: 8 Do not rebel like that rebellious **h;**
33: 7 a watchman for the **h** of Israel;
39:29 pour out my Spirit on the **h** of Israel,
Joel 3:18 will flow out of the LORD's **h**
Hag 1: 4 while this **h** remains a ruin?"
2: 7 and I will fill this **h** with glory,'
Zec 8: 9 the foundation was laid for the **h** of
13: 6 'The wounds I was given at the **h**
Mt 7:24 like a wise man who built his **h** on
10:11 and stay at his **h** until you leave.
12:29 can anyone enter a strong man's **h**
13:57 his own **h** is a prophet without honor.
21:13 " 'My **h** will be called a **h** of prayer,'
Mk 3:25 If a **h** is divided against itself,
11:17 " 'My **h** will be called a **h** of prayer
Lk 6:48 He is like a man building a **h,**
10: 7 Do not move around from **h** to **h.**
11:17 a **h** divided against itself will fall.
11:24 it says, 'I will return to the **h** I left.'
15: 8 sweep the **h** and search carefully
19: 9 "Today salvation has come to this **h,**
Jn 2:16 How dare you turn my Father's **h**
2:17 "Zeal for your **h** will consume me."
12: 3 the **h** was filled with the fragrance of
14: 2 In my Father's **h** are many rooms;
Ac 5:42 in the temple courts and from **h** to **h,**
16:15 she said, "come and stay at my **h.**"
20:20 taught you publicly and from **h** to **h.**
28:30 Paul stayed there in his own rented **h**
Ro 16: 5 also the church that meets at their **h.**
2Co 5: 1 an eternal **h** in heaven,
Heb 3: 2 as Moses was faithful in all God's **h.**
8: 8 a new covenant with the **h** of Israel
10:21 a great priest over the **h** of God,
1Pe 2: 5 are being built into a spiritual **h** to be
2Jn 1:10 do not take him into your **h**

FATHER'S HOUSE Ge 24:23; 28:21; 31:30;
38:11, 11; Lev 22:13; Nu 30:3; Dt 22:21, 21; Jdg
11:7; 14:19; 19:2, 3; 1Sa 2:27, 28, 30, 31; 18:2;
2Sa 3:29; 1Ki 2:31; 2Ch 21:13; Ne 1:6; Ps 45:10;
Pr 4:3; Lk 2:49; 16:27; Jn 2:16; 14:2; Ac 7:20

HOUSE OF DAVID 1Sa 20:16; 2Sa 3:1, 6; 1Ki
12:19, 20, 26; 13:2; 14:8; 2Ki 17:21; 2Ch 10:19;
21:7; Ne 12:37; Ps 122:5; Isa 7:2, 13; 16:5;
22:22; Jer 21:12; Zec 12:7, 8, 10, 12; 13:1

HOUSE OF GOD Ge 28:17; Jdg 18:31; 1Ch
6:48; 9:11, 13, 26, 27; 22:2; 23:28; 25:6; 26:20;
Ezr 2:68; 3:8, 9; 4:24; 5:2, 13, 14, 15, 16, 17; 6:5,
5, 7, 8, 16, 17, 22; 7:24; 8:36; 10:1, 6, 9; Ne 6:10;
8:16; 11:11, 16, 22; 12:40; 13:7, 9, 11; Ps 42:4;
52:8; 55:14; Ecc 5:1; Mt 12:4; Mk 2:26; Lk 6:4;
Heb 10:21

HOUSE OF ISRAEL Ex 40:38; Lev 10:6; Nu
20:29; Jos 21:45; Ru 4:11; 1Sa 7:3; 2Sa 1:12;
6:5, 15; 12:8; 16:3; 1Ki 12:21; 20:31; Ps 98:3;
115:9, 12; 135:19; Isa 5:7; 14:2; 46:3; 63:7; Jer
2:4, 26; 3:18, 20; 5:11, 15; 9:26; 10:1; 11:10, 17;
13:11; 18:6, 6; 31:27, 31, 33; 33:14, 17; 48:13;
Eze 3:1, 4, 5, 7, 7, 17; 4:3, 4, 5; 5:4; 6:11; 8:6, 10,
11, 12; 9:9; 11:5, 15; 12:6, 9, 10, 27; 13:5, 9;
14:6; 17:2; 18:6, 15, 25, 29, 29, 30, 31; 20:30, 31,
39, 40, 44; 22:18; 24:21; 29:6, 21; 33:7, 10, 11,
20; 34:30; 35:15; 36:10, 21, 22, 22, 32, 37; 37:11,
16; 39:12, 22, 29; 40:4; 43:7; 44:6, 6, 12; 45:6, 8,
17, 17; Hos 1:6; 6:10; 11:12; Am 5:1, 4, 25; 6:14;
9:9; Mic 1:5; 3:1, 9; Ac 7:42; Heb 8:8, 10

HOUSE OF JACOB Ex 19:3; Ps 114:1; Isa
2:5, 6; 8:17; 10:20; 14:1; 29:22; 46:3; 48:1; 58:1;
Jer 2:4; 5:20; Eze 20:5; Am 3:13; 9:8; Ob 1:17,
18; Mic 2:7; 3:9; Lk 1:33

HOUSE OF JUDAH 2Sa 2:4, 7, 10, 11; 1Ki
12:21, 23; 2Ki 19:30; 1Ch 28:4; 2Ch 11:1; 22:10;
Isa 22:21; 37:31; Jer 3:18; 5:11; 11:10, 17; 12:14;
13:11; 21:11; 31:27, 31; 33:14; Eze 4:6; 8:17;
25:8, 12; Hos 1:7; Zep 2:7; Zec 10:3, 6; 12:4;
Heb 8:8

HOUSE OF THE †LORD Ex 23:19; 34:26;
Dt 23:18; Jdg 19:18; 1Sa 1:7, 24; 3:15; 2Sa
12:20; 1Ch 6:31; 9:23; 22:1, 11; Ezr 1:5; 2:68;
3:8, 11; 7:27; 8:29; Ne 10:35; Ps 23:6; 27:4;
92:13; 116:19; 118:26; 122:1, 9; 134:1; 135:2;
Jer 17:26; 26:2, 7, 9, 10; 27:18, 21; 28:1, 5;
29:26; 33:11; 35:2, 4; 36:6; 41:5; La 2:7; Eze
8:14, 16; 11:1; Hos 8:1; Joel 1:9, 14; Hag 1:14;
Zec 7:3; 8:9; 11:13; 14:21

HOUSEHOLD [HOUSE]

Ge 12: 1 people and your father's **h** and go
15: 3 so a servant in my **h** will be my heir.
17:12 including those born in your **h**
31:19 Rachel stole her father's **h** gods.
39: 4 Potiphar put him in charge of his **h,**
Ex 12: 3 one for each **h.**
Lev 16: 6 atonement for himself and his **h.**
Jos 24:15 But as for me and my **h,**
Pr 31:21 it snows, she has no fear for her **h;**
31:27 She watches over the affairs of her **h**
Mic 7: 6 are the members of his own **h.**
Mt 10:36 will be the members of his own **h.**'
12:25 **h** divided against itself will not stand
Jn 4:53 So he and all his **h** believed.
Ac 16:31 be saved—you and your **h.**"
Eph 2:19 and members of God's **h,**
1Ti 3:12 manage his children and his **h** well.

3:15 to conduct themselves in God's **h,**

HOUSEHOLDS [HOUSE]
Nu 16:32 with their **h** and all Korah's men
Dt 11: 6 and swallowed them up with their **h,**
Tit   1:11 they are ruining whole **h**

HOUSES [HOUSE]
Ex 12: 7 and tops of the doorframes of the **h**
    12:27 the **h** of the Israelites in Egypt
Dt   6: 9 them on the doorframes of your **h**
    11:20 them on the doorframes of your **h**
Isa 65:21 They will build **h** and dwell in them;
Jer 29:28 Therefore build **h** and settle down;
Eze 11: 3 'Will it not soon be time to build **h?**
Mt 19:29 And everyone who has left **h**
Mk 12:40 They devour widows' **h** and for
Ac   4:34 who owned lands or **h** sold them,

HOVERING* [HOVERS]
Ge   1: 2 Spirit of God was **h** over the waters.
Isa 31: 5 Like birds **h** overhead,

HOVERS* [HOVERING]
Dt 32:11 an eagle that stirs up its nest and **h**

HOW [HOWEVER, SOMEHOW]
Ge   6:12 God saw **h** corrupt the earth
    6:15 This is **h** you are to build it:
   28:17 "**H** awesome is this place!
   39: 9 **H** then could I do such a wicked
Ex 12:11 This is **h** you are to eat it:
Nu   6:23 'This is **h** you are to bless
   23: 8 **H** can I curse those whom God has
Dt 31:27 For I know **h** rebellious
2Sa   1:19 **H** the mighty have fallen!
    7:22 "**H** great you are,
1Ki   3: 7 not know **h** to carry out my duties.
2Ch   6:18 **H** much less this temple I have built!
   32:14 then can your god deliver you
Job   2:13 they saw **h** great his suffering was.
   25: 4 can one born of woman be pure?
   40: 4 **h** can I reply to you?
Ps   6: 3 **H** long, O LORD, **h** long?
    8: 1 **h** majestic is your name in all
  31:19 **H** great is your goodness,
  36: 7 **H** priceless is your unfailing love!
  47: 2 **H** awesome is the LORD Most High,
  92: 5 **H** great are your works, O LORD,
 116:12 **H** can I repay the LORD
 119: 9 **H** can a young man keep his way
 147: 1 **h** pleasant and fitting to praise him!
Pr 15:23 and **h** good is a timely word!
SS   1:15 **H** beautiful you are, my darling!
   1:16 **H** handsome you are, my lover!
Isa   1:21 See **h** the faithful city has become
  14:12 **H** you have fallen from heaven,
Jer   1: 6 I said, "I do not know **h** to speak;
  38:28 This is **h** Jerusalem was taken:
La   1: 1 **H** deserted lies the city,
Eze 33:10 **H** then can we live?" '
Hos 11: 8 "**H** can I give you up, Ephraim?
Mal   1: 2 But you ask, '**H** have you loved us?'
Mk   9:50 **h** can you make it salty again?

  10:23 "**H** hard it is for the rich to enter
Lk 12:27 "Consider **h** the lilies grow.
  20:44 **H** then can he be his son?"
Jn   3: 4 "**H** can a man be born
   7:15 "**H** did this man get such learning
Eph   5: 8 Be very careful, then, **h** you live—
1Ti   3: 5 **h** can he take care of God's church?)
Heb   2: 3 **h** shall we escape if we ignore such
2Pe   2: 9 the Lord knows **h** to rescue godly

HOW LONG Ex 10:3, 7; 16:28; Nu 14:11, 11,
  27; Jos 18:3; 1Sa 1:14; 16:1; 2Sa 2:26; 1Ki
  18:21; Ne 2:6; Job 7:4; 8:2; 19:2; Ps 4:2, 2; 6:3,
  3; 13:1, 1, 2, 2; 35:17; 62:3; 74:9, 10; 79:5, 5;
  80:4; 82:2; 89:46, 46; 90:13; 94:3, 3; 119:84; Pr
  1:22, 22; 6:9; Ecc 6:3; Isa 6:11; Jer 4:14, 21;
  12:4; 13:27; 23:26; 31:22; 47:5, 6; Da 8:13; 12:6;
  Hos 8:5; Hab 1:2; 2:6; Zec 1:12; 2:2; Mt 17:17,
  17; Mk 9:19, 19, 21; Lk 9:41; Jn 10:24; Rev 6:10

HOW MUCH MORE Dt 31:27; 1Sa 21:5; 23:3;
  2Sa 4:11; 16:11; 2Ki 5:13; Job 4:19; Pr 11:31;
  15:11; 19:7; 21:27; SS 4:10; Mt 7:11; 10:25;
  12:12; Lk 11:13; 12:24, 28; Ro 5:9, 10, 15, 17;
  11:24; 1Co 6:3; 2Co 3:9; Heb 9:14; 10:29; 12:9

HOWEVER [HOW]
Ex 16:20 **H,** some of them paid no attention
Dt 15: 4 **H,** there should be no poor
  28:15 **H,** if you do not obey
Jos 14: 8 I, **h,** followed the LORD my God
Jer 34:14 **h,** did not listen to me
Lk 18: 8 **H,** when the Son of Man comes,
Jn 15:22 **h,** they have no excuse for their sin.
Ro   8: 9 **h,** are controlled not by the sinful
1Pe   4:16 **H,** if you suffer as a Christian,

HUGE
2Sa 21:20 **h** man with six fingers on each hand
  23:21 And he struck down a **h** Egyptian.
Da   2:35 the statue became a **h** mountain
Rev   8: 8 and something like a **h** mountain,
  16:21 From the sky **h** hailstones of about

HULDAH
Prophetess inquired by Hilkiah for Josiah (2Ki
22; 2Ch 34:14-28).

HUMAN [HUMANITY]
Lev 24:17 If anyone takes the life of a **h** being,
Nu 19:16 or anyone who touches a **h** bone or
1Ki 13: 2 and **h** bones will be burned on you.'
2Ki 23:14 and covered the sites with **h** bones.
Isa 37:19 fashioned by **h** hands.
  52:14 his form marred beyond **h** likeness—
Da   2:34 but not by **h** hands.
   5: 5 the fingers of a **h** hand appeared
   8:25 but not by **h** power.
Hos 11: 4 I led them with cords of **h** kindness,
Jn   1:13 nor of **h** decision or a husband's will,
   5:34 Not that I accept **h** testimony;
   8:15 You judge by **h** standards;
Ac   5:38 or activity is of **h** origin, it will fail.
Ro   1: 3 as to his **h** nature was a descendant
   9: 5 is traced the **h** ancestry of Christ,
1Co   1:17 not with words of **h** wisdom,

	1:26	of you were wise by **h** standards;
	2:13	by **h** wisdom but in words taught by
2Co	3: 3	of stone but on tablets of **h** hearts.
	5: 1	not built by **h** hands.
Gal	3: 3	to attain your goal by **h** effort?
Php	2: 7	being made in **h** likeness.
Col	2: 8	**h** tradition and the basic principles
	2:22	on **h** commands and teachings.
Heb	12: 9	all had **h** fathers who disciplined us
2Pe	2:18	the lustful desires of sinful **h** nature,
Rev	9: 7	and their faces resembled **h** faces.

HUMANITY* [HUMAN]

Heb 2:14 he too shared in their **h** so that

HUMBLE* [HUMBLED, HUMBLES, HUMBLY, HUMILIATE, HUMILIATED, HUMILITY]

Ex	10: 3	you refuse to **h** yourself before me?
Nu	12: 3	Moses was a very **h** man, more **h**
Dt	8: 2	to **h** you and to test you in order
	8:16	to **h** and to test you so that in
2Sa	22:28	You save the **h,**
1Ki	11:39	I will **h** David's descendants because
2Ch	7:14	will **h** themselves and pray
	33:23	did not **h** himself before the LORD;
	36:12	did not **h** himself before Jeremiah
Ezr	8:21	we might **h** ourselves before our God
Job	8: 7	Your beginnings will seem **h,**
	40:12	look at every proud man and **h** him,
Ps	18:27	You save the **h** but bring low
	25: 9	He guides the **h** in what is right
	147: 6	The LORD sustains the **h** but casts
	149: 4	he crowns the **h** with salvation.
Pr	3:34	but gives grace to the **h.**
	6: 3	Go and **h** yourself;
Isa	13:11	and will **h** the pride of the ruthless.
	23: 9	and to **h** all who are renowned on
	29:19	the **h** will rejoice in the LORD;
	58: 5	only a day for a man to **h** himself?
	66: 2	This is the one I esteem: he who is **h**
Da	4:37	who walk in pride he is able to **h.**
	5:19	and those he wanted to **h,**
	10:12	gain understanding and to **h** yourself
Zep	2: 3	all you **h** of the land,
	3:12	leave within you the meek and **h,**
Mt	11:29	for I am gentle and **h** in heart,
Lk	1:48	for he has been mindful of the **h** state
	1:52	but has lifted up the **h.**
2Co	12:21	I come again my God will **h** me
Eph	4: 2	Be completely **h** and gentle;
Jas	1: 9	The brother in **h** circumstances ought
	4: 6	the proud but gives grace to the **h.**"
	4:10	**H** yourselves before the Lord,
1Pe	3: 8	be compassionate and **h.**
	5: 5	the proud but gives grace to the **h.**"
	5: 6	**H** yourselves, therefore, under God's

HUMBLED [HUMBLE]

Lev	26:41	their uncircumcised hearts are **h**
Dt	8: 3	He **h** you, causing you to hunger
1Ki	21:29	Because he has **h** himself,
2Ch	12: 7	"Since they have **h** themselves,

	33:12	and **h** himself greatly before the God
	34:27	and you **h** yourself before God
Ps	35:13	I put on sackcloth and **h** myself
	44: 9	But now you have rejected and **h** us;
	107:39	and they were **h** by oppression,
Isa	2: 9	will be brought low and mankind **h**
Jer	44:10	not **h** themselves or shown reverence
Da	5:22	O Belshazzar, have not **h** yourself,
Mt	23:12	For whoever exalts himself will be **h,**
Lk	14:11	who exalts himself will be **h,**
Php	2: 8	he **h** himself and became obedient to death—

HUMBLES* [HUMBLE]

1Sa	2: 7	he **h** and he exalts.
Isa	26: 5	He **h** those who dwell on high,
Mt	18: 4	whoever **h** himself like this child is
	23:12	whoever **h** himself will be exalted.
Lk	14:11	he who **h** himself will be exalted."
	18:14	he who **h** himself will be exalted."

HUMBLY [HUMBLE]

| Mic | 6: 8 | and to walk **h** with your God. |
| Jas | 1:21 | **h** accept the word planted in you, |

HUMILIATE* [HUMBLE]

| Pr | 25: 7 | for him to **h** you before a nobleman. |
| 1Co | 11:22 | and **h** those who have nothing? |

HUMILIATED [HUMBLE]

Isa	54: 4	you will not be **h.**
Jer	31:19	I was ashamed and **h** because I bore
Lk	13:17	all his opponents were **h,**
	14: 9	Then, **h,** you will have to take

HUMILITY* [HUMBLE]

Ps	45: 4	**h** and righteousness;
Pr	11: 2	but with **h** comes wisdom.
	15:33	and **h** comes before honor.
	18:12	but **h** comes before honor.
	22: 4	**H** and the fear of the LORD
Zep	2: 3	Seek righteousness, seek **h;**
Ac	20:19	I served the Lord with great **h**
Php	2: 3	in **h** consider others better than
Col	2:18	anyone who delights in false **h**
	2:23	their false **h** and their harsh treatment
	3:12	kindness, **h,** gentleness and patience.
Tit	3: 2	and to show true **h** toward all men.
Jas	3:13	by deeds done in the **h** that comes
1Pe	5: 5	clothe yourselves with **h** toward one

HUNDRED [HUNDREDFOLD]

Ge	6: 3	his days will be a **h** and twenty years
	15:13	enslaved and mistreated four **h** years.
	17:17	a son be born to a man a **h** years old?
Lev	26: 8	Five of you will chase a **h,**
1Ki	18:13	I hid a **h** of the LORD's prophets
Isa	65:20	at a **h** will be thought a mere youth;
Mt	13:23	He produces a crop, yielding a **h,**
	18:12	If a man owns a **h** sheep,
Lk	7:41	One owed him five **h** denarii,
Ac	1:15	(a group numbering about a **h**

HUNDREDFOLD* [HUNDRED]
Ge 26:12 and the same year reaped a **h**,

HUNG [HANG]
Dt   21:23 is **h** on a tree is under God's curse.
Jos   8:29 He **h** the king of Ai on a tree
      10:26 the kings and **h** them on five trees,
Ps 137: 2 There on the poplars we **h** our harps,
Mt   18: 6 a large millstone **h** around his neck
Lk   19:48 because all the people **h** on his words
      23:39 criminals who **h** there hurled insults
Gal   3:13 "Cursed is everyone who is **h**

HUNGER [HUNGRY]
Dt   8: 3 causing you to **h** and then feeding
1Sa   2: 5 those who were hungry **h** no more.
Ne   9:15 In their **h** you gave them bread
Ps   17:14 You still the **h** of those you cherish;
Pr   6:30 to satisfy his **h** when he is starving.
Isa 49:10 They will neither **h** nor thirst,
Mt   5: 6 Blessed are those who **h** and thirst
Lk   6:21 Blessed are you who **h** now,
2Co   6: 5 sleepless nights and **h;**
      11:27 I have known **h**
Rev   7:16 Never again will they **h;**

HUNGRY [HUNGER]
Job 24:10 but still go **h.**
Ps   50:12 If I were **h** I would not tell you,
     107: 9 and fills the **h** with good things.
     146: 7 oppressed and gives food to the **h.**
Pr   10: 3 LORD does not let the righteous go **h**
     19:15 and the shiftless man goes **h.**
     25:21 If your enemy is **h**,
     27: 7 the **h** even what is bitter tastes sweet.
Isa 29: 8 a **h** man dreams that he is eating,
     58: 7 Is it not to share your food with the **h**
Eze 18: 7 but gives his food to the **h**
Mt   4: 2 and forty nights, he was **h.**
     12: 1 His disciples were **h** and began
     15:32 I do not want to send them away **h,**
     25:35 I was **h** and you gave me something
     25:42 For I was **h** and you gave me nothing
Mk   11:12 leaving Bethany, Jesus was **h.**
Lk   1:53 has filled the **h** with good things
Jn   6:35 who comes to me will never go **h,**
Ro   12:20 On the contrary: "If your enemy is **h,**
1Co   4:11 To this very hour we go **h** and thirsty
     11:34 If anyone is **h**, he should eat at home,
Php   4:12 whether well fed or **h,**

HUNT [HUNTED, HUNTER, HUNTS]
Ge   27: 3 to **h** some wild game for me.
Am   9: 3 there I will **h** them down

HUNTED [HUNT]
La   3:52 without cause **h** me like a bird.

HUNTER [HUNT]
Ge   10: 9 a mighty **h** before the LORD;
     25:27 and Esau became a skillful **h,**

HUNTS [HUNT]
Ps   10: 2 the wicked man **h** down the weak,

Mic   7: 2 each **h** his brother with a net.

HUR
Ex   17:12 Aaron and **H** held his hands up—

HURAM [HURAM-ABI]
1Ki   7:14 **H** was highly skilled and
2Ch   4:11 So **H** finished the work

HURAM-ABI [HURAM]
2Ch   2:13 "I am sending you **H,**

HURL [HURLED]
1Sa 25:29 **h** away as from the pocket of a sling.
2Ch 26:15 to shoot arrows and **h** large stones.
Ps   22: 7 who see me mock me; they **h** insults,
Mic   7:19 **h** all our iniquities into the depths

HURLED [HURL]
Ex   15: 1 The horse and its rider he has **h** into
Jos 10:11 the LORD **h** large hailstones down
1Sa 20:33 Saul **h** his spear at him to kill him.
La   2: 1 He has **h** down the splendor of Israel
Jnh   2: 3 You **h** me into the deep,
Mk   15:29 Those who passed by **h** insults
1Pe   2:23 When they **h** their insults at him,
Rev   8: 5 and **h** it on the earth;
     12: 9 The great dragon was **h** down—

HURRIED [HURRY]
Ge   18: 6 So Abraham **h** into the tent to Sarah.
     24:17 The servant **h** to meet her and said,
2Ki   5:21 So Gehazi **h** after Naaman.
Da   6:19 king got up and **h** to the lions' den.
Mt   28: 8 So the women **h** away from the tomb
Lk   2:16 So they **h** off and found Mary

HURRIES* [HURRY]
Ecc   1: 5 and **h** back to where it rises.

HURRY [HURRIED, HURRIES]
Ge   19:15 the angels urged Lot, saying, **"H!**
Ex   12:33 people to **h** and leave the country.

HURT [HURTS]
Ecc   8: 9 lords it over others to his own **h.**
Da   6:22 They have not **h** me,
Mk   16:18 it will not **h** them at all;
Jn   21:17 Peter was **h** because Jesus asked him
2Co   7: 8 I see that my letter **h** you,
Rev   2:11 not be **h** at all by the second death.

HURTS* [HURT]
Ps   15: 4 who keeps his oath even when it **h,**
Pr   26:28 A lying tongue hates those it **h,**

HUSBAND [HUSBAND'S, HUSBANDS]
Ge   3: 6 She also gave some to her **h,**
      3:16 Your desire will be for your **h,**
     16: 3 and gave her to her **h**
Nu   30: 8 But if her **h** forbids her when he
Dt   24: 4 then her first **h,** who divorced her,
Pr   7:19 My **h** is not at home;
     31:11 Her **h** has full confidence in her
     31:23 Her **h** is respected at the city gate,

	31:28	her **h** also, and he praises her:
Isa	54: 1	than of her who has a **h**,"
	54: 5	For your Maker is your **h**—
Jer	3:14	"for I am your **h**.
	3:20	But like a woman unfaithful to her **h**,
	31:32	though I was a **h** to them,"
Hos	2:16	"you will call me 'my **h**';
Mt	1:19	Joseph her **h** was a righteous man
	19:10	"If this is the situation between a **h**
Mk	10:12	And if she divorces her **h**
Jn	4:17	"I have no **h**," she replied.
Ro	7: 2	a married woman is bound to her **h**
1Co	7: 2	and each woman her own **h**.
	7: 3	The **h** should fulfill his marital duty
	7:10	A wife must not separate from her **h**.
	7:11	And a **h** must not divorce his wife.
	7:14	the unbelieving **h** has been sanctified
	7:14	sanctified through her believing **h**.
	7:39	A woman is bound to her **h** as long
2Co	11: 2	I promised you to one **h**, to Christ,
Gal	4:27	than of her who has a **h**."
Eph	5:23	For the **h** is the head of the wife
	5:33	and the wife must respect her **h**.
1Ti	3: 2	the **h** of but one wife, temperate,
	3:12	deacon must be the **h** of but one wife
	5: 9	has been faithful to her **h**,
Tit	1: 6	the **h** of but one wife,
Rev	21: 2	a bride beautifully dressed for her **h**.

HUSBAND'S [HUSBAND]

Dt	25: 5	Her **h** brother shall take her
Ru	2: 1	Naomi had a relative on her **h** side,
Pr	12: 4	wife of noble character is her **h**
Jn	1:13	nor of human decision or a **h** will,
1Co	7: 4	the **h** body does not belong

HUSBANDMAN (KJV) See FARMER, GARDENER

HUSBANDS [HUSBAND]

Jn	4:18	The fact is, you have had five **h**,
1Co	14:35	they should ask their own **h** at home;
Eph	5:22	submit to your **h** as to the Lord.
	5:25	**H**, love your wives,
	5:28	**h** ought to love their wives
Col	3:18	Wives, submit to your **h**,
	3:19	**H**, love your wives and do not
Tit	2: 4	the younger women to love their **h**
	2: 5	and to be subject to their **h**,
1Pe	3: 1	be submissive to your **h** so that,
	3: 7	**H**, in the same way be considerate

HUSHAI

Wise man of David who frustrated Ahithophel's advice and foiled Absalom's revolt (2Sa 15:32-37; 16:15-17:16; 1Ch 27:33).

HUT*

Job	27:18	like a **h** made by a watchman.
Isa	1: 8	like a **h** in a field of melons,
	24:20	it sways like a **h** in the wind;

HYMENAEUS*

A false teacher (1Ti 1:20; 2Ti 2:17).

HYMN* [HYMNS]

Ps	40: 3	a **h** of praise to our God.
Mt	26:30	When they had sung a **h**,
Mk	14:26	When they had sung a **h**,
1Co	14:26	you come together, everyone has a **h**,

HYMNS* [HYMN]

Ac	16:25	and Silas were praying and singing **h**
Ro	15: 9	I will sing **h** to your name."
Eph	5:19	with psalms, **h** and spiritual songs.
Col	3:16	**h** and spiritual songs with gratitude

HYPOCRISY* [HYPOCRITE, HYPOCRITES, HYPOCRITICAL]

Mt	23:28	but on the inside you are full of **h**
Mk	12:15	But Jesus knew their **h**.
Lk	12: 1	yeast of the Pharisees, which is **h**.
Gal	2:13	The other Jews joined him in his **h**,
	2:13	so that by their **h** even Barnabas
1Pe	2: 1	**h**, envy, and slander of every kind.

HYPOCRITE* [HYPOCRISY]

| Mt | 7: 5 | You **h**, first take the plank out |
| Lk | 6:42 | You **h**, first take the plank out |

HYPOCRITES* [HYPOCRISY]

Ps	26: 4	nor do I consort with **h**;
Mt	6: 2	as the **h** do in the synagogues and on
	6: 5	when you pray, do not be like the **h**,
	6:16	do not look somber as the **h** do,
	15: 7	You **h**! Isaiah was right when he
	22:18	their evil intent, said, "You **h**,
	23:13	of the law and Pharisees, you **h**!
	23:15	of the law and Pharisees, you **h**!
	23:23	of the law and Pharisees, you **h**!
	23:25	of the law and Pharisees, you **h**!
	23:27	of the law and Pharisees, you **h**!
	23:29	of the law and Pharisees, you **h**!
	24:51	and assign him a place with the **h**,
Mk	7: 6	when he prophesied about you **h**;
Lk	12:56	**H**! You know how to interpret
	13:15	The Lord answered him, "You **h**!

HYPOCRITICAL* [HYPOCRISY]

| 1Ti | 4: 2 | Such teachings come through **h** liars, |

HYSSOP

Ex	12:22	Take a bunch of **h**,
Lev	14: 4	scarlet yarn and **h** be brought for
Nu	19: 6	some cedar wood, **h** and scarlet wool
Ps	51: 7	Cleanse me with **h**,
Jn	19:29	put the sponge on a stalk of the **h**
Heb	9:19	scarlet wool and branches of **h**,

I

I AM

Ge	15: 1	**I am** your shield, your very great
	17: 1	"**I am** God Almighty; walk before
Ex	3:14	God said to Moses, "**I AM WHO I AM**.

	3:14	Israelites: '**I AM** has sent me to you.'
Ps	46:10	"Be still, and know that **I am** God;
Isa	41:10	So do not fear, for **I am** with you;
	41:10	not be dismayed, for **I am** your God.
	43: 3	For **I am** the LORD, your God,
	43:15	**I am** the LORD, your Holy One,
	44: 6	**I am** the first and **I am** the last;
	48:12	**I am** the first and **I am** the last.
Jer	3:14	"for **I am** your husband.
	32:27	"**I am** the LORD, the God of all
Mt	16:15	he asked. "Who do you say **I am**?"
	28:20	And surely **I am** with you always,
Mk	8:29	he asked. "Who do you say **I am**?"
	14:62	"**I am**," said Jesus. "And you will
Jn	6:35	declared, "**I am** the bread of life.
	6:41	"**I am** the bread that came down
	6:48	**I am** the bread of life.
	6:51	**I am** the living bread that came
	8:12	"**I am** the light of the world.
	8:24	if you do not believe that **I am**
	8:28	then you will know that **I am**
	8:58	"before Abraham was born, **I am!**"
	9: 5	**I am** the light of the world."
	10: 7	**I am** the gate for the sheep.
	10: 9	**I am** the gate; whoever enters
	10:11	"**I am** the good shepherd.
	10:14	"**I am** the good shepherd;
	10:36	because I said, '**I am** God's Son'?
	11:25	"**I am** the resurrection and the life.
	13:19	you will believe that **I am** He.
	14: 6	"**I am** the way and the truth and the life.
	14:10	believe that **I am** in the Father,
	14:11	when I say that **I am** in the Father
	14:20	will realize that **I am** in my Father,
	14:20	and you are in me, and **I am** in you.
	15: 1	"**I am** the true vine,
	15: 5	"**I am** the vine;
	18: 5	"**I am** he," Jesus said.
	18: 6	said, "**I am** he," they drew back
	18: 8	"I told you that **I am** he," Jesus
Ac	9: 5	"**I am** Jesus, whom you are
	18:10	For **I am** with you, and no one is
	22: 8	" '**I am** Jesus of Nazareth, whom
	26:15	" '**I am** Jesus, whom you are
Rev	1: 8	"**I am** the Alpha and the Omega,"
	1:17	**I am** the First and the Last.
	1:18	**I am** the Living One; I was dead, and behold **I am** alive for ever and
	3:11	**I am** coming soon.
	21:' 6	**I am** the Alpha and the Omega,
	22: 7	"Behold, **I am** coming soon!
	22:12	"Behold, **I am** coming soon!
	22:13	**I am** the Alpha and the Omega,
	22:16	**I am** the Root and the Offspring of David,
	22:20	"Yes, **I am** coming soon." Amen.

I AM THE †LORD Ge 15:7; 28:13; Ex 6:2, 6, 7, 8, 29; 7:5, 17; 10:2; 12:12; 14:4, 18; 15:26; 16:12; 20:2; 29:46, 46; 31:13; Lev 11:44, 45; 18:2, 4, 5, 6, 21, 30; 19:3, 4, 10, 12, 14, 16, 18, 25, 28, 30, 31, 32, 34, 36, 37; 20:7, 8, 24; 21:12, 15, 23; 22:2, 3, 8, 9, 16, 30, 31, 32, 33; 23:22, 43; 24:22; 25:17, 38, 55; 26:1, 2, 13, 44, 45; Nu 3:13,

41, 45; 10:10; 15:41, 41; Dt 5:6; 29:6; Jdg 6:10; 1Ki 20:13, 28; Ps 81:10; Isa 41:13; 42:8; 43:3, 11, 15; 44:24; 45:3, 5, 6, 18; 48:17; 49:23; 51:15; 60:22; Jer 9:24; 24:7; 32:27; Eze 6:7, 10, 13, 14; 7:4, 27; 11:10, 12; 12:15, 16, 20; 13:14, 21, 23; 14:8; 15:7; 16:62; 20:5, 7, 19, 20, 26, 38, 42, 44; 22:16; 24:27; 25:5, 7, 11, 17; 26:6; 28:22, 23, 26; 29:6, 9, 21; 30:8, 19, 25, 26; 32:15; 33:29; 34:27; 35:4, 9, 15; 36:11, 23, 38; 37:6, 13; 38:23; 39:6, 22, 28; Hos 12:9; 13:4; Joel 2:27; Zec 10:6

I AM WITH YOU See WITH

IBZAN*

Judge of Israel (Jdg 12:8-10).

ICE [ICY]

| Job | 37:10 | The breath of God produces **i,** |
| Eze | 1:22 | sparkling like **i,** and awesome. |

ICHABOD*

| 1Sa | 4:21 | She named the boy **I,** saying, |

ICONIUM

| Ac | 14: 1 | At **I** Paul and Barnabas went as usual |
| 2Ti | 3:11 | happened to me in Antioch, **I** and |

ICY* [ICE]

| Ps | 147:17 | Who can withstand his **i** blast? |

IDDO

2Ch	9:29	in the visions of **I** the seer
	12:15	and of **I** the seer that deal with
	13:22	in the annotations of the prophet **I.**

IDEA [IDEAS]

| Jn | 18:34 | "Is that your own **i,**" Jesus asked, |
| 2Pe | 2:13 | Their **i** of pleasure is to carouse |

IDEAS [IDEA]

| Ac | 17:21 | and listening to the latest **i.**) |

IDLE* [IDLENESS, IDLERS]

Dt	32:47	They are not just **i** words for you—
Job	11: 3	Will your **i** talk reduce men
Ecc	10:18	if his hands are **i,** the house leaks.
	11: 6	at evening let not your hands be **i,**
Isa	58:13	as you please or speaking **i** words,
Col	2:18	puffs him up with **i** notions.
1Th	5:14	brothers, warn those who are **i,**
2Th	3: 6	away from every brother who is **i**
	3: 7	not **i** when we were with you,
	3:11	We hear that some among you are **i.**
1Ti	5:13	they get into the habit of being **i**

IDLENESS* [IDLE]

| Pr | 31:27 | and does not eat the bread of **i.** |

IDLERS* [IDLE]

| 1Ti | 5:13 | And not only do they become **i,** |

IDOL [CALF-IDOL, IDOL'S, IDOLATER, IDOLATERS, IDOLATRIES, IDOLATRY, IDOLS]

| Ex | 20: 4 | not make for yourself an **i** |

	32: 4	an **i** cast in the shape of a calf,
Dt	27:15	who carves an image or casts an **i**—
Ps	106:19	and worshiped an **i** cast from metal.
Isa	40:19	As for an **i**, a craftsman casts it,
	41: 7	down the **i** so it will not topple.
	44:15	makes an **i** and bows down to it.
	44:17	From the rest he makes a god, his **i**;
Eze	8: 3	the **i** that provokes to jealousy stood.
Hos	4:12	They consult a wooden **i**
Hab	2:18	"Of what value is an **i**,
1Co	8: 4	that an **i** is nothing at all in the world
	10:19	a sacrifice offered to an **i** is anything,

IDOL'S* [IDOL]

1Co 8:10 eating in an **i** temple,

IDOLATER* [IDOL]

1Co 5:11 an **i** or a slanderer,
Eph 5: 5 such a man is an **i**—

IDOLATERS* [IDOL]

1Co	5:10	or the greedy and swindlers, or **i**.
	6: 9	the sexually immoral nor **i**
	10: 7	Do not be **i**, as some of them were;
Rev	21: 8	the **i** and all liars—
	22:15	the murderers, the **i** and everyone

IDOLATRIES* [IDOL]

Jer 14:14 **i** and the delusions of their own

IDOLATRY [IDOL]

1Sa	15:23	and arrogance like the evil of **i**.
Eze	23:49	the consequences of your sins of **i**.
1Co	10:14	my dear friends, flee from **i**.
Gal	5:20	**i** and witchcraft; hatred, discord,
Col	3: 5	evil desires and greed, which is **i**.
1Pe	4: 3	orgies, carousing and detestable **i**.

IDOLS [IDOL]

Ex	34:17	"Do not make cast **i**.
Lev	26:30	on the lifeless forms of your **i**,
Dt	7: 5	and burn their **i** in the fire.
	32:16	angered him with their detestable **i**,
1Ki	15:12	got rid of all the **i** his fathers had
2Ki	17:15	They followed worthless **i** and
1Ch	16:26	For all the gods of the nations are **i**,
Ps	31: 6	I hate those who cling to worthless **i**;
	78:58	aroused his jealousy with their **i**.
	115: 4	But their **i** are silver and gold,
Isa	42: 8	to another or my praise to **i**.
	44: 9	All who make **i** are nothing,
Jer	10: 5	their **i** cannot speak;
	16:19	worthless **i** that did them no good.
Eze	14: 3	men have set up **i** in their hearts
	23:37	committed adultery with their **i**;
	23:39	sacrificed their children to their **i**,
Hab	2:18	he makes a **i** that cannot speak.
Zec	10: 2	The **i** speak deceit,
Ac	15:20	to abstain from food polluted by **i**,
	21:25	abstain from food sacrificed to **i**,
1Co	8: 1	Now about food sacrificed to **i**:
2Co	6:16	between the temple of God and **i**?
1Jn	5:21	keep yourselves from **i**.
Rev	2:14	to sin by eating food sacrificed to **i**

IF

Ge	4: 7	**I** you do what is right,
Ex	19: 5	Now **i** you obey me fully
	33:15	"**I** your Presence does not go
Dt	11:27	the blessing **i** you obey
	11:28	the curse **i** you disobey
1Ki	18:21	**I** the LORD is God, follow him;
1Ch	28: 9	**I** you seek him, he will be found by
Ne	9:29	a man will live **i** he obeys them.
Ps	95: 7	Today, **i** you hear his voice,
Pr	17:28	fool is thought wise **i** he keeps silent,
Jer	18: 8	and **i** that nation I warned repents
Eze	18:21	"But **i** a wicked man turns away
Mt	4: 3	"**I** you are the Son of God,
	27:40	**i** you are the Son of God!"
Mk	3:24	**I** a kingdom is divided against itself,
	5:28	"**I** I just touch his clothes,
	8:38	**I** anyone is ashamed of me
Lk	6:32	"**I** you love those who love you,
Jn	7:17	**I** anyone chooses to do God's will,
	7:37	"**I** anyone is thirsty,
	13:17	you will be blessed **i** you do them.
	14:15	"**I** you love me,
	15: 5	**I** a man remains in me and I in him,
	15:10	**I** you obey my commands,
Ro	6: 8	Now **i** we died with Christ,
	8:31	**I** God is for us, who can be against
Heb	3: 7	**i** you hear his voice,
Jas	1: 5	**I** any of you lacks wisdom,
1Pe	4:16	However, **i** you suffer as a Christian,
1Jn	1: 9	**I** we confess our sins,
Rev	3:20	**I** anyone hears my voice and opens

IGNORANCE [IGNORE]

Ac	3:17	brothers, I know that you acted in **i**,
	17:30	In the past God overlooked such **i**,
1Ti	1:13	because I acted in **i** and unbelief.
Heb	9: 7	sins the people had committed in **i**.

IGNORANT [IGNORE]

Isa	45:20	are those who carry about idols
1Co	15:34	some who are **i** of God—
1Th	4:13	to be **i** about those who fall asleep,
Heb	5: 2	to deal gently with those who are **i**
1Pe	2:15	you should silence the **i** talk
2Pe	3:16	which **i** and unstable people distort,

IGNORE [IGNORANCE, IGNORANT,
   IGNORED, IGNORES]

Dt	22: 1	do not **i** it but be sure to take it back
Ps	9:12	not **i** the cry of the afflicted.
Heb	2: 3	escape if we **i** such a great salvation?

IGNORED [IGNORE]

Pr	1:25	since you **i** all my advice and would
Hos	6: 3	because you have **i** the law
1Co	14:38	he himself will be **i**.

IGNORES* [IGNORE]

Pr	10:17	**i** correction leads others astray.
	13:18	He who **i** discipline comes to poverty
	15:32	He who **i** discipline despises himself,
1Co	14:38	If he **i** this,

ILL [ILLNESS, ILLNESSES]
2Ch 32:24 In those days Hezekiah became **i**
Mt   4:24 brought to him all who were **i**

ILL-GOTTEN [GET]
Pr   1:19 the end of all who go after **i** gain;
     10: 2 **I** treasures are of no value,
Mic   4:13 You will devote their **i** gains to

ILL-TEMPERED* [TEMPER]
Pr   21:19 than with a quarrelsome and **i** wife.

ILLEGITIMATE*
Hos   5: 7 they give birth to **i** children.
Jn   8:41 "We are not **i** children,"
Heb 12: 8 you are **i** children and not true sons.

ILLNESS [ILL]
2Ki   8: 9 'Will I recover from this **i**?' "
2Ch 16:12 **i** he did not seek help from the LORD,
Ps   41: 3 and restore him from his bed of **i**.
Isa 38: 9 of Hezekiah king of Judah after his **i**
Gal   4:13 of an **i** that I first preached the gospel

ILLNESSES* [ILL]
Dt 28:59 and severe and lingering **i**.
Ac 19:12 and their **i** were cured and
1Ti   5:23 of your stomach and your frequent **i**.

ILLUMINATED*
Rev 18: 1 and the earth was **i** by his splendor.

ILLUSIONS*
Isa 30:10 Tell us pleasant things, prophesy **i**.

ILLUSTRATION*
Heb   9: 9 This is an **i** for the present time,

IMAGE [IMAGES]
Ge   1:26 God said, "Let us make man in our **i**,
     1:27 So God created man in his own **i**,
     9: 6 in the **i** of God has God made man.
Lev 26: 1 " 'Do not make idols or set up an **i**
Dt 27:15 "Cursed is the man who carves an **i**
Ps 106:20 They exchanged their Glory for an **i**
Isa 40:18 What **i** will you compare him to?
Da   3: 1 King Nebuchadnezzar made an **i**
1Co 11: 7 since he is the **i** and glory of God;
2Co   4: 4 who is the **i** of God.
Col   1:15 He is the **i** of the invisible God,
     3:10 in knowledge in the **i** of its Creator.
Rev 13:14 He ordered them to set up an **i**
     14:11 who worship the beast and his **i**,
     20: 4 not worshiped the beast or his **i**

IMAGES [IMAGE]
Nu 33:52 Destroy all their carved **i**
Ps 97: 7 All who worship **i** are put to shame,
Isa 42:17 who say to **i**, 'You are our gods,'
Jer 10:14 His **i** are a fraud;
Eze   5:11 my sanctuary with all your vile **i**
Ro   1:23 for **i** made to look like mortal man

IMAGINATION* [IMAGINE]
Eze 13: 2 who prophesy out of their own **i**:
     13:17 who prophesy out of their own **i**.

IMAGINE [IMAGINATION]
Eph   3:20 more than all we ask or **i**,

IMITATE* [IMITATED, IMITATORS]
Dt 18: 9 do not learn to **i** the detestable ways
Eze 23:48 may take warning and not **i** you.
1Co   4:16 Therefore I urge you to **i** me.
Heb   6:12 to **i** those who through faith
     13: 7 of their way of life and **i** their faith.
3Jn   1:11 not **i** what is evil but what is good.

IMITATED* [IMITATE]
2Ki 17:15 They **i** the nations around them

IMITATORS* [IMITATE]
Eph   5: 1 Be **i** of God, therefore,
1Th   1: 6 You became **i** of us and of the Lord;
     2:14 became **i** of God's churches in Judea,

IMMANUEL*
Isa   7:14 and will call him **I**.
     8: 8 the breadth of your land, O **I**!"
Mt   1:23 and they will call him **I**"—

IMMEASURABLY* [MEASURE]
Eph   3:20 able to do **i** more than all we ask

IMMORAL* [IMMORALITY]
Pr   6:24 keeping you from the **i** woman,
1Co   5: 9 not to associate with sexually **i**
     5:10 the people of this world who are **i**,
     5:11 himself a brother but is sexually **i**
     6: 9 Neither the sexually **i** nor idolaters
Eph   5: 5 For of this you can be sure: No **i**,
Heb 12:16 See that no one is sexually **i**,
     13: 4 the adulterer and all the sexually **i**.
Rev 21: 8 the murderers, the sexually **i**,
     22:15 the sexually **i**, the murderers,

IMMORALITY* [IMMORAL]
Nu 25: 1 the men began to indulge in sexual **i**
Jer   3: 9 Israel's **i** mattered so little to her,
Mt 15:19 murder, adultery, sexual **i**, theft,
Mk   7:21 come evil thoughts, sexual **i**, theft,
Ac 15:20 sexual **i**, from the meat of strangled
     15:29 strangled animals and from sexual **i**.
     21:25 strangled animals and from sexual **i**."
Ro 13:13 not in sexual **i** and debauchery,
1Co   5: 1 that there is sexual **i** among you,
     6:13 The body is not meant for sexual **i**,
     6:18 Flee from sexual **i**.
     7: 2 But since there is so much **i**,
     10: 8 We should not commit sexual **i**,
Gal   5:19 sinful nature are obvious: sexual **i**,
Eph   5: 3 not be even a hint of sexual **i**,
Col   3: 5 to your earthly nature: sexual **i**,
1Th   4: 3 that you should avoid sexual **i**;
Jude   1: 4 of our God into a license for **i**
     1: 7 gave themselves up to sexual **i** and
Rev   2:14 to idols and by committing sexual **i**.

2:20 misleads my servants into sexual **i**
2:21 given her time to repent of her **i**,
9:21 their sexual **i** or their thefts.

IMMORTAL* [IMMORTALITY]

Ro 1:23 exchanged the glory of the **i** God
1Ti 1:17 Now to the King eternal, **i**, invisible,
    6:16 who alone is **i** and who lives

IMMORTALITY* [IMMORTAL]

Pr 12:28 there is life; along that path is **i**.
Ro 2: 7 honor and **i**, he will give eternal life.
1Co 15:53 and the mortal with **i**.
    15:54 and the mortal with **i**,
2Ti 1:10 and has brought life and **i** to light

IMMOVABLE

Zec 12: 3 I will make Jerusalem an **i** rock

IMPART* [IMPARTS]

Ro 1:11 that I may **i** to you some spiritual gift
Gal 3:21 law had been given that could **i** life,

IMPARTIAL* [IMPARTIALLY]

Jas 3:17 and good fruit, **i** and sincere.

IMPARTIALLY [IMPARTIAL]

1Pe 1:17 who judges each man's work **i**,

IMPARTS* [IMPART]

Pr 29:15 The rod of correction **i** wisdom,

IMPATIENT

Nu 21: 4 But the people grew **i** on the way;

IMPERFECT*

1Co 13:10 perfection comes, the **i** disappears.

IMPERISHABLE

1Co 15:42 sown is perishable, it is raised **i**;
    15:50 nor does the perishable inherit the **i**.
1Pe 1:23 not of perishable seed, but of **i**,

IMPLANTED* [PLANT]

Ps 94: 9 Does he who **i** the ear not hear?

IMPLORE*

Mal 1: 9 "Now I **i** God to be gracious to us.
2Co 5:20 We **i** you on Christ's behalf:

IMPORTANCE* [IMPORTANT]

1Co 15: 3 I passed on to you as of first **i**:

IMPORTANT [IMPORTANCE]

1Ki 3: 4 for that was the most **i** high place,
Jer 52:13 Every **i** building he burned down.
Mt 6:25 Is not life more **i** than food,
    23:23 the more **i** matters of the law—
Mk 12:29 "The most **i** one," answered Jesus,
    12:33 is more **i** than all burnt offerings
Lk 11:43 the most **i** seats in the synagogues
Php 1:18 The **i** thing is that in every way,

IMPOSING

Jos 22:10 half-tribe of Manasseh built an **i** altar

2Ch 7:21 And though this temple is now so **i**,

IMPOSSIBLE

Ge 11: 6 then nothing they plan to do will be **i**
Mt 17:20 Nothing will be **i** for you."
    19:26 "With man this is **i**,
Mk 10:27 "With man this is **i**,
Lk 1:37 For nothing is **i** with God."
    18:27 "What is **i** with men is possible
Ac 2:24 because it was **i** for death
Heb 6: 4 It is **i** for those who have once been
    6:18 in which it is **i** for God to lie,
    10: 4 because it is **i** for the blood of bulls
    11: 6 without faith it is **i** to please God,

IMPOSTORS*

2Co 6: 8 genuine, yet regarded as **i**;
2Ti 3:13 and **i** will go from bad to worse,

IMPRESS* [IMPRESSED, IMPRESSES]

Dt 6: 7 **I** them on your children.

IMPRESSED* [IMPRESS]

Ecc 9:13 example of wisdom that greatly **i** me:

IMPRESSES* [IMPRESS]

Pr 17:10 A rebuke **i** a man of discernment

IMPRISON* [PRISON]

Ac 22:19 to **i** and beat those who believe

IMPRISONED [PRISON]

Jer 37:15 had him beaten and **i** in the house

IMPRISONMENT [PRISON]

Ac 23:29 against him that deserved death or **i**.
    26:31 that deserves death or **i**."

IMPRISONMENTS* [PRISON]

2Co 6: 5 in beatings, **i** and riots;

IMPROPER*

Eph 5: 3 these are **i** for God's holy people.

IMPURE [IMPURITIES, IMPURITY]

Nu 5:14 and he suspects his wife and she is **i**
Ac 10:15 "Do not call anything **i** that God
    11: 9 'Do not call anything **i** that God
Eph 5: 5 **i** or greedy person—
1Th 2: 3 not spring from error or **i** motives,
    4: 7 For God did not call us to be **i**,
Rev 21:27 Nothing **i** will ever enter it,

IMPURITIES [IMPURE]

Isa 1:25 and remove all your **i**.
Eze 36:25 all your **i** and from all your idols.

IMPURITY [IMPURE]

Zec 13: 1 to cleanse them from sin and **i**.
Ro 1:24 to sexual **i** for the degrading
    6:19 the parts of your body in slavery to **i**
Gal 5:19 sexual immorality, **i** and debauchery;
Eph 4:19 so as to indulge in every kind of **i**,
    5: 3 or of any kind of **i**, or of greed,

Col 3: 5 **i**, lust, evil desires and greed,

INCENSE
Ex 30: 1 an altar of acacia wood for burning **i.**
    40: 5 the gold altar of **i** in front of the ark
Lev 10: 1 put fire in them and added **i;**
Nu 16:17 to take his censer and put **i** in it—
2Ch 26:16 to burn **i** on the altar of **i.**
Ps 141: 2 my prayer be set before you like **i;**
Isa 1:13 Your **i** is detestable to me.
Jer 1:16 in burning **i** to other gods and
Hos 2:13 the days she burned **i** to the Baals;
Mt 2:11 with gifts of gold and of **i** and
Lk 1:10 the time for the burning of **i** came,
Heb 9: 4 which had the golden altar of **i** and
Rev 5: 8 holding golden bowls full of **i,**
    8: 4 The smoke of the **i,**

INCITED
1Sa 26:19 If the LORD has **i** you against me,
1Ch 21: 1 Satan rose up against Israel and **i**

INCLINATION* [INCLINATIONS, INCLINED, INCLINES]
Ge 6: 5 every **i** of the thoughts of his heart
    8:21 though every **i** of his heart is evil

INCLINATIONS* [INCLINATION]
Jer 7:24 the stubborn **i** of their evil hearts.

INCLINED [INCLINATION]
Dt 5:29 that their hearts would be **i** to fear me

INCLINES* [INCLINATION]
Ecc 10: 2 The heart of the wise **i** to the right,

INCOME
Ecc 5:10 is never satisfied with his **i.**
1Co 16: 2 of money in keeping with his **i,**

INCOMPARABLE*
[INCOMPARABLY]
Eph 2: 7 show the **i** riches of his grace,

INCOMPARABLY*
[INCOMPARABLE]
Eph 1:19 his **i** great power for us who believe.

INCREASE [EVER-INCREASING, INCREASED, INCREASES, INCREASING]
Ge 1:22 "Be fruitful and **i** in number and fill
    1:28 "Be fruitful and **i** in number;
    3:16 greatly **i** your pains in childbearing;
    8:17 be fruitful and **i** in number upon it."
    16:10 "I will so **i** your descendants that
Dt 1:11 **i** you a thousand times and bless you
Ps 62:10 though your riches **i,** do not
Pr 22:16 oppresses the poor to **i** his wealth
Isa 9: 7 Of the **i** of his government
Jer 23: 3 they will be fruitful and **i** in number.
Mt 24:12 Because of the **i** of wickedness,
Lk 17: 5 said to the Lord, "I our faith!"

Ac 12:24 But the word of God continued to **i**
Ro 5:20 so that the trespass might **i.**
    6: 1 go on sinning so that grace may **i?**
1Th 3:12 May the Lord make your love **i**

INCREASED [INCREASE]
Ge 7:17 the waters **i** they lifted the ark high
Ex 1:20 the people **i** and became even more
Dt 1:10 LORD your God has **i** your numbers
Ac 6: 7 of disciples in Jerusalem **i** rapidly,
Ro 5:20 But where sin **i,** grace **i** all the more,

INCREASES [INCREASE]
Pr 24: 5 and a man of knowledge **i** strength;
Isa 40:29 and **i** the power of the weak.

INCREASING [INCREASE]
Ac 6: 1 when the number of disciples was **i,**
2Th 1: 3 of you has for each other is **i.**
2Pe 1: 8 possess these qualities in **i** measure,

INCREDIBLE*
Ac 26: 8 it **i** that God raises the dead?

INCURABLE
2Ch 21:18 with an **i** disease of the bowels.
Jer 10:19 My wound is **i!**
Mic 1: 9 her wound is **i;** it has come to Judah.

INDECENT
Dt 24: 1 he finds something **i** about her,
Ro 1:27 Men committed **i** acts with other men

INDEPENDENT*
1Co 11:11 In the Lord, however, woman is not **i** of man, nor is man **i** of woman.

INDESCRIBABLE*
2Co 9:15 Thanks be to God for his **i** gift!

INDESTRUCTIBLE*
Heb 7:16 on the basis of the power of an **i** life.

INDIGNANT [INDIGNATION]
Mt 20:24 they were **i** with the two brothers.
Mk 10:14 When Jesus saw this, he was **i.**
Lk 13:14 **i** because Jesus had healed on

INDIGNATION [INDIGNANT]
Ps 90: 7 by your anger and terrified by your **i.**
Na 1: 6 Who can withstand his **i?**

INDISPENSABLE*
1Co 12:22 body that seem to be weaker are **i,**

INDULGE [INDULGED, INDULGENCE, INDULGING, SELF-INDULGENCE]
Ex 32: 6 and drink and got up to **i** in revelry.
Nu 25: 1 men began to **i** in sexual immorality
1Co 10: 7 and got up to **i** in pagan revelry."
Gal 5:13 But do not use your freedom to **i**

INDULGED* [INDULGE]
2Co 12:21 and debauchery in which they have **i.**

INDULGENCE* [INDULGE]
Col   2:23 any value in restraining sensual **i.**

INDULGING* [INDULGE]
1Ti   3: 8 sincere, not **i** in much wine,

INEFFECTIVE*
2Pe   1: 8 they will keep you from being **i**

INEXPRESSIBLE*
2Co 12: 4 He heard **i** things,
1Pe   1: 8 in him and are filled with an **i**

INFANCY* [INFANT]
2Ti   3:15 from **i** you have known the holy

INFANT [INFANCY, INFANTS]
Nu   11:12 in my arms, as a nurse carries an **i,**
Isa   11: 8 The **i** will play near the hole of
         65:20 be in it an **i** who lives but a few days,

INFANTS [INFANT]
Ps   8: 2 and **i** you have ordained praise
Mt   21:16 and **i** you have ordained praise'?"
1Co   3: 1 as spiritual but as worldly—mere **i**
         14:20 In regard to evil be **i,**
Eph   4:14 Then we will no longer be **i,**

INFIDEL (KJV) See UNBELIEVER

INFILTRATED*
Gal   2: 4 some false brothers had **i** our ranks

INFIRMITIES* [INFIRMITY]
Isa   53: 4 up our **i** and carried our sorrows,
Mt   8:17 up our **i** and carried our diseases."

INFIRMITY* [INFIRMITIES]
Lk   13:12 you are set free from your **i."**

INFLAMED
Ro   1:27 were **i** with lust for one another.

INFLICT [INFLICTED, INFLICTS]
Dt   7:15 will not **i** on you the horrible
                  diseases
Ps 149: 7 to **i** vengeance on the nations
Jer   18: 8 not **i** on it the disaster I had planned.

INFLICTED [INFLICT]
Ge   12:17 But the LORD **i** serious diseases
Isa   30:26 and heals the wounds he **i.**

INFLUENCED* [INFLUENCE]
1Co 12: 2 were **i** and led astray to mute idols.

INFLUENTIAL* [INFLUENCE]
1Co   1:26 human standards; not many were **i;**

INGATHERING* [GATHER]
Ex   23:16 the Feast of **I** at the end of the year,
         34:22 the Feast of **I** at the turn of the year.

INHABITANT [INHABITANTS, INHABITED]
Isa   6:11 the cities lie ruined and without **i,**
Jer   4: 7 towns will lie in ruins without **i.**

INHABITANTS [INHABITANT]
Lev 18:25 and the land vomited out its **i.**
Nu   33:55 you do not drive out the **i** of the land,
Jos   9:24 to wipe out all its **i** from before you.
Rev   6:10 until you judge the **i** of the earth
         8:13 Woe to the **i** of the earth,
         13: 8 All **i** of the earth will worship

INHABITED [INHABITANT]
Isa   45:18 but formed it to be **i—**
Joel   3:20 Judah will be **i** forever and Jerusalem
Zec 14:11 It will be **i;** never again will it

INHERIT [CO-HEIRS, HEIR, HEIRS, HERITAGE, INHERITANCE, INHERITED]
Ge   15: 2 and the one who will **i** my estate
Dt   1:38 because he will lead Israel to **i** it.
Jos   1: 6 **i** the land I swore to their forefathers
2Ki   2: 9 "Let me **i** a double portion
Ps   37:11 But the meek will **i** the land
         37:29 the righteous will **i** the land
Pr   3:35 The wise **i** honor,
         11:29 on his family will **i** only wind,
         14:18 The simple **i** folly,
Isa   61: 7 and so they will **i** a double portion
Zec   2:12 The LORD will **i** Judah
Mt   5: 5 for they will **i** the earth.
         19:29 as much and will **i** eternal life.
Mk   10:17 "what must I do to **i** eternal life?"
Lk   10:25 "what must I do to **i** eternal life?"
         18:18 what must I do to **i** eternal life?"
1Co   6: 9 will not **i** the kingdom of God?
         15:50 and blood cannot **i** the kingdom
Gal   5:21 that those who live like this will not **i**
Heb   1:14 to serve those who will **i** salvation?
Rev 21: 7 He who overcomes will **i** all this,

INHERITANCE [INHERIT]
Ge   21:10 share in the **i** with my son Isaac."
Ex   34: 9 and take us as your **i."**
Lev 20:24 I will give it to you as an **i,**
Nu   18:20 "You will have no **i** in their land,
Dt   4:20 to be the people of his **i,**
         10: 9 the LORD is their **i,**
Jos   14: 1 areas the Israelites received as an **i**
         14: 3 the two-and-a-half tribes their **i** east
Ps   2: 8 and I will make the nations your **i,**
         16: 6 surely I have a delightful **i.**
         33:12 the people he chose for his **i.**
       136:21 and gave their land as an **i,**
Pr   13:22 an **i** for his children's children,
Jer   3:19 the most beautiful **i** of any nation.'
Da   12:13 will rise to receive your allotted **i."**
Joel   2:17 not make your **i** an object of scorn,
Mt   25:34 blessed by my Father; take your **i,**
Lk   12:13 tell my brother to divide the **i**
Gal   3:18 For if the **i** depends on the law,
         4:30 share in the **i** with the free woman's

Eph	1:14	who is a deposit guaranteeing our **i**
	5: 5	You have any **i** in the kingdom of Christ
Col	1:12	you to share in the **i** of the saints
	3:24	an **i** from the Lord as a reward.
Heb	9:15	may receive the promised eternal **i—**
1Pe	1: 4	into an **i** that can never perish, spoil

INHERITED [INHERIT]

Heb 1: 4 as the name he has **i** is superior

INIQUITIES [INIQUITY]

Ps	78:38	he was merciful; he forgave their **i**
	90: 8	You have set our **i** before you,
	103:10	or repay us according to our **i.**
Isa	53: 5	he was crushed for our **i;**
	53:11	and he will bear their **i.**
	59: 2	But your **i** have separated you
Mic	7:19	all our **i** into the depths of the sea.

INIQUITY [INIQUITIES]

Ps	25:11	forgive my **i,** though it is great.
	32: 5	to you and did not cover up my **i.**
	38:18	I confess my **i;**
	51: 2	Wash away all my **i** and cleanse me
	51: 9	from my sins and blot out all my **i.**
Isa	53: 6	and the LORD has laid on him the **i**
Mic	2: 1	Woe to those who plan **i,**

INJURED [INJURY]

Isa	1: 5	Your whole head is **i,**
Eze	34:16	I will bind up the **i** and strengthen
Zec	11:16	or heal the **i,** or feed the healthy,
Mal	1:13	"When you bring **i,** crippled or

INJURES [INJURY]

| Lev | 24:19 | If anyone **i** his neighbor, |
| Job | 5:18 | he **i,** but his hands also heal. |

INJURY [INJURED, INJURES]

Ex	21:23	But if there is serious **i,**
Jer	30:12	your **i** beyond healing.
Na	3:19	can heal your wound; your **i** is fatal.
Rev	9:19	heads with which they inflict **i.**

INJUSTICE

2Ch	19: 7	with the LORD our God there is no **i**
Pr	13:23	but **i** sweeps it away.
	16: 8	righteousness than much gain with **i.**

INK*

Jer	36:18	and I wrote them in **i** on the scroll."
2Co	3: 3	written not with **i** but with the Spirit
2Jn	1:12	but I do not want to use paper and **i.**
3Jn	1:13	I do not want to do so with pen and **i.**

INMOST [INNER]

| Ps | 51: 6 | you teach me wisdom in the **i** place. |
| | 139:13 | For you created my **i** being; |

INN*

| Lk | 2: 7 | there was no room for them in the **i.** |
| | 10:34 | took him to an **i** and took care |

INNER [INMOST]

2Sa 18:24 sitting between the **i** and outer gates,

1Ki	6:16	within the temple an **i** sanctuary,
Ps	51: 6	Surely you desire truth in the **i** parts;
Ro	7:22	in my **i** being I delight in God's law;

INNOCENCE [INNOCENT]

Ps 26: 6 I wash my hands in **i,**

INNOCENT [INNOCENCE, INNOCENTLY]

Ex	23: 7	and do not put an **i** or honest person
Dt	19:10	so that **i** blood will not be shed
	25: 1	the **i** and condemning the guilty.
Job	34: 5	"Job says, 'I am **i,**
Ps	19:13	**i** of great transgression.
Pr	6:17	hands that shed **i** blood,
	16: 2	All a man's ways seem **i** to him,
	17:26	It is not good to punish an **i** man,
Isa	59: 7	they are swift to shed **i** blood.
Mt	10:16	shrewd as snakes and as **i** as doves.
	12: 7	not have condemned the **i.**
	27: 4	"for I have betrayed **i** blood."
	27:24	"I am **i** of this man's blood," he said.
Ac	20:26	to you today that I am **i** of the blood
Ro	16:19	and **i** about what is evil.
1Co	4: 4	but that does not make me **i.**

INQUIRE [INQUIRED, INQUIRING]

Jos	9:14	but did not **i** of the LORD.
1Sa	28: 7	so I may go and **i** of her."
1Ch	10:14	and did not **i** of the LORD.
2Ch	20: 3	Jehoshaphat resolved to **i** of
Isa	8:19	should not a people **i** of their God?
Eze	14: 3	Should I let them **i** of me at all?

INQUIRED [INQUIRE]

| 1Sa | 22:10 | Ahimelech **i** of the LORD for him; |
| | 28: 6 | He **i** of the LORD, |

INQUIRING [INQUIRE]

| Nu | 27:21 | by **i** of the Urim before the LORD. |
| Dt | 12:30 | to be ensnared by **i** about their gods, |

INSANE

1Sa	21:13	pretended to be **i** in their presence;
Ps	34: T	pretended to be **i** before Abimelech,
Ac	26:24	Your great learning is driving you **i."**

INSCRIBE* [INSCRIBED, INSCRIPTION]

Isa 30: 8 **i** it on a scroll,

INSCRIBED [INSCRIBE]

Ex	31:18	the tablets of stone **i** by the finger
Dt	9:10	LORD gave me two stone tablets **i**
Zec	14:20	HOLY TO THE LORD will be **i**

INSCRIPTION [INSCRIBE]

Da	5:24	the hand that wrote the **i.**
Mt	22:20	And whose **i?"**
2Ti	2:19	sealed with this **i:**

INSECTS*

| Lev | 11:20 | " 'All flying **i** that walk on all fours |
| Dt | 14:19 | All flying **i** that swarm are unclean |

INSIDE

Ge	6:14	and coat it with pitch **i** and out.
Ex	4: 6	"Put your hand **i** your cloak."
	12:46	"It must be eaten **i** one house;
1Ki	6:20	He overlaid the **i** with pure gold,
Jnh	1:17	and Jonah was **i** the fish three days
Mt	23:26	First clean the **i** of the cup and dish,
	23:27	on the **i** are full of dead men's bones
Mk	7:23	from **i** and make a man 'unclean.' "
1Co	5:12	Are you not to judge those **i?**
Rev	5: 4	worthy to open the scroll or look **i.**

INSIGHT [INSIGHTS]

1Ki	4:29	Solomon wisdom and very great **i,**
Ps	119:99	I have more **i** than all my teachers,
Pr	5: 1	listen well to my words of no **i,**
	21:30	There is no wisdom, no **i,**
Da	5:11	was found to have **i** and intelligence
	9:22	to give you **i** and understanding.
Eph	3: 4	to understand my **i** into the mystery
Php	1: 9	in knowledge and depth of **i,**
2Ti	2: 7	the Lord will give you **i** into all this.
Rev	13:18	If anyone has **i,**

INSIGHTS* [INSIGHT]

Job	15: 9	What **i** do you have that we do not

INSOLENT

Ro	1:30	God-haters, **i,** arrogant and boastful;

INSPIRE [INSPIRED]

Jer	32:40	and I will **i** them to fear me,

INSPIRED* [INSPIRE]

Hos	9: 7	the **i** man a maniac.
1Th	1: 3	and your endurance **i** by hope

INSTALLED

Ps	2: 6	"I have **i** my King on Zion,

INSTANT [INSTANTLY]

Pr	6:15	disaster will overtake him in an **i;**
Lk	4: 5	showed him in an **i** all the kingdoms

INSTANTLY* [INSTANT]

Lk	8:47	and how she had been **i** healed.
Ac	3: 7	and **i** the man's feet and ankles

INSTEAD

Ge	22:13	and sacrificed it as a burnt offering **i**
2Ch	28:20	but he gave him trouble **i** of help.
Pr	8:10	Choose my instruction **i** of silver,
Isa	60:17	**I** of bronze I will bring you gold,
	61: 7	and **i** of disgrace they will rejoice
Jer	7:24	they did not listen or pay attention; **i,**
Jn	3:19	but men loved darkness **i** of light
	15:15	**I,** I have called you friends,

INSTINCT* [INSTINCTS]

2Pe	2:12	like brute beasts, creatures of **i,**
Jude	1:10	what things they do understand by **i,**

INSTINCTS* [INSTINCT]

Jude	1:19	who follow mere natural **i** and do not

INSTITUTED

Ro	13: 2	rebelling against what God has **i,**
1Pe	2:13	the Lord's sake to every authority **i**

INSTRUCT [INSTRUCTED, INSTRUCTION, INSTRUCTIONS, INSTRUCTOR, INSTRUCTS]

Ne	9:20	You gave your good Spirit to **i** them.
Ps	32: 8	I will **i** you and teach you in
	105:22	to **i** his princes as he pleased
Pr	9: 9	**I** a wise man and he will
Da	11:33	"Those who are wise will **i** many,
Ro	15:14	and competent to **i** one another.
1Co	2:16	of the Lord that he may **i** him?"
	14:19	five intelligible words to **i** others
2Ti	2:25	who oppose him he must gently **i,**

INSTRUCTED [INSTRUCT]

2Ch	26: 5	who **i** him in the fear of God.
Pr	21:11	when a wise man is **i,**
Isa	40:13	or **i** him as his counselor?
	50: 4	LORD has given me an **i** tongue,
Mt	13:52	who has been **i** about the kingdom
	21: 6	and did as Jesus had **i** them.
Ac	18:25	He had been **i** in the way of the Lord,
1Co	14:31	so that everyone may be **i**

INSTRUCTION [INSTRUCT]

Ex	24:12	commands I have written for their **i."**
Pr	1: 8	Listen, my son, to your father's **i**
	4: 1	Listen, my sons, to a father's **i;**
	4:13	Hold on to **i,** do not let it go;
	8:10	Choose my **i** instead of silver,
	8:33	Listen to my **i** and be wise;
	13: 1	A wise son heeds his father's **i,**
	13:13	He who scorns **i** will pay for it,
	16:20	Whoever gives heed to **i** prospers,
	16:21	and pleasant words promote **i.**
	19:20	Listen to advice and accept **i,**
	23:12	Apply your heart to **i** and your ears
	31:26	and faithful **i** is on her tongue.
Isa	29:24	those who complain will accept **i."**
1Co	14: 6	or prophecy or word of **i?**
	14:26	everyone has a hymn, or a word of **i,**
Gal	6: 6	Anyone who receives **i** in the word
Eph	6: 4	bring them up in the training and **i** of
1Th	4: 8	he who rejects this **i** does not
2Th	3:14	If anyone does not obey our **i**
1Ti	1:18	I give you this **i** in keeping with
	6: 3	the sound **i** of our Lord Jesus Christ
2Ti	4: 2	with great patience and careful **i.**

INSTRUCTIONS [INSTRUCT]

Ex	12:24	"Obey these **i** as a lasting ordinance
Jos	8:33	when he gave **i** to bless the people
Ac	1: 2	after giving **i** through the Holy Spirit
1Ti	3:14	I am writing you these **i** so that,

INSTRUCTOR* [INSTRUCT]

Ro	2:20	**i** of the foolish, a teacher of infants,
Gal	6: 6	must share all good things with his **i.**

INSTRUCTS* [INSTRUCT]

Ps   16: 7 even at night my heart i me.
      25: 8 therefore he i sinners in his ways.
Isa   28:26 His God i him and teaches him

INSTRUMENT* [INSTRUMENTS]

Eze   33:32 a beautiful voice and plays an i well,
Ac   9:15 This man is my chosen i
2Ti   2:21 he will be an i for noble purposes,

INSTRUMENTS [INSTRUMENT]

1Ch   15:16 accompanied by musical i:
      23: 5 with the musical i I have provided
Ro   6:13 body to him as i of righteousness.

INSULT [INSULTED, INSULTS]

Ps   69: 9 insults of those who i you fall on me.
Pr   9: 7 corrects a mocker invites i;
      12:16 but a prudent man overlooks an i.
Isa   37:17 has sent to i the living God.
Jer   20: 8 word of the Lord has brought me i
Mt   5:11 "Blessed are you when people i you,
Lk   6:22 when they exclude you and i you
      18:32 They will mock him, i him,
Heb   10:33 publicly exposed to i and persecution
1Pe   3: 9 Do not repay evil with evil or i
       3: 9 with evil or insult with i,

INSULTED [INSULT]

2Ki   19:22 Who is it you have i
Heb   10:29 and who has i the Spirit of grace?
Jas   2: 6 But you have i the poor.
1Pe   4:14 If you are i because of the name

INSULTS [INSULT]

Ne   4: 4 Turn their i back on their own heads.
Ps   22: 7 All who see me mock me; they hurl i
      69: 9 i of those who insult you fall on me.
Pr   22:10 quarrels and i are ended.
La   3:61 O Lord, you have heard their i,
Mk   15:29 Those who passed by hurled i at him,
Jn   9:28 Then they hurled i at him and said,
Ro   15: 3 "The i of those who insult you have
2Co   12:10 in i, in hardships, in persecutions,
1Pe   2:23 When they hurled their i at him,

INTEGRITY*

Dt   9: 5 of your righteousness or your i
1Ki   9: 4 if you walk before me in i of heart
1Ch   29:17 test the heart and are pleased with i.
Ne   7: 2 because he was a man of i
Job   2: 3 And he still maintains his i,
       2: 9 "Are you still holding on to your i?
       6:29 for my i is at stake.
      27: 5 I will not deny my i.
Ps   7: 8 according to my i, O Most High.
      25:21 May i and uprightness protect me,
      41:12 In my i you uphold me and set me
      78:72 David shepherded them with i
Pr   10: 9 The man of i walks securely,
      11: 3 The i of the upright guides them,
      13: 6 Righteousness guards the man of i,
      17:26 or to flog officials for their i.
      29:10 Bloodthirsty men hate a man of i

Isa   45:23 my mouth has uttered in all i a word
      59: 4 no one pleads his case with i.
Mt   22:16 "we know you are a man of i
Mk   12:14 we know you are a man of i.
Tit   2: 7 In your teaching show i,

INTELLIGENCE [INTELLIGENT]

Isa   29:14 the i of the intelligent will vanish."
Da   5:11 to have insight and i and wisdom
1Co   1:19 the i of the intelligent I will frustrate.

INTELLIGENT [INTELLIGENCE]

1Sa   25: 3 She was an i and beautiful woman,

INTELLIGIBLE*

1Co   14: 9 Unless you speak i words with your
      14:19 I would rather speak five i words

INTEND [INTENDED, INTENT,
  INTENTIONAL, INTENTIONALLY,
  INTENTLY]

1Ki   5: 5 I i, therefore, to build a temple for
2Ch   29:10 Now I i to make a covenant with

INTENDED [INTEND]

Ge   50:20 i to harm me, but God i it for good
Jer   18:10 reconsider the good I had i to do for
Ro   7:10 commandment that was i to bring life

INTENSE [INTENSELY]

1Th   2:17 our i longing we made every effort
Rev   16: 9 They were seared by the i heat

INTENSELY [INTENSE]

Gal   1:13 how i I persecuted the church of God

INTENT [INTEND]

Ex   32:12 with evil i that he brought them out,
Pr   7:10 like a prostitute and with crafty i.
Mt   22:18 But Jesus, knowing their evil i, said,

INTENTIONAL* [INTEND]

Nu   15:25 they will be forgiven, for it was not i

INTENTIONALLY* [INTEND]

Ex   21:13 However, if he does not do it i,
Nu   35:20 or throws something at him i so

INTENTLY* [INTEND]

Ac   1:10 They were looking i up into the sky
       6:15 in the Sanhedrin looked i at Stephen,
Jas   1:25 who looks i into the perfect law
1Pe   1:10 searched i and with the greatest care,

INTERCEDE [INTERCEDES,
  INTERCEDING, INTERCESSION,
  INTERCESSOR]

1Sa   2:25 who will i for him?"
Heb   7:25 he always lives to i for them.

INTERCEDES* [INTERCEDE]

Ro   8:26 but the Spirit himself i for us
       8:27 because the Spirit i for the saints

INTERCEDING* [INTERCEDE]
Ro   8:34 at the right hand of God and is also **i**

INTERCESSION* [INTERCEDE]
Isa 53:12 and made **i** for the transgressors.
1Ti   2: 1 **i** and thanksgiving be made for

INTERCESSOR* [INTERCEDE]
Job 16:20 My **i** is my friend

INTEREST [INTERESTS]
Lev 25:36 Do not take **i** of any kind from him,
Dt   23:19 Do not charge your brother **i,**
      23:20 You may charge a foreigner **i,**
Lk   19:23 I could have collected it with **i?'**
Php   2:20 takes a genuine **i** in your welfare
1Ti   6: 4 an unhealthy **i** in controversies

INTERESTS [INTEREST]
1Co 7:34 and his **i** are divided.
Php   2: 4 your own **i,** but also to the **i** of others
      2:21 For everyone looks out for his own **i,**

INTERFERE*
Ezr   6: 7 not **i** with the work on this temple

INTERMARRY* [MARRY]
Ge 34: 9 **I** with us; give us your daughters
Dt   7: 3 Do not **i** with them.
Jos 23:12 and if you **i** with them and associate
1Ki 11: 2 "You must not **i** with them,
Ezr   9:14 **i** with the peoples who commit such

INTERPRET [INTERPRETATION, INTERPRETATIONS, INTERPRETER, INTERPRETS]
Ge 41:15 "I had a dream, and no one can **i** it.
Da   2: 6 So tell me the dream and **i** it for me."
      4: 9 Here is my dream; **i** it for me.
Mt   16: 3 you cannot **i** the signs of the times.
1Co 12:30 Do all **i?**
      14:13 that he may **i** what he says.
      14:27 one at a time, and someone must **i.**

INTERPRETATION [INTERPRET]
Ge 40:16 that Joseph had given a favorable **i,**
Jdg   7:15 Gideon heard the dream and its **i,**
1Co 12:10 and to still another the **i** of tongues.
      14:26 a revelation, a tongue or an **i.**
2Pe   1:20 came about by the prophet's own **i.**

INTERPRETATIONS* [INTERPRET]
Ge 40: 8 "Do not **i** belong to God?
Da   5:16 that you are able to give **i** and

INTERPRETER [INTERPRET]
1Co 14:28 If there is no **i,**

INTERPRETS* [INTERPRET]
Dt 18:10 **i** omens, engages in witchcraft,
1Co 14: 5 who speaks in tongues, unless he **i,**

INTOXICATED*
Rev 17: 2 **i** with the wine of her adulteries."

INVADE [INVADED, INVADING]
Dt 12:29 the nations you are about to **i**
Da 11:41 He will also **i** the Beautiful Land.
Na   1:15 No more will the wicked **i** you;

INVADED [INVADE]
2Ki 17: 5 The king of Assyria **i** the entire land,
      24: 1 Nebuchadnezzar king of Babylon **i**

INVADING [INVADE]
Hab   3:16 calamity to come on the nation **i** us.

INVENT* [INVENTED]
Ro   1:30 they **i** ways of doing evil;

INVENTED* [INVENT]
2Pe   1:16 We did not follow cleverly **i** stories

INVESTIGATED
Lk   1: 3 I myself have carefully **i** everything

INVISIBLE*
Ro   1:20 God's **i** qualities—his eternal power
Col   1:15 He is the image of the **i** God,
      1:16 in heaven and on earth, visible and **i,**
1Ti   1:17 Now to the King eternal, immortal, **i,**
Heb 11:27 because he saw him who is **i.**

INVITE [INVITED, INVITES]
Mt   22: 9 Go to the street corners and **i** to
      25:38 we see you a stranger and **i** you in,
Lk   14:12 do not **i** your friends,
      14:13 when you give a banquet, **i** the poor,

INVITED [INVITE]
Zep   1: 7 he has consecrated those he has **i.**
Mt   22:14 many are **i,** but few are chosen."
      25:35 I was a stranger and you **i** me in,
Lk   7:36 Now one of the Pharisees **i** Jesus
      11:37 a Pharisee **i** him to eat with him;
      14:10 But when you are **i,**
Rev 19: 9 "Write: 'Blessed are those who are **i**

INVITES [INVITE]
Pr   9: 7 "Whoever corrects a mocker **i** insult;
     10:14 but the mouth of a fool **i** ruin.
     18: 6 and his mouth **i** a beating.
1Co 10:27 If some unbeliever **i** you to a meal

INVOKE [INVOKED]
Ex   23:13 Do not **i** the names of other gods;
Ac   19:13 tried to **i** the name of the Lord Jesus

INVOKED* [INVOKE]
Hos   2:17 no longer will their names be **i.**

INVOLVED
2Ti   2: 4 as a soldier gets **i** in civilian affairs—

INWARDLY
Mt   7:15 but **i** they are ferocious wolves.
Ro   2:29 No, a man is a Jew if he is one **i;**

8:23 groan **i** as we wait eagerly for our
2Co 4:16 **i** we are being renewed day by day.

IRON [IRON-SMELTING]

Ge 4:22 all kinds of tools out of bronze and **i.**
Lev 26:19 and make the sky above you like **i**
2Ki 6: 6 and made the **i** float.
Ps   2: 9 You will rule them with an **i** scepter;
Pr 27:17 As **i** sharpens **i**, so one man sharpens
Isa 60:17 and silver in place of **i.**
Da   2:33 its legs of **i**, its feet partly of **i**
7: 7 It had large **i** teeth;
1Ti 4: 2 have been seared as with a hot **i.**
Rev 2:27 'He will rule them with an **i** scepter;
12: 5 rule all the nations with an **i** scepter.
19:15 "He will rule them with an **i** scepter."

IRON-SMELTING [IRON]

Dt   4:20 and brought you out of the **i** furnace,

IRRELIGIOUS*

1Ti 1: 9 ungodly and sinful, the unholy and **i;**

IRREVOCABLE*

Ro 11:29 for God's gifts and his call are **i.**

ISAAC

Son of Abraham by Sarah (Ge 17:19; 21:1-7;
1Ch 1:28). Abrahamic covenant perpetuated
through (Ge 17:21; 26:2-5). Offered up by
Abraham (Ge 22; Heb 11:17-19). Rebekah taken
as wife (Ge 24). Inherited Abraham's estate (Ge
25:5). Fathered Esau and Jacob (Ge 25:19-26;
1Ch 1:34). Nearly lost Rebekah to Abimelech (Ge
26:1-11). Covenant with Abimelech (Ge 26:12-
31). Tricked into blessing Jacob (Ge 27). Death
(Ge 35:27-29). Father of Israel (Ex 3:6; Dt 29:13;
Ro 9:10).

ISAIAH

Prophet to Judah (Isa 1:1). Called by the LORD
(Isa 6). Announced judgment to Ahaz (Isa 7),
deliverance from Assyria to Hezekiah (2Ki 19; Isa
36-37), deliverance from death to Hezekiah (2Ki
20:1-11; Isa 38). Chronicler of Judah's history
(2Ch 26:22; 32:32).

ISCARIOT [JUDAS]

Mt 10: 4 and Judas **I,** who betrayed him.
Lk 22: 3 Then Satan entered Judas, called **I,**

ISH-BOSHETH

Son of Saul who attempted to succeed him as
king (2Sa 2:8-4:12; 1Ch 8:33).

ISHMAEL [ISHMAELITES]

Son of Abraham by Hagar (Ge 16; 1Ch 1:28).
Blessed, but not son of covenant (Ge 17:18-21;
Gal 4:21-31). Sent away by Sarah (Ge 21:8-21).
Children (Ge 25:12-18; 1Ch 1:29-31). Death (Ge
25:17).

ISHMAELITES [ISHMAEL]

Ge 37:27 Come, let's sell him to the **I**

ISLAND [ISLANDS]

Rev 1: 9 the **i** of Patmos because of the word
16:20 Every **i** fled away and

ISLANDS [ISLAND]

Isa 42: 4 In his law the **i** will put their hope."
66:19 to the distant **i** that have not heard

ISRAEL [ISRAEL'S, ISRAELITE, ISRAELITES, JACOB]

1. Name given to Jacob (Ge 32:28; 35:10; see
JACOB).

2. Corporate name of Jacob's descendants;
often specifically Northern Kingdom.

Ge 49:24 the Rock of **I,**
49:28 All these are the twelve tribes of **I,**
Ex 28:11 Engrave the names of the sons of **I**
28:29 will bear the names of the sons of **I**
Nu 19:13 That person must be cut off from **I.**
24:17 a scepter will rise out of **I.**
Dt   6: 4 Hear, O **I:** The LORD our God,
10:12 And now, O **I**, what does the LORD
18: 1 no allotment or inheritance with **I.**
Jos 4:22 'I crossed the Jordan on dry ground.'
24:31 **I** served the LORD throughout
Jdg 17: 6 In those days **I** had no king;
21: 3 "why has this happened to **I**
Ru   4:14 May he become famous throughout **I**
1Sa 3:20 And all **I** from Dan to Beersheba
4:21 "The glory has departed from **I**"—
14:23 So the LORD rescued **I** that day,
15:26 rejected you as king over **I!**"
17:46 that there is a God in **I.**
18:16 But all **I** and Judah loved David,
2Sa 5: 2 'You will shepherd my people **I,**
5: 3 and they anointed David king over **I.**
7:26 LORD Almighty is God over **I!**'
14:25 In all **I** there was not a man so
1Ki 1:35 I have appointed him ruler over **I**
8:25 to sit before me on the throne of **I,**
10: 9 of the LORD's eternal love for **I,**
12:19 So **I** has been in rebellion against
18:17 "Is that you, you troubler of **I?**"
19:18 Yet I reserve seven thousand in **I**—
2Ki 5: 8 that there is a prophet in **I.**"
17:20 LORD rejected all the people of **I;**
1Ch 17:22 your people **I** your very own forever,
21: 1 Satan rose up against **I** and incited
29:25 as no king over **I** ever had before.
2Ch 9: 8 of the love of your God for **I**
Ps 22: 3 you are the praise of **I.**
73: 1 Surely God is good to **I,**
78:21 and his wrath rose against **I,**
81: 8 if you would but listen to me, O **I!**
98: 3 to the house of **I;**
99: 8 you were to **I** a forgiving God,
125: 5 Peace be upon **I.**
Isa 1: 3 but **I** does not know,
11:12 and gather the exiles of **I;**
27: 6 **I** will bud and blossom and fill all
44:21 made you, you are my servant; O **I,**
46:13 my splendor to **I.**
Jer 2: 3 **I** was holy to the LORD,

23: 6 be saved and **I** will live in safety.
31: 2 I will come to give rest to **I.**"
31:10 'He who scattered **I** will gather them
31:31 a new covenant with the house of **I**
33:17 to sit on the throne of the house of **I,**
La 2: 5 he has swallowed up **I.**
Eze 3:17 a watchman for the house of **I;**
33: 7 a watchman for the house of **I;**
34: 2 prophesy against the shepherds of **I;**
36: 1 'O mountains of **I,**
37:28 know that I the LORD make **I** holy,
39:23 that the people of **I** went into exile
Da 9:20 and the sin of my people **I**
Hos 7: 1 whenever I would heal **I,**
11: 1 "When **I** was a child, I loved him,
Am 4:12 prepare to meet your God, O **I.**"
7:11 and **I** will surely go into exile,
8: 2 "The time is ripe for my people **I;**
9:14 I will bring back my exiled people **I;**
Mic 5: 2 for me one who will be ruler over **I,**
Zep 3:13 The remnant of **I** will do no wrong;
Zec 11:14 the brotherhood between Judah and **I**
Mal 1: 5 even beyond the borders of **I!'**
Mt 2: 6 be the shepherd of my people **I.' "**
10: 6 Go rather to the lost sheep of **I.**
15:24 sent only to the lost sheep of **I.**"
Mk 12:29 O **I,** the Lord our God,
15:32 Let this Christ, this King of **I,**
Lk 1:54 He has helped his servant **I,**
2:34 the falling and rising of many in **I,**
22:30 judging the twelve tribes of **I.**
Jn 12:13 "Blessed is the King of **I!**"
Ac 1: 6 to restore the kingdom to **I?**"
9:15 and before the people of **I.**
Ro 9: 6 For not all who are descended from **I** are **I.**
9:31 but **I,** who pursued a law of
11: 7 What **I** sought so earnestly it did
11:26 so all **I** will be saved, as it is written:
Gal 6:16 even to the **I** of God.
Eph 2:12 excluded from citizenship in **I**
3: 6 the Gentiles are heirs together with **I,**
Heb 8: 8 a new covenant with the house of **I**
Rev 7: 4 from all the tribes of **I.**
21:12 the names of the twelve tribes of **I.**

ALL ISRAEL Ex 18:25; Dt 1:1; 5:1; 11:6; 13:11; 21:21; 27:9; 31:1, 7, 11; 32:45; 34:12; Jos 3:7, 17; 4:14; 7:24, 25; 8:15, 21, 33; 10:15, 29, 31, 34, 36, 38, 43; 23:2; Jdg 8:27; 1Sa 2:22; 3:20; 4:1, 5; 7:5; 11:2; 12:1; 13:4, 20; 18:16; 19:5; 24:2; 25:1; 28:3; 2Sa 2:9; 3:12, 21, 37; 4:1; 5:5; 8:15; 10:17; 12:12; 14:25; 16:21, 22; 17:10, 11, 13; 1Ki 1:20; 2:15; 3:28; 4:1, 7; 5:13; 8:62, 65; 11:42; 12:16, 18, 20; 14:13, 18; 15:27, 33; 18:20; 22:17; 2Ki 3:6; 9:14; 1Ch 9:1; 11:1, 10; 12:38; 14:8; 15:3, 28; 18:14; 19:17; 21:5; 28:4, 8; 29:21, 23, 25, 26; 2Ch 1:2; 7:8; 9:30; 10:3, 16; 12:1; 13:4, 15; 18:16; 24:5; 28:23; 29:24, 24; 30:1; 35:3; Ezr 6:17; 8:25, 35; 10:5; Ne 12:47; 13:26; Da 9:7, 11; Mal 4:4; Ac 2:36; Ro 11:26

GOD OF ISRAEL See GOD

HOLY ONE OF ISRAEL 2Ki 19:22; Ps 71:22; 78:41; 89:18; Isa 1:4; 5:19, 24; 10:20; 12:6; 17:7;

29:19; 30:11, 12, 15; 31:1; 37:23; 41:14, 16, 20; 43:3, 14; 45:11; 47:4; 48:17; 49:7, 7; 54:5; 55:5; 60:9, 14; Jer 50:29; 51:5

HOUSE OF ISRAEL See HOUSE

ISRAEL AND JUDAH 1Sa 17:52; 18:16; 2Sa 3:10; 5:5; 11:11; 12:8; 21:2; 24:1; 1Ki 1:35; 2Ki 17:13; 2Ch 27:7; 30:1, 6; 31:6; 34:21; 35:27; 36:8; Jer 30:3, 4; 32:30, 32; 51:5; Eze 9:9

KING OF ISRAEL See KING

KINGS OF ISRAEL See KINGS

MEN OF ISRAEL Nu 26:51; Dt 29:10; Jos 9:6, 7, 14; 10:24; Jdg 20:11, 20, 22, 33, 36, 38, 39, 39, 41, 42, 48; 21:1; 1Sa 7:11; 8:22; 11:8; 13:6; 14:24; 17:19, 52; 26:2; 2Sa 2:17; 15:6, 13; 16:15, 18; 17:14, 24; 19:41, 42, 43, 43; 20:2; 23:9; 24:4; 1Ki 8:2; 1Ch 21:14; 2Ch 5:3; 13:12, 18; 31:6; Ne 7:7; Ps 78:31; Ac 2:22; 3:12; 5:35; 13:16; 21:28

PEOPLE OF ISRAEL Ex 16:31; 19:3; Nu 32:4; Dt 27:14; 32:52; Jos 4:7; 8:33; 1Sa 7:2; 10:17; 1Ki 16:21; 2Ki 17:20, 23; 2Ch 6:11; 30:6; Ezr 2:2; 6:16; 9:1; Ne 1:6; 10:39; Ps 78:71; 103:7; Jer 3:21; 32:30, 30, 32; 50:4, 33; Eze 4:13; 12:24; 14:5, 11; 20:13, 27; 28:24, 25; 29:16; 36:17; 39:23, 25; 43:10; Hos 1:11; Joel 3:16; Am 2:11; 3:1; 6:1; Mt 27:9; Lk 1:16; Ac 4:10, 27; 9:15; 10:36; 13:17, 24; Ro 9:4; 1Co 10:18; Php 3:5

TRIBES OF ISRAEL Ge 49:16, 28; Ex 24:4; Nu 30:1; 31:4; Dt 29:21; 33:5; Jos 3:12; 12:7; 22:14; 24:1; Jdg 18:1; 20:2, 10, 12; 21:5, 8, 15; 1Sa 2:28; 10:20; 15:17; 2Sa 5:1; 15:2, 10; 19:9; 20:14; 24:2; 1Ki 11:32; 14:21; 2Ki 21:7; 1Ch 27:16, 22; 29:6; 2Ch 12:13; 33:7; Ezr 6:17; Ps 78:55; Eze 47:13, 21, 22; 48:19, 29, 31; Hos 5:9; Zec 9:1; Mt 19:28; Lk 22:30; Rev 7:4; 21:12

ISRAEL'S [ISRAEL]

Jdg 10:16 he could bear **I** misery no longer.
2Sa 23: 1 **I** singer of songs:
Isa 44: 6 LORD says—**I** King and Redeemer,
Jer 3: 9 **I** immorality mattered so little to her,
31: 9 because I am **I** father,
Hos 5: 5 **I** arrogance testifies against them;
Jn 3:10 "You are **I** teacher," said Jesus,

ISRAELITE [ISRAEL]

Ex 16: 1 The whole **I** community set out
35:29 **I** men and women who were willing
Nu 8:16 the first male offspring from every **I**
20: 1 the whole **I** community arrived at
20:22 The whole **I** community set out
Ne 9: 2 **I** descent had separated themselves
Jn 1:47 he said of him, "Here is a true **I,**
Ro 11: 1 I am an **I** myself,

ISRAELITES [ISRAEL]

Ex 1: 7 **I** were fruitful and multiplied greatly
2:23 They groaned in their slavery
3: 9 now the cry of the **I** has reached me,
12:35 The **I** did as Moses instructed
12:37 The **I** journeyed from Rameses
14:22 and the **I** went through the sea
16:12 "I have heard the grumbling of the **I.**

	16:35	The **I** ate manna forty years,
	24:17	the **I** the glory of the LORD looked
	28:30	means of making decisions for the **I**
	29:45	Then I will dwell among the **I** and
	31:16	The **I** are to observe the Sabbath,
	33: 5	"Tell the **I**, 'You are a stiff-necked
	39:42	The **I** had done all the work just as
Lev	22:32	be acknowledged as holy by the **I**.
	25:46	not rule over your fellow **I** ruthlessly
	25:55	for the **I** belong to me as servants.
Nu	2:32	These are the **I**, counted according to
	6:23	'This is how you are to bless the **I**.
	9: 2	"Have the **I** celebrate the Passover at
	9:17	the cloud settled, the **I** encamped.
	10:12	the **I** set out from the Desert of Sinai
	14: 2	All the **I** grumbled against Moses
	20:12	honor me as holy in the sight of the **I**
	21: 6	bit the people and many **I** died.
	26:65	**I** they would surely die in the desert,
	27:12	and see the land I have given the **I**.
	33: 3	The **I** set out from Rameses on
	35:10	"Speak to the **I** and say to them:
Dt	4:44	the law Moses set before the **I**.
	33: 1	the man of God pronounced on the **I**
Jos	1: 2	about to give to them—to the **I**.
	5: 6	The **I** had moved about in the desert
	7: 1	But the **I** acted unfaithfully in regard
	8:32	There, in the presence of the **I**,
	18: 1	assembly of the **I** gathered at Shiloh
	21: 3	the **I** gave the Levites
	22: 9	the half-tribe of Manasseh left the **I**
Jdg	2:11	Then the **I** did evil in the eyes of
	3:12	Once again the **I** did evil in the eyes
	4: 1	the **I** once again did evil in the eyes
	6: 1	Again the **I** did evil in the eyes of
	10: 6	Again the **I** did evil in the eyes of
	13: 1	Again the **I** did evil in the eyes of
1Sa	7: 4	So the **I** put away their Baals
	17: 2	and the **I** assembled and camped in
1Ki	8:63	and all the **I** dedicated the temple
	9:22	did not make slaves of any of the **I**;
	12: 1	for all the **I** had gone there
	12:17	**I** who were living in the towns of
2Ki	17: 7	because the **I** had sinned against
1Ch	9: 2	in their own towns were some **I**,
	10: 1	the **I** fled before them,
	11: 4	and all the **I** marched to Jerusalem
	21: 2	count the **I** from Beersheba to Dan.
2Ch	7: 6	and all the **I** were standing.
Ezr	2:70	rest of the **I** settled in their towns.
Ne	1: 6	I confess the sins we **I**,
	8:17	the **I** had not celebrated it like this.
Jer	16:14	who brought the **I** up out of Egypt,'
Hos	1:10	"Yet the **I** will be like the sand on
	3: 1	Love her as the LORD loves the **I**,
Am	4: 5	you **I**, for this is what you love
Mic	5: 3	of his brothers return to join the **I**.
Ro	9:27	"Though the number of the **I** be like
	10: 1	desire and prayer to God for the **I**
	10:16	not all the **I** accepted the good news.
2Co	11:22	Are they **I**? So am I.

ISSACHAR

Son of Jacob by Leah (Ge 30:18; 35:23; 1Ch

2:1). Tribe of blessed (Ge 49:14-15; Dt 33:18-19), numbered (Nu 1:29; 26:25), allotted land (Jos 19:17-23; Eze 48:25), assisted Deborah (Jdg 5:15), 12,000 from (Rev 7:7).

ISSUED [ISSUES, ISSUING]
Lk   2: 1 Augustus **i** a decree that a census

ISSUES* [ISSUED]
Da   6:15 edict that the king **i** can be changed."

ISSUING* [ISSUED]
Da   9:25 the **i** of the decree to restore

ITALIAN* [ITALY]
Ac   10: 1 what was known as the **I** Regiment.

ITALY [ITALIAN]
Ac   27: 1 decided that we would sail for **I**,
Heb 13:24 from **I** send you their greetings.

ITCHING*
2Ti   4: 3 to say what their **i** ears want to hear.

ITHAMAR
Son of Aaron (Ex 6:23; 1Ch 6:3). Duties at tabernacle (Ex 38:21; Nu 4:21-33; 7:8).

ITTAI
2Sa 15:19 The king said to **I** the Gittite,

IVORY
1Ki 10:22 silver and **i**, and apes and baboons.
       22:39 the palace he built and inlaid with **i**,
Am   3:15 the houses adorned with **i** will
Rev 18:12 and articles of every kind made of **i**,

J

JABBOK
Ge   32:22 and crossed the ford of the **J**.
Dt   3:16 the border) and out to the **J** River,

JABESH [JABESH GILEAD]
1Sa 11: 1 And all the men of **J** said to him,
       31:12 the wall of Beth Shan and went to **J**,
1Ch 10:12 bones under the great tree in **J**,

JABESH GILEAD [GILEAD, JABESH]
2Sa   2: 4 the men of **J** who had buried Saul,

JABIN
Jos 11: 1 When **J** king of Hazor heard of this,
Jdg   4:23 On that day God subdued **J**,

JACKALS
Ps   63:10 to the sword and become food for **j**.
Isa 13:21 **j** will fill her houses;
       35: 7 In the haunts where **j** once lay,
Mal   1: 3 his inheritance to the desert **j**."

JACOB [ISRAEL]

1. Second son of Isaac, twin of Esau (Ge 26:21-26; 1Ch 1:34). Bought Esau's birthright (Ge 26:29-34); tricked Isaac into blessing him (Ge 27:1-37). Fled to Haran (Ge 28:1-5). Abrahamic covenant perpetuated through (Ge 28:13-15; Mal 1:2). Vision at Bethel (Ge 28:10-22). Served Laban for Rachel and Leah (Ge 29:1-30). Children (Ge 29:31-30:24; 35:16-26; 1Ch 2-9). Flocks increased (Ge 30:25-43). Returned to Canaan (Ge 31). Wrestled with God; name changed to Israel (Ge 32:22-32). Reconciled to Esau (Ge 33). Returned to Bethel (Ge 35:1-15). Favored Joseph (Ge 37:3). Sent sons to Egypt during famine (Ge 42-43). Settled in Egypt (Ge 46). Blessed Ephraim and Manasseh (Ge 48). Blessed sons (Ge 49:1-28; Heb 11:21). Death (Ge 49:29-33). Burial (Ge 50:1-14).

2. Corporate name of Jacob's descendants; often specifically Northern Kingdom.

Ps	53: 6	let **J** rejoice and Israel be glad!
	59:13	of the earth that God rules over **J.**
	135: 4	LORD has chosen **J** to be his own,
Isa	44: 1	"But now listen, O **J,** my servant,
Jer	30:10	" 'So do not fear, O **J** my servant;
Eze	39:25	now bring **J** back from captivity
Mic	7:20	You will be true to **J,**
Mal	1: 2	"Yet I have loved **J,**
Ro	9:13	Just as it is written: **"J** I loved,

GOD OF JACOB See GOD

HOUSE OF JACOB See HOUSE

JAEL*

Woman who killed Canaanite general, Sisera (Jdg 4:17-22; 5:6, 24-27).

JAH (KJV) See †LORD

JAIL [JAILER]

Ac	4: 3	they put them in **j** until the next day.
	5:18	apostles and put them in the public **j.**

JAILER [JAIL]

Ac	16:34	The **j** brought them into his house

JAIR

Judge from Gilead (Jdg 10:3-5).

JAIRUS*

Synagogue ruler whose daughter Jesus raised (Mk 5:22-43; Lk 8:41-56).

JAKIN

1Ki	7:21	The pillar to the south he named **J**

JAMBRES*

2Ti	3: 8	Just as Jannes and **J** opposed Moses,

JAMES

1. Apostle; brother of John (Mt 4:21-22; 10:2; Mk 3:17; Lk 5:1-10). At transfiguration (Mt 17:1-13; Mk 9:1-13; Lk 9:28-36). Killed by Herod (Ac 12:2).

2. Apostle; son of Alphaeus (Mt 10:3; Mk 3:18; Lk 6:15).

3. Brother of Jesus (Mt 13:55; Mk 6:3; Lk 24:10; Gal 1:19) and Judas (Jude 1). With believers before Pentecost (Ac 1:13). Leader of church at Jerusalem (Ac 12:17; 15; 21:18; Gal 2:9, 12). Author of epistle (Jas 1:1).

JANNES*

2Ti	3: 8	as **J** and Jambres opposed Moses,

JAPHETH

Son of Noah (Ge 5:32; 1Ch 1:4-5). Blessed (Ge 9:18-28). Sons of (Ge 10:2-5).

JAR [JARS]

Ge	24:14	'Please let down your **j** that I may
Ex	16:33	"Take a **j** and put an omer of manna
1Ki	17:14	'The **j** of flour will not be used up
Jer	19: 1	"Go and buy a clay **j** from a potter.
Mk	14: 3	a woman came with an alabaster **j**
Lk	8:16	lights a lamp and hides it in a **j**
	22:10	man carrying a **j** of water will meet
Heb	9: 4	This ark contained the gold **j**

JARS [JAR]

Jdg	7:19	blew their trumpets and broke the **j**
Jn	2: 6	Nearby stood six stone water **j,**
2Co	4: 7	we have this treasure in **j** of clay

JASHAR*

Jos	10:13	as it is written in the Book of **J.**
2Sa	1:18	(it is written in the Book of **J):**

JASON

Ac	17: 7	**J** has welcomed them into his house.

JASPER

Ex	28:20	an onyx and a **j.**
Eze	28:13	chrysolite, onyx and **j,** sapphire,
Rev	4: 3	the appearance of **j** and carnelian.
	21:19	The first foundation was **j,**

JAVELIN

Jos	8:18	"Hold out toward Ai the **j** that is in
1Sa	17:45	with sword and spear and **j,**

JAWBONE

Jdg	15:15	Finding a fresh **j** of a donkey,

JAZER

Nu	21:32	After Moses had sent spies to **J,**
	32: 1	**J** and Gilead were suitable for

JEALOUS* [JEALOUSY]

Ge	30: 1	she became **j** of her sister.
	37:11	His brothers were **j** of him,
Ex	20: 5	the LORD your God, am a **j** God,
	34:14	whose name is **J,** is a **j** God.
Nu	5:14	or if he is **j** and suspects her even
	11:29	"Are you **j** for my sake?
Dt	4:24	God is a consuming fire, a **j** God.
	5: 9	the LORD your God, am a **j** God,
	6:15	is a **j** God and his anger will burn
	32:16	made him **j** with their foreign gods

32:21 They made me **j** by what is no god
Jos   24:19 He is a holy God; he is a **j** God.
1Sa   18: 9 Saul kept a **j** eye on David.
1Ki   14:22 his **j** anger more than their fathers
Isa   11:13 Ephraim will not be **j** of Judah,
Eze   16:38 vengeance of my wrath and **j** anger.
16:42 and my **j** anger will turn away
23:25 I will direct my **j** anger against you,
36: 6 I speak in my **j** wrath
Joel   2:18 the LORD will be **j** for his land
Na   1: 2 LORD is a **j** and avenging God;
Zep   3: 8 consumed by the fire of my **j** anger.
Zec   1:14 'I am very **j** for Jerusalem and Zion,
8: 2 "I am very **j** for Zion."
Ac   7: 9 the patriarchs were **j** of Joseph,
17: 5 But the Jews were **j;**
2Co   11: 2 I am **j** for you with a godly jealousy.

JEALOUSY [JEALOUS]

Nu   5:14 feelings of **j** come over her husband
Ps   79: 5 How long will your **j** burn like fire?
Pr   6:34 for arouses a husband's fury,
27: 4 but who can stand before **j?**
SS   8: 6 its **j** unyielding as the grave.
Eze   8: 3 the idol that provokes to **j**
35:11 and **j** you showed in your hatred
Zep   1:18 the fire of his **j** the whole world will
Zec   8: 2 I am burning with **j** for her."
Ac   5:17 of the Sadducees, were filled with **j.**
13:45 they were filled with **j**
Ro   13:13 not in dissension and **j.**
1Co   3: 3 there is **j** and quarreling among you,
10:22 to arouse the Lord's **j?**
2Co   11: 2 I am jealous for you with a godly **j.**
12:20 **j,** outbursts of anger, factions,
Gal   5:20 **j,** fits of rage, selfish ambition,

JEBUS [JEBUSITE, JEBUSITES, JERUSALEM]

1Ch   11: 4 marched to Jerusalem (that is, **J).**

JEBUSITE [JEBUS]

Jos   18:28 the **J** city (that is, Jerusalem),
2Sa   24:18 the threshing floor of Araunah the **J.**
2Ch   3: 1 the threshing floor of Araunah the **J,**

JEBUSITES [JEBUS]

Ge   15:21 Canaanites, Girgashites and **J."**
Ex   3: 8 Amorites, Perizzites, Hivites and **J.**
Jos   15:63 Judah could not dislodge the **J,**
2Sa   5: 6 marched to Jerusalem to attack the **J,**

JECONIAH* [JEHOIACHIN]

A form of Jehoiachin (Mt 1:11-12).

JEDIDIAH* [SOLOMON]

2Sa   12:25 Nathan the prophet to name him **J.**

JEDUTHUN

1Ch   16:41 With them were Heman and **J** and
2Ch   35:15 Asaph, Heman and **J** the king's seer.
Ps   39: T For **J.**
62: T For **J.**
77: T For **J.**

JEER* [JEERED, JEERS]

Job   16:10 Men open their mouths to **j** at me;

JEERED* [JEER]

2Ki   2:23 youths came out of the town and **j** at

JEERS* [JEER]

Heb   11:36 Some faced **j** and flogging,

JEHOAHAZ

1. Son of Jehu; king of Israel (2Ki 13:1-9).
2. Son of Josiah; king of Judah (2Ki 23:31-34; 2Ch 36:1-4).

JEHOASH [JOASH]

1. See JOASH.
2. Son of Jehoahaz; king of Israel. Defeat of Aram prophesied by Elisha (2Ki 13:10-25). Defeated Amaziah in Jerusalem (2Ki 14:1-16; 2Ch 25:17-24).

JEHOIACHIN [JECONIAH]

Son of Jehoiakim; king of Judah exiled by Nebuchadnezzar (2Ki 24:8-17; 2Ch 36:8-10; Jer 22:24-30; 24:1). Raised from prisoner status (2Ki 25:27-30; Jer 52:31-34).

JEHOIADA

Priest who sheltered Joash from Athaliah (2Ki 11-12; 2Ch 22:11-24:16).

JEHOIAKIM [ELIAKIM]

Son of Josiah; made king of Judah by Nebuchadnezzar (2Ki 23:34-24:6; 2Ch 36:4-8; Jer 22:18-23). Burned scroll of Jeremiah's prophecies (Jer 36).

JEHORAM [JORAM]

1. Son of Jehoshaphat; king of Judah (2Ki 8:16-24). Prophesied against by Elijah; killed by the LORD (2Ch 21).
2. See JORAM.

JEHOSHAPHAT

Son of Asa; king of Judah. Strengthened his kingdom (2Ch 17). Joined with Ahab against Aram (2Ki 22; 2Ch 18). Established judges (2Ch 19). Joined with Joram against Moab (2Ki 3; 2Ch 20).
Valley of judgment (Joel 3:2, 12).

JEHOVAH (KJV) See †LORD

JEHOZADAK

1Ch   6:15 **J** was deported when the LORD sent
Hag   1:12 Joshua son of **J,** the high priest,

JEHU

1. Prophet against Baasha (2Ki 16:1-7).
2. King of Israel. Anointed by Elijah to obliterate house of Ahab (1Ki 19:16-17); anointed by servant of Elisha (2Ki 9:1-13). Killed Joram and Ahaziah (2Ki 9:14-29; 2Ch 22:7-9), Jezebel (2Ki 9:30-37), relatives of Ahab (2Ki 10:1-17;

Hos 1:4), ministers of Baal (2Ki 10:18-29). Death (2Ki 10:30-36).

JEPHTHAH

Judge from Gilead who delivered Israel from Ammon (Jdg 10:6-12:7). Made rash vow concerning his daughter (Jdg 11:30-40).

JEREMIAH

Prophet to Judah (Jer 1:1-3). Called by the LORD (Jer 1). Put in stocks (Jer 20:1-3). Threatened for prophesying (Jer 11:18-23; 26). Opposed by Hananiah (Jer 28). Scroll burned (Jer 36). Imprisoned (Jer 37). Thrown into cistern (Jer 38). Forced to Egypt with those fleeing Babylonians (Jer 43).

JEREMIAS, JEREMY (KJV)

See JEREMIAH

JERICHO

Nu	22: 1	along the Jordan across from **J**.
Dt	34: 3	whole region from the Valley of **J**,
Jos	3:16	the people crossed over opposite **J**.
	5:10	camped at Gilgal on the plains of **J**,
	6: 2	I have delivered **J** into your hands,
	6:26	undertakes to rebuild this city, **J**:
1Ki	16:34	Hiel of Bethel rebuilt **J**.
2Ki	25: 5	and overtook him in the plains of **J**.
Lk	10:30	going down from Jerusalem to **J**,
	18:35	As Jesus approached **J**,
	19: 1	Jesus entered **J** and was passing
Heb	11:30	By faith the walls of **J** fell,

JEROBOAM

1. Official of Solomon; rebelled to become first king of Israel (1Ki 11:26-40; 12:1-20; 2Ch 10). Idolatry (1Ki 12:25-33); judgment for (1Ki 13-14; 2Ch 13).

2. Son of Jehoash; king of Israel (1Ki 14:23-29).

JERUB-BAAL [GIDEON]

Jdg	6:32	So that day they called Gideon "**J**,"
1Sa	12:11	Then the LORD sent **J**, Barak,

JERUSALEM [JEBUS]

Jos	10: 1	king of **J** heard that Joshua had taken
	15: 8	of the Jebusite city (that is, **J**).
Jdg	1: 8	of Judah attacked **J** also and took it.
1Sa	17:54	and brought it to **J**,
2Sa	5: 5	and in **J** he reigned over all Israel
	9:13	And Mephibosheth lived in **J**,
	11: 1	But David remained in **J**.
	15:29	ark of God back to **J** and stayed there
	24:16	stretched out his hand to destroy **J**,
1Ki	3: 1	and the wall around **J**.
	9:15	the wall of **J**, and Hazor,
	9:19	to build in **J**, in Lebanon
	10:26	and also with him in **J**.
	10:27	silver as common in **J** as stones,
	11: 7	On a hill east of **J**,
	11:13	and for the sake of **J**,
	11:36	always have a lamp before me in **J**,
	11:42	in **J** over all Israel forty years.

	12:27	at the temple of the LORD in **J**,
	14:21	and he reigned seventeen years in **J**,
	14:25	Shishak king of Egypt attacked **J**.
	15: 2	and he reigned in **J** three years.
	15:10	and he reigned in **J** forty-one years.
	22:42	he reigned in **J** twenty-five years.
2Ki	8:17	and he reigned in **J** eight years.
	8:26	and he reigned in **J** one year.
	12: 1	and he reigned in **J** forty years.
	12:17	Then he turned to attack **J**.
	14: 2	he reigned in **J** twenty-nine years.
	14: 2	Jehoaddin; she was from **J**.
	14:13	to **J** and broke down the wall of **J**
	15: 2	and he reigned in **J** fifty-two years.
	15: 2	Jecoliah; she was from **J**.
	15:33	and he reigned in **J** sixteen years.
	16: 2	and he reigned in **J** sixteen years.
	16: 5	marched up to fight against **J**
	18: 2	he reigned in **J** twenty-nine years.
	18:17	from Lachish to King Hezekiah at **J**.
	18:35	How then can the LORD deliver **J**
	19:31	For out of **J** will come a remnant,
	21: 1	and he reigned in **J** fifty-five years.
	21: 4	"In **J** I will put my Name."
	21:12	to bring such disaster on **J**
	21:19	and he reigned in **J** two years.
	22: 1	and he reigned in **J** thirty-one years.
	23:27	and I will reject **J**, the city I chose,
	23:31	and he reigned in **J** three months.
	23:36	and he reigned in **J** eleven years.
	24: 8	and he reigned in **J** three months.
	24: 8	she was from **J**.
	24:10	king of Babylon advanced on **J**
	24:14	He carried into exile all **J**:
	24:18	and he reigned in **J** eleven years.
	24:20	anger that all this happened to **J**
	25: 1	king of Babylon marched against **J**
	25:10	broke down the walls around **J**.
1Ch	11: 4	marched to **J** (that is, Jebus).
	21:16	sword in his hand extended over **J**.
2Ch	1: 4	he had pitched a tent for it in **J**.
	3: 1	to build the temple of the LORD in **J**
	6: 6	now I have chosen **J** for my Name
	9: 1	to **J** to test him with hard questions.
	20:15	and all who live in Judah and **J**!
	20:27	Judah and **J** returned joyfully to **J**,
	29: 8	on Judah and **J**;
	36:19	and broke down the wall of **J**;
Ezr	1: 2	to build a temple for him at **J**
	2: 1	to Babylon (they returned to **J**
	3: 1	people assembled as one man in **J**.
	4:12	have gone to **J** and are rebuilding
	4:24	work on the house of God in **J** came
	6:12	or to destroy this temple in **J**.
	7: 8	Ezra arrived in **J** in the fifth month
	9: 9	a wall of protection in Judah and **J**.
	10: 7	for all the exiles to assemble in **J**.
Ne	1: 2	and also about **J**.
	1: 3	The wall of **J** is broken down,
	2:11	I went to **J**,
	2:17	Come, let us rebuild the wall of **J**,
	2:20	you have no share in **J** or any claim
	3: 8	They restored **J** as far as
	4: 8	together to come and fight against **J**

	11: 1	leaders of the people settled in **J**,
	12:27	At the dedication of the wall of **J**,
	12:43	The sound of rejoicing in **J** could
Ps	51:18	build up the walls of **J**.
	79: 1	they have reduced **J** to rubble.
	122: 2	feet are standing in your gates, O **J**.
	122: 3	**J** is built like a city
	122: 6	Pray for the peace of **J**:
	125: 2	As the mountains surround **J**,
	128: 5	may you see the prosperity of **J**,
	137: 5	If I forget you, O **J**,
	147: 2	The LORD builds up **J**;
	147:12	Extol the LORD, O **J**;
Ecc	1:12	was king over Israel in **J**.
SS	6: 4	my darling, as Tirzah, lovely as **J**,
Isa	1: 1	The vision concerning Judah and **J**
	2: 1	saw concerning Judah and **J**:
	3: 1	is about to take from **J** and Judah
	3: 8	**J** staggers, Judah is falling;
	4: 3	who remain in **J**,
	8:14	for the people of **J** he will be a trap
	27:13	on the holy mountain in **J**.
	31: 5	the LORD Almighty will shield **J**;
	33:20	your eyes will see **J**,
	40: 2	Speak tenderly to **J**,
	40: 9	You who bring good tidings to **J**,
	52: 1	O **J**, the holy city.
	52: 2	sit enthroned, O **J**.
	62: 6	posted watchmen on your walls, O **J**;
	62: 7	give him no rest till he establishes **J**
	65:18	for I will create **J** to be a delight
	66:13	and you will be comforted over **J**."
Jer	2: 2	and proclaim in the hearing of **J**:
	3:17	will call **J** The Throne of the LORD,
	4: 5	in Judah and proclaim in **J** and say:
	4:14	O **J**, wash the evil from your heart
	5: 1	"Go up and down the streets of **J**,
	6: 6	and build siege ramps against **J**.
	8: 5	Why does **J** always turn away?
	9:11	"I will make **J** a heap of ruins,
	13:27	Woe to you, O **J**!
	23:14	the people of **J** are like Gomorrah."
	24: 1	were carried into exile from **J**
	26:18	**J** will become a heap of rubble,
	32: 2	of Babylon was then besieging **J**,
	33:10	and the streets of **J** that are deserted,
	39: 1	king of Babylon marched against **J**
	51:50	and think on **J**."
	52:14	broke down all the walls around **J**.
La	1: 8	**J** has sinned greatly and so
Eze	8: 3	in visions of God he took me to **J**,
	14:21	**J** my four dreadful judgments
	16: 2	"Son of man, confront **J** with her
	21: 2	set your face against **J** and preach
	23: 4	and Oholibah is **J**.
Da	5: 3	taken from the temple of God in **J**,
	6:10	where the windows opened toward **J**.
	9: 2	desolation of **J** would last seventy
	9:12	like what has been done to **J**.
	9:25	of the decree to restore and rebuild **J**
Joel	3: 1	restore the fortunes of Judah and **J**,
	3:16	from Zion and thunder from **J**;
	3:17	**J** will be holy;
Am	2: 5	consume the fortresses of **J**."

Ob	1:11	and cast lots for **J**,
Mic	1: 5	Is it not **J**?
	4: 2	the word of the LORD from **J**.
Zep	3:16	On that day they will say to **J**,
Zec	1:14	'I am very jealous for **J** and Zion,
	1:17	comfort Zion and choose **J**.' "
	2: 2	He answered me, "To measure **J**,
	2: 4	'**J** will be a city without walls
	8: 3	**J** will be called the City of Truth,
	8: 8	I will bring them back to live in **J**;
	8:15	to do good again to **J** and Judah.
	8:22	and powerful nations will come to **J**
	9: 9	Shout, Daughter of **J**!
	9:10	and the war-horses from **J**,
	12: 3	I will make **J** an immovable rock
	12:10	and the inhabitants of **J**
	14: 2	the nations to **J** to fight against it;
	14: 8	living water will flow out from **J**,
	14:16	that have attacked **J** will go up year
Mt	2: 1	Magi from the east came to **J**
	16:21	to his disciples that he must go to **J**
	20:18	"We are going up to **J**,
	21:10	When Jesus entered **J**,
	23:37	"O **J**, **J**, you who kill the prophets
Mk	10:33	"We are going up to **J**," he said,
	15:41	who had come up with him to **J**
Lk	2:22	Joseph and Mary took him to **J**
	2:41	Every year his parents went to **J** for
	2:43	the boy Jesus stayed behind in **J**,
	4: 9	The devil led him to **J** and
	9:31	about to bring to fulfillment at **J**.
	9:51	Jesus resolutely set out for **J**.
	13:34	"O **J**, **J**, you who kill the prophets
	18:31	"We are going up to **J**,
	19:41	As he approached **J** and saw
	21:20	"When you see **J** being surrounded
	21:24	**J** will be trampled on by the Gentiles
	23:28	"Daughters of **J**, do not weep for me;
	24:47	to all nations, beginning at **J**.
Jn	1:19	when the Jews of **J** sent priests
	4:20	where we must worship is in **J**."
	5: 1	Jesus went up to **J** for a feast of
	10:22	came the Feast of Dedication at **J**
Ac	1: 4	not leave **J**, but wait for the gift
	1: 8	and you will be my witnesses in **J**,
	6: 7	of disciples in **J** increased rapidly,
	9:13	harm he has done to your saints in **J**.
	9:28	and moved about freely in **J**,
	11:27	some prophets came down from **J** to
	15: 2	up to **J** to see the apostles and elders
	20:22	I am going to **J**,
	21: 4	urged Paul not to go on to **J**.
	23:11	As you have testified about me in **J**,
Ro	15:19	So from **J** all the way around
Gal	1:17	to **J** to see those who were apostles
	2: 1	years later I went up again to **J**,
	4:25	corresponds to the present city of **J**,
	4:26	But the **J** that is above is free,
Heb	12:22	to the heavenly **J**,
Rev	3:12	the new **J**, which is coming down
	21: 2	I saw the Holy City, the new **J**,
	21:10	and showed me the Holy City, **J**,

DAUGHTER OF JERUSALEM
See DAUGHTER

DAUGHTERS OF JERUSALEM
See DAUGHTERS

PEOPLE OF JERUSALEM 2Ki 23:2; 2Ch
20:20; 21:11, 13; 22:1; 32:18, 22, 26, 33; 33:9;
34:30, 32; 35:18; Isa 8:14; Jer 1:3; 4:4; 8:1;
11:12; 19:3; 23:14; 32:32; 35:13; Eze 11:15; Da
9:7; Zec 12:5; Mk 1:5; Jn 7:25; Ac 13:27

JESHUA
Ezr   4: 3 Zerubbabel, **J** and the rest of the
10:18 the descendants of **J** son of Jozadak,
Ne   12: 1 son of Shealtiel and with **J**:

JESSE
Father of David (Ru 4:17-22; 1Sa 16; 1Ch 2:12-
17).

SON OF JESSE See SON

JESUS [JESUS']
LIFE: Genealogy (Mt 1:1-17; Lk 3:21-37).
Birth announced (Mt 1:18-25; Lk 1:26-45). Birth
(Mt 2:1-12; Lk 2:1-40). Escape to Egypt (Mt 2:13-
23). As a boy in the temple (Lk 2:41-52). Baptism
(Mt 3:13-17; Mk 1:9-11; Lk 3:21-22; Jn 1:32-34).
Temptation (Mt 4:1-11; Mk 1:12-13; Lk 4:1-13).
Ministry in Galilee (Mt 4:12-18:35; Mk 1:14-
9:50; Lk 4:14-13:9; Jn 1:35-2:11; 4; 6), Transfiguration (Mt 17:1-8; Mk 9:2-8; Lk 9:28-36), on
the way to Jerusalem (Mt 19-20; Mk 10; Lk
13:10-19:27), in Jerusalem (Mt 21-25; Mk 11-13;
Lk 19:28-21:38; Jn 2:12-3:36; 5; 7-12). Last supper (Mt 26:17-35; Mk 14:12-31; Lk 22:1-38; Jn
13-17). Arrest and trial (Mt 26:36-27:31; Mk
14:43-15:20; Lk 22:39-23:25; Jn 18:1-19:16).
Crucifixion (Mt 27:32-66; Mk 15:21-47; Lk
23:26-55; Jn 19:28-42). Resurrection and ap-
pearances (Mt 28; Mk 16; Lk 24; Jn 20-21; Ac
1:1-11; 7:56; 9:3-6; 1Co 15:1-8; Rev 1:1-20).
MIRACLES. *Healings:* official's son (Jn 4:43-
54), demoniac in Capernaum (Mk 1:23-26; Lk
4:33-35), Peter's mother-in-law (Mt 8:14-17; Mk
1:29-31; Lk 4:38-39), leper (Mt 8:2-4; Mk 1:40-
45; Lk 5:12-16), paralytic (Mt 9:1-8; Mk 2:1-12;
Lk 5:17-26), cripple (Jn 5:1-9), shriveled hand
(Mt 12:10-13; Mk 3:1-5; Lk 6:6-11), centurion's
servant (Mt 8:5-13; Lk 7:1-10), widow's son
raised (Lk 7:11-17), demoniac (Mt 12:22-23; Lk
11:14), Gadarene demoniacs (Mt 8:28-34; Mk
5:1-20; Lk 8:26-39), woman's bleeding and
Jairus' daughter (Mt 9:18-26; Mk 5:21-43; Lk
8:40-56), blind man (Mt 9:27-31), mute man (Mt
9:32-33), Canaanite woman's daughter (Mt 15:21-
28; Mk 7:24-30), deaf man (Mk 7:31-37), blind
man (Mk 8:22-26), demoniac boy (Mt 17:14-18;
Mk 9:14-29; Lk 9:37-43), ten lepers (Lk 17:11-
19), man born blind (Jn 9:1-7), Lazarus raised (Jn
11), crippled woman (Lk 13:11-17), man with
dropsy (Lk 14:1-6), two blind men (Mt 20:29-34;
Mk 10:46-52; Lk 18:35-43), Malchus' ear (Lk
22:50-51). *Other Miracles:* water to wine (Jn 2:1-
11), catch of fish (Lk 5:1-11), storm stilled (Mt
8:23-27; Mk 4:37-41; Lk 8:22-25), 5,000 fed (Mt
14:15-21; Mk 6:35-44; Lk 9:10-17; Jn 6:1-14),
walking on water (Mt 14:25-33; Mk 6:48-52; Jn

6:15-21), 4,000 fed (Mt 15:32-39; Mk 8:1-9),
money from fish (Mt 17:24-27), fig tree cursed
(Mt 21:18-22; Mk 11:12-14), catch of fish (Jn
21:1-14).
MAJOR TEACHING: Sermon on the Mount
(Mt 5-7; Lk 6:17-49), to Nicodemus (Jn 3), to
Samaritan woman (Jn 4), Bread of Life (Jn 6:22-
59), at Feast of Tabernacles (Jn 7-8), woes to
Pharisees (Mt 23; Lk 11:37-54), Good Shepherd
(Jn 10:1-18), Olivet Discourse (Mt 24-25; Mk 13;
Lk 21:5-36), Upper Room Discourse (Jn 13-16).
PARABLES: Sower (Mt 13:3-23; Mk 4:3-25;
Lk 8:5-18), seed's growth (Mk 4:26-29), wheat
and weeds (Mt 13:24-30, 36-43), mustard seed
(Mt 13:31-32; Mk 4:30-32), yeast (Mt 13:33; Lk
13:20-21), hidden treasure (Mt 13:44), valuable
pearl (Mt 13:45-46), net (Mt 13:47-51), house
owner (Mt 13:52), good Samaritan (Lk 10:25-37),
unmerciful servant (Mt 18:15-35), lost sheep (Mt
18:10-14; Lk 15:4-7), lost coin (Lk 15:8-10),
prodigal son (Lk 15:11-32), dishonest manager
(Lk 16:1-13), rich man and Lazarus (Lk 16:19-
31), persistent widow (Lk 18:1-8), Pharisee and
tax collector (Lk 18:9-14), payment of workers
(Mt 20:1-16), tenants and the vineyard (Mt 21:28-
46; Mt 12:1-12; Lk 20:9-19), wedding banquet
(Mt 22:1-14), faithful servant (Mt 24:45-51), ten
virgins (Mt 25:1-13), talents (Mt 25:1-30; Lk
19:12-27).
DISCIPLES see APOSTLES. Call (Jn 1:35-51;
Mt 4:18-22; 9:9; Mk 1:16-20; 2:13-14; Lk 5:1-11,
27-28). Named Apostles (Mk 3:13-19; Lk 6:12-
16). Twelve sent out (Mt 10; Mk 6:7-11; Lk 9:1-
5). Seventy sent out (Lk 10:1-24). Defection of (Jn
6:60-71; Mt 26:56; Mk 14:50-52). Final commission (Mt 28:16-20; Jn 21:15-23; Ac 1:3-8).
Ac   2:32 God has raised this **J** to life,
9: 5 "I am **J**, whom you are persecuting,"
9:34 "**J** Christ heals you.
15:11 grace of our Lord **J** that we are saved
16:31 "Believe in the Lord **J**,
20:24 the task the Lord **J** has given me—
Ro   5: 1 redemption that came by Christ **J**.
5:17 in life through the one man, **J** Christ.
8: 1 no condemnation for those who are
in Christ **J**,
1Co   1: 7 as you eagerly wait for our Lord **J**
2: 2 while I was with you except **J** Christ
6:11 justified in the name of the Lord **J**
8: 6 and there is but one Lord, **J** Christ,
12: 3 "**J** be cursed," and no one can say,
"**J** is Lord," except by the Holy
2Co   4: 5 but **J** Christ as Lord,
13: 5 not realize that Christ **J** is in you—
Gal   2:16 but by faith in **J** Christ.
2:16 in Christ **J** that we may be justified
3:28 for you are all one in Christ **J**.
5: 6 For in Christ **J** neither circumcision
6:17 I bear on my body the marks of **J**.
Eph   1: 5 adopted as his sons through **J** Christ
2:10 created in Christ **J** to do good works,
2:20 **J** himself as the chief cornerstone.
Php   1: 6 completion until the day of Christ **J**.
2: 5 be the same as that of Christ **J**:

	2:10	name of **J** every knee should bow,
Col	3:17	do it all in the name of the Lord **J**,
1Th	1:10	**J**, who rescues us from the coming wrath.
	4:14	with **J** those who have fallen asleep
	5:23	at the coming of our Lord **J** Christ.
2Th	1: 7	the Lord **J** is revealed from heaven
	2: 1	the coming of our Lord **J** Christ
1Ti	1:15	Christ **J** came into the world to save
2Ti	1:10	Christ **J**, who has destroyed death
	2: 3	like a good soldier of Christ **J**.
	3:12	wants to live a godly life in Christ **J**
Tit	2:13	our great God and Savior, **J** Christ,
Heb	2: 9	see **J**, who was made a little lower
	2:11	So **J** is not ashamed to call
	3: 1	fix your thoughts on **J**,
	3: 3	**J** has been found worthy of greater
	4:14	**J** the Son of God,
	6:20	where **J**, who went before us,
	7:22	**J** has become the guarantee of a
	7:24	but because **J** lives forever,
	8: 6	ministry **J** has received is as superior
	12: 2	Let us fix our eyes on **J**,
	12:24	to **J** the mediator of a new covenant,
	13: 8	**J** Christ is the same yesterday
1Pe	1: 3	through the resurrection of **J** Christ
2Pe	1:16	and coming of our Lord **J** Christ,
1Jn	1: 7	and the blood of **J**, his Son,
	2: 1	the Father in our defense—**J** Christ,
	2: 6	to live in him must walk as **J** did.
	4:15	If anyone acknowledges that **J** is
Rev	1: 1	The revelation of **J** Christ,
	12:17	and hold to the testimony of **J**.
	17: 6	of those who bore testimony to **J**.
	22:16	"I, **J**, have sent my angel
	22:20	Come, Lord **J**.

See JUSTUS

CHRIST JESUS Ac 24:24; Ro 1:1; 3:24; 6:3, 11, 23; 8:1, 2, 34, 39; 15:5, 16, 17; 16:3; 1Co 1:1, 2, 4, 30; 4:15, 17; 15:31; 16:24; 2Co 1:1; 3:15; Gal 2:4, 16; 3:14, 26, 28; 4:14; 5:6, 24; Eph 1:1, 1; 2:6, 7, 10, 13, 20; 3:1, 6, 11, 21; Php 1:1, 1, 6, 8, 26; 2:5; 3:3, 8, 12, 14; 4:7, 19, 21; Col 1:1, 4; 2:6; 4:12; 1Th 2:14; 5:18; 1Ti 1:1, 1, 2, 12, 14, 15, 16; 2:5; 3:13; 4:6; 5:21; 6:13; 2Ti 1:1, 1, 2, 9, 10, 13; 2:1, 3, 10; 3:12, 15; 4:1; Tit 1:4; Phm 1:1, 9, 23

JESUS CHRIST Mt 1:1, 18; Mk 1:1; Jn 1:17; 17:3; Ac 2:38; 3:6; 4:10; 8:12; 9:34; 10:36, 48; 11:17; 15:26; 16:18; 28:31; Ro 1:4, 6, 7, 8; 2:16; 3:22; 5:1, 11, 15, 17, 21; 7:25; 13:14; 15:6, 30; 16:25, 27; 1Co 1:2, 3, 7, 8, 9, 10; 2:2; 3:11; 6:11; 8:6; 15:57; 2Co 1:2, 3, 19; 4:5; 8:9; 13:14; Gal 1:1, 3, 12; 2:16; 3:1, 22; 6:14, 18; Eph 1:2, 3, 5, 17; 5:20; 6:23, 24; Php 1:2, 11, 19; 2:11, 21; 3:20; 4:23; Col 1:3; 1Th 1:1, 3; 5:9, 23, 28; 2Th 1:1, 2, 12; 2:1, 14, 16; 3:6, 12, 18; 1Ti 6:3, 14; 2Ti 2:8; Tit 1:1; 2:13; Phm 1:3, 25; Heb 10:10; 13:8, 21; Jas 1:1; 2:1; 1Pe 1:1, 2, 3, 7, 13; 2:5; 3:21; 4:11; 2Pe 1:1, 8, 11, 14, 16; 2:20; 3:18; 1Jn 1:3; 2:1; 3:16, 23; 4:2; 5:6, 20; 2Jn 1:3, 7; Jude 1:1, 1, 4, 17, 21, 25; Rev 1:1, 2, 5

JESUS OF NAZARETH Mt 26:71; Mk 1:24;

10:47; Lk 4:34; 18:37; 24:19; Jn 1:45; 18:5, 7; 19:19; Ac 2:22; 6:14; 10:38; 22:8; 26:9

LORD JESUS Mk 16:19; Lk 24:3; Ac 1:21; 4:33; 7:59; 8:16; 9:17; 11:17, 20; 15:11, 26; 16:31; 19:5, 13, 17; 20:21, 24, 35; 21:13; 28:31; Ro 1:7; 5:1, 11; 13:14; 14:14; 15:6, 30; 16:20; 1Co 1:2, 3, 7, 8, 10; 5:4, 4; 6:11; 8:6; 11:23; 15:57; 16:23; 2Co 1:2, 3, 14; 4:14; 8:9; 11:31; 13:14; Gal 1:3; 6:14, 18; Eph 1:2, 3, 15, 17; 5:20; 6:23, 24; Php 1:2; 2:19; 3:20; 4:23; Col 1:3; 3:17; 1Th 1:1, 3; 2:15, 19; 3:11, 13; 4:1, 2; 5:9, 23, 28; 2Th 1:1, 2, 7, 8, 12, 12; 2:1, 8, 14, 16; 3:6, 12, 18; 1Ti 6:3, 14; Phm 1:3, 5, 25; Heb 13:20; Jas 1:1; 2:1; 1Pe 1:3; 2Pe 1:8, 14, 16; Jude 1:17, 21; Rev 22:20, 21

LORD JESUS CHRIST Ac 11:17; 15:26; 28:31; Ro 1:7; 5:1, 11; 13:14; 15:6, 30; 1Co 1:2, 3, 7, 8, 10; 6:11; 8:6; 15:57; 2Co 1:2, 3; 8:9; 13:14; Gal 1:3; 6:14, 18; Eph 1:2, 3, 17; 5:20; 6:23, 24; Php 1:2; 3:20; 4:23; Col 1:3; 1Th 1:1, 3; 5:9, 23, 28; 2Th 1:1, 2; 2:1, 14, 16; 3:6, 12, 18; 1Ti 6:3, 14; Phm 1:3, 25; Jas 1:1; 2:1; 1Pe 1:3; 2Pe 1:8, 14, 16; Jude 1:17, 21

NAME OF JESUS See NAME

JESUS' [JESUS]

Mt	27:58	he asked for **J** body,
Lk	8:35	sitting at **J** feet,
Jn	12:41	said this because he saw **J** glory
	19:34	one of the soldiers pierced **J** side
Ac	3:16	It is **J** name and the faith

JETHRO* [REUEL]

Father-in-law and adviser of Moses (Ex 3:1; 4:18; 18). Also known as Reuel (Ex 2:18).

JEW [JEWESS, JEWISH, JEWS, JEWS', JUDAISM]

Est	2: 5	a **J** of the tribe of Benjamin, named
	10: 3	Mordecai the **J** was second in rank
Zec	8:23	nations will take firm hold of one **J**
Jn	4: 9	"You are a **J** and I am a Samaritan
	18:35	"Am I a **J**?"
Ac	21:39	Paul answered, "I am a **J**,
Ro	1:16	first for the **J**, then for the Gentile.
	2: 9	for the **J**, then for the Gentile;
	2:29	a man is a **J** if he is one inwardly;
	10:12	no difference between **J** and Gentile
1Co	9:20	To the Jews I became like a **J**,
Gal	2:14	"You are a **J**, yet you live like a Gentile and not like a **J**.
	3:28	There is neither **J** nor Greek,
Col	3:11	Here there is no Greek or **J**,

JEWEL* [JEWELRY, JEWELS]

Pr	20:15	that speak knowledge are a rare **j**.
SS	4: 9	with one **j** of your necklace.
Isa	13:19	Babylon, the **j** of kingdoms,
Rev	21:11	like that of a very precious **j**,

JEWELRY [JEWEL]

Ex	35:22	and brought gold **j** of all kinds:
Jer	2:32	Does a maiden forget her **j**,

Eze 16:11 I adorned you with **j:**
1Pe 3: 3 wearing of gold **j** and fine clothes.

JEWELS [JEWEL]

Job 28:17 nor can it be had for **j** of gold.
Isa 54:12 your gates of sparkling **j,**
61:10 as a bride adorns herself with her **j.**
Zec 9:16 They will sparkle in his land like **j** in

JEWESS* [JEW]

Ac 16: 1 mother was a **J** and a believer,
24:24 his wife Drusilla, who was a **J.**

JEWISH [JEW]

Ezr 6: 7 and the **J** elders rebuild this house
Ne 1: 2 about the **J** remnant that survived
Jn 3: 1 a member of the **J** ruling council.
11:51 that Jesus would die for the **J** nation,
Ac 13: 6 There they met a **J** sorcerer
Gal 2:14 force Gentiles to follow **J** customs?

JEWS [JEW]

Ezr 5: 5 watching over the elders of the **J,**
Ne 4: 1 He ridiculed the **J,**
Est 3:13 kill and annihilate all the **J—**
4:14 and deliverance for the **J** will arise
10: 3 spoke up for the welfare of all the **J.**
Da 3: 8 came forward and denounced the **J.**
Mt 2: 2 who has been born king of the **J?**
27:11 "Are you the king of the **J?"**
27:37 THIS IS JESUS, THE KING OF THE **J.**
Jn 4: 9 **J** do not associate with Samaritans.)
4:22 for salvation is from the **J.**
7:13 about him for fear of the **J.**
9:22 because they were afraid of the **J,**
19: 3 saying, "Hail, king of the **J!"**
19:21 "Do not write 'The King of the **J,'**
Ac 17: 4 Some of the **J** were persuaded
20:21 **J** and Greeks that they must turn to
21:20 many thousands of **J** have believed,
Ro 3:29 Is God the God of **J** only?
9:24 he also called, not only from the **J**
15:27 they owe it to the **J** to share
1Co 1:22 **J** demand miraculous signs and
9:20 To the **J** I became like a Jew,
12:13 into one body—whether **J** or Greeks,
Gal 2: 8 of Peter as an apostle to the **J,**
1Th 2:14 those churches suffered from the **J,**
Rev 2: 9 who say they are **J** and are not,
3: 9 claim to be **J** though they are not,

KING OF THE JEWS See KING

JEWS'* [JEW]

Ro 15:27 shared in the **J** spiritual blessings,

JEZEBEL*

Sidonian wife of Ahab (1Ki 16:31). Promoted Baal worship (1Ki 16:32-33). Killed prophets of the LORD (1Ki 18:4, 13). Opposed Elijah (1Ki 19:1-2). Had Naboth killed (1Ki 21). Death prophesied (1Ki 21:17-24). Killed by Jehu (2Ki 9:30-37). Metaphor of immorality (Rev 2:20).

JEZREEL [JEZREELITE]

1Ki 21:23 will devour Jezebel by the wall of **J.'**
2Ki 9:36 at **J** dogs will devour Jezebel's flesh.
10: 7 and sent them to Jehu in **J.**
Hos 1: 4 LORD said to Hosea, "Call him **J,**
1:11 for great will be the day of **J.**
2:22 and Jezreel will respond to **J.**

JEZREELITE [JEZREEL]

1Ki 21: 1 vineyard belonging to Naboth the **J.**
2Ki 9:25 field that belonged to Naboth the **J.**

JOAB

Nephew of David (1Ch 2:16). Commander of his army (2Sa 8:16). Victorious over Ammon (2Sa 10; 1Ch 19), Rabbah (2Sa 11; 1Ch 20), Jerusalem (1Ch 11:6), Absalom (2Sa 18), Sheba (2Sa 20). Killed Abner (2Sa 3:22-39), Amasa (2Sa 20:1-13). Numbered David's army (2Sa 24; 1Ch 21). Sided with Adonijah (1Ki 1:17, 19). Killed by Benaiah (1Ki 2:5-6, 28-35).

JOANNA*

Lk 8: 3 **J** the wife of Cuza, the manager of
24:10 It was Mary Magdalene, **J,**

JOASH [JEHOASH]

Son of Ahaziah; king of Judah. Sheltered from Athaliah by Jehoiada (2Ki 11; 2Ch 22:10-23:21). Repaired temple (2Ki 12; 2Ch 24).

JOB

Wealthy man from Uz; feared God (Job 1:1-5). Integrity tested by disaster (Job 1:6-22), personal affliction (Job 2). Maintained innocence in debate with three friends (Job 3-31), Elihu (Job 32-37). Rebuked by the LORD (Job 38-41). Vindicated and restored to greater stature by the LORD (Job 42). Example of righteousness (Eze 14:14, 20).

JOCHEBED*

Mother of Moses and Aaron (Ex 6:20; Nu 26:59).

JOEL

1. Son of Samuel (1Sa 8:2; 1Ch 6:28).
2. Prophet (Joel 1:1; Ac 2:16).

JOHANAN

1. First high priest in Solomon's temple (1Ch 6:9-10).
2. Jewish leader who tried to save Gedaliah from assassination (Jer 40:13-14); took Jews, including Jeremiah, to Egypt (Jer 40-43).

JOHN

1. Son of Zechariah and Elizabeth (Lk 1). Called the Baptist (Mt 3:1-12; Mk 1:2-8). Witness to Jesus (Mt 3:11-12; Mk 1:7-8; Lk 3:15-18; Jn 1:6-35; 3:27-30; 5:33-36). Doubts about Jesus (Mt 11:2-6; Lk 7:18-23). Arrest (Mt 4:12; Mk 1:14). Execution (Mt 14:1-12; Mk 6:14-29; Lk 9:7-9). Ministry compared to Elijah (Mt 11:7-19; Mk 9:11-13; Lk 7:24-35).
2. Apostle; brother of James (Mt 4:21-22; 10:2;

Mk 3:17; Lk 5:1-10). At transfiguration (Mt 17:1-13; Mk 9:1-13; Lk 9:28-36). Desire to be greatest (Mk 10:35-45). Leader of church at Jerusalem (Ac 4:1-3; Gal 2:9). Elder who wrote epistles (2Jn 1; 3Jn 1). Prophet who wrote Revelation (Rev 1:1; 22:8).

3. Cousin of Barnabas, co-worker with Paul, (Ac 12:12-13:13; 15:37; see MARK).

JOIN [JOINED, JOINS]

Ex	1:10	if war breaks out, will j our enemies,
Ne	10:29	these now j their brothers the nobles,
Pr	23:20	not j those who drink too much wine
	24:21	and do not j with the rebellious,
Jer	3:18	of Judah will j the house of Israel,
Eze	37:17	J them together into one stick so
Da	11:34	many who are not sincere will j them
Ac	5:13	No one else dared j them,
	9:26	he tried to j the disciples,
Ro	15:30	to j me in my struggle by praying
2Ti	1:8	j with me in suffering for the gospel,

JOINED [JOIN]

1Sa	10:10	and he j in their prophesying.
Hos	4:17	Ephraim is j to idols;
Zec	2:11	be j with the LORD in that day
Mt	19:6	Therefore what God has j together,
Mk	10:9	Therefore what God has j together,
Ac	1:14	j together constantly in prayer,
Eph	2:21	the whole building is j together
	4:16	j and held together by every

JOINS* [JOIN]

Hos	7:5	and he j hands with the mockers.
1Co	16:16	and to everyone who j in the work,

JOINT* [JOINTS]

Job	31:22	let it be broken off at the j.
Ps	22:14	and all my bones are out of j.

JOINTS* [JOINT]

Heb	4:12	soul and spirit, j and marrow;

JOKING*

Ge	19:14	his sons-in-law thought he was j.
Pr	26:19	"I was only j!"
Eph	5:4	foolish talk or coarse j,

JONADAB

2Sa	13:3	Now Amnon had a friend named J
Jer	35:8	obeyed everything our forefather J

JONAH

Prophet in days of Jeroboam II (2Ki 14:25). Called to Nineveh; fled to Tarshish (Jnh 1:1-3). Cause of storm; thrown into sea (Jnh 1:4-16). Swallowed by fish (Jnh 1:17). Prayer (Jnh 2). Preached to Nineveh (Jnh 3). Attitude reproved by the LORD (Jnh 4). Sign of (Mt 12:39-41; Lk 11:29-32).

JONAS (KJV) See JONAH

JONATHAN

Son of Saul (1Sa 13:16; 1Ch 8:33). Valiant war-rior (1Sa 13-14). Relation to David (1Sa 18:1-4; 19-20; 23:16-18). Killed at Gilboa (1Sa 31). Mourned by David (2Sa 1).

JOPPA

2Ch	2:16	in rafts by sea down to J.
Ezr	3:7	cedar logs by sea from Lebanon to J,
Jnh	1:3	He went down to J,
Ac	9:43	Peter stayed in J for some time with

JORAM

1. Son of Ahab; king of Israel. With Jehoshaphat fought against Moab (2Ki 3). Killed with Ahaziah by Jehu (2Ki 8:25-29; 9:14-26; 2Ch 22:5-9).

2. See JEHORAM.

JORDAN

Ge	13:10	plain of the J was well watered,
Nu	22:1	of Moab and camped along the J
	34:12	along the J and end at the Salt Sea.
Dt	1:1	in the desert east of the J—
	3:27	you are not going to cross this J.
Jos	1:2	get ready to cross the J River into
	3:11	will go into the J ahead of you.
	3:17	on dry ground in the middle of the J,
	4:8	stones from the middle of the J,
	4:22	'Israel crossed the J on dry ground.'
	23:4	between the J and the Great Sea
2Ki	2:7	and Elisha had stopped at the J.
	2:13	and stood on the bank of the J.
	5:10	wash yourself seven times in the J,
	6:4	to the J and began to cut down trees.
Ps	114:3	the J turned back;
Isa	9:1	by the way of the sea, along the J—
Jer	12:5	in the thickets by the J?
Mt	3:6	baptized by him in the J River.
	4:15	the way to the sea, along the J,
Mk	1:9	and was baptized by John in the J.
Jn	1:28	Bethany on the other side of the J,

JOSEPH [BARNABAS]

1. Son of Jacob by Rachel (Ge 30:24; 1Ch 2:2). Favored by Jacob, hated by brothers (Ge 37:3-4). Dreams (Ge 37:5-11). Sold by brothers (Ge 37:12-36). Served Potiphar; imprisoned by false accusation (Ge 39). Interpreted dreams of Pharaoh's servants (Ge 40), of Pharaoh (Ge 41:4-40). Made greatest in Egypt (Ge 41:41-57). Sold grain to brothers (Ge 42-45). Brought Jacob and sons to Egypt (Ge 46-47). Sons Ephraim and Manasseh blessed (Ge 48). Blessed (Ge 49:22-26; Dt 33:13-17). Death (Ge 50:22-26; Ex 13:19; Heb 11:22). 12,000 from (Rev 7:8).

2. Husband of Mary mother of Jesus (Mt 1:16-24; 2:13-19; Lk 1:27; 2; Jn 1:45).

3. Disciple from Arimathea, who gave his tomb for Jesus' burial (Mt 27:57-61; Mk 15:43-47; Lk 24:50-52).

4. Original name of Barnabas (Ac 4:36).

JOSES

Mt	27:56	Mary the mother of James and J,

JOSHUA [HOSHEA]

1. Son of Nun; name changed from Hoshea (Nu 13:8, 16; 1Ch 7:27). Fought Amalekites under Moses (Ex 17:9-14). Servant of Moses on Sinai (Ex 24:13; 32:17). Spied Canaan (Nu 13). With Caleb, allowed to enter land (Nu 14:6, 30). Succeeded Moses (Dt 1:38; 31:1-8; 34:9).

Charged Israel to conquer Canaan (Jos 1). Crossed Jordan (Jos 3-4). Circumcised sons of wilderness wanderings (Jos 5). Conquered Jericho (Jos 6), Ai (Jos 7-8), five kings at Gibeon (Jos 10:1-28), southern Canaan (Jos 10:29-43), northern Canaan (Jos 11-12). Defeated at Ai (Jos 7). Deceived by Gibeonites (Jos 9). Renewed covenant (Jos 8:30-35; 24:1-27). Divided land among tribes (Jos 13-22). Last words (Jos 23). Death (Jos 24:28-31).

2. High priest during rebuilding of temple (Hag 1-2; Zec 3:1-9; 6:11).

JOSIAH

Son of Amon; king of Judah (2Ki 21:26; 1Ch 3:14). Prophesied (1Ki 13:2). Book of the Law discovered during his reign (2Ki 22; 2Ch 34:14-31). Reforms (2Ki 23:1-25; 2Ch 34:1-13; 35:1-19). Killed by Pharaoh Neco (2Ki 23:29-30; 2Ch 35:20-27).

JOT (KJV) See SMALLEST LETTER

JOTHAM

1. Son of Gideon (Jdg 9).

2. Son of Azariah (Uzziah); king of Judah (2Ki 15:32-38; 2Ch 26:21-27:9).

JOURNEY

Ge	24:21	LORD had made his **j** successful.
Ex	3:18	a three-day **j** into the desert
Nu	33: 1	the stages in the **j** of the Israelites
Dt	1:33	who went ahead of you on your **j**,
	2: 7	over your **j** through this vast desert.
Jdg	18: 6	Your **j** has the LORD's approval."
Ezr	8:21	and ask him for a safe **j**
Job	16:22	before I go on the **j** of no return.
Isa	35: 8	The unclean will not **j** on it;
Mt	25:14	it will be like a man going on a **j**,
Lk	9: 3	"Take nothing for the **j**—
Ac	9:27	how Saul on his **j** had seen the Lord
Ro	15:24	to have you assist me on my **j** there,

JOY* [ENJOY, ENJOYED, ENJOYMENT, JOYFUL, JOYOUS, JOYFULLY, OVERJOYED, REJOICE, REJOICED, REJOICES, REJOICING]

Ge	31:27	so I could send you away with **j**
Lev	9:24	they shouted for **j** and fell facedown.
Dt	16:15	and your **j** will be complete.
Jdg	9:19	may Abimelech and your **j**,
1Ch	12:40	for there was **j** in Israel.
	16:27	strength and **j** in his dwelling place.
	16:33	they will sing for **j** before
	29:17	And now I have seen with **j**
	29:22	They ate and drank with great **j** in
2Ch	30:26	There was great **j** in Jerusalem,
Ezr	3:12	while many others shouted for **j**.
	3:13	the sound of the shouts of **j**
	6:16	dedication of the house of God with **j**
	6:22	with **j** the Feast of Unleavened Bread
	6:22	the LORD had filled them with **j**
Ne	8:10	**j** of the LORD is your strength."
	8:12	of food and to celebrate with great **j**,
	8:17	And their **j** was very great.
	12:43	because God had given them great **j**.
Est	8:16	a time of happiness and **j**,
	8:17	**j** and gladness among the Jews,
	9:17	and made it a day of feasting and **j**.
	9:18	and made it a day of feasting and **j**.
	9:19	of the month of Adar as a day of **j**
	9:22	when their sorrow was turned into **j**
	9:22	of feasting and **j** and giving presents
Job	3: 7	may no shout of **j** be heard in it.
	6:10	my **j** in unrelenting pain—
	8:21	and your lips with shouts of **j**.
	9:25	they fly away without a glimpse of **j**.
	10:20	from me so I can have a moment's **j**
	20: 5	**j** of the godless lasts but a moment.
	33:26	he sees God's face and shouts for **j**,
	38: 7	and all the angels shouted for **j**?
Ps	4: 7	have filled my heart with greater **j**
	5:11	let them ever sing for **j**.
	16:11	you will fill me with **j**
	19: 8	giving **j** to the heart.
	20: 5	for **j** when you are victorious
	21: 1	How great is his **j** in the victories
	21: 6	and made him glad with the **j**
	27: 6	will I sacrifice with shouts of **j**;
	28: 7	for **j** and I will give thanks to him
	30:11	and clothed me with **j**,
	33: 3	and shout for **j**;
	35:27	delight in my vindication shout for **j**
	42: 4	with shouts of **j** and thanksgiving
	43: 4	to God, my **j** and my delight.
	45: 7	by anointing you with the oil of **j**.
	45:15	They are led in with **j** and gladness;
	47: 1	shout to God with cries of **j**,
	47: 5	God has ascended amid shouts of **j**,
	48: 2	the **j** of the whole earth.
	51: 8	Let me hear **j** and gladness;
	51:12	Restore to me the **j** of your salvation
	65: 8	you call forth songs of **j**.
	65:13	they shout for **j** and sing.
	66: 1	Shout with **j** to God, all the earth!
	67: 4	the nations be glad and sing for **j**,
	71:23	for **j** when I sing praise to you—
	81: 1	Sing for **j** to God our strength;
	86: 4	Bring **j** to your servant, for to you,
	89:12	Tabor and Hermon sing for **j**
	90:14	sing for **j** and be glad all our days.
	92: 4	I sing for **j** at the works
	94:19	consolation brought **j** to my soul.
	95: 1	let us sing for **j** to the LORD;
	96:12	the trees of the forest will sing for **j**;
	97:11	and **j** on the upright in heart.
	98: 4	Shout for **j** to the LORD,
	98: 6	shout for **j** before the LORD, the King
	98: 8	the mountains sing together for **j**;
	100: 1	Shout for **j** to the LORD,

105:43	his chosen ones with shouts of **j;**
106: 5	in the **j** of your nation
107:22	and tell of his works with songs of **j.**
118:15	Shouts of **j** and victory resound
119:111	they are the **j** of my heart.
126: 2	our tongues with songs of **j.**
126: 3	and we are filled with **j.**
126: 5	sow in tears will reap with songs of **j**
126: 6	will return with songs of **j,**
132: 9	may your saints sing for **j."**
132:16	and her saints will ever sing for **j.**
137: 3	our tormentors demanded songs of **j;**
137: 6	not consider Jerusalem my highest **j.**
149: 5	and sing for **j** on their beds.

Pr		
	10: 1	A wise son brings **j** to his father,
	10:28	The prospect of the righteous is **j,**
	11:10	there are shouts of **j.**
	12:20	but **j** for those who promote peace.
	14:10	and no one else can share its **j.**
	14:13	and **j** may end in grief.
	15:20	A wise son brings **j** to his father,
	15:23	man finds **j** in giving an apt reply—
	15:30	A cheerful look brings **j** to the heart,
	17:21	there is no **j** for the father of a fool.
	21:15	When justice is done, it brings **j** to
	23:24	of a righteous man has great **j;**
	27: 9	and incense bring **j** to the heart,
	27:11	my son, and bring **j** to my heart;
	29: 3	A man who loves wisdom brings **j**

Ecc		
	8:15	Then **j** will accompany him
	11: 9	and let your heart give you **j** in

Isa		
	9: 3	the nation and increased their **j;**
	12: 3	With **j** you will draw water from
	12: 6	Shout aloud and sing for **j,**
	16: 9	of **j** over your ripened fruit and
	16:10	**J** and gladness are taken away from
	22:13	But see, there is **j** and revelry,
	24:11	all **j** turns to gloom,
	24:14	they shout for **j;**
	26:19	wake up and shout for **j.**
	35: 2	rejoice greatly and shout for **j.**
	35: 6	and the mute tongue shout for **j.**
	35:10	everlasting **j** will crown their heads.
	35:10	Gladness and **j** will overtake them,
	42:11	Let the people of Sela sing for **j;**
	44:23	Sing for **j,** O heavens,
	48:20	with shouts of **j** and proclaim it.
	49:13	Shout for **j,** O heavens;
	51: 3	**J** and gladness will be found in her,
	51:11	everlasting **j** will crown their heads.
	51:11	Gladness and **j** will overtake them,
	52: 8	together they shout for **j.**
	52: 9	Burst into songs of **j** together,
	54: 1	for **j,** you who were never in labor,
	55:12	You will go out in **j** and be led forth
	56: 7	and give them **j** in my house
	58:14	you will find your **j** in the LORD,
	60: 5	heart will throb and swell with **j;**
	60:15	and the **j** of all generations.
	61: 7	and everlasting **j** will be theirs.
	65:14	My servants will sing out of the **j**
	65:18	to be a delight and its people a **j.**
	66: 5	that we may see your **j!'**

Jer		
	7:34	the sounds of **j** and gladness

15:16	were my **j** and my heart's delight,
16: 9	end to the sounds of **j** and gladness
25:10	the sounds of **j** and gladness,
31: 7	"Sing with **j** for Jacob;
31:12	They will come and shout for **j** on
31:13	and **j** instead of sorrow.
33: 9	this city will bring me renown, **j,**
33:11	the sounds of **j** and gladness,
48:33	**J** and gladness are gone from
48:33	treads them with shouts of **j.**
48:33	they are not shouts of **j.**
51:48	will shout for **j** over Babylon,

La		
	2:15	the **j** of the whole earth?"
	5:15	**J** is gone from our hearts;

Eze		
	7: 7	not **j,** upon the mountains.
	24:25	their **j** and glory,

Joel		
	1:12	the **j** of mankind is withered away.
	1:16	**j** and gladness from the house of our

Mt		
	13:20	and at once receives it with **j.**
	13:44	then in his **j** went and sold all he had
	28: 8	afraid yet filled with **j,**

Mk		
	4:16	and at once receive it with **j.**

Lk		
	1:14	He will be a **j** and delight to you,
	1:44	the baby in my womb leaped for **j.**
	1:58	and they shared her **j.**
	2:10	I bring you good news of great **j**
	6:23	"Rejoice in that day and leap for **j,**
	8:13	the word with **j** when they hear it,
	10: 17	The seventy-two returned with **j**
	10:21	full of **j** through the Holy Spirit,
	24:41	because of **j** and amazement,
	24:52	returned to Jerusalem with great **j.**

Jn		
	3:29	and is full of **j** when he hears
	3:29	**j** is mine, and it is now complete.
	15:11	so that my **j** may be in you and that
		your **j** may be complete.
	16:20	but your grief will turn to **j.**
	16:21	forgets the anguish because of her **j.**
	16:22	and no one will take away your **j.**
	16:24	and your **j** will be complete.
	17:13	the full measure of my **j** within them.

Ac		
	2:28	you will fill me with **j**
	8: 8	So there was great **j** in that city.
	13:52	And the disciples were filled with **j**
	14:17	of food and fills your hearts with **j."**
	16:34	**j** because he had come to believe

Ro		
	14:17	peace and **j** in the Holy Spirit,
	15:13	the God of hope fill you with all **j**
	15:32	God's will I may come to you with **j**
	16:19	so I am full of **j** over you;

2Co		
	1:24	but we work with you for your **j,**
	2: 3	that you would all share my **j.**
	7: 4	our troubles my **j** knows no bounds.
	7: 7	so that my **j** was greater than ever.
	8: 2	their overflowing **j** and their extreme

Gal		
	4:15	What has happened to all your **j?**
	5:22	But the fruit of the Spirit is love, **j,**

Php		
	1: 4	I always pray with **j**
	1:25	for your progress and **j** in the faith,
	1:26	your **j** in Christ Jesus will overflow
	2: 2	then make my **j** complete.
	2:29	in the Lord with great **j,**
	4: 1	my **j** and crown,

1Th		
	1: 6	with the **j** given by the Holy Spirit.

2:19 For what is our hope, our **j,**
2:20 Indeed, you are our glory and **j.**
3: 9 for all the **j** we have in the presence
2Ti 1: 4 so that I may be filled with **j.**
Phm 1: 7 Your love has given me great **j**
Heb 1: 9 by anointing you with the oil of **j."**
12: 2 who for the **j** set before him endured
13:17 so that their work will be a **j,**
Jas 1: 2 Consider it pure **j,** my brothers,
4: 9 to mourning and your **j** to gloom.
1Pe 1: 8 with an inexpressible and glorious **j,**
1Jn 1: 4 to make our **j** complete.
2Jn 1: 4 It has given me great **j** to find some
1:12 so that our **j** may be complete.
3Jn 1: 3 It gave me great **j**
1: 4 I have no greater **j** than to hear
Jude 1:24 without fault and with great **j—**

JOYFUL* [JOY]

Dt 16:14 Be **j** at your Feast—
1Sa 18: 6 with **j** songs and with tambourines
1Ki 8:66 **j** and glad in heart for all the good
1Ch 15:16 as singers to sing **j** songs,
2Ch 7:10 **j** and glad in heart for the good
Ps 68: 3 may they be happy and **j.**
100: 2 come before him with **j** songs.
Ecc 9: 7 and drink your wine with a **j** heart,
Isa 24: 8 the **j** harp is silent.
Jer 31: 4 and go out to dance with the **j.**
Hab 3:18 I will be **j** in God my Savior.
Zec 8:19 will become **j** and glad occasions
10: 7 Their children will see it and be **j;**
Ro 12:12 Be **j** in hope, patient in affliction,
1Th 5:16 Be **j** always;
Heb 12:22 thousands of angels in **j** assembly,

JOYFULLY* [JOY]

Dt 28:47 did not serve {the Lord your God **j**
2Ch 20:27 of Judah and Jerusalem returned **j**
30:23 another seven days they celebrated **j.**
Ne 12:27 celebrate **j** the dedication with songs
Job 39:13 "The wings of the ostrich flap **j,**
Ps 33: 1 Sing **j** to the Lord, you righteous;
145: 7 your abundant goodness and **j** sing
Lk 15: 5 he **j** puts it on his shoulders
19:37 the whole crowd of disciples began **j**
Col 1:11 great endurance and patience, and **j**
Heb 10:34 **j** accepted the confiscation of your

JOYOUS* [JOY]

Est 8:15 the city of Susa held a **j** celebration.

JOZABAD

2Ki 12:21 officials who murdered him were **J**
Ezr 8:33 so were the Levites **J** son of Jeshua

JUBILANT*

1Ch 16:32 let the fields be **j,**
Ps 94: 3 how long will the wicked be **j?**
96:12 let the fields be **j,**
98: 4 burst into **j** song with music;
Hos 9: 1 Do not rejoice, O Israel; do not be **j**

JUBILEE

Lev 25:11 The fiftieth year shall be a **j** for you;

27:17 his field during the Year of **J,**
Nu 36: 4 Year of **J** for the Israelites comes,

JUDAH [JUDEA, JUDEAN]

1. Son of Jacob by Leah (Ge 29:35; 35:23; 1Ch 2:1). Did not want to kill Joseph (Ge 37:26-27). Among Canaanites, fathered Perez by Tamar (Ge 38). Tribe of blessed as ruling tribe (Ge 49:8-12; Dt 33:7), numbered (Nu 1:27; 26:22), allotted land (Jos 15; Eze 48:7), failed to fully possess (Jos 15:63; Jdg 1:1-20).

2. Name used for people and land of Southern Kingdom.

Ru 1: 7 take them back to the land of **J.**
2Sa 2: 4 David king over the house of **J.**
5: 5 over **J** seven years and six months,
24: 1 and take a census of Israel and **J."**
1Ch 28: 4 He chose **J** as leader, and from the house of **J** he chose my family,
Ne 6: 7 'There is a king in **J!'**
Isa 1: 1 vision concerning **J** and Jerusalem
3: 8 Jerusalem staggers, **J** is falling;
Jer 2:28 many gods as you have towns, O **J.**
13:19 All **J** will be carried into exile,
30: 3 and **J** back from captivity
31:31 of Israel and with the house of **J.**
La 1: 3 **J** has gone into exile.
Hos 1: 7 I will show love to the house of **J;**
Joel 3: 1 restore the fortunes of **J** and
Mic 5: 2 you are small among the clans of **J,**
Zec 1:19 the horns that scattered **J,**
8:15 to do good again to Jerusalem and **J.**
10: 4 From **J** will come the cornerstone,
11:14 breaking the brotherhood between **J**
Mal 2:11 **J** has broken faith.
Mt 2: 6 Bethlehem, in the land of **J,**
Heb 7:14 that our Lord descended from **J,**
8: 8 of Israel and with the house of **J.**
Rev 5: 5 See, the Lion of the tribe of **J,**

HOUSE OF JUDAH See HOUSE

ISRAEL AND JUDAH See ISRAEL

KING OF JUDAH See KING

KINGS OF JUDAH See KINGS

MEN OF JUDAH Jos 14:6; Jdg 1:3, 8, 9, 16, 17, 18, 19; 15:10; 1Sa 11:8; 2Sa 1:18; 2:4; 19:14, 15, 16, 41, 42, 43, 43; 20:2, 4; 1Ki 1:9; 2Ki 16:6; 23:2; 25:25; 1Ch 12:24; 2Ch 13:15, 18; 14:13; 16:6; 20:13, 24, 27; 23:8; 34:30; Ezr 10:9; Ne 13:23; Isa 5:3, 7; Jer 4:3, 4; 17:25; 32:32; 35:13; Da 9:7

PEOPLE OF JUDAH Nu 2:3; Jos 15:12, 63; 18:14; 1Ki 4:20; 2Ki 14:21; 1Ch 2:10; 4:27; 9:1; 2Ch 20:4, 18; 25:5; 26:1; 32:9; 34:9; Ezr 4:4, 6; Ne 4:16; 11:25; 13:16; Isa 11:12; Jer 7:2, 30; 11:2, 9; 17:20; 18:11; 25:1, 2; 26:18; 36:3, 6, 31; 44:24; 50:4, 33; Eze 25:3; Hos 1:11; 5:12; Joel 3:6, 8, 19; Ob 1:12

TRIBE OF JUDAH Ex 31:2; 35:30; 38:22; Nu 1:27; 7:12; 13:6; 34:19; Jos 7:1, 18; 15:1, 20, 21; 1Ki 12:20; 2Ki 17:18; 2Ch 19:11; Ps 78:68; Rev 5:5; 7:5

JUDAISM* [JEW]

Ac   2:11 (both Jews and converts to **J**);
      6: 5 Nicolas from Antioch, a convert to **J**.
   13:43 to **J** followed Paul and Barnabas,
Gal 1:13 heard of my previous way of life in **J**
     1:14 I was advancing in **J** beyond many

JUDAS [ISCARIOT]

  1. Apostle; son of James (Lk 6:16; Jn 14:22; Ac 1:13). Probably also called Thaddaeus (Mt 10:3; Mk 3:18).

  2. Brother of James and Jesus (Mt 13:55; Mk 6:3), also called Jude (Jude 1).

  3. Christian prophet (Ac 15:22-32).

  4. Apostle, also called Iscariot, who betrayed Jesus (Mt 10:4; 26:14-56; Mk 3:19; 14:10-50; Lk 6:16; 22:3-53; Jn 6:71; 12:4; 13:2-30; 18:2-11). Suicide of (Mt 27:3-5; Ac 1:16-25).

JUDE*

Jude 1: 1 **J**, a servant of Jesus Christ and

JUDEA [JUDAH]

Mt   2: 1 Jesus was born in Bethlehem in **J**,
    3: 1 preaching in the Desert of **J**
  24:16 then let those who are in **J** flee to
Mk 3: 8 many people came to him from **J**,
Lk   1: 5 In the time of Herod king of **J**
    3: 1 Pontius Pilate was governor of **J**,
   7:17 about Jesus spread throughout **J**
Ac   1: 8 and in all **J** and Samaria,
    8: 1 scattered throughout **J** and Samaria.
   9:31 Then the church throughout **J**,
1Th 2:14 imitators of God's churches in **J**,

JUDEAN [JUDAH]

Mk 1: 5 The whole **J** countryside and all the

JUDGE [JUDGE'S, JUDGED, JUDGES, JUDGING, JUDGMENT, JUDGMENTS]

Ge 16: 5 the LORD **j** between you and me."
  18:25 not the **J** of all the earth do right?"
  19: 9 and now he wants to play the **j**!
  31:53 the God of their father, **j** between us.
Ex   2:14 "Who made you ruler and **j** over us?
  18:14 Why do you alone sit as **j**,
Lev 19:15 but **j** your neighbor fairly.
Dt   1:16 between your brothers and **j** fairly,
  17: 9 to the **j** who is in office at that time.
  32:36 The LORD will **j** his people
Jdg 2:18 Whenever the LORD raised up a **j**
  11:27 the LORD, the **J**, decide the dispute
1Sa 2:10 LORD will **j** the ends of the earth.
   3:13 that I would **j** his family forever
   7:15 Samuel continued as **j** over Israel all
  24:12 the LORD **j** between you and me.
1Ki 8:32 **J** between your servants,
1Ch 16:33 for he comes to **j** the earth.
2Ch 6:23 **J** between your servants,
  19: 7 **J** carefully, for with the LORD our
Job 9:15 plead with my **J** for mercy.
Ps   7: 8 let the LORD **j** the peoples.
   7:11 God is a righteous **j**,

   9: 8 He will **j** the world in righteousness;
  50: 6 for God himself is **j**.
  51: 4 and justified when you **j**.
  75: 2 it is I who **j** uprightly.
  76: 9 O God, rose up to **j**,
  82: 8 Rise up, O God, **j** the earth,
  94: 2 Rise up, O **J** of the earth;
  96:10 he will **j** the peoples
  96:13 he comes to **j** the earth.
  96:13 He will **j** the world in righteousness
  98: 9 for he comes to **j** the earth.
  98: 9 He will **j** the world in righteousness
 110: 6 He will **j** the nations,
Pr 31: 9 Speak up and **j** fairly;
Isa 2: 4 He will **j** between the nations
   3:13 he rises to **j** the people.
  11: 3 not **j** by what he sees with his eyes,
  33:22 For the LORD is our **j**,
Jer 11:20 you who **j** righteously and test
Eze 7: 3 will **j** you according to your conduct
   7:27 by their own standards I will **j** them.
  18:30 O house of Israel, I will **j** you,
  20:36 so I will **j** you,
  22: 2 Will you **j** this city of bloodshed?
  33:20 But I will **j** each of you according
  34:17 **j** between one sheep and another,
Joel 3:12 for there I will sit to **j** all the nations
Mic 3:11 Her leaders **j** for a bribe,
   4: 3 He will **j** between many peoples
Mt   7: 1 "Do not **j**, or you too will be judged.
Lk   6:37 "Do not **j**, and you will not be
  12:14 who appointed me a **j** or an arbiter
  18: 2 a **j** who neither feared God nor cared
  19:22 'I will **j** you by your own words,
Jn   5:27 And he has given him authority to **j**
   5:30 I **j** only as I hear,
   8:16 But if I do **j**, my decisions are right,
  12:47 For I did not come to **j** the world,
  12:48 a **j** for the one who rejects me
  18:31 and **j** him by your own law."
Ac   4:19 "**J** for yourselves whether it is right
   7:27 'Who made you ruler and **j** over us?
  10:42 the one whom God appointed as **j** of
  17:31 when he will **j** the world with justice
Ro   2: 1 for at whatever point you **j** the other,
   2:16 when God will **j** men's secrets
   3: 4 and prevail when you **j**."
   3: 6 how could God **j** the world?
  14:10 then, why do you **j** your brother?
1Co 4: 3 I do not even **j** myself.
   4: 5 **j** nothing before the appointed time;
   5:12 Are you not to **j** those inside?
   6: 2 that the saints will **j** the world?
   6: 3 not know that we will **j** angels?
Gal 2: 6 not **j** by external appearance—
Col 2:16 not let anyone **j** you by what you eat
2Ti 4: 1 who will **j** the living and the dead,
   4: 8 which the Lord, the righteous **J**,
Heb 10:30 "The Lord will **j** his people."
  12:23 the **j** of all men,
  13: 4 for God will **j** the adulterer and all
Jas 4:12 There is only one Lawgiver and **J**,
   4:12 who are you to **j** your neighbor?
   5: 9 The **J** is standing at the door!

1Pe	4: 5	to him who is ready to **j** the living
Jude	1:15	to **j** everyone, and to convict
Rev	6:10	until you **j** the inhabitants of the
	20: 4	who had been given authority to **j**.

JUDGE'S* [JUDGE]

Mt	27:19	While Pilate was sitting on the **j** seat,
Jn	19:13	and sat down on the **j** seat

JUDGED [JUDGE]

1Sa	7:17	and there he also **j** Israel.
Ps	9:19	let the nations be **j**
Eze	20:36	As I **j** your fathers in the desert of
	24:14	be **j** according to your conduct
Mt	7: 1	"Do not judge, or you too will be **j**.
Ro	2:12	sin under the law will be **j** by the law
1Co	4: 3	I care very little if I am **j** by you or
	10:29	For why should my freedom be **j**
	11:31	But if we **j** ourselves,
	14:24	that he is a sinner and will be **j** by all
Jas	2:12	to be **j** by the law that gives freedom,
	3: 1	who teach will be **j** more strictly.
	5: 9	brothers, or you will be **j**.
Rev	16: 5	because you have so **j**;
	18:20	God has **j** her for the way
	20:12	The dead were **j** according

JUDGES [JUDGE]

The Judges of Israel			
Judge	Oppressor	Peace	Text
Othniel	Aram	40 years	Jdg 3:7-11
Ehud	Moab	80 years	Jdg 3:12-30
Shamgar	Philistia		Jdg 3:31
Deborah	Canaan	40 years	Jdg 4-5
Gideon	Midian	40 years	Jdg 6-8
Tola		23 years	Jdg 10:1-2
Jair		22 years	Jdg 10:3-5
Jephthah	Ammon	6 years	Jdg 10:6-12:7
Ibzan		7 years	Jdg 12:8-10
Elon		10 years	Jdg 12:11-12
Abdon		8 years	Jdg 12:13-15
Samson	Philistia	20 years	Jdg 13-16
See also each judge by name			

Ex	18:22	Have them serve as **j** for the people
Jdg	2:16	Then the LORD raised up **j**,
Ru	1: 1	In the days when the **j** ruled,
1Sa	8: 1	he appointed his sons as **j** for Israel.
Job	9:24	he blindfolds its **j**.
Ps	58:11	surely there is a God who **j**
	75: 7	But it is God who **j**:
Pr	29:14	If a king **j** the poor with fairness,
Lk	11:19	So then, they will be your **j**.
Jn	5:22	Moreover, the Father **j** no one,
1Co	4: 4	It is the Lord who **j** me.
Heb	4:12	it **j** the thoughts and attitudes of the
Jas	4:11	**j** him speaks against the law and **j** it.

1Pe	1:17	Father who **j** each man's work
	2:23	to him who **j** justly.
Rev	18: 8	mighty is the Lord God who **j** her.
	19:11	With justice he **j** and makes war.

JUDGING [JUDGE]

Dt	1:17	Do not show partiality in **j**;
Ps	9: 4	sat on your throne, **j** righteously.
Pr	24:23	To show partiality in **j** is not good:
Isa	16: 5	one who in **j** seeks justice
Mt	19:28	**j** the twelve tribes of Israel.
Jn	7:24	Stop **j** by mere appearances,
Rev	11:18	The time has come for **j** the dead,

JUDGMENT [JUDGE]

Ex	6: 6	and with mighty acts of **j**.
	12:12	bring **j** on all the gods of Egypt.
Nu	33: 4	LORD had brought **j** on their gods.
Dt	1:17	for **j** belongs to God.
	32:41	and my hand grasps it in **j**,
1Sa	25:33	be blessed for your good **j**
Job	24: 1	the Almighty not set times for **j**?
Ps	1: 5	the wicked will not stand in the **j**,
	9: 7	he has established his throne for **j**.
	76: 8	From heaven you pronounced **j**,
	82: 1	he gives **j** among the "gods":
	119:66	Teach me knowledge and good **j**,
	122: 5	There the thrones for **j** stand,
	143: 2	Do not bring your servant into **j**,
Pr	3:21	preserve sound **j** and discernment,
	6:32	man who commits adultery lacks **j**;
	7: 7	a youth who lacked **j**.
	8:14	Counsel and sound **j** are mine;
	9: 4	she says to those who lack **j**.
	10:21	but fools die for lack of **j**.
	11:12	who lacks **j** derides his neighbor,
	12:11	but he who chases fantasies lacks **j**.
	15:21	Folly delights a man who lacks **j**,
	17:18	in **j** strikes hands in pledge and puts
	18: 1	selfish ends; he defies all sound **j**.
	28:16	A tyrannical ruler lacks **j**,
Ecc	3:17	God will bring to **j** both the righteous
	11: 9	these things God will bring you to **j**.
	12:14	God will bring every deed into **j**,
Isa	3:14	into **j** against the elders and leaders
	28: 6	spirit of justice to him who sits in **j**,
	53: 8	By oppression and **j** he was taken
	66:16	the LORD will execute **j** upon all
Jer	2:35	I will pass **j** on you because you say,
	25:31	he will bring **j** on all mankind
	51:18	when their **j** comes,
Eze	11:10	and I will execute **j** on you at
Da	7:22	of Days came and pronounced **j**
Joel	3: 2	There I will enter into **j** against them
Am	7: 4	LORD was calling for **j** by fire;
Hab	1:12	have appointed them to execute **j**;
Zec	8:16	and render true and sound **j**
Mal	3: 5	"So I will come near to you for **j**.
Mt	5:21	who murders will be subject to **j**.'
	5:22	with his brother will be subject to **j**,
	10:15	Sodom and Gomorrah on the day of **j**
	11:24	bearable for Sodom on the day of **j**
	12:36	to give account on the day of **j**
	12:41	of Nineveh will stand up at the **j**

Jn	5:22	but has entrusted all **j** to the Son,
	5:30	and my **j** is just,
	7:24	and make a right **j**."
	8:26	"I have much to say in **j** of you.
	9:39	"For **j** I have come into this world,
	12:31	Now is the time for **j** on this world;
	16: 8	to sin and righteousness and **j**:
	16:11	and in regard to **j**, because
Ac	24:25	self-control and the **j** to come,
Ro	2: 1	you who pass **j** do the same things.
	2: 2	we know that God's **j** against those
	5:16	The **j** followed one sin
	12: 3	rather think of yourself with sober **j**,
	14: 1	without passing **j** on disputable
	14:10	we will all stand before God's **j** seat.
	14:13	let us stop passing **j** on one another.
1Co	7:40	In my **j**, she is happier if she stays
	11:29	eats and drinks **j** on himself.
2Co	5:10	all appear before the **j** seat of Christ,
2Th	1: 5	that God's **j** is right,
1Ti	3: 6	under the same **j** as the devil.
	5:12	Thus they bring **j** on themselves,
Heb	6: 2	resurrection of the dead, and eternal **j**
	9:27	and after that to face **j**,
	10:27	a fearful expectation of **j**
Jas	2:13	Mercy triumphs over **j**!
	4:11	but sitting in **j** on it.
1Pe	4:17	for **j** to begin with the family of God;
2Pe	2: 4	gloomy dungeons to be held for **j**;
	2: 9	hold the unrighteous for the day of **j**,
	3: 7	of **j** and destruction of ungodly men.
1Jn	4:17	will have confidence on the day of **j**,
Jude	1: 6	bound with everlasting chains for **j**
Rev	14: 7	because the hour of his **j** has come.

JUDGMENTS [JUDGE]

1Ch	16:14	his **j** are in all the earth.
Jer	1:16	I will pronounce my **j** on my people
Eze	14:21	against Jerusalem my four dreadful **j**
Da	9:11	sworn **j** written in the Law of Moses,
Hos	6: 5	my **j** flashed like lightning upon you.
Ro	11:33	How unsearchable his **j**,
1Co	2:15	The spiritual man makes **j** about
Rev	16: 5	"You are just in these **j**,
	16: 7	true and just are your **j**."
	19: 2	for true and just are his **j**.

JUG

1Sa	26:12	So David took the spear and water **j**
1Ki	17:12	of flour in a jar and a little oil in a **j**.

JUICE

Nu	6: 3	He must not drink grape **j** or eat

JUMPED* [JUMPING]

Mk	10:50	he **j** to his feet and came to Jesus.
Jn	21: 7	and **j** into the water.
Ac	3: 8	He **j** to his feet and began to walk.
	14:10	the man **j** up and began to walk.
	19:16	**j** on them and overpowered them all.

JUMPING* [JUMPED]

Ac	3: 8	walking and **j**, and praising God.

JUPITER (KJV) See ZEUS

JUST [JUSTICE, JUSTIFICATION, JUSTIFIED, JUSTIFIES, JUSTIFY, JUSTIFYING, JUSTLY]

Ge	18:19	by doing what is right and **j**,
Dt	32: 4	and all his ways are **j**.
	32: 4	upright and **j** is he.
	32:47	They are not **j** idle words for you—
2Sa	8:15	doing what was **j** and right
1Ch	18:14	doing what was **j** and right
2Ch	12: 6	"The LORD is **j**."
Ne	9:13	and laws that are **j** and right,
	9:33	you have been **j**;
Job	34:17	Will you condemn the **j**
	35: 2	"Do you think this is **j**?
Ps	37:28	For the LORD loves the **j**
	37:30	and his tongue speaks what is **j**.
	99: 4	in Jacob you have done what is **j**
	111: 7	works of his hands are faithful and **j**;
	119:121	I have done what is righteous and **j**;
Pr	1: 3	doing what is right and **j** and fair;
	2: 8	for he guards the course of the **j**
	2: 9	understand what is right and **j**
	8: 8	All the words of my mouth are **j**;
	8:15	and rulers make laws that are **j**;
	12: 5	The plans of the righteous are **j**,
	21: 3	To do what is right and **j**
Isa	32: 7	even when the plea of the needy is **j**.
	58: 2	They ask me for **j** decisions
Jer	4: 2	**j** and righteous way you swear,
	22: 3	Do what is **j** and right.
	22:15	He did what was right and **j**,
	23: 5	and do what is **j** and right in
	33:15	he will do what is **j**
Eze	18: 5	a righteous man who does what is **j**
	18:19	the son has done what is **j** and right
	18:21	and does what is **j** and right,
	18:25	'The way of the Lord is not **j**.'
	18:27	and does what is **j** and right,
	18:29	'The way of the Lord is not **j**.'
	33:14	and does what is **j** and right—
	33:16	He has done what is **j** and right;
	33:17	'The way of the Lord is not **j**.'
	33:17	But it is their way that is not **j**.
	33:19	and does what is **j** and right,
	33:20	'The way of the Lord is not **j**.'
	45: 9	and do what is **j** and right.
Da	4:37	and all his ways are **j**.
Lk	8:50	"Don't be afraid; I believe,
Jn	5:30	and my judgment is **j**,
Ro	3:26	as to be **j** and the one who justifies
2Th	1: 6	God is **j**: He will pay back
Heb	2: 2	received its **j** punishment,
1Jn	1: 9	and **j** and will forgive us our sins
Rev	15: 3	**J** and true are your ways,
	16: 5	"You are **j** in these judgments,
	16: 7	true and **j** are your judgments."
	19: 2	for true and **j** are his judgments.

JUSTICE* [JUST]

Ge	49:16	"Dan will provide **j** for his people
Ex	23: 2	do not pervert **j** by siding with
	23: 6	"Do not deny **j** to your poor people
Lev	19:15	" 'Do not pervert **j**;

Dt	16:19	Do not pervert **j** or show partiality.
	16:20	Follow **j** and justice alone,
	16:20	Follow justice and **j** alone,
	24:17	deprive the alien or the fatherless of **j**
	27:19	"Cursed is the man who withholds **j**
1Sa	8: 3	and accepted bribes and perverted **j**.
2Sa	15: 4	to me and I would see that he gets **j**."
	15: 6	who came to the king asking for **j**,
1Ki	3:11	for discernment in administering **j**,
	3:28	wisdom from God to administer **j**.
	7: 7	the Hall of **J**,
	10: 9	to maintain **j** and righteousness."
2Ch	9: 8	to maintain **j** and righteousness."
Ezr	7:25	and judges to administer **j** to all
Est	1:13	experts in matters of law and **j**,
Job	8: 3	Does God pervert **j**?
	9:19	And if it is a matter of **j**,
	19: 7	there is no **j**.
	27: 2	who has denied me **j**, the Almighty,
	29:14	**j** was my robe and my turban.
	31:13	"If I have denied **j**
	34: 5	'I am innocent, but God denies me **j**.
	34:12	that the Almighty would pervert **j**.
	34:17	Can he who hates **j** govern?
	36: 3	I will ascribe **j** to my Maker.
	36:17	and **j** have taken hold of you.
	37:23	in his **j** and great righteousness,
	40: 8	"Would you discredit my **j**?
Ps	7: 6	Awake, my God; decree **j**.
	9: 8	he will govern the peoples with **j**.
	9:16	The LORD is known by his **j**;
	11: 7	the LORD is righteous, he loves **j**;
	33: 5	LORD loves righteousness and **j**;
	36: 6	your **j** like the great deep.
	37: 6	the **j** of your cause like the noonday
	45: 6	a scepter of **j** will be the scepter of
	72: 1	Endow the king with your **j**, O God,
	72: 2	your afflicted ones with **j**.
	89:14	**j** are the foundation of your throne;
	97: 2	**j** are the foundation of his throne.
	99: 4	The King is mighty, he loves **j**—
	101: 1	I will sing of your love and **j**;
	103: 6	and **j** for all the oppressed.
	106: 3	Blessed are they who maintain **j**,
	112: 5	who conducts his affairs with **j**.
	140:12	that the LORD secures **j** for the poor
Pr	8:20	along the paths of **j**,
	16:10	and his mouth should not betray **j**.
	17:23	in secret to pervert the course of **j**.
	18: 5	or to deprive the innocent of **j**.
	19:28	A corrupt witness mocks at **j**,
	21:15	When **j** is done,
	28: 5	Evil men do not understand **j**,
	29: 4	By **j** a king gives a country stability,
	29: 7	righteous care about **j** for the poor,
	29:26	from the LORD that man gets **j**.
Ecc	3:16	in the place of **j**—
	5: 8	and **j** and rights denied,
Isa	1:17	Seek **j**, encourage the oppressed.
	1:21	She once was full of **j**;
	1:27	Zion will be redeemed with **j**,
	5: 7	he looked for **j**, but saw bloodshed;
	5:16	Almighty will be exalted by his **j**,
	5:23	but deny **j** to the innocent.
	9: 7	upholding it with **j** and righteousness
	10: 2	and withhold **j** from the oppressed
	11: 4	with **j** he will give decisions for
	16: 5	in judging seeks **j** and speeds the
	28: 6	of **j** to him who sits in judgment,
	28:17	I will make **j** the measuring line
	29:21	deprive the innocent of **j**.
	30:18	For the LORD is a God of **j**.
	32: 1	and rulers will rule with **j**.
	32:16	**J** will dwell in the desert
	33: 5	he will fill Zion with **j**
	42: 1	and he will bring **j** to the nations.
	42: 3	In faithfulness he will bring forth **j**;
	42: 4	or be discouraged till he establishes **j**
	51: 4	**j** will become a light to the nations.
	51: 5	my arm will bring **j** to the nations.
	56: 1	"Maintain **j** and do what is right,
	59: 4	No one calls for **j**;
	59: 8	there is no **j** in their paths.
	59: 9	So **j** is far from us,
	59:11	We look for **j**, but find none;
	59:14	So **j** is driven back,
	59:15	displeased that there was no **j**.
	61: 8	"For I, the LORD, love **j**;
Jer	9:24	**j** and righteousness on earth,
	10:24	Correct me, LORD, but only with **j**—
	12: 1	speak with you about your **j**:
	21:12	says: " 'Administer **j** every morning;
	30:11	I will discipline you but only with **j**;
	46:28	I will discipline you but only with **j**;
La	3:36	to deprive a man of **j**—
Eze	22:29	mistreat the alien, denying them **j**.
	34:16	I will shepherd the flock with **j**.
Hos	2:19	betroth you in righteousness and **j**,
	12: 6	maintain love and **j**,
Am	2: 7	and deny **j** to the oppressed.
	5: 7	You who turn **j** into bitterness
	5:12	and you deprive the poor of **j** in
	5:15	Hate evil, love good; maintain **j** in
	5:24	But let **j** roll on like a river,
	6:12	But you have turned **j** into poison
Mic	3: 1	Should you not know **j**,
	3: 8	and with **j** and might,
	3: 9	who despise **j** and distort all
Hab	1: 4	and **j** never prevails.
	1: 4	so that **j** is perverted.
Zep	3: 5	by morning he dispenses his **j**,
Zec	7: 9	Almighty says: 'Administer true **j**;
Mal	2:17	or "Where is the God of **j**?"
	3: 5	and deprive aliens of **j**,
Mt	12:18	and he will proclaim **j** to the nations.
	12:20	till he leads **j** to victory.
	23:23	important matters of the law—**j**,
Lk	11:42	you neglect **j** and the love of God.
	18: 3	'Grant me **j** against my adversary.'
	18: 5	I will see that she gets **j**,
	18: 7	And will not God bring about **j**
	18: 8	I tell you, he will see that they get **j**,
Ac	8:33	his humiliation he was deprived of **j**.
	17:31	when he will judge the world with **j**
	28: 4	**J** has not allowed him to live."
Ro	3:25	He did this to demonstrate his **j**,
	3:26	he did it to demonstrate his **j** at
2Co	7:11	what readiness to see **j** done.

Heb 11:33 administered **j**, and gained what was
Rev 19:11 With **j** he judges and makes war.

JUSTIFICATION* [JUST]

Eze 16:52 furnished some **j** for your sisters.
Ro 4:25 and was raised to life for our **j.**
    5:16 many trespasses and brought **j.**
    5:18 was **j** that brings life for all men.

JUSTIFIED* [JUST]

Ps 51: 4 and **j** when you judge.
Lk 18:14 went home **j** before God.
Ac 13:39 him everyone who believes is **j**
    13:39 not be **j** from by the law of Moses.
Ro 3:24 and are **j** freely by his grace through
    3:28 that a man is **j** by faith apart from
    4: 2 If, in fact, Abraham was **j** by works,
    5: 1 since we have been **j** through faith,
    5: 9 we have now been **j** by his blood,
    8:30 those he called, he also **j**; those he **j,**
    10:10 that you believe and are **j,**
1Co 6:11 you were **j** in the name of the Lord
Gal 2:16 a man is not **j** by observing the law,
    2:16 that we may be **j** by faith in Christ
    2:16 by observing the law no one will be **j**
    2:17 "If, while we seek to be **j** in Christ,
    3:11 no one is **j** before God by the law,
    3:24 to Christ that we might be **j** by faith.
    5: 4 to be **j** by law have been alienated
Tit 3: 7 having been **j** by his grace,
Jas 2:24 that a person is **j** by what he does

JUSTIFIES* [JUST]

Ro 3:26 the one who **j** those who have faith
    4: 5 but trusts God who **j** the wicked,
    8:33 It is God who **j.**

JUSTIFY* [JUST]

Est 4: 7 no such distress would **j** disturbing
Job 40: 8 you condemn me to **j** yourself?
Isa 53:11 my righteous servant will **j** many,
Lk 10:29 But he wanted to **j** himself,
    16:15 "You are the ones who **j** yourselves
Ro 3:30 who will **j** the circumcised by faith
Gal 3: 8 God would **j** the Gentiles by faith,

JUSTIFYING* [JUST]

Job 32: 2 Job for **j** himself rather than God.

JUSTLY* [JUST]

Ps 58: 1 Do you rulers indeed speak **j?**
    67: 4 for you rule the peoples **j** and guide
Jer 7: 5 and deal with each other **j,**
Mic 6: 8 To act **j** and to love mercy and
Lk 23:41 We are punished **j,**
1Pe 2:23 himself to him who judges **j.**

JUSTUS* [JOSEPH]

Ac 1:23 called Barsabbas (also known as **J**)
    18: 7 next door to the house of Titius **J,**
Col 4:11 Jesus, who is called **J,**

K

KADESH [KADESH BARNEA, MERIBAH KADESH]

Nu 20: 1 and they stayed at **K.**
Dt 1:46 And so you stayed in **K** many days

KADESH BARNEA [KADESH]

Nu 32: 8 when I sent them from **K** to look

KEBAR

Eze 1: 1 among the exiles by the **K** River,
    3:23 the glory I had seen by the **K** River,
    43: 3 the visions I had seen by the **K** River

KEDESH

Jos 12:22 the king of **K** one
Jdg 4: 6 for Barak son of Abinoam from **K**

KEDORLAOMER

Ge 14:17 Abram returned from defeating **K**

KEEP [KEEPER, KEEPING, KEEPS, KEPT]

Ge 6:19 to **k** them alive with you.
    17: 9 you must **k** my covenant,
    31:49 the LORD **k** watch between you
Ex 15:26 his commands and **k** his decrees,
    19: 5 obey me fully and **k** my covenant,
    20: 6 love me and **k** my commandments.
Lev 15:31 " 'You must **k** the Israelites separate
Nu 6:24 " ' "The LORD bless you and **k** you;
Dt 4: 2 but **k** the commands of the LORD
    5:10 love me and **k** my commandments.
    6:17 Be sure to **k** the commands of
    7: 9 who love him and **k** his commands.
    7:12 LORD your God will **k** his covenant
    11: 1 and **k** his requirements, his decrees,
    13: 4 **K** his commands and obey him;
    30:10 and **k** his commands and decrees
    30:16 and to **k** his commands,
Jos 22: 5 very careful to **k** the commandment
2Sa 7:25 **k** forever the promise you have made
1Ki 8:25 **k** for your servant David my father
    8:58 all his ways and to **k** the commands,
2Ki 17:19 even Judah did not **k** the commands
    23: 3 the LORD and **k** his commands,
1Ch 29:18 and **k** their hearts loyal to you.
2Ch 6:14 you who **k** your covenant
    34:31 the LORD and **k** his commands,
Job 14:16 but not **k** track of my sin.
Ps 18:28 You, O LORD, **k** my lamp burning;
    19:13 **K** your servant also from willful sins
    37:34 Wait for the LORD and **k** his way.
    78:10 they did not **k** God's covenant
    119: 2 Blessed are they who **k** his statutes
    119: 9 a young man **k** his way pure?
    121: 7 LORD will **k** you from all harm—
    141: 3 **k** watch over the door of my lips.
Pr 4:21 **k** them within your heart;

	4:24	**k** corrupt talk far from your lips.
	7: 2	**K** my commands and you will live;
	7: 5	they will **k** you from the adulteress,
	30: 8	**K** falsehood and lies far from me;
Ecc	3: 6	a time to **k** and a time to throw away,
	12:13	and **k** his commandments,
Isa	26: 3	You will **k** in perfect peace him
	42: 6	I will **k** you and will make you to be
	58:13	"If you **k** your feet from breaking
Jer	16:11	and did not **k** my law.
Eze	20:19	and be careful to **k** my laws.
Mt	10:10	for the worker is worth his **k.**
Lk	12:35	and **k** your lamps burning,
	17:33	Whoever tries to **k** his life will lose it
Jn	9:16	for he does not **k** the Sabbath."
	10:24	How long will you **k** us in suspense?
	12:25	in this world will **k** it for eternal life.
Ac	2:24	for death to **k** its hold on him.
	18: 9	"Do not be afraid; **k** on speaking,
Ro	7:19	do not want to do—this **I k** on doing.
	12:11	but **k** your spiritual fervor,
	14:22	**k** between yourself and God.
	16:17	**K** away from them.
1Co	1: 8	He will **k** you strong to the end,
2Co	12: 7	To **k** me from becoming conceited
Gal	5:25	let us **k** in step with the Spirit.
Eph	4: 3	Make every effort to **k** the unity of
2Th	3: 6	to **k** away from every brother who
1Ti	5:22	**K** yourself pure.
2Ti	1:13	**k** as the pattern of sound teaching,
	4: 5	But you, **k** your head in all situations
Heb	9:20	which God has commanded you to **k.**
	10:26	If we deliberately **k** on sinning
	13: 1	**K** on loving each other as brothers.
	13: 5	**K** your lives free from the love of money
Jas	1:26	not **k** a tight rein on his tongue,
	2: 8	If you really **k** the royal law found
	3: 2	able to **k** his whole body in check.
1Pe	3:10	must **k** his tongue from evil
2Pe	1: 8	will **k** you from being ineffective
1Jn	5:21	**k** yourselves from idols.
Jude	1: 6	not **k** their positions of authority
	1:21	**K** yourselves in God's love
	1:24	who is able to **k** you from falling
Rev	3:10	also **k** you from the hour of trial
	22: 9	of all who **k** the words

KEEPER [KEEP]

Ge	4: 9	"Am I my brother's **k?**"
Jn	12: 6	as **k** of the money bag,

KEEPING [KEEP]

Ex	20: 8	the Sabbath day by **k** it holy.
Dt	5:12	the Sabbath day by **k** it holy,
	6: 2	by **k** all his decrees and commands
	13:18	**k** all his commands that I am giving
Ps	19:11	in **k** them there is great reward.
	119:112	My heart is set on **k** your decrees to
Pr	6:24	**k** you from the immoral woman,
	15: 3	**k** watch on the wicked and the good.
Mt	3: 8	Produce fruit in **k** with repentance.
Lk	2: 8	**k** watch over their flocks at night.
	3: 8	Produce fruit in **k** with repentance.

1Co	7:19	**K** God's commands is what counts.
	16: 2	sum of money in **k** with his income,
2Co	8: 5	and then to us in **k** with God's will.
Jas	4:11	you judge the law, you are not **k** it,
1Pe	3:16	**k** a clear conscience,
2Pe	3: 9	Lord is not slow in **k** his promise,
	3:13	But in **k** with his promise

KEEPS [KEEP]

Ne	1: 5	who **k** his covenant of love
	9:32	who **k** his covenant of love,
Ps	15: 4	who **k** his oath even when it hurts,
Pr	11:13	but a trustworthy man **k** a secret.
	12:23	A prudent man **k** his knowledge
	15:21	of understanding **k** a straight course.
	17:24	A discerning man **k** wisdom in view,
	17:28	a fool is thought wise if he **k** silent,
	28: 7	who **k** the law is a discerning son,
	29:11	a wise man **k** himself under control.
	29:18	but blessed is he who **k** the law.
Isa	33:15	and **k** his hand from accepting bribes
	56: 2	who **k** the Sabbath without desecrating it, and **k** his hand from
Da	9: 4	who **k** his covenant of love
Am	5:13	Therefore the prudent man **k** quiet
Jn	7:19	Yet not one of you **k** the law.
	8:51	if anyone **k** my word,
1Co	13: 5	it **k** no record of wrongs.
Jas	2:10	For whoever **k** the whole law and
1Jn	3: 6	one who lives in him **k** on sinning.
Rev	22: 7	Blessed is he who **k** the words of

KEILAH

1Sa	23: 5	So David and his men went to **K,**

KENITE

Jdg	1:16	of Moses' father-in-law, the **K,**
	4:17	the wife of Heber the **K,**

KEPT [KEEP]

Ge	4: 2	Now Abel **k** flocks,
	7:17	For forty days the flood **k** coming on
	37:11	but his father **k** the matter in mind.
Ex	12:42	Because the LORD **k** vigil that night
	16:33	to be **k** for the generations to come."
Lev	6: 9	fire must be **k** burning on the altar.
Nu	17:10	to be **k** as a sign to the rebellious.
Dt	7: 8	the LORD loved you and **k** the oath
2Sa	22:22	For I have **k** the ways of the LORD;
2Ki	18: 6	he **k** the commands the LORD had
Ne	9: 8	You have **k** your promise
Ps	130: 3	If you, O LORD, **k** a record of sins,
Pr	28:18	whose walk is blameless is **k** safe,
	28:26	he who walks in wisdom is **k** safe.
	29:25	whoever trusts in the LORD is **k** safe.
Isa	38:17	In your love you **k** me from the pit
Mt	13:35	"All these I have **k,**"
2Co	11: 9	I have **k** myself from being a burden
2Ti	4: 7	I have **k** the faith.
Heb	13: 4	and the marriage bed **k** pure,
1Pe	1: 4	**k** in heaven for you,
2Pe	3: 7	being **k** for the day of judgment
Rev	3: 8	yet you have **k** my word and have
	3:10	Since you have **k** my command

9:15 four angels who had been **k** ready
14: 4 for they **k** themselves pure.

KERNEL* [KERNELS]

Mk   4:28 then the full **k** in the head.
Jn 12:24 unless a **k** of wheat falls to the

KERNELS [KERNEL]

Dt 23:25 you may pick **k** with your hands,
Lk   6: 1 rub them in their hands and eat the **k.**

KETTLES*

Mk   7: 4 the washing of cups, pitchers and **k.)**

KETURAH*

Wife of Abraham (Ge 25:1-4; 1Ch 1:32-33).

KEY [KEYS]

Isa 22:22 the **k** to the house of David;
    33: 6 fear of the LORD is the **k** to this
Lk 11:52 have taken away the **k** to knowledge.
Rev 3: 7 who holds the **k** of David.
     9: 1 given the **k** to the shaft of the Abyss.
    20: 1 having the **k** to the Abyss

KEYS* [KEY]

Mt 16:19 I will give you the **k** of the kingdom
Rev 1:18 And I hold the **k** of death and Hades.

KICK*

Ac 26:14 for you to **k** against the goads.'

KIDNAPPER* [KIDNAPS]

Dt 24: 7 the **k** must die.

KIDNAPS* [KIDNAPPER]

Ex 21:16 "Anyone who **k** another and

KIDRON

2Sa 15:23 The king also crossed the **K** Valley,
Jn 18: 1 disciples and crossed the **K** Valley.

KILION

Ru   1: 5 both Mahlon and **K** also died.

KILL [KILLED, KILLING, KILLS]

Ge   4:14 and whoever finds me will **k** me."
    12:12 they will **k** me but will let you live.
    20:11 they will **k** me because of my wife.'
    26: 7 might **k** me on account of Rebekah,
    37:18 they plotted to **k** him.
Ex   2:15 he tried to **k** Moses,
     4:19 who wanted to **k** you are dead."
     4:23 so I will **k** your firstborn son.' "
1Sa 19: 1 and all the attendants to **k** David.
    20:33 that his father intended to **k** David.
1Ki 11:40 Solomon tried to **k** Jeroboam,
Pr   1:32 waywardness of the simple will **k**
Ecc 3: 3 a time to **k** and a time to heal,
Mt   2:13 to search for the child to **k** him."
    10:28 Do not be afraid of those who **k** the
          body but cannot **k** the soul.
    14: 5 Herod wanted to **k** John,
    17:23 They will **k** him,
Mk   9:31 They will **k** him,

14: 1 to arrest Jesus and **k** him.
Lk 18:32 spit on him, flog him and **k** him.
Jn 10:10 The thief comes only to steal and **k**

KILLED [KILL]

Ge   4: 8 attacked his brother Abel and **k** him.
Ex   2:12 he **k** the Egyptian and hid him in
    13:15 the LORD **k** every firstborn in Egypt,
Nu 35:11 has **k** someone accidentally may flee.
1Sa 17:50 struck down the Philistine and **k** him.
Ne   9:26 They **k** your prophets,
Hos 6: 5 I **k** you with the words of my mouth;
Mk   8:31 be **k** and after three days rise again.
Lk 11:48 forefathers did; they **k** the prophets,
Ac   3:15 You **k** the author of life,
    23:12 to eat or drink until they had **k** Paul.
2Co 6: 9 beaten, and yet not **k;**
Rev 9:18 A third of mankind was **k** by
    19:21 **k** with the sword that came out of

KILLING [KILL]

1Ki 18: 4 Jezebel was **k** off the LORD's
Est   3: 6 scorned the idea of **k** only Mordecai.

KILLS [KILL]

Ge   4:15 if anyone **k** Cain,
Ex 21:12 **k** him shall surely be put to death.
Lev 24:21 **k** an animal must make restitution,
    24:21 **k** a man must be put to death.
2Co 3: 6 the letter **k,** but the Spirit gives life.

KIND [KINDEST, KINDHEARTED, KINDNESS, KINDNESSES, KINDS]

Ge   1:24 each according to its **k."**
     6:20 Two of every **k** of bird,
     7: 2 Take with you seven of every **k**
Ex   1:20 So God was **k** to the midwives and
2Ch 10: 7 be **k** to these people and please them
Pr 11:17 A **k** man benefits himself,
    12:25 but a **k** word cheers him up.
    14:21 blessed is he who is **k** to the needy.
    14:31 but whoever is **k** to the needy
    19:17 He who is **k** to the poor lends to
Isa 58: 5 Is this the **k** of fast I have chosen,
Da   4:27 and your wickedness by being **k** to
Zec 1:13 LORD spoke **k** and comforting words
Mt   8:27 "What **k** of man is this?"
Lk   6:35 he is **k** to the ungrateful and wicked.
Jn   4:23 the **k** of worshipers the Father seeks.
1Co 13: 4 Love is patient, love is **k.**
    15:35 With what **k** of body will they
Eph 4:32 Be **k** and compassionate to one
1Th 5:15 but always try to be **k** to each other
     5:22 Avoid every **k** of evil.
2Ti 2:24 he must be **k** to everyone,
Tit 2: 5 to be busy at home, to be **k,**
2Pe 3:11 what **k** of people ought you to be?

KINDEST* [KIND]

Pr 12:10 the **k** acts of the wicked are cruel.

KINDHEARTED* [KIND, HEART]

Pr 11:16 A **k** woman gains respect,

KINDLE [KINDLED]

Jer 15:14 for my anger will **k** a fire

KINDLED [KINDLE]

Dt 32:22 For a fire has been **k** by my wrath,
Lk 12:49 and how I wish it were already **k!**

KINDNESS [KIND]

Ge 24:12 and show **k** to my master Abraham.
32:10 I am unworthy of all the **k**
39:21 was with him; he showed him **k**
Jos 2:12 by the LORD that you will show **k**
Jdg 8:35 to show **k** to the family of Jerub-Baal
Ru 1: 8 May the LORD show **k** to you,
2:20 "He has not stopped showing his **k** to
2Sa 2: 6 May the LORD now show you **k**
9: 3 to whom I can show God's **k?"**
22:51 he shows unfailing **k** to his anointed,
Ps 141: 5 righteous man strike me—it is a **k;**
Isa 54: 8 everlasting **k** I will have compassion
Jer 9:24 who exercises **k,**
Hos 11: 4 I led them with cords of human **k,**
Ac 14:17 He has shown **k** by giving you rain
Ro 2: 4 not realizing that God's **k** leads you
11:22 therefore the **k** and sternness of God:
2Co 6: 6 understanding, patience and **k;**
Gal 5:22 patience, **k,** goodness, faithfulness,
Eph 2: 7 in his **k** to us in Christ Jesus.
Col 3:12 **k,** humility, gentleness and patience.
Tit 3: 4 But when the **k** and love of God
2Pe 1: 7 brotherly **k;** and to brotherly **k,** love.

KINDNESSES* [KIND]

Ps 106: 7 not remember your many **k,**
Isa 63: 7 I will tell of the **k** of the LORD,
63: 7 his compassion and many **k.**

KINDS [KIND]

Ge 1:11 according to their various **k."**
1:21 according to their **k,**
1:24 living creatures according to their **k:**
Lev 19:19 " 'Do not mate different **k** of animals
Dt 12:31 they do all **k** of detestable things
Jer 15: 3 "I will send four **k** of destroyers
Da 3: 5 lyre, harp, pipes and all **k** of music,
Mt 5:11 falsely say all **k** of evil against you
1Co 12: 4 There are different **k** of gifts,
2Th 2: 9 the work of Satan displayed in all **k**
1Ti 6:10 of money is a root of all **k** of evil.
Jas 1: 2 whenever you face trials of many **k,**
1Pe 1: 6 to suffer grief in all **k** of trials.

KING [KING'S, KINGDOM, KINGDOMS, KINGS, KINGSHIP]

The Kings of the United Kingdom

	Names	Ruled	Dates B.C.
1.	Saul	40 years	1050-1010
2.	David	40 years	1010-970
3.	Solomon	40 years	970-930

The Kings of Israel

	Names	Ruled	Dates B.C.
1.	Jeroboam I	22 years	930-909
2.	Nadab	2 years	909-908
3.	Baasha	24 years	908-886
4.	Elah	2 years	886-885
5.	Zimri	7 days	885
6.	Omri	12 years	885-874
7.	Ahab	22 years	874-853
8.	Ahaziah	2 years	853-852
9.	Joram	12 years	852-841
10.	Jehu	28 years	841-814
11.	Jehoahaz	17 years	814-798
12.	Jehoash	16 years	798-782
13.	Jeroboam II	41 years	793-753
14.	Zechariah	6 months	753
15.	Shallum	1 month	752
16.	Menahem	10 years	752-742
17.	Pekahiah	2 years	742-740
18.	Pekah	20 years	752-732
19.	Hoshea	9 years	732-722

The Kings (and Queen) of Judah

	Name	Ruled	Dates B.C.
1.	Rehoboam	17 years	930-913
2.	Abijah	3 years	913-910
3.	Asa	41 years	910-869
4.	Jehoshaphat	25 years	872-848
5.	Jehoram	8 years	848-841
6.	Ahaziah	1 year	841
7.	Queen Athaliah	6 years	841-835
8.	Joash	40 years	835-796
9.	Amaziah	29 years	796-767
10.	Uzziah / Azariah	52 years	792-740
11.	Jotham	16 years	750-735
12.	Ahaz	16 years	732-715
13.	Hezekiah	29 years	715-686
14.	Manasseh	55 years	697-642
15.	Amon	2 years	642-640
16.	Josiah	31 years	640-609
17.	Jehoahaz	3 months	609
18.	Jehoiakim	11 years	609-598
19.	Jehoiachin	3 months	598-597
20.	Zedekiah / Mattaniah	11 years	597-586

See also each king by name.

Ge	14:18	Then Melchizedek **k** of Salem
	20: 2	Then Abimelech **k** of Gerar sent
	26: 8	Abimelech **k** of the Philistines
Ex	1: 8	Then a new **k,** who did not know
Nu	21:26	the city of Sihon **k** of the Amorites,
	21:33	and Og **k** of Bashan
	22:10	"Balak son of Zippor, **k** of Moab,
	23:21	the shout of the **K** is among them.
Dt	17:14	set a **k** over us like all the nations
Jdg	9: 8	the trees went out to anoint a **k**
	17: 6	In those days Israel had no **k;**
	18: 1	In those days Israel had no **k.**
	19: 1	In those days Israel had no **k.**
	21:25	In those days Israel had no **k;**
1Sa	8: 5	now appoint a **k** to lead us,
	11:15	confirmed Saul as **k** in the presence
	12:12	the LORD your God was your **k.**
	15:11	grieved that I have made Saul **k,**
	16: 1	I have chosen one of his sons to be **k.**
2Sa	2: 4	and there they anointed David **k** over
1Ki	1:30	be **k** after me,
Ps	2: 6	"I have installed my **K** on Zion,
	10:16	The LORD is **K** for ever and ever;
	24: 7	that the **K** of glory may come in.
	33:16	No **k** is saved by the size of his army
	44: 4	You are my **K** and my God,
	47: 7	For God is the **K** of all the earth;
	48: 2	the city of the Great **K.**
Isa	6: 5	and my eyes have seen the **K,**
	32: 1	a **k** will reign in righteousness
	43:15	Israel's Creator, your **K."**
Jer	10:10	he is the living God, the eternal **K.**
	30: 9	and David their **k,**
Eze	37:24	" 'My servant David will be **k**
Hos	3: 5	and David their **k.**
Mic	2:13	Their **k** will pass through
Zep	3:15	LORD, the **K** of Israel, is with you;
Zec	9: 9	See, your **k** comes to you,
	14: 9	LORD will be **k** over the whole earth.
Mal	1:14	For I am a great **k,"**
Mt	2: 2	who has been born **k** of the Jews?
	21: 5	'See, your **k** comes to you,
	27:11	"Are you the **k** of the Jews?"
	27:37	THIS IS JESUS, THE **K** OF THE JEWS.
Mk	15:32	Let this Christ, this **K** of Israel,
Lk	19:38	the **k** who comes in the name of
	23: 3	"Are you the **k** of the Jews?"
Jn	1:49	you are the **K** of Israel."
	12:13	"Blessed is the **K** of Israel!"
	18:37	"You are right in saying I am a **k.**
	19:15	"We have no **k** but Caesar,"
	19:21	"Do not write 'The **K** of the Jews,'
Ac	17: 7	saying that there is another **k,**
1Ti	1:17	Now to the **K** eternal, immortal,
	6:15	the **K** of kings and Lord of lords,
Heb	7: 1	This Melchizedek was **k** of Salem
1Pe	2:13	to the **k,** as the supreme authority,
	2:17	fear God, honor the **k.**
Rev	15: 3	**K** of the ages.
	17:14	he is Lord of lords and **K** of kings—
	19:16	**K** OF KINGS AND LORD OF LORDS.

GREAT KING See GREAT

KING OF ASSYRIA 2Ki 15:19, 20, 20, 29; 16:7, 8, 9, 10, 18; 17:3, 4, 4, 5, 6, 24, 26, 27; 18:7, 9, 11, 13, 14, 14, 16, 17, 19, 23, 28, 30, 31, 33; 19:4, 6, 8, 10, 20, 32, 36; 20:6; 23:29; 1Ch 5:6, 26, 26; 2Ch 28:16, 20, 21; 32:1, 7, 9, 10, 11, 22; 33:11; Ezr 4:2; 6:22; Isa 7:17, 20; 8:4, 7; 10:12; 20:1, 4, 6; 36:1, 2, 4, 8, 13, 15, 16, 18; 37:4, 6, 8, 10, 21, 33, 37; 38:6; Jer 50:17, 18; Na 3:18

KING OF BABYLON 2Ki 20:12, 18; 24:1, 7, 10, 12, 16, 20; 25:1, 6, 8, 8, 11, 20, 22, 23, 24, 27; 2Ch 36:6; Ezr 2:1; 5:12, 13; Ne 7:6; 13:6; Est 2:6; Isa 14:4; 39:1, 7; Jer 20:4; 21:2, 4, 7, 10; 22:25; 24:1; 25:1, 9, 11, 12; 27:6, 8, 9, 11, 12, 13, 14, 17, 20; 28:2, 3, 4, 11, 14; 29:21, 22; 32:2, 3, 4, 28, 36; 34:1, 2, 3, 7, 21; 35:11; 36:29; 37:1, 17, 19; 38:3, 17, 18, 22, 23; 39:1, 3, 3, 5, 6, 11, 13; 40:5, 7, 9, 11; 41:2, 18; 42:11; 43:10; 44:30; 46:2, 13, 26; 49:28, 30; 50:17, 18, 43; 51:31, 34; 52:3, 4, 9, 10, 12, 12, 15, 26, 31, 34; Eze 17:12; 19:9; 21:19, 21; 24:2; 26:7; 29:18, 19; 30:10, 24, 25, 25; 32:11; Da 1:1; 7:1

KING OF EGYPT Ge 40:1, 1, 5; 41:46; Ex 1:15, 17, 18; 2:23; 3:18, 19; 5:4; 6:11, 13, 27, 29; 14:5, 8; Dt 7:8; 11:3; 1Ki 3:1; 9:16; 11:18; 14:25; 2Ki 17:4, 7; 18:21; 19:9; 23:29; 24:7; 2Ch 12:2, 9; 35:20; 36:3, 4; Isa 36:6; 37:9; Jer 25:19; 44:30; 46:2, 17; Eze 29:2, 3; 30:21, 22; 31:2; 32:2; Ac 7:10

KING OF ISRAEL 1Sa 24:14; 26:20; 29:3; 2Sa 6:20; 1Ki 15:9, 16, 17, 19, 25, 32, 33; 16:8, 23, 29; 20:2, 4, 7, 11, 13, 21, 22, 28, 31, 32, 40, 41, 43; 21:18; 22:2, 3, 4, 5, 6, 8, 9, 10, 18, 26, 29, 30, 31, 32, 33, 34, 41, 44, 51; 2Ki 3:1, 4, 5, 9, 10, 11, 12, 13, 13; 5:5, 6, 7, 8; 6:9, 10, 11, 12, 21, 26; 7:6; 8:16, 25, 26; 9:21; 13:1, 10, 14, 16; 14:1, 8, 9, 11, 13, 17, 23; 15:1, 8, 17, 23, 27, 29, 32; 16:5, 7; 17:1; 18:1, 9, 10; 21:3; 23:13; 24:13; 1Ch 5:17; 2Ch 8:11; 16:1, 3; 18:3, 4, 5, 7, 8, 9, 17, 19, 25, 28, 29, 30, 31, 32, 33, 34; 20:35; 21:2; 22:5; 25:17, 18, 21, 23, 25; 28:5, 19; 29:27; 30:26; 35:3, 4; Ezr 3:10; 5:11; Ne 13:26; Pr 1:1; Isa 7:1; Jer 41:9; Hos 1; 10:15; Am 1:1; 7:10; Zep 3:15; Mt 27:42; Mk 15:32; Jn 1:49; 12:13

KING OF JUDAH 1Ki 12:23, 27; 15:1, 9, 17, 25, 28, 33; 16:8, 10, 15, 23, 29; 22:2, 10, 29, 41, 51; 2Ki 1:17; 3:1, 7, 9, 14; 8:16, 16, 25, 29; 9:16, 21, 27, 29; 10:13; 12:18; 13:1, 10, 12; 14:1, 9, 11, 13, 15, 17, 23; 15:1, 8, 13, 17, 23, 27, 32; 16:1; 17:1; 18:1, 14, 14, 16; 19:10; 21:11; 22:16, 18; 24:12; 25:27; 1Ch 4:41; 5:17; 2Ch 11:3; 13:1; 16:1, 7; 18:3, 9, 28; 19:1; 20:31, 35; 21:12; 22:1, 6; 25:17, 18, 21, 23, 25; 30:24; 32:8, 9, 23; 34:24, 26; 35:21; Est 2:6; Pr 25:1; Isa 7:1; 37:10; 38:9; Jer 1:2, 3, 1; 15:4; 21:7; 22:1, 2, 6, 11, 18, 24; 24:1, 8; 25:1, 3; 26:1, 18, 19; 27:1, 3, 12, 18, 20, 21; 28:1, 4; 29:3; 32:1, 3, 4; 34:2, 4, 6, 21; 35:1; 36:1, 9, 28, 29, 30, 32; 37:1, 7; 38:22; 39:1, 4; 44:30; 45:1; 46:2; 49:34; 51:59; 52:31, 31; Da 1:1, 2; Am 1:1; Zep 1:1; Zec 14:5

KING OF KINGS Ezr 7:12; Eze 26:7; Da 2:37; 1Ti 6:15; Rev 17:14; 19:16

KING OF THE JEWS Mt 2:2; 27:11, 29, 37; Mk 15:2, 9, 12, 18, 26; Lk 23:3, 37, 38; Jn 18:33, 39; 19:3, 19, 21, 21

KING'S [KING]

Nu	20:17	We will travel along the **k** highway
1Sa	18:18	I should become the **k** son-in-law?"
2Sa	9:13	because he always ate at the **k** table,
Pr	21:1	**k** heart is in the hand of the LORD;
Ecc	8:2	Obey the **k** command, I say,
Jer	52:33	ate regularly at the **k** table.
Heb	11:23	they were not afraid of the **k** edict.

KINGDOM [KING]

Ex	19:6	you will be for me a **k** of priests and
Dt	17:18	When he takes the throne of his **k,**
1Sa	13:14	But now your **k** will not endure;
	28:17	The LORD has torn the **k** out of your
2Sa	7:12	and I will establish his **k.**
1Ki	11:31	to tear the **k** out of Solomon's hand
1Ch	17:11	and I will establish his **k.**
	29:11	Yours, O LORD, is the **k;**
Ps	45:6	will be the scepter of your **k.**
	103:19	and his **k** rules over all.
	145:13	Your **k** is an everlasting **k,**
Isa	9:7	on David's throne and over his **k,**
Jer	18:7	that a nation or **k** is to be uprooted,
Eze	29:14	There they will be a lowly **k.**
Da	2:39	"After you, another **k** will rise,
	2:44	a **k** that will never be destroyed,
	4:3	His **k** is an eternal **k;**
	5:28	*Peres:* Your **k** is divided and given
	7:18	of the Most High will receive the **k**
	7:27	His **k** will be an everlasting **k,**
Ob	1:21	And the **k** will be the LORD's.
Mt	3:2	"Repent, for the **k** of heaven is near."
	4:17	"Repent, for the **k** of heaven is near."
	4:23	preaching the good news of the **k,**
	5:3	for theirs is the **k** of heaven.
	5:10	for theirs is the **k** of heaven.
	5:19	called least in the **k** of heaven,
	5:20	you will certainly not enter the **k**
	6:10	your **k** come, your will be done
	6:33	seek first his **k** and his righteousness,
	7:21	Lord,' will enter the **k** of heaven,
	8:12	subjects of the **k** will be thrown
	9:35	preaching the good news of the **k**
	10:7	'The **k** of heaven is near.'
	11:11	least in the **k** of heaven is greater
	11:12	**k** of heaven has been forcefully
	12:25	"Every **k** divided against itself will
	12:28	the **k** of God has come upon you.
	13:11	knowledge of the secrets of the **k** of
	13:19	hears the message about the **k**
	13:24	"The **k** of heaven is like a man
	13:31	"The **k** of heaven is like a mustard
	13:33	"The **k** of heaven is like yeast that
	13:38	seed stands for the sons of the **k.**
	13:44	"The **k** of heaven is like treasure
	13:45	the **k** of heaven is like a merchant
	13:47	the **k** of heaven is like a net
	13:52	instructed about the **k** of heaven
	16:19	I will give you the keys of the **k**
	16:28	the Son of Man coming in his **k.**"

	18:1	the greatest in the **k** of heaven?"
	18:3	you will never enter the **k** of heaven.
	18:4	like this child is the greatest in the **k**
	18:23	the **k** of heaven is like a king
	19:12	renounced marriage because of the **k**
	19:14	for the **k** of heaven belongs to such
	19:23	it is hard for a rich man to enter the **k**
	20:1	the **k** of heaven is like a landowner
	20:21	and the other at your left in your **k.**"
	21:31	and the prostitutes are entering the **k**
	21:43	that the **k** of God will be taken away
	22:2	**k** of heaven is like a king
	23:13	shut the **k** of heaven in men's faces.
	24:14	this gospel of the **k** will be preached
	25:1	**k** of heaven will be like ten virgins
	25:34	the **k** prepared for you since
	26:29	with you in my Father's **k.**"
Mk	1:15	"The **k** of God is near.
	3:24	If a **k** is divided against itself,
	4:11	"The secret of the **k** of God has been
	4:26	"This is what the **k** of God is like.
	6:23	up to half my **k.**"
	9:1	not taste death before they see the **k**
	9:47	It is better for you to enter the **k**
	10:14	the **k** of God belongs to such as these
	10:15	not receive the **k** of God like
	10:23	for the rich to enter the **k** of God!"
	10:24	how hard it is to enter the **k** of God!
	11:10	the coming **k** of our father David!"
	12:34	"You are not far from the **k** of God."
	13:8	and **k** against **k.**
	14:25	when I drink it anew in the **k** of God.
	15:43	who was himself waiting for the **k**
Lk	1:33	his **k** will never end."
	4:43	the good news of the **k** of God
	6:20	for yours is the **k** of God.
	7:28	least in the **k** of God is greater than
	8:1	proclaiming the good news of the **k**
	8:10	the **k** of God has been given to you,
	9:2	sent them out to preach the **k** of God
	9:11	spoke to them about the **k** of God,
	9:27	not taste death before they see the **k**
	9:60	you go and proclaim the **k** of God."
	9:62	fit for service in the **k** of God."
	10:9	'The **k** of God is near you.'
	10:11	sure of this: The **k** of God is near.'
	11:2	hallowed be your name, your **k** come
	11:18	how can his **k** stand?
	11:20	then the **k** of God has come to you.
	12:31	But seek his **k,**
	12:32	pleased to give you the **k.**
	13:18	"What is the **k** of God like?
	13:29	at the feast in the **k** of God.
	14:15	will eat at the feast in the **k** of God."
	16:16	of the **k** of God is being preached,
	17:20	"The **k** of God does not come
	17:21	because the **k** of God is within you."
	18:16	the **k** of God belongs to such as these
	18:24	for the rich to enter the **k** of God!
	18:29	or children for the sake of the **k**
	19:11	the **k** of God was going to appear
	21:31	you know that the **k** of God is near.
	22:16	it finds fulfillment in the **k** of God."
	22:18	of the fruit of the vine until the **k**

	22:29	And I confer on you a **k,**
	22:30	and drink at my table in my **k** and sit
	23:42	when you come into your **k."**
	23:51	and he was waiting for the **k**
Jn	3: 3	see the **k** of God unless he is born
	3: 5	no one can enter the **k** of God unless
	18:36	Jesus said, "My **k** is not of this world
Ac	1: 3	and spoke about the **k** of God
	1: 6	at this time going to restore the **k**
	8:12	the good news of the **k** of God
	14:22	many hardships to enter the **k** of God
	19: 8	persuasively about the **k** of God.
	20:25	I have gone about preaching the **k**
	28:23	and declared to them the **k** of God
	28:31	without hindrance he preached the **k**
Ro	14:17	the **k** of God is not a matter of eating
1Co	4:20	the **k** of God is not a matter of talk
	6: 9	wicked will not inherit the **k** of God?
	15:24	hands over the **k** to God the Father
	15:50	blood cannot inherit the **k** of God,
Gal	5:21	like this will not inherit the **k** of God.
Eph	2: 2	and of the ruler of the **k** of the air,
	5: 5	inheritance in the **k** of Christ and of
Col	1:12	the inheritance of the saints in the **k**
	1:13	us into the **k** of the Son he loves,
	4:11	among my fellow workers for the **k**
1Th	2:12	who calls you into his **k** and glory.
2Th	1: 5	be counted worthy of the **k** of God,
2Ti	4: 1	in view of his appearing and his **k,**
	4:18	bring me safely to his heavenly **k.**
Heb	1: 8	will be the scepter of your **k.**
	12:28	receiving a **k** that cannot be shaken,
Jas	2: 5	**k** he promised those who love him?
2Pe	1:11	a rich welcome into the eternal **k**
Rev	1: 6	and has made us to be a **k** and priests
	1: 9	and companion in the suffering and **k**
	5:10	be a **k** and priests to serve our God,
	11:15	"The **k** of the world has become the
		k of our Lord and of his Christ,
	12:10	the salvation and the power and the **k**
	16:10	and his **k** was plunged into darkness.
	17:12	who have not yet received a **k,**

KINGDOM OF HEAVEN Mt 3:2; 4:17; 5:3,
10, 19, 19, 20; 7:21; 8:11; 10:7; 11:11, 12; 13:11,
24, 31, 33, 44, 45, 47, 52; 16:19; 18:1, 3, 4, 23;
19:12, 14, 23; 20:1; 22:2; 23:13; 25:1

KINGDOM OF GOD Mt 12:28; 19:24; 21:31,
43; Mk 1:15; 4:11, 26, 30; 9:1, 47; 10:14, 15, 23,
24, 25; 12:34; 14:25; 15:43; Lk 4:43; 6:20; 7:28;
8:1, 10; 9:2, 11, 27, 60, 62; 10:9, 11; 11:20;
13:18, 20, 28, 29; 14:15; 16:16; 17:20, 20, 21;
18:16, 17, 24, 25, 29; 19:11; 21:31; 22:16, 18;
23:51; Jn 3:3, 5; Ac 1:3; 8:12; 14:22; 19:8; 28:23,
31; Ro 14:17; 1Co 4:20; 6:9, 10; 15:50; Gal 5:21;
Col 4:11; 2Th 1:5

KINGDOMS [KING]

Dt	3:21	LORD will do the same to all the **k**
1Ki	4:21	Solomon ruled over all the **k** from
2Ki	19:15	you alone are God over all the **k** of
	19:19	so that all **k** on earth may know
2Ch	20: 6	You rule over all the **k** of the nations
Ps	68:32	Sing to God, O **k** of the earth,

Isa	37:16	you alone are God over all the **k** of
	37:20	so that all **k** on earth may know
Jer	33:24	'The LORD has rejected the two **k** he
Eze	37:22	or be divided into two **k.**
Da	2:44	It will crush all those **k**
	4:17	Most High is sovereign over the **k**
	7:17	'The four great beasts are four **k**
Zep	3: 8	the **k** and to pour out my wrath
Lk	4: 5	showed him in an instant all the **k**
Heb	11:33	who through faith conquered **k,**

KINGS [KING]

Ge	14: 9	four **k** against five.
	17: 6	and **k** will come from you.
Jos	12: 1	These are the **k** of the land whom
2Sa	11: 1	at the time when **k** go off to war,
1Ki	10:23	and wisdom than all the other **k** of
Ps	2: 2	The **k** of the earth take their stand
	47: 9	for the **k** of the earth belong to God;
	68:29	at Jerusalem **k** will bring gifts.
	72:11	All **k** will bow down to him
	89:27	the most exalted of the **k** of the earth.
	110: 5	will crush **k** on the day of his wrath.
	138: 4	May all the **k** of the earth praise you,
	149: 8	to bind their **k** with fetters,
Pr	8:15	By me **k** reign and rulers make laws
	16:12	**K** detest wrongdoing,
	31: 4	not for **k** to drink wine,
Isa	24:21	the **k** on the earth below.
	52:15	and **k** will shut their mouths because
	60:11	their **k** led in triumphal procession.
Da	2:21	he sets up **k** and deposes them.
	2:47	the God of gods and the Lord of **k**
	7:24	ten horns are ten **k** who will come
Lk	10:24	and **k** wanted to see what you see
	21:12	be brought before **k** and governors,
Ac	4:26	The **k** of the earth take their stand
1Co	4: 8	You have become **k**—
1Ti	2: 2	for **k** and all those in authority,
	6:15	the King of **k** and Lord of lords,
Rev	1: 5	and the ruler of the **k** of the earth.
	16:16	Then they gathered the **k** together
	17: 2	the **k** of the earth committed adultery
	17:12	"The ten horns you saw are ten **k**
	17:14	he is Lord of lords and King of **k**—
	19:16	KING OF **K** AND LORD OF LORDS.
	19:19	the **k** of the earth and their armies
	21:24	and the **k** of the earth will bring

KING OF KINGS See KING

KINGS OF ISRAEL 1Ki 14:19; 15:31; 16:5,
14, 20, 27, 33; 22:39; 2Ki 1:18; 8:18; 10:34;
13:8, 12, 13; 14:15, 16, 28, 29; 15:11, 15, 21, 26,
31; 16:3; 17:2, 8; 23:19, 22; 1Ch 9:1; 2Ch 20:34;
21:6, 13; 27:7; 28:2, 27; 33:18; 35:18, 27; 36:8;
Mic 1:14

KINGS OF JUDAH 1Sa 27:6; 1Ki 14:29; 15:7,
23; 22:45; 2Ki 8:23; 12:18, 19; 14:18; 15:6, 36;
16:19; 18:5; 20:20; 21:17, 25; 23:5, 11, 12, 22,
28; 24:5; 2Ch 16:11; 25:26; 28:26; 32:32; 34:11;
Isa 1:1; Jer 1:18; 17:19, 20; 19:3, 4, 13; 20:5; Hos
1:1; Mic 1:1

KINGS OF THE EARTH 1Ki 10:23; 2Ch
9:22, 23; Ps 2:2; 47:9; 76:12; 89:27; 102:15;

138:4; 148:11; La 4:12; Eze 27:33; Mt 17:25; Ac 4:26; Rev 1:5; 6:15; 17:2, 18; 18:3, 9; 19:19; 21:24

KINGSHIP [KING]

1Sa	10:25	to the people the regulations of the **k.**
1Ch	11:10	gave his **k** strong support to extend it
Mic	4: 8	**k** will come to the Daughter of

KINSMAN* [KINSMAN-REDEEMER]

Ru	3: 2	a **k** of ours?
Pr	7: 4	and call understanding your **k**;

KINSMAN-REDEEMER
[KINSMAN, REDEEM]

Ru	3: 9	since you are a **k."**
	4:14	has not left you without a **k.**

KIRIATH ARBA [HEBRON]

Ge	23: 2	She died at **K** (that is, Hebron),
	35:27	near **K** (that is, Hebron),
Jos	21:11	They gave them **K** (that is,

KIRIATH JEARIM

1Sa	7: 1	men of **K** came and took up the ark
1Ch	13: 5	to bring the ark of God from **K**

KISH

1Sa	10:21	Finally Saul son of **K** was chosen.

KISHON

Jdg	5:21	The river **K** swept them away,
Ps	83: 9	to Sisera and Jabin at the river **K,**

KISS [KISSED, KISSES, KISSING]

Ge	27:26	"Come here, my son, and **k** me."
	31:28	even let me **k** my grandchildren
1Ki	19:20	"Let me **k** my father
Ps	2:12	**K** the Son, lest he be angry
	85:10	righteousness and peace **k** each other
Pr	24:26	honest answer is like a **k** on the lips.
SS	1: 2	Let him **k** me with the kisses
	8: 1	if I found you outside, I would **k** you
Hos	13: 2	human sacrifice and **k** the calf-idols.
Mt	26:48	"The one I **k** is the man;
Lk	7:45	You did not give me a **k,**
	22:48	betraying the Son of Man with a **k?"**
Ro	16:16	Greet one another with a holy **k.**
1Co	16:20	Greet one another with a holy **k.**
2Co	13:12	Greet one another with a holy **k.**
1Th	5:26	Greet all the brothers with a holy **k.**
1Pe	5:14	Greet one another with a **k** of love.

KISSED [KISS]

Ge	29:11	Then Jacob **k** Rachel and began
	33: 4	arms around his neck and **k** him.
	45:15	And he **k** all his brothers and wept
	50: 1	and wept over him and **k** him.
Ex	4:27	at the mountain of God and **k** him.
Ru	1: 9	she **k** them and they wept aloud
1Sa	10: 1	poured it on Saul's head and **k** him,
	20:41	Then they **k** each other and wept
1Ki	19:18	all whose mouths have not **k** him."
Pr	7:13	She took hold of him and **k** him and
Mk	14:45	Judas said, "Rabbi!" and **k** him.

Lk	7:38	**k** them and poured perfume on them.

KISSES* [KISS]

Pr	27: 6	but an enemy multiplies **k.**
SS	1: 2	Let him kiss me with the **k**

KISSING* [KISS]

Lk	7:45	has not stopped **k** my feet.

KNEADING

Dt	28: 5	and your **k** trough will be blessed.
	28:17	and your **k** trough will be cursed.

KNEE [KNEES]

Isa	45:23	Before me every **k** will bow;
Ro	11: 4	who have not bowed the **k** to Baal."
	14:11	'every **k** will bow before me;
Php	2:10	name of Jesus every **k** should bow,

KNEEL [KNELT]

Est	3: 2	But Mordecai would not **k** down
Ps	95: 6	let us **k** before the LORD our Maker;
Eph	3:14	For this reason I **k** before the Father,

KNEES [KNEE]

Jdg	7: 6	the rest got down on their **k** to drink.
1Ki	19:18	**k** have not bowed down to Baal
Isa	35: 3	steady the **k** that give way;
Da	6:10	a day he got down on his **k**
Lk	5: 8	he fell at Jesus' **k** and said,
Heb	12:12	your feeble arms and weak **k.**

KNELT* [KNEEL]

1Ki	1:16	Bathsheba bowed low and **k** before
2Ch	6:13	**k** down before the whole assembly
	7: 3	they **k** on the pavement
	29:29	with him **k** down and worshiped.
Est	3: 2	the royal officials at the king's gate **k**
Mt	8: 2	man with leprosy came and **k** before
	9:18	a ruler came and **k** before him
	15:25	The woman came and **k** before him.
	17:14	a man approached Jesus and **k** before
	27:29	his right hand and **k** in front of him
Lk	22:41	**k** down and prayed,
Ac	20:36	he **k** down with all of them
	21: 5	and there on the beach we **k** to pray.

KNEW [KNOW]

Dt	34:10	whom the LORD **k** face to face,
Jdg	2:10	who **k** neither the LORD nor
2Ch	33:13	Manasseh **k** that the LORD is God.
Job	23: 3	If only I **k** where to find him;
Pr	24:12	"But we **k** nothing about this,"
Jer	1: 5	in the womb I **k** you,
	19: 4	nor the kings of Judah ever **k,**
Jnh	4: 2	I **k** that you are a gracious
Mt	7:23	'I never **k** you.
	12:25	Jesus **k** their thoughts and said
Lk	4:41	because they **k** he was the Christ.
Jn	2:24	for he **k** all men.
	4:10	"If you **k** the gift of God and who it
	8:19	"If you **k** me,
	13: 1	Jesus **k** that the time had come
	13:11	he **k** who was going to betray him,
	14: 7	If you really **k** me,

Ro   1:21 For although they **k** God,

KNIFE [KNIVES]
Ge   22:10 and took the **k** to slay his son.
Ex   4:25 But Zipporah took a flint **k,**
Pr   23: 2 and put a **k** to your throat if you

KNIT*
Job 10:11 **k** me together with bones and sinews
Ps 139:13 **k** me together in my mother's womb.

KNIVES [KNIFE]
Jos   5: 2 "Make flint **k** and circumcise

KNOCK* [KNOCKING, KNOCKS]
Mt   7: 7 **k** and the door will be opened to you.
Lk   11: 9 **k** and the door will be opened to you.
Rev   3:20 I stand at the door and **k.**

KNOCKING* [KNOCK]
SS   5: 2 Listen! My lover is **k:**
Lk   13:25 you will stand outside **k** and pleading
Ac   12:16 But Peter kept on **k,**

KNOCKS [KNOCK]
Mt   7: 8 who **k,** the door will be opened.
Lk   12:36 so that when he comes and **k**

KNOW [FOREKNEW,
  FOREKNOWLEDGE, KNEW, KNOWING,
  KNOWLEDGE, KNOWN, KNOWS]
Ge   15: 8 "O Sovereign LORD, how can I **k**
     22:12 Now I **k** that you fear God,
Ex   1: 8 who did not **k** about Joseph,
      3:19 I **k** that the king of Egypt will not
      6: 7 you will **k** that I am the LORD
      7: 5 Egyptians will **k** that I am the LORD
     14: 4 Egyptians will **k** that I am the LORD.
     18:11 Now I **k** that the LORD is greater
     33:12 'I **k** you by name
     33:13 teach me your ways so I may **k** you
Nu   16:28 "This is how you will **k** that
Dt   7: 9 **K** therefore that the LORD your God
      8: 2 in order to **k** what was in your heart,
     18:21 "How can we **k** when a message has
Jos   3: 7 so they may **k** that I am with you
      4:24 the peoples of the earth might **k** that
     23:14 You **k** with all your heart and soul
1Sa 17:46 that there is a God in Israel.
1Ki   8:39 (for you alone **k** the hearts
Job 11: 6 **K** this: God has even forgotten
     19:25 I **k** that my Redeemer lives,
     42: 2 "I **k** that you can do all things;
     42: 3 things too wonderful for me to **k.**
Ps   9:10 Those who **k** your name will trust
     36:10 your love to those who **k** you,
     46:10 "Be still, and **k** that I am God;
    100: 3 **K** that the LORD is God.
    139: 1 you have searched me and you **k** me.
    139:23 Search me, O God, and **k** my heart;
    145:12 so that all men may **k**
Pr   27: 1 not **k** what a day may bring forth.
     30: 4 Tell me if you **k!**
Ecc   8: 5 the wise heart will **k** the proper time

      8:16 I applied my mind to **k** wisdom
Isa   1: 3 but Israel does not **k,**
     29:15 Who will **k?"**
     40:21 Do you not **k?**
     44: 8 no other Rock; I **k** not one."
Jer   4:22 they **k** not how to do good."
      6:15 not even **k** how to blush.
     22:16 Is that not what it means to **k** me?"
     24: 7 I will give them a heart to **k** me,
     31:34 because they will all **k** me,
     33: 3 unsearchable things you do not **k.'**
Eze   2: 5 they will **k** that a prophet has been
      6:10 And they will **k** that I am the LORD;
     11:32 who **k** their God will firmly resist
Da   6: 3 your left hand **k** what your right
Mt   7:11 **k** how to give good gifts
      9: 6 **k** that the Son of Man has authority
     22:29 because you do not **k** the Scriptures
     24:42 because you do not **k** on what day
     26:74 "I don't **k** the man!"
Mk   12:24 because you do not **k** the Scriptures
Lk   1: 4 so that you may **k** the certainty of
     11:13 **k** how to give good gifts
     12:48 not **k** and does things deserving
     13:25 'I don't **k** you or where you
     18:20 You **k** the commandments:
     21:31 **k** that the kingdom of God is near.
     22:34 deny three times that you **k** me."
     23:34 they do not **k** what they are doing."
Jn   1:26 among you stands one you do not **k.**
      3:11 we speak of what we **k,**
      4:22 worship what you do not **k;**
      4:42 and we **k** that this man really is
      6:69 and **k** that you are the Holy One
      7:28 cried out, "Yes, you **k** me,
      8:14 for I **k** where I came from and
      8:19 "You do not **k** me or my Father,"
      8:32 Then you will **k** the truth,
      8:55 you do not **k** him, I **k** him.
      9:25 One thing I do **k.**
     10: 4 because they **k** his voice.
     10:14 "I am the good shepherd; I **k** my
            sheep and my sheep **k** me—
     10:27 sheep listen to my voice; I **k** them,
     12:35 does not **k** where he is going.
     13:17 Now that you **k** these things,
     13:35 will **k** that you are my disciples,
     14:17 But you **k** him,
     15:21 they do not **k** the One who sent me.
     16:30 Now we can see that you **k** all things
     17: 3 eternal life: that they may **k** you,
     17:23 to complete unity to let the world **k**
     21:15 he said, "you **k** that I love you."
     21:24 We **k** that his testimony is true.
Ac   1: 7 not for you to **k** the times or dates
      1:24 "Lord, you **k** everyone's heart.
Ro   3:17 and the way of peace they do not **k."**
      6: 3 Or don't you **k** that all of us
      6: 6 we **k** that our old self was crucified
      6:16 Don't you **k** that when you offer
      7: 1 Do you not **k,** brothers—
      7:14 We **k** that the law is spiritual;
      7:18 I **k** that nothing good lives in me,
      8:22 We **k** that the whole creation

8:26 We do not **k** what we ought to pray
8:28 we **k** that in all things God works
11: 2 Don't you **k** what the Scripture says
1Co 1:21 through its wisdom did not **k** him,
2: 2 to **k** nothing while I was with you
3:16 Don't you **k** that you yourselves are
5: 6 Don't you **k** that a little yeast works
6: 2 not **k** that the saints will judge
6:15 not **k** that your bodies are members
6:16 not **k** that he who unites himself with
6:19 not **k** that your body is a temple of
7:16 How do you **k**, wife,
8: 2 not yet **k** as he ought to **k.**
8: 4 We **k** that an idol is nothing
9:13 Don't you **k** that those who work in
9:24 Do you not **k** that in a race all
12: 2 You **k** that when you were pagans,
13: 9 we **k** in part and we prophesy in part,
13:12 Now I **k** in part; then I shall **k** fully,
14: 9 will anyone **k** what you are saying?
15:58 because you **k** that your labor in
2Co 4:14 because we **k** that the one who raised
5: 1 Now we **k** that if the earthly tent
5: 6 and **k** that as long as we are at home
5:11 then, we **k** what it is to fear the Lord,
8: 9 For you **k** the grace of our Lord
12: 2 I **k** a man in Christ who
Gal 1:11 I want you to **k**, brothers,
2:16 **k** that a man is not justified by
4: 9 But now that you **k** God—
Eph 1:17 so that you may **k** him better.
1:18 in order that you may **k** the hope
3:19 and to **k** this love that surpasses
4:20 did not come to **k** Christ that way.
6: 8 you **k** that the Lord will reward
Php 3:10 to **k** Christ and the power
4:12 I **k** what it is to be in need, and I **k**
    what it is to have plenty.
Col 2: 2 that they may **k** the mystery of God,
4: 1 because you **k** that you also have
4: 6 you may **k** how to answer everyone.
1Th 3: 3 You **k** quite well
5: 2 **k** very well that the day of the Lord
2Th 1: 8 punish those who do not **k** God
2: 6 now you **k** what is holding him back,
1Ti 1: 7 not **k** what they are talking about
3: 5 not **k** how to manage his own family,
3:15 you will **k** how people ought
2Ti 1:12 because I **k** whom I have believed,
2:23 because you **k** they produce quarrels.
3:14 you **k** those from whom you learned
Tit 1:16 They claim to **k** God,
Heb 8:11 because they will all **k** me,
11: 8 he did not **k** where he was going.
Jas 1: 3 because you **k** that the testing
3: 1 because you **k** that we who teach
4: 4 don't you **k** that friendship with
4:14 even **k** what will happen tomorrow.
1Pe 1:18 For you **k** that it was not
2Pe 1:12 though you **k** them
1Jn 2: 3 We **k** that we have come to **k** him
2: 4 The man who says, "I **k** him,"
2: 5 This is how we **k** we are in him:
2:11 not **k** where he is going,

2:18 This is how we **k** it is the last hour.
2:20 and all of you **k** the truth.
2:29 If you **k** that he is righteous,
3: 1 The reason the world does not **k** us is
3: 2 But we **k** that when he appears,
3:10 This is how we **k** who the children
3:14 **k** that we have passed from death
3:16 This is how we **k** what love is:
3:19 This then is how we **k** that we belong
3:24 this is how we **k** that he lives in us:
4: 8 does not love does not **k** God,
4:13 We **k** that we live in him and he
4:16 so we **k** and rely on the love God has
5: 2 how we **k** that we love the children
5:13 you may **k** that you have eternal life.
5:15 And if we **k** that he hears us—
5:18 We **k** that anyone born of God does
5:20 We **k** also that the Son of God
5:20 so that we may **k** him who is true.
2Jn 1: 1 but also all who **k** the truth—
3Jn 1:12 and you **k** that our testimony is true.
Jude 1: 5 Though you already **k** all this,
Rev 2: 2 I **k** your deeds, your hard work
2: 9 I **k** your afflictions and your poverty
2:13 I **k** where you live—
2:19 I **k** your deeds, your love and faith,
3: 3 not **k** at what time I will come to you
3: 8 I **k** that you have little strength,
3:15 I **k** your deeds,

KNOW THAT I AM THE †LORD Ex 6:7;
7:5, 17; 10:2; 14:4, 18; 16:12; 29:46; 31:13; Dt
29:6; 1Ki 20:13, 28; Isa 45:3; 49:23; Jer 24:7;
Eze 6:7, 10, 13, 14; 7:4, 27; 11:10, 12; 12:15, 16,
20; 13:14, 21, 23; 14:8; 15:7; 16:62; 20:20, 26,
38, 42, 44; 22:16; 24:27; 25:5, 7, 11, 17; 26:6;
28:22, 23, 26; 29:6, 9, 21; 30:8, 19, 25, 26; 32:15;
33:29; 34:27; 35:4, 9, 15; 36:11, 23, 38; 37:6, 13;
38:23; 39:6, 22, 28

KNOW THAT I THE †LORD Ex 8:22; Isa
49:26; 60:16; Eze 5:13; 17:21, 24; 20:12; 21:5;
22:22; 34:30; 35:12; 36:36; 37:14, 28; 39:7; Joel
3:17

KNOW THAT THE †LORD Ex 11:7; 18:11;
Nu 16:28; Dt 4:35; Jos 2:9; 22:31; Jdg 16:20;
17:13; 1Ki 8:60; 2Ki 2:3, 5; 2Ch 13:5; Ps 4:3;
20:6; 100:3; 135:5; 140:12; Eze 5:13; 17:21, 24;
20:12; 21:5; 22:22; 36:36; 37:14, 28;
39:7; Zec 2:9, 11; 4:9; 6:15

KNOWING [KNOW]
Ge 3: 5 **k** good and evil."
3:22 **k** good and evil.
Pr 7:23 little **k** it will cost him his life.
Mt 22:18 But Jesus, **k** their evil intent, said,
Lk 9:47 Jesus, **k** their thoughts,
Jn 18: 4 **k** all that was going to happen to him
19:28 Later, **k** that all was now completed,
Php 3: 8 greatness of **k** Christ Jesus my Lord,
Phm 1:21 **k** that you will do even more
Heb 13: 2 have entertained angels without **k** it.

KNOWLEDGE [KNOW]
Ge 2: 9 tree of the **k** of good and evil.

2:17 not eat from the tree of the **k** of good
Nu 24:16 who has **k** from the Most High,
2Ch 1:10 Give me wisdom and **k**,
Job 21:22 "Can anyone teach **k** to God,
38: 2 my counsel with words without **k**?
42: 3 that obscures my counsel without **k**?
Ps 19: 2 night after night they display **k**.
73:11 Does the Most High have **k**?"
94:10 Does he who teaches man lack **k**?
119:66 Teach me **k** and good judgment,
139: 6 Such **k** is too wonderful for me,
Pr 1: 4 **k** and discretion to the young—
1: 7 The fear of the LORD is the
    beginning of **k**,
1:29 Since they hated **k** and did not
2: 5 of the LORD and the **k** of God.
2: 6 and from his mouth come **k**
2:10 and **k** will be pleasant to your soul.
3:20 by his **k** the deeps were divided,
8:10 **k** rather than choice gold,
8:12 I possess **k** and discretion.
9:10 **k** of the Holy One is understanding.
9:13 she is undisciplined and without **k**.
10:14 Wise men store up **k**,
11: 9 but through **k** the righteous escape.
12: 1 Whoever loves discipline loves **k**,
12:23 prudent man keeps his **k** to himself,
13:16 Every prudent man acts out of **k**,
14: 6 but **k** comes easily to the discerning.
15: 7 The lips of the wise spread **k**;
15:14 The discerning heart seeks **k**,
17:27 A man of **k** uses words with restraint
18:15 heart of the discerning acquires **k**;
19: 2 It is not good to have zeal without **k**,
19:25 and he will gain **k**.
20:15 but lips that speak **k** are a rare jewel.
23:12 and your ears to words of **k**.
24: 4 through **k** its rooms are filled
24: 5 and a man of **k** increases strength;
Ecc 1:18 the more **k**, the more grief.
2:26 God gives wisdom, **k** and happiness,
7:12 but the advantage of **k** is this:
Isa 11: 2 of **k** and of the fear of the LORD—
11: 9 will be full of the **k** of the LORD
40:14 Who was it that taught him **k**
53:11 by his **k** my righteous servant will
Jer 3:15 lead you with **k** and understanding.
10:14 Everyone is senseless and without **k**;
Da 1:17 To these four young men God gave **k**
Hos 4: 6 "Because you have rejected **k**,
Hab 2:14 with the **k** of the glory of the LORD,
Mal 2: 7 lips of a priest ought to preserve **k**,
Mt 13:11 "The **k** of the secrets of the kingdom
Lk 1:77 to give his people the **k** of salvation
8:10 "The **k** of the secrets of the kingdom
11:52 you have taken away the key to **k**.
Ac 18:24 with a thorough **k** of the Scriptures.
Ro 1:28 think it worthwhile to retain the **k**
2:20 in the law the embodiment of **k** and
10: 2 but their zeal is not based on **k**.
11:33 riches of the wisdom and **k** of God!
15:14 complete in **k** and competent to
1Co 8: 1 **K** puffs up, but love builds up.
8:10 conscience sees you who have this **k**

8:11 is destroyed by your **k**.
12: 8 to another the message of **k** by
13: 2 can fathom all mysteries and all **k**,
13: 8 where there is **k**, it will pass away.
2Co 2:14 the fragrance of the **k** of him.
4: 6 the light of the **k** of the glory
8: 7 everything—in faith, in speech, in **k**,
10: 5 sets itself up against the **k** of God,
11: 6 but I do have **k**.
Eph 3:19 to know this love that surpasses **k**—
4:13 reach unity in the faith and in the **k**
Php 1: 9 may abound more and more in **k** and
Col 1:10 growing in the **k** of God,
2: 3 all the treasures of wisdom and **k**.
3:10 in **k** in the image of its Creator.
1Ti 2: 4 to be saved and to come to a **k** of
6:20 ideas of what is falsely called **k**,
2Ti 2:25 repentance leading them to a **k** of
Tit 1: 2 a faith and **k** resting on the hope
Heb 10:26 sinning after we have received the **k**
2Pe 1: 3 for life and godliness through our **k**
1: 5 faith goodness; and to goodness, **k**;
3:18 grow in the grace and **k** of our Lord

KNOWN [KNOW]

Ex 6: 3 the LORD I did not make myself **k**
Dt 13: 2 (gods you have not **k**)
Ps 9:16 The LORD is **k** by his justice;
16:11 You have made **k** to me the path
67: 2 that your ways may be **k** on earth,
89: 1 I will make your faithfulness **k**
98: 2 The LORD has made his salvation **k**
105: 1 make **k** among the nations what he
119:168 for all my ways are **k** to you.
Pr 20:11 Even a child is **k** by his actions,
Isa 12: 4 make **k** among the nations what he
46:10 I make **k** the end from the beginning,
61: 9 Their descendants will be **k** among
Jer 7: 9 follow other gods you have not **k**,
Eze 38:23 and I will make myself **k** in the sight
39: 7 " 'I will make **k** my holy name
Zec 14: 7 a day **k** to the LORD.
Mt 10:26 or hidden that will not be made **k**.
24:43 If the owner of the house had **k**
Mk 6:14 for Jesus' name had become well **k**.
Lk 19:42 had only **k** on this day what
Jn 1:18 has made him **k**.
15:15 from my Father I have made **k**
16:14 from what is mine and making it **k**
17:26 I have made you **k** to them,
Ac 2:28 You have made **k** to me the paths
Ro 1:19 be **k** about God is plain to them,
3:21 apart from law, has been made **k**,
7: 7 not have **k** what sin was except
9:22 his wrath and make his power **k**,
11:34 "Who has **k** the mind of the Lord?
15:20 the gospel where Christ was not **k**,
16:26 now revealed and made **k** through
1Co 2:16 "For who has **k** the mind of the Lord
8: 3 the man who loves God is **k** by God.
13:12 even as I am fully **k**.
2Co 3: 2 **k** and read by everybody.
6: 9 **k**, yet regarded as unknown;
Gal 4: 9 or rather are **k** by God—

Eph	1: 9	he made **k** to us the mystery
	3: 3	mystery made **k** to me by revelation,
	6:19	I will fearlessly make **k** the mystery
2Ti	3:15	you have **k** the holy Scriptures,
Heb	3:10	and they have not **k** my ways.'
2Pe	2:21	to have **k** the way of righteousness,
1Jn	3: 2	has not yet been made **k.**
Rev	1: 1	He made it **k** by sending his angel

KNOWS [KNOW]

Ge	3: 5	"For God **k** that when you eat
1Sa	2: 3	for the LORD is a God who **k,**
Est	4:14	who **k** but that you have come
Job	23:10	But he **k** the way that I take;
Ps	44:21	since he **k** the secrets of the heart?
	94:11	The LORD **k** the thoughts of man;
	103:14	for he **k** how we are formed,
Pr	14:10	Each heart **k** its own bitterness,
Ecc	2:19	who **k** whether he will be a wise
	8: 7	Since no man **k** the future,
	8:17	Even if a wise man claims he **k,**
	9:12	no man **k** when his hour will come:
Isa	29:16	of the potter, "He **k** nothing"?
Jer	9:24	that he understands and **k** me,
Mt	6: 8	for your Father **k** what you need
	6:32	heavenly Father **k** that you need
	11:27	No one **k** the Son except the Father,
	24:36	"No one **k** about that day or hour,
Lk	12:47	That servant who **k** his master's will
	16:15	but God **k** your hearts.
Ac	15: 8	God, who **k** the heart,
Ro	8:27	And he who searches our hearts **k**
1Co	2:11	no one **k** the thoughts of God except
	3:20	"The Lord **k** that the thoughts of
	8: 2	The man who thinks he **k** something
2Ti	2:19	"The Lord **k** those who are his,"
Jas	4:17	who **k** the good he ought to do
2Pe	2: 9	the Lord **k** how to rescue godly men
1Jn	4: 6	and whoever **k** God listens to us;
	4: 7	has been born of God and **k** God.
Rev	19:12	that no one **k** but he himself.

KOHATH [KOHATHITE, KOHATHITES]

Ge	46:11	The sons of Levi: Gershon, **K** and
Nu	26:58	(**K** was the forefather of Amram;
1Ch	23: 6	**K** and Merari.

KOHATHITE [KOHATH]

Nu	3:29	The **K** clans were to camp on
1Ch	9:32	their **K** brothers were in charge

KOHATHITES [KOHATH]

Nu	3:28	The **K** were responsible for the care
	4:15	the **K** are to come to do the carrying.

KORAH

1. Levite who led rebellion against Moses and Aaron (Nu 16; Jude 11).

2. Psalms of the sons of Korah: Pss 42; 44-49; 84; 85; 87; 88

SONS OF KORAH See KORAH

KORAZIN*

Mt	11:21	"Woe to you, **K!**

Lk	10:13	"Woe to you, **K!**

KOUM*

Mk	5:41	*"Talitha k!"* (which means, "Little

L

LABAN

Brother of Rebekah (Ge 24:29), father of Rachel and Leah (Ge 29:16). Received Abraham's servant (Ge 24:29-51). Provided daughters as wives for Jacob in exchange for Jacob's service (Ge 29:1-30). Provided flocks for Jacob's service (Ge 30:25-43). After Jacob's departure, pursued and covenanted with him (Ge 31).

LABOR [LABORER, LABORER'S, LABORERS, LABORING]

Ex	1:11	to oppress them with forced **l,**
	20: 9	Six days you shall **l** and do all
Dt	5:13	Six days you shall **l** and do all
Jdg	1:30	but they did subject them to forced **l.**
	1:35	they too were pressed into forced **l.**
1Ki	4: 2	but now lighten the harsh **l** and
Ps	48: 6	pain like that of a woman in **l.**
	107:12	So he subjected them to bitter **l;**
	127: 1	its builders **l** in vain.
	128: 2	You will eat the fruit of your **l;**
Pr	12:24	but laziness ends in slave **l.**
Ecc	1: 3	What does man gain from all his **l**
	4: 4	that all **l** and all achievement spring
	5:18	to find satisfaction in his toilsome **l**
Isa	54: 1	you who were never in **l;**
	55: 2	and your **l** on what does not satisfy?
Jer	51:58	the nations' **l** is only fuel for
Hab	2:13	that the people's **l** is only fuel
Mt	6:28	They do not **l** or spin.
Jn	4:38	reaped the benefits of their **l."**
1Co	3: 8	rewarded according to his own **l.**
	15:58	you know that your **l** in the Lord
Gal	4:27	you who have no **l** pains;
Php	2:16	that I did not run or **l** for nothing.
Rev	14:13	"they will rest from their **l,**

LABORER* [LABOR]

Ecc	5:12	The sleep of a **l** is sweet,

LABORER'S* [LABOR]

Pr	16:26	The **l** appetite works for him;

LABORERS [LABOR]

Ne	4:10	"The strength of the **l** is giving out,
Mal	3: 5	against those who defraud **l**

LABORING* [LABOR]

2Th	3: 8	**l** and toiling so that we would not

LACHISH

Jos	10:32	The LORD handed **L** over to Israel,
2Ch	25:27	after him to **L** and killed him there.

LACK [LACKED, LACKING, LACKS]

Dt   8: 9 not be scarce and you will l nothing;
Ps 34: 9 for those who fear him l nothing.
    94:10 he who teaches man l knowledge?
Pr   5:23 He will die for l of discipline,
    9: 4 she says to those who l judgment.
  10:21 but fools die for l of judgment.
  11:14 For l of guidance a nation falls,
  15:22 Plans fail for l of counsel,
  28:27 gives to the poor will l nothing,
Isa 5:13 go into exile for l of understanding,
Hos 4: 6 are destroyed from l of knowledge.
Zec 10: 2 sheep oppressed for l of a shepherd.
Mt 13:58 because of their l of faith.
Mk 6: 6 he was amazed at their l of faith.
  16:14 for their l of faith
Lk 18:22 "You still l one thing.
Ro 3: 3 Will their l of faith nullify God's
1Co 1: 7 not l any spiritual gift
   7: 5 because of your l of self-control.
Col 2:23 but they l any value in restraining

LACKED [LACK]

Dt 2: 7 and you have not l anything.
Ne 9:21 in the desert; they l nothing,
1Co 12:24 greater honor to the parts that l it,

LACKING [LACK]

Pr 17:18 A man l in judgment strikes hands
Ecc 1:15 what is l cannot be counted.
Ro 12:11 Never be l in zeal,
Col 1:24 in my flesh what is still l in regard
Jas 1: 4 not l anything.

LACKS [LACK]

Pr 6:32 who commits adultery l judgment;
  11:12 who l judgment derides his neighbor,
  12:11 he who chases fantasies l judgment.
  15:21 Folly delights a man who l judgment,
  24:30 vineyard of the man who l judgment;
  25:28 is a man who l self-control.
  28:16 A tyrannical ruler l judgment,
  31:11 full confidence in her and l nothing
Ecc 10: 3 the fool l sense and shows everyone
Eze 34: 8 because my flock l a shepherd and
Jas 1: 5 If any of you l wisdom,

LADY*

2Jn 1: 1 To the chosen l and her children,
   1: 5 And now, dear l,

LAID [LAY]

Ge 22: 9 his son Isaac and l him on the altar,
Nu 27:23 Then he l his hands on him
Dt 34: 9 Moses had l his hands on him.
1Ki 6:37 of the temple of the LORD was l
Ezr 3:11 of the house of the LORD was l.
Job 38: 4 when I l the earth's foundation?
Ps 18:15 the foundations of the earth l bare
 102:25 the beginning you l the foundations
Pr 3:19 By wisdom the LORD l the earth's
Ecc 1:13 a heavy burden God has l on men!
Isa 14: 8 "Now that you have been l low,
  44:28 "Let its foundations be l." '

  53: 6 and the LORD has l on him
Jer 18:16 Their land will be l waste,
Eze 24: 2 the king of Babylon has l siege
Zec 4: 9 of Zerubbabel have l the foundation
Mk 6:29 and took his body and l it in a tomb.
  16: 6 See the place where they l him.
Lk 6:48 and l the foundation on rock.
Jn 11:38 It was a cave with a stone l across
  19:42 they l Jesus there.
Ac 6: 6 prayed and l their hands on them.
   7:58 the witnesses l their clothes at
1Co 3:11 other than the one already l,
  14:25 secrets of his heart will be l bare
1Ti 4:14 body of elders l their hands on you.
Heb 1:10 you l the foundations of the earth,
   4:13 uncovered and l bare before the eyes
2Pe 3:10 and everything in it will be l bare.
1Jn 3:16 Jesus Christ l down his life for us.

LAKE

Mt 4:18 They were casting a net into the l,
   8:24 a furious storm came up on the l,
  14:25 went out to them, walking on the l.
Mk 4: 1 Again Jesus began to teach by the l.
Lk 8:33 rushed down the steep bank into the l
Jn 6:25 on the other side of the l,
Rev 19:20 thrown alive into the fiery l of
  20:10 thrown into the l of burning sulfur,
  20:14 and Hades were thrown into the l
  20:14 The l of fire is the second death.

LAMA*

Mt 27:46 "Eloi, Eloi, l sabachthani?"—
Mk 15:34 "Eloi, Eloi, l sabachthani?"—

LAMB [LAMB'S, LAMBS]

Ge 22: 8 "God himself will provide the l for
  30:32 every dark-colored l and every
Ex 12:21 and slaughter the Passover l.
Lev 3: 7 If he offers a l,
   4:32 a l as his sin offering,
   5: 7 " 'If he cannot afford a l,
Nu 9:11 They are to eat the l,
2Sa 12: 6 He must pay for that l four times
Isa 11: 6 The wolf will live with the l,
  53: 7 he was led like a l to the slaughter,
  65:25 wolf and the l will feed together,
Jer 11:19 like a gentle l led to the slaughter;
Mk 14:12 to sacrifice the Passover l,
Jn 1:29 "Look, the L of God,
Ac 8:32 as a l before the shearer is silent,
1Co 5: 7 For Christ, our Passover l,
1Pe 1:19 a l without blemish or defect.
Rev 5: 6 Then I saw a L,
   5:12 "Worthy is the L, who was slain,
   6: 1 I watched as the L opened the first
   7:14 them white in the blood of the L.
  12:11 overcame him by the blood of the L
  13: 8 the book of life belonging to the L
  14: 1 and there before me was the L,
  15: 3 of God and the song of the L:
  17:14 They will make war against the L,
  19: 7 For the wedding of the L has come,
  21: 9 the wife of the L."

21:14 of the twelve apostles of the **L.**
21:23 and the **L** is its lamp.
22: 1 from the throne of God and of the **L**

LAMB'S* [LAMB]

Rev 21:27 are written in the **L** book of life.

LAMBS [LAMB]

Ex 29:38 on the altar regularly each day: two **l**
Ps 114: 4 skipped like rams, the hills like **l.**
Isa 40:11 He gathers the **l** in his arms
Lk 10: 3 sending you out like **l** among wolves.
Jn 21:15 Jesus said, "Feed my **l.**"

LAME

2Sa 4: 4 a son who was **l** in both feet.
5: 6 the blind and the **l** can ward you off."
Isa 33:23 even the **l** will carry off plunder.
35: 6 Then will the **l** leap like a deer,
Mic 4: 6 "I will gather the **l;**
Zep 3:19 I will rescue the **l**
Mt 11: 5 The blind receive sight, the **l** walk,
15:31 the **l** walking and the blind seeing.
Lk 14:13 invite the poor, the crippled, the **l,**
Ac 14: 8 **l** from birth and had never walked.

LAMECH

Ge 4:19 **L** married two women,

LAMENT [LAMENTATION, LAMENTS]

2Sa 1:17 David took up this **l** concerning Saul
3:33 The king sang this **l** for Abner:
Ps 56: 8 Record my **l;** list my tears
Eze 19: 1 "Take up a **l** concerning the princes

LAMENTATION [LAMENT]

La 2: 5 He has multiplied mourning and **l**

LAMENTS [LAMENT]

2Ch 35:25 Jeremiah composed **l** for Josiah,

LAMP [LAMPS, LAMPSTAND, LAMPSTANDS]

1Sa 3: 3 The **l** of God had not yet gone out,
2Sa 22:29 You are my **l,** O LORD;
1Ki 11:36 a **l** before me in Jerusalem,
15: 4 gave him a **l** in Jerusalem by raising
2Ki 8:19 He had promised to maintain a **l**
Job 18: 5 "The **l** of the wicked is snuffed out;
Ps 18:28 You, O LORD, keep my **l** burning;
119:105 Your word is a **l** to my feet and
132:17 and set up a **l** for my anointed one.
Pr 6:23 For these commands are a **l,**
20:27 The **l** of the LORD searches the spirit
31:18 and her **l** does not go out at night.
Mt 5:15 light a **l** and put it under a bowl.
6:22 "The eye is the **l** of the body.
Lk 8:16 "No one lights a **l** and hides it in
Jn 5:35 John was a **l** that burned and
Rev 21:23 and the Lamb is its **l.**
22: 5 not need the light of a **l** or the light

LAMPS [LAMP]

Ex 27:21 keep the **l** burning before the LORD

Mt 25: 1 be like ten virgins who took their **l**
Lk 12:35 for service and keep your **l** burning,
Rev 4: 5 seven **l** were blazing.

LAMPSTAND [LAMP]

Ex 25:31 a **l** of pure gold and hammer it out,
Nu 3:31 the table, the **l,** the altars,
Zec 4: 2 "I see a solid gold **l** with a bowl
4:11 trees on the right and the left of the **l**
Heb 9: 2 In its first room were the **l,**
Rev 2: 5 and remove your **l** from its place.

LAMPSTANDS [LAMP]

2Ch 4: 7 He made ten gold **l** according to
Rev 1:12 when I turned I saw seven golden **l,**
1:20 the seven **l** are the seven churches.
11: 4 the two **l** that stand before the Lord

LAND [LANDOWNER, LANDS, WASTELAND, WASTELANDS]

Ge 1:10 God called the dry ground **"l,"**
1:11 "Let the **l** produce vegetation:
1:24 "Let the **l** produce living creatures
7:22 on dry **l** that had the breath of life
12: 1 and go to the **l** I will show you.
12: 7 "To your offspring I will give this **l.**"
12:10 Now there was a famine in the **l,**
13:15 the **l** that you see I will give to you
15:18 "To your descendants I give this **l,**
17: 8 The whole **l** of Canaan,
24: 7 'To your offspring I will give this **l'**
26: 1 Now there was a famine in the **l—**
28:15 and I will bring you back to this **l.**
31:13 and go back to your native **l.**' "
40:15 carried off from the **l** of the Hebrews,
41:30 and the famine will ravage the **l.**
42: 6 Joseph was the governor of the **l,**
50:24 out of this **l** to the land he promised
Ex 1: 7 so that the **l** was filled with them.
3: 8 a **l** flowing with milk and honey—
6: 8 to the **l** I swore with uplifted hand
8:22 I, the LORD, am in this **l.**
20: 2 out of the **l** of slavery.
20:12 so that you may live long in the **l**
34:12 a treaty with those who live in the **l**
Lev 18:25 the **l** vomited out its inhabitants.
25: 5 The **l** is to have a year of rest.
25:23 the **l** is mine and you are but aliens
26:34 the **l** will enjoy its sabbath years all
Nu 13: 2 "Send some men to explore the **l**
13:30 go up and take possession of the **l,**
14: 9 not be afraid of the people of the **l,**
14:23 not one of them will ever see the **l**
26:55 Be sure that the **l** is distributed
35:33 Bloodshed pollutes the **l,**
Dt 1: 8 See, I have given you this **l.**
8: 7 God is bringing you into a good **l—**
11:10 The **l** you are entering to take over is not like the **l** of Egypt.
28:21 until he has destroyed you from the **l**
29:24 has the LORD done this to this **l?**
34: 1 the LORD showed him the whole **l—**
Jos 1: 6 will lead these people to inherit the **l**
2: 1 "Go, look over the **l,**" he said,

	5:12	after they ate this food from the l;
	11:23	So Joshua took the entire l,
	13: 2	"This is the l that remains:
	14: 4	Levites received no share of the l
	14: 9	l on which your foot have walked
Jdg	1:27	were determined to live in that l.
Ru	1: 1	there was a famine in the l,
2Sa	21:14	answered prayer in behalf of the l,
	24:25	answered prayer in behalf of the l,
1Ki	8:34	bring them back to the l you gave
	17: 7	there had been no rain in the l.
2Ki	17: 5	king of Assyria invaded the entire l,
	24: 1	king of Babylon invaded the l,
	25:21	went into captivity, away from her l.
1Ch	14:17	fame spread throughout every l,
2Ch	7:14	and will heal their l.
	7:20	then I will uproot Israel from my l,
	32:21	withdrew to his own l in disgrace.
	36:21	The l enjoyed its sabbath rests;
Ezr	9:11	'The l you are entering to possess is
Ne	9:36	slaves in the l you gave our
Ps	25:13	his descendants will inherit the l.
	37:11	But the meek will inherit the l
	37:29	the righteous will inherit the l
	44: 3	not by their sword that they won the l
	65: 9	You care for the l and water it;
	136:21	and gave their l as an inheritance,
	142: 5	my portion in the l of the living."
Pr	2:21	For the upright will live in the l,
	12:11	works his l will have abundant food,
Isa	2: 8	Their l is full of idols;
	6:13	holy seed will be the stump in the l."
	9: 2	in the l of the shadow of death
	36:18	god of any nation ever delivered his l
	53: 8	cut off from the l of the living;
Jer	2: 7	I brought you into a fertile l
	2: 7	But you came and defiled my l
	22:29	O l, l, l, hear the word of the LORD!
	31:17	children will return to their own l.
Eze	7:23	because the l is full of bloodshed
	36:24	and bring you back into your own l,
	39:28	I will gather them to their own l,
	43: 2	and the l was radiant with his glory.
Da	11:41	He will also invade the Beautiful L.
Hos	2:23	I will plant her for myself in the l;
Zec	3: 9	'and I will remove the sin of this l
Mal	4: 6	or else I will come and strike the l
Mt	4:16	in the l of the shadow of death
Mk	15:33	darkness came over the whole l
Lk	21:23	There will be great distress in the l
Jas	5:17	and it did not rain on the l for three
Rev	7: 3	not harm the l or the sea or the trees
	16: 2	and poured out his bowl on the l,

LAND FLOWING WITH MILK AND HONEY See FLOWING

LANDMARK (KJV) See BOUNDARY STONE

LANDOWNER* [LAND]

Mt	20: 1	the kingdom of heaven is like a l
	20:11	they began to grumble against the l.
	21:33	There was a l who planted a vineyard

LANDS [LAND]

Ge	26: 3	descendants I will give all these l
Ps	106:27	and scatter them throughout the l.
	107: 3	those he gathered from the l,
	111: 6	giving them the l of other nations.
Eze	20: 6	the most beautiful of all l.
Hab	2: 8	you have destroyed l
	2:17	you have destroyed l
Zec	10: 9	in distant l they will remember me.

LANGUAGE [LANGUAGES]

Ge	11: 1	Now the whole world had one l and
	11: 9	there the LORD confused the l of
Dt	28:49	whose l you will not understand,
Ne	13:24	not know how to speak the l of Judah
Ps	19: 3	or l where their voice is not heard.
	81: 5	we heard a l we did not know,
Jer	5:15	a people whose l you do not know,
Jn	8:44	he lies, he speaks his native l,
Ac	2: 6	heard them speaking in his own l.
Col	3: 8	slander, and filthy l from your lips.
Rev	5: 9	men for God from every tribe and l
	7: 9	and l, standing before the throne
	13: 7	over every tribe, people, l and nation.
	14: 6	to every nation, tribe, l and people.

LANGUAGES [LANGUAGE]

Zec	8:23	"In those days ten men from all l

LANTERNS*

Jn	18: 3	carrying torches, l and weapons.

LAODICEA

Col	4:16	in turn read the letter from L.
Rev	3:14	the angel of the church in L write:

LAP

Jdg	7: 5	"Separate those who l the water
Pr	6:27	Can a man scoop fire into his l
	16:33	The lot is cast into the l,
Lk	6:38	will be poured into your l.

LARGE [ENLARGE, ENLARGED, ENLARGES, LARGER, LARGEST]

Nu	13:28	the cities are fortified and very l.
Dt	6:10	a land with l, flourishing cities
	17:17	He must not accumulate l amounts
Jos	10:11	the LORD hurled l hailstones down
Eze	23:32	a cup l and deep;
Da	2:31	there before you stood a l statue—
	4:11	The tree grew l and strong
	7: 7	It had l iron teeth;
	8:21	and the l horn between his eyes is
Gal	6:11	See what l letters I use as I write
Rev	6: 4	To him was given a l sword.
	18:21	a boulder the size of a l millstone

LARGER [LARGE]

Nu	33:54	To a l group give a l inheritance,
Dt	11:23	and you will dispossess nations l

LARGEST* [LARGE]

Mt	13:32	it grows, it is the l of garden plants
Mk	4:32	becomes the l of all garden plants,

LASHES

Dt   25: 3 not give him more than forty **l.**
Pr   17:10 more than a hundred **l** a fool.
2Co 11:24 from the Jews the forty **l** minus one.

LAST [LASTING, LASTS, LATTER]

Ex   14:24 During the **l** watch of the night
2Sa 23: 1 These are the **l** words of David:
1Ch 23:27 to the **l** instructions of David,
Ps   45: 6 O God, will **l** for ever and ever;
    119:152 you established them to **l** forever.
Isa   2: 2 In the **l** days the mountain of the
    41: 4 with the first of them and with the **l**
    44: 6 the first and I am the **l;**
    48:12 the first and I am the **l.**
    51: 6 But my salvation will **l** forever,
Da   9: 2 of Jerusalem would **l** seventy years.
Hos   3: 5 and to his blessings in the **l** days.
Mic   4: 1 In the **l** days the mountain of the
Mt   19:30 But many who are first will be **l,** and
    many who are **l** will be first.
    20: 8 with the **l** ones hired and going on
    21:37 **L** of all, he sent his son to them.
    27:64 This **l** deception will be worse than
Mk   9:35 he must be the very **l,**
    10:31 who are first will be **l,** and the **l** first.
    15:37 Jesus breathed his **l.**
Jn   6:40 and I will raise him up at the **l** day."
    7:37 the **l** and greatest day of the Feast,
    11:24 in the resurrection at the **l** day."
    15:16 bear fruit—fruit that will **l.**
Ac   2:17 " 'In the **l** days, God says,
Ro   1:17 that is by faith from first to **l,**
1Co   9:25 to get a crown that will **l** forever.
    15: 8 and **l** of all he appeared to me also,
    15:26 **l** enemy to be destroyed is death.
    15:52 at the **l** trumpet.
2Ti   3: 1 will be terrible times in the **l** days.
Heb   1: 2 in these **l** days he has spoken to us
    1: 8 O God, will **l** for ever and ever,
1Pe   1: 5 to be revealed in the **l** time.
2Pe   3: 3 in the **l** days scoffers will come,
1Jn   2:18 Dear children, this is the **l** hour;
Jude   1:18 "In the **l** times there will
Rev   1:17 I am the First and the **L.**
    2: 8 of him who is the First and the **L,**
    15: 1 seven angels with the seven **l** plagues
    21: 9 bowls full of the seven **l** plagues
    22:13 the First and the **L,**

LASTING [LAST]

Ex   12:14 festival to the Lord—a **l** ordinance.
    28:43 "This is to be a **l** ordinance for Aaron
Lev   24: 8 as a **l** covenant.
Nu   25:13 a covenant of a **l** priesthood,
Heb   10:34 had better and **l** possessions.

A LASTING ORDINANCE Ex 12:14, 17, 24;
27:21; 28:43; 29:9; 30:21; Lev 3:17; 10:9; 16:29,
31, 34; 17:7; 23:14, 21, 31, 41; 24:3; Nu 10:8;
15:15; 18:23; 19:10, 21; 2Ch 2:4; Eze 46:14

LASTS [LAST]

Job   20: 5 joy of the godless **l** but a moment.

Ps   30: 5 For his anger **l** only a moment, but
    his favor **l** a lifetime;
Pr   12:19 but a lying tongue **l** only a moment.
2Co   3:11 greater is the glory of that which **l!**

LATCHET (KJV) See THONGS

LATE [LATER]

Ps   127: 2 In vain you rise early and stay up **l,**

LATER [LATE]

Mk   10:34 Three days **l** he will rise."
Jn   13: 7 but **l** you will understand."
Gal   3:17 The law, introduced 430 years **l,**
1Ti   4: 1 that in **l** times some will abandon
Rev   1:19 is now and what will take place **l.**

LATIN*

Jn   19:20 sign was written in Aramaic, **L** and

LATTER [LAST]

Job   42:12 Lord blessed the **l** part of Job's life
Mt   23:23 You should have practiced the **l,**
Php   1:16 The **l** do so in love,

LAUD (KJV) See SING PRAISES

LAUGH [LAUGHED, LAUGHINGSTOCK, LAUGHS, LAUGHTER]

Ge   18:13 "Why did Sarah **l** and say,
    21: 6 who hears about this will **l** with me."
Ps   59: 8 But you, O Lord, **l** at them;
Pr   31:25 she can **l** at the days to come.
Ecc   3: 4 a time to weep and a time to **l,**
Lk   6:21 for you will **l.**
    6:25 Woe to you who **l** now,

LAUGHED [LAUGH]

Ge   17:17 Abraham fell facedown; he **l**
    18:12 So Sarah **l** to herself as she thought,
La   1: 7 Her enemies looked at her and **l**
Lk   8:53 They **l** at him,

LAUGHINGSTOCK [LAUGH]

La   3:14 I became the **l** of all my people;

LAUGHS [LAUGH]

Ps   2: 4 The One enthroned in heaven **l;**
    37:13 but the Lord **l** at the wicked,

LAUGHTER [LAUGH]

Ge   21: 6 Sarah said, "God has brought me **l,**
Ps   126: 2 Our mouths were filled with **l,**
Pr   14:13 Even in **l** the heart may ache,
Ecc   7: 3 Sorrow is better than **l,**
    10:19 A feast is made for **l,**
Jas   4: 9 Change your **l** to mourning

LAUNDERER'S*

Mal   3: 2 be like a refiner's fire or a **l** soap.

LAVER (KJV) See BASIN

LAVISHED

Eph 1: 8 that he **l** on us with all wisdom
1Jn 3: 1 the love the Father has **l** on us,

LAW [LAW'S, LAWFUL, LAWGIVER, LAWS, LAWSUITS]

Ex 15:25 the LORD made a decree and a **l**
Lev 24:22 the same **l** for the alien and the
Nu 5:29 is the **l** of jealousy when
6:13 this is the **l** for the Nazirite
Dt 1: 5 Moses began to expound this **l**,
6:25 if we are careful to obey all this **l**
17:18 himself on a scroll a copy of this **l**,
27:26 does not uphold the words of this **l**
31: 9 So Moses wrote down this **l**
31:11 you shall read this **l** before them
31:26 "Take this Book of the **L** and place it
Jos 1: 7 Be careful to obey all the **l** my
1: 8 Do not let this Book of the **L** depart
8:32 Joshua copied on stones the **l** of
22: 5 to keep the commandment and the **l**
2Ki 22: 8 "I have found the Book of the **L**
2Ch 6:16 to walk before me according to my **l**,
17: 9 taking with them the Book of the **L**
34:14 the priest found the Book of the **L** of
Ezr 7: 6 a teacher well versed in the **L**
Ne 8: 2 Ezra the priest brought the **L** before
8: 8 They read from the Book of the **L**
Ps 1: 2 his delight is in the **l** of the LORD,
1: 2 on his **l** he meditates day and night.
19: 7 The **l** of the LORD is perfect,
37:31 The **l** of his God is in his heart;
40: 8 your **l** is within my heart."
89:30 "If his sons forsake my **l** and do
119:18 may see wonderful things in your **l**.
119:70 but I delight in your **l**.
119:72 The **l** from your mouth is more
119:77 for your **l** is my delight.
119:97 Oh, how I love your **l**!
119:142 and your **l** is true.
119:163 but I love your **l**.
119:165 peace have they who love your **l**,
Pr 28: 9 If anyone turns a deaf ear to the **l**,
29:18 but blessed is he who keeps the **l**.
Isa 2: 3 The **l** will go out from Zion,
8:20 To the **l** and to the testimony!
42:21 to make his **l** great and glorious.
Jer 2: 8 Those who deal with the **l** did
8: 8 for we have the **l** of the LORD,"
31:33 "I will put my **l** in their minds
La 2: 9 the **l** is no more,
Da 9:11 All Israel has transgressed your **l**
Hos 4: 6 because you have ignored the **l**
Mic 4: 2 The **l** will go out from Zion,
Hab 1: 4 Therefore the **l** is paralyzed,
1: 4 they are a **l** to themselves
Zec 7:12 as flint and would not listen to the **l**
Mal 2: 9 shown partiality in matters of the **l**."
Mt 5:17 that I have come to abolish the **L** or
7:12 this sums up the **L** and the Prophets.
22:36 greatest commandment in the **L**?"
22:40 All the **L** and the Prophets hang
23:23 the more important matters of the **l**—

Lk 2:23 (as it is written in the **L** of the Lord,
2:39 done everything required by the **L**
10:26 "What is written in the **L**?"
11:52 "Woe to you experts in the **l**,
16:17 stroke of a pen to drop out of the **L**.
24:44 that is written about me in the **L**
Jn 1:17 For the **l** was given through Moses;
7:19 Yet not one of you keeps the **l**.
18:31 and judge him by your own **l**."
Ac 6:13 this holy place and against the **l**.
13:39 be justified from by the **l** of Moses.
15: 5 and required to obey the **l**
28:23 about Jesus from the **L** of Moses and
Ro 2:12 All who sin apart from the **l** will
2:12 and all who sin under the **l** will
2:15 of the **l** are written on their hearts,
2:20 the **l** the embodiment of knowledge
2:25 has value if you observe the **l**,
3:19 we know that whatever the **l** says,
3:20 the **l** we become conscious of sin.
3:21 righteousness from God, apart from **l**
3:28 by faith apart from observing the **l**.
3:31 then, nullify the **l** by this faith?
4:13 It was not through **l** that Abraham
4:15 because **l** brings wrath.
4:15 there is no **l** there is no transgression.
5:13 into account when there is no **l**.
5:20 The **l** was added so that
6:14 because you are not under **l**,
6:15 because we are not under **l** but
7: 1 the **l** has authority over a man only
7: 4 died to the **l** through the body of
7: 5 the sinful passions aroused by the **l**
7: 6 we have been released from the **l** so
7: 7 Is the **l** sin?
7: 8 For apart from **l**, sin is dead.
7: 9 Once I was alive apart from **l**;
7:12 So then, the **l** is holy,
7:14 We know that the **l** is spiritual;
7:22 I delight in God's **l**;
7:25 in my mind am a slave to God's **l**,
8: 2 the **l** of the Spirit of life set me free
8: 3 the **l** was powerless to do
8: 4 of the **l** might be fully met in us,
8: 7 It does not submit to God's **l**,
9: 4 the receiving of the **l**,
9:31 who pursued a **l** of righteousness,
10: 4 Christ is the end of the **l**
13: 8 his fellowman has fulfilled the **l**.
13:10 love is the fulfillment of the **l**.
1Co 6: 6 one brother goes to **l** against another
9: 9 For it is written in the **L** of Moses:
9:20 To those under the **l** I became like
one under the **l**
9:21 so as to win those not having the **l**.
15:56 and the power of sin is the **l**.
Gal 2:16 not justified by observing the **l**,
2:16 by observing the **l** no one will
2:19 For through the **l** I died to the **l**
3: 2 the Spirit by observing the **l**,
3: 5 because you observe the **l**,
3:10 All who rely on observing the **l** are
3:11 is justified before God by the **l**,
3:13 redeemed us from the curse of the **l**

3:19 then, was the purpose of the **l**?
3:21 **l**, therefore, opposed to the promises
3:23 we were held prisoners by the **l**,
3:24 So the **l** was put in charge to lead us
4: 4 born of a woman, born under **l**,
4:21 you who want to be under the **l**,
5: 3 obligated to obey the whole **l**.
5: 4 be justified by **l** have been alienated
5:14 The entire **l** is summed up in
5:18 you are not under **l**.
6: 2 you will fulfill the **l** of Christ.
Eph 2:15 by abolishing in his flesh the **l**
Php 3: 5 in regard to the **l**, a Pharisee;
3: 9 of my own that comes from the **l**,
1Ti 1: 8 the **l** is good if one uses it properly.
Tit 3: 9 arguments and quarrels about the **l**,
Heb 7:12 there must also be a change of the **l**.
7:19 (for the **l** made nothing perfect),
10: 1 The **l** is only a shadow of the good
Jas 1:25 the perfect **l** that gives freedom,
2: 8 If you really keep the royal **l** found
2:10 the whole **l** and yet stumbles
4:11 or judges him speaks against the **l**
1Jn 3: 4 Everyone who sins breaks the **l**;

BOOK OF THE LAW Dt 28:61; 29:21; 30:10;
31:26; Jos 1:8; 8:31, 34; 23:6; 24:26; 2Ki 14:6;
22:8, 11; 2Ch 17:9; 34:14, 15; Ne 8:1, 3, 8, 18;
9:3; Gal 3:10

LAW OF MOSES Jos 8:31, 32; 23:6; 1Ki 2:3;
2Ki 14:6; 23:25; 2Ch 23:18; 30:16; Ezr 3:2; 7:6;
Ne 8:1; Da 9:11, 13; Lk 2:22; 24:44; Jn 7:23; Ac
13:39; 15:5; 28:23; 1Co 9:9; Heb 10:28

LAW OF THE †LORD Ex 13:9; 2Ki 10:31;
1Ch 16:40; 22:12; 2Ch 12:1; 17:9; 19:8; 31:3, 4;
34:14; 35:26; Ezr 7:10; Ne 9:3; Ps 1:2; 19:7;
119:1; Isa 5:24; Jer 8:8; Am 2:4

TEACHERS OF THE LAW Mt 2:4; 5:20;
7:29; 9:3; 12:38; 15:1; 16:21; 17:10; 20:18;
21:15; 23:2, 13, 15, 23, 25, 27, 29; 26:57; 27:41;
Mk 1:22; 2:6, 16; 3:22; 7:1, 5; 8:31; 9:11, 14;
10:33; 11:18, 27; 12:28, 35, 38; 14:1, 43, 53;
15:1, 31; Lk 5:17, 21, 30; 6:7; 9:22; 11:53; 15:2;
19:47; 20:1, 19, 39, 46; 22:2, 66; 23:10; Jn 8:3;
Ac 4:5; 6:12; 23:9; 1Ti 1:7

LAW'S* [LAW]

Ro 2:26 circumcised keep the **l** requirements,

LAWBREAKER* [BREAK]

Ro 2:27 code and circumcision, are a **l**.
Gal 2:18 I prove that I am a **l**.
Jas 2:11 you have become a **l**.

LAWBREAKERS* [BREAK]

1Ti 1: 9 not for the righteous but for **l** and
Jas 2: 9 and are convicted by the law as **l**.

LAWFUL [LAW]

Mt 12:12 it is **l** to do good on the Sabbath."
19: 3 "Is it **l** for a man to divorce his wife
Mk 2:26 which is **l** only for priests to eat.
Lk 14: 3 "Is it **l** to heal on the Sabbath

LAWGIVER* [LAW]

Isa 33:22 the LORD is our **l**,
Jas 4:12 There is only one **L** and Judge,

LAWLESS [LAWLESSNESS]

2Th 2: 8 And then the **l** one will be revealed,
Heb 10:17 **l** acts I will remember no more."
2Pe 3:17 be carried away by the error of **l** men

LAWLESSNESS* [LAWLESS]

2Th 2: 3 and the man of **l** is revealed,
2: 7 secret power of **l** is already at work;
1Jn 3: 4 breaks the law; in fact, sin is **l**.

LAWS [LAW]

Ge 26: 5 my decrees and my **l**."
Ex 21: 1 the **l** you are to set before them:
Lev 25:18 and be careful to obey my **l**,
26:43 their sins because they rejected my **l**
Dt 4: 1 and I **l** am about to teach you.
30:16 to keep his commands, decrees and **l**;
Jos 24:25 he drew up for them decrees and **l**.
1Ki 11:33 nor kept my statutes and **l** as David,
Ezr 7:10 teaching its decrees and **l** in Israel.
Job 38:33 Do you know the **l** of the heavens?
Ps 18:22 All his **l** are before me;
119:30 I have set my heart on your **l**.
119:43 for I have put my hope in your **l**.
119:120 I stand in awe of your **l**.
119:164 I praise you for your righteous **l**.
119:175 and may your **l** sustain me.
147:20 they do not know his **l**.
Pr 8:15 and rulers make **l** that are just;
Isa 10: 1 Woe to those who make unjust **l**,
Eze 5: 6 She has rejected my **l** and has
36:27 and be careful to keep my **l**.
Da 6: 8 the **l** of the Medes and Persians,
Heb 8:10 I will put my **l** in their minds
10:16 I will put my **l** in their hearts,

LAWSUITS [LAW]

Hos 10: 4 therefore **l** spring up like poisonous
1Co 6: 7 The very fact that you have **l**

LAY [LAID, LAYING, LAYS]

Ge 22:12 "Do not **l** a hand on the boy,"
Ex 7: 4 Then I will **l** my hand on Egypt and
29:10 and his sons shall **l** their hands
Lev 1: 4 He is to **l** his hand on the head of
4:15 the community are to **l** their hands
Nu 8:10 the Israelites are to **l** their hands
27:18 and **l** your hand on him.
Dt 9:25 I **l** prostrate before the LORD
1Sa 26: 9 can **l** a hand on the LORD's anointed
Job 1:12 on the man himself do not **l** a finger.
22:22 and **l** up his words in your heart.
Pr 4: 4 "**L** hold of my words
Ecc 10: 4 calmness can **l** great errors
Isa 28:16 I **l** a stone in Zion, a tested stone,
Mt 8:20 of Man has no place to **l** his head."
28: 6 Come and see the place where he **l**.
Mk 6: 5 except **l** his hands on a few sick
Lk 9:58 of Man has no place to **l** his head."
Jn 10:15 I **l** down my life for the sheep.

	10:18	but I l it down of my own accord.
	13:37	I will l down my life for you."
	15:13	he l down his life for his friends.
Ac	8:19	on whom I I my hands may receive
Ro	9:33	I l in Zion a stone that causes men
1Co	3:11	no one can l any foundation other
	7:17	the rule I l down in all the churches.
1Ti	6:19	In this way they will l up treasure
1Pe	2: 6	I l a stone in Zion,
1Jn	3:16	to l down our lives for our brothers.
Rev	4:10	They l their crowns before

LAYING [LAY]

Lk	4:40	and l his hands on each one,
Ac	8:18	that the Spirit was given at the l on
1Ti	5:22	not be hasty in the l on of hands,
2Ti	1: 6	which is in you through the l on
Heb	6: 1	not l again the foundation
	6: 2	the l on of hands,

LAYS [LAY]

| Jn | 10:11 | The good shepherd l down his life |

LAZARUS*

1. Poor man in Jesus' parable (Lk 16:19-31).
2. Brother of Mary and Martha whom Jesus raised from the dead (Jn 11:1-12:19).

LAZINESS* [LAZY]

| Pr | 12:24 | but l ends in slave labor. |
| | 19:15 | L brings on deep sleep, |

LAZY* [LAZINESS]

Ex	5: 8	They are l; that is why
	5:17	said, "L, that's what you are—l!
Pr	10: 4	L hands make a man poor,
	12:27	The l man does not roast his game,
	26:15	he is too l to bring it back
Ecc	10:18	If a man is l, the rafters sag;
Mt	25:26	'You wicked, l servant!
Tit	1:12	evil brutes, l gluttons."
Heb	6:12	We do not want you to become l,

LEAD [LEADER, LEADERS, LEADERSHIP, LEADING, LEADS, LED]

Ex	15:13	"In your unfailing love you will l
	32:34	l the people to the place I spoke of,
Nu	14: 8	he will l us into that land,
Dt	31: 2	and I am no longer able to l you.
Jos	1: 6	because you will l these people
1Sa	8: 5	now appoint a king to l us,
2Ch	1:10	that I may l this people,
	8:14	and the Levites to l the praise and
Ps	27:11	l me in a straight path because
	61: 2	l me to the rock that is higher than I.
	139:24	and l me in the way everlasting.
	143:10	may your good Spirit l me
Pr	4:11	and l you along straight paths.
	5: 5	her steps l straight to the grave.
	21: 5	The plans of the diligent l to profit
Ecc	5: 6	not let your mouth l you into sin.
Isa	3:12	your guides l you astray;
	11: 6	and a little child will l them.
	49:10	on them will guide them and l them

Jer	31: 9	I will l them beside streams
Da	12: 3	those who l many to righteousness,
Mt	6:13	And l us not into temptation,
Lk	6:39	"Can a blind man l a blind man?
	11: 4	And l us not into temptation.' "
Gal	3:24	law was put in charge to l us to
1Th	4:11	your ambition to l a quiet life,
1Jn	2:26	who are trying to l you astray.
	3: 7	do not let anyone l you astray.
	5:16	a sin that does not l to death,
Rev	7:17	will l them to springs of living water.

LEADER [LEAD]

Lev	4:22	" 'When a l sins unintentionally
1Sa	7: 6	Samuel was l of Israel at Mizpah.
	10: 1	"Has not the LORD anointed you l
	12: 2	Now you have a king as your l.
	13:14	and appointed him l of his people,
1Ch	28: 4	He chose Judah as l,

LEADERS [LEAD]

Nu	1:16	the l of their ancestral tribes.
	7:10	the l brought their offerings
1Ch	29: 9	at the willing response of their l,
Isa	3:14	against the elders and l of his people:
Jer	25:34	you l of the flock.
Mic	3: 1	Then I said, "Listen, you l of Jacob,
Heb	13: 7	Remember your l,
	13:17	Obey your l and submit to their

LEADERSHIP* [LEAD]

Nu	33: 1	under the l of Moses and Aaron.
Ps	109: 8	may another take his place of l.
Ac	1:20	" 'May another take his place of l.'
Ro	12: 8	if it is l, let him govern diligently;

LEADING [LEAD]

Dt	1:15	So I took the l men of your tribes,
Mk	14:48	"Am I l a rebellion," said Jesus,
Ro	6:19	to righteousness l to holiness.
2Ti	2:25	God will grant them repentance l

LEADS [LEAD]

Dt	27:18	the man who l the blind astray on
Ps	23: 2	he l me beside quiet waters,
	37: 8	do not fret—it l only to evil.
	68: 6	he l forth the prisoners with singing;
Pr	2:18	For her house l down to death
	10:17	ignores correction l others astray.
	12:26	way of the wicked l them astray
	14:12	but in the end it l to death.
	14:23	but mere talk l only to poverty.
	16:25	but in the end it l to death.
	19:23	The fear of the LORD l to life:
	20: 7	righteous man l a blameless life;
	21: 5	as surely as haste l to poverty.
Isa	40:11	he gently l those that have young.
Mt	7:13	broad is the road that l to destruction,
	7:14	narrow the road that l to life,
	12:20	till he l justice to victory.
	15:14	If a blind man l a blind man,
Jn	10: 3	sheep by name and l them out.
Ro	2: 4	kindness l you toward repentance?
	6:16	obedience, which l to righteousness?

	6:22	the benefit you reap l to holiness,
	14:19	every effort to do what l to peace
2Co	2:14	always l us in triumphal procession
	7:10	repentance that l to salvation
Tit	1: 1	the knowledge of the truth that l
1Jn	5:16	There is a sin that l to death.
Rev	12: 9	who l the whole world astray.

LEAF [LEAVES]

Ge	8:11	beak was a freshly plucked olive l!
Ps	1: 3	and whose l does not wither.
Pr	11:28	righteous will thrive like a green l.

LEAH

Wife of Jacob (Ge 29:16-30); bore six sons and one daughter (Ge 29:31-30:21; 34:1; 35:23).

LEAN [LEANED, LEANING]

Ge	41:20	The l, ugly cows ate up the seven
Pr	3: 5	l not on your own understanding;

LEANED [LEAN]

Ge	47:31	and Israel worshiped as he l on
Jn	21:20	the one who had l back against Jesus
Heb	11:21	and worshiped as he l on the top

LEANING [LEAN]

Jn	13:25	L back against Jesus, he asked him,

LEAP [LEAPED, LEAPS]

Isa	35: 6	Then will the lame l like a deer,
Mal	4: 2	l like calves released from the stall.
Lk	6:23	"Rejoice in that day and l for joy,

LEAPED [LEAP]

Lk	1:41	the baby l in her womb,

LEAPS* [LEAP]

Job	37: 1	my heart pounds and l from its place.
Ps	28: 7	My heart l for joy

LEARN [LEARNED, LEARNING, LEARNS]

Dt	4:10	so that they may l to revere me
	5: 1	L them and be sure to follow them.
	18: 9	not l to imitate the detestable ways
	31:12	and l to fear the LORD your God
Ps	14: 4	Will evildoers never l—
	119: 7	as I l your righteous laws.
Pr	19:25	and the simple will l prudence;
Isa	1:17	l to do right!
	26: 9	people of the world l righteousness.
Jer	35:13	not l a lesson and obey my words?'
Mt	11:29	Take my yoke upon you and l
Mk	13:28	"Now l this lesson from the fig tree:
Jn	14:31	but the world must l that I love
1Th	4: 4	that each of you should l to control
1Ti	2:11	A woman should l in quietness
	5: 4	these should l first of all
Tit	3:14	Our people must l to devote
Heb	5:11	because you are slow to l.
Rev	14: 3	could l the song except the 144,000

LEARNED [LEARN]

Ps	119:152	Long ago I l from your statutes
Pr	24:32	and l a lesson from what I saw:
Ecc	1:17	but I l that this, too,
	9:11	to the brilliant or favor to the l;
Mt	11:25	these things from the wise and l,
Jn	15:15	everything that I l from my Father
Php	4: 9	Whatever you have l or received
	4:11	for I have l to be content whatever
2Ti	3:14	continue in what you have l
Heb	5: 8	he l obedience from what he suffered
Rev	2:24	not l Satan's so-called deep secrets

LEARNING [LEARN]

Pr	1: 5	the wise listen and add to their l,
	4: 2	I give you sound l,
	9: 9	and he will add to his l.
Isa	44:25	who overthrows the l of the wise
Jn	7:15	"How did this man get such l
Ac	26:24	"Your great l is driving you insane."
2Ti	3: 7	always l but never able

LEARNS [LEARN]

Jn	6:45	Father and l from him comes to me.

LEAST [LESS]

1Sa	9:21	not my clan the l of all the clans of
Isa	60:22	l of you will become a thousand,
Mt	5:18	not the l stroke of a pen,
	5:19	same will be called l in the kingdom
	25:40	did for one of the l of these brothers
Lk	7:28	yet the one who is l in the kingdom
	9:48	For he who is l among you all—
1Co	15: 9	I am the l of the apostles and do
2Co	11: 5	I do not think I am in the l inferior
Eph	3: 8	less than the l of all God's people,

LEATHER

Lev	13:48	any l or anything made of l—
2Ki	1: 8	and with a l belt around his waist."
Mt	3: 4	and he had a l belt around his waist.

LEAVE [LEAVES]

Ge	2:24	a man will l his father and mother
	12: 1	I said to Abram, "L your country,
Ex	12:10	Do not l any of it till morning;
	12:33	to hurry and l the country.
	34: 7	he does not l the guilty unpunished;
Lev	19:10	L them for the poor and the alien.
Nu	11:20	"Why did we ever l Egypt?" '"
Dt	31: 6	he will never l you nor forsake you."
Jos	1: 5	I will never l you nor forsake you.
Ru	1:16	Ruth replied, "Don't urge me to l
Mk	10: 7	a man will l his father and mother
Jn	8:11	"Go now and l your life of sin."
	14:18	I will not l you as orphans;
	14:27	Peace I l with you;
Eph	5:31	a man will l his father and mother
Heb	13: 5	"Never will I l you;

LEAVEN (KJV) See YEAST

LEAVES [LEAF, LEAVE]

Ge	3: 7	so they sewed fig l together

Pr 13:22 A good man l an inheritance
    15:10 Stern discipline awaits him who l
Jer 17: 8 its l are always green.
Eze 47:12 for food and their l for healing."
Mk 11:13 he found nothing but l,
1Co 7:15 if the unbeliever l, let him do so.
Rev 22: 2 the l of the tree are for the healing

LEBANON

Dt 11:24 will extend from the desert to L,
1Ki 4:33 from the cedar of L to the hyssop
     5: 6 "So give orders that cedars of L
2Ki 14: 9 "A thistle in L sent a message to
Ps 29: 6 He makes L skip like a calf,
    92:12 they will grow like a cedar of L;
Isa 40:16 is not sufficient for altar fires,
Hab 2:17 The violence you have done to L

LEBBAEUS (KJV) See THADDAEUS

LEBO HAMATH

Nu 34: 8 and from Mount Hor to L
2Ki 14:25 the boundaries of Israel from L

LECTURE*

Jn   9:34 how dare you l us!"
Ac 19: 9 daily in the l hall of Tyrannus.

LED [LEAD]

Ex   3: 1 and he l the flock to the far side of
    32:21 you l them into such great sin?"
Dt   8: 2 the LORD your God l you all the way
    17:17 or his heart will be l astray.
1Ki 11: 3 and his wives l him astray.
2Ki 21: 9 Manasseh l them astray,
2Ch 26:16 his pride l to his downfall.
Ne 13:26 he was l into sin by foreign women.
Job 31: 7 if my heart has been l by my eyes,
Ps 68:18 you l captives in your train;
    77:19 Your path l through the sea,
    78:52 he l them like sheep through
Pr   7:21 persuasive words she l him astray;
    20: 1 whoever is l astray by them is
Isa 53: 7 he was l like a lamb to the slaughter,
    55:12 in joy and be l forth in peace;
Jer 11:19 like a gentle lamb l to the slaughter,
    50: 6 their shepherds have l them astray
Hos 11: 4 I l them with cords of human
Am   2:10 and I l you forty years in the desert
Mt   4: 1 Then Jesus was l by the Spirit into
    27:31 they l him away to crucify him.
Lk   4: 1 was l by the Spirit in the desert,
     4: 5 The devil l him up to a high place
     4: 9 The devil l him to Jerusalem
Ac   8:32 "He was l like a sheep
Ro   8:14 who are l by the Spirit of God are
2Co 7: 9 your sorrow l you to repentance.
Gal 5:18 But if you are l by the Spirit,
Eph 4: 8 he l captives in his train

LEECH*

Pr 30:15 "The l has two daughters.

LEEKS*

Nu 11: 5 melons, l, onions and garlic.

LEFT [LEFT-HANDED, LEFTOVER]

Ge   7:23 Only Noah was l,
    13: 9 If you go to the l,
Ex 12:41 all the LORD's divisions l Egypt.
Nu 26:65 and not one of them was l except
Dt 28:14 to the right or to the l,
Jos 1: 7 from it to the right or to the l,
    23: 6 turning aside to the right or to the l.
Jdg 3: 4 They were l to test the Israelites
2Ki 22: 2 aside to the right or to the l.
Pr   4:27 Do not swerve to the right or the l;
Isa 30:21 turn to the right or to the l,
Mt   6: 3 do not let your l hand know what
    25:33 on his right and the goats on his l.
Mk   8: 8 of broken pieces that were l over.
    10:28 "We have l everything to follow you!
    10:40 to sit at my right or l is not for me
Lk 17:34 one will be taken and the other l.
1Th 4:15 l till the coming of the Lord,
Heb 10:26 no sacrifice for sins is l,
2Pe 2:15 They have l the straight way

LEFT-HANDED* [HAND]

Jdg 3:15 Ehud, a l man,
    20:16 hundred chosen men who were l,
1Ch 12: 2 or to sling stones right-handed or l;

LEFTOVER* [LEFT]

Ru   2: 2 and pick up the l grain

LEGALISTIC*

Php 3: 6 as for l righteousness, faultless.

LEGION [LEGIONS]

Mk   5: 9 "My name is L," he replied,

LEGIONS* [LEGION]

Mt 26:53 more than twelve l of angels?

LEGS

Ps 147:10 nor his delight in the l of a man;
Da   2:33 its l of iron, its feet partly of iron
    10: 6 his arms and l like the gleam
Jn 19:33 they did not break his l.
Rev 10: 1 and his l were like fiery pillars.

LEMUEL*

Pr 31: 1 The sayings of King L—
    31: 4 "It is not for kings, O L—

LEND [LENDER, LENDS, MONEYLENDER]

Lev 25:37 You must not l him money
Dt 15: 8 and freely l him whatever he needs.
    28:12 You will l to many nations
    28:44 but you will not l to him.
Ps 37:26 always generous and l freely;
Eze 18: 8 He does not l at usury
Lk   6:34 Even 'sinners' l to 'sinners,'

LENDER* [LEND]

Pr 22: 7 and the borrower is servant to the l.
Isa 24: 2 for borrower as for l,

LENDS* [LEND]

Ps	15: 5	who l his money without usury
	112: 5	to him who is generous and l freely,
Pr	19:17	He who is kind to the poor l to
Eze	18:13	He l at usury and takes

LENGTH [LONG]

Ge	13:17	through the l and breadth of the land,
Ps	90:10	The l of our days is seventy years—
Pr	10:27	fear of the LORD adds l to life,

LENGTHY* [LONG]

Mk	12:40	and for a show make l prayers.
Lk	20:47	and for a show make l prayers.

LEOPARD

Isa	11: 6	the l will lie down with the goat,
Jer	13:23	change his skin or the l its spots?
Da	7: 6	one that looked like a l.
Rev	13: 2	The beast I saw resembled a l,

LEPROSY [LEPROUS]

Nu	12:10	toward her and saw that she had l;
2Ki	5: 1	but he had l.
	7: 3	Now there were four men with l at
2Ch	26:21	King Uzziah had l until the day
Mt	8: 3	Immediately he was cured of his l.
	11: 5	those who have l are cured,
Lk	4:27	in Israel with l in the time of Elisha
	17:12	ten men who had l met him.

LEPROUS [LEPROSY]

Ex	4: 6	and when he took it out, it was l,

LESS [LEAST]

Ex	30:15	and the poor are not to give l
2Ch	6:18	much l this temple I have built!
	32:15	much l will your god deliver you
Ezr	9:13	you have punished us l than our sins
Jn	3:30	become greater; I must become l.

LESSON

Mk	13:28	"Now learn this l from the fig tree:

LEST

Ps	2:12	Kiss the Son, l he be angry
Pr	31: 5	l they drink and forget what the law
1Co	1:17	l the cross of Christ be emptied

LET

Ge	1: 3	And God said, "L there be light,"
	1: 6	"L there be an expanse between
	1: 9	and l dry ground appear."
	1:11	"L the land produce vegetation:
	1:14	"L there be lights in the expanse of
	1:20	"L the water teem
	1:24	"L the land produce living creatures
	1:26	"L us make man in our image,
	11: 7	l us go down and confuse their
Ex	1:16	but if it is a girl, l her live."
	5: 1	God of Israel, says: 'L my people go,
	5: 2	and I will not l Israel go."
	13:17	When Pharaoh l the people go,
Ps	22: 8	l the LORD rescue him.
	25: 2	Do not l me be put to shame,

	33: 8	L all the earth fear the LORD;
	95: 1	l us sing for joy to the LORD;
	118:24	l us rejoice and be glad in it.
Jer	9:24	l him who boasts boast about this:
La	3:40	and l us return to the LORD.
Joel	3:10	L the weakling say, "I am strong!"
Mt	5:37	Simply l your 'Yes' be 'Yes,'
	27:43	L God rescue him now if he wants
Mk	4: 9	ears to hear, l him hear."
	10: 9	l man not separate."
Jn	7:37	l him come to me and drink.
	14: 1	"Do not l your hearts be troubled.
Ro	3: 4	L God be true, and every man a liar.
2Co	10:17	"L him who boasts boast in the Lord.
Eph	4:26	Do not l the sun go down
Col	3:15	L the peace of Christ rule
	3:16	L the word of Christ dwell
Heb	10:22	l us draw near to God with
Jas	5:12	l your "Yes" be yes,
1Jn	4: 7	Dear friends, l us love one another,
Rev	22:17	Whoever is thirsty, l him come;

LETTER [LETTERS]

Mt	5:18	not the smallest l,
2Co	3: 2	You yourselves are our l,
	3: 6	for the l kills, but the Spirit
2Th	3:14	not obey our instruction in this l,

LETTERS [LETTER]

2Ch	32:17	also wrote l insulting the LORD,
2Co	3: 7	which was engraved in l on stone,
	10:10	"His l are weighty and forceful,
Gal	6:11	See what large l I use as I write
2Th	3:17	the distinguishing mark in all my l.
2Pe	3:16	l contain some things that are hard to

LEVEL

Ps	143:10	good Spirit lead me on l ground.
Pr	4:26	Make l paths for your feet
Isa	26: 7	The path of the righteous is l;
	40: 4	the rough ground shall become l,
	45: 2	before you and will l the mountains;
Jer	31: 9	beside streams of water on a l path
Lk	6:17	with them and stood on a l place.
Heb	12:13	"Make l paths for your feet,"

LEVI [LEVITE, LEVITES, LEVITICAL]

1. Son of Jacob by Leah (Ge 29:34; 46:11; 1Ch 2:1). With Simeon avenged rape of Dinah (Ge 34). Tribe of blessed (Ge 49:5-7; Dt 33:8-11), chosen as priests (Nu 3-4), numbered (Nu 3:39; 26:62), given cities, but not land (Nu 18; 35; Dt 10:9; Jos 13:14; 21), land (Eze 48:8-22), 12,000 from (Rev 7:7).

2. See MATTHEW.

LEVIATHAN*

Job	3: 8	those who are ready to rouse L.
	41: 1	Can you pull in the l with a fishhook
Ps	74:14	was you who crushed the heads of L
	104:26	and the l, which you formed to frolic
Isa	27: 1	L the gliding serpent,
	27: 1	L the coiling serpent;

LEVITE [LEVI]

Nu	3:20	These were the **L** clans,
Dt	26:12	you shall give it to the **L**, the alien,
Jdg	19: 1	Now a **L** who lived in a remote area
Ac	4:36	Joseph, a **L** from Cyprus,

LEVITES [LEVI]

Ex	32:26	And all the **L** rallied to him.
Nu	1:53	The **L**, however, are to set
	1:53	The **L** are to be responsible for
	3:12	The **L** are mine,
	8: 6	"Take the **L** from among the other
	16: 7	You **L** have gone too far!"
	18:21	to the **L** all the tithes in Israel
	35: 7	give the **L** forty-eight towns,
Jos	14: 4	The **L** received no share of the land
1Ch	15: 2	"No one but the **L** may carry the ark
	23: 6	David divided the **L** into groups
2Ch	31: 2	Hezekiah assigned the priests and **L**
Ezr	6:18	and the **L** who were instructing
Ne	8: 9	and the **L** who were instructing
Mal	3: 3	he will purify the **L**

PRIESTS AND LEVITES See PRIESTS

LEVITICAL [LEVI]

Heb	7:11	attained through the **L** priesthood

LEWD [LEWDNESS]

Jdg	20: 6	because they committed this **l**

LEWDNESS [LEWD]

Eze	16:58	bear the consequences of your **l**
	23:48	I will put an end to **l** in the land,
Mk	7:22	malice, deceit, **l**, envy, slander,

LIAR* [LIE]

Dt	19:18	and if the witness proves to be a **l**,
Job	34: 6	I am right, I am considered a **l**;
Pr	17: 4	**l** pays attention to a malicious tongue
	19:22	better to be poor than a **l**,
	30: 6	rebuke you and prove you a **l**.
Mic	2:11	If a **l** and deceiver comes and says,
Jn	8:44	for he is a **l** and the father of lies.
	8:55	I would be a **l** like you,
Ro	3: 4	Let God be true, and every man a **l**.
1Jn	1:10	we make him out to be a **l**
	2: 4	does not do what he commands is a **l**,
	2:22	Who is the **l**?
	4:20	yet hates his brother, he is a **l**,
	5:10	made him out to be a **l**,

LIARS* [LIE]

Ps	63:11	the mouths of **l** will be silenced.
	116:11	in my dismay I said, "All men are **l**."
Isa	57: 4	the offspring of **l**?
Mic	6:12	rich men are violent; her people are **l**
1Ti	1:10	slave traders and **l** and perjurers—
	4: 2	come through hypocritical **l**,
Tit	1:12	"Cretans are always **l**, evil brutes,
Rev	3: 9	though they are not, but are **l**—
	21: 8	the idolaters and all **l**—

LIBATIONS*

Ps	16: 4	I will not pour out their **l** of blood

LIBERAL* [LIBERALLY]

2Co	8:20	of the way we administer this **l** gift.

LIBERALLY* [LIBERAL]

Dt	15:14	Supply him **l** from your flock,

LIBERATED* [LIBERTY]

Ro	8:21	be **l** from its bondage to decay

LIBERTY* [LIBERATED]

Lev	25:10	and proclaim **l** throughout the land

LICE (KJV) See GNATS

LICENSE*

Jude	1: 4	of our God into a **l** for immorality

LICK

Ps	72: 9	and his enemies will **l** the dust.
Isa	49:23	they will **l** the dust at your feet.
Mic	7:17	They will **l** dust like a snake,

LIE [LIAR, LIARS, LIED, LIES, LYING]

Lev	18:22	" 'Do not **l** with a man as one lies
	19:11	" 'Do not **l**.
Nu	23:19	God is not a man, that he should **l**,
Dt	6: 7	when you **l** down and
	11:19	when you **l** down and
Ru	3: 4	go and uncover his feet and **l** down.
1Sa	15:29	who is the Glory of Israel does not **l**
Ps	4: 8	I will **l** down and sleep in peace,
	23: 2	makes me **l** down in green pastures,
	89:35	and I will not **l** to David—
Pr	3:24	you **l** down, you will not be afraid;
Isa	11: 6	leopard will **l** down with the goat,
	28:15	for we have made a **l** our refuge
Jer	9: 5	They have taught their tongues to **l**;
	23:14	They commit adultery and live a **l**.
Eze	13: 6	and their divinations a **l**.
	34:14	There they will **l** down in good
Zep	3:13	They will eat and **l** down
Ro	1:25	exchanged the truth of God for a **l**,
Col	3: 9	Do not **l** to each other,
2Th	2:11	so that they will believe the **l**
Tit	1: 2	which God, who does not **l**,
Heb	6:18	in which it is impossible for God to **l**,
1Jn	1: 6	we **l** and do not live by the truth.
	2:21	because no **l** comes from the truth.
Rev	14: 5	No **l** was found in their mouths;

LIED [LIE]

Ge	18:15	Sarah was afraid, so she **l** and said,
Jer	5:12	They have **l** about the LORD;
Ac	5: 4	You have not **l** to men but to God."

LIES [LIE]

Lev	6: 3	if he finds lost property and **l**
	20:13	" 'If a man **l** with a man as one **l** with a woman,
Ps	5: 6	You destroy those who tell **l**;
	10: 7	His mouth is full of curses and **l**
	12: 2	Everyone **l** to his neighbor;
	34:13	and your lips from speaking **l**.
	58: 3	they are wayward and speak **l**.

144: 8 whose mouths are full of l,
Pr   6:19 a false witness who pours out l and
     12:17 but a false witness tells l.
     19: 5 he who pours out l will not go free.
     19: 9 and he who pours out l will perish.
     29:12 If a ruler listens to l,
     30: 8 Keep falsehood and l far from me;
Isa 59: 3 Your lips have spoken l,
Jer   5:31 The prophets prophesy l,
      9: 3 their tongue like a bow, to shoot l;
     14:14 "The prophets are prophesying l
La   1: 1 How deserted l the city,
Eze 13:22 the righteous with your l,
Hos 11:12 Ephraim has surrounded me with l,
Na   3: 1 Woe to the city of blood, full of l,
Hab   2:18 Or an image that teaches l?
Jn   8:44 for he is a liar and the father of l.

LIFE [LIVE]

Ge   1:30 that has the breath of l in it—
      2: 7 into his nostrils the breath of l,
      2: 9 of the garden were the tree of l
      6:17 to destroy all l under the heavens,
      9: 5 for the l of his fellow man.
      9:11 Never again will all l be cut off by
Ex   21: 6 Then he will be his servant for l.
     21:23 you are to take l for l,
     23:26 I will give you a full l span.
Lev 17:14 the l of every creature is its blood.
     24:17 " 'If anyone takes the l of a human
     24:18 who takes the l of someone's animal
Nu   35:31 " 'Do not accept a ransom for the l
Dt   4:42 one of these cities and save his l.
     12:23 because the blood is the l,
     19:21 Show no pity: l for l, eye for eye,
     30:15 before you today l and prosperity,
     30:19 Now choose l, so that you
     30:20 For the LORD is your l,
     32:39 I put to death and I bring to l,
     32:47 idle words for you—they are your l.
1Sa 19: 5 He took his l in his hands
Ne   9: 6 You give l to everything,
Job   2: 4 will give all he has for his own l.
      2: 6 but you must spare his l."
     10: 1 "I loathe my very l;
     33: 4 breath of the Almighty gives me l.
     33:30 that the light of l may shine on him.
     42:12 LORD blessed the latter part of Job's l
Ps   16:11 made known to me the path of l;
     17:14 whose reward is in this l.
     23: 6 follow me all the days of my l,
     27: 1 LORD is the stronghold of my l—
     34:12 Whoever of you loves l and desires
     36: 9 For with you is the fountain of l;
     39: 5 Each man's l is but a breath.
     41: 2 protect him and preserve his l;
     49: 7 No man can redeem the l of another
     49: 8 the ransom for a l is costly,
     63: 3 Because your love is better than l,
     69:28 be blotted out of the book of l
     91:16 With long l will I satisfy him
    104:33 I will sing to the LORD all my l;
    119:25 preserve my l according to your
Pr   1: 3 acquiring a disciplined and prudent l,

      3: 2 they will prolong your l many years
      3:16 Long l is in her right hand;
      3:18 She is a tree of l to those who
      4:23 for it is the wellspring of l.
      6:23 of discipline are the way to l,
      6:26 adulteress preys upon your very l.
      7:23 little knowing it will cost him his l.
      8:35 For whoever finds me finds l
     10:11 of the righteous is a fountain of l,
     10:27 fear of the LORD adds length to l,
     11:30 fruit of the righteous is a tree of l,
     13: 3 He who guards his lips guards his l,
     13:12 but a longing fulfilled is a tree of l.
     13:14 of the wise is a fountain of l,
     14:27 fear of the LORD is a fountain of l,
     15: 4 that brings healing is a tree of l,
     16:22 Understanding is a fountain of l
     18:21 The tongue has the power of l
     19: 3 A man's own folly ruins his l,
     19:23 The fear of the LORD leads to l:
     21:21 righteousness and love finds l,
Ecc   2:17 So I hated l,
      7:12 that wisdom preserves the l
      9: 9 Enjoy l with your wife,
     10:19 and wine makes l merry,
Isa 53:10 LORD makes his l a guilt offering,
     53:11 see the light [of l] and be satisfied;
     53:12 he poured out his l unto death,
Jer 10:23 that a man's l is not his own;
La   3:58 you redeemed my l.
Eze 18:27 he will save his l.
     37: 5 and you will come to l.
Da   12: 2 to everlasting l, others to shame
Jnh   2: 6 you brought my l up from the pit,
Mal   2: 5 a covenant of l and peace,
Mt   6:25 do not worry about your l,
      7:14 and narrow the road that leads to l,
     10:39 Whoever finds his l will lose it,
     16:21 and on the third day be raised to l.
     16:25 but whoever loses his l for me
     18: 8 to enter l maimed or crippled than
     19:16 must I do to get eternal l?"
     19:29 as much and will inherit eternal l.
     20:28 to give his l as a ransom for many."
     25:46 but the righteous to eternal l."
Mk   3: 4 to save l or to kill?"
      8:35 wants to save his l will lose it,
      9:43 for you to enter l maimed than
     10:17 must I do to inherit eternal l?"
     10:30 and in the age to come, eternal l.
     10:45 to give his l as a ransom for many."
Lk   6: 9 to save l or to destroy it?"
      9:22 and on the third day be raised to l."
      9:24 loses his l for me will save it.
     12:15 a man's l does not consist in
     12:22 do not worry about your l,
     12:25 can add a single hour to his l?
     14:26 even his own l—
     17:33 whoever loses his l will preserve it.
     21:19 By standing firm you will gain l.
Jn   1: 4 In him was l, and that l was the ligh
      3:15 believes in him may have eternal l.
      3:36 believes in the Son has eternal l,
      3:36 rejects the Son will not see l,

4:14 of water welling up to eternal l."
5:21 raises the dead and gives them l,
5:24 he has crossed over from death to l.
5:26 For as the Father has l in himself,
5:39 that by them you possess eternal l.
5:40 you refuse to come to me to have l.
6:27 for food that endures to eternal l,
6:33 comes down from heaven and gives l
6:35 Jesus declared, "I am the bread of l.
6:40 believes in him shall have eternal l,
6:47 he who believes has everlasting l.
6:48 I am the bread of l.
6:51 which I will give for the l of
6:53 you have no l in you.
6:63 The Spirit gives l;
6:68 You have the words of eternal l.
8:12 but will have the light of l."
10:10 that they may have l,
10:11 The good shepherd lays down his l
10:15 and I lay down my l for the sheep.
10:28 I give them eternal l,
11:25 "I am the resurrection and the l.
12:25 man who loves his l will lose it,
12:50 that his command leads to eternal l.
13:37 I will lay down my l for you."
14: 6 the way and the truth and the l.
15:13 he lay down his l for his friends.
17: 2 that he might give eternal l
17: 3 Now this is eternal l:
20:31 that by believing you may have l
Ac   2:28 made known to me the paths of l;
2:32 God has raised this Jesus to l,
3:15 You killed the author of l,
11:18 even the Gentiles repentance unto l."
13:48 appointed for eternal l believed.
Ro   2: 7 he will give eternal l.
4:25 raised to l for our justification.
5:10 shall we be saved through his l!
5:18 justification that brings l
5:21 righteousness to bring eternal l
6: 4 we too may live a new l.
6:13 have been brought from death to l;
6:22 and the result is eternal l
6:23 but the gift of God is eternal l
7:10 to bring l actually brought death.
8: 2 the law of the Spirit of l set me free
8: 6 controlled by the Spirit is l and peace
8:11 also give l to your mortal bodies
8:38 that neither death nor l,
1Co 15:19 for this l we have hope in Christ,
15:36 What you sow does not come to l
2Co 2:16 the fragrance of l.
3: 6 but the Spirit gives l.
4:10 the l of Jesus may also be revealed
5: 4 mortal may be swallowed up by l.
Gal 2:20 The l I live in the body,
3:21 had been given that could impart l,
6: 8 from the Spirit will reap eternal l.
Eph 4: 1 I urge you to live a l worthy of
6: 3 and that you may enjoy long l on
Php 2:16 as you hold out the word of l—
4: 3 whose names are in the book of l.
Col 1:10 that you may live a l worthy of
3: 3 your l is now hidden with Christ

1Th 4:12 that your daily l may win
1Ti 1:16 believe on him and receive eternal l.
4: 8 holding promise for both the present
l and the l to come.
4:12 in l, in love, in faith and in purity.
4:16 Watch your l and doctrine closely.
6:12 Take hold of the eternal l
6:19 may take hold of the l that is truly l.
2Ti 1: 9 and called us to a holy l—
1:10 and has brought l and immortality
3:12 to live a godly l in Christ Jesus will
Tit 1: 2 resting on the hope of eternal l,
3: 7 having the hope of eternal l.
Heb 7:16 of the power of an indestructible l.
Jas 1:12 the crown of l that God
3:13 Let him show it by his good l,
1Pe 3: 7 with you of the gracious gift of l,
3:10 "Whoever would love l
4: 2 not live the rest of his earthly l
2Pe 1: 3 everything we need for l and
1Jn 1: 1 proclaim concerning the Word of l.
2:25 what he promised us—even eternal l.
3:14 we have passed from death to l,
3:16 Jesus Christ laid down his l for us.
5:11 God has given us eternal l,
5:11 and this l is in his Son.
5:20 He is the true God and eternal l.
Jude 1:21 to bring you to eternal l.
Rev 2: 7 the right to eat from the tree of l,
2: 8 who died and came to l again.
2:10 and I will give you the crown of l.
3: 5 his name from the book of l,
11:11 a breath of l from God entered them,
13: 8 the book of l belonging to the Lamb
17: 8 not been written in the book of l
20: 4 came to l and reigned with Christ
20:12 which is the book of l.
20:15 not found written in the book of l,
21: 6 from the spring of the water of l.
21:27 written in the Lamb's book of l.
22: 1 of the water of l, as clear as crystal,
22: 2 side of the river stood the tree of l,
22:14 may have the right to the tree of l
22:17 take the free gift of the water of l.
22:19 his share in the tree of l

ETERNAL LIFE Mt 19:16, 29; 25:46; Mk
10:17, 30; Lk 10:25; 18:18, 30; Jn 3:15, 16, 36;
4:14, 36; 5:24, 39; 6:27, 40, 54, 68; 10:28; 12:25,
50; 17:2, 3; Ac 13:46, 48; Ro 2:7; 5:21; 6:22, 23;
Gal 6:8; 1Ti 1:16; 6:12; Tit 1:2; 3:7; 1Jn 1:2;
2:25; 3:15; 5:11, 13, 20; Jude 1:21

LIFE'S* [LIVE]

Ps 39: 4 my l end and the number of my days;
Lk   8:14 they are choked by l worries,

LIFE-GIVING* [GIVE]

Pr 15:31 He who listens to a l rebuke will be
1Co 15:45 the last Adam, a l spirit.

LIFEBLOOD [BLOOD]

Ge   9: 4 not eat meat that has its l still in it.

LIFELESS [LIVE]

Ps 106:28 and ate sacrifices offered to l gods;
Jer 16:18 with the l forms of their vile images
Hab 2:19 Or to l stone, 'Wake up!'

LIFETIME [LIVE]

1Ki 3:13 in your l you will have no equal
Ps 30: 5 but his favor lasts a l;
Lk 16:25 in your l you received your good

LIFT [LIFTED, LIFTING, LIFTS, UPLIFTED]

Ge 13:14 "**L** up your eyes from where you are
Dt 32:40 I I my hand to heaven and declare:
Ps 3: 3 glory on me and I up my head.
24: 7 L up your heads, O you gates;
25: 1 To you, O Lᴏʀᴅ, I l up my soul;
28: 2 as I I up my hands
63: 4 in your name I will l up my hands.
91:12 they will l you up in their hands,
121: 1 I I up my eyes to the hills—
123: 1 I l up my eyes to you,
134: 2 L up your hands in the sanctuary
143: 8 for to you I I up my soul.
Isa 40: 9 l up your voice with a shout,
La 2:19 L up your hands to him for the lives
3:41 Let us l up our hearts and our hands
Mt 4: 6 they will l you up in their hands,
Lk 11:46 will not l one finger to help them.
21:28 stand up and l up your heads,
1Ti 2: 8 to l up holy hands in prayer,
Jas 4:10 and he will l you up.
1Pe 5: 6 that he may l you up in due time.

LIFTED [LIFT]

Ex 17:16 "For hands were l up to the throne
Nu 9:21 whenever the cloud l, they set out.
1Sa 2: 1 in the Lᴏʀᴅ my horn is l high.
Ne 8: 6 and all the people l their hands
Ps 30: 1 for you l me out of the depths
40: 2 He l me out of the slimy pit,
41: 9 has l up his heel against me.
93: 3 The seas have l up, O Lᴏʀᴅ,
112: 9 be l high in honor.
118:16 The Lᴏʀᴅ's right hand is l high;
Isa 52:13 he will be raised and l up
63: 9 he redeemed them; he l them up
Eze 3:12 Then the Spirit l me up,
8: 3 The Spirit l me up between earth
11: 1 the Spirit l me up and brought me
Mt 11:23 will you be l up to the skies?
Lk 24:50 he l up his hands and blessed them.
Jn 3:14 so the Son of Man must be l up,
8:28 "When you have l up the Son
12:32 when I am l up from the earth,
12:34 'The Son of Man must be l up'?
13:18 'He who shares my bread has l

LIFTING [LIFT]

Ps 141: 2 may the l up of my hands

LIFTS [LIFT]

1Sa 2: 8 and l the needy from the ash heap;

Ps 113: 7 and l the needy from the ash heap;
145:14 and l up all who are bowed down.

LIGAMENT* [LIGAMENTS]

Eph 4:16 held together by every supporting l,

LIGAMENTS* [LIGAMENT]

Col 2:19 held together by its l and sinews,

LIGHT [DAYLIGHT, ENLIGHTEN, ENLIGHTENED, LIGHTEN, LIGHTENED, LIGHTS, TWILIGHT]

Ge 1: 3 And God said, "Let there be l,"
1: 5 God called the l "day,"
1:16 the greater l to govern the day and
Ex 13:21 in a pillar of fire to give them l,
25:37 so that they l the space
Dt 25:13 in your bag—one heavy, one l.
2Sa 22:29 the Lᴏʀᴅ turns my darkness into l.
Ezr 9: 8 and so our God gives l to our eyes
Job 3:20 "Why is l given to those in misery,
38:19 "What is the way to the abode of l?
Ps 4: 6 Let the l of your face shine upon us,
18:28 my God turns my darkness into l.
19: 8 giving l to the eyes.
27: 1 Lᴏʀᴅ is my l and my salvation—
36: 9 in your l we see l.
56:13 that I may walk before God in the l
76: 4 You are resplendent with l,
89:15 who walk in the l of your presence,
104: 2 He wraps himself in l as with
119:105 to my feet and a l for my path.
119:130 unfolding of your words gives l;
139:12 for darkness is as l to you.
Pr 4:18 shining ever brighter till the full l
13: 9 l of the righteous shines brightly,
Ecc 2:13 just as l is better than darkness.
Isa 2: 5 let us walk in the l of the Lᴏʀᴅ.
9: 2 in darkness have seen a great l;
42: 6 and a l for the Gentiles.
45: 7 I form the l and create darkness,
49: 6 also make you a l for the Gentiles,
53:11 see the l [of life] and be satisfied;
58:10 then your l will rise in the darkness,
60: 1 "Arise, shine, for your l has come,
60:19 Lᴏʀᴅ will be your everlasting l,
Eze 1:27 and brilliant l surrounded him.
Am 5:18 That day will be darkness, not l.
Mic 7: 8 the Lᴏʀᴅ will be my l.
Zec 14: 6 On that day there will be no l,
Mt 4:16 in darkness have seen a great l;
5:14 "You are the l of the world.
5:16 let your l shine before men,
6:22 your whole body will be full of l.
11:30 my yoke is easy and my burden is l."
17: 2 as white as the l.
24:29 and the moon will not give its l;
Mk 13:24 and the moon will not give its l;
Lk 2:32 a l for revelation to the Gentiles and
8:16 those who come in can see the l.
11:33 those who come in may see the l.
Jn 1: 4 and that life was the l of men.
1: 5 The l shines in the darkness,

	1: 7	to testify concerning that **l,**
	1: 9	The true **l** that gives **l** to every man
	3:19	but men loved darkness instead of **l**
	3:20	Everyone who does evil hates the **l,**
	5:35	you chose for a time to enjoy his **l.**
	8:12	he said, "I am the **l** of the world.
	8:12	but will have the **l** of life."
	9: 5	I am the **l** of the world."
	12:35	Walk while you have the **l,**
	12:46	I have come into the world as a **l,**
Ac	9: 3	suddenly a **l** from heaven flashed
	13:47	I have made you a **l** for the Gentiles.
Ro	13:12	and put on the armor of **l.**
1Co	3:13	because the Day will bring it to **l.**
2Co	4: 6	"Let **l** shine out of darkness,"
	4:17	For our **l** and momentary troubles
	6:14	Or what fellowship can **l** have
	11:14	masquerades as an angel of **l.**
Eph	5: 8	but now you are **l** in the Lord.
	5: 9	fruit of the **l** consists in all goodness,
Col	1:12	of the saints in the kingdom of **l.**
1Th	5: 5	You are all sons of the **l** and sons of
1Ti	6:16	and who lives in unapproachable **l,**
Heb	12: 5	not make **l** of the Lord's discipline,
1Pe	2: 9	out of darkness into his wonderful **l.**
2Pe	1:19	as to a **l** shining in a dark place,
1Jn	1: 5	declare to you: God is **l;**
	1: 7	if we walk in the **l,** as he is in the **l,**
	2: 8	and the true **l** is already shining.
	2: 9	Anyone who claims to be in the **l**
Rev	8:12	A third of the day was without **l,**
	21:23	for the glory of God gives it **l,**
	22: 5	will not need the **l** of a lamp or the **l**

LIGHTEN [LIGHT]

2Ch	10: 9	'L the yoke your father put on us'?"
Jnh	1: 5	the cargo from the sea to **l** the ship.

LIGHTENED* [LIGHT]

Ac	27:38	they **l** the ship by throwing the grain

LIGHTNING

Ex	9:23	and **l** flashed down to the ground.
	19:16	there was thunder and **l,**
	20:18	the people saw the thunder and **l**
2Sa	22:15	bolts of **l** and routed them.
Job	37:15	the clouds and makes his **l** flash?
Ps	18:12	with hailstones and bolts of **l.**
	97: 4	His **l** lights up the world;
Jer	10:13	He sends **l** with the rain
Eze	1:13	and **l** flashed out of it.
Da	10: 6	his face like **l,**
Mt	24:27	For as **l** that comes from the east
	28: 3	His appearance was like **l,**
Lk	9:29	became as bright as a flash of **l.**
	10:18	"I saw Satan fall like **l** from heaven.
Rev	4: 5	From the throne came flashes of **l,**
	8: 5	flashes of **l** and an earthquake.
	11:19	And there came flashes of **l,**
	16:18	Then there came flashes of **l,**

LIGHTS [LIGHT]

Ge	1:14	"Let there be **l** in the expanse of
	1:16	God made two great **l**—

Ps	136: 7	who made the great **l**—
Lk	8:16	"No one **l** a lamp and hides it in
Jas	1:17	from the Father of the heavenly **l,**

LIKE [LIKE-MINDED, LIKENESS]

Ge	3: 5	and you will be **l** God,
	3:22	man has now become **l** one of us,
	13:16	I will make your offspring **l** the dust
	28:14	Your descendants will be **l** the dust
Ex	7: 1	I have made you **l** God to Pharaoh,
	8:10	there is no one **l** the LORD our God.
	15:11	"Who among the gods is **l** you,
	24:17	the glory of the LORD looked **l**
	34: 1	two stone tablets **l** the first ones,
Nu	11: 7	The manna was **l** coriander seed and looked **l** resin.
	13:33	We seemed **l** grasshoppers
Dt	8:20	**L** the nations the LORD destroyed
	18:15	will raise up for you a prophet **l** me
	32:31	For their rock is not **l** our Rock,
	33:29	Who is **l** you,
1Sa	2: 2	"There is no one holy **l** the LORD;
	25:25	He is just **l** his name—
2Sa	7:22	There is no one **l** you,
1Ki	8:23	there is no God **l** you in heaven
	14: 8	not been **l** my servant David,
	21:25	(There was never a man **l** Ahab,
1Ch	17:21	And who is **l** your people Israel—
Job	1: 8	There is no one on earth **l** him;
	9:32	"He is not a man **l** me
	40: 9	Do you have an arm **l** God's,
Ps	1: 3	He is **l** a tree planted by streams
	1: 4	They are **l** chaff that
	18:33	He makes my feet **l** the feet of
	22:14	I am poured out **l** water,
	35:10	"Who is **l** you, O LORD?
	48:10	**L** your name, O God,
	86: 8	Among the gods there is none **l**
	103:15	As for man, his days are **l** grass,
	113: 5	Who is **l** the LORD our God,
	114: 4	the mountains skipped **l** rams,
	144: 4	Man is **l** a breath; his days are **l** a fleeting shadow.
Pr	7:22	**l** a deer stepping into a noose
	11:22	**L** a gold ring in a pig's snout is
	25:11	A word aptly spoken is **l** apples
Ecc	2:16	For the wise man, **l** the fool,
	12:11	The words of the wise are **l** goads,
SS	2: 2	**L** a lily among thorns is my darling
	8: 6	Place me **l** a seal over your heart,
Isa	1: 9	we would have become **l** Sodom,
	1:18	"Though your sins are **l** scarlet,
	11: 7	and the lion will eat straw **l** the ox.
	40: 6	"All men are **l** grass,
	46: 9	and there is none **l** me.
	53: 2	and **l** a root out of dry ground.
	53: 6	We all, **l** sheep, have gone astray,
	64: 6	all our righteous acts are **l** filthy rags;
Jer	10: 6	No one is **l** you, O LORD;
	23:29	"Is not my word **l** fire,"
La	1:12	Is any suffering **l** my suffering
	2: 5	The Lord is **l** an enemy;
Eze	1: 4	of the fire looked **l** glowing metal,
	1:10	Their faces looked **l** this:

	1:26	throne was a figure I that of a man.
	8: 2	and I saw a figure I that of a man.
Da	3:25	the fourth looks I a son of the gods."
	7: 4	"The first was I a lion,
	7:13	before me was one I a son of man,
	10: 6	his face I lightning,
Hos	1:10	"Yet the Israelites will be I the sand
	6: 4	Your love is I the morning mist,
	14: 5	I will be I the dew to Israel;
Mic	7:18	Who is a God I you,
Na	1: 6	His wrath is poured out I fire;
Zec	1: 4	Do not be I your forefathers,
	13: 9	I will refine them I silver and test them I gold.
Mt	9:36	I sheep without a shepherd.
	10:16	you out I sheep among wolves.
Lk	6:48	He is I a man building a house,
	13:18	"What is the kingdom of God I?
	22:26	one who rules I the one who serves.
Ac	3:22	raise up for you a prophet I me
Ro	5:15	But the gift is not I the trespass.
	9:29	we would have become I Sodom,
1Co	9:20	To the Jews I became I a Jew,
	13:11	I was a child, I talked I a child,
1Pe	1:24	For, "All men are I grass,
2Pe	3: 8	and a thousand years are I a day.
	3:10	day of the Lord will come I a thief.
Rev	1:13	someone "I a son of man,"
	2:18	whose eyes are I blazing fire
	3: 3	I will come I a thief,
	4: 7	The first living creature was I
	10: 1	his face I the sun,
	13: 4	"Who is I the beast?
	16:15	"Behold, I come I a thief!
	19:12	His eyes are I blazing fire,

LIKE-MINDED* [LIKE, MIND]

Php 2: 2 make my joy complete by being I,

LIKENESS [LIKE]

Ge	1:26	man in our image, in our I,
	5: 1	he made him in the I of God.
Ps	17:15	be satisfied with seeing your I.
Isa	52:14	his form marred beyond human I—
Ro	8: 3	by sending his own Son in the I
	8:29	predestined to be conformed to the I
1Co	15:49	bear the I of the man from heaven.
2Co	3:18	are being transformed into his I
Php	2: 7	being made in human I.
Jas	3: 9	who have been made in God's I.

LILIES [LILY]

1Ki	7:22	capitals on top were in the shape of I.
SS	2:16	he browses among the I.
Lk	12:27	"Consider how the I grow.

LILY [LILIES]

2Ch	4: 5	like a I blossom.
SS	2: 1	a I of the valleys.
	2: 2	Like a I among thorns is my darling
Hos	14: 5	he will blossom like a I.

LIMIT [LIMITS]

Job 15: 8 Do you I wisdom to yourself?

Ps	147: 5	his understanding has no I.
Jer	5:28	Their evil deeds have no I;
Jn	3:34	for God gives the Spirit without I.

LIMITS [LIMIT]

Ex	19:23	'Put I around the mountain
Job	11: 7	you probe the I of the Almighty?
2Co	10:13	will not boast beyond proper I,

LIMP

Isa	13: 7	Because of this, all hands will go I,
Zep	3:16	not let your hands hang I.

LINE

Ge	19:32	our family I through our father."
Dt	25: 9	not build up his brother's family I."
Ru	4: 4	and I am next in I."
Ps	89:29	I will establish his I forever,
Isa	28:17	I will make justice the measuring I
Jer	33:15	Branch sprout from David's I;
Mt	17:27	go to the lake and throw out your I.
Lk	2: 4	belonged to the house and I of David.

LINEN

Ex	26: 1	with ten curtains of finely twisted I
	28:39	"Weave the tunic of fine I
Lev	16: 4	He is to put on the sacred I tunic,
Pr	31:22	she is clothed in fine I and purple.
	31:24	She makes I garments
Jer	13: 1	"Go and buy a I belt and put it
Eze	9: 2	a man clothed in I who had a writing
Da	10: 5	before me was a man dressed in I,
Mk	15:46	wrapped it in the I,
Jn	20: 6	He saw the strips of I lying there,
Rev	15: 6	shining I and wore golden sashes
	19: 8	(Fine I stands for the righteous acts

LINGER

Pr	23:30	Those who I over wine,
Hab	2: 3	Though it I, wait for it;

LINTEL (KJV) See TOP

LION [LION'S, LIONS, LIONS']

Ge	49: 9	Like a I he crouches and lies down,
Jdg	14: 5	so that he tore the I apart
1Sa	17:34	a I or a bear came and carried off
Ps	91:13	You will tread upon the I and
Ecc	9: 4	live dog is better off than a dead I!
Isa	11: 7	and the I will eat straw like the ox.
	65:25	and the I will eat straw like the ox,
Jer	4: 7	A I has come out of his lair.
	25:38	Like a I he will leave his lair,
Eze	1:10	each had the face of a I,
	10:14	the third the face of a I,
Da	7: 4	"The first was like a I,
Hos	13: 7	So I will come upon them like a I,
1Pe	5: 8	devil prowls around like a roaring I
Rev	4: 7	The first living creature was like a I,
	5: 5	See, the L of the tribe of Judah,
	13: 2	and a mouth like that of a I.

LION'S [LION]

Ge	49: 9	You are a I cub, O Judah;
2Ti	4:17	I was delivered from the I mouth.

LIONS [LION]

Ps 22:21 Rescue me from the mouth of the **l**;
Da 6:20 to rescue you from the **l**?"

LIONS' [LION]

Da 6: 7 shall be thrown into the **l** den.
Na 2:11 Where now is the **l** den,

LIPS

Ex 6:12 since I speak with faltering **l**?"
Dt 23:23 Whatever your **l** utter you must
Ps 8: 2 From the **l** of children and infants
   34: 1 his praise will always be on my **l**.
   40: 9 I do not seal my **l**,
   63: 3 my **l** will glorify you.
  119:171 May my **l** overflow with praise,
   140: 3 the poison of vipers is on their **l**.
   141: 3 keep watch over the door of my **l**.
Pr 5: 3 the **l** of an adulteress drip honey,
   10:13 Wisdom is found on the **l** of
   10:18 who conceals his hatred has lying **l**,
   10:21 **l** of the righteous nourish many,
   10:32 **l** of the righteous know what is
   12:22 The LORD detests lying **l**,
   13: 3 He who guards his **l** guards his life,
   14: 7 not find knowledge on his **l**.
   15: 7 **l** of the wise spread knowledge;
   24:26 honest answer is like a kiss on the **l**.
   26:23 are fervent **l** with an evil heart.
   27: 2 and not your own **l**.
Ecc 10:12 a fool is consumed by his own **l**.
SS 4:11 Your **l** drop sweetness as
Isa 6: 5 For I am a man of unclean **l**,
   28:11 with foreign **l** and strange tongues
   29:13 and honor me with their **l**,
Jer 12: 2 on their **l** but far from their hearts.
Hos 14: 2 that we may offer the fruit of our **l**.
Mal 2: 7 "For the **l** of a priest ought
Mt 15: 8 'These people honor me with their **l**,
   21:16 " 'From the **l** of children and infants
Lk 4:22 gracious words that came from his **l**.
Ro 3:13 "The poison of vipers is on their **l**."
1Co 14:21 for of foreigners I will speak
Col 3: 8 and filthy language from your **l**.
Heb 13:15 the fruit of **l** that confess his name.
1Pe 3:10 and his **l** from deceitful speech.

LIQUOR (KJV) See JUICE, WINE

LIST [LISTED]

1Ch 11:11 this is the **l** of David's mighty men:
   27: 1 This is the **l** of the Israelites—
Ezr 2: 2 The **l** of the men of the people
Ne 7: 7 The **l** of the men of Israel:
Ps 56: 8 **l** my tears on your scroll—
1Ti 5: 9 on the **l** of widows unless she is

LISTED [LIST]

Nu 1:18 were **l** by name, one by one,

LISTEN [LISTENED, LISTENING, LISTENS]

Ex 4: 1 "What if they do not believe me or **l**
   6:30 why would Pharaoh **l** to me?"

   7:13 and he would not **l** to them,
   15:26 "If you **l** carefully to the voice of
   23:22 If you **l** carefully to what he says
Lev 26:14 " 'But if you will not **l** to me
Dt 18:15 You must **l** to him.
   30:20 to his voice, and hold fast to him.
1Ki 4:34 came to **l** to Solomon's wisdom,
2Ki 17:40 They would not **l**, however,
   21: 9 But the people did not **l**.
Ps 5: 2 **L** to my cry for help,
   34:11 Come, my children, **l** to me;
   55: 1 **L** to my prayer, O God,
  143: 1 **l** to my cry for mercy;
Pr 1: 5 the wise **l** and add to their learning,
   4: 1 **L**, my sons, to a father's instruction;
   8:33 **L** to my instruction and be wise;
   13: 1 but a mocker does not **l** to rebuke.
Ecc 5: 1 Go near to **l** rather than to offer
Isa 44: 1 "But now **l**, O Jacob, my servant,
Jer 7:24 But they did not **l** or pay attention,
Eze 2: 5 And whether they **l** or fail to **l**—
Zec 7:13 " 'When I called, they did not **l**;
Mt 12:42 the earth to **l** to Solomon's wisdom,
Mk 9: 7 **L** to him!"
Jn 10:27 My sheep **l** to my voice;
Ac 3:22 you must **l** to everything he tells you.
Jas 1:19 Everyone should be quick to **l**,
   1:22 Do not merely **l** to the word,
1Jn 4: 6 not from God does not **l** to us.

LISTENED [LISTEN]

Ge 3:17 you **l** to your wife and ate from the
   30:17 God **l** to Leah,
   30:22 Then God remembered Rachel; he **l**
Nu 21: 3 The LORD **l** to Israel's plea
Dt 9:19 But again the LORD **l** to me.
   10:10 the LORD **l** to me at this time also.
   34: 9 the Israelites **l** to him and did what
Ne 8: 3 the people **l** attentively to the Book
Isa 66: 4 when I spoke, no one **l**.
Da 9: 6 not **l** to your servants the prophets,

LISTENING [LISTEN]

1Sa 3:10 "Speak, for your servant is **l**."
Pr 18:13 He who answers before **l**—
Lk 10:39 at the Lord's feet **l** to what he said.

LISTENS [LISTEN]

Pr 1:33 whoever **l** to me will live in safety
   8:34 Blessed is the man who **l** to me,
   12:15 but a wise man **l** to advice.
   17: 4 A wicked man **l** to evil lips;
Lk 10:16 "He who **l** to you **l** to me;
Jn 6:45 Everyone who **l** to the Father
   18:37 on the side of truth **l** to me."
1Jn 4: 6 and whoever knows God **l** to us;

LITTLE

Ex 16:18 who gathered **l** did not have too **l**.
   23:30 **L** by **l** I will drive them out
1Ki 17:12 and a **l** oil in a jug.
2Ki 4: 2 she said, "except a **l** oil."
Ps 8: 5 a **l** lower than the heavenly beings
Pr 6:10 A **l** sleep, a **l** slumber,

	13:11	gathers money I by I makes it grow.
	15:16	Better a I with the fear of the LORD
	16: 8	Better a I with righteousness
Ecc	10: 1	so a I folly outweighs wisdom
Isa	11: 6	and a I child will lead them.
Mt	6:30	O you of I faith?
	8:26	He replied, "You of I faith,
	14:31	"You of I faith," he said,
	16: 8	Jesus asked, "You of I faith,
	17:20	"Because you have so I faith.
	19:14	"Let the I children come to me,
Mk	9:37	welcomes one of these I children
Lk	7:47	he who has been forgiven I loves I."
	18:17	the kingdom of God like a I child
1Co	5: 6	a I yeast works through the whole
2Co	8:15	who gathered I did not have too I."
Gal	5: 9	"A I yeast works through the whole
1Ti	5:23	a I wine because of your stomach
Heb	2: 7	a I lower than the angels;
Rev	3: 8	I know that you have I strength,
	10: 2	He was holding a I scroll,

LIVE [ALIVE, LIFE, LIFE'S, LIFELESS, LIFETIME, LIVED, LIVES, LIVING]

Ge	3:22	and eat, and I forever."
	12:12	they will kill me but will let you I.
Ex	1:16	if it is a girl, let her I."
	20:12	so that you may I long in the land
	33:20	for no one may see me and I."
Lev	23:42	L in booths for seven days:
Nu	21: 8	can look at it and I."
Dt	4: 1	Follow them so that you may I
	5:24	that a man can I even if God speaks
	6: 2	as you I by keeping all his decrees
	8: 3	that man does not I on bread alone
	30: 6	and with all your soul, and I.
Jdg	1:27	the Canaanites were determined to I
Job	14:14	If a man dies, will he I again?
Ps	15: 1	Who may I on your holy hill?
	24: 1	the world, and all who I in it;
	26: 8	I love the house where you I,
	63: 4	I will praise you as long as I I,
	119:175	Let me I that I may praise you,
Pr	2:21	For the upright will I in the land,
	4: 4	keep my commands and you will I.
	15:27	but he who hates bribes will I.
	21: 9	to I on a corner of the roof
	21:19	Better to I in a desert than
Ecc	3:12	be happy and do good while they I.
	9: 4	even a I dog is better off than
Isa	6: 5	I I among a people of unclean lips,
	11: 6	The wolf will I with the lamb,
	26:19	But your dead will I;
	55: 3	that your soul may I.
Eze	18: 9	man is righteous; he will surely I,
	18:32	Repent and I!
	20:11	who obeys them will I by them.
	37: 3	"Son of man, can these bones I?"
Am	5: 6	Seek the LORD and I,
Jnh	4: 3	for me to die than to I."
	4: 8	be better for me to die than to I."
Hab	2: 4	the righteous will I by his faith—
Zec	2:11	I will I among you
Mt	4: 4	does not I on bread alone,

Lk	4: 4	does not I on bread alone.' "
	10:28	"Do this and you will I."
Jn	6:51	he will I forever.
	6:58	on this bread will I forever."
	11:25	He who believes in me will I,
	14:19	Because I I, you also will I.
Ac	17:24	does not I in temples built by hands.
	17:28	'For in him we I and move
Ro	1:17	"The righteous will I by faith."
	6: 8	that we will also I with him.
	8: 4	not I according to the sinful nature
	14: 8	If we I, we I to the Lord;
1Co	8: 6	and through whom we I.
2Co	5: 7	We I by faith, not by sight.
	5:15	those who I should no longer I for
	6:16	As God has said: "I will I with them
Gal	2:20	I I by faith in the Son of God,
	3:11	"The righteous will I by faith."
	3:12	who does these things will I by them.
	5:16	So I say, I by the Spirit,
	5:25	Since we I by the Spirit,
Eph	4: 1	I urge you to I a life worthy of
	4:17	that you must no longer I as
	5: 8	L as children of light
Php	1:21	to I is Christ and to die is gain.
Col	1:10	that you may I a life worthy of
1Th	4: 1	we instructed you how to I in order
	5:13	L in peace with each other.
1Ti	2: 2	that we may I peaceful
2Ti	3:12	wants to I a godly life in Christ Jesus
Tit	2:12	and to I self-controlled,
Heb	10:38	my righteous one will I by faith.
	12:14	effort to I in peace with all men
1Pe	1:17	I your lives as strangers here
	2:12	L such good lives among the pagans
	3: 8	I in harmony with one another;
2Pe	3:11	You ought to I holy and godly lives
1Jn	3:24	who obey his commands I in him,
Rev	21: 3	and he will I with them.

AS I LIVE Nu 14:21, 28; Dt 32:40; 1Sa 20:14; Job 27:6; Ps 63:4; 104:33; 116:2; 146:2; Isa 49:18; Jer 22:24; 46:18; Eze 5:11; 14:16, 18, 20; 16:48; 17:16, 19; 18:3; 20:3, 31, 33; 33:11, 27; 34:8; 35:6, 11; Zep 2:9; Ro 14:11; 2Pe 1:13

LIVED [LIVE]

Ex	6: 4	Canaan, where they I as aliens.
	12:40	Israelite people I in Egypt was 430
Dt	26: 5	Egypt with a few people and I there
Jos	24: 2	I beyond the River and worshiped
	24: 7	you I in the desert for a long time.
Jdg	3: 5	Israelites I among the Canaanites
Lk	1:80	and he I in the desert
Col	3: 7	in the life you once I.
Tit	3: 3	We I in malice and envy,

LIVES [LIVE]

Ge	9: 3	Everything that I and moves will
	45: 7	a remnant on earth and to save your I
	50:20	the saving of many I.
Ex	1:14	They made their I bitter
	30:16	making atonement for your I."
2Sa	18: 8	the forest claimed more I that day
Job	19:25	I know that my Redeemer I,

Ps   18:46   The LORD l!
Pr   1:19   takes away the l of those who get it.
     14:25   A truthful witness saves l,
Isa   57:15   he who l forever,
     65:20   an infant who l but a few days,
Da   3:28   to give up their l rather than serve
     4:34   and glorified him who l forever.
     12: 7   swear by him who l forever,
Jn   11:26   whoever l and believes in me
     14:17   for he l with you and will be in you.
Ro   6:10   but the life he l, he l to God.
     7:18   I know that nothing good l in me,
     8: 9   if the Spirit of God l in you.
     14: 7   For none of us l to himself alone
1Co   3:16   and that God's Spirit l in you?
Gal   2:20   but Christ l in me.
Eph   2:22   in which God l by his Spirit.
Col   2: 9   fullness of the Deity l in bodily form,
1Th   2: 8   not only the gospel of God but our l
     2:12   urging you to live l worthy of God,
1Ti   2: 2   peaceful and quiet l in all godliness
     6:16   and who l in unapproachable light,
2Ti   1:14   help of the Holy Spirit who l in us.
Tit   2:12   and godly l in this present age,
Heb   7:24   but because Jesus l forever,
     7:25   he always l to intercede for them.
     13: 5   your l free from the love of money
1Pe   1:17   live your l as strangers here
     3: 2   the purity and reverence of your l.
2Pe   3:11   You ought to live holy and godly l
1Jn   2:10   Whoever loves his brother l in
     2:14   and the word of God l in you,
     2:17   does the will of God l forever.
     3:16   to lay down our l for our brothers.
     4:16   Whoever l in love l in God,
Rev   4: 9   and who l for ever and ever,
     4:10   and worship him who l for ever
     10: 6   swore by him who l for ever and ever
     15: 7   who l for ever and ever.

AS SURELY AS THE †LORD LIVES
See †LORD

LIVESTOCK

Ge   1:25   the l according to their kinds,
     2:20   So the man gave names to all the l,
     3:14   "Cursed are you above all the l
Ex   34:19   all the firstborn males of your l,

LIVING [LIVE]

Ge   2: 7   and the man became a l being.
     3:20   the mother of all the l.
     6:19   into the ark two of all l creatures,
     8:21   And never again will I destroy all l
Dt   5:26   the voice of the l God speaking out
Jos   3:10   the l God is among you
1Sa   17:26   defy the armies of the l God?"
2Ki   19: 4   has sent to ridicule the l God,
Ps   84: 2   and my flesh cry out for the l God.
     119: 9   By l according to your word.
     142: 5   my portion in the land of the l."
Ecc   9: 4   who is among the l has hope—
Isa   53: 8   cut off from the land of the l;
Jer   2:13   forsaken me, the spring of l water,
     10:10   he is the l God, the eternal King.

     17:13   the LORD, the spring of l water.
Eze   1: 5   what looked like four l creatures.
     10:17   spirit of the l creatures was in them.
Da   6:26   "For he is the l God
Hos   1:10   be called 'sons of the l God.'
Zec   14: 8   On that day l water will flow out
Mt   4:16   the people l in darkness have seen
     16:16   the Son of the l God."
     22:32   not the God of the dead but of the l."
Jn   4:10   he would have given you l water."
     6:51   I am the l bread that came down
     7:38   streams of l water will flow from
Ro   8:11   Jesus from the dead is l in you,
     9:26   be called 'sons of the l God.' "
     12: 1   to offer your bodies as l sacrifices,
     14: 9   the Lord of both the dead and the l.
1Co   9:14   should receive their l from the gospel
2Co   6:16   For we are the temple of the l God.
1Ti   4:10   we have put our hope in the l God,
2Ti   4: 1   who will judge the l and the dead,
Heb   4:12   For the word of God is l and active.
     10:20   by a new and l way opened for us
     10:31   to fall into the hands of the l God.
     11:13   All these people were still l by faith
1Pe   1:23   the l and enduring word of God.
     2: 4   As you come to him, the l Stone—
Rev   1:18   I am the L One;
     4: 6   were four l creatures,
     7:17   lead them to springs of l water.

LIVING GOD See GOD

LIVING WATER Jer 2:13; 17:13; Zec 14:8; Jn 4:10, 11; 7:38; Rev 7:17

LOAD [LOADED, LOADS]

Ne   13:19   I could be brought in on the Sabbath
Jer   17:24   and bring no l through the gates
Lk   11:46   because you l people down
Gal   6: 5   for each one should carry his own l.

LOADED [LOAD]

Isa   1: 4   sinful nation, a people l with guilt,
2Ti   3: 6   who are l down with sins

LOADS [LOAD]

Mt   23: 4   They tie up heavy l and put them

LOAF [LOAVES]

Jdg   7:13   "A round l of barley bread
Pr   6:26   prostitute reduces you to a l of bread,
1Co   10:17   for we all partake of the one l.

LOAN

Dt   15: 2   Every creditor shall cancel the l
     24:10   When you make a l of any kind

LOAVES [LOAF]

Mk   6:41   Taking the five l and the two fish
     8: 6   When he had taken the seven l
     8:19   the five l for the five thousand,
     8:20   the seven l for the four thousand,
Lk   11: 5   'Friend, lend me three l of bread,

LOBE

Dt   15:17   an awl and push it through his ear l

LOCKED

SS	4:12	You are a garden I up, my sister,
Lk	3:20	He I John up in prison.
Jn	20:19	the doors I for fear of the Jews,
	20:26	Though the doors were I,
Ac	5:23	"We found the jail securely I,
Gal	3:23	I up until faith should be revealed.
Rev	20: 3	and I and sealed it over him,

LOCUSTS

Ex	10: 4	I will bring I
2Ch	7:13	or command I to devour the land
Joel	2:25	repay you for the years the I have
Mt	3: 4	His food was I and wild honey.
Rev	9: 3	And out of the smoke I came down

LOFTY

Ps	139: 6	too I for me to attain.
Isa	26: 5	he lays the I city low;
	57:15	the high and I One says—
Eze	16:24	a I shrine in every public square.

LOGS

2Ch	2: 3	"Send me cedar I as you did for my
Ezr	3: 7	that they would bring cedar I by sea

LOIS*

2Ti	1: 1	first lived in your grandmother L

LONELY* [ALONE]

Ps	25:16	for I am I and afflicted.
	68: 6	God sets the I in families,
Mk	1:45	but stayed outside in I places.
Lk	5:16	But Jesus often withdrew to I places

LONG [LENGTH, LENGTHY, LONGED, LONGER, LONGING, LONGINGS, LONGS]

Ex	17:11	As I as Moses held up his hands,
	20:12	so that you may live I in the land
Nu	6: 5	the hair of his head grow I.
	14:11	How I will they refuse to believe
Dt	6: 2	and so that you may enjoy I life.
1Ki	18:21	"How I will you waver
2Ch	1:11	not asked for a I life but for wisdom
Ps	93: 2	Your throne was established I ago;
	116: 2	I will call on him as I as I live.
	119:97	I meditate on it all day I.
	119:174	I I for your salvation, O LORD,
Pr	3:16	L life is in her right hand;
Isa	48: 3	I foretold the former things I ago,
Jer	44:14	to which they I to return and live;
La	5:20	Why do you forsake us so I?
Hos	7:13	I I to redeem them
Am	5:18	Woe to you who I for the day of
Mt	25: 5	The bridegroom was a I time
Lk	10:13	they would have repented I ago,
Jn	9: 4	As I as it is day,
1Co	11:14	that if a man has I hair,
	11:15	but that if a woman has I hair,
Eph	3:18	and I and high and deep is the love
Php	1: 8	God can testify how I I for all
1Pe	1:12	angels I to look into these things.
Rev	6:10	"How I, Sovereign Lord,

HOW LONG See HOW

LONG-SUFFERING* [SUFFER]

Jer	15:15	You are I—do not take me away;

LONGED [LONG]

Mt	13:17	prophets and righteous men I to see
	23:37	how often I have I to gather
Lk	13:34	how often I have I to gather
2Ti	4: 8	to all who have I for his appearing.

LONGER [LONG]

Ge	17: 5	No I will you be called Abram;
	17:15	you are no I to call her Sarai;
	32:28	"Your name will no I be Jacob,
Lev	26:13	so that you would no I be slaves
Dt	32: 5	their shame they are no I his children
Isa	29:22	"No I will Jacob be ashamed;
	62:12	the City No L Deserted.
Eze	14:11	the people of Israel will no I stray
	39:29	I will no I hide my face from them,
Mt	5:13	It is no I good for anything,
Mk	10: 8	So they are no I two, but one.
Jn	13:33	I will be with you only a little I.
Ro	6: 6	we should no I be slaves to sin—
Gal	2:20	crucified with Christ and I no I live,
	4: 7	So you are no I a slave, but a son;
Eph	2:19	you are no I foreigners and aliens,
	4:14	Then we will no I be infants,
Heb	8:11	No I will a man teach his neighbor,
Rev	21: 1	and there was no I any sea.
	22: 3	No I will there be any curse.

LONGING* [LONG]

Dt	28:65	eyes weary with I,
Job	7: 2	a slave I for the evening shadows,
Ps	119:20	with I for your laws at all times.
	119:81	with I for your salvation,
	119:131	I for your commands.
Pr	13:12	but a I fulfilled is a tree of life.
	13:19	A I fulfilled is sweet to the soul,
Eze	23:27	will not look on these things with I
Lk	16:21	and I to eat what fell from
Ro	15:23	I for many years to see you,
2Co	5: 2	I to be clothed with our heavenly
	7: 7	He told us about your I for me,
	7:11	what alarm, what I, what concern,
1Th	2:17	out of our intense I we made every
Heb	11:16	they were I for a better country—

LONGINGS* [LONG]

Ps	38: 9	All my I lie open before you,
	112:10	I of the wicked will come to nothing.

LONGS* [LONG]

Ps	63: 1	my body I for you,
Isa	26: 9	in the morning my spirit I for you.
	30:18	the LORD I to be gracious to you;
Php	2:26	For he I for all of you

LONGSUFFERING (KJV)

See PATIENCE

LOOK [LOOKED, LOOKING, LOOKS]

Ge 15: 5 **"L** up at the heavens and count
19:17 Don't **l** back, and don't stop
Ex 3: 6 because he was afraid to **l** at God.
Nu 21: 8 anyone who is bitten can **l**
32: 8 Kadesh Barnea to **l** over the land.
Dt 3:27 **L** at the land with your own eyes,
4:29 if you **l** for him with all your heart
26:15 **L** down from heaven,
Jos 2: 1 "Go, **l** over the land," he said,
1Sa 16: 7 does not **l** at the things man looks at.
1Ch 16:11 **L** to the LORD and his strength;
Job 31: 1 not to **l** lustfully at a girl.
Ps 34: 5 Those who **l** to him are radiant;
80:14 **L** down from heaven and see!
105: 4 **L** to the LORD and his strength;
113: 6 who stoops down to **l** on the heavens
123: 2 our eyes **l** to the LORD our God,
Pr 1:28 they will **l** for me
4:25 Let your eyes **l** straight ahead,
15:30 A cheerful **l** brings joy to the heart,
Isa 3: 9 The **l** on their faces testifies
17: 7 that day men will **l** to their Maker
31: 1 do not **l** to the Holy One of Israel,
40:26 Lift your eyes and **l** to the heavens:
42:18 "Hear, you deaf; **l**, you blind,
60: 5 Then you will **l** and be radiant,
Jer 3: 3 Yet you have the brazen **l** of
6:16 "Stand at the crossroads and **l**;
Eze 5:11 not **l** on you with pity or spare you.
34:11 for my sheep and **l** after them.
Da 9:17 with favor on your desolate
Hab 1:13 Your eyes are too pure to **l** on evil;
Zec 12:10 They will **l** on me,
Mt 6:26 **L** at the birds of the air;
18:10 "See that you do not **l** down on one
18:12 to **l** for the one that wandered off?
23:27 which **l** beautiful on the outside but
Mk 8:24 "I see people; they **l** like trees
13:21 **'L**, here is the Christ!'
Lk 6:41 "Why do you **l** at the speck
24:39 **L** at my hands and my feet.
Jn 1:36 he said, **"L**, the Lamb of God!"
4:35 open your eyes and **l** at the fields!
7:34 You will **l** for me,
13:33 You will **l** for me,
19:37 "They will **l** on the one
Ro 14:10 Or why do you **l** down
Php 2: 4 Each of you should **l** not only
1Ti 4:12 Don't let anyone **l** down on you
Jas 1:27 to **l** after orphans and widows
1Pe 1:12 angels long to **l** into these things.
2Pe 3:12 as you **l** forward to the day of God

LOOKED [LOOK]

Ge 4: 4 The LORD **l** with favor on Abel
19:26 But Lot's wife **l** back,
Ex 2:25 So God **l** on the Israelites
24:17 glory of the LORD **l** like a consuming
1Sa 6:19 because they had **l** into the ark of
Ps 102:19 The LORD **l** down from his sanctuary
SS 3: 1 I **l** for the one my heart loves;
Eze 1: 5 what **l** like four living creatures.

1:26 what **l** like a throne of sapphire,
10: 1 I **l**, and I saw the likeness of a throne
22:30 "I **l** for a man among them
34: 6 and no one searched or **l** for them.
37: 8 I **l**, and tendons and flesh appeared
44: 4 I **l** and saw the glory of the LORD
Da 7: 2 "In my vision at night I **l**,
7: 9 "As I **l**, "thrones were set in place,
8: 3 I **l** up, and there before me
10: 5 I **l** up and there before me was
Hab 3: 6 he **l**, and made the nations tremble.
Zec 1:18 Then I **l** up—
2: 1 Then I **l** up—
5: 1 I **l** again—
5: 9 Then I **l** up—
6: 1 I **l** up again—
Mt 25:36 I was sick and you **l** after me,
Mk 10:21 Jesus **l** at him and loved him.
Lk 18: 9 and **l** down on everybody else,
22:61 turned and **l** straight at Peter.
Ac 7:55 **l** up to heaven and saw the glory
1Jn 1: 1 which we have **l** at and our hands
Rev 4: 1 After this I **l**,
5:11 Then I **l** and heard the voice
6: 2 I **l**, and there before me was
7: 9 After this I **l** and there
14: 1 Then I **l**, and there before me
15: 2 And I saw what **l** like a sea

LOOKING [LOOK]

Ps 69: 3 My eyes fail, **l** for my God.
119:82 My eyes fail, **l** for your promise;
119:123 My eyes fail, **l** for your salvation,
119:123 **l** for your righteous promise.
Mk 3: 2 **l** for a reason to accuse Jesus,
16: 6 "You are **l** for Jesus the Nazarene,
Ac 1:10 They were **l** intently up into the sky
2Co 10: 7 You are **l** only on the surface
Php 4:17 Not that I am **l** for a gift,
1Th 2: 6 We were not **l** for praise from men,
Heb 11:26 he was **l** ahead to his reward.
13:14 we are **l** for the city that is to come.
1Pe 5: 8 like a roaring lion **l** for someone
2Pe 3:13 we are **l** forward to a new heaven
Rev 5: 6 **l** as if it had been slain,

LOOKINGGLASSES (KJV)

See MIRROR

LOOKS [LOOK]

1Sa 16: 7 Man **l** at the outward appearance,
but the LORD **l** at the heart."
Ezr 8:22 on everyone who **l** to him,
Ps 14: 2 The LORD **l** down from heaven on
33:13 From heaven the LORD **l** down
85:11 righteousness **l** down from heaven.
104:32 he who **l** at the earth,
138: 6 he **l** upon the lowly,
Pr 27:18 and he who **l** after his master will
Eze 34:12 a shepherd **l** after his scattered flock
Mt 5:28 who **l** at a woman lustfully
16: 4 generation **l** for a miraculous sign,
Lk 9:62 the plow and **l** back is fit for service
Jn 6:40 that everyone who **l** to the Son

12:45 When he I at me,
Php 2:21 everyone I out for his own interests,
Jas 1:25 who I intently into the perfect law

LOOSE

Jdg 16: 3 and tore them I, bar and all.
Isa 33:23 Your rigging hangs I:
Mt 16:19 and whatever you I on earth will
18:18 and whatever you I on earth will
Ac 16:26 and everybody's chains came I.

LOOT

Isa 42:24 handed Jacob over to become I,
Eze 39:10 and I those who looted them,

*LORD [*LORD'S, LORDED, LORDING, LORDS]

Ge 18:27 so bold as to speak to the L,
45: 8 I of his entire household and ruler
Ex 4:10 Moses said to the LORD, "O L,
15:17 O L, your hands established.
34: 9 "O L, if I have found favor
Nu 12:11 my I, do not hold against us
16:13 now you also want to I it over us?
Dt 10:17 God of gods and L of lords,
Jos 3:11 the covenant of the L of all the earth
1Ki 3:10 The L was pleased that Solomon
Ne 1:11 O L, let your ear be attentive to
4:14 Remember the L, who is great
10:29 and decrees of the LORD our L.
Job 28:28 he said to man, 'The fear of the L—
Ps 2: 4 the L scoffs at them.
8: 1 O LORD, our L,
16: 2 "You are my L;
30: 8 to the L I cried for mercy:
35:23 Contend for me, my God and L.
37:13 but the L laughs at the wicked,
38:22 O L my Savior.
40:17 may the L think of me.
54: 4 the L is the one who sustains me.
57: 9 I will praise you, O L,
62:12 O L, are loving.
69: 6 O L, the LORD Almighty;
86: 5 You are forgiving and good, O L,
86: 8 there is none like you, O L;
97: 5 before the L of all the earth.
110: 1 The LORD says to my L:
135: 5 that our L is greater than all gods.
136: 3 Give thanks to the L of lords:
147: 5 Great is our L and mighty in power;
Isa 6: 1 I saw the L seated on a throne,
7:14 the L himself will give you a sign:
49:14 the L has forgotten me."
Jer 46:10 But that day belongs to the L,
La 3:31 not cast off by the L forever.
Eze 18:25 'The way of the L is not just.'
Da 2:47 the God of gods and the L of kings
5:23 up against the L of heaven.
9: 3 So I turned to the L God and pleaded
9: 7 "L, you are righteous,
9: 9 L our God is merciful and forgiving,
9:19 O L, hear and act!
Am 9: 1 I saw the L standing by the altar,

Mic 1: 2 the L from his holy temple.
Mal 3: 1 the L you are seeking will come
Mt 1:20 an angel of the L appeared to him in
3: 3 'Prepare the way for the L,
4: 7 'Do not put the L your God to
4:10 'Worship the L your God,
7:21 everyone who says to me, 'L, L,'
9:38 Ask the L of the harvest, therefore,
12: 8 Son of Man is L of the Sabbath."
20:25 rulers of the Gentiles I it over them,
21: 9 who comes in the name of the L!"
21:42 the L has done this,
22:37 "'Love the L your God with all
22:44 "'The L said to my L: "Sit at my
23:39 who comes in the name of the L.'"
Mk 1: 3 'Prepare the way for the L,
5:19 how much the L has done for you,
12:11 the L has done this,
12:29 the L our God, the L is one.
12:30 Love the L your God with all your
12:37 David himself calls him 'L.'
Lk 1:11 an angel of the L appeared to him,
1:32 The L God will give him the throne
1:46 Mary said: "My soul glorifies the L
2: 9 glory of the L shone around them,
2:11 he is Christ the L.
4:18 "The Spirit of the L is on me,
5:12 "L, if you are willing,
5:17 And the power of the L was present
6: 5 Son of Man is L of the Sabbath."
6:46 "Why do you call me, 'L, L,'
10:21 Father, L of heaven and earth,
10:27 "'Love the L your God with all
19:31 tell him, 'The L needs it.'"
19:38 who comes in the name of the L!"
24:34 The L has risen and has appeared
Jn 1:23 'Make straight the way for the L.'"
9:38 Then the man said, "L, I believe,"
13:13 "You call me 'Teacher' and 'L,'
20:18 "I have seen the L!"
20:28 "My L and my God!"
21:17 He said, "L, you know all things;
Ac 2:21 on the name of the L will be saved.'
2:34 "'The L said to my L:
2:36 both L and Christ."
4:26 rulers gather together against the L
5:19 an angel of the L opened the doors
7:59 "L Jesus, receive my spirit."
8:16 into the name of the L Jesus.
9: 5 "Who are you, L?" Saul asked.
9:31 living in the fear of the L.
10:36 Jesus Christ, who is L of all.
11:23 them all to remain true to the L
16:31 "Believe in the L Jesus,
22:10 "'What shall I do, L?'
Ro 4:24 raised Jesus our L from the dead.
5: 1 through our L Jesus Christ,
6:23 eternal life in Christ Jesus our L.
8:39 of God that is in Christ Jesus our L.
10: 9 "Jesus is L," and believe
10:12 the same L is L of all
10:13 on the name of the L will be saved."
12:11 your spiritual fervor, serving the L.

*LORD indicates words translated "Lord" and "lord"; the proper name LORD is indexed under †LORD.

13:14 clothe yourselves with the **L** Jesus
14: 4 for the **L** is able to make him stand.
14: 8 If we live, we live to the **L**;
14: 9 the **L** of both the dead and the living.
1Co 1:31 who boasts boast in the **L**."
2: 8 not have crucified the **L** of glory.
2:16 who has known the mind of the **L**
3: 5 the **L** has assigned to each his task.
4: 4 It is the **L** who judges me.
6:13 but for the **L**, and the **L** for the body.
6:14 By his power God raised the **L** from
7:10 this command (not I, but the **L**):
7:12 To the rest I say this (I, not the **L**):
7:25 I have no command from the **L**,
7:32 how he can please the **L**.
7:34 to be devoted to the **L** in both body
7:39 but he must belong to the **L**,
8: 6 and there is but one **L**, Jesus Christ,
10: 9 We should not test the **L**,
10:21 cup of the **L** and the cup of demons
11:23 For I received from the **L** what I also
11:27 cup of the **L** in an unworthy manner
12: 3 and no one can say, "Jesus is **L**,"
15:57 victory through our **L** Jesus Christ.
15:58 yourselves fully to the work of the **L**,
16:22 If anyone does not love the **L**—
2Co 1:24 Not that we **l** it over your faith,
2:12 that the **L** had opened a door
3:17 Now the **L** is the Spirit,
4: 5 ourselves, but Jesus Christ as **L**,
5: 8 the body and at home with the **L**.
8: 5 they gave themselves first to the **L**
10:17 "Let him who boasts boast in the **L**."
10:18 but the one whom the **L** commends.
13:10 authority the **L** gave me for building
Gal 6:14 in the cross of our **L** Jesus Christ,
Eph 2:21 to become a holy temple in the **L**.
4: 5 one **L**, one faith, one baptism;
5: 8 but now you are light in the **L**.
5:10 and find out what pleases the **L**.
5:19 make music in your heart to the **L**,
5:22 submit to your husbands as to the **L**.
6: 1 obey your parents in the **L**,
6: 8 that the **L** will reward everyone
6:10 Finally, be strong in the **L**
Php 2:11 tongue confess that Jesus Christ is **L**,
3: 1 my brothers, rejoice in the **L**!
3: 8 of knowing Christ Jesus my **L**,
4: 1 how you should stand firm in the **L**,
4: 4 Rejoice in the **L** always.
4: 5 The **L** is near.
Col 1:10 may live a life worthy of the **L**
2: 6 as you received Christ Jesus as **L**,
3:13 Forgive as the **L** forgave you.
3:17 do it all in the name of the **L** Jesus,
3:18 as is fitting in the **L**.
3:20 for this pleases the **L**.
3:23 as working for the **L**, not for men,
3:24 receive an inheritance from the **L**.
4:17 the work you have received in the **L**.
1Th 1: 6 imitators of us and of the **L**;
3: 8 since you are standing firm in the **L**.
3:12 May the **L** make your love increase

4: 1 in the **L** Jesus to do this more
4: 6 **L** will punish men for all such sins,
4:15 who are left till the coming of the **L**,
4:17 so we will be with the **L** forever.
5: 2 day of the **L** will come like a thief
5:23 blameless at the coming of our **L**
2Th 1: 7 the **L** Jesus is revealed from heaven
1:12 name of our **L** Jesus may be glorified
2: 1 the coming of our **L** Jesus Christ
2: 8 whom the **L** Jesus will overthrow
3: 3 But the **L** is faithful,
3: 5 May the **L** direct your hearts into
1Ti 1:14 The grace of our **L** was poured out
6:14 the appearing of our **L** Jesus Christ,
6:15 the King of kings and **L** of lords,
2Ti 1: 8 not be ashamed to testify about our **L**
2:19 "The **L** knows those who are his,"
4: 8 which the **L**, the righteous Judge,
4:17 But the **L** stood at my side
Phm 1:25 The grace of the **L** Jesus Christ be
Heb 1:10 "In the beginning, O **L**,
8: 2 the true tabernacle set up by the **L**,
8:11 saying, 'Know the **L**,'
10:30 "The **L** will judge his people."
12: 6 the **L** disciplines those he loves,
12:14 holiness no one will see the **L**.
13: 6 "The **L** is my helper;
Jas 1: 7 he will receive anything from the **L**;
3: 9 With the tongue we praise our **L**
4:10 Humble yourselves before the **L**,
5:11 The **L** is full of compassion
5:15 the **L** will raise him up.
1Pe 1:25 the word of the **L** stands forever."
2: 3 you have tasted that the **L** is good.
3:12 the **L** is against those who do evil."
3:15 in your hearts set apart Christ as **L**.
2Pe 1:11 into the eternal kingdom of our **L**
1:16 and coming of our **L** Jesus Christ,
2: 1 denying the sovereign **L** who bought
2: 9 then the **L** knows how to rescue
3: 9 **L** is not slow in keeping his promise,
3:10 day of the **L** will come like a thief.
3:18 in the grace and knowledge of our **L**
Jude 1: 4 Christ our only Sovereign and **L**.
1:14 the **L** is coming with thousands
Rev 4: 8 holy, holy is the **L** God Almighty,
6:10 Sovereign **L**, holy and true,
11: 8 where also their **L** was crucified.
11:15 has become the kingdom of our **L**
11:17 **L** God Almighty, the One who is
14:13 the dead who die in the **L** from
15: 4 Who will not fear you, O **L**,
17:14 he is **L** of lords and King of kings—
19: 6 For our **L** God Almighty reigns.
19:16 KING OF KINGS AND **L** OF LORDS.
21:22 because the **L** God Almighty and
22: 5 for the **L** God will give them light.
22:20 Come, **L** Jesus.

ANGEL OF THE *LORD See ANGEL

*LORD GOD Da 9:3; Lk 1:32; Rev 1:8; 4:8;
11:17; 15:3; 16:7; 18:8; 19:6; 21:22; 22:5

*LORD JESUS See JESUS

*LORD indicates words translated "Lord" and "lord"; the proper name LORD is indexed under †**LORD**.

*LORD JESUS CHRIST See JESUS

THE *LORD THE †LORD ALMIGHTY Isa
1:24; 3:1, 15; 10:16, 23, 24, 33; 19:4; 22:5, 12,
14, 15; 28:22; Jer 2:19; 46:10, 10; 49:5; 50:31;
Am 3:13; 5:16; 9:5

MY/OUR *LORD THE KING 1Sa   24:8;
26:15, 15, 17, 19; 29:8; 2Sa 3:21; 4:8; 9:11;
13:33; 14:9, 12, 15, 17, 17, 18, 19, 19, 22; 15:15,
21, 21; 16:4, 9; 18:28, 31, 32; 19:19, 20, 26, 27,
27, 28, 30, 35, 37; 24:3, 3, 21, 22; 1Ki 1:2, 13,
18, 20, 20, 21, 24, 27, 27, 36, 37; 2:38; 20:4, 9;
2Ki 6:12, 26; 8:5; 1Ch 21:3, 23; Jer 37:20; 38:9;
Da 1:10; 4:24

NAME OF THE *LORD See NAME

*LORD'S [*LORD]

Nu 14:17 may the **L** strength be displayed,
Mal 1:12 profane it by saying of the **L** table,
Lk 1:38 "I am the **L** servant,"
  1:66 For the **L** hand was with him.
  4:19 to proclaim the year of the **L** favor."
  10:39 the **L** feet listening to what he said.
Ac 11:21 The **L** hand was with them,
  21:14 "The **L** will be done."
1Co 7:32 concerned about the **L** affairs—
  10:21 the **L** table and the table of demons.
  10:22 trying to arouse the **L** jealousy?
  10:26 "The earth is the **L,**
  11:20 it is not the **L** Supper you eat,
  11:26 proclaim the **L** death until he comes.
2Co 3:18 unveiled faces all reflect the **L** glory,
Gal 1:19 only James, the **L** brother.
Eph 5:17 but understand what the **L** will is.
2Ti 2:24 And the **L** servant must not quarrel;
Heb 12:5 not make light of the **L** discipline,
Jas 4:15 you ought to say, "If it is the **L** will,
  5:8 because the **L** coming is near.
1Pe 2:13 Submit yourselves for the **L** sake
2Pe 3:15 that our **L** patience means salvation,
Rev 1:10 On the **L** Day I was in the Spirit,

†LORD [†LORD'S (YAHWEH'S)]

Ge 2:4 When the **L** God made the earth
  2:7 the **L** God formed the man from
  2:16 the **L** God commanded the man,
  2:22 the **L** God made a woman
  3:9 But the **L** God called to the man,
  3:13 the **L** God said to the woman,
  3:14 So the **L** God said to the serpent,
  3:23 the **L** God banished him from
  4:4 The **L** looked with favor on Abel
  4:15 the **L** put a mark on Cain so
  4:26 began to call on the name of the **L.**
  6:6 **L** was grieved that he had made man
  6:8 found favor in the eyes of the **L.**
  7:16 Then the **L** shut him in.
  8:20 Noah built an altar to the **L** and,
  9:26 He also said, "Blessed be the **L,**
  10:9 a mighty hunter before the **L;**
  11:9 the **L** confused the language of the
  12:1 The **L** had said to Abram,

12:7 The **L** appeared to Abram
13:4 Abram called on the name of the **L.**
15:6 Abram believed the **L,**
15:18 the **L** made a covenant with Abram
17:1 the **L** appeared to him and said,
18:1 The **L** appeared to Abraham near
18:14 Is anything too hard for the **L?**
18:19 to keep the way of the **L**
19:14 the **L** is about to destroy the city!"
21:1 Now the **L** was gracious to Sarah
22:14 called that place The **L** Will Provide.
24:1 **L** had blessed him in every way.
25:21 Isaac prayed to the **L** on behalf
26:2 The **L** appeared to Isaac and said,
26:25 and called on the name of the **L.**
28:16 "Surely the **L** is in this place,
31:49 the **L** keep watch between you
39:2 The **L** was with Joseph
39:23 the **L** was with Joseph
Ex 3:2 the angel of the **L** appeared to him
  3:15 'The **L,** the God of your fathers—
  4:11 Is it not I, the **L?**
  4:31 the **L** was concerned about them
  5:2 Pharaoh said, "Who is the **L,**
  6:2 "I am the **L.**
  6:7 know that I am the **L** your God,
  8:10 there is no one like the **L** our God.
  9:12 the **L** hardened Pharaoh's heart
  9:30 still do not fear the **L** God."
  10:16 "I have sinned against the **L**
  10:20 the **L** hardened Pharaoh's heart,
  10:27 the **L** hardened Pharaoh's heart,
  11:10 the **L** hardened Pharaoh's heart,
  12:27 'It is the Passover sacrifice to the **L,**
  12:29 the **L** struck down all the firstborn
  13:9 For the **L** brought you out of Egypt
  13:12 give over to the **L** the first offspring
  13:21 the **L** went ahead of them in a pillar
  14:4 The **L** hardened the heart
  14:13 deliverance the **L** will bring you
  14:18 Egyptians will know that I am the **L**
  14:30 That day the **L** saved Israel from
  15:3 The **L** is a warrior; the **L** is his name.
  15:11 among the gods is like you, O **L?**
  15:26 for I am the **L,** who heals you."
  16:12 know that I am the **L** your God.' "
  16:29 the **L** has given you the Sabbath;
  17:7 because they tested the **L** saying,
  17:15 and called it The **L** is my Banner.
  18:10 He said, "Praise be to the **L,**
  19:8 We will do everything the **L** has said
  19:20 The **L** descended to the top of Mount
  20:2 "I am the **L** your God,
  20:5 the **L** your God, am a jealous God,
  20:7 the name of the **L** your God,
  20:10 a Sabbath to the **L** your God.
  20:11 in six days the **L** made the heavens
  20:12 land the **L** your God is giving you.
  23:25 Worship the **L** your God,
  24:3 Everything the **L** has said we will do.
  24:12 The **L** said to Moses, "Come up
  24:16 glory of the **L** settled on Mount Sinai

---

*LORD'S indicates words translated "Lord's"; the proper name LORD's is indexed under **†LORD'S.**
†LORD indicates the proper name LORD; words translated "Lord" and "lord" are indexed under ***LORD.**

25: 1	The L said to Moses,
28:36	as on a seal: HOLY TO THE L.
30:11	Then the L said to Moses,
31:13	so you may know that I am the L,
31:18	the L finished speaking to Moses
32:11	But Moses sought the favor of the L
33: 9	while the L spoke with Moses.
34: 5	the L came down in the cloud
34: 6	proclaiming, "The L, the L,
34:10	the L, will do for you.
34:14	for the L, whose name is Jealous,
34:29	because he had spoken with the L.
40:34	glory of the L filled the tabernacle.
40:38	of the L was over the tabernacle

Lev 1: 2 of you brings an offering to the L,
  1: 9 an aroma pleasing to the L.
  8:36 did everything the L commanded
  9:23 glory of the L appeared to all the
  10: 2 and they died before the L.
  19: 2 'Be holy because I, the L your God,
  20: 8 I am the L, who makes you holy.
  20:26 be holy to me because I, the L,
  23:40 and rejoice before the L your God
  24:16 who blasphemes the name of the L

Nu 6:24 " ' "The L bless you and keep you;
  8: 5 The L said to Moses:
  10:29 for the L has promised good things
  11: 1 hardships in the hearing of the L,
  14:14 O L, have been seen face to face,
  14:18 'The L is slow to anger,
  14:21 glory of the L fills the whole earth,
  16: 7 The man the L chooses will be
  20:13 the Israelites quarreled with the L
  21: 6 Then the L sent venomous snakes
  21:14 Book of the Wars of the L says:
  22:31 Then the L opened Balaam's eyes,
  23:12 "Must I not speak what the L puts
  30: 2 When a man makes a vow to the L
  32:12 they followed the L wholeheartedly.'

Dt 1:21 L your God has given you the land.
  2: 7 the L your God has been with you,
  4:29 there you seek the L your God,
  4:39 that the L is God in heaven
  5: 6 "I am the L your God,
  5: 9 the L your God, am a jealous God,
  5:11 the name of the L your God,
  5:14 a Sabbath to the L your God.
  6: 4 The L our God, the L is one.
  6: 5 Love the L your God with all your
  6:16 not test the L your God as you did
  6:25 obey all this law before the L
  7: 1 L your God brings you into the land
  7: 6 a people holy to the L your God.
  7: 8 because the L loved you
  7: 9 that the L your God is God;
  7:12 L your God will keep his covenant
  7:22 The L your God will drive out those
  8: 5 so the L your God disciplines you.
  9:10 The L gave me two stone tablets
  10:12 what does the L your God ask
  10:14 To the L your God belong
  10:17 For the L your God is God of gods
  10:20 the L your God and serve him.

10:22 now the L your God has made you
  11: 1 Love the L your God
  11:13 to love the L your God and to serve
  13: 3 The L your God is testing you
  14: 1 the children of the L your God.
  16: 1 the Passover of the L your God,
  17:15 the king the L your God chooses.
  18: 2 the L is their inheritance,
  18:15 The L your God will raise up
  28: 1 If you fully obey the L your God
  28:15 do not obey the L your God
  29: 1 covenant the L commanded Moses
  29:29 The secret things belong to the L
  30: 4 the L your God will gather you
  30: 6 The L your God will circumcise
  30:10 if you obey the L your God
  30:16 to love the L your God, to walk
  30:20 For the L is your life,
  31: 6 for the L your God goes with you;
  34: 5 Moses the servant of the L died

Jos 1:13 'The L your God is giving you rest
  2:11 the L your God is God in heaven
  7:20 I have sinned against the L,
  10:14 the L was fighting for Israel!
  21:44 The L gave them rest
  22: 5 to love the L your God,
  22:22 The Mighty One, God, the L!
  22:34 Between Us that the L is God.
  23:11 careful to love the L your God.
  24:15 my household, we will serve the L."
  24:18 We too will serve the L,

Jdg 2:12 They forsook the L,
  3: 9 But when they cried out to the L,

Ru 1: 8 May the L show kindness to you,
  4:13 and the L enabled her to conceive,

1Sa 1:11 then I will give him to the L for all
  1:19 and the L remembered her.
  1:28 So now I give him to the L.
  2: 2 "There is no one holy like the L;
  2:25 but if a man sins against the L,
  2:26 and in favor with the L
  3: 1 the word of the L was rare;
  3: 8 that the L was calling the boy.
  3:19 The L was with Samuel as he grew
  4: 3 "Why did the L bring defeat upon us
  5: 3 the ground before the ark of the L!
  7:12 "Thus far has the L helped us."
  10: 1 "Has not the L anointed you leader
  11:15 as king in the presence of the L.
  12: 5 "The L is witness against you,
  12:18 the people stood in awe of the L
  12:22 the L will not reject his people,
  12:24 But be sure to fear the L
  13:14 the L has sought out a man
  14: 6 Nothing can hinder the L from
  15:22 the L delight in burnt offerings
  15:28 "The L has torn the kingdom
  16:13 Spirit of the L came upon David
  17:45 in the name of the L Almighty,

2Sa 5:10 the L Almighty was with him.
  6:14 danced before the L with all his
  7:22 How great you are, O Sovereign L!
  8: 6 The L gave David victory wherever

†**LORD** indicates the proper name LORD; words translated "Lord" and "lord" are indexed under ***LORD.**

12:13 "I have sinned against the **L.**"
22: 2 He said: "The **L** is my rock,
22:29 You are my lamp, O **L;**
22:31 the word of the **L** is flawless.
24:14 Let us fall into the hands of the **L,**
1Ki 1:30 I swore to you by the **L,** the God
2: 3 observe what the **L** your God
3: 3 Solomon showed his love for the **L**
5: 5 a temple for the Name of the **L**
5:12 The **L** gave Solomon wisdom,
8:11 the glory of the **L** filled his temple.
8:23 and said: "O **L,** God of Israel,
8:61 fully committed to the **L** our God,
9: 3 The **L** said to him: "I have heard the
10: 9 Praise be to the **L** your God,
11: 4 not fully devoted to the **L** his God,
15:14 committed to the **L** all his life.
18:21 If the **L** is God, follow him.
18:36 "O **L,** God of Abraham, Isaac and
18:39 "The **L**—he is God! The **L**—he is
19:11 for the **L** is about to pass by."
19:11 but the **L** was not in the wind.
21:23 also concerning Jezebel the **L** says:
22: 5 "First seek the counsel of the **L.**"
2Ki 3:18 an easy thing in the eyes of the **L;**
13:23 the **L** was gracious to them
17:20 **L** rejected all the people of Israel;
18: 5 Hezekiah trusted in the **L,**
19: 1 and went into the temple of the **L.**
19:31 The zeal of the **L** Almighty will
20:11 the **L** made the shadow go back
21:12 Therefore this is what the **L,**
22: 2 right in the eyes of the **L**
22: 8 of the Law in the temple of the **L.**"
23: 3 to follow the **L** and keep his
23:21 the Passover to the **L** your God,
23:25 a king like him who turned to the **L**
24: 2 The **L** sent Babylonian, Aramean,
24: 4 the **L** was not willing to forgive.
25: 9 He set fire to the temple of the **L,**
1Ch 10:13 because he was unfaithful to the **L;**
11: 3 with them at Hebron before the **L,**
11: 9 the **L** Almighty was with him.
13: 6 up from there the ark of God the **L,**
16: 8 Give thanks to the **L,**
16:11 Look to the **L** and his strength;
16:23 Sing to the **L,** all the earth;
17: 1 the ark of the covenant of the **L** is
17:20 "There is no one like you, O **L,**
21:24 not take for the **L** what is yours,
22: 1 house of the **L** God is to be here,
22:11 build the house of the **L** your God,
22:13 laws that the **L** gave Moses
22:16 and the **L** be with you."
22:19 Begin to build the sanctuary of the **L**
25: 7 and skilled in music for the **L**—
28: 9 for the **L** searches every heart
28:20 for the **L** God, my God, is with you.
29: 1 not for man but for the **L** God.
29:11 O **L,** is the greatness and the power
29:11 Yours, O **L,** is the kingdom;
29:25 The **L** highly exalted Solomon in
2Ch 1: 1 for the **L** his God was with him

2:11 "Because the **L** loves his people,
5:14 the glory of the **L** filled the temple
6:17 And now, O **L,** God of Israel,
7: 1 the glory of the **L** filled the temple.
7:12 the **L** appeared to him at night
7:21 'Why has the **L** done such a thing
9: 8 as king to rule for the **L** your God.
13:12 do not fight against the **L,**
14: 6 for the **L** gave him rest.
15:15 the **L** gave them rest on every side.
16: 9 the eyes of the **L** range throughout
17: 9 the Book of the Law of the **L;**
18:15 but the truth in the name of the **L?**"
19: 6 not judging for man but for the **L,**
19: 9 wholeheartedly in the fear of the **L.**
20:15 This is what the **L** says to you:
20:20 Have faith in the **L** your God
21: 7 the **L** was not willing to destroy
26: 5 As long as he sought the **L,**
26:16 He was unfaithful to the **L**
29:31 now dedicated yourselves to the **L.**
30: 9 If you return to the **L,**
31:20 and faithful before the **L** his God.
32: 8 with us is the **L** our God to help us
33:13 the **L** was moved by his entreaty
34:14 found the Book of the Law of the **L**
34:31 to follow the **L** and keep his
36:22 to fulfill the word of the **L** spoken
Ezr 3:10 foundation of the temple of the **L,**
7: 6 hand of the **L** his God was on him.
7:10 and observance of the Law of the **L,**
9: 8 hands spread out to the **L** my God
9: 8 the **L** our God has been gracious
Ne 1: 5 Then I said: "O **L,** God of heaven,
8: 1 the **L** had commanded for Israel.
8:10 the joy of the **L** is your strength."
9: 6 You alone are the **L.**
Job 1: 6 to present themselves before the **L,**
1:21 The **L** gave and the **L** has taken
38: 1 answered Job out of the storm.
42:12 The **L** blessed the latter part of Job's
Ps 1: 2 his delight is in the law of the **L,**
1: 6 For the **L** watches over the way of
2: 2 rulers gather together against the **L**
3: 8 From the **L** comes deliverance.
4: 6 light of your face shine upon us, O **L**
5: 3 In the morning, O **L,**
6: 1 O **L,** do not rebuke me
7: 1 O **L** my God, I take refuge in you;
8: 1 O **L,** our Lord,
9: 9 **L** is a refuge for the oppressed,
9:19 Arise, O **L,** let not man triumph;
10:16 The **L** is King for ever and ever;
11: 5 The **L** examines the righteous,
12: 6 the words of the **L** are flawless,
13: 1 How long, O **L?**
14: 6 but the **L** is their refuge.
15: 4 but honors those who fear the **L,**
16: 2 I said to the **L,** "You are my Lord;
16: 8 I have set the **L** always before me.
17: 1 Hear, O **L,** my righteous plea;
18: 1 I love you, O **L,** my strength.
18: 6 In my distress I called to the **L;**

---

†**LORD** indicates the proper name **LORD**; words translated "Lord" and "lord" are indexed under *****LORD.**

18:31 For who is God besides the **L**?	91: 2 I will say of the **L**, "He is my refuge
19: 7 The law of the **L** is perfect,	92: 1 It is good to praise the **L**
19:14 O **L**, my Rock and my Redeemer.	92: 4 make me glad by your deeds, O **L**;
20: 5 May the **L** grant all your requests.	93: 1 **L** reigns, he is robed in majesty;
20: 7 trust in the name of the **L** our God.	93: 5 your house for endless days, O **L**.
21:13 Be exalted, O **L**, in your strength;	94: 1 O **L**, the God who avenges,
22: 8 let the **L** rescue him.	94:12 the man you discipline, O **L**,
23: 1 The **L** is my shepherd.	94:18 your love, O **L**, supported me.
23: 6 dwell in the house of the **L** forever.	95: 1 Come, let us sing for joy to the **L**;
24: 3 may ascend the hill of the **L**?	95: 3 For the **L** is the great God,
24: 8 The **L** strong and mighty,	96: 1 Sing to the **L** a new song;
25:10 All the ways of the **L** are loving	96: 5 but the **L** made the heavens.
26: 2 Test me, O **L**, and try me,	96: 9 Worship the **L** in the splendor
27: 1 **L** is my light and my salvation—	97: 1 The **L** reigns, let the earth be glad;
27: 4 to gaze upon the beauty of the **L**	97:10 Let those who love the **L** hate evil,
27: 6 and make music to the **L**.	98: 2 **L** has made his salvation known
28: 7 **L** is my strength and my shield;	99: 1 **L** reigns, let the nations tremble;
29: 1 ascribe to the **L** glory and strength.	99: 5 Exalt the **L** our God and worship
29: 4 The voice of the **L** is powerful;	100: 2 Worship the **L** with gladness;
30: 4 Sing to the **L**, you saints of his;	101: 1 O **L**, I will sing praise.
31: 5 O **L**, the God of truth.	102:12 you, O **L**, sit enthroned forever;
32: 2 whose sin the **L** does not count	103: 1 Praise the **L**, O my soul;
33: 1 Sing joyfully to the **L**,	103: 8 **L** is compassionate and gracious,
33: 6 word of the **L** were the heavens	103:19 The **L** has established his throne
33:12 the nation whose God is the **L**,	104: 1 O **L** my God, you are very great;
33:20 We wait in hope for the **L**;	104:24 How many are your works, O **L**!
34: 1 I will extol the **L** at all times;	104:33 I will sing to the **L** all my life;
34: 4 I sought the **L**,	105: 4 Look to the **L** and his strength;
34: 7 The angel of the **L** encamps	105:24 The **L** made his people very fruitful;
34: 8 Taste and see that the **L** is good;	106:47 Save us, O **L** our God,
34: 9 Fear the **L**, you his saints,	107: 1 Give thanks to the **L**, for he is good;
34:15 eyes of the **L** are on the righteous	107: 8 to the **L** for his unfailing love
34:18 The **L** is close to the brokenhearted	107:43 consider the great love of the **L**.
35:10 "Who is like you, O **L**?	108: 3 I will praise you, O **L**,
36: 6 O **L**, you preserve both man	109:26 Help me, O **L** my God;
37: 4 Delight yourself in the **L**	110: 1 The **L** says to my Lord:
37: 5 Commit your way to the **L**;	110: 4 The **L** has sworn and will not
38:21 O **L**, do not forsake me;	111: 2 Great are the works of the **L**;
40: 1 I waited patiently for the **L**;	111: 4 the **L** is gracious
40:13 Be pleased, O **L**, to save me;	111:10 The fear of the **L** is the beginning of
41:10 But you, O **L**, have mercy on me;	112: 1 the man who fears the **L**,
46: 7 The **L** Almighty is with us;	113: 1 praise the name of the **L**.
47: 2 How awesome is the **L** Most High,	113: 5 Who is like the **L** our God,
48: 1 Great is the **L**, and most worthy	115: 1 Not to us, O **L**,
50: 1 The Mighty One, God, the **L**,	115:18 it is we who extol the **L**,
55:22 Cast your cares on the **L**	116: 5 The **L** is gracious and righteous;
59: 8 But you, O **L**, laugh at them;	116:12 How can I repay the **L** for all
68: 4 his name is the **L**—	116:15 Precious in the sight of the **L** is
68:20 from the Sovereign **L** comes escape	117: 1 Praise the **L**, all you nations;
69:31 This will please the **L** more than	118: 7 The **L** is with me; he is my helper.
70: 5 O **L**, do not delay.	118: 8 to take refuge in the **L** than to trust
71: 1 In you, O **L**, I have taken refuge;	118:18 The **L** has chastened me severely,
73:28 made the Sovereign **L** my refuge;	118:24 This is the day the **L** has made;
75: 8 In the hand of the **L** is a cup full	118:26 he who comes in the name of the **L**.
78: 4 the praiseworthy deeds of the **L**,	119: 1 according to the law of the **L**.
81:10 I am the **L** your God,	119:64 earth is filled with your love, O **L**;
83:18 whose name is the **L**—	119:89 Your word, O **L**, is eternal;
84:11 For the **L** God is a sun and shield;	119:126 It is time for you to act, O **L**;
85: 7 Show us your unfailing love, O **L**,	119:159 O **L**, according to your love.
86:11 Teach me your way, O **L**,	120: 1 I call on the **L** in my distress,
87: 2 the **L** loves the gates of Zion	121: 2 My help comes from the **L**,
88: 1 O **L**, the God who saves me,	121: 5 The **L** watches over you—
89: 6 above can compare with the **L**?	122: 1 "Let us go to the house of the **L**."

†**LORD** indicates the proper name LORD; words translated "Lord" and "lord" are indexed under *****LORD**.

18: 7 place of the Name of the **L** Almighty
24: 1 the **L** is going to lay waste the earth
25: 1 O **L**, you are my God;
25: 6 the **L** Almighty will prepare a feast
25: 8 Sovereign **L** will wipe away the tears
26: 4 Trust in the **L** forever,
26: 8 **L**, walking in the way of your laws,
26:13 O **L**, our God, other lords besides
26:21 the **L** is coming out of his dwelling
27: 1 the **L** will punish with his sword,
27:12 In that day the **L** will thresh from
28: 5 **L** Almighty will be a glorious crown,
29: 6 **L** Almighty will come with thunder
29:15 to hide their plans from the **L**,
29:19 the humble will rejoice in the **L**;
30:18 the **L** longs to be gracious to you;
30:26 when the **L** binds up the bruises
30:30 The **L** will cause men to hear
33: 2 O **L**, be gracious to us;
33: 6 fear of the **L** is the key to this
33:22 For the **L** is our judge,
34: 2 The **L** is angry with all nations;
35: 2 they will see the glory of the **L**,
35:10 the ransomed of the **L** will return.
37:15 And Hezekiah prayed to the **L**:
38: 7 the **L** will do what he has promised:
40: 3 the desert prepare the way for the **L**;
40: 5 the glory of the **L** will be revealed,
40: 7 the breath of the **L** blows on them.
40:10 Sovereign **L** comes with power,
40:14 Whom did the **L** consult to enlighten
40:27 "My way is hidden from the **L**;
40:28 The **L** is the everlasting God,
40:31 in the **L** will renew their strength.
41:14 declares the **L**, your Redeemer,
41:20 the hand of the **L** has done this,
42: 8 "I am the **L**; that is my name!
42:10 Sing to the **L** a new song,
42:13 The **L** will march out like
42:21 It pleased the **L** for the sake
43: 3 For I am the **L**, your God,
43:11 I, even I, am the **L**,
44: 6 King and Redeemer, the **L** Almighty:
44:23 for the **L** has redeemed Jacob,
45: 5 I am the **L**, and there is no other;
45: 7 I, the **L**, do all these things.
45:17 the **L** with an everlasting salvation;
45:21 Was it not I, the **L**?
48:17 the **L** your God, who teaches you
49: 7 because of the **L**, who is faithful,
49:14 Zion said, "The **L** has forsaken me,
50: 5 Sovereign **L** has opened my ears,
50:10 Who among you fears the **L** and
51: 1 and who seek the **L**:
51:11 The ransomed of the **L** will return.
51:15 the **L** Almighty is his name.
52:10 The **L** will lay bare his holy arm in
53: 1 has the arm of the **L** been revealed?
53: 6 the **L** has laid on him the iniquity
53:10 **L** makes his life a guilt offering,
54: 5 the **L** Almighty is his name—
55: 6 Seek the **L** while he may be found;
55: 7 Let him turn to the **L**,

56: 6 to love the name of the **L**,
58: 5 a day acceptable to the **L**?
58:11 The **L** will guide you always;
59: 1 arm of the **L** is not too short to save,
59:19 men will fear the name of the **L**,
60: 1 the glory of the **L** rises upon you.
60:19 **L** will be your everlasting light,
61: 1 Spirit of the Sovereign **L** is on me,
61: 3 a planting of the **L** for the display
61: 8 "For I, the **L**, love justice;
61:10 I delight greatly in the **L**;
62: 4 for the **L** will take delight in you,
63: 7 I will tell of the kindnesses of the **L**,
64: 8 Yet, O **L**, you are our Father.
65:23 will be a people blessed by the **L**,
66:15 See, the **L** is coming with fire,

Jer 1: 9 Then the **L** reached out his hand
2:19 when you forsake the **L** your God
3:12 for I am merciful,' declares the **L**,
3:25 not obeyed the **L** our God."
4: 4 Circumcise yourselves to the **L**,
6:10 The word of the **L** is offensive
8: 7 not know the requirements of the **L**.
9:24 I am the **L**, who exercises kindness,
10: 6 No one is like you, O **L**;
10:10 But the **L** is the true God;
10:21 and do not inquire of the **L**;
12: 1 You are always righteous, O **L**,
14: 7 our sins testify against us, O **L**,
14:20 **L**, we acknowledge our wickedness
16:19 O **L**, my strength and my fortress,
17: 7 the man who trusts in the **L**,
17:10 "I the **L** search the heart and
17:13 O **L**, the hope of Israel,
20:11 **L** is with me like a mighty warrior;
23: 6 The **L** Our Righteousness.
24: 7 a heart to know me, that I am the **L**.
28: 9 as one truly sent by the **L** only if
31:11 For the **L** will ransom Jacob
31:22 The **L** will create a new thing
31:34 saying, 'Know the **L**,'
32:27 "I am the **L**, the God of all
33:16 The **L** Our Righteousness.'
36: 6 the words of the **L** that you wrote
40: 3 now the **L** has brought it about;
42: 3 the **L** your God will tell us
42: 4 I will tell you everything the **L** says
42: 6 we will obey the **L** our God,
50: 4 go in tears to seek the **L** their God.
51:10 " 'The **L** has vindicated us;
51:56 For the **L** is a God of retribution;

La 1: 5 The **L** has brought her grief
3:24 "The **L** is my portion;
3:25 The **L** is good to those whose hope
3:26 wait quietly for the salvation of the **L**
3:40 and let us return to the **L**.

Eze 1: 3 the hand of the **L** was upon him.
1:28 the likeness of the glory of the **L**.
3:23 glory of the **L** was standing there,
4:14 Then I said, "Not so, Sovereign **L!**
10: 4 the radiance of the glory of the **L**.
10:18 Then the glory of the **L** departed
15: 7 you will know that I am the **L**.

---

†**LORD** indicates the proper name LORD; words translated "Lord" and "lord" are indexed under ***LORD**.

30: 3 the day of the L is near—
34:24 I the L will be their God,
36:23 nations will know that I am the L,
37: 4 'Dry bones, hear the word of the L!
43: 4 glory of the L entered the temple
44: 4 the glory of the L filling the temple
48:35 that time on will be: THE L IS THERE."
Da   9: 2 word of the L given to Jeremiah
9:14 for the L our God is righteous
Hos 1: 7 but by the L their God."
2:13 but me she forgot," declares the L.
2:20 and you will acknowledge the L.
3: 1 as the L loves the Israelites,
3: 5 They will come trembling to the L
4: 1 because the L has a charge to bring
6: 1 "Come, let us return to the L.
6: 3 Let us acknowledge the L;
10:12 for it is time to seek the L,
12: 5 the L is his name of renown!
14: 1 O Israel, to the L your God.
Joel 1:15 For the day of the L is near;
2:11 The day of the L is great;
2:13 Return to the L your God,
2:21 Surely the L has done great things.
2:23 rejoice in the L your God,
2:31 great and dreadful day of the L.
2:32 on the name of the L will be saved;
3:14 For the day of the L is near in
3:16 L will be a refuge for his people,
Am   1: 2 He said: "The L roars from Zion
4:13 the L God Almighty is his name.
5: 6 Seek the L and live,
5:15 Perhaps the L God Almighty will
5:18 who long for the day of the L!
7:15 the L took me from tending the flock
8:11 famine of hearing the words of the L.
9: 5 The Lord, the L Almighty,
Ob   1:15 "The day of the L is near for all
Jnh 1: 3 But Jonah ran away from the L
1: 4 the L sent a great wind on the sea,
1:17 But the L provided a great fish
2: 9 Salvation comes from the L."
4: 2 He prayed to the L, "O L,
4: 6 Then the L God provided a vine
Mic 1:12 disaster has come from the L,
4: 2 the word of the L from Jerusalem.
5: 4 his flock in the strength of the L,
6: 2 the L has a case against his people;
6: 8 what does the L require of you?
7: 7 as for me, I watch in hope for the L,
Na   1: 2 L is a jealous and avenging God;
1: 3 The L is slow to anger and great
Hab 1:12 O L, are you not from everlasting?
2:14 the knowledge of the glory of the L,
2:20 But the L is in his holy temple;
3: 2 I stand in awe of your deeds, O L.
Zep 1: 7 Be silent before the Sovereign L,
1:14 "The great day of the L is near—
3:17 The L your God is with you,
Hag 1:12 And the people feared the L.
2:23 declares the L, 'and I will make you
Zec 1: 2 "The L was very angry with
1:17 and the L will again comfort Zion

3: 1 standing before the angel of the L,
3: 2 "The L rebuke you, Satan!
4: 6 by my Spirit,' says the L Almighty.
6:12 and build the temple of the L.
8:21 'Let us go at once to entreat the L
9:16 The L their God will save them on
14: 5 Then the L my God will come,
14: 7 a day known to the L.
14: 9 On that day there will be one L,
14:20 HOLY TO THE L will be inscribed
Mal 1: 2 "I have loved you," says the L.
3: 6 "I the L do not change.
4: 5 and dreadful day of the L comes.

THE ANGEL OF THE †LORD See ANGEL

ANGER OF THE †LORD See ANGER

ARK OF THE †LORD See ARK

AS SURELY AS THE †LORD LIVES   Jdg
8:19; Ru 3:13; 1Sa 14:45; 19:6; 20:3, 21; 25:26;
26:10, 16; 28:10; 29:6; 2Sa 4:9; 12:5; 14:11;
15:21; 1Ki 1:29; 2:24; 22:14; 2Ki 2:2, 4, 6; 4:30;
5:16, 20; 2Ch 18:13; Jer 4:2; 5:2; 12:16; 16:14,
15; 23:7, 8; 38:16; Hos 4:15

AS THE †LORD COMMANDED Ex 7:6, 10,
20; 16:34; 17:1; 34:4; 36:1; 39:1, 5, 7, 21, 26, 29,
31, 32, 42, 43; 40:16, 19, 21, 23, 25, 27, 29, 32;
Lev 8:4, 9, 13, 17, 21, 29; 9:7, 10; 10:15; 16:34;
24:23; Nu 1:19, 54; 2:33; 3:42; 4:49; 8:3, 20, 22;
9:5; 15:36; 17:11; 20:27; 26:4; 27:11, 22; 31:7,
31, 41, 47; 36:10; Dt 10:5; Jos 11:15, 20; 14:2, 5;
19:50; 21:3, 8; 2Sa 5:25; 24:19; Ps 106:34

COMMANDS OF THE †LORD
See COMMANDS

COVENANT OF THE †LORD
See COVENANT

DAY OF THE †LORD See DAY

DECLARES THE †LORD Ge   22:16; Nu
14:28; 2Ki 9:26, 26; 19:33; 22:19; 2Ch 34:27; Isa
14:22, 22, 23; 17:3, 6; 22:25; 30:1; 31:9; 37:34;
41:14; 43:10, 12; 49:18; 52:5, 5; 54:17; 55:8;
59:20; 66:2, 17, 22; Jer 1:8, 15, 19; 2:3, 9, 12, 29;
3:1, 10, 12, 12, 13, 14, 16, 20; 4:1, 9, 17; 5:9, 11,
15, 18, 22, 29; 6:12; 7:11, 13, 19, 30, 32; 8:1, 3,
13, 17; 9:3, 6, 9, 24, 25; 12:17; 13:11, 14, 25;
15:3, 6, 9, 20; 16:5, 11, 14, 16; 17:24; 18:6; 19:6,
12; 21:7, 10, 13, 14; 22:5, 16, 24; 23:1, 2, 4, 5, 7,
11, 12, 23, 24, 24, 28, 29, 30, 31, 32, 32, 33; 25:7,
9, 12, 29, 31; 27:8, 11, 15, 22; 28:4; 29:9, 11, 14,
14, 19, 19, 23, 32; 30:3, 8, 10, 11, 17, 21; 31:1,
14, 16, 17, 20, 27, 28, 31, 32, 33, 34, 36, 37, 38;
32:5, 30, 44; 33:14; 34:5, 17, 22; 35:13; 39:17,
18; 42:11; 44:29; 45:5; 46:5, 23, 26, 28; 48:12,
25, 30, 35, 38, 43, 44, 47; 49:2, 6, 13, 16, 26, 30,
31, 32, 37, 38, 39; 50:4, 10, 20, 21, 30, 35, 40;
51:24, 25, 26, 39, 48, 52, 53; Eze 16:58; 37:14;
Hos 2:13, 16, 21; 11:11; Joel 2:12; Am 2:11, 16;
3:10, 15; 4:3, 6, 8, 9, 10, 11; 9:7, 8, 12, 13; Ob
1:4, 8; Mic 4:6; 5:10; Na 2:13; 3:5; Zep 1:2, 3,
10; 2:9; 3:8; Hag 1:9, 13; 2:4, 4, 4, 8, 9, 14, 17,
23, 23, 23; Zec 1:3, 4, 16; 2:5, 6, 6, 10; 3:10; 8:6,
11, 17; 10:12; 11:6; 12:4; 13:2, 7, 8

---

†**LORD** indicates the proper name LORD; words translated "Lord" and "lord" are indexed under *****LORD**.

DECLARES THE SOVEREIGN †LORD
Jer 2:22; Eze 5:11; 11:8, 21; 12:25, 28; 13:8, 16; 14:11, 14, 16, 18, 20, 23; 15:8; 16:8, 14, 19, 23, 30, 43, 48, 63; 17:16; 18:3, 9, 23, 30, 32; 20:3, 31, 33, 36, 40, 44; 21:7, 13; 22:12, 31; 23:34; 24:14; 25:14; 26:5, 14, 21; 28:10; 29:20; 30:6; 31:18; 32:8, 14, 16, 31, 32; 33:11; 34:8, 15, 30, 31; 35:6, 11; 36:14, 15, 23, 32; 38:18, 21; 39:5, 8, 10, 13, 20, 29; 43:19, 27; 44:12, 15, 27; 45:9, 15; 47:23; 48:29; Am 4:5; 8:3, 9, 11

THE EYES OF THE †LORD See EYES

FEAR OF THE †LORD See FEAR

FEAR THE †LORD See FEAR

GIVE THANKS TO THE †LORD 1Ch 16:8, 34, 41; 2Ch 20:21; Ps 7:17; 105:1; 106:1; 107:1, 8, 15, 21, 31; 118:1, 19, 29; 136:1; Isa 12:4; Jer 33:11

GLORY OF THE †LORD See GLORY

HAND OF THE †LORD See HAND

HOLY TO THE †LORD See HOLY

THE HOUSE OF THE †LORD
See HOUSE

I AM THE †LORD See I AM

KNOW THAT I AM THE †LORD
See KNOW

KNOW THAT I THE †LORD See KNOW

KNOW THAT THE †LORD See KNOW

LAW OF THE †LORD See LAW

THE *LORD THE †LORD ALMIGHTY
See *LORD

†LORD ALMIGHTY 1Sa 1:3, 11; 4:4; 15:2; 17:45; 2Sa 6:2, 18; 7:8, 26, 27; 1Ki 18:15; 2Ki 3:14; 19:31; 1Ch 11:9; 17:7, 24; Ps 24:10; 46:7, 11; 48:8; 69:6; 84:1, 3, 12; Isa 1:9, 24; 2:12; 3:1, 15; 5:7, 9, 16, 24; 6:3, 5; 8:13, 18; 9:7, 13, 19; 10:16, 23, 24, 26, 33; 13:4, 13; 14:22, 23, 24, 27; 17:3; 18:7, 7; 19:4, 12, 16, 17, 18, 20, 25; 21:10; 22:5, 12, 14, 14, 15, 25; 23:9; 24:23; 25:6; 28:5, 22, 29; 29:6; 31:4, 5; 37:16, 32; 39:5; 44:6; 45:13; 47:4; 48:2; 51:15; 54:5; Jer 2:19; 6:6, 9; 7:3, 21; 8:3; 9:7, 15, 17; 10:16; 11:17, 20, 22; 16:9; 19:3, 11, 15; 20:12; 23:15, 16, 36; 25:8, 27, 28, 29, 32; 26:18; 27:4, 18, 19, 21; 28:2, 14; 29:4, 8, 17, 21, 25; 30:8; 31:23, 35; 32:14, 15, 18; 33:11, 12; 35:13, 18, 19; 39:16; 42:15, 18; 43:10; 44:2, 11, 25; 46:10, 10, 18, 25; 48:1, 15; 49:5, 7, 26, 35; 50:18, 25, 31, 33, 34; 51:5, 14, 19, 33, 57, 58; Am 9:5; Mic 4:4; Na 2:13; 3:5; Hab 2:13; Zep 2:9, 10; Hag 1:2, 5, 7, 9, 14; 2:4, 6, 7, 8, 9, 9, 11, 23, 23; Zec 1:3, 3, 3, 4, 6, 12, 14, 16, 17; 2:8, 9, 11; 3:7, 9, 10; 4:6, 9; 5:4; 6:12, 15; 7:3, 4, 9, 12, 13; 8:1, 2, 3, 4, 6, 6, 7, 9, 9, 11, 14, 14, 18, 19, 20, 21, 22, 23; 9:15; 10:3; 12:5; 13:2, 7; 14:16, 17, 21; Mal 1:4, 6, 8, 9, 10, 11, 13, 14; 2:2, 4, 7, 8, 12, 16; 3:1, 5, 7, 10, 11, 12, 14, 17; 4:1, 3

†LORD ALMIGHTY SAYS 1Sa 15:2; 2Sa 7:8; 1Ch 17:7; Isa 10:24; 22:15; Jer 6:6, 9; 9:7, 17; 11:22; 19:11; 23:15, 16; 25:8, 28, 32; 26:18;

27:19; 29:17; 33:12; 49:7, 35; 50:33; 51:58; Hag 1:2, 5, 7; 2:6, 11; Zec 1:3, 4, 14, 17; 2:8; 3:7; 6:12; 7:9; 8:2, 4, 6, 9, 14, 19, 20, 23; Mal 1:4

†LORD GOD Ge 2:4, 5, 7, 8, 9, 15, 16, 18, 19, 21, 22; 3:1, 8, 8, 9, 13, 14, 21, 22, 23; 14:22; 24:12, 42; Ex 9:30; Nu 22:18; Dt 4:5, 35, 39; 26:14; Jos 14:8, 9; 22:34; 1Sa 23:10, 11; 2Sa 5:10; 7:25; 24:24; 1Ki 3:7; 5:4, 5; 8:23, 25, 28, 60; 17:20, 21; 18:21, 36; 19:10, 14; 2Ki 19:15; 1Ch 17:16, 17; 21:17; 22:1, 7, 19; 28:20; 29:1, 10, 18; 2Ch 1:9; 2:4; 6:14, 16, 17, 19, 41, 41, 42; 20:6; 26:5, 18; 32:16; 33:13; Ezr 7:28; 9:5, 15; Ne 1:5; 9:7; Ps 7:1, 3; 13:3; 30:2, 12; 35:24; 40:5; 59:5; 68:18; 72:18; 80:4, 19; 84:8, 11; 89:8; 100:3; 104:1; 109:26; 118:27; Ser 5:14; 15:16; 31:18; 35:17; 38:17; 44:7; Da 9:4, 20; Hos 12:5; Am 3:13; 4:13; 5:14, 15, 16; 6:8, 14; Jnh 2:6; 4:6; Zec 11:4; 14:5; Mal 2:16

†LORD GOD ALMIGHTY 2Sa 5:10; 1Ki 19:10, 14; Ps 59:5; 80:4, 19; 84:8; 89:8; Jer 5:14; 15:16; 35:17; 38:17; 44:7; Hos 12:5; Am 3:13; 4:13; 5:14, 15, 16; 6:8, 14

†LORD HIS GOD Ex 32:11; Lev 4:22; Dt 17:19; 18:7; 1Sa 30:6; 2Sa 14:11; 1Ki 5:3; 11:4; 15:3, 4; 2Ki 5:11; 16:2; 2Ch 1:1; 14:2, 11; 15:9; 26:16; 27:6; 28:5; 31:20; 33:12; 34:8; 36:5, 12, 23; Ezr 7:6; Ps 146:5; Hos 7:10; Jnh 2:1; Mic 5:4

†LORD MY GOD Nu 22:18; Dt 4:5; 26:14; Jos 14:8, 9; 2Sa 24:24; 1Ki 3:7; 5:4, 5; 8:28; 17:20, 21; 1Ch 21:17; 22:7; 2Ch 2:4; 6:19; Ezr 7:28; 9:5; Ps 7:1, 3; 13:3; 30:2, 12; 35:24; 40:5; 104:1; 109:26; Jer 31:18; Da 9:4, 20; Jnh 2:6; Zec 11:4; 14:5

†LORD OUR GOD Ex 3:18; 5:3; 8:10, 26, 27; 10:25, 26; Dt 1:6, 19, 20, 25, 41; 2:29, 33, 36, 37; 3:3; 4:7; 5:2, 24, 25, 27, 27; 6:4, 20, 24, 25; 18:16; 29:15, 18, 29; Jos 18:6; 22:19, 29; 24:17, 24; Jdg 11:24; 1Sa 7:8; 1Ki 8:57, 59, 61, 65; 2Ki 18:22; 19:19; 1Ch 13:2; 15:13; 16:14; 29:16; 2Ch 2:4; 13:11; 14:7, 11; 19:7; 29:6; 32:8, 11; Ezr 9:8; Ne 10:34; Ps 20:7; 94:23; 99:5, 8, 9, 9; 105:7; 106:47; 113:5; 122:9; 123:2; Isa 26:13; 36:7; 37:20; Jer 3:22, 23, 25, 25; 5:19, 24; 8:14; 14:22; 16:10; 26:16; 31:6; 37:3; 42:6, 6, 20; 43:2; 50:28; 51:10; Da 9:10, 13, 14; Mic 4:5; 7:17

†LORD THEIR GOD Ex 10:7; 29:46, 46; Lev 26:44; Nu 23:21; Jdg 3:7; 8:34; 1Sa 12:9; 1Ki 9:9; 2Ki 17:7, 9, 14, 16, 19; 18:12; 2Ch 31:6; 33:17; 34:33; Ne 9:3, 3, 4; Jer 3:21; 22:9; 30:9; 43:1; 50:4; Eze 28:26; 34:30; 39:22, 28; Hos 1:7; 3:5; Zep 2:7; Hag 1:12, 12; Zec 9:16; 10:6

†LORD YOUR GOD Ge 27:20; Ex 6:7; 8:28; 10:8, 16, 17; 15:26; 16:12; 20:2, 5, 7, 10, 12; 23:19, 25; 34:24, 26; Lev 11:44; 18:2, 4, 30; 19:2, 3, 4, 10, 25, 31, 34, 36; 20:7, 24; 23:22, 28, 40, 43; 24:22; 25:17, 38, 55; 26:1, 13; Nu 10:9, 10; 15:41, 41; Dt 1:10, 21, 26, 30, 31, 32; 2:7, 7, 30; 3:18, 20, 21, 22; 4:2, 3, 4, 10, 19, 21, 23, 23, 24, 25, 29, 30, 31, 34, 40; 5:6, 9, 11, 12, 14, 15, 15, 16, 16, 32, 33; 6:1, 2, 5, 10, 13, 15, 16, 17; 7:1, 2, 6, 6, 9, 12, 16, 18, 19, 19, 20, 21, 22, 23,

25; 8:2, 5, 6, 7, 10, 11, 14, 18, 19, 20; 9:3, 4, 5, 6, 7, 16, 23; 10:9, 12, 12, 12, 14, 17, 20, 22; 11:1, 2, 12, 12, 13, 22, 25, 27, 28, 29, 31; 12:4, 5, 7, 7, 9, 10, 11, 12, 15, 18, 18, 18, 20, 21, 27, 27, 28, 29, 31; 13:3, 4, 5, 5, 10, 12, 16, 18; 14:1, 2, 21, 23, 23, 24, 25, 26, 29; 15:4, 5, 6, 7, 10, 14, 15, 18, 19, 20, 21; 16:1, 2, 5, 7, 8, 10, 10, 11, 15, 15, 16, 17, 18, 20, 21, 22; 17:1, 2, 8, 12, 14, 15; 18:5, 9, 12, 13, 14, 15, 16; 19:1, 2, 3, 8, 9, 10, 14; 20:1, 4, 13, 14, 16, 17, 18; 21:1, 5, 10, 23; 22:5; 23:5, 5, 14, 18, 18, 20, 21, 21, 23; 24:4, 9, 13, 18, 19; 25:15, 16, 19; 26:1, 2, 2, 3, 4, 5, 10, 11, 13, 16, 19; 27:2, 3, 5, 6, 6, 7, 9, 10; 28:1, 1, 2, 8, 9, 13, 15, 45, 47, 52, 53, 58, 62; 29:6, 10, 12; 30:1, 2, 3, 4, 6, 7, 9, 10, 10, 16, 16, 20; 31:3, 6, 11, 12, 13, 26; Jos 1:9, 11, 13, 15, 17; 2:11; 3:3, 9; 4:5, 23, 23, 24; 8:7; 9:9, 24; 10:19; 22:3, 4, 5; 23:3, 3, 5, 5, 8, 10, 11, 13, 13, 14, 15, 16; Jdg 6:10, 26; 1Sa 12:12, 14, 19; 13:13; 15:15, 21, 30; 25:29; 2Sa 14:17; 18:28; 24:3, 23; 1Ki 1:17; 2:3; 10:9; 13:6, 21; 17:12; 18:10; 2Ki 17:39; 19:4, 4; 23:21; 1Ch 11:2; 22:11, 12, 18, 19; 28:8; 29:20; 2Ch 9:8, 8; 16:7; 20:20; 28:10; 30:8, 9; 35:3; Ne 8:9; 9:5; Ps 76:11; 81:10; Isa 7:11; 37:4, 4; 41:13; 43:3; 48:17; 51:15; 55:5; 60:9; Jer 2:17, 19; 3:13; 13:16; 26:13; 40:2; 42:2, 3, 4, 5, 13, 20, 21; Eze 20:5, 7, 19, 20; Hos 12:9; 13:4; 14:1; Joel 1:14; 2:13, 14, 23, 26, 27; 3:17; Am 9:15; Mic 7:10; Zep 3:17; Zec 6:15

LOVE THE †LORD See LOVE

THE NAME OF THE †LORD See NAME

PRAISE BE TO THE †LORD See PRAISE

PRAISE THE †LORD See PRAISE

PRESENCE OF THE †LORD
See PRESENCE

SAYS THE †LORD 2Ki 20:17; Ps 12:5; 91:14; Isa 1:11, 18; 33:10; 39:6; 41:21; 45:13; 48:22; 54:1, 8, 10; 57:19; 59:21, 21; 65:7, 25; 66:9, 20, 21, 23; Jer 6:15; 8:12; 24:8; 30:3; 33:11, 13; 44:26; 49:2, 18; Am 1:5, 15; 2:3; 5:17, 27; 9:15; Zep 3:20; Hag 1:8; 2:7, 9; Zec 1:3; 3:9; 4:6; 7:13; 8:14; Mal 1:2, 6, 8, 9, 10, 11, 13, 13, 14; 2:2, 4, 8, 16, 16; 3:1, 5, 7, 10, 11, 12, 13, 17; 4:1, 3

SERVANT OF THE †LORD See SERVANT

SOVEREIGN †LORD Ge 15:2, 8; Ex 23:17; 34:23; Dt 3:24; 9:26; Jos 7:7; Jdg 6:22; 16:28; 2Sa 7:18, 19, 19, 20, 22, 28, 29; 1Ki 2:26; 8:53; Ps 68:20; 71:5, 16; 73:28; 109:21; 140:7; 141:8; Isa 7:7; 25:8; 28:16; 30:15; 40:10; 48:16; 49:22; 50:4, 5, 7, 9; 51:22; 52:4; 56:8; 61:1, 11; 65:13, 15; Jer 1:6; 2:22; 4:10; 7:20; 14:13; 32:17, 25; 44:26; 50:25; Eze 2:4; 3:11, 27; 4:14; 5:5, 7, 8, 11; 6:3, 3, 11; 7:2, 5; 8:1; 9:8; 11:7, 8, 13, 16, 17, 21; 12:10, 19, 23, 25, 28, 28; 13:3, 8, 8, 9, 13, 16, 18, 20; 14:4, 6, 11, 14, 16, 18, 20, 21, 23; 15:6, 8; 16:3, 8, 14, 19, 23, 30, 36, 43, 48, 59, 63; 17:3, 9, 16, 19, 22; 18:3, 9, 23, 30, 32; 20:3, 3, 5, 27, 30, 31, 33, 36, 39, 40, 44, 47, 49; 21:7, 13, 24, 26, 28; 22:3, 12, 19, 28, 31; 23:22, 28, 32, 34, 35, 46, 49; 24:3, 6, 9, 14, 21, 24; 25:3, 3, 6, 8, 12, 13, 14, 15,

16; 26:3, 5, 7, 14, 15, 19, 21; 27:3; 28:2, 6, 10, 12, 22, 24, 25; 29:3, 8, 13, 16, 19, 20; 30:2, 6, 10, 13, 22; 31:10, 15, 18; 32:3, 8, 11, 14, 16, 31, 32; 33:11, 25, 27; 34:2, 8, 10, 11, 15, 17, 20, 30, 31; 35:3, 6, 11, 14; 36:2, 3, 4, 4, 5, 6, 7, 13, 14, 15, 22, 23, 32, 33, 37; 37:3, 5, 9, 12, 19, 21; 38:3, 10, 14, 17, 18, 21; 39:1, 5, 8, 10, 13, 17, 20, 25, 29; 43:18, 19, 27; 44:6, 9, 12, 15, 27; 45:9, 9, 15, 18; 46:1, 16; 47:13, 23; 48:29; Am 1:8; 3:7, 8, 11; 4:2, 5; 5:3; 6:8; 7:1, 2, 4, 4, 5, 6; 8:1, 3, 9, 11; 9:8; Ob 1:1; Mic 1:2; Hab 3:19; Zep 1:7; Zec 9:14

SPIRIT OF THE †LORD See SPIRIT

TEMPLE OF THE †LORD See TEMPLE

THE VOICE OF THE †LORD See VOICE

WHAT THE †LORD SAYS Ex 4:22; 7:17; 8:1, 20; 11:4; Nu 24:13; 1Sa 2:27; 2Sa 7:5; 12:11; 24:12; 1Ki 12:24; 13:2, 21; 20:13, 14, 28, 42; 21:19, 19; 22:11; 2Ki 1:4, 6, 16; 2:21; 3:16, 17; 4:43; 7:1; 9:3, 12; 19:6, 32; 20:1; 22:16; 1Ch 17:4; 21:10, 11; 2Ch 11:4; 12:5; 18:10; 20:15; 34:24; Isa 18:4; 31:4; 37:6, 33; 38:1; 43:1, 14, 16; 44:2, 6, 24; 45:1, 11, 14, 18; 48:17; 49:7, 8, 25; 50:1; 52:3; 56:1, 4; 65:8; 66:1, 12; Jer 2:5; 4:3, 27; 6:16, 21, 22; 8:4; 9:23; 10:1, 2; 18: 11:11, 21; 12:14; 13:9, 13; 14:10, 15; 15:2, 19; 16:3, 5; 17:5, 21; 18:11, 13; 19:1; 20:4; 21:8, 12; 22:1, 3, 6, 11, 18, 30; 23:38; 26:2, 4; 27:16; 28:11, 13, 16; 29:10, 16, 31, 32; 30:5, 12, 18; 31:2, 7, 15, 16, 35, 37; 32:3, 28, 42; 33:2, 10, 17, 20, 25; 34:2, 4, 17; 36:29, 30; 37:9; 38:2, 3; 44:30; 45:4; 47:2; 48:40; 49:1, 12, 28; 51:1, 36; Eze 11:5; 21:3; 30:6; Am 1:3, 6, 9, 11, 13; 2:1, 4, 6; 3:12; 5:4; 7:17; Mic 3:5; 6:1; Na 1:12; Zec 1:16; 8:3

WHAT THE SOVEREIGN †LORD SAYS
Isa 7:7; 28:16; 49:22; 52:4; 65:13; Jer 7:20; Eze 2:4; 3:11, 27; 5:5, 7, 8; 6:3, 11; 7:2, 5; 11:7, 16, 17; 12:10, 19, 23, 28; 13:3, 8, 13, 18, 20; 14:4, 6, 21; 15:6; 16:3, 36, 59; 17:3, 9, 19, 22; 20:3, 5, 27, 30, 39, 47; 21:24, 26, 28; 22:3, 19, 28; 23:22, 28, 32, 35, 46; 24:3, 6, 9, 21; 25:3, 6, 8, 12, 13, 15, 16; 26:3, 7, 15, 19; 27:3; 28:2, 6, 12, 22, 25; 29:3, 8, 13, 19; 30:2, 10, 13, 22; 31:10, 15; 32:3, 11; 33:25, 27; 34:2, 10, 11, 17, 20; 35:3, 14; 36:2, 3, 4, 5, 6, 7, 13, 22, 33, 37; 37:5, 9, 12, 19, 21; 38:3, 10, 14, 17, 25; 39:1, 17, 25; 43:18; 44:6, 9; 45:9, 18; 46:1, 16; 47:13; Am 3:11; 5:3; Ob 1:1

WORD OF THE †LORD See WORD

†LORD'S [†LORD (YAHWEH)]

Ex	4:14	the **L** anger burned against Moses
	9:29	may know that the earth is the **L**.
	12:11	Eat it in haste; it is the **L** Passover.
	34:34	whenever he entered the **L** presence
Lev	23:4	" 'These are the **L** appointed feasts,
Nu	9:23	At the **L** command they encamped,
	11:23	"Is the **L** arm too short?
	14:41	are you disobeying the **L** command?
	31:3	and to carry out the **L** vengeance
	32:13	The **L** anger burned against Israel
Dt	6:18	right and good in the **L** sight,

10:13 and to observe the **L** commands
32: 9 For the **L** portion is his people,
33:21 he carried out the **L** righteous will,
Jos 21:45 Not one of all the **L** good promises
Jdg 3: 4 they would obey the **L** commands,
1Sa 17:47 for the battle is the **L,**
24:10 because he is the **L** anointed.'
1Ki 10: 9 of the **L** eternal love for Israel,
Ps 24: 1 The earth is the **L,**
32:10 but the **L** unfailing love surrounds
89: 1 sing of the **L** great love forever;
103:17 the **L** love is with those who fear him
118:15 **L** right hand has done mighty things!
Pr 3:11 son, do not despise the **L** discipline
3:33 The **L** curse is on the house of
19:21 it is the **L** purpose that prevails.
Isa 2: 2 mountain of the **L** temple will be
24:14 they acclaim the **L** majesty.
30: 9 unwilling to listen to the **L**
40: 2 the **L** hand double for all her sins.
49: 4 what is due me is in the **L** hand,
53:10 Yet it was the **L** will to crush him
55:13 This will be for the **L** renown,
61: 2 the year of the **L** favor and the day
62: 3 a crown of splendor in the **L** hand,
Jer 13:17 the **L** flock will be taken captive.
25:17 So I took the cup from the **L** hand
48:10 who is lax in doing the **L** work!
51: 6 It is time for the **L** vengeance;
La 3:22 Because of the **L** great love we are
Eze 7:19 in the day of the **L** wrath.
Joel 3:18 fountain will flow out of the **L** house
Ob 1:21 And the kingdom will be the **L.**
Mic 4: 1 mountain of the **L** temple will be
6: 2 O mountains, the **L** accusation;
Hab 2:16 The cup from the **L** right hand
Zep 2: 3 sheltered on the day of the **L** anger.

LORDED* [*LORD]

Ne 5:15 Their assistants also **l** it over

LORDING* [*LORD]

1Pe 5: 3 not **l** it over those entrusted to you,

LORDS [*LORD]

Dt 10:17 God is God of gods and Lord of **l,**
Ps 136: 3 Give thanks to the Lord of **l:**
Isa 26:13 other **l** besides you have ruled
1Co 8: 5 many "gods" and many "**l**"),
Rev 17:14 he is Lord of **l** and King of kings—
19:16 KING OF KINGS AND LORD OF **L.**

LOSE [LOSES, LOSS, LOST]

Ge 26: 9 "Because I thought I might **l** my life
Dt 1:28 Our brothers have made us **l** heart.
1Sa 17:32 "Let no one **l** heart on account
Isa 7: 4 Do not **l** heart because
Mt 10:39 Whoever finds his life will **l** it,
Mk 8:35 wants to save his life will **l** it,
Lk 9:25 and yet **l** or forfeit his very self?
Jn 6:39 that I shall **l** none of all
12:25 The man who loves his life will **l** it,
2Co 4: 1 we do not **l** heart.
4:16 Therefore we do not **l** heart.

Heb 12: 3 not grow weary and **l** heart.
12: 5 do not **l** heart when he rebukes you,
2Jn 1: 8 not **l** what you have worked for,

LOSES [LOSE]

Mt 5:13 But if the salt **l** its saltiness,
Mk 8:35 but whoever **l** his life for me and
Lk 15: 4 a hundred sheep and **l** one of them.
15: 8 woman has ten silver coins and **l** one.

LOSS [LOSE]

Ro 11:12 their **l** means riches for the Gentiles,
1Co 3:15 If it is burned up, he will suffer **l;**
Php 3: 8 I consider everything a **l** compared
Heb 6: 6 to their **l** they are crucifying

LOST [LOSE]

Nu 17:12 We are **l,** we are all **l!**
Ps 73: 2 I had nearly **l** my foothold.
119:176 I have strayed like a **l** sheep.
Jer 50: 6 "My people have been **l** sheep;
Eze 34: 4 back the strays or searched for the **l.**
34:16 for the **l** and bring back the strays.
Mt 10: 6 Go rather to the **l** sheep of Israel.
15:24 "I was sent only to the **l** sheep
18:14 of these little ones should be **l.**
Lk 15: 4 and go after the **l** sheep
15: 6 with me; I have found my **l** sheep.'
15: 9 with me; I have found my **l** coin.'
15:24 he was **l** and is found.'
19:10 to seek and to save what was **l.**"
Jn 17:12 None has been **l** except the one
18: 9 not **l** one of those you gave me."
Php 3: 8 for whose sake I have **l** all things.
Col 2:19 He has **l** connection with the Head,

LOT [LOT'S, LOTS, PUR]

Nephew of Abraham (Ge 11:27; 12:5). Chose to
live in Sodom (Ge 13). Rescued from four kings
(Ge 14). Rescued from Sodom (Ge 19:1-29; 2Pe
2:7). Fathered Moab and Ammon by his daughters
(Ge 19:30-38).

Lev 16: 9 the goat whose **l** falls to the LORD
Nu 33:54 Distribute the land by **l,**
1Sa 14:42 Saul said, "Cast the **l** between me
Est 3: 7 And the **l** fell on the twelfth month,
9:24 the **l**) for their ruin and destruction.
Job 31: 2 what is man's **l** from God above,
Ps 16: 5 have made my **l** secure.
Pr 16:33 The **l** is cast into the lap,
18:18 Casting the **l** settles disputes
Ecc 3:22 because that is his **l.**
5:19 to accept his **l** and be happy
Jnh 1: 7 and the **l** fell on Jonah.
Ac 1:26 and the **l** fell to Matthias;

LOT'S* [LOT]

Ge 19:26 But **L** wife looked back,
19:36 **L** daughters became pregnant by
Lk 17:32 Remember **L** wife!

LOTS [LOT]

Lev 16: 8 He is to cast **l** for the two goats—
Jos 18:10 Joshua then cast **l** for them in Shiloh

1Ch 25: 8 cast l for their duties.
Ps 22:18 and cast l for my clothing.
Joel 3: 3 They cast l for my people
Ob 1:11 and cast l for Jerusalem.
Mt 27:35 divided up his clothes by casting l.
Ac 1:26 Then they cast l,

LOUD

Ex 12:30 and there was l wailing in Egypt,
    19:16 and a very l trumpet blast.
Jos 6: 5 have all the people give a l shout;
Pr 9:13 The woman Folly is l;
Eze 9: 1 I heard him call out in a l voice,
Da 4:14 He called in a l voice:
Mk 15:34 Jesus cried out in a l voice,
Jn 11:43 Jesus called in a l voice, "Lazarus,
Rev 1:10 and I heard behind me a l voice like
    21: 3 a l voice from the throne saying,

LOVE* [BELOVED, LOVED, LOVELY, LOVER, LOVER'S, LOVERS, LOVES, LOVING, LOVING-KINDNESS]

Ge 20:13 'This is how you can show your l
    22: 2 your only son, Isaac, whom you l,
    29:18 Jacob was in l with Rachel
    29:20 a few days to him because of his l
    29:32 Surely my husband will l me now."
Ex 15:13 "In your unfailing l you will lead
    20: 6 but showing l to a thousand
        [generations] of those who l me and
    21: 5 'I l my master and my wife and
    34: 6 abounding in l and faithfulness,
    34: 7 maintaining l to thousands, and
Lev 19:18 but l your neighbor as yourself.
    19:34 L him as yourself,
Nu 14:18 abounding in l and forgiving sin
    14:19 In accordance with your great l,
Dt 5:10 but showing l to a thousand
        [generations] of those who l me and
    6: 5 L the Lord your God with all your
    7: 9 keeping his covenant of l to a
        thousand generations of those who l
    7:12 keep his covenant of l with you,
    7:13 He will l you and bless you
    10:12 to walk in all his ways, to l him,
    10:19 you are to l those who are aliens,
    11: 1 L the Lord your God and keep
    11:13 to l the Lord your God and to serve
    11:22 to l the Lord your God, to walk
    13: 3 to find out whether you l him
    13: 6 or the wife you l,
    19: 9 to l the Lord your God and to walk
    21:15 the son of the wife he does not l,
    21:16 the son of the wife he does not l.
    30: 6 so that you may l him with all
    30:16 to l the Lord your God, to walk
    30:20 you may l the Lord your God,
    33: 3 Surely it is you who l the people;
Jos 22: 5 to l the Lord your God, to walk
    23:11 careful to l the Lord your God.
Jdg 5:31 But may they who l you be like
    14:16 You don't really l me.
    16: 4 in l with a woman in the Valley

16:15 "How can you say, 'I l you,'
1Sa 18:20 daughter Michal was in l with David,
    20:17 reaffirm his oath out of l for him,
2Sa 1:26 Your l for me was wonderful,
    7:15 But my l will never be taken away
    13: 1 son of David fell in l with Tamar,
    13: 4 "I'm in l with Tamar,
    16:17 "Is this the l you show your friend?
    19: 6 You l those who hate you and hate
        those who l you.
1Ki 3: 3 Solomon showed his l for the Lord
    8:23 who keep your covenant of l
    10: 9 of the Lord's eternal l for Israel,
    11: 2 Solomon held fast to them in l.
1Ch 16:34 for he is good; his l endures forever.
    16:41 "for his l endures forever."
    17:13 I will never take my l away
2Ch 5:13 "He is good; his l endures forever."
    6:14 you who keep your covenant of l
    6:42 Remember the great l promised
    7: 3 "He is good; his l endures forever."
    7: 6 saying, "His l endures forever."
    9: 8 of the l of your God for Israel
    19: 2 and l those who hate the Lord?
    20:21 for his l endures forever."
Ezr 3:11 his l to Israel endures forever."
Ne 1: 5 keeps his covenant of l with those
        who l him and obey his commands,
    9:17 slow to anger and abounding in l.
    9:32 who keeps his covenant of l,
    13:22 to me according to your great l.
Job 15:34 the tents of those who l bribes.
    19:19 those I l have turned against me.
    37:13 or to water his earth and show his l.
Ps 4: 2 How long will you l delusions
    5:11 those who l your name may rejoice
    6: 4 save me because of your unfailing l.
    11: 5 those who l violence his soul hates.
    13: 5 But I trust in your unfailing l;
    17: 7 Show the wonder of your great l,
    18: 1 I l you, O Lord, my strength.
    21: 7 the unfailing l of the Most High
    23: 6 and I will follow me all the days
    25: 6 O Lord, your great mercy and l,
    25: 7 according to your l remember me,
    26: 3 for your l is ever before me,
    26: 8 I l the house where you live,
    31: 7 I will be glad and rejoice in your l,
    31:16 save me in your unfailing l.
    31:21 for he showed his wonderful l
    31:23 L the Lord, all his saints!
    32:10 the Lord's unfailing l surrounds
    33: 5 the earth is full of his unfailing l.
    33:18 whose hope is in his unfailing l,
    33:22 May your unfailing l rest upon us,
    36: 5 Your l, O Lord,
    36: 7 How priceless is your unfailing l!
    36:10 Continue your l to those who
    40:10 not conceal your l and your truth
    40:11 your l and your truth always protect
    40:16 who l your salvation always say,
    42: 8 By day the Lord directs his l,
    44:26 because of your unfailing l.
    45: 7 You l righteousness and hate

48: 9	we meditate on your unfailing **l**.
51: 1	according to your unfailing **l**;
52: 3	You **l** evil rather than good,
52: 4	You **l** every harmful word,
52: 8	in God's unfailing **l** for ever
57: 3	God sends his **l** and his faithfulness.
57:10	For great is your **l**,
59:16	in the morning I will sing of your **l**;
60: 5	that those you **l** may be delivered.
61: 7	your **l** and faithfulness to protect him
63: 3	Because your **l** is better than life,
66:20	or withheld his **l** from me!
69:13	in your great **l**, O God, answer me
69:16	out of the goodness of your **l**;
69:36	who **l** his name will dwell there.
70: 4	who **l** your salvation always say,
77: 8	Has his unfailing **l** vanished forever?
85: 7	Show us your unfailing **l**,
85:10	**L** and faithfulness meet together;
86: 5	abounding in **l** to all who call
86:13	For great is your **l** toward me;
86:15	abounding in **l** and faithfulness.
88:11	Is your **l** declared in the grave,
89: 1	sing of the LORD's great **l** forever;
89: 2	that your **l** stands firm forever,
89:14	**l** and faithfulness go before you.
89:24	My faithful **l** will be with him,
89:28	I will maintain my **l** to him forever,
89:33	but I will not take my **l** from him,
89:49	where is your former great **l**,
90:14	in the morning with your unfailing **l**,
92: 2	to proclaim your **l** in the morning
94:18	your **l**, O LORD, supported me.
97:10	Let those who **l** the LORD
98: 3	He has remembered his **l**
100: 5	and his **l** endures forever;
101: 1	I will sing of your **l** and justice;
103: 4	from the pit and crowns you with **l**
103: 8	slow to anger, abounding in **l**.
103:11	great is his **l** for those who fear him;
103:17	LORD's **l** is with those who fear him,
106: 1	for he is good; his **l** endures forever.
106:45	and out of his great **l** he relented.
107: 1	for he is good; his **l** endures forever.
107: 8	to the LORD for his unfailing **l**
107:15	to the LORD for his unfailing **l**
107:21	to the LORD for his unfailing **l**
107:31	to the LORD for his unfailing **l**
107:43	consider the great **l** of the LORD.
108: 4	For great is your **l**,
108: 6	that those you **l** may be delivered.
109:21	out of the goodness of your **l**,
109:26	save me in accordance with your **l**.
115: 1	because of your **l** and faithfulness.
116: 1	I **l** the LORD,
117: 2	For great is his **l** toward us,
118: 1	for he is good; his **l** endures forever.
118: 2	Israel say: "His **l** endures forever."
118: 3	Aaron say: "His **l** endures forever."
118: 4	say: "His **l** endures forever."
118:29	for he is good; his **l** endures forever.
119:41	May your unfailing **l** come to me,
119:47	in your commands because I **l** them.
119:48	to your commands, which I **l**,

119:64	The earth is filled with your **l**,
119:76	May your unfailing **l**
119:88	my life according to your **l**,
119:97	Oh, how I **l** your law!
119:113	but I **l** your law.
119:119	therefore I **l** your statutes.
119:124	with your servant according to your **l**
119:127	I **l** your commands more than gold,
119:132	do to those who **l** your name.
119:149	in accordance with your **l**;
119:159	See how I **l** your precepts;
119:159	O LORD, according to your **l**.
119:163	abhor falsehood but I **l** your law.
119:165	peace have they who **l** your law,
119:167	for I **l** them greatly.
122: 6	"May those who **l** you be secure.
130: 7	for with the LORD is unfailing **l**
136: 1	*His l endures forever.*
136: 2	*His l endures forever.*
136: 3	*His l endures forever.*
136: 4	*His l endures forever.*
136: 5	*His l endures forever.*
136: 6	*His l endures forever.*
136: 7	*His l endures forever.*
136: 8	*His l endures forever.*
136: 9	*His l endures forever.*
136:10	*His l endures forever.*
136:11	*His l endures forever.*
136:12	*His l endures forever.*
136:13	*His l endures forever.*
136:14	*His l endures forever.*
136:15	*His l endures forever.*
136:16	*His l endures forever.*
136:17	*His l endures forever.*
136:18	*His l endures forever.*
136:19	*His l endures forever.*
136:20	*His l endures forever.*
136:21	*His l endures forever.*
136:22	*His l endures forever.*
136:23	*His l endures forever.*
136:24	*His l endures forever.*
136:25	*His l endures forever.*
136:26	*His l endures forever.*
138: 2	and will praise your name for your **l**
138: 8	your **l**, O LORD, endures forever—
143: 8	bring me word of your unfailing **l**,
143:12	In your unfailing **l**,
145: 8	slow to anger and rich in **l**.
145:20	LORD watches over all who **l** him,
147:11	put their hope in his unfailing **l**.
Pr 1:22	simple ones **l** your simple ways?
3: 3	Let **l** and faithfulness never leave
4: 6	**l** her, and she will watch over you.
5:19	be captivated by her **l**.
7:18	let's drink deep of **l** till morning;
7:18	let's enjoy ourselves with **l**!
8:17	I **l** those who **l** me,
8:21	bestowing wealth on those who **l** me
8:36	all who hate me **l** death."
9: 8	a wise man and he will **l** you.
10:12	but **l** covers over all wrongs.
14:22	those who plan what is good find **l**
15:17	a meal of vegetables where there is **l**
16: 6	**l** and faithfulness sin is atoned for;

	17: 9	covers over an offense promotes l,
	18:21	and those who l it will eat its fruit.
	19:22	What a man desires is unfailing l;
	20: 6	a man claims to have unfailing l,
	20:13	not I sleep or you will grow poor;
	20:28	L and faithfulness keep a king safe;
	20:28	through I his throne is made secure.
	21:21	pursues righteousness and I finds life
	27: 5	Better is open rebuke than hidden l.
Ecc	3: 8	a time to I and a time to hate,
	9: 1	but no man knows whether I
	9: 6	Their l, their hate and their jealousy
	9: 9	with your wife, whom you l,
SS	1: 2	your I is more delightful than wine.
	1: 3	No wonder the maidens I you!
	1: 4	we will praise your I more than wine.
	1: 7	Tell me, you whom I l,
	2: 4	and his banner over me is l.
	2: 5	for I am faint with l.
	2: 7	or awaken I until it so desires.
	3: 5	or awaken I until it so desires.
	4:10	How delightful is your l, my sister,
	4:10	more pleasing is your I than wine,
	5: 8	Tell him I am faint with l.
	7: 6	O I, with your delights!
	7:12	there I will give you my l.
	8: 4	or awaken I until it so desires.
	8: 6	for I is as strong as death,
	8: 7	Many waters cannot quench l;
	8: 7	the wealth of his house for l,
Isa	1:23	they all I bribes and chase
	5: 1	I will sing for the one I I a song
	16: 5	In I a throne will be established;
	38:17	In your I you kept me from the pit
	43: 4	and because I I you,
	54:10	yet my unfailing I for you will not
	55: 3	my faithful I promised to David.
	56: 6	to I the name of the LORD,
	56:10	they I to sleep.
	57: 8	a pact with those whose beds you l,
	61: 8	"For I, the LORD, I justice;
	63: 9	In his I and mercy he redeemed them
	66:10	all you who I her;
Jer	2:25	I I foreign gods,
	2:33	How skilled you are at pursuing l!
	5:31	and my people I it this way.
	12: 7	I will give the one I I
	14:10	"They greatly I to wander;
	16: 5	my I and my pity from this people,"
	31: 3	have loved you with an everlasting l;
	32:18	You show I to thousands but bring
	33:11	LORD is good; his I endures forever."
La	3:22	Because of the LORD's great I we
	3:32	so great is his unfailing l.
Eze	16: 8	that you were old enough for l,
	23:17	to the bed of l,
	33:32	more than one who sings I songs
Da	9: 4	who keeps his covenant of I with all
		who I him and obey his commands,
Hos	1: 6	for I will no longer show I to
	1: 7	I will show I to the house of Judah,
	2: 4	I will not show my I to her children,
	2:19	in I and compassion.
	2:23	I will show my I to the one I called

	3: 1	show your I to your wife again,
	3: 1	L her as the LORD loves
	3: 1	though they turn to other gods and I
	4: 1	no I, no acknowledgment of God in
	4:18	their rulers dearly I shameful ways.
	6: 4	Your I is like the morning mist,
	9: 1	been unfaithful to your God; you I
	9:15	I will no longer I them;
	10:12	reap the fruit of unfailing l,
	11: 4	of human kindness, with ties of l;
	12: 6	must return to your God; maintain I
	14: 4	and I them freely,
Joel	2:13	slow to anger and abounding in l,
Am	4: 5	for this is what you I to do,"
	5:15	Hate evil, I good;
Jnh	4: 2	slow to anger and abounding in l,
Mic	3: 2	you who hate good and I evil;
	6: 8	and to I mercy and to walk humbly
Zep	3:17	he will quiet you with his l,
Zec	8:17	and do not I to swear falsely.
	8:19	Therefore I truth and peace."
Mt	3:17	"This is my Son, whom I I;
	5:43	'L your neighbor and hate your
	5:44	But I tell you: L your enemies
	5:46	If you I those who I you,
	6: 5	for they I to pray standing in
	6:24	he will hate the one and I the other,
	12:18	the one I I, in whom I delight;
	17: 5	"This is my Son, whom I I;
	19:19	and 'I your neighbor as yourself.' "
	22:37	" 'L the Lord your God with all
	22:39	second is like it: 'L your neighbor
	23: 6	they I the place of honor
	23: 7	I to be greeted in the marketplaces
	24:12	the I of most will grow cold,
Mk	1:11	"You are my Son, whom I I;
	9: 7	"This is my Son, whom I I.
	12:30	L the Lord your God with all
	12:31	The second is this: 'L your neighbor
	12:33	To I him with all your heart,
	12:33	to I your neighbor as yourself
Lk	3:22	"You are my Son, whom I I;
	6:27	you who hear me: L your enemies,
	6:32	"If you I those who I you,
	6:32	'sinners' I those who I them.
	6:35	But I your enemies,
	7:42	which of them will I him more?"
	10:27	" 'L the Lord your God with all
	10:27	'L your neighbor as yourself.' "
	11:42	you neglect justice and the I of God.
	11:43	you I the most important seats
	16:13	he will hate the one and I the other,
	20:13	I will send my son, whom I I;
	20:46	I to be greeted in the marketplaces
Jn	5:42	that you do not have the I of God
	8:42	you would I me,
	11: 3	"Lord, the one you I is sick."
	13: 1	showed them the full extent of his l.
	13:34	command I give you: L one another.
	13:34	so you must I one another.
	13:35	if you I one another."
	14:15	"If you I me,
	14:21	and I too will I him
	14:23	My Father will I him,

14:24 not l me will not obey my teaching.
14:31 world must learn that l I the Father
15: 9 Now remain in my l.
15:10 you will remain in my l,
15:10 and remain in his l.
15:12 My command is this: L each other
15:13 Greater l has no one than this,
15:17 This is my command: L each other.
15:19 it would l you as its own.
17:26 the l you have for me may be in them
21:15 do you truly l me more than these?"
21:15 he said, "you know that I l you."
21:16 do you truly l me?"
21:16 "Yes, Lord, you know that I l you."
21:17 "Simon son of John, do you l me?"
21:17 "Do you l me?"
21:17 you know that I l you."

Ro 5: 5 because God has poured out his l
5: 8 But God demonstrates his own l
8:28 God works for the good of those
who l him,
8:35 Who shall separate us from the l
8:39 be able to separate us from the l
12: 9 L must be sincere.
12:10 devoted to one another in brotherly l.
13: 8 the continuing debt to l one another,
13: 9 in this one rule: "L your neighbor
13:10 L does no harm to its neighbor.
13:10 l is the fulfillment of the law.
14:15 you are no longer acting in l.
15:30 and by the l of the Spirit,
16: 8 whom I l in the Lord.

1Co 2: 9 God has prepared for those who l
4:17 my son whom I l,
4:21 or in l and with a gentle spirit?
8: 1 but l builds up.
13: 1 but have not l, I am only a
13: 2 but have not l, I am nothing.
13: 3 but have not l, I gain nothing.
13: 4 L is patient, l is kind.
13: 6 L does not delight in evil
13: 8 L never fails.
13:13 these three remain: faith, hope and l.
13:13 But the greatest of these is l.
14: 1 Follow the way of l and eagerly
16:14 Do everything in l.
16:22 If anyone does not l the Lord—
16:24 My l to all of you in Christ Jesus.

2Co 2: 4 to let you know the depth of my l
2: 8 to reaffirm your l for him.
5:14 For Christ's l compels us,
6: 6 in the Holy Spirit and in sincere l;
8: 7 and in your l for us—
8: 8 the sincerity of your l by comparing
8:24 show these men the proof of your l
11:11 Because I do not l you?
12:15 I l you more, will you l me less?
13:11 And the God of l and peace will be
13:14 and the l of God,

Gal 5: 6 is faith expressing itself through l.
5:13 serve one another in l.
5:14 a single command: "L your neighbor
5:22 But the fruit of the Spirit is l, joy,

Eph 1: 4 and blameless in his sight. In l

1:15 and your l for all the saints,
2: 4 But because of his great l for us,
3:17 being rooted and established in l,
3:18 and high and deep is the l of Christ,
3:19 know this l that surpasses knowledge
4: 2 bearing with one another in l.
4:15 Instead, speaking the truth in l,
4:16 grows and builds itself up in l,
5: 2 and live a life of l, just as Christ
5:25 Husbands, l your wives,
5:28 husbands ought to l their wives as
5:33 each one of you also must l his wife
6:23 and l with faith from God the Father
6:24 Grace to all who l our Lord Jesus
Christ with an undying l.

Php 1: 9 that your l may abound more
1:16 The latter do so in l,
2: 1 if any comfort from his l,
2: 2 having the same l,
4: 1 you whom I l and long for,

Col 1: 4 the l you have for all the saints—
1: 5 and l that spring from the hope
1: 8 also told us of your l in the Spirit.
2: 2 encouraged in heart and united in l,
3:14 And over all these virtues put on l,
3:19 l your wives and do not be harsh

1Th 1: 3 your labor prompted by l,
3: 6 good news about your faith and l.
3:12 May the Lord make your l increase
4: 9 brotherly l we do not need to write
4: 9 taught by God to l each other.
4:10 you do l all the brothers
5: 8 putting on faith and l as a breastplate.
5:13 Hold them in the highest regard in l

2Th 1: 3 and the l every one of you has
2:10 because they refused to l the truth
3: 5 Lord direct your hearts into God's l

1Ti 1: 5 The goal of this command is l,
1:14 faith and l that are in Christ Jesus.
2:15 l and holiness with propriety.
4:12 in life, in l, in faith and in purity.
6:10 the l of money is a root of all kinds
6:11 faith, l, endurance and gentleness.

2Ti 1: 7 of l and of self-discipline.
1:13 with faith and l in Christ Jesus.
2:22 faith, l and peace,
3: 3 without l, unforgiving, slanderous,
3:10 my purpose, faith, patience, l,

Tit 2: 2 in l and in endurance.
2: 4 to l their husbands and children,
3: 4 and l of God our Savior appeared,
3:15 Greet those who l us in the faith.

Phm 1: 5 and your l for all the saints.
1: 7 Your l has given me great joy
1: 9 yet I appeal to you on the basis of l.

Heb 6:10 the l you have shown him
10:24 we may spur one another on toward l
13: 5 your lives free from the l of money

Jas 1:12 has promised to those who l him.
2: 5 kingdom he promised those who l
2: 8 "L your neighbor as yourself,"

1Pe 1: 8 you have not seen him, you l him;
1:22 the truth so that you have sincere l
1:22 l one another deeply,

2:17 **L** the brotherhood of believers,
3: 8 **l** as brothers, be compassionate
3:10 "Whoever would **l** life
4: 8 Above all, **l** each other deeply,
4: 8 **l** covers over a multitude of sins.
5:14 Greet one another with a kiss of **l**.
2Pe 1: 7 and to brotherly kindness, **l**,
1:17 saying, "This is my Son, whom I **l**;
1Jn 2: 5 God's **l** is truly made complete in
2:15 Do not **l** the world or anything in
2:15 the **l** of the Father is not in him.
3: 1 the **l** the Father has lavished on us,
3:10 who does not **l** his brother.
3:11 beginning: We should **l** one another.
3:14 because we **l** our brothers.
3:14 Anyone who does not **l** remains
3:16 This is how we know what **l** is:
3:17 how can the **l** of God be in him?
3:18 let us not **l** with words or tongue
3:23 to **l** one another as he commanded us
4: 7 Dear friends, let us **l** one another,
4: 7 for **l** comes from God.
4: 8 Whoever does not **l** does not know
      God, because God is **l**.
4: 9 how God showed his **l** among us:
4:10 This is **l**: not that we loved God,
4:11 we also ought to **l** one another.
4:12 but if we **l** one another,
4:12 and his **l** is made complete in us.
4:16 and rely on the **l** God has for us.
4:16 God is **l**.
4:16 Whoever lives in **l** lives in God,
4:17 **l** is made complete among us so
4:18 There is no fear in **l**.
4:18 But perfect **l** drives out fear,
4:18 who fears is not made perfect in **l**.
4:19 We **l** because he first loved us.
4:20 If anyone says, "I **l** God,"
4:20 anyone who does not **l** his brother,
4:20 whom he has seen, cannot **l** God,
4:21 must also **l** his brother.
5: 2 how we know that we **l** the children
5: 3 This is **l** for God:
2Jn 1: 1 whom I **l** in the truth—
1: 3 will be with us in truth and **l**.
1: 5 I ask that we **l** one another.
1: 6 And this is **l**:
1: 6 his command is that you walk in **l**.
3Jn 1: 1 whom I **l** in the truth.
1: 6 have told the church about your **l**.
Jude 1: 2 peace and **l** be yours in abundance.
1:12 are blemishes at your **l** feasts,
1:21 Keep yourselves in God's **l** as you
Rev 2: 4 You have forsaken your first **l**.
2:19 I know your deeds, your **l** and faith,
3:19 Those whom I **l** I rebuke
12:11 not **l** their lives so much as

HIS LOVE ENDURES FOREVER
1Ch 16:34, 41; 2Ch 5:13; 7:3, 6; 20:21; Ps 100:5;
106:1; 107:1; 118:1-4, 29; 136:1-26; Jer 33:11.

LOVE THE †LORD Dt 6:5; 11:1, 13, 22; 19:9;
30:16, 20; Jos 22:5; 23:11; Ps 31:23; 97:10;
116:1

LOVE YOUR NEIGHBOR Lev 19:18; Mt
5:43; 19:19; 22:39; Mk 12:31, 33; Lk 10:27; Ro
13:9; Gal 5:14; Jas 2:8

UNFAILING LOVE Ex 15:13; Ps 6:4; 13:5;
21:7; 31:16; 32:10; 33:5, 18, 22; 36:7; 44:26;
48:9; 51:1; 52:8; 77:8; 85:7; 90:14; 107:8, 15, 21,
31; 119:41, 76; 130:7; 143:8, 12; 147:11; Pr
19:22; 20:6; Isa 54:10; La 3:32; Hos 10:12

LOVED* [LOVE]
Ge 24:67 she became his wife, and he **l** her;
25:28 **l** Esau, but Rebekah **l** Jacob.
29:30 and he **l** Rachel more than Leah.
29:31 LORD saw that Leah was not **l**,
29:33 the LORD heard that I am not **l**,
34: 3 and he **l** the girl and spoke tenderly
37: 3 Now Israel **l** Joseph more than any
37: 4 their father **l** him more than any
Dt 4:37 Because he **l** your forefathers
7: 8 because the LORD **l** you and kept
10:15 on your forefathers and **l** them,
1Sa 1: 5 a double portion because he **l** her,
18: 1 and he **l** him as himself.
18: 3 a covenant with David because he **l**
18:16 But all Israel and Judah **l** David,
18:28 that his daughter Michal **l** David,
20:17 he **l** him as he **l** himself.
2Sa 1:23 in life they were **l** and gracious,
12:24 The LORD **l** him;
12:25 and because the LORD **l** him,
13:15 he hated her more than he had **l** her.
1Ki 11: 1 however, **l** many foreign women
2Ch 11:21 Rehoboam **l** Maacah daughter of
26:10 for he **l** the soil.
Ne 13:26 He was **l** by his God,
Ps 44: 3 for you **l** them.
47: 4 the pride of Jacob, whom he **l**.
78:68 Mount Zion, which he **l**.
88:18 and **l** ones from me;
109:17 He **l** to pronounce a curse—
Isa 5: 1 My **l** one had a vineyard on a fertile
Jer 2: 2 how as a bride you **l** me and
8: 2 which they have **l** and served
31: 3 I have **l** you with an everlasting love;
Eze 16:37 those you **l** as well as those
Hos 2: 1 and of your sisters, 'My **l** one.'
2:23 to the one I called 'Not my **l** one.'
3: 1 though she is **l** by another and is
9:10 became as vile as the thing they **l**.
11: 1 "When Israel was a child, I **l** him,
Mal 1: 2 "I have **l** you," says the LORD.
1: 2 "But you ask, 'How have you **l** us?'
1: 2 "Yet I have **l** Jacob,
Mk 10:21 Jesus looked at him and **l** him.
12: 6 a son, whom he **l**.
Lk 7:47 for she **l** much.
16:14 The Pharisees, who **l** money,
Jn 3:16 "For God so **l** the world that
3:19 but men **l** darkness instead of light
11: 5 Jesus **l** Martha and her sister
11:36 the Jews said, "See how he **l** him!"
12:43 for they **l** praise from men more
13: 1 Having **l** his own who were in
13:23 the disciple whom Jesus **l**,

13:34 As I have I you,
14:21 who loves me will be I by my Father,
14:28 If you I me,
15: 9 the Father has I me, so have I I you.
15:12 Love each other as I have I you.
16:27 loves you because you have I me
17:23 have I them even as you have I me.
17:24 because you I me before the creation
19:26 disciple whom he I standing nearby,
20: 2 the one Jesus I, and said,
21: 7 disciple whom Jesus I said to Peter,
21:20 disciple whom Jesus I was following
Ro   1: 7 To all in Rome who are I by God
       8:37 conquerors through him who I us.
       9:13 Just as it is written: "Jacob I I,
       9:25 her 'my I one' who is not my I one,"
      11:28 I on account of the patriarchs,
Gal   2:20 who I me and gave himself for me.
Eph   5: 1 therefore, as dearly I children
       5: 2 just as Christ I us and gave himself
       5:25 just as Christ I the church
Col   3:12 holy and dearly I,
1Th   1: 4 For we know, brothers I by God,
       2: 8 We I you so much that we
2Th   2:13 brothers I by the Lord,
       2:16 who I us and by his grace gave us
2Ti   4:10 because he I this world,
Heb   1: 9 You have I righteousness
2Pe   2:15 who I the wages of wickedness.
1Jn   4:10 This is love: not that we I God, but
             that he I us and sent his Son as
       4:11 Dear friends, since God so I us,
       4:19 We love because he first I us.
Jude 1: 1 who are I by God the Father
Rev   3: 9 and acknowledge that I have I you.

LOVELY* [LOVE]

Ge   29:17 but Rachel was I in form,
Est   1:11 for she was I to look at.
       2: 7 was I in form and features,
Ps   84: 1 How I is your dwelling place,
SS   1: 5 Dark am I, yet I,
       2:14 and your face is I.
       4: 3 like a scarlet ribbon; your mouth is I.
       5:16 is sweetness itself; he is altogether I.
       6: 4 as Tirzah, I as Jerusalem,
Am   8:13 "the I young women
Php   4: 8 whatever is pure, whatever is I,

LOVER* [LOVE]

SS   1:13 My I is to me a sachet of myrrh
       1:14 My I is to me a cluster of henna
       1:16 How handsome you are, my I!
       2: 3 is my I among the young men.
       2: 8 Listen! My I! Look! Here he comes,
       2: 9 My I is like a gazelle or a young stag.
       2:10 My I spoke and said to me, "Arise,
       2:16 My I is mine and I am his;
       2:17 turn, my I,and be like a gazelle
       4:16 Let my I come into his garden
       5: 2 My I is knocking:
       5: 4 My I thrust his hand through
       5: 5 I arose to open for my I,
       5: 6 I opened for my I,

5: 6 but my I had left; he was gone.
5: 8 if you find my I,
5:10 My I is radiant and ruddy,
5:16 This is my I, this my friend,
6: 1 Where has your I gone,
6: 1 Which way did your I turn,
6: 2 My I has gone down to his garden,
6: 3 I am my lover's and my I is mine;
7: 9 May the wine go straight to my I,
7:10 I belong to my I,
7:11 my I, let us go to the countryside,
7:13 that I have stored up for you, my I.
8: 5 from the desert leaning on her I?
8:14 Come away, my I,
1Ti   3: 3 not quarrelsome, not a I of money.

LOVER'S* [LOVE]

SS   6: 3 I am my I and my lover is mine;

LOVERS* [LOVE]

SS   5: 1 and drink; drink your fill, O I.
Jer   3: 1 as a prostitute with many I—
       3: 2 the roadside you sat waiting for I,
       4:30 Your I despise you;
La   1: 2 Among all her I there is none
Eze 16:33 but you give gifts to all your I,
      16:36 in your promiscuity with your I,
      16:37 I am going to gather all your I,
      16:39 Then I will hand you over to your I,
      16:41 and you will no longer pay your I.
      23: 5 she lusted after her I, the Assyrians–
      23: 9 I handed her over to her I,
      23:20 There she lusted after her I,
      23:22 I will stir up your I against you,
Hos   2: 5 She said, 'I will go after my I,
       2: 7 after her I but not catch them;
       2:10 her lewdness before the eyes of her I;
       2:12 she said were her pay from her I;
       2:13 and went after her I,
       8: 9 Ephraim has sold herself to I.
2Ti   3: 2 People will be I of themselves,
       3: 2 I of money, boastful, proud,
       3: 3 brutal, not I of the good,
       3: 4 I of pleasure rather than I of God—

LOVES* [LOVE]

Ge   44:20 and his father I him.'
Dt   10:18 and I the alien,
      15:16 because he I you and your family
      21:15 and he I one but not the other,
      21:16 to the son of the wife he I
      23: 5 the LORD your God I you.
      28:54 on his own brother or the wife he I
      28:56 the husband she I and her own son
      33:12 and the one the LORD I rests
Ru   4:15 who I you and who is better
2Ch   2:11 "Because the LORD I his people,
Ps   11: 7 LORD is righteous, he I justice;
      33: 5 LORD I righteousness and justice;
      34:12 Whoever of you I life and desires
      37:28 For the LORD I the just and will
      87: 2 the LORD I the gates of Zion
      91:14 "Because he I me,"
      99: 4 The King is mighty, he I justice—

119:140 and your servant I them.
127: 2 for he grants sleep to those he l.
146: 8 the LORD I the righteous.
Pr   3:12 the LORD disciplines those he l,
12: 1 Whoever I discipline I knowledge,
13:24 but he who I him is careful
15: 9 he I those who pursue righteousness.
17:17 A friend I at all times,
17:19 He who I a quarrel I sin;
19: 8 He who gets wisdom I his own soul;
21:17 He who I pleasure will become poor;
21:17 I wine and oil will never be rich.
22:11 He who I a pure heart
29: 3 A man who I wisdom brings joy
Ecc 5:10 I money never has money enough;
whoever I wealth is never satisfied
SS   3: 1 I looked for the one my heart l;
3: 2 search for the one my heart l.
3: 3 you seen the one my heart l?"
3: 4 when I found the one my heart l.
Hos 3: 1 as the LORD I the Israelites.
10:11 Ephraim is a trained heifer that I
12: 7 dishonest scales; he I to defraud.
Mal 2:11 the sanctuary the LORD l,
Mt 10:37 "Anyone who I his father or mother
10:37 anyone who I his son or daughter
Lk   7: 5 because he I our nation
7:47 who has been forgiven little I little."
Jn   3:35 The Father I the Son
5:20 For the Father I the Son
10:17 The reason my Father I me is
12:25 The man who I his life will lose it,
14:21 he is the one who I me.
14:21 He who I me will be loved
14:23 Jesus replied, "If anyone I me,
16:27 the Father himself I you
Ro 13: 8 I his fellowman has fulfilled the law.
1Co 8: 3 But the man who I God is known
2Co 9: 7 for God I a cheerful giver.
Eph 1: 6 in the One he l.
5:28 He who I his wife I himself.
5:33 love his wife as he I himself,
Col 1:13 into the kingdom of the Son he l,
Tit 1: 8 one who I what is good,
Heb 12: 6 the Lord disciplines those he l,
1Jn 2:10 Whoever I his brother lives in
2:15 If anyone I the world,
4: 7 Everyone who I has been born
4:21 Whoever I God must must also love
5: 1 everyone who I the father I his child
3Jn 1: 9 but Diotrephes, who I to be first,
Rev 1: 5 To him who I us and has freed us
20: 9 the city he l.
22:15 who I and practices falsehood.

LOVING* [LOVE]

Ps 25:10 All the ways of the LORD are I
59:10 my I God. God will go before me
59:17 O God, are my fortress, my I God.
62:12 O Lord, are I.
144: 2 He is my I God and my fortress,
145:13 and I toward all he has made.
145:17 and I toward all he has made.
Pr   5:19 A I doe, a graceful deer—

Heb 13: 1 Keep on I each other as brothers.
1Jn 5: 2 by I God and carrying out his

LOVING-KINDNESS* [LOVE]

Jer 31: 3 I have drawn you with l.

LOVINGKINDNESS (KJV)

See LOVE, UNFAILING LOVE

LOW [BELOW, LOWER, LOWERED, LOWEST, LOWLY]

2Sa 22:28 on the haughty to bring them l.
Job 40:11 at every proud man and bring him l,
Ps 36: 7 high and I among men find refuge in
136:23 who remembered us in our I estate
Pr 29:23 A man's pride brings him l,
Isa 2:11 and the pride of men brought l;
40: 4 every mountain and hill made l;
Lk   3: 5 every mountain and hill made l.
Ro 12:16 to associate with people of I position.
Jas 1:10 should take pride in his I position,

LOWER [LOW]

Dt 28:43 but you will sink I and l.
Ps   8: 5 a little I than the heavenly beings
2Co 11: 7 to I myself in order to elevate you
Eph 4: 9 that he also descended to the l,
Heb 2: 7 You made him a little I than

LOWERED [LOW]

Ex 17:11 but whenever he I his hands,
Jer 38: 6 I Jeremiah by ropes into the cistern;
Mk   2: 4 I the mat the paralyzed man was
Ac   9:25 I him in a basket through an opening
2Co 11:33 I was I in a basket from a window

LOWEST [LOW]

Ge   9:25 The I of slaves will he be
Ps 88: 6 You have put me in the I pit,
Lk 14:10 you are invited, take the I place,

LOWING

1Sa 15:14 What is this I of cattle that I hear?"

LOWLY [LOW]

Job 5:11 The I he sets on high,
Ps 119:141 Though I am I and despised,
138: 6 he looks upon the l,
Pr 16:19 Better to be I in spirit and among
29:23 but a man of I spirit gains honor.
Isa 57:15 with him who is contrite and I in
spirit, to revive the spirit of the l
Eze 21:26 It will not be as it was: The I will
1Co 1:28 He chose the I things of this world
Php 3:21 will transform our I bodies so

LOYAL

1Ki 12:20 Only the tribe of Judah remained I
1Ch 29:18 and keep their hearts I to you.
Ps 78: 8 whose hearts were not I to God,

LUCIFER (KJV) See MORNING STAR

LUCRE (KJV) See DISHONEST GAIN, MONEY

LUKE*
Associate of Paul (Col 4:14; 2Ti 4:11; Phm 24).

LUKEWARM* [WARM]
Rev 3:16 So, because you are l—

LUMP*
Ro 9:21 the right to make out of the same l

LUNATICK (KJV) See SEIZURES

LURK* [LURKED, LURKS]
Ps 56: 6 They conspire, they l,
Hos 13: 7 like a leopard I will l by the path.

LURKED* [LURK]
Job 31: 9 or if I have l at my neighbor's door,

LURKS* [LURK]
Pr 7:12 at every corner she l.)

LUST* [LUSTED, LUSTFUL, LUSTFULLY, LUSTS]
Pr 6:25 not l in your heart after her beauty
Isa 57: 5 You burn with l among the oaks
Eze 20:30 and l after their vile images?
     23: 8 and poured out their l upon her.
     23:11 yet in her l and prostitution she was
     23:17 and in their l they defiled her.
Na 3: 4 because of the wanton l of a harlot,
Ro 1:27 were inflamed with l for one another.
Eph 4:19 with a continual l for more.
Col 3: 5 impurity, l, evil desires and greed,
1Th 4: 5 not in passionate l like the heathen,
1Pe 4: 3 l, drunkenness, orgies,
1Jn 2:16 the l of his eyes and the boasting

LUSTED* [LUST]
Eze 6: 9 which have l after their idols.
    23: 5 she l after her lovers, the Assyrians

LUSTFUL* [LUST]
Jer 13:27 your adulteries and l neighings,
Eze 16:26 with the Egyptians, your l neighbors,
2Pe 2:18 the l desires of sinful human nature,

LUSTFULLY* [LUST]
Job 31: 1 with my eyes not to look l at a girl.
Mt 5:28 who looks at a woman l has already

LUSTS* [LUST]
Nu 15:39 yourselves by going after the l
Ro 1:26 God gave them over to shameful l.

LUTES*
1Sa 18: 6 songs and with tambourines and l.
2Ch 20:28 temple of the LORD with harps and l

LUXURY
Pr 19:10 It is not fitting for a fool to live in l—
Lk 16:19 and lived in l every day.
Jas 5: 5 on earth in l and self-indulgence.
Rev 18: 7 as the glory and l she gave herself.

LUZ [BETHEL]
Ge 28:19 though the city used to be called L.
    48: 3 "God Almighty appeared to me at L

LYDDA
Ac 9:32 he went to visit the saints in L.

LYDIA [LYDIA'S]
Jer 46: 9 men of L who draw the bow.
Ac 16:14 listening was a woman named L,

LYDIA'S* [LYDIA]
Ac 16:40 they went to L house,

LYING [LIE]
Ge 28:13 the land on which you are l.
Ex 14:30 and Israel saw the Egyptians l dead
Jdg 16:13 making a fool of me and l to me.
Ru 3: 8 discovered a woman l at his feet.
1Sa 3: 3 Samuel was l down in the temple
     5: 4 and were l on the threshold;
    26: 5 Saul was l inside the camp,
1Ki 22:23 the LORD has put a l spirit in
Ps 31:18 Let their l lips be silenced,
   120: 2 Save me, O LORD, from l lips
Pr 6:17 haughty eyes, a l tongue,
    12:19 but a l tongue lasts only a moment.
    12:22 the LORD detests l lips,
    21: 6 A fortune made by a l tongue is
    26:28 A l tongue hates those it hurts,
Jer 23:26 in the hearts of these l prophets,
Eze 13: 9 false visions and utter l divinations.
Da 4:10 the visions I saw while l in my bed:
Hos 4: 2 There is only cursing, l and murder,
Mt 8:14 he saw Peter's mother-in-law l in bed
Mk 2: 4 the mat the paralyzed man was l on.
     7:30 and found her child l on the bed,
Lk 2:12 wrapped in cloths and l in a manger."
Jn 5: 6 When Jesus saw him l there
    20: 6 He saw the strips of linen l there,
Ro 9: 1 speak the truth in Christ—I am not l

LYRE [LYRES]
Ps 33: 2 music to him on the ten-stringed l.
    57: 8 Awake, harp and l!
   150: 3 praise him with the harp and l,
Da 3: 7 l, harp and all kinds of music,

LYRES [LYRE]
1Sa 10: 5 down from the high place with l,
1Ch 15:16 by musical instruments: l,

LYSTRA
Ac 14: 8 In L there sat a man crippled
2Ti 3:11 and L, the persecutions I endured.

M

MAACAH
2Sa 3: 3 Absalom the son of M daughter
1Ki 15: 2 His mother's name was M daughter

15:10 His grandmother's name was **M**

MACEDONIA

Ac 16: 9 Paul had a vision of a man of **M**
18: 5 Silas and Timothy came from **M,**
20: 3 he decided to go back through **M.**

MACHPELAH

Ge 23: 9 so he will sell me the cave of **M,**
49:30 the cave in the field of **M,**
50:13 in the cave in the field of **M,**

MAD [MADDENING, MADMAN, MADMEN, MADNESS]

Dt 28:34 The sights you see will drive you **m.**
Jer 51: 7 therefore they have now gone **m.**
Jn 10:20 is demon-possessed and raving **m.**

MADDENING* [MAD]

Rev 14: 8 drink the **m** wine of her adulteries."
18: 3 drunk the **m** wine of her adulteries.

MADE [MAKE]

Ge 1: 7 So God **m** the expanse and separated
1:16 God **m** two great lights—
1:16 He also **m** the stars.
1:25 God **m** the wild animals according
1:31 God saw all that he had **m,**
2: 3 the seventh day and **m** it holy,
2:22 LORD God **m** a woman from the rib
3:21 The LORD God **m** garments of skin
6: 6 LORD was grieved that he had **m** man
9: 6 in the image of God has God **m** man.
15:18 the LORD **m** a covenant with Abram
24:21 LORD had **m** his journey successful.
45: 9 God has **m** me lord
Ex 1:14 They **m** their lives bitter
2:14 Who **m** you ruler and judge over us?
7: 1 I have **m** you like God to Pharaoh,
12: 8 and bread **m** without yeast.
12:36 **m** the Egyptians favorably disposed
15:25 There the LORD **m** a decree and
20:11 the Sabbath day and **m** it holy.
24: 8 the covenant that the LORD has **m**
32: 4 and **m** it into an idol cast in the shape
36: 8 the workmen **m** the tabernacle
37: 1 Bezalel **m** the ark of acacia wood—
37:10 They **m** the table of acacia wood—
37:17 They **m** the lampstand of pure gold
37:25 They **m** the altar of incense out
37:29 They also **m** the sacred anointing oil
38: 9 Next they **m** the courtyard.
39: 1 also **m** sacred garments for Aaron,
Lev 16:34 Atonement is to be **m** once
Nu 14:36 **m** the whole community grumble
21: 2 Israel **m** this vow to the LORD:
21: 9 So Moses **m** a bronze snake and put
Dt 1:28 Our brothers have **m** us lose heart.
5: 2 The LORD our God **m** a covenant
32: 6 who **m** you and formed you?
32:21 **m** me jealous by what is no god
Jos 24:25 On that day Joshua **m** a covenant for
Jdg 11:30 Jephthah **m** a vow to the LORD:
1Sa 1:11 And she **m** a vow, saying,

15:11 grieved that I have **m** Saul king,
20:16 So Jonathan **m** a covenant with
2Sa 23: 5 **m** with me an everlasting covenant,
1Ki 12:28 the king **m** two golden calves.
2Ki 17:38 Do not forget the covenant I have **m**
18: 4 the bronze snake Moses had **m,**
19:15 You have **m** heaven and earth.
1Ch 22: 5 So David **m** extensive preparations
2Ch 2:12 who **m** heaven and earth!
3:10 the Most Holy Place he **m** a pair
4:19 Solomon also **m** all the furnishings
Ne 9: 6 You **m** the heavens,
9:10 You **m** a name for yourself,
Job 7:20 Why have you **m** me your target?
31: 1 "I **m** a covenant with my eyes not
33: 4 The Spirit of God has **m** me;
42:10 the LORD **m** him prosperous again
Ps 8: 5 You **m** him a little lower than
33: 6 of the LORD were the heavens **m,**
73:28 **m** the Sovereign LORD my refuge;
95: 5 The sea is his, for he **m** it,
96: 5 but the LORD **m** the heavens.
98: 2 LORD has **m** his salvation known
100: 3 It is he who **m** us, and we are his;
118:24 This is the day the LORD has **m;**
136: 7 who **m** the great lights—
139:14 I am fearfully and wonderfully **m;**
145:13 and loving toward all he has **m.**
Pr 8:26 before he **m** the earth or its fields
Ecc 3:11 He has **m** everything beautiful
7:13 straighten what he has **m** crooked?
Isa 22:11 did not look to the One who **m** it,
43: 7 whom I formed and, **m.**"
44:21 I have **m** you, you are my servant;
45:12 It is I who **m** the earth
53:12 **m** intercession for the transgressors.
66: 2 Has not my hand **m** all these things,
Jer 10:12 But God **m** the earth by his power;
25: 6 anger with what your hands have **m.**
27: 5 and outstretched arm I **m** the earth
31:32 It will not be like the covenant I **m**
33: 2 he who **m** the earth,
51:15 "He **m** the earth by his power;
La 3:12 drew his bow and **m** me the target
Eze 3:17 I have **m** you a watchman for
16:60 I will remember the covenant I **m**
33: 7 I have **m** you a watchman for
Da 2:38 he has **m** you ruler over them all.
3: 1 King Nebuchadnezzar **m** an image
Hos 14: 3 to what our own hands have **m,**
Am 5: 8 (he who **m** the Pleiades and Orion,
Jnh 1: 9 who **m** the sea and the land."
Mt 2:36 the oaths you have **m** to the Lord.'
Mk 1: 6 John wore clothing **m** of camel's hair
2:27 "The Sabbath was **m** for man,
15: 5 But Jesus still **m** no reply,
Lk 17:19 your faith has **m** you well."
19:46 you have **m** it 'a den of robbers.' "
Jn 1: 3 Through him all things were **m;**
1:18 has **m** him known.
9: 6 some mud with the saliva,
Ac 2:36 assured of this: God has **m** this Jesus,
10:15 that God has **m** clean."
17:24 "The God who **m** the world

Ro	1:19	because God has **m** it plain to them.
1Co	1:20	Has not God **m** foolish the wisdom
	3: 6	but God **m** it grow.
	12:14	the body is not **m** up of one part
	15:22	so in Christ all will be **m** alive.
	15:28	the Son himself will be **m** subject
2Co	3: 6	He has **m** us competent as ministers
	5:21	God **m** him who had no sin to be sin
	12: 9	my power is **m** perfect in weakness."
Eph	2: 5	**m** us alive with Christ even
	2:14	who has **m** the two one
Php	2: 7	being **m** in human likeness.
Heb	1: 2	through whom he **m** the universe.
	2: 7	You **m** him a little lower than
	8: 9	It will not be like the covenant I **m**
Jas	2:22	and his faith was **m** complete
	3: 9	who have been **m** in God's likeness.
1Jn	2: 5	God's love is truly **m** complete
Rev	5:10	You have **m** them to be a kingdom
	14: 7	Worship him who **m** the heavens,
	19: 7	and his bride has **m** herself ready.

MADMAN [MAD]

1Sa 21:13 in their hands he acted like a **m**,

MADMEN [MAD]

1Sa 21:15 so short of **m** that you have to bring

MADNESS [MAD]

Dt	28:28	The LORD will afflict you with **m**,
Ecc	7:25	of wickedness and the **m** of folly.
	9: 3	is **m** in their hearts while they live,

MAGDALENE

Mt	27:56	Among them were Mary **M**,
Mk	16: 1	Mary **M**, Mary the mother of James,
Lk	8: 2	and diseases: Mary (called **M**)
Jn	20: 1	Mary **M** went to the tomb and saw

MAGI

Mt 2: 1 **M** from the east came to Jerusalem

MAGIC* [MAGICIAN, MAGICIANS]

Isa	47:12	"Keep on, then, with your **m** spells
Eze	13:18	to the women who sew **m** charms
	13:20	I am against your **m** charms
Ac	8:11	for a long time with his **m**.
Rev	9:21	of their murders, their **m** arts,
	18:23	By your **m** spell all the nations
	21: 8	those who practice **m** arts,
	22:15	those who practice **m** arts,

MAGICIAN* [MAGIC]

Da 2:10 has ever asked such a thing of any **m**
    2:27 **m** or diviner can explain to the king

MAGICIANS [MAGIC]

Ge	41: 8	so he sent for all the **m** and wise men
Ex	7:11	and the Egyptian **m** also did
	7:22	the Egyptian **m** did the same things
	8: 7	But the **m** did the same things
	8:18	when the **m** tried to produce gnats
	9:11	The **m** could not stand before Moses
Da	2: 2	So the king summoned the **m**,
	5:11	appointed him chief of the **m**,

MAGNIFICENCE* [MAGNIFY]

1Ch 22: 5 for the LORD should be of great **m**

MAGNIFICENT* [MAGNIFY]

1Ki	8:13	I have indeed built a **m** temple
2Ch	2: 9	temple I build must be large and **m**.
	6: 2	I have built a **m** temple for you,
Isa	28:29	in counsel and **m** in wisdom.
Mk	13: 1	What **m** buildings!"

MAGNIFY* [MAGNIFICENCE, MAGNIFICENT]

Da 11:36 and **m** himself above every god

MAGOG

Eze	38: 2	against Gog, of the land of **M**,
	39: 6	I will send fire on **M**
Rev	20: 8	corners of the earth—Gog and **M**—

MAHANAIM

Ge 32: 2 So he named that place **M**.
2Sa 17:24 David went to **M**,

MAHER-SHALAL-HASH-BAZ

Isa 8: 3 LORD said to me, "Name him **M**.

MAHLON [MAHLON'S]

Ru 1: 5 both **M** and Kilion also died,

MAHLON'S* [MAHLON]

Ru 4:10 Ruth the Moabitess, **M** widow, as

MAID* [MAIDEN, MAIDENS, MAIDS]

Ps 123: 2 as the eyes of a **m** look to the hand
Isa 24: 2 for mistress as for **m**,

MAIDEN* [MAID]

Ge	24:43	if a **m** comes out to draw water
Pr	30:19	and the way of a man with a **m**.
Isa	62: 5	As a young man marries a **m**,
Jer	2:32	Does a **m** forget her jewelry,
	51:22	with you I shatter young man and **m**,

MAIDENS [MAID]

Ps	68:25	the **m** playing tambourines.
	78:63	and their **m** had no wedding songs;
SS	1: 3	No wonder the **m** love you!
	2: 2	is my darling among the **m**.
La	2:21	and **m** have fallen by the sword.

MAIDS [MAID]

Ge	24:61	Then Rebekah and her **m** got ready
1Sa	25:42	attended by her five **m**,
Est	2: 9	He assigned to her seven **m** selected

MAIDSERVANT [SERVANT]

Ge	16: 1	she had an Egyptian **m** named Hagar
	21:13	the son of the **m** into a nation also,
	35:25	The sons of Rachel's **m** Bilhah:
	35:26	The sons of Leah's **m** Zilpah:
Ex	21:26	"If a man hits a manservant or **m** in
Dt	5:14	nor your manservant or **m**,

MAIMED
Mk   9:43 It is better for you to enter life **m**

MAIN
1Ki   7:50 the doors of the **m** hall of the temple.

MAINTAIN [MAINTAINED, MAINTAINING, MAINTAINS]
Ru   4: 5 in order to **m** the name of the dead
1Ki 10: 9 to **m** justice and righteousness."
2Ki   8:19 He had promised to **m** a lamp
Ps   82: 3 **m** the rights of the poor
     106: 3 Blessed are they who **m** justice,
Isa 56: 1 "**M** justice and do what is right,
Hos 12: 6 return to your God; **m** love and
Am   5:15 Hate evil, love good; **m** justice in
Ro   3:28 For we **m** that a man is justified

MAINTAINED* [MAINTAIN]
Rev   6: 9 and the testimony they had **m.**

MAINTAINING* [MAINTAIN]
Ex   34: 7 **m** love to thousands, and forgiving

MAINTAINS [MAINTAIN]
Job   2: 3 And he still **m** his integrity,

MAJESTIC* [MAJESTY]
Ex   15: 6 O LORD, was **m** in power.
     15:11 Who is like you—**m** in holiness,
Job 37: 4 he thunders with his **m** voice.
Ps   8: 1 how **m** is your name in all the earth!
      8: 9 how **m** is your name in all the earth!
     29: 4 the voice of the LORD is **m.**
     68:15 The mountains of Bashan are **m**
     76: 4 more **m** than mountains rich
    111: 3 Glorious and **m** are his deeds,
SS   6: 4 **m** as troops with banners.
      6:10 **m** as the stars in procession?
Isa 30:30 will cause men to hear his **m** voice
Eze 31: 7 It was **m** in beauty,
2Pe   1:17 voice came to him from the **M** Glory

MAJESTY* [MAJESTIC]
Ex   15: 7 In the greatness of your **m** you threw
Dt   5:24 shown us his glory and his **m,**
     11: 2 his **m,** his mighty hand, his
     33:17 In **m** he is like a firstborn bull;
     33:26 and on the clouds in his **m.**
1Ch 16:27 Splendor and **m** are before him;
     29:11 the glory and the **m** and the splendor,
Est   1: 4 and the splendor and glory of his **m.**
      7: 3 O king, and if it pleases your **m,**
Job 37:22 God comes in awesome **m.**
     40:10 and clothe yourself in honor and **m.**
Ps   21: 5 bestowed on him splendor and **m.**
     45: 3 clothe yourself with splendor and **m.**
     45: 4 In your **m** ride forth victoriously
     68:34 whose **m** is over Israel,
     93: 1 The LORD reigns, he is robed in **m;**
          the LORD is robed in **m**
     96: 6 Splendor and **m** are before him;
    104: 1 you are clothed with splendor and **m.**
    110: 3 Arrayed in holy **m,**

145: 5 of the glorious splendor of your **m,**
Isa   2:10 and the splendor of his **m!**
      2:19 and the splendor of his **m,**
      2:21 and the splendor of his **m,**
     24:14 they acclaim the LORD's **m.**
     26:10 and regard not the **m** of the LORD.
     53: 2 He had no beauty or **m** to attract us
Eze 31: 2 be compared with you in **m?**
     31:18 with you in splendor and **m?**
Da   4:30 and for the glory of my **m?"**
Mic   5: 4 in the **m** of the name of the LORD
Zec   6:13 and he will be clothed with **m**
Ac   19:27 will be robbed of her divine **m."**
     25:26 to write to His **M** about him.
2Th   1: 9 Lord and from the **m** of his power
Heb   1: 3 at the right hand of the **M** in heaven.
      8: 1 the right hand of the throne of the **M**
2Pe   1:16 but we were eyewitnesses of his **m.**
Jude 1:25 **m,** power and authority,

MAKE [MADE, MAKER, MAKERS, MAKES, MAKING, MAN-MADE]
Ge   1:26 "Let us **m** man in our image,
      2:18 I will **m** a helper suitable for him.
      6:14 **m** yourself an ark of cypress wood;
     11: 4 that we may **m** a name for ourselves
     12: 2 **m** you into a great nation and I will
          bless you; I will **m** your name great,
     13:16 I will **m** your offspring like the dust
     17: 6 I will **m** you very fruitful; I will **m**
          nations of you,
     21:18 for I will **m** him into a great nation."
     22:17 and **m** your descendants as numerous
     24:40 and **m** your journey a success,
     26: 4 your descendants as numerous
     28: 3 and **m** you fruitful and increase
     32: 9 and I will **m** you prosper,'
     46: 3 I will **m** you into a great nation there.
     48: 4 'I am going to **m** you fruitful
Ex   6: 3 the LORD I did not **m** myself known
      9: 4 But the LORD will **m** a distinction
     20: 4 "You shall not **m** for yourself an idol
     20:23 not **m** any gods to be alongside me;
     22: 3 "A thief must certainly **m** restitution,
     25: 9 **M** this tabernacle and all its
     25:10 "Have them **m** a chest
     25:23 "**M** a table of acacia wood—
     25:31 "**M** a lampstand of pure gold
     25:40 See that you **m** them according to
     28: 2 **M** sacred garments for your brother
     32: 1 **m** us gods who will go before us.
     32:10 I will **m** you into a great nation."
Lev   1: 4 his behalf to **m** atonement for him.
      4:20 the priest will **m** atonement for them,
      8:15 So he consecrated it to **m** atonement
     20:25 'You must therefore **m** a distinction
Nu   6:25 the LORD **m** his face shine
     21: 8 "**M** a snake and put it up on a pole;
Dt   7: 2 **M** no treaty with them,
     30: 9 God will **m** you most prosperous
Jos   9: 7 then can we **m** a treaty with you?"
2Sa   7: 9 Now I will **m** your name great,
     22:36 you stoop down to **m** me great.
Ezr 10: 3 Now let us **m** a covenant

	10:11	Now **m** confession to the LORD,
Job	7:17	"What is man that you **m** so much
Ps	4: 8	O LORD, **m** me dwell in safety.
	20: 4	and **m** all your plans succeed.
	27: 6	and **m** music to the LORD.
	51:18	your good pleasure **m** Zion prosper;
	80: 7	O God Almighty; **m** your face shine
	108: 1	and **m** music with all my soul.
	110: 1	until I **m** your enemies
	115: 8	Those who **m** them will be like them,
	119:165	and nothing can **m** them stumble.
Pr	3: 6	and he will **m** your paths straight.
	4:26	**M** level paths for your feet
	10: 4	Lazy hands **m** a man poor,
	11:14	but many advisers **m** victory sure.
	20:18	**M** plans by seeking advice;
Ecc	5: 4	When you **m** a vow to God,
Isa	6:10	**M** the heart of this people calloused;
		m their ears dull
	14:14	I will **m** myself like the Most High."
	29:16	"He did not **m** me"?
	40: 3	**m** straight in the wilderness a
	44: 9	All who **m** idols are nothing,
	49: 6	also **m** you a light for the Gentiles,
	49: 8	and will **m** you to be a covenant for
	55: 3	I will **m** an everlasting covenant
	61: 8	and **m** an everlasting covenant
	66:22	the new earth that I **m** will endure
Jer	10:11	gods, who did not **m** the heavens
	16:20	Do men **m** their own gods?
	30:10	and no one will **m** him afraid.
	31:31	"when I will **m** a new covenant with
	32:40	I will **m** an everlasting covenant
	33:15	I will **m** a righteous Branch sprout
Eze	34:25	" 'I will **m** a covenant of peace
	37: 5	bones: 'I will **m** breath enter you,
	37:26	I will **m** a covenant of peace
	39: 7	" 'I will **m** known my holy name
Hos	2:18	that day I will **m** a covenant for them
Jnh	2: 9	What I have vowed I will **m** good.
Mt	3: 3	**m** straight paths for him.' "
	27:65	"Go, **m** the tomb as secure
	28:19	go and **m** disciples of all nations,
Mk	1:17	"and I will **m** you fishers of men."
	7:18	the outside can **m** him 'unclean'?
Lk	1:17	to **m** ready a people prepared for
	13:24	"**M** every effort to enter through
	14:23	and country lanes and **m** them come
Jn	1:23	'M straight the way for the Lord.' "
Ac	2:35	until I **m** your enemies a footstool
Ro	9:20	'Why did you **m** me like this?' "
	14: 4	for the Lord is able to **m** him stand.
	14:19	Let us therefore **m** every effort
1Co	9:27	I beat my body and **m** it my slave so
2Co	5: 9	So we **m** it our goal to please him,
	9: 8	to **m** all grace abound to you,
Eph	4: 3	**M** every effort to keep the unity of
	5:19	Sing and **m** music in your heart to
Col	4: 5	**m** the most of every opportunity.
1Th	4:11	**M** it your ambition to lead a quiet
2Ti	3:15	able to **m** you wise for salvation
Heb	1:13	until I **m** your enemies a footstool
	2:17	and that he might **m** atonement for
	4:11	**m** every effort to enter that rest,

	8: 8	when I will **m** a new covenant with
	12: 5	not **m** light of the Lord's discipline,
	12:14	**M** every effort to live in peace
2Pe	1: 5	**m** every effort to add to your faith
	1:10	to **m** your calling and election sure.
	3:14	**m** every effort to be found spotless,
1Jn	1:10	we **m** him out to be a liar
Rev	17:14	They will **m** war against the Lamb,
	19:19	**m** war against the rider on the horse

MAKER* [MAKE]

Job	4:17	a man be more pure than his **M?**
	9: 9	He is the **M** of the Bear and Orion,
	32:22	my **M** would soon take me away.
	35:10	no one says, 'Where is God my **M,**
	36: 3	I will ascribe justice to my **M.**
	40:19	yet his **M** can approach him
Ps	95: 6	kneel before the LORD our **M;**
	115:15	the **M** of heaven and earth.
	121: 2	the **M** of heaven and earth.
	124: 8	the **M** of heaven and earth.
	134: 3	the **M** of heaven and earth,
	146: 6	the **M** of heaven and earth, the sea,
	149: 2	Let Israel rejoice in their **M;**
Pr	14:31	shows contempt for their **M,**
	17: 5	shows contempt for their **M;**
	22: 2	The LORD is the **M** of them all.
Ecc	11: 5	the **M** of all things.
Isa	17: 7	In that day men will look to their **M**
	27:11	so their **M** has no compassion
	45: 9	to him who quarrels with his **M,**
	45:11	the Holy One of Israel, and its **M:**
	51:13	that you forget the LORD your **M,**
	54: 5	For your **M** is your husband—
Jer	10:16	for he is the **M** of all things,
	51:19	for he is the **M** of all things,
Hos	8:14	Israel has forgotten his **M**

MAKERS* [MAKE]

Isa	45:16	the **m** of idols will be put to shame

MAKES [MAKE]

Ex	4:11	Who **m** him deaf or mute?
	11: 7	that the LORD **m** a distinction
Lev	20: 8	I am the LORD, who **m** you holy.
1Sa	2: 6	LORD brings death and **m** alive;
Ps	18:33	He **m** my feet like the feet of a deer;
	23: 2	He **m** me lie down in green pastures,
	40: 4	the man who **m** the LORD his trust,
Pr	13:12	Hope deferred **m** the heart sick,
	15:13	A happy heart **m** the face cheerful,
	16: 7	he **m** even his enemies live at peace
Ecc	10:19	and wine **m** life merry,
Isa	44: 8	and a rock that **m** them fall.
	53:10	the LORD **m** his life a guilt offering,
Mk	7:15	out of a man that **m** him 'unclean.' "
	7:37	"He even **m** the deaf hear and
Ro	9:33	and a rock that **m** them fall,
1Co	3: 7	but only God, who **m** things grow.
1Pe	2: 8	and a rock that **m** them fall."

MAKING [MAKE]

Ne	8: 8	**m** it clear and giving the meaning so
Ps	19: 7	**m** wise the simple.

Ecc	12:12	Of **m** many books there is no end,
Isa	43:19	I am **m** a way in the desert
Mt	21:13	but you are **m** it a 'den of robbers.' "
Mk	2:21	**m** the tear worse.
Jn	5:18	**m** himself equal with God.
Eph	5:16	**m** the most of every opportunity,
Col	1:20	by **m** peace through his blood,
Rev	21:5	"I am **m** everything new!"

MALACHI*

| Mal | 1:1 | of the LORD to Israel through **M.** |

MALE [MALES]

Ge	1:27	**m** and female he created them.
	5:2	He created them **m** and female
	6:19	two of all living creatures, **m** and
	17:10	**m** among you shall be circumcised.
Ex	13:2	"Consecrate to me every firstborn **m.**
Nu	8:16	first **m** offspring from every Israelite
2Ki	23:7	quarters of the **m** shrine prostitutes.
Mt	19:4	Creator 'made them **m** and female,'
Lk	2:23	firstborn **m** is to be consecrated
1Co	6:9	nor adulterers nor **m** prostitutes
Gal	3:28	slave nor free, **m** nor female,
Rev	12:5	She gave birth to a son, a **m** child,

MALEFACTOR(S) (KJV)

See CRIMINAL(S)

MALES [MALE]

| Ex | 12:48 | the **m** in his household circumcised; |
| | 34:19 | the firstborn **m** of your livestock, |

MALICE [MALICIOUS]

Nu	35:20	with **m** aforethought shoves another
Dt	4:42	his neighbor without **m** aforethought.
Mk	7:22	**m**, deceit, lewdness, envy, slander,
Ro	1:29	murder, strife, deceit and **m.**
1Co	5:8	the yeast of **m** and wickedness,
Eph	4:31	along with every form of **m.**
Col	3:8	such things as these: anger, rage, **m,**
Tit	3:3	We lived in **m** and envy,
1Pe	2:1	rid yourselves of all **m** and all deceit,

MALICIOUS [MALICE]

Ex	23:1	a wicked man by being a **m** witness.
Dt	19:16	a **m** witness takes the stand to accuse
Pr	17:4	a liar pays attention to a **m** tongue.
	26:24	A **m** man disguises himself
1Ti	3:11	not **m** talkers but temperate
	6:4	that result in envy, strife, **m** talk,

MALIGN*

| Ps | 12:5 | protect them from those who **m** them |
| Tit | 2:5 | that no one will **m** the word of God. |

MAMMON (KJV) See MONEY, WEALTH

MAMRE

| Ge | 13:18 | to live near the great trees of **M** |
| | 25:9 | in the cave of Machpelah near **M,** |

MAN [COUNTRYMEN, FELLOWMAN, HORSEMAN, HORSEMEN, MAN'S,

MAN-MADE, MANKIND, MEN, MEN'S, WORKMAN, WORKMEN]

Ge	1:26	"Let us make **m** in our image,
	2:7	the **m** from the dust of the ground
	2:7	and the **m** became a living being.
	2:15	the **m** and put him in the Garden
	2:18	"It is not good for the **m** to be alone.
	2:20	the **m** gave names to all the livestock
	2:23	for she was taken out of **m.**"
	2:25	The **m** and his wife were both naked,
	3:9	But the LORD God called to the **m,**
	3:22	**m** has now become like one of us,
	4:1	of the LORD I have brought forth a **m**
	6:3	will not contend with **m** forever,
	6:6	was grieved that he had made **m**
	9:6	"Whoever sheds the blood of **m,** by
		m shall his blood be shed; for in the
		image of God has God made **m.**
	32:24	a **m** wrestled with him till daybreak.
Ex	4:11	"Who gave **m** his mouth?
	33:11	as a **m** speaks with his friend.
Lev	18:5	the **m** who obeys them will live by
	20:10	" 'If a **m** commits adultery
	20:13	" 'If a **m** lies with a **m** as one lies
	24:21	kills a **m** must be put to death.
Nu	1:2	listing every **m** by name, one by one.
	23:19	God is not a **m,** that he should lie,
Dt	8:3	that **m** does not live on bread alone
	22:5	nor a **m** wear women's clothing,
	32:30	How could one **m** chase a thousand,
Jos	10:14	a day when the LORD listened to a **m.**
Jdg	8:21	'As is the **m,** so is his strength.' "
	16:7	I'll become as weak as any other **m.**"
1Sa	2:25	If a **m** sins against another **m,**
	13:14	a **m** after his own heart
	15:29	for he is not a **m,**
	16:7	M looks at the outward appearance,
2Sa	7:19	your usual way of dealing with **m,**
1Ki	2:4	never fail to have a **m** on the throne
	8:25	never fail to have a **m** to sit before
	9:5	never fail to have a **m** on the throne
1Ch	29:1	not for **m** but for the LORD God.
Est	6:7	"For the **m** the king delights to honor
Job	2:4	"A **m** will give all he has
	4:17	a **m** be more pure than his Maker?
	5:7	Yet **m** is born to trouble as surely
	9:32	a **m** like me that I might answer him,
	14:1	"M born of woman is of few days
	14:14	If a **m** dies, will he live again?
	38:3	Brace yourself like a **m;**
	40:7	"Brace yourself like a **m;**
Ps	1:1	the **m** who does not walk
	8:4	what is **m** that you are mindful
	32:2	the **m** whose sin the LORD does not
	34:8	blessed is the **m** who takes refuge
	40:4	Blessed is the **m** who makes
	84:12	blessed is the **m** who trusts in you.
	94:11	LORD knows the thoughts of **m;**
	103:15	As for **m,** his days are like grass,
	112:1	the **m** who fears the LORD,
	119:9	a young **m** keep his way pure?
	127:5	Blessed is the **m** whose quiver is full
	144:3	the son of **m** that you think of him?

Pr   3:13 Blessed is the **m** who finds wisdom,
        6:32 **m** who commits adultery lacks
        9: 9 Instruct a wise **m** and he will be
       10: 9 The **m** of integrity walks securely,
       11:12 **m** of understanding holds his tongue.
       11:17 A kind **m** benefits himself,
       11:25 A generous **m** will prosper;
       12: 8 **m** is praised according to his wisdom
       14: 7 Stay away from a foolish **m,**
       14:12 a way that seems right to a **m,**
       14:16 A wise **m** fears the LORD
       16:25 a way that seems right to a **m,**
       26:12 you see a **m** wise in his own eyes?
       28:20 A faithful **m** will be richly blessed,
       29:23 but a **m** of lowly spirit gains honor.
       30:19 and the way of a **m** with a maiden.
Ecc   2:14 The wise **m** has eyes in his head,
       12:13 for this is the whole [duty] of **m.**
Isa   2:22 Stop trusting in **m,**
       53: 3 a **m** of sorrows,
Jer   17: 5 the one who trusts in **m,**
       17: 7 is the **m** who trusts in the LORD,
Eze   20:11 **m** who obeys them will live by them.
       22:30 a **m** among them who would build
Da   7: 4 and the heart of a **m** was given to it.
        7:13 before me was one like a son of **m,**
Hos   11: 9 For I am God, and not **m—**
Mic   6: 8 has showed you, O **m,** what is good.
Zec   6:12 the **m** whose name is the Branch,
Mal   3: 8 "Will a **m** rob God?"
Mt   4: 4 '**M** does not live on bread alone,
        9: 6 the Son of **M** has authority on earth
       12:12 How much more valuable is a **m**
       19: 5 a **m** will leave his father and mother
       19:26 "With **m** this is impossible.
Mk   2:27 "The Sabbath was made for **m,**
        8:36 for a **m** to gain the whole world,
        9:12 that the Son of **M** must suffer much
       10: 9 let **m** not separate."
Lk   4: 4 "It is written: '**M** does not live on
        6: 5 Son of **M** is Lord of the Sabbath."
        9:25 for a **m** to gain the whole world,
Jn   2:25 not need man's testimony about **m,**
        9:35 "Do you believe in the Son of **M?"**
Ac   7:56 Son of **M** standing at the right hand
       10:26 he said, "I am only a **m** myself."
       16: 9 had a vision of a **m** of Macedonia
Ro   3: 4 Let God be true, and every **m** a liar.
        5:12 sin entered the world through one **m,**
        9:20 But who are you, O **m,**
       10: 5 **m** who does these things will live by
1Co   2:15 The spiritual **m** makes judgments
        3:12 If any **m** builds
        7: 1 for a **m** not to marry.
        7: 2 each **m** should have his own wife,
       10:13 except what is common to **m.**
       11: 3 that the head of every **m** is Christ,
       11: 7 A **m** ought not to cover his head,
       11:14 that if a **m** has long hair,
       13:11 When I became a **m,**
       15:21 of the dead comes also through a **m.**
       15:47 first **m** was of the dust of the earth,
       15:49 the likeness of the **m** from heaven.
2Co   12: 2 I know a **m** in Christ who

Eph   2:15 to create in himself one new **m** out of
        5:31 a **m** will leave his father and mother
Php   2: 8 being found in appearance as a **m,**
1Ti   2: 5 the **m** Christ Jesus,
2Ti   3:17 the **m** of God may be thoroughly
Heb   2: 6 "What is **m** that you are mindful of
        9:27 Just as **m** is destined to die once,
       13: 6 What can **m** do to me?"
Jas   5:17 Elijah was a **m** just like us.
2Pe   1:21 never had its origin in the will of **m,**
Rev   1:13 someone "like a son of **m,"**
        4: 7 the third had a face like a **m,**
       14:14 the cloud was one "like a son of **m"**

MAN OF GOD Dt 33:1; Jos 14:6; Jdg 13:6, 8;
1Sa 2:27; 9:6, 7, 8, 10; 1Ki 12:22; 13:1, 3, 4, 5, 6,
6, 7, 8, 11, 12, 14, 14, 16, 19, 21, 23, 26, 29, 31;
17:18, 24; 20:28; 2Ki 1:9, 10, 11, 12, 13; 4:7, 9,
16, 21, 22, 25, 25, 27, 27, 40, 42; 5:8, 14, 15, 20;
6:6, 9, 10, 15; 7:2, 17, 18, 19, 19; 8:2, 4, 7, 8, 11;
13:19; 23:16, 17; 1Ch 23:14; 2Ch 8:14; 11:2;
25:7, 9, 9; 30:16; Ezr 3:2; Ne 12:24, 36; Ps 90:T;
Jer 35:4; 1Ti 6:11; 2Ti 3:17

SON OF MAN See SON

MAN'S [MAN]

Ge   2:21 he took one of the **m** ribs and
Ps   37:23 If the LORD delights in a **m** way,
       66: 5 how awesome his works in **m** behalf!
Pr   5:21 For a **m** ways are in full view of
       16: 2 All a **m** ways seem innocent to him,
       20:24 **m** steps are directed by the LORD.
Ecc   3:19 **M** fate is like that of the animals;
        8: 1 Wisdom brightens a **m** face
Jer   10:23 that a **m** life is not his own;
Hab   2: 8 For you have shed **m** blood;
        2:17 For you have shed **m** blood;
1Co   1:25 foolishness of God is wiser than **m**
        3:13 fire will test the quality of each **m**
1Pe   1:17 who judges each **m** work impartially,
Rev   13:18 for it is **m** number.

MAN-MADE* [MAN, MAKE]

Dt   4:28 There you will worship **m** gods
Mk   14:58 'I will destroy this **m** temple and
Ac   19:26 He says that **m** gods are no gods
Heb   9:11 more perfect tabernacle that is not **m,**
        9:24 Christ did not enter a **m** sanctuary

MANAGE* [MANAGER]

Jer   12: 5 how will you **m** in the thickets by
1Ti   3: 4 He must **m** his own family well
        3: 5 not know how to **m** his own family,
        3:12 but one wife and must **m** his children
        5:14 to **m** their homes and to give

MANAGER [MANAGE]

Lk   12:42 "Who then is the faithful and wise **m**
       16: 1 a rich man whose **m** was accused

MANASSEH

1. Firstborn of Joseph (Ge 41:51; 46:20).
Blessed by Jacob but not as firstborn (Ge 48).
Tribe of blessed (Dt 33:17), numbered (Nu 1:35;
26:34), half allotted land east of Jordan (Nu 32;

Jos 13:8-33), half west (Jos 16; Eze 48:4), failed to fully possess (Jos 17:12-13; Jdg 1:27), 12,000 from (Rev 7:6).

2. Son of Hezekiah; king of Judah (2Ki 21:1-18; 2Ch 33:1-20). Judah exiled for his detestable sins (2Ki 21:10-15). Repentance (2Ch 33:12-19).

MANDRAKES

Ge	30:14	give me some of your son's **m**."
SS	7:13	The **m** send out their fragrance,

MANGER

Isa	1: 3	the donkey his owner's **m**,
Lk	2:12	in cloths and lying in a **m**."

MANIFESTATION*

1Co	12: 7	the **m** of the Spirit is given for the

MANKIND [MAN]

Ge	6: 7	So the LORD said, "I will wipe **m**,
Nu	16:22	"O God, God of the spirits of all **m**,
	27:16	the God of the spirits of all **m**,
Dt	32: 8	when he divided all **m**,
Ps	33:13	the LORD looks down and sees all **m**;
Pr	8:31	his whole world and delighting in **m**.
Ecc	7:29	have I found: God made **m** upright,
Isa	40: 5	and all **m** together will see it.
	45:12	made the earth and created **m** upon it
Jer	32:27	the God of all **m**.
Zec	2:13	Be still before the LORD, all **m**,
Lk	3: 6	And all **m** will see God's salvation.'
Rev	9:15	were released to kill a third of **m**.

MANNA

Ex	16:31	people of Israel called the bread **m**.
Nu	11: 6	we never see anything but this **m**!"
Dt	8:16	He gave you **m** to eat in the desert,
Jos	5:12	The **m** stopped the day after they ate
Ps	78:24	he rained down **m** for the people
Jn	6:49	Your forefathers ate the **m** in
Heb	9: 4	This ark contained the gold jar of **m**,
Rev	2:17	I will give some of the hidden **m**.

MANNER

1Co	11:27	cup of the Lord in an unworthy **m**
Php	1:27	a **m** worthy of the gospel of Christ.

MANOAH*

Father of Samson (Jdg 13:2-21; 16:31).

MANSERVANT [SERVANT]

Ex	20:10	nor your **m** or maidservant,
Dt	5:14	your **m** and maidservant may rest,

MANSIONS*

Ps	49:14	far from their princely **m**.
Isa	5: 9	the fine **m** left without occupants.
Am	3:15	and the **m** will be demolished,"
	5:11	though you have built stone **m**,

MANY

Ge	17: 4	You will be the father of **m** nations.
	50:20	the saving of **m** lives.
Dt	1:10	that today you are as **m** as the stars
	15: 6	and you will lend to **m** nations

	15: 6	You will rule over **m** nations
	17:17	He must not take **m** wives,
Jdg	16:30	Thus he killed **m** men
1Ki	8: 5	so **m** sheep and cattle that they could
	11: 1	loved **m** foreign women besides
Ps	32:10	**M** are the woes of the wicked,
	34:12	and desires to see **m** good days,
	104:24	How **m** are your works, O LORD!
Pr	3: 2	they will prolong your life **m** years
	9:11	For through me your days will be **m**,
	10:19	When words are **m**, sin is not absent,
	11:14	but **m** advisers make victory sure.
	15:22	but with **m** advisers they succeed.
	31:29	"**M** women do noble things,
Ecc	5: 3	dream comes when there are **m** cares
	12:12	Of making **m** books there is no end,
SS	8: 7	**M** waters cannot quench love;
Isa	52:14	as there were **m** who were appalled
	52:15	so will he sprinkle **m** nations,
	53:11	my righteous servant will justify **m**,
	53:12	For he bore the sin of **m**,
Jer	11:13	as **m** gods as you have towns,
Da	9:27	He will confirm a covenant with **m**
	12: 3	those who lead **m** to righteousness,
Mt	10:31	you are worth more than **m** sparrows
	18:21	how **m** times shall I forgive my
	22:14	**m** are invited, but few are chosen."
	24: 5	For **m** will come in my name,
	26:28	poured out for **m** for the forgiveness
Mk	10:31	But **m** who are first will be last,
	10:45	to give his life as a ransom for **m**."
Lk	2:34	the falling and rising of **m** in Israel,
	10:41	worried and upset about **m** things,
Jn	20:30	Jesus did **m** other miraculous signs
	21:25	Jesus did **m** other things as well.
Ac	1: 3	and gave **m** convincing proofs
	5:12	apostles performed **m** miraculous
	14:22	"We must go through **m** hardships
Ro	5:19	the **m** will be made righteous.
	12: 5	in Christ we who are **m** form one
1Co	1:26	Not **m** of you were wise
	12:12	though it is made up of **m** parts;
Heb	2:10	In bringing **m** sons to glory,
	9:28	to take away the sins of **m** people;
Jas	1: 2	whenever you face trials of **m** kinds,
	3: 1	Not **m** of you should presume to
1Jn	2:18	even now **m** antichrists have come.
2Jn	1: 7	**M** deceivers, who do not
Rev	5:11	and heard the voice of **m** angels,
	19:12	and on his head are **m** crowns.

MAON

1Sa	23:24	and his men were in the Desert of **M**,

MARA*

Ru	1:20	Naomi," she told them. "Call me **M**,

MARAH

Ex	15:23	When they came to **M**,

MARANATHA (KJV)

See COME O LORD

MARCH [MARCHED, MARCHING]

Jos	6: 4	**m** around the city seven times,

Isa 42:13 LORD will **m** out like a mighty man,

MARCHED [MARCH]
Nu 33: 3 They **m** out boldly in full view of all

MARCHING [MARCH]
Ex 14: 8 who were **m** out boldly.
Jos   6:13 **m** before the ark of the LORD
2Sa 5:24 As soon as you hear the sound of **m**

MARITAL* [MARRY]
Ex 21:10 clothing and **m** rights.
Mt   5:32 except for **m** unfaithfulness,
     19: 9 except for **m** unfaithfulness,
1Co   7: 3 husband should fulfill his **m** duty

MARK [MARKED, MARKS]
   Cousin of Barnabas (Ac 12:12; 15:37-39; Col
4:10; 2Ti 4:11; Phm 24; 1Pe 5:13), see JOHN.
Ge   1:14 to **m** seasons and days and years,
     4:15 the LORD put a **m** on Cain so
Eze 9: 6 do not touch anyone who has the **m.**
Rev 13:16 to receive a **m** on his right hand or
    14: 9 and receives his **m** on the forehead
    16: 2 people who had the **m** of the beast
    19:20 received the **m** of the beast
    20: 4 and had not received his **m**

MARKED [MARK]
Job 38: 5 Who **m** off its dimensions?
Pr   8:27 when he **m** out the horizon on
Eph 1:13 you were **m** in him with a seal,
Heb 12: 1 run with perseverance the race **m** out

MARKET [MARKETPLACE, MARKETPLACES]
Jn   2:16 turn my Father's house into a **m!**"

MARKETPLACE [MARKET]
Lk   7:32 are like children sitting in the **m**

MARKETPLACES [MARKET]
Mt 23: 7 they love to be greeted in the **m** and

MARKS [MARK]
Lev 19:28 or put tattoo **m** on yourselves.
Jn 20:25 I see the nail **m** in his hands
Gal 6:17 for I bear on my body the **m** of Jesus.

MARRED*
Isa 52:14 his form **m** beyond human likeness
Jer 18: 4 from the clay was **m** in his hands;

MARRIAGE [MARRY]
Ge 29:26 to give the younger daughter in **m**
Dt 23: 2 No one born of a forbidden **m** nor
Jdg 3: 6 They took their daughters in **m** and
Ezr 9:12 do not give your daughters in **m**
Ne 13:25 not to give your daughters in **m**
Mt 22:30 will neither marry nor be given in **m;**
    24:38 marrying and giving in **m,**
Ro   7: 2 she is released from the law of **m.**
Heb 13: 4 **M** should be honored by all, and the
            m bed kept pure,

MARRIAGES* [MARRY]
Ne 13:26 Was it not because of **m** like these

MARRIED [MARRY]
Ge   4:19 Lamech **m** two women,
Dt 24: 5 If a man has recently **m,**
Ezr 10:10 you have **m** foreign women,
Pr 30:23 an unloved woman who is **m,**
Isa 62: 4 and your land will be **m.**
Mt   1:18 Mary was pledged to be **m** to Joseph,
Mk 12:23 since the seven were **m** to her?"
Lk   1:27 to a virgin pledged to be **m**
Ro   7: 2 a **m** woman is bound to her husband
1Co 7:10 To the **m** I give this command (not I,
     7:27 Are you **m?** Do not seek a divorce.
     7:33 But a **m** man is concerned about
     7:36 They should get **m.**

MARRIES [MARRY]
Dt 24: 1 If a man **m** a woman who becomes
Jer 3: 1 leaves him and **m** another man,
Mt   5:32 anyone who **m** the divorced woman
    19: 9 **m** another woman commits adultery.
Mk 10:11 **m** another woman commits adultery,
Lk 16:18 **m** another woman commits adultery,
Ro   7: 3 if she **m** another man while her
1Co 7:28 if a virgin **m,** she has not sinned.

MARROW
Heb 4:12 dividing soul and spirit, joints and **m**

MARRY [INTERMARRY, MARITAL, MARRIAGE, MARRIAGES, MARRIED, MARRIES, MARRYING]
Dt 25: 5 his widow must not **m** outside
Jdg 11:37 because I will never **m.**"
Mt 19:10 it is better not to **m.**"
    22:30 resurrection people will neither **m**
Mk 12:19 the man must **m** the widow
1Co 7: 1 It is good for a man not to **m.**
     7: 9 for it is better to **m** than to burn
     7:28 But if you do **m,** you have not sinned
1Ti 4: 3 They forbid people to **m** and order
     5:14 So I counsel younger widows to **m,**

MARRYING* [MARRY]
Ezr 10: 2 unfaithful to our God by **m** foreign
Ne 13:27 unfaithful to our God by **m** foreign
Mal 2:11 by **m** the daughter of a foreign god.
Mt 24:38 **m** and giving in marriage,
Lk 17:27 **m** and being given in marriage up to

MARS' (KJV) See AREOPAGUS

MARTHA*
   Sister of Mary and Lazarus (Lk 10:38-42; Jn 11; 12:2).

MARTYR*
Ac 22:20 blood of your **m** Stephen was shed,

MARVELED* [MARVELOUS]
Lk   2:33 The child's father and mother **m**
2Th 1:10 and to be **m** at among all those

MARVELING* [MARVELOUS]

Lk   9:43 everyone was **m** at all that Jesus did,

MARVELOUS* [MARVELED, MARVELING]

1Ch 16:24 his **m** deeds among all peoples.
Job 37: 5 God's voice thunders in **m** ways;
Ps 71:17 to this day I declare your **m** deeds.
    72:18 who alone does **m** deeds.
    86:10 For you are great and do **m** deeds;
    96: 3 his **m** deeds among all peoples.
    98: 1 for he has done **m** things;
  118:23 and it is **m** in our eyes.
Isa 25: 1 faithfulness you have done **m** things,
Zec 8: 6 "It may seem **m** to the remnant
    8: 6 but will it seem **m** to me?"
Mt 21:42 and it is **m** in our eyes'?
Mk 12:11 and it is **m** in our eyes'?"
Rev 15: 1 in heaven another great and **m** sign:
    15: 3 "Great and **m** are your deeds,

MARY

1. Mother of Jesus (Mt 1:16-25; Lk 1:27-56; 2:1-40). With Jesus at Cana (Jn 2:1-5), questioning his sanity (Mk 3:21), at the cross (Jn 19:25-27). Among disciples after Ascension (Ac 1:14).

2. Magdalene; former demoniac (Lk 8:2). Helped support Jesus' ministry (Lk 8:1-3). At the cross (Mt 27:56; Mk 15:40), burial (Mt 27:61; Mk 15:47). Saw angel after resurrection (Mt 28:1-10; Mk 16:1-9; Lk 24:1-12); also Jesus (Jn 20:1-18).

3. Sister of Martha and Lazarus (Jn 11). Washed Jesus' feet (Jn 12:1-8).

4. Mother of James and Joses; witnessed crucifixion (Mt 27:56; Mk 15:40) and empty tomb (Mk 16:1; Lk 24:10).

MASONS

1Ch 22:15 stonecutters, **m** and carpenters,
2Ch 24:12 hired **m** and carpenters to restore
Ezr   3: 7 Then they gave money to the **m**

MASQUERADE* [MASQUERADES, MASQUERADING]

2Co 11:15 **m** as servants of righteousness.

MASQUERADES* [MASQUERADE]

2Co 11:14 Satan himself **m** as an angel of light.

MASQUERADING* [MASQUERADE]

2Co 11:13 **m** as apostles of Christ.

MASSAH

Ex 17: 7 And he called the place **M**
Dt 33: 8 You tested him at **M;**
Ps 95: 8 as you did that day at **M** in the desert

MASTER [MASTER'S, MASTERED, MASTERS, MASTERY]

Ge   4: 7 but you must **m** it."

24:12 "O LORD, God of my **m** Abraham,
Ex 21: 5 'I love my **m** and my wife
1Sa 24:10 'I will not lift my hand against my **m**
Ps 12: 4 we own our lips—who is our **m?"**
Isa   1: 3 The ox knows his **m,**
Hos 2:16 you will no longer call me 'my **m.'**
Mal 1: 6 If I am a **m,**
Mt 10:24 nor a servant above his **m.**
    23: 8 for you have only one **M**
    24:46 servant whose **m** finds him doing
    25:21 "His **m** replied, 'Well done,
    25:23 "His **m** replied, 'Well done,
Jn 13:16 no servant is greater than his **m,**
    15:20 'No servant is greater than his **m.'**
Ro   6:14 For sin shall not be your **m,**
    14: 4 To his own **m** he stands or falls.
Eph 6: 9 both their **M** and yours is in heaven,
Col   4: 1 that you also have a **M** in heaven.
2Ti 2:21 useful to the **M** and prepared

MASTER'S [MASTER]

Mt 25:21 Come and share your **m** happiness!'
Lk 12:47 "That servant who knows his **m** will

MASTERED* [MASTER]

1Co 6:12 but I will not be **m** by anything.
2Pe 2:19 a slave to whatever has **m** him.

MASTERS [MASTER]

Ex   1:11 So they put slave **m** over them
Pr 25:13 the spirit of his **m.**
Mt   6:24 "No one can serve two **m.**
Lk 16:13 "No servant can serve two **m.**
Eph 6: 5 obey your earthly **m** with respect
    6: 9 **m,** treat your slaves in the same way.
Col   3:22 obey your earthly **m** in everything;
    4: 1 **M,** provide your slaves with what
1Ti   6: 1 should consider their **m** worthy
    6: 2 Those who have believing **m** are not
Tit   2: 9 be subject to their **m** in everything,
1Pe 2:18 submit yourselves to your **m**

MASTERY* [MASTER]

Ro   6: 9 death no longer has **m** over him.

MAT [MATS]

Mk   2: 9 'Get up, take your **m** and walk'?
Jn   5: 8 Pick up your **m** and walk."
Ac   9:34 Get up and take care of your **m."**

MATCHED*

2Co 8:11 may be **m** by your completion

MATERIAL

Ro 15:27 to share with them their **m** blessings.
1Co 9:11 is it too much if we reap a **m** harvest
1Jn 3:17 If anyone has **m** possessions

MATS* [MAT]

Mk 6:55 on **m** to wherever they heard he was.
Ac   5:15 and laid them on beds and **m** so that

MATTANIAH [ZEDEKIAH]

Original name of King Zedekiah (2Ki 24:17).

MATTER [MATTERS]

Dt   19:15 A **m** must be established by
Ecc 12:13 here is the conclusion of the **m:**
Mt   18:16 that 'every **m** may be established by
2Co 13: 1 "Every **m** must be established by

MATTERS [MATTER]

Mt   23:23 the more important **m** of the law—

MATTHEW [LEVI]

Apostle; former tax collector (Mt 9:9-13; 10:3;
Mk 3:18; Lk 6:15; Ac 1:13). Also called Levi (Mk
2:14-17; Lk 5:27-32).

MATTHIAS*

Disciple chosen to replace Judas (Ac 1:23-26).

MATURE* [MATURITY, PREMATURELY]

Lk   8:14 and they do not **m.**
1Co   2: 6 a message of wisdom among the **m,**
Eph   4:13 of the Son of God and become **m,**
Php   3:15 All of us who are **m** should take such
Col   4:12 **m** and fully assured.
Heb   5:14 But solid food is for the **m,**
Jas   1: 4 so that you may be **m** and complete,

MATURITY* [MATURE]

Heb   6: 1 about Christ and go on to **m,**

MEAL

Pr   15:17 Better a **m** of vegetables where
Lk   11:38 did not first wash before the **m,**
1Co   10:27 If some unbeliever invites you to a **m**
Heb   12:16 for a single **m** sold his inheritance

MEAN [MEANING, MEANINGLESS, MEANS]

Ex   12:26 What does this ceremony **m** to you?'
Jos   4: 6 'What do these stones **m?'**
Da   5:26 "This is what these words **m:**
Mt   12: 7 you had known what these words **m,**

MEANING [MEAN]

Ne   8: 8 making it clear and giving the **m**
Ecc   6:11 The more the words, the less the **m,**

MEANINGLESS [MEAN]

Ecc   1: 2 **"M! M!"** says the Teacher. "Utterly
                  m! Everything is **m."**
        2:11 everything was **m,** a chasing after
      12: 8 **"M! M!"** says the Teacher.
                  "Everything is **m!"**
1Ti   1: 6 from these and turned to **m** talk.

MEANS [MEAN]

Ge   40:12 "This is what it **m,"**
Da   2:25 tell the king what his dream **m."**
        4:18 Belteshazzar, tell me what it **m,**
        5:17 for the king and tell him what it **m.**
Mt   13:18 to what the parable of the sower **m:**
1Co   9:22 by all possible **m** I might save some.
Heb   9:12 not enter by **m** of the blood of goats

2Pe   3:15 that our Lord's patience **m** salvation,

MEASURE [IMMEASURABLY, MEASURED, MEASURES]

Ge   15:16 has not yet reached its full **m."**
Ps   71:15 though I know not its **m.**
Eze   45: 3 **m** off a section 25,000
Zec   2: 2 He answered me, "To **m** Jerusalem,
Mk   4:24 "With the **m** you use,
Lk   6:38 A good **m,** pressed down,
Eph   3:19 to the **m** of all the fullness of God.
        4:13 the whole **m** of the fullness of Christ.
2Pe   1: 8 these qualities in increasing **m,**
Rev   11: 1 "Go and **m** the temple of God and

MEASURED [MEASURE]

Isa   40:12 Who has **m** the waters in the hollow
Jer   31:37 be **m** and the foundations of the earth
Mk   4:24 it will be **m** to you—and even more.

MEASURES [MEASURE]

Dt   25:14 Do not have two differing **m**
Pr   20:10 Differing weights and differing **m—**

MEAT

Ge   9: 4 must not eat **m** that has its lifeblood
Ex   16:12 'At twilight you will eat **m,**
Nu   11:13 'Give us **m** to eat!'
Pr   23:20 or gorge themselves on **m,**
Ac   15:20 from the **m** of strangled animals and
Ro   14: 6 He who eats **m,** eats to the Lord,
        14:21 to eat **m** or drink wine or to do
1Co   8:13 I will never eat **m** again,
      10:25 Eat anything sold in the **m** market

MEDAD

Nu   11:27 and **M** are prophesying in the camp."

MEDDLER* [MEDDLES]

1Pe   4:15 or even as a **m.**

MEDDLES* [MEDDLER]

Pr   26:17 is a passer-by who **m** in a quarrel

MEDE [MEDIA]

Da   5:31 Darius the **M** took over the kingdom,

MEDES [MEDIA]

Da   5:28 and given to the **M** and Persians."
        6:15 in accordance with the laws of the **M**
Ac   2: 9 Parthians, **M** and Elamites;

MEDIA [MEDE, MEDES]

Ezr   6: 2 of Ecbatana in the province of **M,**
Da   8:20 represents the kings of **M** and Persia.

MEDIATE* [MEDIATOR]

1Sa   2:25 God may **m** for him;

MEDIATOR [MEDIATE]

Gal   3:19 put into effect through angels by a **m**
1Ti   2: 5 and one **m** between God and men,
Heb   8: 6 of which he is **m** is superior to the
        9:15 Christ is the **m** of a new covenant,
      12:24 to Jesus the **m** of a new covenant,

MEDICINE*

Pr 17:22 A cheerful heart is good **m,**

MEDITATE* [MEDITATED, MEDITATES, MEDITATION]

Ge 24:63 to the field one evening to **m,**
Jos 1: 8 **m** on it day and night,
Ps 48: 9 O God, we **m** on your unfailing love.
77:12 I will **m** on all your works
119:15 I **m** on your precepts
119:23 your servant will **m** on your decrees.
119:27 then I will **m** on your wonders.
119:48 and I **m** on your decrees.
119:78 but I will **m** on your precepts.
119:97 I **m** on it all day long.
119:99 for I **m** on your statutes.
119:148 that I may **m** on your promises.
143: 5 I **m** on all your works
145: 5 I will **m** on your wonderful works.

MEDITATED* [MEDITATE]

Ps 39: 3 and as I **m,** the fire burned;

MEDITATES* [MEDITATE]

Ps 1: 2 and on his law he **m** day and night.

MEDITATION* [MEDITATE]

Ps 19:14 the **m** of my heart be pleasing in
104:34 May my **m** be pleasing to him,

MEDIUM* [MEDIUMS]

Lev 20:27 " 'A man or woman who is a **m**
Dt 18:11 a **m** or spiritist or who consults the
1Sa 28: 7 "Find me a woman who is a **m,**
1Ch 10:13 and even consulted a **m** for guidance,

MEDIUMS [MEDIUM]

Lev 19:31 not turn to **m** or seek out spiritists,
2Ki 21: 6 and consulted **m** and spiritists.
23:24 Josiah got rid of the **m** and spiritists,
Isa 8:19 When men tell you to consult **m**

MEEK* [MEEKNESS]

Ps 37:11 But the **m** will inherit the land
Zep 3:12 But I will leave within you the **m**
Mt 5: 5 Blessed are the **m,**

MEEKNESS* [MEEK]

2Co 10: 1 By the **m** and gentleness of Christ,

MEET [MEETING, MEETINGS, MEETS, MET]

Ex 19:17 out of the camp to **m** with God,
30:36 where I will **m** with you.
Ps 42: 2 When can I go and **m** with God?
79: 8 your mercy come quickly to **m** us,
85:10 Love and faithfulness **m** together;
Pr 7:10 Then out came a woman to **m** him,
Am 4:12 prepare to **m** your God, O Israel."
Ac 2:46 to **m** together in the temple courts.
5:12 the believers used to **m** together
1Co 11:34 so that when you **m** together it may
1Th 4:17 in the clouds to **m** the Lord in the air.

MEETING [MEET]

Ex 27:21 In the Tent of **M,**
29:44 "So I will consecrate the Tent of **M**
33: 7 calling it the "tent of **m."**
40:34 the cloud covered the Tent of **M,**
Jos 18: 1 and set up the Tent of **M** there.
Heb 10:25 Let us not give up **m** together,
TENT OF MEETING See TENT

MEETINGS* [MEET]

1Co 11:17 for your **m** do more harm than good.

MEETS [MEET]

Ro 16: 5 also the church that **m** at their house.
1Co 16:19 does the church that **m** at their house.
Phm 1: 2 to the church that **m** in your home:
Heb 7:26 Such a high priest **m** our need—

MEGIDDO

Jos 12:21 the king of **M** one
Jdg 1:27 or Taanach or Dor or Ibleam or **M**

MELCHIZEDEK

Ge 14:18 Then **M** king of Salem brought out
Ps 110: 4 in the order of **M."**
Heb 5:10 to be high priest in the order of **M.**
6:20 high priest forever, in the order of **M**
7: 1 This **M** was king of Salem and priest
7:11 in the order of **M,** not in the order

MELON* [MELONS]

Jer 10: 5 Like a scarecrow in a **m** patch,

MELONS* [MELON]

Nu 11: 5 **m,** leeks, onions and garlic.
Isa 1: 8 like a hut in a field of **m,**

MELT [MELTED, MELTING, MELTS]

Ex 15:15 the people of Canaan will **m** away;
Jos 14: 8 made the hearts of the people **m**
Mic 1: 4 The mountains **m** beneath him and
Na 1: 5 before him and the hills **m** away.
2Pe 3:12 and the elements will **m** in the heat.

MELTED [MELT]

Jos 2:11 we heard of it, our hearts **m**

MELTS [MELT]

Ps 147:18 He sends his word and **m** them;
Am 9: 5 he who touches the earth and it **m,**

MEMBER [MEMBERS]

Mk 15:43 a prominent **m** of the Council,
Jn 3: 1 a **m** of the Jewish ruling council.
Ac 17:34 a **m** of the Areopagus,
Ro 12: 5 and each **m** belongs to all the others.

MEMBERS [MEMBER]

Mic 7: 6 are the **m** of his own household.
Mt 10:36 be the **m** of his own household.'
Ro 7:23 I see another law at work in the **m**
12: 4 of us has one body with many **m,**
1Co 6:15 your bodies are **m** of Christ himself?
12:24 But God has combined the **m** of

Eph	2:19	and **m** of God's household,
	3: 6	**m** together of one body,
	4:25	for we are all **m** of one body.
	5:30	for we are **m** of his body.
Col	3:15	as **m** of one body you were called

MEMORABLE* [MEMORY]

Eze	39:13	day I am glorified will be a **m** day

MEMORIAL [MEMORY]

Ex	28:12	as **m** stones for the sons of Israel.
Lev	2: 2	burn this as a **m** portion on the altar,
Jos	4: 7	These stones are to be a **m**

MEMORIES* [MEMORY]

1Th	3: 6	you always have pleasant **m** of us

MEMORY [MEMORABLE, MEMORIAL, MEMORIES]

Ex	17:14	completely blot out the **m** of Amalek
Pr	10: 7	**m** of the righteous will be a blessing,
Mt	26:13	will also be told, in **m** of her."

MEN [MAN]

Ge	4:26	**m** began to call on the name of the
	6: 2	the daughters of **m** were beautiful,
	6: 4	of God went to the daughters of **m**
	18: 2	Abraham looked up and saw three **m**
Nu	1:44	These were the **m** counted by Moses
	13: 2	"Send some **m** to explore the land
	16:29	If these **m** die a natural death
	26:51	of the **m** of Israel was 601,730.
Dt	16:16	Three times a year all your **m** must
Jdg	15:15	and struck down a thousand **m**.
1Sa	2:26	in favor with the LORD and with **m**.
2Sa	7:14	I will punish him with the rod of **m**,
	23: 8	the names of David's mighty **m:**
	24: 2	and enroll the fighting **m**,
1Ki	4:34	**M** of all nations came to listen
	8:39	you alone know the hearts of all **m**),
	12:10	young **m** who had grown up with
2Ki	4:43	can I set this before a hundred **m?**"
1Ch	17:17	though I were the most exalted of **m**,
	21:13	not let me fall into the hands of **m**."
Job	13: 9	him as you might deceive **m**?
	34:23	God has no need to examine **m**
Ps	9:20	the nations know they are but **m**.
	11: 4	He observes the sons of **m**;
	11: 7	upright **m** will see his face.
	37: 1	Do not fret because of evil **m** or
	37: 9	For evil **m** will be cut off,
	78:25	**M** ate the bread of angels;
	90: 3	You turn **m** back to dust, saying,
	107: 8	and his wonderful deeds for **m**,
Pr	10:14	Wise **m** store up knowledge,
	11:16	but ruthless **m** gain only wealth.
	12:22	but he delights in **m** who are truthful.
	24: 1	Do not envy wicked **m**,
Ecc	1:13	a heavy burden God has laid on **m!**
	3:11	also set eternity in the hearts of **m**;
	3:12	that there is nothing better for **m** than
	8:12	it will go better with God-fearing **m**,
Isa	29:13	made up only of rules taught by **m**.
	40: 6	"All **m** are like grass,

	53: 3	He was despised and rejected by **m**,
Jer	16:20	Do **m** make their own gods?
La	3:31	**m** are not cast off by the Lord
Da	1:17	four young **m** God gave knowledge
	3:25	four **m** walking around in the fire,
Mt	4:19	"and I will make you fishers of **m**."
	5:16	let your light shine before **m**,
	6:14	For if you forgive **m** when they sin
	10:32	acknowledges me before **m**,
	12:31	and blasphemy will be forgiven **m**,
	12:36	that **m** will have to give account on
	23: 5	"Everything they do is done for **m**
Mk	6:44	**m** who had eaten was five thousand.
	7: 7	teachings are but rules taught by **m**.'
	8: 9	About four thousand **m** were present.
	11:30	was it from heaven, or from **m?**
Lk	2:14	and on earth peace to **m**
	2:52	and in favor with God and **m**.
	6:22	Blessed are you when **m** hate you,
	9:30	Two **m**, Moses and Elijah,
Jn	1: 4	and that life was the light of **m**.
	1: 7	that through him all **m** might believe.
	2:24	for he knew all **m**.
	3:19	but **m** loved darkness instead of light
	12:32	will draw all **m** to myself."
	13:35	By this all **m** will know that you
Ac	4: 4	of **m** grew to about five thousand.
	4:13	that these **m** had been with Jesus.
	5: 4	You have not lied to **m** but to God."
	5:29	"We must obey God rather than **m!**
Ro	1:18	and wickedness of **m** who suppress
	1:27	**M** committed indecent acts with other **m**,
	5:12	and in this way death came to all **m**,
	5:18	justification that brings life for all **m**.
1Co	2:11	among **m** knows the thoughts of a
	3: 3	Are you not acting like mere **m?**
	3:21	So then, no more boasting about **m!**
	9:22	I have become all things to all **m**
	13: 1	in the tongues of **m** and of angels,
	16:13	be **m** of courage; be strong.
	16:18	Such **m** deserve recognition.
2Co	5:11	we try to persuade **m**.
	8:21	of the Lord but also in the eyes of **m**.
Gal	1: 1	Paul, an apostle—sent not from **m**
	1:10	now trying to win the approval of **m**,
Eph	4: 8	in his train and gave gifts to **m**."
1Th	2: 4	not trying to please **m** but God,
	2:13	you accepted it not as the word of **m**,
	4:13	or to grieve like the rest of **m**,
1Ti	2: 4	who wants all **m** to be saved and
	2: 5	one mediator between God and **m**,
	2: 6	gave himself as a ransom for all **m**—
	2: 8	I want **m** everywhere to lift up
	4:10	who is the Savior of all **m**,
2Ti	2: 2	entrust to reliable **m** who will also
Tit	2: 2	Teach the older **m** to be temperate,
	2: 6	the young **m** to be self-controlled.
	2:11	salvation has appeared to all **m**.
Heb	5: 1	high priest is selected from among **m**
	7:28	as high priests **m** who are weak;
	12:14	in peace with all **m** and to be holy;
	12:23	the judge of all **m**,
1Pe	1:24	For, "All **m** are like grass,

2: 8 "A stone that causes **m** to stumble
2Pe 1:21 but **m** spoke from God
2: 9 how to rescue godly **m** from trials
Rev 5: 9 with your blood you purchased **m**
13: 4 **M** worshiped the dragon because
18:13 and bodies and souls of **m.**
21: 3 "Now the dwelling of God is with **m,**

MEN OF ISRAEL See ISRAEL

MEN OF JUDAH See JUDAH

MEN'S [MAN]

Dt 22: 5 A woman must not wear **m** clothing,
2Ki 19:18 fashioned by **m** hands.
2Ch 32:19 the work of **m** hands.
Mt 23: 4 loads and put them on **m** shoulders,
23:27 the inside are full of dead **m** bones
Mk 7:21 For from within, out of **m** hearts,
Ro 2:16 when God will judge **m** secrets
1Co 2: 5 faith might not rest on **m** wisdom,
2Co 5:19 not counting **m** sins against them.

MENAHEM*

King of Israel (2Ki 15:14-23).

MEND*

Ps 60: 2 **m** its fractures, for it is quaking.
Ecc 3: 7 a time to tear and a time to **m,**

MENE*

Da 5:25 that was written: **M, M,** TEKEL. PARSIN
5:26 **M:** God has numbered the days of

MENPLEASERS (KJV)

See WIN FAVOR

MENTION

Eph 5:12 shameful even to **m** what the

MEPHIBOSHETH

Son of Jonathan shown kindness by David (2Sa
4:4; 9; 21:7). Accused of siding with Absalom
(2Sa 16:1-4; 19:24-30).

MERAB*

Daughter of Saul (1Sa 14:49; 18:17-19; 2Sa
21:8).

MERARI [MERARITE, MERARITES]

Ge 46:11 of Levi: Gershon, Kohath and **M.**
Jos 21: 7 The descendants of **M,** clan by clan,
1Ch 6:19 The sons of **M:** Mahli and Mushi.
2Ch 34:12 Levites descended from **M,**

MERARITE [MERARI]

Nu 3:20 The **M** clans: Mahli and Mushi.
4:45 the total of those in the **M** clans.

MERARITES [MERARI]

Nu 3:36 The **M** were appointed to take care

MERCHANDISE

Ne 10:31 the neighboring peoples bring **m**
Mk 11:16 to carry **m** through the temple courts.

MERCHANT [MERCHANTS]

Pr 31:14 She is like the **m** ships,
Hos 12: 7 The **m** uses dishonest scales;
Mt 13:45 like a **m** looking for fine pearls.

MERCHANTS [MERCHANT]

Ge 37:28 So when the Midianite **m** came by,
Ps 107:23 they were **m** on the mighty waters.
Na 3:16 have increased the number of your **m**
Rev 18:11 "The **m** of the earth will weep

MERCIFUL* [MERCY]

Ge 19:16 for the LORD was **m** to them.
Dt 4:31 For the LORD your God is a **m** God;
1Ki 20:31 kings of the house of Israel are **m.**
Ne 9:31 for you are a gracious and **m** God.
Ps 4: 1 be **m** to me and hear my prayer.
6: 2 Be **m** to me, LORD, for I am faint;
26:11 redeem me and be **m** to me.
27: 7 be **m** to me and answer me.
30:10 Hear, O LORD, and be **m** to me;
31: 9 Be **m** to me, O LORD,
56: 1 Be **m** to me, O God,
77: 9 Has God forgotten to be **m?**
78:38 Yet he was **m;**
Jer 3:12 for I am **m,**' declares the LORD.
Da 9: 9 The LORD our God is **m** and forgiving
Mt 5: 7 Blessed are the **m,**
Lk 1:54 remembering to be **m**
6:36 Be **m,** just as your Father is merciful.
6:36 Be merciful, just as your Father is **m.**
Heb 2:17 **m** and faithful high priest in service
Jas 2:13 to anyone who has not been **m.**
Jude 1:22 Be **m** to those who doubt;

MERCY* [MERCIFUL]

Ge 43:14 And may God Almighty grant you **m**
Ex 33:19 I will have **m** on whom I will have **m**
Dt 7: 2 and show them no **m.**
13:17 he will show you **m,**
Jos 11:20 exterminating them without **m,**
2Sa 24:14 for his **m** is great;
1Ki 8:28 and his plea for **m,**
8:50 to show them **m;**
1Ch 21:13 for his **m** is very great;
2Ch 6:39 and his plea for **m,**
Ne 9:31 But in your great **m** you did not put
13:22 and show **m** to me according
Est 4: 8 into the king's presence to beg for **m**
Job 9:15 plead with my Judge for **m.**
27:22 It hurls itself against him without **m**
41: 3 Will he keep begging you for **m?**
Ps 5: 7 But I, by your great **m,**
6: 9 The LORD has heard my cry for **m;**
9:13 Have **m** and lift me up from the gates
25: 6 O LORD, your great **m** and love,
28: 2 Hear my cry for **m** as I call to you
28: 6 for he has heard my cry for **m.**
30: 8 to the Lord I cried for **m:**
31:22 for when I called to you for help.
40:11 Do not withhold your **m** from me,
41: 4 I said, "O LORD, have **m** on me;
41:10 But you, O LORD, have **m** on me;
51: 1 Have **m** on me, O God,

57: 1 Have **m** on me, O God,
57: 1 O God, have **m** on me,
59: 5 show no **m** to wicked traitors.
69:16 in your great **m** turn to me.
79: 8 may your **m** come quickly
86: 3 Have **m** on me, O Lord,
86: 6 listen to my cry for **m.**
86:16 Turn to me and have **m** on me;
116: 1 he heard my cry for **m.**
119:132 Turn to me and have **m** on me,
123: 2 till he shows us his **m.**
123: 3 Have **m** on us, O LORD,
123: 3 O LORD, have **m** on us,
130: 2 ears be attentive to my cry for **m.**
140: 6 Hear, O LORD, my cry for **m.**
142: 1 I lift up my voice to the LORD for **m.**
143: 1 listen to my cry for **m;**
Pr 6:34 and he will show no **m**
18:23 A poor man pleads for **m,**
21:10 his neighbor gets no **m** from him.
28:13 and renounces them finds **m.**
Isa 13:18 they will have no **m** on infants
47: 6 and you showed them no **m.**
55: 7 and he will have **m** on him,
63: 9 In his love and **m** he redeemed them;
Jer 6:23 they are cruel and show no **m.**
13:14 or **m** or compassion to keep me
21: 7 he will show them no **m** or pity
50:42 they are cruel and without **m.**
Da 2:18 plead for **m** from the God of heaven
9:18 but because of your great **m.**
Hos 6: 6 For I desire **m,** not sacrifice.
Am 5:15 the LORD God Almighty will have **m**
Mic 6: 8 and to love **m** and to walk humbly
7:18 angry forever but delight to show **m.**
7:20 and show **m** to Abraham,
Hab 1:17 destroying nations without **m?**
3: 2 in wrath remember **m.**
Zec 1:12 how long will you withhold **m**
1:16 'I will return to Jerusalem with **m,**
7: 9 'Administer true justice; show **m**
Mt 5: 7 for they will be shown **m.**
9:13 'I desire **m,** not sacrifice.'
9:27 'Have **m** on us, Son of David!'
12: 7 'I desire **m,** not sacrifice,'
15:22 "Lord, Son of David, have **m** on me!
17:15 "Lord, have **m** on my son," he said.
18:33 Shouldn't you have had **m** on your
20:30 "Lord, Son of David, have **m** on us!"
20:31 "Lord, Son of David, have **m** on us!"
23:23 **m** and faithfulness.
Mk 5:19 and how he has had **m** on you."
10:47 Son of David, have **m** on me!"
10:48 "Son of David, have **m** on me!"
Lk 1:50 His **m** extends to those who fear him,
1:58 that the Lord had shown her great **m,**
1:72 to show **m** to our fathers and
1:78 because of the tender **m** of our God,
10:37 "The one who had **m** on him."
18:13 'God, have **m** on me, a sinner.'
18:38 "Son of David, have **m** on me!"
18:39 "Son of David, have **m** on me!"
Ro 9:15 "I will have **m** on whom I have **m,**
9:16 but on God's **m.**

9:18 has **m** on whom he wants to have **m,**
9:23 glory known to the objects of his **m,**
11:30 have now received **m** as a result
11:31 receive **m** as a result of God's **m** to
11:32 so that he may have **m**
12: 1 brothers, in view of God's **m,**
12: 8 showing **m,** let him do it cheerfully.
15: 9 Gentiles may glorify God for his **m,**
1Co 7:25 who by the Lord's **m** is trustworthy.
2Co 4: 1 God's **m** we have this ministry,
Gal 6:16 and **m** to all who follow this rule,
Eph 2: 4 God, who is rich in **m,**
Php 2:27 But God had **m** on him,
1Ti 1: 2 **m** and peace from God the Father
1:13 I was shown **m** because I acted
1:16 for that very reason I was shown **m**
2Ti 1: 2 **m** and peace from God the Father
1:16 the Lord show **m** to the household
1:18 that he will find **m** from the Lord on
Tit 3: 5 but because of his **m.**
Heb 4:16 we may receive **m** and find grace
10:28 died without **m** on the testimony of
Jas 2:13 judgment without **m** will be shown
2:13 **M** triumphs over judgment!
3:17 submissive, full of **m** and good fruit,
5:11 Lord is full of compassion and **m.**
1Pe 1: 3 his great **m** he has given us new birth
2:10 you had not received **m,** but now
you have received **m.**
2Jn 1: 3 **m** and peace from God the Father
Jude 1: 2 **M,** peace and love be yours
1:21 as you wait for the **m** of our Lord
1:23 to others show **m,** mixed with fear—

MERCYSEAT (KJV)
See PLACE OF ATONEMENT

MERELY
Ro 2:28 nor is circumcision **m** outward
Jas 1:22 Do not **m** listen to the word,

MERIBAH [MERIBAH KADESH]
Ex 17: 7 he called the place Massah and **M**
Nu 20:13 These were the waters of **M,**
Dt 33: 8 with him at the waters of **M.**
Ps 95: 8 harden your hearts as you did at **M,**
106:32 By the waters of **M** they angered

MERIBAH KADESH [MERIBAH]
Nu 27:14 (These were the waters of **M**

MERRY
Ecc 10:19 and wine makes life **m,**
Lk 12:19 Take life easy; eat, drink and be **m."**

MESHACH* [MISHAEL]
Hebrew exiled to Babylon; name changed from
Mishael (Da 1:6-7). Refused defilement by food
(Da 1:8-20). Refused to worship idol (Da 3:1-18);
saved from furnace (Da 3:19-30).

MESHECH
Ge 10: 2 Madai, Javan, Tubal, **M** and Tiras.
10:23 Hul, Gether and **M.**
Ps 120: 5 Woe to me that I dwell in **M,**

Eze 38: 3 O Gog, chief prince of **M** and Tubal.
    39: 1 O Gog, chief prince of **M** and Tubal.

MESOPOTAMIA*

Ac 2: 9 residents of **M**, Judea and
    7: 2 Abraham while he was still in **M**,

MESSAGE [MESSENGER, MESSENGERS]

Nu 23: 5 LORD put a **m** in Balaam's mouth
    23:16 Balaam and put a **m** in his mouth
Dt 18:22 that is a **m** the LORD has not spoken.
2Ch 25:18 "A thistle in Lebanon sent a **m** to
Isa 9: 8 The Lord has sent a **m** against Jacob;
    28: 9 To whom is he explaining his **m?**
    53: 1 Who has believed our **m** and
Jer 23:21 yet they have run with their **m;**
    49:14 I have heard a **m** from the LORD:
Da 9:23 the **m** and understand the vision:
    10: 1 The understanding of the **m** came
Mt 10: 7 As you go, preach this **m:**
Lk 4:32 because his **m** had authority.
Jn 12:38 who has believed our **m** and
    17:20 will believe in me through their **m,**
Ac 2:41 who accepted his **m** were baptized,
    4: 4 But many who heard the **m** believed,
    5:20 "and tell the people the full **m**
    10:36 You know the **m** God sent to
    15:31 and were glad for its encouraging **m.**
    17:11 received the **m** with great eagerness
Ro 10:16 "Lord, who has believed our **m?"**
    10:17 faith comes from hearing the **m,**
1Co 1:18 For the **m** of the cross is foolishness
    2: 4 My **m** and my preaching were not
    12: 8 through the Spirit the **m** of wisdom,
    to another the **m** of knowledge
2Co 5:19 to us the **m** of reconciliation.
2Th 3: 1 the **m** of the Lord may spread rapidly
Tit 1: 9 hold firmly to the trustworthy **m**
Heb 4: 2 but the **m** they heard was of no value
1Pe 2: 8 because they disobey the **m—**
1Jn 1: 5 This is the **m** we have heard from
    3:11 the **m** you heard from the beginning:

MESSENGER [MESSAGE]

Isa 41:27 to Jerusalem a **m** of good tidings.
    42:19 and deaf like the **m** I send?
Da 4:13 and there before me was a **m,**
Hag 1:13 Then Haggai, the LORD's **m,**
Mal 2: 7 he is the **m** of the LORD Almighty.
    3: 1 "See, I will send my **m,**
Mt 11:10 " 'I will send my **m** ahead of you,
Jn 13:16 nor is a **m** greater than the one
2Co 12: 7 a **m** of Satan, to torment me.

MESSENGERS [MESSAGE]

2Sa 15:10 Then Absalom sent secret **m**
2Ch 36:15 through his **m** again and again,
Ps 104: 4 He makes winds his **m,**
Isa 44:26 and fulfills the predictions of his **m,**

MESSIAH* [CHRIST]

Jn 1:41 "We have found the **M"** (that is,
    4:25 that **M"** (called Christ) "is coming.

MET [MEET]

Ge 32: 1 and the angels of God **m** him.
Ex 3:18 God of the Hebrews, has **m** with us.
    5: 3 God of the Hebrews, has **m** with us.
Mt 28: 9 Suddenly Jesus **m** them.
Jn 18: 2 because Jesus had often **m** there

METAL

Lev 19: 4 make gods of cast **m** for yourselves.
1Ki 14: 9 idols made of **m;**
2Ch 4: 2 He made the Sea of cast **m,**
Ps 106:19 and worshiped an idol cast from **m.**
Isa 48: 5 and **m** god ordained them.'
Eze 1:27 he looked like glowing **m,** as if full
    8: 2 was as bright as glowing **m.**

METHUSELAH

Ge 5:27 Altogether, **M** lived 969 years,

MICAH

1. Idolater from Ephraim (Jdg 17-18).
2. Prophet from Moresheth (Jer 26:18-19; Mic 1:1).

MICAIAH

Prophet of the LORD who spoke against Ahab (1Ki 22:1-28; 2Ch 18:1-27).

MICHAEL

Archangel (Jude 9); warrior in angelic realm, protector of Israel (Da 10:13, 21; 12:1; Rev 12:7).

MICHAL*

Daughter of Saul, wife of David (1Sa 14:49; 18:20-28). Warned David of Saul's plot (1Sa 19). Saul gave her to Paltiel (1Sa 25:44); David retrieved her (2Sa 3:13-16). Criticized David for dancing before the ark (2Sa 6:16-23; 1Ch 15:29).

MIDAIR* [AIR]

2Sa 18: 9 He was left hanging in **m,**
Rev 8:13 an eagle that was flying in **m** call out
    14: 6 Then I saw another angel flying in **m**
    19:17 to all the birds flying in **m,**

MIDDAY [DAY]

Dt 28:29 At **m** you will grope about like
Isa 59:10 **m** we stumble as if it were twilight;

MIDDLE [MIDST]

Ge 2: 9 In the **m** of the garden were the tree
Jos 3:17 on dry ground in the **m** of the Jordan,
    4: 3 stones from the **m** of the Jordan
    10:13 The sun stopped in the **m** of the sky
Jdg 16: 3 Samson lay there only until the **m**
Ru 3: 8 the **m** of the night something startled
Da 9:27 In the **m** of the 'seven' he will put
Jn 19:18 one on each side and Jesus in the **m.**

MIDIAN [MIDIANITE, MIDIANITES]

Ex 2:15 from Pharaoh and went to live in **M,**
    18: 1 Now Jethro, the priest of **M** and
Jdg 7: 2 for me to deliver **M** into their hands.
Ps 83: 9 Do to them as you did to **M,**

MIDIANITE [MIDIAN]
Ge 37:28 So when the **M** merchants came by,
Nu 25: 6 a **M** woman right before the eyes

MIDIANITES [MIDIAN]
Ge 37:36 **M** sold Joseph in Egypt to Potiphar,
Nu 31: 2 "Take vengeance on the **M** for the
Jdg 6:16 strike down all the **M** together."

MIDNIGHT [NIGHT]
Ex 11: 4 'About **m** I will go throughout Egypt
    12:29 At **m** the LORD struck down all
Ps 119:62 At **m** I rise to give you thanks
Ac 16:25 About **m** Paul and Silas were praying

MIDST [MIDDLE]
Ps 135: 9 and wonders into your **m**, O Egypt,
    136:14 brought Israel through the **m** of it,

MIDWIVES
Ex 1:17 The **m**, however, feared God and did

MIGHT [ALMIGHTY, MIGHTIER, MIGHTY]
Ex 9:16 that my name **m** be proclaimed in all
    33: 3 and I **m** destroy you on the way."
Dt 5:29 so that it **m** go well with them
Jos 4:24 and so that you **m** always fear
Jdg 16:30 Then he pushed with all his **m,**
2Sa 6: 5 were celebrating with all their **m**
    6:14 before the LORD with all his **m,**
2Ch 6:41 you and the ark of your **m.**
    20: 6 Power and **m** are in your hand,
Ps 21:13 we will sing and praise your **m.**
    54: 1 vindicate me by your **m**
    59:11 In your **m** make them wander about,
    80: 2 Awaken your **m**; come and save us.
    119:11 that I **m** not sin against you.
    119:71 so that I **m** learn your decrees.
    119:101 so that I **m** obey your word.
Ecc 9:10 finds to do, do it with all your **m,**
Isa 63:15 Where are your zeal and your **m?**
Jer 16:21 I will teach them my power and **m**
Mic 3: 8 and with justice and **m,**
Zec 4: 6 'Not by **m** nor by power,
Mt 13:15 Otherwise they **m** see with their eyes
Mk 14:35 if possible the hour **m** pass from him.
Lk 22: 4 with them how he **m** betray Jesus.
Jn 1: 7 that through him all men **m** believe.
Ac 28:27 Otherwise they **m** see with their eyes
1Co 9:22 by all possible means I **m** save some.
2Co 8: 9 through his poverty **m** become rich.
Col 1:11 according to his glorious **m**
1Ti 1:16 To him be honor and **m** forever.
1Pe 2:24 so that we **m** die to sins and live
1Jn 3: 5 so that he **m** take away our sins.

MIGHTIER* [MIGHT]
Ps 93: 4 **M** than the thunder of the great
         waters, **m** than the breakers of the

MIGHTY [MIGHT]
Ge 10: 9 a **m** hunter before the LORD;
    49:24 of the hand of the **M** One of Jacob,

Ex 6: 1 of my **m** hand he will let them go;
    7: 4 and with **m** acts of judgment
    13: 3 brought you out of it with a **m** hand.
Dt 3:24 the deeds and **m** works you do?
    5:15 you out of there with a **m** hand
    7: 8 a **m** hand and redeemed you from
    10:17 the great God, **m** and awesome,
    34:12 no one has ever shown the **m** power
Jos 22:22 "The **M** One, God, the LORD! The
         M One, God, the LORD!
2Sa 1:19 How the **m** have fallen!
    23: 8 the names of David's **m** men:
2Ch 14:11 to help the powerless against the **m.**
Ne 9:32 the great, **m** and awesome God,
Job 36: 5 "God is **m**, but does not despise men;
Ps 24: 8 The LORD strong and **m,**
    29: 1 Ascribe to the LORD, O **m** ones,
    45: 3 sword upon your side, O **m** one;
    50: 1 The **M** One, God, the LORD,
    62: 7 he is my **m** rock, my refuge.
    68:33 who thunders with **m** voice.
    71:16 I will come and proclaim your **m**
         acts,
    77:12 and consider all your **m** deeds.
    77:15 With your **m** arm you redeemed
    89: 8 You are **m**, O LORD,
    93: 4 the LORD on high is **m.**
    99: 4 The King is **m**, he loves justice—
    106: 2 Who can proclaim the **m** acts of
    110: 2 LORD will extend your **m** scepter
    118:15 right hand has done **m** things!
    136:12 with a **m** hand and outstretched arm;
    145: 4 they will tell of your **m** acts.
    145:12 that all men may know of your **m**
    147: 5 Great is our Lord and **m** in power;
    150: 1 praise him in his **m** heavens.
SS 8: 6 like a **m** flame.
Isa 9: 6 **M** God, Everlasting Father,
    33:21 There the LORD will be our **M** One.
    49:26 the **M** One of Jacob."
    60:16 your Redeemer, the **M** One of Jacob.
    63: 1 speaking in righteousness, **m** to save.
Jer 10: 6 and your name is **m** in power.
    20:11 LORD is with me like a **m** warrior;
    32:19 your purposes and **m** are your deeds.
Eze 20:33 a **m** hand and an outstretched arm
Da 4: 3 how **m** his wonders!
    11: 3 Then a **m** king will appear,
Zep 3:17 he is **m** to save.
Mk 14:62 sitting at the right hand of the **M** One
Lk 1:49 for the **M** One has done great things
Eph 1:19 like the working of his **m** strength,
    6:10 in the Lord and in his **m** power.
1Pe 5: 6 therefore, under God's **m** hand,
Rev 18: 8 **m** is the Lord God who judges her.

MIGHTY HAND See HAND

MIGHTY ONE Ge 49:24; Jos 22:22, 22; Job 34:17; Ps 45:3; 50:1; 132:2, 5; Isa 1:24; 10:13, 34; 33:21; 49:26; 60:16; Mt 26:64; Mk 14:62; Lk 1:49

MILCAH
Ge 11:29 the name of Nahor's wife was **M;**

MILDEW

Dt 28:22 with blight and **m**,
2Ch 6:28 or blight or **m**,
Am 4: 9 I struck them with blight and **m**.

MILE*

Mt 5:41 If someone forces you to go one **m**,

MILETUS

2Ti 4:20 and I left Trophimus sick in **M**.

MILK

Ex 3: 8 a land flowing with **m** and honey—
23:19 cook a young goat in its mother's **m**.
Pr 30:33 as churning the **m** produces butter,
SS 4:11 **m** and honey are under your tongue.
Isa 55: 1 buy wine and **m** without money and
Joel 3:18 and the hills will flow with **m**;
1Co 3: 2 I gave you **m**, not solid food,
Heb 5:12 You need **m**, not solid food!
1Pe 2: 2 crave pure spiritual **m**,

LAND FLOWING WITH MILK AND
HONEY See FLOWING

MILL

Mt 24:41 will be grinding with a hand **m**;

MILLSTONE [STONE]

Jdg 9:53 a woman dropped an upper **m**
Lk 17: 2 a **m** tied around his neck than for

MILLSTONES [STONE]

Dt 24: 6 Do not take a pair of **m**—

MIND [DOUBLE-MINDED,
LIKE-MINDED, MINDED, MINDFUL,
MINDS]

Ge 37:11 but his father kept the matter in **m**.
Nu 23:19 that he should change his **m**.
Dt 28:65 LORD will give you an anxious **m**,
29: 4 a **m** that understands or eyes that see
1Sa 15:29 that he should change his **m**."
1Ch 28: 9 devotion and with a willing **m**,
2Ch 30:12 the people to give them unity of **m**
Ps 26: 2 examine my heart and my **m**;
110: 4 has sworn and will not change his **m**:
Ecc 2: 3 embracing folly—my **m** still guiding
Isa 26: 3 peace him whose **m** is steadfast,
40:13 understood the **m** of the LORD,
Jer 17:10 search the heart and examine the **m**,
La 3:21 I call to **m** and therefore I have hope
Da 4:16 Let his **m** be changed from that of
Mt 1:19 he had in **m** to divorce her quietly,
22:37 all your soul and with all your **m**.'
Mk 3:21 for they said, "He is out of his **m**."
5:15 dressed and in his right **m**,
12:30 all your soul and with all your **m**
Lk 10:27 your strength and with all your **m**';
Ac 4:32 believers were one in heart and **m**.
Ro 1:28 he gave them over to a depraved **m**,
7:25 in my **m** am a slave to God's law,
8: 6 The **m** of sinful man is death,
8: 6 the **m** controlled by the Spirit is life

8: 7 the sinful **m** is hostile to God.
11:34 "Who has known the **m** of the Lord?
12: 2 by the renewing of your **m**.
14:13 make up your **m** not to put
1Co 1:10 you may be perfectly united in **m**
2: 9 no **m** has conceived what God has
2:16 who has known the **m** of the Lord
14:14 but my **m** is unfruitful.
2Co 5:13 If we are out of our **m**,
5:13 if we are in our right **m**,
13:11 listen to my appeal, be of one **m**,
Php 3:19 Their **m** is on earthly things.
Col 2:18 and his unspiritual **m** puffs him up
1Th 4:11 to **m** your own business and to work
Heb 7:21 has sworn and will not change his **m**:
Rev 17: 9 "This calls for a **m** with wisdom.

MINDED* [MIND]

1Pe 4: 7 be clear **m** and self-controlled

MINDFUL* [MIND]

Ps 8: 4 what is man that you are **m** of him,
Lk 1:48 he has been **m** of the humble state
Heb 2: 6 "What is man that you are **m** of him,

MINDS [MIND]

Dt 11:18 words of mine in your hearts and **m**;
Ps 7: 9 who searches **m** and hearts,
Jer 23:16 They speak visions from their own **m**
31:33 "I will put my law in their **m**
Lk 24:38 and why do doubts rise in your **m**?
24:45 Then he opened their **m** so they
Ro 8: 5 to the sinful nature have their **m** set
8: 5 with the Spirit have their **m** set on
2Co 3:14 But their **m** were made dull,
4: 4 god of this age has blinded the **m**
Eph 4:23 made new in the attitude of your **m**;
Php 4: 7 will guard your hearts and your **m**
Col 3: 2 Set your **m** on things above,
Heb 8:10 I will put my laws in their **m**
10:16 and I will write them on their **m**."
1Pe 1:13 Therefore, prepare your **m** for action;
Rev 2:23 I am he who searches hearts and **m**,

MINE

Ex 19:: 5 Although the whole earth is **m**,
Nu 3::12 The Levites are **m**,
3::13 for all the firstborn are **m**.
Dt 32::35 It is **m** to avenge; I will repay.
Job 28:: 1 "There is a **m** for silver
Ps 50::10 for every animal of the forest is **m**,
Pr 8::14 Counsel and sound judgment are **m**;
SS 2::16 My lover is **m** and I am his;
Isa 30:: 1 who carry out plans that are not **m**,
Hag 2:: 8 'The silver is **m** and the gold is **m**,'
Mt 7::24 everyone who hears these words **m**
25::40 one of the least of these brothers **m**,
Jn 16::15 All that belongs to the Father is **m**.
Ro 12::19 "It is **m** to avenge; I will repay,"
Heb 10::30 him who said, "It is **m** to avenge;

MINGLED*

Ezr 9: 2 and have **m** the holy race with
Ps 106:35 but they **m** with the nations

MINISTER [MINISTERED, MINISTERING, MINISTERS, MINISTRY]

Nu 16: 9 to stand before the community and **m**
Dt 10: 8 to **m** and to pronounce blessings in
1Ch 15: 2 to carry the ark of the LORD and to **m**
Ps 101: 6 he whose walk is blameless will **m**
    135: 2 who **m** in the house of the LORD,
Ro 15:16 be a **m** of Christ Jesus to the Gentiles
1Ti 4: 6 you will be a good **m** of Christ Jesus,

MINISTERED* [MINISTER]

1Sa 2:11 but the boy **m** before the LORD
     3: 1 The boy Samuel **m** before the LORD
1Ch 6:32 They **m** with music before the

MINISTERING [MINISTER]

1Ch 24: 3 for their appointed order of **m.**
Heb 1:14 Are not all angels **m** spirits sent

MINISTERS [MINISTER]

2Ki 10:19 in order to destroy the **m** of Baal.
2Co 3: 6 He has made us competent as **m** of

MINISTRATION (KJV)
See DISTRIBUTION, MINISTRY, SERVICE

MINISTRY [MINISTER]

Lk   3:23 thirty years old when he began his **m**
Ac   1:17 of our number and shared in this **m."**
     6: 4 to prayer and the **m** of the word."
Ro 11:13 I make much of my **m**
2Co 3: 7 Now if the **m** that brought death,
     4: 1 through God's mercy we have this **m**
     5:18 gave us the **m** of reconciliation:
     6: 3 so that our **m** will not be discredited.
Gal 2: 8 **m** of Peter as an apostle to the Jews,
     2: 8 my **m** as an apostle to the Gentiles.
2Ti 4: 5 discharge all the duties of your **m.**
Heb 8: 6 But the **m** Jesus has received is

MIRACLE* [MIRACLES, MIRACULOUS]

Ex   7: 9 'Perform a **m,**' then say to Aaron,
Mk   9:39 "No one who does a **m** in my name
Lk 23: 8 hoped to see him perform some **m.**
Jn   7:21 Jesus said to them, "I did one **m,**
Ac   4:16 they have done an outstanding **m,**

MIRACLES* [MIRACLE]

1Ch 16:12 the wonders he has done, his **m,**
Ne   9:17 failed to remember the **m** you
Job 5: 9 **m** that cannot be counted.
     9:10 **m** that cannot be counted.
Ps 77:11 I will remember your **m** of long ago.
    77:14 You are the God who performs **m;**
    78:12 He did **m** in the sight of their fathers
   105: 5 the wonders he has done, his **m,**
   106: 7 gave no thought to your **m;**
   106:22 **m** in the land of Ham
Mt   7:22 and perform many **m?'**
    11:20 most of his **m** had been performed,
    11:21 If the **m** that were performed
    11:23 If the **m** that were performed
    13:58 And he did not do many **m** there
    24:24 great signs and **m** to deceive
Mk   6: 2 that he even does **m!**
     6: 5 He could not do any **m** there,
    13:22 and perform signs and **m**
Lk 10:13 if the **m** that were performed
    19:37 for all the **m** they had seen:
Jn   3: 2 disciples may see the **m** you do.
    10:25 The **m** I do in my Father's name
    10:32 "I have shown you many great **m**
    10:38 not believe me, believe the **m,**
    14:11 on the evidence of the **m** themselves.
    15:24 But now they have seen these **m,**
Ac   2:22 accredited by God to you by **m,**
     8:13 by the great signs and **m** he saw.
    19:11 God did extraordinary **m** through
Ro 15:19 by the power of signs and **m,**
1Co 12:28 third teachers, then workers of **m,**
    12:29 Do all work **m?**
2Co 12:12 an apostle—signs, wonders and **m—**
Gal 3: 5 **m** among you because you observe
2Th 2: 9 in all kinds of counterfeit **m,**
Heb 2: 4 wonders and various **m,**

MIRACULOUS [MIRACLE]

Ex   4: 8 or pay attention to the first **m** sign,
     7: 3 and though I multiply my **m** signs
Nu 14:11 in spite of all the **m** signs I have
Dt   4:34 by testings, by **m** signs and wonders,
    13: 1 and announces to you a **m** sign
    34:11 did all those **m** signs and wonders
Ps 74: 9 We are given no **m** signs;
Mt 12:39 generation asks for a **m** sign!
    13:54 get this wisdom and these **m** powers?
Jn   2:11 This, the first of his **m** signs,
     2:23 many people saw the **m** signs
     3: 2 the **m** signs you are doing if God
     4:48 "Unless you people see **m** signs
     6:14 After the people saw the **m** sign
     7:31 he do more **m** signs than this man?"
     9:16 How can a sinner do such **m** signs?"
    10:41 John never performed a **m** sign,
    12:37 Jesus had done all these **m** signs
    20:30 Jesus did many other **m** signs in
Ac   2:43 **m** signs were done by the apostles.
     5:12 The apostles performed many **m**
    14: 3 by enabling them to do **m** signs
1Co 1:22 Jews demand **m** signs and Greeks
    12:10 to another **m** powers,
Rev 13:13 And he performed great and **m** signs,
    16:14 spirits of demons performing **m**
    19:20 performed the **m** signs on his behalf.

MIRACULOUS SIGNS See SIGNS

MIRE

Ps 40: 2 out of the mud and **m;**
Isa 57:20 whose waves cast up **m** and mud.

MIRIAM

Sister of Moses and Aaron (Nu 26:59). Led dancing at Red Sea (Ex 15:20-21). Struck with leprosy for criticizing Moses (Nu 12). Death (Nu 20:1).

MIRROR*

Job 37:18 hard as a **m** of cast bronze?
1Co 13:12 but a poor reflection as in a **m**;
Jas 1:23 a man who looks at his face in a **m**

MISCARRY

Ex 23:26 none will **m** or be barren in your land

MISDEEDS*

Ps 99: 8 though you punished their **m**.
Ro 8:13 by the Spirit you put to death the **m**

MISERABLE [MISERY]

Gal 4: 9 back to those weak and **m** principles

MISERY [MISERABLE]

Ex 3: 7 seen the **m** of my people in Egypt.
Nu 23:21 no **m** observed in Israel.
Jdg 10:16 he could bear Israel's **m** no longer.
Ps 44:24 and forget our **m** and oppression?
Ecc 8: 6 a man's **m** weighs heavily upon him.
Hos 5:15 their **m** they will earnestly seek me."
Ro 3:16 ruin and **m** mark their ways,
Jas 5: 1 of the **m** that is coming upon you.

MISFORTUNE

Nu 23:21 "No **m** is seen in Jacob,
Pr 13:21 **M** pursues the sinner,
Ob 1:12 on your brother in the day of his **m**,

MISHAEL [MESHACH]

Original name of Meshach (Da 1:6-19; 2:17).

MISLEAD [MISLEADS, MISLED]

Isa 9:16 Those who guide this people **m** them
47:10 Your wisdom and knowledge **m** you

MISLEADS* [MISLEAD]

Isa 44:20 a deluded heart **m** him;
Rev 2:20 By her teaching she **m** my servants

MISLED [MISLEAD]

1Co 15:33 Do not be **m**: "Bad company

MISS* [MISSES, MISSING]

Jdg 20:16 sling a stone at a hair and not **m**.
Pr 19: 2 nor to be hasty and **m** the way.

MISSES [MISS]

Heb 12:15 that no one **m** the grace of God

MISSING [MISS]

Jdg 21: 3 Why should one tribe be **m**
Isa 40:26 not one of them is **m**.

MISSION

Isa 48:15 and he will succeed in his **m**.
Ac 12:25 had finished their **m**,

MIST* [MISTS]

Isa 44:22 your sins like the morning **m**.
Hos 6: 4 Your love is like the morning **m**,
13: 3 they will be like the morning **m**,
Ac 13:11 Immediately **m** and darkness came
Jas 4:14 a **m** that appears for a little while and

MISTAKE

Ecc 5: 6 "My vow was a **m**."

MISTREAT [MISTREATED]

Ex 22:21 "Do not **m** an alien or oppress him,
Eze 22:29 the poor and needy and **m** the alien,
Lk 6:28 pray for those who **m** you.

MISTREATED [MISTREAT]

Ge 15:13 enslaved and **m** four hundred years.
16: 6 Sarai **m** Hagar; so she fled from her.
Nu 20:15 The Egyptians **m** us and our fathers,
Eze 22: 7 and **m** the fatherless and the widow.
Heb 11:25 be **m** along with the people of God
11:37 destitute, persecuted and **m**—
13: 3 and those who are **m** as if you

MISTRESS

Ge 16: 4 she began to despise her **m**.
Ps 123: 2 of a maid look to the hand of her **m**,

MISTS* [MIST]

2Pe 2:17 and **m** driven by a storm.

MISUSE* [MISUSES]

Ex 20: 7 "You shall not **m** the name of
Dt 5:11 "You shall not **m** the name of
Ps 139:20 your adversaries **m** your name.

MISUSES* [MISUSE]

Ex 20: 7 anyone guiltless who **m** his name.
Dt 5:11 anyone guiltless who **m** his name.

MITE(S) (KJV) See PENNY, SMALL COPPER COINS

MIX* [MIXED, MIXES, MIXING, MIXTURE, WELL-MIXED]

Rev 18: 6 **M** her a double portion from her own

MIXED [MIX]

Ex 29: 2 make bread, and cakes **m** with oil,
Lev 7:10 whether **m** with oil or dry,
Ps 75: 8 full of foaming wine **m** with spices;
Pr 9: 5 and drink the wine I have **m**.
Da 2:41 even as you saw iron **m** with clay.
Mk 15:23 they offered him wine **m** with myrrh,
Jude 1:23 to others show mercy, **m** with fear—
Rev 8: 7 came hail and fire **m** with blood,
15: 2 looked like a sea of glass **m** with fire

MIXES* [MIX]

Da 2:43 any more than iron **m** with clay.
Hos 7: 8 "Ephraim **m** with the nations;

MIXING [MIX]

Isa 5:22 and champions at **m** drinks,

MIZPAH

Ge 31:49 It was also called **M**, because he said
1Sa 7: 6 Samuel was leader of Israel at **M**.
Jer 41: 1 to Gedaliah son of Ahikam at **M**.

MOAB [MOABITE, MOABITES, MOABITESS]

Ge	19:37	and she named him **M**;
Nu	22: 3	**M** was filled with dread because of
Dt	34: 5	servant of the LORD died there in **M**,
Jdg	3:12	Eglon king of **M** power over Israel.
Ru	1: 1	live for a while in the country of **M**.
1Sa	22: 4	So he left them with the king of **M**,
2Ki	1: 1	**M** rebelled against Israel.
	23:13	for Chemosh the vile god of **M**,
Isa	15: 1	An oracle concerning **M**:
Jer	48: 1	Concerning **M**: This is what the
	48:16	"The fall of **M** is at hand;
Eze	25: 8	'Because **M** and Seir said,
Am	2: 1	"For three sins of **M**, even for four,
Zep	2: 9	"surely **M** will become like Sodom,

MOABITE [MOAB]

Nu	25: 1	in sexual immorality with **M** women,
Dt	23: 3	No Ammonite or **M** or any of his
Ne	13: 1	that no Ammonite or **M** should ever

MOABITES [MOAB]

Ge	19:37	the father of the **M** of today.

MOABITESS [MOAB]

Ru	1:22	accompanied by Ruth the **M**,

MOAN

Ps	90: 9	we finish our years with a **m**.
Isa	59:11	we **m** mournfully like doves.

MOCK [MOCKED, MOCKER, MOCKERS, MOCKERY, MOCKING, MOCKS]

Ps	22: 7	All who see me **m** me;
	74:22	how fools **m** you all day long.
	119:51	The arrogant **m** me without restraint,
Pr	1:26	I will **m** when calamity overtakes
	14: 9	Fools **m** at making amends for sin,
La	3:63	they **m** me in their songs.
Mk	10:34	who will **m** him and spit on him,

MOCKED [MOCK]

2Ch	36:16	But they **m** God's messengers,
Ps	74:18	how the enemy has **m** you,
	89:51	with which your enemies have **m**,
Mt	27:29	and knelt in front of him and **m** him.
	27:41	of the law and the elders **m** him.
Lk	23:11	and his soldiers ridiculed and **m** him.
Gal	6: 7	God cannot be **m**.

MOCKER [MOCK]

Pr	9: 7	"Whoever corrects a **m** invites insult;
	9:12	if you are a **m**, you alone will suffer.
	20: 1	Wine is a **m** and beer a brawler;
	22:10	Drive out the **m**, and out goes strife;
	24: 9	and men detest a **m**.

MOCKERS [MOCK]

Ps	1: 1	of sinners or sit in the seat of **m**.
Pr	3:34	He mocks proud **m** but gives grace
	29: 8	**M** stir up a city,

MOCKERY* [MOCK]

Pr	1:22	How long will mockers delight in **m**
Jer	10:15	They are worthless, the objects of **m**;
	51:18	They are worthless, the objects of **m**;

MOCKING [MOCK]

Isa	50: 6	not hide my face from **m** and spitting
Lk	22:63	who were guarding Jesus began **m**

MOCKS [MOCK]

Pr	17: 5	He who **m** the poor shows contempt
	19:28	A corrupt witness **m** at justice,
	30:17	"The eye that **m** a father,

MODEL*

Eze	28:12	" 'You were the **m** of perfection,
1Th	1: 7	a **m** to all the believers in Macedonia
2Th	3: 9	but in order to make ourselves a **m**

MODERATION (KJV)
See GENTLENESS

MODESTLY* [MODESTY]

1Ti	2: 9	I also want women to dress **m**,

MODESTY* [MODESTY]

1Co	12:23	we treat with special **m**,

MOLDED*

Job	10: 9	Remember that you **m** me like clay.

MOLDY

Jos	9: 5	of their food supply was dry and **m**.

MOLECH

Lev	20: 2	who gives any of his children to **M**
1Ki	11:33	and **M** the god of the Ammonites,
2Ki	23:10	son or daughter in the fire to **M**.
Jer	32:35	their sons and daughters to **M**,

MOMENT [MOMENTARY]

Ex	33: 5	If I were to go with you even for a **m**
Nu	4:20	even for a **m**, or they will die."
Job	20: 5	the joy of the godless lasts but a **m**.
Ps	2:12	for his wrath can flare up in a **m**.
	30: 5	For his anger lasts only a **m**,
Pr	12:19	but a lying tongue lasts only a **m**.
Isa	54: 7	"For a brief **m** I abandoned you,
	66: 8	or a nation be brought forth in a **m**?
Mt	9:22	the woman was healed from that **m**.
Jn	18:27	at that **m** a rooster began to crow.
Ac	5:10	At that **m** she fell down at his feet
Gal	2: 5	We did not give in to them for a **m**,

MOMENTARY* [MOMENT]

2Co	4:17	For our light and **m** troubles are

MONEY

Ex	22:25	"If you lend **m** to one of my people
	30:16	the atonement **m** from the Israelites
2Ki	12: 4	**m** that is brought as sacred offerings
Ps	15: 5	who lends his **m** without usury
Pr	13:11	Dishonest **m** dwindles away,
	13:11	but he who gathers **m** little by
Ecc	5:10	loves **m** never has **m** enough;

	7:12	Wisdom is a shelter as **m** is a shelter,
	10:19	but **m** is the answer for everything.
Isa	55: 1	you who have no **m**, come,
Mic	3:11	and her prophets tell fortunes for **m**.
Mt	6:24	You cannot serve both God and **M.**
	27: 5	So Judas threw the **m** into the temple
Lk	3:14	He replied, "Don't extort **m**
	9: 3	no bread, no **m**, no extra tunic.
	16:13	You cannot serve both God and **M."**
Jn	2:14	others sitting at tables exchanging **m**.
	12: 6	as keeper of the **m** bag,
Ac	5: 2	part of the **m** for himself,
1Co	16: 2	of you should set aside a sum of **m**
1Ti	3: 3	not quarrelsome, not a lover of **m**.
	6:10	love of **m** is a root of all kinds of evil
	6:10	Some people, eager for **m**,
2Ti	3: 2	lovers of **m**, boastful, proud, abusive,
Heb	13: 5	your lives free from the love of **m**
1Pe	5: 2	not greedy for **m**, but eager to serve;

MONEYLENDER* [LEND]

Ex	22:25	do not be like a **m**;
Lk	7:41	men owed money to a certain **m**.

MONSTER*

Job	7:12	Am I the sea, or the **m** of the deep,
Ps	74:13	the heads of the **m** in the waters.
Isa	27: 1	he will slay the **m** of the sea.
	51: 9	who pierced that **m** through?
Eze	29: 3	Pharaoh king of Egypt, you great **m**
	32: 2	like a **m** in the seas thrashing about

[SEA] MONSTERS (KJV)
See JACKALS

MONTH [MONTHLY, MONTHS, MONTHS']

Ex	12: 2	"This **m** is to be for you the first **m**,
	40: 2	on the first day of the first **m**.
Lev	23:24	'On the first day of the seventh **m**
	23:27	"The tenth day of this seventh **m** is
	23:34	On the fifteenth day of the seventh **m**
	25: 9	on the tenth day of the seventh **m**;
Nu	3:15	Count every male a **m** old or more."
	11:21	meat to eat for a whole **m**!'
Ezr	6:19	On the fourteenth day of the first **m**,
Ne	8: 2	the first day of the seventh **m** Ezra
Est	9:21	and fifteenth days of the **m**
Eze	47:12	Every **m** they will bear,
Rev	9:15	for this very hour and day and **m**
	22: 2	yielding its fruit every **m**.

MONTHLY [MONTH]

Lev	15:19	of her **m** period will last seven days,
Nu	28:14	the **m** burnt offering to be made

MONTHS [MONTH]

Ex	2: 2	she hid him for three **m**.
Jdg	11:37	"Give me two **m** to roam the hills
1Sa	6: 1	been in Philistine territory seven **m**,
1Ch	13:14	in his house for three **m**,
Mk	6:37	take eight **m** of a man's wages!
Jn	4:35	'Four **m** more and then the harvest'?
Gal	4:10	are observing special days and **m**

Rev	9: 5	but only to torture them for five **m**.
	11: 2	on the holy city for 42 **m**.
	13: 5	his authority for forty-two **m**.

MONTHS'* [MONTH]

Jn	6: 7	"Eight **m** wages would not

MOON [MOONS]

Ge	37: 9	and **m** and eleven stars were bowing
Nu	28:14	offering to be made at each new **m**
Dt	17: 3	down to them or to the sun or the **m**
Jos	10:13	the sun stood still, and the **m** stopped
Ps	8: 3	the **m** and the stars,
	72: 7	abound till the **m** is no more.
	74:16	you established the sun and **m**.
	89:37	be established forever like the **m**,
	104:19	The **m** marks off the seasons,
	121: 6	nor the **m** by night.
	136: 9	the **m** and stars to govern the night;
	148: 3	Praise him, sun and **m**, praise him,
SS	6:10	fair as the **m**, bright as the sun,
Isa	13:10	and the **m** will not give its light.
Jer	31:35	who decrees the **m** and stars to shine
Eze	32: 7	and the **m** will not give its light.
Joel	2:31	to darkness and the **m** to blood
Hab	3:11	Sun and **m** stood still in the heavens
Mt	24:29	and the **m** will not give its light;
Ac	2:20	to darkness and the **m** to blood
1Co	15:41	the **m** another and the stars another;
Col	2:16	New **M** celebration or a Sabbath day.
Rev	6:12	the whole **m** turned blood red,
	8:12	a third of the **m**,
	12: 1	the **m** under her feet and a crown
	21:23	not need the sun or the **m** to shine

MOONS [MOON]

2Ch	8:13	New **M** and the three annual feasts—
	31: 3	New **M** and appointed feasts
Isa	1:13	New **M**, Sabbaths and convocations

MORAL*

Jas	1:21	get rid of all **m** filth and the evil

MORDECAI
Benjamite exile who raised Esther (Est 2:5-15). Exposed plot to kill Xerxes (Est 2:19-23). Refused to honor Haman (Est 3:1-6; 5:9-14). Charged Esther to foil Haman's plot against the Jews (Est 4). Xerxes forced Haman to honor Mordecai (Est 6). Mordecai exalted (Est 8-10). Established Purim (Est 9:18-32).

MORE [MUCH]

Ge	3: 1	the serpent was **m** crafty than any of
	4:13	My punishment is **m** than I can bear.
	5:24	then he was no **m**,
	37: 3	Now Israel loved Joseph **m** than any
Ex	1:12	But the **m** they were oppressed, the
		m they multiplied and spread;
Nu	1:18	twenty years old or **m** were listed by
	3:15	Count every male a month old or **m**.
	12: 3	**m** humble than anyone else on
Dt	7:14	be blessed **m** than any other people;
Jos	10:11	**m** of them died from the hailstones

Jdg 16:30 he killed many **m** when he died
2Sa 1:26 **m** wonderful than that of women.
18: 8 and the forest claimed **m** lives
1Ki 16:33 and did **m** to provoke the LORD,
2Ki 2:12 And Elisha saw him no **m**.
1Ch 11: 9 David became **m** and **m** powerful,
Job 4:17 a mortal be **m** righteous than God?
42:12 blessed the latter part of Job's life **m**
Ps 19:10 They are **m** precious than gold,
37:10 and the wicked will be no **m**;
69:31 This will please the LORD **m** than
71:14 I will praise you **m** and **m**.
119:127 I love your commands **m** than gold,
130: 6 My soul waits for the Lord **m** than
Pr 3:14 for she is **m** profitable than silver
8:11 wisdom is **m** precious than rubies,
21: 3 right and just is **m** acceptable to
22: 1 name is **m** desirable than great riches
31:10 She is worth far **m** than rubies.
Ecc 1:18 the **m** knowledge, the **m** grief.
SS 1: 2 your love is **m** delightful than wine.
Isa 54: 1 **m** are the children of the desolate
60:19 sun will no **m** be your light by day,
Jer 31:34 and will remember their sins no **m**."
La 5: 7 Our fathers sinned and are no **m**,
Hos 13: 2 Now they sin **m** and **m**;
Jnh 3: 4 "Forty **m** days and Nineveh will be
Na 1:15 No **m** will the wicked invade you;
Mt 2:18 because they are no **m**."
Mk 4:25 Whoever has will be given **m**;
12:43 this poor widow has put **m** into
Lk 13: 2 But one **m** powerful than I will come
12:23 Life is **m** than food,
Jn 16:12 "I have much **m** to say to you,
16:16 a little while you will see me no **m**,
21:15 do you truly love me **m** than these?"
Ac 17:11 Bereans were of **m** noble character
Ro 5: 9 how much **m** shall we be saved
8:37 we are **m** than conquerors through
14: 5 One man considers one day **m** sacred
2Co 3: 9 how much **m** glorious is the ministry
Heb 8:12 and will remember their sins no **m**."
10:17 lawless acts I will remember no **m**."
Jas 4: 6 But he gives us **m** grace.
2Pe 1:19 word of the prophets made **m** certain
Rev 10: 6 and said, "There will be no **m** delay!
21: 4 no **m** death or mourning or crying
22: 5 There will be no **m** night.

HOW MUCH MORE See HOW

MORIAH*

Ge 22: 2 and go to the region of **M.**
2Ch 3: 1 the LORD in Jerusalem on Mount **M,**

MORNING [MORNINGS]

Ge 1: 5 there was evening, and there was **m**
Ex 12:10 Do not leave any of it till **m**;
16:12 you will be filled with bread.
29:39 in the **m** and the other at twilight.
Dt 28:67 In the **m** you will say,
2Sa 23: 4 is like the light of **m** at sunrise on
23: 4 at sunrise on a cloudless **m,**
Ezr 3: 3 both the **m** and evening sacrifices.
Job 38: 7 while the **m** stars sang together

Ps 5: 3 the **m**, O LORD, you hear my voice;
5: 3 in the **m** I lay my requests
30: 5 but rejoicing comes in the **m**.
130: 6 more than watchmen wait for the **m**.
Pr 27:14 blesses his neighbor early in the **m**,
Ecc 11: 6 Sow your seed in the **m**,
Isa 14:12 O **m** star, son of the dawn!
50: 4 He wakens me **m** by **m**,
La 3:23 They are new every **m**;
Hos 6: 4 Your love is like the **m** mist,
13: 3 they will be like the **m** mist,
Zep 3: 5 **M** by **m** he dispenses his justice,
Lk 24: 1 very early in the **m,**
24:22 They went to the tomb early this **m**
Ac 2:15 It's only nine in the **m**!
2Pe 1:19 and the **m** star rises in your hearts.
Rev 2:28 I will also give him the **m** star.
22:16 and the bright **M** Star."

MORNINGS* [MORNING]

Da 8:14 "It will take 2,300 evenings and **m**;
8:26 "The vision of the evenings and **m**

MORTAL

Ge 6: 3 with man forever, for he is **m**;
Dt 5:26 For what **m** man has ever heard
Job 4:17 a **m** be more righteous than God?
10: 4 Do you see as a **m** sees?
Ps 56: 4 What can **m** man do to me?
146: 3 in **m** men, who cannot save.
Isa 51:12 Who are you that you fear **m** men,
Ro 1:23 for images made to look like **m** man
6:12 do not let sin reign in your **m** body
8:11 will also give life to your **m** bodies
1Co 15:53 and the **m** with immortality.
2Co 5: 4 is **m** may be swallowed up by life.

MORTGAGING*

Ne 5: 3 "We are **m** our fields,

MORTIFY (KJV) See PUT TO DEATH

MOSES

Levite; brother of Aaron (Ex 6:20; 1Ch 6:3). Put in basket into Nile; discovered and raised by Pharaoh's daughter (Ex 2:1-10). Fled to Midian after killing Egyptian (Ex 2:11-15). Married to Zipporah, fathered Gershom (Ex 2:16-22).

Called by the LORD to deliver Israel (Ex 3-4). Pharaoh's resistance (Ex 5). Ten plagues (Ex 7-11). Passover and Exodus (Ex 12-13). Led Israel through Red Sea (Ex 14). Song of deliverance (Ex 15:1-21). Brought water from rock (Ex 17:1-7). Raised hands to defeat Amalekites (Ex 17:8-16). Delegated judges (Ex 18; Dt 1:9-18).

Received Law at Sinai (Ex 19-23; Jn 1:17). Announced Law to Israel (Ex 19:7-8; 24; 35). Broke tablets because of golden calf (Ex 32; Dt 9). Saw glory of the LORD (Ex 33-34). Supervised building of tabernacle (Ex 36-40). Set apart Aaron and priests (Lev 8-9). Numbered tribes (Nu 1-4; 26). Opposed by Aaron and Miriam (Nu 12). Sent spies into Canaan (Nu 13). Announced forty years of wandering for failure to enter land (Nu 14). Opposed by Korah (Nu 16). Forbidden to enter land for striking rock (Nu 20:1-13; Dt 1:37). Lifted bronze snake for healing (Nu 21:4-9; Jn 3:14). Final address to Israel (Dt 1-33). Succeeded by Joshua (Nu 27:12-23; Dt 34). Death and burial by God (Dt 34:5-12).

"Law of Moses" (1Ki 2:3; Ezr 3:2; Mk 12:26; Lk 24:44). "Book of Moses" (2Ch 25:12; Ne 13:1). "Song of Moses" (Ex 15:1-21; Rev 15:3). "Prayer of Moses" (Ps 90).

LAW OF MOSES See LAW

MOST [INMOST, MUCH]

Ge	14:18	He was priest of God **M** High,
Ex	26:33	Holy Place from the **M** Holy Place.
Nu	4: 4	the care of the **m** holy things.
	24:16	has knowledge from the **M** High,
Jdg	5:24	"**M** blessed of women be Jael,
1Ki	3: 4	that was the **m** important high place,
1Ch	16:25	the LORD and **m** worthy of praise;
Ps	7:10	My shield is God **M** High,
	46: 4	holy place where the **M** High dwells.
	48: 1	and **m** worthy of praise,
	78:35	God **M** High was their Redeemer.
	91: 1	dwells in the shelter of the **M** High
SS	1: 8	**m** beautiful of women,
Isa	14:14	I will make myself like the **M** High."
Jer	3:19	the **m** beautiful inheritance
Eze	20: 6	the **m** beautiful of all lands.
Da	4:17	that the **M** High is sovereign over
	7:25	He will speak against the **M** High
Mk	5: 7	Jesus, Son of the **M** High God?
	12:28	which is the **m** important?"
Lk	1:32	be called the Son of the **M** High.
	1:76	be called a prophet of the **M** High;
	20:47	will be punished **m** severely."
Eph	5:16	making the **m** of every opportunity.
Col	4: 5	make the **m** of every opportunity.
Jude	1:20	yourselves up in your **m** holy faith

MOST HIGH See HIGH

MOST HOLY See HOLY

MOTE (KJV) See SPECK OF SAWDUST

MOTH

Ps	39:11	you consume their wealth like a **m**—
Isa	51: 8	the **m** will eat them up like a garment
Mt	6:19	where **m** and rust destroy,

MOTHER [GRANDMOTHER, MOTHER-IN-LAW, MOTHER'S, MOTHERS]

Ge	2:24	a man will leave his father and **m**
	3:20	because she would become the **m**
	17:16	so that she will be the **m** of nations;
Ex	20:12	"Honor your father and your **m**,
	21:15	who attacks his father or his **m**
	21:17	"Anyone who curses his father or **m**
Lev	18: 7	having sexual relations with your **m**.
	19: 3	of you must respect his **m** and father,
	20: 9	" 'If anyone curses his father or **m**,
Dt	5:16	"Honor your father and your **m**,
	21:18	who does not obey his father and **m**
	22: 6	do not take the **m** with the young.

	27:16	who dishonors his father or his **m**."
Jdg	5: 7	Deborah, arose, arose a **m** in Israel.
1Sa	2:19	his **m** made him a little robe
2Sa	20:19	to destroy a city that is a **m** in Israel.
1Ki	19:20	kiss my father and **m** good-by,"
Ps	27:10	Though my father and **m** forsake me,
	51: 5	sinful from the time my **m** conceived
	113: 9	in her home as a happy **m** of children
Pr	10: 1	but a foolish son grief to his **m**.
	15:20	but a foolish man despises his **m**.
	20:20	If a man curses his father or **m**,
	23:22	not despise your **m** when she is old.
	23:25	May your father and **m** be glad;
	29:15	child left to himself disgraces his **m**.
	30:17	that scorns obedience to a **m**,
	31: 1	an oracle his **m** taught him:
SS	6: 9	unique, the only daughter of her **m**,
Isa	8: 4	how to say 'My father' or 'My **m**,'
	49:15	Can a **m** forget the baby at her breast
	66:13	As a **m** comforts her child,
Jer	20:17	with my **m** as my grave,
Hos	2: 2	"Rebuke your **m**, rebuke her,
Mic	7: 6	a daughter rises up against her **m**,
Mt	2:11	they saw the child with his **m** Mary,
	10:35	a daughter against her **m**,
	10:37	who loves his father or **m** more
	12:48	He replied to him, "Who is my **m**,
	19: 5	a man will leave his father and **m**
	19:19	honor your father and **m**,'
Mk	7:10	'Honor your father and your **m**,' and,
	10:19	honor your father and **m**.' "
Lk	11:27	Blessed is the **m** who gave you birth
	12:53	**m** against daughter and daughter against **m**,
	14:26	not hate his father and **m**,
	18:20	honor your father and **m**.' "
Jn	19:27	"Here is your **m**."
Gal	4:26	and she is our **m**.
Eph	5:31	a man will leave his father and **m**
	6: 2	"Honor your father and **m**"—
1Th	2: 7	like a **m** caring for her little children.
2Ti	1: 5	and in your **m** Eunice and,
Heb	7: 3	Without father or **m**,
Rev	17: 5	BABYLON THE GREAT THE **M** OF PROSTITUTES

MOTHER'S [MOTHER]

Ex	23:19	not cook a young goat in its **m** milk.
Job	1:21	"Naked I came from my **m** womb,
Ps	22:10	from my **m** womb you have been my
Pr	1: 8	and do not forsake your **m** teaching.
	6:20	and do not forsake your **m** teaching.
Ecc	5:15	Naked a man comes from his **m**
	11: 5	the body is formed in a **m** womb,
Isa	50: 1	is your **m** certificate of divorce
Jn	3: 4	enter a second time into his **m** womb

MOTHER-IN-LAW [MOTHER]

Dt	27:23	the man who sleeps with his **m**."
Ru	2:11	what you have done for your **m**
Mic	7: 6	a daughter-in-law against her **m**—
Mt	10:35	a daughter-in-law against her **m**—
Mk	1:30	Simon's **m** was in bed with a fever,

MOTHERS [MOTHER]

Pr   30:11 and do not bless their **m;**
Hos   10:14 when **m** were dashed to the ground
Mk   13:17 for pregnant women and nursing **m!**
1Ti   1: 9 for those who kill their fathers or **m,**
          5: 2 older women as **m,** and younger

MOTIONED

Jn   13:24 Simon Peter **m** to this disciple
Ac   12:17 Peter **m** with his hand for them to
         13:16 Paul **m** with his hand and said:
         19:33 He **m** for silence in order to make
         26: 1 So Paul **m** with his hand

MOTIVE* [MOTIVES]

1Ch   28: 9 and understands every **m** behind

MOTIVES* [MOTIVE]

Pr   16: 2 but **m** are weighed by the LORD.
1Co   4: 5 will expose the **m** of men's hearts.
Php   1:18 whether from false **m** or true,
1Th   2: 3 not spring from error or impure **m,**
Jas   4: 3 because you ask with wrong **m,**

MOUND

Jer   26:18 the temple hill a **m** overgrown
Mic   3:12 the temple hill a **m** overgrown

MOUNT [MOUNTAIN, MOUNTAINS, MOUNTAINSIDE, MOUNTAINTOPS, MOUNTED]

Ex   19:20 descended to the top of **M** Sinai
         34:29 from **M** Sinai with the two tablets
Nu   33:39 when he died on **M** Hor.
Dt   11:29 on **M** Gerizim the blessings, and on
                    M Ebal the curses.
          34: 1 Moses climbed **M** Nebo from
Jos   8:30 Then Joshua built on **M** Ebal an altar
1Ch   10: 8 and his sons fallen on **M** Gilboa.
2Ch   3: 1 in Jerusalem on **M** Moriah,
Ps   78:68 **M** Zion, which he loved.
         89: 9 when its waves **m** up,
Isa   14:13 on the **m** of assembly,
Eze   28:14 You were on the holy **m** of God;
Ob   1:17 But on **M** Zion will be deliverance;
Mic   4: 7 LORD will rule over them in **M** Zion
Zec   14: 4 the **M** of Olives will be split in two
Mk   13: 3 Jesus was sitting on the **M** of Olives
Gal   4:24 One covenant is from **M** Sinai
Heb   12:22 But you have come to **M** Zion,
Rev   14: 1 standing on **M** Zion,

MOUNT OF OLIVES 2Sa 15:30; Zec 14:4, 4;
Mt 21:1; 24:3; 26:30; Mk 11:1; 13:3; 14:26; Lk
19:29, 37; 21:37; 22:39; Jn 8:1; Ac 1:12

MOUNT SINAI Ex 19:11, 18, 20, 23; 24:16;
31:18; 34:2, 4, 29, 32; Lev 7:38; 25:1; 26:46;
27:34; Nu 3:1; 28:6; Ne 9:13; Ac 7:30, 38; Gal
4:24, 25

MOUNT ZION 2Ki 19:31; Ps 48:2, 11; 74:2;
78:68; 125:1; 133:3; Isa 4:5; 8:18; 10:12; 18:7;
24:23; 29:8; 31:4; 37:32; La 5:18; Joel 2:32; Ob
1:17, 21; Mic 4:7; Heb 12:22; Rev 14:1

MOUNTAIN [MOUNT]

Ge   22:14 "On the **m** of the LORD it will
Ex   3: 1 came to Horeb, the **m** of God.
          19: 2 there in the desert in front of the **m.**
          19:20 and called Moses to the top of the **m.**
          24:18 on the **m** forty days and forty nights.
          32:19 them to pieces at the foot of the **m.**
Dt   5: 4 face to face out of the fire on the **m.**
1Ki   19: 8 he reached Horeb, the **m** of God.
Job   14:18 "But as a **m** erodes and crumbles and
Ps   48: 1 in the city of our God, his holy **m.**
          68:16 at the **m** where God chooses to reign,
Isa   2: 2 the **m** of the LORD's temple will
          11: 9 nor destroy on all my holy **m,**
          40: 4 every **m** and hill made low;
          65:25 nor destroy on all my holy **m,"**
Da   2:45 the vision of the rock cut out of a **m,**
Mic   4: 1 the **m** of the LORD's temple will
Zec   14: 4 with half of the **m** moving north
Mt   4: 8 the devil took him to a very high **m**
          17:20 you can say to this **m,**
Mk   9: 2 with him and led them up a high **m,**
Lk   3: 5 every **m** and hill made low.
Jn   4:21 worship the Father neither on this **m**
2Pe   1:18 we were with him on the sacred **m.**
Rev   6:14 and every **m** and island was removed
           8: 8 and something like a huge **m,**
          21:10 in the Spirit to a **m** great and high,

HOLY MOUNTAIN See HOLY

MOUNTAINS [MOUNT]

Ge   7:20 The waters rose and covered the **m**
           8: 4 the ark came to rest on the **m**
Ps   36: 6 righteousness is like the mighty **m,**
          46: 2 the **m** fall into the heart of the sea,
          90: 2 Before the **m** were born or
          97: 5 **m** melt like wax before the LORD,
          98: 8 let the **m** sing together for joy;
         125: 2 As the **m** surround Jerusalem,
Isa   2: 2 be established as chief among the **m;**
          52: 7 How beautiful on the **m** are the feet
          54:10 Though the **m** be shaken and the
          55:12 the **m** and hills will burst into song
Eze   34: 6 over all the **m** and on every high hill.
          39: 4 On the **m** of Israel you will fall,
Hos   10: 8 Then they will say to the **m,** "Cover
Mic   4: 1 be established as chief among the **m;**
Na   1:15 Look, there on the **m,**
Mk   13:14 who are in Judea flee to the **m.**
Lk   23:30 Then " 'they will say to the **m,** "Fall
1Co   13: 2 and if I have a faith that can move **m,**
Rev   6:16 They called to the **m** and the rocks,
          16:20 and the **m** could not be found.

MOUNTAINSIDE [MOUNT]

Mt   5: 1 he went up on a **m** and sat down.
Mk   6:46 he went up on a **m** to pray.

MOUNTAINTOPS [MOUNT]

Isa   42:11 let them shout from the **m.**
Eze   6:13 on every high hill and on all the **m,**

MOUNTED [MOUNT]

Ex   25: 7 be **m** on the ephod and breastpiece.
2Sa 22:11 He **m** the cherubim and flew;
SS   5:12 washed in milk, **m** like jewels.

MOURN [MOURNED, MOURNING, MOURNS]

Ge 23: 2 and Abraham went to **m** for Sarah
Ezr 10: 6 because he continued to **m** over
Ne   8: 9 Do not **m** or weep."
Ecc 3: 4 a time to **m** and a time to dance,
Isa 61: 2 to comfort all who **m,**
Zec 12:10 and they will **m** for him
Mt   5: 4 Blessed are those who **m,**
     9:15 can the guests of the bridegroom **m**
Lk   6:25 for you will **m** and weep.
Ro 12:15 **m** with those who **m,**
1Co 7:30 those who **m,** as if they did not;
Rev 1: 7 all the peoples of the earth will **m**
   18: 7 and I will never **m.'**

MOURNED [MOURN]

Nu 14:39 all the Israelites, they **m** bitterly.
1Sa 7: 2 the people of Israel **m** and sought
Ne   1: 4 For some days I **m** and fasted
Da 10: 2 Daniel, **m** for three weeks.
Lk 23:27 including women who **m** and wailed
Ac   8: 2 Stephen and **m** deeply for him.

MOURNING [MOURN]

Est 4: 3 there was great **m** among the Jews,
    9:22 and their **m** into a day
Ecc 7: 2 It is better to go to a house of **m**
Isa 61: 3 the oil of gladness instead of **m,**
Jer 31:13 I will turn their **m** into gladness;
La   5:15 our dancing has turned to **m.**
Rev 21: 4 There will be no more death or **m**

MOURNS [MOURN]

Zec 12:10 they will mourn for him as one **m**

MOUTH [MOUTHS]

Ex   4:11 "Who gave man his **m?**
Nu 16:30 earth opens its **m** and swallows them
   22:38 what God puts in my **m."**
Dt   8: 3 that comes from the **m** of the LORD.
   18:18 I will put my words in his **m,**
   30:14 it is in your **m** and in your heart
Jos   1: 8 Book of the Law depart from your **m**
2Ki 4:34 **m** to **m,** eyes to eyes,
Job 23:12 of his **m** more than my daily bread.
   40: 4 I put my hand over my **m.**
Ps 10: 7 His **m** is full of curses and lies
   17: 3 resolved that my **m** will not sin.
   19:14 May the words of my **m** and
   37:30 The **m** of the righteous man utters
   40: 3 He put a new song in my **m,**
   71: 8 My **m** is filled with your praise,
   78: 2 I will open my **m** in parables,
 119:103 sweeter than honey to my **m!**
 141: 3 Set a guard over my **m,** O LORD;
Pr   2: 6 and from his **m** come knowledge
   4:24 Put away perversity from your **m;**

    8: 7 My **m** speaks what is true,
  10:11 The **m** of the righteous is a fountain
  10:31 The **m** of the righteous brings
  15: 2 but the **m** of the fool gushes folly.
  16:23 A wise man's heart guides his **m,**
  18: 7 A fool's **m** is his undoing,
  26:28 and a flattering **m** works ruin.
  27: 2 and not your own **m;**
Ecc 5: 2 Do not be quick with your **m,**
   6: 7 All man's efforts are for his **m,**
SS   1: 2 kiss me with the kisses of his **m—**
   5:16 His **m** is sweetness itself;
Isa 29:13 people come near to me with their **m**
  40: 5 For the **m** of the LORD has spoken."
  45:23 my **m** has uttered in all integrity
  48: 3 my **m** announced them
  49: 2 made my **m** like a sharpened sword,
  51:16 I have put my words in your **m**
  53: 7 yet he did not open his **m;**
  55:11 is my word that goes out from my **m:**
  59:21 my words that I have put in your **m**
Jer   1: 9 I have put my words in your **m.**
Eze 3: 2 So I opened my **m,**
Da   7: 8 and a **m** that spoke boastfully.
Hos 6: 5 I killed you with the words of my **m;**
Mal 2: 7 from his **m** men should seek
Mt   4: 4 word that comes from the **m** of God.'
  12:34 overflow of the heart the **m** speaks.
  15:11 but what comes out of his **m,**
Lk   6:45 overflow of his heart his **m** speaks.
Ac   8:32 so he did not open his **m.**
Ro 10: 8 The word is near you; it is in your **m**
  10: 9 That if you confess with your **m,**
  15: 6 and **m** you may glorify
2Th 2: 8 overthrow with the breath of his **m**
Jas 3:10 the same **m** come praise and cursing.
1Pe 2:22 and no deceit was found in his **m."**
Rev 1:16 and out of his **m** came a sharp
   2:16 them with the sword of my **m.**
   3:16 about to spit you out of my **m.**
  10:10 It tasted as sweet as honey in my **m,**
  13: 6 He opened his **m** to blaspheme God,
  19:15 Out of his **m** comes a sharp sword

MOUTHS [MOUTH]

Ps 73: 9 Their **m** lay claim to heaven,
  78:36 they would flatter him with their **m,**
 115: 5 They have **m,** but cannot speak,
 135:17 nor is there breath in their **m.**
Isa 52:15 and kings will shut their **m** because
Eze 33:31 With their **m** they express devotion,
Da   6:22 and he shut the **m** of the lions.
Ro   3:14 "Their **m** are full of cursing
Eph 4:29 talk come out of your **m,**
Jas 3: 3 we put bits into the **m** of horses
Rev 9:17 and out of their **m** came fire,
  11: 5 fire comes from their **m**
  14: 5 No lie was found in their **m;**

MOVE [MOVED, MOVES]

Ge 1:24 creatures that **m** along the ground,
Lev 11:29 " 'Of the animals that **m** about on
Nu   1:51 Whenever the tabernacle is to **m,**
Dt 19:14 Do not **m** your neighbor's boundary

Job   24: 2 Men **m** boundary stones;
Pr   23:10 not **m** an ancient boundary stone
Isa   46: 7 From that spot it cannot **m**.
Mt   17:20 'M from here to there' and it will **m**.
Ac   17:28 live and **m** and have our being.'
1Co   13: 2 if I have a faith that can **m** mountains
      15:58 Let nothing **m** you.

MOVED [MOVE]

Ge   7:21 that **m** on the earth perished—
Ex   35:21 and whose heart **m** him came
1Ch   16:30 firmly established; it cannot be **m**.
2Ch   33:19 and how God was **m** by his entreaty,
      36:22 the LORD **m** the heart of Cyrus king
Ezr   1: 5 everyone whose heart God had **m**—
Ps   93: 1 firmly established; it cannot be **m**.
Isa   33:20 a tent that will not be **m**;
Eze   1:19 When the living creatures **m**,
Jn   11:33 he was deeply **m** in spirit
Col   1:23 not **m** from the hope held out in

MOVES [MOVE]

Ge   9: 3 that lives and **m** will be food for you.
Lev   11:41 " 'Every creature that **m** about on
Dt   23:14 For the LORD your God **m** about
      27:17 **m** his neighbor's boundary stone."

MUCH [MORE, MOST]

Ex   16:18 Each one gathered as **m** as he needed
Dt   28:38 You will sow **m** seed in the field
1Ki   8:27 How **m** less this temple I have built!
Job   7:17 "What is man that you make so **m**
      42:10 and gave him twice as **m**
Ps   19:10 than **m** pure gold;
Pr   16:16 **m** better to get wisdom than gold,
      23:20 not join those who drink too **m** wine
Ecc   1:18 with **m** wisdom comes **m** sorrow;
       9:18 but one sinner destroys **m** good.
      12:12 and **m** study wearies the body.
Hag   1: 9 "You expected **m**, but see,
Mt   6:26 not **m** more valuable than they?
      23:15 twice as **m** a son of hell as you are.
Mk   9:12 that the Son of Man must suffer **m**
Lk   12:48 From everyone who has been given
             m, **m** will be demanded;
      16:10 little can also be trusted with **m**,
Jn   8:26 "I have **m** to say in judgment of you.
      15: 5 he will bear **m** fruit;
      16:12 "I have **m** more to say to you,
Ac   2:13 "They have had too **m** wine."
2Co   3:11 how **m** greater is the glory of
       8:15 who gathered **m** did not have too **m**,
1Ti   3: 8 sincere, not indulging in **m** wine,
Tit   2: 3 be slanderers or addicted to **m** wine,
Heb   1: 4 as **m** superior to the angels
Rev   12:11 not love their lives so **m** as to shrink
      18: 7 as **m** torture and grief as the glory

HOW MUCH MORE See HOW

MUD [MUDDIED]

Ps   40: 2 out of the **m** and mire;
Isa   57:20 whose waves cast up mire and **m**.
Jer   38: 6 and Jeremiah sank down into the **m**.
Jn   9: 6 made some **m** with the saliva,

2Pe   2:22 goes back to her wallowing in the **m**.

MUDDIED* [MUD]

Pr   25:26 Like a **m** spring or a polluted well is
Eze   32:13 be stirred by the foot of man or **m** by
      34:19 and drink what you have **m**

MULBERRY*

Lk   17: 6 you can say to this **m** tree,

MULE

2Sa   18: 9 He was riding his **m**,
1Ki   1:38 and put Solomon on King David's **m**
Ps   32: 9 Do not be like the horse or the **m**,

MULTIPLIED [MULTIPLY]

Ex   1: 7 Israelites were fruitful and **m** greatly
      11: 9 that my wonders may be **m** in Egypt.

MULTIPLIES [MULTIPLY]

Pr   27: 6 but an enemy **m** kisses.
Ecc   10:14 and the fool **m** words.

MULTIPLY [MULTIPLIED, MULTIPLIES, MULTIPLYING]

Ge   9: 7 increase in number; **m** on the earth
Ex   7: 3 and though I **m** my miraculous signs
Lev   26:21 I will **m** your afflictions seven times

MULTIPLYING* [MULTIPLY]

Mk   4: 8 grew and produced a crop, **m** thirty,

MULTITUDE [MULTITUDES]

Isa   31: 1 who trust in the **m** of their chariots
Da   10: 6 and his voice like the sound of a **m**.
Jas   5:20 and cover over a **m** of sins.
1Pe   4: 8 because love covers over a **m** of sins.
Rev   7: 9 and there before me was a great **m**
      19: 6 I heard what sounded like a great **m**,

MULTITUDES [MULTITUDE]

Ne   9: 6 and the **m** of heaven worship you.
Da   12: 2 **M** who sleep in the dust of
Joel   3:14 **M**, **m** in the valley of decision!

MURDER [MURDERED, MURDERER, MURDERERS, MURDEROUS, MURDERS]

Ex   20:13 "You shall not **m**.
Nu   35:12 a person accused of **m** may not die
Dt   5:17 "You shall not **m**.
Hos   4: 2 There is only cursing, lying and **m**,
Mt   5:21 to the people long ago, 'Do not **m**,
      15:19 **m**, adultery, sexual immorality, theft,
Mk   10:19 the commandments: 'Do not **m**,
Ro   1:29 They are full of envy, **m**, strife,
      13: 9 "Do not **m**," "Do not steal,"
Jas   2:11 also said, "Do not **m**."
1Jn   3:12 And why did he **m** him?

MURDERED [MURDER]

Jdg   9:18 **m** his seventy sons on a single stone,
Mt   23:31 of those who **m** the prophets.
Ac   7:52 now you have betrayed and **m** him—

1Jn 3:12 to the evil one and **m** his brother.

MURDERER [MURDER]

Nu 35:16 the **m** shall be put to death.
35:31 a ransom for the life of a **m**,
Jn 8:44 He was a **m** from the beginning.
Ac 3:14 and asked that a **m** be released
1Jn 3:15 Anyone who hates his brother is a **m**,

MURDERERS [MURDER]

1Ti 1: 9 kill their fathers or mothers, for **m**,
Rev 21: 8 the vile, the **m**, the sexually immoral,
22:15 the sexually immoral, the **m**,

MURDEROUS* [MURDER]

Ac 9: 1 Saul was still breathing out **m** threats

MURDERS [MURDER]

Mt 5:21 who **m** will be subject to judgment.'
Rev 9:21 Nor did they repent of their **m**,

MUSHI

Nu 3:20 The Merarite clans: Mahli and **M**.

MUSIC* [MUSICAL, MUSICIAN, MUSICIANS]

Ge 31:27 and singing to the **m** of tambourines
Jdg 5: 3 I will make **m** to the LORD.
1Ch 6:31 the men David put in charge of the **m**
6:32 They ministered with **m** before
25: 6 the **m** of the temple of the LORD,
25: 7 all of them trained and skilled in **m**
Ne 12:27 and with the **m** of cymbals,
Job 21:12 They sing to the **m** of tambourine
Ps 27: 6 and make **m** to the LORD.
33: 2 make **m** to him on the ten-stringed
45: 8 the **m** of the strings makes you glad.
57: 7 I will sing and make **m**.
81: 2 Begin the **m**, strike the tambourine,
87: 7 As they make **m** they will sing,
92: 1 make **m** to your name, O Most High,
92: 3 to the **m** of the ten-stringed lyre and
95: 2 and extol him with **m** and song.
98: 4 burst into jubilant song with **m**;
98: 5 make **m** to the LORD with the harp,
108: 1 and make **m** with all my soul.
144: 9 the ten-stringed lyre I will make **m**
147: 7 the LORD with thanksgiving; make **m**
149: 3 and make **m** to him with tambourine
Isa 30:32 to the **m** of tambourines and harps,
La 5:14 the young men have stopped their **m**.
Eze 26:13 **m** of your harps will be heard no
Da 3: 5 lyre, harp, pipes and all kinds of **m**,
3: 7 zither, lyre, harp and all kinds of **m**,
3:10 and all kinds of **m** must fall down
3:15 lyre, harp, pipes and all kinds of **m**,
Am 5:23 not listen to the **m** of your harps.
Lk 15:25 he heard **m** and dancing.
Eph 5:19 make **m** in your heart to the Lord,
Rev 18:22 The **m** of harpists and musicians,

FOR THE DIRECTOR OF MUSIC Ps 4:T;
5:T; 6:T; 8:T; 9:T; 11:T; 12:T; 13:T; 14:T; 18:T;
19:T; 20:T; 21:T; 22:T; 31:T; 36:T; 39:T; 40:T;
41:T; 42:T; 44:T; 45:T; 46:T; 47:T; 49:T; 51:T;
52:T; 53:T; 54:T; 55:T; 56:T; 57:T; 58:T; 59:T;
60:T; 61:T; 62:T; 64:T; 65:T; 66:T; 67:T; 68:T;
69:T; 70:T; 75:T; 76:T; 77:T; 80:T; 81:T; 84:T;
85:T; 88:T; 109:T; 139:T; 140:T; Hab 3:19

MUSICAL* [MUSIC]

1Ch 15:16 accompanied by **m** instruments:
23: 5 the **m** instruments I have provided
2Ch 7: 6 with the LORD's **m** instruments,
23:13 with **m** instruments were leading
34:12 in playing **m** instruments—
Ne 12:36 with **m** instruments [prescribed
Am 6: 5 and improvise on **m** instruments.

MUSICIAN* [MUSIC]

1Ch 6:33 From the Kohathites: Heman, the **m**,

MUSICIANS* [MUSIC]

1Ki 10:12 to make harps and lyres for the **m**.
1Ch 9:33 Those who were **m**,
15:19 The **m** Heman, Asaph and Ethan
2Ch 5:12 All the Levites who were **m**—
9:11 to make harps and lyres for the **m**.
35:15 The **m**, the descendants of Asaph,
Ps 68:25 after them the **m**;
Rev 18:22 The music of harpists and **m**,

MUST

Ge 2:17 but you **m** not eat from the tree of
3: 1 'You **m** not eat from any tree in
4: 7 but you **m** master it."
9: 4 "But you **m** not eat meat that
17:12 eight days old **m** be circumcised,
Ex 22: 3 A thief **m** certainly make restitution.
Dt 7: 2 then you **m** destroy them totally.
13: 4 the LORD your God **m** follow,
18:13 You **m** be blameless before
Ps 119:84 How long **m** your servant wait?
Pr 19:19 hot-tempered man **m** pay the penalty
Hos 12: 6 But you **m** return to your God;
Mt 16:21 and that he **m** be killed and on
Mk 8:34 **m** deny himself and take up his cross
10:17 "what **m** I do to inherit eternal life?"
13: 7 Such things **m** happen,
14:49 But the Scriptures **m** be fulfilled."
Lk 9:22 Son of Man **m** suffer many things
Jn 3: 7 'You **m** be born again.'
3:14 so the Son of Man **m** be lifted up,
4:24 his worshipers **m** worship in spirit
13:34 so you **m** love one another.
15: 4 it **m** remain in the vine.
Ac 20:21 they **m** turn to God in repentance
Ro 12: 9 Love **m** be sincere.
1Co 7:10 A wife **m** not separate from her
7:11 a husband **m** not divorce his wife.
2Co 5:10 we **m** all appear before the judgment
Eph 5:33 each one of you also **m** love his wife
5:33 and the wife **m** respect her husband.
1Ti 3: 2 the overseer **m** be above reproach,
3:12 A deacon **m** be the husband of
Tit 1: 6 An elder **m** be blameless,
Heb 11: 6 who comes to him **m** believe that he
Rev 4: 1 I will show you what **m** take place
22: 6 the things that **m** soon take place."

MUST BE CUT OFF Ex 12:15, 19; 30:33, 38;
31:14; Lev 7:20, 21, 25, 27; 17:4, 9, 14; 18:29;
19:8; 20:17, 18; 22:3; 23:29; Nu 9:13; 15:30;
19:13, 20

MUST BE PUT TO DEATH Ex 21:15, 16, 17,
29; 22:19; 31:14, 15; 35:2; Lev 20:2, 9, 10, 11,
12, 13, 15, 16, 27; 24:16, 16, 17, 21; 27:29; Nu
3:10; 18:7; Dt 13:5; 17:12; 18:20; 2Ki 11:8; 2Ch
23:7; Mt 15:4; Mk 7:10

MUST DIE Nu 15:35; Dt 22:22; 24:7; Jdg 6:30;
1Sa 14:39; 20:31; 2Sa 14:14; Ecc 2:16; Jer 26:8;
Zec 13:3; Jn 19:7; Rev 11:5

MUST NOT EAT Ge 2:17; 3:1, 3, 17; 9:4; Lev
3:17; 7:24, 26; 11:4, 8, 11; 17:14; 22:6, 8; 23:14;
Nu 6:4; Dt 12:16, 17, 23, 24; 15:23; Jdg 13:14;
1Ki 13:9, 17; Eze 44:31

MUST PURGE Dt 13:5; 17:7, 12; 19:13, 19;
21:21; 22:21, 22, 24; 24:7

MUST WASH Lev 6:27; 11:25, 28, 40, 40; 13:6,
34; 14:8, 9, 47; 15:5, 6, 7, 8, 10, 11, 13, 21, 22,
27; 16:26, 28; 17:15; Nu 19:7, 19

MUSTARD*

Mt   13:31 kingdom of heaven is like a **m** seed,
     17:20 if you have faith as small as a **m** seed
Mk   4:31 It is like a **m** seed,
Lk   13:19 It is like a **m** seed,
     17: 6 you have faith as small as a **m** seed,

MUTE

Ex   4:11 Who makes him deaf or **m?**
Isa 35: 6 and the **m** tongue shout for joy.
Mt   9:33 the man who had been **m** spoke.
Mk   7:37 the deaf hear and the **m** speak."
1Co 12: 2 and led astray to **m** idols.

MUTILATORS*

Php   3: 2 those **m** of the flesh.

MUTTER

Isa   8:19 and spiritists, who whisper and **m,**

MUTUAL* [MUTUALLY]

Ro   14:19 leads to peace and to **m** edification.
1Co   7: 5 except by **m** consent and for a time,

MUTUALLY* [MUTUAL]

Ro   1:12 that you and I may be **m** encouraged

MUZZLE*

Dt   25: 4 not **m** an ox while it is treading out
Ps   39: 1 I will put a **m** on my mouth
1Co   9: 9 not **m** an ox while it is treading out
1Ti   5:18 not **m** the ox while it is treading out

MYRRH

Ps   45: 8 All your robes are fragrant with **m**
SS   1:13 My lover is to me a sachet of **m**
Mt   2:11 gifts of gold and of incense and of **m**
Mk   15:23 they offered him wine mixed with **m,**
Jn   19:39 Nicodemus brought a mixture of **m**
Rev 18:13 of incense, **m** and frankincense,

MYRTLE

Isa 55:13 instead of briers the **m** will grow.
Zec   1: 8 He was standing among the **m** trees

MYSTERIES* [MYSTERY]

Job 11: 7 "Can you fathom the **m** of God?
Da   2:28 a God in heaven who reveals **m.**
      2:29 and the revealer of **m** showed you
      2:47 Lord of kings and a revealer of **m,**
1Co 13: 2 of prophecy and can fathom all **m**
     14: 2 he utters **m** with his spirit.

MYSTERY* [MYSTERIES]

Da   2:18 God of heaven concerning this **m,**
      2:19 During the night the **m** was revealed
      2:27 explain to the king the **m** he has
      2:30 this **m** has been revealed to me,
      2:47 for you were able to reveal this **m."**
      4: 9 and no **m** is too difficult for you.
Ro   11:25 not want you to be ignorant of this **m**
     16:25 of the **m** hidden for long ages past,
1Co 15:51 Listen, I tell you a **m:**
Eph   1: 9 made known to us the **m** of his will
      3: 3 **m** made known to me by revelation,
      3: 4 to understand my insight into the **m**
      3: 6 This **m** is that through the gospel
      3: 9 the administration of this **m,**
      5:32 This is a profound **m—**
      6:19 I will fearlessly make known the **m**
Col   1:26 the **m** that has been kept hidden
      1:27 the glorious riches of this **m,**
      2: 2 know the **m** of God, namely, Christ,
      4: 3 we may proclaim the **m** of Christ,
1Ti   3:16 the **m** of godliness is great:
Rev   1:20 The **m** of the seven stars that you
     10: 7 the **m** of God will be accomplished,
     17: 5 her forehead: M BABYLON THE GREAT
     17: 7 explain to you the **m** of the woman

MYTHS*

1Ti   1: 4 nor to devote themselves to **m**
      4: 7 Have nothing to do with godless **m**
2Ti   4: 4 from the truth and turn aside to **m.**
Tit   1:14 will pay no attention to Jewish **m**

N

NAAMAN

Aramean general whose leprosy was cleansed
by Elisha (2Ki 5; Lk 4:27).

NABAL

Wealthy Carmelite the LORD killed for refusing
to help David (1Sa 25). David married Abigail, his
widow (1Sa 25:39-42).

NABOTH*

Jezreelite killed by Jezebel for his vineyard
(1Ki 21). Ahab's family destroyed for this (1Ki
21:17-24; 2Ki 9:21-37).

NADAB

1. Firstborn of Aaron (Ex 6:23); killed with Abihu for offering unauthorized fire (Lev 10; Nu 3:4).

2. Son of Jeroboam I; king of Israel (1Ki 15:25-32).

NAHASH

1Sa 11: 1 **N** the Ammonite went up and

NAHOR

Ge 11:26 the father of Abram, **N** and Haran.
22:23 eight sons to Abraham's brother **N**.
24:15 the wife of Abraham's brother **N**.

NAHUM

Prophet against Nineveh (Na 1:1).

NAIL* [NAILING, NAILS]

Jn 20:25 I see the **n** marks in his hands

NAILING* [NAIL]

Ac 2:23 to death by **n** him to the cross.
Col 2:14 he took it away, **n** it to the cross.

NAILS [NAIL]

Ecc 12:11 sayings like firmly embedded **n—**
Isa 41: 7 He **n** down the idol so it will
Jn 20:25 and put my finger where the **n** were,

NAIOTH

1Sa 19:18 Then he and Samuel went to **N**

NAIVE*

Ro 16:18 they deceive the minds of **n** people.

NAKED [NAKEDNESS]

Ge 2:25 The man and his wife were both **n**,
Job 1:21 **"N** I came from my mother's womb,
and **n** I will depart.
Ecc 5:15 **N** a man comes from his mother's
Isa 58: 7 when you see the **n**, to clothe him,
Mk 14:52 he fled **n**, leaving his garment behind
2Co 5: 3 we will not be found **n**.
11:27 I have been cold and **n**.
Rev 3:17 pitiful, poor, blind and **n**.

NAKEDNESS [NAKED]

Ge 9:22 father of Canaan, saw his father's **n**
Ex 20:26 lest your **n** be exposed on it.'
Eze 16: 8 over you and covered your **n**.
Ro 8:35 persecution or famine or **n** or danger
Rev 3:18 so you can cover your shameful **n;**

NAME [NAME'S, NAMED, NAMES]

Ge 2:19 man to see what he would **n** them;
4:26 began to call on the **n** of the LORD.
11: 4 that we may make a **n** for ourselves,
12: 2 I will make your **n** great,
12: 8 called on the **n** of the LORD.
13: 4 Abram called on the **n** of the LORD.
16:13 She gave this **n** to the LORD
17: 5 Abram; your **n** will be Abraham,
17:15 Sarai; her **n** will be Sarah.
21:33 he called upon the **n** of the LORD,

26:25 called on the **n** of the LORD.
32:28 "Your **n** will no longer be Jacob,
32:29 Jacob said, "Please tell me your **n."**
Ex 3:15 This is my **n** forever, the **n** by which
I am to be remembered
6: 3 but by my **n** the LORD I did not
20: 7 misuse the **n** of the LORD your God,
33:17 with you and I know you by **n."**
33:19 and I will proclaim my **n,**
34: 5 there with him and proclaimed his **n,**
34:14 whose **n** is Jealous, is a jealous God.
Lev 19:12 " 'Do not swear falsely by my **n** and
so profane the **n** of your God.
24:11 blasphemed the **N** with a curse;
Nu 1: 2 listing every man by **n,** one by one.
17: 2 Write the **n** of each man on his staff.
Dt 5:11 misuse the **n** of the LORD your God,
10: 8 and to pronounce blessings in his **n,**
12:11 will choose as a dwelling for his **N—**
18: 5 in the LORD's **n** always.
25: 6 so that his **n** will not be blotted out
28:58 revere this glorious and awesome **n**
Jos 7: 9 will you do for your own great **n?"**
Jdg 13:17 "What is your **n,**
Ru 4: 5 in order to maintain the **n** of the dead
1Sa 12:22 For the sake of his great **n** the LORD
17:45 against you in the **n** of the LORD
25:25 He is just like his **n—**his is Fool,
and folly goes with him.
2Sa 6: 2 which is called by the **N,**
7: 9 Now I will make your **n** great,
1Ki 5: 5 temple for the **N** of the LORD my
8:29 'My **N** shall be there,'
18:24 I will call on the **n** of the LORD.
1Ch 17: 8 Now I will make your **n** like
2Ch 7:14 who are called by my **n,**
Ezr 6:12 who has caused his **N** to dwell there,
Ne 9:10 You made a **n** for yourself,
Ps 5:11 those who love your **n** may rejoice
8: 1 majestic is your **n** in all the earth!
9: 5 you have blotted out their **n**
9:10 Those who know your **n** will trust
20: 7 trust in the **n** of the LORD our God.
29: 2 to the LORD the glory due his **n;**
34: 3 let us exalt his **n** together.
44:20 If we had forgotten the **n** of our God
54: 1 Save me, O God, by your **n;**
66: 2 Sing the glory of his **n;**
68: 4 his **n** is the LORD—
74:10 Will the foe revile your **n** forever?
74:21 the poor and needy praise your **n.**
79: 9 for the glory of your **n;**
96: 8 to the LORD the glory due his **n;**
103: 1 praise his holy **n.**
113: 1 praise the **n** of the LORD.
115: 1 not to us but to your **n** be the glory,
124: 8 Our help is in the **n** of the LORD,
138: 2 and will praise your **n** for your love
145: 1 I will praise your **n** for ever and ever.
147: 4 of the stars and calls them each by **n.**
149: 3 Let them praise his **n** with dancing
Pr 3: 4 and a good **n** in the sight of God
10: 7 but the **n** of the wicked will rot.
18:10 **n** of the LORD is a strong tower;

	22: 1	**n** is more desirable than great riches;
	30: 4	and the **n** of his son?
Ecc	7: 1	A good **n** is better than fine perfume,
SS	1: 3	your **n** is like perfume poured out.
Isa	12: 4	and proclaim that his **n** is exalted.
	26: 8	your **n** and renown are the desire of
	40:26	and calls them each by **n**.
	42: 8	"I am the LORD; that is my **n!**
	50:10	trust in the **n** of the LORD and rely
	56: 5	a memorial and a **n** better than sons
	57:15	whose **n** is holy:
	63:14	to make for yourself a glorious **n**.
Jer	7:11	Has this house, which bears my **N,**
	10: 6	and your **n** is mighty in power.
	14: 7	do something for the sake of your **n**.
	15:16	for I bear your **n,**
	27:15	'They are prophesying lies in my **n**.
Eze	20: 9	the sake of my **n** I did what
	20:14	the sake of my **n** I did what
	20:22	the sake of my **n** I did what would
	36:22	but for the sake of my holy **n,**
	48:35	"And the **n** of the city from that time
Da	2:20	to the **n** of God for ever and ever;
	12: 1	everyone whose **n** is found written
Hos	12: 5	the LORD is his **n** of renown!
Joel	2:32	calls on the **n** of the LORD will
Am	9:12	and all the nations that bear my **n,"**
Mic	5: 4	of the **n** of the LORD his God.
	6: 9	and to fear your **n** is wisdom—
Zep	3: 9	may call on the **n** of the LORD
Zec	6:12	the man whose **n** is the Branch,
	13: 9	call on my **n** and I will answer them;
	14: 9	and his **n** the only **n**.
Mal	1: 6	who show contempt for my **n**.
	4: 2	But for you who revere my **n,**
Mt	1:21	and you are to give him the **n** Jesus,
	6: 9	hallowed be your **n,**
	7:22	Lord, did we not prophesy in your **n,**
	12:21	In his **n** the nations will put
	18:20	two or three come together in my **n,**
	24: 5	Many will come in my **n,**
	28:19	baptizing them in the **n** of the Father
Mk	9:41	gives you a cup of water in my **n**
	11: 9	"Blessed is he who comes in the **n** of
Lk	1:31	and you are to give him the **n** Jesus.
	11: 2	hallowed be your **n,**
	19:38	is the king who comes in the **n** of the
Jn	1:12	to those who believed in his **n,**
	5:43	I have come in my Father's **n,**
	10: 3	He calls his own sheep by **n**
	12:28	Father, glorify your **n!"**
	14:13	I will do whatever you ask in my **n,**
	15:16	whatever you ask in my **n**.
	16:23	whatever you ask in my **n**.
	16:24	not asked for anything in my **n**.
	17:11	protect them by the power of your **n**
	20:31	believing you may have life in his **n**.
Ac	2:21	And everyone who calls on the **n** of
	3:16	By faith in the **n** of Jesus,
	4:12	for there is no other **n** under heaven
	4:17	speak no longer to anyone in this **n**."
	5:40	not to speak in the **n** of Jesus,
	15:17	and all the Gentiles who bear my **n,**
Ro	10:13	who calls on the **n** of the Lord will

1Co	6:11	justified in the **n** of the Lord Jesus
Eph	3:15	in heaven and on earth derives its **n**.
Php	2: 9	gave him the **n** that is above every **n,**
	2:10	that at the **n** of Jesus every knee
Col	3:17	do it all in the **n** of the Lord Jesus,
2Ti	2:19	"Everyone who confesses the **n** of
Heb	1: 4	as the **n** he has inherited is superior
	13:15	the fruit of lips that confess his **n**.
Jas	5:14	and anoint him with oil in the **n**
1Pe	4:16	but praise God that you bear that **n**.
1Jn	2:12	forgiven on account of his **n**.
	3:23	to believe in the **n** of his Son,
	5:13	believe in the **n** of the Son of God
Rev	2: 3	have endured hardships for my **n,**
	2:13	Yet you remain true to my **n**.
	2:17	a white stone with a new **n** written
	3: 5	I will never blot out his **n** from
	3: 5	but will acknowledge his **n**
	3: 8	and have not denied my **n**.
	3:12	I will write on him the **n** of my God
	11:18	and those who reverence your **n,**
	13: 1	and on each head a blasphemous **n**.
	13:17	which is the **n** of the beast or the
		number of his **n**.
	14: 1	had his **n** and his Father's **n** written
	16: 9	and they cursed the **n** of God,
	19:12	a **n** written on him that no one knows
	19:13	and his **n** is the Word of God.
	19:16	on his thigh he has this **n** written:
	20:15	If anyone's **n** was not found written
	22: 4	and his **n** will be on their foreheads.

HOLY NAME See HOLY

NAME OF JESUS Ac 2:38; 3:6, 16; 4:10, 18; 5:40; 8:12; 9:27; 10:48; 16:18; 19:13; 26:9; Php 2:10

NAME OF THE †LORD Ge 4:26; 12:8; 13:4; 21:33; 26:25; Ex 20:7; Lev 24:16; Dt 5:11; 18:7, 22; 21:5; 28:10; 32:3; 1Sa 17:45; 20:42; 2Sa 6:2, 18; 1Ki 3:2; 5:3, 5; 8:17, 20; 10:1; 18:24, 32; 22:16; 2Ki 2:24; 5:11; 1Ch 16:2; 21:19; 22:7, 19; 2Ch 2:1, 4; 6:7, 10; 18:15; 33:18; Job 1:21; Ps 7:17; 20:7; 102:15, 21; 113:1, 2, 3; 116:4, 13, 17; 118:10, 11, 12, 26; 122:4; 124:8; 129:8; 135:1; 148:5, 13; Pr 18:10; Isa 18:7; 24:15; 30:27; 48:1; 50:10; 56:6; 59:19; Jer 3:17; 11:21; 26:16, 20; 44:16; Joel 2:26, 32; Am 6:10; Mic 4:5; 5:4; Zep 3:9, 12

NAME OF THE *LORD Mt 21:9; 23:39; Mk 11:9; Lk 13:35; 19:38; Jn 12:13; Ac 2:21; 8:16; 9:28; 19:5, 13, 17; 21:13; Ro 10:13; 1Co 6:11; Col 3:17; 2Th 3:6; 2Ti 2:19; Jas 5:10, 14

NAME'S [NAME]

Ps	23: 3	of righteousness for his **n** sake.
	79: 9	and forgive our sins for your **n** sake.
	106: 8	Yet he saved them for his **n** sake,
Eze	20:44	when I deal with you for my **n** sake

NAMED [NAME]

Ge	3:20	Adam **n** his wife Eve,
	5:29	He **n** him Noah and said,
	27:36	Esau said, "Isn't he rightly **n** Jacob?
Ex	2:10	She **n** him Moses, saying,

1Sa   4:21 She **n** the boy Ichabod, saying,
       7:12 He **n** it Ebenezer, saying,
Lk   2:21 he was **n** Jesus,

NAMES [NAME]

Ge   2:20 the man gave **n** to all the livestock,
Ex   28: 9 on them the **n** of the sons of Israel
Dt   7:24 and you will wipe out their **n** from
2Sa   7: 9 like the **n** of the greatest men of the
Hos 2:17 I will remove the **n** of the Baals
Mt   10: 2 the **n** of the twelve apostles:
Lk 10:20 that your **n** are written in heaven."
Php   4: 3 whose **n** are in the book of life.
Heb 12:23 whose **n** are written in heaven.
Rev 17: 3 was covered with blasphemous **n**
     17: 8 whose **n** have not been written in the
   21:12 the **n** of the twelve tribes of Israel.
   21:14 the **n** of the twelve apostles of the
   21:27 whose **n** are written in the Lamb's

NAOMI

Wife of Elimelech, mother-in-law of Ruth (Ru 1:2, 4). Left Bethlehem for Moab during famine (Ru 1:1). Returned a widow, with Ruth (Ru 1:6-22). Advised Ruth to seek marriage with Boaz (Ru 2:17-3:4). Cared for Ruth's son Obed (Ru 4:13-17).

NAPHTALI [NAPHTALITES]

Son of Jacob by Bilhah (Ge 30:8; 35:25; 1Ch 2:2). Tribe of blessed (Ge 49:21; Dt 33:23), numbered (Nu 1:43; 26:50), allotted land (Jos 19:32-39; Eze 48:3), failed to fully possess (Jdg 1:33), supported Deborah (Jdg 4:10; 5:18), David (1Ch 12:34), 12,000 from (Rev 7:6).

NAPHTALITES* [NAPHTALI]

Jdg   1:33 the **N** too lived among the Canaanite

NAPKIN (KJV) See [BURIAL] CLOTH

NARD

Jn   12: 3 Mary took about a pint of pure **n**,

NARROW

Nu 22:24 in a **n** path between two vineyards,
Mt   7:13 "Enter through the **n** gate.
Lk 13:24 to enter through the **n** door,

NATHAN

Prophet and chronicler of Israel's history (1Ch 29:29; 2Ch 9:29). Announced the Davidic covenant (2Sa 7; 1Ch 17). Denounced David's sin with Bathsheba (2Sa 12). Supported Solomon (1Ki 1).

NATHANAEL*

Apostle (Jn 1:45-49; 21:2). Probably also called Bartholomew (Mt 10:3).

NATION [NATIONAL, NATIONALITY, NATIONS]

Ge 12: 2 "I will make you into a great **n**
   15:14 But I will punish the **n** they serve
   35:11 A **n** and a community of nations
Ex 19: 6 a kingdom of priests and a holy **n**.'

   32:10 Then I will make you into a great **n**."
Nu 14:12 but I will make you into a **n** greater
Dt   4: 7 What other **n** is so great as
Jos   4: 1 the whole **n** had finished crossing
     5: 8 the whole **n** had been circumcised,
2Sa   7:23 the one **n** on earth that God went out
2Ki 18:33 Has the god of any **n** ever delivered
1Ch 16:20 they wandered from **n** to **n**,
Ps 33:12 the **n** whose God is the LORD,
  147:20 He has done this for no other **n**;
Pr 11:14 For lack of guidance a **n** falls,
   14:34 Righteousness exalts a **n**,
Isa   2: 4 **N** will not take up sword against **n**,
     9: 3 enlarged the **n** and increased their
   26: 2 that the righteous **n** may enter,
   60:12 **n** or kingdom that will not serve you
   65: 1 To a **n** that did not call on my name,
   66: 8 or a **n** be brought forth in a moment?
Jer   2:11 Has a **n** ever changed its gods?
   18: 8 if that **n** I warned repents of its evil,
Eze 37:22 I will make them one **n** in the land,
Mic 4: 3 **N** will not take up sword against **n**,
Mal 3: 9 You are under a curse—the whole **n**
Mt 24: 7 **N** will rise against **n**,
Jn 11:50 than that the whole **n** perish."
Ac 17:26 From one man he made every **n**
1Pe 2: 9 a holy **n**, a people belonging to God,
Rev 5: 9 tribe and language and people and **n**.
     7: 9 from every **n**, tribe,
   14: 6 to every **n**, tribe, language

NATIONAL* [NATION]

2Ki 17:29 each **n** group made its own gods in

NATIONALITY [NATION]

Est   2:10 Esther had not revealed her **n**

NATIONS [NATION]

Ge 17: 4 You will be the father of many **n**.
   18:18 and all **n** on earth will be blessed
   22:18 all **n** on earth will be blessed,
Ex 19: 5 then out of all **n** you will be my
   34:24 I will drive out **n** before you
Lev 18:28 as it vomited out the **n** that were
   20:26 and I have set you apart from the **n**
Dt   7: 1 seven **n** larger and stronger than you
   15: 6 You will rule over many **n** but
   32:43 Rejoice, O **n**, with his people,
Jos 23: 7 Do not associate with these **n** that
Jdg   3: 1 These are the **n** the LORD left
1Sa   8:20 Then we will be like all the other **n**,
1Ki 4:34 Men of all **n** came to listen
2Ki 17:15 They imitated the **n** around them
2Ch 20: 6 rule over all the kingdoms of the **n**.
Ne   1: 8 I will scatter you among the **n**,
Ps   2: 1 the **n** conspire and the peoples plot
     2: 8 I will make the **n** your inheritance,
     9: 5 You have rebuked the **n** and
   22:28 the LORD and he rules over the **n**.
   33:10 The LORD foils the plans of the **n**;
   46:10 I will be exalted among the **n**,
   47: 8 God reigns over the **n**;
   66: 7 his eyes watch the **n**—
   67: 2 your salvation among all **n**.

68:30 Scatter the **n** who delight in war.
72:17 All **n** will be blessed through him,
96: 5 For all the gods of the **n** are idols,
99: 2 he is exalted over all the **n**.
106:35 but they mingled with the **n**
110: 6 He will judge the **n**,
113: 4 The LORD is exalted over all the **n**,
Isa 2: 2 and all **n** will stream to it.
5:26 He lifts up a banner for the distant **n**,
11:10 the **n** will rally to him,
12: 4 among the **n** what he has done,
40:15 the **n** are like a drop in a bucket;
42: 1 and he will bring justice to the **n**.
51: 4 will become a light to the **n**.
52:15 so will he sprinkle many **n**,
56: 7 be called a house of prayer for all **n**."
60: 3 **N** will come to your light,
66:18 to come and gather all **n** and tongues,
Jer 1: 5 as a prophet to the **n**."
3:17 and all **n** will gather in Jerusalem
31:10 "Hear the word of the LORD, O **n**;
33: 9 praise and honor before all **n** on
46:28 the **n** among which I scatter you,
La 1: 1 who once was great among the **n**!
Eze 22: 4 make you an object of scorn to the **n**
34:13 I will bring them out from the **n**
36:23 **n** will know that I am the LORD,
37:22 and they will never again be two **n**
39:21 I will display my glory among the **n**,
Hos 7: 8 "Ephraim mixes with the **n**;
Joel 2:17 a byword among the **n**,
3: 2 I will gather all **n** and bring them
Am 9:12 and all the **n** that bear my name,"
Ob 1:15 of the LORD is near for all **n**.
Zep 3: 8 I have decided to assemble the **n**,
Hag 2: 7 and the desired of all **n** will come,
Zec 8:13 an object of cursing among the **n**,
8:23 and **n** will take firm hold of one Jew
9:10 He will proclaim peace to the **n**.
14: 2 the **n** to Jerusalem to fight against it;
Mal 1:11 My name will be great among the **n**,
3:12 "Then all the **n** will call you blessed,
Mt 12:18 and he will proclaim justice to the **n**.
24: 9 be hated by all **n** because of me.
24:14 as a testimony to all **n**,
25:32 the **n** will be gathered before him,
28:19 go and make disciples of all **n**,
Mk 11:17 a house of prayer for all **n**'?
Ac 4:25 the **n** rage and the peoples plot
Ro 4:18 and so became the father of many **n**,
15:12 who will arise to rule over the **n**,
Gal 3: 8 "All **n** will be blessed through you."
1Ti 3:16 was preached among the **n**,
Rev 2:26 I will give authority over the **n**—
12: 5 who will rule all the **n** with
15: 4 All **n** will come and worship
18:23 all the **n** were led astray.
19:15 with which to strike down the **n**.
20: 8 and go out to deceive the **n**
21:24 The **n** will walk by its light,
22: 2 the tree are for the healing of the **n**.

NATIVE [NATIVE-BORN]

Jn 8:44 he lies, he speaks his **n** language,

Ac 2: 8 hears them in his own **n** language?

NATIVE-BORN [BEAR, NATIVE]

Ex 12:49 The same law applies to the **n** and to

NATURAL [NATURE]

Nu 16:29 If these men die a **n** death
Jn 1:13 children born not of **n** descent,
Ro 1:26 their women exchanged **n** relations
6:19 you are weak in your **n** selves.
11:21 if God did not spare the **n** branches,
1Co 15:44 it is sown a **n** body, it is raised

NATURE [NATURAL]

Ro 1: 3 as to his human **n** was a descendant
1:20 his eternal power and divine **n**—
7:18 that is, in my sinful **n**.
7:25 the sinful **n** a slave to the law of sin.
8: 4 do not live according to the sinful **n**
8: 5 set on what that **n** desires;
8: 8 by the sinful **n** cannot please God.
13:14 to gratify the desires of the sinful **n**.
Gal 5:13 your freedom to indulge the sinful **n**;
5:19 The acts of the sinful **n** are obvious:
5:24 crucified the sinful **n** with its
Eph 2: 3 we were by **n** objects of wrath.
Php 2: 6 being in very **n** God,
Col 2: 9 in the putting off of the sinful **n**,
3: 5 whatever belongs to your earthly **n**:
2Pe 1: 4 you may participate in the divine **n**

SINFUL NATURE See SINFUL

NAUGHTINESS, NAUGHTY

(KJV) See EVIL, MALICIOUS, POOR,
SCOUNDREL, WICKED

NAZARENE* [NAZARETH]

Mt 2:23 "He will be called a **N**."
Mk 14:67 "You also were with that **N**, Jesus,"
16: 6 "You are looking for Jesus the **N**,
Ac 24: 5 He is a ringleader of the **N** sect

NAZARETH [NAZARENE]

Mt 2:23 he went and lived in a town called **N**.
Mk 1:24 do you want with us, Jesus of **N**?
Lk 1:26 God sent the angel Gabriel to **N**,
4:16 He went to **N**,
Jn 1:46 "**N**! Can anything good come from
19:19 JESUS OF **N**, THE KING OF THE JEWS.
Ac 2:22 Jesus of **N** was a man accredited by
10:38 how God anointed Jesus of **N** with

JESUS OF NAZARETH See JESUS

NAZIRITE [NAZIRITES]

Nu 6: 2 of separation to the LORD as a **N**,
Jdg 13: 5 because the boy is to be a **N**,

NAZIRITES [NAZIRITE]

Am 2:12 you made the **N** drink wine

NEAR [NEARBY, NEARER, NEARSIGHTED]

Dt 4: 7 as to have their gods **n** them the way
the LORD our God is **n** us

30:14 No, the word is very **n** you;
Ps 69:18 Come **n** and rescue me;
73:28 But as for me, it is good to be **n** God.
85: 9 his salvation is **n** those who fear him,
145:18 LORD is **n** to all who call on him,
Isa 11: 8 The infant will play **n** the hole of
55: 6 call on him while he is **n**.
Eze 7: 7 The time has come, the day is **n;**
Joel 1:15 For the day of the LORD is **n;**
Zep 1: 7 for the day of the LORD is **n**.
Mal 3: 5 I will come **n** to you for judgment.
Mk 1:15 "The kingdom of God is **n**.
Lk 10: 9 'The kingdom of God is **n** you.'
21:28 your redemption is drawing **n**."
Ro 10: 8 "The word is **n** you;
1Co 8: 8 But food does not bring us **n** to God;
Php 4: 5 The Lord is **n**.
Heb 10:22 let us draw **n** to God with a sincere
Jas 4: 8 Come **n** to God and he will come **n**
to you.
1Pe 4: 7 The end of all things is **n**.
Rev 1: 3 because the time is **n**.
22:10 because the time is **n**.

NEARBY [NEAR]

Jer 23:23 "Am I only a God **n**,"

NEARER [NEAR]

Ro 13:11 because our salvation is **n** now than

NEARSIGHTED* [NEAR, SEE]

2Pe 1: 9 he is **n** and blind, and has forgotten

NEBO

Dt 34: 1 Moses climbed Mount **N** from
Isa 46: 1 Bel bows down, **N** stoops low;

NEBUCHADNEZZAR

Babylonian king. Subdued and exiled Judah (2Ki 24-25; 2Ch 36; Jer 39). Dreams interpreted by Daniel (Da 2; 4). Worshiped God (Da 3:28-29; 4:34-37).

NEBUZARADAN

2Ki 25: 8 **N** commander of the imperial guard,
Jer 52:12 **N** commander of the imperial guard,

NECESSARY* [NECESSITIES]

Ac 1:21 Therefore it is **n** to choose one of
Ro 13: 5 it is **n** to submit to the authorities,
2Co 9: 5 So I thought it **n** to urge the brothers
Php 1:24 but it is more **n** for you that I remain
2:25 But I think it is **n** to send back
Heb 8: 3 and so it was **n** for this one also
9:16 it is **n** to prove the death of
9:23 It was **n**, then, for the copies

NECESSITIES* [NECESSARY]

Tit 3:14 that they may provide for daily **n** and

NECK [NECKS, STIFF-NECKED]

Ge 27:16 and the smooth part of his **n** with
Ps 75: 5 not speak with outstretched **n**.' "
Pr 1: 9 and a chain to adorn your **n**.
3:22 an ornament to grace your **n**.

6:21 fasten them around your **n**.
SS 7: 4 Your **n** is like an ivory tower.
Jer 28:10 off the **n** of the prophet Jeremiah
Hos 10:11 so I will put a yoke on her fair **n**.
11: 4 the yoke from their **n** and bent down
Mt 18: 6 a large millstone hung around his **n**

NECKS [NECK]

Isa 3:16 walking along with outstretched **n**,

NECO

Pharaoh who killed Josiah (2Ki 23:29-30; 2Ch 35:20-22), deposed Jehoahaz (2Ki 23:33-35; 2Ch 36:3-4).

NEED [NEEDED, NEEDS, NEEDY]

Ex 14:14 you **n** only to be still."
1Ki 8:59 according to each day's **n**,
Job 34:23 God has no **n** to examine men further
Ps 50: 9 I have no **n** of a bull from your stall
79: 8 for we are in desperate **n**.
116: 1 when I was in great **n**,
142: 6 for I am in desperate **n;**
Mt 3:14 saying, "I **n** to be baptized by you,
6: 8 for your Father knows what you **n**
Mk 2:17 "It is not the healthy who **n** a doctor,
Lk 12:30 your Father knows that you **n** them.
15:14 and he began to be in **n**.
Jn 2:25 not **n** man's testimony about man,
Ac 2:45 they gave to anyone as he had **n**.
4:35 distributed to anyone as he had **n**.
Ro 12:13 with God's people who are in **n**.
1Co 12:21 "I don't **n** you!"
2Co 8:14 their plenty will supply what you **n**.
Eph 4:28 something to share with those in **n**.
1Th 5: 1 about times and dates we do not **n**
1Ti 5: 3 to those widows who are really in **n**.
2Ti 2:15 who does not **n** to be ashamed
Heb 4:16 to help us in our time of **n**.
7:26 Such a high priest meets our **n—**
2Pe 1: 3 power has given us everything we **n**
1Jn 2:27 you do not **n** anyone to teach you.
3:17 and sees his brother in **n**
Rev 21:23 not **n** the sun or the moon to shine
22: 5 They will not **n** the light of a lamp or

NEEDED [NEED]

Ex 16:18 Each one gathered as much as he **n**.
Mt 25:36 I **n** clothes and you clothed me,
Ac 17:25 as if he **n** anything,

NEEDLE

Lk 18:25 a camel to go through the eye of a **n**

NEEDS [NEED]

Ex 16:16 to gather as much as he **n**.
Dt 15: 8 and freely lend him whatever he **n**.
Pr 12:10 A righteous man cares for the **n**
Isa 58:11 he will satisfy your **n** in
Mk 15:41 followed him and cared for his **n**.
Jn 13:10 "A person who has had a bath **n** only
Ro 12: 8 if it is contributing to the **n**
Eph 4:29 others up according to their **n**,
Php 2:25 whom you sent to take care of my **n**.
4:19 And my God will meet all your **n**

Jas 2:16 does nothing about his physical **n,**

NEEDY [NEED]

Ex 22:25 of my people among you who is **n,**
Dt 15:11 and toward the poor and **n**
1Sa 2: 8 and lifts the **n** from the ash heap;
Job 29:16 I was a father to the **n;**
Ps 9:18 the **n** will not always be forgotten,
35:10 and **n** from those who rob them."
69:33 The LORD hears the **n** and does
70: 5 Yet I am poor and **n;**
72:12 For he will deliver the **n** who cry out,
74:21 the poor and **n** praise your name.
113: 7 and lifts the **n** from the ash heap;
140:12 and upholds the cause of the **n.**
Pr 14:21 blessed is he who is kind to the **n.**
14:31 whoever is kind to the **n** honors God.
22:22 and do not crush the **n** in court,
31: 9 defend the rights of the poor and **n."**
31:20 and extends her hands to the **n.**
Isa 11: 4 righteousness he will judge the **n,**
Am 8: 4 you who trample the **n** and do away
Mt 6: 2 "So when you give to the **n,**

NEGEV [RAMOTH NEGEV]

Ge 13: 1 Abram went up from Egypt to the **N,**
24:62 for he was living in the **N.**
Jos 11:16 the hill country, all the **N,**
Ps 126: 4 O LORD, like streams in the **N.**

NEGLECT* [NEGLECTED]

Dt 12:19 Be careful not to **n** the Levites
14:27 And do not **n** the Levites living
Ezr 4:22 Be careful not to **n** in this matter.
Ne 10:39 not **n** the house of our God."
Est 6:10 **n** anything you have recommended."
Ps 119:16 I will not **n** your word.
Lk 11:42 you **n** justice and the love of God.
Ac 6: 2 not be right for us to **n** the ministry
1Ti 4:14 Do not **n** your gift,

NEGLECTED* [NEGLECT]

Ne 13:11 "Why is the house of God **n?"**
SS 1: 6 my own vineyard I have **n.**
Mt 23:23 But you have **n** the more important

NEHEMIAH

Cupbearer of Artaxerxes (Ne 2:1); governor of Israel (Ne 8:9). Returned to Jerusalem to rebuild walls (Ne 2-6). With Ezra, reestablished worship (Ne 8). Prayer confessing nation's sin (Ne 9). Dedicated wall (Ne 12).

NEHUSHTAN*

2Ki 18: 4 (It was called **N.**)

NEIGHBOR [NEIGHBOR'S, NEIGHBORS]

Ex 20:16 false testimony against your **n.**
20:17 or anything that belongs to your **n."**
Lev 19:13 " 'Do not defraud your **n** or rob him.
19:17 Rebuke your **n** frankly so you will
19:18 but love your **n** as yourself.
Dt 4:42 if he had unintentionally killed his **n**
5:20 false testimony against your **n.**
19:11 if a man hates his **n** and lies in wait
2Ch 6:22 a man wrongs his **n** and is required
Ps 15: 3 who does his **n** no wrong
Pr 3:29 Do not plot harm against your **n,**
11:12 who lacks judgment derides his **n,**
14:21 He who despises his **n** sins,
16:29 A violent man entices his **n**
24:28 against your **n** without cause,
25:18 false testimony against his **n.**
27:10 a **n** nearby than a brother far away.
27:14 a man loudly blesses his **n** early in
29: 5 Whoever flatters his **n** is spreading
Ecc 4: 4 from man's envy of his **n.**
Isa 19: 2 **n** against **n,** city against city,
Jer 31:34 No longer will a man teach his **n,**
Zec 8:17 do not plot evil against your **n,**
Mt 5:43 'Love your **n** and hate your enemy.'
19:19 and 'love your **n** as yourself.' "
Mk 12:31 The second is this: 'Love your **n**
Lk 10:27 'Love your **n** as yourself.' "
10:29 "And who is my **n?"**
Ro 13: 9 in this one rule: "Love your **n**
13:10 Love does no harm to its **n.**
15: 2 Each of us should please his **n**
Gal 5:14 in a single command: "Love your **n**
Eph 4:25 and speak truthfully to his **n,**
Heb 8:11 No longer will a man teach his **n,**
Jas 2: 8 "Love your **n** as yourself,"

LOVE YOUR NEIGHBOR See LOVE

NEIGHBOR'S [NEIGHBOR]

Ex 20:17 "You shall not covet your **n** house.
20:17 You shall not covet your **n** wife,
22:26 If you take your **n** cloak as a pledge,
Lev 19:16 anything that endangers your **n** life.
Dt 5:21 "You shall not covet your **n** wife.
5:21 not set your desire on your **n** house
19:14 not move your **n** boundary stone set
27:17 who moves his **n** boundary stone."
Pr 25:17 Seldom set foot in your **n** house—

NEIGHBORS [NEIGHBOR]

Ex 11: 2 are to ask their **n** for articles
1Sa 15:28 and has given it to one of your **n**—
2Ki 4: 3 and ask all your **n** for empty jars.
Ezr 1: 6 All their **n** assisted them with articles
6:21 unclean practices of their Gentile **n**
Ps 79: 4 We are objects of reproach to our **n,**
79:12 into the laps of our **n** seven times

NEPHEW*

Ge 12: 5 He took his wife Sarai, his **n** Lot,
14:12 They also carried off Abram's **n** Lot

NEST [NESTED, NESTING, NESTS]

Dt 22: 6 If you come across a bird's **n** beside
Isa 11: 8 child put his hand into the viper's **n.**
Ob 1: 4 make your **n** among the stars,
Hab 2: 9 by unjust gain to set his **n** on high,

NESTED* [NEST]

Eze 31: 6 the birds of the air **n** in its boughs,

NESTING* [NEST]

Da   4:21 and having **n** places in its branches

NESTS [NEST]

Mt   8:20 and birds of the air have **n,**

NET [NETS]

Ps   35: 8 the **n** they hid entangle them,
Pr   1:17 a **n** in full view of all the birds!
La   1:13 a **n** for my feet and turned me back.
Hab   1:15 he catches them in his **n,**
Mt   13:47 a **n** that was let down into the lake
Mk   1:16 Andrew casting a **n** into the lake,
Jn   21: 6 "Throw your **n** on the right side of

NETS [NET]

Ps   141:10 Let the wicked fall into their own **n,**
Mt   4:20 At once they left their **n**
Lk   5: 4 and let down the **n** for a catch."

NEVER

Ge   8:21 And **n** again will I destroy all living
Dt   9: 7 and **n** forget how you provoked
      31: 6 he will **n** leave you
Jdg   1:28 but **n** drove them out completely.
2Sa   7:15 But my love will **n** be taken away
1Ki   2: 4 you will **n** fail to have a man on
      8:25 'You shall **n** fail to have a man to sit
      9: 5 'You shall **n** fail to have a man on
2Ch 18: 7 he **n** prophesies anything good
Ps   14: 4 Will evildoers **n** learn—
      30: 6 I said, "I will **n** be shaken."
      89:28 my covenant with him will **n** fail.
      95:11 "They shall **n** enter my rest."
Pr   3: 3 and faithfulness **n** leave you;
      30:15 four that **n** say, 'Enough!':
Ecc   1: 8 The eye **n** has enough of seeing,
            whoever loves wealth is **n** satisfied
Isa   6: 9 ever hearing, but **n** understanding;
      28:16 who trusts will **n** be dismayed.
      51: 6 my righteousness will **n** fail.
Jer 33:17 David will **n** fail to have a man to sit
La   3:22 for his compassions **n** fail.
Da   2:44 a kingdom that will **n** be destroyed,
      6:26 his dominion will **n** end.
Hos 14: 3 We will **n** again say 'Our gods'
Mk   3:29 against the Holy Spirit will **n** be
      4:12 ever seeing but **n** perceiving,
Lk   21:33 but my words will **n** pass away.
Jn   4:14 the water I give him will **n** thirst.
      6:35 comes to me will **n** go hungry,
      8:51 he will **n** see death."
      10:28 and they shall **n** perish;
      11:26 and believes in me will **n** die.
Ro   9:33 and the one who trusts in him will **n**
1Co 13: 8 Love **n** fails.
Gal   6:14 May I **n** boast except in the cross
2Th   3:13 **n** tire of doing what is right.
Heb   3:11 'They shall **n** enter my rest.' "
      4: 3 'They shall **n** enter my rest.' "
      13: 5 "**N** will I leave you;
1Pe   1: 4 an inheritance that can **n** perish, spoil
      2: 6 and the one who trusts in him will **n**
      5: 4 crown of glory that will **n** fade away.

2Pe   1:10 you do these things, you will **n** fall,
Rev   7:16 **N** again will they hunger;

NEVER-FAILING*

Am   5:24 righteousness like a **n** stream!

NEW

Ex   1: 8 Then a **n** king, who did not know
Jdg   5: 8 When they chose **n** gods,
Ezr   9: 9 He has granted us **n** life
Ne   13: 5 the tithes of grain, **n** wine and oil
Ps   33: 3 Sing to him a **n** song;
      40: 3 He put a **n** song in my mouth,
      98: 1 Sing to the LORD a **n** song,
Pr   3:10 your vats will brim over with **n** wine.
Ecc   1: 9 there is nothing **n** under the sun.
Isa 42: 9 and **n** things I declare;
      42:10 Sing to the LORD a **n** song,
      43:19 See, I am doing a **n** thing!
      62: 2 you be called by a **n** name
      65:17 I will create **n** heavens and a **n** earth.
      66:22 "As the **n** heavens and the **n** earth
Jer 31:31 a **n** covenant with the house of Israel
La   3:23 They are **n** every morning;
Eze 11:19 an undivided heart and put a **n** spirit
      18:31 and get a **n** heart and a **n** spirit.
      36:26 a **n** heart and put a **n** spirit in you;
Joel 3:18 the mountains will drip **n** wine,
Am   9:13 **N** wine will drip from the mountains
Zep   3: 5 and every **n** day he does not fail,
Mt   9:17 they pour **n** wine into **n** wineskins,
      13:52 of his storeroom **n** treasures as well
Mk   1:27 A **n** teaching—and with authority!
Lk   5:39 after drinking old wine wants the **n,**
      22:20 cup is the **n** covenant in my blood,
Jn   13:34 "A **n** command I give you:
Ac   5:20 the full message of this **n** life."
      17:19 "May we know what this **n** teaching
Ro   6: 4 we too may live a **n** life.
1Co   5: 7 you may be a **n** batch without yeast
      11:25 cup is the **n** covenant in my blood;
2Co   3: 6 as ministers of a **n** covenant—
      5:17 in Christ, he is a **n** creation.
Gal   6:15 what counts is a **n** creation.
Eph   2:15 to create in himself one **n** man out of
      4:23 to be made **n** in the attitude
      4:24 and to put on the **n** self,
Col   3:10 and have put on the **n** self,
Heb   8: 8 a **n** covenant with the house of Israel
      9:15 is the mediator of a **n** covenant,
      10:20 by a **n** and living way opened for us
      12:24 Jesus the mediator of a **n** covenant,
1Pe   1: 3 great mercy he has given us **n** birth
2Pe   3:13 to a **n** heaven and a **n** earth,
1Jn   2: 7 I am not writing you a **n** command
2Jn   1: 5 not writing you a **n** command
Rev   2:17 a white stone with a **n** name written
      3:12 the **n** Jerusalem, which is coming
      3:12 also write on him my **n** name.
      5: 9 And they sang a **n** song:
      14: 3 a **n** song before the throne
      21: 1 I saw a **n** heaven and a **n** earth,
      21: 2 I saw the Holy City, the **n** Jerusalem,
      21: 5 "I am making everything **n**!"

NEW MOON Nu 10:10; 28:14; 1Sa 20:5, 18, 24;
2Ki 4:23; 1Ch 23:31; Ezr 3:5; Ne 10:33; Ps 81:3;
Isa 1:14; 66:23; Eze 46:1, 6; Hos 5:7; Am 8:5;
Col 2:16

NEW WINE Ge 27:28, 37; Nu 18:12; Dt 7:13;
11:14; 12:17; 14:23; 18:4; 28:51; 33:28; 2Ki
18:32; 2Ch 31:5; 32:28; Ne 5:11; 10:37, 39; 13:5,
12; Ps 4:7; Pr 3:10; Isa 24:7; 36:17; 62:8; Jer
31:12; Hos 2:8, 9, 22; 7:14; 9:2; Joel 1:5, 10;
2:19, 24; 3:18; Am 9:13; Hag 1:11; Zec 9:17; Mt
9:17, 17; Mk 2:22, 22; Lk 5:37, 37, 38

NEWBORN [BEAR]
1Pe 2: 2 Like **n** babies, crave pure spiritual

NEWS
2Ki 7: 9 This is a day of good **n**
Ps 112: 7 He will have no fear of bad **n;**
Pr 15:30 and good **n** gives health to the bones.
    25:25 is good **n** from a distant land.
Isa 52: 7 the feet of those who bring good **n,**
    61: 1 to preach good **n** to the poor.
Na 1:15 the feet of one who brings good **n,**
Mt 4:23 preaching the good **n** of the kingdom
     9:35 the good **n** of the kingdom
    11: 5 the good **n** is preached to the poor.
Mk 1:15 Repent and believe the good **n!"**
Lk 1:19 to you and to tell you this good **n.**
     2:10 I bring you good **n** of great joy
     3:18 and preached the good **n** to them.
     4:43 the good **n** of the kingdom of God to
     8: 1 the good **n** of the kingdom of God.
    16:16 the good **n** of the kingdom of God
Jn 20:18 went to the disciples with the **n:**
Ac 5:42 proclaiming the good **n** that Jesus is
    10:36 telling the good **n** of peace
    14: 7 to preach the good **n.**
    14:21 They preached the good **n** in that city
    17:18 preaching the good **n** about Jesus
Ro 10:15 the feet of those who bring good **n!"**

GOOD NEWS See GOOD

NEXT
Ge 18:10 return to you about this time **n** year,
Ps 78: 4 we will tell the **n** generation

NICODEMUS*
Pharisee who visted Jesus at night (Jn 3). Ar-
gued for fair treatment of Jesus (Jn 7:50-52). With
Joseph, prepared Jesus for burial (Jn 19:38-42).

NICOLAITANS*
Rev 2: 6 You hate the practices of the **N,**
     2:15 who hold to the teaching of the **N.**

NIGER*
Ac 13: 1 Simeon called **N,** Lucius of Cyrene,

NIGH (KJV) See NEAR

NIGHT [MIDNIGHT, NIGHTS,
NIGHTTIME, OVERNIGHT]
Ge 1: 5 and the darkness he called **"n."**
     1:16 and the lesser light to govern the **n.**

     8:22 day and **n** will never cease."
Ex 13:21 by **n** in a pillar of fire to give them
    40:38 and fire was in the cloud by **n,**
Dt 28:66 filled with dread both **n** and day,
Jos 1: 8 meditate on it day and **n,**
Job 35:10 who gives songs in the **n,**
Ps   1: 2 on his law he meditates day and **n.**
    16: 7 even at **n** my heart instructs me.
    19: 2 **n** after **n** they display knowledge.
    42: 8 at **n** his song is with me—
    63: 6 of you through the watches of the **n.**
    74:16 day is yours, and yours also the **n;**
    77: 6 I remembered my songs in the **n.**
    90: 4 or like a watch in the **n.**
    91: 5 You will not fear the terror of **n,**
   119:55 In the **n** I remember your name,
   121: 6 nor the moon by **n.**
   136: 9 the moon and stars to govern the **n;**
Pr 31:18 and her lamp does not go out at **n.**
Ecc 2:23 even at **n** his mind does not rest.
Isa 21:11 "Watchman, what is left of the **n?**
    58:10 your **n** will become like the noonday.
Jer 33:20 so that day and **n** no longer come
Mt 24:43 what time of **n** the thief was coming,
Lk   2: 8 keeping watch over their flocks at **n.**
     6:12 and spent the **n** praying to God.
Jn   3: 2 He came to Jesus at **n** and said,
     9: 4 **N** is coming, when no one can work.
    11:10 when he walks by **n** that he stumbles,
1Th 5: 2 will come like a thief in the **n.**
     5: 5 We do not belong to the **n** or to
Rev 8:12 and also a third of the **n.**
    20:10 They will be tormented day and **n**
    21:25 for there will be no **n** there.
    22: 5 There will be no more **n.**

NIGHTS [NIGHT]
Ge   7:12 on the earth forty days and forty **n.**
Ex 24:18 the mountain forty days and forty **n.**
1Ki 19: 8 he traveled forty days and forty **n**
Jnh 1:17 inside the fish three days and three **n.**
Mt   4: 2 After fasting forty days and forty **n,**
    12:40 as Jonah was three days and three **n**
2Co 6: 5 sleepless **n** and hunger;

NIGHTTIME* [NIGHT]
Zec 14: 7 without daytime or **n**—

NILE
Ex   1:22 you must throw into the **N,**
     2: 5 went down to the **N** to bathe,
     7:17 I will strike the water of the **N,**

NIMROD
Ge 10: 9 **N,** a mighty hunter before the LORD.

NINE [NINTH]
Nu 34:13 be given to the **n** and a half tribes,
Jos 13: 7 as an inheritance among the **n** tribes
1Sa 17: 4 He was over **n** feet tall.
Ac   2:15 It's only **n** in the morning!

NINETY
Ge 17:17 Sarah bear a child at the age of **n?"**

NINETY-NINE

Ge   17: 1   When Abram was **n** years old,
Lk   15: 4   Does he not leave the **n** in the open

NINEVEH [NINEVITES]

Jnh   1: 2   "Go to the great city of **N** and preach
Na   1: 1   An oracle concerning **N.**
Mt   12:41   of **N** will stand up at the judgment

NINEVITES* [NINEVEH]

Jnh   3: 5   The **N** believed God.
Lk   11:30   For as Jonah was a sign to the **N,**

NINTH [NINE]

Mt   27:46   About the **n** hour Jesus cried out in

NO [NONE, NOTHING]

Ex   20: 3   shall have **n** other gods before me.
Dt   4:35   LORD is God; besides him there is **n**
      5: 7   shall have **n** other gods before me.
     15: 4   there should be **n** poor among you,
     32: 4   A faithful God who does **n** wrong,
1Ki   8:23   there is **n** God like you in heaven
Ecc 12:12   making many books there is **n** end,
Isa 43:11   apart from me there is **n** savior.
Jer 31:34   will remember their sins **n** more."
Eze 13:10   "Peace," when there is **n** peace,
Mt   5:37   'Yes' be 'Yes,' and your **'N,' 'N';**
     24:36   "**N** one knows about that day or hour
Mk   8:12   **n** sign will be given to it."
     10:18   "**N** one is good—except God alone.
Lk   16:13   "**N** servant can serve two masters.
Jn   1:18   **N** one has ever seen God,
      4:44   a prophet has **n** honor in his own
Ro   8: 1   there is now **n** condemnation for
Jas   5:12   your "Yes" be yes, and your **"N,"** n,
Rev 21: 1   there was **n** longer any sea.
     21: 4   **n** more death or mourning or crying
     22: 3   **N** longer will there be any curse.
     22: 5   There will be **n** more night.

NOAH

Righteous man (Eze 14:14, 20) called to build ark (Ge 6-8; Heb 11:7; 1Pe 3:20; 2Pe 2:5). God's covenant with (Ge 9:1-17). Drunkenness of (Ge 9:18-23). Blessed sons, cursed Canaan (Ge 9:24-27).

NOB

1Sa 21: 1   David went to **N,**

NOBLE

Ru   3:11   that you are a woman of **n** character.
Ps   45: 1   My heart is stirred by a **n** theme
Pr   12: 4   wife of **n** character is her husband's
     31:10   A wife of **n** character who can find?
     31:29   "Many women do **n** things.
Isa 32: 8   But the **n** man makes **n** plans,
Lk   8:15   on good soil stands for those with a **n**
Ac   17:11   Bereans were of more **n** character
Ro   9:21   clay some pottery for **n** purposes
1Co   1:26   not many were of **n** birth.
Php   4: 8   whatever is **n**, whatever is right,
1Ti   3: 1   he desires a **n** task.

2Ti   2:20   for **n** purposes and some for ignoble.
Jas   2: 7   are slandering the **n** name of him

NOBODY

Jn   9:32   **N** has ever heard of opening the eyes
1Co 10:24   **N** should seek his own good,
1Th   5:15   that **n** pays back wrong for wrong,

NOISE

Ex   32:17   the **n** of the people shouting,
Isa 13: 4   Listen, a **n** on the mountains,
     29: 6   thunder and earthquake and great **n,**

NONE [NO]

Dt   15: 6   over many nations but **n** will rule
1Sa   3:19   and he let **n** of his words fall to
Ps   86: 8   Among the gods there is **n** like you,
Pr   2:19   **N** who go to her return or attain
Isa 46: 9   and there is **n** like me.
     47: 8   'I am, and there is **n** besides me.
Mt   12:39   But **n** will be given it except the sign
     16: 4   but **n** will be given it except the sign
Jn   6:39   that I shall lose **n** of all
     17:12   **N** has been lost except the one

NORTH

Ge   13:14   where you are and look **n** and south,
Nu   34: 9   This will be your boundary on the **n.**
Ps   89:12   You created the **n** and the south;
Isa 41:25   "I have stirred up one from the **n,**
Jer   4: 6   I am bringing disaster from the **n,**
Eze   1: 4   a windstorm coming out of the **n—**
Da   11: 6   will go to the king of the **N** to make
Zec   2: 6   Flee from the land of the **n,"**
     14: 4   with half of the mountain moving **n**

NOSE [NOSES]

2Ki 19:28   I will put my hook in your **n**
2Ch 33:11   put a hook in his **n,**

NOSES* [NOSE]

Ps 115: 6   **n,** but they cannot smell;
Eze 23:25   They will cut off your **n**

NOSTRILS

Ge   2: 7   breathed into his **n** the breath
      7:22   the breath of life in its **n** died.
Ex   15: 8   blast of your **n** the waters piled up.
Ps   18:15   at the blast of breath from your **n.**
Isa   2:22   who has but a breath in his **n.**

NOTE

Ac   4:13   **n** that these men had been with Jesus
Php   3:17   and take **n** of those who live

NOTHING [NO, THING]

Ge   14:23   that I will accept **n** belonging to you,
2Sa 24:24   burnt offerings that cost me **n.**"
2Ch   9: 2   was too hard for him to explain to
Ne   9:21   in the desert; they lacked **n,**
Job   1: 9   "Does Job fear God for **n?**"
Ps   34: 9   for those who fear him lack **n.**
     73:25   And earth has **n** I desire besides you.
     82: 5   "They know **n**, they understand **n.**
Pr   8:11   **n** you desire can compare with her.

10:28 the hopes of the wicked come to **n.**
13: 4 The sluggard craves and gets **n,**
28:27 He who gives to the poor will lack **n,**
Ecc 1: 9 there is **n** new under the sun.
3:22 **n** better for a man than to enjoy his
8:15 is **n** better for a man under the sun
Isa 44: 9 All who make idols are **n,**
53: 2 **n** in his appearance that we should
Jer 32:17 **N** is too hard for you.
Da 9:26 will be cut off and will have **n.**
Mt 17:20 **N** will be impossible for you."
Lk 1:37 For **n** is impossible with God."
23:15 he has done **n** to deserve death.
Jn 5:30 By myself I can do **n;**
15: 5 apart from me you can do **n.**
Ro 7:18 I know that **n** good lives in me,
1Co 8: 4 We know that an idol is **n**
13: 2 but have not love, I am **n.**
Gal 2:21 Christ died for **n!"**
3: 4 if it really was for **n?**
Php 2: 7 but made himself **n,**
1Ti 6: 7 For we brought **n** into the world,
Heb 4:13 **N** in all creation is hidden
7:19 (for the law made **n** perfect),

NOTORIOUS*

Mt 27:16 At that time they had a **n** prisoner,

NOURISH [NOURISHED, NOURISHING, NOURISHMENT]

Pr 10:21 The lips of the righteous **n** many,

NOURISHED [NOURISH]

Dt 32:13 He **n** him with honey from the rock,
Da 1:15 better **n** than any of the young men

NOURISHING* [NOURISH]

Ro 11:17 now share in the **n** sap from

NOURISHMENT* [NOURISH]

Pr 3: 8 to your body and **n** to your bones.

NOVICE (KJV) See RECENT CONVERT

NOW

Ge 22:12 **N** I know that you fear God,
Ezr 9: 8 "But **n,** for a brief moment,
Ps 20: 6 **N** I know that the LORD saves
131: 3 hope in the LORD both **n** and
Hab 2:16 **N** it is your turn!
Zec 1: 5 Where are your forefathers **n?**
Mt 12:42 **n** one greater than Solomon is here.
Lk 1:48 From **n** on all generations will call
Jn 2:10 but you have saved the best till **n."**
5:25 a time is coming and has **n** come
9:25 I was blind but **n** I see!"
13:19 "I am telling you **n** before it happens,
13:36 you cannot follow **n,**
16:12 more than you can **n** bear.
Ro 3:21 But **n** a righteousness from God,
5: 9 Since we have **n** been justified
8: 1 there is **n** no condemnation
13:11 because our salvation is nearer **n**
1Co 13:13 And **n** these three remain:

2Co 6: 2 **n** is the time of God's favor,
Gal 4: 9 But **n** that you know God—
Eph 2: 2 the spirit who is **n** at work
3: 5 as it has **n** been revealed by the Spirit
Col 1:26 but is **n** disclosed to the saints.
1Pe 1: 8 even though you do not see him **n,**
2:10 but **n** you are the people of God;
1Jn 2:18 even **n** many antichrists have come.
Rev 1:19 what is **n** and what will take place
21: 3 **"N** the dwelling of God is with men,

NULLIFY

Mt 15: 6 Thus you **n** the word of God for
Ro 3: 3 lack of faith **n** God's faithfulness?
3:31 Do we, then, **n** the law by this faith?

NUMBER [NUMBERED, NUMBERING, NUMBERLESS, NUMBERS, NUMEROUS]

Ge 1:22 "Be fruitful and increase in **n**
1:28 "Be fruitful and increase in **n;**
9: 1 "Be fruitful and increase in **n** and fill
Nu 1: 3 to **n** by their divisions all the men
26:51 The total **n** of the men of Israel
Dt 32: 8 to the **n** of the sons of Israel.
1Ki 3: 8 too numerous to count or **n.**
1Ch 21: 5 the **n** of the fighting men to David:
Ps 90:12 Teach us to **n** our days aright,
105:12 When they were but few in **n,**
147: 4 the **n** of the stars and calls them each
Jer 23: 3 will be fruitful and increase in **n.**
Mt 14:21 The **n** of those who ate was
15:38 The **n** of those who ate was
Jn 21: 6 because of the large **n** of fish.
Ac 2:47 And the Lord added to their **n** daily
5:14 the Lord and were added to their **n.**
6: 1 the **n** of disciples was increasing,
11:21 and a great **n** of people believed
Ro 11:25 a hardening in part until the full **n** of
Rev 6:11 until the **n** of their fellow servants
7: 4 the **n** of those who were sealed:
13:18 His **n** is 666.
20: 8 In **n** they are like the sand on

NUMBERED [NUMBER]

Ex 1: 5 The descendants of Jacob **n** seventy
Lk 12: 7 the very hairs of your head are all **n.**
22:37 he was **n** with the transgressors';

NUMBERING [NUMBER]

1Ch 27:24 came on Israel on account of this **n,**

NUMBERLESS* [NUMBER]

Isa 48:19 your children like its **n** grains;

NUMBERS [NUMBER]

Ge 17: 2 and will greatly increase your **n."**
28: 3 you fruitful and increase your **n**
48: 4 you fruitful and will increase your **n.**
Lev 26: 9 you fruitful and increase your **n**
Dt 1:10 LORD your God has increased your **n**

NUMEROUS [NUMBER]

Ge 16:10 that they will be too **n** to count."

22:17 as **n** as the stars in the sky
Ex   1: 9 Israelites have become much too **n**
     23:29 and the wild animals too **n** for you.
Ne   9:23 You made their sons as **n** as the stars
Zec 10: 8 they will be as **n** as before.
Heb 11:12 came descendants as **n** as the stars in

NURSE [NURSED, NURSING]

Ge 21: 7 that Sarah would **n** children?
Ex   2: 7 of the Hebrew women to **n** the baby
Isa 66:11 For you will **n** and be satisfied

NURSED [NURSE]

Ex   2: 9 the woman took the baby and **n** him.
Lk 11:27 who gave you birth and **n** you."

NURSING [NURSE]

Lk 21:23 for pregnant women and **n** mothers!

O

OAK [OAKS]

Ge 35: 4 and Jacob buried them under the **o**
2Sa 18:10 Absalom hanging in an **o** tree."
Eze 6:13 spreading tree and every leafy **o**—

OAKS [OAK]

Ps 29: 9 The voice of the LORD twists the **o**
Isa 57: 5 You burn with lust among the **o**

OATH [OATHS]

Ge 21:31 the two men swore an **o** there.
     24: 7 and promised me on **o**, saying,
     26: 3 and will confirm the **o** I swore
Ex 13:11 as he promised on **o** to you
     33: 1 go up to the land I promised on **o**
Nu 30: 2 takes an **o** to obligate himself
Dt   6:18 land that the LORD promised on **o**
     7: 8 the **o** he swore to your forefathers
     29:12 and sealing with an **o**,
Jos 2:17 "This **o** you made us swear will not
     6:22 in accordance with your **o** to her."
1Sa 14:24 bound the people under an **o**,
     24:22 So David gave his **o** to Saul.
Ezr 10: 5 who keeps his **o** even when it hurts,
Ne 13:25 an **o** in God's name and said:
Ps 15: 4 who keeps his **o** even when it hurts,
     95:11 So I declared on **o** in my anger,
     119:106 I have taken an **o** and confirmed it,
     132:11 The LORD swore an **o** to David,
Ecc 8: 2 because you took an **o** before God.
Mt   5:33 'Do not break your **o**,
Heb 4: 3 "So I declared on **o** in my anger,
     7:20 that was not without an **o**!

OATHS [OATH]

Dt   6:13 and take your **o** in his name.
Mt   5:33 the **o** you have made to the Lord.'

OBADIAH

1. Believer who sheltered 100 prophets from
Jezebel (1Ki 18:1-16).
2. Prophet against Edom (Ob 1).

OBED

Ru   4:22 **O** the father of Jesse,
Lk   3:32 the son of **O**, the son of Boaz,

OBED-EDOM

2Sa 6:10 he took it aside to the house of **O**
1Ch 26: 5 (For God had blessed **O**.)

OBEDIENCE* [OBEY]

Ge 49:10 and the **o** of the nations is his.
Jdg 2:17 way of **o** to the LORD's commands.
1Ch 21:19 So David went up in **o** to the word
2Ch 31:21 the service of God's temple and in **o**
Pr 30:17 that scorns **o** to a mother,
Lk 23:56 But they rested on the Sabbath in **o**
Ac 21:24 but that you yourself are living in **o**
Ro   1: 5 from among all the Gentiles to the **o**
     5:19 so also through the **o** of the one man
     6:16 which leads to death, or to **o**,
     16:19 Everyone has heard about your **o**,
2Co 9:13 men will praise God for the **o**
     10: 6 once your **o** is complete.
Phm 1:21 Confident of your **o**, I write to you,
Heb 5: 8 he learned **o** from what he suffered
1Pe 1: 2 for **o** to Jesus Christ and sprinkling
2Jn 1: 6 that we walk in **o** to his commands.

OBEDIENT* [OBEY]

Dt 30:17 turns away and you are not **o**,
Isa 1:19 If you are willing and **o**,
Lk   2:51 to Nazareth with them and was **o**
Ac   6: 7 a large number of priests became **o**
2Co 2: 9 if you would stand the test and be **o**
     7:15 he remembers that you were all **o**,
     10: 5 every thought to make it **o** to Christ.
Php 2: 8 himself and became **o** to death
Tit 3: 1 to rulers and authorities, to be **o**,
1Pe 1:14 As **o** children, do not conform

OBEISANCE (KJV) See BOWED

OBEY [OBEDIENCE, OBEDIENT, OBEYED, OBEYING, OBEYS]

Ex 12:24 "**O** these instructions as a lasting
     19: 5 Now if you **o** me fully and keep
     24: 7 the LORD has said; we will **o**."
Lev 18: 4 You must **o** my laws and be careful
     25:18 and be careful to **o** my laws,
Nu 15:40 Then you will remember to **o** all my
Dt   4:30 to the LORD your God and **o** him.
     5:27 We will listen and **o**."
     6: 3 to **o** so that it may go well
     6:24 commanded us to **o** all these decrees
     11:13 So if you faithfully **o** the commands
     11:27 the blessing if you **o** the commands
     12:28 to **o** all these regulations I am giving
     13: 4 Keep his commands and **o** him;
     21:18 who does not **o** his father and mother
     28: 1 If you fully **o** the LORD your God

28:15 not **o** the LORD your God
30: 2 to the LORD your God and **o** him
30:10 if you **o** the LORD your God
30:14 and in your heart so you may **o** it.
32:46 to **o** carefully all the words
Jos　1: 7 Be careful to **o** all the law
22: 5 to **o** his commands,
24:24 the LORD our God and **o** him."
Jdg　3: 4 to see whether they would **o** the
1Sa 12:14 and serve and **o** him and do not rebel
15:22 To **o** is better than sacrifice,
1Ki　8:61 by his decrees and **o** his commands,
2Ki 17:13 that I commanded your fathers to **o**
2Ch 34:31 and to **o** the words of the covenant
Ne　1: 5 and **o** his commands,
Ps 103:18 and remember to **o** his precepts.
103:20 who **o** his word.
119:17 I will **o** your word.
119:34 and I will keep your law and **o** it
119:57 I have promised to **o** your words.
119:67 but now I **o** your word.
119:100 for I **o** your precepts.
119:129 wonderful; therefore I **o** them.
119:167 I **o** your statutes,
Pr　5:13 I would not **o** my teachers or listen
Jer　7:23 I gave them this command: **O** me,
11: 4 I said, '**O** me and do everything
11: 7 and again, saying, "**O** me."
18:10 evil in my sight and does not **o** me,
42: 6 we will **o** the LORD our God,
Da　9: 4 who love him and **o** his commands,
Mt　8:27 the winds and the waves **o** him!"
19:17 to enter life, **o** the commandments."
28:20 to **o** everything I have commanded
Lk 11:28 hear the word of God and **o** it."
Jn 14:15 you will **o** what I command.
14:24 not love me will not **o** my teaching.
15:10 If you **o** my commands,
Ac　5:29 "We must **o** God rather than men!
5:32 has given to those who **o** him."
15: 5 and required to **o** the law of Moses."
Ro　2:13 but it is those who **o** the law who
6:12 so that you **o** its evil desires.
6:16 to **o** him as slaves, you are slaves to
the one whom you **o**—
15:18 in leading the Gentiles to **o** God
16:26 all nations might believe and **o** him
Gal　5: 3 circumcised that he is obligated to **o**
Eph　6: 1 Children, **o** your parents in the Lord,
6: 5 just as you would **o** Christ.
Col　3:20 **o** your parents in everything,
3:22 **o** your earthly masters in everything;
2Th　3:14 If anyone does not **o** our instruction
1Ti　3: 4 and see that his children **o** him
Heb　5: 9 of eternal salvation for all who **o** him
13:17 **O** your leaders and submit
1Pe　4:17 who do not **o** the gospel of God?
1Jn　3:24 Those who **o** his commands live
5: 3 love for God: to **o** his commands.
Rev 12:17 those who **o** God's commandments
14:12 saints who **o** God's commandments

OBEYED [OBEY]

Ge 22:18 because you have **o** me."

26: 5 because Abraham **o** me
Jos　1:17 Just as we fully **o** Moses,
2Ki 18:12 they had not **o** the LORD their God,
Ps 119: 4 precepts that are to be fully **o**.
Jer　3:13 and have not **o** me,' "
Da　9:10 we have not **o** the LORD our God
Jnh　3: 3 Jonah **o** the word of the LORD
Mic　5:15 upon the nations that have not **o** me."
Jn 15:10 as I have **o** my Father's commands
15:20 If they **o** my teaching,
17: 6 and they have **o** your word.
Ac　7:53 through angels but have not **o** it."
Ro　6:17 you wholeheartedly **o** the form of
Php　2:12 as you have always **o**—
Heb 11: 8 **o** and went, even though he did not
1Pe　3: 6 who **o** Abraham and called him

OBEYING* [OBEY]

Dt　8:20 so you will be destroyed for not **o**
1Sa 15:22 as in **o** the voice of the LORD?
Ps 119: 5 were steadfast in **o** your decrees!
Jer 16:12 of his evil heart instead of **o** me.
Gal　5: 7 and kept you from **o** the truth?
1Pe　1:22 purified yourselves by **o** the truth

OBEYS [OBEY]

Lev 18: 5 who **o** them will live by them.
Ne　9:29 by which a man will live if he **o**
Pr 19:16 He who **o** instructions guards his life,
Eze 20:11 man who **o** them will live by them.
Jn 14:21 has my commands and **o** them,
Ro　2:27 yet **o** the law will condemn you who,
1Jn　2: 5 But if anyone **o** his word,

OBJECTS

Ro　9:23 glory known to the **o** of his mercy,
Eph　2: 3 we were by nature **o** of wrath.

OBLATION(S) (KJV) See GIFTS, OFFERING(S), PORTION, SACRIFICE

OBLIGATE* [OBLIGATED, OBLIGATION, OBLIGATIONS]

Nu 30: 2 an oath to **o** himself by a pledge,

OBLIGATED [OBLIGATE]

Ro　1:14 I am **o** both to Greeks
Gal　5: 3 be circumcised that he is **o**

OBLIGATION [OBLIGATE]

Ro　8:12 Therefore, brothers, we have an **o**—

OBLIGATIONS* [OBLIGATE]

Nu　3: 8 fulfilling the **o** of the Israelites
1Ki　9:25 and so fulfilled the temple **o**.

OBSCENITY*

Eph　5: 4 Nor should there be **o**,

OBSCURES*

Job 42: 3 'Who is this that **o** my counsel

OBSERVANCE* [OBSERVE]

Ex 13: 9 This **o** will be for you like a sign
Ezr　7:10 and **o** of the Law of the LORD,

OBSERVATION* [OBSERVE]

Lk 17:20 does not come with your careful **o,**

OBSERVE [OBSERVANCE, OBSERVATION, OBSERVES, OBSERVING]

Ex 31:13 'You must **o** my Sabbaths.
Lev 25: 2 the land itself must **o** a sabbath to
Dt   4: 6 **O** them carefully, for this will show
     5:12 "**O** the Sabbath day
     8: 6 the commands of the LORD
    11:22 If you carefully **o** all these
    26:16 carefully **o** them with all your heart
Ps 37:37 Consider the blameless, **o** the upright
Mk   7: 9 in order to **o** your own traditions!
Ro   2:25 Circumcision has value if you **o**
Gal 3: 5 among you because you **o** the law,

OBSERVES* [OBSERVE]

Ps 11: 4 He **o** the sons of men;

OBSERVING [OBSERVE]

Ro   3:20 righteous in his sight by **o** the law;
     3:27 On that of **o** the law?
Gal 2:16 know that a man is not justified by **o**
     3: 2 Did you receive the Spirit by **o**
     3:10 All who rely on **o** law are under

OBSOLETE*

Heb 8:13 made the first one **o;** and what is **o**
              and aging will soon disappear.

OBSTACLE* [OBSTACLES]

Ro 14:13 not to put any stumbling block or **o**

OBSTACLES* [OBSTACLE]

Isa 57:14 the **o** out of the way of my people."
Jer   6:21 "I will put **o** before this people.
Ro   16:17 and put **o** in your way that are

OBSTINATE

Isa 65: 2 held out my hands to an **o** people,
Eze   3: 7 house of Israel is hardened and **o.**
Ro   10:21 hands to a disobedient and **o** people."

OBTAIN [OBTAINED, OBTAINS]

Ro 11: 7 Israel sought so earnestly it did not **o,**
2Ti 2:10 that they too may **o** the salvation

OBTAINED [OBTAIN]

Ro   9:30 have **o** it, a righteousness that
Php 3:12 Not that I have already **o** all this,
Heb 9:12 having **o** eternal redemption.

OBTAINS* [OBTAIN]

Pr 12: 2 good man **o** favor from the LORD,

OBVIOUS*

Mt   6:18 be **o** to men that you are fasting,
Gal 5:19 The acts of the sinful nature are **o:**
1Ti 5:24 The sins of some men are **o,**
     5:25 In the same way, good deeds are **o,**

OCCASIONS*

Zec 8:19 joyful and glad **o** and happy festivals
Eph 6:18 And pray in the Spirit on all **o**

ODED

2Ch 28: 9 prophet of the LORD named **O** was

ODOR*

Jn 11:39 "by this time there is a bad **o,**

ODOUR (KJV) See AROMA

OFFEND* [OFFENDED, OFFENDERS, OFFENSE, OFFENSES, OFFENSIVE]

Job 34:31 'I am guilty but will **o** no more.
Mt 17:27 "But so that we may not **o** them,
Jn   6:61 Jesus said to them, "Does this **o** you?

OFFENDED [OFFEND]

Pr 18:19 An **o** brother is more unyielding than

OFFENDERS* [OFFEND]

1Co 6: 9 male prostitutes nor homosexual **o**

OFFENSE [OFFEND]

Dt 19:15 or **o** he may have committed.
    21:22 If a man guilty of a capital **o** is put
Pr 17: 9 over an **o** promotes love,
    19:11 to his glory to overlook an **o.**
Mk   6: 3 And they took **o** at him.
Gal 5:11 the **o** of the cross has been abolished.

OFFENSES [OFFEND]

Job 7:21 Why do you not pardon my **o**
Isa 44:22 I have swept away your **o** like
    59:12 For our **o** are many in your sight,
Eze 18:30 Turn away from all your **o;**
    33:10 "Our **o** and sins weigh us down,

OFFENSIVE [OFFEND]

Ps 139:24 See if there is any **o** way in me,

OFFER [OFFERED, OFFERING, OFFERINGS, OFFERS]

Ex 29:38 to **o** on the altar regularly each day:
Dt 12:14 **O** them only at the place the LORD
Ps   4: 5 **O** right sacrifices and trust in
Isa 1:15 even if you **o** many prayers,
Jer 7:16 nor **o** any plea or petition for them;
Hos 14: 2 that we may **o** the fruit of our lips.
Mic 6: 7 Shall I **o** my firstborn for my
Mt   5:24 then come and **o** your gift.
Ro   6:13 not **o** the parts of your body to sin,
    12: 1 to **o** your bodies as living sacrifices,
Heb 9:25 to **o** himself again and again,
    13:15 let us continually **o** to God a sacrifice

OFFERED [OFFER]

Lev 10: 1 and they **o** unauthorized fire before
1Sa 13: 9 And Saul **o** up the burnt offering.
1Ki 3: 4 and Solomon **o** a thousand burnt
Ps 106:28 ate sacrifices **o** to lifeless gods;
Isa 50: 6 I **o** my back to those who beat me,
Mt 27:34 There they **o** Jesus wine to drink,

1Co 9:13 serve at the altar share in what is **o**,
    10:20 sacrifices of pagans are **o** to demons,
Heb 7:27 once for all when he **o** himself.
    9:14 through the eternal Spirit **o** himself
    11: 4 By faith Abel **o** God a better
    11:17 of Isaac as a sacrifice.
Jas 5:15 And the prayer **o** in faith will make

OFFERING [OFFER]

Ge 4: 4 looked with favor on Abel and his **o**,
    22: 2 Sacrifice him there as a burnt **o**
    22: 8 provide the lamb for the burnt **o**,
Ex 29:14 It is a sin **o**.
    29:18 It is a burnt **o** to the LORD,
    29:18 an **o** made to the LORD by fire.
    29:24 before the LORD as a wave **o**.
    29:40 quarter of a hin of wine as a drink **o**.
Lev 1: 3 **o** is a burnt **o** from the herd,
    2: 1 " 'When someone brings a grain **o** to
    3: 1 " 'If someone's **o** is a fellowship **o**,
    4: 3 a young bull without defect as a sin **o**
    5:15 It is a guilt **o**.
    7:37 the regulations for the burnt **o**, the
        grain **o**, the sin **o**, the guilt **o**, the
        ordination **o** and the fellowship **o**,
    9:24 consumed the burnt **o** and the fat
1Sa 13: 9 And Saul offered up the burnt **o**.
1Ch 21:26 from heaven on the altar of burnt **o**.
2Ch 7: 1 and consumed the burnt **o** and
Ezr 6:17 as a sin **o** for all Israel,
Ps 40: 6 Sacrifice and **o** you did not desire,
    116:17 I will sacrifice a thank **o** to you
Isa 53:10 the LORD makes his life a guilt **o**,
Mt 5:23 if you are **o** your gift at the altar
Ro 8: 3 likeness of sinful man to be a sin **o**.
Eph 5: 2 gave himself up for us as a fragrant **o**
Php 2:17 I am being poured out like a drink **o**
    4:18 They are a fragrant **o**,
2Ti 4: 6 being poured out like a drink **o**,
Heb 10: 5 "Sacrifice and **o** you did not desire,
1Pe 2: 5 **o** spiritual sacrifices acceptable to

BURNT OFFERING See BURNT

DRINK OFFERING See DRINK

FELLOWSHIP OFFERING
See FELLOWSHIP

GRAIN OFFERING See GRAIN

GUILT OFFERING See GUILT

SIN OFFERING See SIN

WAVE OFFERING See WAVE

OFFERINGS [OFFER]

Ge 8:20 he sacrificed burnt **o** on it.
Ex 40:29 offered on it burnt **o** and grain **o**,
1Sa 15:22 "Does the LORD delight in burnt **o**
Ps 40: 6 and sin **o** you did not require.
    50:14 Sacrifice thank **o** to God,
Isa 1:13 Stop bringing meaningless **o**!
Jer 6:20 Your burnt **o** are not acceptable;
Hos 6: 6 of God rather than burnt **o**.
Mal 3: 8 "In tithes and **o**.
Mk 12:33 is more important than all burnt **o**
Heb 10: 6 with burnt **o** and sin **o** you were not

BURNT OFFERINGS See BURNT

DRINK OFFERINGS See DRINK

FELLOWSHIP OFFERINGS
See FELLOWSHIP

GRAIN OFFERINGS See GRAIN

GUILT OFFERINGS See GUILT

SIN OFFERINGS See SIN

OFFERS [OFFER]

Heb 10:11 and again he **o** the same sacrifices,

OFFICER [OFFICERS, OFFICIAL]

2Ti 2: 4 wants to please his commanding **o**.

OFFICERS [OFFICER]

Ex 15: 4 The best of Pharaoh's **o** are drowned

OFFICIALS [OFFICER]

Ex 5:21 us a stench to Pharaoh and his **o**
    9:20 Those **o** of Pharaoh who feared
Pr 17:26 or to flog **o** for their integrity.
    29:12 all his **o** become wicked.
Jer 52:10 also killed all the **o** of Judah.
Mk 10:42 and their high **o** exercise authority

OFFSCOURING (KJV) See SCUM

OFFSPRING

Ge 3:15 and between your **o** and hers;
    12: 7 "To your **o** I will give this land."
    13:16 I will make your **o** like the dust of
    26: 4 through your **o** all nations on earth
    28:14 be blessed through you and your **o**.
Ex 13:12 the LORD the first **o** of every womb.
Ru 4:12 Through the **o** the LORD gives you
2Sa 7:12 I will raise up your **o** to succeed you,
Isa 44: 3 I will pour out my Spirit on your **o**,
    53:10 he will see his **o** and prolong
Mal 2:15 Because he was seeking godly **o**.
Ac 3:25 'Through your **o** all peoples on earth
    17:28 'We are his **o**.'
    17:29 "Therefore since we are God's **o**,
Ro 4:18 "So shall your **o** be."
    9: 8 who are regarded as Abraham's **o**.
Rev 22:16 I am the Root and the **O** of David,

OFTEN

Lk 13:34 how **o** I have longed to gather your
Jn 18: 2 because Jesus had **o** met there

OG

Nu 21:33 **O** king of Bashan and his whole
Dt 31: 4 to them what he did to Sihon and **O**,
Ps 136:20 and **O** king of Bashan—

OHOLIAB⁺

Craftsman who worked on the tabernacle (Ex 31:6; 35:34; 36:1-2; 38:23).

OIL

Ge 28:18 and poured **o** on top of it.
    35:14 he also poured **o** on it.
Ex 25: 6 olive **o** for the light; spices for the
        anointing **o**

29: 7 Take the anointing **o** and anoint him
30:25 It will be the sacred anointing **o.**
Dt 14:23 tithe of your grain, new wine and **o,**
1Sa 10: 1 Samuel took a flask of **o** and
16:13 So Samuel took the horn of **o**
1Ki 17:16 the jug of **o** did not run dry.
2Ki 4: 6 Then the **o** stopped flowing.
Ps 23: 5 You anoint my head with **o;**
45: 7 by anointing you with the **o** of joy.
104:15 **o** to make his face shine,
133: 2 like precious **o** poured on the head,
Pr 5: 3 and her speech is smoother than **o;**
21:17 and **o** will never be rich.
Isa 1: 6 or bandaged or soothed with **o.**
61: 3 **o** of gladness instead of mourning,
Joel 2:24 will overflow with new wine and **o.**
Mt 25: 3 but did not take any **o** with them.
Heb 1: 9 by anointing you with the **o** of joy."
Jas 5:14 and anoint him with **o** in the name of

ANOINTING OIL Ex 25:6; 29:7, 21; 30:25, 25, 31; 31:11; 35:8, 15, 28; 37:29; 39:38; 40:9; Lev 8:2, 10, 12, 30; 10:7; 21:10, 12; Nu 4:16

OLIVE OIL Ex 25:6; 30:24; 35:8, 28; Nu 11:8; 18:12; Dt 8:8; 1Ki 5:11; 1Ch 27:28; 2Ch 2:10, 15; 11:11; Ezr 7:22; Job 29:6; Isa 57:9; Eze 16:13, 19; Hos 12:1; Lk 16:6; Rev 18:13

OLD [OLDER]

Ge 17:12 eight days **o** must be circumcised,
17:17 born to a man a hundred years **o?**
21: 7 I have borne him a son in his **o** age."
Nu 1: 3 in Israel twenty years **o** or more
14:29 every one of you twenty years **o**
Dt 32: 7 Remember the days of **o;**
Ps 71: 9 Do not cast me away when I am **o;**
74:12 you, O God, are my king from of **o;**
Pr 20:29 gray hair the splendor of the **o.**
22: 6 when he is **o** he will not turn from it.
La 5:21 renew our days as of **o**
Joel 2:28 your **o** men will dream dreams,
Mic 5: 2 whose origins are from of **o,**
Mk 2:22 pours new wine into **o** wineskins.
Jn 3: 4 can a man be born when he is **o?**"
Ac 2:17 your **o** men will dream dreams.
Ro 4:19 since he was about a hundred years **o**
1Co 5: 7 Get rid of the **o** yeast that you
2Co 5:17 the **o** has gone, the new has come!
Eph 4:22 to put off your **o** self,
Heb 8: 6 is superior to the **o** one,
1Jn 2: 7 a new command but an **o** one,
Rev 21: 4 for the **o** order of things has passed

OLDER [OLD]

1Ti 5: 1 Do not rebuke an **o** man harshly,
5: 2 **o** women as mothers,
Tit 2: 2 Teach the **o** men to be temperate,
2: 3 teach the **o** women to be reverent in
1Pe 5: 5 be submissive to those who are **o.**

OLIVE [OLIVES]

Ge 8:11 a freshly plucked **o** leaf!
Ex 25: 6 **o** oil for the light;
Jdg 9: 8 They said to the **o** tree,
Ps 52: 8 like an **o** tree flourishing in the house

Jer 11:16 LORD called you a thriving **o** tree
Hab 3:17 though the **o** crop fails and
Zec 4: 3 Also there are two **o** trees by it,
Ro 11:17 and you, though a wild **o** shoot,
11:24 grafted into a cultivated **o** tree,
Rev 11: 4 two **o** trees and the two lampstands

OLIVE OIL See OIL

OLIVES [OLIVE]

Dt 24:20 When you beat the **o** from your trees,
Zec 14: 4 the Mount of **O** will be split in two
Mt 24: 3 Jesus was sitting on the Mount of **O,**
Jas 3:12 My brothers, can a fig tree bear **o,**

MOUNT OF OLIVES See MOUNT

OMEGA*

Rev 1: 8 "I am the Alpha and the **O,**"
21: 6 I am the Alpha and the **O,**
22:13 I am the Alpha and the **O,**

OMENS*

Dt 18:10 interprets **o,** engages in witchcraft,

OMIT*

Jer 26: 2 do not **o** a word.

OMNIPOTENT (KJV) See ALMIGHTY

OMRI

King of Israel (1Ki 16:21-26).

ONAN

Ge 38: 8 Then Judah said to **O,**
46:12 The sons of Judah: Er, **O,** Shelah,

ONCE [ONE]

Ge 18:32 but let me speak just **o** more.
Ex 30:10 **O** a year Aaron shall make
Job 40: 5 I spoke **o,** but I have no answer—
La 1: 1 so full of people!
Ro 6:10 he died to sin **o** for all;
7: 9 **O** I was alive apart from law;
Eph 5: 8 For you were **o** darkness,
Heb 7:27 He sacrificed for their sins **o** for all
9:12 but he entered the Most Holy Place **o**
9:27 Just as man is destined to die **o,**
1Pe 2:10 **O** you were not a people,
3:18 For Christ died for sins **o** for all,

ONE [ONCE, ONES]

Ge 2:24 and they will become **o** flesh.
Ex 12: 3 **o** for each household.
Nu 1: 2 listing every man by name, **o** by **o.**
Dt 6: 4 The LORD our God, the LORD is **o.**
Jos 23:10 **O** of you routs a thousand,
Ps 14: 3 no **o** who does good, not even **o.**
Ecc 4: 9 Two are better than **o,**
Isa 30:17 thousand will flee at the threat of **o;**
Eze 34:23 I will place over them **o** shepherd,
37:22 I will make them **o** nation in the land
Zec 14: 9 On that day there will be **o** LORD,
Mal 2:10 Have we not all **o** Father?
Mk 10: 8 and the two will become **o** flesh.'
10:21 "**O** thing you lack," he said.

12:29 "The most important **o**,"
Lk 10:42 but only **o** thing is needed.
Jn 1:14 the glory of the **O** and Only,
1:18 but God the **O** and Only,
3:16 that he gave his **o** and only Son,
10:16 there shall be **o** flock and **o** shepherd.
10:30 I and the Father are **o**."
Ro 3:10 "There is no **o** righteous, not even **o**;
5:15 that came by the grace of the **o** man,
13: 9 are summed up in this **o** rule:
1Co 6:16 "The two will become **o** flesh."
8: 4 and that there is no God but **o**.
10:17 we, who are many, are **o** body,
12:13 For we were all baptized by **o** Spirit
into **o** body—
Eph 4: 5 **o** Lord, **o** faith, **o** baptism;
1Ti 2: 5 For there is **o** God and **o** mediator
3: 2 the husband of but **o** wife, temperate,
3:12 be the husband of but **o** wife
Tit 1: 6 the husband of but **o** wife,
2Pe 3: 8 But do not forget this **o** thing,

ANOINTED ONE See ANOINTED

HOLY ONE See HOLY

MIGHTY ONE See MIGHTY

ONE ANOTHER Ge 42:21; Lev 19:11; 26:37;
Jdg 20:22; 2Ki 7:6; 2Ch 20:23; Est 9:22; Job
41:17; Isa 6:3; Jer 9:20; 22:8; 23:27, 30; Eze 1:9;
Zec 7:9; Mal 2:10; Mk 8:16; 12:7; 14:4; Lk 2:15;
6:11; 8:25; 12:1; Jn 5:44; 7:35; 11:56; 12:19;
13:22, 34, 34, 35; 16:17, 19; 19:24; Ac 2:12;
26:31; Ro 1:24, 27; 12:10, 10, 16; 13:8; 14:13;
15:7, 14; 16:16; 1Co 1:10; 16:20; 2Co 13:12; Gal
5:13; Eph 4:2, 32; 5:19, 21; Col 3:13, 16; 1Th
5:11; Tit 3:3; Heb 3:13; 10:24, 25; Jas 4:11; 1Pe
1:22; 3:8; 4:9; 5:5, 14; 1Jn 1:7; 3:11, 23; 4:7, 11,
12; 2Jn 1:5

ONES [ONE]
Dt 33: 3 the holy **o** are in your hand.
1Ch 16:13 O sons of Jacob, his chosen, **o**.
Ps 37:28 and will not forsake his faithful **o**.
105:15 "Do not touch my anointed **o**;
Mt 18: 6 of these little **o** who believe in me
1Th 3:13 Lord Jesus comes with all his holy **o**.
Jude 1:14 upon thousands of his holy **o**

HOLY ONES See HOLY

ONESIMUS*
Col 4: 9 He is coming with **O**,
Phm 1:10 I appeal to you for my son **O**,

ONESIPHORUS*
2Ti 1:16 show mercy to the household of **O**,
4:19 and Aquila and the household of **O**.

ONIONS*
Nu 11: 5 melons, leeks, **o** and garlic.

ONLY
Ge 6: 5 of his heart was **o** evil all the time.
7:23 O Noah was left,
22: 2 your **o** son, Isaac, whom you love,
Nu 11: 4 "If **o** we had meat to eat!"

14: 2 "If **o** we had died in Egypt!
20: 3 "If **o** we had died when our
Dt 15: 5 if **o** you fully obey the LORD
1Ki 18:22 "I am the **o** one of the LORD's
Job 23: 3 If **o** I knew where to find him;
Ps 30: 5 For his anger lasts **o** a moment,
Pr 30: 8 but give me **o** my daily bread.
Jer 23:23 "Am I a **o** God nearby,"
Mt 4:10 and serve him **o**.' "
7:14 and **o** a few find it.
Mk 13:32 nor the Son, but **o** the Father.
Jn 1:14 the glory of the One and **O**,
1:18 but God the One and **O**,
3:16 that he gave his one and **o** Son,
Ro 3:29 Is God the God of Jews **o**?
1Ti 1:17 immortal, invisible, the **o** God,
1Jn 4: 9 He sent his one and **o** Son

ONYX
Ex 28: 9 "Take two **o** stones and engrave
28:20 an **o** and a jasper.

OPEN [OPENED, OPENHANDED,
OPENING, OPENS]
Dt 28:12 The LORD will **o** the heavens,
Ps 78: 2 I will **o** my mouth in parables,
118:19 **O** for me the gates of righteousness;
145:16 You **o** your hand and satisfy
Pr 15:11 Death and Destruction lie **o** before
27: 5 Better is **o** rebuke than hidden love.
SS 5: 2 My lover is knocking: "**O** to me,
Isa 42: 7 to **o** eyes that are blind,
53: 7 yet he did not **o** his mouth;
Mal 3:10 throw **o** the floodgates of heaven
Mt 13:35 "I will **o** my mouth in parables,
17:27 the first fish you catch; **o** its mouth
Mk 1:10 he saw heaven being torn **o** and
Ac 7:56 "I see heaven **o** and the Son of Man
Rev 3: 8 I have placed before you an **o** door
4: 1 before me was a door standing **o**
5: 2 to break the seals and **o** the scroll?"
19:11 I saw heaven standing **o** and there

OPENED [OPEN]
Ge 3: 7 the eyes of both of them were **o**,
Nu 16:32 and the earth **o** its mouth
Ne 8: 5 Ezra **o** the book.
Ps 105:41 He **o** the rock, and water gushed out;
Isa 35: 5 Then will the eyes of the blind be **o**
50: 5 Sovereign LORD has **o** my ears,
Da 7:10 and the books were **o**.
Zec 13: 1 "On that day a fountain will be **o** to
Mt 3:16 At that moment heaven was **o**,
Lk 11: 9 knock and the door will be **o** to you.
24:45 Then he **o** their minds
Ac 10:11 He saw heaven **o** and something like
Heb 10:20 by a new and living way **o** for us
Rev 6: 1 I watched as the Lamb **o** the first of
11:19 Then God's temple in heaven was **o**,
20:12 and books were **o**.

OPENHANDED* [OPEN, HAND]
Dt 15: 8 Rather be **o** and freely lend him
15:11 to be **o** toward your brothers

OPENING [OPEN]

Mk 2: 4 made an **o** in the roof above Jesus

OPENS [OPEN]

Isa 22:22 what he **o** no one can shut,
Rev 3: 7 What he **o** no one can shut,
    3:20 hears my voice and **o** the door,

OPHIR

1Ki 10:11 Hiram's ships brought gold from **O**;
Isa 13:12 more rare than the gold of **O**.

OPINIONS*

1Ki 18:21 will you waver between two **o**?
Pr 18: 2 but delights in airing his own **o**.

OPPONENTS* [OPPOSE]

Pr 18:18 and keeps strong **o** apart.
Lk 13:17 all his **o** were humiliated,

OPPORTUNE* [OPPORTUNITY]

Mk 6:21 Finally the **o** time came.
Lk 4:13 he left him until an **o** time.

OPPORTUNITY [OPPORTUNE]

Mt 26:16 From then on Judas watched for an **o**
Ac 25:16 and has had an **o** to defend himself
Ro 7: 8 But sin, seizing the **o** afforded by
2Co 5: 5 giving you an **o** to take pride in us,
    11:12 an **o** to be considered equal with us
Gal 6:10 Therefore, as we have **o**,
Eph 5:16 making the most of every **o**,
Php 4:10 but you had no **o** to show it.
Col 4: 5 make the most of every **o**.
1Ti 5:14 to give the enemy no **o** for slander.
Heb 11:15 they would have had **o** to return.

OPPOSE [OPPONENTS, OPPOSED, OPPOSES, OPPOSING, OPPOSITION]

Ex 23:22 and will **o** those who **o** you.
Nu 16: 3 They came as a group to **o** Moses
1Sa 2:10 who **o** the Lᴏʀᴅ will be shattered.
Job 23:13 he stands alone, and who can **o** him?
Ps 55:18 even though many **o** me.
Ac 11:17 to think that I could **o** God?"
2Ti 2:25 who **o** him he must gently instruct,
    3: 8 so also these men **o** the truth—
Tit 1: 9 and refute those who **o** it.
    2: 8 so that those who **o** you may

OPPOSED [OPPOSE]

Gal 2:11 I **o** him to his face,
    3:21 therefore, **o** to the promises of God?
2Ti 3: 8 Just as Jannes and Jambres **o** Moses,

OPPOSES* [OPPOSE]

Mk 3:26 if Satan **o** himself and is divided,
Lk 23: 2 He **o** payment of taxes to Caesar
Jn 19:12 claims to be a king **o** Caesar."
Jas 4: 6 "God **o** the proud but gives grace to
1Pe 5: 5 "God **o** the proud but gives grace to

OPPOSING [OPPOSE]

1Ti 6:20 the **o** ideas of what is falsely called

OPPOSITION [OPPOSE]

Nu 16:42 the assembly gathered in **o** to Moses
    20: 2 the people gathered in **o** to Moses
Heb 12: 3 Consider him who endured such **o**

OPPRESS [OPPRESSED, OPPRESSES, OPPRESSION, OPPRESSOR, OPPRESSORS]

Ex 1:11 to **o** them with forced labor,
    22:21 "Do not mistreat an alien or **o** him,
1Ch 17: 9 Wicked people will not **o** them
Ps 105:14 He allowed no one to **o** them;
Isa 3: 5 People will **o** each other—
Eze 22:29 they **o** the poor and needy and
Da 7:25 the Most High and **o** his saints
Am 5:12 You **o** the righteous and take bribes
Zec 7:10 Do not **o** the widow or the fatherless,
Mal 3: 5 who **o** the widows and the fatherless,

OPPRESSED [OPPRESS]

Ex 1:12 But the more they were **o**,
Jdg 2:18 as they groaned under those who **o**
Ne 9:27 they were **o** they cried out to you.
Ps 9: 9 The Lᴏʀᴅ is a refuge for the **o**,
    82: 3 the rights of the poor and **o**.
    103: 6 and justice for all the **o**.
    146: 7 He upholds the cause of the **o**
Pr 16:19 among the **o** than to share plunder
    31: 5 and deprive all the **o** of their rights.
Isa 1:17 Seek justice, encourage the **o**.
    53: 7 He was **o** and afflicted,
    58:10 and satisfy the needs of the **o**,
Zep 3:19 I will deal with all who **o** you;
Zec 10: 2 like sheep **o** for lack of a shepherd.
Lk 4:18 to release the **o**,

OPPRESSES* [OPPRESS]

Pr 14:31 He who **o** the poor shows contempt
    22:16 He who **o** the poor to increase
    28: 3 A ruler who **o** the poor is like
Eze 18:12 He **o** the poor and needy.

OPPRESSION [OPPRESS]

Dt 26: 7 and saw our misery, toil and **o**.
Ps 12: 5 "Because of the **o** of the weak
    72:14 He will rescue them from **o**
    119:134 Redeem me from the **o** of men,
Isa 53: 8 By **o** and judgment he was taken
    58: 9 "If you do away with the yoke of **o**,
Eze 45: 9 and **o** and do what is just and right.

OPPRESSOR [OPPRESS]

Ps 72: 4 he will crush the **o**.
Isa 51:13 For where is the wrath of the **o**?
Jer 22: 3 Rescue from the hand of his **o**

OPPRESSORS [OPPRESS]

Jdg 6: 9 and from the hand of all your **o**.
Zep 3: 1 Woe to the city of **o**,

ORACLE [ORACLES]

Nu 23: 7 Then Balaam uttered his **o**:
2Sa 23: 1 "The **o** of David son of Jesse,

Ps   36: 1 An **o** is within my heart concerning
Jer   23:33 'What is the **o** of the LORD?'

ORACLES* [ORACLE]

La   2:14 The **o** they gave you were false

ORDAIN [ORDAINED, ORDINATION]

Ex   29: 9 In this way you shall **o** Aaron

ORDAINED [ORDAIN]

Ps   8: 2 and infants you have **o** praise
      111: 9 he **o** his covenant forever—
      139:16 All the days **o** for me were written
Isa   37:26 Long ago I **o** it.
Eze   28:14 for so I **o** you.
Hab   1:12 you have **o** them to punish.
Mt   21:16 and infants you have **o** praise'?"

ORDER [ORDERLY, ORDERS]

Nu   9:23 They obeyed the LORD's **o**,
Dt   8: 2 in **o** to know what was in your heart,
2Ch   36:22 in **o** to fulfill the word of the LORD
Ps   110: 4 in the **o** of Melchizedek."
Mk   7: 9 in **o** to observe your own traditions!
Ro   7: 4 in **o** that we might bear fruit to God.
Heb   5:10 high priest in the **o** of Melchizedek.
       9:10 until the time of the new **o**.
Rev   21: 4 the old **o** of things has passed away."

ORDERLY* [ORDER]

Lk   1: 3 to me to write an **o** account for you,
1Co   14:40 be done in a fitting and **o** way.
Col   2: 5 and delight to see how **o** you are and

ORDERS [ORDER]

Mk   1:27 He even gives **o** to evil spirits
       3:12 But he gave them strict **o** not
       9: 9 Jesus gave them **o** not to tell
Ac   5:28 "We gave you strict **o** not to teach

ORDINANCE [ORDINANCES]

Ex   12:17 Celebrate this day as a lasting **o** for
      29: 9 priesthood is theirs by a lasting **o**.

A LASTING ORDINANCE See LASTING

ORDINANCES [ORDINANCE]

Ps   19: 9 The **o** of the LORD are sure

ORDINARY

Ac   4:13 that they were unschooled, **o** men,
Heb   11:23 because they saw he was no **o** child,

ORDINATION [ORDAIN]

Ex   29:22 (This is the ram for the **o**.)

OREB

Jdg   7:25 the Midianite leaders, **O** and Zeeb.
Ps   83:11 Make their nobles like **O** and Zeeb.

ORGIES*

Ro   13:13 not in **o** and drunkenness,
Gal   5:21 envy; drunkenness, **o**, and the like.
1Pe   4: 3 **o**, carousing and detestable idolatry.

ORIGIN* [ORIGINAL, ORIGINATE, ORIGINS]

Est   6:13 of Jewish **o**, you cannot stand against
Ac   5:38 or activity is of human **o**, it will fail.
2Pe   1:21 For prophecy never had its **o** in

ORIGINAL* [ORIGIN]

2Ch   24:13 the temple of God according to its **o**

ORIGINATE* [ORIGIN]

1Co   14:36 Did the word of God **o** with you?

ORIGINS* [ORIGIN]

Mic   5: 2 whose **o** are from of old,

ORION

Job   9: 9 He is the Maker of the Bear and **O**,

ORNAMENT* [ORNAMENTED, ORNAMENTS]

Pr   3:22 an **o** to grace your neck.
      25:12 Like an earring of gold or an **o**

ORNAMENTED [ORNAMENT]

Ge   37: 3 and he made a richly **o** robe for him.

ORNAMENTS [ORNAMENT]

Ex   33: 6 So the Israelites stripped off their **o**

ORPAH

Ru   1: 4 one named **O** and the other Ruth.

ORPHAN* [ORPHANS]

Ex   22:22 take advantage of a widow or an **o**.

ORPHANS [ORPHAN]

Jn   14:18 I will not leave you as **o**;
Jas   1:27 after **o** and widows in their distress

OSEE (KJV) See HOSEA

OSHEA (KJV) See JOSHUA

OTHER [OTHER'S, OTHERS, OTHERWISE]

Ge   28:17 none **o** than the house of God;
Ex   20: 3 "You shall have no **o** gods
      23:13 Do not invoke the names of **o** gods;
Dt   4:35 besides him there is no **o**.
Jdg   2:19 following **o** gods and serving
1Sa   8:20 we will be like all the **o** nations,
1Ki   11: 4 turned his heart after **o** gods,
2Ki   17: 7 They worshiped **o** gods
2Ch   2: 5 our God is greater than all **o** gods.
Ps   147:20 He has done this for no **o** nation;
Isa   44: 8 No, there is no **o** Rock;
      45: 5 I am the LORD, and there is no **o**;
Jer   7: 6 not follow **o** gods to your own harm,
Da   3:29 for no **o** god can save in this way."
Mt   6:24 he will hate the one and love the **o**,
Lk   17:34 one will be taken and the **o** left.
Jn   20:30 Jesus did many **o** miraculous signs in
      21:25 Jesus did many **o** things as well.
1Pe   4: 8 Above all, love each **o** deeply,

2Pe 3:16 as they do the **o** Scriptures,
Rev 3:15 I wish you were either one or the **o**!

NO OTHER Ex 20:3; Nu 5:19; Dt 4:35, 39; 5:7;
1Sa 18:25; 1Ki 8:60; 1Ch 23:17; Ps 147:20; Isa
44:8; 45:5, 6, 14, 14, 18, 22; 46:9; Eze 31:14, 14;
Da 3:29; Joel 2:27; Mk 12:32; Ac 4:12; 1Co
11:16; Gal 5:10

OTHER GODS Ex 18:11; 20:3; 23:13; Dt 5:7;
6:14; 7:4; 8:19; 11:16, 28; 13:2, 6, 13; 17:3;
18:20; 28:14, 36, 64; 29:26; 30:17; 31:18, 20; Jos
23:16; 24:2, 16; Jdg 2:17, 19; 10:13; 1Sa 8:8;
26:19; 1Ki 9:6, 9; 11:4, 10; 14:9; 2Ki 17:7, 35,
37, 38; 22:17; 2Ch 2:5; 7:19, 22; 28:25; 34:25; Ps
16:4; Jer 1:16; 7:6, 9, 18; 11:10; 13:10; 16:11, 13;
19:13; 22:9; 25:6; 32:29; 35:15; 44:3, 5, 8, 15;
Hos 3:1

OTHER'S* [OTHER]

Ro 1:12 mutually encouraged by each **o** faith.
Gal 6: 2 Carry each **o** burdens,

OTHERS [OTHER]

1Sa 9: 2 a head taller than any of the **o**.
Pr 10:17 ignores correction leads **o** astray.
SS 5: 9 How is your beloved better than **o**,
Da 12: 2 **o** to shame and everlasting contempt.
Mt 7: 2 For in the same way you judge **o**,
7:12 do to **o** what you would have them
Lk 6:31 Do to **o** as you would have them do
Php 2: 3 consider **o** better than yourselves.

OTHERWISE [OTHER]

Isa 6:10 **O** they might see with their eyes,
Mt 13:15 **O** they might see with their eyes,
Ac 28:27 **O** they might see with their eyes,

OTHNIEL

Nephew of Caleb (Jos 15:15-19; Jdg 1:12-15).
Judge who freed Israel from Aram (Jdg 3:7-11).

OUGHT

Ro 1:28 to do what **o** not to be done.
12: 3 of yourself more highly than you **o**,
Jas 4:17 the good he **o** to do and doesn't do it,
2Pe 3:11 what kind of people **o** you to be?
1Jn 3:16 And we **o** to lay down our lives
3Jn 1: 8 We **o** therefore to show hospitality

OUTBURSTS*

2Co 12:20 **o** of anger, factions, slander, gossip,

OUTCOME

Isa 41:22 and know their final **o**.
Da 12: 8 what will the **o** of all this be?"
Heb 13: 7 Consider the **o** of their way of life
1Pe 4:17 what will the **o** be for those who do

OUTNUMBER [NUMBER]

Ps 139:18 they would **o** the grains of sand.

OUTPOURED* [POUR]

Ps 79:10 avenge the **o** blood of your servants.
Eze 20:33 outstretched arm and with **o** wrath.
20:34 outstretched arm and with **o** wrath.

OUTPOURING* [POUR]

Eze 9: 8 this **o** of your wrath on Jerusalem?"

OUTSIDE [OUTSIDERS]

Pr 22:13 sluggard says, "There is a lion **o**!"
Mt 22:13 and throw him **o**, into the darkness,
Lk 11:39 you Pharisees clean the **o** of the cup
13:33 no prophet can die **o** Jerusalem!
1Co 5:13 God will judge those **o**.
Heb 13:12 so Jesus also suffered **o** the city gate
Rev 22:15 **O** are the dogs,

OUTSIDE THE CAMP See CAMP

OUTSIDERS* [OUTSIDE]

Col 4: 5 Be wise in the way you act toward **o**;
1Th 4:12 the respect of **o** and so that you will
1Ti 3: 7 also have a good reputation with **o**,

OUTSTANDING

SS 5:10 **o** among ten thousand.
Ac 4:16 knows they have done an **o** miracle,
Ro 13: 8 Let no debt remain **o**,

OUTSTRETCHED [STRETCH]

Ex 6: 6 and I will redeem you with an **o** arm
Dt 4:34 by a mighty hand and an **o** arm,
1Ki 8:42 and your **o** arm—
Ps 136:12 with a mighty hand and an **o** arm;
Isa 3:16 walking along with **o** necks,
Jer 27: 5 and **o** arm I made the earth
32:17 by your great power and **o** arm.
Eze 20:33 with a mighty hand and an **o** arm and

OUTSTRETCHED ARM Ex 6:6; Dt 4:34;
5:15; 7:19; 9:29; 11:2; 26:8; 1Ki 8:42; 2Ki 17:36;
2Ch 6:32; Ps 136:12; Jer 27:5; 32:17, 21; Eze
20:33, 34

OUTWARD* [OUTWARDLY]

1Sa 16: 7 Man looks at the **o** appearance,
Ro 2:28 nor is circumcision merely **o**
1Pe 3: 3 beauty should not come from **o**

OUTWARDLY [OUTWARD]

Ro 2:28 not a Jew if he is only one **o**,
2Co 4:16 Though **o** we are wasting away,

OUTWEIGHS* [WEIGH]

Ecc 10: 1 so a little folly **o** wisdom and honor.
2Co 4:17 an eternal glory that far **o** them all.

OUTWIT* [OUTWITTED]

2Co 2:11 in order that Satan might not **o** us.

OUTWITTED* [OUTWIT]

Mt 2:16 that he had been **o** by the Magi,

OVER

Ex 12:13 I will pass **o** you.
12:23 and will pass **o** that doorway,
Ps 1: 6 For the LORD watches **o** the way of
8: 6 You made him ruler **o** the works
113: 4 LORD is exalted **o** all the nations,
145:20 LORD watches **o** all who love him,
Isa 31: 5 he will 'pass **o**' it and will rescue it."

Mk   15:15 and handed him **o** to be crucified.

OVERAWED* [AWE]
Ps   49:16 not be **o** when a man grows rich,

OVERBEARING*
Tit   1: 7 he must be blameless—not **o,**

OVERCAME [OVERCOME]
Hos   12: 4 struggled with the angel and **o** him;
Rev   3:21 as I **o** and sat down with my Father
      12:11 They **o** him by the blood of

OVERCOME [OVERCAME, OVERCOMES]
Ge   32:28 with God and with men and have **o."**
Mt   16:18 and the gates of Hades will not **o** it.
Mk   9:24 I do believe; help me **o** my unbelief!
Lk   10:19 and to **o** all the power of the enemy;
Jn   16:33 I have **o** the world."
Ro   12:21 Do not be **o** by evil,
      12:21 but **o** evil with good.
1Ti   5:11 sensual desires **o** their dedication
2Pe   2:20 and are again entangled in it and **o,**
1Jn   2:13 because you have **o** the evil one.
       4: 4 are from God and have **o** them,
       5: 4 the victory that has **o** the world,
Rev   17:14 but the Lamb will **o** them

OVERCOMES* [OVERCOME]
1Jn   5: 4 everyone born of God **o** the world.
       5: 5 Who is it that **o** the world?
Rev   2: 7 To him who **o,**
       2:11 He who **o** will not be hurt at all by
       2:17 To him who **o,**
       2:26 To him who **o** and does my will to
       3: 5 He who **o** will, like them,
       3:12 Him who **o** I will make a pillar in
       3:21 To him who **o,**
      21: 7 He who **o** will inherit all this,

OVERFLOW [OVERFLOWING, OVERFLOWS]
Ps   65:11 and your carts **o** with abundance.
      119:171 May my lips **o** with praise,
La   1:16 "This is why I weep and my eyes **o**
Mt   12:34 the **o** of the heart the mouth speaks.
Lk   6:45 the **o** of his heart his mouth speaks.
Ro   5:15 Jesus Christ, **o** to the many!
      15:13 so that you may **o** with hope by
2Co   4:15 may cause thanksgiving to **o** to
1Th   3:12 love increase and **o** for each other

OVERFLOWING [OVERFLOW]
Pr   3:10 then your barns will be filled to **o,**
2Co   8: 2 their **o** joy and their extreme poverty
       9:12 also **o** in many expressions of thanks
Col   2: 7 and **o** with thankfulness.

OVERFLOWS* [OVERFLOW]
Ps   23: 5 anoint my head with oil; my cup **o.**
2Co   1: 5 so also through Christ our comfort **o.**

OVERJOYED* [JOY]
Da   6:23 The king was **o** and gave orders
Mt   2:10 When they saw the star, they were **o.**
Jn   20:20 The disciples were **o** when they saw
Ac   12:14 so **o** she ran back without opening it
1Pe   4:13 be **o** when his glory is revealed.

OVERLOOK* [OVERLOOKED, OVERLOOKS]
Dt   9:27 **O** the stubbornness of this people,
      24:19 in your field and you **o** a sheaf,
Pr   19:11 to his glory to **o** an offense.

OVERLOOKED* [OVERLOOK]
Ac   6: 1 because their widows were being **o**
      17:30 In the past God **o** such ignorance,

OVERLOOKS [OVERLOOK]
Pr   12:16 but a prudent man **o** an insult.

OVERNIGHT [NIGHT]
Lev   19:13 back the wages of a hired man **o.**
Jnh   4:10 It sprang up **o** and died **o.**

OVERPOWER [POWER]
Ge   32:25 the man saw that he could not **o** him,
Rev   11: 7 and **o** and kill them.

OVERRIGHTEOUS* [RIGHTEOUS]
Ecc   7:16 Do not be **o,** neither be overwise—

OVERSEER* [OVERSEERS]
Pr   6: 7 It has no commander, no **o** or ruler,
1Ti   3: 1 If anyone sets his heart on being an **o**
       3: 2 Now the **o** must be above reproach,
Tit   1: 7 an **o** is entrusted with God's work,
1Pe   2:25 to the Shepherd and **O** of your souls.

OVERSEERS* [OVERSEER]
Ac   20:28 the Holy Spirit has made you **o.**
Php   1: 1 together with the **o** and deacons:
1Pe   5: 2 under your care, serving as **o—**

OVERSHADOW* [OVERSHADOWING]
Lk   1:35 power of the Most High will **o** you.

OVERSHADOWING [OVERSHADOW]
Ex   25:20 **o** the cover with them.
Heb   9: 5 **o** the atonement cover.

OVERTHREW [OVERTHROW]
Ge   19:25 Thus he **o** those cities and
Jer   50:40 As God **o** Sodom and Gomorrah

OVERTHROW [OVERTHREW, OVERTHROWN, OVERTHROWS]
2Th   2: 8 whom the Lord Jesus will **o** with the

OVERTHROWN [OVERTHROW]
Isa   13:19 will be **o** by God like Sodom

OVERTHROWS [OVERTHROW]

Pr 13: 6 but wickedness **o** the sinner.
Isa 44:25 who **o** the learning of the wise

OVERTURNED

Mk 11:15 **o** the tables of the money changers

OVERWHELMED
[OVERWHELMING]

2Sa 22: 5 The torrents of destruction **o** me.
1Ki 10: 5 at the temple of the LORD, she was **o.**
Ps 38: 4 My guilt has **o** me like
       65: 3 When we were **o** by sins,
Mt 26:38 "My soul is **o** with sorrow to
Mk 7:37 People were **o** with amazement.
      9:15 they were **o** with wonder and ran
2Co 2: 7 he will not be **o** by excessive sorrow.

OVERWHELMING
[OVERWHELMED]

Pr 27: 4 Anger is cruel and fury **o,**
Isa 10:22 Destruction has been decreed, **o** and
      28:15 When an **o** scourge sweeps by,
Na 1: 8 with an **o** flood he will make an end

OVERWICKED* [WICKED]

Ecc 7:17 Do not be **o,** and do not be a fool—

OVERWISE* [WISE]

Ecc 7:16 Do not be overrighteous, neither be **o**

OWE [OWES]

Ro 13: 7 Give everyone what you **o** him:
Phm 1:19 that you **o** me your very self.

OWES* [OWE]

Dt 15: 3 cancel any debt your brother **o** you.
Phm 1:18 or **o** you anything, charge it to me.

OWN [OWNER, OWNER'S, OWNERSHIP, OWNS]

Ge 1:27 So God created man in his **o** image,
      15: 4 from your **o** body will be your heir."
Ex 6: 7 I will take you as my **o** people,
      32:13 to whom you swore by your **o** self:
Dt 18:15 prophet like me from among your **o**
      24:16 each is to die for his **o** sin.
1Sa 13:14 a man after his **o** heart
Pr 3: 7 Do not be wise in your **o** eyes;
      26:12 Do you see a man wise in his **o** eyes?
Isa 48:11 For my **o** sake, for my **o** sake,
      53: 6 each of us has turned to his **o** way;
Jer 10:23 that a man's life is not his **o;**
      31:30 everyone will die for his **o** sin;
Eze 33: 4 his blood will be on his **o** head.
Jn 1:11 He came to that which was his **o,**
      7:16 "My teaching is not my **o.**
      10:18 but I lay it down of my **o** accord.
Ro 8:32 He who did not spare his **o** Son,
1Co 6:19 You are not your **o;**
      7: 7 each man has his **o** gift from God;
Gal 6: 5 for each one should carry his **o** load.
Php 2: 4 look not only to your **o** interests,

OWNER [OWN]

Mt 21:40 when the **o** of the vineyard comes,
      24:43 If the **o** of the house had known

OWNER'S [OWN]

Isa 1: 3 the donkey his **o** manger,

OWNERSHIP* [OWN]

2Co 1:22 set his seal of **o** on us,

OWNS [OWN]

Mt 18:12 If a man **o** a hundred sheep,
Jn 10:12 not the shepherd who **o** the sheep.

OX [OXEN]

Ex 20:17 his **o** or donkey,
Dt 22:10 Do not plow with an **o** and a
      25: 4 Do not muzzle an **o** while it is
Pr 7:22 like an **o** going to the slaughter,
Isa 11: 7 and the lion will eat straw like the **o.**
      65:25 and the lion will eat straw like the **o,**
Eze 1:10 and on the left the face of an **o;**
Lk 13:15 on the Sabbath untie his **o** or donkey
1Co 9: 9 "Do not muzzle an **o** while it is
1Ti 5:18 "Do not muzzle the **o** while it is
Rev 4: 7 the second was like an **o,**

OXEN [OX]

1Ki 19:20 Elisha then left his **o** and ran after
Lk 14:19 'I have just bought five yoke of **o,**
1Co 9: 9 Is it about **o** that God is concerned?

OZIAS (KJV) See UZZIAH

P

PADDAN ARAM [ARAM]

Ge 28: 2 Go at once to **P**
      35: 9 After Jacob returned from **P**

PAGAN [PAGANS]

2Ki 23: 5 the **p** priests appointed by the kings
Isa 57: 8 you have put your **p** symbols.
Mt 18:17 as you would a **p** or a tax collector.
Lk 12:30 the **p** world runs after all such things,
1Co 10: 7 and got up to indulge in **p** revelry."

PAGANS* [PAGAN]

Isa 2: 6 and clasp hands with **p.**
Mt 5:47 Do not even **p** do that?
      6: 7 do not keep on babbling like **p,**
      6:32 For the **p** run after all these things,
1Co 5: 1 that does not occur even among **p:**
      10:20 but the sacrifices of **p** are offered
      12: 2 You know that when you were **p,**
1Pe 2:12 Live such good lives among the **p**
      4: 3 the past doing what **p** choose to do—
3Jn 1: 7 receiving no help from the **p.**

PAID [PAY]

Jdg 1: 7 Now God has **p** me back

1Sa 25:21 He has **p** me back evil for good.
Ne 9:30 Yet they **p** no attention,
Isa 40: 2 that her sin has been **p** for,
Zec 11:12 So they **p** me thirty pieces of silver.
2Pe 2:13 They will be **p** back with harm for

PAIN [PAINFUL, PAINS]

Ge 3:16 with **p** you will give birth
    6: 6 and his heart was filled with **p.**
Job 6:10 my joy in unrelenting **p—**
    33:19 man may be chastened on a bed of **p**
Isa 26:18 We were with child, we writhed in **p,**
Jer 4:19 I writhe in **p.**
    15:18 Why is my **p** unending
Mt 4:24 those suffering severe **p,**
Jn 16:21 woman giving birth to a child has **p**
1Pe 2:19 under the **p** of unjust suffering
Rev 21: 4 death or mourning or crying or **p,**

PAINFUL [PAIN]

Ge 3:17 through **p** toil you will eat of it all
    5:29 and **p** toil of our hands caused by
Job 6:25 How **p** are honest words!
Eze 28:24 malicious neighbors who are **p** briers
2Co 2: 1 that I would not make another **p** visit
Heb 12:11 seems pleasant at the time, but **p.**
1Pe 4:12 at the **p** trial you are suffering,

PAINS [PAIN]

Ge 3:16 "I will greatly increase your **p**
Mk 13: 8 These are the beginning of birth **p.**
Ro 8:22 groaning as in the **p** of childbirth
Gal 4:19 I am again in the **p** of childbirth
1Th 5: 3 as labor **p** on a pregnant woman,

PAIRS

Ge 7: 8 **P** of clean and unclean animals,

PALACE [PALACES]

2Sa 5:11 and they built a **p** for David.
    7: 2 "Here I am, living in a **p** of cedar,
1Ki 7: 2 the **P** of the Forest of Lebanon
    9: 1 temple of the LORD and the royal **p,**
Est 9: 4 Mordecai was prominent in the **p;**
Jer 22:13 "Woe to him who builds his **p**
    52:13 the royal **p** and all the houses of
Jn 18:28 to the **p** of the Roman governor.
Ac 23:35 be kept under guard in Herod's **p.**

PALACES [PALACE]

Hos 8:14 forgotten his Maker and built **p;**
Lk 7:25 and indulge in luxury are in **p.**

PALE

Isa 29:22 no longer will their faces grow **p.**
Jer 30: 6 every face turned deathly **p?**
Da 10: 8 my face turned deathly **p**
Rev 6: 8 and there before me was a **p** horse!

PALESTINA, PALESTINE (KJV)
See PHILISTIA, PHILISTINE

PALM [PALMS]

Ex 15:27 twelve springs and seventy **p** trees,
Lev 23:40 fruit from the trees, and **p** fronds,

Jdg 4: 5 under the **P** of Deborah between
1Ki 6:29 **p** trees and open flowers.
Ps 92:12 righteous will flourish like a **p** tree,
Jn 12:13 They took **p** branches and went out
Rev 7: 9 and were holding **p** branches

PALMS [PALM]

Ne 8:15 **p** and shade trees, to make booths"—
Isa 49:16 engraved you on the **p** of my hands;

PALSY (KJV) See PARALYZED, PARALYTIC

PAMPERS*

Pr 29:21 If a man **p** his servant from youth,

PANELED [PANELING]

Hag 1: 4 to be living in your **p** houses,

PANELING* [PANELED]

1Ki 6:15 **p** them from the floor of the temple
Ps 74: 6 They smashed all the carved **p**

PANIC

Dt 20: 3 do not be terrified or give way to **p**
1Sa 14:15 It was a **p** sent by God.
Eze 7: 7 the day is near; there is **p,**
Zec 14:13 stricken by the LORD with great **p.**

PANTS*

Ps 42: 1 As the deer **p** for streams of water,
        so my soul **p** for you, O God.

PAPER*

2Jn 1:12 but I do not want to use **p** and ink.

PAPYRUS

Ex 2: 3 she got a **p** basket for him

PARABLE [PARABLES]

Eze 17: 2 and tell the house of Israel a **p.**
Mt 13:18 to what the **p** of the sower means:
    15:15 Peter said, "Explain the **p** to us."
    21:33 "Listen to another **p:**
Lk 20:19 he had spoken this **p** against them.

PARABLES [PARABLE]
See also JESUS: PARABLES

Ps 78: 2 I will open my mouth in **p,**
Mt 13:35 "I will open my mouth in **p,**
Lk 8:10 but to others I speak in **p,** so that,

PARADISE*

Lk 23:43 today you will be with me in **p.**"
2Co 12: 4 was caught up to **p.**
Rev 2: 7 which is in the **p** of God.

PARALYTIC [PARALYZED]

Mt 9: 2 Some men brought to him a **p,**
Mk 2: 3 bringing to him a **p,**
Ac 9:33 a **p** who had been bedridden for eight

PARALYZED [PARALYTIC]

Hab 1: 4 Therefore the law is **p,**
Jn 5: 3 the blind, the lame, the **p.**

PARAN
Ge 21:21 he was living in the Desert of **P,**
Nu 10:12 came to rest in the Desert of **P.**
Hab 3: 3 the Holy One from Mount **P.**

PARCHED
Ps 143: 6 my soul thirsts for you like a **p** land.
Isa 41:18 and the **p** ground into springs.

PARCHMENTS*
2Ti 4:13 and my scrolls, especially the **p.**

PARDON* [PARDONED, PARDONS]
2Ch 30:18 the LORD, who is good, **p** everyone
Job 7:21 Why do you not **p** my offenses
Isa 55: 7 and to our God, for he will freely **p.**
Joel 3:21 which I have not pardoned, I will **p."**

PARDONED* [PARDON]
Nu 14:19 just as you have **p** them from
Joel 3:21 Their bloodguilt, which I have not **p,**

PARDONS* [PARDON]
Mic 7:18 **p** sin and forgives the transgression

PARENTS
Pr 17: 6 and **p** are the pride of their children.
  19:14 and wealth are inherited from **p,**
Mk 13:12 Children will rebel against their **p**
Lk 2:27 the **p** brought in the child Jesus to do
  18:29 or wife or brothers or **p** or children
  21:16 You will be betrayed even by **p,**
Jn 9: 3 "Neither this man nor his **p** sinned,"
Ro 1:30 of doing evil; they disobey their **p;**
2Co 12:14 not have to save up for their **p,** but **p**
      for their children.
Eph 6: 1 Children, obey your **p** in the Lord,
Col 3:20 Children, obey your **p** in everything,
1Ti 5: 4 so repaying their **p** and grandparents,
2Ti 3: 2 disobedient to their **p,** ungrateful,

PARSIN* [PERES]
Da 5:25 was written: MENE, MENE, TEKEL, **P**

PART [APART, PARTED, PARTLY, PARTS]
Nu 18:29 LORD's portion the best and holiest **p**
2Sa 20: 1 no **p** in Jesse's son!
1Ki 12:16 what **p** in Jesse's son?
Job 42:12 blessed the latter **p** of Job's life more
Ps 144: 5 **P** your heavens, O LORD,
Mt 5:29 It is better for you to lose one **p**
Jn 13: 8 you have no **p** with me."
1Co 12:14 the body is not made up of one **p** but
  13: 9 we know in **p** and we prophesy in **p,**
Rev 20: 6 who have **p** in the first resurrection.

PARTAKE*
1Co 10:17 for we all **p** of the one loaf.

PARTED [PART]
Ge 13:11 The two men **p** company:
2Sa 22:10 He **p** the heavens and came down;
Ac 15:39 disagreement that they **p** company.

PARTIAL* [PARTIALITY]
Pr 18: 5 It is not good to be **p** to the wicked

PARTIALITY* [PARTIAL]
Lev 19:15 not show **p** to the poor or favoritism
Dt 1:17 Do not show **p** in judging;
  10:17 shows no **p** and accepts no bribes.
  16:19 Do not pervert justice or show **p.**
2Ch 19: 7 or **p** or bribery."
Job 13: 8 Will you show him **p?**
  13:10 if you secretly showed **p.**
  32:21 I will show **p** to no one,
  34:19 who shows no **p** to princes and does
Ps 82: 2 the unjust and show **p** to the wicked?
Pr 24:23 To show **p** in judging is not good:
  28:21 To show **p** is not good—
Mal 2: 9 have shown **p** in matters of the law."
Lk 20:21 and that you do not show **p**
1Ti 5:21 to keep these instructions without **p,**

PARTICIPANTS* [PARTICIPATE]
1Co 10:20 not want you to be **p** with demons.

PARTICIPATE [PARTICIPANTS, PARTICIPATION]
1Co 10:18 who eat the sacrifices **p** in the altar?
1Pe 4:13 that you **p** in the sufferings of Christ,
2Pe 1: 4 through them you may **p** in

PARTICIPATION* [PARTICIPATE]
1Co 10:16 a **p** in the blood of Christ?
  10:16 a **p** in the body of Christ?

PARTLY [PART]
Da 2:33 its feet **p** of iron and **p** of baked clay.

PARTNER [PARTNERS, PARTNERSHIP]
Pr 2:17 who has left the **p** of her youth
Mal 2:14 though she is your **p,**
1Pe 3: 7 as the weaker **p** and as heirs with you

PARTNERS [PARTNER]
Eph 5: 7 Therefore do not be **p** with them.

PARTNERSHIP* [PARTNER]
Php 1: 5 because of your **p** in the gospel from

PARTS [PART]
Ps 51: 6 you desire truth in the inner **p;**
Pr 18: 8 go down to a man's inmost **p.**
1Co 12:20 there are many **p,** but one body.

PASHHUR
Priest; opponent of Jeremiah (Jer 20:1-6).

PASS [PASSED, PASSER-BY, PASSES, PASSING]
Ex 12:13 I will **p** over you.
  12:23 and will **p** over that doorway,
  33:19 "I will cause all my goodness to **p**
Nu 20:17 Please let us **p** through your country.
  21:22 "Let us **p** through your country.

1Ki 9: 8 all who **p** by will be appalled
    19:11 for the LORD is about to **p** by."
Ps 90:10 for they quickly **p,** and we fly away.
   105:19 till what he foretold came to **p,**
Isa 31: 5 he will '**p** over' it and will rescue it."
    43: 2 When you **p** through the waters,
    43: 2 and when you **p**
    62:10 **P** through, **p** through the gates!
Jer 22: 8 from many nations will **p** by this city
La   1:12 all you who **p** by?
Da   7:14 dominion that will not **p** away,
Am   5:17 for I will **p** through your midst,"
Mt 24:35 Heaven and earth will **p** away, but
           my words will never **p** away.
Mk 14:35 that if possible the hour might **p**
Ro   2: 1 because you who **p** judgment do
1Co 13: 8 it will **p** away.
Jas 1:10 he will **p** away like a wild flower.
1Jn 2:17 The world and its desires **p** away,

PASSED [PASS]

Ge 15:17 appeared and **p** between the pieces.
Ex 12:27 **p** over the houses of the Israelites
    33:22 with my hand until I have **p** by.
    34: 6 in front of Moses,
Nu 33: 8 and **p** through the sea into the desert,
Jos 3:17 all Israel **p** by until the whole nation
2Ch 21:20 He **p** away, to no one's regret,
Ps 37:36 he soon **p** away and was no more;
    57: 1 until the disaster has **p.**
Lk 10:32 **p** by on the other side.
1Co 15: 3 For what I received I **p** on to you as
Heb 11:29 the people **p** through the Red Sea as
1Jn 3:14 We know that we have **p** from death
Rev 21: 1 and the first earth had **p** away,
    21: 4 the old order of things has **p** away."

PASSER-BY* [PASS]

Pr 26:10 he who hires a fool or any **p.**
    26:17 is a **p** who meddles in a quarrel

PASSES [PASS]

Ex 33:22 When my glory **p** by,
Ecc 6:12 he **p** through like a shadow?

PASSING [PASS]

Ro 14:13 Therefore let us stop **p** judgment
1Co 7:31 world in its present form is **p** away.
1Jn 2: 8 because the darkness is **p** and

PASSION* [PASSIONATE, PASSIONS]

Hos 7: 6 Their **p** smolders all night;
1Co 7: 9 better to marry than to burn with **p.**

PASSIONATE* [PASSION]

1Th 4: 5 not in **p** lust like the heathen, who do

PASSIONS* [PASSION]

Ro   7: 5 the sinful **p** aroused by the law were
Gal 5:24 crucified the sinful nature with its **p**
Tit 2:12 "No" to ungodliness and worldly **p,**
     3: 3 enslaved by all kinds of **p** and

PASSOVER

Ex 12:11 Eat it in haste; it is the LORD's **P.**

Lev 23: 5 The LORD's **P** begins at twilight
Nu   9: 2 "Have the Israelites celebrate the **P**
Dt 16: 1 celebrate the **P** of the LORD your
Jos 5:10 the Israelites celebrated the **P.**
2Ki 23:21 "Celebrate the **P** to the LORD your
2Ch 30: 1 celebrate the **P** to the LORD,
Ezr 6:19 the exiles celebrated the **P.**
Mk 14:12 customary to sacrifice the **P** lamb,
    14:12 for you to eat the **P?**"
Lk 22: 8 preparations for us to eat the **P.**"
1Co 5: 7 For Christ, our **P** lamb,
Heb 11:28 By faith he kept the **P** and the

PAST

Ge 18:11 Sarah was **p** the age of childbearing.
Ecc 3:15 and God will call the **p** to account.
Isa 43:18 do not dwell on the **p.**
    65:16 For the **p** troubles will be forgotten
Ac 14:16 In the **p,** he let all nations
    17:30 In the **p** God overlooked
Ro 15: 4 that was written in the **p** was written
    16:25 the mystery hidden for long ages **p,**
Eph 3: 9 for ages **p** was kept hidden in God
Heb 1: 1 the **p** God spoke to our forefathers
    11:11 even though he was **p** age—
1Pe 3: 5 of the **p** who put their hope in God
2Pe 1: 9 he has been cleansed from his **p** sins.

PASTORS*

Eph 4:11 and some to be **p** and teachers,

PASTURE [PASTURELANDS, PASTURES]

Ps 37: 3 dwell in the land and enjoy safe **p.**
    79:13 we your people, the sheep of your **p,**
    95: 7 and we are the people of his **p,**
   100: 3 the sheep of his **p.**
Jer 23: 1 and scattering the sheep of my **p!**"
    50: 7 sinned against the LORD, their true **p,**
Eze 34:13 I will **p** them on the mountains
Zec 11: 4 "**P** the flock marked for slaughter.
Jn 10: 9 will come in and go out, and find **p.**

PASTURELANDS [PASTURE]

Nu 35: 2 And give them **p** around the towns.

PASTURES [PASTURE]

Ps 23: 2 He makes me lie down in green **p,**

PATCH

Jer 10: 5 Like a scarecrow in a melon **p,**
Mk   2:21 "No one sews a **p** of unshrunk cloth

PATH [PATHS]

Nu 22:24 a narrow **p** between two vineyards,
2Sa 22:37 You broaden the **p** beneath me,
Ne   9:19 not cease to guide them on their **p,**
Ps 16:11 made known to me the **p** of life;
    27:11 lead me in a straight **p**
   119:32 I run in the **p** of your commands,
   119:105 and a light for my **p.**
Pr   2: 9 and just and fair—every good **p.**
     5: 8 Keep to a **p** far from her,
    12:28 along that **p** is immortality.

15:10 awaits him who leaves the **p**;
15:19 but the **p** of the upright is a highway.
15:24 The **p** of life leads upward for
21:16 strays from the **p** of understanding
Isa 26: 7 The **p** of the righteous is level;
Jer 31: 9 beside streams of water on a level **p**
Mt 13: 4 some fell along the **p,**
Lk 1:79 to guide our feet into the **p** of peace."
2Co 6: 3 no stumbling block in anyone's **p,**

PATHS [PATH]

Ps 17: 5 My steps have held to your **p**;
   23: 3 He guides me in **p** of righteousness
   25: 4 O LORD, teach me your **p**;
Pr 2:13 leave the straight **p** to walk in dark
   2:18 her **p** to the spirits of the dead.
   3: 6 and he will make your **p** straight.
   4:11 and lead you along straight **p.**
   4:26 Make level **p** for your feet
   5:21 and he examines all his **p.**
   8:20 along the **p** of justice,
   22: 5 In the **p** of the wicked lie thorns
Isa 2: 3 so that we may walk in his **p."**
Jer 6:16 ask for the ancient **p,**
Mic 4: 2 so that we may walk in his **p."**
Mt 3: 3 make straight **p** for him.' "
Ac 2:28 made known to me the **p** of life;
Ro 11:33 and his **p** beyond tracing out!
Heb 12:13 "Make level **p** for your feet,"

PATIENCE* [PATIENT]

Pr 19:11 A man's wisdom gives him **p**;
   25:15 Through **p** a ruler can be persuaded,
Ecc 7: 8 and **p** is better than pride.
Isa 7:13 Is it not enough to try the **p** of men?
   7:13 Will you try the **p** of my God also?
Ro 2: 4 tolerance and **p,**
   9:22 bore with great **p** the objects
2Co 6: 6 understanding, **p** and kindness;
Gal 5:22 **p,** kindness, goodness, faithfulness,
Col 1:11 you may have great endurance and **p,**
   3:12 kindness, humility, gentleness and **p.**
1Ti 1:16 Jesus might display his unlimited **p**
2Ti 3:10 my way of life, my purpose, faith, **p,**
   4: 2 with great **p** and careful instruction.
Heb 6:12 **p** inherit what has been promised.
Jas 5:10 example of **p** in the face of suffering,
2Pe 3:15 that our Lord's **p** means salvation,

PATIENT* [PATIENCE, PATIENTLY]

Ne 9:30 For many years you were **p**
Job 6:11 What prospects, that I should be **p?**
Pr 14:29 A **p** man has great understanding,
   15:18 but a **p** man calms a quarrel.
   16:32 Better a **p** man than a warrior,
Mt 18:26 'Be **p** with me,' he begged,
   18:29 'Be **p** with me,
Ro 12:12 Be joyful in hope, **p** in affliction,
1Co 13: 4 Love is **p,** love is kind.
2Co 1: 6 which produces in you **p** endurance
Eph 4: 2 be **p,** bearing with one another
1Th 5:14 help the weak, be **p** with everyone.
Jas 5: 7 Be **p,** then, brothers,
   5: 7 and how **p** he is for the autumn

5: 8 You too, be **p** and stand firm,
2Pe 3: 9 He is **p** with you,
Rev 1: 9 **p** endurance that are ours in Jesus,
   13:10 for **p** endurance and faithfulness
   14:12 for **p** endurance on the part

PATIENTLY* [PATIENT]

Ps 37: 7 Be still before the LORD and wait **p**
   40: 1 I waited **p** for the LORD;
Isa 38:13 I waited **p** till dawn,
Hab 3:16 I will wait **p** for the day of calamity
Ac 26: 3 I beg you to listen to me **p.**
Ro 8:25 we wait for it **p.**
Heb 6:15 And so after waiting **p,**
1Pe 3:20 God waited **p** in the days of Noah
Rev 3:10 kept my command to endure **p,**

PATMOS*

Rev 1: 9 was on the island of **P**

PATRIARCH* [PATRIARCHS]

Ac 2:29 that the **p** David died and was buried,
Heb 7: 4 the **p** Abraham gave him a tenth

PATRIARCHS [PATRIARCH]

Jn 7:22 from Moses, but from the **p**),
Ro 9: 5 Theirs are the **p,**
   15: 8 confirm the promises made to the **p**

PATTERN

Ex 25:40 to the **p** shown you on the mountain.
Nu 8: 4 the **p** the LORD had shown Moses.
Ro 5:14 who was a **p** of the one to come.
   12: 2 Do not conform any longer to the **p**
Php 3:17 according to the **p** we gave you.
2Ti 1:13 keep as the **p** of sound teaching,
Heb 8: 5 the **p** shown you on the mountain."

PAUL [SAUL]

Also called Saul (Ac 13:9). Pharisee from Tarsus (Ac 9:11; Php 3:5). Apostle (Gal 1). At stoning of Stephen (Ac 8:1). Persecuted Church (Ac 9:1-2; Gal 1:13). Vision of Jesus on road to Damascus (Ac 9:4-9; 26:12-18). In Arabia (Gal 1:17). Preached in Damascus; escaped death through the wall in a basket (Ac 9:19-25). In Jerusalem; sent back to Tarsus (Ac 9:26-30).

Brought to Antioch by Barnabas (Ac 11:22-26). First missionary journey to Cyprus and Galatia (Ac 13-14). Stoned at Lystra (Ac 14:19-20). At Jerusalem council (Ac 15). Split with Barnabas over Mark (Ac 15:36-41).

Second missionary journey with Silas (Ac 16-20). Called to Macedonia (Ac 16:6-10). Freed from prison in Philippi (Ac 16:16-40). In Thessalonica (Ac 17:1-9). Speech in Athens (Ac 17:16-33). In Corinth (Ac 18). In Ephesus (Ac 19). Return to Jerusalem (Ac 20). Farewell to Ephesian elders (Ac 20:13-38). Arrival in Jerusalem (Ac 21:1-26). Arrested (Ac 21:27-36). Addressed crowds (Ac 22), Sanhedrin (Ac 23:1-11). Sent to Caesarea (Ac 23:12-35). Trial before Felix (Ac 24), Festus (Ac 25:1-12). Before Agrippa (Ac

25:13-26:32). Voyage to Rome; shipwreck (Ac 27). Arrival in Rome (Ac 28).

Letters: Romans, 1 and 2 Corinthians, Galatians, Ephesians, Philippians, Colossians, 1 and 2 Thessalonians, 1 and 2 Timothy, Titus, Philemon.

PAVEMENT
Ex 24:10 something like a **p** made of sapphire,
Jn 19:13 seat at a place known as the Stone **P**

PAW*
1Sa 17:37 the **p** of the lion and the **p** of the bear

PAY [PAID, PAYING, PAYMENT, PAYS, REPAID, REPAY, REPAYING]
Ge 23:13 I will **p** the price of the field.
Ex   4: 8 not believe you or **p** attention to
    15:26 if you **p** attention to his commands
    22: 3 he must be sold to **p** for his theft.
    22: 4 he must **p** back double.
    30:12 each one must **p** the LORD
Lev 26:43 They will **p** for their sins
Dt   7:12 If you **p** attention to these laws
Ps 94: 2 **p** back to the proud what they
Pr   4: 1 to a father's instruction; **p** attention
     4:20 My son, **p** attention to what I say;
     5: 1 My son, **p** attention to my wisdom,
     6:31 if he is caught, he must **p** sevenfold,
    19:19 A hot-tempered man must **p**
    22:17 **P** attention and listen to the sayings
    24:29 I'll **p** that man back
Jer 7:24 But they did not listen or **p** attention;
Eze 40: 4 and **p** attention to everything I am
Zec 11:12 "If you think it best, give me my **p;**
Mt 20: 4 and I will **p** you whatever is right.'
    22:16 you **p** no attention to who they are.
    22:17 Is it right to **p** taxes to Caesar
Lk   3:14 be content with your **p."**
    19: 8 I will **p** back four times the amount."
Ro 13: 6 This is also why you **p** taxes,
2Th 1: 6 God is just: He will **p** back trouble
2Pe 1:19 you will do well to **p** attention to it,
Rev 18: 6 **p** her back double for what she has

PAYING [PAY]
1Ch 21:24 "No, I insist on **p** the full price.
Mt 22:19 Show me the coin used for **p** the tax.

PAYMENT [PAY]
Ps 49: 8 no **p** is ever enough—
Isa 65: 7 the full **p** for their former deeds."
Php 4:18 I have received full **p** and even more;

PAYS [PAY]
Ps 31:23 but the proud he **p** back in full.
Pr 17:13 If a man **p** back evil for good,
1Th 5:15 that nobody **p** back wrong for wrong,

PEACE [PEACE-LOVING, PEACEABLE, PEACEFUL, PEACEMAKERS]
Lev 26: 6 " 'I will grant **p** in the land,

Nu   6:26 toward you and give you **p."** '
    25:12 making my covenant of **p** with him.
Dt 20:10 make its people an offer of **p.**
Jos 9:15 Then Joshua made a treaty of **p**
    11:19 not one city made a treaty of **p** with
Jdg 3:11 So the land had **p** for forty years,
     3:30 and the land had **p** for eighty years.
     5:31 Then the land had **p** forty years.
     6:24 and called it The LORD is **P.**
     8:28 the land enjoyed **p** forty years.
1Sa 1:17 Eli answered, "Go in **p,**
     7:14 And there was **p** between Israel and
    20:42 Jonathan said to David, "Go in **p,**
2Sa 10:19 they made **p** with the Israelites
1Ki 2:33 may there be the LORD's **p** forever."
2Ki 9:17 'Do you come in **p?'** "
1Ch 19:19 they made **p** with David
    22: 9 a son who will be a man of **p**
2Ch 14: 1 and in his days the country was at **p**
    20:30 kingdom of Jehoshaphat was at **p,**
Job 3:26 I have no **p,** no quietness;
    22:21 "Submit to God and be at **p**
Ps 29:11 the LORD blesses his people with **p.**
    34:14 Turn from evil and do good; seek **p.**
    37:11 inherit the land and enjoy great **p.**
    37:37 a future for the man of **p.**
    85: 8 he promises **p** to his people,
    85:10 righteousness and **p** kiss each other.
   119:165 Great **p** have they who love your law
   120: 7 I am a man of **p;**
   122: 6 Pray for the **p** of Jerusalem:
   147:14 He grants **p** to your borders
Pr   3:17 and all her paths are **p.**
    12:20 but joy for those who promote **p.**
    14:30 A heart at **p** gives life to the body,
    16: 7 even his enemies live at **p** with him.
    17: 1 with **p** and quiet than a house full
Ecc 3: 8 a time for war and a time for **p.**
Isa 9: 6 Everlasting Father, Prince of **P.**
    14: 7 All the lands are at rest and at **p;**
    26: 3 in perfect **p** him whose mind is
    32:17 The fruit of righteousness will be **p;**
    48:18 your **p** would have been like a river,
    48:22 "There is no **p,"** says the LORD,
    52: 7 proclaim **p,** who bring good tidings,
    53: 5 the punishment that brought us **p** was
    54:10 not be shaken nor my covenant of **p**
    55:12 in joy and be led forth in **p;**
    57: 2 who walk uprightly enter into **p;**
    57:19 **P, p,** to those far and near,"
    57:21 "There is no **p,"** says my God,
    59: 8 The way of **p** they do not know;
    59: 8 in them will know **p.**
    66:12 "I will extend **p** to her like a river,
Jer 6:14 '**P, p,**' they say, when there is no **p.**
     8:11 "**P, p,**" they say, when there is no **p.**
    30:10 Jacob will again have **p** and security,
    33: 6 and will let them enjoy abundant **p**
    46:27 Jacob will again have **p** and security,
La   3:17 I have been deprived of **p;**
Eze 13:10 saying, "**P,"** when there is no **p,**
    34:25 " 'I will make a covenant of **p** with
    37:26 I will make a covenant of **p** with
Mic 5: 5 And he will be their **p.**

Na 1:15 brings good news, who proclaims **p**!
Hag 2: 9 'And in this place I will grant **p,**'
Zec 8:19 Therefore love truth and **p.**"
 9:10 He will proclaim **p** to the nations.
Mal 2: 5 a covenant of life and **p,**
 2: 6 walked with me in **p** and uprightness
Mt 10:13 let your **p** rest on it;
 10:34 I did not come to bring **p,**
Mk 9:50 and be at **p** with each other."
Lk 1:79 to guide our feet into the path of **p.**"
 2:14 and on earth **p** to men
 7:50 "Your faith has saved you; go in **p.**"
 19:38 "**P** in heaven and glory in
 19:42 on this day what would bring you **p**
Jn 14:27 **P** I leave with you; my **p** I give you.
 16:33 so that in me you may have **p.**
Ac 10:36 telling the good news of **p**
Ro 2:10 and **p** for everyone who does good:
 3:17 and the way of **p** they do not know."
 5: 1 we have **p** with God
 8: 6 controlled by the Spirit is life and **p;**
 12:18 live at **p** with everyone.
 14:19 to do what leads to **p** and
 16:20 The God of **p** will soon crush Satan
1Co 7:15 God has called us to live in **p.**
 14:33 not a God of disorder but of **p.**
2Co 13:11 be of one mind, live in **p.**
 13:11 God of love and **p** will be with you.
Gal 5:22 the fruit of the Spirit is love, joy, **p,**
 6:16 **P** and mercy to all who follow
Eph 2:14 For he himself is our **p,**
 2:15 out of the two, thus making **p,**
 2:17 preached **p** to you who were far
 away and **p** to those who were near.
 4: 3 of the Spirit through the bond of **p.**
 6:15 that comes from the gospel of **p.**
Php 4: 7 the **p** of God, which transcends all
Col 1:20 by making **p** through his blood,
 3:15 the **p** of Christ rule in your hearts,
 3:15 of one body you were called to **p.**
1Th 5: 3 people are saying, "**P** and safety,"
 5:13 Live in **p** with each other.
 5:23 May God himself, the God of **p,**
2Th 3:16 the Lord of **p** himself give you **p**
2Ti 2:22 faith, love and **p,**
Heb 7: 2 "king of Salem" means "king of **p.**"
 12:11 a harvest of righteousness and **p**
 12:14 every effort to live in **p** with all men
 13:20 May the God of **p,**
Jas 3:18 Peacemakers who sow in **p** raise
1Pe 3:11 he must seek **p** and pursue it.
2Pe 3:14 blameless and at **p** with him.
Rev 6: 4 to take **p** from the earth

GRACE AND PEACE See GRACE

PEACE-LOVING* [PEACE, LOVE]
Jas 3:17 heaven is first of all pure; then **p,**

PEACEABLE* [PEACE]
Tit 3: 2 to be **p** and considerate,

PEACEFUL [PEACE]
1Ti 2: 2 that we may live **p** and quiet lives

PEACEMAKERS* [PEACE]
Mt 5: 9 Blessed are the **p,**
Jas 3:18 **P** who sow in peace raise a harvest

PEARL* [PEARLS]
Rev 21:21 each gate made of a single **p.**

PEARLS [PEARL]
Mt 7: 6 do not throw your **p** to pigs.
 13:45 like a merchant looking for fine **p.**
1Ti 2: 9 or gold or **p** or expensive clothes,
Rev 21:21 The twelve gates were twelve **p,**

PEBBLE*
Am 9: 9 and not a **p** will reach the ground.

PEDDLE*
2Co 2:17 do not **p** the word of God for profit.

PEG
Jdg 4:21 She drove the **p** through his temple
Isa 22:23 I will drive him like a **p** into
Zec 10: 4 from him the tent **p,**

PEKAH
 King of Israel (2Ki 15:25-31; 2Ch 28:6; Isa 7:1).

PEKAHIAH*
 Son of Menahem; king of Israel (2Ki 15:22-26).

PELETHITES
2Sa 20: 7 and **P** and all the mighty warriors
1Ch 18:17 over the Kerethites and **P;**

PEN [PENS]
Ps 45: 1 the **p** of a skillful writer.
Isa 8: 1 and write on it with an ordinary **p:**
Hab 3:17 though there are no sheep in the **p**
Mt 5:18 not the least stroke of a **p,**
Jn 10: 1 not enter the sheep **p** by the gate,
3Jn 1:13 do not want to do so with **p** and ink.

PENALTIES* [PENALTY]
Pr 19:29 **P** are prepared for mockers,

PENALTY [PENALTIES]
Lev 5: 6 as a **p** for the sin he has committed,
Pr 19:19 A hot-tempered man must pay the **p;**
Eze 23:49 will suffer the **p** for your lewdness
Lk 23:22 in him no grounds for the death **p.**
Ro 1:27 the due **p** for their perversion.

PENCE (KJV) See DENARII, COINS, A YEAR'S WAGES

PENETRATES*
Heb 4:12 it **p** even to dividing soul and spirit,

PENIEL
Ge 32:30 So Jacob called the place **P,** saying,

PENINNAH
1Sa 1: 2 was called Hannah and the other **P.**

PENITENT* [REPENT]

Isa 1:27 her **p** ones with righteousness.

PENNIES* [PENNY]

Lk 12: 6 not five sparrows sold for two **p**?

PENNY* [PENNIES]

Mt 5:26 until you have paid the last **p.**
10:29 Are not two sparrows sold for a **p**?
Mk 12:42 worth only a fraction of a **p.**
Lk 12:59 until you have paid the last **p."**

PENS [PEN]

Ps 50: 9 or of goats from your **p,**
78:70 and took him from the sheep **p;**

PENTECOST*

Ac 2: 1 When the day of **P** came,
20:16 if possible, by the day of **P.**
1Co 16: 8 But I will stay on at Ephesus until **P,**

PEOPLE [PEOPLE'S, PEOPLES]

Ge 6:13 "I am going to put an end to all **p,**
11: 6 as one **p** speaking the same language
12: 1 "Leave your country, your **p** and
18:24 What if there are fifty righteous **p** in
Ex 3:10 my **p** the Israelites out of Egypt."
5: 1 the God of Israel, says: 'Let my **p** go,
6: 7 I will take you as my own **p,**
8:23 distinction between my **p** and your **p.**
13:17 When Pharaoh let the **p** go,
15:13 the **p** you have redeemed.
15:24 So the **p** grumbled against Moses,
19: 8 The **p** all responded together,
24: 3 When Moses went and told the **p** all
32: 1 the **p** saw that Moses was so long
32: 9 "and they are a stiff-necked **p.**
32:12 and do not bring disaster on your **p.**
33:13 Remember that this nation is your **p.**
Lev 9: 7 atonement for yourself and the **p;**
16:24 and the burnt offering for the **p,**
26:12 and you will be my **p.**
Nu 11:11 that you put the burden of all these **p**
14:11 "How long will these **p** treat me
14:19 forgive the sin of these **p,**
20: 2 and the **p** gathered in opposition
21: 7 So Moses prayed for the **p.**
22: 5 Balak said: "A **p** has come out
Dt 4: 6 a wise and understanding **p."**
4:20 to be the **p** of his inheritance,
5:28 "I have heard what this **p** said to you.
7: 6 a **p** holy to the LORD your God.
26:18 that you are his **p,**
31: 7 go with this **p** into the land
31:16 these **p** will soon prostitute
32: 9 For the LORD's portion is his **p,**
32:43 Rejoice, O nations, with his **p,**
32:43 make atonement for his land and **p.**
33:29 a **p** saved by the LORD?
Jos 1: 6 because you will lead these **p**
3:16 the **p** crossed over opposite Jericho.
24:25 Joshua made a covenant for the **p,**
Jdg 2: 7 The **p** served the LORD throughout
2:19 the **p** returned to ways even more

Ru 1:16 Your **p** will be my **p**
1Sa 8: 7 to all that the **p** are saying to you;
10:24 no one like him among all the **p."**
12:22 the LORD will not reject his **p,**
2Sa 5: 2 'You will shepherd my **p** Israel,
7:10 a place for my **p** Israel
7:23 And who is like your **p** Israel—
24:17 angel who was striking down the **p,**
1Ki 3: 8 here among the **p** you have chosen,
8:30 and of your **p** Israel when they pray
8:56 who has given rest to his **p** Israel just
18:39 When all the **p** saw this,
2Ki 17:23 So the **p** of Israel were taken from
23: 3 Then all the **p** pledged themselves to
25:11 carried into exile the **p** who remained
1Ch 17:21 to redeem a **p** for himself,
29:17 willingly your **p** who are here have
2Ch 2:11 "Because the LORD loves his **p,**
7: 5 So the king and all the **p** dedicated
7:14 if my **p,** who are called by my name,
30: 6 "P of Israel, return to the LORD,
36:16 the LORD was aroused against his **p**
Ezr 2: 1 the **p** of the province who came up
3: 1 the **p** assembled as one man
Ne 1:10 "They are your servants and your **p,**
4: 6 for the **p** worked with all their heart.
8: 1 all the **p** assembled as one man in
Est 3: 6 to destroy all Mordecai's **p,** the Jews,
7: 3 And spare my **p**—this is my request.
Job 12: 2 "Doubtless you are the **p,**
Ps 3: 8 May your blessing be on your **p.**
29:11 the LORD blesses his **p** with peace.
33:12 the **p** he chose for his inheritance.
50: 4 that he may judge his **p:**
53: 6 God restores the fortunes of his **p,**
81:13 "If my **p** would but listen to me,
94:14 For the LORD will not reject his **p;**
95: 7 we are the **p** of his pasture,
95:10 a **p** whose hearts go astray,
125: 2 the LORD surrounds his **p** both now
135:14 For the LORD will vindicate his **p**
144:15 the **p** whose God is the LORD.
149: 4 the LORD takes delight in his **p;**
Pr 14:34 but sin is a disgrace to any **p.**
29: 2 the righteous thrive, the **p** rejoice;
29:18 the **p** cast off restraint;
Isa 1: 3 my **p** do not understand."
1: 4 sinful nation, a **p** loaded with guilt,
5:13 Therefore my **p** will go into exile
6:10 Make the heart of this **p** calloused;
9: 2 The **p** walking in darkness have seen
19:25 saying, "Blessed be Egypt my **p,**
25: 8 he will remove the disgrace of his **p**
29:13 **p** come near to me with their mouth
40: 1 Comfort, comfort my **p,**
40: 7 Surely the **p** are grass.
42: 6 make you to be a covenant for the **p**
49: 8 to be a covenant for the **p,**
49:13 the LORD comforts his **p**
51: 4 "Listen to me, my **p;**
52: 6 Therefore my **p** will know my name;
53: 8 of my **p** he was stricken.
60:21 Then will all your **p** be righteous
62:12 They will be called the Holy **P,**

	65: 2	held out my hands to an obstinate **p,**
	65:23	a **p** blessed by the LORD,
Jer	2:11	my **p** have exchanged their Glory
	2:13	"My **p** have committed two sins:
	2:32	Yet my **p** have forgotten me,
	4:22	"My **p** are fools;
	5:14	and these **p** the wood it consumes.
	5:31	and my **p** love it this way.
	6:27	a tester of metals and my **p** the ore,
	7:16	"So do not pray for this **p**
	7:23	be your God and you will be my **p.**
	18:15	Yet my **p** have forgotten me;
	23: 2	to the shepherds who tend my **p:**
	30: 3	'when I will bring my **p** Israel
	31:33	and they will be my **p.**
	50: 6	"My **p** have been lost sheep;
La	1: 1	once so full of **p!**
Eze	12: 2	you are living among a rebellious **p.**
	13:23	I will save my **p** from your hands.
	36: 8	and fruit for my **p** Israel,
	36:28	you will be my **p,**
	36:38	cities will be filled with flocks of **p.**
	37:13	my **p,** will know that I am the LORD,
	38:14	when my **p** Israel are living in safety,
	39: 7	my holy name among my **p** Israel.
Da	7:27	the **p** of the Most High.
	8:24	the mighty men and the holy **p.**
	9:19	and your **p** bear your Name."
	9:24	'sevens' are decreed for your **p**
	9:26	The **p** of the ruler who will come
	10:14	to you what will happen to your **p**
	11:32	**p** who know their God will firmly
	12: 1	the great prince who protects your **p,**
Hos	1:10	'You are not my **p,'**
	2:23	I will say to those called 'Not my **p,'**
	4:14	a **p** without understanding will come
Joel	2:18	for his land and take pity on his **p.**
	3:16	a stronghold for the **p** of Israel.
Am	9:14	I will bring back my exiled **p** Israel;
Jnh	4:11	**p** who cannot tell their right hand
Mic	3: 5	the prophets who lead my **p** astray,
	6: 2	the LORD has a case against his **p;**
	7:14	Shepherd your **p** with your staff,
Zep	2: 9	remnant of my **p** will plunder them;
Hag	1:12	And the **p** feared the LORD.
Zec	2:11	in that day and will become my **p.**
	8: 7	"I will save my **p** from
	13: 9	'They are my **p,'** and they will say,
Mt	1:21	he will save his **p** from their sins."
	2: 6	be the shepherd of my **p** Israel.' "
	4:16	the **p** living in darkness have seen
Mk	7: 6	" 'These **p** honor me with their lips,
	8:27	"Who do **p** say I am?"
Lk	1:17	a **p** prepared for the Lord."
	1:68	he has come and has redeemed his **p.**
	2:10	of great joy that will be for all the **p.**
	13:23	are only a few **p** going to be saved?"
	21:23	in the land and wrath against this **p.**
Jn	7:43	the **p** were divided because of Jesus.
	11:50	that one man die for the **p** than
	18:14	be good if one man died for the **p.**
Ac	2:17	I will pour out my Spirit on all **p.**
	2:47	and enjoying the favor of all the **p.**
	3:22	like me from among your own **p;**

	5:13	they were highly regarded by the **p.**
	15:14	by taking from the Gentiles a **p**
	18:10	because I have many **p** in this city."
Ro	9:25	in Hosea: "I will call them 'my **p'**
	11: 1	I ask then: Did God reject his **p?**
	15:10	"Rejoice, O Gentiles, with his **p.''**
2Co	6:16	and they will be my **p.''**
Eph	2:19	but fellow citizens with God's **p**
Col	3:12	Therefore, as God's chosen **p,**
1Ti	6: 9	**P** who want to get rich fall
Tit	1:10	For there are many rebellious **p,**
	2:14	for himself a **p** that are his very own,
Heb	2:17	make atonement for the sins of the **p.**
	4: 9	then, a Sabbath-rest for the **p** of God;
	5: 3	as well as for the sins of the **p.**
	8:10	and they will be my **p.**
	10:30	"The Lord will judge his **p.''**
	11:13	All these **p** were still living by faith
	13:12	the **p** holy through his own blood.
1Pe	2: 9	But you are a chosen **p,**
	2:10	Once you were not a **p,**
2Pe	2: 1	also false prophets among the **p,**
	3:11	what kind of **p** ought you to be?
Rev	18: 4	"Come out of her, my **p,**
	21: 3	They will be his **p,**
	22:21	of the Lord Jesus be with God's **p.**

ALL PEOPLE Ge 6:13; Jer 17:20; 45:5; Eze 21:5; Joel 2:28; Lk 2:31; Jn 17:2; Ac 2:17; 17:30; Gal 6:10; Rev 19:18

ALL THE PEOPLE Ge 6:12; 26:11; 29:22; 35:6; Ex 11:8; 12:6; 18:21; 19:11; 33:8; 33:8; Lev 9:23, 24; 10:3; 16:33; Nu 13:32; 14:1; 15:26; 31:26; Dt 13:9; 17:7, 13; 20:11; 27:14, 15, 16, 17, 18, 19, 20, 21, 22, 23, 24, 25, 26; Jos 2:24; 5:5, 5; 6:5; 7:3, 3; 8:25; 11:14; 24:2, 27; Jdg 9:49, 51; 16:30; 20:2, 8, 26; Ru 4:9; 1Sa 2:23; 7:2; 10:24, 24; 11:15; 12:18; 18:5; 2Sa 3:31, 32, 34, 36, 37; 6:19; 15:17, 23, 23, 24, 30; 16:14; 17:2, 3, 3, 16, 22; 19:39; 20:22; 1Ki 1:39, 40; 9:20; 12:12; 18:24, 30, 39; 2Ki 10:9, 18; 11:14, 18, 19, 20; 14:21; 16:15; 17:20; 23:2, 3, 21; 25:26; 1Ch 13:4; 16:36, 43; 28:21; 2Ch 7:4, 5; 8:7; 10:12; 20:18; 23:13, 17, 20, 21; 24:10; 26:1; 29:36; 32:9; 34:9, 30; 35:13; Ezr 3:11; 7:25; 10:9; Ne 4:16; 8:1, 3, 5, 6, 9, 11, 12; 10:9; Est 1:5; Job 1:3; Ps 33:8; 106:48; Ecc 4:16; Isa 9:9; Jer 19:14; 25:1, 2; 26:2, 7, 8, 8, 9, 11, 12, 16, 18; 28:1, 5, 7, 11; 29:16, 25; 34:8, 19; 36:6, 9, 10; 38:1, 4; 41:13, 14; 42:1, 8; 43:4; 44:15, 20, 24; Eze 38:20; 39:13, 25; 45:16, 22; Da 9:6; Am 9:1; Zec 7:5; Mal 2:9; Mt 12:23; 13:2; 22:10; 27:25; Mk 1:5; 4:1; 5:20; 6:39; 9:15; Lk 2:10; 3:21; 4:28, 36; 7:29; 8:37, 47, 52; 18:43; 19:7, 48; 20:6, 45; 21:38; 23:48; 24:19; Jn 8:2; Ac 2:47; 3:9, 11; 4:10, 21; 5:34; 8:9, 10; 10:41; 13:24; Heb 9:19, 19

PEOPLE OF ISRAEL See ISRAEL

PEOPLE OF JERUSALEM
See JERUSALEM

PEOPLE OF JUDAH See JUDAH

PEOPLE'S [PEOPLE]
2Ch 25:15 "Why do you consult this **p** gods,

Mt 13:15 this **p** heart has become calloused;
Ac 28:27 this **p** heart has become calloused;

PEOPLES [PEOPLE]

Ge 12: 3 and all **p** on earth will be blessed
17:16 kings of **p** will come from her."
25:23 and two **p** from within you will
27:29 May nations serve you and **p** bow
28: 3 until you become a community of **p**.
48: 4 I will make you a community of **p**,
Dt 4:27 LORD will scatter you among the **p**,
7: 7 for you were the fewest of all **p**.
14: 2 of all the **p** on the face of the earth,
28:10 all the **p** on earth will see
Jos 4:24 the **p** of the earth might know
Jdg 2:12 and worshiped various gods of the **p**
1Ki 8:43 that all the **p** of the earth may know
2Ch 7:20 an object of ridicule among all **p**.
Ezr 3: 3 Despite their fear of the **p** around
10: 2 foreign women from the **p** around us.
Ne 10:30 in marriage to the **p** around us
Ps 2: 1 conspire and the **p** plot in vain?
9: 8 he will govern the **p** with justice.
67: 3 May the **p** praise you, O God;
87: 6 will write in the register of the **p**:
96:10 he will judge the **p**
117: 1 extol him, all you **p**.
Isa 2: 4 and will settle disputes for many **p**.
11:10 will stand as a banner for the **p**;
17:12 Oh, the uproar of the **p**—
25: 6 prepare a feast of rich food for all **p**,
34: 1 and listen; pay attention, you **p**!
49:22 I will lift up my banner to the **p**;
55: 4 I have made him a witness to the **p**,
Jer 10: 3 the customs of the **p** are worthless;
Da 7:14 all **p**, nations and men of every
Mic 4: 1 and **p** will stream to it.
5: 7 will be in the midst of many **p**
Zep 3: 9 "Then will I purify the lips of the **p**,
3:20 honor and praise among all the **p**
Zec 8:20 "Many **p** and the inhabitants of many
12: 2 sends all the surrounding **p** reeling.
Ac 3:25 all **p** on earth will be blessed.'
4:25 rage and the **p** plot in vain?
Rev 1: 7 **p** of the earth will mourn because of
10:11 must prophesy again about many **p**,

ALL PEOPLES Ge 12:3; 28:14; Dt 7:7; 1Ki
9:7; 1Ch 16:24; 2Ch 7:20; Ps 96:3; Isa 25:6, 7;
Da 7:14; Ac 3:25

ALL THE PEOPLES Dt 7:6, 16, 19; 14:2;
28:10; Jos 4:24; 1Ki 8:43, 60; 2Ch 6:33; 32:13;
Ps 67:3, 5; 97:6; Jer 1:15; 25:9; Da 3:7; 4:35;
5:19; 6:25; Hab 2:5; Zep 3:20; Rev 1:7

PEOR

Nu 25: 3 joined in worshiping the Baal of **P**.
Dt 4: 3 everyone who followed the Baal of **P**
Jos 22:17 Was not the sin of **P** enough for us?

PERCEIVE [PERCEIVED,
PERCEIVING]

Ps 139: 2 you **p** my thoughts from afar.
Pr 24:12 not he who weighs the heart **p** it?

PERCEIVED* [PERCEIVE]

Isa 64: 4 no one has heard, no ear has **p**,

PERCEIVING* [PERCEIVE]

Isa 6: 9 be ever seeing, but never **p**.'
Mt 13:14 be ever seeing but never **p**,
Mk 4:12 be ever seeing but never **p**,
Ac 28:26 be ever seeing but never **p**."

PERES* [PARSIN]

Da 5:28 **P**: Your kingdom is divided and

PEREZ

Ge 38:29 And he was named **P**.
Ru 4:12 may your family be like that of **P**,
Mt 1: 3 Judah the father of **P** and Zerah,

PERFECT* [PERFECTER,
PERFECTING, PERFECTION]

Dt 32: 4 He is the Rock, his works are **p**,
2Sa 22:31 "As for God, his way is **p**;
22:33 with strength and makes my way **p**.
Job 36: 4 one **p** in knowledge is with you.
37:16 of him who is **p** in knowledge?
Ps 18:30 As for God, his way is **p**;
18:32 with strength and makes my way **p**.
19: 7 The law of the LORD is **p**,
50: 2 From Zion, **p** in beauty,
64: 6 "We have devised a **p** plan!"
SS 6: 9 my **p** one, is unique,
Isa 25: 1 in **p** faithfulness you have done
26: 3 in **p** peace him whose mind is
Eze 16:14 I had given you made your beauty **p**,
27: 3 O Tyre, "I am **p** in beauty."
28:12 full of wisdom and **p** in beauty.
Mt 5:48 Be **p**, therefore, as your heavenly
Father is **p**.
19:21 "If you want to be **p**, go,
Ro 12: 2 his good, pleasing and **p** will.
2Co 12: 9 my power is made **p** in weakness."
Php 3:12 or have already been made **p**,
Col 1:28 we may present everyone **p** in Christ.
3:14 binds them all together in **p** unity.
Heb 2:10 the author of their salvation **p**
5: 9 once made **p**, he became the source
7:19 (for the law made nothing **p**),
7:28 who has been made **p** forever.
9:11 the greater and more **p** tabernacle
10: 1 make **p** those who draw near
10:14 by one sacrifice he has made **p**
11:40 with us would they be made **p**.
12:23 the spirits of righteous men made **p**,
Jas 1:17 Every good and **p** gift is from above,
1:25 into the **p** law that gives freedom,
3: 2 he is a **p** man,
1Jn 4:18 But **p** love drives out fear.
4:18 who fears is not made **p** in love.

PERFECTER* [PERFECT]

Heb 12: 2 the author and **p** of our faith,

PERFECTING* [PERFECT]

2Co 7: 1 **p** holiness out of reverence for God.

PERFECTION* [PERFECT]

Ps 119:96 To all I see a limit;
La 2:15 city that was called the **p** of beauty,
Eze 27: 4 builders brought your beauty to **p**.
    27:11 they brought your beauty to **p**.
    28:12 the model of **p**, full of wisdom
1Co 13:10 but when **p** comes, the imperfect
2Co 13: 9 and our prayer is for your **p**.
    13:11 Aim for **p**, listen to my appeal,
Heb 7:11 If **p** could have been attained through

PERFORM [PERFORMED, PERFORMS]

Ex 3:20 with all the wonders that I will **p**
2Sa 7:23 and to **p** great and awesome wonders
1Ki 8:11 the priests could not **p** their service
Jer 21: 2 the LORD will **p** wonders for us as
Mk 13:22 will appear and **p** signs and miracles
Jn 3: 2 For no one could **p** the miraculous

PERFORMED [PERFORM]

Ex 4:30 also **p** the signs before the people,
Nu 14:11 signs I have **p** among them?
Dt 11: 3 the signs he **p** and the things he did
Ne 9:17 to remember the miracles you **p**
Mt 11:21 If the miracles that were **p** in you
Jn 10:41 John never **p** a miraculous sign,
Ac 5:12 apostles **p** many miraculous signs
Rev 13:13 And he **p** great and miraculous signs,
    19:20 the false prophet who had **p** the

PERFORMS [PERFORM]

Ps 77:14 You are the God who **p** miracles;

PERFUME

Ex 30:33 Whoever makes **p** like it and
Ecc 7: 1 A good name is better than fine **p**,
SS 1: 3 your name is like **p** poured out.
Mk 14: 3 an alabaster jar of very expensive **p**,
Jn 12: 7 save this **p** for the day of my burial.

PERGAMUM*

Rev 1:11 Smyrna, **P**, Thyatira, Sardis,
    2:12 the angel of the church in **P** write:

PERIL

2Co 1:10 delivered us from such a deadly **p**,

PERISH [PERISHABLE, PERISHED, PERISHES, PERISHING]

Ge 6:17 Everything on earth will **p**.
Lev 26:38 You will **p** among the nations;
Jos 23:13 until you **p** from this good land,
Est 4:16 And if I **p**, I **p**."
Ps 1: 6 but the way of the wicked will **p**.
    37:20 But the wicked will **p**:
    73:27 Those who are far from you will **p**;
    102:26 They will **p**, but you remain;
Pr 11:10 when the wicked **p**,
    19: 9 and he who pours out lies will **p**.
    21:28 A false witness will **p**,
    28:28 but when the wicked **p**,
Isa 1:28 those who forsake the LORD will **p**.

    29:14 the wisdom of the wise will **p**,
    60:12 that will not serve you will **p**;
Jer 51:18 their judgment comes, they will **p**.
Jnh 1: 6 and we will not **p**."
    3: 9 so that we will not **p**."
Zec 11: 9 and the perishing to **p**.
Lk 13: 3 unless you repent, you too will all **p**.
    13: 5 unless you repent, you too will all **p**.
    21:18 But not a hair of your head will **p**.
Jn 3:16 shall not **p** but have eternal life.
    10:28 and they shall never **p**;
    11:50 than that the whole nation **p**."
Ac 8:20 "May your money **p** with you,
Ro 2:12 will also **p** apart from the law,
Col 2:22 These are all destined to **p** with use,
2Th 2:10 They **p** because they refused to love
Heb 1:11 They will **p**, but you remain;
1Pe 1: 4 an inheritance that can never **p**, spoil
2Pe 3: 9 not wanting anyone to **p**,

PERISHABLE [PERISH]

1Co 15:42 The body that is sown is **p**,
1Pe 1:18 not with **p** things such as silver or
    1:23 not of **p** seed, but of imperishable,

PERISHED [PERISH]

Ge 7:21 that moved on the earth **p**—
Dt 2:14 generation of fighting men had **p**
Job 4: 7 Who, being innocent, has ever **p**?
Ps 119:92 I would have **p** in my affliction.
Jer 7:28 Truth has **p**; it has vanished

PERISHES [PERISH]

Job 8:13 so **p** the hope of the godless.
1Pe 1: 7 which **p** even though refined

PERISHING [PERISH]

Ecc 7:15 righteous man **p** in his righteousness,
1Co 1:18 is foolishness to those who are **p**,
2Co 2:15 being saved and those who are **p**.
    4: 3 it is veiled to those who are **p**.

PERIZZITES

Ge 13: 7 and **P** were also living in the land at
Ex 3: 8 Amorites, **P**, Hivites and Jebusites.
Jos 24:11 **P**, Canaanites, Hittites, Girgashites,

PERJURERS* [PERJURY]

Mal 3: 5 against sorcerers, adulterers and **p**,
1Ti 1:10 for slave traders and liars and **p**—

PERJURY* [PERJURERS]

Jer 7: 9 commit adultery and **p**,

PERMANENT* [PERMANENTLY]

Lev 25:34 it is their **p** possession.
Jos 8:28 and made it a **p** heap of ruins,
Jn 8:35 a slave has no **p** place in the family,
Heb 7:24 he has a **p** priesthood.

PERMANENTLY [PERMANENT]

Lev 25:23 " 'The land must not be sold **p**,

PERMISSIBLE* [PERMIT]

1Co 6:12 "Everything is **p** for me"—

6:12   "Everything is **p** for me"—
10:23   "Everything is **p"**—
10:23   "Everything is **p"**—

PERMIT* [PERMISSIBLE, PERMITTED]

Ex   12:23   and he will not **p** the destroyer
Hos   5: 4   "Their deeds do not **p** them to return
Ac   24:23   **p** his friends to take care of his needs
1Ti   2:12   I do not **p** a woman to teach or

PERMITTED [PERMIT]

Mt   19: 8   "Moses **p** you to divorce your wives
2Co   12: 4   things that man is not **p** to tell.

PERPLEXED

2Co   4: 8   **p**, but not in despair;

PERSECUTE [PERSECUTED, PERSECUTING, PERSECUTION, PERSECUTIONS, PERSECUTORS]

Dt   30: 7   on your enemies who hate and **p** you.
Ps   119:86   for men **p** me without cause.
Mt   5:11   when people insult you, **p** you
      5:44   and pray for those who **p** you,
Lk   11:49   and others they will **p.'**
      21:12   will lay hands on you and **p** you.
Jn   15:20   they will **p** you also.
Ac   9: 4   "Saul, Saul, why do you **p** me?"
      22: 7   Why do you **p** me?'
      26:11   even went to foreign cities to **p** them.
Ro   12:14   Bless those who **p** you;

PERSECUTED [PERSECUTE]

Mt   5:10   Blessed are those who are **p** because
      5:12   in the same way they **p** the prophets
Jn   15:20   If they **p** me, they will persecute you
Ac   22: 4   I **p** the followers of this Way
1Co   4:12   when we are **p**, we endure it;
      15: 9   because I **p** the church of God.
2Co   4: 9   **p**, but not abandoned;
Gal   1:13   how intensely I **p** the church of God
1Th   3: 4   kept telling you that we would be **p**,
2Ti   3:12   a godly life in Christ Jesus will be **p**,
Heb   11:37   destitute, **p** and mistreated—

PERSECUTING* [PERSECUTE]

Ac   9: 5   "I am Jesus, whom you are **p**,"
      22: 8   whom you are **p**,' he replied.
      26:15   " 'I am Jesus, whom you are **p**,'
Php   3: 6   as for zeal, **p** the church;

PERSECUTION [PERSECUTE]

Mt   13:21   When trouble or **p** comes because of
Ac   8: 1   that day a great **p** broke out against
Ro   8:35   Shall trouble or hardship or **p**
Heb   10:33   publicly exposed to insult and **p**;

PERSECUTIONS* [PERSECUTE]

Mk   10:30   and fields—and with them, **p**)
2Co   12:10   in hardships, in **p**, in difficulties.
2Th   1: 4   the **p** and trials you are enduring.
2Ti   3:11   **p**, sufferings—what kinds of things
      3:11   Iconium and Lystra, the **p** I endured.

PERSECUTORS [PERSECUTE]

Ps   119:84   When will you punish my **p**?
Jer   15:15   Avenge me on my **p**.

PERSEVERANCE* [PERSEVERE]

Ro   5: 3   we know that suffering produces **p**;
      5: 4   **p**, character; and character, hope.
2Co   12:12   were done among you with great **p**.
2Th   1: 4   about your **p** and faith in all
      3: 5   hearts into God's love and Christ's **p**
Heb   12: 1   run with **p** the race marked out for us
Jas   1: 3   the testing of your faith develops **p**.
      1: 4   **P** must finish its work so
      5:11   You have heard of Job's **p**
2Pe   1: 6   and to self-control; and to **p**,
Rev   2: 2   your hard work and your **p**.
      2:19   your service and **p**,

PERSEVERE* [PERSEVERANCE, PERSEVERED, PERSEVERES, PERSEVERING]

1Ti   4:16   **P** in them, because if you do,
Heb   10:36   to **p** so that when you have done

PERSEVERED* [PERSEVERE]

Heb   11:27   he **p** because he saw him who is
Jas   5:11   consider blessed those who have **p**.
Rev   2: 3   You have **p** and have endured

PERSEVERES* [PERSEVERE]

1Co   13: 7   always hopes, always **p**.
Jas   1:12   Blessed is the man who **p** under trial,

PERSEVERING* [PERSEVERE]

Lk   8:15   retain it, and by **p** produce a crop.

PERSIA [PERSIANS]

Ezr   1: 1   In the first year of Cyrus king of **P**,
Da   8:20   the kings of Media and **P**.
      10:20   return to fight against the prince of **P**

PERSIANS [PERSIA]

Da   6:15   law of the Medes and **P** no decree

PERSIST [PERSISTENCE]

Isa   1: 5   Why do you **p** in rebellion?
Ro   11:23   And if they do not **p** in unbelief,

PERSISTENCE* [PERSIST]

Ro   2: 7   by **p** in doing good seek glory,

PERSON

Ex   23: 7   an innocent or honest **p** to death,
Ps   62:12   Surely you will reward each **p**
Pr   24:12   Will he not repay each **p** according
Mt   16:27   then he will reward each **p** according
Ro   2: 6   God "will give to each **p** according
Rev   20:13   and each **p** was judged according

PERSUADE [PERSUADED, PERSUASIVE]

Ac   18: 4   trying to **p** Jews and Greeks.
      26:28   in such a short time you can **p** me to

2Co 5:11 we try to **p** men.

PERSUADED [PERSUADE]
Mt 27:20 and the elders **p** the crowd
Ro 4:21 being fully **p** that God had power

PERSUASIVE* [PERSUADE]
Pr 7:21 With **p** words she led him astray;
1Co 2: 4 not with wise and **p** words,

PERVERSE [PERVERT]
Dt 32:20 for they are a **p** generation,
Pr 3:32 for the LORD detests a **p** man
  17:20 A man of **p** heart does not prosper;
Lk 9:41 "O unbelieving and **p** generation,"

PERVERSION* [PERVERT]
Lev 18:23 sexual relations with it; that is a **p.**
  20:12 What they have done is a **p;**
Ro 1:27 the due penalty for their **p.**
Jude 1: 7 up to sexual immorality and **p.**

PERVERT* [PERVERSE, PERVERSION, PERVERTED, PERVERTING, PERVERTS]
Ex 23: 2 do not **p** justice by siding with
Lev 19:15 " 'Do not **p** justice;
Dt 16:19 Do not **p** justice or show partiality.
Job 8: 3 Does God **p** justice?
  8: 3 Does the Almighty **p** what is right?
  34:12 that the Almighty would **p** justice.
Pr 17:23 in secret to **p** the course of justice.
Gal 1: 7 trying to **p** the gospel of Christ.

PERVERTED [PERVERT]
1Sa 8: 3 and accepted bribes and **p** justice.
Jer 3:21 because they have **p** their ways

PERVERTING* [PERVERT]
Ac 13:10 Will you never stop **p** the right ways

PERVERTS* [PERVERT]
1Ti 1:10 for adulterers and **p,** for slave traders

PESTILENCE [PESTILENCES]
Dt 32:24 consuming **p** and deadly plague;
Ps 91: 6 nor the **p** that stalks in the darkness,

PESTILENCES* [PESTILENCE]
Lk 21:11 famines and **p** in various places,

PETER [CEPHAS, SIMON]
Apostle, brother of Andrew, also called Simon (Mt 10:2; Mk 3:16; Lk 6:14; Ac 1:13), and Cephas (Jn 1:42). Confession of Christ (Mt 16:13-20; Mk 8:27-30; Lk 9:18-27). At transfiguration (Mt 17:1-8; Mk 9:2-8; Lk 9:28-36; 2Pe 1:16-18). Caught fish with coin (Mt 17:24-27). Denial of Jesus predicted (Mt 26:31-35; Mk 14:27-31; Lk 22:31-34; Jn 13:31-38). Denied Jesus (Mt 26:69-75; Mk 14:66-72; Lk 22:54-62; Jn 18:15-27). Commissioned by Jesus to shepherd his flock (Jn 21:15-23).

Speech at Pentecost (Ac 2). Healed beggar (Ac 3:1-10). Speech at temple (Ac 3:11-26), before Sanhedrin (Ac 4:1-22). In Samaria (Ac 8:14-25). Sent by vision to Cornelius (Ac 10). Announced salvation of Gentiles in Jerusalem (Ac 11; 15). Freed from prison (Ac 12). Inconsistency at Antioch (Gal 2:11-21). At Jerusalem Council (Ac 15).

Letters: 1-2 Peter.

PETITION [PETITIONS]
1Ch 16: 4 to make **p,** to give thanks,
Est 7: 3 grant me my life—this is my **p.**
Jer 7:16 nor offer any plea or **p** for them;
Da 9: 3 pleaded with him in prayer and **p,**
Php 4: 6 by prayer and **p,** with thanksgiving,

PETITIONS* [PETITION]
Da 9:17 the prayers and **p** of your servant.
Heb 5: 7 and **p** with loud cries and tears to

PHANTOM*
Ps 39: 6 Man is a mere **p** as he goes

PHARAOH [PHARAOH'S]
Ge 12:15 they praised her to **P,**
  41:14 So **P** sent for Joseph,
  47:10 Then Jacob blessed **P** and went out
Ex 1:22 **P** gave this order to all his people:
  2:15 When **P** heard of this,
  3:11 "Who am I, that I should go to **P**
  5: 2 **P** said, "Who is the LORD,
  11: 1 "I will bring one more plague on **P**
  14:17 And I will gain glory through **P**
Dt 7: 8 from the power of **P** king of Egypt.
Isa 36: 6 Such is **P** king of Egypt to all
Ro 9:17 For the Scripture says to **P:**

PHARAOH'S [PHARAOH]
Ex 2: 5 **P** daughter went down to the Nile
  7: 3 But I will harden **P** heart,
  7:13 Yet **P** heart became hard
  7:22 and **P** heart became hard;
  8:19 But **P** heart was hard and he would
  9:12 the LORD hardened **P** heart
  9:35 So **P** heart was hard and he would
  10:20 But the LORD hardened **P** heart,
  10:27 But the LORD hardened **P** heart,
  11:10 But the LORD hardened **P** heart,
  14: 4 And I will harden **P** heart,
1Ki 11: 1 foreign women besides **P** daughter—
Heb 11:24 be known as the son of **P** daughter.

PHARISEE [PHARISEES]
Lk 11:37 a **P** invited him to eat with him;
Ac 5:34 But a **P** named Gamaliel,
  23: 6 I am a **P,** the son of a **P.**
Php 3: 5 in regard to the law, a **P;**

PHARISEES [PHARISEE]
Mt 5:20 righteousness surpasses that of the **P**
  16: 6 your guard against the yeast of the **P**
  23:13 teachers of the law and **P**
Mk 2:18 and the disciples of the **P** are fasting,
Lk 11:42 "Woe to you **P,**

Jn   3: 1 a man of the **P** named Nicodemus,
Ac   23: 7 a dispute broke out between the **P**

PHILADELPHIA*

Rev 1:11 Thyatira, Sardis, **P** and Laodicea."
       3: 7 the angel of the church in **P** write:

PHILEMON*

Phm 1: 1 To **P** our dear friend

PHILIP

   1. Apostle (Mt 10:3; Mk 3:18; Lk 6:14; Jn 1:43-48; 14:8; Ac 1:13).
   2. Deacon (Ac 6:1-7); evangelist in Samaria (Ac 8:4-25), to Ethiopian (Ac 8:26-40).
   3. Herod Philip I (Mt 14:3; Mk 6:17).
   4. Herod Philip II (Lk 3:1).

PHILIPPI

Mt   16:13 to the region of Caesarea **P,**
Ac   16:12 From there we traveled to **P,**
Php   1: 1 To all the saints in Christ Jesus at **P,**

PHILISTIA [PHILISTINE]

Ex   15:14 anguish will grip the people of **P.**
Ps   60: 8 over **P** I shout in triumph."

PHILISTINE [PHILISTIA, PHILISTINES]

Jos 13: 3 (the territory of the five **P** rulers
1Sa   6: 1 had been in **P** territory seven months,
      14: 1 to the **P** outpost on the other side."
      17:23 Goliath, the **P** champion from Gath,
      17:37 deliver me from the hand of this **P."**

PHILISTINES [PHILISTINE]

Ge   21:34 Abraham stayed in the land of the **P**
      26: 1 to Abimelech king of the **P** in Gerar.
Ex   23:31 from the Red Sea to the Sea of the **P,**
Jdg 10: 7 He sold them into the hands of the **P**
      13: 1 into the hands of the **P** for forty years
      16: 5 The rulers of the **P** went to her
      16:30 "Let me die with the **P!"**
1Sa   4: 1 went out to fight against the **P.**
       5: 1 the **P** had captured the ark of God,
      13:20 So all Israel went down to the **P** to
      17: 1 the **P** gathered their forces for war
      17:51 the **P** saw that their hero was dead,
      23: 1 the **P** are fighting against Keilah
      27: 1 to escape to the land of the **P.**
      31: 1 Now the **P** fought against Israel;
2Sa   5:17 When the **P** heard that David had
       8: 1 David defeated the **P** and subdued
      21:15 a battle between the **P** and Israel.
2Ki 18: 8 he defeated the **P,**
Isa 14:31 Melt away, all you **P!**
Jer 47: 1 The LORD is about to destroy the **P,**
Eze 25:16 to stretch out my hand against the **P,**
Am   1: 8 till the last of the **P** is dead,"

PHILOSOPHER* [PHILOSOPHY]

1Co   1:20 Where is the **p** of this age?

PHILOSOPHERS* [PHILOSOPHY]

Ac   17:18 A group of Epicurean and Stoic **p**

PHILOSOPHY* [PHILOSOPHER, PHILOSOPHERS]

Col   2: 8 through hollow and deceptive **p,**

PHINEHAS

   1. Grandson of Aaron (Ex 6:25; Jos 22:30-32). Zeal for the LORD stopped plague (Nu 25:7-13; Ps 106:30).
   2. Son of Eli; a wicked priest (1Sa 1:3; 2:12-17; 4:1-19).

PHOEBE*

Ro   16: 1 I commend to you our sister **P,**

PHYLACTERIES*

Mt   23: 5 They make their **p** wide

PHYSICAL*

Da   1: 4 without any **p** defect, handsome,
Ro   2:28 circumcision merely outward and **p.**
Col   1:22 reconciled you by Christ's **p** body
1Ti   4: 8 For **p** training is of some value,
Jas   2:16 but does nothing about his **p** needs,

PHYSICIAN* [PHYSICIANS]

Jer   8:22 Is there no **p** there?
Lk   4:23 this proverb to me: '**P,** heal yourself!

PHYSICIANS [PHYSICIAN]

Job 13: 4 you are worthless **p,** all of you!

PICK [PICKED]

Lev 19:10 or **p** up the grapes that have fallen.
Dt   23:25 you may **p** kernels with your hands,
Ru   2:16 and leave them for her to **p** up,
Mk   2:23 they began to **p** some heads of grain.
Jn   5: 8 **P** up your mat and walk."

PICKED [PICK]

Lk   14: 7 how the guests **p** the places of honor
Jn   5: 9 he **p** up his mat and walked.
       8:59 they **p** up stones to stone him,

PIECE [PIECES]

Ex   15:25 the LORD showed him a **p** of wood.
1Sa 24:11 at this **p** of your robe in my hand!
1Ki 17:11 "And bring me, please, a **p** of bread."
Mk   2:21 the new **p** will pull away from
Jn   13:26 to whom I will give this **p** of bread
      19:23 woven in one **p** from top to bottom.

PIECES [PIECE]

Ge   15:17 and passed between the **p.**
Ex   32:19 breaking them to **p** at the foot of
Jdg 20: 6 cut her into **p** and sent one piece
1Ki 11:30 and tore it into twelve **p.**
2Ki 18: 4 He broke into **p** the bronze snake
Ps   2: 9 you will dash them to **p**
Jer 34:18 and then walked between its **p.**
Hos   6: 5 I cut you in **p** with my prophets,
Mic   1: 7 All her idols will be broken to **p;**

Zec 11:12 So they paid me thirty **p** of silver.
Mt 14:20 twelve basketfuls of broken **p**
     15:37 seven basketfuls of broken **p**
Lk 20:18 falls on that stone will be broken to **p**
Rev 2:27 he will dash them to **p**

PIERCE [PIERCED]

Ex 21: 6 doorpost and **p** his ear with an awl.
Pr 12:18 Reckless words **p** like a sword,
Lk 2:35 a sword will **p** your own soul too."

PIERCED [PIERCE]

Ps 22:16 they have **p** my hands and my feet.
     40: 6 but my ears you have **p;**
Isa 53: 5 But he was **p** for our transgressions,
Zec 12:10 look on me, the one they have **p,**
Jn 19:37 look on the one they have **p."**
Rev 1: 7 even those who **p** him;

PIG* [PIG'S, PIGS]

Lev 11: 7 And the **p**, though it has a split hoof
Dt 14: 8 The **p** is also unclean;

PIG'S* [PIG]

Pr 11:22 a gold ring in a **p** snout is
Isa 66: 3 like one who presents **p** blood,

PIGEONS

Lev 5: 7 to bring two doves or two young **p** to
     12: 8 to bring two doves or two young **p,**
Lk 2:24 "a pair of doves or two young **p."**

PIGS [PIG]

Isa 66:17 of those who eat the flesh of **p**
Mt 7: 6 do not throw your pearls to **p.**
Mk 5:11 A large herd of **p** was feeding on
Lk 15:16 with the pods that the **p** were eating,

PILATE [PONTIUS]

Governor of Judea. Questioned Jesus (Mt 27:1-26; Mk 15:15; Lk 22:66-23:25; Jn 18:28-19:16); sent him to Herod (Lk 23:6-12); consented to his crucifixion when crowds chose Barabbas (Mt 27:15-26; Mk 15:6-15; Lk 23:13-25; Jn 19:1-10).

PILGRIMS (KJV) See STRANGERS

PILLAR [PILLARS]

Ge 19:26 and she became a **p** of salt.
     28:18 and set it up as a **p** and poured oil
     31:52 and this **p** is a witness,
Ex 13:21 in a **p** of cloud to guide them on
               their way and by night in a **p** of fire
Nu 14:14 before them in a **p** of cloud by day
               and a **p** of fire by night.
1Ti 3:15 the **p** and foundation of the truth.
Rev 3:12 Him who overcomes I will make a **p**

PILLARS [PILLAR]

Ex 24: 4 set up twelve stone **p** representing
Jdg 16:29 reached toward the two central **p**
1Ki 7:15 He cast two bronze **p,**
2Ki 25:13 Babylonians broke up the bronze **p,**
Ps 75: 3 it is I who hold its **p** firm.
     144:12 our daughters will be like **p** carved

Pr 9: 1 she has hewn out its seven **p.**
SS 5:15 His legs are **p** of marble set on bases
Gal 2: 9 those reputed to be **p,**
Rev 10: 1 and his legs were like fiery **p.**

PINE

1Ki 5: 8 in providing the cedar and **p** logs.
Isa 60:13 the **p,** the fir and the cypress together
Hos 14: 8 I am like a green **p** tree;

PINIONS

Dt 32:11 and carries them on its **p.**

PIPES

Da 3: 5 lyre, harp, **p** and all kinds of music,

PISGAH

Dt 3:27 Go up to the top of **P** and look west

PIT [PITS]

Ex 21:33 a **p** or digs one and fails to cover it
Ps 7:15 falls into the **p** he has made.
     35: 8 may they fall into the **p,** to their ruin.
     40: 2 He lifted me out of the slimy **p,**
     103: 4 who redeems your life from the **p**
Pr 23:27 for a prostitute is a deep **p**
     26:27 If a man digs a **p,** he will fall into it;
Isa 24:17 Terror and **p** and snare await you,
     38:17 In your love you kept me from the **p**
Eze 19: 4 and he was trapped in their **p.**
Jnh 2: 6 you brought my life up from the **p,**
Mt 15:14 both will fall into a **p."**

PITCH

Ge 6:14 and coat it with **p** inside and out.
Ex 2: 3 and coated it with tar and **p.**

PITIED* [PITY]

Ps 106:46 to be **p** by all who held them captive.
1Co 15:19 we are to be **p** more than all men.

PITIFUL* [PITY]

Rev 3:17 **p,** poor, blind and naked.

PITY [PITIED, PITIFUL]

Dt 7:16 Do not look on them with **p** and do
2Ch 36:15 because he had **p** on his people and
Ps 72:13 He will take **p** on the weak and
Ecc 4:10 But **p** the man who falls
Eze 7: 4 not look on you with **p** or spare you;
Joel 2:14 He may turn and have **p** and leave
Lk 10:33 he took **p** on him.
1Jn 3:17 brother in need but has no **p** on him,

PLACE [PLACED, PLACES]

Ge 22:14 called that **p** The LORD Will Provide.
     28:16 "Surely the LORD is in this **p,**
     50:19 Am I in the **p** of God?
Ex 3: 5 the **p** where you are standing is holy
     26:33 The curtain will separate the Holy **P**
               from the Most Holy **P.**
     32:34 lead the people to the **p** I spoke of,
Lev 26:11 I will put my dwelling **p** among you,
Dt 12: 5 to seek the **p** the LORD your God
Jos 5:15 the **p** where you are standing is holy.

1Ki 8:13 a **p** for you to dwell forever."
2Ki 17:11 At every high **p** they burned incense,
2Ch 6:21 Hear from heaven, your dwelling **p;**
Ezr 9: 8 giving us a firm **p** in his sanctuary,
Est 4:14 the Jews will arise from another **p,**
Ps 24: 3 Who may stand in his holy **p?**
     26: 8 the **p** where your glory dwells.
     32: 7 You are my hiding **p;**
     84: 1 How lovely is your dwelling **p,**
    132:14 "This is my resting **p** for ever
Pr   8:27 when he set the heavens in **p,**
Ecc 6: 6 Do not all go to the same **p?**
SS   8: 6 **P** me like a seal over your heart,
Isa 42: 9 See, the former things have taken **p,**
Eze 37:27 My dwelling **p** will be with them;
Da   7: 9 "As I looked, "thrones were set in **p,**
Hag 2: 9 'And in this **p** I will grant peace,'
Mt   8:20 Son of Man has no **p** to lay his head.
    27:33 (which means The **P** of the Skull).
Jn 14: 2 I am going there to prepare a **p**
Php 2: 9 God exalted him to the highest **p**
2Pe 1:19 as to a light shining in a dark **p,**
Rev 1: 1 his servants what must soon take **p.**
    20:11 and there was no **p** for them.
    22: 6 the things that must soon take **p."**

HIGH PLACE See HIGH

HOLY PLACE See HOLY

PLACED [PLACE]
Mk 15:46 and **p** it in a tomb cut out of rock.
Lk   2: 7 in cloths and **p** him in a manger,
Jn   6:27 the Father has **p** his seal of approval.
Eph 1:22 And God **p** all things under his feet

PLACES [PLACE]
Dt 33:29 you will trample down their high **p."**
1Ki 3: 2 were still sacrificing at the high **p,**
2Ki 18: 4 He removed the high **p,**
Ps 78:58 They angered him with their high **p;**
Jer 19: 5 the high **p** of Baal to burn their sons
Mt 13: 5 Some fell on rocky **p,**

HIGH PLACES See HIGH

PLAGUE [PLAGUED, PLAGUES]
Ex 11: 1 "I will bring one more **p** on Pharaoh
    32:35 the LORD struck the people with a **p**
Nu 11:33 and he struck them with a severe **p.**
    14:37 struck down and died of a **p** before
    16:48 and the **p** stopped.
    25: 8 **p** against the Israelites was stopped;
Dt 28:21 The LORD will **p** you with diseases
2Sa 24:13 Or three days of **p** in your land?
2Ch 6:28 famine or **p** comes to the land,
Ps 91: 6 nor the **p** that destroys at midday.
Jer 14:12 with the sword, famine and **p."**
Zec 14:12 This is the **p** with which the LORD
Rev 11: 6 strike the earth with every kind of **p**
    16:21 because the **p** was so terrible.

PLAGUED* [PLAGUE]
Ps 73: 5 they are not **p** by human ills.
    73:14 All day long I have been **p;**

PLAGUES [PLAGUE]
Hos 13:14 Where, O death, are your **p?**
Rev 9:18 was killed by the three **p** of fire,
    15: 1 seven angels with the seven last **p—**
    21: 9 seven bowls full of the seven last **p**
    22:18 God will add to him the **p** described

PLAIN [PLAINS]
Ge 13:12 Lot lived among the cities of the **p**
    19:29 God destroyed the cities of the **p,**
Isa 40: 4 the rugged places a **p.**
Ro   1:19 because God has made it **p** to them.

PLAINS [PLAIN]
Dt 34: 8 grieved for Moses in the **p** of Moab
1Ki 20:23 But if we fight them on the **p,**

PLAITING (KJV) See BRAIDED

PLAN [PLANNED, PLANS]
Ge 11: 6 then nothing they **p** to do will be
Ex 26:30 to the **p** shown you on the mountain.
Est 8: 3 to put an end to the evil **p** of Haman
Job 42: 2 no **p** of yours can be thwarted.
Pr 14:22 those who **p** what is good find love
    21:30 no **p** that can succeed against the
Isa 8:10 propose your **p,** but it will not stand,
Am   3: 7 revealing his **p** to his servants
Eph 1:11 been predestined according to the **p**

PLANK
Mt   7: 3 and pay no attention to the **p**
Lk   6:42 first take the **p** out of your eye,

PLANNED [PLAN]
Ps 40: 5 The things you **p** for us
Isa 14:24 "Surely, as I have **p,** so it will be,
    23: 9 The LORD Almighty **p** it,
    46:11 what I have **p,** that will I do.
La   2:17 The LORD has done what he **p;**
Heb 11:40 God had **p** something better for us so

PLANS [PLAN]
Ps 20: 4 and make all your **p** succeed.
    33:11 **p** of the LORD stand firm forever,
Pr 12: 5 The **p** of the righteous are just,
    15:22 **P** fail for lack of counsel,
    16: 3 and your **p** will succeed.
    19:21 Many are the **p** in a man's heart,
    20:18 Make **p** by seeking advice;
Isa 29:15 to great depths to hide their **p** from
    30: 1 "to those who carry out **p** that are
    32: 8 But the noble man makes noble **p,**
Jer 29:11 For I know the **p** I have for you,"
2Co 1:17 Or do I make my **p** in a worldly

PLANT [IMPLANTED, PLANTED, PLANTING, PLANTS, REPLANTED]
Ge   1:29 "I give you every seed-bearing **p** on
Ex   9:25 You will bring them in and **p** them
Lev 19:19 " 'Do not **p** your field with two kinds
Ecc 3: 2 a time to uproot,
Hos 2:23 I will **p** her for myself in the land;
Am   9:15 I will **p** Israel in their own land,

Mt   15:13 "Every **p** that my heavenly Father
1Co   15:37 you do not **p** the body that will be,

PLANTED [PLANT]

Ge   2: 8 Now the LORD God had **p** a garden
Ps   1: 3 like a tree **p** by streams of water,
      92:13 **p** in the house of the LORD.
Isa   60:21 They are the shoot I have **p,**
Jer   17: 8 He will be like a tree **p** by the water
      18: 9 or kingdom is to be built up and **p,**
Mt   15:13 that my heavenly Father has not **p**
      21:33 a landowner who **p** a vineyard.
Lk   13: 6 **p** in his vineyard,
1Co   3: 6 I **p** the seed, Apollos watered it,
Jas   1:21 and humbly accept the word **p**

PLANTING [PLANT]

Isa   61: 3 a **p** of the LORD for the display

PLANTS [PLANT]

Ge   1:11 produce vegetation: seed-bearing **p**
       9: 3 Just as I gave you the green **p,**
Ps   144:12 youth will be like well-nurtured **p,**
Pr   31:16 out of her earnings she **p** a vineyard.
Mk   4:32 becomes the largest of all garden **p,**
1Co   9: 7 Who **p** a vineyard and does not eat

PLASTER

Dt   27: 2 large stones and coat them with **p.**
Da   5: 5 hand appeared and wrote on the **p**

PLATE [PLATES, PLATTER]

Ex   28:36 "Make a **p** of pure gold and engrave

PLATES [PLATE]

Ex   25:29 make its **p** and dishes of pure gold,

PLATFORM

2Ch   6:13 Now he had made a bronze **p,**
Ne   8: 4 the scribe stood on a high wooden **p**

PLATTER [PLATE]

Mk   6:25 the head of John the Baptist on a **p."**

PLAY [PLAYED, PLAYING]

Ge   19: 9 and now he wants to **p** the judge!
1Sa   16:23 David would take his harp and **p.**
Ps   33: 3 Sing to him a new song; **p** skillfully,
Isa   11: 8 The infant will **p** near the hole of

PLAYED [PLAY]

Mt   11:17 " 'We **p** the flute for you,
1Co   14: 7 anyone know what tune is being **p**

PLAYING [PLAY]

1Sa   18:10 while David was **p** the harp,
      19: 9 While David was **p** the harp,
Zec   8: 5 be filled with boys and girls **p** there."
Rev   14: 2 like that of harpists **p** their harps.

PLEA [PLEAD, PLEADED, PLEADS, PLEAS]

1Ki   8:28 servant's prayer and his **p** for mercy,
       9: 3 the prayer and **p** you have made

Ps   17: 1 Hear, O LORD, my righteous **p;**
     102:17 he will not despise their **p.**
Jer   7:16 nor offer any **p** or petition for them;
La   3:56 You heard my **p:**

PLEAD [PLEA]

2Ch   6:37 and repent and **p** with you in the land
Ps   43: 1 and **p** my cause against an ungodly
Isa   1:17 **p** the case of the widow.
Jer   30:13 There is no one to **p** your cause,
Mic   6: 1 **p** your case before the mountains;

PLEADED [PLEA]

Dt   3:23 At that time I **p** with the LORD:
Est   8: 3 Esther again **p** with the king,
Da   9: 3 So I turned to the Lord God and **p**
2Co   12: 8 Three times I **p** with the Lord

PLEADS [PLEA]

Job   16:21 **p** with God as a man **p** for his friend.

PLEAS* [PLEA]

2Ch   6:39 hear their prayer and their **p,**
Isa   19:22 will respond to their **p** and heal them.

PLEASANT [PLEASE]

Ge   49:15 and how **p** is his land,
Ps   16: 6 have fallen for me in **p** places;
     106:24 Then they despised the **p** land;
     133: 1 How good and **p** it is when brothers
     135: 3 sing praise to his name, for that is **p.**
     147: 1 how **p** and fitting to praise him!
Pr   2:10 knowledge will be **p** to your soul.
       3:17 Her ways are **p** ways,
      16:21 and **p** words promote instruction.
      16:24 **P** words are a honeycomb,
Isa   30:10 Tell us **p** things, prophesy illusions.
Heb   12:11 No discipline seems **p** at the time,

PLEASANTNESS* [PLEASE]

Pr   27: 9 the **p** of one's friend springs from

PLEASE [PLEASANT, PLEASANTNESS, PLEASED, PLEASES, PLEASING, PLEASURE, PLEASURES]

Ex   21: 8 If she does not **p** the master
Dt   12:13 your burnt offerings anywhere you **p.**
Job   10: 3 Does it **p** you to oppress me,
Ps   69:31 This will **p** the LORD more than
Pr   20:23 and dishonest scales do not **p** him.
Isa   44:28 and will accomplish all that I **p;**
      46:10 and I will do all that I **p.**
Jer   6:20 your sacrifices do not **p** me."
      27: 5 and I give it to whoever I **p.**
Hos   10:10 When I **p,** I will punish them;
Jn   5:30 not to **p** myself but him who sent me.
Ro   8: 8 by the sinful nature cannot **p** God.
      15: 1 of the weak and not to **p** ourselves.
      15: 2 Each of us should **p** his neighbor
1Co   7:32 how he can **p** the Lord.
       7:33 how he can **p** his wife—
      10:33 as I try to **p** everybody in every way.
2Co   5: 9 So we make it our goal to **p** him,
Gal   1:10 Or am I trying to **p** men?

     6: 8 the one who sows to **p** the Spirit,
Col 1:10 and may **p** him in every way:
1Th 2: 4 We are not trying to **p** men but God,
     4: 1 how to live in order to **p** God,
2Ti 2: 4 wants to **p** his commanding officer.
Tit 2: 9 to try to **p** them,
Heb 11: 6 without faith it is impossible to **p**

PLEASED [PLEASE]

Ex 33:13 If you are **p** with me,
Nu 14: 8 If the LORD is **p** with us,
    24: 1 that it **p** the LORD to bless Israel,
Dt 28:63 Just as it **p** the LORD
1Sa 12:22 LORD was **p** to make you his own.
1Ki 3:10 The Lord was **p** that Solomon
1Ch 29:17 test the heart and are **p** with integrity.
Ps 40:13 Be **p**, O LORD, to save me;
Isa 42:21 It **p** the LORD for the sake
Eze 18:23 not **p** when they turn from their ways
Da 8: 4 He did as he **p** and became great.
Mic 6: 7 Will the LORD be **p** with thousands
Mal 1:10 I am not **p** with you,"
Mt 3:17 with him I am well **p."**
   17: 5 with him I am well **p.**
Mk 1:11 with you I am well **p."**
Lk 3:22 with you I am well **p."**
Jn 5:21 so the Son gives life to whom he is **p**
1Co 1:21 God was **p** through the foolishness
  10: 5 God was not **p** with most of them;
Col 1:19 For God was **p** to have all his
Heb 10: 6 and sin offerings you were not **p.**
  10: 8 nor were you **p** with them"
  10:38 I will not be **p** with him."
  11: 5 was commended as one who **p** God.
  13:16 for with such sacrifices God is **p.**
2Pe 1:17 with him I am well **p."**

PLEASES [PLEASE]

Job 23:13 He does whatever he **p.**
Ps 115: 3 he does whatever he **p.**
  135: 6 The LORD does whatever **p** him,
Pr 15: 8 but the prayer of the upright **p** him.
  21: 1 like a watercourse wherever he **p.**
Ecc 2:26 To the man who **p** him,
  2:26 to hand it over to the one who **p** God.
  7:26 The man who **p** God will escape her,
Isa 56: 4 who choose what **p** me and hold fast
Da 4:35 as he **p** with the powers of heaven
  11: 3 with great power and do as he **p.**
  11:36 "The king will do as he **p.**
Jn 3: 8 The wind blows wherever it **p.**
  8:29 for I always do what **p** him."
Eph 5:10 and find out what **p** the Lord.
Col 3:20 for this **p** the Lord.
1Ti 2: 3 This is good, and **p** God our Savior,
1Jn 3:22 and do what **p** him.

PLEASING [PLEASE]

Ge 2: 9 that were **p** to the eye and good
  8:21 The LORD smelled the **p** aroma
Ex 29:18 offering to the LORD, a **p** aroma,
Lev 1: 9 an aroma **p** to the LORD.
Ezr 6:10 so that they may offer sacrifices **p** to
Ps 19:14 and the meditation of my heart be **p**

104:34 May my meditation be **p** to him,
Pr 15:26 but those of the pure are **p** to him.
  16: 7 a man's ways are **p** to the LORD,
SS 1: 3 **P** is the fragrance of your perfumes;
  4:10 much more **p** is your love than wine,
  7: 6 How beautiful you are and how **p,**
Ro 12: 1 holy and **p** to God—
  14:18 in this way is **p** to God and approved
Php 4:18 an acceptable sacrifice, **p** to God.
1Ti 5: 4 for this is **p** to God.
Heb 13:21 may he work in us what is **p** to him,

AROMA PLEASING

Lev 1:9, 13, 17; 2:2, 9;
3:5; 4:31; 6:15, 21; 17:6; 23:18; Nu 15:3, 7, 10,
13, 14, 24; 18:17; 28:2, 8, 24, 27; 29:2, 8, 13, 36

PLEASING AROMA

Ge 8:21; Ex 29:18, 25,
41; Lev 2:12; 3:16; 8:21, 28; 23:13; 26:31; Nu
28:6, 13; 29:6

PLEASURE [PLEASE]

Ge 18:12 will I now have this **p?"**
Ps 5: 4 not a God who takes **p** in evil;
  51:16 not take **p** in burnt offerings.
  147:10 His **p** is not in the strength of
Pr 10:23 A fool finds **p** in evil conduct,
  18: 2 A fool finds no **p** in understanding
  21:17 He who loves **p** will become poor;
Ecc 2: 2 And what does **p** accomplish?"
  7: 4 the heart of fools is in the house of **p.**
Isa 1:11 I have no **p** in the blood of bulls
Jer 6:10 they find no **p** in it.
Eze 18:32 I take no **p** in the death of anyone,
  33:11 I take no **p** in the death of
Hag 1: 8 I may take **p** in it and be honored,"
Lk 10:21 Father, for this was your good **p.**
Eph 1: 5 in accordance with his **p** and will—
  1: 9 of his will according to his good **p,**
1Ti 5: 6 the widow who lives for **p** is dead
2Ti 3: 4 lovers of **p** rather than lovers of God
2Pe 2:13 of **p** is to carouse in broad daylight.

PLEASURES* [PLEASE]

Ps 16:11 with eternal **p** at your right hand.
Lk 8:14 riches and **p,** and they do not mature.
Tit 3: 3 by all kinds of passions and **p.**
Heb 11:25 to enjoy the **p** of sin for a short time.
Jas 4: 3 spend what you get on your **p.**
2Pe 2:13 in their **p** while they feast with you.

PLEDGE [PLEDGED]

Ge 38:17 "Will you give me something as a **p**
Ex 22:26 take your neighbor's cloak as a **p,**
Nu 30: 2 an oath to obligate himself by a **p,**
Dt 24:17 take the cloak of the widow as a **p.**
Pr 6: 1 if you have struck hands in **p**
  22:26 not be a man who strikes hands in a **p**
Eze 18: 7 returns what he took in **p** for a loan.
1Pe 3:21 but the **p** of a good conscience

PLEDGED [PLEDGE]

Mt 1:18 His mother Mary was **p** to be
Lk 1:27 to a virgin **p** to be married to a man

PLEIADES

Job 38:31 "Can you bind the beautiful **P?**

Am 5: 8 (he who made the **P** and Orion,

PLENTIFUL [PLENTY]

Mt 9:37 "The harvest is **p** but the workers
Lk 10: 2 He told them, "The harvest is **p,**

PLENTY [PLENTIFUL]

Mic 2:11 'I will prophesy for you **p** of wine
2Co 8:14 your **p** will supply what they need,
Php 4:12 whether living in **p** or in want.

PLOT [PLOTS, PLOTTED]

Ne 4:15 that we were aware of their **p** and
Est 2:22 But Mordecai found out about the **p**
Ps 2: 1 and the peoples **p** in vain?
    64: 6 They **p** injustice and say,
Pr 3:29 not **p** harm against your neighbor,
    14:22 Do not those who **p** evil go astray?
Jer 11:18 the LORD revealed their **p** to me,
Na 1: 9 Whatever they **p** against the LORD
Zec 8:17 do not **p** evil against your neighbor,
Mk 3: 6 and began to **p** with the Herodians
Ac 4:25 and the peoples **p** in vain?
    23:16 son of Paul's sister heard of this **p,**

PLOTS [PLOT]

Pr 6:14 who **p** evil with deceit in his heart—
Na 1:11 who **p** evil against the LORD

PLOTTED [PLOT]

Est 9:24 had **p** against the Jews
Jn 11:53 that day on they **p** to take his life.

PLOW [PLOWED, PLOWMAN, PLOWSHARES]

Dt 22:10 Do not **p** with an ox and a donkey
Pr 20: 4 A sluggard does not **p** in season;
Lk 9:62 the **p** and looks back is fit for service

PLOWED [PLOW]

Jdg 14:18 "If you had not **p** with my heifer,

PLOWMAN* [PLOW]

Am 9:13 the reaper will be overtaken by the **p**
1Co 9:10 **p** plows and the thresher threshes,

PLOWSHARES [PLOW]

1Sa 13:20 to the Philistines to have their **p,**
Isa 2: 4 They will beat their swords into **p**
Joel 3:10 Beat your **p** into swords
Mic 4: 3 They will beat their swords into **p**

PLUCK*

Mk 9:47 your eye causes you to sin, **p** it out.

PLUMB

2Ki 21:13 and the **p** line used against
Isa 28:17 and righteousness the **p** line;
Am 7: 8 a **p** line among my people Israel;
Zec 4:10 the **p** line in the hand of Zerubbabel.

PLUNDER [PLUNDERED]

Ex 3:22 And so you will **p** the Egyptians."
Nu 14:31 that you said would be taken as **p,**
Dt 20:14 you may take these as **p**
Jos 7:21 When I saw in the **p** a beautiful robe
Est 3:13 and to **p** their goods.
    8:11 to **p** the property of their enemies.
    9:10 they did not lay their hands on the **p.**
Pr 12:12 The wicked desire the **p** of evil men,
    22:23 and will **p** those who **p** them.
Isa 3:14 **p** from the poor is in your houses.
Jer 30:16 Those who **p** you will be plundered;
Eze 39:10 will **p** those who plundered them
Hab 2: 8 the peoples who are left will **p** you.
Zep 2: 9 remnant of my people will **p** them;

PLUNDERED [PLUNDER]

Ex 12:36 so they **p** the Egyptians.
Jdg 2:14 handed them over to raiders who **p**
Eze 34: 8 lacks a shepherd and so has been **p**

PLUNGE

1Ti 6: 9 harmful desires that **p** men into ruin
1Pe 4: 4 not **p** with them into the same flood

POCKET*

1Sa 25:29 hurl away as from the **p** of a sling.

PODS

Lk 15:16 with the **p** that the pigs were eating,

POETS*

Nu 21:27 That is why the **p** say:
Ac 17:28 As some of your own **p** have said,

POINT

Pr 9: 3 calls from the highest **p** of the city.
Mt 4: 5 and had him stand on the highest **p**
    26:38 with sorrow to the **p** of death.
Ro 2: 1 at whatever **p** you judge the other,
Heb 12: 4 not yet resisted to the **p** of shedding
Jas 2:10 yet stumbles at just one **p** is guilty
Rev 2:10 Be faithful, even to the **p** of death,

POISON

Dt 32:32 Their grapes are filled with **p,**
Ps 140: 3 the **p** of vipers is on their lips.
Am 6:12 But you have turned justice into **p**
Mk 16:18 and when they drink deadly **p,**
Ro 3:13 "The **p** of vipers is on their lips."
Jas 3: 8 It is a restless evil, full of deadly **p.**

POLE [POLES]

Nu 21: 8 "Make a snake and put it up on a **p;**
Dt 16:21 Do not set up any wooden Asherah **p**
Jdg 6:25 cut down the Asherah **p** beside it.
1Ki 16:33 Ahab also made an Asherah **p**

POLES [POLE]

Ex 25:13 Then make **p** of acacia wood
Dt 12: 3 and burn their Asherah **p** in the fire;
2Ki 17:10 and Asherah **p** on every high hill and

POLISHED

Isa 49: 2 he made me into a **p** arrow
Eze 21:11 " 'The sword is appointed to be **p,**

POLLUTE* [POLLUTED, POLLUTES]

Nu 35:33 " 'Do not **p** the land where you are.
Jude 1: 8 these dreamers **p** their own bodies,

POLLUTED* [POLLUTE]

Ezr 9:11 a land **p** by the corruption
Pr 25:26 Like a muddied spring or a **p** well is
Ac 15:20 to abstain from food **p** by idols,
Jas 1:27 oneself from being **p** by the world.

POLLUTES* [POLLUTE]

Nu 35:33 Bloodshed **p** the land,

POMEGRANATES

Ex 28:33 Make **p** of blue,
Dt 8: 8 **p**, olive oil and honey;
1Ki 7:18 He made **p** in two rows
SS 8: 2 the nectar of my **p**.

PONDER [PONDERED, PONDERS]

Ps 64: 9 of God and **p** what he has done.
119:95 but I will **p** your statutes.

PONDERED [PONDER]

Ps 111: 2 they are **p** by all who delight in them
Ecc 12: 9 He **p** and searched out and set
Lk 2:19 He and **p** them in her heart.

PONDERS* [PONDER]

Isa 57: 1 and no one **p** it in his heart;

PONTIUS [PILATE]

Lk 3: 1 when **P** Pilate was governor

POOL [POOLS]

2Sa 2:13 and met them at the **p** of Gibeon.
1Ki 22:38 washed the chariot at a **p** in Samaria
Ps 114: 8 who turned the rock into a **p**,
Jn 5: 2 Jerusalem near the Sheep Gate a **p**,
9: 7 "wash in the **P** of Siloam"

POOLS [POOL]

Dt 8: 7 and **p** of water, with springs flowing
Ps 107:35 the desert into **p** of water

POOR [POOREST, POVERTY]

Ex 23: 3 not show favoritism to a **p** man
23: 6 not deny justice to your **p** people
Lev 19:10 Leave them for the **p** and the alien.
23:22 Leave them for the **p** and the alien.
27: 8 If anyone making the vow is too **p**
Dt 15: 4 there should be no **p** among you,
15: 7 or tightfisted toward your **p** brother.
15:11 There will always be **p** people in
24:12 If the man is **p**,
24:14 of a hired man who is **p** and needy,
1Sa 2: 8 He raises the **p** from the dust
2Sa 12: 1 one rich and the other **p**.
Job 5:16 So the **p** have hope,
24: 4 force all the **p** of the land into hiding.
30:25 Has not my soul grieved for the **p**?
Ps 14: 6 evildoers frustrate the plans of the **p**,
34: 6 This **p** man called,
35:10 the **p** from those too strong for them,

40:17 Yet I am **p** and needy;
68:10 O God, you provided for the **p**.
69:32 The **p** will see and be glad—
82: 3 maintain the rights of the **p**
112: 9 scattered abroad his gifts to the **p**,
113: 7 He raises the **p** from the dust
140:12 the LORD secures justice for the **p**
Pr 10: 4 Lazy hands make a man **p**,
13: 7 another pretends to be **p**,
14:20 The **p** are shunned even by their
14:31 He who oppresses the **p** shows
17: 5 He who mocks the **p** shows contempt
19: 1 **p** man whose walk is blameless than
19:17 He who is kind to the **p** lends to
19:22 better to be **p** than a liar.
20:13 not love sleep or you will grow **p**;
21:13 shuts his ears to the cry of the **p**,
21:17 who loves pleasure will become **p**;
22: 2 Rich and **p** have this in common:
22: 9 for he shares his food with the **p**.
22:22 not exploit the **p** because they are **p**
28: 6 **p** man whose walk is blameless than
28:27 who gives to the **p** will lack nothing,
29: 7 righteous care about justice for the **p**,
31: 9 defend the rights of the **p** and needy.
31:20 She opens her arms to the **p**
Ecc 4:13 a **p** but wise youth than an old
Isa 3:14 from the **p** is in your houses.
10: 2 to deprive the **p** of their rights
14:30 poorest of the **p** will find pasture,
25: 4 You have been a refuge for the **p**,
32: 7 schemes to destroy the **p** with lies,
61: 1 to preach good news to the **p**.
Jer 22:16 He defended the cause of the **p**,
24: 2 the other basket had very **p** figs,
Eze 18:12 He oppresses the **p** and needy.
Am 2: 7 They trample on the heads of the **p**
4: 1 you women who oppress the **p**
5:11 You trample on the **p** and force him
Zec 7:10 the alien or the **p**.
Mt 5: 3 "Blessed are the **p** in spirit,
11: 5 the good news is preached to the **p**.
Mk 10:21 and give to the **p**,
12:42 But a **p** widow came and put
14: 7 The **p** you will always have
Lk 4:18 to preach good news to the **p**.
6:20 "Blessed are you who are **p**,
11:41 give what is inside (the dish) to the **p**
14:13 you give a banquet, invite the **p**,
19: 8 half of my possessions to the **p**,
21: 2 He also saw a **p** widow put
Jn 12: 8 You will always have the **p**
Ac 9:36 doing good and helping the **p**.
10: 4 "Your prayers and gifts to the **p**
24:17 to bring my people gifts for the **p** and
Ro 15:26 contribution for the **p** among the
1Co 13: 3 If I give all I possess to the **p**
2Co 6:10 **p**, yet making many rich;
8: 9 yet for your sakes his became **p**,
9: 9 scattered abroad his gifts to the **p**;
Gal 2:10 should continue to remember the **p**,
Jas 2: 2 and a **p** man in shabby clothes
2: 5 not God chosen those who are **p** in
Rev 3:17 pitiful, **p**, blind and naked.

POOREST [POOR]

2Ki 24:14 the **p** people of the land were left,
Jer 52:16 of the **p** people of the land to work

POPULATION*

Pr 14:28 A large **p** is a king's glóry,

PORCIUS* [FESTUS]

Ac 24:27 Felix was succeeded by **P** Festus,

PORTENT*

Ps 71: 7 I have become like a **p** to many,
Isa 20: 3 a sign and **p** against Egypt and Cush,

PORTICO

1Ki 6: 3 The **p** at the front of the main hall of
1Ch 28:11 the plans for the **p** of the temple,

PORTION [PORTIONS]

Lev 2: 2 and burn this as a memorial **p** on
5:12 a memorial **p** and burn it on the altar
Nu 18:29 as the LORD's **p** the best
Dt 32: 9 For the LORD's **p** is his people,
Jos 18: 7 however, do not get a **p** among you,
1Sa 1: 5 But to Hannah he gave a double **p**
2Ki 2: 9 inherit a double **p** of your spirit,"
Ps 16: 5 you have assigned me my **p**
73:26 of my heart and my **p** forever.
119:57 You are my **p**, O LORD;
142: 5 my **p** in the land of the living."
Isa 53:12 Therefore I will give him a **p** among
61: 7 my people will receive a double **p,**
Jer 10:16 He who is the **P** of Jacob is not
La 3:24 "The LORD is my **p;**
Zec 2:12 as his **p** in the holy land
Rev 18: 6 a double **p** from her own cup.

PORTIONS [PORTION]

Ge 4: 4 But Abel brought fat **p** from some of
Lev 9:24 the burnt offering and the fat **p**
Jos 19:49 dividing the land into its allotted **p,**

PORTRAIT

Lk 20:24 Whose **p** and inscription are on it?"

PORTRAYED

Gal 3: 1 Christ was clearly **p** as crucified.

POSITION [POSITIONS]

Est 4:14 to royal **p** for such a time as this?"
Da 2:48 the king placed Daniel in a high **p**
Ro 12:16 to associate with people of low **p.**
Jas 1:10 rich should take pride in his low **p,**
2Pe 3:17 and fall from your secure **p.**

POSITIONS [POSITION]

2Ch 20:17 Take up your **p;**
Ecc 10: 6 Fools are put in many high **p,**
Jude 1: 6 not keep their **p** of authority

POSSESS [POSSESSED,
POSSESSING, POSSESSION,
POSSESSIONS, POSSESSOR]

Lev 20:24 I said to you, "You will **p** their land;

Nu 33:53 for I have given you the land to **p.**
Dt 4:14 that you are crossing the Jordan to **p.**
28:21 from the land you are entering to **p.**
Ezr 9:11 'The land you are entering to **p** is
Pr 8:12 I **p** knowledge and discretion.
Isa 14: 2 the house of Israel will **p** the nations
60:21 and they will **p** the land forever.
Da 7:18 the kingdom and will **p** it forever—
Jn 5:39 that by them you **p** eternal life.
1Co 13: 3 If I give all I **p** to the poor
2Pe 1: 8 For if you **p** these qualities

POSSESSED [POSSESS]

Jer 16:19 fathers **p** nothing but false gods,
Mk 3:22 "He is **p** by Beelzebul!
Lk 4:33 a man **p** by a demon, an evil spirit,
Jn 8:49 "I am not **p** by a demon," said Jesus,
10:21 the sayings of a man **p** by a demon.

POSSESSING* [POSSESS]

2Co 6:10 and yet **p** everything.

POSSESSION [POSSESS]

Ge 15: 7 to give you this land to take **p**
17: 8 I will give as an everlasting **p** to you
Ex 6: 8 I will give it to you as a **p.**
19: 5 you will be my treasured **p.**
Nu 13:30 "We should go up and take **p** of
Dt 1: 8 Go in and take **p** of the land that
7: 6 to be his people, his treasured **p.**
Jos 1:11 and take **p** of the land
21:43 they took **p** of it and settled there.
Ps 2: 8 the ends of the earth your **p.**
135: 4 Israel to be his treasured **p.**
Eze 44:28 I will be their **p.**
Mal 3:17 when I make up my treasured **p.**
Eph 1:14 redemption of those who are God's **p**

POSSESSIONS [POSSESS]

Ge 15:14 they will come out with great **p.**
Ecc 5:19 God gives any man wealth and **p,**
Mt 19:21 go, sell your **p** and give to the poor,
Lk 11:21 guards his own house, his **p** are safe.
12:15 not consist in the abundance of his **p.**
19: 8 Here and now I give half of my **p** to
Ac 4:32 that any of his **p** was his own,
2Co 12:14 what I want is not your **p** but you.
Heb 10:34 had better and lasting **p.**
1Jn 3:17 If anyone has material **p**

POSSESSOR* [POSSESS]

Ecc 7:12 wisdom preserves the life of its **p.**

POSSIBLE

Mt 19:26 but with God all things are **p."**
26:39 "My Father, if it is **p,**
Mk 9:23 is **p** for him who believes."
10:27 all things are **p** with God."
14:35 if **p** the hour might pass from him.
Lk 18:27 impossible with men is **p** with God."
Ro 12:18 If it is **p,** as far as it depends on you,
1Co 9:19 to win as many as **p.**
9:22 by all **p** means I might save some.

POSTS

Ex   27:17 All the **p** around the courtyard are
Jdg 16: 3 together with the two **p,**

POT [POTSHERD, POTTER, POTTER'S, POTTERY]

2Ki   4:40 there is death in the **p!"**
Isa 29:16 Can the **p** say of the potter,
Jer   1:13 "I see a boiling **p,**
      18: 4 the potter formed it into another **p,**
Eze 11: 3 This city is a cooking **p,**

POTENTATE (KJV) See RULER

POTIPHAR*

Egyptian who bought Joseph (Ge 37:36), set him over his house (Ge 39:1-6), sent him to prison (Ge 39:7-30).

POTSHERD [POT]

Isa 45: 9 but a **p** among the potsherds on

POTTAGE (KJV) See STEW

POTTER [POT]

Isa 29:16 Can the pot say of the **p,**
      45: 9 Does the clay say to the **p,**
      64: 8 We are the clay, you are the **p;**
Jer 18: 6 not do with you as this **p** does?"
Zec 11:13 "Throw it to the **p"**—
Ro   9:21 not the **p** have the right to make

POTTER'S [POT]

Jer 18: 2 "Go down to the **p** house,
Mt   27: 7 to use the money to buy the **p** field

POTTERY [POT]

Ps   2: 9 you will dash them to pieces like **p."**
Ro   9:21 some **p** for noble purposes and some
Rev   2:27 he will dash them to pieces like **p'**—

POUR [OUTPOURED, OUTPOURING, POURED, POURING, POURS]

Lev   4: 7 he shall **p** out at the base of the altar
Nu   20: 8 and it will **p** out its water.
Dt   12:16 **p** it out on the ground like water.
2Ki   4: 4 **P** oil into all the jars,
Ps   19: 2 Day after day they **p** forth speech;
      62: 8 pour out your hearts to him,
      79: 6 **P** out your wrath on the nations
Isa 44: 3 I will **p** out my Spirit
Eze 20: 8 So I said I would **p** out my wrath
      39:29 for I will **p** out my Spirit on
Joel 2:28 I will **p** out my Spirit on all people.
Zec 12:10 I will **p** out on the house of David
Mal   3:10 and **p** out so much blessing
Mt   9:17 they **p** new wine into new wineskins,
Ac   2:17 I will **p** out my Spirit on all people.
Rev 16: 1 **p** out the seven bowls of God's
            wrath on the earth."

POURED [POUR]

Ge   28:18 set it up as a pillar and **p** oil
      35:14 and he **p** out a drink offering on it;
Lev   8:12 He **p** some of the anointing oil
2Sa 23:16 he **p** it out before the LORD.
2Ch 34:25 my anger will be **p** out on this place
Ps   22:14 I am **p** out like water,
     133: 2 It is like precious oil **p** on the head,
SS   1: 3 your name is like perfume **p** out.
Isa 19:14 The LORD has **p** into them a spirit
      32:15 the Spirit is **p** upon us from on high,
La   4:11 he has **p** out his fierce anger.
Mt   26:28 **p** out for many for the forgiveness
Mk   14: 3 She broke the jar and **p** the perfume
Lk   6:38 will be **p** into your lap.
      22:20 which is **p** out for you.
Ac   2:33 and has **p** out what you now see
      10:45 gift of the Holy Spirit had been **p** out
Ro   5: 5 because God has **p** out his love
Php   2:17 I am being **p** out like a drink offering
1Ti   1:14 The grace of our Lord was **p** out
2Ti   4: 6 being **p** out like a drink offering,
Tit   3: 6 whom he **p** out on us generously
Rev 14:10 **p** full strength into the cup of his
      16: 2 and **p** out his bowl on the land,

POURING [POUR]

1Sa   1:15 I was **p** out my soul to the LORD.
2Ki   4: 5 the jars to her and she kept **p.**
Lk   10:34 **p** on oil and wine.

POURS [POUR]

Pr   14: 5 but a false witness **p** out lies.
Lk   5:37 one **p** new wine into old wineskins.

POVERTY* [POOR]

Dt   28:48 in nakedness and dire **p,**
1Sa   2: 7 The LORD sends **p** and wealth;
Pr   6:11 and **p** will come on you like a bandit
      10:15 but **p** is the ruin of the poor.
      11:24 but comes to **p.**
      13:18 who ignores discipline comes to **p**
      14:23 but mere talk leads only to **p.**
      21: 5 to profit as surely as haste leads to **p.**
      22:16 both come to **p.**
      24:34 and **p** will come on you like a bandit
      28:19 fantasies will have his fill of **p.**
      28:22 and is unaware that **p** awaits him.
      30: 8 give me neither **p** nor riches,
      31: 7 let them drink and forget their **p**
Ecc   4:14 or he may have been born in **p**
Mk   12:44 out of her **p,** put in everything—
Lk   21: 4 of her **p** put in all she had to live on."
2Co   8: 2 their extreme **p** welled up in rich
       8: 9 through his **p** might become rich.
Rev   2: 9 I know your afflictions and your **p**—

POWDER

Ex   32:20 then he ground it to **p,**
2Ki 23:15 the high place and ground it to **p,**

POWER [OVERPOWER, OVERPOWERS, POWERFUL, POWERLESS, POWERS]

Ex   9:16 that I might show you my **p** and
      15: 6 O LORD, was majestic in **p.**
      32:11 with great **p** and a mighty hand?

Dt	8:17	"My **p** and the strength of my hands
	34:12	no one has ever shown the mighty **p**
Jdg	14:19	of the LORD came upon him in **p.**
	15:14	of the LORD came upon him in **p.**
1Sa	10:10	Spirit of God came upon him in **p,**
	11: 6	Spirit of God came upon him in **p,**
	16:13	of the LORD came upon David in **p.**
1Ki	18:46	The **p** of the LORD came
1Ch	29:11	the greatness and the **p** and the glory
2Ch	20: 6	**P** and might are in your hand,
	32: 7	for there is a greater **p** with us than
Job	9: 4	his **p** is vast.
	12:13	"To God belong wisdom and **p;**
	36:22	"God is exalted in his **p.**
	37:23	beyond our reach and exalted in **p;**
Ps	20: 6	with the saving **p** of his right hand.
	37:17	the **p** of the wicked will be broken,
	63: 2	in the sanctuary and beheld your **p**
	66: 3	So great is your **p**
	68:34	Proclaim the **p** of God,
	77:14	you display your **p** among
	89:13	Your arm is endued with **p;**
	145: 6	tell of the **p** of your awesome works,
	147: 5	Great is our Lord and mighty in **p;**
	150: 2	Praise him for his acts of **p;**
Pr	3:27	when it is in your **p** to act.
	8:14	I have understanding and **p.**
	18:21	tongue has the **p** of life and death,
	24: 5	A wise man has great **p**
	28:12	but when the wicked rise to **p,**
Ecc	8: 8	No man has **p** over the wind
Isa	11: 2	the Spirit of counsel and of **p,**
	40:10	the Sovereign LORD comes with **p,**
	40:26	of his great **p** and mighty strength,
	40:29	and increases the **p** of the weak.
	63:12	who sent his glorious arm of **p** to be
Jer	10: 6	and your name is mighty in **p.**
	10:12	But God made the earth by his **p;**
	27: 5	my great **p** and outstretched arm
	32:17	and the earth by your great **p**
Da	2:20	wisdom and **p** are his.
	6:27	Daniel from the **p** of the lions."
	11: 3	with great **p** and do as he pleases.
Hos	13:14	ransom them from the **p** of the grave;
Mic	3: 8	But as for me, I am filled with **p,**
Na	1: 3	slow to anger and great in **p;**
Zec	4: 6	'Not by might nor by **p,**
Mt	22:29	know the Scriptures or the **p** of God.
	24:30	with **p** and great glory.
Mk	9: 1	the kingdom of God come with **p."**
	13:26	coming in clouds with great **p**
Lk	1:17	in the spirit and **p** of Elijah,
	1:35	and the **p** of the Most High
	4:14	to Galilee in the **p** of the Spirit,
	6:19	because **p** was coming from him
	8:46	that **p** has gone out from me."
	9: 1	he gave them **p** and authority
	10:19	to overcome all the **p** of the enemy;
	21:27	Son of Man coming in a cloud with **p**
	24:49	until you have been clothed with **p**
Jn	19:11	"You would have no **p** over me
Ac	1: 8	But you will receive **p** when
	4:28	They did what your **p** and will
	4:33	With great **p** the apostles continued

	8:10	"This man is the divine **p** known as the Great **P.**"
	10:38	with the Holy Spirit and **p,**
	26:18	and from the **p** of Satan to God,
Ro	1:16	the **p** of God for the salvation
	1:20	invisible qualities—his eternal **p**
	4:21	being fully persuaded that God had **p**
	9:17	that I might display my **p** in you and
	15:13	hope by the **p** of the Holy Spirit.
	15:19	by the **p** of signs and miracles,
	15:19	through the **p** of the Spirit.
1Co	1:17	cross of Christ be emptied of its **p.**
	1:18	are being saved it is the **p** of God.
	1:24	Christ the **p** of God and the wisdom
	2: 4	a demonstration of the Spirit's **p,**
	6:14	By his **p** God raised the Lord from
	15:24	all dominion, authority and **p.**
	15:56	and the **p** of sin is the law.
2Co	4: 7	that this all-surpassing **p** is from God
	6: 7	truthful speech and in the **p** of God;
	10: 4	divine to demolish strongholds.
	12: 9	my **p** is made perfect in weakness."
	12: 9	so that Christ's **p** may rest on me.
	13: 4	yet he lives by God's **p.**
	13: 4	yet by God's **p** we will live with him
Eph	1:19	and his incomparably great **p** for us
	1:19	That **p** is like the working
	1:21	**p** and dominion, and every title
	3:16	you with **p** through his Spirit
	3:20	to his **p** that is at work within us,
	6:10	in the Lord and in his mighty **p.**
Php	3:10	Christ and the **p** of his resurrection
	3:21	by the **p** that enables him to bring
Col	1:11	being strengthened with all **p**
	2:10	the head over every **p** and authority.
1Th	1: 5	but also with **p,**
2Th	1: 9	and from the majesty of his **p**
	2: 7	the secret **p** of lawlessness is already
2Ti	1: 7	but a spirit of **p,**
	3: 5	a form of godliness but denying its **p.**
Heb	2:14	who holds the **p** of death—
	7:16	of the **p** of an indestructible life.
1Pe	1: 5	through faith are shielded by God's **p**
2Pe	1: 3	His divine **p** has given us everything
	1:16	when we told you about the **p**
Jude	1:25	majesty, **p** and authority,
Rev	4:11	to receive glory and honor and **p,**
	5:12	to receive **p** and wealth and wisdom
	6: 4	Its rider was given **p** to take peace
	6: 8	They were given **p** over a fourth of
	7: 2	four angels who had been given **p**
	9: 5	They were not given **p** to kill them,
	11: 3	I will give **p** to my two witnesses,
	11:17	because you have taken your great **p**
	12:10	the **p** and the kingdom of our God,
	13: 2	The dragon gave the beast his **p**
	16: 8	the sun was given **p** to scorch people
	17:17	by agreeing to give the beast their **p**
	19: 1	and glory and **p** belong to our God,
	20: 6	second death has no **p** over them,

POWERFUL [POWER]

Ge	18:18	surely become a great and **p** nation,
Nu	13:28	But the people who live there are **p,**

Jos 4:24 know that the hand of the LORD is **p**
1Ch 11: 9 David became more and more **p,**
2Ch 26:16 But after Uzziah became **p,**
      27: 6 Jotham grew **p** because he walked
Est   9: 4 and he became more and more **p.**
Ps   29: 4 The voice of the LORD is **p;**
Ecc   7:19 makes one wise man more **p** than
Jer 32:18 O great and **p** God,
Zec   8:22 and **p** nations will come to Jerusalem
Mk   1: 7 "After me will come one more **p**
Lk   24:19 **p** in word and deed before God
Ac   9:22 Yet Saul grew more and more **p**
2Th   1: 7 in blazing fire with his **p** angels.
Heb   1: 3 sustaining all things by his **p** word.
Jas   5:16 The prayer of a righteous man is **p**

POWERLESS [POWER]

2Ch 14:11 there is no one like you to help the **p**
Ro   5: 6 when we were still **p,**
      8: 3 For what the law was **p** to do in

POWERS [POWER]

Isa 24:21 will punish the **p** in the heavens
Da   4:35 as he pleases with the **p** of heaven
Mt   13:54 wisdom and these miraculous **p?"**
Ro   8:38 the present nor the future, nor any **p,**
1Co 12:10 to another miraculous **p,**
Eph   6:12 against the **p** of this dark world and
Col   1:16 thrones or **p** or rulers or authorities;
      2:15 And having disarmed the **p**
Heb   6: 5 and the **p** of the coming age,
1Pe   3:22 authorities and **p** in submission

PRACTICE [PRACTICED, PRACTICES]

Lev 19:26 " 'Do not **p** divination or sorcery.
Ps 119:56 This has been my **p:**
Jer   6:13 and priests alike, all **p** deceit.
Eze 13:23 see false visions or **p** divination.
     33:31 but they do not put them into **p.**
Mt   7:24 and puts them into **p** is like
     23: 3 for they do not **p** what they preach.
Lk   8:21 God's word and put it into **p."**
Ro   12:13 **P** hospitality.
Php   4: 9 or seen in me—put it into **p.**
1Ti   5: 4 to put their religion into **p** by caring
Rev 21: 8 those who **p** magic arts,
     22:15 those who **p** magic arts,

PRACTICED [PRACTICE]

Lev 18:30 of the detestable customs that were **p**
Mt   23:23 You should have **p** the latter,
Ac   8: 9 a man named Simon had **p** sorcery in
     19:19 A number who had **p** sorcery

PRACTICES [PRACTICE]

Ex   23:24 or worship them or follow their **p.**
Lev 18: 3 Do not follow their **p.**
Jdg   2:19 They refused to give up their evil **p**
2Ki 17: 8 and followed the **p** of the nations
Ps 101: 7 No one who **p** deceit will dwell
Eze   7: 3 repay you for all your detestable **p.**
Mt   5:19 but whoever **p** and teaches these
Col   3: 9 taken off your old self with its **p**

Rev 22:15 everyone who loves and **p** falsehood.

PRAETORIUM*

Mt   27:27 soldiers took Jesus into the **P**
Mk   15:16 into the palace (that is, the **P**)

PRAISE [PRAISED, PRAISES, PRAISEWORTHY, PRAISING]

Ex   15: 2 He is my God, and I will **p** him,
Lev 19:24 an offering of **p** to the LORD.
Dt   10:21 He is your **p;**
     26:19 that he will set you in **p,**
     32: 3 Oh, **p** the greatness of our God!
Ru   4:14 "**P** be to the LORD,
2Sa 22: 4 who is worthy of **p,**
     22:47 **P** be to my Rock!
1Ch 16:25 the LORD and most worthy of **p;**
     23: 5 to **p** the LORD with the musical
     29:10 saying, "**P** be to you, O LORD
2Ch 5:13 to give **p** and thanks to the LORD.
      5:13 voices in **p** to the LORD and sang:
     20:21 **p** him for the splendor of his holiness
     29:30 **p** the LORD with the words of David
Ezr   3:10 took their places to **p** the LORD,
Ne   9: 5 be exalted above all blessing and **p.**
Ps   8: 2 and infants you have ordained **p**
      9: 1 I will **p** you, O LORD,
     16: 7 I will **p** the LORD,
     22:23 You who fear the LORD, **p** him!
     26: 7 proclaiming aloud your **p** and telling
     30: 4 **p** his holy name.
     33: 1 fitting for the upright to **p** him.
     34: 1 his **p** will always be on my lips.
     40: 3 a hymn of **p** to our God.
     42: 5 for I will yet **p** him,
     43: 5 for I will yet **p** him,
     45:17 therefore the nations will **p** you
     47: 7 sing to him a psalm of **p.**
     48: 1 and most worthy of **p,**
     51:15 and my mouth will declare your **p.**
     56: 4 In God, whose word I **p,**
     57: 9 I will **p** you, O Lord,
     63: 4 I will **p** you as long as I live,
     65: 1 **P** awaits you, O God, in Zion;
     66: 2 make his **p** glorious!
     66: 8 **P** our God, O peoples,
     68:19 **P** be to the Lord, to God our Savior,
     68:26 **P** God in the great congregation;
     69:30 I will **p** God's name in song
     69:34 Let heaven and earth **p** him,
     71: 8 My mouth is filled with your **p,**
     71:14 I will **p** you more and more.
     71:22 I will **p** you with the harp
     74:21 the poor and needy **p** your name.
     86:12 I will **p** you, O Lord my God,
     89: 5 The heavens **p** your wonders,
     92: 1 It is good to **p** the LORD
     96: 2 Sing to the LORD, **p** his name;
    100: 4 and his courts with **p;**
    100: 4 thanks to him and **p** his name.
    101: 1 O LORD, I will sing **p.**
    102:18 that a people not yet created may **p**
    103: 1 **p** his holy name.
    103:20 **P** the LORD, you his angels,

104:	1	**P** the LORD, O my soul.
105:	2	Sing to him, sing **p** to him;
106:	2	the LORD or fully declare his **p?**
108:	3	I will **p** you, O LORD,
111:10		To him belongs eternal **p.**
113:	1	**p** the name of the LORD.
117:	1	**P** the LORD, all you nations;
119:175		Let me live that I may **p** you,
135:	1	**P** the name of the LORD;
135:20		who fear him, **p** the LORD.
138:	1	before the "gods" I will sing your **p.**
139:14		I **p** you because I am fearfully
144:	1	**P** be to the LORD my Rock,
145:	3	the LORD and most worthy of **p;**
145:10		All you have made will **p** you,
145:21		Let every creature **p** his holy name
146:	1	**P** the LORD, O my soul.
147:	1	how pleasant and fitting to **p** him!
148:	1	**P** the LORD from the heavens,
148:	1	**p** him in the heights above.
148:13		Let them **p** the name of the LORD,
149:	1	his **p** in the assembly of the saints.
149:	6	the **p** of God be in their mouths
150:	2	**P** him for his acts of power;
150:	6	Let everything that has breath **p**
Pr 27:	2	Let another **p** you,
27:21		man is tested by the **p** he receives.
31:31		and let her works bring her **p** at
SS 1:	4	**p** your love more than wine.
Isa 12:	1	that day you will say: "I will **p** you
38:18		For the grave cannot **p** you,
42:10		his **p** from the ends of the earth,
61:	3	and a garment of **p** instead of a spirit
Jer 33:	9	**p** and honor before all nations
Da 2:20		and said: "**P** be to the name of God
4:37		**p** and exalt and glorify the King
Hab 3:	3	the heavens and his **p** filled the earth.
Mt 5:16		and **p** your Father in heaven.
21:16		and infants you have ordained **p'?"**
Lk 19:37		of disciples began joyfully to **p** God
Jn 5:41		"I do not accept **p** from men,
5:44		the **p** that comes from the only God?
12:43		for they loved **p** from men more
		than **p** from God.
Ac 12:23		because Herod did not give **p** to God,
Ro 2:29		Such a man's **p** is not from men,
15:	7	in order to bring **p** to God.
1Co 4:	5	At that time each will receive his **p**
2Co 1:	3	**P** be to the God and Father
Eph 1:	3	**P** be to the God and Father
1:	6	to the **p** of his glorious grace,
1:12		might be for the **p** of his glory.
1:14		to the **p** of his glory.
1Th 2:	6	not looking for **p** from men,
Heb 13:15		offer to God a sacrifice of **p—**
Jas 3:	9	the tongue we **p** our Lord and Father,
5:13		Let him sing songs of **p.**
1Pe 4:16		but **p** God that you bear that name.
Rev 5:13		to the Lamb be **p** and honor and
7:12		**P** and glory and wisdom and thanks
19:	5	from the throne, saying: "**P** our God,

PRAISE BE TO THE †LORD Ge 24:27; Ex 18:10; Ru 4:14; 1Sa 25:32, 39; 2Sa 18:28; 1Ki 1:48; 5:7; 8:15, 56; 10:9; 1Ch 16:36; 2Ch 2:12; 6:4; 9:8; Ezr 7:27; Ps 28:6; 31:21; 41:13; 72:18; 89:52; 106:48; 124:6; 135:21; 144:1

PRAISE THE †LORD Ge 29:35; Dt 8:10; Jdg 5:2, 9; 1Ch 16:4, 36; 23:5, 30; 29:20; 2Ch 29:30; Ezr 3:10; Ne 9:5; Ps 16:7; 26:12; 33:2; 68:26; 92:1; 102:18; 103:1, 2, 20, 21, 22, 22; 104:1, 35, 35; 105:45; 106:1, 48; 111:1; 112:1; 113:1, 9; 115:17, 18; 116:19; 117:1, 2; 134:1, 2; 135:1, 3, 19, 19, 20, 20, 21; 146:1, 1, 2, 10; 147:1, 20; 148:1, 1, 7, 14; 149:1, 9; 150:1, 6, 6; Isa 62:9; Zec 11:5

SING PRAISE 1Ch 16:9; Ps 7:17; 9:2; 59:17; 61:8; 66:4, 4; 68:4, 32; 71:22, 23; 75:9; 101:1; 104:33; 105:2; 135:3; 146:2

PRAISED [PRAISE]

Ge 12:15		they **p** her to Pharaoh,
Jdg 16:24		the people saw him, they **p** their god,
2Sa 14:25		there was not a man so highly **p**
1Ch 29:10		David **p** the LORD in the presence
Ne 8:	6	Ezra **p** the LORD, the great God;
Job 1:21		the name of the LORD be **p."**
Ps 113:	2	Let the name of the LORD be **p,**
Pr 12:	8	A man is **p** according to his wisdom,
31:30		but a woman who fears the LORD is
		to be **p.**
Isa 63:	7	the deeds for which he is to be **p,**
Da 2:19		Then Daniel **p** the God of heaven
4:34		Then I **p** the Most High;
5:	4	they **p** the gods of gold and silver,
Lk 18:43		they also **p** God.
23:47		seeing what had happened, **p** God
Ro 1:25		the Creator—who is forever **p.**
9:	5	who is God over all, forever **p!**
Gal 1:24		And they **p** God because of me.
1Pe 4:11		so that in all things God may be **p**

PRAISES* [PRAISE]

2Sa 22:50		I will sing **p** to your name.
2Ch 23:13		instruments were leading the **p.**
29:30		So they sang **p** with gladness
31:	2	give thanks and to sing **p** at the gates
Ps 6:	5	Who **p** you from the grave?
9:11		Sing **p** to the LORD,
9:14		that I may declare your **p** in the gates
18:49		I will sing **p** to your name.
35:28		and of your **p** all day long.
47:	6	Sing **p** to God, sing **p;** sing **p** to our
		King, sing **p.**
147:	1	How good it is to sing **p** to our God,
Pr 31:28		her husband also, and he **p** her:
Jer 31:	7	Make your **p** heard, and say,
Ro 15:11		and sing **p** to him, all you peoples."
Heb 2:12		the congregation I will sing your **p."**
1Pe 2:	9	the **p** of him who called you out

PRAISEWORTHY* [PRAISE]

Ps 78:	4	the **p** deeds of the LORD,
Php 4:	8	if anything is excellent or **p—**

PRAISING [PRAISE]

1Ch 25:	3	using the harp in thanking and **p**
2Ch 7:	6	which King David had made for **p**
Lk 2:13		**p** God and saying,

2:20   glorifying and **p** God for all the
24:53   continually at the temple, **p** God.
Ac   2:47   **p** God and enjoying the favor of all
3: 8   walking and jumping, and **p** God.
10:46 speaking in tongues and **p** God.
1Co 14:16 If you are **p** God with your spirit,

PRAY [PRAYED, PRAYER, PRAYERS, PRAYING, PRAYS]

Ex   8: 9   for me to **p** for you and your officials
Nu   21: 7   **P** that the LORD will take the snakes
Dt   4: 7   near us whenever we **p** to him?
1Sa 12:23   sin against the LORD by failing to **p**
1Ki   8:30   Israel when they **p** toward this place.
2Ch 6:38   and **p** toward the land you gave their
7:14   and **p** and seek my face and turn
Ezr   6:10   **p** for the well-being of the king
Job 42: 8   My servant Job will **p** for you,
Ps   5: 2   my King and my God, for to you I **p.**
32: 6   let everyone who is godly **p** to you
122: 6   **P** for the peace of Jerusalem:
Isa   37: 4   **p** for the remnant that still survives."
45:20   who **p** to gods that cannot save.
Jer   7:16   "So do not **p** for this people
29: 7   **P** to the LORD for it,
29:12   call upon me and come and **p** to me,
42: 3   **P** that the LORD your God will tell us
Da   9:23   As soon as you began to **p,**
Mt   5:44   and **p** for those who persecute you,
6: 5   "And when you **p,**
6: 9   "This, then, is how you should **p:**
14:23   on a mountainside by himself to **p.**
19:13   to place his hands on them and **p**
26:36   Sit here while I go over there and **p."**
Lk   5:33   "John's disciples often fast and **p,**
6:28   **p** for those who mistreat you.
11: 1   "Lord, teach us to **p,**
18: 1   that they should always **p** and ,
18:10   Two men went up to the temple to **p,**
22:40   **"P** that you will not fall
Jn   17:20   I **p** also for those who will believe
Ro   8:26   We do not know what we ought to **p**
1Co 11:13   **p** to God with her head uncovered?
14:13   who speaks in a tongue should **p**
14:15   but I will also **p** with my mind;
Eph   1:18   I **p** also that the eyes of your heart
3:16   I **p** that out of his glorious riches
6:18   And **p** in the Spirit on all occasions
1Th   5:17   **p** continually;
2Th   1:11   we constantly **p** for you,
1Ti   5: 5   and continues night and day to **p**
Jas   5:13   He should **p.**
5:16   and **p** for each other so
1Pe   4: 7   and self-controlled so that you can **p.**
1Jn   5:16   I am not saying that he should **p**
Jude 1:20   and **p** in the Holy Spirit.

PRAYED [PRAY]

Ge   20:17   Then Abraham **p** to God,
24:12   Then he **p,** "O LORD,
25:21   Isaac **p** to the LORD on behalf
Nu   11: 2   to Moses, he **p** to the LORD
21: 7   So Moses **p** for the people.
Jdg 16:28   Then Samson **p** to the LORD,

1Sa   1:27   I **p** for this child,
1Ki 18:36   Elijah stepped forward and **p:**
19: 4   and **p** that he might die.
2Ki   6:17   And Elisha **p,** "O LORD,
2Ch 30:18   But Hezekiah **p** for them, saying,
Ne   1: 4   and **p** before the God of heaven.
4: 9   But we **p** to our God and posted
Job 42:10   After Job had **p** for his friends,
Da   6:10   he got down on his knees and **p,**
9: 4   I **p** to the LORD my God
Jnh   2: 1   From inside the fish Jonah **p** to
Mt   26:39   with his face to the ground and **p,**
Mk   1:35   to a solitary place, where he **p.**
14:35   **p** that if possible the hour might pass
Lk   5:16   withdrew to lonely places and **p.**
18:11   The Pharisee stood up and **p**
22:41   knelt down and **p,**
Jn   17: 1   he looked toward heaven and **p:**
Ac   4:31   After they **p,** the place where they
6: 6   who **p** and laid their hands on them.
8:15   **p** for them that they might receive
13: 3   So after they had fasted and **p,**
Jas   5:17   He **p** earnestly that it would not rain,

PRAYER [PRAY]

Ge   25:21   The LORD answered his **p,**
2Sa 21:14   answered **p** in behalf of the land.
24:25   answered **p** in behalf of the land,
1Ki   8:49   hear their **p** and their plea,
2Ch   7:12   and said: "I have heard your **p**
30:27   for their **p** reached heaven,
33:19   His **p** and how God was moved
Ezr   8:23   and he answered our **p.**
Job 42: 8   and I will accept his **p** and not deal
Ps   4: 1   be merciful to me and hear my **p.**
6: 9   the LORD accepts my **p.**
17: 1   Give ear to my **p—**
55: 1   Listen to my **p,** O God,
65: 2   O you who hear **p,**
66:20   who has not rejected my **p**
86: T   A **p** of David.
90: T   A **p** of Moses the man of God.
Pr   15: 8   but the **p** of the upright pleases him.
15:29   he hears the **p** of the righteous.
Isa   56: 7   called a house of **p** for all nations."
Hab   3: 1   A **p** of Habakkuk the prophet.
Mt   21:13   will be called a house of **p,'**
21:22   whatever you ask for in **p."**
Mk   9:29   "This kind can come out only by **p."**
11:24   whatever you ask for in **p,**
Jn   17:15   My **p** is not that you take them out of
Ac   1:14   all joined together constantly in **p,**
2:42   to the breaking of bread and to **p.**
6: 4   and will give our attention to **p** and
10:31   God has heard your **p**
16:13   we expected to find a place of **p.**
Ro   10: 1   and **p** to God for the Israelites
12:12   patient in affliction, faithful in **p.**
1Co   7: 5   that you may devote yourselves to **p.**
2Co 13: 9   our **p** is for your perfection.
Php   1: 9   And this is my **p:**
4: 6   by **p** and petition, with thanksgiving,
Col   4: 2   Devote yourselves to **p,**
1Ti   2: 8   to lift up holy hands in **p,**

4: 5 by the word of God and **p.**
Jas 5:15 And the **p** offered in faith will make
5:16 The **p** of a righteous man is powerful
1Pe 3:12 and his ears are attentive to their **p,**

PRAYERS [PRAY]

1Ch 5:20 He answered their **p,**
Ps 35:13 my **p** returned to me unanswered,
Isa 1:15 even if you offer many **p,**
Mk 12:40 and for a show make lengthy **p.**
2Co 1:11 as you help us by your **p.**
Eph 6:18 on all occasions with all kinds of **p**
1Ti 2: 1 then, first of all, that requests, **p,**
Heb 5: 7 offered up **p** and petitions with loud
1Pe 3: 7 so that nothing will hinder your **p.**
Rev 5: 8 which are the **p** of the saints,
8: 3 with the **p** of all the saints,

PRAYING [PRAY]

Ge 24:45 "Before I finished **p** in my heart,
1Sa 1:13 Hannah was **p** in her heart,
2Ch 7: 1 When Solomon finished **p,**
Da 6:11 and found Daniel **p** and asking God
Mk 11:25 And when you stand **p,**
Lk 3:21 And as he was **p,**
6:12 and spent the night **p** to God.
9:29 As he was **p,**
Jn 17: 9 I am not **p** for the world,
Ac 9:11 named Saul, for he is **p.**
16:25 Paul and Silas were **p** and singing
Ro 15:30 in my struggle by **p** to God for me.
Eph 6:18 be alert and always keep on **p** for all

PRAYS [PRAY]

2Ch 6:32 he comes and **p** toward this temple,
Da 6: 7 that anyone who **p** to any god or man
1Co 11: 4 Every man who **p** or prophesies
14:14 For if I pray in a tongue, my spirit **p,**

PREACH [PREACHED, PREACHER, PREACHING]

Isa 61: 1 me to **p** good news to the poor.
Mt 4:17 From that time on Jesus began to **p,**
10: 7 As you go, **p** this message:
23: 3 for they do not practice what they **p.**
Lk 4:18 me to **p** good news to the poor.
Ac 9:20 he began to **p** in the synagogues
16:10 God had called us to **p** the gospel
Ro 1:15 to **p** the gospel also to you who are
10:15 how can they **p** unless they are sent?
15:20 It has always been my ambition to **p**
1Co 1:17 but to **p** the gospel—
1:23 but we **p** Christ crucified:
9:14 who **p** the gospel should receive
9:16 Woe to me if I do not **p** the gospel!
2Co 4: 5 For we do not **p** ourselves,
10:16 so that we can **p** the gospel in
Gal 1: 8 or an angel from heaven should **p**
Php 1:15 It is true that some **p** Christ out
2Ti 4: 2 **P** the Word; be prepared in season

PREACHED [PREACH]

Dt 13: 5 because he **p** rebellion against
Jer 28:16 because you have **p** rebellion against

Mk 6:12 and **p** that people should repent.
13:10 gospel must first be **p** to all nations.
14: 9 the gospel is **p** throughout the world,
Lk 7:22 and the good news is **p** to the poor.
24:47 and forgiveness of sins will be **p**
Ac 8: 4 Those who had been scattered **p**
15:21 For Moses has been **p** in every city
28:31 without hindrance he **p** the kingdom
1Co 9:27 so that after I have **p** to others,
15: 1 remind you of the gospel I **p** to you,
15:12 if it is **p** that Christ has been raised
2Co 11: 4 a Jesus other than the Jesus we **p,**
Gal 1: 8 a gospel other than the one we **p**
Eph 2:17 and **p** peace to you who were far
Php 1:18 false motives or true, Christ is **p.**
1Ti 3:16 was **p** among the nations,
1Pe 1:25 this is the word that was **p** to you.
3:19 and **p** to the spirits in prison

PREACHER* [PREACH]

2Pe 2: 5 protected Noah, a **p** of righteousness,

PREACHING [PREACH]

Ezr 6:14 and prosper under the **p** of Haggai
Am 7:16 stop **p** against the house of Isaac.'
Mt 12:41 for they repented at the **p** of Jonah,
Lk 9: 6 **p** the gospel and healing people
Ac 18: 5 devoted himself exclusively to **p**
Ro 10:14 hear without someone **p** to them?
1Co 2: 4 My message and my **p** were not
9:18 **p** the gospel I may offer it free of
Gal 1: 9 If anybody is **p** to you
1Ti 4:13 reading of Scripture, to **p** and to
5:17 especially those whose work is **p**

PRECEDE*

1Th 4:15 not **p** those who have fallen asleep.

PRECEPTS*

Dt 33:10 He teaches your **p** to Jacob
Ps 19: 8 The **p** of the LORD are right,
103:18 and remember to obey his **p.**
105:45 that they might keep his **p**
111: 7 all his **p** are trustworthy.
111:10 all who follow his **p** have good
119: 4 **p** that are to be fully obeyed.
119:15 on your **p** and consider your ways.
119:27 understand the teaching of your **p;**
119:40 How I long for your **p!**
119:45 for I have sought out your **p.**
119:56 been my practice: I obey your **p.**
119:63 to all who follow your **p.**
119:69 I keep your **p** with all my heart.
119:78 but I will meditate on your **p.**
119:87 but I have not forsaken your **p.**
119:93 I will never forget your **p,**
119:94 I have sought out your **p.**
119:100 for I obey your **p.**
119:104 I gain understanding from your **p;**
119:110 but I have not strayed from your **p.**
119:128 because I consider all your **p** right,
119:134 that I may obey your **p.**
119:141 I do not forget your **p.**
119:159 See how I love your **p;**

119:168 I obey your **p** and your statutes,
119:173 for I have chosen your **p.**

PRECIOUS

Ex   28:17 mount four rows of **p** stones on it.
1Sa 26:21 you considered my life **p** today,
2Ch   3: 6 He adorned the temple with **p** stones.
Ps   19:10 They are more **p** than gold,
     35:17 my **p** life from these lions.
     72:14 for **p** is their blood in his sight.
    116:15 **P** in the sight of the LORD is the
    119:72 from your mouth is more **p**
    139:17 How **p** to me are your thoughts,
Pr   3:15 She is more **p** than rubies;
      8:11 for wisdom is more **p** than rubies,
Isa 28:16 **p** cornerstone for a sure foundation;
Eze 28:13 every **p** stone adorned you:
1Pe   1:19 but with the **p** blood of Christ,
      2: 4 but chosen by God and **p** to him—
      2: 6 a chosen and **p** cornerstone,
2Pe   1: 1 have received a faith as **p** as ours:
      1: 4 his very great and **p** promises,
Rev 21:11 was like that of a very **p** jewel,
     21:19 decorated with every kind of **p** stone.

PREDESTINED* [DESTINE]

Ro   8:29 those God foreknew he also **p** to be
      8:30 And those he **p,** he also called;
Eph   1: 5 he **p** us to be adopted as his sons
      1:11 having been **p** according to the plan

PREDICTED* [PREDICTION]

1Sa 28:17 The LORD has done what he **p**
Ac   7:52 even killed those who **p** the coming
     11:28 through the Spirit **p** that a severe
     16:16 a spirit by which she **p** the future.
1Pe   1:11 when he **p** the sufferings of Christ

PREDICTING* [PREDICTION]

1Ki 22:13 the other prophets are **p** success for
2Ch 18:12 the other prophets are **p** success for

PREDICTION* [PREDICTED,
PREDICTING, PREDICTIONS]

Jer 28: 9 by the LORD only if his **p** comes true.

PREDICTIONS* [PREDICTION]

Isa 44:26 and fulfills the **p** of his messengers,
     47:13 stargazers who make **p** month by

PREGNANT

Ge   19:36 So both of Lot's daughters became **p**
     21: 2 Sarah became **p** and bore a son
     25:21 and his wife Rebekah became **p.**
Ex   21:22 men who are fighting hit a **p** woman
Ps   7:14 He who is **p** with evil
Mt   24:19 for pregnant women and nursing mothers!
1Th   5: 3 as labor pains on a **p** woman,
Rev 12: 2 She was **p** and cried out in pain

PREMATURELY* [MATURE]

Ex   21:22 and she gives birth **p**

PREPARATION [PREPARE]

Mt   27:62 The next day, the one after **P** Day,
Jn   19:14 the day of **P** of Passover Week,

PREPARATIONS [PREPARE]

1Ch 22: 5 So David made extensive **p**
Mk   14:12 make **p** for you to eat the Passover?"

PREPARE [PREPARATION,
PREPARATIONS, PREPARED]

Ps   23: 5 You **p** a table before me in
Isa 25: 6 the LORD Almighty will **p** a feast
     40: 3 the desert **p** the way for the LORD;
Am   4:12 **p** to meet your God, O Israel."
Mal   3: 1 who will **p** the way before me.
Mt   3: 'P **p** the way for the Lord,
     11:10 who will **p** your way before you.'
     26:12 she did it to **p** me for burial.
Jn   14: 2 I am going there to **p** a place for you.
Eph   4:12 to **p** God's people for works
1Pe   1:13 Therefore, **p** your minds for action;

PREPARED [PREPARE]

Ex   23:20 to bring you to the place I have **p.**
1Ch 15: 1 he **p** a place for the ark of God
2Ch   1: 4 to the place he had **p** for it,
Pr   19:29 Penalties are **p** for mockers,
Mt   20:23 to those for whom they have been **p**
     25:34 kingdom **p** for you since the creation
Lk   1:17 ready a people **p** for the Lord."
Ro   9:23 whom he **p** in advance for glory—
1Co   2: 9 mind has conceived what God has **p**
Eph   2:10 which God **p** in advance for us to do.
2Ti   2:21 and **p** to do any good work.
      4: 2 be **p** in season and out of season;
Heb 10: 5 but a body you **p** for me;
     11:16 for he has **p** a city for them.
1Pe   3:15 be **p** to give an answer to everyone
Rev   1: 2 to a place **p** for her by God,
     21: 2 **p** as a bride beautifully dressed

PRESBYTERY (KJV) See ELDERS

PRESCRIBED

1Ch 24:19 according to the regulations **p**
2Ch 29:25 and lyres in the way **p** by David
Ezr   3: 4 of burnt offerings **p** for each day.
      3:10 as **p** by David king of Israel.
      7:23 Whatever the God of heaven has **p,**
Ne   12:24 as **p** by David the man of God.
Heb   8: 4 who offer the gifts **p** by the law.

PRESENCE [PRESENT]

Ex   18:12 in the **p** of God.
     25:30 Put the bread of the **P** on this table
     33:14 "My **P** will go with you,
     34:34 the LORD's **p** to speak with him,
Lev   9:24 Fire came out from the **p** of the
     10: 2 fire came out from the **p** of the LORD
Nu   4: 7 "Over the table of the **P**
Dt   4:37 he brought you out of Egypt by his **P**
1Sa   2:21 Samuel grew up in the **p** of the LORD
      6:20 can stand in the **p** of the LORD,
     21: 6 bread of the **P** that had been removed

2Sa	22:13	Out of the brightness of his **p** bolts
2Ki	17:23	the LORD removed them from his **p**,
	23:27	"I will remove Judah also from my **p**
	24:20	in the end he thrust them from his **p**.
Ezr	9:15	not one of us can stand in your **p**."
Job	1:12	Satan went out from the **p** of the
	2: 7	Satan went out from the **p** of the
Ps	5: 5	The arrogant cannot stand in your **p**;
	16:11	with joy in your **p**,
	21: 6	glad with the joy of your **p**.
	23: 5	before me in the **p** of my enemies.
	31:20	In the shelter of your **p** you hide
	41:12	and set me in your **p** forever.
	51:11	Do not cast me from your **p**
	52: 9	I will praise you in the **p**
	89:15	who walk in the light of your **p**,
	90: 8	our secret sins in the light of your **p**.
	114: 7	O earth, at the **p** of the Lord,
	139: 7	Where can I flee from your **p**?
Isa	26:17	so were we in your **p**, O LORD.
	63: 9	and the angel of his **p** saved them.
Jer	5:22	"Should you not tremble in my **p**?
Eze	38:20	of the earth will tremble at my **p**.
Da	7:13	of Days and was led into his **p**.
Hos	6: 2	that we may live in his **p**.
Na	1: 5	The earth trembles at his **p**,
Mal	3:16	of remembrance was written in his **p**
Jn	8:38	what I have seen in the Father's **p**,
	17: 5	glorify me in your **p** with the glory I
Ac	2:28	fill me with joy in your **p**.'
1Th	2:19	in which we will glory in the **p** of our Lord Jesus
	3:13	holy in the **p** of our God and Father
2Th	1: 9	and shut out from the **p**
Heb	9:24	now to appear for us in God's **p**.
1Jn	3:19	how we set our hearts at rest in his **p**
Jude	1:24	to present you before his glorious **p**
Rev	14:10	sulfur in the **p** of the holy angels
	20:11	Earth and sky fled from his **p**,

PRESENCE OF THE †LORD Ge 27:7; Ex 28:30; Lev 9:24; 10:2; Dt 12:7, 18; 14:23, 26; 15:20; 18:7; 19:17; 27:7; 29:10, 15; Jos 18:6, 8, 10; 19:51; 1Sa 2:21; 6:20; 11:15; 12:3; 26:20; 1Ki 19:11; 2Ki 23:3; 1Ch 29:22; 2Ch 34:31; Job 1:12; 2:7; Eze 44:3; 46:3

†LORD'S PRESENCE Ge 4:16; Ex 29:11; 34:34; Nu 17:9; 20:9

PRESENT [EVER-PRESENT, PRESENCE, PRESENTED]

Lev	18:23	A woman must not **p** herself to
Nu	16:17	and **p** it before the LORD.
	18:29	You must **p** as the LORD's portion
Ezr	6: 3	be rebuilt as a place to **p** sacrifices,
Job	1: 6	the angels came to **p** themselves
	2: 1	the angels came to **p** themselves
	2: 1	Satan also came with them to **p**
Ps	14: 5	God is **p** in the company of the
Isa	41:21	"**P** your case," says the LORD.
Mk	10:30	hundred times as much in this **p** age
Lk	2:22	to Jerusalem to **p** him to the Lord
Ro	8:18	I consider that our **p** sufferings are
	8:38	neither the **p** nor the future,

1Co	3:22	the world or life or death or the **p** or
	7:26	Because of the **p** crisis,
	7:31	world in its **p** form is passing away.
2Co	11: 2	I might **p** you as a pure virgin to him.
Gal	1: 4	to rescue us from the **p** evil age,
Eph	1:21	the **p** age but also in the one to come.
	5:27	and to **p** her to himself as
Col	1:22	to **p** you holy in his sight,
1Ti	4: 8	both the **p** life and the life to come.
2Ti	2:15	to **p** yourself to God as one approved
Tit	2:12	upright and godly lives in this **p** age,
2Pe	3: 7	**p** heavens and earth are reserved for
Jude	1:24	to **p** you before his glorious presence

PRESENTED [PRESENT]

Mt	2:11	and **p** him with gifts of gold and
Ac	9:41	the widows and **p** her to them alive.
Ro	3:25	God **p** him as a sacrifice

PRESERVE [PRESERVES]

Ge	19:32	**p** our family line through our father."
Ps	36: 6	you **p** both man and beast.
	119:25	**p** my life according to your word.
Pr	3:21	**p** sound judgment and discernment,
	5: 2	and your lips may **p** knowledge.
Eze	7:13	not one of them will **p** his life.
Lk	17:33	and whoever loses his life will **p** it.

PRESERVES* [PRESERVE]

Ps	31:23	The LORD **p** the faithful,
	119:50	Your promise **p** my life.
Ecc	7:12	wisdom **p** the life of its possessor.

PRESS [PRESSED, PRESSURE]

Php	3:12	but I **p** on to take hold of that
	3:14	I **p** on toward the goal to win

PRESSED [PRESS]

Lk	6:38	A good measure, **p** down,
2Co	4: 8	We are hard **p** on every side,

PRESSURE [PRESS]

2Co	1: 8	We were under great **p**,
	11:28	I face daily the **p** of my concern

PRESUME* [PRESUMES, PRESUMPTION, PRESUMPTUOUSLY]

Jas	3: 1	many of you should **p** to be teachers,

PRESUMES* [PRESUME]

Dt	18:20	prophet who **p** to speak in my name

PRESUMPTION* [PRESUME]

Nu	14:44	in their **p** they went up toward the

PRESUMPTUOUSLY*

Dt	18:22	That prophet has spoken **p**.

PRETENDED [PRETENSION]

Ge	42: 7	but he **p** to be a stranger
1Sa	21:13	he **p** to be insane in their presence;

PRETENSION* [PRETENDED]

2Co	10: 5	We demolish arguments and every **p**

PREVAIL [PREVAILS]

2Ch 14:11 do not let man **p** against you."
Isa 54:17 no weapon forged against you will **p,**
Ro   3: 4 and **p** when you judge."

PREVAILS* [PREVAIL]

1Sa 2: 9 "It is not by strength that one **p;**
Pr 19:21 but it is the LORD's purpose that **p.**
Hab 1: 4 and justice never **p.**

PREY [PREYS]

Ge 15:11 Then birds of **p** came down on
Na   2:13 I will leave you no **p** on the earth.

PREYS* [PREY]

Pr   6:26 the adulteress **p** upon your very life.

PRICE [PRICELESS]

Ge 23: 9 Ask him to sell it to me for the full **p**
Lev 25:50 The **p** for his release is to be based
1Ch 21:22 Sell it to me at the full **p."**
Job 28:18 the **p** of wisdom is beyond rubies.
Zec 11:13 the handsome **p** at which they priced
Mt 27: 9 **p** set on him by the people of Israel,
Ac   5: 8 is this the **p** you and Ananias got for
1Co 6:20 you were bought at a **p.**
     7:23 you were bought at a **p;**

PRICELESS* [PRICE]

Ps 36: 7 How **p** is your unfailing love!

PRIDE [PROUD]

Lev 26:19 I will break down your stubborn **p**
2Ch 26:16 his **p** led to his downfall.
    32:26 Hezekiah repented of the **p** of his
Ps 47: 4 the **p** of Jacob, whom he loved.
Pr   8:13 I hate **p** and arrogance,
    11: 2 When **p** comes, then comes disgrace,
    13:10 **P** only breeds quarrels,
    16:18 **P** goes before destruction,
    17: 6 parents are the **p** of their children.
    29:23 A man's **p** brings him low,
Ecc 7: 8 and patience is better than **p.**
Isa 2:11 and the **p** of men brought low;
    25:11 God will bring down their **p** despite
    60:15 I will make you the everlasting **p** and
Eze 28: 2 " 'In the **p** of your heart you say,
Da   4:37 who walk in **p** he is able to humble.
Am   8: 7 LORD has sworn by the **P** of Jacob:
1Co 4: 6 Then you will not take **p** in one man
2Co 5:12 you can answer those who take **p**
     7: 4 I take great **p** in you.
Gal 6: 4 Then he can take **p** in himself,
Jas 1: 9 ought to take **p** in his high position.

PRIEST [PRIEST'S, PRIESTHOOD, PRIESTLY, PRIESTS]

Ge 14:18 He was **p** of God Most High,
Ex   2:16 a **p** of Midian had seven daughters,
    18: 1 Now Jethro, the **p** of Midian and
    18: 3 so he may serve me as **p.**
Lev 4: 3 " 'If the anointed **p** sins,
     4:20 the **p** will make atonement for them,

     5: 6 the **p** shall make atonement for him
     5:13 of the offering will belong to the **p,**
Nu   5:10 but what he gives to the **p** will
         belong to the **p.' "**
Jdg 17:10 with me and be my father and **p,**
1Sa 2:11 before the LORD under Eli the **p.**
     2:35 I will raise up for myself a faithful **p,**
    21: 6 **p** gave him the consecrated bread,
2Ch 13: 9 become a **p** of what are not gods.
Ne   8: 9 Ezra the **p** and scribe,
Ps 110: 4 "You are a **p** forever,
Jer 23:11 "Both prophet and **p** are godless;
Eze 1: 3 of the LORD came to Ezekiel the **p,**
Zec 6:13 And he will be a **p** on his throne.
Mk 14:63 The high **p** tore his clothes.
Heb 2:17 a merciful and faithful high **p** in
     3: 1 and high **p** whom we confess.
     4:14 a great high **p** who has gone through
     4:15 a high **p** who is unable to sympathize
     5: 6 "You are a **p** forever,
     6:20 He has become a high **p** forever,
     7: 3 Son of God he remains a **p** forever.
     7:15 if another **p** like Melchizedek
     7:26 Such a high **p** meets our need—
     8: 1 We do have such a high **p,**
     9:11 Christ came as high **p** of the good
    10:21 and since we have a great **p** over
    13:11 The high **p** carries the blood

HIGH PRIEST See HIGH

PRIEST'S [PRIEST]

Lev 6:29 Any male in a **p** family may eat it;
    21: 9 " 'If a **p** daughter defiles herself
    22:10 " 'No one outside a **p** family may eat

PRIESTHOOD [PRIEST]

Ex 29: 9 **p** is theirs by a lasting ordinance.
Nu 16:10 now you are trying to get the **p** too.
    25:13 a covenant of a lasting **p,**
Ezr 2:62 and so were excluded from the **p**
Heb 7:24 he has a permanent **p.**
1Pe 2: 5 into a spiritual house to be a holy **p,**
     2: 9 you are a chosen people, a royal **p,**

PRIESTLY [PRIEST]

Jos 18: 7 the **p** service of the LORD is their
Ro 15:16 the **p** duty of proclaiming the gospel

PRIESTS [PRIEST]

Ex 19: 6 a kingdom of **p** and a holy nation.'
    28: 1 so they may serve me as **p.**
    40:15 so they may serve me as **p.**
Lev 21: 7 because **p** are holy to their God.
Dt 31: 9 this law and gave it to the **p,**
Jos 3:15 as the **p** who carried the ark reached
     6: 4 Have seven **p** carry trumpets
1Sa 22:17 and kill the **p** of the LORD.
2Ch 5: 7 The **p** then brought the ark of the
    31: 2 Hezekiah assigned the **p** and Levites
    34: 5 the bones of the **p** on their altars,
Ezr 6:20 The **p** and Levites had purified
    10: 5 So Ezra rose up and put the leading **p**
Ne   3:28 the **p** made repairs,
    13:30 So I purified the **p** and the Levites

Ps 99: 6 Moses and Aaron were among his **p,**
Isa 28: 7 **P** and prophets stagger from beer
Jer 5:31 the **p** rule by their own authority,
Eze 22:26 Her **p** do violence to my law
44:28 to be the only inheritance the **p** have.
Hos 4: 6 I also reject you as my **p;**
Mic 3:11 her **p** teach for a price,
Mal 1: 6 "It is you, O **p,**
Mt 20:18 will be betrayed to the chief **p**
27: 3 the thirty silver coins to the chief **p**
Mk 2:26 which is lawful only for **p** to eat.
15: 3 The chief **p** accused him
Ac 6: 7 a large number of **p** became obedient
Heb 7:27 Unlike the other high **p,**
Rev 1: 6 be a kingdom and **p** to serve his God
5:10 a kingdom and **p** to serve our God,
20: 6 **p** of God and of Christ and will reign

CHIEF PRIESTS See CHIEF

PRIESTS AND LEVITES 1Ki 8:4; 1Ch 13:2;
15:14; 23:2; 24:6, 31; 28:13, 21; 2Ch 11:13;
23:4, 6; 24:5; 29:4; 30:15, 25, 27; 31:2, 4, 9;
34:30; 35:8; Ezr 1:5; 3:8, 12; 6:20; 7:13; 8:29,
30; 9:1; 10:5; Ne 8:13; 11:20; 12:1, 30, 44, 44;
13:30; Isa 66:21; Jn 1:19

PRINCE [PRINCES, PRINCESS]

Ge 49:26 of the **p** among his brothers.
Dt 33:16 of the **p** among his brothers.
Isa 9: 6 Everlasting Father, **P** of Peace.
Eze 34:24 and my servant David will be **p**
37:25 and David my servant will be their **p**
45:17 It will be the duty of the **p** to provide
46: 8 When the **p** enters,
Da 8:11 to be as great as the **P** of the host;
8:25 his stand against the **P** of princes.
10:20 to fight against the **p** of Persia,
10:21 against them except Michael, your **p.**
11:22 a **p** of the covenant will be destroyed
12: 1 the great **p** who protects your people,
Lk 11:15 "By Beelzebub, the **p** of demons,
Jn 12:31 the **p** of this world will be driven out.
14:30 for the **p** of this world is coming.
16:11 the **p** of this world now stands
condemned.
Ac 5:31 as **P** and Savior that he might give

PRINCES [PRINCE]

Jdg 5: 9 My heart is with Israel's **p,**
1Sa 2: 8 he seats them with **p**
Job 34:19 who shows no partiality to **p**
Ps 113: 8 he seats them with **p,**
118: 9 in the LORD than to trust in **p.**
146: 3 Do not put your trust in **p,**
148:11 you **p** and all rulers on earth,
Pr 8:16 by me **p** govern,
Isa 40:23 He brings **p** to naught and reduces
Eze 19: 1 "Take up a lament concerning the **p**
Da 8:25 his stand against the Prince of **p.**
10:13 Then Michael, one of the chief **p,**
Rev 6:15 Then the kings of the earth, the **p,**

PRINCESS* [PRINCE]

Ps 45:13 All glorious is the **p** within

PRINCIPLES*

Gal 4: 3 we were in slavery under the basic **p**
4: 9 to those weak and miserable **p?**
Col 2: 8 on human tradition and the basic **p**
2:20 died with Christ to the basic **p** of this

PRISCILLA

Wife of Aquila; co-worker with Paul (Ac 18; Ro
16:3; 1Co 16:19; 2Ti 4:19); instructor of Apollos
(Ac 18:24-28).

PRISON [IMPRISON, IMPRISONED,
IMPRISONMENT, IMPRISONMENTS,
PRISONER, PRISONERS]

Ge 39:20 But while Joseph was there in the **p,**
Jdg 16:25 So they called Samson out of the **p,**
2Ki 25:29 So Jehoiachin put aside his **p** clothes
Ps 66:11 You brought us into **p**
142: 7 Set me free from my **p,**
Isa 42: 7 to free captives from **p** and to release
Mt 4:12 that John had been put in **p,**
14:10 and had John beheaded in the **p.**
25:36 I was in **p** and you came to visit me.'
Lk 22:33 I am ready to go with you to **p** and
Ac 8: 3 men and women and put them in **p.**
12: 5 So Peter was kept in **p,**
16:26 At once all the **p** doors flew open,
2Co 11:23 been in **p** more frequently,
Heb 11:36 others were chained and put in **p.**
13: 3 Remember those in **p** as
1Pe 3:19 and preached to the spirits in **p**
Rev 2:10 the devil will put some of you in **p**
20: 7 Satan will be released from his **p**

PRISONER [PRISON]

Jdg 15:10 "We have come to take Samson **p,"**
2Ki 24:12 he took Jehoiachin **p.**
2Ch 33:11 who took Manasseh **p,**
Mk 15: 6 the custom at the Feast to release a **p**
Ro 7:23 and making me a **p** of the law of sin
Gal 3:22 that the whole world is a **p** of sin,
Eph 3: 1 Paul, the **p** of Christ Jesus for the

PRISONERS [PRISON]

Ps 68: 6 he leads forth the **p** with singing;
79:11 the groans of the **p** come before you;
107:10 **p** suffering in iron chains,
146: 7 The LORD sets **p** free,
Isa 51:14 The cowering **p** will soon be set free;
61: 1 and release from darkness for the **p,**
Zec 9:12 Return to your fortress, O **p** of hope;
Lk 4:18 to proclaim freedom for the **p**
Ac 9: 2 might take them as **p** to Jerusalem.
Gal 3:23 we were held **p** by the law,

PRIVATE

Mt 17:19 disciples came to Jesus in **p** and
Lk 9:18 Once when Jesus was praying in **p**

PRIVILEGE*

2Co 8: 4 for the **p** of sharing in this service to

PRIZE*

1Co	9:24	but only one gets the **p**?
	9:24	Run in such a way as to get the **p**.
	9:27	not be disqualified for the **p**.
Php	3:14	on toward the goal to win the **p**
Col	2:18	of angels disqualify you for the **p**.

PROBE

Job	11:7	you **p** the limits of the Almighty?
Ps	17:3	Though you **p** my heart
Jer	20:12	and **p** the heart and mind,

PROBLEMS*

Dt	1:12	how can I bear your **p** and your
Da	5:12	explain riddles and solve difficult **p**.
	5:16	and to solve difficult **p**.

PROCEDURE* [PROCESSION]

Ecc	8:5	will know the proper time and **p**.
	8:6	a proper time and **p** for every matter,

PROCESSION [PROCEDURE]

1Sa	10:10	a **p** of prophets met him;
Ne	12:36	Ezra the scribe led the **p**.
Ps	42:4	leading the **p** to the house of God,
	68:24	Your **p** has come into view, O God,
	118:27	join in the festal **p** up to the horns of
Isa	60:11	their kings led in triumphal **p**.
1Co	4:9	on display at the end of the **p**,
2Co	2:14	in triumphal **p** in Christ

PROCLAIM [PROCLAIMED, PROCLAIMING, PROCLAIMS, PROCLAMATION]

Ex	33:19	and I will **p** my name, the LORD,
Lev	25:10	and **p** liberty throughout the land
Dt	30:12	and **p** it to us so we may obey it?"
	32:3	I will **p** the name of the LORD.
2Sa	1:20	**p** it not in the streets of Ashkelon,
1Ch	16:23	**p** his salvation day after day.
Ne	8:15	and that they should **p** this word
Ps	2:7	I will **p** the decree of the LORD:
	9:11	**p** among the nations what he has
	19:1	the skies **p** the work of his hands.
	22:31	They will **p** his righteousness to
	30:9	Will it **p** your faithfulness?
	40:9	I **p** righteousness in the great
	50:6	And the heavens **p** his righteousness,
	64:9	they will **p** the works of God
	68:34	**P** the power of God,
	71:16	I will come and **p** your mighty acts,
	92:2	to **p** your love in the morning
	96:2	**p** his salvation day after day.
	97:6	The heavens **p** his righteousness,
	106:2	can **p** the mighty acts of the LORD
	118:17	will **p** what the LORD has done.
	145:6	and I will **p** your great deeds.
Isa	12:4	and **p** that his name is exalted.
	40:2	and **p** to her that her hard service
	42:12	and **p** his praise in the islands.
	43:21	that they may **p** my praise.
	44:8	Did I not **p** this and foretell it
	52:7	who **p** peace, who bring good tidings

	61:1	to **p** freedom for the captives
	66:19	They will **p** my glory among
Jer	7:2	and there **p** this message:
	50:2	"Announce and **p** among the nations,
Hos	5:9	the tribes of Israel I **p** what is certain.
Jnh	3:2	and **p** to it the message I give you."
Mic	3:5	if one feeds them, they **p** 'peace';
Zec	9:10	He will **p** peace to the nations.
Mt	10:27	**p** from the roofs.
	12:18	and he will **p** justice to the nations.
Lk	4:19	to **p** the year of the Lord's favor."
	9:60	you go and **p** the kingdom of God."
Ac	17:23	I am going to **p** to you.
	20:27	For I have not hesitated to **p** to you
1Co	11:26	**p** the Lord's death until he comes.
Col	1:28	We **p** him, admonishing and teaching
	4:4	Pray that I may **p** it clearly,
1Jn	1:1	we **p** concerning the Word of life.
Rev	14:6	and he had the eternal gospel to **p**

PROCLAIMED [PROCLAIM]

Ex	9:16	my name might be **p** in all the earth.
	34:5	stood there with him and **p** his name,
Dt	10:4	the Ten Commandments he had **p**
Ps	68:11	the company of those who **p** it:
Isa	43:9	Which of them foretold this and **p**
	43:12	I have revealed and saved and **p**—
Lk	16:16	and the Prophets were **p** until John.
Ro	9:17	and that my name might be **p** in all
	15:19	I have fully **p** the gospel of Christ.
Col	1:23	and that has been **p** to every creature
2Ti	4:17	the message might be fully **p** and all

PROCLAIMING [PROCLAIM]

Ex	34:6	And he passed in front of Moses, **p**,
Ps	26:7	**p** aloud your praise and telling
	92:15	**p**, "The LORD is upright;
Mk	1:14	**p** the good news of God.
Ac	4:2	and **p** in Jesus the resurrection of
	5:42	they never stopped teaching and **p**
	17:3	"This Jesus I am **p** to you is
Ro	10:8	that is, the word of faith we are **p**:
2Th	2:4	**p** himself to be God.

PROCLAIMS* [PROCLAIM]

Dt	18:22	If what a prophet **p** in the name
Na	1:15	who brings good news, who **p** peace!

PROCLAMATION [PROCLAIM]

Ezr	1:1	Cyrus king of Persia to make a **p**
Isa	62:11	The LORD has made **p** to the ends
Ro	16:25	and the **p** of Jesus Christ,

PROCONSUL

Ac	13:12	When the **p** saw what had happened,

PRODUCE [PRODUCED, PRODUCES]

Ge	1:11	God said, "Let the land **p** vegetation:
	1:24	"Let the land **p** living creatures
	3:18	It will **p** thorns and thistles for you,
Dt	14:22	tenth of all that your fields **p** each
Jos	5:11	they ate some of the **p** of the land:
Eze	36:8	**p** branches and fruit for my people
Mt	3:8	**P** fruit in keeping with repentance.

Lk   3: 9 not **p** good fruit will be cut down
Jas   3:12 can a salt spring **p** fresh water.

PRODUCED [PRODUCE]

Nu   17: 8 blossomed and **p** almonds.
Mk   4: 8 It came up, grew and **p** a crop,

PRODUCES [PRODUCE]

Pr   30:33 so stirring up anger **p** strife."
Mt   13:23 He **p** a crop, yielding a hundred,
Jn   12:24 But if it dies, it **p** many seeds.
Ro   5: 3 that suffering **p** perseverance,
2Co   1: 6 which **p** in you patient endurance of
Heb   6: 8 that **p** thorns and thistles is worthless
     12:11 it **p** a harvest of righteousness

PROFANE [PROFANED]

Lev 18:21 must not **p** the name of your God.
     19:12 and so **p** the name of your God.
     22:32 Do not **p** my holy name.
Eze 20:39 and no longer **p** my holy name
Zep   3: 4 Her priests **p** the sanctuary
Mal   2:10 Why do we **p** the covenant

PROFANED [PROFANE]

Jer 34:16 have turned around and **p** my name;
Eze 20: 9 did what would keep it from being **p**
     36:20 the nations they **p** my holy name,
     39: 7 no longer let my holy name be **p,**

PROFESS* [PROFESSED]

1Ti   2:10 for women who **p** to worship God.
Heb   4:14 let us hold firmly to the faith we **p.**
     10:23 hold unswervingly to the hope we **p,**

PROFESSED* [PROFESS]

1Ti   6:21 which some have **p** and in so doing

PROFIT [PROFITABLE]

Lev 25:37 at interest or sell him food at a **p.**
Pr   14:23 All hard work brings a **p,**
     21: 5 The plans of the diligent lead to **p** as
Isa 44:10 which can **p** him nothing?
2Co   2:17 not peddle the word of God for **p.**
Php   3: 7 to my **p** I now consider loss for

PROFITABLE* [PROFIT]

Pr   3:14 for she is more **p** than silver
     31:18 She sees that her trading is **p,**
Tit   3: 8 These things are excellent and **p**

PROFOUND*

Job   9: 4 His wisdom is **p,** his power is vast.
Ps   92: 5 O LORD, how **p** your thoughts!
Ecc   7:24 it is far off and most **p—**
Ac   24: 3 acknowledge this with **p** gratitude.
Eph   5:32 This is a **p** mystery—

PROGRESS*

Ezr   5: 8 with diligence and is making rapid **p**
Php   1:25 of you for your **p** and joy in the faith,
1Ti   4:15 so that everyone may see your **p.**

PROLONG*

Dt   5:33 and prosper and **p** your days in

Ps   85: 5 Will you **p** your anger
Pr   3: 2 for they will **p** your life many years
Isa 53:10 see his offspring and **p** his days,
La   4:22 he will not **p** your exile.

PROMINENT

Est   9: 4 Mordecai was **p** in the palace;
Da   8: 5 suddenly a goat with a **p** horn
Mk   15:43 a **p** member of the Council,
Lk   14: 1 to eat in the house of a **p** Pharisee,
Ac   17: 4 and not a few **p** women.
     17:12 also a number of **p** Greek women

PROMISCUITY [PROMISCUOUS]

Eze 16:25 offering your body with increasing **p**
     23:29 Your lewdness and **p**

PROMISCUOUS* [PROMISCUITY]

Dt   22:21 by being **p** while still in her father's
Eze 23:19 Yet she became more and more **p**

PROMISE [PROMISED, PROMISES]

Nu   23:19 Does he **p** and not fulfill?
     30: 6 or after her lips utter a rash **p**
Jos   9:21 So the leaders' **p** to them was kept.
     23:14 Every **p** has been fulfilled;
2Sa   7:25 keep forever the **p** you have made
1Ki   6:12 I will fulfill through you the **p** I gave
     8:20 "The LORD has kept the **p**
     8:24 You have kept your **p** to your servant
Ne   5:13 every man who does not keep this **p.**
     9: 8 You have kept your **p**
Ps   77: 8 Has his **p** failed for all time?
    105:42 For he remembered his holy **p** given
    106:24 they did not believe his **p.**
    119:41 your salvation according to your **p;**
    119:50 Your **p** preserves my life.
    119:58 gracious to me according to your **p.**
    119:162 I rejoice in your **p**
Ac   2:39 The **p** is for you and your children
     26: 7 the **p** our twelve tribes are hoping
Ro   4:13 and his offspring received the **p**
     4:20 through unbelief regarding the **p**
     9: 8 children of the **p** who are regarded
Gal   3:14 that by faith we might receive the **p**
Eph   2:12 foreigners to the covenants of the **p,**
     6: 2 the first commandment with a **p—**
1Ti   4: 8 holding **p** for both the present life
2Ti   1: 1 to the **p** of life that is in Christ Jesus,
Heb   4: 1 the **p** of entering his rest still stands,
     6:13 When God made his **p** to Abraham,
     11:11 him faithful who had made the **p.**
2Pe   2:19 They **p** them freedom,
     3: 9 Lord is not slow in keeping his **p,**
     3:13 in keeping with his **p** we are looking

PROMISED [PROMISE]

Ge   18:19 for Abraham what he has **p** him."
     21: 1 LORD did for Sarah what he had **p.**
     24: 7 to me and **p** me on oath, saying,
     28:15 until I have done what I have **p** you."
Ex   3:17 And I have **p** to bring you up out
     32:13 descendants all this land I **p** them,
Nu   10:29 for the LORD has **p** good things

	14:23	of them will ever see the land I **p**
Dt	15: 6	God will bless you as he has **p,**
	26:18	his treasured possession as he **p,**
	34: 4	the land I **p** on oath to Abraham,
Jos	23: 5	as the LORD your God **p** you.
2Sa	7:28	and you have **p** these good things
1Ki	8:15	his own hand has fulfilled what he **p**
	9: 5	as I **p** David your father when I said,
2Ch	6:15	with your mouth you have **p** and
Ps	119:57	I have **p** to obey your words.
Isa	55: 3	my faithful love **p** to David.
Mk	6:23	And he **p** her with an oath,
Lk	24:49	to send you what my Father has **p;**
Ac	1: 4	but wait for the gift my Father **p,**
	2:33	from the Father the **p** Holy Spirit
	13:23	to Israel the Savior Jesus, as he **p.**
	13:32	good news: What God **p** our fathers
Ro	4:21	power to do what he had **p.**
2Co	11: 2	I **p** you to one husband, to Christ,
Eph	1:13	the **p** Holy Spirit,
Tit	1: 2	**p** before the beginning of time,
Heb	6:15	Abraham received what was **p.**
	10:23	for he who **p** is faithful.
	10:36	you will receive what he has **p;**
	11:13	They did not receive the things **p;**
Jas	1:12	the crown of life that God has **p**
	2: 5	kingdom he **p** those who love him?
2Pe	3: 4	"Where is this 'coming' he **p?**
1Jn	2:25	And this is what he **p** us—

PROMISES [PROMISE]

Jos	21:45	Not one of all the LORD's good **p**
	23:14	that not one of all the good **p**
1Ki	8:56	of all the good **p** he gave through
1Ch	17:19	and made known all these great **p.**
Ps	85: 8	he **p** peace to his people,
	106:12	Then they believed his **p**
	119:140	Your **p** have been thoroughly tested,
	119:148	that I may meditate on your **p.**
	145:13	The LORD is faithful to all his **p**
Ro	9: 4	the temple worship and the **p.**
2Co	1:20	how many **p** God has made,
	7: 1	Since we have these **p,** dear friends,
Gal	3:21	therefore, opposed to the **p** of God?
Heb	8: 6	and it is founded on better **p.**
2Pe	1: 4	us his very great and precious **p,**

PROMOTE [PROMOTES]

Pr	12:20	but joy for those who **p** peace.
	16:21	and pleasant words **p** instruction.
1Ti	1: 4	**p** controversies rather than God's

PROMOTES* [PROMOTE]

Pr	17: 9	who covers over an offense **p** love,
Gal	2:17	does that mean that Christ **p** sin?

PROMPTED*

Mt	14: 8	**P** by her mother, she said,
Jn	13: 2	devil have already **p** Judas Iscariot,
1Th	1: 3	your labor **p** by love,
2Th	1:11	and every act **p** by your faith.

PRONE*

Ex	32:22	how **p** these people are to evil.

PRONOUNCE [PRONOUNCED]

Ge	48:20	your name will Israel **p** this blessing:
Dt	10: 8	and to **p** blessings in his name,
Jdg	12: 6	he could not **p** the word correctly,
1Ch	23:13	to **p** blessings in his name forever.
Ps	109:17	He loved to **p** a curse—
Jer	1:16	I will **p** my judgments on my people

PRONOUNCED [PRONOUNCE]

1Ch	16:12	his miracles, and the judgments he **p,**
Ps	76: 8	From heaven you **p** judgment,
Da	7:22	and **p** judgment in favor of the saints

PROOF [PROVE]

Dt	22:14	I did not find **p** of her virginity,"
Ac	17:31	He has given **p** of this to all men
2Co	8:24	the **p** of your love and the reason

PROOFS* [PROVE]

Ac	1: 3	many convincing **p** that he was alive.

PROPER [PROPERLY]

Ps	104:27	to give them their food at the **p** time.
	145:15	give them their food at the **p** time.
Ecc	5:18	and **p** for a man to eat and drink,
	8: 5	the wise heart will know the **p** time
Mt	3:15	it is **p** for us to do this
	24:45	to give them their food at the **p** time?
Lk	1:20	will come true at their **p** time."
1Co	11:13	Is it **p** for a woman to pray to God
2Co	10:13	will not boast beyond **p** limits,
Gal	6: 9	at the **p** time we will reap a harvest
2Th	2: 6	he may be revealed at the **p** time.
1Ti	2: 6	the testimony given in its **p** time.
	3: 4	his children obey him with **p** respect.
	5: 3	Give **p** recognition to those widows
1Pe	2:17	Show **p** respect to everyone:

PROPERLY* [PROPER]

1Ti	1: 8	that the law is good if one uses it **p.**

PROPERTY

Ge	23: 4	Sell me some **p** for a burial site here
Lev	25:10	of you is to return to his family **p**
Ru	4: 5	the name of the dead with his **p."**
Lk	15:12	So he divided his **p** between them.
Ac	5: 1	also sold a piece of **p.**
Heb	10:34	accepted the confiscation of your **p,**

PROPHECIES [PROPHESY]

1Co	13: 8	where there are **p,** they will cease;
1Th	5:20	do not treat **p** with contempt.

PROPHECY [PROPHESY]

2Ki	9:25	the LORD made this **p** about him:
Eze	14: 9	if the prophet is enticed to utter a **p,**
Da	9:24	to seal up vision and **p** and to anoint
1Co	12:10	to another **p,** to another
	13: 2	If I have the gift of **p** and can
	14: 1	especially the gift of **p.**
	14: 6	or **p** or word of instruction?
	14:22	**p,** however, is for believers,
2Th	2: 2	unsettled or alarmed by some **p,**
2Pe	1:20	that no **p** of Scripture came about by

Rev	1: 3	who reads the words of this **p,**
	19:10	testimony of Jesus is the spirit of **p."**
	22: 7	keeps the words of the **p** in this book
	22:18	hears the words of the **p** of this book:

PROPHESIED [PROPHESY]

Nu	11:25	they **p,** but they did not do so again.
1Sa	19:24	He stripped off his robes and also **p**
Jer	2: 8	The prophets **p** by Baal,
	26:11	because he has **p** against this city.
Mt	11:13	For all the Prophets and the Law **p**
Mk	7: 6	when he **p** about you hypocrites;
Jn	11:51	that year he **p** that Jesus would die
Ac	19: 6	and they spoke in tongues and **p.**
	21: 9	had four unmarried daughters who **p.**
Jude	1:14	**p** about these men:

PROPHESIES [PROPHESY]

2Ch	18: 7	because he never **p** anything good
Jer	28: 9	But the prophet who **p** peace will
Eze	12:27	and he **p** about the distant future.'
1Co	11: 4	Every man who prays or **p**
	14: 3	But everyone who **p** speaks to men

PROPHESY [PROPHECIES, PROPHECY, PROPHESIED, PROPHESIES, PROPHESYING, PROPHET, PROPHET'S, PROPHETESS, PROPHETS]

1Sa	10: 6	and you will **p** with them;
Isa	30:10	Tell us pleasant things, **p** illusions.
Jer	5:31	The prophets **p** lies,
Eze	13: 2	**p** against the prophets of Israel
	13:17	who **p** out of their own imagination.
	34: 2	**p** against the shepherds of Israel;
	37: 4	"**P** to these bones and say to them,
Joel	2:28	Your sons and daughters will **p,**
Am	2:12	commanded the prophets not to **p.**
	7:16	You say, " 'Do not **p** against Israel,
Mic	2: 6	"Do not **p,**" their prophets say.
Mt	7:22	Lord, did we not **p** in your name,
Lk	22:64	and demanded, "**P!** Who hit you?"
Ac	2:17	Your sons and daughters will **p,**
1Co	13: 9	we know in part and we **p** in part,
	14: 5	but I would rather have you **p.**
	14:39	my brothers, be eager to **p,**
Rev	11: 3	and they will **p** for 1,260 days,

PROPHESYING [PROPHESY]

1Sa	10:13	After Saul stopped **p,**
	19:20	they saw a group of prophets **p,**
1Ki	18:29	and they continued their frantic **p**
1Ch	25: 1	and Jeduthun for the ministry of **p,**
Jer	14:14	"The prophets are **p** lies in my name.
Ro	12: 6	If a man's gift is **p,**
1Co	14:24	comes in while everybody is **p,**
Rev	11: 6	not rain during the time they are **p;**

PROPHET [PROPHESY]

Ex	7: 1	your brother Aaron will be your **p.**
Nu	12: 6	a **p** of the LORD is among you,
Dt	13: 1	If a **p,** or one who foretells
	18:18	I will raise up for them a **p** like you

	18:22	That **p** has spoken presumptuously.
	34:10	no **p** has risen in Israel like Moses,
1Sa	3:20	Samuel was attested as a **p** of the
	9: 9	**p** of today used to be called a seer.)
1Ki	1: 8	son of Jehoiada, Nathan the **p,**
	18:36	the **p** Elijah stepped forward and
	22: 7	"Is there not a **p** of the LORD here
2Ki	5: 8	will know that there is a **p** in Israel."
	6:12	"but Elisha, the **p** who is in Israel,
	20: 1	The **p** Isaiah son of Amoz went
2Ch	35:18	since the days of the **p** Samuel;
	36:12	himself before Jeremiah the **p,**
Ezr	5: 1	Haggai the **p** and Zechariah the **p,**
	6:14	under the preaching of Haggai the **p**
Ps	51: T	When the **p** Nathan came to him
Jer	1: 5	you as a **p** to the nations."
	23:11	"Both **p** and priest are godless;
	28: 1	the **p** Hananiah son of Azzur,
Eze	2: 5	that a **p** has been among them.
	33:33	know that a **p** has been among them.
Da	9: 2	of the LORD given to Jeremiah the **p,**
Hos	9: 7	the **p** is considered a fool,
Am	7:14	a **p** nor a prophet's son,
Hab	1: 1	oracle that Habakkuk the **p** received.
Hag	1: 1	the **p** Haggai to Zerubbabel son of
Zec	1: 1	to the **p** Zechariah son of Berekiah,
	13: 4	that day every **p** will be ashamed
Mal	4: 5	I will send you the **p** Elijah before
Mt	10:41	Anyone who receives a **p**
	11: 9	Yes, I tell you, and more than a **p.**
	12:39	except the sign of the **p** Jonah.
Mk	6: 4	his own house is a **p** without honor."
Lk	1:76	will be called a **p** of the Most High;
	4:24	"no **p** is accepted in his hometown.
	7:16	"A great **p** has appeared among us,"
	20: 6	they are persuaded that John was a **p.**
	24:19	"He was a **p,** powerful in word and
Jn	1:21	"Are you the **P?**"
	7:40	"Surely this man is the **P.**"
Ac	7:37	a **p** like me from your own people.'
	13: 6	and false **p** named Bar-Jesus,
	21:10	a **p** named Agabus came down
1Co	14:37	If anybody thinks he is a **p**
Rev	16:13	and out of the mouth of the false **p.**
	19:20	the false **p** who had performed
	20:10	and the false **p** had been thrown.

PROPHET'S [PROPHESY]

Am	7:14	"I was neither a prophet nor a **p** son,
2Pe	1:20	about by the **p** own interpretation.

PROPHETESS* [PROPHESY]

Ex	15:20	Then Miriam the **p,** Aaron's sister,
Jdg	4: 4	Deborah, a **p,** the wife of Lappidoth,
2Ki	22:14	went to speak to the **p** Huldah,
2Ch	34:22	went to speak to the **p** Huldah,
Ne	6:14	also the **p** Noadiah and the rest of
Isa	8: 3	Then I went to the **p,**
Lk	2:36	There was also a **p,** Anna,
Rev	2:20	who calls herself a **p.**

PROPHETS [PROPHESY]

Nu	11:29	that all the LORD's people were **p**
1Sa	10:11	Is Saul also among the **p?**"

	19:24	"Is Saul also among the **p?**"
	28: 6	answer him by dreams or Urim or **p.**
1Ki	18: 4	Jezebel was killing off the LORD's **p,**
	18:40	"Seize the **p** of Baal.
	19:10	put your **p** to death with the sword.
2Ki	17:23	warned through all his servants the **p**
1Ch	16:22	anointed ones; do my **p** no harm."
2Ch	18:22	a lying spirit in the mouths of these **p**
Ne	9:30	admonished them through your **p.**
Ps	105:15	anointed ones; do my **p** no harm."
Isa	44:25	who foils the signs of false **p**
Jer	5:13	The **p** are but wind and the word is
	14:14	**p** are prophesying lies in my name.
	23: 9	Concerning the **p:**
	23:30	against the **p** who steal from one
La	2: 9	and her **p** no longer find visions from
Eze	13: 2	prophesy against the **p** of Israel
Hos	6: 5	I cut you in pieces with my **p,**
Mic	3: 6	The sun will set for the **p,**
Zep	3: 4	Her **p** are arrogant;
Zec	1: 5	And the **p,** do they live forever?
Mt	5:17	to abolish the Law or the **P;**
	7:12	for this sums up the Law and the **P.**
	7:15	"Watch out for false **p.**
	22:40	All the Law and the **P** hang
	24:24	and false **p** will appear and perform
Lk	6:23	that is how their fathers treated the **p.**
	10:24	that many **p** and kings wanted to see
	11:49	'I will send them **p** and apostles,
	16:29	'They have Moses and the **P;**
	24:25	to believe all that the **p** have spoken!
	24:44	the **P** and the Psalms."
Ac	3:24	"Indeed, all the **p** from Samuel on,
	10:43	All the **p** testify about him
	13: 1	In the church at Antioch there were **p**
	26:22	saying nothing beyond what the **p**
	28:23	the Law of Moses and from the **P.**
Ro	1: 2	through his **p** in the Holy Scriptures
	3:21	to which the Law and the **P** testify.
	11: 3	they have killed your **p** and torn
1Co	12:28	second **p,** third teachers,
	12:29	Are all **p?** Are all teachers?
	14:32	The spirits of **p** are subject to the
		control of **p.**
Eph	2:20	the foundation of the apostles and **p,**
	3: 5	Spirit to God's holy apostles and **p.**
	4:11	some to be **p,** some to be evangelists,
1Th	2:15	who killed the Lord Jesus and the **p**
Heb	1: 1	through the **p** at many times and
1Pe	1:10	Concerning this salvation, the **p,**
2Pe	1:19	the word of the **p** made more certain,
	2: 1	But there were also false **p** among
	3: 2	in the past by the holy **p**
1Jn	4: 1	because many false **p** have gone out
Rev	11:10	these two **p** had tormented those
	16: 6	shed the blood of your saints and **p,**
	18:20	Rejoice, saints and apostles and **p!**
	22: 6	the God of the spirits of the **p,**

FALSE PROPHETS See FALSE

PROPORTION
Dt	16:10	by giving a freewill offering in **p** to
	16:17	a gift in **p** to the way the LORD
Ro	12: 6	let him use it in **p** to his faith.

PROPOSE* [PROPOSED]
| Dt | 1:14 | "What you **p** to do is good." |
| Isa | 8:10 | **p** your plan, but it will not stand, |

PROPOSED [PROPOSE]
| Ezr | 10:16 | So the exiles did as was **p.** |
| Ac | 1:23 | So they **p** two men: |

PROPRIETY*
| 1Ti | 2: 9 | with decency and **p,** |
| | 2:15 | love and holiness with **p.** |

PROSELYTE (KJV) See CONVERT

PROSPECT*
| Pr | 10:28 | The **p** of the righteous is joy, |

PROSPER [PROSPERED, PROSPERITY, PROSPEROUS, PROSPERS]
Ge	32: 9	and I will make you **p,**'
Dt	5:33	so that you may live and **p**
	28:63	to make you **p** and increase
	29: 9	that you may **p** in everything you do.
1Ki	2: 3	so that you may **p** in all you do
Ezr	6:14	and **p** under the preaching of Haggai
Ps	51:18	In your good pleasure make Zion **p;**
Pr	11:10	the righteous **p,** the city rejoices;
	11:25	A generous man will **p;**
	17:20	A man of perverse heart does not **p;**
	28:13	He who conceals his sins does not **p,**
	28:25	he who trusts in the LORD will **p.**
Isa	53:10	will of the LORD will **p** in his hand.
Jer	12: 1	the way of the wicked **p?**
	29:11	"plans to **p** you and not to harm you,

PROSPERED* [PROSPER]
Ge	39: 2	LORD was with Joseph and he **p,**
1Ch	29:23	He **p** and all Israel obeyed him.
2Ch	14: 7	So they built and **p.**
	31:21	And so he **p.**
Da	6:28	So Daniel **p** during the reign
	8:12	It **p** in everything it did,
Hos	10: 1	as his land **p,** he adorned his sacred

PROSPERITY [PROSPER]
Dt	28:11	The LORD will grant you abundant **p**
	30:15	I set before you today life and **p,**
Job	21:16	But their **p** is not in their own hands,
	36:11	in **p** and their years in contentment.
Ps	25:13	He will spend his days in **p,**
	73: 3	when I saw the **p** of the wicked.
	122: 9	I will seek your **p.**
	128: 2	blessings and **p** will be yours.
Pr	3: 2	many years and bring you **p.**
	8:18	enduring wealth and **p.**
	13:21	but **p** is the reward of the righteous.
	21:21	and love finds life, **p** and honor.
Ecc	6: 6	but fails to enjoy his **p.**
Isa	45: 7	I bring **p** and create disaster;
La	3:17	I have forgotten what **p** is.

PROSPEROUS [PROSPER]

Dt	30: 9	your God will make you most **p**
	30: 9	again delight in you and make you **p,**
Jos	1: 8	Then you will be **p** and successful.
Job	42:10	the LORD made him **p** again
Ps	10: 5	His ways are always **p;**

PROSPERS [PROSPER]

Ps	1: 3	Whatever he does **p.**
Pr	16:20	Whoever gives heed to instruction **p,**
	19: 8	who cherishes understanding **p.**

PROSTITUTE [PROSTITUTED, PROSTITUTES, PROSTITUTION]

Ge	34:31	have treated our sister like a **p?"**
	38:15	he thought she was a **p,**
Ex	34:15	when they **p** themselves to their gods
Lev	19:29	your daughter by making her a **p,**
	20: 6	spiritists to **p** himself by following
Nu	15:39	not **p** yourselves by going after the
Dt	23:17	or woman is to become a shrine **p.**
Jos	2: 1	a **p** named Rahab and stayed there.
	6:25	But Joshua spared Rahab the **p,**
Pr	6:26	the **p** reduces you to a loaf of bread,
	7:10	like a **p** and with crafty intent.
	23:27	for a **p** is a deep pit and
Jer	3: 3	Yet you have the brazen look of a **p;**
Eze	16:15	and used your fame to become a **p.**
	23: 7	as a **p** to all the elite of the Assyrians
Hos	3: 3	you must not be a **p**
1Co	6:15	of Christ and unite them with a **p?**
	6:16	with a **p** is one with her in body?
Heb	11:31	By faith the **p** Rahab,
Jas	2:25	Rahab the **p** considered righteous
Rev	17: 1	the punishment of the great **p,**
	19: 2	He has condemned the great **p**

PROSTITUTED [PROSTITUTE]

Jdg	2:17	but **p** themselves to other gods
Ps	106:39	by their deeds they **p** themselves.

PROSTITUTES [PROSTITUTE]

1Ki	3:16	Now two **p** came to the king
	14:24	There were even male shrine **p** in
	15:12	He expelled the male shrine **p** from
Pr	29: 3	companion of **p** squanders his wealth
Isa	57: 3	you offspring of adulterers and **p!**
Joel	3: 3	for my people and traded boys for **p;**
Mic	1: 7	as the wages of **p** they will again
Mt	21:31	and the **p** are entering the kingdom
Lk	15:30	your property with **p** comes home,
1Co	6: 9	idolaters nor adulterers nor male **p**
Rev	17: 5	THE MOTHER OF **P**

PROSTITUTION [PROSTITUTE]

Lev	19:29	or the land will turn to **p** and
Jer	3: 2	have defiled the land with your **p**
Eze	16:16	where you carried on your **p.**
	23: 3	engaging in **p** from their youth.
Hos	4:10	engage in **p** but not increase,
	4:12	A spirit of **p** leads them astray;
Na	3: 4	who enslaved nations by her **p**

PROSTRATE

Dt	9:18	Then once again I fell **p** before
1Ki	18:39	they fell **p** and cried, "The LORD—
Da	2:46	Then King Nebuchadnezzar fell **p**
	8:17	I was terrified and fell **p.**

PROTECT [PROTECTED, PROTECTION, PROTECTS]

Dt	23:14	God moves about in your camp to **p**
Est	9:16	also assembled to **p** themselves
Ps	12: 7	and **p** us from such people forever.
	20: 1	the name of the God of Jacob **p** you.
	25:21	May integrity and uprightness **p** me,
	32: 7	you will **p** me from trouble
	40:11	and your truth always **p** me.
	41: 2	The LORD will **p** him
	61: 7	your love and faithfulness to **p** him.
	91:14	"I will rescue him; I will **p** him,
	140: 1	**p** me from men of violence,
Pr	2:11	Discretion will **p** you,
	4: 6	and she will **p** you;
	14: 3	but the lips of the wise **p** them.
Jn	17:11	**p** them by the power of your name—
	17:15	that you **p** them from the evil one.
2Th	3: 3	and **p** you from the evil one.

PROTECTED* [PROTECT]

Jos	24:17	He **p** us on our entire journey and
1Sa	30:23	He has **p** us and handed over to us
Ezr	8:31	and he **p** us from enemies
Job	5:21	be **p** from the lash of the tongue,
Ps	37:28	They will be **p** forever,
Mk	6:20	Herod feared John and **p** him,
Jn	17:12	I **p** them and kept them safe by
2Pe	2: 5	**p** Noah, a preacher of righteousness,

PROTECTION [PROTECT]

Ge	19: 8	come under the **p** of my roof."
Jos	20: 3	find **p** from the avenger of blood.
Ezr	9: 9	a wall of **p** in Judah and Jerusalem.
Ps	5:11	Spread your **p** over them,

PROTECTS* [PROTECT]

Ps	34:20	he **p** all his bones, not one
	116: 6	The LORD **p** the simplehearted;
Pr	2: 8	the course of the just and **p** the way
Da	12: 1	the great prince who **p** your people,
1Co	13: 7	It always **p,** always trusts,

PROTEST

Ac	13:51	shook the dust from their feet in **p**
	18: 6	he shook out his clothes in **p** and said

PROUD [PRIDE]

Dt	8:14	then your heart will become **p**
2Ch	32:25	Hezekiah's heart was **p**
Ps	31:23	but the **p** he pays back in full.
	94: 2	pay back to the **p** what they deserve.
	101: 5	haughty eyes and a **p** heart,
	131: 1	My heart is not **p,** O LORD,
	138: 6	but the **p** he knows from afar.
Pr	3:34	He mocks **p** mockers but gives grace
	16: 5	The LORD detests all the **p** of heart.
	16:19	than to share plunder with the **p.**

18:12 his downfall a man's heart is **p,**
21: 4 Haughty eyes and a **p** heart,
Isa 2:12 a day in store for all the **p** and lofty,
Eze 28:17 Your heart became **p** on account
Hos 13: 6 they became **p;** then they forgot me.
Ro 12:16 Do not be **p,**
1Co 13: 4 it does not boast, it is not **p.**
2Ti 3: 2 lovers of money, boastful, **p,**
Jas 4: 6 "God opposes the **p** but gives grace
1Pe 5: 5 "God opposes the **p** but gives grace
Rev 13: 5 to utter **p** words and blasphemies and

PROVE [PROOF, PROOFS, PROVED, PROVING]

Ge 44:16 How can we **p** our innocence?
Pr 29:25 Fear of man will **p** to be a snare,
Hab 2: 3 of the end and will not **p** false.
Jn 2:18 can you show us to **p** your authority
8:46 Can any of you **p** me guilty of sin?
Ac 26:20 turn to God and **p** their repentance
1Co 4: 2 given a trust must **p** faithful.

PROVED [PROVE]

Dt 13:14 And if it is true and it has been **p**
17: 5 If it is true and it has been **p**
Job 32:12 But not one of you has **p** Job wrong;
Ps 51: 4 that you are **p** right when you speak
105:19 the word of the LORD **p** him true.
Mt 11:19 wisdom is **p** right by her actions."
Ro 3: 4 "So that you may be **p** right
1Pe 1: 7 genuine and may result in praise,

PROVERB [PROVERBS]

Ps 49: 4 I will turn my ear to a **p;**
Pr 26: 7 is a **p** in the mouth of a fool.
26: 9 is a **p** in the mouth of a fool.
Eze 18: 3 you will no longer quote this **p**
Lk 4:23 "Surely you will quote this **p** to me:

PROVERBS [PROVERB]

1Ki 4:32 He spoke three thousand **p**
Pr 1: 1 The **p** of Solomon son of David,
10: 1 The **p** of Solomon:
25: 1 These are more **p** of Solomon,
Ecc 12: 9 and set in order many **p.**

PROVIDE [PROVIDED, PROVIDES, PROVISION, PROVISIONS]

Ge 22: 8 "God himself will **p** the lamb for
22:14 that place The LORD Will **P.**
1Ch 17: 9 And I will **p** a place for my people
22:14 to **p** for the temple of the LORD
Isa 43:20 because I **p** water in the desert
61: 3 and **p** for those who grieve in Zion—
Ac 27: 3 friends so they might **p** for his needs.
1Co 10:13 he will also **p** a way out so
1Ti 5: 8 If anyone does not **p** for his relatives,
Tit 3:14 that they may **p** for daily necessities

PROVIDED [PROVIDE]

Ge 22:14 mountain of the LORD it will be **p."**
1Ki 8:21 I have **p** a place there for the ark,
1Ch 29: 2 With all my resources I have **p** for
Ps 68:10 O God, you **p** for the poor.

111: 9 He **p** redemption for his people;
Jnh 1:17 But the LORD **p** a great fish
4: 6 the LORD God **p** a vine
4: 7 at dawn the next day God **p** a worm,
4: 8 God **p** a scorching east wind,
Ro 11:22 **p** that you continue in his kindness.
Gal 4:18 **p** the purpose is good,
Heb 1: 3 After he had **p** purification for sins,

PROVIDES [PROVIDE]

Ps 111: 5 He **p** food for those who fear him;
147: 9 He **p** food for the cattle and for
Pr 31:15 she **p** food for her family and
Eze 18: 7 and **p** clothing for the naked.
1Ti 6:17 who richly **p** us with everything
1Pe 4:11 should do it with the strength God **p,**

PROVING* [PROVE]

Ac 9:22 by **p** that Jesus is the Christ.
17: 3 **p** that the Christ had to suffer
18:28 **p** from the Scriptures that Jesus was

PROVISION [PROVIDE]

Ps 144:13 be filled with every kind of **p.**
Ro 5:17 those who receive God's abundant **p**

PROVISIONS [PROVIDE]

Ps 132:15 I will bless her with abundant **p;**
Pr 6: 8 yet it stores its **p** in summer

PROVOCATION* [PROVOKE]

Pr 27: 3 but **p** by a fool is heavier than both.

PROVOKE [PROVOCATION, PROVOKED, PROVOKES]

Dt 31:29 in the sight of the LORD and **p** him
1Ki 16:33 and did more to **p** the LORD,
Jer 25: 6 do not **p** me to anger
Eze 8:17 and continually **p** me to anger?

PROVOKED [PROVOKE]

Dt 9: 7 you **p** the LORD your God to anger
Jdg 2:12 They **p** the LORD to anger
1Sa 1: 7 her rival **p** her till she wept
2Ki 17:11 They did wicked things that **p**
Ecc 7: 9 Do not be quickly **p** in your spirit,
Jer 8:19 "Why have they **p** me to anger
32:32 **p** me by all the evil they have done

PROVOKES* [PROVOKE]

Eze 8: 3 the idol that **p** to jealousy stood.

PROWLS

1Pe 5: 8 Your enemy the devil **p** around like

PRUDENCE* [PRUDENT]

Pr 1: 4 for giving **p** to the simple,
8: 5 You who are simple, gain **p;**
8:12 "I, wisdom, dwell together with **p;**
15: 5 whoever heeds correction shows **p.**
19:25 and the simple will learn **p;**

PRUDENT* [PRUDENCE]

Pr 1: 3 for acquiring a disciplined and **p** life,

12:16 but a **p** man overlooks an insult.
12:23 A **p** man keeps his knowledge
13:16 Every **p** man acts out of knowledge,
14: 8 the **p** is to give thought to their ways,
14:15 a **p** man gives thought to his steps.
14:18 the **p** are crowned with knowledge.
19:14 but a **p** wife is from the LORD.
22: 3 **p** man sees danger and takes refuge,
27:12 The **p** see danger and take refuge,
Jer 49: 7 Has counsel perished from the **p?**
Am 5:13 the **p** man keeps quiet in such times,

PRUNES* [PRUNING]

Jn 15: 2 that does bear fruit he **p** so

PRUNING [PRUNES]

Isa 2: 4 and their spears into **p** hooks.
Joel 3:10 into swords and your **p** hooks

PSALM [PSALMS]

1Ch 16: 7 to Asaph and his associates this **p**
Ps 47: 7 sing to him a **p** of praise.
Ac 13:33 As it is written in the second **P:**

PSALMS* [PSALM]

Lk 20:42 declares in the Book of **P:**
24:44 the Prophets and the **P."**
Ac 1:20 "it is written in the book of **P,**
Eph 5:19 Speak to one another with **p,**
Col 3:16 and as you sing **p,**

PUBLIC [PUBLICLY]

Pr 1:20 she raises her voice in the **p** squares;
Eze 16:24 a lofty shrine in every **p** square.
Mt 1:19 not want to expose her to **p** disgrace,
Lk 20:26 in what he had said there in **p.**
Col 2:15 he made a **p** spectacle of them,
1Ti 4:13 to the **p** reading of Scripture.
Heb 6: 6 and subjecting him to **p** disgrace.

PUBLICAN (KJV) See PAGANS, TAX COLLECTOR

PUBLICLY [PUBLIC]

Lk 1:80 in the desert until he appeared **p**
Jn 7:13 But no one would say anything **p**
Ac 20:20 to you but have taught you **p** and
1Ti 5:20 Those who sin are to be rebuked **p,**
Heb 10:33 you were **p** exposed to insult

PUFFED* [PUFFS]

Hab 2: 4 "See, he is **p** up;

PUFFS* [PUFFED]

1Co 8: 1 Knowledge **p** up, but love builds up.
Col 2:18 and his unspiritual mind **p** him up

PUL [TIGLATH-PILESER]

2Ki 15:19 **P** king of Assyria invaded the land,

PULL [PULLED, PULLING]

Ru 2:16 **p** out some stalks for her from
Mk 2:21 the new piece will **p** away from

PULLED [PULL]

Ge 19:10 inside reached out and **p** Lot back
37:28 his brothers **p** Joseph up out of
Ezr 9: 3 **p** hair from my head and beard
Ne 13:25 some of the men and **p** out their hair.
Mt 15:13 not planted will be **p** up by

PULLING* [PULL]

Mt 13:29 'because while you are **p** the weeds,
2Co 10: 8 for building you up rather than **p** you

PUNISH [PUNISHED, PUNISHES, PUNISHING, PUNISHMENT]

Ge 15:14 But I will **p** the nation they serve
Ex 32:34 I will **p** them for their sin."
Lev 26:18 I will **p** you for your sins seven times
2Sa 7:14 I will **p** him with the rod of men,
Pr 17:26 It is not good to **p** an innocent man,
23:13 if you **p** him with the rod,
Isa 13:11 I will **p** the world for its evil,
Jer 2:19 Your wickedness will **p** you;
21:14 I will **p** you as your deeds deserve,
Hos 10:10 When I please, I will **p** them;
Zep 1:12 and **p** those who are complacent,
Ac 4:21 could not decide how to **p** them,
7: 7 But I will **p** the nation they serve
1Th 4: 6 The Lord will **p** men
2Th 1: 8 He will **p** those who do not know
1Pe 2:14 by him to **p** those who do wrong and

PUNISHED [PUNISH]

Ge 19:15 be swept away when the city is **p."**
Ezr 9:13 you have **p** us less than our sins
Ps 99: 8 though you **p** their misdeeds.
La 3:39 complain when **p** for his sins?
Mk 12:40 Such men will be **p** most severely."
Lk 23:41 We are **p** justly,
2Th 1: 9 be **p** with everlasting destruction
Heb 10:29 to be **p** who has trampled the Son

PUNISHES [PUNISH]

Ex 34: 7 he **p** the children and their children
Nu 14:18 he **p** the children for the sin
Heb 12: 6 he **p** everyone he accepts as a son."

PUNISHING [PUNISH]

Ex 20: 5 **p** the children for the sin of the
Dt 5: 9 **p** the children for the sin of the

PUNISHMENT [PUNISH]

Ge 4:13 "My **p** is more than I can bear.
Ps 91: 8 and see the **p** of the wicked.
Pr 16:22 but folly brings **p** to fools.
Isa 53: 5 the **p** that brought us peace was
Jer 4:18 This is your **p.**
La 4: 6 The **p** of my people is greater than
Eze 39:21 all the nations will see the **p** I inflict
Hos 9: 7 The days of **p** are coming,
Zep 3:15 The LORD has taken away your **p,**
Mt 25:46 they will go away to eternal **p,**
Lk 12:48 and does things deserving **p** will
21:22 For this is the time of **p** in fulfillment
Ro 13: 4 an agent of wrath to bring **p** on

Heb 2: 2 and disobedience received its just **p**,
2Pe 2: 9 while continuing their **p.**
1Jn 4:18 because fear has to do with **p.**
Jude 1: 7 an example of those who suffer the **p**
Rev 17: 1 the **p** of the great prostitute,

PUR [LOT, PURIM]

Est 3: 7 they cast the **p** (that is, the lot)

PURCHASED

Ps 74: 2 Remember the people you **p** of old,
Rev 5: 9 with your blood you **p** men for God
     14: 4 They were **p** from among men

PURE [PURIFICATION, PURIFIED, PURIFIES, PURIFY, PURITY]

Ex 25:11 Overlay it with **p** gold,
     25:31 "Make a lampstand of **p** gold
     37: 6 the atonement cover of **p** gold—
2Sa 22:27 to the **p** you show yourself **p,**
1Ki 6:21 the inside of the temple with **p** gold,
Job 4:17 a man be more **p** than his Maker?
     14: 4 bring what is **p** from the impure?
Ps 19: 9 The fear of the LORD is **p,**
     19:10 than much **p** gold;
     24: 4 clean hands and a **p** heart,
     51:10 Create in me a **p** heart, O God,
    119: 9 a young man keep his way **p?**
Pr 15:26 those of the **p** are pleasing to him.
     20: 9 "I have kept my heart **p;**
     20:11 by whether his conduct is **p**
Isa 52:11 Come out from it and be **p,**
Hab 1:13 Your eyes are too **p** to look on evil;
Mt   5: 8 Blessed are the **p** in heart,
2Co 11: 2 that I might present you as a **p** virgin
Php 1:10 may be **p** and blameless until the day
      2:15 you may become blameless and **p,**
      4: 8 whatever is **p,** whatever is lovely,
1Ti 1: 5 from a **p** heart and a good conscience
      5:22 Keep yourself **p.**
2Ti 2:22 who call on the Lord out of a **p** heart.
Tit 1:15 To the **p,** all things are **p,**
      2: 5 be self-controlled and **p,**
Heb 7:26 blameless, **p,** set apart from sinners,
     10:22 our bodies washed with **p** water.
     13: 4 and the marriage bed kept **p,**
Jas 1:27 that God our Father accepts as **p**
      3:17 comes from heaven is first of all **p;**
1Jn 3: 3 just as he is **p.**
Rev 14: 4 for they kept themselves **p.**
     21:18 and the city of **p** gold,

PURGE

Dt 13: 5 You must **p** the evil from
     19:19 You must **p** the evil from
Pr 20:30 and beatings **p** the inmost being.

MUST PURGE See MUST

PURIFICATION [PURE]

Lev 12: 6 " 'When the days of her **p** for a son
Lk   2:22 time of their **p** according to the Law
Ac 21:24 Take these men, join in their **p** rites
Heb 1: 3 After he had provided **p** for sins,

PURIFIED [PURE]

Ezr 6:20 The priests and Levites had **p**
Ne 12:30 they **p** the people,
Ps 12: 6 in a furnace of clay, **p** seven times.
Da 12:10 Many will be **p,**
Ac 15: 9 for he **p** their hearts by faith.
1Pe 1:22 Now that you have **p** yourselves

PURIFIES* [PURE]

1Jn 1: 7 his Son, **p** us from all sin.
      3: 3 who has this hope in him **p** himself,

PURIFY [PURE]

Ex 29:36 **P** the altar by making atonement
Nu 19:12 He must **p** himself with the water on
Zep 3: 9 "Then will I **p** the lips of the peoples,
2Co 7: 1 let us **p** ourselves from everything
Tit 2:14 and to **p** for himself a people
Jas 4: 8 you sinners, **p** your hearts,
1Jn 1: 9 and **p** us from all unrighteousness.

PURIM [PUR]

Est 9:26 (Therefore these days were called **P,**

PURITY* [PURE]

Hos 8: 5 will they be incapable of **p?**
2Co 6: 6 in **p,** understanding, patience
1Ti 4:12 in life, in love, in faith and in **p.**
      5: 2 as sisters, with absolute **p.**
1Pe 3: 2 when they see the **p** and reverence

PURPLE

Ex 25: 4 **p** and scarlet yarn and fine linen;
Pr 31:22 she is clothed in fine linen and **p.**
Da   5:29 Daniel was clothed in **p,**
Mk 15:17 They put a **p** robe on him,
Rev 17: 4 The woman was dressed in **p**
     18:16 dressed in fine linen, **p** and scarlet,

PURPOSE [PURPOSED, PURPOSES]

Ex   9:16 I have raised you up for this very **p,**
Job 36: 5 and firm in his **p.**
Pr 19:21 but it is the LORD's **p** that prevails.
Isa 46:10 I say: My **p** will stand,
     55:11 and achieve the **p** for which I sent it.
Jer 51:12 The LORD will carry out his **p,**
Ac   2:23 by God's set **p** and foreknowledge;
Ro   8:28 have been called according to his **p.**
      9:11 that God's **p** in election might stand:
      9:17 "I raised you up for this very **p,**
1Co 3: 8 and the man who waters have one **p,**
2Co 5: 5 who has made us for this very **p**
Gal 3:19 What, then, was the **p** of the law?
      4:18 provided the **p** is good,
Eph 1:11 in conformity with the **p** of his will,
      2:15 His **p** was to create in himself one
      3:11 his eternal **p** which he accomplished
Php 2: 2 being one in spirit and **p.**
      2:13 and to act according to his good **p.**
2Ti 1: 9 but because of his own **p** and grace.
Heb 6:17 unchanging nature of his **p** very clear
Rev 17:17 into their hearts to accomplish his **p**

PURPOSED* [PURPOSE]

Isa 14:24 and as I have **p**, so it will stand.
   14:27 For the LORD Almighty has **p**,
Jer 49:20 what he has **p** against those who live
   50:45 what he has **p** against the land of
Eph 1: 9 which he **p** in Christ,

PURPOSES [PURPOSE]

Ps 33:10 he thwarts the **p** of the peoples.
Pr 20: 5 **p** of a man's heart are deep waters,
Jer 23:20 until he fully accomplishes the **p**
   32:19 great are your **p** and mighty are your
Ro   9:21 some pottery for noble **p** and some
2Ti 2:20 for noble **p** and some for ignoble.

PURSE [PURSES]

Hag 1: 6 to put them in a **p** with holes in it."
Lk 10: 4 Do not take a **p** or bag or sandals;
   22:36 "But now if you have a **p**, take it,

PURSES [PURSE]

Lk 12:33 Provide **p** for yourselves that will

PURSUE [PURSUED, PURSUES, PURSUING]

Lev 26: 7 You will **p** your enemies.
Dt 19: 6 the avenger of blood might **p** him in
Ps 34:14 seek peace and **p** it.
Pr 15: 9 he loves those who **p** righteousness.
Isa 51: 1 who **p** righteousness and who seek
Jer 9:16 and I will **p** them with the sword
Eze 5: 2 For I will **p** them with drawn sword.
Ro   9:30 who did not **p** righteousness,
1Ti 6:11 and **p** righteousness, godliness, faith,
2Ti 2:22 and **p** righteousness, faith,
1Pe 3:11 he must seek peace and **p** it.

PURSUED [PURSUE]

Ex 14:23 The Egyptians **p** them,
Ps 18:37 I **p** my enemies and overtook them;
Ro   9:32 Because they **p** it not by faith but as

PURSUES [PURSUE]

Jos 20: 5 If the avenger of blood **p** him,
Pr 11:19 but he who **p** evil goes to his death.
   13:21 Misfortune **p** the sinner,
   21:21 He who **p** righteousness
   28: 1 wicked man flees though no one **p**,

PURSUING [PURSUE]

Lev 26:17 even when no one is **p** you.
Hos 5:11 intent on **p** idols.
1Ti 3: 8 and not **p** dishonest gain.
Tit 1: 7 not violent, not **p** dishonest gain.

PUSH

Dt 15:17 an awl and **p** it through his ear lobe

PUT [PUTS, PUTTING]

Ge   2:15 the man and **p** him in the Garden
    3:12 "The woman you **p** here with me—
    3:15 And I will **p** enmity between you and
    4:15 the LORD **p** a mark on Cain
    6:13 "I am going to **p** an end to all people,
   24: 2 "**P** your hand under my thigh.
   47:29 **p** your hand under my thigh
Ex   4: 6 So Moses **p** his hand into his cloak,
   16:34 Aaron **p** the manna in front of
Nu 14:15 If you **p** these people to death all
   17:10 "**P** back Aaron's staff in front of
   21: 8 "Make a snake and **p** it up on a pole;
   22: 6 and **p** a curse on these people,
Dt 32:39 I **p** to death and I bring to life,
1Sa 5: 3 They took Dagon and **p** him back
    7: 4 Israelites **p** away their Baals
1Ki 11:36 city where I chose to **p** my Name.
2Ch 10: 4 "Your father **p** a heavy yoke on us,
   33: 7 I will **p** my Name forever.
Job 40: 4 I **p** my hand over my mouth.
Ps 22: 4 In you our fathers **p** their trust;
   25: 2 Do not let me be **p** to shame,
   33:22 even as we **p** our hope in you.
   40: 3 He **p** a new song in my mouth,
   42: 5 **P** your hope in God,
   78:18 They willfully **p** God to the test
  119:43 for I have **p** my hope in your laws.
Isa 8:17 I will **p** my trust in him.
   11: 8 and the young child **p** his hand into
   42: 1 I will **p** my Spirit
   59:17 He **p** on righteousness as his
Jer 1: 9 I have **p** my words in your mouth.
   32:14 and **p** them in a clay jar
   38: 6 So they took Jeremiah and **p** him
Eze 36:27 And I will **p** my Spirit in you
   37:14 I will **p** my Spirit in you
Mt   4: 7 not **p** the Lord your God to
   12:18 I will **p** my Spirit
Mk 12:44 out of her poverty, **p** in everything—
Jn   8:30 he spoke, many **p** their faith in him.
   11:45 **p** their faith in him.
   20:25 **p** my finger where the nails were,
Ro   7:11 the commandment **p** me to death.
    8:13 but if by the Spirit you **p** to death
    9:33 in him will never be **p** to shame."
   10:11 in him will never be **p** to shame."
1Co 4: 9 that God has **p** us apostles on display
   13:11 I **p** childish ways behind me.
   15:25 until he has **p** all his enemies under
2Co 1:22 **p** his Spirit in our hearts as a deposit,
Eph 4:24 and to **p** on the new self,
    6:11 **P** on the full armor of God so
Php 3: 3 who **p** no confidence in the flesh—
Col 3:14 And over all these virtues **p** on love,
1Th 5:19 Do not **p** out the Spirit's fire;
Heb 2: 8 and **p** everything under his feet."
Rev 7: 3 until we **p** a seal on the foreheads of

PUT ... TO DEATH Ge 26:11; 38:7, 10; 42:37;
   Ex 19:12; 21:12, 14, 15, 16, 17, 29; 22:19; 31:14,
   15; 35:2; Lev 19:20; 20:2, 4, 9, 10, 11, 12, 13, 15,
   16, 27; 24:16, 16, 17, 21; 27:29; Nu 1:51; 3:10,
   38; 11:15; 14:15; 18:7; 25:5, 15; 35:16, 17, 18,
   19, 21, 21, 23, 30, 30, 31; Dt 9:28; 13:5, 9; 17:6,
   6, 12; 18:20; 21:22; 24:16, 16; 32:39; Jos 1:18;
   Jdg 6:31; 20:13; 21:5; 1Sa 2:25; 11:12, 13;
   14:45; 15:3, 33; 19:6; 20:32; 2Sa 4:10; 8:2; 14:7,
   32; 19:21, 22; 21:1, 4, 9; 1Ki 1:51; 2:8, 24, 26;
   18:9; 19:10, 14, 17, 17; 2Ki 11:8, 15, 16; 14:6, 6;
   16:9; 19:35; 1Ch 2:3; 10:14; 2Ch 15:13; 22:9;

23:7, 14, 15; 25:4, 4, 4; Est 4:11; 9:15; Ps 78:31;
Isa 37:36; 65:15; Jer 18:21; 26:15, 19, 21, 24;
29:21; 38:4; Eze 18:13; Da 2:13, 13, 14; 5:19, 19;
Mt 10:21; 15:4; 24:9; 26:59; 27:1; Mk 7:10;
13:12; 14:55; Lk 21:16; Ac 2:23; 5:33; 12:2;
26:10; Ro 7:11; 8:13; Eph 2:16; Col 3:5; Heb
11:37; 1Pe 3:18; Rev 2:13

PUT ... TO THE SWORD   Nu 21:24;   Dt
13:15; 20:13; Jos 8:24; 10:28, 30, 32, 35, 37, 39;
11:10, 11, 12, 14; 13:22; 19:47; Jdg 1:8, 25;
20:37, 48; 21:10; 1Sa 22:19; 2Sa 15:14; 2Ki
11:15; 2Ch 21:4; 23:14; Job 1:15, 17; Ps 78:64;
Jer 15:9; 20:4; 21:7; 25:31

PUTS [PUT]
Nu 23:12 speak what the Lord **p** in my
          mouth?
Mt 7:24 **p** them into practice is like a wise
Lk 9:62 "No one who **p** his hand to the plow

PUTTING [PUT]
1Ki 9: 3 by **p** my Name there forever.
Jn 12:11 over to Jesus and **p** their faith in him.
Col 2:11 in the **p** off of the sinful nature,
1Th 5: 8 **p** on faith and love as a breastplate,
Heb 2: 8 In **p** everything under him,
2Pe 2: 4 **p** them into gloomy dungeons to

Q

QUAIL*
Ex 16:13 That evening **q** came and covered
Nu 11:31 and drove **q** in from the sea.
   11:32 the people went out and gathered **q.**
Ps 105:40 and he brought them **q**

QUAKE [EARTHQUAKE,
EARTHQUAKES, QUAKED]
Ps 46: 3 the mountains **q** with their surging.
   75: 3 When the earth and all its people **q,**
Na 1: 5 The mountains **q** before him and
Rev 16:18 so tremendous was the **q.**

QUAKED* [QUAKE]
Jdg 5: 5 The mountains **q** before the Lord,
2Sa 22: 8 "The earth trembled and **q,**
Ps 18: 7 The earth trembled and **q,**
   77:18 the earth trembled and **q.**

QUALIFIED
Col 1:12 has **q** you to share in the inheritance
2Ti 2: 2 who will also be **q** to teach others.

QUALITIES* [QUALITY]
Da 6: 3 the satraps by his exceptional **q** that
Ro 1:20 God's invisible **q**—his eternal power
2Pe 1: 8 For if you possess these **q**

QUALITY [QUALITIES]
1Co 3:13 fire will test the **q** of each man's

QUARREL [QUARRELED,
QUARRELING, QUARRELS,
QUARRELSOME]
Pr 15:18 but a patient man calms a **q.**
   17:14 Starting a **q** is like breaching a dam;
   17:19 He who loves a **q** loves sin;
   20: 3 but every fool is quick to **q.**
   26:17 a passer-by who meddles in a **q**
   26:20 without gossip a **q** dies down.
Mt 12:19 He will not **q** or cry out;
2Ti 2:24 And the Lord's servant must not **q;**
Jas 4: 2 You **q** and fight.

QUARRELED [QUARREL]
Ex 17: 7 and Meribah because the Israelites **q**
Nu 20: 3 They **q** with Moses and said,

QUARRELING [QUARREL]
Ge 13: 7 **q** arose between Abram's herdsmen
1Co 3: 3 there is jealousy and **q** among you,
2Co 12:20 I fear that there may be **q,** jealousy,
2Ti 2:14 before God against **q** about words;

QUARRELS [QUARREL]
Pr 13:10 Pride only breeds **q,**
Isa 45: 9 "Woe to him who **q** with his Maker,
1Ti 6: 4 controversies and **q** about words
2Ti 2:23 because you know they produce **q.**
Tit 3: 9 genealogies and arguments and **q**
Jas 4: 1 What causes fights and **q**

QUARRELSOME [QUARREL]
Pr 19:13 a **q** wife is like a constant dripping.
   21: 9 than share a house with a **q** wife.
   21:19 to live in a desert than with a **q** and
   26:21 so is a **q** man for kindling strife.
1Ti 3: 3 not violent but gentle, not **q,**

QUEEN
1Ki 10: 1 the **q** of Sheba heard about the fame
2Ch 9: 1 **q** of Sheba heard of Solomon's fame,
   15:16 from her position as **q** mother,
Est 1:12 **Q** Vashti refused to come.
   2:17 and made her **q** instead of Vashti.
Isa 47: 7 continue forever—the eternal **q!'**
Jer 7:18 cakes of bread for the **Q** of Heaven.
La 1: 1 She who was **q** among the provinces
Eze 16:13 and rose to be a **q.**
Mt 12:42 The **Q** of the South will rise at
Ac 8:27 Candace, **q** of the Ethiopians.
Rev 18: 7 In her heart she boasts, 'I sit as **q;**

QUENCH [QUENCHED]
SS 8: 7 Many waters cannot **q** love;
Isa 1:31 with no one to **q** the fire."
Jer 4: 4 burn with no one to **q** it.

QUENCHED [QUENCH]
2Ki 22:17 against this place and will not be **q.'**
Isa 66:24 nor will their fire be **q,**
Jer 7:20 and it will burn and not be **q.**
Mk 9:48 and the fire is not **q.'**
Heb 11:34 **q** the fury of the flames, and escaped

QUESTION [QUESTIONS]

Job	38: 3	Brace yourself like a man; I will **q**
	40: 7	"Brace yourself like a man; I will **q**
Mt	22:35	tested him with this **q:**
Mk	11:29	Jesus replied, "I will ask you one **q.**
Jn	8: 6	They were using this **q** as a trap,

QUESTIONS [QUESTION]

2Ch	9: 1	to Jerusalem to test him with hard **q.**
Mt	22:46	no one dared to ask him any more **q.**
1Co	10:25	without raising **q** of conscience,

QUICK [QUICK-TEMPERED, QUICKLY]

Pr	6:18	feet that are **q** to rush into evil,
	20: 3	but every fool is **q** to quarrel.
Ecc	5: 2	Do not be **q** with your mouth,
Jas	1:19	Everyone should be **q** to listen,

QUICK, QUICKEN (KJV)
See also GIVE LIFE, LIVING

QUICK-TEMPERED* [QUICK, TEMPER]

Pr	14:17	A **q** man does foolish things,
	14:29	but a **q** man displays folly.
Tit	1: 7	not **q**, not given to drunkenness,

QUICKLY [QUICK]

Dt	4:26	that you will **q** perish from the land
Jos	23:16	you will **q** perish from the good land
Jdg	2:17	they **q** turned from the way
Ps	22:19	come **q** to help me.
	69:17	answer me, **q**, for I am in trouble.
	71:12	Be not far from me, O God; come **q,**
	90:10	for they **q** pass, and we fly away.
Ecc	4:12	of three strands is not **q** broken.
	7: 9	Do not be **q** provoked in your spirit,
	8:11	sentence for a crime is not **q** carried
Jn	13:27	"What you are about to do, do **q,"**
Gal	1: 6	**q** deserting the one who called you

QUIET [QUIETED, QUIETLY, QUIETNESS]

Ps	23: 2	he leads me beside **q** waters,
	83: 1	O God, do not keep silent; be not **q,**
Pr	17: 1	Better a dry crust with peace and **q**
Ecc	9:17	The **q** words of the wise are more to
Isa	62: 1	Jerusalem's sake I will not remain **q,**
Am	5:13	Therefore the prudent man keeps **q**
Zep	3:17	he will **q** you with his love,
Mk	4:39	the wind and said to the waves, "**Q!**
	6:31	"Come with me by yourselves to a **q**
Lk	19:40	he replied, "if they keep **q,**
1Th	4:11	your ambition to lead a **q** life,
1Ti	2: 2	that we may live peaceful and **q** lives
1Pe	3: 4	beauty of a gentle and **q** spirit,

QUIETED [QUIET]

Ps	131: 2	But I have stilled and **q** my soul;

QUIETLY [QUIET]

La	3:26	it is good to wait **q** for the salvation
Mt	1:19	he had in mind to divorce her **q.**

QUIETNESS* [QUIET]

Job	3:26	I have no peace, no **q;**
Isa	30:15	and trust is your strength,
	32:17	the effect of righteousness will be **q**
1Ti	2:11	A woman should learn in **q**

QUIRINIUS*

Lk	2: 2	first census that took place while **Q**

QUIVER

Ps	127: 5	Blessed is the man whose **q** is full
Isa	49: 2	and concealed me in his **q.**

QUOTE [QUOTES]

Eze	16:44	will **q** this proverb about you:
	18: 3	you will no longer **q** this proverb
Lk	4:23	you will **q** this proverb to me:

R

RABBI [RABBONI]

Mt	23: 8	"But you are not to be called '**R,**'
	26:49	Judas said, "Greetings, **R!**"
Jn	1:38	"**R**" (which means Teacher),

RABBONI* [RABBI]

Jn	20:16	and cried out in Aramaic, "**R!**"

RACE*

Ezr	9: 2	and have mingled the holy **r** with
Ecc	9:11	The **r** is not to the swift or the battle
Ac	20:24	if only I may finish the **r**
Ro	9: 3	those of my own **r,**
1Co	9:24	Do you not know that in a **r** all
Gal	2: 2	running or had run my **r** in vain.
	5: 7	You were running a good **r.**
2Ti	4: 7	I have finished the **r,**
Heb	12: 1	let us run with perseverance the **r**

RACHEL
Daughter of Laban (Ge 29:16); wife of Jacob (Ge 29:28); bore two sons (Ge 30:22-24; 35:16-24; 46:19). Stole Laban's gods (Ge 31:19, 32-35). Death (Ge 35:19-20).

RADIANCE* [RADIANT]

Job	31:26	if I have regarded the sun in its **r** or
Eze	1:28	so was the **r** around him.
	10: 4	full of the **r** of the glory of the LORD.
2Co	3:13	gazing at it while the **r** was fading
Heb	1: 3	The Son is the **r** of God's glory and

RADIANT [RADIANCE]

Ex	34:29	not aware that his face was **r**
Ps	19: 8	The commands of the LORD are **r,**
	34: 5	Those who look to him are **r;**
SS	5:10	My lover is **r** and ruddy,
Isa	60: 5	Then you will look and be **r,**
Eze	43: 2	and the land was **r** with his glory.
Eph	5:27	to himself as a **r** church,

RAGE [RAGING]

Dt	19: 6	of blood might pursue him in a **r,**
Job	15:13	you vent your **r** against God
Isa	41:11	"All who **r** against you will surely
Ac	4:25	" 'Why do the the nations **r** and
Gal	5:20	jealousy, fits of **r,** selfish ambition,
Eph	4:31	Get rid of all bitterness, **r** and anger,
Col	3: 8	anger, **r,** malice, slander, and filthy

RAGING [RAGE]

Jnh	1:15	and the **r** sea grew calm.
Lk	8:24	the wind and the **r** waters;

RAGS

Isa	64: 6	all our righteous acts are like filthy **r**
Jer	38:12	"Put these old **r** and worn-out clothes

RAHAB

Prostitute of Jericho who hid Israelite spies (Jos 2; 6:22-25; Heb 11:31; Jas 2:25). Mother of Boaz (Mt 1:5).

RAIDERS

Jdg	2:14	the LORD handed them over to **r**

RAIMENT (KJV) See CLOTHING, DRESS, GARMENT

RAIN [RAINBOW, RAINED, RAINS]

Ge	2: 5	the LORD God had not sent **r**
	7: 4	from now I will send **r** on the earth
Ex	16: 4	"I will **r** down bread from heaven
Lev	26: 4	I will send you **r** in its season,
Dt	11:14	then I will send **r** on your land
1Ki	17: 1	nor **r** in the next few years except
	18: 1	and I will send **r** on the land."
2Ch	6:26	no **r** because your people have
Job	38:28	Does the **r** have a father?
Ps	147: 8	he supplies the earth with **r**
Isa	45: 8	heavens above, **r** down righteousness
Jer	14:22	idols of the nations bring **r?**
Zec	14:17	they will have no **r.**
Mt	5:45	and sends **r** on the righteous and
	7:25	The **r** came down, the streams rose,
Jas	5:17	prayed earnestly that it would not **r,**
Jude	1:12	They are clouds without **r,**
Rev	11: 6	to shut up the sky so that it will not **r**

RAINBOW [RAIN]

Ge	9:13	I have set my **r** in the clouds,
Eze	1:28	the appearance of a **r** in the clouds
Rev	4: 3	A **r,** resembling an emerald,
	10: 1	with a **r** above his head;

RAINED* [RAIN]

Ge	19:24	the LORD **r** down burning sulfur
Ex	9:23	LORD **r** hail on the land of Egypt;
Ps	78:24	he **r** down manna for the people
	78:27	He **r** meat down on them like dust,
Lk	17:29	fire and sulfur **r** down from heaven

RAINS [RAIN]

Dt	11:14	both autumn and spring **r,**
Jer	5:24	who gives autumn and spring **r**
Joel	2:23	both autumn and spring **r,** as before.

Jas	5: 7	for the autumn and spring **r.**

RAISE [RISE]

Dt	18:15	will **r** up for you a prophet like me
1Sa	2:35	**r** up for myself a faithful priest,
Pr	8: 1	Does not understanding **r** her voice?
Isa	11:12	He will **r** a banner for the nations
	14:13	I will **r** my throne above
Mt	3: 9	of these stones God can **r** up children
Jn	2:19	and I will **r** it again in three days."
	6:39	but **r** them up at the last day.
Ac	3:22	will **r** up for you a prophet like me
1Co	6:14	and he will **r** us also.
2Co	4:14	also **r** us with Jesus and present us
Heb	11:19	Abraham reasoned that God could **r**

RAISED [RISE]

Ex	9:16	But I have **r** you up for this
Jdg	2:18	Whenever the LORD **r** up a judge
Isa	40: 4	Every valley shall be **r** up,
	52:13	he will be **r** and lifted up
Mt	17:23	on the third day he will be **r** to life."
Lk	7:22	the deaf hear, the dead are **r,**
Ac	2:24	But God **r** him from the dead,
	10:40	but God **r** him from the dead on
	13:30	But God **r** him from the dead,
Ro	4:25	and was **r** to life for our justification.
	6: 4	just as Christ was **r** from the dead
	8:11	he who **r** Christ from the dead will
	9:17	"I **r** you up for this very purpose,
	10: 9	believe in your heart that God **r** him
1Co	15: 4	that he was **r** on the third day
	15:20	But Christ has indeed been **r** from
2Co	5:15	died for them and was **r** again.
Eph	2: 6	And God **r** us up with Christ
Col	2:12	and **r** with him through your faith

RAISES [RISE]

1Sa	2: 8	He **r** the poor from the dust and lifts
Ps	113: 7	He **r** the poor from the dust and lifts
Jn	5:21	For just as the Father **r** the dead

RAISINS

Nu	6: 3	grape juice or eat grapes or **r.**
SS	2: 5	Strengthen me with **r,**

RALLY*

Isa	11:10	the nations will **r** to him,

RAM [RAMS, RAMS']

Ge	22:13	he saw a **r** caught by its horns.
Ex	25: 5	**r** skins dyed red and hides
	29:22	(This is the **r** for the ordination.)
Lev	8:22	the **r** for the ordination,
Da	8: 3	before me was a **r** with two horns,

RAMAH

Jer	31:15	"A voice is heard in **R,**
Mt	2:18	"A voice is heard in **R,**

RAMESES

Ex	1:11	and **R** as store cities for Pharaoh.

RAMOTH GILEAD [GILEAD]

1Ki	22: 6	"Shall I go to war against **R**

RAMPART* [RAMPARTS]
Ps   91: 4 faithfulness will be your shield and **r**

RAMPARTS [RAMPART]
Ps   48:13 consider well her **r,**
Hab   2: 1 and station myself on the **r;**

RAMS [RAM]
1Sa 15:22 and to heed is better than the fat of **r.**
Ps 114: 4 the mountains skipped like **r,**
Mic   6: 7 LORD be pleased with thousands of **r,**

RAMS'* [RAM]
Jos   6: 4 of **r** horns in front of the ark.
1Ch 15:28 with the sounding of **r** horns

RAN [RUN]
Ge   39:12 in her hand and **r** out of the house.
1Ki 18:46 he **r** ahead of Ahab all the way
       19: 3 Elijah was afraid and **r** for his life.
Jnh   1: 3 But Jonah **r** away from the LORD

RANGE
2Ch 16: 9 eyes of the LORD **r** throughout the
Zec   4:10 which **r** throughout the earth.)"

RANK [RANKS]
1Sa 18: 5 Saul gave him a high **r** in the army.
Est   10: 3 Mordecai the Jew was second in **r**

RANKS [RANK]
1Sa 17:10 "This day I defy the **r** of Israel!
Gal   2: 4 false brothers had infiltrated our **r**

RANSOM [RANSOMED]
Nu   35:31 " 'Do not accept a **r** for the life of
Ps   49: 8 the **r** for a life is costly,
Isa   50: 2 Was my arm too short to **r** you?
Hos 13:14 "I will **r** them from the power of
Mt   20:28 and to give his life as a **r** for many."
Mk   10:45 and to give his life as a **r** for many."
1Ti   2: 6 who gave himself as a **r**
Heb   9:15 as a **r** to set them free from

RANSOMED [RANSOM]
Isa   35:10 and the **r** of the LORD will return.
      51:11 The **r** of the LORD will return.

RARE
1Sa   3: 1 the word of the LORD was **r;**
Pr   20:15 that speak knowledge are a **r** jewel.

RASH [RASHLY]
Nu   30: 6 or after her lips utter a **r** promise
Ps 106:33 and **r** words came from Moses' lips.

RASHLY* [RASH]
Pr   13: 3 he who speaks **r** will come to ruin.
      20:25 for a man to dedicate something **r**

RATHER
Job 32: 2 Job for justifying himself **r** than God
Mt   10: 6 Go **r** to the lost sheep of Israel.
Mk   7:15 **R,** it is what comes out of a man
Ac   5:29 "We must obey God **r** than men!

1Co   9:12 put up with anything **r** than hinder
      14: 5 but I would **r** have you prophesy.
      14:19 would **r** speak five intelligible words
1Pe   4: 2 but **r** for the will of God.

RAVEN [RAVENS]
Ge   8: 7 and sent out a **r,** and it kept flying
Job 38:41 the **r** when its young cry out to God

RAVENS [RAVEN]
1Ki 17: 6 The **r** brought him bread and meat in
Ps 147: 9 and for the young **r** when they call.
Lk   12:24 Consider the **r:** They do not sow

RAW
Ex   12: 9 Do not eat the meat **r** or cooked
1Sa   2:15 boiled meat from you, but only **r."**

RAZOR
Nu   6: 5 of his vow of separation no **r** may
Jdg 16:17 "No **r** has ever been used
1Sa   1:11 no **r** will ever be used on his head."

REACH [REACHES]
Dt   30:11 difficult for you or beyond your **r.**
Job 37:23 The Almighty is beyond our **r** and
Ps 144: 7 **R** down your hand from on high;
Isa   11:11 that day the Lord will **r** out his hand
Mic   5: 4 then his greatness will **r** to the ends
Rev 12:14 out of the serpent's **r.**

REACHES [REACH]
Ge   11: 4 with a tower that **r** to the heavens,
Ps   57:10 your faithfulness **r** to the skies.
      71:19 Your righteousness **r** to the skies,
Da   12:12 and **r** the end of the 1,335 days.

READ [READER, READING, READS]
Ex   24: 7 the Book of the Covenant and **r** it to
Dt   17:19 and he is to **r** it all the days of his life
Jos   8:34 Joshua **r** all the words of the law—
2Ki 23: 2 He **r** in their hearing all the words of
Ne   8: 8 They **r** from the Book of the Law
       8: 8 could understand what was being **r.**
Isa   34:16 in the scroll of the LORD and **r:**
Jer   36: 6 and **r** to the people from the scroll
      36:23 Whenever Jehudi had **r** three or
Da   5:16 If you can **r** this writing
Mk   12:10 Haven't you **r** this scripture:
Lk   4:16 And he stood up to **r.**
2Co   3: 2 known and **r** by everybody.
       3:15 Even to this day when Moses is **r,**

READER* [READ]
Mt   24:15 let the **r** understand—
Mk   13:14 let the **r** understand—

READINESS* [READY]
2Co   7:11 what **r** to see justice done.
Eph   6:15 and with your feet fitted with the **r**

READING [READ]
Ac   8:30 Do you understand what you are **r?**
1Ti   4:13 to the public **r** of Scripture,

READS* [READ]

Da   5: 7 "Whoever **r** this writing and tells
Rev   1: 3 Blessed is the one who **r** the words

READY [ALREADY, READINESS]

Ps 119:173 May your hand be **r** to help me,
Mt 24:44 So you also must be **r,**
      25:10 The virgins who were **r** went in
Lk   1:17 **r** a people prepared for the Lord."
      12:38 servants whose master finds them **r,**
1Pe   1: 5 the salvation that is **r** to be revealed
Rev   9:15 the four angels who had been kept **r**
     19: 7 and his bride has made herself **r.**

REAFFIRM

2Co   2: 8 therefore, to **r** your love for him.

REAL* [REALITIES, REALITY, REALLY]

Jn   6:55 For my flesh is **r** food and my blood
          is **r** drink.
1Jn   2:27 and as that anointing is **r,**

REALITIES* [REAL]

Heb 10: 1 not the **r** themselves.

REALITY* [REAL]

Col   2:17 the **r,** however, is found in Christ.

REALIZE [REALIZED]

Hos   7: 2 they do not **r** that I remember
Jn 12:16 after Jesus was glorified did they **r**
     13: 7 "You do not **r** now what I am doing,
     20:14 but she did not **r** that it was Jesus.
     21: 4 disciples did not **r** that it was Jesus.

REALIZED [REALIZE]

Ge   3: 7 and they **r** they were naked;
Jdg   6:22 When Gideon **r** that it was the angel
     13:21 Manoah **r** that it was the angel of
1Sa   3: 8 Then Eli **r** that the LORD
     18:28 When Saul **r** that the LORD was
1Ki   3:15 and he **r** it had been a dream.
Mk   5:30 At once Jesus **r** that power had gone

REALLY [REAL]

Ge   3: 1 "Did God **r** say,
Jdg   6:31 If Baal **r** is a god,
1Ki   8:27 "But will God **r** dwell on earth?
Jn 13:38 "Will you **r** lay down your life
1Jn   2:19 but they did not **r** belong to us.

REALM [REALMS]

Hab   2: 9 "Woe to him who builds his **r**

REALMS* [REALM]

Eph   1: 3 who has blessed us in the heavenly **r**
     1:20 at his right hand in the heavenly **r,**
     2: 6 with him in the heavenly **r**
     3:10 and authorities in the heavenly **r,**
     6:12 forces of evil in the heavenly **r.**

REAP [REAPER, REAPS]

Lev 19: 9 " 'When you **r** the harvest
Job   4: 8 and those who sow trouble **r** it.

Ps 126: 5 in tears will **r** with songs of joy.
Hos   8: 7 sow the wind and **r** the whirlwind.
     10:12 **r** the fruit of unfailing love,
Lk 12:24 They do not sow or **r,**
Jn   4:38 to **r** what you have not worked for.
Ro   6:22 the benefit you **r** leads to holiness,
1Co   9:11 if we **r** a material harvest from you?
2Co   9: 6 sows sparingly will also **r** sparingly,
Gal   6: 8 from the Spirit will **r** eternal life.
Rev 14:15 "Take your sickle and **r,**

REAPER [REAP]

Am   9:13 "when the **r** will be overtaken by
Jn   4:36 Even now the **r** draws his wages,

REAPS* [REAP]

Pr 11:18 but he who sows righteousness **r**
     22: 8 He who sows wickedness **r** trouble,
Jn   4:37 'One sows and another **r'** is true.
Gal   6: 7 A man **r** what he sows.

REAR

Nu 10:25 as the **r** guard for all the units,
Jos   6: 9 and the **r** guard followed the ark.
Isa 52:12 God of Israel will be your **r** guard.

REASON [REASONED]

Ge   2:24 For this **r** a man will leave his father
Ps 38:19 those who hate me without **r**
Isa   1:18 "Come now, let us **r** together,"
Mt 19: 5 this **r** a man will leave his father
Lk   6: 7 looking for a **r** to accuse Jesus,
Jn 12:27 for this very **r** I came to this hour.
     15:25 'They hated me without **r.'**
     18:37 In fact, for this **r** I was born,
1Pe   3:15 the **r** for the hope that you have.
2Pe   1: 5 For this very **r,** make every effort to
1Jn   3: 8 The **r** the Son of God appeared was

REASONED [REASON]

Ac 17:17 So he **r** in the synagogue with
1Co 13:11 I thought like a child, I **r** like a child.

REBEKAH

Sister of Laban, secured as bride for Isaac (Ge 24). Mother of Esau and Jacob (Ge 25:19-26). Taken by Abimelech as sister of Isaac; returned (Ge 26:1-11). Encouraged Jacob to trick Isaac out of blessing (Ge 27:1-17).

REBEL [REBELLED, REBELLING, REBELLION, REBELLIOUS, REBELS]

Ex 23:21 Do not **r** against him;
Nu 14: 9 Only do not **r** against the LORD.
Jos 22:18 " 'If you **r** against the LORD today,
1Sa 12:14 and serve and obey him and do not **r**
Mk 13:12 Children will **r** against their parents

REBELLED [REBEL]

Nu 20:24 both of you **r** against my command
Dt   1:26 **r** against the command of the LORD
Ne   9:26 "But they were disobedient and **r**
Ps 78:56 the test and **r** against the Most High;
   106:33 for they **r** against the Spirit of God,

Isa 63:10 they **r** and grieved his Holy Spirit.

REBELLING [REBEL]

Ro 13: 2 **r** against what God has instituted,

REBELLION [REBEL]

Ex 23:21 he will not forgive your **r,**
   34: 7 and forgiving wickedness, **r** and sin.
Nu 14:18 in love and forgiving sin and **r.**
Jos 24:19 not forgive your **r** and your sins.
1Sa 15:23 For **r** is like the sin of divination,
Da   8:13 the **r** that causes desolation,
Mk 14:48 "Am I leading a **r,"** said Jesus,
2Th 2: 3 until the **r** occurs and the man of
Heb 3: 8 as you did in the **r,**

REBELLIOUS [REBEL]

Dt 21:18 a stubborn and **r** son who does
Ps 25: 7 the sins of my youth and my **r** ways;
Pr 24:21 my son, and do not join with the **r,**
Eze 2: 5 for they are a **r** house—

REBELS [REBEL]

Jos 1:18 Whoever **r** against your word
Ro 13: 2 he who **r** against the authority
1Ti 1: 9 for lawbreakers and **r,** the ungodly

REBIRTH* [BEAR]

Tit 3: 5 of **r** and renewal by the Holy Spirit,

REBUILD [BUILD]

Jos 6:26 who undertakes to **r** this city, Jericho
Ezr 5: 2 to **r** the house of God in Jerusalem.
Ne 2:17 Come, let us **r** the wall of Jerusalem,
Ps 102:16 the LORD will **r** Zion and appear
Isa 58:12 Your people will **r** the ancient ruins
Da 9:25 the decree to restore and **r** Jerusalem
Am 9:14 they will **r** the ruined cities
Mt 26:61 to destroy the temple of God and **r** it
Ac 15:16 I will return and **r** David's fallen tent

REBUILT [BUILD]

2Ch 24:13 They **r** the temple of God according
Ezr 6: 3 the temple be **r** as a place to present
Ne 7: 1 the wall had been **r** and I had set
Eze 36:36 LORD have **r** what was destroyed
Zec 1:16 and there my house will be **r.**

REBUKE [REBUKED, REBUKES, REBUKING]

Lev 19:17 **R** your neighbor frankly so you will
Ps 6: 1 do not **r** me in your anger
   50: 8 I do not **r** you for your sacrifices
   119:21 You **r** the arrogant,
   141: 5 let him **r** me—it is oil on my head.
Pr 3:11 and do not resent his **r,**
    9: 8 not **r** a mocker or he will hate you;
    15:31 He who listens to a life-giving **r** will
    17:10 A **r** impresses a man of discernment
    19:25 **r** a discerning man, and he will gain
    25:12 a wise man's **r** to to a listening ear.
    27: 5 Better is open **r** than hidden love.
    30: 6 or he will **r** you and prove you a liar.
Ecc 7: 5 It is better to heed a wise man's **r**

Isa 54: 9 never to **r** you again.
Jer 2:19 your backsliding will **r** you.
Hos 2: 2 "**R** your mother, **r** her,
Zec 3: 2 "The LORD **r** you, Satan!"
Mk 8:32 and began to **r** him.
Lk 17: 3 "If your brother sins, **r** him,
1Ti 5: 1 Do not **r** an older man harshly,
2Ti 4: 2 correct, **r** and encourage—
Tit 1:13 Therefore, **r** them sharply,
    2:15 Encourage and **r** with all authority.
Jude 1: 9 but said, "The Lord **r** you!"
Rev 3:19 Those whom I love I **r** and

REBUKED [REBUKE]

Ps 106: 9 He **r** the Red Sea, and it dried up;
Mt 8:26 and **r** the winds and the waves,
    17:18 Jesus **r** the demon,
Lk 3:19 But when John **r** Herod the tetrarch
    4:39 So he bent over her and **r** the fever,
1Ti 5:20 Those who sin are to be **r** publicly,
2Pe 2:16 **r** for his wrongdoing by a donkey—

REBUKES [REBUKE]

Job 22: 4 "Is it for your piety that he **r** you
Ps 2: 5 Then he **r** them in his anger
Pr 28:23 He who **r** a man will in the end
    29: 1 after many **r** will suddenly
Heb 12: 5 and do not lose heart when he **r** you,

REBUKING [REBUKE]

2Ti 3:16 and is useful for teaching, **r,**

RECAB [RECABITES]

Jer 35: 6 son of **R** gave us this command:

RECABITES [RECAB]

Jer 35: 3 the whole family of the **R.**

RECALL* [RECALLED]

2Pe 3: 2 to **r** the words spoken in the past by

RECALLED* [RECALL]

Isa 63:11 Then his people **r** the days of old,
Eze 23:19 and more promiscuous as she **r**
Jn 2:22 his disciples **r** what he had said.

RECEDED

Ge 8: 3 The water **r** steadily from the earth.
Rev 6:14 The sky **r** like a scroll, rolling up,

RECEIVE [RECEIVED, RECEIVES, RECEIVING]

Ge 4:11 to **r** your brother's blood from your
Nu 18:23 They will **r** no inheritance among
Dt 9: 9 the mountain to **r** the tablets of stone,
Ps 24: 5 He will **r** blessing from the LORD
    27:10 the LORD will **r** me.
Pr 28:10 blameless will **r** a good inheritance.
Isa 61: 7 my people will **r** a double portion,
Da 12:13 to **r** your allotted inheritance."
Hos 14: 2 and **r** us graciously,
Mt 10:41 because he is a righteous man will **r**
Mk 10:15 **r** the kingdom of God like a little
    10:30 to **r** a hundred times as much in this

Lk	7:22	The blind **r** sight, the lame walk,
Jn	1:11	but his own did not **r** him.
	16:24	Ask and you will **r**,
	20:22	"**R** the Holy Spirit.
Ac	1: 8	But you will **r** power when
	2:38	you will **r** the gift of the Holy Spirit.
	19: 2	"Did you **r** the Holy Spirit
	20:35	more blessed to give than to **r.'** "
Ro	11:31	that they too may now **r** mercy as
1Co	4: 5	At that time each will **r** his praise
	9:14	the gospel should **r** their living from
2Co	6:17	and I will **r** you."
Gal	3:14	that by faith we might **r** the promise
1Ti	1:16	believe on him and **r** eternal life.
Heb	4:16	that we may **r** mercy and find grace
	11:13	They did not **r** the things promised;
Jas	1: 7	not think he will **r** anything from
	1:12	he will **r** the crown of life
1Pe	5: 4	you will **r** the crown of glory
2Pe	1:11	and you will **r** a rich welcome into
1Jn	3:22	and **r** from him anything we ask,
Rev	4:11	to **r** glory and honor and power,
	5:12	to **r** power and wealth and wisdom
	13:16	to **r** a mark on his right hand or
	18: 4	you will not **r** any of her plagues;

RECEIVED [RECEIVE]

Nu	23:20	I have **r** a command to bless;
Jos	14: 1	the Israelites **r** as an inheritance in
	14: 4	The Levites **r** no share of the land
Mt	6: 2	they have **r** their reward in full.
	10: 8	Freely you have **r**, freely give.
Mk	11:24	believe that you have **r** it,
Jn	1:12	Yet to all who **r** him,
	1:16	the fullness of his grace we have all **r**
Ac	8:17	and they **r** the Holy Spirit.
	10:47	They have **r** the Holy Spirit just
Ro	8:15	but you **r** the Spirit of sonship.
	11:30	to God have now **r** mercy
1Co	2:12	We have not **r** the spirit of the world
	11:23	For I **r** from the Lord what I
2Co	1: 4	with the comfort we ourselves have **r**
Eph	4: 1	worthy of the calling you have **r**.
Col	2: 6	just as you **r** Christ Jesus as Lord,
	4:17	complete the work you have **r**
1Ti	4: 4	if it is **r** with thanksgiving,
Heb	8: 6	the ministry Jesus has **r** is as superior
1Pe	2:10	but now you have **r** mercy.
	4:10	should use whatever gift he has **r**
2Pe	1: 1	have **r** a faith as precious as ours:
	1:17	For he **r** honor and glory from God
Rev	2:27	as I have **r** authority from my Father.
	19:20	who had **r** the mark of the beast
	20: 4	or his image and had not **r** his mark

RECEIVES [RECEIVE]

Pr	18:22	and **r** favor from the LORD.
	27:21	but man is tested by the praise he **r**.
Mt	10:40	"He who **r** you **r** me, and he who **r**
		me **r** the one who sent me.
Lk	11:10	For everyone who asks **r**;
Ac	10:43	believes in him **r** forgiveness of sins
Rev	14:11	anyone who **r** the mark of his name."

RECEIVING [RECEIVE]

Ro	9: 4	the covenants, the **r** of the law,
1Pe	1: 9	for you are **r** the goal of your faith,
3Jn	1: 7	**r** no help from the pagans.

RECENT*

1Ti	3: 6	He must not be a **r** convert,

RECITE [RECITED, RECITING]

Dt	27:14	The Levites shall **r** to all the people
Ps	45: 1	as I **r** my verses for the king;

RECITED* [RECITE]

Dt	31:30	And Moses **r** the words of this song

RECITING* [RECITE]

Dt	32:45	Moses finished **r** all these words

RECKLESS

Pr	12:18	**R** words pierce like a sword,
	14:16	but a fool is hotheaded and **r**.

RECKONED [RECKONING]

Ge	21:12	Isaac that your offspring will be **r**.
Ro	9: 7	Isaac that your offspring will be **r**."
Heb	11:18	Isaac that your offspring will be **r**."

RECKONING* [RECKONED]

Isa	10: 3	What will you do on the day of **r**,
Hos	5: 9	be laid waste on the day of **r**.
	9: 7	the days of **r** are at hand.

RECLAIM* [CLAIM]

Isa	11:11	a second time to **r** the remnant

RECLINED* [RECLINING]

Lk	7:36	to the Pharisee's house and **r** at
	11:37	so he went in and **r** at the table.
	22:14	Jesus and his apostles **r** at the table.

RECLINING [RECLINED]

Est	7: 8	on the couch where Esther was **r**.
Jn	13:23	was **r** next to him.

RECOGNITION* [RECOGNIZE]

Est	6: 3	honor and **r** has Mordecai received
1Co	16:18	Such men deserve **r**.
1Ti	5: 3	Give proper **r**

RECOGNIZE [RECOGNITION, RECOGNIZED, RECOGNIZING]

Ge	42: 8	they did not **r** him.
Job	2:12	they could hardly **r** him;
Mt	7:16	By their fruit you will **r** them.
Lk	19:44	not **r** the time of God's coming
Jn	1:10	the world did not **r** him.
1Jn	4: 2	how you can **r** the Spirit of God:
	4: 6	This is how we **r** the Spirit of truth

RECOGNIZED [RECOGNIZE]

Mt	12:33	for a tree is **r** by its fruit.
Lk	24:31	eyes were opened and they **r** him,
Ac	12:14	When she **r** Peter's voice,
Ro	7:13	in order that sin might be **r** as sin,

RECOGNIZING* [RECOGNIZE]

Lk   24:16 but they were kept from **r** him.
1Co 11:29 without **r** the body of the Lord eats

RECOMMENDATION*

2Co 3: 1 letters of **r** to you or from you?

RECOMPENSE*

Isa 40:10 and his **r** accompanies him.
     62:11 and his **r** accompanies him.' "

RECONCILE* [RECONCILED,
RECONCILIATION, RECONCILING]

Ac   7:26 He tried to **r** them by saying, 'Men,
Eph 2:16 in this one body to **r** both of them
Col 1:20 him to **r** to himself all things,

RECONCILED* [RECONCILE]

Mt   5:24 First go and be **r** to your brother;
Lk 12:58 try hard to be **r** to him on the way,
Ro   5:10 we were **r** to him through the death
     5:10 how much more, having been **r**,
1Co 7:11 or else be **r** to her husband.
2Co 5:18 who **r** us to himself through Christ
     5:20 on Christ's behalf: Be **r** to God.
Col 1:22 But now he has **r** you by Christ's

RECONCILIATION* [RECONCILE]

Ro   5:11 whom we have now received **r**.
    11:15 if their rejection is the **r** of the world,
2Co 5:18 and gave us the ministry of **r**:
     5:19 committed to us the message of **r**.

RECONCILING* [RECONCILE]

2Co 5:19 that God was **r** the world to himself

RECORD [RECORDED, RECORDS]

Ps   56: 8 **R** my lament; list my tears
    130: 3 If you, O LORD, kept a **r** of sins,
Hos 13:12 his sins are kept on **r**.
1Co 13: 5 it keeps no **r** of wrongs.

RECORDED [RECORD]

Nu 33: 2 At the LORD's command Moses **r**
Jos 24:26 And Joshua **r** these things in
1Ch 9: 1 Israel was listed in the genealogies **r**
Est 9:20 Mordecai **r** these events,
Job 19:23 "Oh, that my words were **r**,
Jn 20:30 which are not **r** in this book.
Rev 20:12 according to what they had done as **r**

RECORDS [RECORD]

1Ch 4:22 (These **r** are from ancient times.)
Ezr 2:62 These searched for their family **r**,
Ne   7:64 These searched for their family **r**,

RECOUNT*

Ps   40: 5 for us no one can **r** to you;
     79:13 to generation we will **r** your praise.
    119:13 With my lips I **r** all the laws

RECOVER [RECOVERED,
RECOVERY]

Isa 38: 1 you will not **r**."

RECOVERY [RECOVER]

Isa 38: 9 after his illness and **r**:
Ro 11:11 stumble so as to fall beyond **r**?

RED

Ge 25:25 The first to come out was **r**,
Ex 15: 4 officers are drowned in the **R** Sea.
     25: 5 ram skins dyed **r** and hides
Nu 19: 2 a **r** heifer without defect or blemish
2Ki 3:22 the water looked **r**—like blood.
Ps 106: 9 He rebuked the **R** Sea,
Pr 23:31 Do not gaze at wine when it is **r**,
Isa 1:18 though they are **r** as crimson,
Zec 1: 8 a man riding a **r** horse!
     6: 2 The first chariot had **r** horses,
Mt 16: 3 for the sky is **r** and overcast.'
Heb 11:29 the people passed through the **R** Sea
Rev 6: 4 a fiery **r** one.
     6:12 the whole moon turned blood **r**,
     9:17 Their breastplates were fiery **r**,
    12: 3 enormous **r** dragon with seven heads

REDEEM [KINSMAN-REDEEMER,
REDEEMED, REDEEMER, REDEEMS,
REDEMPTION]

Ex   6: 6 I will **r** you with an outstretched arm
    13:13 **R** every firstborn among your sons.
Lev 25:25 and **r** what his countryman has sold.
Ru   4: 6 You **r** it yourself.
2Sa 7:23 that God went out to **r** as a people
Ps 31: 5 **r** me, O LORD, the God of truth.
    44:26 **r** us because of your unfailing love.
    49: 7 No man can **r** the life of another
    49:15 God will **r** my life from the grave;
   130: 8 He himself will **r** Israel
Hos 13:14 I will **r** them from death.
Lk 24:21 the one who was going to **r** Israel.
Gal 4: 5 to **r** those under law,
Tit 2:14 for us to **r** us from all wickedness

REDEEMED [REDEEM]

Ex 15:13 lead the people you have **r**.
Dt 15:15 and the LORD your God **r** you.
Ne   1:10 whom you have **r** by your great strength
Job 33:28 He **r** my soul from going down to
Ps 71:23 whom you have **r**.
   107: 2 Let the **r** of the LORD say this—
Isa 1:27 Zion will be **r** with justice,
    35: 9 But only the **r** will walk there,
    44:22 Return to me, for I have **r** you."
    63: 9 In his love and mercy he **r** them;
Lk   1:68 he has come and has **r** his people.
Gal 3:13 Christ **r** us from the curse of the law
1Pe 1:18 as silver or gold that you were **r**
Rev 14: 3 who had been **r** from the earth.

REDEEMER [REDEEM]

Job 19:25 I know that my **R** lives,
Ps 19:14 O LORD, my Rock and my **R**.

78:35 that God Most High was their **R.**
Isa 44: 6 Israel's King and **R,**
     48:17 your **R,** the Holy One of Israel:
     59:20 "The **R** will come to Zion,

REDEEMS [REDEEM]
Ps 34:22 The LORD **r** his servants;
    103: 4 who **r** your life from the pit

REDEMPTION [REDEEM]
Ru   4: 7 for the **r** and transfer of property
Ps 130: 7 and with him is full **r.**
Lk   2:38 looking forward to the **r** of Jerusalem
    21:28 because your **r** is drawing near."
Ro   3:24 the **r** that came by Christ Jesus.
     8:23 the **r** of our bodies.
1Co 1:30 our righteousness, holiness and **r.**
Eph 1: 7 In him we have **r** through his blood,
     1:14 our inheritance until the **r** of those
     4:30 you were sealed for the day of **r.**
Col 1:14 in whom we have **r,**
Heb 9:12 having obtained eternal **r.**

REDUCE [REDUCED]
2Ki 10:32 the LORD began to **r** the size of Israel
Jer 10:24 lest you **r** me to nothing.

REDUCED [REDUCE]
Ps 79: 1 they have **r** Jerusalem to rubble.
Eze 16:27 against you and **r** your territory;

REED [REEDS]
2Ki 18:21 that splintered **r** of a staff,
Isa 42: 3 A bruised **r** he will not break,
Mt 12:20 A bruised **r** he will not break,
Lk   7:24 A **r** swayed by the wind?

REEDS [REED]
Ex   2: 3 the child in it and put it among the **r**

REEL [REELED, REELING, REELS]
Isa 28: 7 stagger from wine and **r** from beer:

REELED* [REEL]
Ps 107:27 They **r** and staggered like drunken

REELING* [REEL]
Zec 12: 2 sends all the surrounding peoples **r.**

REELS* [REEL]
Isa 24:20 The earth **r** like a drunkard,

REFINE* [REFINED, REFINER]
Jer 9: 7 I will **r** and test them,
Zec 13: 9 I will **r** them like silver and test them
Mal 3: 3 the Levites and **r** them like gold

REFINED [REFINE]
Job 28: 1 and a place where gold is **r.**
Ps 12: 6 like silver **r** in a furnace of clay,
Isa 48:10 See, I have **r** you,
Da 12:10 made spotless and **r,**
1Pe 1: 7 perishes even though **r** by fire—

REFINER* [REFINE]
Mal 3: 3 He will sit as a **r** and purifier

REFLECT [REFLECTION, REFLECTS]
2Co 3:18 unveiled faces all **r** the Lord's glory,

REFLECTION* [REFLECT]
1Co 13:12 Now we see but a poor **r** as in

REFLECTS* [REFLECT]
Pr 27:19 As water **r** a face,
    27:19 so a man's heart **r** the man.
Ecc 5:20 He seldom **r** on the days of his life,

REFORM
Jer 18:11 and **r** your ways and your actions.'

REFRAIN
Ps 37: 8 **R** from anger and turn from wrath;
Ecc 3: 5 a time to embrace and a time to **r,**

REFRESH [REFRESHED, REFRESHING]
Jer 31:25 I will **r** the weary and satisfy
Phm 1:20 **r** my heart in Christ.

REFRESHED [REFRESH]
Ps 68: 9 you **r** your weary inheritance.
Pr 11:25 refreshes others will himself be **r.**

REFRESHING* [REFRESH]
Ac   3:19 times of **r** may come from the Lord,

REFUGE
Nu 35:11 towns to be your cities of **r,**
Dt 33:27 The eternal God is your **r,**
Jos 20: 2 to designate the cities of **r,**
Ru   2:12 you have come to take **r."**
2Sa 22: 3 my **r** and my savior—
     22:31 a shield for all who take **r** in him.
Ps   2:12 Blessed are all who take **r** in him.
     5:11 But let all who take **r** in you be glad;
     9: 9 The LORD is a **r** for the oppressed,
    11: 1 In the LORD I take **r.**
    16: 1 O God, for in you I take **r.**
    17: 7 by your right hand those who take **r**
    31: 2 be my rock of **r,**
    34: 8 blessed is the man who takes **r**
    36: 7 Both high and low among men find **r**
    46: 1 God is our **r** and strength,
    59:16 my **r** in times of trouble.
    62: 8 for God is our **r.**
    71: 1 In you, O LORD, I have taken **r;**
    91: 2 "He is my **r** and my fortress,
   118: 8 to take **r** in the LORD than to trust
   144: 2 my shield, in whom I take **r,**
Pr 14:26 and for his children it will be a **r.**
    14:32 even in death the righteous have a **r.**
    30: 5 a shield to those who take **r** in him.
Isa 25: 4 You have been a **r** for the poor,
Jer 16:19 my **r** in time of distress,
Na   1: 7 a **r** in times of trouble.

REFUSE [REFUSED]

Ex   8: 2 If you **r** to let them go,
Lev 26:21 toward me and **r** to listen to me,
Nu 14:11 How long will they **r** to believe
Eze 3:27 and whoever will **r** let him **r;**
Jn   5:40 yet you **r** to come to me to have life.
Heb 12:25 that you do not **r** him who speaks.

REFUSED [REFUSE]

Ex 13:15 Pharaoh stubbornly **r** to let us go,
Jdg 2:19 They **r** to give up their evil practices
Jer 5: 3 but they **r** correction.
2Th 2:10 **r** to love the truth and so be saved.
Heb 12:25 when they **r** him who warned them
Rev 16: 9 but they **r** to repent and glorify him.

REFUTE [REFUTED]

Job 32: 3 they had found no way to **r** Job,
Tit 1: 9 and **r** those who oppose it.

REFUTED* [REFUTE]

Ac 18:28 **r** the Jews in public debate,

REGARD [REGARDED, REGARDS]

1Sa 2:12 they had no **r** for the LORD.
Ps 41: 1 Blessed is he who has **r** for the weak;
   74:20 Have **r** for your covenant,
Isa 8:13 the one you are to **r** as holy,
1Co 14:20 In **r** to evil be infants,
1Th 5:13 Hold them in the highest **r** in love

REGARDED [REGARD]

Ex 11: 3 and Moses himself was highly **r**
Isa 40:17 they are **r** by him as worthless
Ac 5:13 they were highly **r** by the people.
2Co 5:16 Though we once **r** Christ in this way,
Heb 11:26 He **r** disgrace for the sake of Christ

REGARDS [REGARD]

Ro 14: 6 He who **r** one day as special,
   14:14 if anyone **r** something as unclean,

REGENERATION (KJV)

See REBIRTH

REGIONS

2Co 10:16 preach the gospel in the **r** beyond
Eph 4: 9 descended to the lower, earthly **r?**

REGISTER

Lk 2: 5 He went there to **r** with Mary,

REGRET

2Co 7:10 leads to salvation and leaves no **r,**

REGULAR

Ex 29:28 This is always to be the **r** share from
Nu 28: 3 as a **r** burnt offering each day.
2Ki 25:30 a **r** allowance as long as he lived.

REGULATION [REGULATIONS]

Heb 7:18 The former **r** is set aside

REGULATIONS [REGULATION]

Ex 12:43 "These are the **r** for the Passover:

Lev 26:46 and the **r** that the LORD established
Dt 12:28 to obey all these **r** I am giving you,
Col 2:23 Such **r** indeed have an appearance
Heb 9:10 external **r** applying until the time

REHOBOAM

Son of Solomon (1Ki 11:43; 1Ch 3:10). Harsh treatment of subjects caused divided kingdom (1Ki 12:1-24; 14:21-31; 2Ch 10-12).

REIGN [REIGNED, REIGNS]

Ex 15:18 LORD will **r** for ever and ever."
Dt 17:20 Then he and his descendants will **r**
1Sa 8:11 the king who will **r** over you will do:
Ps 68:16 where God chooses to **r,**
Pr 8:13 By me kings **r** and rulers make laws
Isa 9: 7 He will **r** on David's throne and
   24:23 for the LORD Almighty will **r**
   32: 1 a king will **r** in righteousness
Jer 23: 5 a King who will **r** wisely
La 5:19 You, O LORD, **r** forever;
Lk 1:33 and he will **r** over the house
Ro 6:12 do not let sin **r** in your mortal body
1Co 15:25 For he must **r** until he has put all
2Ti 2:12 we will also **r** with him.
Rev 5:10 and they will **r** on the earth."
   11:15 and he will **r** for ever and ever."
   11:17 and have begun to **r.**
   20: 6 will **r** with him for a thousand years.
   22: 5 And they will **r** for ever and ever.

REIGNED [REIGN]

Ro 5:21 just as sin **r** in death,
Rev 20: 4 and **r** with Christ a thousand years.

REIGNS [REIGN]

Ps 9: 7 The LORD **r** forever;
   47: 8 God **r** over the nations;
   93: 1 LORD **r,** he is robed in majesty;
   96:10 among the nations, "The LORD **r.**"
   97: 1 The LORD **r,** let the earth be glad;
   99: 1 LORD **r,** let the nations tremble;
  146:10 The LORD **r** forever, your God,
Isa 52: 7 who say to Zion, "Your God **r!**"
Lk 22:53 this is your hour—when darkness **r.**"
Rev 19: 6 For our Lord God Almighty **r.**

REIN

Jas 1:26 not keep a tight **r** on his tongue,

REJECT [REJECTED, REJECTION, REJECTS]

Lev 26:15 and if you **r** my decrees
1Sa 12:22 the LORD will not **r** his people,
2Ch 7:20 will **r** this temple I have consecrated
Ps 44:23 Do not **r** us forever.
   94:14 For the LORD will not **r** his people;
Isa 31: 7 will **r** the idols of silver and gold
Hos 4: 6 I also **r** you as my priests;
Ro 11: 1 I ask then: Did God **r** his people?
1Th 4: 8 does not **r** man but God,

REJECTED [REJECT]

Nu 11:20 because you have **r** the LORD,

Dt   32:15 and **r** the Rock his Savior.
1Sa   8: 7 not you they have **r**, but they have **r**
             me as their king.
      15:23 he has **r** you as king."
1Ki   12: 8 Rehoboam **r** the advice the elders
      19:10 The Israelites have **r** your covenant,
2Ki   17:15 They **r** his decrees and the covenant
      17:20 the LORD **r** all the people of Israel;
Ps   60: 1 You have **r** us, O God,
      66:20 not **r** my prayer or withheld his love
     118:22 The stone the builders **r** has become
Isa   5:24 they have **r** the law of the LORD
      41: 9 have chosen you and have not **r** you.
      53: 3 He was despised and **r** by men,
Jer   8: 9 they have **r** the word of the LORD,
      14:19 Have you **r** Judah completely?
Hos   8: 3 But Israel has **r** what is good;
Zec   10: 6 be as though I had not **r** them,
Mt   21:42 " 'The stone the builders **r** has
Mk   9:12 of Man must suffer much and be **r**?
Ac   4:11 He is " 'the stone you builders **r**,
1Ti   4: 4 and nothing is to be **r** if it is received
Heb   10:28 Anyone who **r** the law of Moses died
1Pe   2: 4 the living Stone—**r** by men but
       2: 7 "The stone the builders **r** has become

REJECTION* [REJECT]

Ro   11:15 For if their **r** is the reconciliation of

REJECTS [REJECT]

Lk   10:16 who **r** you **r** me; but he who **r** me
             r him who sent me."
Jn   3:36 whoever **r** the Son will not see life,
      12:48 a judge for the one who **r** me
1Th   4: 8 he who **r** this instruction does not

REJOICE [JOY]

Dt   12: 7 and shall **r** in everything you
      32:43 **R**, O nations, with his people,
1Ch   16:10 hearts of those who seek the LORD **r**.
      16:31 Let the heavens **r**,
2Ch   6:41 may your saints **r** in your goodness.
Ps   2:11 Serve the LORD with fear and **r**
       5:11 that those who love your name may **r**
       9:14 of Zion and there **r** in your salvation.
      14: 7 let Jacob **r** and Israel be glad!
      31: 7 I will be glad and **r** in your love,
      34: 2 let the afflicted hear and **r**.
      51: 8 let the bones you have crushed **r**.
      63:11 But the king will **r** in God;
      64:10 Let the righteous **r** in the LORD
      66: 6 let us **r** in him.
      68: 3 righteous be glad and **r** before God;
      89:16 They **r** in your name all day long;
      97: 1 let the distant shores **r**.
     104:31 may the LORD **r** in his works—
     105: 3 of those who seek the LORD **r**.
     118:24 the day the LORD has made; let us **r**
     119:14 I **r** in following your statutes
     119:162 I **r** in your promise
     149: 2 Let Israel **r** in their Maker;
Pr   5:18 may you **r** in the wife of your youth.
      23:25 may she who gave you birth **r**!
      24:17 do not let your heart **r**,

29: 2 the righteous thrive, the people **r**;
Isa   9: 3 they **r** before you as people **r** at the
             harvest,
      29:19 the humble will **r** in the LORD;
      35: 1 the wilderness will **r**
      61: 7 and instead of disgrace they will **r**
      62: 5 so will your God **r** over you.
Jer   31:12 they will **r** in the bounty of the LORD
Hab   3:18 yet I will **r** in the LORD,
Zep   3:17 he will **r** over you with singing."
Zec   9: 9 **R** greatly, O Daughter of Zion!
Lk   6:23 "**R** in that day and leap for joy,
      10:20 but **r** that your names are written
      15: 6 '**R** with me; I have found
      15: 9 '**R** with me; I have found
Ro   5: 2 we **r** in the hope of the glory of God.
      12:15 **R** with those who **r**;
Php   2:17 I am glad and **r** with all of you.
       3: 1 Finally, my brothers, **r** in the Lord!
       4: 4 **R** in the Lord always.
1Pe   4:13 But **r** that you participate in
Rev   18:20 **R**, saints and apostles and prophets!
      19: 7 Let us **r** and be glad

REJOICED [JOY]

1Ch   29: 9 The people **r** at the willing response
Job   31:25 if I have **r** over my great wealth,
Ps   122: 1 I **r** with those who said to me,
Jn   8:56 Your father Abraham **r** at the

REJOICES [JOY]

1Sa   2: 1 "My heart **r** in the LORD;
Ps   13: 5 my heart **r** in your salvation.
      16: 9 heart is glad and my tongue **r**;
Pr   11:10 the righteous prosper, the city **r**;
Isa   61:10 in the LORD; my soul **r** in my God.
      62: 5 as a bridegroom **r** over his bride,
Lk   1:47 and my spirit **r** in God my Savior,
Ac   2:26 my heart is glad and my tongue **r**;
1Co   12:26 every part **r** with it.
      13: 6 but **r** with the truth.

REJOICING [JOY]

2Sa   6:12 to the City of David with **r**.
Ne   12:43 The sound of **r** in Jerusalem could
Ps   30: 5 but **r** comes in the morning.
Pr   8:30 **r** always in his presence,
Lk   15: 7 in the same way there will be more **r**
Ac   5:41 **r** because they had been counted
2Co   6:10 sorrowful, yet always **r**;

RELATIONS

Ex   22:19 who has sexual **r** with an animal
Lev   18: 6 any close relative to have sexual **r**.
Ro   1:26 their women exchanged natural **r**

RELATIVE [RELATIVES]

Lev   18: 6 " 'No one is to approach any close **r**
      25:25 his nearest **r** is to come and
Ru   2:20 She added, "That man is our close **r**;

RELATIVES [RELATIVE]

Lev   25:48 One of his **r** may redeem him:
Pr   19: 7 A poor man is shunned by all his **r**—

Mk 6: 4 among his **r** and in his own house is
Lk 21:16 brothers, **r** and friends,
1Ti 5: 8 If anyone does not provide for his **r**,

RELEASE [RELEASED]

Isa 61: 1 **r** from darkness for the prisoners,
Mt 27:15 at the Feast to **r** a prisoner chosen by
Lk 4:18 to **r** the oppressed,

RELEASED [RELEASE]

Lev 25:54 to be **r** in the Year of Jubilee,
  27:21 When the field is **r** in the Jubilee,
2Ki 25:27 he **r** Jehoiachin from prison on
Mal 4: 2 and leap like calves **r** from the stall.
Mk 15:15 Pilate **r** Barabbas to them.
Ac 3:14 and asked that a murderer be **r**
Ro 7: 2 she is **r** from the law of marriage.
  7: 6 we have been **r** from the law so
Rev 20: 7 Satan will be **r** from his prison

RELENT [RELENTED, RELENTS]

Ex 32:12 Turn from your fierce anger; **r**
Jer 18: 8 then I will **r** and not inflict on it
  26: 3 Then I will **r** and not bring on them
Jnh 3: 9 yet **r** and with compassion turn

RELENTED* [RELENT]

Ex 32:14 LORD and did not bring
Ps 106:45 and out of his great love he **r.**
Am 7: 3 So the LORD **r.**
  7: 6 So the LORD **r.**

RELENTS* [RELENT]

Joel 2:13 and he **r** from sending calamity.
Jnh 4: 2 a God who **r** from sending calamity.

RELIABLE [RELY]

Pr 22:21 teaching you true and **r** words,
Jn 8:26 But he who sent me is **r**,
2Ti 2: 2 entrust to **r** men who will also be

RELIANCE* [RELY]

Pr 25:19 **r** on the unfaithful in times of trouble

RELIED [RELY]

2Ch 13:18 because they **r** on the LORD,
  16: 8 Yet when you **r** on the LORD,
Ps 71: 6 From birth I have **r** on you;

RELIEF

1Sa 8:18 for **r** from the king you have chosen,
Est 4:14 **r** and deliverance for the Jews
  9:22 the Jews got **r** from their enemies.
Job 35: 9 for **r** from the arm of the powerful.
Ps 94:13 you grant him **r** from days of trouble,
  143: 1 and righteousness come to my **r.**
La 3:49 eyes will flow unceasingly, without **r**
  3:56 not close your ears to my cry for **r.''**
2Th 1: 7 and give **r** to you who are troubled,

RELIGION* [RELIGIOUS]

Ac 25:19 dispute with him about their own **r**
  26: 5 according to the strictest sect of our **r**
1Ti 5: 4 to put their **r** into practice by caring
Jas 1:26 and his **r** is worthless.

1:27 **R** that God our Father accepts as

RELIGIOUS [RELIGION]

Am 5:21 "I hate, I despise your **r** feasts;
Col 2:16 or with regard to a **r** festival,
Jas 1:26 If anyone considers himself **r** and

RELY [RELIABLE, RELIANCE, RELIED]

2Ch 14:11 O LORD our God, for we **r** on you,
Isa 50:10 of the LORD and **r** on his God.
Eze 33:26 You **r** on your sword,
Ro 2:17 if you **r** on the law and brag
2Co 1: 9 that we might not **r** on ourselves but
Gal 3:10 All who **r** on observing the law are
1Jn 4:16 and **r** on the love God has for us.

REMAIN [REMAINED, REMAINS]

Nu 33:55 allow to **r** will become barbs in your
Jos 23: 7 with these nations that **r** among you;
Jdg 2:23 LORD had allowed those nations to **r**;
2Ch 33: 4 Name will **r** in Jerusalem forever."
Ps 102:27 But you **r** the same,
Jn 1:32 from heaven as a dove and **r** on him.
  15: 4 **R** in me, and I will **r** in you.
  15: 4 bear fruit unless you **r** in me.
  15: 7 If you **r** in me and my words **r** in you
  15: 9 Now **r** in my love.
Ro 13: 8 Let no debt **r** outstanding,
1Co 7:20 Each one should **r** in the situation
  13:13 these three **r**: faith, hope and love.
2Ti 2:13 he will **r** faithful,
Heb 1:11 They will perish, but you **r**;
1Jn 2:27 as it has taught you, **r** in him.
Rev 2:13 Yet you **r** true to my name.
  14:12 and **r** faithful to Jesus.

REMAINED [REMAIN]

Jdg 1:30 who **r** among them;
2Sa 11: 1 But David **r** in Jerusalem.
Mk 14:61 But Jesus **r** silent
1Jn 2:19 they would have **r** with us;

REMAINS [REMAIN]

Dt 24:20 Leave what **r** for the alien,
Jos 13: 2 "This is the land that **r**:
Ps 146: 6 who **r** faithful forever.
Hag 2: 5 And my Spirit **r** among you.
Jn 3:36 for God's wrath **r** on him."
  6:56 and drinks my blood **r** in me,
  15: 5 If a man **r** in me and I in him,
2Co 3:14 for to this day the same veil **r** when
Heb 7: 3 the Son of God he **r** a priest forever.
1Jn 3: 9 because God's seed **r** in him;

REMARKABLE*

Lk 5:26 "We have seen **r** things today."
Jn 9:30 The man answered, "Now that is **r**!

REMEDY

2Ch 36:16 and there was no **r**.
Pr 6:15 suddenly be destroyed—without **r**.
  29: 1 suddenly be destroyed—without **r**.
Isa 3: 7 "I have no **r**.
Jer 30:13 no **r** for your sore,

Mic 2:10 it is ruined, beyond all **r.**

REMEMBER [REMEMBERED, REMEMBERS, REMEMBRANCE]

Ge   9:15 I will **r** my covenant between me
Ex 20: 8 "**R** the Sabbath day
    33:13 **R** that this nation is your people."
Lev 26:42 I will **r** my covenant with Jacob
Dt   5:15 **R** that you were slaves in Egypt and
     8:18 But **r** the LORD your God,
Jos 1:13 "**R** the command that Moses
1Ch 16:12 the wonders he has done,
Ne   5:19 **R** me with favor, O my God,
    13:31 **R** me with favor, O my God.
Job 10: 9 **R** that you molded me like clay.
    36:24 **R** to extol his work,
Ps 25: 6 **R,** O LORD, your great mercy
    63: 6 On my bed I **r** you;
    74: 2 **R** the people you purchased of old,
    77:11 I will **r** the deeds of the LORD;
Ecc 12: 1 **R** your Creator in the days of your
Isa 46: 8 "**R** this, fix it in mind, take it to heart
    64: 9 do not **r** our sins forever.
Jer 31:34 and will **r** their sins no more."
La   5: 1 **R,** O LORD, what has happened
Eze 36:31 Then you will **r** your evil ways
Hos 7: 2 that I **r** all their evil deeds.
Hab 3: 2 in wrath **r** mercy.
Mk   8:18 And don't you **r?**
Lk   1:72 and to **r** his holy covenant,
    17:32 **R** Lot's wife!
    23:42 "Jesus, **r** me when you come
Gal 2:10 should continue to **r** the poor,
Php 1: 3 I thank my God every time I **r** you.
2Ti 2: 8 **R** Jesus Christ, raised from the dead,
Heb 8:12 and will **r** their sins no more."
Jas 5:20 **r** this: Whoever turns a sinner from
Rev 3: 3 **R,** therefore, what you have received

REMEMBERED [REMEMBER]

Ge   8: 1 But God **r** Noah and all
    19:29 he **r** Abraham, and he brought Lot
    30:22 Then God **r** Rachel;
Ex   2:24 and he **r** his covenant with Abraham,
     3:15 be **r** from generation to generation.
     6: 5 and I have **r** my covenant.
1Sa 1:19 and the LORD **r** her.
Ps 78:35 They **r** that God was their Rock,
    98: 3 He has **r** his love and his faithfulness
   106:45 for their sake he **r** his covenant
   111: 4 He has caused his wonders to be **r;**
   136:23 to the One who **r** us
Isa 17:10 you have not **r** the Rock,
    65:17 The former things will not be **r,**
Eze 18:22 committed will be **r** against him.
    33:13 things he has done will be **r;**
Mt 26:75 Peter **r** the word Jesus had spoken:
Jn   2:17 His disciples **r** that it is written:
Rev 16:19 God **r** Babylon the Great
    18: 5 and God has **r** her crimes.

REMEMBERS [REMEMBER]

1Ch 16:15 He **r** his covenant forever,
Ps 103:14 he **r** that we are dust.

111: 5 he **r** his covenant forever.
Isa 43:25 and **r** your sins no more.

REMEMBRANCE [REMEMBER]

Lk 22:19 do this in **r** of me."
1Co 11:24 do this in **r** of me."

REMIND [REMINDER]

Jn 14:26 will **r** you of everything I have said
2Pe 1:12 I will always **r** you of these things,

REMINDER [REMIND]

Ex 13: 9 your hand and a **r** on your forehead
Heb 10: 3 sacrifices are an annual **r** of sins,

REMISSION (KJV) See FORGIVENESS

REMNANT

Ge 45: 7 to preserve for you a **r** on earth
2Ki 19:31 For out of Jerusalem will come a **r,**
2Ch 36:20 carried into exile to Babylon the **r,**
Ezr 9: 8 has been gracious in leaving us a **r**
Ne   1: 2 the Jewish **r** that survived the exile,
Isa 10:21 A **r** will return, a **r** of Jacob will
    11:11 a second time to reclaim the **r**
Jer 23: 3 the **r** of my flock out of all
    50:20 for I will forgive the **r** I spare.
Zep 3:13 The **r** of Israel will do no wrong;
Zec 8:12 an inheritance to the **r** of this people.
Ro   9:27 only the **r** will be saved.
    11: 5 at the present time there is a **r** chosen

REMOVAL* [REMOVE]

Isa '27: 9 be the full fruitage of the **r** of his sin:
1Pe 3:21 not the **r** of dirt from the body

REMOVE [REMOVAL, REMOVED]

Ex 12:15 On the first day **r** the yeast
Job 9:34 someone to **r** God's rod from me,
Ps 39:10 **R** your scourge from me;
   119:22 **R** from me scorn and contempt,
Isa 1:25 and **r** all your impurities.
Eze 36:26 I will **r** from you your heart of stone
Zec 3: 9 'and I will **r** the sin of this land in
Lk   6:42 **r** the speck from your brother's eye.

REMOVED [REMOVE]

2Ki 17:18 and **r** them from his presence.
Ps 30:11 you **r** my sackcloth and clothed me
   103:12 so far has he **r** our transgressions
Jn 20: 1 and saw that the stone had been **r**
2Co 3:14 It has not been **r,**
Rev 6:14 every mountain and island was **r**

REND*

Isa 64: 1 that you would **r** the heavens
Joel 2:13 **R** your heart and not your garments,

RENEW [RENEWAL, RENEWED, RENEWING]

Ps 51:10 and **r** a steadfast spirit within me.
Isa 40:31 in the LORD will **r** their strength.
La   5:21 **r** our days as of old
Hab 3: 2 **R** them in our day,

RENEWAL* [RENEW]

Job 14:14 I will wait for my **r** to come.
Isa 57:10 You found **r** of your strength,
Mt 19:28 at the **r** of all things,
Tit 3: 5 of rebirth and **r** by the Holy Spirit,

RENEWED [RENEW]

2Ch 34:31 and **r** the covenant in the presence of
Ps 103: 5 that your youth is **r** like the eagle's.
2Co 4:16 inwardly we are being **r** day by day.
Col 3:10 **r** in knowledge in the image of its

RENEWING* [RENEW]

Ro 12: 2 transformed by the **r** of your mind.

RENOUNCE* [RENOUNCED, RENOUNCES]

Eze 14: 6 and **r** all your detestable practices!
Da 4:27 to accept my advice: **R** your sins
Rev 2:13 You did not **r** your faith in me,

RENOUNCED* [RENOUNCE]

Ps 89:39 You have **r** the covenant
Mt 19:12 **r** marriage because of the kingdom
2Co 4: 2 we have **r** secret and shameful ways;

RENOUNCES* [RENOUNCE]

Pr 28:13 and **r** them finds mercy.

RENOWN*

Ge 6: 4 the heroes of old, men of **r.**
Ps 102:12 **r** endures through all generations.
135:13 endures forever, your **r,** O LORD.
Isa 26: 8 and **r** are the desire of our hearts.
55:13 This will be for the LORD's **r,**
63:12 to gain for himself everlasting **r,**
Jer 13:11 'to be my people for my **r** and praise
32:20 have gained the **r** that is still yours.
33: 9 Then this city will bring me **r,** joy,
49:25 the city of **r** not been abandoned,
Eze 26:17 How you are destroyed, O city of **r,**
Hos 12: 5 the LORD is his name of **r!**

REPAID [PAY]

Pr 14:14 faithless will be fully **r** for their ways
Jer 18:20 Should good be **r** with evil?
Lk 6:34 expecting to be **r** in full.
14:14 you will be **r** at the resurrection of
Col 3:25 Anyone who does wrong will be **r**

REPAIR [REPAIRED, REPAIRER, REPAIRING]

2Ch 24: 5 to **r** the temple of your God.
Ezr 9: 9 the house of our God and **r** its ruins,
Am 9:11 I will **r** its broken places,

REPAIRED [REPAIR]

2Ch 15: 8 He **r** the altar of the LORD that was
29: 3 the temple of the LORD and **r** them.
Ne 3: 4 **r** the next section.
Jer 19:11 smashed and cannot be **r.**

REPAIRER* [REPAIR]

Isa 58:12 be called **R** of Broken Walls,

REPAIRING [REPAIR]

2Ki 12: 7 "Why aren't you **r** the damage done
Ezr 4:12 They are restoring the walls and **r**

REPAY [PAY]

Dt 7:10 But those who hate him he will **r**
32: 6 Is this the way you **r** the LORD,
32:35 It is mine to avenge; I will **r.**
Ru 2:12 May the LORD **r** you for what
Ps 28: 4 **R** them for their deeds and
35:12 They **r** me evil for good
103:10 or **r** us according to our iniquities.
116:12 How can I **r** the LORD
Isa 59:18 so will he **r** wrath to his enemies
Jer 25:14 I will **r** them according
51:56 he will **r** in full.
Eze 7: 3 according to your conduct and **r** you
Joel 2:25 "I will **r** you for the years
Ro 12:17 Do not **r** anyone evil for evil.
12:19 "It is mine to avenge; I will **r,**"
Heb 10:30 "It is mine to avenge; I will **r,**"
1Pe 3: 9 Do not **r** evil with evil or insult
Rev 2:23 and I will **r** each of you according

REPAYING [PAY]

2Ch 6:23 **r** the guilty by bringing down
1Ti 5: 4 so **r** their parents and grandparents,

REPEALED

Est 1:19 which cannot be **r,**
Da 6: 8 which cannot be **r."**

REPEATED [REPEATS]

Heb 10: 1 the same sacrifices **r** endlessly year

REPEATS* [REPEATED]

Pr 17: 9 but whoever **r** the matter separates
26:11 so a fool **r** his folly.

REPENT [PENITENT, REPENTANCE, REPENTED, REPENTS]

1Ki 8:47 and **r** and plead with you in the land
Job 36:10 commands them to **r** of their evil.
42: 6 Therefore I despise myself and **r**
Isa 59:20 to those in Jacob who **r** of their sins,
Jer 15:19 "If you **r,** I will restore you
Eze 18:32 **R** and live!
Mt 3: 2 **R,** for the kingdom of heaven is near.
4:17 Jesus began to preach, **"R,**
Mk 6:12 and preached that people should **r.**
Lk 13: 3 unless you **r,** you too will all perish.
Ac 2:38 Peter replied, **"R** and be baptized,
3:19 **R,** then, and turn to God,
17:30 all people everywhere to **r.**
26:20 that they should **r** and turn to God
Rev 2: 5 **R** and do the things you did at first.
2:21 I have given her time to **r**
9:20 still did not **r** of the work
16: 9 but they refused to **r** and glorify him.

REPENTANCE [REPENT]
Isa	30:15	"In **r** and rest is your salvation,
Mt	3: 8	Produce fruit in keeping with **r.**
Mk	1: 4	a baptism of **r** for the forgiveness
Lk	3: 8	Produce fruit in keeping with **r.**
	5:32	the righteous, but sinners to **r.**"
	24:47	and **r** and forgiveness of sins will
Ac	5:31	that he might give **r** and forgiveness
	11:18	granted even the Gentiles **r** unto life.
	20:21	that they must turn to God in **r**
	26:20	and prove their **r** by their deeds.
Ro	2: 4	God's kindness leads you toward **r?**
2Co	7:10	Godly sorrow brings **r** that leads
2Ti	2:25	the hope that God will grant them **r**
Heb	6: 1	not laying again the foundation of **r**
2Pe	3: 3	but everyone to come to **r.**

REPENTED [REPENT]
2Ch	32:26	Hezekiah **r** of the pride of his heart,
Zec	1: 6	"Then they **r** and said,
Mt	11:21	they would have **r** long ago
Lk	11:32	for they **r** at the preaching of Jonah,

REPENTS* [REPENT]
Jer	8: 6	No one **r** of his wickedness, saying,
	18: 8	if that nation I warned **r** of its evil,
Lk	15: 7	in heaven over one sinner who **r**
	15:10	angels of God over one sinner who **r.**
	17: 3	rebuke him, and if he **r,** forgive him.

REPHAITES
Ge	15:20	Hittites, Perizzites, **R,**
Dt	2:11	they too were considered **R,**
1Ch	20: 4	one of the descendants of the **R,**

REPLANTED* [PLANT]
Eze	36:36	and have **r** what was desolate.

REPLY
Pr	15:23	A man finds joy in giving an apt **r—**
	16: 1	but from the LORD comes the **r** of
Mt	27:14	But Jesus made no **r,**

REPORT [REPORTS]
Ge	37: 2	and he brought their father a bad **r**
Nu	13:32	among the Israelites a bad **r** about
1Ki	10: 7	that exceeded the **r** I heard.
Lk	7:22	and **r** to John what you have seen

REPORTS [REPORT]
Ex	23: 1	"Do not spread false **r.**
Mt	14: 1	the tetrarch heard the **r** about Jesus,
Ac	9:13	"I have heard many **r** about this man

REPOSES*
Pr	14:33	Wisdom **r** in the heart of the

REPRESENT [REPRESENTATION]
Da	8:22	**r** four kingdoms that will emerge
Gal	4:24	for the women **r** two covenants.
Heb	5: 1	and is appointed to **r** them

REPRESENTATION*
[REPRESENT]
Heb	1: 3	glory and the exact **r** of his being,

REPROACH
Jos	5: 9	"Today I have rolled away the **r**
Job	27: 6	not **r** me as long as I live.
Isa	51: 7	not fear the **r** of men or be terrified
Jer	20: 8	insult and **r** all day long.
1Ti	3: 2	Now the overseer must be above **r,**

REPROBATE(S) (KJV)
See DEPRAVED, FAIL, FAILED, REJECTED, UNFIT

REPUTATION
1Ti	3: 7	also have a good **r** with outsiders,
Rev	3: 1	you have a **r** of being alive, but you

REQUEST [REQUESTS]
Est	7: 3	And spare my people—this is my **r.**
Ps	21: 2	not withheld the **r** of his lips.

REQUESTS [REQUEST]
Ps	20: 5	May the LORD grant all your **r.**
Php	4: 6	present your **r** to God.
1Ti	2: 1	I urge, then, first of all, that **r,**

REQUIRE [REQUIRED,
REQUIREMENTS, REQUIRES]
Ps	40: 6	and sin offerings you did not **r.**
Mic	6: 8	And what does the LORD **r** of you?

REQUIRED [REQUIRE]
Ac	15: 5	and **r** to obey the law of Moses."
Ro	2:14	do by nature things **r** by the law,
1Co	4: 2	Now it is **r** that those who have
Heb	10: 8	(although the law **r** them to be made)

REQUIREMENTS [REQUIRE]
Dt	11: 1	and keep his **r,** his decrees,
2Ki	23:24	the **r** of the law written in the book
Jer	8: 7	But my people do not know the **r** of
Ro	2:15	**r** of the law are written on their
	8: 4	**r** that the righteous **r** of the law might

REQUIRES [REQUIRE]
1Ki	2: 3	the LORD your God **r:**
Jn	6:28	to do the works God **r?"**
Heb	9:22	the law **r** that nearly everything

REQUITE(ED) (KJV) See PAID BACK,
PAY, PAYS BACK, REPAY, REPAYING

RESCUE [RESCUED, RESCUES]
Ge	37:21	he tried to **r** him from their hands.
Ex	3: 8	I have come down to **r** them
Dt	28:29	with no one to **r** you.
Job	5:19	From six calamities he will **r** you;
Ps	22: 8	let the LORD **r** him.
	31: 2	come quickly to my **r;**
	35:10	You **r** the poor from those too strong
	69:14	**R** me from the mire,
	82: 4	**R** the weak and needy;

91:14 says the LORD, "I will r him;
143: 9 **R** me from my enemies, O LORD,
Isa 31: 5 he will 'pass over' it and will r it."
Jer 1: 8 for I am with you and will r you,"
Eze 34:10 I will r my flock from their mouths,
Da 6:20 been able to r you from the lions?"
Mt 27:43 Let God r him now if he wants him,
Ro 7:24 Who will r me from this body
Gal 1: 4 who gave himself for our sins to r us
2Pe 2: 9 how to r godly men from trials

RESCUED [RESCUE]

Ex 18:10 and who r the people from the hand
1Sa 11:13 for this day the LORD has r Israel."
14:23 So the LORD r Israel that day,
Ps 18:17 He r me from my powerful enemy,
81: 7 your distress you called and I r you,
Pr 11: 8 The righteous man is r from trouble,
Da 3:28 sent his angel and r his servants!
6:27 r Daniel from the power of the lions.
Ac 12:11 and r me from Herod's clutches
Col 1:13 For he has r us from the dominion

RESCUES* [RESCUE]

1Sa 14:39 as the LORD who r Israel lives,
Pr 12: 6 but the speech of the upright r them.
Jer 20:13 He r the life of the needy from
Da 6:27 He r and he saves;
1Th 1:10 who r us from the coming wrath.

RESEMBLED* [RESEMBLING]

Rev 9: 7 and their faces r human faces.
9:17 of the horses r the heads of lions,
13: 2 The beast I saw r a leopard,

RESEMBLING* [RESEMBLED]

Rev 4: 3 A rainbow, r an emerald,

RESENT* [RESENTFUL, RESENTMENT, RESENTS]

Pr 3:11 and do not r his rebuke,

RESENTFUL* [RESENT]

2Ti 2:24 able to teach, not r.

RESENTMENT [RESENT]

Job 5: 2 **R** kills a fool,
36:13 "The godless in heart harbor r;

RESENTS* [RESENT]

Pr 15:12 A mocker r correction;

RESERVE [RESERVED]

1Ki 19:18 Yet I r seven thousand in Israel—

RESERVED [RESERVE]

Ge 27:36 "Haven't you r any blessing
Ro 11: 4 "I have r for myself seven thousand
2Pe 2:17 Blackest darkness is r for them.
3: 7 heavens and earth are r for fire,

RESETTLE* [SETTLE]

1Ch 9: 2 first to r on their own property
Eze 36:33 I will r your towns,

RESIST [RESISTED, RESISTS]

Jdg 2:14 whom they were no longer able to r.
Pr 28: 4 but those who keep the law r them.
Da 11:32 know their God will firmly r him.
Mt 5:39 I tell you, Do not r an evil person.
Lk 21:15 of your adversaries will be able to r
Ac 7:51 You always r the Holy Spirit!
Jas 4: 7 **R** the devil, and he will flee from
1Pe 5: 9 **R** him, standing firm in the faith,

RESISTED* [RESIST]

Job 9: 4 has r him and come out unscathed?
Da 10:13 Persian kingdom r me twenty-one
Heb 12: 4 not yet r to the point of shedding

RESISTS* [RESIST]

Ro 9:19 For who r his will?"

RESOLVED*

2Ch 20: 3 Jehoshaphat r to inquire of the LORD,
Ps 17: 3 I have r that my mouth will not sin.
Da 1: 8 But Daniel r not to defile himself
1Co 2: 2 For I r to know nothing while I was

RESOUND [RESOUNDED, RESOUNDING]

Ps 98: 7 Let the sea r, and everything in it,
118:15 victory r in the tents of the righteous:

RESOUNDED* [RESOUND]

2Sa 22:14 the voice of the Most High r.
Ps 18:13 the voice of the Most High r.
77:17 the skies r with thunder;

RESOUNDING* [RESOUND]

Ps 150: 5 praise him with r cymbals.
1Co 13: 1 I am only a r gong or

RESPECT [RESPECTABLE, RESPECTED, RESPECTS]

Lev 19: 3 of you must r his mother and father,
19:32 show r for the elderly
Pr 11:16 A kindhearted woman gains r,
Mal 1: 6 where is the r due me?"
Mk 12: 6 saying, 'They will r my son.'
Ro 13: 7 if r, then r; if honor, then honor.
Eph 5:33 and the wife must r her husband.
6: 5 obey your earthly masters with r
1Th 4:12 daily life may win the r of outsiders
5:12 to r those who work hard among you
1Ti 3: 3 his children obey him with proper r.
3: 8 likewise, are to be men worthy of r,
3:11 wives are to be women worthy of r,
6: 1 their masters worthy of full r,
Tit 2: 2 worthy of r, self-controlled,
1Pe 2:17 Show proper r to everyone:
3: 7 with r as the weaker partner and

RESPECTABLE* [RESPECT]

1Ti 3: 2 self-controlled, r, hospitable,

RESPECTED [RESPECT]

Dt 1:13 understanding and r men from each

Pr   31:23 Her husband is **r** at the city gate,
Heb 12: 9 disciplined us and we **r** them for it.

RESPECTER (KJV) See FAVORITISM

RESPECTS [RESPECT]

Pr   13:13 who **r** a command is rewarded.

RESPLENDENT*

Ps   76: 4 You are **r** with light,
     132:18 but the crown on his head will be **r."**

RESPOND [RESPONSE]

2Ch 32:25 not **r** to the kindness shown him;
Ps 102:17 He will **r** to the prayer of
Isa 19:22 he will **r** to their pleas and heal them.
Jer   2:30 they did not **r** to correction.
     17:23 not listen or **r** to discipline.
Hos   2:21 "In that day I will **r**,"
Ac   16:14 The Lord opened her heart to **r**

RESPONSE [RESPOND]

1Ki 18:26 there was no **r**; no one answered.
1Ch 29: 9 The people rejoiced at the willing **r**

RESPONSIBILITIES

[RESPONSIBLE]

Nu   8:26 to assign the **r** of the Levites."

RESPONSIBILITY [RESPONSIBLE]

Ac   18: 6 I am clear of my **r.**

RESPONSIBLE

[RESPONSIBILITIES, RESPONSIBILITY]

Nu   1:53 to be **r** for the care of the tabernacle
     14:37 men **r** for spreading the bad report
Jnh   1: 8 who is **r** for making all this trouble
Lk   11:50 **r** for the blood of all the prophets
1Co   7:24 Brothers, each man, as **r** to God,

REST [RESTED, RESTING, RESTLESS, RESTS, SABBATH-REST]

Ge   8: 4 the ark came to **r** on the mountains
Ex   16:23 a day of **r**, a holy Sabbath
     31:15 but the seventh day is a Sabbath of **r**,
     33:14 and I will give you **r."**
Lev 23:24 you are to have a day of **r**,
     25: 4 the land is to have a sabbath of **r**,
     25: 5 The land is to have a year of **r**,
Nu   10:36 Whenever it came to **r**, he said,
Dt   12:10 and he will give you **r** from all
Jos   1:13 LORD your God is giving you **r**
     11:23 Then the land had **r** from war.
     14:15 Then the land had **r** from war.
     21:44 The LORD gave them **r** on every side,
2Sa   7:11 I will also give you **r** from all
1Ki   5: 4 the LORD my God has given me **r**
1Ch 22: 9 who will be a man of peace and **r**,
     28: 2 a house as a place of **r** for the ark of
Job   3:17 and there the weary are at **r.**
Ps   16: 9 my body also will **r** secure,
     33:22 May your unfailing love **r** upon us,
     62: 1 My soul finds **r** in God alone;
     62: 5 Find **r**, O my soul, in God alone;

90:17 May the favor of the Lord our God be
91: 1 in the shelter of the Most High will **r**
95:11 "They shall never enter my **r."**
Pr   6:10 a little folding of the hands to r—
Isa 11: 2 The Spirit of the LORD will **r**
     11:10 and his place of **r** will be glorious.
     30:15 repentance and **r** is your salvation,
     32:18 in undisturbed places of **r**.
     44:17 From the **r** he makes a god, his idol;
     57:20 like the tossing sea, which cannot **r**,
Jer   6:16 and you will find **r** for your souls.
     47: 6 [you cry,] 'how long till you **r**?
Mt   11:28 and I will give you **r**.
Mk   6:31 to a quiet place and get some **r."**
1Co   2: 5 faith might not **r** on men's wisdom,
2Co 12: 9 so that Christ's power may **r** on me.
1Th   4:13 or to grieve like the **r** of men,
Heb   3:11 'They shall never enter my **r.'** "
      4: 3 we who have believed enter that **r**,
      4:10 for anyone who enters God's **r**
Rev 14:11 There is no **r** day or night
     14:13 "they will **r** from their labor,

RESTED [REST]

Ge   2: 2 so on the seventh day he **r**
Ex   16:30 So the people **r** on the seventh day.
     20:11 but he **r** on the seventh day.
Nu   11:25 When the Spirit **r** on them,
2Ch 36:21 all the time of its desolation it **r**,
Heb   4: 4 "And on the seventh day God **r**

RESTING [REST]

2Ki   2:15 "The spirit of Elijah is **r** on Elisha."
Ps   132: 8 O LORD, and come to your **r** place,
Isa 28:12 "This is the **r** place,

RESTITUTION

Ex   22: 3 "A thief must certainly make **r**,
Lev   6: 5 He must make **r** in full,
Nu   5: 8 whom **r** can be made for the wrong,

RESTLESS [REST]

Ge   4:12 be a **r** wanderer on the earth."
Jas   3: 8 It is a **r** evil, full of deadly poison.

RESTORE [RESTORED, RESTORES]

Dt   30: 3 LORD your God will **r** your fortunes
2Ch 24: 4 Joash decided to **r** the temple of the
Ezr   5: 3 this temple and **r** this structure?"
Ne   4: 2 Will they **r** their wall?
Ps   51:12 **R** to me the joy of your salvation
     80: 3 **R** us, O God;
     126: 4 **R** our fortunes, O LORD,
Isa 49: 6 be my servant to **r** the tribes
Jer 15:19 I will **r** you that you may serve me;
     31:18 **R** me, and I will return,
La   5:21 **R** us to yourself, O LORD,
Da   9:25 the decree to **r** and rebuild Jerusalem
Hos   6: 2 on the third day he will **r** us,
Am   9:11 that day I will **r** David's fallen tent.
Na   2: 2 LORD will **r** the splendor of Jacob
Zec   9:12 now I announce that I will **r** twice
Mt   17:11 Elijah comes and will **r** all things.
Ac   1: 6 at this time going to **r** the kingdom

15:16 Its ruins I will rebuild, and I will **r** it,
Gal 6: 1 who are spiritual should **r** him gently
1Pe 5:10 **r** you and make you strong,

RESTORED [RESTORE]

Ex   4: 7 and when he took it out, it was **r**,
2Ki 5:10 and your flesh will be **r** and you will
Ps 85: 1 you **r** the fortunes of Jacob.
Eze 21:27 It will not be **r** until he comes
Mk   3: 5 and his hand was completely **r**.
     8:25 his sight was **r**,

RESTORES* [RESTORE]

Ps 14: 7 Lord **r** the fortunes of his people,
    23: 3 he **r** my soul.
    53: 6 God **r** the fortunes of his people,
Mk   9:12 Elijah does come first, and **r** all

RESTRAIN [RESTRAINED,
RESTRAINING, RESTRAINT]

Job 9:13 God does not **r** his anger;

RESTRAINED [RESTRAIN]

Ps 78:38 Time after time he **r** his anger
2Pe 2:16 and the prophet's madness.

RESTRAINING* [RESTRAIN]

Pr 27:16 **r** her is like **r** the wind
Col 2:23 any value in **r** sensual indulgence.

RESTRAINT [RESTRAIN]

Pr 17:27 of knowledge uses words with **r**,
    23: 4 have the wisdom to show **r**.
    29:18 the people cast off **r**;

RESTS [REST]

Dt 33:12 and the one the Lord loves **r**
2Ch 28:11 the Lord's fierce anger **r** on you."
    36:21 The land enjoyed its sabbath **r**;
Pr 19:23 one **r** content, untouched by trouble.
Lk   2:14 to men on whom his favor **r**."
1Pe 4:14 Spirit of glory and of God **r** on you.

RESULT

Nu 25:18 the plague came as a **r** of Peor."
Ezr 9:13 "What has happened to us is a **r**
Lk 21:13 This will **r** in your being witnesses
Ro   5:18 **r** of one act of righteousness
     6:22 and the **r** is eternal life.
    11:31 receive mercy as a **r** of God's mercy
2Co 3: 3 the **r** of our ministry,
2Th 1: 5 as a **r** you will be counted worthy of
1Pe 1: 2 proved genuine and may **r** in praise,

RESURRECTION*

Mt 22:23 who say there is no **r**,
    22:28 Now then, at the **r**,
    22:30 At the **r** people will neither marry
    22:31 But about the **r** of the dead—
    27:53 after Jesus' **r** they went into
Mk 12:18 The Sadducees, who say there is no **r**,
    12:23 At the **r** whose wife will she be,
Lk 14:14 be repaid at the **r** of the righteous."
    20:27 who say there is no **r**,

20:33 then, at the **r** whose wife will she be,
20:35 of taking part in that age and in the **r**
20:36 since they are children of the **r**.
Jn 11:24 "I know he will rise again in the **r** at
    11:25 "I am the **r** and the life.
Ac   1:22 a witness with us of his **r**."
     2:31 he spoke of the **r** of the Christ,
     4: 2 and proclaiming in Jesus the **r** of
     4:33 apostles continued to testify to the **r**
    17:18 the good news about Jesus and the **r**.
    17:32 When they heard about the **r** of
    23: 6 on trial because of my hope in the **r**
    23: 8 Sadducees say that there is no **r**,
    24:15 be a **r** of both the righteous and
    24:21 the **r** of the dead that I am on trial
Ro   1: 4 to be the Son of God by his **r** from
     6: 5 also be united with him in his **r**.
1Co 15:12 some of you say that there is no **r** of
    15:13 If there is no **r** of the dead,
    15:21 the **r** of the dead comes also through
    15:29 Now if there is no **r**,
    15:42 So will it be with the **r** of the dead.
Php 3:10 know Christ and the power of his **r**
     3:11 to attain to the **r** from the dead.
2Ti 2:18 that the **r** has already taken place,
Heb 6: 2 the **r** of the dead,
    11:35 so that they might gain a better **r**.
1Pe 1: 3 the **r** of Jesus Christ from the dead,
     3:21 It saves you by the **r** of Jesus Christ,
Rev 20: 5 This is the first **r**.
    20: 6 those who have part in the first **r**.

RETAIN

Lk   8:15 who hear the word, **r** it,
1Co 7:17 each one should **r** the place in life

RETALIATE*

1Pe 2:23 their insults at him, he did not **r**;

RETIRE*

Nu   8:25 must **r** from their regular service

RETREAT

Ps 44:10 You made us **r** before the enemy,
    74:21 not let the oppressed **r** in disgrace;

RETRIBUTION*

Ps 69:22 may it become **r** and a trap.
Isa 34: 8 a year of **r**, to uphold Zion's cause.
    35: 4 with divine **r** he will come
    59:18 to his enemies and **r** to his foes;
Jer 51:56 For the Lord is a God of **r**;
Ro 11: 9 a stumbling block and a **r** for them.

RETURN [RETURNED, RETURNS]

Ge   3:19 dust you are and to dust you will **r**."
    18:10 "I will surely **r** to you about this time
    29:18 "I'll work for you seven years in **r**
Lev 25:10 of you is to **r** to his family property
Nu 10:36 he said, **"R,** O Lord,
Dt 30: 2 you and your children **r** to the Lord
2Sa 12:23 but he will not **r** to me."
2Ch 30: 9 If you **r** to the Lord,
Ne   1: 9 if you **r** to me and obey my
     9:29 "You warned them to **r** to your law,

Job	10:21	before I go to the place of no **r**,
	16:22	before I go on the journey of no **r**.
	22:23	If you **r** to the Almighty,
Ps	80:14	**R** to us, O God Almighty!
	90: 3	saying, "**R** to dust, O sons of men."
	126: 6	will **r** with songs of joy,
Pr	2:19	None who go to her **r** or
Ecc	3:20	and to dust all **r**.
Isa	10:21	A remnant will **r**,
	35:10	the ransomed of the LORD will **r**.
	44:22	**R** to me, for I have redeemed you."
	55:11	It will not **r** to me empty,
Jer	3:12	" '**R**, faithless Israel,'
	4: 1	"If you will **r**, O Israel, **r** to me,"
	24: 7	they will **r** to me with all their heart.
	31: 8	a great throng will **r**.
La	3:40	and let us **r** to the LORD.
Hos	5: 4	"Their deeds do not permit them to **r**
	6: 1	"Come, let us **r** to the LORD.
	12: 6	But you must **r** to your God;
	14: 1	**R**, O Israel, to the LORD your God.
Joel	2:12	"**r** to me with all your heart,
Zec	1: 3	'and I will **r** to you,'
	10: 9	and they will **r**.
Mal	3: 7	**R** to me, and I will **r** to you,"
Ro	9: 9	"At the appointed time I will **r**,

RETURNED [RETURN]

Ge	8: 9	so it **r** to Noah in the ark.
Nu	13:25	they **r** from exploring the land.
1Ki	17:22	and the boy's life **r** to him,
Ezr	2: 1	(they **r** to Jerusalem and Judah,
Ps	35:13	my prayers **r** to me unanswered,
Am	4: 6	yet you have not **r** to me,"
Mt	27: 3	and **r** the thirty silver coins to the
Ro	14: 9	and **r** to life so that he might be
1Pe	2:25	but now you have **r** to the Shepherd

RETURNS [RETURN]

Pr	3:14	and yields better **r** than gold.
	26:11	As a dog **r** to its vomit,
Ecc	12: 7	dust **r** to the ground it came from,
Isa	52: 8	When the LORD **r** to Zion,
Mt	24:46	master finds him doing so when he **r**.
2Pe	2:22	"A dog **r** to its vomit,"

REUBEN [REUBENITES]

Firstborn of Jacob by Leah (Ge 29:32; 46:8; 1Ch 2:1). Attempted to rescue Joseph (Ge 37:21-30). Lost birthright for sleeping with Bilhah (Ge 35:22; 49:4). Tribe of blessed (Ge 49:3-4; Dt 33:6), numbered (Nu 1:21; 26:7), allotted land east of Jordan (Nu 32; 34:14; Jos 13:15), west (Eze 48:6), failed to help Deborah (Jdg 5:15-16), supported David (1Ch 12:37), 12,000 from (Rev 7:5).

REUBENITES [REUBEN]

Nu	32: 1	The **R** and Gadites,
Dt	29: 8	as an inheritance to the **R**,
Jos	13: 8	the **R** and the Gadites had received

REUNITED* [UNITE]

Hos	1:11	and the people of Israel will be **r**,

REVEAL [REVEALED, REVEALS, REVELATION, REVELATIONS]

Nu	12: 6	I **r** myself to him in visions,
Da	2:11	No one can **r** it to the king except
Mt	11:27	to whom the Son chooses to **r** him.
Gal	1:16	to **r** his Son in me so that

REVEALED [REVEAL]

Dt	29:29	but the things **r** belong to us and
Est	2:10	Esther had not **r** her nationality
Isa	40: 5	the glory of the LORD will be **r**,
	43:12	I have **r** and saved and proclaimed—
	53: 1	the arm of the LORD been **r**?
	65: 1	"I **r** myself to those who did not ask
Da	2:19	mystery was **r** to Daniel in a vision.
Mt	11:25	and **r** them to little children.
	16:17	for this was not **r** to you by man,
Lk	17:30	on the day the Son of Man is **r**.
Jn	2:11	He thus **r** his glory,
	12:38	the arm of the Lord been **r**?"
	17: 6	"I have **r** you to those whom
Ro	1:17	a righteousness from God is **r**,
	8:18	with the glory that will be **r** in us.
	10:20	I **r** myself to those who did not ask
	16:26	now **r** and made known through
1Co	2:10	but God has **r** it to us by his Spirit.
	3:13	It will be **r** with fire,
2Co	4:11	his life may be **r** in our mortal body.
Eph	3: 5	as it has now been **r** by the Spirit
2Th	1: 7	the Lord Jesus is **r** from heaven
	2: 3	and the man of lawlessness is **r**,
1Pe	1: 7	and honor when Jesus Christ is **r**.
	1:20	but was **r** in these last times
	4:13	be overjoyed when his glory is **r**.
Rev	15: 4	for your righteous acts have been **r**."

REVEALS* [REVEAL]

Nu	23: 3	Whatever he **r** to me I will tell you."
Job	12:22	He **r** the deep things of darkness
Da	2:22	He **r** deep and hidden things;
	2:28	a God in heaven who **r** mysteries.
Am	4:13	and **r** his thoughts to man,

REVELATION* [REVEAL]

2Sa	7:17	all the words of this entire **r**.
1Ch	17:15	all the words of this entire **r**.
Pr	29:18	Where there is no **r**,
Da	10: 1	a **r** was given to Daniel
Hab	2: 2	"Write down the **r** and make it plain
	2: 3	For the **r** awaits an appointed time;
Lk	2:32	a light for **r** to the Gentiles
Ro	16:25	according to the **r** of the mystery
1Co	14: 6	I bring you some **r**
	14:26	a **r**, a tongue or an interpretation.
	14:30	if a **r** comes to someone who is
Gal	1:12	I received it by **r** from Jesus Christ.
	2: 2	I went in response to a **r** and
Eph	1:17	give you the Spirit of wisdom and **r**,
	3: 3	the mystery made known to me by **r**,
Rev	1: 1	The **r** of Jesus Christ,

REVELATIONS* [REVEAL]

2Co	12: 1	on to visions and **r** from the Lord.

12: 7 because of these surpassingly great **r,**

REVELED* [REVELRY]
Ne 9:25 they **r** in your great goodness.

REVELING [REVELRY]
2Pe 2:13 **r** in their pleasures while they feast

REVELRY [REVELED, REVELING]
Ex 32: 6 and drink and got up to indulge in **r.**
1Co 10: 7 and got up to indulge in pagan **r."**

REVENGE [VENGEANCE]
Lev 19:18 " 'Do not seek **r** or bear a grudge
Jdg 16:28 and let me with one blow get **r** on
Ro 12:19 Do not take **r,** my friends,

REVENUE
Ro 13: 7 owe taxes, pay taxes; if **r,** then **r;**

REVERE* [REVERED, REVERENCE, REVERENT, REVERING]
Lev 19:32 for the elderly and **r** your God.
Dt 4:10 that they may learn to **r** me as long
13: 4 and him you must **r.**
14:23 learn to **r** the LORD your God always
17:19 to **r** the LORD his God
28:58 and do not **r** this glorious
Job 37:24 Therefore, men **r** him,
Ps 22:23 **R** him, all you descendants of Israel!
33: 8 the people of the world **r** him.
102:15 kings of the earth will **r** your glory.
Ecc 3:14 God does it so that men will **r** him.
Isa 25: 3 cities of ruthless nations will **r** you.
59:19 they will **r** his glory.
63:17 so we do not **r** you?
Jer 10: 7 Who should not **r** you,
Hos 10: 3 because we did not **r** the LORD.
Mal 4: 2 But for you who **r** my name,

REVERED [REVERE]
Jos 4:14 just as they had **r** Moses.
Mal 2: 5 **r** me and stood in awe of my name.

REVERENCE [REVERE]
Lev 19:30 and have **r** for my sanctuary.
Ne 5:15 of **r** for God I did not act like that.
Ps 5: 7 in **r** will I bow down
Jer 44:10 not humbled themselves or shown **r,**
Da 6:26 must fear and **r** the God
2Co 7: 1 perfecting holiness out of **r** for God.
Eph 5:21 to one another out of **r** for Christ.
Col 3:22 sincerity of heart and **r** for the Lord.
1Pe 3: 2 when they see the purity and **r**
Rev 11:18 and those who **r** your name,

REVERENT* [REVERE]
Ecc 8:12 who are **r** before God.
Tit 2: 3 teach the older women to be **r** in
Heb 5: 7 because of his **r** submission.
1Pe 1:17 as strangers here in **r** fear.

REVERING* [REVERE]
Dt 8: 6 walking in his ways and **r** him.

Ne 1:11 who delight in **r** your name.

REVERSE*
Isa 43:13 When I act, who can **r** it?"

REVILE
Ps 10:13 Why does the wicked man **r** God?
74:10 Will the foe **r** your name forever?

REVIVE* [REVIVING]
Ps 80:18 **r** us, and we will call on your name.
85: 6 Will you not **r** us again,
Isa 57:15 to **r** the spirit of the lowly and to **r** the heart of the contrite.
Hos 6: 2 After two days he will **r** us;

REVIVING* [REVIVE]
Ps 19: 7 law of the LORD is perfect, **r** the soul

REVOKE* [REVOKED, REVOKING]
Ps 132:11 a sure oath that he will not **r:**

REVOKED* [REVOKE]
Est 8: 8 and sealed with his ring can be **r."**
Isa 45:23 a word that will not be **r:**
Zec 11:11 It was **r** on that day,

REVOKING* [REVOKE]
Zec 11:10 **r** the covenant I had made with all

REVOLUTIONS*
Lk 21: 9 When you hear of wars and **r,**

REWARD [REWARDED, REWARDING, REWARDS]
Ge 15: 1 I am your shield, your very great **r."**
1Sa 24:19 May the LORD **r** you well for
Ps 17:14 of this world whose **r** is in this life.
19:11 in keeping them there is great **r.**
62:12 Surely you will **r** each person
127: 3 children a **r** from him.
Pr 9:12 your wisdom will **r** you;
11:18 sows righteousness reaps a sure **r.**
13:21 prosperity is the **r** of the righteous.
19:17 he will **r** him for what he has done.
25:22 and the LORD will **r** you.
31:31 Give her the **r** she has earned,
Isa 40:10 See, his **r** is with him,
49: 4 and my **r** is with my God."
61: 8 In my faithfulness I will **r** them
62:11 See, his **r** is with him,
Jer 17:10 to **r** a man according to his conduct,
32:19 you **r** everyone according to
Mt 5:12 because great is your **r** in heaven,
6: 1 you will have no **r** from your Father
6: 5 they have received their **r** in full.
10:41 a prophet will receive a prophet's **r,**
16:27 then he will **r** each person according
Lk 6:23 because great is your **r** in heaven.
6:35 Then your **r** will be great,
1Co 3:14 he will receive his **r.**
9:17 If I preach voluntarily, I have a **r;**
Eph 6: 8 that the Lord will **r** everyone
Col 3:24 an inheritance from the Lord as a **r.**

Heb 11:26 he was looking ahead to his **r.**
Rev 22:12 My **r** is with me,

REWARDED [REWARD]

Ru   2:12 May you be richly **r** by the LORD,
2Sa 22:21 cleanness of my hands he has **r** me.
2Ch 15: 7 for your work will be **r.**"
Ps   18:24 The LORD has **r** me according
Pr   13:13 but he who respects a command is **r.**
14:14 and the good man **r** for his.
Jer 31:16 for your work will be **r,**"
1Co   3: 8 be **r** according to his own labor.
Heb 10:35 confidence; it will be richly **r.**
2Jn   1: 8 but that you may be **r** fully.

REWARDING* [REWARD]

Rev 11:18 and for **r** your servants the prophets

REWARDS [REWARD]

1Sa 26:23 The LORD **r** every man
Pr   12:14 as the work of his hands **r** him.
Heb 11: 6 he **r** those who earnestly seek him.

REZIN

Isa   7: 1 King **R** of Aram and Pekah son of

RHODA*

Ac   12:13 and a servant girl named **R** came

RIB* [RIBS]

Ge   2:22 LORD God made a woman from the **r**

RIBLAH

2Ki 25: 6 to the king of Babylon at **R,**

RIBS* [RIB]

Ge   2:21 he took one of the man's **r** and
Da   7: 5 and it had three **r** in its mouth

RICH [ENRICH, ENRICHED, RICHES, RICHEST, RICHLY]

Ge   26:13 The man became **r,**
2Sa 12: 1 one **r** and the other poor.
Job 34:19 does not favor the **r** over the poor,
Ps   21: 3 You welcomed him with **r** blessings
49:16 when a man grows **r,**
145: 8 slow to anger and **r** in love.
Pr   13: 7 One man pretends to be **r,**
21:17 wine and oil will never be **r.**
22: 2 **R** and poor have this in common:
23: 4 Do not wear yourself out to get **r;**
28: 6 a **r** man whose ways are perverse.
28:20 to get **r** will not go unpunished.
28:22 A stingy man is eager to get **r**
Ecc   5:12 a **r** man permits him no sleep.
Isa 33: 6 a **r** store of salvation and wisdom
53: 9 and with the **r** in his death,
Jer   9:23 or the **r** man boast of his riches,
Eze 34:14 and there they will feed in a **r** pasture
Zec   3: 4 and I will put **r** garments on you."
Mt   19:23 for a **r** man to enter the kingdom
Lk   1:53 but has sent the **r** away empty.
6:24 "But woe to you who are **r,**
12:21 for himself but is not **r** toward God."

16: 1 a **r** man whose manager was accused
16:19 "There was a **r** man who was dressed
21: 1 Jesus saw the **r** putting their gifts
2Co   6:10 poor, yet making many **r;**
8: 2 poverty welled up in **r** generosity.
8: 9 through his poverty might become **r.**
9:11 be made **r** in every way so
Eph   2: 4 God, who is **r** in mercy,
1Ti   6: 9 want to get **r** fall into temptation
6:17 Command those who are **r**
6:18 to be **r** in good deeds,
Jas   1:10 the one who is **r** should take pride
2: 5 the eyes of the world to be **r** in faith
5: 1 Now listen, you **r** people,
2Pe   1:11 **r** welcome into the eternal kingdom
Rev   2: 9 your poverty—yet you are **r!**
3:17 You say, 'I am **r;**
3:18 so you can become **r;**

RICHES [RICH]

1Ki   3:13 you have not asked for—both **r**
10:23 King Solomon was greater in **r**
Job 36:18 that no one entices you by **r;**
Ps   49: 6 and boast of their great **r?**
49:12 man, despite his **r,** does not endure;
62:10 though your **r** increase,
119:14 as one rejoices in great **r.**
Pr   3:16 in her left hand are **r** and honor.
11:28 Whoever trusts in his **r** will fall,
22: 1 name is more desirable than great **r;**
27:24 for **r** do not endure forever,
30: 8 give me neither poverty nor **r,**
Isa 10: 3 Where will you leave your **r?**
60: 5 to you the **r** of the nations will come.
Jer   9:23 or the rich man boast of his **r,**
Lk   8:14 choked by life's worries, **r** and
Ro   9:23 to make the **r** of his glory known to
11:12 their loss means **r** for the Gentiles,
11:33 Oh, the depth of the **r** of the wisdom
Eph   2: 7 show the incomparable **r** of his grace
3: 8 to the Gentiles the unsearchable **r**
Col   1:27 the glorious **r** of this mystery,
2: 2 the full **r** of complete understanding,

RICHEST [RICH]

Isa 55: 2 your soul will delight in the **r** of fare.

RICHLY [RICH]

Pr   28:20 A faithful man will be **r** blessed,
Ro   10:12 and **r** blesses all who call on him,
Col   3:16 the word of Christ dwell in you **r**
1Ti   6:17 who **r** provides us with everything

RID

Ge   21:10 "Get **r** of that slave woman
35: 2 "Get **r** of the foreign gods you have
Jdg 10:16 Then they got **r** of the foreign gods
1Sa   7: 3 then **r** yourselves of the foreign gods
Lk   22: 2 for some way to get **r** of Jesus,
1Co   5: 7 Get **r** of the old yeast that you may
Gal   4:30 "Get **r** of the slave woman
Eph   4:31 Get **r** of all bitterness,
Col   3: 8 But now you must **r** yourselves
Jas   1:21 get **r** of all moral filth and the evil

1Pe 2: 1 **r** yourselves of all malice

RIDDLE [RIDDLES]

Jdg 14:12 "Let me tell you a **r**,"
Ps 49: 4 with the harp I will expound my **r**:

RIDDLES* [RIDDLE]

Nu 12: 8 clearly and not in **r**;
Pr 1: 6 the sayings and **r** of the wise.
Da 5:12 dreams, explain **r** and solve difficult

RIDE [RIDER, RIDERS, RIDES, RIDING, RODE]

Ps 45: 4 In your majesty **r** forth victoriously

RIDER [RIDE]

Ex 15: 1 The horse and its **r** he has hurled into
Rev 6: 2 Its **r** held a bow,
19:11 whose **r** is called Faithful and True.

RIDERS [RIDE]

Rev 9:17 and **r** I saw in my vision looked

RIDES* [RIDE]

Dt 33:26 who **r** on the heavens to help you
Ps 68: 4 extol him who **r** on the clouds—
68:33 to him who **r** the ancient skies above,
104: 3 and **r** on the wings of the wind.
Isa 19: 1 the LORD **r** on a swift cloud
Rev 17: 7 of the woman and of the beast she **r**,

RIDICULE [RIDICULED]

2Ki 19: 4 has sent to **r** the living God,
Ps 123: 4 We have endured much **r** from

RIDICULED [RIDICULE]

Jer 20: 7 I am **r** all day long;
Lk 23:11 and his soldiers **r** and mocked him.

RIDING [RIDE]

Zec 9: 9 gentle and **r** on a donkey, on a colt,
Mt 21: 5 gentle and **r** on a donkey, on a colt,
Rev 19:14 **r** on white horses and dressed

RIGGING*

Pr 23:34 lying on top of the **r**.
Isa 33:23 Your **r** hangs loose:

RIGHT [RIGHTFULLY, RIGHTS]

Ge 4: 7 If you do what is **r**,
4: 7 But if you do not do what is **r**,
13: 9 If you go to the left, I'll go to the **r**;
18:19 of the LORD by doing what is **r**
18:25 not the Judge of all the earth do **r**?"
Ex 14:22 Ephraim on his **r** toward Israel's left
14:22 with a wall of water on their **r** and on
15: 6 "Your **r** hand, O LORD,
15: 6 and do what is **r** in his eyes,
Dt 5:32 not turn aside to the **r** or to the left.
6:18 Do what is **r** and good in
13:18 and doing what is **r**
28:14 to the **r** or to the left,
Jos 1: 7 not turn from it to the **r** or to the left,
1Sa 12:23 teach you the way that is good and **r**.

1Ki 3: 9 and to distinguish between **r**
8:36 Teach them the **r** way to live,
15: 5 For David had done what is **r** in
2Ki 7: 9 "We're not doing **r**.
Ne 9:13 and laws that are just and **r**,
Job 40:14 that your own **r** hand can save you.
42: 7 you have not spoken of me what is **r**,
Ps 4: 5 Offer **r** sacrifices and trust in
16: 8 Because he is at my **r** hand,
16:11 with eternal pleasures at your **r** hand.
17: 7 your **r** hand those who take refuge
18:35 and your **r** hand sustains me;
19: 8 The precepts of the LORD are **r**,
25: 9 He guides the humble in what is **r**
33: 4 the word of the LORD is **r** and true;
44: 3 it was your **r** hand,
45: 4 your **r** hand display awesome deeds.
51: 4 so that you are proved **r**
63: 8 your **r** hand upholds me.
73:23 you hold me by my **r** hand.
80:17 on the man at your **r** hand,
89:13 your **r** hand exalted.
91: 7 ten thousand at your **r** hand,
106: 3 who constantly do what is **r**.
110: 1 "Sit at my **r** hand until I make
110: 5 The Lord is at your **r** hand;
118:15 LORD's **r** hand has done mighty
119:144 Your statutes are forever **r**;
137: 5 may my **r** hand forget [its skill].
139:10 your **r** hand will hold me fast.
Pr 1: 3 doing what is **r** and just and fair;
3:16 Long life is in her **r** hand;
4:27 Do not swerve to the **r** or the left;
12:15 The way of a fool seems **r** to him,
14:12 There is a way that seems **r** to a man,
16:25 There is a way that seems **r** to a man,
18:17 The first to present his case seems **r**,
21: 2 All a man's ways seem **r** to him,
Ecc 7:20 who does what is **r** and never sins.
SS 1: 4 How **r** they are to adore you!
Isa 1:17 learn to do **r**!
7:15 to reject the wrong and choose the **r**.
30:10 no more visions of what is **r**!
30:21 Whether you turn to the **r** or to
41:10 uphold you with my righteous **r** hand
41:13 God, who takes hold of your **r** hand
48:13 my **r** hand spread out the heavens;
64: 5 to the help of those who gladly do **r**,
Jer 22: 3 Do what is just and **r**.
23: 5 and do what is just and **r** in the land.
Eze 1:10 the **r** side each had the face of a lion,
18: 5 who does what is just and **r**.
18:21 and does what is just and **r**, he will
33:14 and does what is just and **r**—
Hos 14: 9 The ways of the LORD are **r**;
Am 3:10 "They do not know how to do **r**,"
Jnh 4:11 people who cannot tell their **r** hand
Zec 3: 1 and Satan standing at his **r** side
Mt 5:29 If your **r** eye causes you to sin,
6: 3 know what your **r** hand is doing,
22:44 "Sit at my **r** hand until I put
25:33 He will put the sheep on his **r** and
Mk 7:27 not **r** to take the children's bread
14:62 the Son of Man sitting at the **r** hand

Jn	1:12	the **r** to become children of God—
	8:16	But if I do judge, my decisions are **r**,
	18:37	"You are **r** in saying I am a king.
Ac	2:34	to my Lord: "Sit at my **r** hand
	7:55	Jesus standing at the **r** hand of God.
Ro	3: 4	"So that you may be proved **r**
	8:34	is at the **r** hand of God
	9:21	the potter have the **r** to make
	12:17	Be careful to do what is **r** in the eyes
1Co	7:35	in a **r** way in undivided devotion to
	9: 4	Don't we have the **r** to food
2Co		we are taking pains to do what is **r**,
Eph	1:20	the dead and seated him at his **r** hand
	6: 1	for this is **r**.
Php	4: 8	whatever is noble, whatever is **r**,
Col	3: 1	Christ is seated at the **r** hand of God.
2Th	3:13	never tire of doing what is **r**.
Heb	1: 3	the **r** hand of the Majesty in heaven.
	1:13	"Sit at my **r** hand until I make
	10:12	he sat down at the **r** hand of God.
Jas	2: 8	you are doing **r**.
1Pe	3:14	if you should suffer for what is **r**,
	3:22	into heaven and is at God's **r** hand—
1Jn	2:29	who does what is **r** has been born
	3: 7	He who does what is **r** is righteous,
Rev	1:16	In his **r** hand he held seven stars,
	2: 7	the **r** to eat from the tree of life,
	3:21	the **r** to sit with me on my throne,
	22:11	let him who does **r** continue to do **r**;
	22:14	the **r** to the tree of life

RIGHT HAND See HAND

RIGHT IN THE EYES OF THE †LORD
See EYES

RIGHT-HANDED* [HAND]

1Ch	12: 2	to shoot arrows or to sling stones **r**

RIGHTEOUS [OVERRIGHTEOUS, RIGHTEOUSLY, RIGHTEOUSNESS]

Ge	6: 9	Noah was a **r** man,
	18:23	"Will you sweep away the **r**
	38:26	"She is more **r** than I,
Nu	23:10	Let me die the death of the **r**,
Dt	4: 8	as to have such **r** decrees and laws
1Sa	24:17	"You are more **r** than I," he said.
Ne	9: 8	kept your promise because you are **r**.
Job	4:17	'Can a mortal be more **r** than God?
	36: 7	He does not take his eyes off the **r**;
Ps	1: 5	nor sinners in the assembly of the **r**.
	5:12	surely, O LORD, you bless the **r**;
	7:11	God is a **r** judge,
	11: 7	For the LORD is **r**, he loves justice;
	15: 2	and who does what is **r**,
	34:15	The eyes of the LORD are on the **r**
	37:16	Better the little that the **r** have than
	37:21	but the **r** give generously;
	37:25	yet I have never seen the **r** forsaken
	37:30	mouth of the **r** man utters wisdom,
	55:22	he will never let the **r** fall.
	64:10	Let the **r** rejoice in the LORD
	68: 3	the **r** be glad and rejoice before God;
	72: 7	In his days the **r** will flourish;
	112: 4	and compassionate and **r** man.
	116: 5	The LORD is gracious and **r**;
	118:20	through which the **r** may enter.
	119: 7	as I learn your **r** laws.
	119:137	**R** are you, O LORD,
	140:13	Surely the **r** will praise your name
	143: 2	for no one living is **r** before you.
	145:17	The LORD is **r** in all his ways
	146: 8	the LORD loves the **r**.
Pr	3:33	but he blesses the home of the **r**.
	4:18	the **r** is like the first gleam of dawn,
	10: 6	Blessings crown the head of the **r**,
	10: 7	memory of the **r** will be a blessing,
	10:11	mouth of the **r** is a fountain of life,
	10:16	The wages of the **r** bring them life,
	10:20	The tongue of the **r** is choice silver,
	10:24	the **r** desire will
	10:28	The prospect of the **r** is joy,
	10:32	lips of the **r** know what is fitting,
	11: 9	but through knowledge the **r** escape,
	11:23	desire of the **r** ends only in good,
	11:30	The fruit of the **r** is a tree of life,
	12:10	A **r** man cares for the needs
	12:21	No harm befalls the **r**,
	13: 5	The **r** hate what is false,
	13: 9	The light of the **r** shines brightly,
	14:32	but even in death the **r** have a refuge.
	15:28	heart of the **r** weighs its answers,
	15:29	but he hears the prayer of the **r**.
	16:31	it is attained by a **r** life.
	18:10	the **r** run to it and are safe.
	20: 7	The **r** man leads a blameless life;
	21:15	joy to the **r** but terror to evildoers.
	23:24	The father of a **r** man has great joy;
	24:16	for though a **r** man falls seven times,
	28: 1	but the **r** are as bold as a lion.
	29: 2	the **r** thrive, the people rejoice;
	29: 6	but a **r** one can sing and be glad.
	29: 7	The **r** care about justice for the poor,
	29:27	The **r** detest the dishonest;
Ecc	7:15	**r** man perishing in his righteousness,
	7:20	There is not a **r** man on earth who
	8:14	men who get what the **r** deserve.
Isa	26: 7	The path of the **r** is level;
	41:10	uphold you with my **r** right hand.
	45:21	a **r** God and a Savior;
	53:11	my **r** servant will justify many,
	64: 6	and all our **r** acts are like filthy rags;
Jer	12: 1	You are always **r**, O LORD,
	23: 5	I will raise up to David a **r** Branch,
	33:15	a **r** Branch sprout from David's line;
La	1:18	"The LORD is **r**,
Eze	3:20	a **r** man turns from his righteousness
	18: 5	a **r** man who does what is just
	18:20	of the **r** man will be credited to him,
	33:12	The **r** man, if he sins,
Da	9:14	the LORD our God is **r** in everything
Hab	2: 4	but the **r** will live by his faith—
Zep	3: 5	The LORD within her is **r**;
Zec	9: 9	**r** and having salvation,
Mal	3:18	the distinction between the **r** and
Mt	5:45	rain on the **r** and the unrighteous.
	13:43	Then the **r** will shine like the sun in
	13:49	and separate the wicked from the **r**
	25:37	"Then the **r** will answer him, 'Lord,

	25:46	but the **r** to eternal life."
Mk	2:17	I have not come to call the **r**,
Lk	23:47	"Surely this was a **r** man."
Ac	3:14	You disowned the Holy and **R** One
	24:15	be a resurrection of both the **r** and
Ro	1:17	"The **r** will live by faith."
	2: 5	his **r** judgment will be revealed.
	2:13	not those who hear the law who are **r**
	3:10	As it is written: "There is no one **r**,
	3:20	**r** in his sight by observing the law;
	5:19	one man the many will be made **r**.
	7:12	commandment is holy, **r** and good.
	8: 4	the **r** requirements of the law might
Gal	3:11	because, "The **r** will live by faith."
1Ti	1: 9	that law is made not for the **r** but
2Ti	4: 8	which the Lord, the **r** Judge,
Tit	3: 5	not because of **r** things we had done,
Heb	10:38	But my **r** one will live by faith.
Jas	2:21	our ancestor Abraham considered **r**
	2:25	Rahab the prostitute considered **r**
	5:16	The prayer of a **r** man is powerful
1Pe	3:12	the eyes of the Lord are on the **r**
	3:18	the **r** for the unrighteous,
	4:18	"If it is hard for the **r** to be saved,
1Jn	2: 1	Jesus Christ, the **R** One.
	3: 7	He who does what is right is **r**,
Rev	15: 4	for your **r** acts have been revealed."
	19: 8	(Fine linen stands for the **r** acts of

RIGHTEOUSLY* [RIGHTEOUS]

Ps	9: 4	sat on your throne, judging **r**.
Isa	33:15	He who walks **r** and test the heart
Jer	11:20	you who judge **r** and test the heart

RIGHTEOUSNESS [RIGHTEOUS]

Ge	15: 6	and he credited it to him as **r**.
Dt	6:25	that will be our **r**."
	9: 4	of this land because of my **r**."
1Sa	26:23	LORD rewards every man for his **r**
1Ki	10: 9	to maintain justice and **r**."
Job	27: 6	I will maintain my **r** and never let go
	37:23	in his justice and great **r**,
Ps	7:17	because of his **r** and will sing praise
	9: 8	He will judge the world in **r**;
	17:15	And I—in **r** I will see your face;
	18:20	dealt with me according to my **r**;
	22:31	They will proclaim his **r** to a people
	23: 3	in paths of **r** for his name's sake.
	33: 5	The LORD loves **r** and justice;
	35:24	Vindicate me in your **r**,
	35:28	My tongue will speak of your **r** and
	36: 6	Your **r** is like the mighty mountains,
	37: 6	He will make your **r** shine like
	40: 9	I proclaim **r** in the great assembly;
	45: 4	in behalf of truth, humility and **r**;
	45: 7	You love **r** and hate wickedness;
	48:10	your right hand is filled with **r**.
	50: 6	And the heavens proclaim his **r**,
	65: 5	answer us with awesome deeds of **r**,
	71: 2	Rescue me and deliver me in your **r**;
	71:15	My mouth will tell of your **r**,
	71:19	Your **r** reaches to the skies, O God,
	72: 2	He will judge your people in **r**,
	85:10	**r** and peace kiss each other.

	89:14	**R** and justice are the foundation
	96:13	He will judge the world in **r** and
	98: 2	and revealed his **r** to the nations.
	98: 9	He will judge the world in **r** and
	103: 6	The LORD works **r** and justice
	103:17	his **r** with their children's children—
	106:31	This was credited to him as **r** for
	111: 3	and his **r** endures forever.
	118:19	Open for me the gates of **r**;
	132: 9	May your priests be clothed with **r**;
	145: 7	and joyfully sing of your **r**.
Pr	8:20	I walk in the way of **r**,
	10: 2	but **r** delivers from death.
	11: 5	The **r** of the blameless makes
	11: 6	The **r** of the upright delivers them,
	11:18	he who sows **r** reaps a sure reward.
	12:28	In the way of **r** there is life;
	13: 6	**R** guards the man of integrity,
	14:34	**R** exalts a nation,
	15: 9	but he loves those who pursue **r**.
	16:12	for a throne is established through **r**.
	21:21	He who pursues **r** and love finds life,
Ecc	7:15	a righteous man perishing in his **r**,
Isa	1:26	you will be called the City of **R**,
	5:16	will show himself holy by his **r**.
	9: 7	and **r** from that time on and forever.
	11: 4	but with **r** he will judge the needy,
	11: 5	**R** will be his belt and faithfulness
	16: 5	and speeds the cause of **r**.
	26: 9	the people of the world learn **r**.
	28:17	and **r** the plumb line;
	32: 1	See, a king will reign in **r**
	32:17	The fruit of **r** will be peace;
	33: 5	he will fill Zion with justice and **r**.
	42: 6	the LORD, have called you in **r**;
	42:21	the LORD for the sake of his **r**
	45: 8	"You heavens above, rain down **r**;
	45:24	'In the LORD alone are **r**
	46:13	I am bringing my **r** near,
	51: 5	My **r** draws near speedily,
	51: 6	my **r** will never fail.
	51: 8	But my **r** will last forever,
	56: 1	and my **r** will soon be revealed.
	58: 8	then your **r** will go before you,
	59:17	He put on **r** as his breastplate,
	61:10	and arrayed me in a robe of **r**,
	62: 1	till her **r** shines out like the dawn,
	63: 1	"It is I, speaking in **r**,
Jer	9:24	justice and **r** on earth,
	23: 6	The LORD Our **R**.
	33:16	The LORD Our **R**.'
Eze	3:20	a righteous man turns from his **r**
	14:20	save only themselves by their **r**.
	18:20	The **r** of the righteous man will
	33:12	'The **r** of the righteous man will
Da	9:24	to bring in everlasting **r**,
	12: 3	and those who lead many to **r**,
Hos	2:19	I will betroth you in **r** and justice,
	10:12	Sow for yourselves **r**,
	10:12	until he comes and showers **r** on you.
Am	5:24	**r** like a never-failing stream!
Mic	7: 9	I will see his **r**.
Zep	2: 3	Seek **r**, seek humility;
Mal	4: 2	the sun of **r** will rise with healing

Mt   3:15 for us to do this to fulfill all **r**."
      5: 6 those who hunger and thirst for **r**,
      5:10 who are persecuted because of **r**,
      5:20 unless your **r** surpasses that of
      6: 1 not to do your 'acts of **r**' before men,
      6:33 But seek first his kingdom and his **r**,
Jn   16: 8 in regard to sin and **r** and judgment:
Ac   24:25 As Paul discoursed on **r**,
Ro   1:17 a **r** that is by faith from first to last,
      3: 5 unrighteousness brings out God's **r**
      3:22 This **r** from God comes through faith
      4: 3 and it was credited to him as **r**."
      4: 5 his faith is credited as **r**.
      4: 6 the man to whom God credits **r** apart
      4: 9 faith was credited to him as **r**.
      4:13 but through the **r** that comes by faith.
      4:22 "it was credited to him as **r**."
      5:18 of **r** was justification that brings life
      6:13 body to him as instruments of **r**.
      6:16 or to obedience, which leads to **r**?
      6:18 and have become slaves to **r**.
      6:19 in slavery to **r** leading to holiness.
      8:10 yet your spirit is alive because of **r**.
      9:30 have obtained it, a **r** that is by faith;
     10: 3 they did not submit to God's **r**.
     10: 4 end of the law so that there may be **r**
     14:17 of eating and drinking, but of **r**,
1Co   1:30 our **r**, holiness and redemption.
2Co   3: 9 the ministry that brings **r**!
      5:21 we might become the **r** of God.
      6: 7 with weapons of **r** in the right hand
      6:14 For what do **r** and wickedness have
      9: 9 his **r** endures forever."
      9:10 enlarge the harvest of your **r**.
     11:15 masquerade as servants of **r**.
Gal   2:21 if **r** could be gained through the law,
      3: 6 and it was credited to him as **r**."
      3:21 then **r** would certainly have come by
Eph   4:24 to be like God in true **r** and holiness.
      5: 9 consists in all goodness, **r** and truth)
      6:14 with the breastplate of **r** in place,
Php   1:11 filled with the fruit of **r** that comes
      3: 6 as for legalistic **r**, faultless.
      3: 9 not having a **r** of my own that comes
1Ti   6:11 and pursue **r**, godliness, faith, love,
2Ti   2:22 and pursue **r**, faith, love and peace,
      3:16 correcting and training in **r**,
      4: 8 in store for me the crown of **r**,
Heb   1: 8 and **r** will be the scepter
      5:13 acquainted with the teaching about **r**.
      7: 1 First, his name means "king of **r**";
     11: 7 and became heir of the **r** that comes
     12:11 it produces a harvest of **r** and peace
Jas   2:23 and it was credited to him as **r**,"
      3:18 sow in peace raise a harvest of **r**.
1Pe   2:24 we might die to sins and live for **r**;
2Pe   2:21 not to have known the way of **r**,
      3:13 and a new earth, the home of **r**.

RIGHTFULLY* [RIGHT]

Eze 21:27 until he comes to whom it **r** belongs;

RIGHTS [RIGHT]

Ex   21: 9 he must grant her the **r** of a daughter.

     21:10 her food, clothing and marital **r**.
Dt   21:16 not give the **r** of the firstborn to
Job 36: 6 but gives the afflicted their **r**.
Ps   82: 3 maintain the **r** of the poor
Pr   31: 8 for the **r** of all who are destitute.
Isa 10: 2 to deprive the poor of their **r**
Jer   5:28 they do not defend the **r** of the poor.
La   3:35 a man his **r** before the Most High,
1Co   9:15 But I have not used any of these **r**.
Gal   4: 5 we might receive the full **r** of sons.
Heb 12:16 a single meal sold his inheritance **r**

RING

Ge   41:42 Pharaoh took his signet **r**
Est   3:12 and sealed with his own **r**.
      8:10 dispatches with the king's signet **r**,
Pr   11:22 a gold **r** in a pig's snout is
Jer 22:24 were a signet **r** on my right hand,
Da   6:17 sealed it with his own signet **r**
Hag   2:23 I will make you like my signet **r**,
Lk   15:22 Put a **r** on his finger and sandals

RIOT [RIOTS]

Mk   14: 2 they said, "or the people may **r**."
Ac   17: 5 a mob and started a **r** in the city.

RIOTS* [RIOT]

Ac   24: 5 stirring up **r** among the Jews all over
2Co   6: 5 imprisonments and **r**;

RIPE

Joel 3:13 Swing the sickle, for the harvest is **r**.
Am   8: 2 "The time is **r** for my people Israel;
Na   3:12 like fig trees with their first **r** fruit;
Mk   4:29 As soon as the grain is **r**,
Jn   4:35 They are **r** for harvest.
Rev 14:15 for the harvest of the earth is **r**."

RISE [ARISE, RAISE, RAISED, RAISES, RISEN, RISES, RISING, ROSE]

Lev 19:32 " '**R** in the presence of the aged,
Nu   10:35 Moses said, "**R** up, O Lord!
     24:17 a scepter will **r** out of Israel.
Ps   7: 6 **r** up against the rage of my enemies;
     27:12 for false witnesses **r** up against me,
     74:22 **R** up, O God, and defend your cause;
     94: 2 **R** up, O Judge of the earth;
    139:19 If I **r** on the wings of the dawn,
Isa 26:19 dead will live; their bodies will **r**.
Da   7:17 kingdoms that will **r** from the earth.
     12:13 **r** to receive your allotted inheritance.
Am   8:14 never to **r** again."
Mal   4: 2 of righteousness will **r** with healing
Mt   5:45 He causes his sun to **r** on the evil and
     27:63 'After three days I will **r** again.'
Mk   8:31 be killed and after three days **r** again.
     13: 8 Nation will **r** against nation,
Lk   18:33 On the third day he will **r** again."
Jn   5:29 who have done good will **r** to live,
     20: 9 that Jesus had to **r** from
Ac   17: 3 the Christ had to suffer and **r** from
Eph   5:14 O sleeper, **r** from the dead,
1Th   4:16 and the dead in Christ will **r** first.

RISEN [RISE]

Dt	34:10	no prophet has **r** in Israel like Moses,
Mt	28: 6	He is not here; he has **r,**
Mk	16: 6	He has **r!** He is not here.
Lk	24:34	The Lord has **r** and has appeared

RISES [RISE]

Ecc	1: 5	The sun **r** and the sun sets,
Isa	2:19	when he **r** to shake the earth.
	30:18	he **r** to show you compassion.
	60: 1	the glory of the LORD **r** upon you.
Lk	16:31	even if someone **r** from the dead.' ''
2Pe	1:19	and the morning star **r** in your hearts.

RISING [RISE]

Ps	113: 3	From the **r** of the sun to the place
Mk	9:10	what "**r** from the dead" meant.
Lk	2:34	the falling and **r** of many in Israel,

RIVAL [RIVALRY]

1Sa	1: 7	her **r** provoked her till she wept

RIVALRY* [RIVAL]

Php	1:15	some preach Christ out of envy and **r**

RIVER [RIVERS]

Ge	2:10	A **r** watering the garden flowed
	15:18	from the **r** of Egypt to the great **r,**
	41: 2	of the **r** there came up seven cows,
Dt	1: 7	as far as the great **r,** the Euphrates.
	11:24	from the Euphrates **R** to the western
Jos	1: 2	get ready to cross the Jordan **R**
	24: 2	lived beyond the **R** and worshiped
Ps	46: 4	a **r** whose streams make glad the city
Isa	48:18	your peace would have been like a **r,**
	66:12	"I will extend peace to her like a **r,**
La	2:18	let your tears flow like a **r** day
Eze	47:12	grow on both banks of the **r.**
Da	7:10	A **r** of fire was flowing,
Am	5:24	But let justice roll on like a **r,**
Mt	3: 6	baptized by him in the Jordan **R.**
Rev	12:15	the serpent spewed water like a **r,**
	22: 1	the **r** of the water of life,

RIVERS [RIVER]

Ps	78:16	and made water flow down like **r.**
	78:44	He turned their **r** to blood;
	137: 1	By the **r** of Babylon we sat and wept
Rev	8:10	fell from the sky on a third of the **r**
	16: 4	angel poured out his bowl on the **r**

ROAD [CROSSROADS, ROADS]

Nu	22:22	angel of the LORD stood in the **r**
Mt	7:13	is the **r** that leads to destruction,
Mk	11: 8	people spread their cloaks on the **r,**

ROADS [ROAD]

Lk	3: 5	The crooked **r** shall become straight,

ROAR [ROARING, ROARS]

Ps	46: 3	though its waters **r** and foam and
Isa	17:13	peoples **r** like the **r** of surging waters
Jer	25:30	" 'The LORD will **r** from on high;
Hos	11:10	the LORD; he will **r** like a lion.

Joel	3:16	The LORD will **r** from Zion
2Pe	3:10	The heavens will disappear with a **r;**
Rev	10: 3	a loud shout like the **r** of a lion.
	14: 2	like the **r** of rushing waters
	19: 6	like the **r** of rushing waters and

ROARING [ROAR]

Ps	65: 7	who stilled the **r** of the seas,
1Pe	5: 8	like a **r** lion looking for someone

ROARS [ROAR]

Hos	11:10	When he **r,** his children will come
Am	1: 2	He said: "The LORD **r** from Zion

ROB [ROBBER, ROBBERS, ROBBERY, ROBS]

Lev	19:13	not defraud your neighbor or **r** him.
Mal	3: 8	"Will a man **r** God?
Mk	3:27	Then he can **r** his house.

ROBBER* [ROB]

Jn	10: 1	by some other way, is a thief and a **r.**

ROBBERS [ROB]

Jer	7:11	become a den of **r** to you?
Mt	21:13	but you are making it a 'den of **r.** ''
Mk	15:27	They crucified two **r** with him,
Lk	10:30	when he fell into the hands of **r.**
	19:46	but you have made it 'a den of **r.** ''
Jn	10: 8	before me were thieves and **r,**

ROBBERY [ROB]

Isa	61: 8	I, the LORD, love justice; I hate **r**
Eze	22:29	practice extortion and commit **r;**

ROBE [ROBED, ROBES]

Ge	37: 3	and he made a richly ornamented **r**
Ex	28: 4	an ephod, a **r,** a woven tunic,
Jos	7:21	a beautiful **r** from Babylonia,
1Sa	2:19	his mother made him a little **r**
	15:27	Saul caught hold of the hem of his **r,**
	24: 4	and cut off a corner of Saul's **r.**
2Sa	13:18	wearing a richly ornamented **r,**
Isa	6: 1	the train of his **r** filled the temple.
	61:10	arrayed me in a **r** of righteousness,
Zec	8:23	hold of one Jew by the hem of his **r**
Lk	15:22	Bring the best **r** and put it on him.
Jn	19: 5	the crown of thorns and the purple **r,**
Heb	1:12	You will roll them up like a **r;**
Rev	1:13	in a **r** reaching down to his feet and
	6:11	each of them was given a white **r,**
	19:13	He is dressed in a **r** dipped in blood,

ROBED* [ROBE]

Est	6:11	He **r** Mordecai, and led him
Ps	93: 1	he is **r** in majesty; the LORD is **r** in
Isa	63: 1	Who is this, **r** in splendor,
Rev	10: 1	He was **r** in a cloud,

ROBES [ROBE]

Ps	45: 8	All your **r** are fragrant with myrrh
Mk	12:38	like to walk around in flowing **r**
Rev	7:13	"These in white **r**—who are they,
	22:14	"Blessed are those who wash their **r,**

ROBS* [ROB]

Pr   19:26 He who **r** his father and drives out
        28:24 He who **r** his father or mother

ROCK [ROCKS, ROCKY]

Ge   49:24 the **R** of Israel,
Ex   17: 6 Strike the **r**, and water will
        33:22 I will put you in a cleft in the **r**
Nu   20: 8 Speak to that **r** before their eyes
Dt   32: 4 He is the **R**, his works are perfect,
        32:13 nourished him with honey from the **r**
        32:15 and rejected the **R** his Savior.
        32:31 For their **r** is not like our **R**,
1Sa   2: 2 there is no **R** like our God.
2Sa 22: 2 He said: "The LORD is my **r**,
Ps   18: 2 The LORD is my **r**,
       19:14 O LORD, my **R** and my Redeemer.
       27: 5 and set me high upon a **r**.
       40: 2 he set my feet on a **r**
       61: 2 to the **r** that is higher than I.
       62: 2 He alone is my **r** and my salvation;
       92:15 "The LORD is upright; he is my **R**,
Isa 26: 4 the LORD, is the **R** eternal.
       44: 8 No, there is no other **R**;
       48:21 made water flow for them from the **r**
       51: 1 to the **r** from which you were cut
Da   2:34 you were watching, a **r** was cut out,
Zec 12: 3 an immovable **r** for all the nations.
Mt   7:24 man who built his house on the **r**.
       16:18 and on this **r** I will build my church,
Mk 15:46 and placed it in a tomb cut out of **r**.
Ro   9:33 and a **r** that makes them fall,
1Co 10: 4 for they drank from the spiritual **r**
       10: 4 and that **r** was Christ.
1Pe   2: 8 and a **r** that makes them fall."

ROCKS [ROCK]

Ps   78:15 He split the **r** in the desert
     137: 9 and dashes them against the **r**.
Isa   2:19 to caves in the **r** and to holes
Ob   1: 3 you who live in the clefts of the **r**
Na   1: 6 the **r** are shattered before him.
Mt 27:51 The earth shook and the **r** split.
Rev   6:15 hid in caves and among the **r**

ROCKY [ROCK]

Mk   4: 5 Some fell on **r** places,

ROD [RODS]

2Sa   7:14 I will punish him with the **r** of men,
Ps   23: 4 your **r** and your staff, they comfort
Pr   13:24 He who spares the **r** hates his son,
       14: 3 A fool's talk brings a **r** to his back,
       22:15 but the **r** of discipline will drive it far
       23:13 if you punish him with the **r**,
       29:15 The **r** of correction imparts wisdom,
Isa 11: 4 He will strike the earth with the **r**

RODE [RIDE]

Hab   3: 8 when you **r** with your horses
Rev   6: 2 and he **r** out as a conqueror bent

RODS [ROD]

2Co 11:25 Three times I was beaten with **r**,

ROLL [ROLLED, ROLLING]

Am   5:24 But let justice **r** on like a river,
Mk 16: 3 "Who will **r** the stone away from
Heb   1:12 You will **r** them up like a robe;

ROLLED [ROLL]

Jos   5: 9 "Today I have **r** away the reproach
Lk   24: 2 They found the stone **r** away from

ROLLING [ROLL]

Rev   6:14 The sky receded like a scroll, **r** up,

ROMAN [ROME]

Ac 16:37 even though we are **R** citizens,
       22:25 "Is it legal for you to flog a **R** citizen

ROMANS [ROME]

Jn 11:48 then the **R** will come and take away

ROME [ROMAN, ROMANS]

Ac 18: 2 had ordered all the Jews to leave **R**.
       28:14 And so we came to **R**.
Ro   1:15 the gospel also to you who are at **R**.

ROOF [ROOFS]

Ge 19: 8 under the protection of my **r**."
Jos   2: 6 up to the **r** and hidden them
2Sa 11: 2 From the **r** he saw a woman bathing.
Ps 22:15 and my tongue sticks to the **r**
Pr 21: 9 to live on a corner of the **r** than share
Mt   8: 8 to have you come under my **r**.
Mk   2: 4 an opening in the **r** above Jesus
Ac 10: 9 Peter went up on the **r** to pray.

ROOFS [ROOF]

Mt 10:27 proclaim from the **r**.

ROOM [ROOMS, STOREROOM]

Mt   6: 6 But when you pray, go into your **r**,
Mk 14:15 He will show you a large upper **r**,
Lk   2: 7 there was no **r** for them in the inn.
Jn   8:37 because you have no **r** for my word.
      21:25 not have **r** for the books that would
Ro 12:19 but leave **r** for God's wrath,
2Co 7: 2 Make **r** for us in your hearts.

ROOMS [ROOM]

Mt 24:26 in the inner **r**,' do not believe it.
Lk 12: 3 in the inner **r** will be proclaimed
Jn 14: 2 In my Father's house are many **r**;

ROOSTER

Mt 26:34 "this very night, before the **r** crows,
       26:75 "Before the **r** crows,

ROOT [ROOTED, ROOTS]

Pr 12:12 but the **r** of the righteous flourishes.
Isa 11:10 the **R** of Jesse will stand as a banner
       53: 2 and like a **r** out of dry ground.
Mt   3:10 The ax is already at the **r** of the trees,
       13:21 But since he has no **r**,
Ro 11:16 if the **r** is holy, so are the branches.
       15:12 "The **R** of Jesse will spring up,
1Ti   6:10 the love of money is a **r** of all kinds

Rev 5: 5 the **R** of David, has triumphed.
22:16 the **R** and the Offspring of David,

ROOTED* [ROOT]

Eph 3:17 being **r** and established in love,
Col 2: 7 **r** and built up in him,

ROOTS [ROOT]

Isa 11: 1 from his **r** a Branch will bear fruit.
Jer 17: 8 that sends out its **r** by the stream.
Eze 17: 9 to pull it up by the **r.**
Hos 14: 5 of Lebanon he will send down his **r;**
Mt 15:13 will be pulled up by the **r.**

ROSE [RISE]

Ge 7:18 The waters **r** and increased greatly
1Ch 21: 1 Satan **r** up against Israel
SS 2: 1 I am a **r** of Sharon,
Eze 1:19 and when the living creatures **r** from
Mt 7:25 The rain came down, the streams **r,**
Ac 10:41 with him after he **r** from the dead.
1Th 4:14 that Jesus died and **r** again and

ROT [ROTS, ROTTED]

Pr 10: 7 but the name of the wicked will **r.**
Hos 5:12 like **r** to the people of Judah.
Zec 14:12 Their flesh will **r** while they are

ROTS* [ROT]

Pr 14:30 but envy **r** the bones.

ROTTED* [ROT]

Jas 5: 2 Your wealth has **r,**

ROUGH* [ROUGHER]

Isa 40: 4 the **r** ground shall become level,
42:16 and make the **r** places smooth.
Lk 3: 5 the **r** ways smooth.
Jn 6:18 and the waters grew **r.**

ROUGHER* [ROUGH]

Jnh 1:11 The sea was getting **r** and **r.**

ROUND

Ecc 1: 6 **r** and **r** it goes,

ROUSE [AROUSE, AROUSED]

Job 3: 8 those who are ready to **r** Leviathan.
Ps 59: 5 **r** yourself to punish all the nations;

ROUTED [ROUTS]

Ps 18:14 great bolts of lightning and **r** them.
Heb 11:34 in battle and **r** foreign armies.

ROUTS* [ROUTED]

Jos 23:10 One of you **r** a thousand,

ROW

Jnh 1:13 men did their best to **r** back to land.

ROYAL

Jos 11:12 Joshua took all these **r** cities
1Ki 9: 5 I will establish your **r** throne
2Ch 22:10 to destroy the whole **r** family of
Ps 45: 9 at your right hand is the **r** bride

Isa 62: 3 a **r** diadem in the hand of your God.
Da 1: 8 not to defile himself with the **r** food
Jas 2: 8 If you really keep the **r** law found
1Pe 2: 9 a **r** priesthood, a holy nation,

RUBBISH* [RUBBLE]

Php 3: 8 I consider them **r,**

RUBBLE [RUBBISH]

Jer 26:18 Jerusalem will become a heap of **r,**
Mic 3:12 Jerusalem will become a heap of **r,**

RUBIES [RUBY]

Job 28:18 the price of wisdom is beyond **r.**
Pr 3:15 She is more precious than **r;**
8:11 for wisdom is more precious than **r,**
31:10 She is worth far more than **r.**

RUBY [RUBIES]

Ex 28:17 In the first row there shall be a **r,**

RUDDER*

Jas 3: 4 they are steered by a very small **r**

RUDDY

1Sa 16:12 He was **r,** with a fine appearance
SS 5:10 My lover is radiant and **r,**

RUDE*

1Co 13: 5 It is not **r,** it is not self-seeking,

RUDIMENTS (KJV)

See BASIC PRINCIPLES

RUGGED

Ps 68:16 Why gaze in envy, O **r** mountains,
Isa 40: 4 the **r** places a plain.

RUIN [RUINED, RUINING, RUINS]

Dt 28:20 and come to sudden **r** because of
Job 22:19 righteous see their **r** and rejoice;
Pr 10: 8 but a chattering fool comes to **r.**
10:14 but the mouth of a fool invites **r.**
10:29 but it is the **r** of those who do evil.
18:24 of many companions may come to **r,**
19:13 A foolish son is his father's **r,**
26:28 and a flattering mouth works **r.**
SS 2:15 the little foxes that **r** the vineyards,
Isa 25: 2 the fortified town a **r,**
Eze 21:27 A **r!** A **r!** I will make it a **r!**
Hos 4:14 without understanding will come to **r**
Mic 6:13 to **r** you because of your sins.
Zep 1:15 a day of trouble and **r,**
Hag 1: 4 while this house remains a **r?"**
1Ti 6: 9 desires that plunge men into **r**
Rev 18:19 one hour she has been brought to **r!**

RUINED [RUIN]

Ex 10: 7 not yet realize that Egypt is **r?"**
Isa 3:14 "It is you who have **r** my vineyard;
6: 5 "I am **r!** For I am a man of unclean
Jer 4:27 "The whole land will be **r,**
Mt 12:25 divided against itself will be **r,**
Mk 2:22 the wine and the wineskins will be **r.**

RUINING* [RUIN]

Tit   1:11   they are **r** whole households

RUINS [RUIN]

Ezr   9: 9   the house of our God and repair its **r**,
Ne   2:17   Jerusalem lies in **r**,
Pr   19: 3   A man's own folly **r** his life,
Ecc   4: 5   fool folds his hands and **r** himself.
Isa   51: 3   look with compassion on all her **r**;
Jer   9:11   "I will make Jerusalem a heap of **r**,
Am   9:11   restore its **r**, and build it
Ac   15:16   Its **r** I will rebuild,
2Ti   2:14   and only **r** those who listen.

RULE [RULER, RULER'S, RULERS, RULES, RULING]

Ge   1:26   and let them **r** over the fish of the sea
      3:16   and he will **r** over you."
    37: 8   Will you actually **r** us?"
Dt   15: 6   You will **r** over many nations
Jdg   8:22   said to Gideon, "**R** over us—
1Sa 12:12   'No, we want a king to **r** over us'—
2Ch   6: 6   chosen David to **r** my people Israel.'
Ps   2: 9   You will **r** them with an iron scepter;
    7: 7   **R** over them from on high;
   67: 4   for you **r** the peoples justly
  119:133   let no sin **r** over me.
Pr   12:24   Diligent hands will **r**,
   17: 2   A wise servant will **r** over
Isa   28:10   **r** on **r**, **r** on **r**; a little here,
   32: 1   and rulers will **r** with justice.
Eze 20:33   I will **r** over you with a mighty hand
Mic   4: 7   The LORD will **r** over them
Zec   6:13   and will sit and **r** on his throne.
   9:10   His **r** will extend from sea to sea and
Ro   13: 9   are summed up in this one **r**:
   15:12   one who will arise to **r** over
1Co   7:17   the **r** I lay down in all the churches.
Gal   6:16   and mercy to all who follow this **r**,
Eph   1:21   far above all **r** and authority,
Col   3:15   the peace of Christ **r** in your hearts,
2Th   3:10   we gave you this **r**:
Rev   2:27   'He will **r** them with an iron scepter;
   12: 5   will **r** all the nations with an iron
   17:17   to give the beast their power to **r**,
   19:15   "He will **r** them with an iron

RULER [RULE]

Ex   2:14   "Who made you **r** and judge
2Sa   7: 8   and from following the flock to be **r**
Ps   8: 6   You made him **r** over the works
   82: 7   you will fall like every other **r**."
Pr   19: 6   Many curry favor with a **r**,
   23: 1   When you sit to dine with a **r**,
   25:15   patience a **r** can be persuaded,
   29:12   If a **r** listens to lies,
   29:26   Many seek an audience with a **r**,
Ecc   9:17   to be heeded than the shouts of a **r**
Isa   60:17   and righteousness your **r**.
Da   5:29   the third highest **r** in the kingdom.
   9:25   until the Anointed One, the **r**, comes,
Mic   5: 2   for me one who will be **r** over Israel,
Mt   2: 6   for out of you will come a **r**

Lk   8:41   Jairus, a **r** of the synagogue,
Ac   7:27   'Who made you **r** and judge over us?
Eph   2: 2   of the **r** of the kingdom of
1Ti   6:15   the blessed and only **R**,
Rev   1: 5   and the **r** of the kings of the earth.
   3:14   the **r** of God's creation.

RULER'S [RULE]

Ge   49:10   nor the **r** staff from between his feet,

RULERS [RULE]

Jdg   16: 5   The **r** of the Philistines went to her
Ps   2: 2   **r** gather together against the LORD
  119:161   **R** persecute me without cause,
Pr   8:15   By me kings reign and **r** make laws
   31: 4   not for **r** to crave beer,
Isa   1:10   you **r** of Sodom;
   32: 1   and **r** will rule with justice.
   40:23   and reduces the **r** of this world
Da   7:27   and all **r** will worship and obey him.'
Mt   2: 6   are by no means least among the **r**
   20:25   that the **r** of the Gentiles lord it
Ac   4:26   the **r** gather together against the Lord
   13:27   and their **r** did not recognize Jesus,
Ro   13: 3   For **r** hold no terror for those
1Co   2: 6   or of the **r** of this age,
Eph   3:10   the **r** and authorities in the heavenly
   6:12   flesh and blood, but against the **r**,
Col   1:16   whether thrones or powers or **r**

RULES [RULE]

Nu   15:15   the same **r** for you and for the alien
2Sa   23: 3   when he **r** in the fear of God,
Ps   22:28   and he **r** over the nations.
   66: 7   He **r** forever by his power,
  103:19   and his kingdom **r** over all.
Isa   29:13   made up only of **r** taught by men.
   40:10   and his arm **r** for him.
Mk   7: 7   are but **r** taught by men.'
Lk   22:26   one who **r** like the one who serves.
Col   2:20   do you submit to its **r**:
2Ti   2: 5   he competes according to the **r**.
Rev 17:18   the great city that **r** over the kings of

RULING [RULE]

Jn   3: 1   a member of the Jewish **r** council.

RUMOR [RUMORS]

Eze   7:26   calamity will come, and **r** upon **r**.
Jn   21:23   the **r** spread among the brothers

RUMORS [RUMOR]

Jer   51:46   or be afraid when **r** are heard in
Mt   24: 6   You will hear of wars and **r** of wars,

RUN [RAN, RUNNERS, RUNNING, RUNS]

1Sa   31: 4   "Draw your sword and **r** me through,
Ps   19: 5   a champion rejoicing to **r** his course.
  119:32   I **r** in the path of your commands,
Pr   4:12   when you **r**, you will not stumble.
   18:10   the righteous **r** to it and are safe.
Isa   10: 3   To whom will you **r** for help?
   40:31   they will **r** and not grow weary,

Jer 51:45 **R** from the fierce anger of
Joel 3:18 ravines of Judah will **r** with water.
Hab 2: 2 so that a herald may **r** with it.
Mt 6:32 the pagans **r** after all these things,
1Co 9:24 **R** in such a way as to get the prize.
Gal 2: 2 running or had **r** my race in vain.
Php 2:16 that I did not **r** or labor for nothing.
Heb 12: 1 let us **r** with perseverance the race

RUNNERS* [RUN]

1Co 9:24 not know that in a race all the **r** run,

RUNNING [RUN]

Ps 133: 2 **r** down on Aaron's beard,
Pr 5:15 **r** water from your own well.
Jnh 1:10 he was **r** away from the LORD,
Lk 17:23 Do not go **r** off after them.
1Co 9:26 I do not run like a man **r** aimlessly;
Gal 2: 2 **r** or had run my race in vain.
    5: 7 You were **r** a good race.

RUNS [RUN]

Jn 10:12 he abandons the sheep and **r** away.
2Jn 1: 9 Anyone who **r** ahead and does not

RUSH [RUSHING]

Pr 1:16 for their feet **r** into sin,
    6:18 feet that are quick to **r** into evil,
Isa 59: 7 Their feet **r** into sin;

RUSHING [RUSH]

Eze 1:24 like the roar of **r** waters,
    43: 2 like the roar of **r** waters,
Rev 1:15 like the sound of **r** waters.
    14: 2 from heaven like the roar of **r** waters
    19: 6 like the roar of **r** waters

RUST

Mt 6:19 where moth and **r** destroy,

RUTH

Moabitess; widow who went to Bethlehem with mother-in-law Naomi (Ru 1). Gleaned in field of Boaz; shown favor (Ru 2). Proposed marriage to Boaz (Ru 3). Married (Ru 4:1-12); bore Obed, ancestor of David (Ru 4:13-22), Jesus (Mt 1:5).

RUTHLESS [RUTHLESSLY]

Ps 37:35 a wicked and **r** man flourishing like
Pr 11:16 but **r** men gain only wealth.
Isa 29:20 The **r** will vanish,
Ro 1:31 faithless, heartless, **r**.

RUTHLESSLY [RUTHLESS]

Ex 1:14 the Egyptians used them **r**.
Lev 25:43 Do not rule over them **r**,

S

SABACHTHANI*

Mt 27:46 *"Eloi, Eloi, lama s?"*—

Mk 15:34 *"Eloi, Eloi, lama s?"*—

SABAOTH (KJV) See ALMIGHTY

SABBATH [SABBATHS]

Ex 16:23 a holy **S** to the LORD.
    20: 8 the **S** day by keeping it holy.
    31:14 " 'Observe the **S**, because it is holy
Lev 23:16 up to the day after the seventh **S**,
    25: 2 the land itself must observe a **s** to
Nu 15:32 found gathering wood on the **S** day.
Dt 5:12 the **S** day by keeping it holy,
2Ch 36:21 The land enjoyed its **s** rests;
Ne 13:17 desecrating the **S** day?
Ps 92: T A psalm. A song. For the **S** day.
Isa 56: 2 keeps the **S** without desecrating it,
    58:13 if you call the **S** a delight and
Jer 17:21 not to carry a load on the **S** day
Mt 12: 1 through the grainfields on the **S**.
Mk 2:28 Son of Man is Lord even of the **S**."
Lk 6: 9 "I ask you, which is lawful on the **S**:
    13:10 On a **S** Jesus was teaching in one of
    14: 3 "Is it lawful to heal on the **S** or not?"
Col 2:16 a New Moon celebration or a **S** day.

SABBATH-REST* [REST]

Heb 4: 9 then, a **S** for the people of God;

SABBATHS [SABBATH]

Ex 31:13 'You must observe my **S**.
Lev 26:34 then the land will rest and enjoy its **s**.
Eze 20:12 Also I gave them my **S** as a sign

SACKCLOTH

1Ch 21:16 David and the elders, clothed in **s**,
Ps 30:11 you removed my **s** and clothed me
Da 9: 3 in fasting, and in **s** and ashes.
Joel 1:13 Come, spend the night in **s**,
Jnh 3: 5 greatest to the least, put on **s**.
Mt 11:21 repented long ago in **s** and ashes.

SACRED

Ex 12:16 On the first day hold a **s** assembly,
    23:24 and break their **s** stones to pieces.
    28: 2 **s** garments for your brother Aaron,
    30:31 'This is to be my **s** anointing oil for
Lev 23: 2 to proclaim as **s** assemblies.
Ne 8:10 This day is **s** to our Lord.
Isa 1:29 be ashamed because of the **s** oaks
Hos 3: 4 without sacrifice or **s** stones,
Joel 1:14 Declare a holy fast; call a **s** assembly
Mt 7: 6 "Do not give dogs what is **s**;
Ro 14: 5 One man considers one day more **s**
1Co 3:17 for God's temple is **s**,
2Pe 1:18 with him on the **s** mountain.
    2:21 to turn their backs on the **s** command

SACRIFICE [SACRIFICED, SACRIFICES]

Ge 22: 2 **S** him there as a burnt offering
Ex 5:17 'Let us go and **s** to the LORD.'
    12:27 'It is the Passover **s** to the LORD,
Jdg 11:31 and I will **s** it as a burnt offering."
1Sa 2:13 that whenever anyone offered a **s**

	15:22	To obey is better than **s**,
1Ki	18:38	of the LORD fell and burned up the **s**,
1Ch	21:24	**s** a burnt offering that costs me
Ps	40: 6	**S** and offering you did not desire,
	50:14	**S** thank offerings to God,
	51:16	You do not delight in **s**,
	54: 6	I will **s** a freewill offering to you;
	107:22	Let them **s** thank offerings and tell
	141: 2	of my hands be like the evening **s**.
Pr	15: 8	LORD detests the **s** of the wicked,
	21: 3	acceptable to the LORD than **s**.
	21:27	The **s** of the wicked is detestable—
Eze	20:26	the **s** of every firstborn—
Da	8:13	the vision concerning the daily **s**,
	9:27	of the 'seven' he will put an end to **s**
	11:31	the daily **s** is abolished
Hos	6: 6	For I desire mercy, not **s**,
Zep	1: 7	The LORD has prepared a **s**;
Mt	9:13	'I desire mercy, not **s**.'
Ro	3:25	God presented him as a **s**
Eph	5: 2	up for us as a fragrant offering and **s**
Php	2:17	like a drink offering on the **s**
	4:18	an acceptable **s**, pleasing to God.
Heb	9:26	do away with sin by the **s** of himself.
	10: 5	"**S** and offering you did not desire,
	10:10	the **s** of the body of Jesus Christ once
	10:14	by one **s** he has made perfect forever
	10:18	there is no longer any **s** for sin.
	11: 4	a better **s** than Cain did.
	11:17	offered Isaac as a **s**.
	13:15	continually offer to God a **s** of praise
1Jn	2: 2	He is the atoning **s** for our sins,
	4:10	and sent his Son as an atoning **s**

SACRIFICED [SACRIFICE]

Ge	8:20	he **s** burnt offerings on it.
	22:13	and **s** it as a burnt offering instead
Lev	18:21	not give any of your children to be **s**
2Ki	17:17	They **s** their sons and daughters in
Lk	22: 7	the Passover lamb had to be **s**.
Ac	15:29	to abstain from food **s** to idols,
1Co	5: 7	our Passover lamb, has been **s**.
	8: 1	Now about food **s** to idols:
Heb	7:27	for his sins once for all
	9:28	so Christ was **s** once to take away
Rev	2:14	to sin by eating food **s** to idols
	2:20	and the eating of food **s** to idols.

SACRIFICES [SACRIFICE]

Ex	3:18	to offer **s** to the LORD our God.'
	22:20	"Whoever **s** to any god other than
Lev	17: 7	offer any of their **s** to the goat idols
Dt	12:31	sons and daughters in the fire as **s**
Jos	22:26	but not for burnt offerings or **s**.'
2Ch	7: 1	the burnt offering and the **s**,
	7:12	place for myself as a temple for **s**.
Ezr	6: 3	be rebuilt as a place to present **s**,
Ps	4: 5	Offer right **s** and trust in the LORD.
	50: 8	I do not rebuke you for your **s**
	50:23	He who **s** thank offerings honors me,
	51:17	The **s** of God are a broken spirit;
Isa	1:11	"The multitude of your **s**—
	56: 7	and **s** will be accepted on my altar;
Jer	6:20	your **s** do not please me."

Am	5:25	"Did you bring me **s** and
Mk	12:33	than all burnt offerings and **s**."
Ro	12: 1	to offer your bodies as living **s**,
1Co	10:20	**s** of pagans are offered to demons,
Heb	7:27	not need to offer **s** day after day,
	9:23	with better **s** than these.
	13:16	for with such **s** God is pleased.
1Pe	2: 5	offering spiritual **s** acceptable to God

SAD [SADDENED]

Ne	2: 1	not been **s** in his presence before;
Ecc	7: 3	because a **s** face is good for the heart.
Lk	18:23	he heard this, he became very **s**,

SADDENED* [SAD]

Mk	14:19	They were **s**, and one by one

SADDUCEES

Mt	16: 1	and **S** came to Jesus and tested him
	16: 6	the yeast of the Pharisees and **S**."
	22:34	that Jesus had silenced the **S**,
Mk	12:18	**S**, who say there is no resurrection,
Ac	23: 7	between the Pharisees and the **S**,

SAFE [SAVE]

Ezr	8:21	a **s** journey for us and our children,
Ps	12: 7	you will keep us **s** and protect us
	27: 5	the day of trouble he will keep me **s**
	37: 3	in the land and enjoy **s** pasture.
Pr	18:10	the righteous run to it and are **s**.
	28:18	whose walk is blameless is kept **s**,
	28:26	he who walks in wisdom is kept **s**.
	29:25	trusts in the LORD is kept **s**.
Jer	12: 5	If you stumble in **s** country,
Jn	17:12	I protected them and kept them **s** by
1Jn	5:18	who was born of God keeps him **s**,

SAFE-CONDUCT* [CONDUCT]

Ne	2: 7	so that they will provide me **s**

SAFEGUARD* [GUARD]

Php	3: 1	and it is a **s** for you.

SAFELY [SAVE]

Ge	19:16	and led them **s** out of the city,
	28:21	that I return **s** to my father's house,
Lev	25:18	and you will live **s** in the land.

SAFETY [SAVE]

Dt	12:10	around you so that you will live in **s**.
Ps	4: 8	O LORD, make me dwell in **s**.
Pr	3:23	Then you will go on your way in **s**,
Isa	14:30	and the needy will lie down in **s**.
Jer	33:16	and Jerusalem will live in **s**.
Eze	34:28	They will live in **s**,
Hos	2:18	so that all may lie down in **s**.
1Th	5: 3	people are saying, "Peace and **s**,"

SAIL [SAILED, SAILORS]

2Ch	20:37	and were not able to set **s** to trade.

SAILED [SAIL]

Jnh	1: 3	**s** for Tarshish to flee from the LORD.
Lk	8:23	As they **s**, he fell asleep.

SAILORS [SAIL]
Jnh 1: 5 the **s** were afraid and each cried out

SAINTS
1Sa 2: 9 He will guard the feet of his **s,**
2Ch 6:41 may your **s** rejoice in your goodness.
Ps 16: 3 As for the **s** who are in the land,
30: 4 Sing to the LORD, you **s** of his;
31:23 Love the LORD, all his **s!**
34: 9 Fear the LORD, you his **s,**
116:15 of the LORD is the death of his **s.**
149: 1 his praise in the assembly of the **s.**
149: 5 Let the **s** rejoice in this honor
149: 9 This is the glory of all his **s.**
Da 7:18 **s** of the Most High will receive
7:21 against the **s** and defeating them,
Ac 9:13 the harm he has done to your **s**
Ro 8:27 because the Spirit intercedes for the **s**
1Co 6: 2 that the **s** will judge the world?
Eph 1:15 and your love for all the **s,**
1:18 of his glorious inheritance in the **s,**
6:18 always keep on praying for all the **s.**
Col 1:12 to share in the inheritance of the **s**
1:26 but is now disclosed to the **s.**
1Ti 5:10 washing the feet of the **s,**
Phm 1: 7 have refreshed the hearts of the **s.**
Jude 1: 3 once for all entrusted to the **s.**
Rev 5: 8 which are the prayers of the **s.**
8: 3 with the prayers of all the **s,**
13: 7 war against the **s** and to conquer
14:12 **s** who obey God's commandments
16: 6 the blood of your **s** and prophets,
17: 6 was drunk with the blood of the **s,**
18:20 Rejoice, **s** and apostles and prophets!
19: 8 for the righteous acts of the **s.**)

SAKE [SAKES]
Ge 12:16 He treated Abram well for her **s,**
18:24 for the **s** of the fifty righteous people
Lev 26:45 But for their **s** I will remember
Jos 23: 3 to all these nations for your **s;**
1Sa 12:22 For the **s** of his great name
1Ki 11:12 for the **s** of David your father,
Ps 23: 3 of righteousness for his name's **s.**
25:11 For the **s** of your name, O LORD,
44:22 for your **s** we face death all day long;
69: 7 For I endure scorn for your **s,**
106: 8 Yet he saved them for his name's **s,**
109:21 deal well with me for your name's **s;**
132:10 For the **s** of David your servant,
Isa 42:21 It pleased the LORD for the **s**
43:25 for my own **s,**
48: 9 my own name's **s** I delay my wrath;
48:11 For my own **s,** for my own **s,**
62: 1 For Zion's **s** I will not keep silent,
Jer 14: 7 do something for the **s** of your name.
14:21 the **s** of your name do not despise us;
Eze 20: 9 for the **s** of my name I did
20:14 for the **s** of my name I did
20:22 for the **s** of my name I did
36:32 that I am not doing this for your **s,**
Da 9:17 For your **s,** O Lord,
Mt 10:39 loses his life for my **s** will find it.
19:29 for my **s** will receive a hundred times

Ro 8:36 "For your **s** we face death all day
9: 3 for the **s** of my brothers,
14:20 work of God for the **s** of food.
1Co 9:23 I do all this for the **s** of the gospel,
2Co 4:11 given over to death for Jesus' **s,**
12:10 That is why, for Christ's **s,**
Php 3: 7 now consider loss for the **s** of Christ.
Heb 11:26 disgrace for the **s** of Christ
1Pe 2:13 Submit yourselves for the Lord's **s**
3Jn 1: 7 the **s** of the Name that they went out,

SAKES* [SAKE]
2Co 8: 9 yet for your **s** he became poor,

SALE [SELL]
Dt 28:68 There you will offer yourselves for **s**
Ps 44:12 gaining nothing from their **s.**

SALEM
Ge 14:18 Then Melchizedek king of **S** brought
Heb 7: 2 "king of **S**" means "king of peace."

SALIVA*
1Sa 21:13 and letting **s** run down his beard.
Jn 9: 6 made some mud with the **s,**

SALT [SALTED, SALTINESS, SALTY]
Ge 19:26 and she became a pillar of **s.**
Lev 2:13 Season all your grain offerings with **s**
Nu 18:19 It is an everlasting covenant of **s**
2Ki 2:20 he said, "and put **s** in it."
Mt 5:13 "You are the **s** of the earth.
Mk 9:50 "**S** is good, but if it loses
Col 4: 6 full of grace, seasoned with **s,**
Jas 3:11 both fresh water and **s** water flow

SALTED [SALT]
Mk 9:49 Everyone will be **s** with fire.

SALTINESS [SALT]
Lk 14:34 "Salt is good, but if it loses its **s,**

SALTY [SALT]
Mt 5:13 how can it be made **s** again?

SALVATION* [SAVE]
Ex 15: 2 he has become my **s.**
2Sa 22: 3 my shield and the horn of my **s.**
23: 5 Will he not bring to fruition my **s**
1Ch 16:23 proclaim his **s** day after day.
2Ch 6:41 O LORD God, be clothed with **s,**
Ps 9:14 and there rejoice in your **s.**
13: 5 my heart rejoices in your **s.**
14: 7 **s** for Israel would come out of Zion!
18: 2 and the horn of my **s,**
27: 1 The LORD is my light and my **s—**
28: 8 a fortress of **s** for his anointed one.
35: 3 Say to my soul, "I am your **s."**
35: 9 in the LORD and delight in his **s.**
37:39 The **s** of the righteous comes from
40:10 I speak of your faithfulness and **s.**
40:16 who love your **s** always say,
50:23 that I may show him the **s** of God."
51:12 Restore to me the joy of your **s**
53: 6 **s** for Israel would come out of Zion!

62: 1 in God alone; my **s** comes from him.
62: 2 He alone is my rock and my **s;**
62: 6 He alone is my rock and my **s;**
62: 7 My **s** and my honor depend on God;
67: 2 your **s** among all nations.
69:13 O God, answer me with your sure **s.**
69:27 not let them share in your **s.**
69:29 may your **s,** O God, protect me.
70: 4 who love your **s** always say,
71:15 of your **s** all day long,
74:12 you bring **s** upon the earth.
85: 7 O LORD, and grant us your **s.**
85: 9 his **s** is near those who fear him,
91:16 and show him my **s."**
95: 1 to the Rock of our **s.**
96: 2 proclaim his **s** day after day.
98: 1 and his holy arm have worked **s**
98: 2 The LORD has made his **s** known
98: 3 the earth have seen the **s** of our God.
116:13 I will lift up the cup of **s** and
118:14 he has become my **s.**
118:21 you have become my **s.**
119:41 your **s** according to your promise;
119:81 faints with longing for your **s,**
119:123 My eyes fail, looking for your **s,**
119:155 **S** is far from the wicked,
119:166 I wait for your **s,** O LORD,
119:174 I long for your **s,** O LORD,
132:16 I will clothe her priests with **s,**
149: 4 he crowns the humble with **s.**
Isa 12: 2 Surely God is my **s;**
12: 2 he has become my **s."**
12: 3 draw water from the wells of **s.**
25: 9 and be glad in his **s."**
26: 1 God makes **s** its walls
26:18 We have not brought **s** to the earth;
30:15 "In repentance and rest is your **s,**
33: 2 our **s** in time of distress.
33: 6 a rich store of **s** and wisdom
45: 8 let **s** spring up,
45:17 by the LORD with an everlasting **s;**
46:13 and my **s** will not be delayed.
46:13 I will grant **s** to Zion,
49: 6 that you may bring my **s** to the ends
49: 8 and in the day of **s** I will help you;
51: 5 my **s** is on the way,
51: 6 But my **s** will last forever,
51: 8 my **s** through all generations."
52: 7 who proclaim **s,** who say to Zion,
52:10 of the earth will see the **s** of our God.
56: 1 for my **s** is close at hand
59:16 so his own arm worked **s** for him,
59:17 and the helmet of **s** on his head;
60:18 but you will call your walls **S**
61:10 he has clothed me with garments of **s**
62: 1 her **s** like a blazing torch.
63: 5 so my own arm worked **s** for me.
Jer 3:23 the LORD our God is the **s** of Israel.
La 3:26 wait quietly for the **s** of the LORD.
Jnh 2: 9 **S** comes from the LORD."
Zec 9: 9 righteous and having **s,**
Lk 1:69 He has raised up a horn of **s** for us in
1:71 **s** from our enemies and from
1:77 to give his people the knowledge of **s**

2:30 For my eyes have seen your **s,**
3: 6 And all mankind will see God's **s.' "**
19: 9 "Today **s** has come to this house,
Jn 4:22 for **s** is from the Jews.
Ac 4:12 **S** is found in no one else,
13:26 that this message of **s** has been sent.
13:47 that you may bring **s** to the ends of
28:28 to know that God's **s** has been sent to
Ro 1:16 for the **s** of everyone who believes:
11:11 **s** has come to the Gentiles
13:11 because our **s** is nearer now than
2Co 1: 6 it is for your comfort and **s;**
6: 2 and in the day of **s** I helped you."
6: 2 now is the day of **s.**
7:10 brings repentance that leads to **s**
Eph 1:13 the gospel of your **s.**
6:17 Take the helmet of **s** and the sword
Php 2:12 to work out your **s** with fear
1Th 5: 8 and the hope of **s** as a helmet.
5: 9 to suffer wrath but to receive **s**
2Ti 2:10 that they too may obtain the **s** that is
3:15 to make you wise for **s** through faith
Tit 2:11 that brings **s** has appeared to all men.
Heb 1:14 to serve those who will inherit **s?**
2: 3 if we ignore such a great **s?**
2: 3 This **s,** which was first announced by
2:10 of their **s** perfect through suffering.
5: 9 he became the source of eternal **s**
6: 9 things that accompany **s.**
9:28 to bring **s** to those who are waiting
1Pe 1: 5 until the coming of the **s**
1: 9 the **s** of your souls.
1:10 Concerning this **s,** the prophets,
2: 2 that by it you may grow up in your **s,**
2Pe 3:15 that our Lord's patience means **s,**
Jude 1: 3 to write to you about the **s** we share,
Rev 7:10 **"S** belongs to our God,
12:10 "Now have come the **s** and
19: 1 **S** and glory and power belong

SAMARIA [SAMARITAN, SAMARITANS]

1Ki 16:24 calling it **S,** after Shemer,
16:32 the temple of Baal that he built in **S.**
20:43 king of Israel went to his palace in **S.**
2Ki 17: 6 captured **S** and deported the
Israelites to Assyria.
Isa 7: 9 The head of Ephraim is **S,**
36:19 Have they rescued **S** from my hand?
Eze 23: 4 Oholah is **S,** and Oholibah
Hos 8: 5 Throw out your calf-idol, O **S!**
Am 6: 1 to you who feel secure on Mount **S,**
Mic 1: 6 I will make **S** a heap of rubble,
Jn 4: 4 Now he had to go through **S.**
Ac 1: 8 and in all Judea and **S,**
8: 1 scattered throughout Judea and **S.**
8:14 that **S** had accepted the word of God,

SAMARITAN [SAMARIA]

Lk 10:33 But a **S,** as he traveled,
17:16 and he was a **S.**
Jn 4: 7 a **S** woman came to draw water,
8:48 a **S** and demon-possessed?"
Ac 8:25 the gospel in many **S** villages.

SAMARITANS [SAMARIA]

Jn 4: 9 (For Jews do not associate with **S.**)

SAME

Ge	11: 6	one people speaking the **s** language
Ex	5: 8	the **s** number of bricks as before;
	7:11	the **s** things by their secret arts:
	7:22	the **s** things by their secret arts,
	8: 7	did the **s** things by their secret arts;
	34:16	they will lead your sons to do the **s.**
Dt	7:19	the **s** to all the peoples you now fear.
1Sa	2:34	both die on the **s** day.
Ps	102:27	But you remain the **s,**
Ecc	2:14	that the **s** fate overtakes them both.
	9: 3	The **s** destiny overtakes all.
Mt	5:12	for in the **s** way they persecuted
	7: 2	For in the **s** way you judge others,
Ac	1:11	will come back in the **s** way
	11:17	So if God gave them the **s** gift
Ro	2: 1	pass judgment do the **s** things.
	10:12	the **s** Lord is Lord of all
	12: 4	do not all have the **s** function,
1Co	10: 3	They all ate the **s** spiritual food
	12: 4	kinds of gifts, but the **s** Spirit.
	12: 5	kinds of service, but the **s** Lord.
Php	2: 5	Your attitude should be the **s** as that
1Ti	3: 6	under the **s** judgment as the devil.
Heb	1:12	But you remain the **s,**
	13: 8	Jesus Christ is the **s** yesterday

SAMSON*

Danite judge. Birth promised (Jdg 13). Married to Philistine, but wife given away (Jdg 14). Vengeance on the Philistines (Jdg 15). Betrayed by Delilah (Jdg 16:1-22). Death (Jdg 16:23-31). Feats of strength: killed lion (Jdg 14:6), 30 Philistines (Jdg 14:19), 1,000 Philistines with jawbone (Jdg 15:13-17), carried off gates of Gaza (Jdg 16:3), pushed down temple of Dagon (Jdg 16:25-30; Heb 11:32).

SAMUEL

Ephraimite judge and prophet (Heb 11:32). Birth prayed for (1Sa 1:10-18). Dedicated to temple by Hannah (1Sa 1:21-28). Raised by Eli (1Sa 2:11, 18-26). Called as prophet (1Sa 3). Led Israel to victory over Philistines (1Sa 7). Asked by Israel for a king (1Sa 8). Anointed Saul as king (1Sa 9-10). Farewell speech (1Sa 12). Rebuked Saul for sacrifice (1Sa 13). Announced rejection of Saul (1Sa 15). Anointed David as king (1Sa 16). Protected David from Saul (1Sa 19:18-24). Death (1Sa 25:1). Returned from dead to condemn Saul (1Sa 28).

SANBALLAT

Led opposition to Nehemiah's rebuilding of Jerusalem (Ne 2:10, 19; 4; 6).

SANCTIFIED* [SANCTIFY]

Jn	17:19	that they too may be truly **s.**
Ac	20:32	among all those who are **s.**
	26:18	and a place among those who are **s**
Ro	15:16	**s** by the Holy Spirit.

1Co	1: 2	to those **s** in Christ Jesus and called
	6:11	But you were washed, you were **s,**
	7:14	the unbelieving husband has been **s**
	7:14	and the unbelieving wife has been **s**
1Th	4: 3	It is God's will that you should be **s:**
Heb	10:29	the blood of the covenant that **s** him,

SANCTIFY* [SANCTIFIED, SANCTIFYING]

Jn	17:17	**S** them by the truth;
	17:19	For them **I** sanctify myself,
1Th	5:23	**s** you through and through.
Heb	9:13	who are ceremonially unclean **s** them

SANCTIFYING* [SANCTIFY]

2Th	2:13	to be saved through the **s** work
1Pe	1: 2	through the **s** work of the Spirit,

SANCTUARIES [SANCTUARY]

Lev 26:31 into ruins and lay waste your **s,**

SANCTUARY [SANCTUARIES]

Ex	15:17	you made for your dwelling, the **s,**
	25: 8	"Then have them make a **s** for me,
Lev	16: 3	how Aaron is to enter the **s** area:
	19:30	and have reverence for my **s.**
Nu	3:28	responsible for the care of the **s.**
	18: 1	for offenses against the **s,**
1Ki	6:19	the inner **s** within the temple
1Ch	22:19	to build the **s** of the LORD God,
Ezr	9: 8	and giving us a firm place in his **s,**
Ps	15: 1	LORD, who may dwell in your **s?**
	20: 2	May he send you help from the **s**
	60: 6	God has spoken from his **s:**
	63: 2	I have seen you in the **s**
	68:24	of my God and King into the **s.**
	68:35	You are awesome, O God, in your **s;**
	73:17	till I entered the **s** of God;
	74: 7	They burned your **s** to the ground;
	102:19	"The LORD looked down from his **s**
	114: 2	Judah became God's **s,**
	134: 2	Lift up your hands in the **s** and praise
	150: 1	Praise God in his **s;**
Isa	8:14	and he will be a **s;**
La	1:10	she saw pagan nations enter her **s—**
Eze	5:11	because you have defiled my **s**
	37:26	I will put my **s** among them forever.
	41: 1	the man brought me to the outer **s**
Da	8:11	the place of his **s** was brought low.
	9:26	will destroy the city and the **s.**
Heb	6:19	the inner **s** behind the curtain,
	8: 2	and who serves in the **s,**
	8: 5	at a **s** that is a copy and shadow
	9:24	Christ did not enter a man-made **s**

SAND

Ge	22:17	and as the **s** on the seashore.
	32:12	descendants like the **s** of the sea,
	41:49	like the **s** of the sea;
Ex	2:12	the Egyptian and hid him in the **s.**
1Ki	4:20	as numerous as the **s** on the seashore;
Jer	33:22	measureless as the **s** on the seashore.
Hos	1:10	"Yet the Israelites will be like the **s**
Mt	7:26	foolish man who built his house on **s.**

Ro   9:27   the Israelites be like the **s** by the sea,
Heb 11:12   as countless as the **s** on the seashore.
Rev 20: 8   In number they are like the **s** on

SANDAL [SANDALS]

Ge 14:23   not even a thread or the thong of a **s,**
Ru   4: 7   one party took off his **s** and gave it to

SANDALS [SANDAL]

Ex   3: 5   "Take off your **s,**
      12:11   your **s** on your feet and your staff
Dt 25: 9   take off one of his **s,**
      29: 5   nor did the **s** on your feet.
Jos   5:15   "Take off your **s,**
Mt   3:11   whose **s** I am not fit to carry.

SANG [SING]

Ex 15: 1   and the Israelites **s** this song to
      15:21   Miriam **s** to them:
Nu 21:17   Then Israel **s** this song:
Jdg   5: 1   son of Abinoam **s** this song:
1Sa 18: 7   As they danced, they **s:**
      29: 5   Isn't this the David they **s** about
2Sa   3:33   The king **s** this lament for Abner:
      22: 1   David **s** to the LORD the words
2Ch   5:13   in praise to the LORD and **s:**
      29:30   So they **s** praises with gladness
Ezr   3:11   With praise and thanksgiving they **s**
Ne 12:42   The choirs **s** under the direction
Job 38: 7   while the morning stars **s** together
Ps 106:12   his promises and **s** his praise.
Mt 11:17   we **s** a dirge,
Rev   5: 9   And they **s** a new song:
      5:12   In a loud voice they **s:**
      14: 3   And they **s** a new song before
      15: 3   and **s** the song of Moses the servant

SANHEDRIN

Mt 26:59   **S** were looking for false evidence
Jn 11:47   called a meeting of the **S.**
Ac   4:15   the **S** and then conferred together.
      5:21   they called together the **S—**
      6:12   and brought him before the **S.**

SANK [SINK]

Ex 15: 5   they **s** to the depths like a stone.
1Sa 17:49   The stone **s** into his forehead,
Jer 38: 6   and Jeremiah **s** down into the mud.
Jnh   2: 6   the roots of the mountains I **s** down;

SAP*

Hos   7: 9   Foreigners **s** his strength,
Ro 11:17   the nourishing **s** from the olive root,

SAPPHIRA*

Ac   5: 1   together with his wife **S,**

SAPPHIRE [SAPPHIRES]

Ex 24:10   like a pavement made of **s,**
      28:18   a **s** and an emerald;
Eze   1:26   what looked like a throne of **s,**
      10: 1   the likeness of a throne of **s** above
Rev 21:19   the second **s,** the third chalcedony,

SARAH [SARAI]

Wife of Abraham, originally named Sarai; barren (Ge 11:29-31; 1Pe 3:6). Taken by Pharaoh as Abraham's sister; returned (Ge 12:10-20). Gave Hagar to Abraham; sent her away in pregnancy (Ge 16). Name changed; Isaac promised (Ge 17:15-21; 18:10-15; Heb 11:11). Taken by Abimelech as Abraham's sister; returned (Ge 20). Isaac born; Hagar and Ishmael sent away (Ge 21:1-21; Gal 4:21-31). Death (Ge 23).

SARAI [SARAH]

Ge 17:15   you are no longer to call her **S;**

SARDIS

Rev   3: 1   the angel of the church in **S** write:

SASH [SASHES]

Ex 28: 4   a woven tunic, a turban and a **s.**
Isa 11: 5   faithfulness the **s** around his waist.
Rev   1:13   and with a golden **s** around his chest.

SASHES [SASH]

Rev 15: 6   wore golden **s** around their chests.

SAT [SIT]

Ge 48: 2   and **s** up on the bed.
Ex   2:15   where he **s** down by a well.
Jdg 19:15   They went and **s** in the city square,
Ru   4: 1   up to the town gate and **s** there.
1Ki 19: 4   **s** down under it and prayed
Ne   1: 4   I **s** down and wept.
Ps 137: 1   the rivers of Babylon we **s** and wept
Mt   5: 1   up on a mountainside and **s** down.
      13: 2   that he got into a boat and **s** in it,
      28: 2   rolled back the stone and **s** on it.
Lk   7:15   The dead man **s** up and began to talk,
      10:39   who **s** at the Lord's feet listening
Jn   4: 6   **s** down by the well.
      12:14   Jesus found a young donkey and **s**
Heb   1: 3   he **s** down at the right hand of
      8: 1   who **s** down at the right hand of
      10:12   he **s** down at the right hand of God.
      12: 2   and **s** down at the right hand of
Rev   3:21   just as I overcame and **s** down
      4: 3   And the one who **s** there had
      5: 1   of him who **s** on the throne

SATAN

1Ch 21: 1   **S** rose up against Israel
Job   1: 6   and **S** also came with them.
      2: 1   and **S** also came with them
Zec   3: 2   "The LORD rebuke you, **S!**
Mt   4:10   "Away from me, **S!**
      12:26   If **S** drives out **S,**
      16:23   "Get behind me, **S!**
Mk   4:15   **S** comes and takes away the word
Lk 10:18   "I saw **S** fall like lightning
      22: 3   Then **S** entered Judas,
Jn 13:27   **S** entered into him.
Ac   5: 3   that **S** has so filled your heart
      26:18   and from the power of **S** to God,
Ro 16:20   The God of peace will soon crush **S**
1Co   5: 5   hand this man over to **S,**

7: 5 so that **S** will not tempt you because
2Co 2:11 in order that **S** might not outwit us.
11:14 for **S** himself masquerades as
12: 7 a messenger of **S,** to torment me.
2Th 2: 9 in accordance with the work of **S**
1Ti 1:20 to **S** to be taught not to blaspheme.
5:15 already turned away to follow **S.**
Rev 2: 9 but are a synagogue of **S.**
2:13 where **S** has his throne.
3: 9 who are of the synagogue of **S,**
12: 9 **S,** who leads the whole world astray.
20: 2 who is the devil, or **S,**
20: 7 **S** will be released from his prison

SATISFACTION [SATISFY]

Ecc 2:24 and drink and find **s** in his work.
3:13 and find **s** in all his toil—

SATISFIED [SATISFY]

Lev 26:26 You will eat, but you will not be **s.**
Dt 6:11 then when you eat and are **s,**
Ps 17:15 I will be **s** with seeing your likeness.
22:26 The poor will eat and be **s;**
63: 5 My soul will be **s** as with the richest
104:28 they are **s** with good things.
105:40 and **s** them with the bread of heaven.
Pr 13: 4 the desires of the diligent are fully **s.**
18:20 with the harvest from his lips he is **s.**
27:20 Death and Destruction are never **s,**
30:15 three things that are never **s,**
Ecc 5:10 whoever loves wealth is never **s**
Isa 53:11 will see the light [of life] and be **s;**
Hos 13: 6 they were **s,** they became proud;
Mt 14:20 They all ate and were **s,**
15:37 They all ate and were **s.**
Lk 6:21 for you will be **s.**

SATISFIES* [SATISFY]

Ps 103: 5 who **s** your desires with good things
107: 9 for he **s** the thirsty and fills
147:14 and **s** you with the finest of wheat.

SATISFY [SATISFACTION, SATISFIED, SATISFIES]

Ps 90:14 **S** us in the morning with
91:16 With long life will I **s** him
132:15 her poor will I **s** with food.
145:16 open your hand and **s** the desires
Pr 5:19 may her breasts **s** you always,
6:30 if he steals to **s** his hunger
Isa 55: 2 and your labor on what does not **s?**
58:10 and **s** the needs of the oppressed,
Jer 31:25 refresh the weary and **s** the faint."
Joel 2:19 enough to **s** you fully;

SATYRS (KJV) See WILD GOATS

SAUL [PAUL]

1. Benjamite; anointed by Samuel as first king of Israel (1Sa 9-10). Defeated Ammonites (1Sa 11). Rebuked for offering sacrifice (1Sa 13:1-15). Defeated Philistines (1Sa 14). Rejected as king for failing to annihilate Amalekites (1Sa 15). Soothed from evil spirit by David (1Sa 16:14-23). Sent

David against Goliath (1Sa 17). Jealousy and attempted murder of David (1Sa 18:1-11). Gave David Michal as wife (1Sa 18:12-30). Second attempt to kill David (1Sa 19). Anger at Jonathan (1Sa 20:26-34). Pursued David: killed priests at Nob (1Sa 22), went to Keilah and Ziph (1Sa 23), life spared by David at En Gedi (1Sa 24) and in his tent (1Sa 26). Rebuked by Samuel's spirit for consulting witch at Endor (1Sa 28). Wounded by Philistines; took his own life (1Sa 31; 1Ch 10). Lamented by David (2Sa 1:17-27). Children (1Sa 14:49-51; 1Ch 8).

2. See PAUL

SAVAGE*

Lev 26: 6 I will remove **s** beasts from the land,
Ac 20:29 **s** wolves will come in among you

SAVE [SAFE, SAFELY, SAFETY, SALVATION, SAVED, SAVES, SAVING, SAVIOR]

Ge 45: 5 to **s** lives that God sent me ahead
Dt 4:42 into one of these cities and **s** his life.
2Sa 22:28 You **s** the humble,
1Ch 16:35 Cry out, "**S** us, O God our Savior;
Job 40:14 that your own right hand can **s** you.
Ps 6: 4 **s** me because of your unfailing love.
17: 7 you who **s** by your right hand
18:27 You **s** the humble but bring low
28: 9 **S** your people and bless
31:16 **s** me in your unfailing love.
51:14 **S** me from bloodguilt, O God,
69:35 for God will **s** Zion and rebuild
71: 2 turn your ear to me and **s** me.
72:13 and **s** the needy from death.
86: 2 **s** your servant who trusts in you.
89:48 or **s** himself from the power of
91: 3 he will **s** you from the fowler's snare
109:31 to **s** his life from those who
146: 3 in mortal men, who cannot **s.**
Pr 2:12 Wisdom will **s** you from the ways
2:16 It will **s** you also from the adulteress,
Isa 33:22 it is he who will **s** us.
35: 4 he will come to **s** you."
36:20 to **s** his land from me?
38:20 The LORD will **s** me,
45:20 who pray to gods that cannot **s.**
46: 7 it cannot **s** him from his troubles.
59: 1 arm of the LORD is not too short to **s,**
63: 1 in righteousness, mighty to **s.**"
Jer 15:20 I am with you to rescue and **s** you,"
17:14 **s** me and I will be saved,
La 4:17 for a nation that could not **s** us.
Eze 3:18 in order to **s** his life,
7:19 and gold will not be able to **s** them in
14:14 they could **s** only themselves
33:12 of the righteous man will not **s** him
34:22 I will **s** my flock,
Da 3:17 the God we serve is able to **s** us
Hos 1: 7 and I will **s** them—
Zep 1:18 nor their gold will be able to **s** them
3:17 he is mighty to **s.**
Zec 8: 7 "I will **s** my people from

Mt	1:21	he will **s** his people from their sins."
	16:25	wants to **s** his life will lose it,
	27:42	they said, "but he can't **s** himself!"
Lk	6: 9	to **s** life or to destroy it?"
	19:10	to seek and to **s** what was lost."
	23:37	the king of the Jews, save '?
Jn	3:17	but to **s** the world through him.
	12:27	'Father, **s** me from this hour'?
	12:47	to judge the world, but to **s** it.
Ac	2:40	"**S** yourselves from this corrupt
Ro	11:14	to envy and **s** some
1Co	7:16	whether you will **s** your husband?
	7:16	whether you will **s** your wife?
	9:22	by all possible means I might **s** some.
1Ti	1:15	came into the world to **s** sinners—
Heb	7:25	Therefore he is able to **s** completely
Jas	2:14	Can such faith **s** him?
	5:20	from the error of his way will **s** him
Jude	1:23	others from the fire and **s** them;

SAVED [SAVE]

Ex	14:30	That day the LORD **s** Israel
Dt	33:29	a people **s** by the LORD?
Jdg	2:16	judges, who **s** them out of the hands
2Ch	32:22	So the LORD **s** Hezekiah and
Ps	18: 3	and I am **s** from my enemies.
	22: 5	They cried to you and were **s**;
	33:16	No king is **s** by the size of his army;
	34: 6	the LORD heard him; he **s** him
	106: 8	Yet he **s** them for his name's sake,
	106:21	They forgot the God who **s** them,
	116: 6	I was in great need, he **s** me.
Isa	25: 9	we trusted in him, and he **s** us.
	45:17	But Israel will be **s** by the LORD
	45:22	"Turn to me and be **s**,
	64: 5	How then can we be **s**?
Jer	4:14	the evil from your heart and be **s**.
	8:20	and we are not **s**."
	17:14	save me and I will be **s**,
Eze	3:19	but you will have **s** yourself.
	33: 5	he would have **s** himself.
Joel	2:32	on the name of the LORD will be **s**;
Mt	10:22	stands firm to the end will be **s**.
	19:25	"Who then can be **s**?"
	24:13	stands firm to the end will be **s**.
Mk	15:31	"He **s** others," they said,
Lk	7:50	"Your faith has **s** you; go in peace."
	13:23	are only a few people going to be **s**?"
Jn	10: 9	whoever enters through me will be **s**.
Ac	2:21	on the name of the Lord will be **s**.'
	2:47	daily those who were being **s**.
	4:12	to men by which we must be **s**."
	15:11	of our Lord Jesus that we are **s**,
	16:30	"Sirs, what must I do to be **s**?"
Ro	5: 9	be **s** from God's wrath through him!
	8:24	For in this hope we were **s**.
	9:27	only the remnant will be **s**.
	10: 1	the Israelites is that they may be **s**.
	10: 9	from the dead, you will be **s**.
	10:13	on the name of the Lord will be **s**."
	11:26	so all Israel will be **s**, as it is written:
1Co	1:18	to us who are being **s** it is the power
	3:15	he himself will be **s**,
	5: 5	be destroyed and his spirit **s** on

	10:33	so that they may be **s**.
	15: 2	By this gospel you are **s**,
Eph	2: 5	it is by grace you have been **s**.
	2: 8	For it is by grace you have been **s**,
2Th	2:10	refused to love the truth and so be **s**.
	2:13	the beginning God chose you to be **s**
1Ti	2: 4	who wants all men to be **s**
	2:15	will be **s** through childbearing—
2Ti	1: 9	who has **s** us and called us to
Tit	3: 5	he **s** us, not because of righteous
	3: 5	He **s** us through the washing
Heb	10:39	but of those who believe and are **s**.
1Pe	4:18	"If it is hard for the righteous to be **s**,

SAVES [SAVE]

1Sa	17:47	by sword or spear that the LORD **s**;
Ps	7:10	who is the upright in heart.
	34:18	**s** those who are crushed in spirit.
	55:16	I call to God, and the LORD **s** me.
	68:20	Our God is a God who **s**;
	145:19	he hears their cry and **s** them.
Pr	14:25	A truthful witness **s** lives,
1Pe	3:21	It **s** you by the resurrection

SAVING [SAVE]

Ge	50:20	the **s** of many lives.
1Sa	14: 6	Nothing can hinder the LORD from **s**,

SAVIOR* [SAVE]

Dt	32:15	and rejected the Rock his **S**.
2Sa	22: 3	my refuge and my **s**—
	22:47	Exalted be God, the Rock, my **S**!
1Ch	16:35	Cry out, "Save us, O God our **S**;
Ps	18:46	Exalted be God my **S**!
	24: 5	and vindication from God his **S**.
	25: 5	for you are God my **S**,
	27: 9	O God my **S**.
	38:22	O Lord my **S**.
	42: 5	I will yet praise him, my **S** and
	42:11	my **S** and my God.
	43: 5	my **S** and my God.
	65: 5	O God our **S**,
	68:19	Praise be to the Lord, to God our **S**,
	79: 9	Help us, O God our **S**,
	85: 4	Restore us again, O God our **S**,
	89:26	my God, the Rock my **S**.'
Isa	17:10	You have forgotten God your **S**;
	19:20	he will send them a **s** and defender,
	43: 3	the Holy One of Israel, your **S**;
	43:11	and apart from me there is no **s**.
	45:15	O God and **S** of Israel.
	45:21	a righteous God and a **S**;
	49:26	am your **S**, your Redeemer,
	60:16	am your **S**, your Redeemer,
	62:11	'See, your **S** comes!
	63: 8	and so he became their **S**.
Jer	14: 8	its **S** in times of distress,
Hos	13: 4	no **S** except me.
Mic	7: 7	I wait for God my **S**;
Hab	3:18	I will be joyful in God my **S**.
Lk	1:47	and my spirit rejoices in God my **S**,
	2:11	the town of David a **S** has been born
Jn	4:42	that this man really is the **S** of
Ac	5:31	to his own right hand as Prince and **S**

	13:23	brought to Israel the **S** Jesus,
Eph	5:23	his body, of which he is the **S**.
Php	3:20	we eagerly await a **S** from there,
1Ti	1: 1	by the command of God our **S** and
	2: 3	This is good, and pleases God our **S**,
	4:10	who is the **S** of all men,
2Ti	1:10	through the appearing of our **S**,
Tit	1: 3	by the command of God our **S**,
	1: 4	the Father and Christ Jesus our **S**.
	2:10	teaching about God our **S** attractive.
	2:13	appearing of our great God and **S**,
	3: 4	and love of God our **S** appeared,
	3: 6	through Jesus Christ our **S**,
2Pe	1: 1	of our God and **S** Jesus Christ
	1:11	of our Lord and **S** Jesus Christ.
	2:20	by knowing our Lord and **S** Jesus
	3: 2	command given by our Lord and **S**
	3:18	of our Lord and **S** Jesus Christ.
1Jn	4:14	has sent his Son to be the **S**
Jude	1:25	to the only God our **S** be glory,

SAW [SEE]

Ge	1: 4	God **s** that the light was good,
	1:31	God **s** all that he had made,
	3: 6	the woman **s** that the fruit of the tree
	6: 2	the sons of God **s** that the daughters
	6:12	God **s** how corrupt the earth
	22:13	in a thicket he **s** a ram caught
Ex	2: 2	When she **s** that he was a fine child,
	2: 5	She **s** the basket among the reeds
	2:11	He **s** an Egyptian beating a Hebrew,
	3: 2	Moses **s** that though the bush was
	24:10	and **s** the God of Israel.
	34:35	they **s** that his face was radiant.
Nu	22:23	When the donkey **s** the angel of
Dt	4:15	You **s** no form of any kind the day
	32:19	The LORD **s** this and rejected them
2Sa	11: 2	From the roof he **s** a woman bathing.
Ps	31: 7	for you **s** my affliction and knew
	73: 3	when I **s** the prosperity of the wicked
	139:16	your eyes **s** my unformed body.
Ecc	2:13	I **s** that wisdom is better than folly,
	8:17	then I **s** all that God has done.
Isa	6: 1	I **s** the Lord seated on a throne,
Eze	1: 1	and I **s** visions of God.
Da	2:26	"Are you able to tell me what I **s**
	4:10	the visions I **s** while lying in my bed:
	8: 2	In my vision I **s** myself in the citadel
	10: 7	was the only one who **s** the vision;
Am	9: 1	I **s** the Lord standing by the altar,
Mt	2: 2	We **s** his star in the east
	3:16	he **s** the Spirit of God descending
	9: 2	When Jesus **s** their faith,
Mk	1:10	he **s** heaven being torn open and
	3:11	Whenever the evil spirits **s** him,
Lk	9:32	they **s** his glory and
Jn	1:29	The next day John **s** Jesus coming
	19:35	man who **s** it has given testimony,
	20: 1	**s** that the stone had been removed
	20: 8	He **s** and believed.
Ac	2: 3	They **s** what seemed to be tongues
	7:55	up to heaven and **s** the glory of God,
	10:11	He **s** heaven opened and something
Heb	11:27	because he **s** him who is invisible.

Rev	1: 2	who testifies to everything he **s**—
	1:12	I turned I **s** seven golden lampstands,
	5: 6	Then I **s** a Lamb,
	21: 1	I **s** a new heaven and a new earth,
	22: 8	the one who heard and **s** these things.

SAY [SAYING, SAYINGS, SAYS]

Ge	3: 1	"Did God really **s**, 'You must not eat
	12:19	Why did you **s**, 'She is my sister,'
	18:13	"Why did Sarah laugh and **s**,
	26: 9	Why did you **s**, 'She is my sister'?"
Ex	7: 2	to **s** everything I command you,
Job	40: 5	but I will **s** no more."
Pr	4:10	Listen, my son, accept what I **s**,
	5: 7	not turn aside from what I **s**.
	8: 6	Listen, for I have worthy things to **s**;
Mt	10:19	worry about what to **s** or how to **s** it.
	16:15	"Who do you **s** I am?"
Mk	2: 9	Which is easier: to **s** to the paralytic,
	8:27	"Who do people **s** I am?"
Lk	11:54	to catch him in something he might **s**
Jn	8:26	"I have much to **s** in judgment
	8:43	you are unable to hear what I **s**.
	12:49	commanded me what to **s** and how to **s** it,
	16:12	"I have much more to **s** to you,
1Co	15:12	of you **s** that there is no resurrection
Tit	2:12	to **s** "No" to ungodliness
Rev	22:17	The Spirit and the bride **s**, "Come!"

SAYING [SAY]

1Ti	1:15	Here is a trustworthy **s**
	3: 1	Here is a trustworthy **s:**
	4: 9	This is a trustworthy **s**
2Ti	2:11	Here is a trustworthy **s:**
Tit	3: 8	This is a trustworthy **s.**

SAYINGS [SAY]

Pr	1: 6	the **s** and riddles of the wise.
	22:17	listen to the **s** of the wise;
Ecc	12:11	collected **s** like firmly embedded
Jn	10:21	are not the **s** of a man possessed

SAYS [SAY]

Ex	23:22	If you listen carefully to what he **s**
1Sa	9: 6	and everything he **s** comes true.
Ps	14: 1	fool **s** in his heart, "There is no God.
	53: 1	fool **s** in his heart, "There is no God.
Ac	19:26	**s** that man-made gods are no gods
Ro	3:19	we know that whatever the law **s**,
Jas	1:23	the word but does not do what it **s** is

WHAT THE SOVEREIGN †LORD SAYS
See †LORD

WHAT THE †LORD SAYS See †LORD

THE †LORD ALMIGHTY SAYS
See †LORD

SAYS THE †LORD See †LORD

SCABBARD

Jer	47: 6	Return to your **s**; cease and be still.'
Eze	21: 3	I will draw my sword from its **s**

SCALE [SCALES]

| 1Sa | 17: 5 | and wore a coat of **s** armor |

Ps   18:29   with my God I can **s** a wall.

SCALES [SCALE]

Lev	11: 9	you may eat any that have fins and **s.**
	19:36	Use honest **s** and honest weights,
Pr	11: 1	The LORD abhors dishonest **s,**
	16:11	Honest **s** and balances are from
Da	5:27	something like **s** fell from Saul's
Ac	9:18	something like **s** fell from Saul's
Rev	6: 5	Its rider was holding a pair of **s**

SCAPEGOAT [GOAT]

Lev   16:10   by sending it into the desert as a **s.**

SCARECROW*

Jer   10: 5   Like a **s** in a melon patch,

SCARLET

Ge	38:28	a **s** thread and tied it on his wrist
Ex	25: 4	purple and **s** yarn and fine linen;
Lev	14: 4	**s** yarn and hyssop be brought for
Nu	19: 6	hyssop and **s** wool and throw them
Jos	2:21	she tied the **s** cord in the window.
Isa	1:18	"Though your sins are like **s,**
Mt	27:28	They stripped him and put a **s** robe
Heb	9:19	**s** wool and branches of hyssop,
Rev	17: 3	a **s** beast that was covered with

SCATTER [SCATTERED, SCATTERING, SCATTERS]

Lev	26:33	I will **s** among the nations
Dt	4:27	The LORD will **s** you among
Ne	1: 8	I will **s** you among the nations,
Ecc	3: 5	to **s** stones and a time to gather them,
Jer	9:16	I will **s** them among nations
	30:11	the nations among which I **s** you,
Zec	10: 9	Though I **s** them among the peoples,

SCATTERED [SCATTER]

Ge	11: 4	a name for ourselves and not be **s**
Nu	10:35	May your enemies be **s;**
Dt	30: 3	from all the nations where he **s** you.
2Ch	18:16	"I saw all Israel **s** on the hills
Ps	89:10	your strong arm you **s** your enemies.
	112: 9	He has **s** abroad his gifts to the poor,
Isa	11:12	the **s** people of Judah from
Jer	31:10	'He who **s** Israel will gather them
La	4:16	The LORD himself has **s** them;
Eze	34:12	As a shepherd looks after his **s** flock
Zep	3:19	and gather those who have been **s.**
Zec	1:19	"These are the horns that **s** Judah,
	2: 6	"for I have **s** you to the four winds
	13: 7	and the sheep will be **s,**
Mt	26:31	and the sheep of the flock will be **s.**'
Jn	11:52	but also for the **s** children of God,
Ac	8: 1	were **s** throughout Judea and Samaria
	8: 4	Those who had been **s** preached
2Co	9: 9	"He has **s** abroad his gifts
Jas	1: 1	To the twelve tribes **s** among
1Pe	1: 1	**s** throughout Pontus, Galatia,

SCATTERING [SCATTER]

Jer	23: 1	and **s** the sheep of my pasture!"
Mk	4: 4	As he was **s** the seed,

SCATTERS [SCATTER]

Mt	12:30	he who does not gather with me **s.**
Jn	10:12	the wolf attacks the flock and **s** it.

SCEPTER

Ge	49:10	The **s** will not depart from Judah,
Nu	24:17	a **s** will rise out of Israel.
Est	4:11	the king to extend the gold **s** to him
Ps	2: 9	You will rule them with an iron **s;**
	45: 6	a **s** of justice will be the **s** of your
	125: 3	The **s** of the wicked will not remain
Heb	1: 8	and righteousness will be the **s**
Rev	2:27	'He will rule them with an iron **s;**
	12: 5	rule all the nations with an iron **s.**
	19:15	"He will rule them with an iron **s.**"

SCHEME [SCHEMES, SCHEMING]

Est	9:25	the evil **s** Haman had devised against
Ecc	7:27	to discover the **s** of things—

SCHEMES [SCHEME]

Ex	21:14	But if a man **s** and kills another
Ps	21:11	against you and devise wicked **s,**
Pr	6:18	a heart that devises wicked **s,**
	24: 9	The **s** of folly are sin,
2Co	2:11	For we are not unaware of his **s.**
Eph	6:11	stand against the devil's **s.**

SCHEMING* [SCHEME]

Ne	6: 2	But they were **s** to harm me;
Eph	4:14	of men in their deceitful **s.**

SCHOOL (KJV) See LECTURE HALL

SCHOOLMASTER (KJV)
See SUPERVISION, PUT IN CHARGE

SCHOLAR*

1Co   1:20   Where is the **s?**

SCOFF [SCOFFED, SCOFFERS, SCOFFS]

Ps	59: 8	you **s** at all those nations.
La	2:15	they **s** and shake their heads

SCOFFED* [SCOFF]

2Ch   36:16   and **s** at his prophets until the wrath

SCOFFERS [SCOFF]

Isa	28:14	you **s** who rule this people
2Pe	3: 3	that in the last days **s** will come,

SCOFFS* [SCOFF]

Ps	2: 4	the Lord **s** at them.
Pr	29: 9	the fool rages and **s,**

SCOOP*

Pr   6:27   Can a man **s** fire into his lap

SCORCH* [SCORCHED, SCORCHING]

Rev   16: 8   the sun was given power to **s** people

SCORCHED [SCORCH]

Ge   41:27   the seven worthless heads of grain **s**

Pr	6:28	hot coals without his feet being **s?**
Da	3:27	not **s,** and there was no smell of fire
Mk	4: 6	the sun came up, the plants were **s,**

SCORCHING [SCORCH]

Jnh	4: 8	God provided a **s** east wind,
Jas	1:11	the sun rises with **s** heat and withers

SCORN [SCORNED, SCORNING, SCORNS]

Ps	39: 8	not make me the **s** of fools.
	69: 7	For I endure **s** for your sake,
	69:20	**S** has broken my heart
	89:41	he has become the **s** of his neighbors.
	109:25	I am an object of **s** to my accusers;
	119:22	Remove from me **s** and contempt,
Isa	43:28	to destruction and Israel to **s.**
Eze	36: 7	nations around you will also suffer **s.**
Mic	6:16	you will bear the **s** of the nations."

SCORNED [SCORN]

Ps	22: 6	**s** by men and despised by the people.
SS	8: 7	it would be utterly **s.**

SCORNING* [SCORN]

Heb	12: 2	endured the cross, **s** its shame,

SCORNS* [SCORN]

Pr	13:13	He who **s** instruction will pay for it,
	30:17	that **s** obedience to a mother,

SCORPION [SCORPIONS]

Lk	11:12	for an egg, will give him a **s?**
Rev	9: 5	was like that of the sting of a **s**

SCORPIONS [SCORPION]

1Ki	12:11	I will scourge you with **s.'** "
Rev	9:10	They had tails and stings like **s,**

SCOUNDREL [SCOUNDREL'S, SCOUNDRELS]

Pr	6:12	A **s** and villain,
	16:27	A **s** plots evil,

SCOUNDREL'S* [SCOUNDREL]

Isa	32: 7	The **s** methods are wicked,

SCOUNDRELS [SCOUNDREL]

1Ki	21:10	But seat two **s** opposite him

SCOURGE

Ps	39:10	Remove your **s** from me;
Isa	28:15	When an overwhelming **s** sweeps by,
	28:18	the overwhelming **s** sweeps by,

SCREAM*

Ge	39:15	When he heard me **s** for help,
Dt	22:24	in a town and did not **s** for help,

SCRIBE [SCRIBE'S]

Ne	8: 1	They told Ezra the **s** to bring out
	12:36	Ezra the **s** led the procession.
Jer	36:32	and gave it to the **s** Baruch

SCRIBE'S* [SCRIBE]

Jer	36:23	the king cut them off with a **s** knife

SCRIPTURE [SCRIPTURES]

Mk	12:10	Haven't you read this **s:**
Lk	4:21	"Today this **s** is fulfilled
Jn	2:22	Then they believed the **S** and
	7:42	the **S** say that the Christ will come
	10:35	and the **S** cannot be broken—
Ac	1:16	the **S** had to be fulfilled which
	8:32	was reading this passage of **S:**
1Ti	4:13	to the public reading of **S,**
2Ti	3:16	All **S** is God-breathed and is useful
2Pe	1:20	that no prophecy of **S** came about by

SCRIPTURES [SCRIPTURE]

Da	9: 2	I, Daniel, understood from the **S,**
Mt	22:29	not know the **S** or the power of God.
Mk	14:49	But the **S** must be fulfilled."
Lk	24:27	to them what was said in all the **S**
	24:45	so they could understand the **S.**
Jn	5:39	You diligently study the **S** because
	5:39	These are the **S** that testify about me,
Ac	17:11	and examined the **S** every day to see
	18:28	from the **S** that Jesus was the Christ.
1Co	15: 3	died for our sins according to the **S,**
	15: 4	on the third day according to the **S,**
2Ti	3:15	you have known the holy **S,**
2Pe	3:16	as they do the other **S,**

SCROLL [SCROLLS]

Ex	17:14	a **s** as something to be remembered
Dt	17:18	for himself on a **s** a copy of this law,
1Sa	10:25	He wrote them down on a **s**
Ps	40: 7	it is written about me in the **s.**
Isa	8: 1	"Take a large **s** and write on it with
	29:11	but words sealed in a **s.**
	34: 4	and the sky rolled up like a **s;**
Jer	36: 4	Baruch wrote them on the **s.**
	45: 1	after Baruch had written on a **s**
Eze	3: 1	eat what is before you, eat this **s;**
Da	12: 4	close up and seal the words of the **s**
Zec	5: 1	and there before me was a flying **s!**
Mal	3:16	A **s** of remembrance was written
Lk	4:17	The **s** of the prophet Isaiah
Heb	10: 7	it is written about me in the **s—**
Rev	1:11	"Write on a **s** what you see and send
	5: 2	to break the **s** and open the **s?"**
	6:14	The sky receded like a **s,** rolling up,
	10: 8	take the **s** that lies open in the hand

SCROLLS [SCROLL]

Ac	19:19	had practiced sorcery brought their **s**
2Ti	4:13	and my **s,** especially the parchments.

SCUM*

La	3:45	You have made us **s** and refuse
1Co	4:13	we have become the **s** of the earth,

SEA [SEAS, SEASHORE]

Ge	1:26	let them rule over the fish of the **s**
	32:12	like the sand of the **s,**
	41:49	like the sand of the **s;**
Ex	14:16	the Israelites can go through the **s**

14:27 the LORD swept them into the **s**.
15: 1 and its rider he has hurled into the **s**.
Nu 11:31 and drove quail in from the **s**.
34: 6 will be the coast of the Great **S**.
Dt 11:24 the Euphrates River to the western **s**.
30:13 Nor is it beyond the **s**,
1Ki 7:23 He made the **S** of cast metal,
2Ki 25:13 the movable stands and the bronze **S**
Ne 9:11 You divided the **s** before them,
Job 11: 9 the earth and wider than the **s**.
Ps 46: 2 fall into the heart of the **s**,
74:13 It was you who split open the **s**
93: 4 mightier than the breakers of the **s**—
95: 5 The **s** is his, for he made it,
106: 7 and they rebelled by the **s**, the Red **S**.
139: 9 if I settle on the far side of the **s**,
Ecc 1: 7 yet the **s** is never full.
Isa 10:22 O Israel, be like the sand by the **s**,
48:18 righteousness like the waves of the **s**.
57:20 But the wicked are like the tossing **s**,
Da 7: 3 came up out of the **s**.
Jnh 1: 4 LORD sent a great wind on the **s**,
Mic 7:19 iniquities into the depths of the **s**.
Hab 2:14 as the waters cover the **s**.
Zec 9:10 His rule will extend from **s** to **s**
Mt 18: 6 to be drowned in the depths of the **s**,
Mk 11:23 'Go, throw yourself into the **s**,'
1Co 10: 1 that they all passed through the **s**.
Heb 11:29 the people passed through the Red **S**
Jas 1: 6 who doubts is like a wave of the **s**,
Jude 1:13 They are wild waves of the **s**,
Rev 4: 6 what looked like a **s** of glass,
8: 8 A third of the **s** turned into blood,
10: 2 on the **s** and his left foot on the land,
13: 1 I saw a beast coming out of the **s**.
15: 2 like a **s** of glass mixed with fire and,
20:13 The **s** gave up the dead that were
21: 1 and there was no longer any **s**.

SEAL [SEALED, SEALS]

Ex 28:21 each engraved like a **s** with the name
Est 8: 8 and **s** it with the king's signet ring—
Ps 40: 9 I do not **s** my lips,
SS 8: 6 Place me like a **s** over your heart,
Isa 8:16 and **s** up the law among my disciples.
Da 8:26 but **s** up the vision,
9:24 to **s** up vision and prophecy and
12: 4 close up and **s** the words of the scroll
Mt 27:66 secure by putting a **s** on the stone
Jn 6:27 him God the Father has placed his **s**
1Co 9: 2 the **s** of my apostleship in the Lord.
2Co 1:22 set his **s** of ownership on us,
Eph 1:13 you were marked in him with a **s**,
Rev 6: 3 When the Lamb opened the second **s**,
6: 5 When the Lamb opened the third **s**,
6: 7 When the Lamb opened the fourth **s**,
6: 9 When he opened the fifth **s**,
6:12 I watched as he opened the sixth **s**.
7: 2 having the **s** of the living God.
7: 3 a **s** on the foreheads of the servants
8: 1 When he opened the seventh **s**,
9: 4 who did not have the **s** of God on
10: 4 "**S** up what the seven thunders have
22:10 not **s** up the words of the prophecy

SEALED [SEAL]

Isa 29:11 but words **s** in a scroll.
Da 6:17 the king **s** it with his own signet ring
12: 9 the words are closed up and **s** until
Eph 4:30 with whom you were **s** for the day
2Ti 2:19 **s** with this inscription:
Rev 5: 1 on both sides and **s** with seven seals.
7: 4 the number of those who were **s**:
20: 3 and locked and **s** it over him,

SEALS [SEAL]

Rev 5: 2 "Who is worthy to break the **s**
6: 1 Lamb opened the first of the seven **s**.

SEAMLESS*

Jn 19:23 This garment was **s**,

SEARCH [SEARCHED, SEARCHES, SEARCHING]

Ezr 5:17 let a **s** be made in the royal archives
Est 2: 2 "Let a **s** be made for beautiful
Ps 4: 4 **s** your hearts and be silent.
139:23 **S** me, O God, and know my heart;
Pr 2: 4 and **s** for it as for hidden treasure,
25: 2 to **s** out a matter is the glory
Ecc 3: 6 a time to **s** and a time to give up,
SS 3: 2 I will **s** for the one my heart loves.
Jer 17:10 "I the LORD **s** the heart
Eze 34:11 I myself will **s** for my sheep
34:16 I will **s** for the lost and bring back
Mt 2: 8 and make a careful **s** for the child.
Lk 15: 8 and **s** carefully until she finds it?

SEARCHED [SEARCH]

1Sa 23:14 Day after day Saul **s** for him,
Ps 139: 1 you have **s** me and you know me.
Ecc 12:10 Teacher **s** to find just the right words,
1Pe 1:10 **s** intently and with the greatest care,

SEARCHES [SEARCH]

1Ch 28: 9 for the LORD **s** every heart
Ps 7: 9 who **s** minds and hearts,
Pr 11:27 but evil comes to him who **s** for it.
20:27 lamp of the LORD **s** the spirit
Ro 8:27 And he who **s** our hearts knows
1Co 2:10 The Spirit **s** all things,
Rev 2:23 that I am he who **s** hearts and minds,

SEARCHING [SEARCH]

Jdg 5:15 of Reuben there was much **s** of heart.
Am 8:12 **s** for the word of the LORD,
Lk 2:49 "Why were you **s** for me?"

SEARED*

1Ti 4: 2 whose consciences have been **s** as
Rev 16: 9 They were **s** by the intense heat

SEAS [SEA]

Ge 1:10 the gathered waters he called "**s**."
Ps 65: 7 who stilled the roaring of the **s**,
93: 3 The **s** have lifted up, O LORD,
Jnh 2: 3 into the very heart of the **s**,

SEASHORE [SEA]

Ge 22:17 in the sky and the sand on the **s**.
Jos 11: 4 as numerous as the sand on the **s**.
1Ki 4:20 as numerous as the sand on the **s;**
       4:29 as measureless as the sand on the **s**.
Jer 33:22 measureless as the sand on the **s**.' "
Hos 1:10 will be like the sand on the **s**,
Heb 11:12 and as countless as the sand on the **s**.
Rev 20: 8 they are like the sand on the **s**.

SEASON [SEASONED, SEASONS]

Lev 2:13 **S** all your grain offerings with salt.
      26: 4 I will send you rain in its **s**,
Dt 28:12 to send rain on your land in **s** and
Ps   1: 3 which yields its fruit in **s**
Pr 20: 4 A sluggard does not plow in **s;**
Ecc 3: 1 a **s** for every activity under heaven:
2Ti 4: 2 be prepared in **s** and out of **s;**
Tit 1: 3 his appointed **s** he brought his word

SEASONED* [SEASON]

Col 4: 6 always full of grace, **s** with salt,

SEASONS [SEASON]

Ge   1:14 and let them serve as signs to mark **s**
Ps 104:19 The moon marks off the **s,**
Gal 4:10 and months and **s** and years!

SEAT [SEATED, SEATS]

Ex 18:13 The next day Moses took his **s**
2Ki 25:28 a **s** of honor higher than those of
Ps   1: 1 or sit in the **s** of mockers.
Pr 31:23 he takes his **s** among the elders
Da   7: 9 and the Ancient of Days took his **s**.
Mt 23: 2 and the Pharisees sit in Moses' **s**.
Lk 14: 9 'Give this man your **s**.'
Ro 14:10 all stand before God's judgment **s**.
2Co 5:10 before the judgment **s** of Christ,

SEATED [SEAT]

Ps 47: 8 God is **s** on his holy throne.
Isa 6: 1 I saw the Lord **s** on a throne,
Lk 22:69 the Son of Man will be **s** at the right
Jn 12:15 **s** on a donkey's colt."
     20:12 **s** where Jesus' body had been,
Eph 1:20 the dead and **s** him at his right hand
      2: 6 **s** us with him in the heavenly realms
Col 3: 1 Christ is **s** at the right hand of God.
Rev 4: 4 **s** on them were twenty-four elders.
     11:16 who were **s** on their thrones
     14:14 **s** on the cloud was one "like a son of
     19: 4 who was **s** on the throne.
     20: 4 I saw thrones on which were **s** those
     20:11 and him who was **s** on it.
     21: 5 He who was **s** on the throne said,

SEATS [SEAT]

1Sa 2: 8 he **s** them with princes
Ps 113: 8 he **s** them with princes,
Lk 11:43 the most important **s** in

SECLUSION*

Lk   1:24 and for five months remained in **s**.

SECOND [TWO]

Ge 22:15 to Abraham from heaven a **s** time
     41: 5 and had a **s** dream:
Ex   4: 8 they may believe the **s**.
Lev 19:10 not go over your vineyard a **s** time
Nu   9:11 on the fourteenth day of the **s** month
Dt 24:20 do not go over the branches a **s** time.
1Ki 9: 2 the LORD appeared to him a **s** time,
Est 10: 3 Mordecai the Jew was **s** in rank
Eze 10:14 the **s** the face of a man,
Da   7: 5 "And there before me was a **s** beast,
Jnh 3: 1 the LORD came to Jonah a **s** time:
Hag 2:20 the LORD came to Haggai a **s** time,
Zec 11:14 Then I broke my **s** staff called Union,
Mt 22:39 And the **s** is like it:
Jn   3: 4 a **s** time into his mother's womb to
1Co 12:28 **s** prophets, third teachers,
     15:47 the **s** man from heaven.
Tit 3:10 and then warn him a **s** time.
Heb 9:28 and he will appear a **s** time,
Rev 2:11 not be hurt at all by the **s** death.
      4: 7 the **s** was like an ox,
      6: 3 When the Lamb opened the **s** seal,
      8: 8 The **s** angel sounded his trumpet,
     11:14 The **s** woe has passed;
     16: 3 The **s** angel poured out his bowl on
     20: 6 The **s** death has no power over them,
     20:14 The lake of fire is the **s** death.
     21: 8 This is the **s** death."

SECRET [SECRETLY, SECRETS]

Ex   7:11 the same things by their **s** arts:
      7:22 the same things by their **s** arts,
      8: 7 the same things by their **s** arts,
      8:18 to produce gnats by their **s** arts,
Dt 29:29 The **s** things belong to the LORD
Jdg 16: 6 the **s** of your great strength
Est 2:20 Esther had kept **s** her family
Ps 90: 8 our **s** sins in the light of your
    139:15 when I was made in the **s** place.
Pr   9:17 food eaten in **s** is delicious!"
     11:13 but a trustworthy man keeps a **s**.
     21:14 A gift given in **s** soothes anger,
Jer 23:24 in **s** places so that I cannot see him?"
Mt   6: 4 so that your giving may be in **s**.
      6: 4 who sees what is done in **s,**
      6: 6 who sees what is done in **s,**
      6:18 who sees what is done in **s,**
Mk   4:11 "The **s** of the kingdom of God has
1Co 2: 7 No, we speak of God's **s** wisdom,
      4: 1 as those entrusted with the **s** things
2Co 4: 2 renounced **s** and shameful ways;
Eph 5:12 what the disobedient do in **s**.
Php 4:12 I have learned the **s** of being content
2Th 2: 7 the **s** power of lawlessness is already

SECRETLY [SECRET]

Dt 13: 6 or your closest friend **s** entices you,
2Ki 17: 9 The Israelites **s** did things against
Mt   2: 7 Then Herod called the Magi **s**
Jn 19:38 but **s** because he feared the Jews.
2Pe 2: 1 will **s** introduce destructive heresies,
Jude 1: 4 about long ago have **s** slipped in

SECRETS [SECRET]

Ps 44:21 since he knows the **s** of the heart?
Mt 13:11 of the **s** of the kingdom of heaven
Ro   2:16 the day when God will judge men's **s**
1Co 14:25 the **s** of his heart will be laid bare.
Rev 2:24 not learned Satan's so-called deep **s**

SECT

Ac 24: 5 He is a ringleader of the Nazarene **s**
     26: 5 to the strictest **s** of our religion,

SECURE [SECURELY, SECURES, SECURITY]

Dt 33:12 the beloved of the LORD rest **s**
1Ki 2:45 and David's throne will remain **s**
Ps 16: 5 you have made my lot **s.**
     16: 9 my body also will rest **s,**
  112: 8 His heart is **s,** he will have no fear;
  122: 6 "May those who love you be **s.**
Pr 14:26 fears the LORD has a **s** fortress,
Am   6: 1 to you who feel **s** on Mount Samaria,
Zec 1:15 with the nations that feel **s.**
Mt 27:64 the order for the tomb to be made **s**
Heb 6:19 an anchor for the soul, firm and **s.**
2Pe 3:17 and fall from your **s** position.

SECURELY [SECURE]

Pr 10: 9 The man of integrity walks **s,**

SECURES* [SECURE]

Ps 140:12 that the LORD **s** justice for the poor

SECURITY [SECURE]

Dt 24: 6 be taking a man's livelihood as **s.**
Job 31:24 'You are my **s,'**
Ps 122: 7 and **s** within your citadels."
Pr 17:18 and puts up **s** for his neighbor.
   22:26 in pledge or puts up **s** for debts;
Jer 30:10 Jacob will again have peace and **s,**

SEDUCE* [SEDUCED, SEDUCES, SEDUCTIVE]

2Pe 2:14 they **s** the unstable;

SEDUCED* [SEDUCE]

Pr 7:21 she **s** him with her smooth talk.

SEDUCES* [SEDUCE]

Ex 22:16 "If a man **s** a virgin who is not

SEDUCTIVE* [SEDUCE]

Pr 2:16 the wayward wife with her **s** words.
    7: 5 the wayward wife with her **s** words.

SEE [NEARSIGHTED, SAW, SEEING, SEEN, SEES, SIGHT]

Ge 2:19 to **s** what he would name them;
    8: 8 a dove to **s** if the water had receded
    9:16 I will **s** it and remember
  13:15 the land that you **s** I will give to you
Ex 12:13 and when I **s** the blood,
  14:13 and you will **s** the deliverance
  16: 4 and **s** whether they will follow my

Nu 14:23 not one of them will ever **s**
Dt 34: 4 I have let you **s** it with your eyes,
Jdg 2:22 and **s** whether they will keep the way
Job 19:26 yet in my flesh I will **s** God;
Ps 11: 7 upright men will **s** his face.
  16:10 will you let your Holy One **s** decay.
  34: 8 Taste and **s** that the LORD is good;
 115: 5 eyes, but they cannot **s;**
Isa 40: 5 and all mankind together will **s** it.
  53:10 he will **s** his offspring
  53:11 he will **s** the light [of life] and
Eze 8:12 They say, 'The LORD does not **s** us;
Da 3:25 I **s** four men walking around in
Joel 2:28 your young men will **s** visions,
Mic 7: 9 I will **s** his righteousness.
Mt 5: 8 for they will **s** God.
    7: 5 and then you will **s** clearly to remove
  13:16 blessed are your eyes because they **s,**
Mk 8:18 Do you have eyes but fail to **s,**
  14:62 you will **s** the Son of Man
  16: 6 **S** the place where they laid him.
Lk 3: 6 all mankind will **s** God's salvation.'
Jn 9:25 I was blind but now I **s!"**
  14:19 the world will not **s** me anymore,
  16:16 a little while you will **s** me no more,
Ac 2:17 your young men will **s** visions,
   2:27 will you let your Holy One **s** decay.
1Co 13:12 then we shall **s** face to face.
2Co 13: 5 to **s** whether you are in the faith;
Heb 12:14 without holiness no one will **s**
1Jn 3: 2 for we shall **s** him as he is.
Rev 1: 7 and every eye will **s** him,
  22: 4 They will **s** his face,

SEED [SEED-BEARING, SEEDS, SEEDTIME]

Ge 1:11 on the land that bear fruit with **s** in it,
Lev 19:19 your field with two kinds of **s.**
Ecc 11: 6 Sow your **s** in the morning,
Isa 6:13 holy **s** will be the stump in the land."
  55:10 so that it yields **s** for the sower
Mt 13: 3 "A farmer went out to sow his **s.**
  13:31 of heaven is like a mustard **s,**
  17:20 faith as small as a mustard **s,**
Mk 4:31 which is the smallest **s** you plant in
Lk 8:11 The **s** is the word of God.
Jn 12:24 it remains only a single **s.**
1Co 3: 6 I planted the **s,** Apollos watered it,
  9:11 we have sown spiritual **s** among you,
2Co 9:10 Now he who supplies **s** to the sower
Gal 3:16 spoken to Abraham and to his **s.**
   3:29 then you are Abraham's **s,**
1Pe 1:23 not of perishable **s,**
1Jn 3: 9 because God's **s** remains in him;

SEED-BEARING* [SEED]

Ge 1:11 the land produce vegetation: **s** plants
   1:29 "I give you every **s** plant on the face

SEEDS [SEED]

Jn 12:24 But if it dies, it produces many **s.**
Gal 3:16 Scripture does not say "and to **s,"**

SEEDTIME* [SEED]

Ge   8:22 **s** and harvest, cold and heat,

SEEING [SEE]

Isa   6: 9 be ever **s**, but never perceiving.'
Mt 13:14 be ever **s** but never perceiving.
      15:31 the lame walking and the blind **s**.
Jn   8:56 rejoiced at the thought of **s** my day;

SEEK [SEEKING, SEEKS, SELF-SEEKING, SOUGHT]

Ex 18:15 come to me to **s** God's will.
Lev 19:18 " 'Do not **s** revenge or bear a grudge
      19:31 to mediums or **s** out spiritists,
Dt   4:29 But if from there you **s** the Lord
      23: 6 not **s** a treaty of friendship with them
1Ki 22: 5 "First **s** the counsel of the Lord."
1Ch 28: 9 you **s** him, he will be found by you;
2Ch 7:14 and pray and **s** my face and turn
      15: 2 If you **s** him, he will be found
Ezr 9:12 not **s** a treaty of friendship with them
Ps   4: 2 and **s** false gods?
      9:10 never forsaken those who **s** you.
    24: 6 who **s** your face, O God of Jacob.
    34:10 but those who **s** the Lord
    63: 1 you are my God, earnestly I **s** you;
   105: 3 of those who **s** the Lord rejoice.
   105: 4 and his strength; **s** his face always.
   119: 2 and **s** him with all their heart.
   119: 10 I **s** you with all my heart;
  119:176 **S** your servant,
Pr   8:17 and those who **s** me find me.
    18:15 the ears of the wise **s** it out.
    25:27 is it honorable to **s** one's own honor.
    28: 5 who **s** the Lord understand it fully.
Isa   1:17 **S** justice, encourage the oppressed.
    55: 6 **S** the Lord while he may be found;
    65: 1 by those who did not **s** me.
Jer 29:13 You will **s** me and find me when
            you **s** me with all your heart.
Hos 10:12 for it is time to **s** the Lord,
Am   5: 6 **S** the Lord and live,
Zep   2: 3 **S** the Lord, all you humble
      2: 3 **S** righteousness, **s** humility;
Mt   6:33 But **s** first his kingdom and his
      7: 7 **s** and you will find;
Lk 12:31 But **s** his kingdom,
    19:10 Son of Man came to **s** and to save
Jn   5:30 for I **s** not to please myself
Ac 15:17 the remnant of men may **s** the Lord,
Ro 10:20 by those who did not **s** me;
1Co 7:27 Do not **s** a divorce.
           Nobody should **s** his own good,
Heb 11: 6 rewards those who earnestly **s** him.
1Pe 3:11 he must **s** peace and pursue it.

SEEKING [SEEK]

1Ch 22:19 Now devote your heart and soul to **s**
2Ch 30:19 who sets his heart on **s** God—
Pr 20:18 Make plans by **s** advice;
Mal 3: 1 the Lord you are **s** will come
Jn   8:50 I am not **s** glory for myself;
1Co 10:33 not **s** my own good but the good

SEEKS [SEEK]

Pr 11:27 He who **s** good finds goodwill,
    14: 6 mocker **s** wisdom and finds none,
    15:14 The discerning heart **s** knowledge,
Mt   7: 8 who asks receives; he who **s** finds;
Jn   4:23 the kind of worshipers the Father **s**.
Ro   3:11 no one who **s** God.

SEEM [SEEMED, SEEMS]

Pr 16: 2 All a man's ways **s** innocent to him,
    21: 2 All a man's ways **s** right to him,
Zec 8: 6 but will it **s** marvelous to me?"

SEEMED [SEEM]

Ge 29:20 but they **s** like only a few days to
Nu 13:33 We **s** like grasshoppers
Ac   2: 3 They saw what **s** to be tongues of fire
Rev 13: 3 the beast **s** to have had a fatal wound,

SEEMS [SEEM]

Jos 24:15 if serving the Lord **s** undesirable
Pr 12:15 The way of a fool **s** right to him,
    14:12 There is a way that **s** right to a man,
    16:25 There is a way that **s** right to a man,
Heb 12:11 No discipline **s** pleasant at the time,

SEEN [SEE]

Ge 16:13 "I have now **s** the One who sees me."
Ex   3: 7 "I have indeed **s** the misery
    33:23 but my face must not be **s**."
Nu 14:14 O Lord, have been **s** face to face,
Dt   4: 9 not forget the things your eyes have **s**
Jos 23: 3 You yourselves have **s** everything
Jdg 6:22 I have **s** the angel of the Lord face
    13:22 "We have **s** God!"
Ezr 3:12 who had **s** the former temple,
Ps 37:25 I have never **s** the righteous forsaken
    37:35 I have **s** a wicked and ruthless man
    98: 3 have **s** the salvation of our God.
Ecc 1:14 I have **s** all the things that are done
Isa   6: 5 and my eyes have **s** the King,
    9: 2 in darkness have **s** a great light;
    64: 4 no eye has **s** any God besides you,
Mt   2: 9 the star they had **s** in the east
    4:16 in darkness have **s** a great light;
Lk   2:30 For my eyes have **s** your salvation,
Jn   1:14 We have **s** his glory,
    1:18 No one has ever **s** God,
    6:46 No one has **s** the Father except
    14: 9 who has **s** me has **s** the Father.
    20:25 "We have **s** the Lord!"
    20:29 not **s** and yet have believed."
Ro   8:24 But hope that is **s** is no hope at all.
1Co 2: 9 as it is written: "No eye has **s**,
Php 4: 9 or **s** in me—put it into practice.
1Ti 3:16 was **s** by angels,
1Pe 1: 8 you have not **s** him, you love him;
1Jn 1: 3 We proclaim to you what we have **s**
    4:12 No one has ever **s** God;
3Jn 1:11 does what is evil has not **s** God.
Rev 1:19 "Write, therefore, what you have **s**,

SEER [SEERS]

1Sa 9: 9 prophet of today used to be called a **s**

2Sa 24:11 to Gad the prophet, David's **s:**
1Ch 29:29 in the records of Samuel the **s,**
     29:29 and the records of Gad the **s,**
2Ch 9:29 and in the visions of Iddo the **s**
     29:30 words of David and of Asaph the **s.**
Am   7:12 "Get out, you **s!**

SEERS [SEER]

2Ki 17:13 through all his prophets and **s:**
Mic 3: 7 The **s** will be ashamed and

SEES [SEE]

Ge 16:13 now seen the One who **s** me."
Nu 24: 3 the oracle of one whose eye **s** clearly,
     24:15 the oracle of one whose eye **s** clearly,
Dt 12: 8 everyone as he **s** fit,
Ps 33:13 LORD looks down and **s** all mankind;
Isa 11: 3 not judge by what he **s** with his eyes,
     47:10 and have said, 'No one **s** me.'
Mt   6: 4 who **s** what is done in secret,
     6: 6 who **s** what is done in secret,
     6:18 who **s** what is done in secret,
Jn   5:19 do only what he **s** his Father doing,
1Jn 3:17 and **s** his brother in need
     5:16 If anyone **s** his brother commit a sin

SEIR

Ge 32: 3 to his brother Esau in the land of **S,**
Dt   2: 4 descendants of Esau, who live in **S.**
Eze 35: 2 set your face against Mount **S;**

SELAH

Ps 3:2, 4, 8; 4:2, 4; 7:5; 9:16, 20; 20:3; 21:2;
24:6, 10; 32:4, 5, 7; 39:5, 11; 44:8; 46:3, 7, 11;
47:4; 48:8; 49:13, 15; 50:6; 52:3, 5; 54:3; 55:7,
19; 57:3, 6; 59:5, 13; 60:4; 61:4; 62:4, 8; 66:4, 7,
15; 67:1, 4; 68:7, 19, 32; 75:3; 76:3, 9; 77:3, 9,
15; 81:7; 82:2; 83:8; 84:4, 8; 85:2; 87:3, 6; 88:7,
10; 89:4, 37, 45, 48; 140:3, 5, 8; 143:6; Hab 3:3,
9, 13

SELECT [SELECTED]

Ex 12:21 and **s** the animals for your families
     18:21 **s** capable men from all the people—

SELECTED [SELECT]

Nu 18: 6 I myself have **s** your fellow Levites

SELF [SELFISH]

Lk   9:25 and yet lose or forfeit his very **s?**
Ro   6: 6 that our old **s** was crucified with him
Eph 4:22 to put off your old **s,**
Col 3:10 and have put on the new **s,**
1Pe 3: 4 it should be that of your inner **s,**

SELF-CONDEMNED* [CONDEMN]

Tit 3:11 warped and sinful; he is **s.**

SELF-CONTROL* [CONTROL]

Pr 25:28 broken down is a man who lacks **s.**
Ac 24:25 **s** and the judgment to come,
1Co 7: 5 tempt you because of your lack of **s.**
Gal 5:23 gentleness and **s.**
2Ti 3: 3 unforgiving, slanderous, without **s,**
2Pe 1: 6 knowledge, **s;** and to **s,** perseverance;

SELF-CONTROLLED* [CONTROL]

1Th 5: 6 but let us be alert and **s.**
     5: 8 we belong to the day, let us be **s,**
1Ti 3: 2 temperate, **s,** respectable, hospitable,
Tit 1: 8 who is **s,** upright,
     2: 2 **s,** and sound in faith,
     2: 5 to be **s** and pure, to be busy at home,
     2: 6 encourage the young men to be **s.**
     2:12 and to live **s,** upright and godly lives
1Pe 1:13 prepare your minds for action; be **s;**
     4: 7 Therefore be clear minded and **s** so
     5: 8 Be **s** and alert.

SELF-DISCIPLINE* [DISCIPLINE]

2Ti 1: 7 of love and of **s.**

SELF-INDULGENCE* [INDULGE]

Mt 23:25 inside they are full of greed and **s.**
Jas 5: 5 on earth in luxury and **s.**

SELF-SEEKING* [SEEK]

Ro   2: 8 for those who are **s** and who reject
1Co 13: 5 It is not rude, it is not **s,**

SELFISH* [SELF]

Ps 119:36 and not toward **s** gain.
Pr 18: 1 An unfriendly man pursues **s** ends;
Gal 5:20 fits of rage, **s** ambition, dissensions,
Php 1:17 preach Christ out of **s** ambition,
     2: 3 Do nothing out of **s** ambition
Jas 3:14 envy and **s** ambition in your hearts,
     3:16 where you have envy and **s** ambition,

SELL [SALE, SELLING, SELLS, SOLD]

Ge 23: 9 he will **s** me the cave of Machpelah,
     25:31 "First **s** me your birthright."
Lev 25:14 " 'If you **s** land to one of your
Pr 23:23 Buy the truth and do not **s** it;
Mk 10:21 **s** everything you have and give to
Rev 13:17 buy or **s** unless he had the mark,

SELLING [SELL]

Ge 25:33 **s** his birthright to Jacob.
Mk 11:15 those who were buying and **s** there.
Lk 17:28 buying and **s,** planting and building.
Jn   2:14 temple courts he found men **s** cattle,

SELLS [SELL]

Pr 31:24 She makes linen garments and **s**

SEND [SENDING, SENDS, SENT]

Ge   7: 4 from now I will **s** rain on the earth
Ex 23:27 "I will **s** my terror ahead of you
     33: 2 I will **s** an angel before you
Lev 16:21 He shall **s** the goat away into
Dt 11:14 then I will **s** rain on your land
     28:20 The LORD will **s** on you curses,
1Sa 5:11 "**S** the ark of the god of Israel away;
Ps 43: 3 **S** forth your light and your truth,
    104:30 When you **s** your Spirit,
Isa 6: 8 "Whom shall I **s?**
     6: 8 And I said, "Here am I. **S** me!"
Mal 3: 1 "See, I will **s** my messenger,
     4: 5 I will **s** you the prophet Elijah before

Mt	9:38	to **s** out workers into his harvest field
	11:10	" 'I will **s** my messenger ahead
	24:31	And he will **s** his angels with
Mk	1: 2	"I will **s** my messenger ahead of you,
	10: 4	certificate of divorce and **s** her away.
Lk	11:49	'I will **s** them prophets and apostles,
	20:13	I will **s** my son, whom I love;
Jn	3:17	For God did not **s** his Son into
	14:26	whom the Father will **s** in my name,
	15:26	whom I will **s** to you from the Father
	16: 7	I will **s** him to you.
Ac	3:20	and that he may **s** the Christ,
1Co	1:17	For Christ did not **s** me to baptize,

SENDING [SEND]

Ex	3:10	I am **s** you to Pharaoh
	23:20	I am **s** an angel ahead of you
Joel	2:13	and he relents from **s** calamity.
Jnh	4: 2	a God who relents from **s** calamity.
Mt	10:16	I am **s** you out like sheep
Jn	20:21	the Father has sent me, I am **s** you."
Ro	8: 3	by **s** his own Son in the likeness

SENDS [SEND]

Ps	57: 3	He **s** from heaven and saves me,
Mt	5:45	and **s** rain on the righteous and

SENNACHERIB

Assyrian king whose siege of Jerusalem was overthrown by the LORD following prayer of Hezekiah and Isaiah (2Ki 18:13-19:37; 2Ch 32:1-21; Isa 36-37).

SENSE [SENSES, SENSITIVE, SENSITIVITY]

Dt	32:28	They are a nation without **s,**
Ecc	10: 3	the fool lacks **s** and shows everyone

SENSES* [SENSE]

Lk	15:17	"When he came to his **s,** he said,
1Co	15:34	Come back to your **s** as you ought,
2Ti	2:26	to their **s** and escape from the trap of

SENSITIVE [SENSE]

Dt	28:56	The most gentle and **s** woman

SENSITIVITY* [SENSE]

Eph	4:19	Having lost all **s,** they have given

SENSUAL* [SENSUALITY]

Col	2:23	any value in restraining **s** indulgence.
1Ti	5:11	**s** desires overcome their dedication

SENSUALITY* [SENSUAL]

Eph	4:19	they have given themselves over to **s**

SENT [SEND]

Ge	2: 5	the LORD God had not **s** rain on
	8: 8	Then he **s** out a dove to see if
	45: 5	to save lives that God **s** me ahead
Ex	3:14	'I AM has **s** me to you.' "
Nu	13:17	Moses **s** them to explore Canaan,
	16:29	then the LORD has not **s** me.
	21: 6	Then the LORD **s** venomous snakes

Jos	2: 1	son of Nun secretly **s** two spies
	24:12	I **s** the hornet ahead of you,
1Sa	14:15	It was a panic **s** by God.
2Sa	24:15	So the LORD **s** a plague on Israel
2Ki	14: 9	"A thistle in Lebanon **s** a message to
Ps	107:20	He **s** forth his word and healed them;
Isa	55:11	achieve the purpose for which I **s** it.
	61: 1	He has **s** me to bind up
Jer	3: 8	certificate of divorce and **s** her away
	28: 9	as one truly **s** by the LORD only if
	44: 4	Again and again I **s** my servants
Eze	39:28	I **s** them into exile among the nations
Da	3:28	who has **s** his angel and rescued
	6:22	My God **s** his angel,
Mt	10:40	receives the one who **s** me.
Mk	1:12	the Spirit **s** him out into the desert,
	6: 7	he **s** them out two by two
Lk	1:26	God **s** the angel Gabriel to Nazareth,
	4:18	He has **s** me to proclaim freedom for
	9: 2	and he **s** them out to preach
	10:16	rejects me rejects him who **s** me."
	13:34	the prophets and stone those **s** to you,
Jn	1: 6	a man who was **s** from God;
	3:28	'I am not the Christ but am **s** ahead
	4:34	to do the will of him who **s** me and
	5:24	believes him who **s** me has eternal
	8:16	I stand with the Father, who **s** me.
	9: 4	the work of him who **s** me.
	16: 5	"Now I am going to him who **s** me,
	17: 3	and Jesus Christ, whom you have **s.**
	17:18	As you **s** me into the world, I have **s**
	20:21	Father has **s** me, I am sending you."
Ro	10:15	can they preach unless they are **s?**
Gal	4: 4	time had fully come, God **s** his Son,
1Jn	4:10	but that he loved us and **s** his Son as
Rev	22:16	"I, Jesus, have **s** my angel

SENTENCE [SENTENCED]

Ecc	8:11	When the **s** for a crime is not
Ac	13:28	no proper ground for a death **s,**
2Co	1: 9	in our hearts we felt the **s** of death.

SENTENCED [SENTENCE]

Jer	26:16	"This man should not be **s** to death!
Lk	24:20	handed him over to be **s** to death,

SEPARATE [SEPARATED, SEPARATES, SEPARATION]

Ex	26:33	The curtain will **s** the Holy Place
Mt	19: 6	has joined together, let man not **s.**"
Ro	8:35	Who shall **s** us from the love
1Co	7:10	A wife must not **s** from her husband.
2Co	6:17	come out from them and be **s,**
Eph	2:12	at that time you were **s** from Christ,

SEPARATED [SEPARATE]

Ge	1: 4	and he **s** the light from the darkness.
	1: 7	and **s** the water under the expanse
Isa	59: 2	But your iniquities have **s** you
Eph	4:18	and **s** from the life of God because of

SEPARATES [SEPARATE]

Pr	16:28	and a gossip **s** close friends.
	17: 9	the matter **s** close friends.

Mt 25:32 as a shepherd **s** the sheep

SEPARATION [SEPARATE]

Nu   6: 2 vow of **s** to the LORD as a Nazirite,

SEPULCHRE(S) (KJV)

See GRAVE(S), TOMB(S)

SERAPHS*

Isa 6: 2 Above him were **s,**
     6: 6 of the **s** flew to me with a live coal

SERIOUS [SERIOUSNESS]

Ex 21:23 But if there is **s** injury,
Jer 6:14 of my people as though it were not **s.**

SERIOUSNESS* [SERIOUS]

Tit 2: 7 In your teaching show integrity, **s**

SERPENT [SERPENT'S]

Ge   3: 1 **s** was more crafty than any
     3:13 "The **s** deceived me, and I ate."
Isa 27: 1 Leviathan the gliding **s,**
Rev 12: 9 that ancient **s** called the devil,
     20: 2 He seized the dragon, that ancient **s,**

SERPENT'S [SERPENT]

Isa 65:25 but dust will be the **s** food.
2Co 11: 3 Eve was deceived by the **s** cunning,

SERVANT [MAIDSERVANT, MANSERVANT, SERVANT'S, SERVANTS]

Ge   16: 5 I put my **s** in your arms,
Ex   14:31 trust in him and in Moses his **s.**
     21: 2 "If you buy a Hebrew **s,**
Nu   12: 7 But this is not true of my **s** Moses,
1Sa   3:10 "Speak, for your **s** is listening."
2Sa   7:19 the future of the house of your **s.**
1Ki   3: 7 you have made your **s** king in place
      8:56 he gave through his **s** Moses.
      8:66 for his **s** David and his people Israel.
     20:40 your **s** was busy here and there,
Job   1: 8 "Have you considered my **s** Job?
      2: 3 "Have you considered my **s** Job?
     42: 8 My **s** Job will pray for you,
Ps   19:11 By them is your **s** warned;
     19:13 Keep your **s** also from willful sins;
     31:16 Let your face shine on your **s;**
     78:70 He chose David his **s** and took him
     89: 3 I have sworn to David my **s,**
    105:26 He sent Moses his **s,** and Aaron,
Pr   11:29 and the fool will be **s** to the wise.
     14:35 but a shameful **s** incurs his wrath.
     17: 2 A wise **s** will rule over
     22: 7 and the borrower is **s** to the lender.
     31:15 and portions for her **s** girls.
Isa 41: 8 "But you, O Israel, my **s,** Jacob,
     42: 1 "Here is my **s,** whom I uphold,
     43:10 "and my **s** whom I have chosen,
     44: 1 "But now listen, O Jacob, my **s,**
     45: 4 For the sake of Jacob my **s,**
     48:20 LORD has redeemed his **s** Jacob."
     49: 3 He said to me, "You are my **s,** Israel,
     52:13 See, my **s** will act wisely;

53:11 my righteous **s** will justify many,
Jer 30:10 " 'So do not fear, O Jacob my **s;**
     33:21 then my covenant with David my **s—**
Eze 34:24 and my **s** David will be prince
Zec   3: 8 I am going to bring my **s,**
Mal   1: 6 and a **s** his master.
Mt   8:13 his **s** was healed at that very hour.
     20:26 great among you must be your **s,**
     24:45 "Who then is the faithful and wise **s,**
     25:21 'Well done, good and faithful **s!**
Lk   1:38 "I am the Lord's **s,**" Mary answered.
      1:54 He has helped his **s** Israel,
      1:69 for us in the house of his **s** David
     16:13 "No **s** can serve two masters.
Jn   12:26 my **s** also will be.
Ac   3:13 has glorified his **s** Jesus.
     12:13 a **s** girl named Rhoda came to answer
Ro   1: 1 Paul, a **s** of Christ Jesus,
     13: 4 For he is God's **s** to do you good.
     14: 4 to judge someone else's **s?**
Php   2: 7 taking the very nature of a **s,**
Col   1:23 Paul, have become a **s.**
2Ti   2:24 And the Lord's **s** must not quarrel,
Heb   3: 5 Moses was faithful as a **s**
Rev 15: 3 sang the song of Moses the **s** of God
     19:10 I am a fellow **s** with you and

SERVANT OF THE †LORD Dt 34:5; Jos 1:1, 13, 15; 8:31, 33; 11:12; 12:6, 6; 13:8; 14:7; 18:7; 22:2, 4, 5; 24:29; Jdg 2:8; 2Ki 18:12; 2Ch 24:6; Ps 18:T; 36:T; Isa 42:19

SERVANT'S [SERVANT]

1Sa   1:11 only look upon your **s** misery
2Ki   6:17 Then the LORD opened the **s** eyes,
2Ch   6:19 your **s** prayer and his plea for mercy,
Ps 119:122 Ensure your **s** well-being;

SERVANTS [SERVANT]

Lev 25:55 for the Israelites belong to me as **s.**
Dt   32:36 and have compassion on his **s**
2Ki 17:23 warned through all his **s** the prophets
Ezr   5:11 the **s** of the God of heaven
Job   4:18 If God places no trust in his **s,**
Ps   34:22 The LORD redeems his **s;**
     90:13 Have compassion on your **s.**
    103:21 you his **s** who do his will.
    104: 4 flames of fire his **s.**
    113: 1 Praise, O **s** of the LORD,
Isa 44:26 who carries out the words of his **s**
     65: 8 so will I do in behalf of my **s;**
     65:14 My **s** will sing out of the joy
Jer   7:25 again and again I sent you my **s**
Da   9: 6 not listened to your **s** the prophets,
Lk   17:10 should say, 'We are unworthy **s;**
Jn   15:15 I no longer call you **s,**
Ac   4:29 and enable your **s** to speak your word
Ro   13: 6 for the authorities are God's **s,**
1Co   3: 5 Only **s,** through whom you came
2Co 11:15 **s** masquerade as **s** of righteousness.
Heb   1: 7 his **s** flames of fire."
Rev   7: 3 on the foreheads of the **s** of our God.
     19: 2 avenged on her the blood of his **s.**"
     22: 3 and his **s** will serve him.

SERVE [SERVANT, SERVED, SERVES, SERVICE, SERVING]

Ge   1:14 and let them **s** as signs
      15:14 But I will punish the nation they **s**
      25:23 and the older will **s** the younger."
Ex   28: 1 so they may **s** me as priests.
Nu   1: 3 who are able to **s** in the army.
Dt   6:13 Fear the LORD your God, **s** him only
      10:12 to **s** the LORD your God
      11:13 and to **s** him with all your heart and
      13: 4 **s** him and hold fast to him.
      28:47 not **s** the LORD your God joyfully
Jos   22: 5 and to **s** him with all your heart
      24:14 "Now fear the LORD and **s** him
      24:15 we will **s** the LORD."
      24:18 We too will **s** the LORD,
1Sa   7: 3 to the LORD and **s** him only,
      12:20 but **s** the LORD with all your heart.
      12:24 to fear the LORD and **s** him
2Ki 17:35 **s** them or sacrifice to them.
2Ch 19: 9 "You must **s** faithfully and
Ne   9:35 they did not **s** you or turn
Job 36:11 If they obey and **s** him,
Ps   2:11 **S** the LORD with fear and rejoice
Isa 60:12 that will not **s** you will perish;
Jer   2:20 'I will not **s** you!'
      25: 6 Do not follow other gods to **s**
Da   3:17 The God we **s** is able to save us
Mt   4:10 and **s** him only.' "
      6:24 You cannot **s** both God and Money.
Mk 10:45 not come to be served, but to **s,**
Lk 16:13 "No servant can **s** two masters.
Ro 12: 7 If it is serving, let him **s;**
Gal   5:13 **s** one another in love.
Eph   6: 7 **S** wholeheartedly, as if you were
1Th   1: 9 to **s** the living and true God,
1Ti   6: 2 they are to **s** them even better,
Heb   9:14 so that we may **s** the living God!
1Pe   4:10 gift he has received to **s** others,
      5: 2 not greedy for money, but eager to **s;**
Rev   1: 6 and priests to **s** his God and Father—
      5:10 a kingdom and priests to **s** our God,
      7:15 and **s** him day and night in his temple

SERVED [SERVE]

Ge 29:20 So Jacob **s** seven years to get Rachel,
Jos 24:15 whether the gods your forefathers **s**
Jdg   2:13 because they forsook him and **s** Baal
Jer   5:19 and **s** foreign gods in your own land,
Mt 20:28 the Son of Man did not come to be **s,**
Jn   12: 2 Martha **s,** while Lazarus was
Ac 17:25 And he is not **s** by human hands,
Ro   1:25 and **s** created things rather than
1Ti   3:13 Those who have **s** well gain

SERVES [SERVE]

Lk 22:26 the one who rules like the one who **s.**
Jn 12:26 Whoever **s** me must follow me;
Ro 14:18 anyone who **s** Christ in this way
1Pe   4:11 If anyone **s,** he should do it

SERVICE [SERVE]

Nu   8:25 they must retire from their regular **s**

     18: 7 the **s** of the priesthood as a gift.
2Ch   5:14 the priests could not perform their **s**
Job   7: 1 "Does not man have hard **s** on earth?
Lk   9:62 the plow and looks back is fit for **s** in
     12:35 "Be dressed ready for **s**
Ro 15:17 in Christ Jesus in my **s** to God.
1Co 12: 5 There are different kinds of **s,**
     16:15 to the **s** of the saints.
2Co   9:12 This **s** that you perform is
Eph   4:12 God's people for works of **s,**
Rev   2:19 your **s** and perseverance,

SERVING [SERVE]

Jos 24:15 if **s** the LORD seems undesirable
Jdg   2:19 following other gods and **s**
2Ch 12: 8 between **s** me and **s** the kings
Ro 12: 7 If it is **s,** let him serve;
     12:11 your spiritual fervor, **s** the Lord.
     16:18 are not **s** our Lord Christ,
Eph   6: 7 as if you were **s** the Lord, not men,
Col   3:24 It is the Lord Christ you are **s.**
2Ti   2: 4 No one **s** as a soldier gets involved
1Pe   1:12 that they were not **s** themselves

SET [SETS, SETTING, SETTINGS]

Ge   9:13 I have **s** my rainbow in the clouds,
     28:18 and **s** it up as a pillar and poured oil
     31:45 So Jacob took a stone and **s** it up as
     35:14 Jacob **s** up a stone pillar at the place
Ex 24: 4 and **s** up twelve stone pillars
     26:30 "**S** up the tabernacle according to
     40:18 When Moses **s** up the tabernacle,
Lev 20:26 I have **s** you apart from the nations
Nu   8:17 I **s** them apart for myself.
     9:23 at the LORD's command they **s** out.
Dt 10:15 Yet the LORD **s** his affection
     16:21 not **s** up any wooden Asherah pole
     27: 2 **s** up some large stones and coat them
     28: 1 the LORD your God will **s** you high
     30:15 I **s** before you today life
Jos   4: 9 Joshua **s** up the twelve stones
Jdg 13: 5 **s** apart to God from birth,
1Sa   5: 2 the ark into Dagon's temple and **s** it
2Ki 25: 9 He **s** fire to the temple of the LORD,
Ps   4: 3 that the LORD has **s** apart the godly
     8: 1 You have **s** your glory above
     16: 8 I have **s** the LORD always
   142: 7 **S** me free from my prison,
Isa 50: 7 Therefore have I **s** my face like flint,
Da   9:27 he will **s** up an abomination that
     11:28 be **s** against the holy covenant.
Mal   2: 2 **s** your heart to honor my name,"
Mk 15:17 a crown of thorns and **s** it on him.
Jn   8:32 and the truth will **s** you free."
Ac   1: 7 the Father has **s** by his own authority.
     2:23 over to you by God's **s** purpose
Ro   8: 2 the law of the Spirit of life **s** me free
2Co   1:22 **s** his seal of ownership on us,
Gal   5: 1 for freedom that Christ has **s** us free.
Col   3: 1 **s** your hearts on things above,
Heb   4: 7 Therefore God again **s** a certain day,
1Pe   3:15 in your hearts **s** apart Christ as Lord.

SETH

Ge   4:25 to a son and named him **S,**

SETS [SET]

2Ch 30:19 who **s** his heart on seeking God—
Job 5:11 The lowly he **s** on high,
Ps   68: 6 God **s** the lonely in families,
    146: 7 The LORD **s** prisoners free,
Ecc 1: 5 The sun rises and the sun **s,**
Eze 14: 4 When any Israelite **s** up idols
2Th 2: 4 that he **s** himself up in God's temple,
1Ti 3: 1 **s** his heart on being an overseer,
Heb 10: 9 He **s** aside the first to establish

SETTING [SET]

Dt 11:26 I am **s** before you today a blessing
Jer 21: 8 I am **s** before you the way of life and
Mk   7: 9 of **s** aside the commands of God

SETTINGS [SET]

Pr 25:11 like apples of gold in **s** of silver.

SETTLE [RESETTLE, SETTLED, SETTLES]

Ge 47: 4 please let your servants **s** in
          Goshen."
Nu 33:53 Take possession of the land and **s**
Isa 2: 4 and will **s** disputes for many peoples.
Jer 29: 5 "Build houses and **s** down;
Eze 37:14 and I will **s** you in your own land.
Mt   5:25 "**S** matters quickly with your
2Th 3:12 **s** down and earn the bread they eat.

SETTLED [SETTLE]

Ex 24:16 glory of the LORD **s** on Mount Sinai.
    40:35 because the cloud had **s** upon it,
Dt 19: 1 when you have driven them out and **s**
2Ki 18:11 deported Israel to Assyria and **s** them

SETTLES [SETTLE]

Ps 113: 9 He **s** the barren woman in her home
Pr 18:18 Casting the lot **s** disputes

SEVEN [SEVENS, SEVENTH]

Ge   4:15 will suffer vengeance **s** times over."
     7: 2 Take with you **s** of every kind
    21:28 Abraham set apart **s** ewe lambs from
    29:18 "I'll work for you **s** years in return
    41: 2 out of the river there came up **s** cows
    41: 5 a second dream: **S** heads of grain,
Ex   2:16 a priest of Midian had **s** daughters,
    12:15 For **s** days you are to eat bread made
    25:37 "Then make its **s** lamps and set them
    29:35 taking **s** days to ordain them.
Lev 4: 6 sprinkle some of it **s** times before
    12: 2 be ceremonially unclean for **s** days,
    15:19 of her monthly period will last **s** days
    15:24 he will be unclean for **s** days;
    23:15 count off **s** full weeks.
    23:42 Live in booths for **s** days:
    25: 8 " 'Count off **s** sabbaths of years—
    26:18 for your sins **s** times over.
Nu 23: 1 Balaam said, "Build me **s** altars here,
Dt   7: 1 **s** nations larger and stronger than

15: 1 every **s** years you must cancel debts.
Jos 6: 4 march around the city **s** times,
Jdg 16:13 Delilah took the **s** braids of his head,
1Sa 2: 5 who was barren has borne **s** children,
1Ki 19:18 Yet I reserve **s** thousand in Israel—
2Ki 5:10 wash yourself **s** times in the Jordan,
Ps 79:12 **s** times the reproach they have hurled
   119:164 **S** times a day I praise you
Pr   6:16 **s** that are detestable to him:
     9: 1 she has hewn out its **s** pillars.
    24:16 though a righteous man falls **s** times,
    26:25 for **s** abominations fill his heart.
Isa 4: 1 In that day **s** women will take hold
Da   3:19 furnace heated **s** times hotter than
     4:16 till **s** times pass by for him.
     9:25 comes, there will be **s** 'sevens,'
Zec 3: 9 There are **s** eyes on that one stone,
     4: 2 a bowl at the top and **s** lights on it,
Mt 18:22 not **s** times, but seventy-seven times.
Mk 12:20 Now there were **s** brothers.
    16: 9 of whom he had driven **s** demons.
Lk 11:26 takes **s** other spirits more wicked
Ro 11: 4 I have reserved for myself **s** thousand
Rev 1: 4 To the **s** churches in the province
     1: 4 from the **s** spirits before his throne,
     1:12 I turned I saw **s** golden lampstands,
     1:16 In his right hand he held **s** stars,
     3: 1 of him who holds the **s** spirits of God
     4: 5 These are the **s** spirits of God.
     5: 1 on both sides and sealed with **s** seals.
     6: 1 Lamb opened the first of the **s** seals.
     8: 2 and to them were given **s** trumpets.
    10: 4 And when the **s** thunders spoke,
    12: 3 an enormous red dragon with **s** heads
    15: 1 **s** angels with the **s** last plagues—
    15: 7 to the **s** angels **s** golden bowls filled
    16: 1 pour out the **s** bowls of God's wrath
    17: 9 The **s** heads are **s** hills on which

SEVENS* [SEVEN]

Da   9:24 "Seventy '**s**' are decreed
     9:25 will be seven '**s,**' and sixty-two '**s.**'
     9:26 After the sixty-two '**s,**'

SEVENTH [SEVEN]

Ge   2: 2 the **s** day he rested from all his work.
Ex 16:30 So the people rested on the **s** day.
    20:10 but the **s** day is a Sabbath,
    23:11 the **s** year let the land lie unplowed
    23:12 do not work on the **s** day do not work,
Lev 16:29 On the tenth day of the **s** month
    23:16 up to the day after the **s** Sabbath,
    23:24 'On the first day of the **s** month
    23:27 "The tenth day of this **s** month is
    23:34 The fifteenth day of the **s** month
    25: 4 in the **s** year the land is to have
Jos 6:16 The **s** time around,
Heb 4: 4 "And on the **s** day God rested
Rev 8: 1 When he opened the **s** seal,
    11:15 The **s** angel sounded his trumpet,
    16:17 The **s** angel poured out his bowl into

SEVENTY

Ge 46:27 which went to Egypt, were **s** in all.

Ex   24: 1 and s of the elders of Israel.
Nu   11:25 and put the Spirit on the s elders.
2Ch 36:21 until the s years were completed
Ps   90:10 The length of our days is s years—
Jer 25:12 "But when the s years are fulfilled,
Da   9: 2 desolation of Jerusalem would last s
      9:24 "S 'sevens' are decreed

SEVENTY-SEVEN

Ge   4:24 then Lamech s times."
Mt   18:22 not seven times, but s times.

SEVENTY-TWO

Lk   10: 1 After this the Lord appointed s others

SEVERE

Ge   12:10 for a while because the famine was s.
     41:57 the famine was s in all the world.
Nu   11:33 and he struck them with a s plague.
1Ki 18: 2 Now the famine was s in Samaria,
2Ki 25: 3 famine in the city had become so s
Lk   4:25 and there was a s famine
     15:14 a s famine in that whole country,
Ac   11:28 predicted that a s famine would
2Co   8: 2 Out of the most s trial,
1Th   1: 6 in spite of s suffering,

SEWED [SEWS]

Ge   3: 7 so they s fig leaves together

SEWS [SEWED]

Mt   9:16 "No one s a patch of unshrunk cloth

SEX* [SEXUAL, SEXUALLY]

Ge   19: 5 so that we can have s with them."
Jdg 19:22 so we can have s with him."

SEXUAL [SEX]

Ex   22:19 "Anyone who has s relations with
Lev 18: 6 close relative to have s relations.
     20:15 a man has s relations with an animal,
Nu   25: 1 to indulge in s immorality
Mt   15:19 murder, adultery, s immorality, theft,
Ac   15:20 from s immorality, from the meat of
Ro   1:24 to s impurity for the degrading
     13:13 not in s immorality and debauchery,
1Co   5: 1 that there is s immorality among you,
      6:13 not meant for s immorality,
      6:18 Flee from s immorality.
     10: 8 We should not commit s immorality,
2Co 12:21 not repented of the impurity, s sin
Gal   5:19 s immorality, impurity and
Eph   5: 3 not be even a hint of s immorality,
Col   3: 5 to your earthly nature: s immorality,
1Th   4: 3 that you should avoid s immorality;
Jude 1: 7 gave themselves up to s immorality
Rev   2:14 and by committing s immorality.
      2:20 my servants into s immorality
      9:21 their s immorality or their thefts.

SEXUALLY* [SEX]

1Co   5: 9 to associate with s immoral people—
      5:11 a brother but is s immoral
      6: 9 Neither the s immoral nor idolaters
      6:18 but he who sins s sins against

Heb 12:16 See that no one is s immoral,
     13: 4 the adulterer and all the s immoral.
Rev 21: 8 the murderers, the s immoral,
     22:15 the s immoral, the murderers,

SHACKLES

2Ch 33:11 bound him with bronze s and took
     36: 6 bound him with bronze s to take him
Na   1:13 and tear your s away."

SHADE

Ps 121: 5 the LORD is your s at your right hand
SS   2: 3 I delight to sit in his s,
Isa 25: 4 from the storm and a s from the heat.
Eze 31: 6 the great nations lived in its s.
Jnh   4: 6 grow up over Jonah to give s
Mk   4:32 the birds of the air can perch in its s.

SHADOW [SHADOWS]

2Ki 20:11 and the LORD made the s go back
1Ch 29:15 Our days on earth are like a s,
Job 14: 2 like a fleeting s,
Ps   17: 8 hide me in the s of your wings
     23: 4 through the valley of the s of death,
     36: 7 among men find refuge in the s
     57: 1 take refuge in the s of your wings
     63: 7 I sing in the s of your wings.
     91: 1 will rest in the s of the Almighty.
Isa   9: 2 living in the land of the s of death
     49: 2 in the s of his hand he hid me;
     51:16 and covered you with the s
Mt   4:16 living in the land of the s of death
Lk   1:79 in darkness and in the s of death,
Ac   5:15 at least Peter's s might fall on some
Col   2:17 These are a s of the things that were
Heb   8: 5 a copy and s of what is in heaven.
     10: 1 law is only a s of the good things

SHADOWS [SHADOW]

Jas   1:17 who does not change like shifting s.

SHADRACH [HANANIAH]

Hebrew exiled to Babylon; name changed from
Hananiah (Da 1:6-7). Refused defilement by food
(Da 1:8-20). Refused to worship idol (Da 3:1-18);
saved from furnace (Da 3:19-30).

SHAGGY*

Da   8:21 The s goat is the king of Greece,

SHAKE [SHAKEN, SHAKES, SHAKING, SHOOK]

Ps   10: 6 "Nothing will s me;
     64: 8 all who see them will s their heads
     99: 1 let the earth s.
Isa   2:19 when he rises to s the earth.
Hag   2: 6 I will once more s the heavens
      2:21 I will s the heavens and the earth.
Mk   6:11 s the dust off your feet
Heb 12:26 "Once more I will s not only

SHAKEN [SHAKE]

Ps   15: 5 does these things will never be s.
     16: 8 he is at my right hand, I will not be s.

```
       30: 6  I said, "I will never be s."
       62: 2  I will never be s.
      112: 6  Surely he will never be s;
Isa    54:10  the mountains be s and the hills
       54:10  unfailing love for you will not be s
Mt     24:29  and the heavenly bodies will be s.'
Lk      6:38  s together and running over,
Ac      2:25  he is at my right hand, I will not be s.
Heb    12:28  a kingdom that cannot be s,
```

SHAKES [SHAKE]

```
Ps     29: 8  The voice of the LORD s the desert;
Isa    30:28  He s the nations in the sieve
```

SHAKING* [SHAKE]

```
Ps     22: 7  they hurl insults, s their heads:
Mt     27:39  hurled insults at him, s their heads
Mk     15:29  hurled insults at him, s their heads
```

SHALLOW

```
Mt     13: 5  because the soil was s.
```

SHALLUM

King of Israel (2Ki 15:10-16).

SHALMANESER*

King of Assyria; conquered and deported Israel
(2Ki 17:3-4; 18:9).

SHAMBLES (KJV) See MEAT MARKET

SHAME [ASHAMED, SHAMED, SHAMEFUL]

```
Ge      2:25  and they felt no s.
Ps      4: 2  will you turn my glory into s?
       25: 3  in you will never be put to s,
       25: 3  be put to s who are treacherous
       34: 5  their faces are never covered with s.
       69: 6  not be put to s because of me,
       97: 7  All who worship images are put to s,
Pr      3:35  but fools he holds up to s.
       13: 5  but the wicked bring s and disgrace.
       13:18  comes to poverty and s,
       18:13  that is his folly and his s.
Isa    30: 5  everyone will be put to s because of
       45:17  never be put to s or disgraced,
       61: 7  Instead of their s my people will
Jer     8: 9  The wise will be put to s;
        8:12  No, they have no s at all;
Eze    39:26  They will forget their s and all
Da      9: 7  but this day we are covered with s—
       12: 2  others to s and everlasting contempt.
Ro      9:33  in him will never be put to s."
       10:11  in him will never be put to s."
1Co     1:27  things of the world to s the wise;
Php     3:19  and their glory is in their s.
Heb    12: 2  endured the cross, scorning its s,
1Pe     2: 6  in him will never be put to s."
```

SHAMED [SHAME]

```
Jer    10:14  every goldsmith is s by his idols.
Joel    2:26  never again will my people be s.
```

SHAMEFUL [SHAME]

```
Jer     3:24  From our youth s gods have
```

```
Ro      1:26  God gave them over to s lusts.
2Co     4: 2  renounced secret and s ways;
Eph     5:12  For it is s even to mention what
2Pe     2: 2  Many will follow their s ways
Rev    21:27  nor will anyone who does what is s
```

SHAMGAR*

Judge; killed 600 Philistines (Jdg 3:31; 5:6).

SHAPE [SHAPED, SHAPES, SHAPING]

```
Ex     32: 4  an idol cast in the s of a calf,
2Ki    17:16  two idols cast in the s of calves,
Job    38:14  earth takes s like clay under a seal;
```

SHAPED [SHAPE]

```
Job    10: 8  "Your hands s me and made me.
```

SHAPES [SHAPE]

```
Isa    44:10  Who s a god and casts an idol,
Jer    10: 3  and a craftsman s it with his chisel.
```

SHAPHAN

```
2Ki    22: 8  high priest said to S the secretary,
```

SHAPING* [SHAPE]

```
Jer    18: 4  But the pot he was s from
       18: 4  s it as seemed best to him.
```

SHARE [SHARED, SHARERS, SHARES, SHARING]

```
Ge     21:10  that slave woman's son will never s
Lev     6:18  It is his regular s of
        6:22  It is the LORD's regular s and is to
       19:17  so you will not s in his guilt.
Nu     18:20  nor will you have any s among
              them; I am your s
Dt     10: 9  the Levites have no s or inheritance
Jos    14: 4  The Levites received no s of the land
       22:25  You have no s in the LORD.'
2Sa    20: 1  "We have no s in David,
2Ch    10:16  "What s do we have
Ne      2:20  you have no s in Jerusalem
Ps     69:27  not let them s in your salvation.
Ecc     9: 2  All s a common destiny—
Eze    18:20  son will not s the guilt of the father,
Mt     25:21  and s your master's happiness!'
Lk      3:11  "The man with two tunics should s
       15:12  'Father, give me my s of the estate.'
Ac      8:21  no part or s in this ministry,
Ro      8:17  indeed we s in his sufferings in
              order that we may also s in his glory.
       12:13  S with God's people who are
       15:27  they owe it to the Jews to s
2Co     1: 7  so also you s in our comfort.
Gal     4:30  the slave woman's son will never s
        6: 6  in the word must s all good things
Eph     4:28  that he may have something to s
Col     1:12  to s in the inheritance of the saints in
2Th     2:14  that you might s in the glory
1Ti     5:22  and do not s in the sins of others.
        6:18  and to be generous and willing to s.
2Ti     2: 6  be the first to receive a s of the crops.
Heb     3:14  to s in Christ if we hold firmly till
       12:10  that we may s in his holiness.
```

13:16 do not forget to do good and to **s**
1Pe 5: 1 also will **s** in the glory to be revealed
Rev 18: 4 so that you will not **s** in her sins,
22:19 God will take away from him his **s** in

SHARED [SHARE]
Ps 41: 9 whom I trusted, he who **s** my bread,
Ac 1:17 of our number and **s** in this ministry.
4:32 but they **s** everything they had.
Heb 2:14 he too **s** in their humanity so that
6: 4 who have **s** in the Holy Spirit,

SHARERS* [SHARE]
Eph 3: 6 and **s** together in the promise

SHARES [SHARE]
Pr 22: 9 for he **s** his food with the poor.
Jn 13:18 'He who **s** my bread has lifted
2Jn 1:11 welcomes him **s** in his wicked work.

SHARING [SHARE]
1Co 9:10 they ought to do so in the hope of **s**
2Co 9:13 for your generosity in **s** with them
Php 3:10 the fellowship of **s** in his sufferings,
Phm 1: 6 be active in **s** your faith,

SHARON
SS 2: 1 I am a rose of **S**, a lily of the valleys.

SHARP [SHARPENED, SHARPENS, SHARPER]
Pr 5: 4 **s** as a double-edged sword.
Isa 5:28 Their arrows are **s**,
Ac 15:39 They had such a **s** disagreement
Rev 1:16 a **s** double-edged sword.
2:12 the words of him who has the **s**,
14:14 his head and a **s** sickle in his hand.
19:15 a **s** sword with which to strike down

SHARPENED [SHARP]
Isa 49: 2 He made my mouth like a **s** sword,
Eze 21: 9 a sword, **s** and polished—

SHARPENS* [SHARP]
Pr 27:17 As iron **s** iron, so one man **s** another.

SHARPER* [SHARP]
Heb 4:12 **S** than any double-edged sword,

SHATTER [SHATTERED, SHATTERS]
Isa 30:31 of the LORD will **s** Assyria;
Jer 51:20 with you I **s** nations,
Hag 2:22 **s** the power of the foreign kingdoms.

SHATTERED [SHATTER]
Ex 15: 6 O LORD, **s** the enemy.
1Sa 2:10 who oppose the LORD will be **s**.
1Ki 19:11 the mountains apart and **s** the rocks
Job 16:12 All was well with me, but he **s** me;
17:11 my plans are **s**,
Ecc 12: 6 before the pitcher is **s** at the spring,
Isa 7: 8 Ephraim will be too **s** to be a people.
Na 1: 6 the rocks are **s** before him.

SHATTERS [SHATTER]
Ps 46: 9 the bow and **s** the spear,

SHAVE [SHAVED]
Nu 6:18 the Nazirite must **s** off the hair
Dt 14: 1 **s** the front of your heads for the dead
Jdg 16:19 to **s** off the seven braids of his hair,

SHAVED [SHAVE]
Nu 6:19 " 'After the Nazirite has **s** off the hair
Jdg 16:17 If my head were **s**,
Ac 21:24 so that they can have their heads **s**.
1Co 11: 5 just as though her head were **s**.

SHEAF [SHEAVES]
Ge 37: 7 suddenly my **s** rose and stood upright
Lev 23:11 to wave the **s** before the LORD
Dt 24:19 in your field and you overlook a **s**,

SHEAR [SHEARER, SHEARERS]
Dt 15:19 not **s** the firstborn of your sheep.

SHEARER* [SHEAR]
Ac 8:32 and as a lamb before the **s** is silent,

SHEARERS [SHEAR]
Isa 53: 7 and as a sheep before her **s** is silent,

SHEAVES [SHEAF]
Ge 37: 7 while your **s** gathered around mine
Ru 2:15 "Even if she gathers among the **s**,
Ps 126: 6 carrying **s** with him.

SHEBA
1. Benjamite; rebelled against David (2Sa 20).
2. Queen of Sheba (1Ki 10; 2Ch 9).

SHECHEM
1. Raped Jacob's daughter Dinah; killed by Simeon and Levi (Ge 34).
2. City where Joshua renewed the covenant (Jos 24). Abimelech as king (Jdg 9).

SHED [SHEDDING, SHEDS]
Ge 9: 6 by man shall his blood be **s**;
Nu 35:33 by the blood of the one who **s** it.
Dt 19:10 so that innocent blood will not be **s**
2Ki 21:16 also **s** so much innocent blood
Ps 106:38 They **s** innocent blood,
Pr 6:17 hands that **s** innocent blood,
Isa 59: 7 they are swift to **s** innocent blood.
Eze 22:12 In you men accept bribes to **s** blood;
Hab 2: 8 For you have **s** man's blood;
2:17 For you have **s** man's blood;
Mt 23:35 the righteous blood that has been **s**
Ro 3:15 "Their feet are swift to **s** blood;
Col 1:20 through his blood, **s** on the cross.
Rev 16: 6 for they have **s** the blood

SHEDDING [SHED]
Heb 9:22 the **s** of blood there is no forgiveness.
12: 4 to the point of **s** your blood.

SHEDS* [SHED]

Ge 9: 6 "Whoever s the blood of man,
Eze 18:10 who s blood or does any

SHEEP [SHEEP'S, SHEEPSKINS]

Lev 1:10 from either the s or the goats,
Nu 27:17 not be like s without a shepherd.
Dt 17: 1 or a s that has any defect
1Sa 15:14 then is this bleating of s in my ears?
    17:35 and rescued the s from its mouth.
2Sa 12: 4 from taking one of his own s or
1Ki 22:17 on the hills like s without a shepherd,
Ps 44:22 as s to to be slaughtered.
    74: 1 against the s of your pasture?
    78:52 he led them like s through
    78:70 and took him from the s pens;
   100: 3 the s of his pasture.
   119:176 I have strayed like a lost s.
SS 4: 2 like a flock of s just shorn,
Isa 13:14 like s without a shepherd,
    53: 6 We all, like s, have gone astray,
    53: 7 as a s before her shearers is silent,
Jer 23: 1 and scattering the s of my pasture!"
    50: 6 "My people have been lost s;
Eze 34:15 I myself will tend my s
Zec 13: 7 and the s will be scattered,
Mt 9:36 like s without a shepherd.
    10: 6 Go rather to the lost s of Israel.
    10:16 I am sending you out like s
    12:11 of you has a s and it falls into a pit
    25:32 separates the s from the goats.
Lk 15: 4 after the lost s until he finds it?
Jn 10: 1 the man who does not enter the s pen
    10: 3 He calls his own s by name
    10: 7 I am the gate for the s.
    10:11 lays down his life for the s.
    10:15 and I lay down my life for the s.
    10:27 My s listen to my voice;
    21:17 Jesus said, "Feed my s.
Ac 8:32 "He was led like a s to
Ro 8:36 as s to be slaughtered."
Heb 13:20 that great Shepherd of the s,
1Pe 2:25 For you were like s going astray,

SHEEP'S* [SHEEP]

Mt 7:15 They come to you in s clothing,

SHEEPSKINS* [SHEEP]

Heb 11:37 They went about in s and goatskins,

SHEET [SHEETS]

Isa 25: 7 the s that covers all nations;
Ac 10:11 and something like a large s being let

SHEETS* [SHEET]

Ex 39: 3 They hammered out thin s of gold
Nu 16:38 Hammer the censers into s to overlay

SHEKEL [SHEKELS]

Ex 30:13 This half s is an offering to

SHEKELS [SHEKEL]

Ge 37:28 and sold him for twenty s of silver to
Lev 27: 3 twenty and sixty at fifty s of silver,

27: 4 set her value at thirty s.
1Ch 21:25 So David paid Araunah six hundred s
Hos 3: 2 So I bought her for fifteen s of silver

SHELAH

Ge 38:11 until my son S grows up."
    46:12 The sons of Judah: Er, Onan, S,

SHELTER [SHELTERED, SHELTERS]

1Ch 28:18 and s the ark of the covenant
Ps 27: 5 in the s of his tabernacle
    31:20 the s of your presence you hide them
    55: 8 I would hurry to my place of s,
    61: 4 and take refuge in the s
    91: 1 who dwells in the s of the Most High
Ecc 7:12 Wisdom is a s as money is a s,
Isa 1: 8 The Daughter of Zion is left like a s
    4: 6 It will be a s and shade from the heat
    25: 4 a s from the storm and a shade from
    32: 2 a s from the wind and a refuge from
    58: 7 to provide the poor wanderer with s
Jnh 4: 5 There he made himself a s,

SHELTERED* [SHELTER]

Zep 2: 3 perhaps you will be s on the day of

SHELTERS [SHELTER]

Mk 9: 5 Let us put up three s—

SHEM

Son of Noah (Ge 5:32; 6:10). Blessed (Ge
9:26). Descendants (Ge 10:21-31; 11:10-32; Lk
3:36).

SHEMAIAH

1Ki 12:22 of God came to S the man of God:
2Ch 12: 5 the prophet S came to Rehoboam
Jer 29:31 Because S has prophesied to you,

SHEMER

1Ki 16:24 calling it Samaria, after S,

SHEPHERD [SHEPHERDED, SHEPHERDS]

Ge 48:15 God who has been my s all my life
    49:24 because of the S, the Rock of Israel,
Nu 27:17 not be like sheep without a s."
1Sa 21: 7 Doeg the Edomite, Saul's head s
2Sa 7: 7 to s my people Israel,
1Ki 22:17 on the hills like sheep without a s,
1Ch 11: 2 'You will s my people Israel,
Ps 23: 1 The LORD is my s,
    28: 9 be their s and carry them forever.
    78:71 to be the s of his people Jacob,
    80: 1 Hear us, O S of Israel,
Ecc 12:11 given by one S.
Isa 13:20 no s will rest his flocks there.
    40:11 He tends his flock like a s
Jer 31:10 will watch over his flock like a s.'
Eze 34: 5 because there was no s,
    34:12 As a s looks after his scattered flock
Mic 5: 4 and s his flock in the strength of
Zec 10: 2 like sheep oppressed for lack of a s.
    11: 9 "I will not be your s.
    11:17 "Woe to the worthless s,

	13: 7 "Strike the **s**, and the sheep will be
Mt	2: 6 be the **s** of my people Israel.' "
	25:32 as a **s** separates the sheep
	26:31 the **s**, and the sheep of the flock will
Mk	6:34 they were like sheep without a **s**.
Jn	10:11 "I am the good **s**. The good **s** lays
	down his life for the sheep.
	10:14 "I am the good **s**;
	10:16 there shall be one flock and one **s**.
Heb	13:20 that great **S** of the sheep,
1Pe	2:25 to the **S** and Overseer of your souls.
	5: 4 And when the Chief **S** appears,
Rev	7:17 of the throne will be their **s**;

SHEPHERDED* [SHEPHERD]

Ps 78:72 David **s** them with integrity of heart;

SHEPHERDS [SHEPHERD]

Ge	46:34 all **s** are detestable to the Egyptians."
Ex	2:19 "An Egyptian rescued us from the **s**.
Nu	14:33 Your children will be **s** here
Isa	56:11 They are **s** who lack understanding;
Jer	3:15 I will give you **s** after my own heart,
	23: 1 "Woe to the **s** who are destroying
	50: 6 their **s** have led them astray
Eze	34: 2 prophesy against the **s** of Israel;
Zec	10: 3 "My anger burns against the **s**,
Lk	2: 8 And there were **s** living out in
Ac	20:28 Be **s** of the church of God,
1Pe	5: 2 Be **s** of God's flock that is
Jude	1:12 **s** who feed only themselves.

SHESHBAZZAR

Ezr	1: 8 to **S** the prince of Judah.
	5:16 **S** came and laid the foundations

SHEWBREAD (KJV) See BREAD OF
THE PRESENCE

SHIBBOLETH* [SIBBOLETH]

Jdg 12: 6 "All right, say **'S.'** "

SHIELD [SHIELDED, SHIELDS]

Ge	15: 1 I am your **s**, your very great reward."
Ex	40: 3 and **s** the ark with the curtain.
Dt	33:29 He is your **s** and helper
2Sa	22:36 You give me your **s** of victory;
Ps	3: 3 you are a **s** around me, O LORD;
	5:12 with your favor as with a **s**.
	7:10 My **s** is God Most High,
	18: 2 He is my **s** and the horn
	28: 7 LORD is my strength and my **s**;
	33:20 he is our help and our **s**.
	84:11 For the LORD God is a sun and **s**;
	91: 4 will be your **s** and rampart.
	115: 9 he is their help and **s**.
	119:114 You are my refuge and my **s**;
	144: 2 my **s**, in whom I take refuge,
Pr	2: 7 a **s** to those whose walk is blameless,
	30: 5 a **s** to those who take refuge in him.
Isa	31: 5 the LORD Almighty will **s** Jerusalem;
Zec	9:15 the LORD Almighty will **s** them.
Eph	6:16 take up the **s** of faith,

SHIELDED [SHIELD]

Dt	32:10 He **s** him and cared for him;
1Pe	1: 5 through faith are **s** by God's power

SHIELDS [SHIELD]

Dt 33:12 for he **s** him all day long,

SHIFTING*

Jas 1:17 who does not change like **s** shadows.

SHIFTLESS*

Pr 19:15 and the **s** man goes hungry.

SHILOH [TAANATH SHILOH]

Jos	18: 1 the Israelites gathered at **S** and set up
1Sa	1:24 to the house of the LORD at **S**.
Ps	78:60 He abandoned the tabernacle of **S**,

SHIMEI

Cursed David (2Sa 16:5-14); spared (2Sa 19:16-23). Killed by Solomon (1Ki 2:8-9, 36-46).

SHINAR

Ge 11: 2 a plain in **S** and settled there.

SHINE [SHINES, SHINING, SHONE]

Nu	6:25 the LORD make his face **s** upon you
Job	33:30 that the light of life may **s** on him.
Ps	4: 6 Let the light of your face **s** upon us,
	37: 6 He will make your righteousness **s**
	67: 1 and make his face **s** upon us,
	80: 1 between the cherubim, **s** forth
	94: 1 O God who avenges, **s** forth.
	118:27 and he has made his light **s** upon us.
Isa	60: 1 "Arise, **s**, for your light has come,
Da	12: 3 Those who are wise will **s** like
Mt	5:16 let your light **s** before men,
	13:43 Then the righteous will **s** like the sun
Lk	1:79 to **s** on those living in darkness and
2Co	4: 6 "Let light **s** out of darkness,"
Eph	5:14 and Christ will **s** on you."
Php	2:15 in which you **s** like stars in
Rev	21:23 not need the sun or the moon to **s**

SHINES* [SHINE]

Ps	50: 2 perfect in beauty, God **s** forth.
Pr	13: 9 The light of the righteous **s** brightly,
Isa	62: 1 till her righteousness **s** out like
Lk	11:36 when the light of a lamp **s** on you."
Jn	1: 5 The light **s** in the darkness,

SHINING [SHINE]

Pr	4:18 **s** ever brighter till the full light
Lk	23:45 for the sun stopped **s**.
2Pe	1:19 as to a light **s** in a dark place,
1Jn	2: 8 and the true light is already **s**.
Rev	1:16 His face was like the sun **s**

SHIP [SHIPS]

Jnh	1: 4 that the **s** threatened to break up.
Ac	27:22 only the **s** will be destroyed.

SHIPS [SHIP]

1Ki 9:26 Solomon also built **s** at Ezion Geber,

22:48 Jehoshaphat built a fleet of trading **s**,
Ps 107:23 Others went out on the sea in **s**;
Pr 31:14 She is like the merchant **s**,
Jas 3: 4 Or take **s** as an example.

SHIPWRECKED*

2Co 11:25 three times I was **s**,
1Ti 1:19 and so have **s** their faith.

SHISHAK

2Ch 12: 2 **S** king of Egypt attacked Jerusalem

SHOCKED* [SHOCKING]

Eze 16:27 who were **s** by your lewd conduct.

SHOCKING* [SHOCKED]

Jer 5:30 "A horrible and **s** thing has happened

SHOE(S) (KJV) See SANDAL(S), SANDALED, UNSANDALED

SHONE [SHINE]

Mt 17: 2 His face **s** like the sun,
Lk 2: 9 the glory of the Lord **s** around them,
Rev 21:11 It **s** with the glory of God,

SHOOK [SHAKE]

Ps 18: 7 the foundations of the mountains **s**;
Isa 6: 4 the doorposts and thresholds **s** and
Mt 27:51 The earth **s** and the rocks split.
Ac 13:51 So they **s** the dust from their feet
18: 6 he **s** out his clothes in protest

SHOOT [SHOOTS]

Isa 11: 1 A **s** will come up from the stump
53: 2 grew up before him like a tender **s**,
60:21 They are the **s** I have planted,
Ro 11:17 and you, though a wild olive **s**,

SHOOTS [SHOOT]

Ps 128: 3 be like olive **s** around your table.
Hos 14: 6 his young **s** will grow.

SHORE [SHORES]

Ex 14:30 the Egyptians lying dead on the **s**.
Zep 2:11 nations on every **s** will worship him,
Lk 5: 3 asked him to put out a little from **s**.
Rev 13: 1 the dragon stood on the **s** of the sea.

SHORES [SHORE]

Ps 72:10 of distant **s** will bring tribute to him;
97: 1 let the distant **s** rejoice.

SHORT [SHORTENED]

Nu 11:23 "Is the Lord's arm too **s**?
Isa 50: 2 Was my arm too **s** to ransom you?
59: 1 of the Lord is not too **s** to save,
Mt 13:21 he has no root, he lasts only a **s** time.
24:22 If those days had not been cut **s**,
Lk 19: 3 but being a **s** man he could not,
Jn 7:33 "I am with you for only a **s** time.
Ac 26:28 in such a **s** time you can persuade me
Ro 3:23 for all have sinned and fall **s** of
1Co 7:29 brothers, is that the time is **s**.
Heb 4: 1 of you be found to have fallen **s** of it.

Rev 12:12 because he knows that his time is **s**."
20: 3 that, he must be set free for a **s** time.

SHORTENED* [SHORT]

Mt 24:22 sake of the elect those days will be **s**.
Mk 13:20 whom he has chosen, he has **s** them.

SHOULD

Mt 23:23 You **s** have practiced the latter,
Lk 18: 1 **s** always pray and not give up.
Php 2:10 the name of Jesus every knee **s** bow,

SHOULDER [SHOULDERS]

Isa 22:22 I will place on his **s** the key to
Zep 3: 9 of the Lord and serve him **s** to **s**.

SHOULDERS [SHOULDER]

Ex 28:12 Aaron is to bear the names on his **s**
Dt 33:12 the Lord loves rests between his **s**."
Ps 81: 6 "I removed the burden from their **s**;
Isa 9: 4 the bar across their **s**,
9: 6 and the government will be on his **s**.
Mt 23: 4 and put them on men's **s**,
Lk 15: 5 he joyfully puts it on his **s**

SHOUT [SHOUTED, SHOUTING, SHOUTS]

Nu 23:21 the **s** of the King is among them.
Jos 6:16 Joshua commanded the people, "**S**!
Ezr 3:11 the people gave a great **s** of praise to
Ps 20: 5 We will **s** for joy when you
35:27 **s** for joy and gladness;
47: 1 **s** to God with cries of joy.
66: 1 **S** with joy to God, all the earth!
95: 1 let us **s** aloud to the Rock
98: 4 **S** for joy to the Lord, all the earth,
100: 1 **S** for joy to the Lord, all the earth.
Isa 12: 6 **S** aloud and sing for joy,
26:19 wake up and **s** for joy.
35: 6 and the mute tongue **s** for joy.
40: 9 lift up your voice with a **s**, lift it up,
42: 2 He will not **s** or cry out,
44:23 **s** aloud, O earth beneath.
54: 1 **s** for joy, you who were never
Jer 31:12 and **s** for joy on the heights of Zion;
Zec 9: 9 **S**, Daughter of Jerusalem!
Rev 10: 3 and he gave a loud **s** like the roar of

SHOUTED [SHOUT]

Lev 9:24 they **s** for joy and fell facedown.
1Sa 17: 8 Goliath stood and **s** to the ranks
Job 38: 7 and all the angels **s** for joy?
Mk 15:13 "Crucify him!" they **s**.
Rev 18: 2 With a mighty voice he **s**: "Fallen!
19: 3 And again they **s**: "Hallelujah!

SHOUTING [SHOUT]

Mt 21:15 things he did and the children **s**
Jn 12:13 to meet him, **s**, "Hosanna!"

SHOUTS [SHOUT]

2Sa 6:15 the ark of the Lord with **s** and
Ps 27: 6 I sacrifice with **s** of joy;
47: 5 God has ascended amid **s** of joy,

Ecc 9:17 than the **s** of a ruler of fools.

SHOW [SHOWED, SHOWING, SHOWN, SHOWS]

Ge 12: 1 and go to the land I will **s** you.
      24:12 **s** kindness to my master Abraham.
Ex   9:16 that I might **s** you my power and
      18:20 and **s** them the way to live and
      25: 9 exactly like the pattern I will **s** you.
      33:18 Moses said, "Now **s** me your glory."
Dt   1:17 Do not **s** partiality in judging;
      4: 6 for this will **s** your wisdom
      7: 2 and **s** them no mercy.
Jos 2:12 that you will **s** kindness to my family
Ru   1: 8 May the LORD **s** kindness to you,
1Sa 20:14 But **s** me unfailing kindness like that
2Sa 9: 1 of Saul to whom I can **s** kindness
      22:26 the faithful you **s** yourself faithful,
1Ki 2: 2 "So be strong, **s** yourself a man,
Ezr 2:59 but they could not **s** that their
Ps   17: 7 **S** the wonder of your great love,
      18:26 to the pure you **s** yourself pure,
      25: 4 **S** me your ways, O LORD,
      39: 4 "**S** me, O LORD, my life's end and
      85: 7 **S** us your unfailing love, O LORD,
      102:13 for it is time to **s** favor to her;
      143: 8 **S** me the way I should go,
Pr   23: 4 have the wisdom to **s** restraint.
SS   2:14 **s** me your face,
Isa 5:16 and the holy God will **s** himself holy
      30:18 he rises to **s** you compassion.
Jer 32:18 You **s** love to thousands but bring
La   3:32 he brings grief, he will **s** compassion,
Eze 28:25 I will **s** myself holy among them in
Hos 1: 6 for I will no longer **s** love to
      2:23 I will **s** my love to the one I called
Joel 2:30 I will **s** wonders in the heavens and
Mic 7:20 and **s** mercy to Abraham,
Zec 7: 9 'Administer true justice; **s** mercy
Mt   22:19 **S** me the coin used for paying
Mk   12:40 and for a **s** make lengthy prayers.
Jn   2:18 "What miraculous sign can you **s** us
      14: 8 "Lord, **s** us the Father
Ac   2:19 I will **s** wonders in the heaven above
      10:34 that God does not **s** favoritism
Ro   2:11 For God does not **s** favoritism.
1Co 12:31 I will **s** you the most excellent way.
2Co 11:30 of the things that **s** my weakness.
Eph 2: 7 he might **s** the incomparable riches
Tit 2: 7 In your teaching **s** integrity,
      3: 2 to **s** true humility toward all men.
Jas 2:18 **S** me your faith without deeds,
1Pe 2:17 **S** proper respect to everyone:
Jude 1:23 to others **s** mercy, mixed with fear—
Rev 1: 1 to **s** his servants what must soon take
      4: 1 and I will **s** you what must take place
      17: 1 I will **s** you the punishment of
      21: 9 "Come, I will **s** you the bride,

SHOWED [SHOW]

Ge 39:21 was with him; he **s** him kindness
Dt   34: 1 the LORD **s** him the whole land—
1Ki 3: 3 Solomon **s** his love for the LORD
Mic 6: 8 He has **s** you, O man, what is good.

Mt   4: 8 and **s** him all the kingdoms of
Lk   24:40 he **s** them his hands and feet.
Jn   20:20 he **s** them his hands and side.
Ac   1: 3 he **s** himself to these men
1Jn 4: 9 This is how God **s** his love among us
Rev 21:10 and **s** me the Holy City, Jerusalem,
      22: 1 the angel **s** me the river of the water

SHOWERS

Dt   32: 2 like **s** on new grass,
Ps   68: 9 You gave abundant **s**, O God;
Jer 3: 3 Therefore the **s** have been withheld,
Eze 34:26 there will be **s** of blessing.
Hos 10:12 until he comes and **s** righteousness

SHOWING [SHOW]

Ex   20: 6 but **s** love to a thousand [generations]
Dt   5:10 but **s** love to a thousand [generations]
Jn   15: 8 **s** yourselves to be my disciples.

SHOWN [SHOW]

Ex   25:40 to the pattern **s** you on the mountain.
Dt   4:35 You were **s** these things so
1Ki 3: 6 "You have **s** great kindness
Ps   78:11 the wonders he had **s** them.
Mt   5: 7 for they will be **s** mercy.
Jn   10:32 "I have **s** you many great miracles
1Co 3:13 his work will be **s** for what it is,

SHOWS [SHOW]

Dt   10:17 who **s** no partiality and accepts no
Ps   123: 2 till he **s** us his mercy.
Pr   10:17 He who heeds discipline **s** the way
      15: 5 whoever heeds correction **s** prudence
Ecc 10: 3 the fool lacks sense and **s** everyone

SHREWD [SHREWDLY]

2Sa 22:27 to the crooked you show yourself **s.**
Mt   10:16 be as **s** as snakes and as innocent

SHREWDLY* [SHREWD]

Ex   1:10 we must deal **s** with them
Lk   16: 8 because he had acted **s.**

SHRINE [SHRINES]

Ge 38:21 "Where is the **s** prostitute who was
Dt   23:17 or woman is to become a **s** prostitute.
1Ki 14:24 There were even male **s** prostitutes in
Hos 4:14 and sacrifice with **s** prostitutes—

SHRINES [SHRINE]

1Ki 12:31 Jeroboam built **s** on high places
Eze 16:25 of every street you built your lofty **s**

SHRINK* [SHRINKS]

Heb 10:39 But we are not of those who **s** back
Rev 12:11 so much as to **s** from death.

SHRINKS* [SHRINK]

Heb 10:38 And if he **s** back,

SHRIVEL [SHRIVELED]

Isa 64: 6 we all **s** up like a leaf,

SHRIVELED [SHRIVEL]

1Ki 13: 4 stretched out toward the man **s** up,
Mk 3: 1 and a man with a **s** hand was there.

SHUDDER

Eze 32:10 and their kings will **s** with horror
Jas 2:19 Even the demons believe that—and **s**

SHUHITE

Job 2:11 Eliphaz the Temanite, Bildad the **S**

SHULAMMITE

SS 6:13 Come back, come back, O **S**;

SHUN* [SHUNNED, SHUNS]

Job 28:28 and to **s** evil is understanding.' "
Pr 3: 7 fear the LORD and **s** evil.

SHUNAMMITE

1Ki 1: 3 a **S**, and brought her to the king.
2Ki 4:12 "Call the **S**."

SHUNNED* [SHUN]

Job 1: 1 he feared God and **s** evil.
Pr 14:20 poor are **s** even by their neighbors,
19: 7 A poor man is **s** by all his relatives—

SHUNS* [SHUN]

Job 1: 8 a man who fears God and **s** evil."
2: 3 a man who fears God and **s** evil.
Pr 14:16 the LORD and **s** evil,
Isa 59:15 and whoever **s** evil becomes a prey.

SHUSHAN (KJV) See SUSA

SHUT [SHUTS]

Ge 7:16 Then the LORD **s** him in.
19: 6 Lot went outside to meet them and **s**
Dt 11:17 and he will **s** the heavens so
Jos 6: 1 Now Jericho was tightly **s** up
2Ch 6:26 the heavens are **s** up
Isa 22:22 what he opens no one can **s**,
52:15 and kings will **s** their mouths because
60:11 they will never be **s**, day or night,
Da 6:22 and he **s** the mouths of the lions.
Mt 23:13 You **s** the kingdom of heaven
Heb 11:33 who **s** the mouths of lions,
Rev 3: 7 What he opens no one can **s**,
11: 6 to **s** up the sky so that it will not rain
21:25 On no day will its gates ever be **s**,

SHUTS [SHUT]

Isa 22:22 and what he **s** no one can open.
Rev 3: 7 and what he **s** no one can open.

SIBBOLETH* [SHIBBOLETH]

Jdg 12: 6 If he said, "**S**,"

SICK [SICKNESS]

Pr 13:12 Hope deferred makes the heart **s**,
Eze 34: 4 strengthened the weak or healed the **s**
Mt 8:16 with a word and healed all the **s**.
9:12 who need a doctor, but the **s**.
10: 8 Heal the **s**, raise the dead,
25:36 I was **s** and you looked after me,

Jn 11: 1 Now a man named Lazarus was **s**.
Ac 19:12 had touched him were taken to the **s**,
1Co 11:30 among you are weak and **s**,
2Ti 4:20 and I left Trophimus **s** in Miletus.
Jas 5:14 Is any one of you **s**?

SICKBED* [BED, SICK]

Ps 41: 3 LORD will sustain him on his **s**

SICKLE

Joel 3:13 Swing the **s**, for the harvest is ripe.
Rev 14:14 on his head and a sharp **s** in his hand.

SICKNESS [SICK]

Ex 23:25 I will take away **s** from among you,
Mt 4:23 and healing every disease and **s**
Jn 11: 4 "This **s** will not end in death.

SIDE [SIDES]

1Ch 22: 9 rest from all his enemies on every **s**.
2Ch 15:15 LORD gave them rest on every **s**.
20:30 given him rest on every **s**.
Ps 91: 7 A thousand may fall at your **s**,
124: 1 If the LORD had not been on our **s**—
Pr 8:30 Then I was the craftsman at his **s**,
Jer 20:10 "Terror on every **s**!
Eze 1:10 the right **s** each had the face of a lion,
4: 4 the number of days you lie on your **s**.
Joel 3:12 to judge all the nations on every **s**.
Zec 3: 1 and Satan standing at his right **s**
Jn 1:18 who is at the Father's **s**,
18:37 Everyone on the **s** of truth listens
19:18 two others—one on each **s**
19:34 one of the soldiers pierced Jesus' **s**
20:20 he showed them his hands and **s**.
2Ti 4:17 But the Lord stood at my **s**
Heb 10:33 at other times you stood **s** by **s**
Rev 22: 2 On each **s** of the river stood the tree

SIDES [SIDE]

Ex 12: 7 and put it on the **s** and tops
29:16 against the altar on all **s**.
Nu 33:55 in your eyes and thorns in your **s**.
Jdg 2: 3 in your **s** and their gods will be
Job 11: 6 for true wisdom has two **s**.
Eze 2:10 On both **s** of it were written words
Da 7: 5 It was raised up on one of its **s**,
Rev 5: 1 a scroll with writing on both **s**

SIDON

Jdg 1:31 living in Acco or **S** or Ahlab or
1Ki 17: 9 to Zarephath of **S** and stay there.
Eze 28:21 set your face against **S**;
Mt 11:21 had been performed in Tyre and **S**,
Mk 7:31 vicinity of Tyre and went through **S**,
Lk 4:26 in Zarephath in the region of **S**.

SIEGE [BESIEGED]

Dt 28:52 They will lay **s** to all the cities
2Ki 6:25 **s** lasted so long that
18: 9 against Samaria and laid **s** to it.
24:10 advanced on Jerusalem and laid **s**

SIEVE*

Isa 30:28 the nations in the **s** of destruction;

Am 9: 9 9 the nations as grain is shaken in a **s,**

SIFT*

Jdg 7: 4 and I will **s** them for you there.
Lk 22:31 Satan has asked to **s** you as wheat.

SIGH* [SIGHED, SIGHING]

Mk 7:34 a deep **s** said to him, "Ephphatha!"

SIGHED* [SIGH]

Mk 8:12 He **s** deeply and said,

SIGHING [SIGH]

Ps 5: 1 O LORD, consider my **s.**
Isa 35:10 and sorrow and **s** will flee away.

SIGHT [SEE]

Ge 6:11 Now the earth was corrupt in God's **s**
Ex 3: 3 "I will go over and see this strange **s**
        4:11 Who gives him **s** or makes him blind
Nu 20:12 as holy in the **s** of
Ps 19:14 of my heart be pleasing in your **s,**
        51: 4 and done what is evil in your **s,**
        72:14 for precious is their blood in his **s.**
        90: 4 a thousand years in your **s** are like
       116:15 in the **s** of the LORD is the death
Pr   3: 4 and a good name in the **s** of God
Jer 18:10 and if it does evil in my **s** and does
Mt 11: 5 The blind receive **s,**
Ac   1: 9 and a cloud hid him from their **s.**
        4:19 right in God's **s** to obey you rather
1Co 3:19 this world is foolishness in God's **s.**
2Co 5: 7 We live by faith, not by **s.**
Eph 1: 4 to be holy and blameless in his **s.**
1Pe 3: 4 which is of great worth in God's **s.**

SIGN [SIGNS]

Ge   9:12 the **s** of the covenant I am making
        17:11 be the **s** of the covenant between me
Ex   4: 8 And this will be the **s** to you
        12:13 The blood will be a **s** for you
        13:16 And it will be like a **s** on your hand
Nu 16:38 Let them be a **s** to the Israelites."
        17:10 to be kept as a **s** to the rebellious.
Dt 13: 1 and announces to you a miraculous **s**
Jdg 6:17 a **s** that it is really you talking to me.
1Ki 13: 3 the man of God gave a **s:**
Isa 7:14 the Lord himself will give you a **s:**
        55:13 for an everlasting **s,**
Eze 20:12 Also I gave them my Sabbaths as a **s**
        24:24 Ezekiel will be a **s** to you;
Mt 12:38 to see a miraculous **s** from you."
        16: 1 by asking him to show them a **s**
        24: 3 the **s** of your coming and of the end
        24:30 the **s** of the Son of Man will appear
Mk   8:12 no **s** will be given to it."
Lk   2:12 This will be a **s** to you:
        11:29 except the **s** of Jonah.
Jn   2:18 "What miraculous **s** can you show us
Ro   4:11 he received the **s** of circumcision.
1Co 11:10 to have a **s** of authority on her head.
        14:22 Tongues, then, are a **s,**
Rev 12: 1 and wondrous **s** appeared in heaven:
        12: 3 Then another **s** appeared in heaven:

        15: 1 another great and marvelous **s:**

SIGNAL

Mk 14:44 betrayer had arranged a **s** with them:

SIGNET

Ge 41:42 Then Pharaoh took his **s** ring
Est 3:10 So the king took his **s** ring
         8: 2 The king took off his **s** ring,
Jer 22:24 were a **s** ring on my right hand,
Da   6:17 the king sealed it with his own **s** ring
Hag 2:23 'and I will make you like my **s** ring,

SIGNS [SIGN]

Ge   1:14 as **s** to mark seasons and days
Ex   4: 9 But if they do not believe these two **s**
         7: 3 though I multiply my miraculous **s**
Ps 78:43 the day he displayed his miraculous **s**
       105:27 They performed his miraculous **s**
Isa 8:18 We are **s** and symbols in Israel from
        44:25 who foils the **s** of false prophets
Da   6:27 rescues and he saves; he performs **s**
Mt 16: 3 but you cannot interpret the **s** of
        24:24 great **s** and miracles to deceive
Mk 13:22 and perform **s** and miracles
Jn   3: 2 one could perform the miraculous **s**
         7:31 do more miraculous **s** than this man?
         9:16 can a sinner do such miraculous **s?"**
        20:30 Jesus did many other miraculous **s** in
Ac   2:19 above and **s** on the earth below,
         5:12 performed many miraculous **s** and
1Co 1:22 Jews demand miraculous **s**
2Co 12:12 The things that mark an apostle—**s,**
2Th 2: 9 in all kinds of counterfeit miracles, **s**
Heb 2: 4 God also testified to it by **s,**
Rev 13:13 he performed great and miraculous **s,**
        16:14 of demons performing miraculous **s,**
        19:20 With these **s** he had deluded those

MIRACULOUS SIGNS Ex 4:17, 28; 7:3; 10:1;
Nu 14:11, 22; Dt 4:34; 6:22; 7:19; 26:8; 29:3;
34:11; Ne 9:10; Ps 74:9; 78:43; 105:27; Jer
32:20; Da 4:2; 2:11, 23; 3:2; 4:48; 6:2, 26;
7:31; 9:16; 11:47; 12:37; 20:30; Ac 2:43; 4:30;
5:12; 6:8; 7:36; 8:6; 14:3; 15:12; 1Co 1:22; Rev
13:13; 16:14; 19:20

SIGNS AND WONDERS Ex 7:3; Dt 4:34;
6:22; 7:19; 26:8; 34:11; Ne 9:10; Ps 135:9; Jer
32:20, 21; Da 4:2; 6:27; Jn 4:48; Ac 4:30; 5:12;
14:3; 15:12; 2Th 2:9

SIHON

Nu 21:21 to say to **S** king of the Amorites:
Dt 31: 4 to them what he did to **S** and Og,
Ps 136:19 **S** king of the Amorites

SILAS*

Prophet (Ac 15:22-32); co-worker with Paul on
second missionary journey (Ac 16-18; 2Co 1:19).
Co-writer with Paul (1Th 1:1; 2Th 1:1); Peter (1Pe
5:12).

SILENCE [SILENCED, SILENT]

Ps   8: 2 to **s** the foe and the avenger.
1Pe 2:15 that by doing good you should **s**

Rev 8: 1 **s** in heaven for about half an hour.

SILENCED [SILENCE]

Ps   63:11 while the mouths of liars will be **s.**
Mt   22:34 that Jesus had **s** the Sadducees,
Ro   3:19 that every mouth may be **s** and
Tit   1:11 They must be **s,**

SILENT [SILENCE]

Est   4:14 For if you remain **s** at this time,
Ps   30:12 sing to you and not be **s.**
      32: 3 When I kept **s,**
      39: 2 But when I was **s** and still,
      50: 3 Our God comes and will not be **s;**
Pr   17:28 a fool is thought wise if he keeps **s,**
Ecc   3: 7 a time to be **s** and a time to speak,
Isa   53: 7 as a sheep before her shearers is **s,**
      62: 1 For Zion's sake I will not keep **s,**
Jer   4:19 I cannot keep **s.**
Hab   2:20 the earth be **s** before him."
Zep   1: 7 Be **s** before the Sovereign LORD,
Mk   14:61 But Jesus remained **s.**
Ac   8:32 and as a lamb before the shearer is **s,**
1Co 14:34 women should remain **s** in
1Ti   2:12 authority over a man; she must be **s.**

SILOAM

Jn   9: 7 he told him, "wash in the Pool of **S**"

SILVER

Ge   37:28 and sold him for twenty shekels of **s**
Ex   11: 2 to ask their neighbors for articles of **s**
      20:23 not make for yourselves gods of **s**
      25: 3 to receive from them: gold, **s** and
Dt   17:17 not accumulate large amounts of **s**
Jos   7:21 two hundred shekels of **s** and
2Ch   1:15 king made **s** and gold as common
Ps   12: 6 like **s** refined in a furnace of clay,
      66:10 you refined us like **s.**
     115: 4 But their idols are **s** and gold,
Pr   2: 4 if you look for it as for **s** and search
      3:14 for she is more profitable than **s**
      8:10 Choose my instruction instead of **s,**
      22: 1 be esteemed is better than **s** or gold.
      25: 4 Remove the dross from the **s,**
      25:11 like apples of gold in settings of **s.**
Isa   48:10 I have refined you, though not as **s;**
Eze   22:18 They are but the dross of **s,**
Da   2:32 its chest and arms of **s,**
      5: 4 they praised the gods of gold and **s,**
Hag   2: 8 'The **s** is mine and the gold is mine,'
Zec 11:12 So they paid me thirty pieces of **s.**
      13: 9 I will refine them like **s**
Mal   3: 3 as a refiner and purifier of **s;**
Mt   26:15 counted out for him thirty **s** coins.
Ac   3: 6 Peter said, "**S** or gold I do not have,
1Co   3:12 **s,** costly stones, wood, hay or straw,
2Ti   2:20 articles not only of gold and **s,**
1Pe   1:18 as **s** or gold that you were redeemed

SILVERSMITH

Ac   19:24 A **s** named Demetrius,

SIMEON

Son of Jacob by Leah (Ge 29:33; 35:23; 1Ch

2:1). With Levi killed Shechem for rape of Dinah (Ge 34:25-29). Held hostage by Joseph in Egypt (Ge 42:24-43:23). Tribe of blessed (Ge 49:5-7), numbered (Nu 1:23; 26:14), allotted land (Jos 19:1-9; Eze 48:24), 12,000 from (Rev 7:7).

SIMON [PETER]

1. See PETER.

2. Apostle, called the Zealot (Mt 10:4; Mk 3:18; Lk 6:15; Ac 1:13).

3. Samaritan sorcerer (Ac 8:9-24).

SIMPLE [SIMPLEHEARTED]

Ex   18:22 **s** cases they can decide themselves.
Ps   19: 7 making wise the **s.**
     119:130 gives understanding to the **s.**
Pr   1:22 will you **s** ones love your **s** ways?
      8: 5 You who are **s,** gain prudence;
      14:15 A **s** man believes anything,

SIMPLEHEARTED* [SIMPLE, HEART]

Ps 116: 6 The LORD protects the **s;**

SIN [SIN'S, SINFUL, SINNED, SINNER, SINNER'S, SINNERS, SINNING, SINS]

Ge   4: 7 **s** is crouching at your door;
Ex   20: 5 the children for the **s** of the fathers
      32:32 But now, please forgive their **s—**
      34: 7 forgiving wickedness, rebellion and **s**
Lev   4: 3 bull without defect as a **s** offering
      5: 6 or goat from the flock as a **s** offering;
Nu   5: 7 must confess the **s** he has committed.
      14:18 abounding in love and forgiving **s**
      32:23 be sure that your **s** will find you out.
Dt   24:16 each is to die for his own **s.**
1Sa 12:23 that I should **s** against the LORD by
      15:23 rebellion is like the **s** of divination,
1Ki   8:46 for there is no one who does not **s—**
      13:34 the **s** of the house of Jeroboam
2Ch   7:14 from heaven and will forgive their **s**
Ne   13:26 he was led into **s** by foreign women.
Job   1:22 Job did not **s** by charging God
      2:10 Job did not **s** in what he said.
Ps   4: 4 In your anger do not **s;**
      17: 3 that my mouth will not **s.**
      32: 2 the man whose **s** the LORD does not
      32: 5 Then I acknowledged my **s** to you
      32: 5 and you forgave the guilt of my **s.**
      36: 2 to detect or hate his **s.**
      38:18 I am troubled by my **s.**
      39: 1 and keep my tongue from **s;**
      51: 2 and cleanse me from my **s.**
      66:18 If I had cherished **s** in my heart,
     119:11 that I might not **s** against you.
     119:133 let no **s** rule over me.
Pr   5:22 the cords of his **s** hold him fast.
      10:19 words are many, **s** is not absent,
      14: 9 Fools mock at making amends for **s,**
      16: 6 love and faithfulness **s** is atoned for;
      17:19 He who loves a quarrel loves **s;**
      20: 9 I am clean and without **s"**?
      29: 6 An evil man is snared by his own **s,**

Ecc 5: 6 not let your mouth lead you into **s.**
Isa 3: 9 they parade their **s** like Sodom;
6: 7 and your **s** atoned for."
53:12 For he bore the **s** of many,
64: 5 when we continued to **s** against them
Jer 16:18 for their wickedness and their **s,**
31:30 everyone will die for his own **s;**
Eze 3:18 that wicked man will die for his **s,**
18:26 his righteousness and commits **s,**
18:26 of the **s** he has committed he will die.
33: 8 that wicked man will die for his **s,**
Da 9:20 confessing my **s** and the **s** of my
Hos 13: 2 Now they **s** more and more;
Mic 6: 7 of my body for the **s** of my soul?
7:18 who pardons **s** and forgives
Zec 3: 4 "See, I have taken away your **s,**
Mt 5:29 If your right eye causes you to **s,**
6:14 For if you forgive men when they **s**
18: 6 who believe in me to **s,**
Mk 3:29 he is guilty of an eternal **s."**
9:43 If your hand causes you to **s,**
Lk 17: 1 "Things that cause people to **s**
Jn 1:29 who takes away the **s** of the world!
8: 7 "If any one of you is without **s,**
8:34 everyone who sins is a slave to **s.**
8:46 any of you prove me guilty of **s?**
16: 9 to **s,** because men do not believe
Ac 7:60 do not hold this **s** against them."
Ro 2:12 All who **s** apart from the law will
4: 8 Blessed is the man whose **s**
5:12 just as **s** entered the world
5:20 But where **s** increased,
6: 2 We died to **s;**
6:11 dead to **s** but alive to God in Christ
6:14 For **s** shall not be your master,
6:23 For the wages of **s** is death,
7: 7 Is the law **s?**
7: 7 not have known what **s** was except
7:25 a slave to the law of **s.**
8: 2 set me free from the law of **s**
14:23 that does not come from faith is **s.**
1Co 8:12 When you **s** against your brothers
15:56 The sting of death is **s,**
2Co 5:21 him who had no **s** to be **s** for us,
Gal 2:17 that mean that Christ promotes **s?**
6: 1 Brothers, if someone is caught in a **s,**
Eph 4:26 "In your anger do not **s":**
1Ti 5:20 who **s** are to be rebuked publicly,
Heb 4:15 just as we are—yet was without **s.**
9:26 the end of the ages to do away with **s**
10:18 there is no longer any sacrifice for **s.**
11:25 the pleasures of **s** for a short time.
12: 1 and the **s** that so easily entangles,
Jas 1:15 it gives birth to **s;** and **s,**
1Pe 2:22 "He committed no **s,**
1Jn 1: 7 his Son, purifies us from all **s.**
1: 8 If we claim to be without **s,**
2: 1 to you so that you will not **s.**
2: 1 But if anybody does **s,**
3: 4 in fact, **s** is lawlessness.
3: 5 And in him is no **s.**
3: 6 No one who continues to **s** has
3: 9 born of God will continue to **s,**
5:16 If anyone sees his brother commit a **s**

5:16 There is a **s** that leads to death.
5:17 there is **s** that does not lead to death.

SIN OFFERING Ex 29:14, 36; 30:10; Lev 4:3, 8, 14, 20, 21, 24, 25, 29, 32, 33, 34; 5:6, 7, 8, 9, 9, 11, 11, 12; 6:17, 25, 25, 30; 7:7, 37; 8:2, 14; 9:2, 3, 7, 8, 10, 15, 15, 22; 10:16, 17, 19, 19; 12:6, 8; 14:13, 13, 19, 22, 31; 15:15, 30; 16:3, 5, 6, 9, 11, 11, 15, 25; 23:19; Nu 6:11, 14, 16; 7:16, 22, 28, 34, 40, 46, 52, 58, 64, 70, 76, 82, 87; 8:8, 12; 15:24, 25, 27; 28:15, 22; 29:5, 11, 11, 16, 19, 22, 25, 28, 31, 34, 38; 2Ch 29:21, 23, 24, 24; Ezr 6:17; 8:35; Eze 43:19, 21, 22, 25; 44:27; 45:19, 22, 23; 46:20; Ro 8:3; Heb 13:11

SIN OFFERINGS Lev 16:27; 2Ki 12:16; Ne 10:33; Ps 40:6; Eze 40:39; 42:13; 44:29; 45:17, 25; Hos 8:11; Heb 10:6, 8

SIN'S* [SIN]
Heb 3:13 be hardened by **s** deceitfulness.

SINAI
Ex 19: 1 they came to the Desert of **S.**
19:20 descended to the top of Mount **S**
31:18 speaking to Moses on Mount **S,**
Lev 27:34 the LORD gave Moses on Mount **S**
Nu 1:19 he counted them in the Desert of **S:**
Ps 68:17 the Lord [has come] from **S**
Gal 4:24 One covenant is from Mount **S**

MOUNT SINAI See MOUNT

SINCERE* [SINCERITY, SINCERELY]
Da 11:34 who are not **s** will join them.
Ac 2:46 ate together with glad and **s** hearts,
Ro 12: 9 Love must be **s.**
2Co 6: 6 in the Holy Spirit and in **s** love;
11: 3 astray from your **s** and pure devotion
1Ti 1: 5 and a good conscience and a **s** faith.
3: 8 are to be men worthy of respect, **s,**
2Ti 1: 5 I have been reminded of your **s** faith,
Heb 10:22 let us draw near to God with a **s** heart
Jas 3:17 and good fruit, impartial and **s.**
1Pe 1:22 you have **s** love for your brothers,

SINCERELY [SINCERE]
Job 33: 3 my lips **s** speak what I know.

SINCERITY* [SINCERE]
1Co 5: 8 the bread of **s** and truth.
2Co 1:12 the holiness and **s** that are from God.
2:17 in Christ we speak before God with **s**
8: 8 but I want to test the **s** of your love
Eph 6: 5 and with **s** of heart,
Col 3:22 but with **s** of heart and reverence for

SINEWS
Col 2:19 held together by its ligaments and **s,**

SINFUL [SIN]
Ps 51: 5 I was **s** at birth, **s** from the time my
Isa 1: 4 nation, a people loaded with guilt,
Eze 37:23 them from all their **s** backsliding,
Lk 5: 8 Lord; I am a **s** man!"
7:37 a woman who had lived a **s** life in
24: 7 be delivered into the hands of **s** men,

Ro   7: 5   we were controlled by the **s** nature,
      7:18   that is, in my **s** nature.
      7:25   the **s** nature a slave to the law of sin.
      8: 3   his own Son in the likeness of **s** man
      8: 4   do not live according to the **s** nature
      8: 8   by the **s** nature cannot please God.
      8: 9   are controlled not by the **s** nature but
      8:13   if you live according to the **s** nature,
    13:14   to gratify the desires of the **s** nature.
1Co   5: 5   the **s** nature may be destroyed
Gal   5:13   freedom to indulge the **s** nature;
      5:16   not gratify the desires of the **s** nature.
      5:19   The acts of the **s** nature are obvious:
      5:24   the **s** nature with its passions
Eph   2: 3   the cravings of our **s** nature
Col   2:11   in the putting off of the **s** nature,
      2:13   the uncircumcision of your **s** nature,
Heb   3:12   brothers, that none of you has a **s,**
    12: 3   endured such opposition from **s** men,
1Pe   2:11   to abstain from **s** desires,
1Jn   3: 8   He who does what is **s** is of the devil,

SINFUL NATURE Ro 7:5, 18, 25; 8:3, 4, 5, 8,
9, 12, 13; 13:14; 1Co 5:5; Gal 5:13, 16, 17, 17,
19, 24; 6:8; Eph 2:3; Col 2:11, 13; 2Pe 2:10

SING [SANG, SINGER, SINGERS, SINGING, SINGS, SONG, SONGS, SUNG]

Ex   15: 1   "I will **s** to the LORD,
Dt   31:19   and have them **s** it,
1Sa   21:11   the one they **s** about in their dances:
Ps   5:11   let them ever **s** for joy.
     13: 6   I will **s** to the LORD,
     30: 4   **S** to the LORD, you saints of his;
    30:12   that my heart may **s** to you and not
     33: 1   **S** joyfully to the LORD,
     33: 3   **S** to him a new song;
     47: 6   **S** praises to God, **s** praises; **s** praises
              to our King, **s** praises.
     57: 7   I will **s** and make music.
    59:16   But I will **s** of your strength,
    59:16   in the morning I will **s** of your love;
     63: 7   I **s** in the shadow of your wings.
     66: 2   **S** the glory of his name;
     68: 4   **S** to God, **s** praise to his name,
     89: 1   I will **s** of the LORD's great love
     95: 1   Come, let us **s** for joy to the LORD;
     96: 1   **S** to the LORD a new song;
     98: 1   **S** to the LORD a new song,
   101: 1   I will **s** of your love and justice;
   108: 1   I will **s** and make music
  119:172   May my tongue **s** of your word,
   137: 3   "**S** us one of the songs of Zion!"
   147: 1   good it is to **s** praises to our God,
   149: 1   **S** to the LORD a new song,
Isa   5: 1   I will **s** for the one I love a song
     27: 2   "**S** about a fruitful vineyard:
     54: 1   "**S,** O barren woman,
Jer   31: 7   "**S** with joy for Jacob;
1Co   14:15   I will **s** with my spirit, but I will also
              s with my mind.
Eph   5:19   **S** and make music in your heart to
Col   3:16   and as you **s** psalms,

Jas   5:13   Let him **s** songs of praise.
SING PRAISE See PRAISE

SINGED*

Da   3:27   nor was a hair of their heads **s;**

SINGER* [SING]

2Sa   23: 1   Israel's **s** of songs:

SINGERS [SING]

1Ch   15:16   to appoint their brothers as **s**
Ezr   2:70   The priests, the Levites, the **s,**
Ps   68:25   In front are the **s,**

SINGING [SING]

Ex   32:18   the sound of **s** that I hear."
Ps   63: 5   with **s** lips my mouth will praise you.
     68: 6   he leads forth the prisoners with **s;**
     98: 5   with the harp and the sound of **s,**
SS   2:12   the season of **s** has come,
Isa   35:10   They will enter Zion with **s;**
     51:11   They will enter Zion with **s;**
Zep   3:17   he will rejoice over you with **s."**
Ac   16:25   and Silas were praying and **s** hymns
Rev   5:13   and all that is in them, **s:**

SINGLE [SINGLED]

Ex   23:29   I will not drive them out in a **s** year,
Nu   13:23   a branch bearing a **s** cluster
Zec   3: 9   the sin of this land in a **s** day.
Mt   6:27   worrying can add a **s** hour to his life?
Jn   12:24   it remains only a **s** seed.
Gal   5:14   law is summed up in a **s** command:
Heb   12:16   for a **s** meal sold his inheritance
Rev   21:21   each gate made of a **s** pearl.

SINGLED* [SINGLE]

1Ki   8:53   For you **s** them out from all

SINGS [SING]

Eze   33:32   more than one who **s** love songs

SINK [SANK, SINKING, SUNK]

Dt   28:43   but you will **s** lower and lower.
Ps   69: 2   I **s** in the miry depths,
Jer   51:64   'So will Babylon **s** to rise no more

SINNED [SIN]

Lev   5: 5   he must confess in what way he has **s**
Nu   14:40   "We have **s,**" they said.
1Sa   15:24   Then Saul said to Samuel, "I have **s.**
2Sa   12:13   "I have **s** against the LORD."
    24:10   "I have **s** greatly in what I have done.
2Ch   6:37   'We have **s,** we have done wrong
Job   1: 5   "Perhaps my children have **s**
    33:27   Then he comes to men and says, 'I **s,**
Ps   51: 4   Against you, you only, have I **s**
Jer   2:35   'I have not **s.'**
    14:20   we have indeed **s**
La   5: 7   Our fathers **s** and are no more,
Da   9: 5   we have **s** and done wrong.
Mic   7: 9   Because I have **s** against him,
Mt   27: 4   "I have **s,**" he said,
Lk   15:18   I have **s** against heaven and

Jn	9: 2	who **s**, this man or his parents,
Ro	3:23	for all have **s** and fall short of
	5:12	to all men, because all **s**—
Jas	5:15	If he has **s**, he will be forgiven.
2Pe	2: 4	not spare angels when they **s**,
1Jn	1:10	If we claim we have not **s**,

SINNER [SIN]

Pr	13: 6	but wickedness overthrows the **s**.
Ecc	9:18	but one **s** destroys much good.
Lk	15: 7	over one **s** who repents than
	18:13	'God, have mercy on me, a **s**.'
Jn	9:16	can a **s** do such miraculous signs?"
1Co	14:24	be convinced by all that he is a **s**
Jas	5:20	Whoever turns a **s** from the error
1Pe	4:18	become of the ungodly and the **s**?"

SINNER'S* [SIN]

Pr	13:22	but a **s** wealth is stored up for

SINNERS [SIN]

Ps	1: 1	the wicked or stand in the way of **s**
	25: 8	therefore he instructs **s** in his ways.
	37:38	But all **s** will be destroyed;
	51:13	and **s** will turn back to you.
Pr	1:10	My son, if **s** entice you,
	23:17	Do not let your heart envy **s**,
Isa	1:28	But rebels and **s** will both be broken,
Mt	9:13	not come to call the righteous, but **s**.
Mk	14:41	is betrayed into the hands of **s**.
Lk	15: 2	"This man welcomes **s** and eats
Ro	5: 8	While we were still **s**,
Gal	2:17	evident that we ourselves are **s**,
1Ti	1:15	Jesus came into the world to save **s**
Heb	7:26	blameless, pure, set apart from **s**,

SINNING [SIN]

Ge	13:13	were **s** greatly against the LORD.
Ex	20:20	be with you to keep you from **s**."
Ps	78:32	In spite of all this, they kept on **s**;
Ro	6: 1	go on **s** so that grace may increase?
1Co	15:34	as you ought, and stop **s**;
Heb	10:26	If we deliberately keep on **s**
1Jn	3: 6	No one who lives in him keeps on **s**.
	3: 8	devil has been **s** from the beginning.

SINS [SIN]

Lev	4: 2	'When anyone **s** unintentionally
	4: 3	" 'If the anointed priest **s**,
	5: 1	a person **s** because he does not speak
	16:30	you will be clean from all your **s**.
	26:40	" 'But if they will confess their **s** and
Nu	15:30	" 'But anyone who **s** defiantly,
1Sa	2:25	but if a man **s** against the LORD,
2Ki	14: 6	each is to die for his own **s**."
	17:22	The Israelites persisted in all the **s**
Ezr	9: 6	our **s** are higher than our heads
	9:13	less than our **s** have deserved
Ps	19:13	Keep your servant also from willful **s**
	32: 1	whose **s** are covered.
	51: 9	Hide your face from my **s**
	79: 9	forgive our **s** for your name's sake.
	85: 2	and covered all their **s**.
	103: 3	who forgives all your **s**

	103:10	not treat us as our **s** deserve
	130: 3	If you, O LORD, kept a record of **s**,
Pr	14:21	He who despises his neighbor **s**,
	28:13	He who conceals his **s** does
	29:22	a hot-tempered one commits many **s**.
Ecc	7:20	does what is right and never **s**.
Isa	1:18	"Though your **s** are like scarlet,
	38:17	put all my **s** behind your back.
	40: 2	double for all her **s**.
	43:25	and remembers your **s** no more.
	59: 2	your **s** have hidden his face
	64: 6	like the wind our **s** sweep us away.
Jer	31:34	and will remember their **s** no more."
La	3:39	when punished for his **s?**
Eze	18: 4	soul who **s** is the one who will die.
	33:10	and **s** weigh us down,
	36:33	the day I cleanse you from all your **s**,
Hos	14: 1	Your **s** have been your downfall!
	14: 2	Say to him: "Forgive all our **s**
Mic	7:19	you will tread our **s** underfoot
Mt	1:21	he will save his people from their **s**."
	6:15	But if you do not forgive men their **s**, your Father will not forgive your **s**.
	9: 6	authority on earth to forgive **s**."
	18:15	"If your brother **s** against you,
	26:28	for many for the forgiveness of **s**.
Mk	1: 5	Confessing their **s**, they were
Lk	5:24	on earth to forgive **s**."
	11: 4	Forgive us our **s**, for we also forgive everyone who **s** against us.
	17: 3	"If your brother **s**, rebuke him,
Jn	8:24	you will indeed die in your **s**."
	20:23	If you forgive anyone his **s**,
Ac	2:38	for the forgiveness of your **s**.
	3:19	so that your **s** may be wiped out,
	10:43	in him receives forgiveness of **s**
	22:16	be baptized and wash your **s** away,
	26:18	they may receive forgiveness of **s**
Ro	4: 7	whose **s** are covered.
	4:25	over to death for our **s** and was raised
1Co	6:18	**s** sexually is against his own body.
	15: 3	that Christ died for our **s** according
2Co	5:19	not counting men's **s** against them.
Gal	1: 4	who gave himself for our **s**
Eph	1: 7	the forgiveness of **s**,
	2: 1	in your transgressions and **s**,
Col	2:13	When you were dead in your **s** and in
	2:13	He forgave us all our **s**,
1Ti	5:22	and do not share in the **s** of others.
Heb	1: 3	he had provided purification for **s**,
	2:17	atonement for the **s** of the people.
	7:27	He sacrificed for their **s** once for all
	8:12	and will remember their **s** no more."
	9:28	to take away the **s** of many people;
	10: 4	of bulls and goats to take away **s**.
	10:12	for all time one sacrifice for **s**,
	10:26	no sacrifice for **s** is left,
Jas	4:17	ought to do and doesn't do it, **s**.
	5:16	Therefore confess your **s**
	5:20	and cover over a multitude of **s**.
1Pe	2:24	He himself bore our **s** in his body on
	3:18	For Christ died for **s** once for all,
	4: 8	love covers over a multitude of **s**.
1Jn	1: 9	and just and will forgive us our **s**

499

2: 2 He is the atoning sacrifice for our **s,**
3: 5 so that he might take away our **s.**
4:10 as an atoning sacrifice for our **s.**
Rev 1: 5 and has freed us from our **s**

SION (KJV) See ZION

SISERA
Jdg 4: 2 The commander of his army was **S,**
5:26 She struck **S,** she crushed his head,

SISTER [SISTERS]
Ge 12:13 Say you are my **s,**
20: 2 "She is my **s."**
26: 7 he said, "She is my **s,"**
Lev 18: 9 not have sexual relations with your **s,**
Pr 7: 4 Say to wisdom, "You are my **s,"**
SS 4: 9 You have stolen my heart, my **s,**
Jer 3: 7 and her unfaithful **s** Judah saw it.
Eze 16:46 who bore you was Samaria,
Mk 3:35 does God's will is my brother and **s**
Lk 10:40 that my **s** has left me to do the work
Jn 11: 5 Jesus loved Martha and her **s**
Ro 16: 1 I commend to you our **s** Phoebe,
2Jn 1:13 of your chosen **s** send their greetings.

SISTERS [SISTER]
Mt 19:29 who has left houses or brothers or **s**
Mk 6: 3 Aren't his **s** here with us?"
1Ti 5: 2 and younger women as **s,**

SIT [SAT, SITS, SITTING]
Ex 18:14 Why do you alone **s** as judge,
Dt 6: 7 Talk about them when you **s** at home
11:19 about them when you **s** at home
1Ki 8:25 to **s** before me on the throne of Israel
Ps 1: 1 or **s** in the seat of mockers.
26: 5 refuse to **s** with the wicked.
80: 1 you who **s** enthroned
110: 1 "**S** at my right hand
139: 2 You know when I **s** and when I rise;
SS 2: 3 I delight to **s** in his shade,
Isa 14:13 I will **s** enthroned
16: 5 in faithfulness a man will **s** on it—
Jer 33:17 never fail to have a man to **s**
Eze 28: 2 I am a god; I **s** on the throne of a god
Mic 4: 4 Every man will **s** under his own vine
Mal 3: 3 He will **s** as a refiner and purifier
Mt 20:23 to **s** at my right or left is not for me
22:44 "**S** at my right hand until I put
23: 2 and the Pharisees **s** in Moses' seat.
Mk 14:32 "**S** here while I pray."
Lk 22:30 in my kingdom and **s** on thrones,
Jn 6:10 "Have the people **s** down."
Ac 2:34 "**S** at my right hand
Heb 1:13 "**S** at my right hand
Rev 3:21 the right to **s** with me on my throne,
18: 7 In her heart she boasts, 'I **s** as queen;

SITS [SIT]
Ps 29:10 LORD **s** enthroned over the flood;
99: 1 he **s** enthroned between the cherubim
113: 5 the One who **s** enthroned on high,
Isa 28: 6 of justice to him who **s** in judgment,
40:22 He **s** enthroned above the circle of

Mt 19:28 Son of Man **s** on his glorious throne,
Rev 4: 2 to him who **s** on the throne
5:13 "To him who **s** on the throne and to
6:16 of him who **s** on the throne and from
17: 1 who **s** on many waters.

SITTING [SIT]
2Ch 18:18 the LORD **s** on his throne with all
Est 2:19 Mordecai was **s** at the king's gate.
Mt 26:64 Son of Man **s** at the right hand
Lk 8:35 **s** at Jesus' feet,
Rev 4: 2 a throne in heaven with someone **s**
17: 3 a woman **s** on a scarlet beast

SITUATION [SITUATIONS]
1Co 7:24 remain in the **s** God called him to.
Php 4:12 of being content in any and every **s,**

SITUATIONS* [SITUATION]
2Ti 4: 5 But you, keep your head in all **s,**

SIX [SIXTH]
Ex 20: 9 **S** days you shall labor
1Ch 20: 6 a huge man with **s** fingers
Pr 6:16 There are **s** things the LORD hates,
Isa 6: 2 each with **s** wings:
Rev 4: 8 the four living creatures had **s** wings

SIXTH [SIX]
Lev 25:21 such a blessing in the **s** year
Mk 15:33 At the **s** hour darkness came over
Rev 6:12 I watched as he opened the **s** seal.
16:12 The **s** angel poured out his bowl on

SIXTY
Mt 13: 8 **s** or thirty times what was sown.

SIZE
2Ki 10:32 LORD began to reduce the **s** of Israel.
Ps 33:16 No king is saved by the **s**

SKIES [SKY]
Ps 19: 1 the **s** proclaim the work of his hands.
36: 5 your faithfulness to the **s.**
68:33 to him who rides the ancient **s** above,
71:19 Your righteousness reaches to the **s,**
89: 6 For who in the **s** above can compare
108: 4 your faithfulness reaches to the **s.**
Jer 51: 9 for her judgment reaches to the **s,**
Mt 11:23 will you be lifted up to the **s?**

SKILL [SKILLED, SKILLFUL, SKILLFULLY]
Ex 31: 3 with **s,** ability and knowledge
Ps 137: 5 may my right hand forget [its **s].**
Ecc 10:10 but **s** will bring success.

SKILLED [SKILL]
Ex 35:10 "All who are **s** among you are
1Ch 28:21 and every willing man **s**
Pr 22:29 Do you see a man **s** in his work?
Jer 4:22 They are **s** in doing evil;
Mic 7: 3 Both hands are **s** in doing evil;

SKILLFUL [SKILL]
Ps 45: 1 my tongue is the pen of a **s** writer.
78:72 with **s** hands he led them.

SKILLFULLY [SKILL]
Ps 33: 3 Sing to him a new song; play **s,**

SKIN [SKINS]
Ge 3:21 The LORD God made garments of **s**
Job 2: 4 "**S** for **s!**" Satan replied.
19:20 I am nothing but **s** and bones;
19:26 And after my **s** has been destroyed,
Jer 13:23 Can the Ethiopian change his **s** or

SKINS [SKIN]
Ex 25: 5 ram **s** dyed red and hides
Lk 5:37 the new wine will burst the **s,**

SKIP* [SKIPPED]
Ps 29: 6 He makes Lebanon **s** like a calf,

SKIPPED [SKIP]
Ps 114: 4 the mountains **s** like rams,

SKIRTS
Isa 47: 2 Lift up your **s,** bare your legs,
La   1: 9 Her filthiness clung to her **s;**

SKULL
2Ki 9:35 they found nothing except her **s,**
Mt 27:33 (which means The Place of the **S**).

SKY [SKIES]
Ge   1: 8 God called the expanse "**s.**"
22:17 as the stars in the **s**
26: 4 as numerous as the stars in the **s**
Ex 24:10 clear as the **s** itself.
Lev 26:19 and make the **s** above you like iron
Dt   1:10 as many as the stars in the **s.**
Ps 89:37 the faithful witness in the **s.**"
Pr 30:19 the way of an eagle in the **s,**
Isa 34: 4 and the **s** rolled up like a scroll;
Jer 33:22 as countless as the stars of the **s**
Mt 16: 3 to interpret the appearance of the **s,**
24:30 the Son of Man will appear in the **s,**
Mk 13:25 the stars will fall from the **s,**
Ac   1:10 up into the **s** as he was going,
Rev 6:13 and the stars in the **s** fell to earth,
6:14 The **s** receded like a scroll,
12: 4 swept a third of the stars out of the **s**
20:11 Earth and **s** fled from his presence,

SLACK*
Pr 18: 9 One who is **s** in his work is brother

SLAIN [SLAY]
1Sa 18: 7 they sang: "Saul has **s** his thousands,
21:11 " 'Saul has **s** his thousands,
29: 5 " 'Saul has **s** his thousands,
1Ch 10: 1 and many fell **s** on Mount Gilboa.
Pr   7:26 her **s** are a mighty throng.
Eze 37: 9 O breath, and breathe into these **s,**
Da   7:11 I kept looking until the beast was **s**
Rev 5: 6 looking as if it had been **s,**

5:12 "Worthy is the Lamb, who was **s,**
6: 9 of those who had been **s** because of
13: 8 belonging to the Lamb that was **s**

SLANDER [SLANDERED, SLANDERER, SLANDERERS, SLANDEROUS, SLANDEROUSLY, SLANDERS]
Lev 19:16 " 'Do not go about spreading **s**
Ps 15: 3 and has no **s** on his tongue,
54: 5 Let evil recoil on those who **s** me;
Pr 10:18 and whoever spreads **s** is a fool.
Mt 15:19 theft, false testimony, **s.**
2Co 12:20 **s,** gossip, arrogance and disorder.
Eph 4:31 rage and anger, brawling and **s,**
Col 3: 8 **s,** and filthy language from your lips.
1Ti 5:14 the enemy no opportunity for **s.**
Tit 3: 2 to **s** no one, to be peaceable
Jas 4:11 Brothers, do not **s** one another.
1Pe 2: 1 hypocrisy, envy, and **s** of every kind.
3:16 in Christ may be ashamed of their **s.**
2Pe 2:10 are not afraid to **s** celestial beings;
Jude 1: 8 reject authority and **s** celestial beings
Rev 13: 6 to **s** his name and his dwelling place

SLANDERED [SLANDER]
1Co 4:13 when we are **s,** we answer kindly.
1Ti 6: 1 and our teaching may not be **s.**

SLANDERER* [SLANDER]
Jer 9: 4 and every friend a **s.**
1Co 5:11 an idolater or a **s,**

SLANDERERS* [SLANDER]
Ps 56: 2 My **s** pursue me all day long;
140:11 Let **s** not be established in the land;
Ro   1:30 **s,** God-haters, insolent, arrogant
1Co 6:10 nor **s** nor swindlers will inherit the
Tit 2: 3 not to be **s** or addicted to much wine,

SLANDEROUS* [SLANDER]
Eze 22: 9 **s** men bent on shedding blood;
2Ti 3: 3 unforgiving, **s,** without self-control,
2Pe 2:11 do not bring **s** accusations
Jude 1: 9 to bring a **s** accusation against him,

SLANDEROUSLY* [SLANDER]
Ro   3: 8 as we are being **s** reported as saying

SLANDERS* [SLANDER]
Dt 22:14 and **s** her and gives her a bad name,
Ps 101: 5 Whoever **s** his neighbor in secret,

SLAPPED [SLAPS]
2Ch 18:23 went up and **s** Micaiah in the face.
Mt 26:67 with their fists. Others **s** him

SLAPS* [SLAPPED]
2Co 11:20 or **s** you in the face.

SLAUGHTER [SLAUGHTERED]
Ex 12: 6 must **s** them at twilight.
29:11 **S** it in the LORD's presence at

Lev   1: 5 He is to **s** the young bull before
      3: 2 and **s** it at the entrance to the Tent of
Dt   12:15 you may **s** your animals in any
Pr   7:22 like an ox going to the **s,**
Isa 53: 7 like a lamb to the **s,**
Jer 11:19 like a gentle lamb led to the **s;**
Zec 11: 4 "Pasture the flock marked for **s.**
Ac   8:32 like a sheep to the **s,**

SLAUGHTERED [SLAUGHTER]

Nu   11:22 if flocks and herds were **s** for them?
     14:16 so he **s** them in the desert.'
Ps   44:22 considered as sheep to be **s,**
Ro   8:36 considered as sheep to be **s."**

SLAVE [ENSLAVED, ENSLAVES, ENSLAVING, SLAVERY, SLAVES]

Ge   9:26 May Canaan be the **s** of Shem.
     21:10 "Get rid of that **s** woman and her son
     39:19 "This is how your **s** treated me,"
Ex   1:11 So they put **s** masters over them
      3: 7 crying out because of their **s** drivers,
Mk   10:44 wants to be first must be **s** of all.
Jn   8:34 everyone who sins is a **s** to sin.
Ac   7: 9 they sold him as a **s** into Egypt.
Ro   7:14 sold as a **s** to sin.
      8:15 that makes you a **s** again to fear,
1Co   7:21 Were you a **s** when you were called?
      9:19 I make myself a **s** to everyone,
     12:13 whether Jews or Greeks, **s** or free—
Gal   3:28 **s** nor free, male nor female,
      4: 7 So you are no longer a **s,** but a son;
      4:30 "Get rid of the **s** woman and her son,
Eph   6: 8 whether he is **s** or free.
Col   3:11 Scythian, **s** or free, but Christ is all,
1Ti   1:10 for **s** traders and liars and perjurers—
Phm   1:16 no longer as a **s,** but better than a **s,**
2Pe   2:19 a **s** to whatever has mastered him.
Rev 13:16 rich and poor, free and **s,**

SLAVERY [SLAVE]

Ex   2:23 The Israelites groaned in their **s**
     20: 2 out of the land of **s.**
Dt   7: 8 and redeemed you from the land of **s,**
Ne   5: 5 subject our sons and daughters to **s.**
Ro   6:19 offer them in **s** to righteousness
Gal   4: 3 in **s** under the basic principles of
1Ti   6: 1 of **s** should consider their masters

SLAVES [SLAVE]

Ge   9:25 lowest of **s** will he be to his brothers.
     15:14 will punish the nation they serve as **s,**
Ex   6: 6 I will free you from being **s** to them,
Dt   5:15 Remember that you were **s** in Egypt
     16:12 Remember that you were **s** in Egypt,
1Ki   9:22 But Solomon did not make **s** of any
Ps 123: 2 As the eyes of **s** look to the hand
Ecc 10: 7 while princes go on foot like **s.**
Jer 34: 9 Everyone was to free his Hebrew **s,**
Jn   8:33 and have never been **s** of anyone.
Ro   6: 6 we should no longer be **s** to sin—
      6:16 you are **s** to the one whom you obey
      6:22 from sin and have become **s** to God,
1Co   7:23 do not become **s** of men.

Gal   2: 4 in Christ Jesus and to make us **s.**
      4: 8 you were **s** to those who
Eph   6: 5 **S,** obey your earthly masters
Col   3:22 **S,** obey your earthly masters
      4: 1 I provide your **s** with what is right
Tit   2: 9 Teach **s** to be subject to their masters
2Pe   2:19 they themselves are **s** of depravity—

SLAY [SLAIN, SLAYS]

Ge   22:10 and took the knife to **s** his son.
Job 13:15 he **s** me, yet will I hope in him;
Ps   34:21 Evil will **s** the wicked;
Isa 11: 4 he will **s** the wicked.
Rev   6: 4 and to make men **s** each other.

SLAYS* [SLAY]

Job   5: 2 and envy **s** the simple.

SLEEK

Ge   41: 4 ate up the seven **s,** fat cows.
Dt   32:15 he became heavy and **s.**

SLEEP [ASLEEP, SLEEPER, SLEEPING, SLEEPLESS, SLEEPS, SLEPT]

Ge   2:21 caused the man to fall into a deep **s;**
     15:12 Abram fell into a deep **s,**
     28:11 under his head and lay down to **s.**
Ex   22:27 What else will he **s** in?
Dt   24:13 by sunset so that he may **s** in it.
1Sa 26:12 had put them into a deep **s.**
Ps   4: 8 I will lie down and **s** in peace,
     13: 3 or I will **s** in death;
     76: 5 they **s** their last **s;**
     78:65 Then the Lord awoke as from **s,**
    121: 4 over Israel will neither slumber nor **s**
    127: 2 for he grants to those he loves.
    132: 4 I will allow no **s** to my eyes,
Pr   6: 9 When will you get up from your **s?**
      6:10 A little **s,** a little slumber,
Ecc   5:12 The **s** of a laborer is sweet,
Isa 29:10 has brought over you a deep **s:**
Da   8:18 I was in a deep **s,**
     10: 9 I fell into a deep **s,**
     12: 2 Multitudes who **s** in the dust of
Jnh   1: 5 lay down and fell into a deep **s.**
Ac   20: 9 a deep **s** as Paul talked on and on.
1Co 15:51 a mystery: We will not all **s,**
1Th   5: 7 For those who **s,** **s** at night,

SLEEPER* [SLEEP]

Eph   5:14 This is why it is said: "Wake up, O **s,**

SLEEPING [SLEEP]

1Ki 18:27 Maybe he is **s** and must
Mt   26:40 to his disciples and found them **s.**
Mk   13:36 do not let him find you **s.**

SLEEPLESS* [SLEEP]

2Co   6: 5 **s** nights and hunger;

SLEEPS [SLEEP]

Dt   27:20 "Cursed is the man who **s** with
Pr   6:29 is he who **s** with another man's wife;

10: 5 but he who **s** during harvest is

SLEPT [SLEEP]
SS   5: 2 I **s** but my heart was awake.

SLIMY*
Ps   40: 2 He lifted me out of the **s** pit,

SLING
Jdg 20:16 of whom could **s** a stone at a hair
1Sa 17:50 the Philistine with a **s** and a stone;
1Ch 12: 2 or to **s** stones right-handed
Pr   26: 8 Like tying a stone in a **s** is

SLIP [SLIPPED, SLIPPERY, SLIPPING]
Dt   4: 9 or let them **s** from your heart
    32:35 In due time their foot will **s**;
Ps   37:31 his feet do not **s**.
    121: 3 He will not let your foot **s**—

SLIPPED [SLIP]
Ps   17: 5 my feet have not **s**.
    73: 2 But as for me, my feet had almost **s**;
Jn   5:13 for Jesus had **s** away into the crowd
2Co 11:33 in the wall and **s** through his hands.

SLIPPERY* [SLIP]
Ps   35: 6 may their path be dark and **s**,
    73:18 Surely you place them on **s** ground;
Jer 23:12 "Therefore their path will become **s**;

SLIPPING [SLIP]
Ps   66: 9 and kept our feet from **s**.
    94:18 When I said, "My foot is **s**,"

SLOW
Ex   4:10 I am **s** of speech and tongue."
    34: 6 and gracious God, **s** to anger,
Nu 14:18 'The LORD is **s** to anger,
Dt   7:10 not be **s** to repay to their face
Ne   9:17 **s** to anger and abounding in love.
Ps   86:15 and gracious God, **s** to anger,
    103: 8 **s** to anger, abounding in love.
    145: 8 **s** to anger and rich in love.
Joel 2:13 **s** to anger and abounding in love,
Jnh 4: 2 **s** to anger and abounding in love,
Na   1: 3 The LORD is **s** to anger and great
Lk 24:25 and how **s** of heart to believe all that
Heb 5:11 to explain because you are **s** to learn.
Jas 1:19 so be quick and **s** to become angry,
2Pe 3: 9 Lord is not **s** in keeping his promise,

SLUGGARD [SLUGGARD'S]
Pr   6: 6 Go to the ant, you **s**;
    6: 9 How long will you lie there, you **s**?
    13: 4 The **s** craves and gets nothing,
    20: 4 A **s** does not plow in season;
    26:14 so a **s** turns on his bed.
    26:15 The **s** buries his hand in the dish;

SLUGGARD'S* [SLUGGARD]
Pr   21:25 **s** craving will be the death of him,

SLUMBER
Ps   121: 3 who watches over you will not **s**;

121: 4 watches over Israel will neither **s**
Pr   6:10 A little sleep, a little **s**,
Ro 13:11 for you to wake up from your **s**,

SLUR*
Ps   15: 3 and casts no **s** on his fellowman,

SLY*
Pr   25:23 so a **s** tongue brings angry looks.
Mt 26: 4 plotted to arrest Jesus in some **s** way
Mk 14: 1 for some **s** way to arrest Jesus and

SMALL [SMALLEST]
1Ki 18:44 "A cloud as **s** as a man's hand
Isa 49: 6 he says: "It is too a **s** thing for you to
Mic 5: 2 you are **s** among the clans of Judah,
Mt   7:14 **s** is the gate and narrow the road
    17:20 you have faith as **s** as a mustard seed,
Mk 12:42 and put in two very **s** copper coins,
Lk 19:17 trustworthy in a very **s** matter,
Jas 3: 5 the tongue is a **s** part of the body,

SMALLEST [SMALL]
Mt   5:18 not the **s** letter,
Mk   4:31 the **s** seed you plant in the ground.

SMASH [SMASHED]
Ex 34:13 **s** their sacred stones and cut
Dt   12: 3 **s** their sacred stones

SMASHED [SMASH]
2Ki 11:18 They **s** the altars and idols to pieces
    18: 4 **s** the sacred stones and cut down
Jer 19:11 as this potter's jar is **s** and cannot
Da   2:34 feet of iron and clay and **s** them.

SMELL
Dt   4:28 which cannot see or hear or eat or **s**.
Ps 115: 6 noses, but they cannot **s**;
Ecc 10: 1 As dead flies give perfume a bad **s**,
Da   3:27 and there was no **s** of fire on them.
2Co 2:16 To the one we are the **s** of death;

SMITTEN*
Isa 53: 4 **s** by him, and afflicted.

SMOKE [SMOKING]
Ex 19:18 Mount Sinai was covered with **s**,
Ps 68: 2 As **s** is blown away by the wind,
    104:32 touches the mountains, and they **s**.
Isa 6: 4 and the temple was filled with **s**.
Joel 2:30 blood and fire and billows of **s**.
Ac   2:19 blood and fire and billows of **s**.
Rev 8: 4 The **s** of the incense,
    9: 2 and sky were darkened by the **s** from
    15: 8 the temple was filled with **s** from

SMOKING* [SMOKE]
Ge 15:17 a **s** firepot with a blazing torch

SMOLDER* [SMOLDERING]
Ps 74: 1 Why does your anger **s** against
    80: 4 how long will your anger **s** against

SMOLDERING [SMOLDER]
Isa 42: 3 and a **s** wick he will not snuff out.
Mt 12:20 and a **s** wick he will not snuff out,

SMOOTH
1Sa 17:40 chose five **s** stones from the stream,
Ps 55:21 His speech is **s** as butter,
Pr 6:24 the **s** tongue of the wayward wife.
    7:21 she seduced him with her **s** talk.
Isa 42:16 and make the rough places **s**.
Lk 3: 5 the rough ways **s**.

SMYRNA
Rev 2: 8 the angel of the church in **S** write:

SNAKE [SNAKES]
Ex 4: 3 on the ground and it became a **s**,
    7:10 and it became a **s**.
Nu 21: 8 "Make a **s** and put it up on a pole;
2Ki 18: 4 the bronze **s** Moses had made,
Pr 23:32 the end it bites like a **s** and poisons
Mic 7:17 They will lick dust like a **s**,
Mt 7:10 he asks for a fish, will give him a **s**?
Jn 3:14 as Moses lifted up the **s** in the desert,
Ac 28: 5 But Paul shook the **s** off into the fire

SNAKES [SNAKE]
Nu 21: 6 Then the LORD sent venomous **s**
Mt 10:16 be as shrewd as **s** and as innocent
Lk 10:19 to trample on **s** and scorpions and
1Co 10: 9 and were killed by **s**.
Rev 9:19 for their tails were like **s**,

SNARE [ENSNARE, ENSNARED, SNARED, SNARES]
Ex 23:33 of their gods will certainly be a **s**
Dt 7:16 for that will be a **s** to you.
Jdg 2: 3 and their gods will be a **s** to you."
Ps 69:22 table set before them become a **s**;
    91: 3 he will save you from the fowler's **s**
    142: 3 where I walk men have hidden a **s**
Pr 6: 5 like a bird from the **s** of the fowler.
    29:25 Fear of man will prove to be a **s**,
Ro 11: 9 "May their table become a **s**

SNARED [SNARE]
Pr 3:26 and will keep your foot from being **s**.
    29: 6 An evil man is **s** by his own sin,

SNARES [SNARE]
Jos 23:13 they will become **s** and traps for you,
Ps 18: 5 the **s** of death confronted me.
Pr 13:14 turning a man from the **s** of death.

SNATCH [SNATCHED, SNATCHES]
Ps 119:43 Do not **s** the word of truth
Jn 10:28 no one can **s** them out
Jude 1:23 **s** others from the fire and save them;

SNATCHED [SNATCH]
Am 4:11 You were like a burning stick **s** from
Zec 3: 2 Is not this man a burning stick **s** from

SNATCHES [SNATCH]
Mt 13:19 and **s** away what was sown

SNEEZED*
2Ki 4:35 The boy **s** seven times

SNIFF*
Mal 1:13 and you **s** at it contemptuously,"

SNOUT*
Pr 11:22 a gold ring in a pig's **s** is

SNOW [SNOWS]
Ex 4: 6 it was leprous, like **s**.
Nu 12:10 there stood Miriam—leprous, like **s**.
2Ki 5:27 as white as **s**.
Ps 51: 7 and I will be whiter than **s**.
Isa 1:18 they shall be as white as **s**;
Da 7: 9 His clothing was as white as **s**;
Mt 28: 3 and his clothes were white as **s**.
Rev 1:14 as white as **s**,

SNOWS* [SNOW]
Pr 31:21 When it **s**, she has no fear

SNUFF [SNUFFED]
Isa 42: 3 a smoldering wick he will not **s** out.
Mt 12:20 a smoldering wick he will not **s** out,

SNUFFED [SNUFF]
Job 21:17 the lamp of the wicked **s** out?
Pr 13: 9 but the lamp of the wicked is **s** out.

SO-CALLED* [CALL]
1Co 8: 5 For even if there are **s** gods,
Rev 2:24 not learned Satan's **s** deep secrets

SOAKED [SOAK]
Jn 19:29 so they **s** a sponge in it,

SOAP*
Job 9:30 Even if I washed myself with **s**
Jer 2:22 and use an abundance of **s**,
Mal 3: 2 like a refiner's fire or a launderer's **s**.

SOAR [SOARED]
Isa 40:31 They will **s** on wings like eagles;
Jer 49:22 An eagle will **s** and swoop down,
Ob 1: 4 Though you **s** like the eagle

SOARED* [SOAR]
2Sa 22:11 he **s** on the wings of the wind.
Ps 18:10 he **s** on the wings of the wind.

SOBER
Ro 12: 3 think of yourself with **s** judgment,

SOCKET
Ge 32:25 he touched the **s** of Jacob's hip so

SODA*
Job 9:30 and my hands with washing **s**,
Pr 25:20 or like vinegar poured on **s**,
Jer 2:22 Although you wash yourself with **s**

SODOM

Ge 13:12 and pitched his tents near **S**.
    13:13 the men of **S** were wicked
    18:20 outcry against **S** and Gomorrah is so
    19:24 rained down burning sulfur on **S**
Isa 1: 9 we would have become like **S,**
Eze 16:49 this was the sin of your sister **S:**
Lk 10:12 more bearable on that day for **S**
Ro   9:29 we would have become like **S,**
Jude 1: 7 **S** and Gomorrah and the surrounding
Rev 11: 8 which is figuratively called **S**

SODOMITE(S) (KJV)

See SHRINE PROSTITUTE(S)

SOIL

Ge   4: 2 and Cain worked the **s.**
     9:20 Noah, a man of the **s,**
Ex 23:19 the best of the firstfruits of your **s** to
Mt 13:23 received the seed that fell on good **s**

SOLD [SELL]

Ge 37:28 **s** him for twenty shekels of silver
Ex 22: 3 he must be **s** to pay for his theft.
Lev 25:23 land must not be **s** permanently,
Dt 32:30 unless their Rock had **s** them,
Jdg 4: 2 So the LORD **s** them into the hands
    10: 7 He **s** them into the hands of
1Ki 21:25 who **s** himself to do evil in the eyes
Mt 10:29 Are not two sparrows **s** for a penny?
    13:44 **s** all he had and bought that field.
    13:46 **s** everything he had and bought it.
Ac   5: 1 also **s** a piece of property.
Ro   7:14 **s** as a slave to sin.
1Co 10:25 Eat anything **s** in the meat market
Heb 12:16 for a single meal **s** his inheritance

SOLDIER [SOLDIERS]

1Co 9: 7 serves as a **s** at his own expense?
2Ti 2: 3 with us like a good **s** of Christ Jesus.

SOLDIERS [SOLDIER]

Mt 27:27 Then the governor's **s** took Jesus into
    28:12 gave the **s** a large sum of money,
Jn 19:23 When the **s** crucified Jesus,
    19:34 one of the **s** pierced Jesus' side

SOLE

Dt 28:65 no resting place for the **s**
Isa 1: 6 From the **s** of your foot to the top

SOLEMN

Jos 6:26 Joshua pronounced this **s** oath:
Eze 16: 8 I gave you my **s** oath and entered

SOLID

1Co 3: 2 I gave you milk, not **s** food,
2Ti 2:19 God's **s** foundation stands firm,
Heb 5:14 But **s** food is for the mature,

SOLITARY

Lev 16:22 on itself all their sins to a **s** place;
Mk   1:35 to a **s** place, where he prayed.
     6:32 by themselves in a boat to a **s** place.

SOLOMON

Son of David by Bathsheba; king of Judah (2Sa 12:24; 1Ch 3:5, 10). Appointed king by David (1Ki 1); adversaries Adonijah, Joab, Shimei killed by Benaiah (1Ki 2). Asked for wisdom (1Ki 3; 2Ch 1). Judged between two prostitutes (1Ki 3:16-28). Built temple (1Ki 5-7; 2Ch 2-5); prayer of dedication (1Ki 8; 2Ch 6). Visited by Queen of Sheba (1Ki 10; 2Ch 9). Wives turned his heart from God (1Ki 11:1-13). Jeroboam rebelled against (1Ki 11:26-40). Death (1Ki 11:41-43; 2Ch 9:29-31).

Proverbs of (1Ki 4:32; Pr 1:1; 10:1; 25:1); psalms of (Ps 72; 127); song of (SS 1:1).

SOMBER*

Mt   6:16 do not look **s** as the hypocrites do,

SOME [SOMEHOW, SOMEONE, SOMETHING]

Ge   3: 6 She also gave **s** to her husband,
Mk   4:15 **S** people are like seed along the path,
     8:28 "**S** say John the Baptist;
1Co 9:22 by all possible means I might save **s.**
Eph 4:11 It was he who gave **s** to be apostles,
1Ti 4: 1 in later times **s** will abandon the faith
2Pe 3:16 **s** things that are hard to understand,

SOMEHOW [HOW, SOME]

Ro 11:14 that I may **s** arouse my own people
Gal 4:11 **s** I have wasted my efforts on you.
Php 3:11 and so, **s**, to attain to the resurrection

SOMEONE [ONE, SOME]

Ex   4:13 "O Lord, please send **s** else to do it."
    12:30 there was not a house without **s** dead.
Nu 35:11 has killed **s** accidentally may flee.
Mt   5:39 If **s** strikes you on the right cheek,
     5:41 If **s** forces you to go one mile,
Lk   7:19 or should we expect **s** else?"
    16:31 not be convinced even if **s** rises from
Ro 10:14 hear without **s** preaching to them?

SOMETHING [SOME, THING]

Ex 24:10 Under his feet was **s** like
Nu 16:30 LORD brings about **s** totally new,
Dt   8:16 **s** your fathers had never known,
Mt 25:35 For I was hungry and you gave me **s**
Ac   3: 5 expecting to get **s** from them.
     9:18 **s** like scales fell from Saul's eyes,
Php 2: 6 did not consider equality with God **s**
Rev 8: 8 and **s** like a huge mountain,
     9: 7 On their heads they wore **s**

SON [SONS, SONS', SONSHIP]

Ge   5: 3 he had a **s** in his own likeness,
    15: 4 a **s** coming from your own body will
    17:19 your wife Sarah will bear you a **s,**
    21: 2 Sarah became pregnant and bore a **s**
    21:10 of that slave woman and her **s,**
    22: 2 Then God said, "Take your **s,**
    22:12 not withheld from me your **s,**
    25:11 God blessed his **s** Isaac,
Ex   4:23 so I will kill your firstborn **s.**' "

	11: 5	Every firstborn **s** in Egypt will die,
Nu	18:15	you must redeem every firstborn **s**
Dt	1:31	as a father carries his **s,**
	6:20	In the future, when your **s** asks you,
	8: 5	that as a man disciplines his **s,**
	18:10	among you who sacrifices his **s**
	21:18	a stubborn and rebellious **s** who does
2Sa	7:14	and he will be my **s.**
1Ki	3:23	'My **s** is alive and your **s** is dead,'
	8:19	to build the temple, but your **s,**
2Ki	6:29	So we cooked my **s** and ate him.
1Ch	22:10	He will be my **s,**
Ps	2: 7	"You are my **S;**
	2:12	Kiss the **S,** lest he be angry
	8: 4	the **s** of man that you care for him?
	80:15	the **s** you have raised up for yourself.
Pr	3: 1	My **s,** do not forget my teaching,
	3:12	as a father the **s** he delights in.
	6:20	My **s,** keep your father's commands
	10: 1	A wise **s** brings joy to his father,
	13:24	He who spares the rod hates his **s,**
	29:17	Discipline your **s,** and he will
Isa	7:14	with child and will give birth to a **s,**
	8: 3	she conceived and gave birth to a **s.**
	9: 6	to us a **s** is given,
Jer	31:20	Is not Ephraim my dear **s,**
Eze	18:20	**s** will not share the guilt of the father
Da	3:25	the fourth looks like a **s** of the gods."
	7:13	was one like a **s** of man,
Hos	11: 1	and out of Egypt I called my **s.**
Am	7:14	neither a prophet nor a prophet's **s,**
Mal	1: 6	"A **s** honors his father,
Mt	1: 1	the genealogy of Jesus Christ the **s**
		of David, the **s** of Abraham:
	1:23	with child and will give birth to a **s,**
	2:15	"Out of Egypt I called my **s.**"
	3:17	"This is my **S,** whom I love;
	4: 3	"If you are the **S** of God,
	8:20	but the **S** of Man has no place
	11:27	No one knows the **S** except
	12: 8	the **S** of Man is Lord of the Sabbath.
	12:32	a word against the **S** of Man will
	12:40	the **S** of Man will be three days
	13:55	"Isn't this the carpenter's **s?**
	14:33	"Truly you are the **S** of God."
	16:16	the **S** of the living God."
	16:27	For the **S** of Man is going to come
	17: 5	"This is my **S,** whom I love;
	19:28	**S** of Man sits on his glorious throne,
	20:18	**S** of Man will be betrayed to
	20:28	just as the **S** of Man did not come to
	21: 9	"Hosanna to the **S** of David!"
	22:42	Whose **s** is he?"
	24:27	will be the coming of the **S** of Man.
	24:30	the sign of the **S** of Man will appear
	24:44	because the **S** of Man will come at
	25:31	the **S** of Man comes in his glory,
	26:63	if you are the Christ, the **S** of God."
	27:54	"Surely he was the **S** of God!"
	28:19	the name of the Father and of the **S**
Mk	1:11	"You are my **S,** whom I love;
	2:28	So the **S** of Man is Lord even of
	8:38	the **S** of Man will be ashamed of him
	9: 7	from the cloud: "This is my **S,**

	10:45	**S** of Man did not come to be served,
	13:32	nor the **S,** but only the Father.
	14:62	the **S** of Man sitting at the right hand
	15:39	"Surely this man was the **S** of God!"
Lk	1:32	be called the **S** of the Most High.
	1:35	will be called the **S** of God.
	2: 7	she gave birth to her firstborn, a **s.**
	3:22	"You are my **S,** whom I love;
	9:35	"This is my **S,** whom I have chosen;
	9:58	but the **S** of Man has no place
	12: 8	the **S** of Man will also acknowledge
	15:21	no longer worthy to be called your **s.**
	18: 8	However, when the **S** of Man comes,
	18:31	written by the prophets about the **S**
	19:10	For the **S** of Man came to seek and
	20:44	How then can he be his **s?**"
Jn	1:34	testify that this is the **S** of God."
	1:49	"Rabbi, you are the **S** of God;
	3:14	so the **S** of Man must be lifted up,
	3:16	that he gave his one and only **S,**
	3:36	believes in the **S** has eternal life,
	5:19	the **S** can do nothing by himself;
	6:40	that everyone who looks to the **S**
	11: 4	for God's glory so that God's **S** may
	12:34	'The **S** of Man must be lifted up'?
	13:31	"Now is the **S** of Man glorified
	17: 1	Glorify your **S,** that your **S** may
		glorify you.
Ac	7:56	"I see heaven open and the **S** of Man
	13:33	the second Psalm: " 'You are my **S;**
Ro	1: 4	be the **S** of God by his resurrection
	5:10	to him through the death of his **S,**
	8: 3	by sending his own **S** in the likeness
	8:29	conformed to the likeness of his **S,**
	8:32	He who did not spare his own **S,**
1Co	15:28	the **S** himself will be made subject
Gal	2:20	I live by faith in the **S** of God,
	4: 4	time had fully come, God sent his **S,**
	4: 7	So you are no longer a slave, but a **s;**
	4:30	of the slave woman and her **s,**
Col	1:13	into the kingdom of the **S** he loves,
1Th	1:10	and to wait for his **S** from heaven,
Heb	1: 2	he has spoken to us by his **S,**
	1: 5	"You are my **S;**
	2: 6	the **s** of man that you care for him?
	4:14	Jesus the **S** of God,
	5: 5	God said to him, "You are my **S;**
	7:28	appointed the **S,** who has been made
	10:29	trampled the **S** of God under foot,
	12: 6	everyone he accepts as a **s.**"
Jas	2:21	when he offered his Isaac on
2Pe	1:17	saying, "This is my **S,** whom I love;
1Jn	1: 3	with the Father and with his **S,**
	1: 7	his **S,** purifies us from all sin.
	2:23	acknowledges the **S** has the Father
	3: 8	The reason the **S** of God appeared
	4: 9	He sent his one and only **S**
	4:14	that the Father has sent his **S** to be
	5: 5	that Jesus is the **S** of God.
	5:11	and this life is in his **S.**
Rev	1:13	someone "like a **s** of man,"
	2:18	These are the words of the **S**
	12: 5	She gave birth to a **s,** a male child,
	14:14	the cloud was one "like a **s** of man"

21: 7 I will be his God and he will be my **s**

MY SON Ge 21:10; 22:7, 8; 24:3, 4, 6, 7, 8, 37, 38, 40; 27:1, 8, 13, 18, 20, 21, 21, 24, 25, 26, 27, 37, 43; 34:8; 37:35; 38:11, 26; 42:38; 43:29; 45:28; 48:19; 49:9; Ex 4:23; Jos 7:19; Jdg 8:23; 17:2, 3; 1Sa 3:6, 16; 4:16; 10:2; 14:39, 40, 42; 22:8, 8; 24:16; 26:17, 21, 25; 2Sa 7:14; 13:25; 14:11, 16; 16:11; 18:22, 33, 33, 33, 33, 33; 19:4, 4, 4; 1Ki 1:21, 33; 3:20, 21, 22, 23; 17:12, 18; 2Ki 6:28, 29; 14:9; 1Ch 17:13; 22:5, 7, 10, 11; 28:5, 6, 9; 29:1, 19; 2Ch 25:18; Ps 2:7; Pr 1:8, 10, 15; 2:1; 3:1, 11, 21; 4:10, 20; 5:1, 20; 6:1, 3, 20; 7:1; 19:27; 23:15, 19, 26; 24:13, 21; 27:11; 31:2; Ecc 12:12; Eze 21:10; Hos 11:1; Mt 2:15; 3:17; 17:5, 15; 21:37; Mk 1:11; 9:7, 17; 12:6; Lk 3:22; 9:35, 38; 15:31; 20:13; Ac 13:33; 1Co 4:17; 1Ti 1:18; 2Ti 2:1; Phm 1:10, 10; Heb 1:5, 5; 5:5; 12:5; 1Pe 5:13; 2Pe 1:17; Rev 21:7

SON OF AARON Ex 6:25; 38:21; Lev 7:33; Nu 3:32; 4:16, 28, 33; 7:8; 16:37; 25:7, 11; 26:1; Jos 24:33; Jdg 20:28; Ezr 7:5

SON OF DAVID 2Sa 13:1, 1; 1Ch 29:22; 2Ch 1:1; 13:6; 30:26; 35:3; Pr 1:1; Ecc 1:1; Mt 1:1, 20; 9:27; 12:23; 15:22; 20:30, 31; 21:9, 15; 22:42; Mk 10:47, 48; 12:35; Lk 3:31; 18:38, 39; 20:41

SON OF GOD Mt 4:3, 6; 8:29; 14:33; 26:63; 27:40, 43, 54; Mk 1:1; 3:11; 15:39; Lk 1:35; 3:38; 4:3, 9, 41; 22:70; Jn 1:34, 49; 5:25; 11:27; 19:7; 20:31; Ac 9:20; Ro 1:4; 2Co 1:19; Gal 2:20; Eph 4:13; Heb 4:14; 6:6; 7:3; 10:29; 1Jn 3:8; 4:15; 5:5, 10, 12, 13, 20; Rev 2:18

SON OF JESSE 1Sa 16:18; 20:27, 30, 31; 22:7, 8, 9, 13; 25:10; 2Sa 23:1; 1Ch 10:14; 12:18; 29:26; Ps 72:20; Lk 3:32; Ac 13:22

SON OF MAN Nu 23:19; Job 25:6; Ps 8:4; 80:17; 144:3; Eze 2:1, 3, 6, 8; 3:1, 3, 4, 10, 17, 25; 4:1, 16; 5:1; 6:2; 7:2; 8:5, 6, 8, 12, 15, 17; 11:2, 4, 15; 12:2, 3, 9, 18, 22, 27; 13:2, 17; 14:3, 13; 15:2; 16:2; 17:2; 20:3, 4, 27, 46; 21:2, 6, 9, 12, 14, 19, 28; 22:2, 18, 24; 23:2, 36; 24:2, 16, 25; 25:2; 26:2; 27:2; 28:2, 12, 21; 29:2, 18; 30:2, 21; 31:2; 32:2, 18; 33:2, 7, 10, 12, 24, 30; 34:2; 35:2; 36:1, 17; 37:3, 9, 11, 16; 38:2, 14; 39:1, 17; 40:4; 43:7, 10, 18; 44:5; 47:6; Da 7:13; 8:17; Mt 8:20; 9:6; 10:23; 11:19; 12:8, 32, 40; 13:37, 41; 16:13, 27, 28; 17:9, 12, 22; 19:28; 20:18, 28; 24:27, 30, 30, 37, 39, 44; 25:31; 26:2, 24, 24, 45, 64; Mk 2:10, 28; 8:31, 38; 9:9, 12, 31; 10:33, 45; 13:26; 14:21, 21, 41, 62; Lk 5:24; 6:5, 22; 7:34; 9:22, 26, 44, 58; 11:30; 12:8, 10, 40; 17:22, 24, 26, 30; 18:8, 31; 19:10; 21:27, 36; 22:22, 48, 69; 24:7; Jn 1:51; 3:13, 14; 5:27; 6:27, 53, 62; 8:28; 9:35; 12:23, 34, 34; 13:31; Ac 7:56; Heb 2:6; Rev 1:13; 14:14

SONG [SING]

Ex 15: 2 LORD is my strength and my **s;**
Dt 31:21 this **s** will testify against them,
    32:44 and spoke all the words of this **s**
Jdg 5: 1 Barak son of Abinoam sang this **s:**
Ps 33: 3 Sing to him a new **s;**
    40: 3 He put a new **s** in my mouth,

69:30 I will praise God's name in **s**
96: 1 Sing to the LORD a new **s;**
98: 4 burst into jubilant **s** with music;
119:54 Your decrees are the theme of my **s**
149: 1 Sing to the LORD a new **s,**
Isa 5: 1 the one I love a **s** about his vineyard:
    12: 2 the LORD, is my strength and my **s;**
    49:13 burst into **s,** O mountains!
    54: 1 who never bore a child; burst into **s,**
    55:12 and hills will burst into **s** before you,
Jnh 2: 9 But I, with a **s** of thanksgiving,
Rev 5: 9 And they sang a new **s:**
    14: 3 No one could learn the **s** except
    15: 3 and sang the **s** of Moses the servant

SONGS [SING]

2Sa 23: 1 Israel's singer of **s:**
1Ki 4:32 and his **s** numbered a thousand
Ne 12:46 for the **s** of praise and thanksgiving
Job 35:10 who gives **s** in the night,
Ps 77: 6 I remembered my **s** in the night.
    100: 2 before him with joyful **s.**
    126: 6 will return with **s** of joy,
    137: 3 there our captors asked us for **s,**
Eph 5:19 with psalms, hymns and spiritual **s.**
Col 3:16 sing psalms, hymns and spiritual **s**
Jas 5:13 Let him sing **s** of praise.

SONS [SON]

Ge 6: 2 the **s** of God saw that the daughters
    9: 1 Then God blessed Noah and his **s,**
    10:32 These are the clans of Noah's **s,**
    35:22 Jacob had twelve **s:**
Ex 13:15 and redeem each of my firstborn **s.'**
    28: 9 on them the names of the **s** of Israel
Nu 18: 7 and your **s** may serve as priests
Dt 7: 3 or take their daughters for your **s,**
Ru 4:15 better to you than seven **s,**
Ps 11: 4 He observes the **s** of men;
    82: 6 you are all **s** of the Most High.'
    89:30 "If his **s** forsake my law and do
    90: 3 "Return to dust, O **s** of men."
    127: 3 **S** are a heritage from the LORD,
    132:12 if your **s** keep my covenant and
Hos 1:10 be called '**s** of the living God.'
Joel 2:28 Your **s** and daughters will prophesy,
Mt 5: 9 for they will be called **s** of God.
    13:38 stands for the **s** of the kingdom.
Lk 6:35 and you will be **s** of the Most High,
Jn 12:36 so that you may become **s** of light."
Ac 2:17 Your **s** and daughters will prophesy,
Ro 8:14 by the Spirit of God are **s** of God.
    9: 4 Theirs is the adoption as **s;**
    9:26 be called '**s** of the living God.' "
2Co 6:18 and you will be my **s** and daughters,
Gal 3:26 You are all **s** of God through faith
    4: 5 we might receive the full rights of **s.**
Eph 1: 5 adopted as his **s** through Jesus Christ,
1Th 5: 5 You are all **s** of the light and **s** of
Heb 2:10 In bringing many **s** to glory,
    12: 7 God is treating you as **s.**

AARON AND HIS SONS Ex 27:21; 28:4, 41, 43; 29:4, 9, 9, 10, 15, 19, 20, 24, 27, 28, 32, 35, 44; 30:19, 30; 39:27; 40:12, 31; Lev 2:3, 10; 6:9,

16, 20, 25; 7:31, 35; 8:2, 6, 14, 18, 22, 27, 31, 31, 36; 9:1; 10:6; 17:2; 21:24; 22:2, 18; 24:9; Nu 3:9, 10, 38, 48, 51; 4:5, 15, 19, 27; 6:23; 8:13, 19, 22

AARON'S SONS Ex 28:40; Lev 1:5, 8, 11; 2:2; 3:2, 5, 8, 13; 6:14; 8:13, 24; 10:1; Nu 3:3

SONS OF AARON Lev 1:7; 7:10; 16:1; 21:1; Nu 3:2; 10:8; 1Ch 6:3; 24:1,1; 2Ch 13:9, 10

SONS OF KORAH Ex 6:24; Ps 42:T; 44:T; 45:T; 46:T; 47:T; 48:T; 49:T; 84:T; 85:T; 87:T; 88:T

SONS' [SON]

Ge 6:18 and your wife and your **s'** wives
Lev 10:13 and your **s'** share of the offerings

SONSHIP* [SON]

Ro 8:15 but you received the Spirit of **s.**

SOON

Ps 37: 2 for like the grass they will **s** wither,
   106:13 But they **s** forgot what he had done
Isa 56: 1 my righteousness will **s** be revealed.
Da   9:23 As **s** as you began to pray,
Ro 16:20 The God of peace will **s** crush Satan
Rev 1: 1 his servants what must **s** take place.
     3:11 I am coming **s.**
    22: 7 "Behold, I am coming **s!**
    22:12 "Behold, I am coming **s!**
    22:20 "Yes, I am coming **s.**"

SORCERER [SORCERY]

Ac 13: 6 There they met a Jewish **s**

SORCERERS [SORCERY]

Ex 7:11 then summoned wise men and **s,**
Jer 27: 9 your mediums or your **s** who tell you
Da   2: 2 enchanters, **s** and astrologers

SORCERESS [SORCERY]

Ex 22:18 "Do not allow a **s** to live.

SORCERIES [SORCERY]

Isa 47: 9 in spite of your many **s**
Na   3: 4 alluring, the mistress of **s,**

SORCERY [SORCERER, SORCERERS, SORCERESS, SORCERIES]

Lev 19:26 " 'Do not practice divination or **s.**
Nu 23:23 There is no **s** against Jacob,
Dt 18:10 who practices divination or **s,**
Ac   8: 9 a man named Simon had practiced **s**
    19:19 A number who had practiced **s**

SORE [SORES]

Jer 30:13 no remedy for your **s,**

SOREK*

Jdg 16: 4 Valley of **S** whose name was Delilah

SORES [SORE]

Job 2: 7 and afflicted Job with painful **s** from
Hos 5:13 not able to heal your **s.**

Rev 16: 2 and painful **s** broke out on the people

SORROW [SORROWFUL, SORROWS]

Ps   6: 7 My eyes grow weak with **s;**
    90:10 yet their span is but trouble and **s,**
   116: 3 I was overcome by trouble and **s.**
Pr 23:29 Who has **s?**
Ecc 1:18 with much wisdom comes much **s;**
Isa 35:10 and **s** and sighing will flee away.
    51:11 and **s** and sighing will flee away.
    60:20 and your days of **s** will end.
Jer 31:12 and they will **s** no more.
Mk 14:34 "My soul is overwhelmed with **s** to
Ro   9: 2 I have great **s** and unceasing anguish
2Co 7:10 Godly **s** brings repentance that leads

SORROWFUL [SORROW]

2Co 6:10 **s,** yet always rejoicing;

SORROWS [SORROW]

Ps 16: 4 The **s** of those will increase who run
Isa 53: 3 man of **s,** and familiar with suffering.

SOUGHT [SEEK]

Ex 32:11 But Moses **s** the favor of
1Sa 13:14 Israel mourned and **s** after the LORD.
    13:14 the LORD has **s** out a man
2Ch 26: 5 As long as he **s** the LORD,
    31:21 he **s** his God and worked
Ps 34: 4 I **s** the LORD, and he answered me;
   119:45 for I have **s** out your precepts.
   119:58 I have **s** your face with all my heart;
Isa 9:13 nor have they **s** the LORD
Ro 11: 7 What Israel **s** so earnestly it did not

SOUL [SOULS]

Dt   6: 5 all your heart and with all your **s**
    10:12 all your heart and with all your **s**
    30: 6 all your heart and with all your **s**
Jos 22: 5 with all your heart and all your **s.**"
1Sa 1:10 In bitterness of **s** Hannah wept and
2Ki 23:25 with all his heart and with all his **s**
Ps 19: 7 is perfect, reviving the **s.**
    23: 3 he restores my **s.**
    25: 1 To you, O LORD, I lift up my **s;**
    34: 2 My **s** will boast in the LORD;
    42: 1 so my **s** pants for you, O God.
    42:11 Why are you downcast, O my **s?**
    62: 5 O my **s,** in God alone;
    63: 8 My **s** clings to you;
    94:19 your consolation brought joy to my **s**
   103: 1 Praise the LORD, O my **s;**
   108: 1 and make music with all my **s.**
   116: 7 Be at rest once more, O my **s,**
   130: 5 I wait for the LORD, my **s** waits,
Pr 13:19 A longing fulfilled is sweet to the **s,**
    16:24 sweet to the **s** and healing to the
    19: 8 who gets wisdom loves his own **s;**
    22: 5 but he who guards his **s** stays far
    24:14 also that wisdom is sweet to your **s;**
Isa 53:11 After the suffering of his **s,**
La   3:20 and my **s** is downcast within me.
Eze 18: 4 **s** who sins is the one who will die.
Mic 6: 7 fruit of my body for the sin of my **s?**

Mt	10:28	of the One who can destroy both **s**
	16:26	a man give in exchange for his **s?**
	22:37	all your heart and with all your **s**
Mk	8:36	yet forfeit his **s?**
Lk	1:46	Mary said: "My **s** glorifies the Lord
	2:35	a sword will pierce your own **s** too."
1Th	5:23	**s** and body be kept blameless at
Heb	4:12	even to dividing **s** and spirit, joints
		this hope as an anchor for the **s**,
1Pe	2:11	which war against your **s**.
3Jn	1: 2	even as your **s** is getting along well.

SOULS [SOUL]

Pr	11:30	and he who wins **s** is wise.
Jer	6:16	and you will find rest for your **s**.
Mt	11:29	and you will find rest for your **s**.
1Pe	2:25	the Shepherd and Overseer of your **s**.
Rev	6: 9	the **s** of those who had been slain
	20: 4	**s** of those who had been beheaded

SOUND [FINE-SOUNDING, SOUNDED, SOUNDING]

Ge	3: 8	heard the **s** of the LORD God as he
Ex	32:18	"It is not the **s** of victory, it is not the
		s of defeat; it is the **s** of singing
Dt	4:12	the **s** of words but saw no form;
Ps	66: 8	let the **s** of his praise be heard;
	115: 7	nor can they utter a **s**
Pr	3:21	My son, preserve **s** judgment
	8:14	Counsel and **s** judgment are mine;
Isa	6: 4	At the **s** of their voices the doorposts
Eze	3:12	I heard behind me a loud rumbling **s**
Joel	2: 1	**s** the alarm on my holy hill.
Jn	3: 8	You hear its **s**,
Ac	2: 2	a **s** like the blowing of a violent wind
1Co	14: 8	if the trumpet does not **s** a clear call,
	15:52	For the trumpet will **s**,
1Ti	1:10	contrary to the **s** doctrine
	6: 3	does not agree to the **s** instruction
2Ti	1:13	keep as the pattern of **s** teaching,
	4: 3	not put up with **s** doctrine.
Tit	1: 9	can encourage others by **s** doctrine.
	2: 1	what is in accord with **s** doctrine.
Rev	1:15	like the **s** of rushing waters.

SOUNDED [SOUND]

| Rev | 6: 6 | Then I heard what **s** like a voice |
| | 19: 6 | I heard what **s** like a great multitude, |

SOUNDING [SOUND]

| Ps | 47: 5 | the LORD amid the **s** of trumpets. |
| | 150: 3 | Praise him with the **s** of the trumpet, |

SOUR

Jer	31:29	'The fathers have eaten **s** grapes,
Eze	18: 2	" 'The fathers eat **s** grapes,
Rev	10: 9	It will turn your stomach **s**,

SOURCE

| Heb | 5: 9 | he became the **s** of eternal salvation |

SOUTH

| Ge | 13:14 | where you are and look north and **s**, |
| Ps | 89:12 | You created the north and the **s**; |

Da	11: 5	king of the **S** will become strong,
Zec	14: 4	and half moving **s**.
Mt	12:42	The Queen of the of the **S** will rise at

SOVEREIGN [SOVEREIGNTY]

Ge	15: 2	But Abram said, "O **S** LORD,
Ex	23:17	to appear before the **S** LORD.
2Sa	7:18	O **S** LORD, and what is my family,
	7:22	"How great you are, O **S** LORD!
Ps	71: 5	you have been my hope, O **S** LORD,
	71:16	your mighty acts, O **S** LORD;
	140: 7	O **S** LORD, my strong deliverer,
Isa	25: 8	The **S** LORD will wipe away
	40:10	the **S** LORD comes with power,
	50: 4	The **S** LORD has given me
	61: 1	The Spirit of the **S** LORD is on me,
	61:11	**S** LORD will make righteousness
Jer	32:17	**S** LORD, you have made the heavens
Da	4:25	Most High is **s** over the kingdoms
Hab	3:19	The **S** LORD is my strength;
Zep	1: 7	Be silent before the **S** LORD,
2Pe	2: 1	denying the **s** Lord who bought them
Jude	1: 4	and deny Jesus Christ our only **S**
Rev	6:10	"How long, **S** Lord, holy and true,

WHAT THE SOVEREIGN †LORD SAYS
See †LORD

SOVEREIGN †LORD See †LORD

DECLARES THE SOVEREIGN †LORD
See †LORD

SOVEREIGNTY [SOVEREIGN]

| Da | 7:27 | the **s**, power and greatness of the |

SOW [SOWED, SOWER, SOWN, SOWS]

Ex	23:10	For six years you are to **s** your fields
Dt	28:38	You will **s** much seed in the field
Job	4: 8	and those who **s** trouble reap it.
Ps	126: 5	Those who **s** in tears will reap
Ecc	11: 6	**S** your seed in the morning,
Hos	8: 7	"They **s** the wind and reap
	10:12	**S** for yourselves righteousness,
Mt	6:26	they do not **s** or reap or store away
	13: 3	"A farmer went out to **s** his seed.
1Co	15:36	What you **s** does not come to life
Jas	3:18	Peacemakers who **s** in peace raise
2Pe	2:22	"A **s** that is washed goes back

SOWED [SOW]

| Mt | 13:24 | like a man who **s** good seed in his |

SOWER [SOW]

Isa	55:10	so that it yields seed for the **s**
Mt	13:18	to what the parable of the **s** means:
Jn	4:36	so that the **s** and the reaper may
2Co	9:10	Now he who supplies seed to the **s**

SOWN [SOW]

Mt	13: 8	sixty or thirty times what was **s**.
Mk	4:15	and takes away the word that was **s**
1Co	9:11	we have **s** spiritual seed among you,
	15:42	The body that is **s** is perishable,

SOWS [SOW]

| Pr | 11:18 | but he who **s** righteousness reaps |

22: 8 He who s wickedness reaps trouble,
Mt   13:39 the enemy who s them is the devil.
Mk   4:14 the farmer s the word.
2Co   9: 6 Whoever s sparingly will also reap
Gal   6: 7 A man reaps what he s.

SPACIOUS
Ex   3: 8 of that land into a good and s land,
Ps   18:19 He brought me out into a s place;

SPAN
Ex   23:26 I will give you a full life s.
Ps   90:10 yet their s is but trouble and sorrow,

SPARE [SPARED, SPARES, SPARING]
Ge   18:24 and not s the place for the sake of
Est   7: 3 s my people—this is my request.
Jer 50:20 for I will forgive the remnant I s.
Eze   6: 8 " 'But I will s some,
Zec 11: 5 Their own shepherds do not s them.
Ro   8:32 He who did not s his own Son,
     11:21 if God did not s the natural branches,
2Pe   2: 4 not s angels when they sinned,
      2: 5 not s the ancient world

SPARED [SPARE]
Ge   12:13 for your sake and my life will be s
     19:20 Then my life will be s."
Jos   6:25 But Joshua s Rahab the prostitute,
Ps   30: 3 you s me from going down

SPARES* [SPARE]
Pr   13:24 He who s the rod hates his son,
Mal   3:17 a man s his son who serves him.

SPARING [SPARE]
Pr   21:26 but the righteous give without s.

SPARKLE*
Zec   9:16 They will s in his land like jewels in

SPARROW [SPARROWS]
Ps   84: 3 Even the s has found a home,

SPARROWS [SPARROW]
Mt   10:29 Are not two s sold for a penny?
Lk   12: 7 you are worth more than many s.

SPEAK [SPEAKER, SPEAKING,
SPEAKS, SPOKE, SPOKEN]
Ge   18:27 "Now that I have been so bold as to s
     37: 4 and could not s a kind word to him.
Ex   4:12 Now go; I will help you s
      6:30 "Since I s with faltering lips,
     33:11 The LORD would s to Moses face
Nu   12: 8 With him I s face to face,
     20: 8 S to that rock before their eyes
     22:35 but s only what I tell you."
Dt   18:20 But a prophet who presumes to s
1Sa   3: 9 and if he calls you, say, 'S, LORD,
2Ki 18:26 Don't s to us in Hebrew in
Job 13: 3 But I desire to s to the Almighty and
Ps   49: 3 My mouth will s words of wisdom,
    135:16 They have mouths, but cannot s,

Pr   20:15 that s knowledge are a rare jewel.
     23: 9 Do not s to a fool,
     31: 8 "S up for those who cannot s for
Ecc   3: 7 a time to be silent and a time to s,
Isa 28:11 and strange tongues God will s
     40: 2 S tenderly to Jerusalem,
Jer 10: 5 their idols cannot s;
Eze   3:18 and you do not warn him or s out
Da   7:25 He will s against the Most High
Zec 10: 2 The idols s deceit,
Mt   13:13 This is why I s to them in parables:
Mk   7:37 the deaf hear and the mute s."
Jn   12:49 For I did not s of my own accord,
Ac   2: 4 began to s in other tongues
      4:18 not to s or teach at all in the name
1Co 12:30 Do all s in tongues?
     14: 2 in a tongue does not s to men but
     14:19 would rather s five intelligible words
Eph   5:19 S to one another with psalms,
Jas   1:19 slow to s and slow to become angry,

SPEAKER [SPEAK]
1Co 14:11 I am a foreigner to the s,

SPEAKING [SPEAK]
Dt   5:26 heard the voice of the living God s
Mt   10:20 Spirit of your Father s through you.
Mk   12:36 David himself, s by the Holy Spirit,
Ac   2: 6 heard them s in his own language.
     10:46 For they heard them s in tongues
1Co 12:10 to another s in different kinds
Eph   4:15 Instead, s the truth in love,

SPEAKS [SPEAK]
Ex   33:11 as a man s with his friend.
Dt   5:24 that a man can live even if God s
     18:19 that the prophet s in my name,
Ps   15: 2 who s the truth from his heart
Pr   8: 7 My mouth s what is true,
     31:26 She s with wisdom,
Mt   12:32 who s against the Holy Spirit
Lk   6:45 the overflow of his heart his mouth s.
1Co 14: 3 everyone who prophesies s to men
     14: 5 greater than one who s in tongues,
Heb 11: 4 And by faith he still s,
     12:25 that you do not refuse him who s.

SPEAR [SPEARS]
1Sa 17: 7 His s shaft was like a weaver's rod,
     19:10 as Saul drove the s into the wall.
     20:33 Saul hurled his s at him to kill him.
Ps   46: 9 the bow and shatters the s,
Jn   19:34 pierced Jesus' side with a s,

SPEARS [SPEAR]
Isa   2: 4 and their s into pruning hooks.
Joel 3:10 and your pruning hooks into s.
Mic   4: 3 and their s into pruning hooks.

SPECIAL
Nu   6: 2 or woman wants to make a s vow,
Dt   12: 6 your tithes and s gifts,
Ro   14: 6 He who regards one day as s,
Gal   4:10 You are observing s days and months

Jas   2: 3 If you show **s** attention to the man

SPECK
Mt   7: 4 'Let me take the **s** out of your eye,'

SPECTACLE
1Co   4: 9 We have been made a **s** to
Col   2:15 he made a public **s** of them,

SPEECH [SPEECHES]
Ge   11: 1 one language and a common **s**.
Ex   4:10 I am slow of **s** and tongue."
Ps   19: 2 Day after day they pour forth **s**;
      19: 3 There is no **s** or language
Pr   22:11 and whose **s** is gracious will have
Jn   10: 6 Jesus used this figure of **s**,
2Co   8: 7 in **s**, in knowledge,
1Ti   4:12 set an example for the believers in **s**,

SPEED* [SPEEDILY]
Ro   9:28 sentence on earth with **s** and finality.
2Pe   3:12 to the day of God and **s** its coming.

SPEEDILY [SPEED]
Isa   51: 5 My righteousness draws near **s**,

SPELL* [SPELLS]
Rev   18:23 By your magic **s** all the nations

SPELLS [SPELL]
Dt   18:11 or casts **s**, or who is a medium
Mic   5:12 and you will no longer cast **s**.

SPEND [SPENT]
Ge   19: 2 "we will **s** the night in the square."
Jdg   19:20 Only don't **s** the night in the square."
Pr   31: 3 do not **s** your strength on women,
Isa   55: 2 Why **s** money on what is not bread,
2Co   12:15 will very gladly **s** for you everything

SPENT [SPEND]
Pr   5:11 when your flesh and body are **s**.
Mk   5:26 and had **s** all she had,
Lk   6:12 and **s** the night praying to God.
      15:14 After he had **s** everything,

SPICES
Ex   25: 6 **s** for the anointing oil and for the
1Ki   10:10 large quantities of **s**,
Mt   23:23 You give a tenth of your **s**—
Jn   19:40 with the **s**, in strips of linen.

SPIED [SPY]
Jos   6:22 the two men who had **s** out the land,

SPIES [SPY]
Ge   42: 9 and said to them, "You are **s**!
Jos   6:17 because she hid the **s** we sent.
Heb   11:31 because she welcomed the **s**,
Jas   2:25 when she gave lodging to the **s**

SPIN
Mt   6:28 They do not labor or **s**.

SPIRIT [SPIRIT'S, SPIRITIST,
SPIRITISTS, SPIRITS, SPIRITUAL,
SPIRITUALLY]
Ge   1: 2 and the **S** of God was hovering over
       6: 3 "My **S** will not contend with man
Ex   31: 3 I have filled him with the **S** of God,
Nu   11:25 he took of the **S** that was on him and
             put the **S** on the seventy elders.
      24: 2 the **S** of God came upon him
Dt   34: 9 was filled with the **s** of wisdom
Jdg   6:34 **S** of the LORD came upon Gideon,
      11:29 Then the **S** of the LORD came
      13:25 and the **S** of the LORD began
      14: 6 The **S** of the LORD came upon him
      15:14 The **S** of the LORD came upon him
1Sa   10: 6 The **S** of the LORD will come upon
      16:13 the **S** of the LORD came upon David
      16:14 the **S** of the LORD had departed
      16:15 evil **s** from God is tormenting you.
      28: 8 "Consult a **s** for me," he said,
2Sa   23: 2 **S** of the LORD spoke through me;
2Ki   2: 9 inherit a double portion of your **s**,"
       2:15 "The **s** of Elijah is resting on Elisha."
2Ch   18:21 and be a lying **s** in the mouths
Ne   9:20 You gave your good **S**
Job   33: 4 The **S** of God has made me;
Ps   31: 5 Into your hands I commit my **s**;
      34:18 and saves those who are crushed in **s**.
      51:10 and renew a steadfast **s** within me.
      51:11 or take your Holy **S** from me.
      51:17 The sacrifices of God are a broken **s**;
     106:33 they rebelled against the **S** of God,
     139: 7 Where can I go from your **S**?
     143:10 may your good **S** lead me
Pr   16:18 a haughty **s** before a fall.
      20:27 the LORD searches the **s** of a man;
      29:23 but a man of lowly **s** gains honor.
Ecc   12: 7 and the **s** returns to God who gave it.
Isa   11: 2 The **S** of the LORD will rest on him—
      30: 1 but not by my **S**,
      32:15 till the **S** is poured upon us from
      42: 1 I will put my **S** on him
      44: 3 I will pour out my **S**
      48:16 LORD has sent me, with his **S**.
      57:15 who is contrite and lowly in **s**,
      59:21 "My **S**, who is on you,
      61: 1 **S** of the Sovereign LORD is on me,
      63:10 they rebelled and grieved his Holy **S**.
Eze   3:12 Then the **S** lifted me up,
      11:19 an undivided heart and put a new **s**
      13: 3 prophets who follow their own **s**
      36:26 a new heart and put a new **s** in you;
Da   4: 8 he has the **s** of the holy gods in him.)
Joel   2:28 I will pour out my **S** on all people.
Zec   4: 6 nor by power, but by my **S**,'
Mt   1:18 to be with child through the Holy **S**.
       3:11 He will baptize you with the Holy **S**
       3:16 and he saw the **S** of God descending
       4: 1 Then Jesus was led by the **S** into
       5: 3 "Blessed are the poor in **s**,
      10:20 but the **S** of your Father speaking
      12:31 but the blasphemy against the **S** will
      26:41 The **s** is willing, but the body is weak
      28:19 and of the Son and of the Holy **S**,

Mk	1: 8	he will baptize you with the Holy **S**."
Lk	1:15	and he will be filled with the Holy **S**
	1:35	"The Holy **S** will come upon you,
	1:80	child grew and became strong in s;
	3:16	He will baptize you with the Holy **S**
	4: 1	Jesus, full of the Holy **S,**
	4:18	"The **S** of the Lord is on me,
	11:13	Father in heaven give the Holy **S**
	23:46	into your hands I commit my s."
Jn	1:33	the **S** come down and remain is he
		who will baptize with the Holy **S.**'
	3: 5	unless he is born of water and the **S.**
	3: 6	but the **S** gives birth to s.
	3:34	for God gives the **S** without limit.
	4:24	God is s, and his worshipers must
		worship in s and in truth."
	6:63	The **S** gives life;
	7:39	By this he meant the **S,**
	14:17	the **S** of truth.
	14:26	But the Counselor, the Holy **S,**
	15:26	the **S** of truth who goes out from
	16:13	But when he, the **S** of truth, comes,
	20:22	"Receive the Holy **S.**
Ac	1: 5	you will be baptized with the Holy **S.**
	1: 8	when the Holy **S** comes on you;
	2: 4	were filled the Holy **S**
	2:17	I will pour out my **S** on all people.
	2:38	receive the gift of the Holy **S.**
	4:31	they were all filled with the Holy **S**
	5: 3	that you have lied to the Holy **S**
	6: 3	known to be full of the **S**
	7:51	You always resist the Holy **S!**
	8:15	that they might receive the Holy **S,**
	9:17	and be filled with the Holy **S.**"
	11:16	be baptized with the Holy **S.**'
	13: 2	the Holy **S** said,
	19: 2	the Holy **S** when you believed?"
	19: 2	not even heard that there is a Holy **S.**
Ro	7: 6	serve in the new way of the **S,**
	8: 4	but according to the **S.**
	8: 5	minds set on what the **S** desires.
	8: 9	And if anyone does not have the **S**
	8:13	the **S** you put to death the misdeeds
	8:15	but you received the **S** of sonship.
	8:16	The **S** himself testifies with our s
	8:23	who have the firstfruits of the **S,**
	8:26	the **S** helps us in our weakness.
1Co	2:10	The **S** searches all things,
	2:14	without the **S** does not accept the
		things that come from the **S** of God,
	5: 3	I am with you in s.
	6:17	with the Lord is one with him in s.
	6:19	your body is a temple of the Holy **S,**
	12: 4	kinds of gifts, but the same **S.**
	12:13	For we were all baptized by one **S**
2Co	1:22	put his **S** in our hearts as a deposit,
	3: 3	written not with ink but with the **S** of
	3: 6	but the **S** gives life.
	3:17	Now the Lord is the **S,**
	5: 5	and has given us the **S** as a deposit,
	7: 1	that contaminates body and s,
Gal	3: 2	Did you receive the **S** by observing
	3:14	receive the promise of the **S.**
	5:16	So I say, live by the **S,**

	5:22	But the fruit of the **S** is love, joy,
	5:25	let us keep in step with the **S.**
	6: 8	the one who sows to please the **S,**
Eph	1:13	the promised Holy **S,**
	2:18	access to the Father by one **S.**
	2:22	in which God lives by his **S.**
	4: 3	unity of the **S** through the bond of
	4: 4	There is one body and one **S**—
	4:30	do not grieve the Holy **S** of God,
	5:18	Instead, be filled with the **S.**
	6:17	of salvation and the sword of the **S,**
Php	2: 2	being one in s and purpose.
Col	2: 5	I am present with you in s
1Th	5:23	May your whole s, soul and body
2Th	2:13	the sanctifying work of the **S**
1Ti	3:16	was vindicated by the **S,**
2Ti	1: 7	God did not give us a s of timidity,
	4:22	The Lord be with your s.
Heb	2: 4	and gifts of the Holy **S** distributed
	4:12	even to dividing soul and s, joints
	6: 4	who have shared in the Holy **S,**
	10:29	and who has insulted the **S** of grace?
1Pe	1: 2	the sanctifying work of the **S,**
	3: 4	beauty of a gentle and quiet s,
2Pe	1:21	carried along by the Holy **S.**
1Jn	3:24	We know it by the **S** he gave us.
	4: 1	Dear friends, do not believe every s,
	4:13	because he has given us of his **S.**
Jude	1:20	and pray in the Holy **S.**
Rev	1:10	On the Lord's Day I was in the **S,**
	2: 7	let him hear what the **S** says to
	4: 2	At once I was in the **S,**

EVIL SPIRIT See EVIL

HOLY SPIRIT See HOLY

MY SPIRIT Ge 6:3; 2Ki 5:26; Job 6:4; 7:11; 10:12; 17:1; Ps 31:5; 73:21; 77:3, 6; 142:3; 143:4, 7; Isa 26:9; 30:1; 38:16; 42:1; 44:3; 59:21; La 1:16; Eze 3:14; 36:27; 37:14; 39:29; Joel 2:28, 29; Hag 2:5; Zec 4:6; 6:8; Mt 12:18; Lk 1:47; 23:46; Ac 2:17, 18; 7:59; 1Co 14:14, 15, 15; 16:18

SPIRIT OF GOD Ge 1:2; 41:38; Ex 31:3; 35:31; Nu 24:2; 1Sa 10:10; 11:6; 19:20, 23; 2Ch 15:1; 24:20; Job 33:4; Ps 106:33; Eze 11:24; Mt 3:16; 12:28; Ro 8:9, 14; 1Co 2:11, 14; 7:40; 12:3; Eph 4:30; Php 3:3; 1Jn 4:2

SPIRIT OF THE †LORD Jdg 3:10; 6:34; 11:29; 13:25; 14:6, 19; 15:14; 1Sa 10:6; 16:13, 14; 2Sa 23:2; 1Ki 18:12; 2Ki 2:16; 2Ch 20:14; Isa 11:2; 63:14; Eze 11:5; 37:1; Mic 2:7; 3:8

SPIRIT'S* [SPIRIT]

1Co	2: 4	with a demonstration of the **S** power,
1Th	5:19	Do not put out the **S** fire;

SPIRITIST* [SPIRIT]

Lev	20:27	or s among you must be put to death.
Dt	18:11	or s or who consults the dead.

SPIRITISTS [SPIRIT]

Lev	19:31	not turn to mediums or seek out s,
1Sa	28: 3	Saul had expelled the mediums and s
2Ki	23:24	Josiah got rid of the mediums and s,

SPIRITS [SPIRIT]

Nu	16:22	"O God, God of the **s** of all mankind,
	27:16	the God of the **s** of all mankind,
Ru	3: 7	and drinking and was in good **s,**
Ps	78: 8	whose **s** were not faithful to him.
Mt	12:45	with it seven other **s** more wicked
Lk	4:36	and power he gives orders to evil **s**
Ac	8: 7	evil **s** came out of many,
1Co	12:10	to another distinguishing between **s,**
	14:32	The **s** of prophets are subject to
Heb	12: 9	to the Father of our **s** and live!
1Pe	3:19	and preached to the **s** in prison
1Jn	4: 1	but test the **s** to see whether they are
Rev	1: 4	from the seven **s** before his throne,
	16:13	Then I saw three evil **s** that looked
	22: 6	the God of the **s** of the prophets,

EVIL SPIRITS See EVIL

SPIRITUAL [SPIRIT]

Ro	1:11	that I may impart to you some **s** gift
	7:14	We know that the law is **s;**
	12: 1	this is your **s** act of worship.
	12:11	but keep your **s** fervor,
	15:27	shared in the Jews' **s** blessings,
1Co	2:13	expressing **s** truths in **s** words.
	3: 1	not address you as **s** but as worldly—
	9:11	If we have sown **s** seed among you,
	10: 3	They all ate the same **s** food
	12: 1	Now about **s** gifts, brothers,
	14: 1	way of love and eagerly desire **s** gifts
	15:44	it is raised a **s** body.
Gal	6: 1	who are **s** should restore him gently.
Eph	1: 3	with every **s** blessing in Christ.
	5:19	hymns and **s** songs.
	6:12	and against the **s** forces of evil in
Col	1: 9	all **s** wisdom and understanding.
	3:16	hymns and **s** songs with gratitude
1Pe	2: 2	crave pure **s** milk,
	2: 5	are being built into a **s** house to be
	2: 5	offering **s** sacrifices acceptable

SPIRITUALLY* [SPIRIT]

1Co	2:14	because they are **s** discerned.
	14:37	thinks he is a prophet or **s** gifted,

SPIT

Dt	25: 9	**s** in his face and say,
Mt	27:30	They **s** on him,
Mk	14:65	Then some began to **s** at him;
Rev	3:16	about to **s** you out of my mouth.

SPLENDOR

1Ch	16:29	worship the LORD in the **s** of
	29:11	the glory and the majesty and the **s,**
Job	37:22	of the north he comes in golden **s;**
Ps	21: 5	bestowed on him **s** and majesty.
	29: 2	worship the LORD in the **s** of
	45: 3	clothe yourself with **s**
	96: 6	**S** and majesty are before him;
	96: 9	the LORD in the **s** of his holiness;
	104: 1	you are clothed with **s** and majesty.
	145: 5	of the glorious **s** of your majesty,
	145:12	your mighty acts and the glorious **s**
	148:13	his **s** is above the earth and the

Pr	4: 9	and present you with a crown of **s."**
	16:31	Gray hair is a crown of **s;**
	20:29	gray hair the **s** of the old.
Isa	2:10	the LORD and the **s** of his majesty!
	49: 3	Israel, in whom I will display my **s."**
	55: 5	for he has endowed you with **s."**
	60:21	for the display of my **s.**
	61: 3	the LORD for the display of his **s.**
	62: 3	a crown of **s** in the LORD's hand,
	63: 1	Who is this, robed in **s,**
Hos	14: 6	His **s** will be like an olive tree,
Hab	3: 4	His **s** was like the sunrise;
Mt	6:29	not even Solomon in all his **s**
Lk	9:31	appeared in glorious **s,**
2Th	2: 8	and destroy by the **s** of his coming.
Rev	21:24	kings of the earth will bring their **s**

SPLINTERED

2Ki	18:21	that **s** reed of a staff,

SPLIT

Lev	11: 3	that has a **s** hoof completely divided
Nu	16:31	the ground under them **s** apart
1Ki	13: 3	The altar will be **s** apart and the
	16:21	of Israel were **s** into two factions;
Ps	74:13	It was you who **s** open the sea
Zec	14: 4	the Mount of Olives will be **s** in two
Mt	27:51	The earth shook and the rocks **s.**
Rev	16:19	The great city **s** into three parts,

SPOIL [SPOILS]

Ps	119:162	like one who finds great **s.**
1Pe	1: 4	that can never perish, **s** or fade—

SPOILS [SPOIL]

Ex	15: 9	I will divide the **s;**
Nu	31:27	Divide the **s** between the soldiers
Isa	53:12	he will divide the **s** with the strong,
Jn	6:27	Do not work for food that **s,**

SPOKE [SPEAK]

Ge	16:13	name to the LORD who **s** to her:
	39:10	though she **s** to Joseph day after day,
Ex	20: 1	And God **s** all these words:
Dt	4:12	the LORD **s** to you out of the fire.
	5: 4	The LORD **s** to you face to face
1Ki	4:32	He **s** three thousand proverbs
Job	42: 3	I **s** of things I did not understand,
Ps	99: 7	He **s** to them from the pillar of cloud;
Jer	35:17	I **s** to them, but they did not listen;
Mt	9:33	the man who had been mute **s.**
Mk	4:33	With many similar parables Jesus **s**
Jn	8:30	as he **s,** many put their faith in him.
Heb	1: 1	God **s** to our forefathers through the
	13: 7	who **s** the word of God to you.
2Pe	1:21	but men **s** from God

SPOKEN [SPEAK]

Ex	34:29	because he had **s** with the LORD.
Nu	12: 2	the LORD **s** only through Moses?"
Dt	18:22	a message the LORD has not **s.**
Ezr	1: 1	to fulfill the word of the LORD **s**
Job	42: 7	you have not **s** of me what is right,
Ps	60: 6	God has **s** from his sanctuary:
Pr	25:11	A word aptly **s** is like apples of gold

Isa 45:19 I have not **s** in secret,
Jer 29:23 and in my name have **s** lies,
Lk 20:19 they knew he had **s** this parable
Jn 2:21 the temple he had **s** of was his body.
Heb 1: 2 last days he has **s** to us by his Son,

SPONGE

Mk 15:36 filled a **s** with wine vinegar,
Jn 19:29 put the **s** on a stalk of the hyssop

SPONTANEOUS*

Phm 1:14 so that any favor you do will be **s**

SPOT [SPOTLESS, SPOTS, SPOTTED]

Isa 28: 8 and there is not a **s** without filth.
  46: 7 From that **s** it cannot move.
1Ti 6:14 keep this command without **s** or

SPOTLESS* [SPOT]

Da 11:35 and made **s** until the time of the end,
  12:10 made **s** and refined,
2Pe 3:14 make every effort to be found **s,**

SPOTS [SPOT]

Jer 13:23 his skin or the leopard its **s?**

SPOTTED [SPOT]

Ge 30:32 from them every speckled or **s** sheep,

SPRANG* [SPRING]

Jnh 4:10 It **s** up overnight and died overnight.
Mt 13: 5 It **s** up quickly,
Mk 4: 5 It **s** up quickly,
Ro 7: 9 sin **s** to life and I died.

SPREAD [SPREADING, SPREADS]

Ge 10:32 the nations **s** out over the earth after
Ex 23: 1 "Do not **s** false reports.
  37: 9 cherubim had their wings **s** upward,
1Ch 14:17 So David's fame **s** throughout
Ps 5:11 **S** your protection over them,
  78:19 "Can God **s** a table in the desert?
  143: 6 I **s** out my hands to you;
Pr 15: 7 The lips of the wise **s** knowledge;
Isa 48:13 and my right hand **s** out the heavens;
Eze 1:11 Their wings were **s** out upward;
Lk 19:36 people **s** their cloaks on the road.
Jn 21:23 the rumor **s** among the brothers
Ac 6: 7 So the word of God **s.**
  12:24 of God continued to increase and **s.**
  13:49 the Lord **s** through the whole region.
  19:20 the Lord **s** widely and grew in power.
2Th 3: 1 message of the Lord may **s** rapidly
2Ti 2:17 Their teaching will **s** like gangrene.

SPREADING [SPREAD]

1Sa 2:24 not a good report that I hear **s** among
1Ki 8:38 out his hands toward this temple—
Pr 29: 5 Whoever flatters his neighbor is **s**
Jer 2:20 and under every **s** tree you lay down
  17: 2 and Asherah poles beside the **s** trees
1Th 3: 2 fellow worker in **s** the gospel of

SPREADS [SPREAD]

Job 36:29 Who can understand how he **s** out

Pr 10:18 and whoever **s** slander is a fool.
2Co 2:14 **s** everywhere the fragrance of

SPRING [SPRANG, SPRINGS, SPRINGTIME]

Ge 16: 7 of the LORD found Hagar near a **s**
Dt 11:14 both autumn and **s** rains,
Ecc 4: 4 all achievement **s** from man's envy
Isa 45: 8 let salvation **s** up,
  58:11 like a **s** whose waters never fail.
Jer 2:13 the **s** of living water,
  9: 1 Oh, that my head were a **s** of water
  17:13 the **s** of living water.
Jn 4:14 in him a **s** of water welling up
Ro 15:12 "The Root of Jesse will **s** up,
Jas 3:12 a salt **s** produce fresh water.
Rev 21: 6 to drink without cost from the **s** of

SPRINGS [SPRING]

Ge 7:11 the **s** of the great deep burst forth,
Ps 114: 8 the hard rock into **s** of water.
Pr 5:16 Should your **s** overflow in the streets,
Isa 49:10 and lead them beside **s**
2Pe 2:17 These men are **s** without water
Rev 7:17 lead them to **s** of living water.

SPRINGTIME* [SPRING]

Zec 10: 1 Ask the LORD for rain in the **s;**

SPRINKLE [SPRINKLED, SPRINKLING]

Ex 29:16 and **s** it against the altar on all sides.
Lev 16:14 and with his finger **s** it on the front
Nu 8: 7 **S** the water of cleansing on them;
Isa 52:15 so will he **s** many nations,
Eze 36:25 I will **s** clean water on you,

SPRINKLED [SPRINKLE]

Heb 10:22 having our hearts **s** to cleanse us

SPRINKLING [SPRINKLE]

Heb 11:28 kept the Passover and the **s** of blood,
1Pe 1: 2 to Jesus Christ and **s** by his blood:

SPROUT

Nu 17: 5 to the man I choose will **s,**
Pr 23: 5 surely **s** wings and fly off to the sky
Jer 33:15 a righteous Branch **s** from David's

SPUR*

Heb 10:24 how we may **s** one another on

SPURNED [SPURNS]

Pr 1:30 my advice and **s** my rebuke,
Isa 1: 4 they have **s** the Holy One of Israel
La 2: 6 he has **s** both king and priest.

SPURNS* [SPURNED]

Pr 15: 5 A fool **s** his father's discipline,

SPY [SPIED, SPIES, SPYING]

Dt 1:22 "Let us send men ahead to **s** out
Jos 2: 2 here tonight to **s** out the land."
Gal 2: 4 to **s** on the freedom we have

SPYING [SPY]
Ge 42:30 and treated us as though we were **s**

SQUANDERED [SQUANDERS]
Lk 15:13 and there **s** his wealth in wild living.

SQUANDERS* [SQUANDERED]
Pr 29: 3 companion of prostitutes **s** his wealth

SQUARE [SQUARES]
Ge 19: 2 spend the night in the **s.**"
Ex 27: 1 it is to be **s,**
    28:16 It is to be **s—**
    30: 2 It is to be **s,**
Jdg 19:20 don't spend the night in the **s.**"
Ne 8: 1 in the **s** before the Water Gate.
Rev 21:16 The city was laid out like a **s,**

SQUARES [SQUARE]
Pr 1:20 she raises her voice in the public **s;**

STABILITY*
Pr 29: 4 By justice a king gives a country **s,**

STAFF [STAFFS]
Ge 38:25 whose seal and cord and **s** these are."
    49:10 the ruler's **s** from between his feet,
Ex 4: 4 the snake and it turned back into a **s**
    7:12 Aaron's **s** swallowed up their staffs.
    14:16 Raise your **s** and stretch out
Nu 17: 6 and Aaron's **s** was among them.
    20:11 and struck the rock twice with his **s.**
Ps 23: 4 and your **s,** they comfort me.
Mic 7:14 Shepherd your people with your **s,**
Zec 11:10 I took my **s** called Favor and broke it
Mk 15:19 they struck him on the head with a **s**
Heb 9: 4 Aaron's **s** that had budded,

STAFFS [STAFF]
Ex 7:12 Aaron's staff swallowed up their **s.**
Nu 17: 7 Moses placed the **s** before the LORD

STAGES
Nu 33: 1 the **s** in the journey of the Israelites

STAGGER [STAGGERED, STAGGERS]
Ps 60: 3 given us wine that makes us **s.**
Isa 28: 7 also **s** from wine and reel from beer:
    29: 9 **s,** but not from beer.
Jer 25:16 they will **s** and go mad because of
Am 8:12 Men will **s** from sea to sea

STAGGERED [STAGGER]
Ps 107:27 They reeled and **s** like drunken men;

STAGGERS [STAGGER]
Isa 3: 8 Jerusalem **s,** Judah is falling;

STAIN* [STAINED]
Jer 2:22 the **s** of your guilt is still before me,"
Eph 5:27 without **s** or wrinkle or any other

STAINED [STAIN]
Isa 63: 1 with his garments **s** crimson?
Jude 1:23 the clothing **s** by corrupted flesh.

STAIRWAY
Ge 28:12 a dream in which he saw a **s** resting
2Ki 20:11 it had gone down on the **s** of Ahaz.

STAKES
Isa 54: 2 your cords, strengthen your **s.**

STALK [STALKS]
Ge 41: 5 were growing on a single **s.**
Jn 19:29 the sponge on a **s** of the hyssop plant,

STALKS* [STALK]
Jos 2: 6 hidden them under the **s** of flax
Ru 2:16 pull out some **s** for her from
Ps 91: 6 the pestilence that **s** in the darkness,

STALL [STALLS]
Ps 50: 9 I have no need of a bull from your **s**
Mal 4: 2 like calves released from the **s.**

STALLS [STALL]
1Ki 4:26 Solomon had four thousand **s**
Hab 3:17 in the pen and no cattle in the **s,**

STAND [STANDING, STANDS, STOOD]
Ex 9:11 magicians could not **s** before Moses
    14:13 **S** firm and you will see the
Lev 26:37 not be able to **s** before your enemies.
Nu 30: 4 by which she obligated herself will **s.**
Dt 10: 8 to **s** before the LORD to minister
    11:25 No man will be able to **s** against you.
Jos 3: 8 go and **s** in the river.' "
    10:12 "O sun, **s** still over Gibeon,
2Ch 20:17 **s** firm and see the deliverance
Job 19:25 in the end he will **s** upon the earth.
Ps 1: 1 or **s** in the way of sinners
    1: 5 wicked will not **s** in the judgment,
    10: 1 O LORD, do you **s** far off?
    24: 3 Who may **s** in his holy place?
    33:11 plans of the LORD **s** firm forever,
    40: 2 a rock and gave me a firm place to **s.**
    76: 7 Who can **s** before you when
    93: 5 Your statutes **s** firm;
   119:120 I **s** in awe of your laws.
   130: 3 O Lord, who could **s?**
Pr 10:25 but the righteous **s** firm forever.
Ecc 5: 7 Therefore **s** in awe of God.
Isa 7: 9 If you do not **s** firm in your faith,
    11:10 In that day the Root of Jesse will **s** as
    29:23 will **s** in awe of the God of Israel.
Jer 15: 1 Even if Moses and Samuel were to **s**
Eze 22:30 and **s** before me in the gap on behalf
Mic 5: 4 He will **s** and shepherd his flock in
Hab 3: 2 I **s** in awe of your deeds, O LORD.
Zec 14: 4 his feet will **s** on the Mount of Olives
Mal 3: 2 Who can **s** when he appears?
Mt 12:25 divided against itself will not **s.**
Lk 4: 9 and had him **s** on the highest point of
Ro 5: 2 into this grace in which we now **s.**
    14: 4 for the Lord is able to make him **s.**

14:10 For we will all **s** before God's
1Co 10:13 a way out so that you can **s** up
15:58 Therefore, my dear brothers, **s** firm.
16:13 Be on your guard; **s** firm in the faith;
2Co 1:24 because it is by faith you **s** firm.
Gal 5: 1 **S** firm, then, and do not let
Eph 6:11 so that you can take your **s** against
Col 4:12 you may **s** firm in all the will of God,
2Th 2:15 **s** firm and hold to the teachings
Jas 5: 8 You too, be patient and **s** firm,
Rev 3:20 I **s** at the door and knock.

STANDARD [STANDARDS]
Nu 1:52 in his own camp under his own **s**.

STANDARDS [STANDARD]
Lev 19:35 " 'Do not use dishonest **s**
Nu 2:34 the way they encamped under their **s**,
Eze 7:27 and by their own **s** I will judge them.

STANDING [STAND]
Ge 18:22 but Abraham remained **s** before
Ex 3: 5 where you are **s** is holy ground."
Nu 22:23 the angel of the LORD **s** in the road
Jos 4:10 the ark remained **s** in the middle of
5:15 the place where you are **s** is holy."
Ru 2: 1 a man of **s**, whose name was Boaz.
4:11 May you have **s** in Ephrathah and
2Ch 18:18 the host of heaven on his right
Eze 3:23 the glory of the LORD was **s** there,
Am 7: 7 The Lord was **s** by a wall
9: 1 I saw the Lord **s** by the altar,
Zec 1: 8 He was **s** among the myrtle trees in
3: 1 and Satan **s** at his right side
Mt 6: 5 to pray **s** in the synagogues and on
Lk 9:32 they saw his glory and the two men **s**
21:19 By **s** firm you will gain life.
Ac 7:55 and Jesus **s** at the right hand of God.
1Co 10:12 So, if you think you are **s** firm,
1Ti 3:13 an excellent **s** and great assurance
Jas 5: 9 The Judge is **s** at the door!
1Pe 5: 9 Resist him, **s** firm in the faith,
Rev 7: 9 **s** before the throne and in front of
20:12 great and small, **s** before the throne,

STANDS [STAND]
1Ki 7:27 also made ten movable **s** of bronze;
2Ki 25:13 the movable **s** and the bronze Sea
Ps 89: 2 that your love **s** firm forever,
119:89 it **s** firm in the heavens.
Pr 12: 7 but the house of the righteous **s** firm.
Isa 40: 8 but the word of our God **s** forever."
Mt 10:22 but he who **s** firm to the end will
Jn 1:26 among you is one you do not know.
16:11 of this world now **s** condemned.
2Ti 2:19 God's solid foundation **s** firm,
Heb 4: 1 promise of entering his rest still **s**,
1Pe 1:25 but the word of the Lord **s** forever."

STAR [STARGAZERS, STARRY, STARS]
Nu 24:17 A **s** will come out of Jacob;
Isa 14:12 O morning **s**, son of the dawn!
Mt 2: 2 We saw his **s** in the east
2Pe 1:19 the morning **s** rises in your hearts.

Rev 2:28 I will also give him the morning **s**.
8:11 the name of the **s** is Wormwood.
9: 1 The **s** was given the key to the shaft
22:16 and the bright Morning **S**."

STARGAZERS* [STAR]
Isa 47:13 those **s** who make predictions month

STARRY [STAR]
2Ki 17:16 They bowed down to all the **s** hosts,
Isa 40:26 He who brings out the **s** host one
Da 8:10 and it threw some of the **s** host down

STARS [STAR]
Ge 1:16 He also made the **s**.
15: 5 up at the heavens and count the **s**—
37: 9 and moon and eleven **s** were bowing
Dt 1:10 that today you are as many as the **s** in
Job 38: 7 while the morning **s** sang together
Ps 148: 3 praise him, all you shining **s**.
Isa 14:13 my throne above the **s** of God;
Da 12: 3 like the **s** for ever and ever.
Joel 2:10 and the **s** no longer shine.
Mk 13:25 the **s** will fall from the sky,
Php 2:15 in which you shine like **s** in
Rev 1:16 In his right hand he held seven **s**,
6:13 and the **s** in the sky fell to earth,
8:12 and a third of the **s**,
12: 1 and a crown of twelve **s** on her head.
12: 4 His tail swept a third of the **s** out of

STARVE [STARVING]
Ex 16: 3 to **s** this entire assembly to death."

STARVING [STARVE]
Pr 6:30 to satisfy his hunger when he is **s**.
Lk 15:17 and here I am **s** to death!

STATE [STATEMENTS]
Job 23: 4 I would **s** my case before him
Isa 43:26 **s** the case for your innocence.
Lk 1:48 of the humble **s** of his servant.

STATEMENTS* [STATE]
Mk 14:56 but their **s** did not agree.

STATUE
Da 2:31 and there before you stood a large **s**

STATURE*
1Sa 2:26 Samuel continued to grow in **s** and
SS 7: 7 Your **s** is like that of the palm,
Lk 2:52 And Jesus grew in wisdom and **s**,

STATUTES
1Ki 3: 3 by walking according to the **s**
11:33 nor kept my **s** and laws as David,
Ps 19: 7 The **s** of the LORD are trustworthy,
93: 5 Your **s** stand firm;
119: 2 Blessed are they who keep his **s**
119: 14 I rejoice in following your **s**
119:24 Your **s** are my delight;
119:36 Turn my heart toward your **s** and not
119:99 for I meditate on your **s**.
119:111 Your **s** are my heritage forever;

119:125 that I may understand your **s.**
119:129 Your **s** are wonderful;
119:138 **s** you have laid down are righteous;
119:152 Long ago I learned from your **s**
119:167 I obey your **s,**
Isa 24: 5 disobeyed the laws, violated the **s**

STAY [STAYED]

Ge 13: 6 that they were not able to **s** together.
Ex 16:29 to **s** where he is on the seventh day;
Pr 7:11 her feet never **s** at home;
14: 7 **S** away from a foolish man,
Mic 7:18 You do not **s** angry forever
Mk 14:34 "**S** here and keep watch."

STAYED [STAY]

Ex 24:18 And he **s** on the mountain forty days
Nu 9:18 as the cloud **s** over the tabernacle,
Lk 2:43 the boy Jesus **s** behind in Jerusalem,

STEADFAST* [STEADFASTLY]

Ps 51:10 and renew a **s** spirit within me.
57: 7 My heart is **s,** O God, my heart is **s;**
108: 1 My heart is **s,** O God;
111: 8 They are **s** for ever and ever,
112: 8 his heart is **s,** trusting in the LORD.
119: 5 that my ways were **s** in obeying
Isa 26: 3 perfect peace him whose mind is **s,**
1Pe 5:10 and make you strong, firm and **s.**

STEADFASTLY* [STEADFAST]

2Ch 27: 6 he walked **s** before the LORD his God

STEADY

Ex 17:12 that his hands remained **s** till sunset.
1Ch 13: 9 Uzzah reached out his hand to **s**
Isa 35: 3 **s** the knees that give way;

STEAL [STEALING, STEALS, STOLE, STOLEN]

Ex 20:15 "You shall not **s.**
Lev 19:11 " 'Do not **s.**
Dt 5:19 "You shall not **s.**
Jer 23:30 against the prophets who **s**
Mt 6:19 and where thieves break in and **s.**
19:18 do not **s,** do not give false testimony,
Jn 10:10 The thief comes only to **s** and kill
Ro 13: 9 "Do not murder," "Do not **s,**"
Eph 4:28 has been stealing must **s** no longer,

STEALING [STEAL]

Ro 2:21 You who preach against **s,**

STEALS [STEAL]

Pr 6:30 a thief if he **s** to satisfy his hunger

STEEL (KJV) See BRONZE

STEERED*

Jas 3: 4 they are **s** by a very small rudder

STEP [FOOTSTEPS, STEPS]

Job 34:21 he sees their every **s.**
Gal 5:25 let us keep in **s** with the Spirit.

STEPHEN*

Deacon (Ac 6:5). Arrested (Ac 6:8-15). Speech to Sanhedrin (Ac 7). Stoned (Ac 7:54-60; 8:2; 11:19; 22:20).

STEPS [STEP]

Ex 20:26 And do not go up to my altar on **s,**
2Ki 20: 9 the shadow go forward ten **s,**
Ps 37:23 he makes his **s** firm;
Pr 5: 5 her **s** lead straight to the grave.
14:15 a prudent man gives thought to his **s.**
16: 9 but the LORD determines his **s.**
20:24 man's **s** are directed by the LORD.
Jer 10:23 not for man to direct his **s.**
1Pe 2:21 that you should follow in his **s.**

STERN [STERNNESS]

Pr 15:10 **S** discipline awaits him who leaves

STERNNESS* [STERN]

Ro 11:22 and **s** of God: **s** to those who fell,

STEW

Ge 25:29 when Jacob was cooking some **s,**
2Ki 4:39 he cut them up into the pot of **s,**

STICK [STICKS, STUCK]

2Ki 6: 6 Elisha cut a **s** and threw it there,
Eze 37:16 take a **s** of wood and write on it,
Hos 4:12 and are answered by a **s** of wood.
Am 4:11 a burning **s** snatched from the fire,
Zec 3: 2 a burning **s** snatched from the fire?"
Mt 27:48 put it on a **s,** and offered it

STICKS [STICK]

Pr 18:24 but there is a friend who **s** closer than

STIFF-NECKED [NECK]

Ex 32: 9 "and they are a **s** people.
34: 9 Although this is a **s** people,
2Ki 17:14 and were as **s** as their fathers,
Pr 29: 1 A man who remains **s**
Ac 7:51 "You **s** people,

STILL [STILLED]

Ge 9: 4 not eat meat that has its lifeblood **s**
Ex 14:14 fight for you; you need only to be **s.**"
Lev 19:26 not eat any meat with the blood **s**
Jos 10:13 So the sun stood **s,**
Ps 37: 7 Be **s** before the LORD
46:10 "Be **s,** and know that I am God;
83: 1 O God, be not **s.**
89: 9 its waves mount up, you **s** them.
Da 11:35 it will **s** come at the appointed time.
Hab 3:11 Sun and moon stood **s** in the heavens
Zec 2:13 Be **s** before the LORD, all mankind,
Mk 4:39 and said to the waves, "Quiet! Be **s!**"
8:17 Do you **s** not see or understand?
Jn 12:37 they **s** would not believe in him.
Ro 5: 8 While we were **s** sinners,
Heb 11: 4 And by faith he **s** speaks,

STILLED [STILL]

Ps 65: 7 who **s** the roaring of the seas,

131: 2 But I have **s** and quieted my soul;

STIMULATE*

2Pe 3: 1 to **s** you to wholesome thinking.

STING

1Co 15:55 Where, O death, is your **s?"**
Rev 9: 5 of the **s** of a scorpion when it strikes

STINGY*

Pr 23: 6 Do not eat the food of a **s** man,
28:22 A **s** man is eager to get rich

STIPULATIONS

Dt 6:20 "What is the meaning of the **s,**
Jer 44:23 or his decrees or his **s,**

STIRRED [STIRRING]

1Ki 14:22 By the sins they committed they **s**
Ps 45: 1 My heart is **s** by a noble theme
Hag 1:14 So the LORD **s** up the spirit
Ac 13:50 They **s** up persecution against Paul

STIRRING [STIRRED, STIR]

Pr 30:33 so **s** up anger produces strife."
Ac 17:13 agitating the crowds and **s** them up.

STIRS [STIRRING]

Pr 6:19 and a man who **s** up dissension
10:12 Hatred **s** up dissension,
15: 1 but a harsh word **s** up anger.
15:18 A hot-tempered man **s** up dissension,
16:28 A perverse man **s** up dissension,
28:25 A greedy man **s** up dissension,
29:22 An angry man **s** up dissension,
Lk 23: 5 "He **s** up the people all over Judea

STOIC*

Ac 17:18 and **S** philosophers began to dispute

STOLE [STEAL]

Ge 31:19 Rachel **s** her father's household gods.
2Sa 15: 6 he **s** the hearts of the men of Israel.
Mt 28:13 during the night and **s** him away

STOLEN [STEAL]

Ex 22: 4 "If the **s** animal is found alive
Lev 6: 4 he must return what he has **s** or taken
Ps 62:10 in extortion or take pride in **s** goods;
Pr 9:17 **"S** water is sweet;
SS 4: 9 You have **s** my heart, my sister,
Eze 33:15 returns what he has **s,**

STOMACH

Eze 3: 3 and fill your **s** with it."
Mk 7:19 go into his heart but into his **s,**
1Co 6:13 "Food for the **s** and the **s** for food"—
Php 3:19 their god is their **s,**
1Ti 5:23 use a little wine because of your **s**
Rev 10: 9 It will turn your **s** sour,

STONE [CAPSTONE, CORNERSTONE, MILLSTONE, MILLSTONES,

SLINGSTONES, STONED, STONES, STONING]

Ge 28:18 the **s** he had placed under his head
31:45 So Jacob took a **s** and set it up as
35:14 Jacob set up a **s** pillar at the place
Ex 17: 4 They are almost ready to **s** me."
24: 4 set up twelve **s** pillars representing
28:10 six names on one **s** and the
31:18 tablets of **s** inscribed by the finger of
34: 1 "Chisel out two **s** tablets like
Lev 26: 1 an image or a sacred **s** for yourselves
Dt 4:13 and then wrote them on two **s** tablets.
16:22 and do not erect a sacred **s,**
19:14 move your neighbor's boundary **s**
28:36 gods of wood and **s.**
1Sa 7:12 Then Samuel took a **s** and set it up
17:50 the Philistine with a sling and a **s;**
2Ki 10:27 They demolished the sacred **s** of Baal
Ps 91:12 not strike your foot against a **s.**
118:22 The **s** the builders rejected has
Isa 8:14 a **s** that causes men to stumble
28:16 I lay a **s** in Zion, a tested **s,**
Jer 3: 9 committed adultery with **s** and wood.
Eze 11:19 from them their heart of **s**
36:26 from you your heart of **s**
Zec 3: 9 There are seven eyes on that one **s,**
Mt 4: 6 not strike your foot against a **s.' "**
7: 9 will give him a **s?**
23:37 the prophets and **s** those sent to you,
24: 2 not one **s** here will be left on another;
Mk 12:10 " 'The **s** the builders rejected has
16: 3 "Who will roll the **s** away from
Lk 4: 3 tell this **s** to become bread."
20:18 falls on that **s** will be broken to
Jn 8: 7 be the first to throw a stone at her."
8:59 they picked up stones to **s** him,
10:32 For which of these do you **s** me?"
19:13 at a place known as the **S** Pavement
Ac 4:11 He is " 'the **s** you builders rejected,
Ro 9:32 stumbled over the "stumbling **s."**
2Co 3: 3 of **s** but on tablets of human hearts.
1Pe 2: 4 As you come to him, the living **S—**
2: 6 I lay a **s** in Zion,
Rev 2:17 a white **s** with a new name written
21:19 with every kind of precious **s.**

STONED [STONE]

Lev 24:23 outside the camp and **s** him.
Nu 15:36 outside the camp and **s** him to death.
Jos 7:25 Then all Israel **s** him.
1Ki 21:13 outside the city and **s** him to death.
2Ch 24:21 they **s** him to death in the courtyard
Ac 14:19 They **s** Paul and dragged him outside
2Co 11:25 once I was **s,**
Heb 11:37 They were **s;** they were sawed in two

STONES [STONE]

Ex 23:24 and break their sacred **s** to pieces.
28: 9 "Take two onyx **s** and engrave
28:21 There are to be twelve **s,**
Dt 27: 2 set up some large **s** and coat them
Jos 4: 3 to take up twelve **s** from the middle
1Sa 17:40 chose five smooth **s** from the stream,

1Ki 18:31 Elijah took twelve **s**,
2Ki 17:10 set up sacred **s** and Asherah poles
      18: 4 smashed the sacred **s** and cut down
Ps 102:14 For her **s** are dear to your servants;
Ecc 3: 5 to scatter **s** and a time to gather them,
Mt   3: 9 of these **s** God can raise up children
      4: 3 tell these **s** to become bread."
Mk 13: 1 What massive **s**!
Lk 19:40 the **s** will cry out."
1Co 3:12 silver, costly **s**, wood, hay or straw,
1Pe 2: 5 like living **s**, are being built into

STONING* [STONE]

Nu 14:10 whole assembly talked about **s** them.
1Sa 30: 6 the men were talking of **s** him;
Jn 10:33 "We are not **s** you for any of these,"
Ac   7:59 While they were **s** him,

STOOD [STAND]

Ge 28:13 There above it **s** the LORD,
Ex 15: 8 The surging waters **s** firm like a wall;
Dt   5: 5 (At that time I **s** between the LORD
Jos 3:17 ark of the covenant of the LORD **s**
     10:13 So the sun **s** still,
Zec 3: 5 while the angel of the LORD **s** by.
Lk 10:25 expert in the law **s** up to test Jesus.
     18:11 The Pharisee **s** up and prayed
     22:28 You are those who have **s** by me
Jn 19:25 Near the cross of Jesus **s** his mother,
     20:19 Jesus came and **s** among them
2Ti 4:17 But the Lord **s** at my side
Jas 1:12 because when he has **s** the test,
Rev 22: 2 of the river **s** the tree of life,

STOOP [STOOPS]

2Sa 22:36 you **s** down to make me great.
Mk   1: 7 not worthy to **s** down and untie.

STOOPS [STOOP]

Ps 113: 6 who **s** down to look on the heavens

STOP [STOPPED]

Job 37:14 **s** and consider God's wonders.
Isa 1:13 **S** bringing meaningless offerings!
      1:16 **S** doing wrong,
      2:22 **S** trusting in man,
Jer 32:40 I will never **s** doing good
Mk   9:39 "Do not **s** him," Jesus said.
Jn   5:14 **S** sinning or something worse may
      6:43 "**S** grumbling among yourselves,"
      7:24 **S** judging by mere appearances,
     20:27 **S** doubting and believe."
Ac   5:39 you will not be able to **s** these men;
Ro 14:13 Therefore let us **s** passing judgment
1Co 14:20 Brothers, **s** thinking like children.
Rev 4: 8 Day and night they never **s** saying:

STOPPED [STOP]

Nu 16:48 and the plague **s**.
Jos 3:16 the water from upstream **s** flowing.
     10:13 the sun stood still, and the moon **s**,
2Sa 24:25 and the plague on Israel was **s**.
2Ki 4: 6 Then the oil **s** flowing.
Mk   5:29 Immediately her bleeding **s**

Lk 23:45 for the sun **s** shining.

STORE [STORED, STORES, STORING]

Pr   2: 1 and **s** up my commands within you,
      2: 7 He holds victory in **s** for the upright,
      7: 1 and **s** up my commands within you.
     10:14 Wise men **s** up knowledge,
Isa 2:12 The LORD Almighty has a day in **s**
     33: 6 a rich **s** of salvation and wisdom
Mt   6:19 "Do not **s** up for yourselves treasures
      6:26 not sow or reap or **s** away in barns,
2Ti 4: 8 Now there is in **s** for me the crown

STORED [STORE]

Pr 13:22 but a sinner's wealth is **s** up for
Lk   6:45 out of the good **s** up in his heart,
Col 1: 5 that spring from the hope that is **s** up

STOREHOUSE [HOUSE]

Dt 28:12 the **s** of his bounty,
Mal 3:10 Bring the whole tithe into the **s**,

STOREHOUSES [HOUSE]

Job 38:22 "Have you entered the **s** of the snow
            or seen the **s** of the hail,
Ps 33: 7 he puts the deep into **s**.
    135: 7 and brings out the wind from his **s**.
Isa 39: 2 and showed them what was in his **s**

STOREROOM* [ROOM]

Mt 13:52 of his **s** new treasures as well as old."
Lk 12:24 they have no **s** or barn;

STORES [STORE]

Pr   6: 8 yet it **s** its provisions in summer
     21:20 In the house of the wise are **s** of
Lk 12:21 who **s** up things for himself but is not

STORIES*

2Pe 1:16 did not follow cleverly invented **s**
      2: 3 exploit you with **s** they have made up

STORING* [STORE]

Ecc 2:26 the task of gathering and **s** up wealth
Ro   2: 5 you are **s** up wrath against yourself

STORM

Ex   9:24 the worst **s** in all the land of Egypt
Job 38: 1 LORD answered Job out of the **s**.
     40: 6 the LORD spoke to Job out of the **s**:
Ps 107:29 He stilled the **s** to a whisper;
Isa 25: 4 a shelter from the **s** and a shade
Jer 30:23 the **s** of the LORD will burst out
Jnh 1:12 that this great **s** has come upon you."
Na   1: 3 His way is in the whirlwind and the **s**
Lk   8:24 the **s** subsided,

STOUTHEARTED* [HEART]

Ps 138: 3 you made me bold and **s**.

STRAIGHT [STRAIGHTEN, STRAIGHTENED]

Ps 27:11 lead me in a **s** path because
    107: 7 He led them by a **s** way to a city

Pr   2:13   the s paths to walk in dark ways,
      3: 6   and he will make your paths s.
      4:11   and lead you along s paths.
      4:25   Let your eyes look s ahead,
      5: 5   her steps lead s to the grave.
     11: 5   makes a s way for them,
     15:21   of understanding keeps a s course.
Isa 40: 3   make s in the wilderness a highway
Mt   3: 3   make s paths for him.' "
Lk   3: 5   The crooked roads shall become s,
Jn   1:23   'Make s the way for the Lord.' "
2Pe   2:15   the s way and wandered off to follow

STRAIGHTEN [STRAIGHT]
Ecc   7:13   can s what he has made crooked?

STRAIGHTENED [STRAIGHT]
Ecc   1:15   What is twisted cannot be s;
Lk   13:13   and immediately she s up

STRAIN* [STRAINING]
Ex   18:23   you will be able to stand the s,
Mt   23:24   You s out a gnat but swallow

STRAINING [STRAIN]
Php   3:13   behind and s toward what is ahead,

STRANGE [STRANGER,
    STRANGER'S, STRANGERS]
Ex   3: 3   "I will go over and see this s sight—
Isa 28:11   s tongues God will speak to this
1Co 14:21   "Through men of s tongues
Heb 13: 9   away by all kinds of s teachings.
1Pe   4: 4   They think it s that you do not

STRANGER [STRANGE]
Ge   23: 4   "I am an alien and a s among you.
Ps 119:19   I am a s on earth;
Mt   25:35   I was a s and you invited me in,
Jn   10: 5   But they will never follow a s;
Heb 11: 9   home in the promised land like a s

STRANGER'S* [STRANGE]
Jn   10: 5   they do not recognize a s voice."

STRANGERS [STRANGE]
Ge   15:13   that your descendants will be s in
1Ch 16:19   few indeed, and s in it,
Pr   5:17   never to be shared with s.
Heb 11:13   that were aliens and s on earth.
     13: 2   Do not forget to entertain s,
1Pe   2:11   as aliens and s in the world,
3Jn   1: 5   even though they are s to you.

STRAW
Ex   5:10   not give you any more s.
Isa 11: 7   and the lion will eat s like the ox.
1Co   3:12   silver, costly stones, wood, hay or s,

STRAY [ASTRAY, STRAYED, STRAYS]
Ps 119:10   not let me s from your commands.
Pr   7:25   to her ways or s into her paths.
Eze 14:11   the people of Israel will no longer s

STRAYED [STRAY]
Ps   44:18   our feet had not s from your path.
    119:176 I have s like a lost sheep.
Jer 31:19   After I s, I repented;

STRAYS [STRAY]
Pr   21:16   A man who s from the path
Eze 34:16   for the lost and bring back the s.

STREAM [STREAMS]
1Sa 17:40   chose five smooth stones from the s,
Isa   2: 2   and all nations will s to it.
Am   5:24   righteousness like a never-failing s!
Mic   4: 1   and peoples will s to it.

STREAMS [STREAM]
Ge   2: 6   s came up from the earth
Dt   10: 7   a land with s of water.
Job   6:15   as undependable as intermittent s,
Ps   1: 3   like a tree planted by s of water,
     42: 1   As the deer pants for s of water,
     46: 4   There is a river whose s make glad
    126: 4   O LORD, like s in the Negev.
Ecc   1: 7   All s flow into the sea,
Isa 35: 6   in the wilderness and s in the desert.
     44: 4   like poplar trees by flowing s.
La   3:48   S of tears flow from my eyes
Mt   7:27   The rain came down, the s rose,
Jn   7:38   s of living water will flow from

STREET [STREETS]
Pr   1:20   Wisdom calls aloud in the s,
Mt   6: 5   on the s corners to be seen by men.
     22: 9   Go to the s corners and invite to
Rev 21:21   great s of the city was of pure gold,
     22: 2   the middle of the great s of the city.

STREETS [STREET]
Ps 144:14   no cry of distress in our s.
Zec   8: 5   The city s will be filled with boys
Mt   12:19   no one will hear his voice in the s.

STRENGTH [STRONG]
Ex   15: 2   The LORD is my s and my song;
Nu   14:17   "Now may the Lord's s be displayed,
Dt   4:37   by his Presence and his great s,
      6: 5   with all your soul and with all your s.
     33:25   and your s will equal your days.
Jdg   7: 2   that her own s has saved her,
     16:15   the secret of your great s."
1Sa   2: 9   "It is not by s that one prevails;
2Sa 22:33   It is God who arms me with s
2Ki 23:25   with all his soul and with all his s,
1Ch 16:11   Look to the LORD and his s;
     16:28   ascribe to the LORD glory and s,
     29:12   In your hands are s and power
Ne   8:10   for the joy of the LORD is your s."
Ps   18: 1   I love you, O LORD, my s.
     21:13   Be exalted, O LORD, in your s;
     28: 7   The LORD is my s and my shield;
     29:11   The LORD gives s to his people;
     33:17   despite all its great s it cannot save.
     46: 1   God is our refuge and s,
     59: 9   O my S, I watch for you;

59:17 O my **S**, I sing praise to you;
65: 6 having armed yourself with **s**,
73:26 but God is the **s** of my heart
84: 5 Blessed are those whose **s** is in you,
84: 7 They go from **s** to **s**,
96: 7 ascribe to the LORD glory and **s**.
105: 4 Look to the LORD and his **s**;
118:14 The LORD is my **s** and my song;
147:10 the **s** of the horse,
Pr 24: 5 and a man of knowledge increases **s**;
30:25 Ants are creatures of little **s**,
31:25 She is clothed with **s** and dignity;
Ecc 9:16 So I said, "Wisdom is better than **s.**"
Isa 12: 2 the LORD, is my **s** and my song;
31: 1 and in the great **s** of their horsemen,
40:26 of his great power and mighty **s**,
40:31 hope in the LORD will renew their **s**.
63: 1 forward in the greatness of his **s**?
Jer 9:23 or the strong man boast of his **s** or
Mic 5: 4 and shepherd his flock in the **s** of
Hab 3:19 The Sovereign LORD is my **s**;
Mk 12:30 and with all your **s**.'
1Co 1:25 of God is stronger than man's **s**.
Eph 1:19 like the working of his mighty **s**,
Php 4:13 through him who gives me **s**.
2Ti 4:17 Lord stood at my side and gave me **s**,
Heb 11:34 whose weakness was turned to **s**;
1Pe 4:11 do it with the **s** God provides,
Rev 3: 8 I know that you have little **s**,
5:12 and wealth and wisdom and **s**
7:12 and power and **s** be to our God

STRENGTHEN [STRONG]

Jdg 16:28 O God, please **s** me just once more,
2Ch 16: 9 to **s** those whose hearts are fully
Ps 89:21 surely my arm will **s** him.
119:28 **s** me according to your word.
Isa 35: 3 **S** the feeble hands,
41:10 I will **s** you and help you;
Eze 34:16 the injured and **s** the weak,
Zec 10:12 I will **s** them in the LORD and
Lk 22:32 have turned back, **s** your brothers."
Ac 15:32 to encourage and **s** the brothers.
Eph 3:16 **s** you with power through his Spirit
1Th 3:13 May he **s** your hearts so that you will
2Th 2:17 **s** you in every good deed and word.
Heb 12:12 **s** your feeble arms and weak knees.

STRENGTHENED [STRONG]

Job 4: 3 how you have **s** feeble hands.
Eze 34: 4 You have not **s** the weak or healed
Lk 22:43 appeared to him and **s** him.
Ac 16: 5 So the churches were **s** in the faith
Col 1:11 being **s** with all power according
2: 7 **s** in the faith as you were taught,
Heb 13: 9 It is good for our hearts to be **s**

STRENGTHENING [STRONG]

1Co 14: 3 prophesies speaks to men for their **s**,
14:26 All of these must be done for the **s** of

STRETCH [OUTSTRETCHED, STRETCHED, STRETCHES]

Ex 3:20 So I will **s** out my hand and strike

14:16 Raise your staff and **s** out your hand
Ps 138: 7 you **s** out your hand against the anger
Zep 1: 4 "I will **s** out my hand against Judah
Mk 3: 5 said to the man, "**S** out your hand."
Ac 4:30 **S** out your hand to heal and

STRETCHED [STRETCH]

Ex 14:21 Moses **s** out his hand over the sea,
2Sa 24:16 When the angel **s** out his hand
1Ki 13: 4 But the hand he **s** out toward
Isa 45:12 My own hands **s** out the heavens;
Jer 10:12 and **s** out the heavens by his

STRETCHES [STRETCH]

Ps 104: 2 he **s** out the heavens like
Zec 12: 1 The LORD, who **s** out the heavens,

STRICKEN [STRIKE]

Isa 53: 4 yet we considered him **s** by God,
53: 8 transgression of my people he was **s**.

STRICT [STRICTEST, STRICTLY]

Mk 3:12 But he gave them **s** orders not
Ac 5:28 "We gave you **s** orders not to teach
1Co 9:25 in the games goes into **s** training.

STRICTEST* [STRICT]

Ac 26: 5 according to the **s** sect of our religion

STRICTLY* [STRICT]

Lk 9:21 Jesus **s** warned them not to tell this
Jas 3: 1 who teach will be judged more **s**.

STRIFE [STRIVE]

Pr 17: 1 a house full of feasting, with **s**.
18: 6 A fool's lips bring him **s**,
20: 3 It is to a man's honor to avoid **s**,
22:10 Drive out the mocker, and out goes **s**
23:29 Who has **s**? Who has complaints?
30:33 so stirring up anger produces **s**."
Ro 1:29 They are full of envy, murder, **s**,
1Ti 6: 4 about words that result in envy, **s**,

STRIKE [STRICKEN, STRIKES, STRIKING, STROKE, STRUCK]

Ge 3:15 and you will **s** his heel."
Ex 3:20 and **s** the Egyptians with all
12:12 and **s** down every firstborn—
17: 6 **S** the rock, and water will come out
Ps 91:12 not **s** your foot against a stone.
Isa 11: 4 He will **s** the earth with the rod
Zec 13: 7 "**S** the shepherd, and the sheep
Mal 4: 6 and **s** the land with a curse."
Mt 4: 6 not **s** your foot against a stone.' "
Mk 14:27 " 'I will **s** and the sheep will
Rev 11: 6 **s** the earth with every kind of plague
19:15 a sharp sword with which to **s** down

STRIKES [STRIKE]

Ex 21:12 "Anyone who **s** a man and kills
Pr 22:26 not be a man who **s** hands in pledge
Mt 5:39 If someone **s** you on the right cheek,

STRIPPED [STRIPS]

Ge 37:23 they s him of his robe—
Ex 33: 6 So the Israelites s off their ornaments
Isa 20: 3 Isaiah has gone s and barefoot
Mt 27:28 They s him and put a scarlet robe
Ac 16:22 ordered them to be s and beaten.

STRIPS [STRIPPED]

Jn 11:44 his hands and feet wrapped with s
    20: 5 looked in at the s of linen lying there

STRIVE* [STRIFE]

Ac 24:16 So I s always to keep my conscience
1Ti 4:10 (and for this we labor and s),

STROKE [STRIKE]

Mt 5:18 not the least s of a pen,
Lk 16:17 for the least s of a pen to drop out of

STRONG [STRENGTH, STRENGTHEN, STRENGTHENED, STRENGTHENING, STRONGER]

Nu 24:18 but Israel will grow s.
Dt 3:24 your greatness and your s hand.
    31: 6 Be s and courageous.
Jos 1: 6 "Be s and courageous,
    10:25 Be s and courageous.
    23: 6 "Be very s; be careful to obey
Jdg 5:21 March on, my soul; be s!
2Sa 10:12 Be s and let us fight bravely
1Ki 2: 2 "So be s, show yourself a man,
1Ch 22:13 Be s and courageous.
    28:20 "Be s and courageous,
2Ch 32: 7 "Be s and courageous.
Ps 24: 8 The LORD s and mighty,
    31: 2 a s fortress to save me.
    35:10 You rescue the poor from those too s
    62:11 O God, are s,
   140: 7 O Sovereign LORD, my s deliverer,
Pr 18:10 The name of the LORD is a s tower;
    31:17 her arms are s for her tasks.
Ecc 9:11 or the battle to the s,
SS 8: 6 for love is as s as death,
Isa 35: 4 "Be s, do not fear;
    53:12 he will divide the spoils with the s,
Jer 9:23 or the s man boast of his strength or
    50:34 Yet their Redeemer is s;
Eze 3:14 the s hand of the LORD upon me.
Da 2:40 a fourth kingdom, s as iron—
Joel 3:10 Let the weakling say, "I am s!"
Hag 2: 4 But now be s, O Zerubbabel,'
Zec 8: 9 be s so that the temple may be built.
Mt 12:29 can anyone enter a s man's house
Lk 1:80 the child grew and became s in spirit;
    2:40 And the child grew and became s;
Ro 15: 1 We who are s ought to bear with
1Co 1: 8 He will keep you s to the end,
    1:27 of the world to shame the s.
    16:13 be men of courage; be s.
2Co 12:10 For when I am weak, then I am s.
Eph 6:10 be s in the Lord and in his mighty
2Ti 2: 1 be s in the grace that is in Christ
1Pe 5:10 make you s, firm and steadfast.

STRONGER [STRONG]

Nu 14:12 into a nation greater and s than they."
Dt 7: 1 seven nations larger and s than you
2Sa 3: 1 David grew s and s,
1Co 1:25 and the weakness of God is s than

STRONGHOLD [STRONGHOLDS]

1Sa 22: 4 as long as David was in the s.
Ps 9: 9 a s in times of trouble.
    18: 2 and the horn of my salvation, my s.
    27: 1 The LORD is the s of my life—
    52: 7 the man who did not make God his s
  144: 2 my s and my deliverer, my shield,

STRONGHOLDS [STRONGHOLD]

Zep 3: 6 nations; their s are demolished.
2Co 10: 4 have divine power to demolish s.

STRUCK [STRIKE]

Ex 12:29 the LORD s down all the firstborn
Nu 20:11 and s the rock twice with his staff.
1Sa 17:49 and s the Philistine on the forehead.
Ps 78:20 When he s the rock,
Da 2:34 It s the statue on its feet of iron
Zec 13: 8 "two-thirds will be s down
Mk 14:65 s him with their fists, and said,
Ac 23: 3 the law by commanding that I be s!"

STRUCTURE

1Ch 29: 1 because this palatial s is not for man
Ezr 5: 3 rebuild this temple and restore this s?

STRUGGLE [STRUGGLED, STRUGGLING]

Ro 15:30 to join me in my s by praying to God
Eph 6:12 our s is not against flesh and blood,
Heb 12: 4 In your s against sin,

STRUGGLED [STRUGGLE]

Ge 32:28 because you have s with God and
Hos 12: 3 as a man he s with God.

STRUGGLING* [STRUGGLE]

Col 1:29 s with all his energy,
    2: 1 how much I am s for you

STUBBLE

Ob 1:18 the house of Esau will be s,
Na 1:10 they will be consumed like dry s.
Mal 4: 1 and every evildoer will be s,

STUBBORN [STUBBORNLY, STUBBORNNESS]

Lev 26:19 I will break down your s pride
Ps 78: 8 a s and rebellious generation,
Mk 3: 5 deeply distressed at their s hearts,

STUBBORNLY [STUBBORN]

Ex 13:15 When Pharaoh s refused to let us go,

STUBBORNNESS [STUBBORN]

Dt 9:27 Overlook the s of this people,
Jer 3:17 No longer will they follow the s
Ro 2: 5 of your s and your unrepentant heart,

STUDENT [STUDY]

Mt 10:24 "A **s** is not above his teacher,

STUDIED* [STUDY]

Jn 7:15 such learning without having **s?"**

STUDY* [STUDENT, STUDIED]

Ezr 7:10 For Ezra had devoted himself to the **s**
Ecc 1:13 I devoted myself to **s** and to explore
12:12 and much **s** wearies the body.
Jn 5:39 You diligently **s** the Scriptures

STUMBLE [STUMBLED, STUMBLES, STUMBLING]

Ps 37:24 though he **s**, he will not fall,
119:165 and nothing can make them **s.**
Pr 3:23 and your foot will not **s;**
Isa 8:14 a stone that causes men to **s**
Jer 13:16 before your feet **s** on
31: 9 on a level path where they will not **s,**
Eze 7:19 for it has made them **s** into sin.
Da 11:35 Some of the wise will **s,**
Hos 14: 9 but the rebellious **s** in them.
Mal 2: 8 teaching have caused many to **s;**
Jn 11: 9 A man who walks by day will not **s,**
Ro 9:33 a stone that causes men to **s**
11:11 **s** so as to fall beyond recovery?
14:20 that causes someone else to **s.**
1Co 10:32 Do not cause anyone to **s,**
Jas 3: 2 We all **s** in many ways.
1Pe 2: 8 "A stone that causes men to **s**
2: 8 They **s** because they disobey
1Jn 2:10 nothing in him to make him **s.**

STUMBLED [STUMBLE]

Ro 9:32 They **s** over the "stumbling stone."

STUMBLES [STUMBLE]

Pr 24:17 when he **s**, do not let your heart
Jn 11:10 when he walks by night that he **s,**
Jas 2:10 and yet **s** at just one point is guilty

STUMBLING [STUMBLE]

Lev 19:14 or put a **s** block in front of the blind,
Ps 56:13 from death and my feet from **s,**
Eze 14: 3 and put wicked **s** blocks before their
Mt 16:23 You are a **s** block to me;
Ro 9:32 They stumbled over the **"s** stone."
11: 9 a **s** block and a retribution for them.
14:13 not to put any a **s** block or obstacle
1Co 1:23 a **s** block to Jews and foolishness
8: 9 not become a **s** block to the weak.
2Co 6: 3 We put no **s** block in anyone's path,

STUMP

Isa 6:13 holy seed will be the **s** in the land."
11: 1 A shoot will come up from the **s**

STUPID [STUPIDITY]

Pr 12: 1 but he who hates correction is **s.**
Ecc 10: 3 and shows everyone how **s** he is.
2Ti 2:23 to do with foolish and **s** arguments,

STUPIDITY* [STUPID]

Ecc 7:25 to understand the **s** of wickedness

STUPOR

Ro 11: 8 "God gave them a spirit of **s,**

SUBDUE [SUBDUED, SUBDUES]

Ge 1:28 fill the earth and **s** it.
1Ch 17:10 I will also **s** all your enemies.

SUBDUED [SUBDUE]

Jos 10:40 So Joshua **s** the whole region,
Ps 47: 3 He **s** nations under us,

SUBDUES [SUBDUE]

Ps 18:47 who **s** nations under me,

SUBJECT [SUBJECTED]

Dt 20:11 be **s** to forced labor and shall work
Jdg 1:30 but they did **s** them to forced labor.
Mt 5:22 angry with his brother will be **s**
9:20 a woman who had been **s** to bleeding
1Co 14:32 The spirits of prophets are **s** to
15:28 be made **s** to him who put everything
Tit 2: 5 and to be **s** to their husbands,
2: 9 Teach slaves to be **s** to their masters
3: 1 Remind the people to be **s** to rulers
Heb 2: 8 God left nothing that is not **s** to him.

SUBJECTED [SUBJECT]

Ro 8:20 For the creation was **s** to frustration,
Heb 2: 5 not to angels that he has **s** the world

SUBMISSION [SUBMIT]

1Co 14:34 but must be in **s**, as the Law says.
1Ti 2:11 should learn in quietness and full **s.**
Heb 5: 7 heard because of his reverent **s.**

SUBMISSIVE* [SUBMIT]

Jas 3:17 **s**, full of mercy and good fruit,
1Pe 3: 1 the same way be **s** to your husbands,
3: 5 They were **s** to their own husbands,
5: 5 be **s** to those who are older.

SUBMIT [SUBMISSION, SUBMISSIVE, SUBMITS]

2Ch 30: 8 as your fathers were; **s** to the LORD.
Ps 81:11 Israel would not **s** to me.
Lk 10:17 the demons **s** to us in your name."
Ro 8: 7 It does not **s** to God's law,
13: 5 it is necessary to **s** to the authorities,
1Co 16:16 to **s** to such as these and
Eph 5:21 **S** to one another out of reverence
Col 3:18 Wives, **s** to your husbands,
Heb 12: 9 How much more should we **s** to
13:17 Obey your leaders and **s**
Jas 4: 7 **S** yourselves, then, to God.
1Pe 2:13 **S** yourselves for the Lord's sake

SUBMITS* [SUBMIT]

Eph 5:24 Now as the church **s** to Christ,

SUBTRACT*

Dt 4: 2 and do not **s** from it,

SUCCEED [SUCCESS, SUCCESSFUL]

2Sa 7:12 raise up your offspring to **s** you,
1Ki 22:22 " 'You will **s** in enticing him,'
Ps   20: 4 and make all your plans **s**.
Pr   15:22 but with many advisers they **s**.
     16: 3 and your plans will **s**.
     21:30 that can **s** against the LORD.
Ecc 11: 6 for you do not know which will **s**,

SUCCESS [SUCCEED]

Ge   24:12 give me **s** today,
     39:23 and gave him **s** in whatever he did.
1Sa 18:14 In everything he did he had great **s**,
1Ch 12:18 **S, s** to you, and **s** to those who help
     22:13 Then you will have **s** if you
2Ch 26: 5 God gave him **s**.
Ne   2:20 "The God of heaven will give us **s**.
Ps 118:25 O LORD, grant us **s**.
Ecc 10:10 but skill will bring **s**.

SUCCESSFUL [SUCCEED]

Jos   1: 7 that you may be **s** wherever you go.
2Ki 18: 7 he was **s** in whatever he undertook.
2Ch 20:20 in his prophets and you will be **s**."

SUCCOTH [SUCCOTH BENOTH]

Ge   33:17 That is why the place is called **S**.
Jdg   8:16 taught the men of **S** a lesson

SUCH

Ex   32:21 that you led them into **s** great sin?"
Lev 25:21 I will send you a **s** blessing in
Ps 139: 6 **S** knowledge is too wonderful for me
Jer   5: 9 "Should I not avenge myself on **s**
Mt   8:10 anyone in Israel with **s** great faith.
Mk   12:40 **s** men will be punished most
     13: 7 **S** things must happen,
Lk   12:30 pagan world runs after all **s** things,
Jn   9:16 can a sinner do **s** miraculous signs?"
1Co   9:24 Run in **s** a way as to get the prize.
2Co   3: 4 **S** confidence as this is ours
Heb   2: 3 if we ignore **s** a great salvation?
      7:26 **S** a high priest meets our need—
     12: 3 him who endured **s** opposition from
1Jn   2:22 **S** a man is the antichrist—
2Jn   1: 7 Any **s** person is the deceiver and
3Jn   1: 8 to show hospitality to **s** men so

SUDDEN [SUDDENLY]

Lev 26:16 I will bring upon you **s** terror,
Dt   28:20 and come to **s** ruin because of
Pr   3:25 Have no fear of **s** disaster or

SUDDENLY [SUDDEN]

Ps   73:19 How are they destroyed,
Mal   3: 1 Then **s** the Lord you are seeking
Mt   28: 9 **S** Jesus met them.
Mk   13:36 If he comes **s**, do not let him find you
Ac   9: 3 a light from heaven flashed
1Th   5: 3 destruction will come on them **s**,

SUE*

Mt   5:40 And if someone wants to **s** you

SUFFER [LONG-SUFFERING, SUFFERED, SUFFERING, SUFFERINGS, SUFFERS]

Job 36:15 But those who **s** he delivers
Pr   9:12 a mocker, you alone will **s**."
Isa 53:10 to crush him and cause him to **s**,
Mk   8:31 the Son of Man must **s** many things
Lk   22:15 Passover with you before I **s**.
     24:26 Did not the Christ have to **s** these
     24:46 The Christ will **s** and rise from
Ac   3:18 saying that his Christ would **s**.
1Co   3:15 If it is burned up, he will **s** loss;
2Co   1: 6 of the same sufferings we **s**.
Php   1:29 but also to **s** for him,
Heb   9:26 Christ would have had to **s** many
1Pe   3:17 **s** for doing good than for doing evil.
      4:16 However, if you **s** as a Christian,
Rev   2:10 be afraid of what you are about to **s**.

SUFFERED [SUFFER]

Mk   5:26 She had **s** a great deal under the care
Gal   3: 4 Have you **s** so much for nothing—
Heb   2: 9 and honor because he **s** death,
      2:18 he himself **s** when he was tempted,
      5: 8 he learned obedience from what he **s**
1Pe   2:21 because Christ **s** for you,
      4: 1 Therefore, since Christ **s** in his body,

SUFFERING [SUFFER]

Ex   3: 7 and I am concerned about their **s**.
Job 21:13 they saw how great his **s** was.
Ps   22:24 or disdained the **s** of the afflicted one
    119:50 My comfort in my **s** is this:
Isa 53: 3 and familiar with **s**.
     53:11 After the **s** of his soul,
La   1:12 Is any **s** like my **s** that was inflicted
Mt   4:24 those **s** severe pain,
      8: 6 at home paralyzed and in terrible **s**."
     15:22 My daughter is **s** terribly
     17:15 "He has seizures and is **s** greatly.
Ac   5:41 worthy of **s** disgrace for the Name.
Ro   5: 3 that **s** produces perseverance;
2Ti   1: 8 But join with me in **s** for the gospel,
Heb   2:10 of their salvation perfect through **s**.
     13: 3 as if you yourselves were **s**.
Jas   5:10 example of patience in the face of **s**,
1Pe   4:12 surprised at the painful trial you are **s**

SUFFERINGS [SUFFER]

Ro   5: 3 but we also rejoice in our **s**,
      8:18 I consider that our present **s** are
2Co   1: 5 For just as the **s** of Christ flow over
      1: 7 that just as you share in our **s**,
Php   3:10 the fellowship of sharing in his **s**,
1Pe   1:11 when he predicted the **s** of Christ
      4:13 that you participate in the **s** of Christ,
      5: 9 undergoing the same kind of **s**.

SUFFERS* [SUFFER]

Job 15:20 the wicked man **s** torment,
Pr   13:20 but a companion of fools **s** harm.
1Co 12:26 If one part **s**, every part **s** with it;

SUFFICIENT

2Co 12: 9 said to me, "My grace is **s** for you,

SUITABLE

Ge 2:18 I will make a helper **s** for him."

SULFUR

Ge 19:24 burning **s** on Sodom and Gomorrah
Ps 11: 6 he will rain fiery coals and burning **s**
Lk 17:29 fire and **s** rained down from heaven
Rev 9:17 mouths came fire, smoke and **s.**
14:10 He will be tormented with burning **s**
19:20 into the fiery lake of burning **s**
20:10 thrown into the lake of burning **s,**
21: 8 be in the fiery lake of burning **s.**

SUMMED* [SUMS]

Ro 13: 9 are **s** up in this one rule:
Gal 5:14 The entire law is **s** up in

SUMMER

Pr 6: 8 yet it stores its provisions in **s**
Mk 13:28 you know that **s** is near.

SUMMON [SUMMONS]

Ps 68:28 **S** your power, O God;
Isa 45: 4 I **s** you by name and bestow on you

SUMMONS [SUMMON]

Ps 50: 1 speaks and **s** the earth
Isa 45: 3 who **s** you by name.

SUMS* [SUMMED]

Mt 7:12 this **s** up the Law and the Prophets.

SUN [SUNDOWN, SUNRISE, SUNSET, SUNSHINE]

Jos 10:13 So the **s** stood still,
Jdg 5:31 the **s** when it rises in its strength."
Ps 72: 5 He will endure as long as the **s,**
84:11 For the LORD God is a **s** and shield;
113: 3 From the rising of the **s** to the place
121: 6 the **s** will not harm you by day,
136: 8 the **s** to govern the day,
148: 3 Praise him, **s** and moon, praise him,
Ecc 1: 9 there is nothing new under the **s.**
SS 6:10 fair as the moon, bright as the **s,**
Isa 60:19 **s** will no more be your light by day,
Joel 2:31 The **s** will be turned to darkness
3:15 The **s** and moon will be darkened,
Mic 3: 6 The **s** will set for the prophets,
Mal 4: 2 the **s** of righteousness will rise
Mt 5:45 He causes his **s** to rise on the evil and
13:43 the righteous will shine like the **s**
17: 2 His face shone like the **s,**
Mk 13:24 " 'the **s** will be darkened,
Lk 23:45 for the **s** stopped shining.
Ac 2:20 The **s** will be turned to darkness and
Eph 4:26 not let the **s** go down while you are
Rev 1:16 His face was like the **s** shining
8:12 and a third of the **s** was struck,
9: 2 The **s** and sky were darkened by
10: 1 his face was like the **s,**
12: 1 a woman clothed with the **s,**

21:23 The city does not need the **s** or
22: 5 light of a lamp or the light of the **s,**

UNDER THE SUN Ecc 1:3, 9, 14; 2:11, 17, 18,
19, 20, 22; 3:16; 4:1, 3, 7, 15; 5:13, 18; 6:1, 12;
8:9, 15, 15, 17; 9:3, 6, 9, 9, 11, 13; 10:5

SUNG [SING]

Mt 26:30 When they had **s** a hymn,

SUNRISE [SUN]

2Sa 23: 4 he is like the light of morning at **s** on
Hab 3: 4 His splendor was like the **s;**

SUNSET [SUN]

Ex 17:12 that his hands remained steady till **s.**
22:26 return it to him by **s,**
Dt 24:15 Pay him his wages each day before **s,**

SUPER-APOSTLES* [APOSTLE]

2Co 11: 5 in the least inferior to those **"s."**
12:11 not in the least inferior to the **"s,"**

SUPERIOR

Ro 2:18 and approve of what is **s**
Heb 1: 4 as much **s** to the angels as the name
he has inherited is **s** to theirs.
8: 6 ministry Jesus has received is as **s**
8: 6 covenant of which he is mediator is **s**

SUPERSTITIONS*

Isa 2: 6 They are full of **s** from the East;

SUPERVISION

Gal 3:25 no longer under the **s** of the law.

SUPPER

Lk 22:20 after the **s** he took the cup, saying,
1Co 11:25 after **s** he took the cup, saying,
Rev 19: 9 to the wedding **s** of the Lamb!' "

SUPPLICATION [SUPPLICATIONS]

1Ki 8:30 Hear the **s** of your servant and
2Ch 6:24 making **s** before you in this temple,
Zec 12:10 of Jerusalem a spirit of grace and **s.**

SUPPLICATIONS* [SUPPLICATION]

1Ki 8:54 prayers and **s** to the LORD,
2Ch 6:21 Hear the **s** of your servant and

SUPPLIED [SUPPLY]

Ac 20:34 hands of mine have **s** my own needs
Php 4:18 and even more; I am amply **s,**

SUPPLIES [SUPPLY]

Ps 147: 8 he **s** the earth with rain
2Co 9:10 Now he who **s** seed to the sower

SUPPLY [SUPPLIED, SUPPLIES, SUPPLYING]

Lev 26:26 When I cut off your **s** of bread,
Ps 78:20 Can he **s** meat for his people?"
2Co 8:14 your plenty will **s** what they need,
1Th 3:10 and **s** what is lacking in your faith.

SUPPLYING* [SUPPLY]

2Co 9:12 not only s the needs of God's people

SUPPORT [SUPPORTED, SUPPORTING, SUPPORTS]

Jdg 16:26 feel the pillars that s the temple,
Ps 18:18 but the LORD was my s.
Ro 11:18 You do not s the root, but
1Co 9:12 others have this right of s from you,

SUPPORTED [SUPPORT]

Ps 94:18 your love, O LORD, s me.
Col 2:19 s and held together by its ligaments

SUPPORTING [SUPPORT]

Eph 4:16 held together by every s ligament,

SUPPORTS [SUPPORT]

Ro 11:18 but the root s you.

SUPPRESS*

Ro 1:18 who s the truth by their wickedness,

SUPREMACY* [SUPREME]

Col 1:18 in everything he might have the s.

SUPREME [SUPREMACY]

Pr 4: 7 Wisdom is s; therefore get wisdom.

SURE [SURELY]

Nu 28:31 Be s the animals are without defect.
    32:23 be s that your sin will find you out.
Dt 6:17 Be s to keep the commands of
    14:22 Be s to set aside a tenth of all
    23:23 lips utter you must be s to do,
    29:18 make s there is no root among you
Jos 23:13 be s that the LORD your God
1Sa 12:24 But be s to fear the LORD
Ps 19: 9 The ordinances of the LORD are s
    69:13 answer me with your s salvation.
    132:11 a s oath that he will not revoke:
Pr 11:14 but many advisers make victory s.
    27:23 Be s you know the condition
Isa 28:16 cornerstone for a s foundation;
Eph 5: 5 For of this you can be s:
Heb 11: 1 faith is being s of what we hope
2Pe 1:10 to make your calling and election s.

SURELY [SURE]

Ge 2:17 when you eat of it you will s die."
    6:13 I am s going to destroy both them
    18:18 Abraham will s become a great
    22:17 I will s bless you and make your
    28:16 "S the LORD is in this place,
    50:24 But God will s come to your aid
Ex 13:19 "God will s come to your aid,
Nu 26:65 they would s die in the desert,
Jos 10:14 S the LORD was fighting for Israel!
Job 1:11 and he will s curse you to your face."
    2: 5 and he will s curse you to your face."
Ps 5:12 s, O LORD, you bless the righteous;
    23: 6 S goodness and love will follow me
    54: 4 S God is my help;
    73: 1 S God is good to Israel,

85: 9 S his salvation is near
Pr 23:18 There is s a future hope for you,
Isa 12: 2 S God is my salvation;
    53: 4 S he took up our infirmities
Eze 33:15 and does no evil, he will s live;
Mt 28:20 And s I am with you always,
Mk 14:19 they said to him, "S not I?"
    15:39 "S this man was the Son of God!"
Lk 23:47 "S this was a righteous man."
2Co 1:18 But as s as God is faithful,

SURFACE

Ge 1: 2 darkness was over the s of the deep,
    7:18 the ark floated on the s of the water.
2Co 10: 7 You are looking only on the s

SURGING

Ex 15: 8 The s waters stood firm like a wall;
Ps 89: 9 You rule over the s sea;
Zec 10:11 the s sea will be subdued

SURPASS* [SURPASSED, SURPASSES, SURPASSING]

Pr 31:29 but you s them all."

SURPASSED* [SURPASS]

Jn 1:15 'He who comes after me has s me
    1:30 A man who comes after me has s me

SURPASSES* [SURPASS]

Pr 8:19 what I yield s choice silver.
Mt 5:20 that unless your righteousness s that
Eph 3:19 to know this love that s knowledge—

SURPASSING* [SURPASS]

Ps 150: 2 praise him for his s greatness.
2Co 3:10 now in comparison with the s glory.
    9:14 of the s grace God has given you.
Php 3: 8 a loss compared to the s greatness

SURPRISE [SURPRISED]

Ps 35: 8 may ruin overtake them by s—
1Th 5: 4 that this day should s you like a thief.

SURPRISED [SURPRISE]

Jn 3: 7 You should not be s at my saying,
1Pe 4:12 do not be s at the painful trial
1Jn 3:13 Do not be s, my brothers,

SURRENDER [SURRENDERED]

1Co 13: 3 and s my body to the flames,

SURRENDERED [SURRENDER]

Lk 23:25 and s Jesus to their will.

SURROUND [SURROUNDED, SURROUNDING, SURROUNDS]

Ps 5:12 you s them with your favor
    22:12 Many bulls s me;
    32: 7 and s me with songs of deliverance.
    89: 7 more awesome than all who s him.
    97: 2 Clouds and thick darkness s him;
    125: 2 As the mountains s Jerusalem,
Jer 31:22 a woman will s a man."

SURROUNDED [SURROUND]

Ge   19: 4 both young and old—s the house.
Jdg 19:22 wicked men of the city s the house.
Ps   22:16 Dogs have s me;
Eze   1:27 and brilliant light s him.
Lk   21:20 "When you see Jerusalem being s
Heb 12: 1 since we are s by such a great cloud
Rev 20: 9 and s the camp of God's people,

SURROUNDING [SURROUND]

Rev   4: 4 S the throne were twenty-four other

SURROUNDS* [SURROUND]

Ps   32:10 but the LORD's unfailing love s
     89: 8 and your faithfulness s you.
    125: 2 so the LORD s his people both now

SURVEYED*

Ecc   2:11 when I s all that my hands had done

SURVIVE [SURVIVED, SURVIVES, SURVIVORS]

Dt   4:27 few of you will s among the nations
Am   7: 2 How can Jacob s?
      7: 5 How can Jacob s?
Mk   13:20 cut short those days, no one would s.

SURVIVED [SURVIVE]

Ex   14:28 Not one of them s.
Nu   14:38 and Caleb son of Jephunneh s.
Ne   1: 2 the Jewish remnant that s the exile,

SURVIVES [SURVIVE]

Isa 37: 4 pray for the remnant that still s."
1Co   3:14 If what he has built s,

SURVIVORS [SURVIVE]

Isa   1: 9 LORD Almighty had left us some s,
Eze 14:22 Yet there will be some s—

SUSA

Ezr   4: 9 the Elamites of S,
Ne   1: 1 while I was in the citadel of S,
Est   1: 2 his royal throne in the citadel of S,

SUSPECTS [SUSPICIONS]

Nu   5:14 or if he is jealous and s her even

SUSPENDS*

Job 26: 7 he s the earth over nothing.

SUSPENSE

Jn   10:24 "How long will you keep us in s?

SUSPICIONS* [SUSPECTS]

1Ti   6: 4 in envy, strife, malicious talk, evil s

SUSTAIN [SUSTAINED, SUSTAINING, SUSTAINS]

Ru   4:15 He will renew your life and s you
Ps   51:12 a willing spirit, to s me.
     55:22 on the LORD and he will s you;
Isa 46: 4 I am he who will s you.
     46: 4 I will s you and I will rescue you.

SUSTAINED [SUSTAIN]

Ne   9:21 For forty years you s them in

SUSTAINING* [SUSTAIN]

Heb   1: 3 s all things by his powerful word.

SUSTAINS [SUSTAIN]

Ps   18:35 and your right hand s me;
    146: 9 and s the fatherless and the widow,
    147: 6 The LORD s the humble but casts
Isa 50: 4 to know the word that s the weary.

SWADDLED, SWADDLING, SWADDLINGBAND (KJV)

See CARED FOR, WRAPPED IN CLOTHS

SWALLOW [SWALLOWED]

Nu   16:34 "The earth is going to s us too!"
Ps   21: 9 In his wrath the LORD will s them
     84: 3 and the s a nest for herself,
Isa 25: 8 he will s up death forever.
Jnh   1:17 provided a great fish to s Jonah,
Mt   23:24 You strain out a gnat but s a camel.

SWALLOWED [SWALLOW]

Ge   41: 7 thin heads of grain s up the seven
Nu   16:32 earth opened its mouth and s them,
Ps 106:17 The earth opened up and s Dathan;
1Co 15:54 "Death has been s up in victory."
2Co   5: 4 what is mortal may be s up by life.

SWARM [SWARMING, SWARMS]

Dt   14:19 All flying insects that s are unclean

SWAYED

Mt   11: 7 A reed s by the wind?
     22:16 You aren't s by men,
2Ti   3: 6 s by all kinds of evil desires,

SWEAR [SWEARING, SWEARS, SWORE, SWORN]

Ge   22:16 "I s by myself, declares the LORD,
Lev 19:12 " 'Do not s falsely by my name and
Jos   2:12 please s to me by the LORD
     23: 7 the names of their gods or s by them.
Ps   24: 4 to an idol or s by what is false.
Isa 45:23 by me every tongue will s.
Mt   5:34 But I tell you, Do not s at all:
Heb   6:13 for him to s by, he swore by himself,
Jas   5:12 Above all, my brothers, do not s—

SWEARING* [SWEAR]

Jer   5: 2 still they are s falsely."

SWEARS [SWEAR]

Zec   5: 3 who s falsely will be banished.
Mt   23:16 You say, 'If anyone s by the temple,

SWEAT*

Ge   3:19 By the s of your brow
Lk   22:44 and his s was like drops

SWEEP [SWEEPS, SWEPT]

Ge   18:23 "Will you s away the righteous

Ps   90: 5   You **s** men away in the sleep
Lk   15: 8   **s** the house and search carefully

SWEEPS [SWEEP]

Pr   1:27   when disaster **s** over you like
Isa 40:24   a whirlwind **s** them away like chaff.
Zep   2: 2   and that day **s** on like chaff,

SWEET [SWEETER, SWEETNESS]

Ex   15:25   and the water became **s.**
Job 20:12   "Though evil is **s** in his mouth
Ps 119:103   How **s** are your words to my taste,
Pr   9:17   "Stolen water is **s**;
     13:19   A longing fulfilled is **s** to the soul,
     16:24   **s** to the soul and healing to the bones
     20:17   Food gained by fraud tastes **s** to
     24:14   also that wisdom is **s** to your soul;
Ecc   5:12   The sleep of a laborer is **s,**
Isa   5:20   who put bitter for **s** and **s** for bitter.
Eze   3: 3   it tasted as **s** as honey in my mouth.
Rev 10:10   It tasted as **s** as honey in my mouth,

SWEETER* [SWEET]

Jdg 14:18   "What is **s** than honey?
Ps   19:10   they are **s** than honey,
    119:103   than honey to my mouth!

SWEETNESS* [SWEET]

SS   4:11   Your lips drop **s** as the honeycomb,
      5:16   His mouth is **s** itself;

SWELL

Dt   8: 4   not wear out and your feet did not **s**

SWEPT [SWEEP]

Ge   19:15   be **s** away when the city is punished.
Ex   14:27   and the LORD **s** them into the sea.
Ps   58: 9   the wicked will be **s** away.
Mt   12:44   **s** clean and put in order.
Rev 12: 4   His tail **s** a third of the stars out of

SWERVE*

Pr   4: 5   not forget my words or **s** from them.
      4:27   Do not **s** to the right or the left;

SWIFT [SWIFTLY]

Pr   1:16   they are **s** to shed blood.
Ecc   9:11   The race is not to the **s**
Isa 59: 7   they are **s** to shed innocent blood.
Jer 46: 6   **s** cannot flee nor the strong escape.
Ro   3:15   "Their feet are **s** to shed blood;
2Pe   2: 1   bringing **s** destruction on themselves.

SWIFTLY [SWIFT]

Ps 147:15   to the earth; his word runs **s.**
Isa 60:22   in its time I will do this **s.**"

SWINDLER* [SWINDLERS]

1Co   5:11   a drunkard or a **s.**

SWINDLERS* [SWINDLER]

1Co   5:10   or the greedy and **s,** or idolaters.
      6:10   nor **s** will inherit the kingdom

SWINE (KJV) See PIG

SWING

Joel 3:13   **S** the sickle, for the harvest is ripe.

SWIRLED*

2Sa 22: 5   "The waves of death **s** about me;
Jnh   2: 3   and the currents **s** about me;

SWORD [SWORDS]

Ge   3:24   a flaming **s** flashing back and forth
Ex   18: 4   saved me from the **s** of Pharaoh."
Lev 26: 7   and they will fall by the **s** before you.
Nu   14: 3   to let us fall by the **s?**
Dt   32:41   when I sharpen my flashing **s**
Jos   5:13   of him with a drawn **s** in his hand.
1Sa 17:45   "You come against me with **s**
     17:47   not by **s** or spear that the LORD saves
     31: 4   so Saul took his own **s** and fell on it.
2Sa 12:10   **s** will never depart from your house,
1Ch 21:30   afraid of the **s** of the angel of the
Ne   4:18   of the builders wore his **s** at his side
Ps   22:20   Deliver my life from the **s,**
     44: 3   not by their **s** that they won the land,
     44: 6   my **s** does not bring me victory;
     45: 3   Gird your **s** upon your side,
    149: 6   and a double-edged **s** in their hands,
Pr   5: 4   sharp as a double-edged **s.**
     12:18   Reckless words pierce like a **s,**
Isa   2: 4   not take up **s** against nation,
     49: 2   my mouth like a sharpened **s,**
Jer 15: 2   those for the **s,** to the **s;**
La   1:20   Outside, the **s** bereaves;
Eze   5: 2   For I will pursue them with drawn **s.**
Hos   2:18   Bow and **s** and battle I will abolish
Mic   4: 3   not take up **s** against nation,
Mt   10:34   did not come to bring peace, but a **s.**
     26:52   all who draw the **s** will die by the **s.**
Lk   2:35   a **s** will pierce your own soul too."
Ac   12: 2   put to death with the **s.**
Ro   13: 4   for he does not bear the **s** for nothing
Eph   6:17   and the **s** of the Spirit,
Heb   4:12   Sharper than any double-edged **s,**
     11:34   and escaped the edge of the **s;**
     11:37   they were put to death by the **s.**
Rev   1:16   a sharp double-edged **s.**
      6: 4   To him was given a large **s.**
     13:14   the beast who was wounded by the **s**
     19:15   Out of his mouth comes a sharp **s**

PUT ... TO THE SWORD See PUT

SWORDS [SWORD]

Ps   37:15   their **s** will pierce their own hearts,
     57: 4   whose tongues are sharp **s.**
     64: 3   They sharpen their tongues like **s**
Isa   2: 4   will beat their **s** into plowshares
Joel 3:10   Beat your plowshares into **s**
Mk   14:48   with **s** and clubs to capture me?

SWORE [SWEAR]

Ge   26: 3   the oath I **s** to your father Abraham.
Ex   6: 8   the land I **s** with uplifted hand to give
     32:13   to whom you **s** by your own self:
Nu   14:30   Not one of you will enter the land I **s**
Dt   6:10   into the land he **s** to your fathers,
Ps   89:49   in your faithfulness you **s** to David?

132:11 The LORD **s** an oath to David,
Lk   1:73 the oath he **s** to our father Abraham:
Heb   6:13 he **s** by himself,
Rev 10: 6 And he **s** by him who lives for ever

SWORN [SWEAR]

Jos 21:43 gave Israel all the land he had **s**
Ps   89:35 I have **s** by my holiness—
     110: 4 The LORD has **s** and will not
Jer 32:22 You gave them this land you had **s**
Eze 20:42 the land I had **s** with uplifted hand
Heb   7:21 "The Lord has **s** and will not

SYCAMORE-FIG [FIG]

Am   7:14 and I also took care of **s** trees.
Lk   19: 4 So he ran ahead and climbed a **s** tree

SYCHAR*

Jn   4: 5 to a town in Samaria called **S**,

SYMBOL* [SYMBOLIC, SYMBOLIZES, SYMBOLS]

Ex   13:16 a **s** on your forehead that the LORD
Nu   6: 7 the **s** of his separation to God is on

SYMBOLIC* [SYMBOL]

Zec   3: 8 who are men **s** of things to come:

SYMBOLIZES* [SYMBOL]

1Pe   3:21 and this water **s** baptism that

SYMBOLS* [SYMBOL]

Dt   6: 8 Tie them as **s** on your hands
     11:18 tie them as **s** on your hands
Isa   8:18 We are signs and **s** in Israel from
     57: 8 doorposts you have put your pagan **s**.

SYMPATHETIC* [SYMPATHY]

1Pe   3: 8 **s**, love as brothers, be compassionate

SYMPATHIZE [SYMPATHY]

Heb   4:15 a high priest who is unable to **s**

SYMPATHIZED* [SYMPATHY]

Heb 10:34 You **s** with those in prison

SYMPATHY [SYMPATHETIC, SYMPATHIZE, SYMPATHIZED]

Ps   69:20 I looked for **s**,
Da   1: 9 to show favor and **s** to Daniel,

SYNAGOGUE [SYNAGOGUES]

Mt   13:54 teaching the people in their **s**,
Lk   4:16 the Sabbath day he went into the **s**,
      8:41 a man named Jairus, a ruler of the **s**,
Jn   16: 2 They will put you out of the **s**;
Ac   13:14 On the Sabbath they entered the **s**
     14: 1 went as usual into the Jewish **s**.
     17: 2 Paul went into the **s**,
     18: 4 Every Sabbath he reasoned in the **s**,
     18:26 He began to speak boldly in the **s**.
Rev   2: 9 but are a **s** of Satan,
      3: 9 who are of the **s** of Satan,

SYNAGOGUES [SYNAGOGUE]

Mt   4:23 teaching in their **s**,
      6: 2 as the hypocrites do in the **s** and on
     10:17 and flog you in their **s**.
Lk   12:11 "When you are brought before **s**,
Jn   18:20 "I always taught in **s** or at the temple,
Ac   13: 5 the word of God in the Jewish **s**.

SYNTYCHE*

Php   4: 2 with **S** to agree with each other

SYRIA [SYRIAN]

Mt   4:24 News about him spread all over **S**,
Gal   1:21 Later I went to **S** and Cilicia.

SYRIAN* [SYRIA]

Lk   4:27 was cleansed—only Naaman the **S**."

T

TABERNACLE [TABERNACLES]

Ex   25: 9 Make this **t** and all its furnishings
     38:21 for the **t**, the **t** of the Testimony,
     40:18 When Moses set up the **t**,
     40:34 the glory of the LORD filled the **t**.
Nu   1:50 the Levites to be in charge of the **t**
Heb   8: 2 the true **t** set up by the Lord,
      9:11 the greater and more perfect **t** that is
Rev 15: 5 the **t** of the Testimony, was opened.

TABERNACLES [TABERNACLE]

Lev 23:34 the LORD's Feast of **T** begins,
Dt   16:16 Feast of Weeks and the Feast of **T**.
Zec 14:16 and to celebrate the Feast of **T**.
Jn   7: 2 the Jewish Feast of **T** was near,

TABITHA* [DORCAS]

Disciple, also known as Dorcas, whom Peter
raised from the dead (Ac 9:36-42).

TABLE [TABLES]

Ex   25:23 "Make a **t** of acacia wood—
Nu   3:31 the **t**, the lampstand, the altars,
Ps   23: 5 You prepare a **t** before me in
     78:19 "Can God spread a **t** in the desert?
1Co 10:21 both the Lord's **t** and the **t** of demons

TABLES [TABLE]

Mk   11:15 the **t** of the money changers and
Jn   2:15 changers and overturned their **t**.
Ac   6: 2 word of God in order to wait on **t**.

TABLET* [TABLETS]

Pr   3: 3 write them on the **t** of your heart.
      7: 3 write them on the **t** of your heart.
Isa 30: 8 Go now, write it on a **t** for them,
Eze   4: 1 "Now, son of man, take a clay **t**,
Lk   1:63 He asked for a writing **t**,

TABLETS [TABLET]

Ex   31:18   the **t** of stone inscribed by the finger
       32:19   and he threw the **t** out of his hands,
Dt   10: 5   put the **t** in the ark I had made,
2Co   3: 3   not on **t** of stone but on **t** of human

TAIL [TAILS]

Dt   28:13   make you the head, not the **t.**
Jdg 15: 4   foxes and tied them **t** to **t**
Rev 12: 4   His **t** swept a third of the stars out of

TAILS [TAIL]

Rev   9:10   They had **t** and stings like scorpions,
        9:19   for their **t** were like snakes,

TAKE [TAKEN, TAKES, TAKING, TOOK]

Ge   15: 7   to give you this land to **t** possession
       22: 2   Then God said, "**T** your son,
       22:17   Your descendants will **t** possession
Ex   3: 5   "**T** off your sandals,
        6: 7   I will **t** you as my own people,
       21:23   you are to **t** life for life,
       22:22   "Do not **t** advantage of a widow or
       34: 9   and **t** us as your inheritance."
Lev 10:17   to **t** away the guilt of the community
       25:14   do not **t** advantage of each other.
Nu   1: 2   "**T** a census of the whole Israelite
       13:30   "We should go up and **t** possession
Dt   1: 8   Go in and **t** possession of the land
       12:32   do not add to it or **t** away from it.
       31:26   "**T** this Book of the Law and place it
1Sa   8:11   He will **t** your sons
1Ki   11:34   " 'But I will not **t** the whole kingdom
       19: 4   "**T** my life; I am no better
1Ch 17:13   I will never **t** my love away
Job 23:10   But he knows the way that I **t;**
Ps   2:12   Blessed are all who **t** refuge in him.
       25:18   and **t** away all my sins.
       27:14   and **t** heart and wait for the LORD.
       31:24   Be strong and **t** heart,
       49:17   for he will **t** nothing with him
       51:11   or **t** your Holy Spirit from me.
       73:24   afterward you will **t** me into glory.
       89:33   but I will not **t** my love from him,
     118: 8   to **t** refuge in the LORD than
Pr   22:23   the LORD will **t** up their case
Isa   62: 4   for the LORD will **t** delight in you,
Jer   51:11   The LORD will **t** vengeance,
Eze   3:10   and **t** to heart all the words I speak
       33:11   I **t** no pleasure in the death of
Da   8:13   "How long will it **t** for the vision to
       11:36   has been determined must **t** place.
Hos   1: 2   to yourself an adulterous wife
       14: 2   **T** words with you and return to
Mic   4: 3   not **t** up sword against nation,
Mt   1:20   do not be afraid to **t** Mary home
        2:13   "**t** the child and his mother
        2:20   **t** the child and his mother and go to
        7: 5   first **t** the plank out of your own eye,
       11:29   **T** my yoke upon you and learn
       16:24   and **t** up his cross and follow me.
       17:27   **T** the first fish you catch;
       26:26   saying, "**T** and eat; this is my body."
Mk   2: 9   'Get up, **t** your mat and walk'?

        8:34   and **t** up his cross and follow me.
       14:36   **T** this cup from me.
Lk   21: 7   that they are about to **t** place?"
Ac   1:20   " 'May another **t** his place
Ro   12:19   Do not **t** revenge, my friends,
2Co   12: 8   with the Lord to **t** it away from me.
Eph   6:11   so that you can **t** your stand against
1Ti   3: 5   how can he **t** care of God's church?)
        6:12   **T** hold of the eternal life
Heb   9:28   to **t** away the sins of many people;
Rev   1: 1   his servants that must soon **t** place.
        4: 1   I will show you what must **t** place
        5: 9   "You are worthy to **t** the scroll and
       22:17   let him **t** the free gift of the water

TAKEN [TAKE]

Ge   2:23   for she was **t** out of man."
       27:36   and now he's **t** my blessing!"
Lev   6: 4   he has stolen or **t** by extortion,
Nu   8:16   I have **t** them as my own in place of
       19: 3   it is to be **t** outside the camp
Jos   7:11   **t** some of the devoted things;
2Sa   7:15   But my love will never be **t** away
       12:13   "The LORD has **t** away your sin.
Ps   31: 1   In you, O LORD, I have **t** refuge;
Ecc   3:14   be added to it and nothing **t** from it.
Isa   6: 7   your guilt is **t** away
Jer   13:17   the LORD's flock will be **t** captive.
       38:28   This is how Jerusalem was **t:**
Da   5: 2   that Nebuchadnezzar his father had **t**
Zec   3: 4   "See, I have **t** away your sin,
Mt   13:12   even what he has will be **t** from him.
       24:40   one will be **t** and the other left.
       26:39   may this cup be **t** from me.
Lk   24:51   and was **t** up into heaven.
Jn   20:13   "They have **t** my Lord away,"
Ac   1: 9   he was **t** up before their very eyes,
Ro   5:13   But sin is not **t** into account
Php   3:12   yet to have **t** hold of it.
1Ti   3:16   was **t** up in glory.
Heb   11: 5   By faith Enoch was **t** from this life,

TAKES [TAKE]

Lev   24:17   " 'If anyone **t** the life of a human
1Ki   20:11   not boast like one who it **t** off.' "
Ps   5: 4   not a God who **t** pleasure in evil;
       34: 1   blessed is the man who **t** refuge
      149: 4   the LORD **t** delight in his people;
Na   1: 2   The LORD **t** vengeance on his foes
Mk   4:15   Satan comes and **t** away the word
Lk   6:30   and if anyone **t** what belongs to you,
Jn   1:29   who **t** away the sin of the world!
       10:18   No one **t** it from me,
Rev   22:19   And if anyone **t** words away

TAKING [TAKE]

Ac   15:14   by **t** from the Gentiles a people
Php   2: 7   **t** the very nature of a servant,

TALEBEARER (KJV) See GOSSIP, SPREADING SLANDER

TALENT [TALENTS]

Mt   25:15   and to another one **t,**

TALENTS [TALENT]
Mt 25:15 To one he gave five **t** of money,

TALES*
1Ti 4: 7 with godless myths and old wives' **t**;

TALK [TALKED, TALKING, TALKS]
Dt   6: 7 **T** about them when you sit at home
Pr 12:13 evil man is trapped by his sinful **t**,
Ro   9:20 O man, to **t** back to God?

TALKED [TALK]
Ge 35:14 where God had **t** with him,
Nu   3: 1 at the time the LORD **t** with Moses
1Co 13:11 When I was a child, I **t** like a child,

TALKING [TALK]
Mt 17: 3 Moses and Elijah, **t** with Jesus.
Jn   4:27 surprised to find him **t** with a woman

TALKS* [TALK]
Pr 20:19 so avoid a man who **t** too much.

TALL [TALLER]
1Sa 17: 4 He was over nine feet **t**.
1Ch 11:23 who was seven and a half feet **t**.

TALLER [TALL]
1Sa 9: 2 a head **t** than any of the others.

TAMAR
1. Wife of Judah's sons Er and Onan (Ge 38:1-10). Tricked Judah into fathering children when he refused her his third son (Ge 38:11-30; Mt 1:3).
2. Daughter of David, raped by Amnon (2Sa 13).

TAMARISK
Ge 21:33 Abraham planted a **t** tree

TAMBOURINE [TAMBOURINES]
Ex 15:20 Aaron's sister, took a **t** in her hand,
Ps 150: 4 praise him with **t** and dancing,

TAMBOURINES [TAMBOURINE]
Jdg 11:34 dancing to the sound of **t**!
Isa 24: 8 The gaiety of the **t** is stilled,
Jer 31: 4 Again you will take up your **t**

TAME*
Jas   3: 8 but no man can **t** the tongue.

TANNER
Ac   9:43 some time with a **t** named Simon.

TAR
Ge 14:10 Valley of Siddim was full of **t** pits,

TARES (KJV) See WEEDS

TARGET
Job 16:12 He has made me his **t**;
La   3:12 He drew his bow and made me the **t**

TARSHISH
Ps 48: 7 You destroyed them like ships of **T**

Isa 60: 9 in the lead are the ships of **T**,
Jnh   1: 3 from the LORD and headed for **T**.

TARSUS
Ac   9:11 for a man from **T** named Saul,
    11:25 Barnabas went to **T** to look for Saul,

TASK [TASKS]
1Ch 29: 1 The **t** is great, because this palatial
Mk 13:34 each with his assigned **t**,
Ac 20:24 the **t** of testifying to the gospel
1Co 3: 5 the Lord has assigned to each his **t**.
2Co 2:16 And who is equal to such a **t**?
1Ti   3: 1 he desires a noble **t**.

TASKS [TASK]
Pr 31:17 her arms are strong for her **t**.

TASSELS
Dt 22:12 Make **t** on the four corners of
Mt 23: 5 and the **t** on their garments long;

TASTE [TASTED, TASTY]
Ps 34: 8 **T** and see that the LORD is good;
   119:103 How sweet are your words to my **t**,
Pr 24:13 from the comb is sweet to your **t**.
SS   2: 3 and his fruit is sweet to my **t**.
Mt 16:28 not **t** death before they see the Son
Col 2:21 "Do not handle! Do not **t**!
Heb 2: 9 by the grace of God he might **t** death

TASTED [TASTE]
Eze 3: 3 it **t** as sweet as honey in my mouth.
Heb 6: 4 who have **t** the heavenly gift,
1Pe 2: 3 you have **t** that the Lord is good.
Rev 10:10 it **t** as sweet as honey in my mouth,

TASTY [TASTE]
Ge 27: 4 Prepare me the kind of **t** food I like

TATTOO*
Lev 19:28 or put **t** marks on yourselves.

TAUGHT [TEACH]
Dt   4: 5 I have **t** you decrees and laws as
    31:22 and **t** it to the Israelites.
1Ki 4:33 He also **t** about animals and birds,
2Ki 17:28 in Bethel and **t** them how to worship
2Ch 17: 9 They **t** throughout Judah,
Ps 119:102 for you yourself have **t** me.
Pr   4: 4 he **t** me and said, "Lay hold
    31: 1 an oracle his mother **t** him:
Isa 29:13 made up only of rules **t** by men.
    40:14 and who **t** him the right way?
    50: 4 my ear to listen like one being **t**.
    54:13 sons will be **t** by the LORD,
Hos 11: 3 It was I who **t** Ephraim to walk,
Mt   7:29 he **t** as one who had authority,
    15: 9 teachings are but rules **t** by men.' "
Mk   4: 2 He **t** them many things by parables,
Lk   4:15 He **t** in their synagogues,
Jn   6:45 'They will all be **t** by God.'
Ac 20:20 have **t** you publicly and from house
1Co 2:13 not in words **t** us by human wisdom
Gal 1:12 nor was I **t** it;

1Ti 1:20 to Satan to be **t** not to blaspheme.
     4: 1 spirits and things **t** by demons.
1Jn 2:27 just as it has **t** you,

TAUNT [TAUNTS]

1Ki 18:27 At noon Elijah began to **t** them.
Ps 102: 8 All day long my enemies **t** me;

TAUNTS [TAUNT]

Ps 119:42 then I will answer the one who **t** me,
Eze 36:15 No longer will I make you hear the **t**

TAX [TAXES]

2Ch 24: 6 the **t** imposed by Moses
Mt   5:46 not even the **t** collectors doing that?
    11:19 friend of **t** collectors and "sinners." '
    17:24 your teacher pay the temple **t**?"
Lk 18:10 a Pharisee and the other a **t** collector.

TAXES [TAX]

Mt 22:17 Is it right to pay **t** to Caesar or not?"
Ro 13: 7 If you owe **t**, pay **t**;

TEACH [TAUGHT, TEACHER, TEACHERS, TEACHES, TEACHING, TEACHINGS]

Ex   4:12 and will **t** you what to say."
    18:20 **T** them the decrees and laws,
    33:13 **t** me your ways so I may know you
Lev 10:11 and you must **t** the Israelites all
Dt   4: 9 **T** them to your children and
     6: 1 to **t** you to observe in the land
     8: 3 to **t** you that man does not live on
    11:19 **T** them to your children,
1Sa 12:23 And I will **t** you the way that is good
1Ki 8:36 **T** them the right way to live,
Job 6:24 "**T** me, and I will be quiet;
    21:22 "Can anyone **t** knowledge to God,
Ps 25: 4 O LORD, **t** me your paths;
    32: 8 and **t** you in the way you should go;
    34:11 I will **t** you the fear of the LORD.
    51:13 I will **t** transgressors your ways,
    78: 5 our forefathers to **t** their children,
    90:12 **T** us to number our days aright,
   143:10 **T** me to do your will,
Pr   9: 9 **t** a righteous man and he will add
    22:17 apply your heart to what I **t**,
Jer 31:34 No longer will a man **t** his neighbor,
Mic 4: 2 He will **t** us his ways,
Mt   5: 2 and he began to **t** them, saying:
Lk 11: 1 "Lord, **t** us to pray,
    12:12 for the Holy Spirit will **t** you at
Jn 14:26 will **t** you all things
Ac   5:28 strict orders not to **t** in this name,"
Ro   2:21 who **t** others, do you not **t** yourself?
    12: 7 if it is teaching, let him **t**;
    15: 4 in the past was written to **t** us,
Col 3:16 as you **t** and admonish one another
1Ti 1: 3 not to **t** false doctrines any longer
     2:12 I do not permit a woman to **t** or
     3: 2 respectable, hospitable, able to **t**,
2Ti 2: 2 also be qualified to **t** others.
     2:24 able to **t**, not resentful.

Tit 2: 1 You must **t** what is in accord
     2:15 then, are the things you should **t**.
Heb 5:12 to **t** you the elementary truths
     8:11 No longer will a man **t** his neighbor,
Jas 3: 1 who **t** will be judged more strictly.
1Jn 2:27 you do not need anyone to **t** you.

TEACHER [TEACH]

Ezr 7: 6 a **t** well versed in the Law of Moses,
Ecc 1: 1 The words of the **T**, son of David,
    12: 9 Not only was the **T** wise,
Mt 10:24 "A student is not above his **t**,
    13:52 "Therefore every **t** of the law who
    22:36 "**T**, which is the greatest
    23:10 for you have one **T**, the Christ.
Lk   6:40 who is fully trained will be like his **t**.
Jn   1:38 "Rabbi" (which means **T**),
     3: 2 we know you are a **t** who has come
    13:14 Now that I, your Lord and **T**,

TEACHERS [TEACH]

Ps 119:99 I have more insight than all my **t**,
Pr   5:13 I would not obey my **t** or listen
Mt   7:29 and not as their **t** of the law.
Mk 12:38 "Watch out for the **t** of the law.
Lk 20:46 "Beware of the **t** of the law.
1Co 12:28 third **t**, then workers of miracles,
Eph 4:11 and some to be pastors and **t**,
2Ti 4: 3 around them a great number of **t**
Heb 5:12 by this time you ought to be **t**,
Jas 3: 1 of you should presume to be **t**,
2Pe 2: 1 as there will be false **t** among you.
     2: 3 In their greed these **t** will exploit you

TEACHERS OF THE LAW See LAW

TEACHES [TEACH]

Ps 25: 9 in what is right and **t** them his way.
    94:10 Does he who **t** man lack knowledge?
Pr 15:33 fear of the LORD **t** a man wisdom,
Isa 48:17 who **t** you what is best for you,
Hab 2:18 Or an image that **t** lies?
Mt   5:19 and **t** others to do the same
1Ti 6: 3 If anyone **t** false doctrines and does
Tit 2:12 It **t** us to say "No" to ungodliness
1Jn 2:27 But as his anointing **t** you about all

TEACHING [TEACH]

Ezr 7:10 to **t** its decrees and laws in Israel.
Ps 78: 1 O my people, hear my **t**;
Pr   1: 8 and do not forsake your mother's **t**.
     3: 1 My son, do not forget my **t**,
     6:23 this **t** is a light,
    13:14 **t** of the wise is a fountain of life,
Mt 28:20 and **t** them to obey everything
Mk   1:27 A new **t**—and with authority!
    11:18 whole crowd was amazed at his **t**.
Lk 19:47 Every day he was **t** at the temple.
Jn   7:17 he will find out whether my **t** comes
     8:31 Jesus said, "If you hold to my **t**,
    14:23 loves me, he will obey my **t**.
Ac   2:42 devoted themselves to the apostles' **t**
     5:42 they never stopped **t** and proclaiming
Ro 12: 7 if it is **t**, let him teach;
Eph 4:14 here and there by every wind of **t**

Col	1:28	and t everyone with all wisdom,
2Th	3: 6	according to the t you received
1Ti	4:13	to preaching and to t.
	5:17	especially those whose work is preaching and t.
	6: 3	Lord Jesus Christ and to godly t,
2Ti	2:17	Their t will spread like gangrene.
	3:16	God-breathed and is useful for t,
Tit	1:11	by t things they ought not to teach—
	2: 7	In your t show integrity,
Heb	5:13	with the t about righteousness.
2Jn	1: 9	not continue in the t of Christ does
	1:10	to you and does not bring this t,
Rev	2:20	By her t she misleads my servants

TEACHINGS [TEACH]

Pr	7: 2	guard my t as the apple of your eye.
Mt	15: 9	their t are but rules taught by men.' '
Col	2:22	based on human commands and t.
2Th	2:15	and hold to the t we passed on
Heb	6: 1	leave the elementary t about Christ
	13: 9	carried away by all kinds of strange t

TEAR [TEARS, TORE, TORN]

1Ki	11:13	not t the whole kingdom from him,
Ecc	3: 3	a time to t down and a time to build,
Mt	7: 6	and then turn and t you to pieces.
Mk	2:21	making the t worse.
Rev	7:17	And God will wipe away every t
	21: 4	He will wipe every t from their eyes.

TEARS [TEAR]

Job	12:14	What he t down cannot be rebuilt;
Ps	42: 3	My t have been my food day
	126: 5	in t will reap with songs of joy.
Pr	15:25	down the proud
Isa	25: 8	Sovereign LORD will wipe away the t
Jer	9: 1	and my eyes a fountain of t!
	31:16	from weeping and your eyes from t,
	50: 4	of Judah together will go in t to seek
La	1:16	and my eyes overflow with t.
Lk	7:38	she began to wet his feet with her t.
2Co	2: 4	anguish of heart and with many t,
Php	3:18	and now say again even with t,
Heb	5: 7	and petitions with loud cries and t to

TEETH [TOOTH]

Nu	11:33	the meat was still between their t
Job	19:20	with only the skin of my t.
Ps	3: 7	break the t of the wicked.
	35:16	they gnashed their t at me.
Jer	31:29	and the children's t are set on edge.'
Da	7: 7	It had large iron t;
Mt	8:12	be weeping and gnashing of t."
Ac	7:54	and gnashed their t at him.
Rev	9: 8	and their t were like lions' t.

TEKEL*

Da	5:25	written: MENE, MENE, T, PARSIN
	5:27	T: You have been weighed on the

TEKOA

2Sa	14: 4	the woman from T went to the king,
Am	1: 1	one of the shepherds of T—

TELL [TELLING, TELLS, TOLD]

Ge	22: 2	of the mountains I will t you about."
Ex	6:11	t Pharaoh king of Egypt to let
Nu	22:35	but speak only what I t you."
Dt	18:18	t them everything I command him.
Jdg	14:12	"Let me t you a riddle,"
Ru	3: 4	He will t you what to do."
1Sa	3:15	He was afraid to t Eli the vision,
2Ch	18:15	swear to t me nothing but the truth
Ps	5: 6	You destroy those who t lies;
	50:12	If I were hungry I would not t you,
	66:16	let me t you what he has done
	78: 4	we will t the next generation
	105: 2	t of all his wonderful acts.
Isa	41:23	t us what the future holds,
Eze	40: 4	T the house of Israel everything you
Da	2: 4	T your servants the dream,
Jnh	4:11	who cannot t their right hand from
Mt	4: 3	t these stones to become bread."
	12:16	warning them not to t who he was.
Jn	20:15	t me where you have put him,
Ac	13:32	"We t you the good news:
1Co	15:51	Listen, I t you a mystery:

I TELL YOU THE TRUTH See TRUTH

TELLING [TELL]

Jn	13:19	"I am t you now before it happens,

TELLS [TELL]

Pr	12:17	but a false witness t lies.
Mt	24:26	"So if anyone t you, 'There he is,
Jn	19:35	He knows that he t the truth,

TEMANITE

Job	2:11	Job's three friends, Eliphaz the T,

TEMPER [EVEN-TEMPERED, HOT-TEMPERED, ILL-TEMPERED, QUICK-TEMPERED]

Pr	16:32	a man who controls his t than one

TEMPERANCE (KJV)
See SELF-CONTROL

TEMPERATE*

1Ti	3: 2	the husband of but one wife, t,
	3:11	but t and trustworthy in everything.
Tit	2: 2	Teach the older men to be t,

TEMPEST

Ps	50: 3	and around him a t rages.
	55: 8	far from the t and storm."

TEMPLE [TEMPLES]

Jdg	4:21	She drove the peg through his t into
	16:30	and down came the t on the rulers
1Sa	3: 3	and Samuel was lying down in the t
	5: 2	they carried the ark into Dagon's t
1Ki	6: 1	he began to build the t of the LORD.
	6:38	the t was finished in all its details
	8:11	the glory of the LORD filled his t.
	8:27	How much less this t I have built!
2Ki	25: 9	He set fire to the t of the LORD,

2Ch	24: 4	to restore the **t** of the Lord.
	36:23	and he has appointed me to build a t
Ezr	3:12	the foundation of this **t** being laid,
	6:15	The **t** was completed on the third day
Ps	27: 4	and to seek him in his **t.**
	30: T	For the dedication of the **t.**
Isa	6: 1	and the train of his robe filled the **t.**
Jer	7:14	the **t** you trust in,
Eze	10: 4	The cloud filled the **t,**
	43: 4	The glory of the Lord entered the **t**
Da	5: 2	taken from the **t** in Jerusalem,
Mic	4: 1	of the Lord's **t** will be established
Hab	2:20	But the Lord is in his holy **t;**
Zec	4: 9	have laid the foundation of this **t;**
Mt	4: 5	stand on the highest point of the **t.**
	12: 6	that one greater than the **t** is here.
	23:35	whom you murdered between the **t**
	26:61	to destroy the **t** of God and rebuild it
	27:51	the curtain of the **t** was torn in two
Mk	15:38	The curtain of the **t** was torn in two
Lk	21: 5	the **t** was adorned
Jn	2:14	**t** courts he found men selling cattle,
	2:21	the **t** he had spoken of was his body.
Ac	2:46	continued to meet together in the **t**
	5:42	Day after day, in the **t** courts
1Co	3:16	that you yourselves are God's **t**
	6:19	your body is a **t** of the Holy Spirit,
2Co	6:16	For we are the **t** of the living God.
Eph	2:21	and rises to become a holy **t**
2Th	2: 4	so that he sets himself up in God's **t,**
Rev	3:12	a pillar in the **t** of my God.
	11:19	Then God's **t** in heaven was opened,
	21:22	the Lord God Almighty and the Lamb are its **t.**

TEMPLE OF ... GOD Jdg 9:27; 2Ki 19:37; 1Ch 28:12, 21; 29:2, 3, 7; 2Ch 3:3; 4:11; 5:14; 7:5; 15:18; 22:12; 23:3, 9; 24:5, 7, 13, 27; 25:24; 28:24; 31:13; 32:21; 34:9; 36:18; Ezr 1:4, 7; 6:3, 7; 7:16, 17, 19, 20, 23; Isa 37:38; Da 1:2, 2; 5:3; Mt 26:61; 2Co 6:16; Rev 3:12; 11:1

TEMPLE OF THE †LORD 1Sa 3:3; 1Ki 3:1; 6:1, 37; 7:12, 40, 45, 51; 8:10, 63, 64; 9:1, 10; 10:5; 12:27; 14:26; 15:15; 2Ki 11:3, 4, 4, 10, 13, 15, 18, 19; 12:4, 9, 9, 10, 11, 12, 13, 16, 18; 14:14; 15:35; 16:8, 14, 18; 18:15, 16; 19:1, 14; 20:5, 8; 21:4, 5; 22:3, 4, 5, 8, 9; 23:2, 2, 4, 6, 7, 11, 12, 24; 24:13, 13; 25:9, 13, 16; 1Ch 6:32; 22:14; 23:4, 24, 28, 32; 24:19; 25:6; 26:12, 22, 27; 28:12, 13, 20; 29:8; 2Ch 3:1; 4:16; 5:1, 13; 7:2, 7, 11, 11; 8:1, 16, 16; 9:4, 11; 12:9; 20:5, 28; 23:5, 6, 12, 14, 18, 20; 24:4, 8, 12, 14, 18; 26:16, 21; 27:2, 3; 28:21; 29:3, 5, 15, 16, 17, 18, 20, 25, 31, 35; 30:1, 15; 31:10, 11, 16; 33:4, 5, 15; 34:8, 14, 15, 17, 30, 30; 36:7, 10, 14; Ezr 1:3, 7; 3:10; Isa 37:1, 14; 38:20, 22; 66:20; Jer 7:4, 4, 4; 20:1; 24:1; 38:14; 52:13, 17, 20; Eze 8:16; 44:4, 5; Hos 9:4; Zec 6:12, 13, 14, 15

TEMPLES [TEMPLE]
Ac 17:24 and does not live in **t** built by hands.

TEMPORARY
2Co 4:18 For what is seen is **t,**

TEMPT* [TEMPTATION, TEMPTED, TEMPTER, TEMPTING]
| 1Co | 7: 5 | so that Satan will not **t** you because |
| Jas | 1:13 | nor does he **t** anyone; |

TEMPTATION* [TEMPT]
Mt	6:13	And lead us not into **t,**
	26:41	so that you will not fall into **t.**
Mk	14:38	so that you will not fall into **t.**
Lk	11: 4	And lead us not into **t.'** "
	22:40	"Pray that you will not fall into **t.**"
	22:46	so that you will not fall into **t.**"
1Co	10:13	No **t** has seized you except what is
1Ti	6: 9	want to get rich fall into **t** and a trap

TEMPTED* [TEMPT]
Mt	4: 1	into the desert to be **t** by the devil.
Mk	1:13	being **t** by Satan.
Lk	4: 2	for forty days he was **t** by the devil.
1Co	10:13	be **t** beyond what you can bear.
	10:13	But when you are **t,**
Gal	6: 1	or you also may be **t.**
1Th	3: 5	the tempter might have **t** you
Heb	2:18	he himself suffered when he was **t,**
	2:18	able to help those who are being **t.**
	4:15	but we have one who has been **t**
Jas	1:13	When **t,** no one should say,
	1:13	For God cannot be **t** by evil,
	1:14	but each one is **t** when,

TEMPTER* [TEMPT]
| Mt | 4: 3 | The **t** came to him and said, |
| 1Th | 3: 5 | the **t** might have tempted you |

TEMPTING* [TEMPT]
| Lk | 4:13 | the devil had finished all this **t,** |
| Jas | 1:13 | no one should say, "God is **t** me." |

TEN [TENS, TENTH, TITHE, TITHES, TWO-TENTHS]
Ge	18:32	What if only **t** can be found there?"
Ex	34:28	covenant—the **T** Commandments.
Lev	26: 8	hundred of you will chase **t** thousand
Dt	4:13	his covenant, the **T** Commandments,
	10: 4	the **T** Commandments he had
1Sa	1: 8	more to you than **t** sons?"
2Ki	20: 9	the shadow go forward **t** steps,
Ps	91: 7	**t** thousand at your right hand,
Da	1:12	"Please test your servants for **t** days:
	7:24	The **t** horns are **t** kings who will
Mt	25: 1	like **t** virgins who took their lamps
	25:28	to the one who has the **t** talents.
Lk	15: 8	suppose a woman has **t** silver coins
Rev	5:11	and **t** thousand times **t** thousand.
	12: 3	and **t** horns and seven crowns
	17:12	"The **t** horns you saw are **t** kings

TENANTS
| Lev | 25:23 | and you are but aliens and my **t.** |
| Mt | 21:34 | he sent his servants to the **t** |

TEND [TENDING, TENDS]
Jer 23: 2 to the shepherds who **t** my people:

Eze 34:14 I will t them in a good pasture,

TENDER [TENDERLY, TENDERNESS]

Isa 53: 2 grew up before him like a t shoot,
Lk 1:78 because of the t mercy of our God,

TENDERLY* [TENDER]

Ge 34: 3 he loved the girl and spoke t to her.
Isa 40: 2 Speak t to Jerusalem,
Hos 2:14 into the desert and speak t to her.

TENDERNESS* [TENDER]

Isa 63:15 Your t and compassion are withheld
Php 2: 1 if any t and compassion,

TENDING [TEND]

Ex 3: 1 Now Moses was t the flock
1Sa 16:11 "but he is t the sheep."

TENDS [TEND]

Isa 40:11 He t his flock like a shepherd:

TENS [TEN]

1Sa 18: 7 and David his t of thousands."
Ps 3: 6 not fear the t of thousands drawn up

TENT [TENTMAKER, TENTS]

Ex 27:21 In the T of Meeting,
    33: 7 calling it the **"t** of meeting."
    40: 2 the T of Meeting,
2Sa 7: 2 while the ark of God remains in a t."
    20: 1 Every man to his t, O Israel!"
Ps 61: 4 to dwell in your t forever
Isa 33:20 a t that will not be moved;
    54: 2 "Enlarge the place of your t,
Am 9:11 I will restore David's fallen t.
Ac 15:16 and rebuild David's fallen t.
2Co 5: 1 the earthly t we live in is destroyed,
2Pe 1:13 as long as I live in the t
Rev 7:15 will spread his t over them.

TENT OF MEETING Ex 27:21; 28:43; 29:4,
10, 11, 30, 32, 42, 44; 30:16, 18, 20, 26, 36; 31:7;
33:7, 7; 35:21; 38:8, 30; 39:32, 40; 40:2, 6, 7, 12,
22, 24, 26, 29, 30, 32, 34, 35; Lev 1:1, 3, 5; 3:2,
8, 13; 4:4, 5, 7, 7, 14, 16, 18, 18; 6:16, 26, 30;
8:3, 4, 31, 33, 35; 9:5, 23; 10:7, 9; 12:6; 14:11,
23; 15:14, 29; 16:7, 16, 17, 20, 23, 33; 17:4, 5, 6,
9; 19:21; 24:3; Nu 1:1; 2:2; 17: 3:7, 8, 25, 25, 38;
4:3, 4, 15, 23, 25, 25, 28, 30, 31, 33, 35, 37, 39,
41, 43, 47; 6:10, 13, 18; 7:5, 89; 8:9, 15, 19, 22,
24, 26; 10:3; 11:16; 12:4; 14:10; 16:18, 19, 42,
43, 50; 17:4; 18:4, 6, 21, 22, 23, 31; 19:4; 20:6;
25:6; 27:2; 31:54; Dt 31:14, 14; Jos 18:1; 19:51;
1Sa 2:22; 1Ki 8:4; 1Ch 6:32; 9:21; 23:32; 2Ch
1:3, 6, 13; 5:5

TENTH [TEN]

Ge 14:20 Abram gave him a t of everything.
Nu 18:26 you must present a t of that tithe as
Dt 14:22 Be sure to set aside a t of all
1Sa 8:15 a t of your grain and of your vintage
Isa 6:13 And though a t remains in the land,
Lk 11:42 you give God a t of your mint,
    18:12 a week and give a t of all I get.'

Heb 7: 4 the patriarch Abraham gave him a t

TENTMAKER* [TENT]

Ac 18: 3 and because he was a t as they were,

TENTS [TENT]

Ge 13:12 and pitched his t near Sodom.
Nu 1:52 The Israelites are to set up their t
Ps 84:10 than dwell in the t of the wicked.

TERAH

Ge 11:27 T became the father of Abram,

TEREBINTH

Isa 6:13 But as the t and oak leave stumps

TERMS

Dt 29: 1 These are the t of the covenant
Jer 11: 3 not obey the t of this covenant—

TERRIBLE [TERROR]

2Ti 3: 1 There will be t times in the last days.

TERRIFIED [TERROR]

Dt 7:21 Do not be t by them,
    20: 3 not be t or give way to panic
Est 7: 6 Then Haman was t before the king
Ps 90: 7 and t by your indignation.
Jer 1:17 Do not be t by them,
Eze 2: 6 not be afraid of what they say or t
Mt 14:26 walking on the lake, they were t.
    17: 6 they fell facedown to the ground, t.
    27:54 they were t, and exclaimed,
Mk 4:41 They were t and asked each other,

TERRIFYING [TERROR]

Heb 12:21 The sight was so t that Moses said,

TERRITORY

Ex 34:24 before you and enlarge your t,
Jos 1: 4 Your t will extend from the desert
1Ch 4:10 bless me and enlarge my t!
2Co 10:16 work already done in another man's t

TERROR [TERRIBLE, TERRIFIED, TERRIFYING, TERRORS]

Ex 23:27 "I will send my t ahead of you
Dt 2:25 to put the t and fear of you on all
    28:67 the t that will fill your hearts
Job 9:34 his t would frighten me no more.
Ps 31:13 there is t on every side;
    91: 5 You will not fear the t of night,
Pr 21:15 joy to the righteous but t to evildoers
Isa 13: 8 T will seize them,
    24:17 T and pit and snare await you,
    51:13 you live in constant t every day
    54:14 T will be far removed;
Jer 20:10 "T on every side!
Lk 21:26 Men will faint from t,
Ro 13: 3 For rulers hold no t for those who

TERRORS [TERROR]

Ps 55: 4 the t of death assail me.
La 2:22 so you summoned against me t

TERTIUS*

Ro 16:22 I, **T,** who wrote down this letter,

TEST [TESTED, TESTER, TESTING, TESTINGS, TESTS]

Ex 16: 4 In this way I will **t** them
Dt 6:16 Do not **t** the LORD your God
8: 2 to humble you and to **t** you in order
Jdg 3: 4 They were left to **t** the Israelites
6:39 one more **t** with the fleece.
1Ki 10: 1 to **t** him with hard questions.
1Ch 29:17 that you **t** the heart and are pleased
Ps 26: 2 **T** me, O LORD, and try me,
78:18 They willfully put God to the **t**
106:14 the wasteland they put God to the **t.**
139:23 **t** me and know my anxious thoughts.
Jer 9: 7 I will refine and **t** them,
11:20 and **t** the heart and mind,
Mal 3:10 **T** me in this,"
Lk 4:12 not put the Lord your God to the **t.'**"
10:25 expert in the law stood up to **t** Jesus.
Ac 5: 9 "How could you agree to **t** the Spirit
Ro 12: 2 Then you will be able to **t**
1Co 3:13 and the fire will **t** the quality
10: 9 We should not **t** the Lord,
2Co 13: 5 you are in the faith; **t** yourselves.
Gal 6: 4 Each one should **t** his own actions.
1Th 5:21 **T** everything. Hold on to the good.
Jas 1:12 because when he has stood the **t,**
1Jn 4: 1 but **t** the spirits to see whether
Rev 2:10 some of you in prison to **t** you,
3:10 to come upon the whole world to **t**

TESTED [TEST]

Ge 22: 1 Some time later God **t** Abraham.
Ex 17: 7 because they **t** the LORD saying,
Nu 14:22 and **t** me ten times—
Job 23:10 when he has **t** me,
34:36 Oh, that Job might be **t** to the utmost
Ps 66:10 For you, O God, **t** us;
Pr 27:21 man is **t** by the praise he receives.
Ecc 7:23 All this I **t** by wisdom and I said,
Isa 28:16 I lay a stone in Zion, a **t** stone,
48:10 I have **t** you in the furnace
Da 1:14 and **t** them for ten days.
Lk 11:16 Others **t** him by asking for a sign
Ro 16:10 **t** and approved in Christ.
1Ti 3:10 They must first be **t;**
Heb 11:17 By faith Abraham, when God **t** him,

TESTER* [TEST]

Jer 6:27 a **t** of metals and my people the ore,

TESTIFIED [TESTIFY]

Mk 14:56 Many **t** falsely against him,
Jn 5:37 has himself **t** concerning me.
Heb 2: 4 God also **t** to it by signs,

TESTIFIES [TESTIFY]

Jn 5:32 There is another who **t** in my favor,
19:35 he **t** so that you also may believe.
21:24 the disciple who **t** to these things
Ro 8:16 The Spirit himself **t** with our spirit

Rev 1: 2 who **t** to everything he saw—
22:20 He who **t** to these things says, "Yes,

TESTIFY [TESTIFIED, TESTIFIES, TESTIMONY]

Dt 31:21 this song will **t** against them,
Pr 24:28 Do not **t** against your neighbor
Isa 59:12 and our sins **t** against us.
Jer 14: 7 Although our sins **t** against us,
Jn 1: 7 a witness to **t** concerning that light,
1:34 and I **t** that this is the Son of God."
5:39 the Scriptures that **t** about me,
7: 7 because I **t** that what it does is evil.
15:26 he will **t** about me.
Ac 4:33 the apostles continued to **t** to
10:43 All the prophets **t** about him
Ro 3:21 to which the Law and the Prophets **t.**
2Ti 1: 8 not be ashamed to **t** about our Lord,
1Jn 4:14 and **t** that the Father has sent his Son
5: 7 For there are three that **t:**

TESTIMONY [TESTIFY]

Ex 16:34 put the manna in front of the **T,**
20:16 "You shall not give false **t**
25:16 Then put in the ark the **T,**
31:18 he gave him the two tablets of the **T,**
Nu 35:30 to death as a murderer only on the **t**
Dt 19:18 giving false **t** against his brother,
Pr 12:17 A truthful witness gives honest **t,**
Isa 8:20 To the law and to the **t!**
Mt 15:19 sexual immorality, theft, false **t,**
24:14 preached in the whole world as a **t**
Mk 14:59 Yet even then their **t** did not agree.
Lk 22:71 "Why do we need any more **t?**
Jn 2:25 He did not need man's **t** about man,
8:17 that the **t** of two men is valid.
21:24 We know that his **t** is true.
1Jn 5: 9 but God's **t** is greater because it is the **t** of God,
Rev 1: 9 the word of God and the **t** of Jesus.
12:11 and by the word of their **t;**
15: 5 the tabernacle of the **T,** was opened.
19:10 **t** of Jesus is the spirit of prophecy."

ARK OF THE TESTIMONY See ARK

TESTING* [TEST]

Dt 13: 3 The LORD your God is **t** you
Eze 21:13 "'**T** will surely come.
Lk 8:13 but in the time of **t** they fall away.
Heb 3: 8 during the time of **t** in the desert,
Jas 1: 3 because you know that the **t**

TESTINGS* [TEST]

Dt 4:34 by **t,** by miraculous signs

TESTS [TEST]

Pr 17: 3 but the LORD **t** the heart.
1Th 2: 4 who **t** our hearts.

TETRARCH

Mt 14: 1 the **t** heard the reports about Jesus,
Lk 3:19 But when John rebuked Herod the **t**

THADDAEUS

Apostle (Mt 10:3; Mk 3:18); probably also known as Judas son of James (Lk 6:16; Ac 1:13).

THANK [THANKFUL, THANKFULNESS, THANKING, THANKS, THANKSGIVING]

Lev	22:29	"When you sacrifice a **t** offering to
2Ch	29:31	and bring sacrifices and **t** offerings
Ps	50:14	Sacrifice **t** offerings to God,
	116:17	I will sacrifice a **t** offering to you
Da	2:23	I **t** and praise you,
Lk	18:11	I **t** you that I am not
Jn	11:41	I **t** you that you have heard me.
1Co	10:30	because of something I **t** God for?
Php	1:3	I **t** my God every time I remember
1Th	3:9	How can we **t** God enough for you

THANKFUL [THANK]

Col	4:2	to prayer, being watchful and **t.**
Heb	12:28	let us be **t,**

THANKFULNESS* [THANK]

Lev	7:12	he offers it as an expression of **t,**
1Co	10:30	If I take part in the meal with **t,**
Col	2:7	and overflowing with **t.**

THANKING* [THANK]

1Ch	25:3	using the harp in **t** and praising

THANKS [THANK]

1Ch	16:8	Give **t** to the LORD, call
Ne	12:31	assigned two large choirs to give **t.**
Ps	7:17	I will give **t** to the LORD because
	28:7	and I will give **t** to him in song.
	30:12	I will give you **t** forever.
	35:18	I will give you **t** in
	75:1	we give **t,** for your Name is near;
	100:	T A psalm. For giving **t.**
	107:1	Give **t** to the LORD, for he is good;
	118:28	and I will give you **t;**
	136:2	Give **t** to the God of gods.
Mt	14:19	he gave **t** and broke the loaves.
Ro	1:21	glorified him as God nor gave **t** to
1Co	11:24	he had given **t,** he broke it
	15:57	But **t** be to God!
2Co	2:14	But **t** be to God,
	9:15	**T** be to God for his indescribable gift
1Th	5:18	give **t** in all circumstances,
Rev	4:9	and **t** to him who sits on the throne
	7:12	and **t** and honor and power
	11:17	saying: "We give **t** to you,

GAVE THANKS 2Ch 7:3, 6; Ne 12:40; Mt 14:19; 26:26, 27; Mk 6:41; 8:7; 14:22, 23; Lk 2:38; 9:16; 22:17, 19; 24:30; Jn 6:11; Ac 27:35; Ro 1:21

GIVE THANKS 1Ch 16:4, 8, 34, 35, 41; 2Ch 20:21; 31:2; Ne 12:31; Ps 7:17; 28:7; 75:1, 1; 100:4; 105:1; 106:1, 47; 107:1, 8, 15, 21, 31; 118:1, 19, 29; 136:1, 2, 3, 26; Isa 12:4; Jer 33:11; 1Co 10:16; 2Co 1:11; 1Th 5:18; Rev 11:17

THANKSGIVING [THANK]

Ezr	3:11	and **t** they sang to the LORD:
Ne	12:27	the dedication with songs of **t**
Ps	95:2	Let us come before him with **t**
	100:4	Enter his gates with **t** and his courts
Jnh	2:9	But I, with a song of **t,**
1Co	10:16	Is not the cup of **t** for which
2Co	9:11	generosity will result in **t** to God.
Php	4:6	with **t,** present your requests to God.
1Ti	4:3	received with **t** by those who believe

THEFT* [THIEF]

Ex	22:3	he must be sold to pay for his **t.**
Mt	15:19	adultery, sexual immorality, **t,**
Mk	7:21	sexual immorality, **t,** murder,

THEFTS* [THIEF]

Rev	9:21	their sexual immorality or their **t.**

THEME*

Ps	22:25	From you comes the **t** of my praise
	45:1	by a noble **t** as I recite my verses for
	119:54	the **t** of my song wherever I lodge.

THEOPHILUS*

Lk	1:3	account for you, most excellent **T,**
Ac	1:1	In my former book, **T,**

THESSALONIANS [THESSALONICA]

Ac	17:11	of more noble character than the **T,**

THESSALONICA [THESSALONIANS]

Ac	17:1	they came to **T,**
Php	4:16	for even when I was in **T,**

THICK

Ge	15:12	and a **t** and dreadful darkness came
Ex	19:16	with a **t** cloud over the mountain,
Ps	97:2	Clouds and **t** darkness surround him;

THIEF [THEFT, THEFTS, THIEVES]

Ex	22:3	"A **t** must certainly make restitution,
Pr	6:30	a **t** if he steals to satisfy his hunger
Lk	12:39	at what hour the **t** was coming,
Jn	10:10	The **t** comes only to steal and kill
1Th	5:2	day of the Lord will come like a **t**
1Pe	4:15	it should not be as a murderer or **t**
Rev	16:15	"Behold, I come like a **t!**

THIEVES [THIEF]

Mt	6:19	where **t** break in and steal.
Jn	10:8	All who ever came before me were **t**
1Co	6:10	nor **t** nor the greedy nor drunkards

THIGH [THIGHS]

Ge	24:2	"Put your hand under my **t.**
	47:29	put your hand under my **t**
Rev	19:16	on his **t** he has this name written:

THIGHS [THIGH]

Da	2:32	its belly and **t** of bronze,

THIN
Ge 41: 7 The **t** heads of grain swallowed up
Ex 16:14 **t** flakes like frost on the ground

THING [SOMETHING, THINGS]
Ge   1:21 and every living and moving **t**
     7:21 Every living **t** that moved on
    19: 7 Don't do this wicked **t.**
Jdg 19:24 don't do such a disgraceful **t."**
2Sa 13:12 Don't do this wicked **t.**
2Ki 3:18 an easy **t** in the eyes of the LORD;
Ps 27: 4 One **t** I ask of the LORD,
    84:11 no good **t** does he withhold
Isa 43:19 See, I am doing a new **t!**
Jer 31:22 The LORD will create a new **t**
Mt 19:16 what good **t** must I do
Mk 10:21 "One **t** you lack," he said.
Lk 10:42 but only one **t** is needed.
Jn   9:25 One **t** I do know.
Php 3:13 But one **t** I do:

THINGS [THING]
Nu 10:29 LORD has promised good **t** to Israel."
2Sa 7:28 promised these good **t** to your
Ps 15: 5 does these **t** will never be shaken.
    71:19 O God, you who have done great **t.**
   118:15 right hand has done mighty **t!**
Pr   6:16 There are six **t** the LORD hates,
    31:29 "Many women do noble **t,**
Isa 66: 2 Has not my hand made all these **t,**
Jer 10:16 for he is the Maker of all **t,**
Joel 2:21 Surely the LORD has done great **t.**
Mt 19:26 but with God all **t** are possible."
Mk 11:33 by what authority I am doing these **t.**
Lk   6:45 The good man brings good **t** out of
     9:22 "The Son of Man must suffer many **t**
Jn   1: 3 Through him all **t** were made;
     1:50 You shall see greater **t** than that."
    14:12 He will do even greater **t** than these,
    21:25 Jesus did many other **t** as well.
1Co 2:10 The Spirit searches all **t,**
Eph 1:22 And God placed all **t** under his feet
Col 1:17 and in him all **t** hold together.
1Pe 4: 7 The end of all **t** is near.
Rev 4:11 for you created all **t,**
    21: 4 the old order of **t** has passed away."
    22: 6 the **t** that must soon take place."

THINK [THINKING, THINKS, THOUGHT, THOUGHTS]
Ps 40:17 may the Lord **t** of me.
    63: 6 I **t** of you through the watches of the
   144: 3 the son of man that you **t** of him?
Isa 44:19 No one stops to **t,**
Eze 28: 2 you **t** you are as wise as a god.
Mt 22:42 "What do you **t** about the Christ?
Jn   5:39 you **t** that by them you possess
Ro 12: 3 Do not **t** of yourself more highly
1Co 10:12 So, if you **t** you are standing firm,
Php 4: 8 praiseworthy—**t** about such things.

THINKING [THINK]
Pr 23: 7 who is always **t** about the cost.

Lk   5:22 Jesus knew what they were **t**
1Co 14:20 but in your **t** be adults.
2Pe 3: 1 to stimulate you to wholesome **t.**

THINKS [THINK]
1Co 8: 2 The man who **t** he knows something
    14:37 If anybody **t** he is a prophet

THIRD [THREE]
Eze 5:12 and a **t** I will scatter to the winds
    10:14 the **t** the face of a lion,
Da   5: 7 the **t** highest ruler in the kingdom."
Hos 6: 2 on the **t** day he will restore us,
Mk 14:41 Returning the **t** time,
Lk 18:33 On the **t** day he will rise again."
Jn 21:17 because Jesus asked him the **t** time,
Ac 20: 9 he fell to the ground from the **t** story
2Co 12: 2 caught up to the **t** heaven.
Rev 4: 7 the **t** had a face like a man,
     6: 5 When the Lamb opened the **t** seal,
     8:10 The **t** angel sounded his trumpet,
    12: 4 His tail swept a **t** of the stars out of

THE THIRD DAY See DAY

THIRST [THIRSTS, THIRSTY]
Ps 69:21 and gave me vinegar for my **t.**
Mt   5: 6 who hunger and **t** for righteousness,
Jn   4:14 the water I give him will never **t.**
2Co 11:27 and **t** and have often gone
Rev 7:16 never again will they **t.**

THIRSTS [THIRST]
Ps 42: 2 My soul **t** for God,

THIRSTY [THIRST]
Ex 17: 3 the people were **t** for water there,
Ps 107: 9 for he satisfies the **t** and fills
Pr 25:21 if he is **t,** give him water to drink.
Isa 55: 1 "Come, all you who are **t,**
Mt 25:35 I was **t** and you gave me something
Jn   6:35 who believes in me will never be **t.**
     7:37 "If anyone is **t,**
    19:28 Jesus said, "I am **t."**
Ro 12:20 if he is **t,** give him something to
Rev 21: 6 To him who is **t** I will give to drink
    22:17 Whoever is **t,** let him come;

THIRTY
Ge 41:46 Joseph was **t** years old when
Lev 27: 4 set her value at **t** shekels.
2Sa 23:24 Among the **T** were:
Pr 22:20 Have I not written **t** sayings for you,
Mt 13: 8 sixty or **t** times what was sown.
Lk   3:23 Jesus himself was about **t** years old

THISTLE [THISTLES]
2Ki 14: 9 "A **t** in Lebanon sent a message to

THISTLES [THISTLE]
Ge   3:18 It will produce thorns and **t** for you,
Heb 6: 8 produces thorns and **t** is worthless

THOMAS*
Apostle (Mt 10:3; Mk 3:18; Lk 6:15; Jn 11:16;

14:5; 21:2; Ac 1:13). Doubted resurrection (Jn 20:24-28).

THONGS
Mk   1: 7 the **t** of whose sandals I am

THORN* [THORNBUSH, THORNBUSHES, THORNS]
Mic   7: 4 most upright worse than a **t** hedge.
2Co 12: 7 there was given me a **t** in my flesh,

THORNBUSH [THORN]
Jdg   9:14 "Finally all the trees said to the **t,**
Isa 55:13 Instead of the **t** will grow the pine

THORNBUSHES [THORN]
Lk   6:44 People do not pick figs from **t,**

THORNS [THORN]
Ge   3:18 It will produce **t** and thistles for you,
Nu 33:55 and **t** in your sides.
Jer 12:13 They will sow wheat but reap **t;**
Mt 13: 7 Other seed fell among **t,**
Jn 19: 2 a crown of **t** and put it on his head.
Heb   6: 8 produces **t** and thistles is worthless

THOROUGH [THOROUGHLY]
Ac 18:24 with a **t** knowledge of the Scriptures.

THOROUGHLY [THOROUGH]
Ps 119:140 Your promises have been **t** tested,
Ac 22: 3 Under Gamaliel I was **t** trained in
2Ti   3:17 be **t** equipped for every good work.

THOUGH
Job 13:15 **T** he slay me, yet will I hope in him;
Ps 17: 3 **t** you test me, you will find nothing;
27:10 **T** my father and mother forsake me,
37:24 **t** he stumble, he will not fall,
Isa   1:18 "**T** your sins are like scarlet,
Hab   2: 3 **T** it linger, wait for it;
3:17 **T** the fig tree does not bud
Lk   8:10 " '**t** seeing, they may not see;
Jn 11:25 even **t** he dies;
Ro   9: 6 It is not as **t** God's word had failed.

THOUGHT [THINK]
1Sa   1:13 Eli **t** she was drunk
Ps 106: 7 they gave no **t** to your miracles;
Pr 14:15 a prudent man gives **t** to his steps.
21:29 an upright man gives **t** to his ways.
1Co 13:11 I talked like a child, I **t** like a child,
2Co 10: 5 and we take captive every **t**

THOUGHTS [THINK]
Ge   6: 5 of the **t** of his heart was only evil all
1Ch 28: 9 every motive behind the **t.**
Ps 92: 5 O LORD, how profound your **t!**
94:11 The LORD knows the **t** of man;
139:23 test me and know my anxious **t.**
Pr 15:26 LORD detests the **t** of the wicked,
Isa 55: 8 "For my **t** are not your **t,**
Mt   9: 4 Knowing their **t,** Jesus said,
15:19 For out of the heart come evil **t,**

Ro   2:15 and their **t** now accusing,
1Co   2:11 no one knows the **t** of God except
Heb   3: 1 fix your **t** on Jesus,
4:12 the **t** and attitudes of the heart.

THOUSAND [THOUSANDS]
Dt   7: 9 **t** generations of those who love him
32:30 How could one man chase a **t,**
Jos 23:10 One of you routs a **t,**
Jdg 15:16 jawbone I have killed a **t** men."
Ps 50:10 and the cattle on a **t** hills.
84:10 in your courts than a **t** elsewhere;
90: 4 **t** years in your sight are like a day
91: 7 A **t** may fall at your side,
105: 8 for a **t** generations,
SS   5:10 outstanding among ten **t.**
Mt 14:21 who ate was about five **t** men,
15:38 of those who ate was four **t,**
2Pe   3: 8 With the Lord a day is like a **t** years,
Rev   5:11 and ten **t** times ten **t.**
20: 4 and reigned with Christ a **t** years.

THOUSANDS [THOUSAND]
Ex 34: 7 maintaining love to **t,** and forgiving
1Sa 18: 7 "Saul has slain his **t,** and David his tens of **t.**"
Ps 68:17 The chariots of God are tens of **t** and **t** of **t;**
Da   7:10 **T** upon **t** attended him;
Heb 12:22 to **t** upon **t** of angels in joyful
Jude   1:14 the Lord is coming with **t** upon **t**
Rev   5:11 numbering **t** upon **t,**

THREAT [THREATENED, THREATS]
Isa 30:17 A thousand will flee at the **t** of one;

THREATENED [THREAT]
Ex 32:14 on his people the disaster he had **t.**
Jnh   3:10 upon them the destruction he had **t.**

THREATS [THREAT]
Ac   4:21 After further **t** they let them go.
9: 1 was still breathing out murderous **t**

THREE [THIRD]
Ge   6:10 Noah had **t** sons:
18: 2 Abraham looked up and saw **t** men
Ex 23:14 "**T** times a year you are to celebrate
Dt 14:28 At the end of every **t** years,
19:15 the testimony of two or **t** witnesses.
1Sa 31: 8 they found Saul and his **t** sons fallen
2Sa 23: 9 As one of the **t** mighty men,
Job   2:11 When Job's **t** friends,
Pr 30:15 "There are **t** things that
30:18 "There are **t** things that
30:21 "Under **t** things the earth trembles,
30:29 "There are **t** things that are stately
Ecc   4:12 of **t** strands is not quickly broken.
Da   3:24 "Weren't there **t** men that we tied up
7: 5 and it had **t** ribs in its mouth
Am   1: 3 "For **t** sins of Damascus,
Jnh   1:17 and Jonah was inside the fish **t** days
Mt 12:40 as Jonah was **t** days and **t** nights
17: 4 you wish, I will put up **t** shelters—

	18:20	two or t come together in my name,
	26:34	you will disown me t times."
	26:75	you will disown me t times.
	27:63	'After t days I will rise again.'
Mk	8:31	be killed and after t days rise again.
	14:30	you yourself will disown me t times.
Jn	2:19	and I will raise it again in t days."
1Co	13:13	these t remain: faith, hope and love.
	14:27	or at the most t—
2Co	12: 8	T times I pleaded with the Lord
	13: 1	the testimony of two or t witnesses."
1Jn	5: 7	For there are t that testify:

THRESH [THRESHED, THRESHER, THRESHING]

Mic 4:13 "Rise and t, O Daughter of Zion,

THRESHED [THRESH]

Ru 2:17 she t the barley she had gathered,

THRESHER* [THRESH]

1Co 9:10 plowman plows and the t threshes,

THRESHING [THRESH]

Ru	3: 3	Then go down to the t floor,
2Sa	24:18	the t floor of Araunah the Jebusite."
Hos	9: 1	wages of a prostitute at every t floor.
Lk	3:17	in his hand to clear his t floor

THRESHOLD

1Sa	5: 4	and were lying on the t;
Eze	10:18	of the LORD departed from over the t
	47: 1	out from under the t of the temple
Zep	1: 9	all who avoid stepping on the t,

THREW [THROW]

Ex	7:10	Aaron t his staff down in front
	15:25	He t it into the water,
	32:19	and he t the tablets out of his hands,
2Ki	6: 6	Elisha cut a stick and t it there,
Da	3:24	that we tied up and t into the fire?"
	6:16	Daniel and t him into the lions' den.
Jnh	1:15	took Jonah and t him overboard,
Mt	27: 5	Judas t the money into the temple
Rev	20: 3	He t him into the Abyss,

THRIVE

Pr	11:28	the righteous will t like a green leaf.
	29: 2	the righteous t, the people rejoice;
	29:16	When the wicked t, so does sin,

THROAT [THROATS]

| Ps | 5: 9 | Their t is an open grave; |
| Pr | 23: 2 | a knife to your t if you are given |

THROATS [THROAT]

Ro 3:13 "Their t are open graves;

THROB*

Isa 60: 5 your heart will t and swell with joy;

THRONE [ENTHRONED, ENTHRONES, THRONES]

Ex 17:16 "For hands were lifted up to the t of

2Sa	7:13	the t of his kingdom forever.
1Ch	17:12	and I will establish his t forever.
Ps	11: 4	the LORD is on his heavenly t.
	45: 6	Your t, O God,
	47: 8	God is seated on his holy t.
	89:14	justice are the foundation of your t;
	123: 1	to you whose t is in heaven.
Pr	20:28	through love his t is made secure.
Isa	6: 1	I saw the Lord seated on a t,
	66: 1	the LORD says: "Heaven is my t,
Jer	33:21	a descendant to reign on his t.
Eze	1:26	what looked like a t of sapphire,
	28: 2	I sit on the on the t of a god
Da	7: 9	His t was flaming with fire,
Mt	5:34	for it is God's t;
	19:28	Son of Man sits on his glorious t,
Lk	1:32	The Lord God will give him the t
Ac	7:49	" 'Heaven is my t,
Heb	1: 8	But about the Son he says, "Your t,
	4:16	Let us then approach the t of grace
	12: 2	at the right hand of the t of God.
Rev	2:13	where Satan has his t.
	3:21	the right to sit with me on my t,
	4: 2	there before me was a t in heaven
	4:10	They lay their crowns before the t
	5:13	on the t and to the Lamb be praise
	20:11	Then I saw a great white t
	22: 3	The t of God and of the Lamb will

THRONES [THRONE]

Mt	19:28	will also sit on twelve t,
Col	1:16	whether t or powers or rulers
Rev	4: 4	the throne were twenty-four other t,
	20: 4	I saw t on which were seated

THRONG

| Ps | 42: 4 | thanksgiving among the festive t. |
| Jer | 31: 8 | a great t will return. |

THROUGH

Ge	12: 3	on earth will be blessed t you."
	21:12	because it is t Isaac that
	22:18	and t your offspring all nations
Ex	14:22	and the Israelites went t the sea
Ps	72:17	All nations will be blessed t him,
Pr	16: 6	T love and faithfulness sin is atoned
Isa	43: 2	When you walk t the fire,
Mt	1:18	to be with child t the Holy Spirit.
Jn	10: 9	whoever enters t me will be saved.
	14: 6	comes to the Father except t me.
Ro	5: 1	since we have been justified t faith,
1Co	8: 6	Jesus Christ, t whom all things came and t whom we live.
Eph	2: 8	by grace you have been saved, t faith

THROW [THREW, THROWN]

Ex	1:22	you must t into the Nile,
	4: 3	"T it on the ground."
Jos	24:23	"t away the foreign gods that are
Zec	11:13	"T it to the potter"—
Mt	5:30	cut it off and t it away.
	7: 6	do not t your pearls to pigs.
Jn	8: 7	be the first to t a stone at her."
Heb	10:35	So do not t away your confidence;

12: 1 let us **t** off everything that hinders

THROWN [THROW]
Da 3:21 and **t** into the blazing furnace.
   6:12 would be **t** into the lions' den?"
Rev 19:20 **t** alive into the fiery lake of burning
   20:10 was **t** into the lake of burning sulfur,
   20:14 Then death and Hades were **t** into

THRUST
2Ki 17:20 until he **t** them from his presence.
Isa 8:22 they will be **t** into utter darkness.

THUMMIM
Ex 28:30 Also put the Urim and the **T** in
Ezr 2:63 ministering with the Urim and **T**.

THUNDER [THUNDERED, THUNDERS]
Ex 9:23 the LORD sent **t** and hail,
   20:18 the people saw the **t** and lightning
Job 40: 9 and can your voice **t** like his?
Ps 93: 4 Mightier than the **t** of the great
Joel 3:16 from Zion and **t** from Jerusalem;
Mk 3:17 which means Sons of **T**);
Rev 4: 5 rumblings and peals of **t**.
   6: 1 in a voice like **t**,
   16:18 peals of **t** and a severe earthquake.

THUNDERCLOUD* [CLOUD]
Ps 81: 7 I answered you out of a **t**;

THUNDERED [THUNDER]
Ps 18:13 The LORD **t** from heaven;
Jn 12:29 and heard it said it had **t**;

THUNDERS [THUNDER]
Job 37: 5 God's voice **t** in marvelous ways;
Ps 29: 3 the God of glory **t**,
Jer 10:13 he **t**, the waters in the heavens roar;
Rev 10: 3 the voices of the seven **t** spoke.

THWART* [THWARTED, THWARTS]
Isa 14:27 and who can **t** him?

THWARTED* [THWART]
Job 42: 2 no plan of yours can be **t**.
Isa 8:10 but it will be **t**;

THWARTS [THWART]
Ps 33:10 he **t** the purposes of the peoples.

THYATIRA
Ac 16:14 in purple cloth from the city of **T**,
Rev 2:18 the angel of the church in **T** write:

TIBERIAS [GALILEE]
Jn 6: 1 Galilee (that is, the Sea of **T**),

TIBERIUS*
Lk 3: 1 of the reign of **T** Caesar—

TIBNI*
   King of Israel (1Ki 16:21-22).

TIDINGS
Isa 40: 9 You who bring good **t** to Zion,
   52: 7 who bring good **t**,

TIE [TIED, TIES]
Dt 6: 8 **T** them as symbols on your hands
   11:18 **t** them as symbols on your hands
Mt 23: 4 They **t** up heavy loads and put them

TIED [TIE]
Ge 38:28 a scarlet thread and **t** it on his wrist
Jos 2:21 she **t** the scarlet cord in the window.
Mk 9:42 into the sea with a large millstone **t**
Lk 19:30 you will find a colt there, **t**

TIES [TIE]
Hos 11: 4 of human kindness, with **t** of love;
Mt 12:29 unless he first **t** up the strong man?

TIGHT* [TIGHTFISTED]
Jas 1:26 not keep a **t** rein on his tongue,

TIGHTFISTED* [TIGHT]
Dt 15: 7 or **t** toward your poor brother.

TIGLATH-PILESER [PUL]
2Ki 16: 7 to say to **T** king of Assyria,
1Ch 5: 6 whom **T** king of Assyria took

TIGRIS*
Ge 2:14 The name of the third river is the **T**;
Da 10: 4 on the bank of the great river, the **T**,

TILES*
Lk 5:19 lowered him on his mat through the **t**

TIME [TIMES]
Ge 4:26 that **t** men began to call on the name
   6: 5 of his heart was only evil all the **t**.
Dt 32:35 In due **t** their foot will slip;
Ne 9:28 you delivered them **t** after **t**.
Est 4:14 to royal position for such a **t** as this?"
Ps 119:126 It is **t** for you to act, O LORD;
Ecc 3: 1 There is a **t** for everything,
   3:11 made everything beautiful in its **t**.
   8: 5 the wise heart will know the proper **t**
Da 7:25 for a **t**, times and half a **t**.
   12: 1 There will be a **t** of distress such
   12: 7 "It will be for a **t**, times and half a **t**.
Hos 10:12 for it is **t** to seek the LORD,
Lk 21: 8 'I am he,' and, 'The **t** is near.'
Jn 2: 4 "My **t** has not yet come."
   17: 1 the **t** has come.
Ro 5: 6 You see, at just the right **t**,
   9: 9 "At the appointed **t** I will return,
1Co 4: 5 At that **t** each will receive his praise
   7:29 brothers, is that the **t** is short.
2Co 6: 2 now is the **t** of God's favor,
Gal 4: 4 But when the **t** had fully come,
2Ti 1: 9 before the beginning of **t**,
Tit 1: 2 promised before the beginning of **t**,
Heb 9:28 and he will appear a second **t**,
   10:12 for all **t** one sacrifice for sins,
1Pe 4:17 For it is **t** for judgment to begin with

Rev 1: 3 because the **t** is near.
     2:21 I have given her **t** to repent
     3: 3 not know at what **t** I will come
   12:14 for a **t**, times and half a **t**,
   22:10 because the **t** is near.

APPOINTED TIME See APPOINTED

TIMES [TIME]

Ge 4:15 he will suffer vengeance seven **t** over."
Ex 23:14 "Three **t** a year you are to celebrate
Jos 6: 4 march around the city seven **t**,
Ps 9: 9 a stronghold in **t** of trouble.
  31:15 My **t** are in your hands;
  62: 8 Trust in him at all **t**, O people;
Pr 17:17 A friend loves at all **t**,
  24: 16 though a righteous man falls seven **t**,
Isa 46:10 from ancient **t**, what is still to come.
Da 7:25 for a time, **t** and half a time.
Am 5:13 quiet in such **t**, for the **t** are evil.
Mt 16: 3 cannot interpret the signs of the **t**.
  18:22 not seven times, but seventy-seven **t**.
Mk 4: 8 sixty, or even a hundred **t**."
  14:30 you yourself will disown me three **t**.
Lk 17: 4 If he sins against you seven **t** in
Ac 1: 7 not for you to know the **t** or dates
1Ti 4: 1 in later **t** some will abandon the faith
2Ti 3: 1 be terrible **t** in the last days.
Rev 5:11 ten thousand **t** ten thousand.
  12:14 for a time, **t** and half a time,

TIMID* [TIMIDITY]

2Co 10: 1 who am "**t**" when face to face
1Th 5:14 encourage the **t**, help the weak,

TIMIDITY* [TIMID]

2Ti 1: 7 For God did not give us a spirit of **t**,

TIMOTHY

Believer from Lystra (Ac 16:1). Joined Paul on second missionary journey (Ac 16-20). Sent to settle problems at Corinth (1Co 4:17; 16:10). Led church at Ephesus (1Ti 1:3). Co-writer with Paul (1Th 1:1; 2Th 1:1; Phm 1).

TIP

Job 33: 2 words are on the **t** of my tongue.

TIRE [TIRED]

2Th 3:13 never **t** of doing what is right.

TIRED [TIRE]

Ex 17:12 When Moses' hands grew **t**,
Isa 40:28 He will not grow **t** or weary,
Jn 4: 6 **t** as he was from the journey,

TIRZAH

1Ki 15:33 became king of all Israel in **T**,

TISHBITE

1Ki 17: 1 Now Elijah the **T**,
2Ki 1: 8 "That was Elijah the **T**."

TITHE [TEN]

Lev 27:30 " 'A **t** of everything from the land,

Nu 18:26 the **t** I give you as your inheritance,
Dt 12:17 the **t** of your grain and new wine
Ne 10:37 And we will bring a **t** of our crops to
Mal 3:10 the whole **t** into the storehouse,

TITHES [TEN]

Nu 18:21 all the **t** in Israel as their inheritance
Ne 10:37 for it is the Levites who collect the **t**
Mal 3: 8 "In **t** and offerings.

TITLE*

Isa 45: 4 and bestow on you a **t** of honor,
Eph 1:21 and every **t** that can be given,
Rev 17: 5 This **t** was written on her forehead:

TITTLE (KJV) See SMALLEST STROKE

TITUS*

Gentile co-worker of Paul (Gal 2:1-3; 2Ti 4:10); sent to Corinth (2Co 2:13; 7-8; 12:18), Crete (Tit 1:4-5).

TOBIAH

Enemy of Nehemiah and the exiles (Ne 2:10-19; 4; 6; 13:4-9).

TOBIJAH

Zec 6:14 The crown will be given to Heldai, **T**

TODAY

Ex 14:13 the deliverance the LORD will bring you **t**.
  34:11 Obey what I command you **t**.
Dt 5: 3 with all of us who are alive here **t**.
  30:15 I set before you **t** life and prosperity,
Ps 2: 7 **t** I have become your Father.
  95: 7 **T**, if you hear his voice,
Mt 6:11 Give us **t** our daily bread.
Lk 2:11 **T** in the town of David a Savior
  4:21 "**T** this scripture is fulfilled
  19: 9 "**T** salvation has come to this house,
  23:43 **t** you will be with me in paradise."
Ac 13:33 **t** I have become your Father.'
Heb 1: 5 **t** I have become your Father"?
  3: 7 "**T**, if you hear his voice,
  3:13 as long as it is called **T**,
  4: 7 set a certain day, calling it **T**,
  13: 8 Christ is the same yesterday and **t**

TOES

Da 2:42 As the **t** were partly iron

TOGETHER

Ge 3: 7 so they sewed fig leaves **t**
Dt 22:10 with an ox and a donkey yoked **t**.
Ps 2: 2 rulers gather **t** against the LORD and
  85:10 Love and faithfulness meet **t**;
  133: 1 when brothers live **t** in unity!
  139:13 you knit me **t** in my mother's womb.
Isa 1:18 "Come now, let us reason **t**,"
  11: 6 and the lion and the yearling **t**;
  65:25 The wolf and the lamb will feed **t**,
Eze 37: 7 and the bones came **t**, bone to bone.
Mt 19: 6 Therefore what God has joined **t**,
Ac 2:44 All the believers were **t**

	4:26	the rulers gather t against the Lord
	5:12	And all the believers used to meet t
2Co	6:14	Do not be yoked t with unbelievers.
Eph	3: 6	the Gentiles are heirs t with Israel,
Rev	16:16	Then they gathered the kings t to

TOIL [TOILED, TOILING]

Ge	3:17	through painful t you will eat
	5:29	and painful t of our hands caused by
Ecc	3:13	and find satisfaction in all his t—

TOILED [TOIL]

| 2Co | 11:27 | I have labored and t and have |

TOILING [TOIL]

| 2Th | 3: 8 | t so that we would not be a burden |

TOLA

A judge of Israel (Jdg 10:1-2).

TOLD [TELL]

Ge	3:11	"Who t you that you were naked?
	22: 9	the place God had t him about,
Dt	1:18	I t you everything you were to do.
Jdg	16:17	So he t her everything.
1Ki	10: 7	Indeed, not even half was t me;
Ps	44: 1	our fathers have t us what you did
Isa	48: 5	I t you these things long ago;
Lk	2:20	which were just as they had been t.
Jn	14:29	I have t you now before it happens,

TOLERANCE* [TOLERATE]

| Ro | 2: 4 | riches of his kindness, t and patience, |

TOLERATE [TOLERANCE]

| Hab | 1:13 | you cannot t wrong. |
| Rev | 2: 2 | that you cannot t wicked men, |

TOMB [TOMBS]

Mt	27:65	the t as secure as you know how."
Mk	15:46	and placed it in a t cut out of rock.
Lk	24: 2	the stone rolled away from the t,

TOMBS [TOMB]

| Mt | 23:29 | You build t for the prophets |
| | 27:52 | The t broke open and the bodies |

TOMORROW

Pr	27: 1	Do not boast about t,
Isa	22:13	you say, "for t we die!"
Mt	6:34	Therefore do not worry about t,
	6:34	for t will worry about itself.
1Co	15:32	"Let us eat and drink, for t we die."
Jas	4:14	not even know what will happen t.

TONGUE [TONGUES]

Ex	4:10	I am slow of speech and t."
Job	33: 2	words are on the tip of my t.
Ps	5: 9	with their t they speak deceit.
	34:13	keep your t from evil and your lips
	37:30	and his t speaks what is just.
	39: 1	and keep my t from sin;
	51:14	my t will sing of your righteousness.
	52: 4	O you deceitful t!
	71:24	My t will tell of your righteous

119:172	May my t sing of your word,
137: 6	May my t cling to the roof
139: 4	on my t you know it completely,
Pr	6:17	haughty eyes, a lying t,
	10:19	but he who holds his t is wise.
	11:12	a man of understanding holds his t.
	12:18	but the t of the wise brings healing.
	15: 4	t that brings healing is a tree of life,
	17:28	and discerning if he holds his t.
	18:21	t has the power of life and death,
	25:15	and a gentle t can break a bone.
	26:28	A lying t hates those it hurts,
	28:23	than he who has a flattering t.
	31:26	and faithful instruction is on her t.
SS	4:11	and honey are under your t.
Isa	32: 4	and the stammering t will be fluent
	45:23	by me every t will swear.
	50: 4	LORD has given me an instructed t,
	59: 3	and your t mutters wicked things.
Mk	7:33	he spit and touched the man's t.
Lk	16:24	of his finger in water and cool my t,
Ro	14:11	every t will confess
1Co	14: 2	For anyone who speaks in a t does
	14: 4	He who speaks in a t edifies himself,
	14: 9	speak intelligible words with your t,
	14:13	who speaks in a t should pray
	14:19	than ten thousand words in a t.
	14:26	a revelation, a t or an interpretation.
	14:27	If anyone speaks in a t, two—
Php	2:11	and every t confess that Jesus
Jas	1:26	not keep a tight rein on his t,
	3: 5	the t is a small part of the body,
	3: 8	but no man can tame the t.
1Jn	3:18	let us not love with words or t but

TONGUES [TONGUE]

Jdg	7: 5	the water with their t like a dog
Ps	12: 4	"We will triumph with our t;
	126: 2	our t with songs of joy.
Isa	28:11	and strange t God will speak
	66:18	to come and gather all nations and t,
Jer	23:31	the prophets who wag their own t
Ac	2: 3	what seemed to be t of fire
	2: 4	and began to speak in other t
	10:46	For they heard them speaking in t
	19: 6	and they spoke in t and prophesied.
Ro	3:13	their t practice deceit."
1Co	12:10	speaking in different kinds of t,
	12:10	another the interpretation of t.
	12:28	speaking in different kinds of t.
	12:30	Do all speak in t?
	13: 1	in the t of men and of angels,
	13: 8	where there are t,
	14: 5	like every one of you to speak in t,
	14: 5	greater than one who speaks in t,
	14:18	that I speak in t more than all
	14:21	"Through men of strange t and
	14:39	and do not forbid speaking in t.

TOOK [TAKE]

Ge	2:21	he t one of the man's ribs
	3: 6	she t some and ate it.
	5:24	because God t him away.
Jos	11:16	So Joshua t this entire land:

Ps   78:70 and t him from the sheep pens;
Isa 53: 4 Surely he t up our infirmities
Da   7: 9 and the Ancient of Days t his seat.
Mt   4: 5 the devil t him to the holy city
      4: 8 the devil t him to a very high
      8:17 "He t up our infirmities
     26:26 Jesus t bread, gave thanks
     26:27 Then he t the cup,
1Co 11:23 the night he was betrayed, t bread,
     11:25 after supper he t the cup, saying,
Php   3:12 for which Christ Jesus t hold of me.

TOOTH [TEETH]

Ex   21:24 eye for eye, t for t,
Lev 24:20 eye for eye, t for t.
Mt   5:38 'Eye for eye, and t for t.'

TOP [TOPS]

Ge   28:12 with its t reaching to heaven,
Ex   19:20 Moses to the t of the mountain.
Dt   28:13 you will always be at the t,
Isa   1: 6 From the sole of your foot to the t
Mt   27:51 of the temple was torn in two from t
Jn   19:23 woven in one piece from t to bottom.

TOPHETH

2Ki 23:10 He desecrated T,
Jer 19:12 I will make this city like T.

TOPPLE

Isa 40:20 to set up an idol that will not t.

TOPS [TOP]

Ex   12: 7 the sides and t of the doorframes

TORCH [TORCHES]

Ge   15:17 with a blazing t appeared and passed
Isa 62: 1 her salvation like a blazing t.
Rev   8:10 and a great star, blazing like a t,

TORCHES [TORCH]

Eze   1:13 like burning coals of fire or like t.
Da   10: 6 his eyes like flaming t,

TORE [TEAR]

Ge   37:34 Then Jacob t his clothes,
Jos   7: 6 Then Joshua t his clothes
1Ki 14: 8 I t the kingdom away from
Mt   26:65 the high priest t his clothes and said,

TORMENT [TORMENTED, TORMENTORS]

Job 15:20 the wicked man suffers t,
Lk   16:28 not also come to this place of t.'
2Co 12: 7 a messenger of Satan, to t me.

TORMENTED [TORMENT]

1Sa 16:14 an evil spirit from the LORD t him.
Rev 11:10 these two prophets had t those who
     20:10 They will be t day and night for ever

TORMENTORS* [TORMENT]

Ps 137: 3 our t demanded songs of joy;
Isa 51:23 I will put it into the hands of your t,

TORN [TEAR]

Ge   37:33 Joseph has surely been t to pieces."
Lev 22: 8 not eat anything found dead or t
1Sa 28:17 The LORD has t the kingdom out
Mk   1:10 he saw heaven being t open and
Lk   23:45 curtain of the temple was t in two.
Gal   4:15 you would have t out your eyes
Php   1:23 I am t between the two:

TORTURE [TORTURED]

Mt   8:29 "Have you come here to t us before
Rev 18: 7 as much t and grief as the glory

TORTURED* [TORTURE]

Mt   18:34 over to the jailers to be t,
Heb 11:35 Others were t and refused to

TOSS [TOSSED, TOSSING]

Mt   15:26 children's bread and t it to their dogs

TOSSED [TOSS]

Eph   4:14 t back and forth by the waves,
Jas   1: 6 blown and t by the wind.

TOSSING [TOSS]

Isa 57:20 But the wicked are like the t sea,

TOTAL [TOTALLY]

Ex   38:26 a t of 603,550 men.
Nu   26:51 t number of the men of Israel

TOTALLY [TOTAL]

Nu   16:30 LORD brings about something t new,
Dt   7: 2 then you must destroy them t.
Am   9: 8 yet I will not t destroy

TOUCH [TOUCHED, TOUCHES]

Ge   3: 3 and you must not t it,
Ex   19:12 not go up the mountain or t the foot
Nu   4:15 not t the holy things or they will die.
Ps 105:15 "Do not t my anointed ones;
Isa 52:11 T no unclean thing!
Eze   9: 6 do not t anyone who has the mark.
Mt   9:21 "If I only t his cloak,
Lk   18:15 to Jesus to have him t them.
     24:39 T me and see;
2Co   6:17 T no unclean thing,
Col   2:21 Do not t!"?
Heb 11:28 would not t the firstborn of Israel.

TOUCHED [TOUCH]

Ge   32:25 he t the socket of Jacob's hip so
1Sa 10:26 valiant men whose hearts God had t.
Isa   6: 7 With it he t my mouth and said,
Jer   1: 9 and t my mouth and said to me,
Da   10:16 one who looked like a man t my lips,
Mt   8: 3 Jesus reached out his hand and t
     14:36 and all who t him were healed.
Mk   5:30 "Who t my clothes?"
Ac   19:12 that had t him were taken to the sick,
1Jn   1: 1 looked at and our hands have t—

TOUCHES [TOUCH]

Ex   19:12 Whoever t the mountain shall surely

Ps   104:32   who **t** the mountains,
Am   9: 5   he who **t** the earth and it melts,
Zec   2: 8   whoever **t** you **t** the apple of his eye

TOWER [WATCHTOWER]

Ge   11: 4   with a **t** that reaches to the heavens,
Ps   61: 3   a strong **t** against the foe.
Pr   18:10   name of the LORD is a strong **t**;
Lk   14:28   one of you wants to build a **t**.

TOWN [HOMETOWN, TOWNS]

Ezr   2: 1   each to his own **t**,
Ne   7: 6   each to his own **t**,
Mt   2:23   and lived in a **t** called Nazareth.
Lk   2: 3   And everyone went to his own **t**
       2:11   Today in the **t** of David

TOWNS [TOWN]

Nu   35: 2   to give the Levites **t** to live in
      35:15   These six **t** will be a place of refuge
Jos   14: 4   of the land but only **t** to live in,
Jer   11:13   as many gods as you have **t**,
Mt   9:35   through all the **t** and villages,

TRACE [TRACED, TRACING]

Heb   7: 6   did not **t** his descent from Levi,

TRACED* [TRACE]

Ro   9: 5   is **t** the human ancestry of Christ,

TRACING* [TRACE]

Ro   11:33   and his paths beyond **t** out!

TRACK

Job   14:16   but not keep **t** of my sin.

TRADE [TRADED, TRADERS, TRADING]

Ge   42:34   and you can **t** in the land.' "
Isa   23:17   as a prostitute and will ply her **t**
Rev   18:22   No workman of any **t** will ever

TRADED [TRADE]

Joel   3: 3   and **t** boys for prostitutes;

TRADERS [TRADE]

1Ti   1:10   for slave **t** and liars and perjurers—

TRADING [TRADE]

1Ki   10:22   The king had a fleet of **t** ships at sea
Pr   31:18   She sees that her **t** is profitable,

TRADITION [TRADITIONS]

Mt   15: 2   "Why do your disciples break the **t**
Mk   7:13   nullify the word of God by your **t**
Col   2: 8   on human **t** and the basic principles

TRADITIONS [TRADITION]

Mk   7: 8   and are holding on to the **t**
Gal   1:14   and was extremely zealous for the **t**

TRAIL

1Ti   5:24   the sins of others **t** behind them.

TRAIN* [TRAINED, TRAINING, TRAINS]

Ps   68:18   you led captives in your **t**;
Pr   22: 6   **T** a child in the way he should go,
Isa   2: 4   nor will they **t** for war anymore.
       6: 1   the **t** of his robe filled the temple.
Mic   4: 3   nor will they **t** for war anymore.
Eph   4: 8   he led captives in his **t**
1Ti   4: 7   **t** yourself to be godly.
Tit   2: 4   Then they can **t** the younger women

TRAINED [TRAIN]

Lk   6:40   but everyone who is fully **t** will be
Ac   22: 3   Under Gamaliel I was thoroughly **t**
2Co   11: 6   I may not be a **t** speaker,
Heb   5:14   by constant use have **t** themselves
      12:11   peace for those who have been **t** by

TRAINING* [TRAIN]

1Co   9:25   in the games goes into strict **t**.
Eph   6: 4   in the **t** and instruction of the Lord.
1Ti   4: 8   For physical **t** is of some value,
2Ti   3:16   correcting and **t** in righteousness,

TRAINS* [TRAIN]

2Sa   22:35   He **t** my hands for battle;
Ps   18:34   He **t** my hands for battle;
     144: 1   who **t** my hands for war,

TRAITOR [TREASON]

Lk   6:16   and Judas Iscariot, who became a **t**.
Jn   18: 5   (And Judas the **t** was standing there

TRAITORS [TREASON]

Ps   59: 5   show no mercy to wicked **t**.

TRAMPLE [TRAMPLED]

Dt   33:29   you will **t** down their high places."
Ps   44: 5   through your name we **t** our foes.
Joel   3:13   Come, **t** the grapes,
Am   2: 7   They **t** on the heads of the poor as
       5:11   You **t** on the poor and force him
       8: 4   you who **t** the needy and do away
Mt   7: 6   they may **t** them under their feet,
Lk   10:19   to **t** on snakes and scorpions and
Rev   11: 2   They will **t** on the holy city

TRAMPLED [TRAMPLE]

2Ki   9:33   the horses as they **t** her underfoot.
Isa   63: 6   I **t** the nations in my anger;
Da   7: 7   and **t** underfoot whatever was left.
       8: 7   to the ground and **t** on him,
       8:10   down to the earth and **t** on them.
Mt   5:13   to be thrown out and **t** by men.
Lk   21:24   be **t** on by the Gentiles until
Heb   10:29   who has **t** the Son of God under foot,
Rev   14:20   They were **t** in the winepress outside

TRANCE*

Ac   10:10   he fell into a **t**.
      11: 5   and in a **t** I saw a vision.
      22:17   at the temple, I fell into a **t**

TRANQUILLITY*

Ecc   4: 6   with **t** than two handfuls with toil

TRANSACTION* [TRANSACTIONS]
Jer 32:25 and have the **t** witnessed.' "

TRANSACTIONS* [TRANSACTION]
Ru   4: 7 the method of legalizing **t** in Israel.)

TRANSCENDS*
Php 4: 7 which **t** all understanding,

TRANSFER*
Ru   4: 7 for the redemption and **t** of property
2Sa 3:10 and **t** the kingdom from the house

TRANSFIGURED*
Mt 17: 2 There he was **t** before them.
Mk   9: 2 There he was **t** before them.

TRANSFORM* [TRANSFORMED]
Php 3:21 will **t** our lowly bodies so

TRANSFORMED [TRANSFORM]
Ro 12: 2 be **t** by the renewing of your mind.
2Co 3:18 are being **t** into his likeness

TRANSGRESSED*
[TRANSGRESSION]
Da   9:11 All Israel has **t** your law

TRANSGRESSION*
[TRANSGRESSED, TRANSGRESSIONS,
TRANSGRESSORS]
Ps 19:13 innocent of great **t.**
Isa 53: 8 the **t** of my people he was stricken.
Da   9:24 and your holy city to finish **t,**
Mic 1: 5 All this is because of Jacob's **t,**
     1: 5 What is Jacob's **t?**
     3: 8 to declare to Jacob his **t,**
     6: 7 Shall I offer my firstborn for my **t,**
     7:18 who pardons sin and forgives the **t**
Ro   4:15 where there is no law there is no **t.**
    11:11 Rather, because of their **t,**
    11:12 if their **t** means riches for the world,

TRANSGRESSIONS*
[TRANSGRESSION]
Ps 32: 1 Blessed is he whose **t** are forgiven,
    32: 1 "I will confess my **t** to
    39: 8 Save me from all my **t;**
    51: 1 your great compassion blot out my **t.**
    51: 3 For I know my **t,**
    65: 3 you forgave our **t.**
   103:12 so far has he removed our **t** from us.
Isa 43:25 even I, am he who blots out your **t**
    50: 1 of your **t** your mother was sent away.
    53: 5 But he was pierced for our **t,**
Mic 1:13 the beginning of sin to the Daughter
Ro   4: 7 are they whose **t** are forgiven,
Gal 3:19 It was added because of **t** until
Eph 2: 1 you were dead in your **t** and sins,
     2: 5 even when we were dead in **t—**

TRANSGRESSORS*
[TRANSGRESSION]
Ps 51:13 Then I will teach **t** your ways,
Isa 53:12 and was numbered with the **t.**
    53:12 and made intercession for the **t.**
Lk 22:37 'And he was numbered with the **t';**

TRANSPARENT*
Rev 21:21 of pure gold, like **t** glass.

TRAP [TRAPPED, TRAPS]
Ps 31: 4 Free me from the **t** that is set for me,
    69:22 may it become retribution and a **t.**
Pr 20:25 It is a **t** for a man to dedicate
    28:10 an evil path will fall into his own **t,**
Isa 8:14 of Jerusalem he will be a **t** and
Mt 22:15 and laid plans to **t** him in his words.
Lk 21:34 close on you unexpectedly like a **t.**
Ro 11: 9 their table become a snare and a **t,**
1Ti 3: 7 into disgrace and into the devil's **t.**
     6: 9 to get rich fall into temptation and a **t**
2Ti 2:26 and escape from the **t** of the devil,

TRAPPED [TRAP]
Pr   6: 2 if you have been **t** by what you said,
    11: 6 the unfaithful are **t** by evil desires.
    12:13 An evil man is **t** by his sinful talk,

TRAPS [TRAP]
Jos 23:13 they will become snares and **t**
La   4:20 was caught in their **t.**

TRAVEL [TRAVELED, TRAVELER]
Ex 13:21 so that they could **t** by day or night.
Pr   4:15 Avoid it, do not **t** on it;
Mt 23:15 You **t** over land and sea to win

TRAVELED [TRAVEL]
Ge 12: 6 Abram **t** through the land as far as
Ex 15:22 For three days they **t** in the desert
1Ki 19: 8 he **t** forty days and forty nights

TRAVELER [TRAVEL]
Job 31:32 my door was always open to the **t—**
Jer 14: 8 like a **t** who stays only a night?

TREACHEROUS [TREASON]
Ps 25: 3 to shame who are **t** without excuse.
Isa 24:16 With treachery the **t** betray!"
Hab 1:13 Why then do you tolerate the **t?**
2Ti 3: 4 **t,** rash, conceited, lovers of pleasure

TREACHERY [TREASON]
Isa 59:13 rebellion and **t** against the LORD,

TREAD [TREADING, TREADS]
Ps 91:13 You will **t** upon the lion and
Mic 7:19 you will **t** our sins underfoot

TREADING [TREAD]
Dt 25: 4 Do not muzzle an ox while it is **t** out
1Co 9: 9 not muzzle an ox while it is **t** out
1Ti 5:18 not muzzle the ox while it is **t** out

TREADS [TREAD]

Am 4:13 and **t** the high places of the earth—
Rev 19:15 He **t** the winepress of the fury of

TREASON [TRAITOR, TRAITORS, TREACHEROUS, TREACHERY]

2Ki 11:14 her robes and called out, "**T! T!**"

TREASURE [TREASURED, TREASURES, TREASURIES, TREASURY]

Pr 2:4 and search for it as for hidden **t,**
Isa 33:6 fear of the LORD is the key to this **t.**
Mt 6:21 For where your **t** is,
     13:44 of heaven is like **t** hidden in a field.
     19:21 and you will have **t** in heaven.
Lk 12:33 a **t** in heaven that will not
2Co 4:7 But we have this **t** in jars of clay
1Ti 6:19 In this way they will lay up **t**

TREASURED* [TREASURE]

Ex 19:5 you will be my **t** possession.
Dt 7:6 his people, his **t** possession.
     14:2 chosen you to be his **t** possession.
     26:18 his **t** possession as he promised,
Job 23:12 I have **t** the words
Ps 135:4 Israel to be his **t** possession.
Isa 64:11 and all that we **t** lies in ruins.
Eze 7:22 and they will desecrate my **t** place;
Mal 3:17 when I make up my **t** possession.
Lk 2:19 But Mary **t** up all these things
     2:51 But his mother **t** all these things

TREASURES [TREASURE]

Dt 33:19 on the **t** hidden in the sand."
2Ki 20:13 and everything found among his **t.**
     24:13 the **t** from the temple of the LORD
1Ch 29:3 of my God I now give my personal **t**
Pr 10:2 Ill-gotten **t** are of no value,
Isa 45:3 I will give you the **t** of darkness,
Mt 2:11 Then they opened their **t**
     6:19 "Do not store up for yourselves **t**
     13:52 new **t** as well as old."
Col 2:3 all the **t** of wisdom and knowledge.
Heb 11:26 as of greater value than the **t**

TREASURIES [TREASURE]

2Ch 16:2 out of the **t** of the LORD's temple
Pr 8:21 and making their **t** full.

TREASURY [TREASURE]

Ezr 2:69 to their ability they gave to the **t**
Mt 27:6 against the law to put this into the **t,**
Mk 12:43 poor widow has put more into the **t**

TREAT [TREATED, TREATING, TREATMENT]

Lev 22:2 to **t** with respect the sacred offerings
Nu 14:11 these people **t** me with contempt?
Ps 103:10 not **t** us as our sins deserve
Mt 18:17 **t** him as you would a pagan or
     18:35 how my heavenly Father will **t** each

Jn 15:21 They will **t** you this way because
Eph 6:9 **t** your slaves in the same way.
1Th 5:20 do not **t** prophecies with contempt.
1Ti 5:1 **T** younger men as brothers,
1Pe 3:7 and **t** them with respect as

TREATED [TREAT]

Ge 12:16 He **t** Abram well for her sake,
Ex 18:11 to those who had **t** Israel arrogantly."
Lev 19:34 The alien living with you must be **t**
     25:40 He is to be **t** as a hired worker or
1Sa 24:17 "You have **t** me well,
Lk 6:23 how their fathers **t** the prophets.
Heb 10:29 who has **t** as an unholy thing
Rev 18:20 judged her for the way she **t** you.' "

TREATING [TREAT]

Ge 18:25 **t** the righteous and the wicked alike.
Heb 12:7 as discipline; God is **t** you as sons.

TREATMENT [TREAT]

Col 2:23 their false humility and their harsh **t**

TREATY

Ex 34:12 not to make a **t** with those who live
Dt 7:2 Make no **t** with them,
     23:6 not seek a **t** of friendship with them
Jos 9:6 make a **t** with us."
Am 1:9 disregarding a **t** of brotherhood,

TREE [TREES]

Ge 1:29 and every **t** that has fruit with seed
     2:9 the **t** of life and the **t** of the
          knowledge of good and evil.
     3:1 not eat from any **t** in the garden'?"
     3:24 to guard the way to the **t** of life.
Dt 21:23 hung on a **t** is under God's curse.
2Sa 18:9 Absalom's head got caught in the **t.**
1Ki 14:23 and under every spreading **t.**
     19:4 He came to a broom **t,**
Ps 1:3 like a **t** planted by streams of water,
     52:8 But I am like an olive **t** flourishing
     92:12 righteous will flourish like a palm **t,**
Pr 3:18 a **t** of life to those who embrace her;
     11:30 fruit of the righteous is a **t** of life,
     27:18 He who tends a fig **t** will eat its fruit,
Isa 65:22 For as the days of a **t,**
Jer 17:8 be like a **t** planted by the water
Eze 17:24 that I the LORD bring down the tall **t**
Da 4:10 and there before me stood a **t**
Hos 9:10 like seeing the early fruit on the fig **t.**
     14:6 His splendor will be like an olive **t,**
Mic 4:4 and under his own fig **t,**
Hab 3:17 Though the fig **t** does not bud
Zec 3:10 to sit under his vine and fig **t,**'
Mt 3:10 and every **t** that does not produce
     12:33 for a **t** is recognized by its fruit.
Mk 11:13 Seeing in the distance a fig **t** in leaf,
Lk 19:4 climbed a sycamore-fig **t** to see him,
Ac 5:30 killed by hanging him on a **t.**
Ro 11:24 grafted into a cultivated olive **t,**
Gal 3:13 who is hung on a **t.**"
Jas 3:12 My brothers, can a fig **t** bear olives,
1Pe 2:24 bore our sins in his body on the **t,**

Rev   2: 7 the right to eat from the **t** of life,
     22: 2 side of the river stood the **t** of life,
     22:14 the right to the **t** of life
     22:19 share in the **t** of life and in the holy

TREES [TREE]

Ge   1:11 and **t** on the land that bear fruit
      3: 2 "We may eat fruit from the **t** in
Dt   20:19 do not destroy its **t** by putting an ax
Jdg   9: 8 One day the **t** went out to anoint
1Ch 14:15 marching in the tops of the balsam **t**,
Ps   96:12 Then all the **t** of the forest will sing
Isa 55:12 **t** of the field will clap their hands.
Eze 47:12 Fruit of all kinds will grow on
Zec   4:11 "What are these two olive **t** on
Mt   3:10 The ax is already at the root of the **t**,
Mk   8:24 they look like **t** walking around."
Jude 1:12 autumn **t**, without fruit and uprooted
Rev   8: 7 a third of the **t** were burned up,
     11: 4 the two olive **t** and the two

TREMBLE [TREMBLED, TREMBLES, TREMBLING]

Ex   15:14 The nations will hear and **t**;
1Ch 16:30 **T** before him, all the earth!
Ps   99: 1 LORD reigns, let the nations **t**;
    114: 7 **T**, O earth, at the presence of
Jer   5:22 "Should you not **t** in my presence?
Eze 38:20 of the earth will **t** at my presence.
Joel 2: 1 Let all who live in the land **t**,
Hab   3: 6 and made the nations **t**.

TREMBLED [TREMBLE]

Ex   19:16 Everyone in the camp **t**.
     20:18 they **t** with fear.
2Sa 22: 8 "The earth **t** and quaked,
Ac   7:32 Moses **t** with fear and did not dare

TREMBLES [TREMBLE]

Ps   97: 4 the earth sees and **t**.
    104:32 who looks at the earth, and it **t**,
    119:161 but my heart **t** at your word.
Isa 66: 2 and **t** at my word.
Jer 10:10 When he is angry, the earth **t**;
Na   1: 5 The earth **t** at his presence,

TREMBLING [TREMBLE]

Ps   2:11 with fear and rejoice with **t**.
Da   10:10 and set me **t** on my hands and knees.
Mk   16: 8 **T** and bewildered, the women went
Php   2:12 your salvation with fear and **t**,
Heb 12:21 "I am **t** with fear."

TRENCH

1Ki 18:38 and also licked up the water in the **t**.
Da   9:25 It will be rebuilt with streets and a **t**,

TRESPASS* [TRESPASSES]

Ro   5:15 But the gift is not like the **t**.
      5:15 many died by the **t** of the one man,
      5:17 For if, by the **t** of the one man,
      5:18 the result of one **t** was condemnation
      5:20 added so that the **t** might increase.

TRESPASSES* [TRESPASS]

Ro   5:16 but the gift followed many **t**

TRIAL [TRIALS]

Nu   35:12 may not die before he stands **t**
Ps   37:33 be condemned when brought to **t**.
Mk   13:11 arrested and brought to **t**,
2Co   8: 2 Out of the most severe **t**,
Jas   1:12 the man who perseveres under **t**,
1Pe   4:12 at the painful **t** you are suffering,
Rev   3:10 of **t** that is going to come

TRIALS* [TRIAL]

Dt   7:19 with your own eyes the great **t**,
     29: 3 your own eyes you saw those great **t**,
Lk   22:28 who have stood by me in my **t**.
1Th   3: 3 would be unsettled by these **t**.
2Th   1: 4 persecutions and **t** you are enduring.
Jas   1: 2 whenever you face **t** of many kinds,
1Pe   1: 6 to suffer grief in all kinds of **t**.
2Pe   2: 9 how to rescue godly men from **t** and

TRIBAL [TRIBE]

Jos 11:23 Israel according to their **t** divisions.

TRIBE [HALF-TRIBE, TRIBAL, TRIBES]

Nu   1: 4 One man from each **t**,
     17: 3 for the head of each ancestral **t**.
     36: 9 No inheritance may pass from **t** to **t**,
Jos 13:14 the **t** of Levi he gave no inheritance,
Jdg 21: 6 "Today one **t** is cut off from Israel,"
1Ki 11:13 but will give him one **t** for the sake
Ps   78:68 but he chose the **t** of Judah,
Heb   7:13 that **t** has ever served at the altar.
Rev   5: 5 See, the Lion of the **t** of Judah,
      5: 9 purchased men for God from every **t**
     11: 9 men from every people, **t**,
     14: 6 **t**, language and people.

TRIBE OF JUDAH See JUDAH

TRIBES [TRIBE]

Ge   49:28 All these are the twelve **t** of Israel,
Ex   24: 4 pillars representing the twelve **t**
     39:14 with the name of one of the twelve **t**.
1Ki 11:31 and give you ten **t**.
     18:31 twelve stones, one for each of the **t**
Ps 122: 4 That is where the **t** go up,
Isa 49: 6 to be my servant to restore the **t**
Mt   19:28 judging the twelve **t** of Israel.
Jas   1: 1 To the twelve **t** scattered among
Rev 21:12 the names of the twelve **t** of Israel.

TRIBES OF ISRAEL See ISRAEL

TRIBULATION*

Rev   7:14 who have come out of the great **t**;

TRIBUTE

Nu   31:28 set apart as **t** for the LORD one out
1Ki   4:21 These countries brought **t**

TRICK* [TRICKERY]

1Th   2: 3 nor are we trying to **t** you.

TRICKERY* [TRICK]
Ac 13:10 of all kinds of deceit and **t**.
2Co 12:16 I caught you by **t**!

TRIED [TRY]
Ge 37:21 he **t** to rescue him from their hands.
Ex   2:15 he **t** to kill Moses,
       8:18 the magicians **t** to produce gnats
Dt   4:34 Has any god ever **t** to take
Ps 73:16 When I **t** to understand all this,
    95: 9 where your fathers tested and **t** me,
Jn   5:18 the Jews **t** all the harder to kill him;
  19:12 Pilate **t** to set Jesus free,
Gal   1:23 the faith he once **t** to destroy."
Heb 3: 9 where your fathers tested and **t** me

TRIES [TRY]
Lk 17:33 **t** to keep his life will lose it,

TRIMMED
Mt 25: 7 woke up and **t** their lamps.

TRIUMPH [TRIUMPHAL, TRIUMPHANT, TRIUMPHED, TRIUMPHING, TRIUMPHS]
Ps   9:19 Arise, O LORD, let not man **t**;
    25: 2 nor let my enemies **t** over me.
    54: 7 and my eyes have looked in **t**
  112: 8 in the end he will look in **t**
  118: 7 I will look in **t** on my enemies.
Pr 28:12 the righteous **t**, there is great elation;
Isa 42:13 and will **t** over his enemies.

TRIUMPHAL* [TRIUMPH]
Isa 60:11 their kings led in **t** procession.
2Co   2:14 in **t** procession in Christ

TRIUMPHANT* [TRIUMPH]
Da 11:12 yet he will not remain **t**.

TRIUMPHED [TRIUMPH]
Dt 32:27 'Our hand has **t**;
Rev   5: 5 the Root of David, has **t**.

TRIUMPHING* [TRIUMPH]
Col   2:15 **t** over them by the cross.

TRIUMPHS* [TRIUMPH]
Jas   2:13 Mercy **t** over judgment!

TRIVIAL*
1Ki 16:31 not only considered it **t** to commit
Eze   8:17 Is it a **t** matter for the house of Judah
1Co   6: 2 not competent to judge **t** cases?

TROOPS
Ex 14: 9 chariots, horsemen and **t**—
Ps 110: 3 Your **t** will be willing on your day
Rev   9:16 mounted **t** was two hundred million.

TROPHIMUS
2Ti   4:20 and I left **T** sick in Miletus.

TROUBLE [TROUBLED, TROUBLER, TROUBLES]
Ge 41:51 God has made me forget all my **t**
Nu 11:11 "Why have you brought this **t**
Jos   7:25 "Why have you brought this **t** on us?
1Ki 18:18 "I have not made **t** for Israel,"
Job   2:10 good from God, and not **t**?"
     5: 7 to **t** as surely as sparks fly upward.
    14: 1 is of few days and full of **t**.
   42:11 and consoled him over all the **t**
Ps   7:14 pregnant with evil and conceives **t**
    7:16 The **t** he causes recoils on himself;
    9: 9 a stronghold in times of **t**.
  10:14 But you, O God, do see **t** and grief;
  22:11 **t** is near and there is no one to help.
  27: 5 in the day of **t** he will keep me safe
  32: 7 you will protect me from **t**
  37:39 their stronghold in time of **t**.
  41: 1 the LORD delivers him in times of **t**.
  46: 1 an ever-present help in **t**.
  50:15 and call upon me in the day of **t**;
  59:16 my refuge in times of **t**.
  66:14 my mouth spoke when I was in **t**.
  86: 7 In the day of my **t** I will call to you,
  90:10 yet their span is but **t** and sorrow,
  91:15 I will be with him in **t**,
 107: 6 cried out to the LORD in their **t**,
 116: 3 I was overcome by **t** and sorrow.
 119:143 **T** and distress have come upon me,
 138: 7 Though I walk in the midst of **t**,
 143:11 bring me out of **t**.
Pr 11: 8 righteous man is rescued from **t**,
  11:17 but a cruel man brings **t** on himself.
  11:29 He who brings **t** on his family
  12:13 but a righteous man escapes **t**.
  12:21 but the wicked have their fill of **t**.
  15:27 A greedy man brings **t** to his family,
  19:23 one rests content, untouched by **t**.
  22: 8 He who sows wickedness reaps **t**,
  24:10 If you falter in times of **t**,
  25:19 on the unfaithful in times of **t**.
  28:14 he who hardens his heart falls into **t**.
Ecc 12: 1 before the days of **t** come
Jer 30: 7 It will be a time of **t** for Jacob,
Da   9:25 but in times of **t**.
Jnh 1: 8 for making all this **t** for us?
Na   1: 7 a refuge in times of **t**.
Zep 1:15 a day of **t** and ruin,
Mt   6:34 Each day has enough **t** of its own.
  13:21 When **t** or persecution comes
Jn 16:33 In this world you will have **t**.
Ro   8:35 Shall **t** or hardship or persecution
2Co 1: 4 that we can comfort those in any **t**
2Th 1: 6 will pay back **t** to those who **t** you
Jas   5:13 Is any one of you in **t**?

TROUBLED [TROUBLE]
Ps 38:18 I am **t** by my sin.
Isa 38:14 I am **t**; O Lord, come to my aid!"
Mk 14:33 to be deeply distressed and **t**.
Lk   1:29 Mary was greatly **t** at his words
Jn 14: 1 "Do not let your hearts be **t**.
  14:27 Do not let your hearts be **t**

2Th   1: 7   and give relief to you who are **t,**

TROUBLER* [TROUBLE]

1Ki 18:17   "Is that you, you **t** of Israel?"

TROUBLES [TROUBLE]

Ps   34: 6   saved him out of all his **t.**
     34:17   delivers them from all their **t.**
     34:19   A righteous man may have many **t,**
     40:12   For **t** without number surround me;
     54: 7   he has delivered me from all my **t,**
Isa   46: 7   cannot save him from his **t.**
1Co   7:28   those who marry will face many **t**
2Co   1: 4   who comforts us in all our **t,**
     4:17   and momentary **t** are achieving
     6: 4   in **t,** hardships and distresses;
     7: 4   in all our **t** my joy knows no bounds.
Php   4:14   it was good of you to share in my **t.**

TRUE [TRUTH]

Nu   11:23   what I say will come **t** for you."
     12: 7   this is not **t** of my servant Moses;
Dt   18:22   does not take place or come **t,**
Jos   23:15   of the LORD your God has come **t,**
1Sa   9: 6   and everything he says comes **t.**
1Ki   10: 6   and your wisdom is **t.**
2Ch   6:17   promised your servant David come **t.**
     15: 3   Israel was without the **t** God,
Job   11: 6   for **t** wisdom has two sides.
Ps   33: 4   word of the LORD is right and **t;**
   119:142   and your law is **t.**
   119:151   and all your commands are **t.**
   119:160   All your words are **t;**
   144:15   the people of whom this is **t;**
Pr   8: 7   My mouth speaks what is **t,**
     22:21   teaching you **t** and reliable words,
Ecc   12:10   what he wrote was upright and **t.**
Jer   10:10   But the LORD is the **t** God;
     28: 9   only if his prediction comes **t."**
     50: 7   their **t** pasture, the LORD,
Eze   33:33   "When all this comes **t—**
Mic   7:20   You will be **t** to Jacob,
Lk   1:20   my words, which will come **t**
     16:11   who will trust you with **t** riches?
Jn   1: 9   The **t** light that gives light
     4:23   when the **t** worshipers will worship
     6:32   the **t** bread from heaven.
     7:28   but he who sent me is **t.**
     15: 1   "I am the **t** vine,
     17: 3   the only **t** God, and Jesus Christ,
     19:35   and his testimony is **t.**
     21:24   We know that his testimony is **t.**
Ac   10:34   "I now realize how **t** it is that
     11:23   to remain **t** to the Lord with all their
     14:22   them to remain **t** to the faith.
     17:11   to see if what Paul said was **t.**
Ro   3: 4   Let God be **t,** and every man a liar.
Eph   4:24   to be like God in **t** righteousness
Php   4: 8   Finally, brothers, whatever is **t,**
1Th   1: 9   to serve the living and **t** God,
1Jn   2: 8   and the **t** light is already shining.
     5:20   so that we may know him who is **t.**
     5:20   And we are in him who is **t—**
     5:20   He is the **t** God and eternal life.

3Jn   1:12   you know that our testimony is **t.**
Rev   2:13   Yet you remain **t** to my name.
     3: 7   the words of him who is holy and **t,**
     3:14   the faithful and **t** witness,
     6:10   Sovereign Lord, holy and **t,**
     15: 3   Just and **t** are your ways,
     16: 7   **t** and just are your judgments."
     19: 2   for **t** and just are his judgments.
     19: 9   "These are the **t** words of God."
     19:11   whose rider is called Faithful and **T.**
     21: 5   these words are trustworthy and **t."**
     22: 6   "These words are trustworthy and **t.**

TRUMPET [TRUMPETERS, TRUMPETS]

Ex   19:16   and a very loud **t** blast.
Lev   23:24   commemorated with **t** blasts.
     25: 9   on the Day of Atonement sound the **t**
Nu   10: 5   When a **t** blast is sounded,
Isa   27:13   And in that day a great **t** will sound.
Eze   33: 5   of the **t** but did not take warning,
Joel   2:15   Blow the **t** in Zion,
Zec   9:14   Sovereign LORD will sound the **t;**
Mt   24:31   send his angels with a loud **t** call,
1Co   14: 8   if the **t** does not sound a clear call,
     15:52   For the **t** will sound,
1Th   4:16   and with the **t** call of God,
Rev   1:10   behind me a loud voice like a **t,**
     8: 7   The first angel sounded his **t,**

TRUMPETERS [TRUMPET]

2Ch   5:13   The **t** and singers joined in unison,

TRUMPETS [TRUMPET]

Nu   10: 2   "Make two **t** of hammered silver,
     29: 1   It is a day for you to sound the **t.**
Jos   6: 8   the seven priests carrying the seven **t**
Jdg   7:19   They blew their **t** and broke the jars
Ps   47: 5   the LORD amid the sounding of **t.**
Mt   6: 2   do not announce it with **t,**
Rev   8: 2   and to them were given seven **t.**

TRUST* [ENTRUST, ENTRUSTED, TRUSTED, TRUSTFULLY, TRUSTING, TRUSTS, TRUSTWORTHY]

Ex   14:31   the LORD and put their **t** in him
     19: 9   will always put their **t** in you."
Nu   20:12   not **t** in me enough to honor me
Dt   1:32   did not **t** in the LORD your God,
     9:23   You did not **t** him or obey him.
     28:52   walls in which you **t** fall down.
Jdg   11:20   did not **t** Israel to pass through
2Ki   17:14   not **t** in the LORD their God.
     18:30   not let Hezekiah persuade you to **t** in
1Ch   9:22   to their positions of **t** by David
Job   4:18   If God places no **t** in his servants,
     15:15   If God places no **t** in his holy ones,
     31:24   "If I have put my **t** in gold or said
     39:12   Can you **t** him to bring in your grain
Ps   4: 5   and **t** in the LORD.
     9:10   Those who know your name will **t**
     13: 5   But I **t** in your unfailing love;
     20: 7   Some **t** in chariots and some

20: 7 but we **t** in the name of
22: 4 In you our fathers put their **t;**
22: 9 you made me **t** in you even
25: 2 in you I **t,** O my God.
31: 6 I **t** in the LORD.
31:14 But I **t** in you, O LORD;
33:21 for we **t** in his holy name.
37: 3 **T** in the LORD and do good;
37: 5 **t** in him and he will do this:
40: 3 and put their **t** in the LORD.
40: 4 who makes the LORD his **t,**
44: 6 I do not **t** in my bow,
49: 6 those who **t** in their wealth and boast
49:13 This is the fate of those who **t**
52: 8 I **t** in God's unfailing love
55:23 But as for me, I **t** in you.
56: 3 When I am afraid, I will **t** in you.
56: 4 whose word I praise, in God I **t;**
56:11 in God I **t;** I will not be afraid.
62: 8 **T** in him at all times, O people;
62:10 Do not **t** in extortion or take pride
78: 7 Then they would put their **t** in God
78:22 for they did not believe in God or **t**
91: 2 my God, in whom I **t."**
115: 8 and so will all who **t** in them.
115: 9 O house of Israel, **t** in the LORD—
115:10 **t** in the LORD—
115:11 **t** in the LORD—
118: 8 in the LORD than to **t** in man.
118: 9 in the LORD than to **t** in princes.
119:42 for I **t** in your word.
125: 1 Those who **t** in the LORD are
135:18 and so will all who **t** in them.
143: 8 for I have put my **t** in you.
146: 3 Do not put your **t** in princes,
Pr 3: 5 **T** in the LORD with all your heart
21:22 down the stronghold in which they **t.**
22:19 So that your **t** may be in the LORD,
Isa 8:17 I will put my **t** in him.
12: 2 I will **t** and not be afraid.
26: 4 **T** in the LORD forever,
30:15 in quietness and **t** is your strength,
31: 1 who **t** in the multitude
36:15 not let Hezekiah persuade you to **t** in
42:17 But those who **t** in idols,
50:10 **t** in the name of the LORD and rely
Jer 2:37 LORD has rejected those you **t;**
5:17 the fortified cities in which you **t.**
7: 4 Do not **t** in deceptive words and say,
7:14 the temple you **t** in,
9: 4 do not **t** your brothers.
12: 6 Do not **t** them,
28:15 persuaded this nation to **t** in lies.
39:18 because you **t** in me,
48: 7 Since you **t** in your deeds and riches,
49: 4 you **t** in your riches and say,
49:11 Your widows too can **t** in me."
Mic 7: 5 Do not **t** a neighbor;
Na 1: 7 He cares for those who **t** in him,
Zep 3: 2 She does not **t** in the LORD,
3:12 who **t** in the name of the LORD.
Lk 16:11 who will **t** you with true riches?
Jn 12:36 Put your **t** in the light
14: 1 **T** in God; **t** also in me.

Ac 14:23 in whom they had put their **t.**
Ro 15:13 all joy and peace as you **t** in him,
1Co 4: 2 been given a **t** must prove faithful.
9:17 discharging the **t** committed to me.
2Co 13: 6 And I **t** that you will discover
Heb 2:13 And again, "I will put my **t** in him."

TRUSTED [TRUST]

1Sa 27:12 Achish **t** David and said to himself,
2Ki 18: 5 Hezekiah **t** in the LORD,
1Ch 5:20 because they **t** in him.
Job 12:20 He silences the lips of **t** advisers
Ps 5: 9 a word from their mouth can be **t;**
22: 4 they **t** and you delivered them.
22: 5 they **t** and were not disappointed.
26: 1 have **t** in the LORD without wavering.
41: 9 Even my close friend, whom I **t,**
52: 7 but **t** in his great wealth
Isa 20: 5 Those who **t** in Cush and boasted
25: 9 this is our God; we **t** in him,
25: 9 This is the LORD, we **t** in him;
47:10 You have **t** in your wickedness
Jer 13:25 and **t** in false gods.
38:22 and overcame you—those **t** friends
48:13 ashamed when they **t** in Bethel.
Eze 16:15 " 'But your **t** in your beauty
Da 3:28 They **t** in him and defied
6:23 because he had **t** in his God.
Lk 11:22 the armor in which the man **t**
16:10 "Whoever can be **t** with very little
can also be **t** with much,
Ac 12:20 a **t** personal servant of the king,
Tit 2:10 but to show that they can be fully **t,**
3: 8 so that those who have **t** in God may

TRUSTFULLY* [TRUST]

Pr 3:29 who lives **t** near you.

TRUSTING* [TRUST]

Job 15:31 by **t** what is worthless,
Ps 112: 7 **t** in the LORD.
Isa 2:22 Stop **t** in man,
Jer 7: 8 you are **t** in deceptive words

TRUSTS* [TRUST]

Job 8:14 What he **t** in is fragile;
Ps 21: 7 For the king **t** in the LORD;
22: 8 "He **t** in the LORD;
28: 7 my heart **t** in him, and I am helped.
32:10 the man who **t** in him.
84:12 blessed is the man who **t** in you.
86: 2 save your servant who **t** in you.
Pr 11:28 Whoever **t** in his riches will fall,
16:20 blessed is he who **t** in the LORD.
28:25 he who **t** in the LORD will prosper.
28:26 He who **t** in himself is a fool,
29:25 but whoever **t** in the LORD
Isa 26: 3 because he **t** in you.
28:16 who **t** will never be dismayed.
Jer 17: 5 "Cursed is the one who **t** in man,
17: 7 blessed is the man who **t** in the LORD
Eze 33:13 but then he **t** in his righteousness
Hab 2:18 who makes it **t** in his own creation;
Mt 27:43 He **t** in God.

Ro   4: 5 but t God who justifies the wicked,
         9:33 and the one who t in him will never
        10:11 "Anyone who t in him will never
1Co   13: 7 It always protects, always t,
1Pe   2: 6 and the one who t in him will never

TRUSTWORTHY* [TRUST]

Ex   18:21 t men who hate dishonest gain—
2Sa   7:28 Your words are t,
Ne   13:13 because these men were considered t
Ps   19: 7 The statutes of the LORD are t,
        111: 7 all his precepts are t.
       119:86 All your commands are t;
       119:138 are righteous; they are fully t.
Pr   11:13 but a t man keeps a secret.
        13:17 but a t envoy brings healing.
        25:13 t messenger to those who send him;
Da   2:45 and the interpretation is t."
         6: 4 because he was t and neither corrupt
Lk   16:11 So if you have not been t
        16:12 And if you have not been t
        19:17 'Because you have been t in
1Co   7:25 as one who by the Lord's mercy is t.
1Ti   1:15 Here is a t saying
         3: 1 Here is a t saying:
         3:11 but temperate and t in everything.
         4: 9 This is a t saying
2Ti   2:11 Here is a t saying:
Tit   1: 9 the t message as it has been taught,
         3: 8 This is a t saying.
Rev   21: 5 for these words are t and true."
        22: 6 "These words are t and true.

TRUTH *[TRUE, TRUTHFUL, TRUTHFULLY, TRUTHFULNESS, TRUTHS]

Ge   42:16 to see if you are telling the t.
1Ki   17:24 from your mouth is the t."
        22:16 swear to tell me nothing but the t
2Ch   18:15 swear to tell me nothing but the t
Ps   15: 2 who speaks the t from his heart
        25: 5 guide me in your t and teach me,
        26: 3 and I walk continually in your t.
        31: 5 O LORD, the God of t.
        40:10 and your t from the great assembly.
        40:11 and your t always protect me.
        43: 3 Send forth your light and your t,
        45: 4 ride forth victoriously in behalf of t,
        51: 6 you desire t in the inner parts;
        52: 3 falsehood rather than speaking the t.
        86:11 and I will walk in your t;
        96:13 and the peoples in his t.
       119:30 I have chosen the way of t;
       119:43 the word of t from my mouth,
       145:18 to all who call on him in t.
Pr   16:13 value a man who speaks the t.
        23:23 Buy the t and do not sell it;
Isa   45:19 I, the LORD, speak the t;
        48: 1 but not in t or righteousness—
        59:14 t has stumbled in the streets,
        59:15 T is nowhere to be found,
        65:16 the land will do so by the God of t;
        65:16 the land will swear by the God of t.

Jer   5: 1 deals honestly and seeks the t,
         5: 3 do not your eyes look for t?
         7:28 T has perished;
         9: 3 it is not by tthat they triumph
         9: 5 and no one speaks the t.
        26:15 in t the LORD has sent me to you
Da   8:12 and t was thrown to the ground.
         9:13 and giving attention to your t.
        10:21 what is written in the Book of T.
Am   5:10 and despise him who tells the t.
Zec   8: 3 be called the City of T,
         8:16 Speak the t to each other,
         8:19 Therefore love t and peace."
Mt   22:16 of God in accordance with the t.
Mk   5:33 told him the whole t.
        12:14 way of God in accordance with the t.
Lk   20:21 way of God in accordance with the t.
Jn   1:14 full of grace and t.
         1:17 grace and t came through Jesus
         3:21 But whoever lives by the t comes
         4:23 worship the Father in spirit and t,
         4:24 worship in spirit and in t."
         5:33 to John and he has testified to the t.
         7:18 the one who sent him is a man of t;
         8:32 Then you will know the t,
         8:32 and the t will set you free."
         8:40 a man who has told you the t
         8:44 not holding to the t,
         8:44 for there is no t in him.
         8:45 I tell the t, you do not believe me!
         8:46 If I am telling the t,
        14: 6 "I am the way and the t and the life.
        14:17 the Spirit of t.
        15:26 the Spirit of t who goes out from
        16:13 But when he, the Spirit of t, comes,
        16:13 comes, he will guide you into all t.
        17:17 Sanctify them by the t; your word
               is t.
        18:23 But if I spoke the t,
        18:37 to testify to the t.
        18:37 Everyone on the side of t listens
        18:38 "What is t?"
        19:35 He knows that he tells the t,
Ac   20:30 men will arise and distort the t
        21:24 no t in these reports about you,
        21:34 the commander could not get at the t
        24: 8 be able to learn the t
        28:25 "The Holy Spirit spoke the t
Ro   1:18 of men who suppress the t by their
         1:25 the t of God for a lie,
         2: 2 who do such things is based on t.
         2: 8 and who reject the t and follow evil,
         2:20 the embodiment of knowledge and t
         9: 1 I speak the t in Christ—
        15: 8 of the Jews on behalf of God's t,
1Co   5: 8 the bread of sincerity and t.
        13: 6 in evil but rejoices with the t.
2Co   4: 2 by setting forth the t plainly
        11:10 As surely as the t of Christ is in me,
        12: 6 because I would be speaking the t,
        13: 8 we cannot do anything against the t,
        13: 8 but only for the t.
Gal   2: 5 that the t of the gospel might remain
         2:14 in line with the t of the gospel,

4:16 your enemy by telling you the **t**?
5: 7 and kept you from obeying the **t**?
Eph 1:13 when you heard the word of **t**,
4:15 Instead, speaking the **t** in love,
4:21 in him in accordance with the **t**
5: 9 all goodness, righteousness and **t**)
6:14 with the belt of **t** buckled around
Col 1: 5 already heard about in the word of **t**,
1: 6 God's grace in all its **t**.
2Th 2:10 because they refused to love the **t**
2:12 who have not believed the **t**
2:13 the Spirit and through belief in the **t**.
1Ti 2: 4 and to come to a knowledge of the **t**.
2: 7 I am telling the **t**,
3:15 the pillar and foundation of the **t**.
4: 3 who believe and who know the **t**.
6: 5 who have been robbed of the **t**
2Ti 2:15 who correctly handles the word of **t**.
2:18 who have wandered away from the **t**.
2:25 leading them to a knowledge of the **t**,
3: 7 but never able to acknowledge the **t**.
3: 8 so also these men oppose the **t**—
4: 4 will turn their ears away from the **t**
Tit 1: 1 and the knowledge of the **t**
1:14 commands of those who reject the **t**.
Heb 10:26 received the knowledge of the **t**,
Jas 1:18 give us birth through the word of **t**,
3:14 do not boast about it or deny the **t**.
5:19 one of you should wander from the **t**
1Pe 1:22 the **t** so that you have sincere love
2Pe 1:12 established in the **t** you now have.
2: 2 bring the way of **t**into disrepute.
1Jn 1: 6 we lie and do not live by the **t**.
1: 8 we deceive ourselves and the **t** is not
2: 4 and the **t** is not in him.
2: 8 its **t** is seen in him and you,
2:20 and all of you know the **t**.
2:21 because you do not know the **t**,
2:21 and because no lie comes from the **t**.
3:18 or tongue but with actions and in **t**.
3:19 we know that we belong to the **t**,
4: 6 how we recognize the Spirit of **t** and
5: 6 because the Spirit is the **t**.
2Jn 1: 1 whom I love in the **t**—
1: 1 but also all who know the **t**—
1: 2 because of the **t**, which lives in us
1: 3 will be with us in **t** and love.
1: 4 of your children walking in the **t**,
3Jn 1: 1 whom I love in the **t**.
1: 3 about your faithfulness to the **t** and
how you continue to walk in the **t**.
1: 4 my children are walking in the **t**.
1: 8 that we may work together for the **t**.
1:12 and even by the **t** itself.

I TELL YOU THE TRUTH Da 11:2; Mt 5:18,
26; 6:2, 5, 16; 8:10; 10:15, 23, 42; 11:11; 13:17;
16:28; 17:20; 18:3, 13, 18; 19:23, 28; 21:21, 31;
23:36; 24:2, 34, 47; 25:12, 40, 45; 26:13, 21, 34;
Mk 3:28; 8:12; 9:1, 41; 10:15, 29; 11:23; 12:43;
13:30; 14:9, 18, 25, 30; Lk 4:24; 9:27; 12:37, 44;
18:17, 29; 21:3, 32; 23:43; Jn 1:51; 3:3, 5, 11;
5:19, 24, 25; 6:26, 32, 47, 53; 8:34, 51, 58; 10:1,
7; 12:24; 13:16, 20, 21, 38; 14:12; 16:7, 20, 23;
21:18

TRUTHFUL* [TRUTH]

Pr 12:17 A **t** witness gives honest testimony,
12:19 **T** lips endure forever,
12:22 but he delights in men who are **t**.
14: 5 A **t** witness does not deceive,
14:25 A **t** witness saves lives,
Jer 4: 2 in a **t**, just and righteous way
Jn 3:33 has certified that God is **t**.
2Co 6: 7 in **t** speech and in the power of God;

TRUTHFULLY* [TRUTH]

Eph 4:25 and speak **t** to his neighbor,

TRUTHFULNESS* [TRUTH]

Ro 3: 7 "If my falsehood enhances God's **t**

TRUTHS* [TRUTH]

1Co 2:13 spiritual **t** in spiritual words.
1Ti 3: 9 They must keep hold of the deep **t** of
4: 6 brought up in the **t** of the faith
Heb 5:12 the elementary **t** of God's word all

TRY [TRIED, TRIES, TRYING]

Ps 26: 2 Test me, O LORD, and **t** me,
Isa 7:13 **t** the patience of my God also?
Lk 12:58 **t** hard to be reconciled to him on
13:24 will **t** to enter and will not
Ac 15:10 why do you **t** to test God by putting
1Co 10:33 even as I **t** to please everybody
14:12 to excel in gifts that build up
2Co 5:11 we **t** to persuade men.
1Th 5:15 but always **t** to be kind to each other
Tit 2: 9 to **t** to please them,

TRYING [TRY]

Nu 16:10 to get the priesthood too.
Da 8:15 the vision and **t** to understand it,
Mt 2:20 **t** to take the child's life are dead."
2Co 5:12 We are not **t** to commend ourselves
Gal 1:10 now **t** to win the approval of men,
3: 3 **t** to attain your goal by human
effort?
1Th 2: 4 We are not **t** to please men but God,
1Pe 1:11 **t** to find out the time and
1Jn 2:26 who are **t** to lead you astray.

TUCK [TUCKED, TUCKING]

2Ki 4:29 "**T** your cloak into your belt,
9: 1 "**T** your cloak into your belt,

TUCKED* [TUCK]

Ex 12:11 with your cloak **t** into your belt,

TUCKING* [TUCK]

1Ki 18:46 **t** his cloak into his belt,

TUMORS

1Sa 5: 6 upon them and afflicted them with **t**.
6: 4 "Five gold **t** and five gold rats,

TUNE [TUNED]

1Co 14: 7 anyone know what **t** is being played

TUNED* [TUNE]

Job 30:31   My harp is t to mourning,

TUNIC [TUNICS]

Ex   28: 4   a woven **t,** a turban and a sash.
Lk   6:29   do not stop him from taking your **t.**
        9: 3   no bread, no money, no extra **t.**

TUNICS [TUNIC]

Lk   3:11   "The man with two t should share

TUNNEL*

2Ki 20:20   the t by which he brought water into

TURBAN

Ex   28: 4   a robe, a woven tunic, a t and a sash.
Zec   3: 5   So they put a clean t on his head

TURMOIL

Ps   65: 7   and the t of the nations.
Pr   15:16   than great wealth with t.

TURN [TURNED, TURNING, TURNS]

Ex   23:27   I will make all your enemies t their
      32:12   **T** from your fierce anger;
Lev 19: 4   " 'Do not t to idols or make gods
Nu   32:15   If you t away from following him,
Dt   5:32   not t aside to the right or to the left.
      28:14   Do not t aside from any of
      30:10   t to the LORD your God with all your
Jos   1: 7   not t from it to the right or
1Ki   8:58   May he t our hearts to him,
2Ch   7:14   and pray and seek my face and t
        30: 9   not t his face from you if you return
Job 33:30   to t back his soul from the pit,
Ps   4: 2   will you t my glory into shame?
        6: 4   **T,** O LORD, and deliver me;
      25:16   **T** to me and be gracious to me,
      28: 1   do not t a deaf ear to me.
      34:14   **T** from evil and do good;
      51:13   and sinners will t back to you.
      78: 6   they in t would tell their children.
    119:36   **T** my heart toward your statutes and
    119:132   **T** to me and have mercy on me,
Pr   7:25   Do not let your heart t to her ways
      22: 6   when he is old he will not t from it.
Isa   6:10   and t and be healed."
      17: 7   and t their eyes to the Holy One
      28: 6   who t back the battle at the gate.
      29:16   You t things upside down,
      30:21   Whether you t to the right or to
      41:18   I will t the desert into pools
      45:22   "**T** to me and be saved,
      55: 7   Let him t to the LORD,
      56:11   they all t to their own way,
Jer   18:11   So t from your evil ways,
      31:13   I will t their mourning into gladness;
Eze   1:17   the wheels did not t about as
      33: 9   if you do warn the wicked man to t
      33:11   that they t from their ways and live.
Joel   2:14   He may t and have pity and leave
Jnh   3: 9   t from his fierce anger so that
Mal   4: 6   He will t the hearts of the fathers
Mt   5:39   t to him the other also.

      10:35   to t " 'a man against his father,
Lk   1:17   to t the hearts of the fathers
Jn   12:40   nor t—and I would heal them."
      16:20   but your grief will t to joy.
Ac   3:19   Repent, then, and t to God,
      26:18   and t them from darkness to light,
1Co 14:31   For you can all prophesy in t so
      15:23   But each in his own t:
1Ti   6:20   **T** away from godless chatter and
2Ti   4: 4   They will t their ears away from the
        truth and t aside to myths.
Heb 12:25   if we t away from him who warns us
1Pe   3:11   He must t from evil and do good;
Rev 10: 9   It will t your stomach sour,

TURNED [TURN]

Ex   4: 4   the snake and it t back into a staff
Dt   23: 5   but t the curse into a blessing for you
1Ki   11: 4   his wives t his heart after other gods,
2Ch 15: 4   in their distress they t to the LORD,
Est   9: 1   tables were t and the Jews got
        9:22   their sorrow was t into joy
Ps   14: 3   All have t aside,
      30:11   You t my wailing into dancing;
      40: 1   he t to me and heard my cry.
      66: 6   He t the sea into dry land,
      114: 3   the Jordan t back;
Ecc   2:12   I t my thoughts to consider wisdom,
Isa   9:12   for all this, his anger is not t away,
      53: 6   each of us has t to his own way;
Hos   7: 8   a flat cake not t over.
Joel   2:31   The sun will be t to darkness and
Jnh   3:10   and how they t from their evil ways,
Zec   7:11   stubbornly they t their backs
Lk   22:32   And when you have t back,
Jn   2: 9   the water that had been t into wine.
Ro   3:12   All have t away,
Rev   6:12   the whole moon t blood red,
      10:10   my stomach t sour.

TURNING [TURN]

2Ki 21:13   wiping it and t it upside down.
Pr   2: 2   t your ear to wisdom
      14:27   t a man from the snares of death.
Gal   4: 9   that you are t back to those weak

TURNS [TURN]

Dt   30:17   But if your heart t away and you are
2Sa 22:29   the LORD t my darkness into light.
Pr   15: 1   A gentle answer t away wrath,
Ecc   7: 7   Extortion t a wise man into a fool,
Isa   44:25   of the wise and t it into nonsense,
Eze   18:21   if a wicked man t away from all
      33:18   a righteous man t from his
2Co   3:16   But whenever anyone t to the Lord,
Jas   5:20   Whoever t a sinner from the error

TURTLE(S), TURTLEDOVE

(KJV) See DOVE(S)

TWELVE [12,000, 144,000]

Ge   35:22   Jacob had t sons:
      49:28   All these are the t tribes of Israel,

Ex 24: 4 set up **t** stone pillars representing the
t tribes of Israel.
28:21 There are to be **t** stones,
Jos 4: 3 to take up **t** stones from the middle
1Ki 11:30 and tore it into **t** pieces.
18:31 Elijah took **t** stones,
Mt 10: 1 He called his **t** disciples to him
Lk 9:17 the disciples picked up **t** basketfuls
Jas 1: 1 To the **t** tribes scattered among
Rev 12: 1 a crown of **t** stars on her head.
21:12 It had a great, high wall with **t** gates,
21:12 the names of the **t** tribes of Israel.
21:14 wall of the city had **t** foundations,
21:14 names of the **t** apostles of the Lamb.
21:21 The **t** gates were **t** pearls,
22: 2 bearing **t** crops of fruit,

TWENTY
Nu 1: 3 all the men in Israel **t** years old

TWICE [TWO]
Ex 16: 5 that is to be **t** as much as they gather
Nu 20:11 and struck the rock **t** with his staff.
1Ki 11: 9 who had appeared to him **t**.
Mk 14:30 before the rooster crows **t** you

TWILIGHT [LIGHT]
Ex 12: 6 of Israel must slaughter them at **t**.
16:12 Tell them, 'At **t** you will eat meat,
Lev 23: 5 The LORD's Passover begins at **t**

TWIN [TWINS]
Ge 25:24 there were **t** boys in her womb.
SS 4: 2 Each has its **t**;

TWINKLING*
1Co 15:52 in the **t** of an eye, at the last trumpet.

TWINS [TWIN]
Ro 9:11 before the **t** were born or had done

TWIST* [TWISTED, TWISTING,
TWISTS]
Ps 56: 5 All day long they **t** my words;

TWISTED [TWIST]
Ex 26: 1 with ten curtains of finely **t** linen
Ecc 1:15 What is **t** cannot be straightened;
Mt 27:29 then **t** together a crown of thorns

TWISTING* [TWIST]
Pr 30:33 and as **t** the nose produces blood,

TWISTS [TWIST]
Ex 23: 8 a bribe blinds those who see and **t**

TWO [SECOND, TWICE]
Ge 1:16 God made **t** great lights—
4:19 Lamech married **t** women,
6:19 into the ark **t** of all living creatures,
Ex 31:18 the **t** tablets of the Testimony,
34: 1 "Chisel out **t** stone tablets like
Lev 16: 8 He is to cast lots for the **t** goats—
Dt 4:13 then wrote them on **t** stone tablets.

17: 6 the testimony of **t** or three witnesses
22: 9 Do not plant **t** kinds of seed
25:13 Do not have **t** differing weights
1Ki 3:16 Now **t** prostitutes came to the king
Ps 62:11 **t** things have I heard:
Pr 30: 7 "**T** things I ask of you, O LORD;
30:15 "The leech has **t** daughters.
Ecc 4: 9 **T** are better than one,
Isa 6: 2 With **t** wings they covered their faces
Eze 1:11 each had **t** wings,
Da 8: 3 before me was a ram with **t** horns,
Zec 4:11 "What are these **t** olive trees on
14: 4 the Mount of Olives will be split in **t**
Mt 6:24 "No one can serve **t** masters.
18:16 be established by the testimony of **t**
19: 5 and the **t** will become one flesh'?
Mk 6: 7 he sent them out **t** by **t**
12:42 and put in **t** very small copper coins,
15:27 They crucified **t** robbers with him,
Lk 9:30 **T** men, Moses and Elijah,
17:35 **T** women will be grinding grain
18:10 "**T** men went up to the temple
1Co 6:16 "The **t** will become one flesh."
Gal 4:24 the women represent **t** covenants.
Eph 2:14 who has made the **t** one
Rev 11: 3 I will give power to my **t** witnesses,
19:20 The **t** of them were thrown alive into

TWO-EDGED (KJV)
See DOUBLE-EDGED

TYCHICUS*
Companion of Paul (Ac 20:4; Eph 6:21; Col
4:7; 2Ti 4:12; Tit 3:12).

TYRANNICAL*
Pr 28:16 A **t** ruler lacks judgment,

TYRANNUS*
Ac 19: 9 in the lecture hall of **T**.

TYRE [TYRIANS]
1Ki 5: 1 When Hiram king of **T** heard
Ps 45:12 The Daughter of **T** will come with
Isa 23: 1 An oracle concerning **T**:
Eze 27: 2 take up a lament concerning **T**.
28:12 a lament concerning the king of **T**
Mt 11:22 be more bearable for **T** and Sidon on

U

UGLY
Ge 41: 3 seven other cows, **u** and gaunt,

UNAPPROACHABLE*
1Ti 6:16 and who lives in **u** light,

UNASHAMED*
1Jn 2:28 and **u** before him at his coming.

UNAUTHORIZED
Lev 10: 1 and they offered **u** fire before

UNAWARE
Lev 4:13 the community is **u** of the matter,
        5: 2 even though he is **u** of it,
2Co 2:11 For we are not **u** of his schemes.

UNBELIEF* [UNBELIEVER,
UNBELIEVERS, UNBELIEVING]
Mk 9:24 believe; help me overcome my **u**!"
Ro 4:20 Yet he did not waver through **u**
        11:20 they were broken off because of **u**,
        11:23 And if they do not persist in **u**,
1Ti 1:13 because I acted in ignorance and **u**.
Heb 3:19 because of their **u**.

UNBELIEVER* [UNBELIEF]
1Co 7:15 But if the **u** leaves, let him do so.
        10:27 If some **u** invites you to a meal
        14:24 But if an **u** or someone who does
2Co 6:15 have in common with an **u**?
1Ti 5: 8 the faith and is worse than an **u**.

UNBELIEVERS* [UNBELIEF]
Lk 12:46 and assign him a place with the **u**.
Ro 15:31 I may be rescued from the **u** in Judea
1Co 6: 6 and this in front of **u**!
        14:22 not for believers but for **u**;
        14:22 however, is for believers, not for **u**.
        14:23 not understand or some **u** come in,
2Co 4: 4 has blinded the minds of **u**,
        6:14 Do not be yoked together with **u**.

UNBELIEVING* [UNBELIEF]
Mt 17:17 "O **u** and perverse generation,"
Mk 9:19 "O **u** generation," Jesus replied,
Lk 9:41 "O **u** and perverse generation,"
1Co 7:14 the **u** husband has been sanctified
        7:14 and the **u** wife has been sanctified
Heb 3:12 a sinful, **u** heart that turns away from
Rev 21: 8 But the cowardly, the **u**, the vile,

UNBLEMISHED*
Heb 9:14 offered himself **u** to God,

UNCEASING [UNCEASINGLY]
Ro 9: 2 I have great sorrow and **u** anguish

UNCEASINGLY* [UNCEASING]
La 3:49 My eyes will flow **u**, without relief,

UNCERTAIN*
1Ti 6:17 in wealth, which is so **u**,

UNCHANGEABLE*
[UNCHANGING]
Heb 6:18 God did this so that, by two **u** things

UNCHANGING* [UNCHANGABLE]
Heb 6:17 the **u** nature of his purpose very clear

UNCIRCUMCISED
[UNCIRCUMCISION]
Ex 12:48 No **u** male may eat of it.
Lev 26:41 then when their **u** hearts are humbled
1Sa 17:26 Who is this **u** Philistine that he
Jer 9:26 whole house of Israel is **u** in heart."
Ac 7:51 with **u** hearts and ears!
Ro 3:30 the circumcised by faith and the **u**
        4:11 by faith while he was still **u**.
1Co 7:18 Was a man **u** when he was called?
Col 3:11 circumcised or **u**, barbarian,

UNCIRCUMCISION
[UNCIRCUMCISED]
1Co 7:19 Circumcision is nothing and **u** is
Gal 5: 6 nor **u** has any value.

UNCLEAN [UNCLEANNESS]
Ge 7: 2 and two of every kind of **u** animal,
Lev 10:10 between the **u** and the clean,
        17:15 be ceremonially **u** till evening;
        20:25 between clean and **u** animals
Ezr 6:21 separated themselves from the **u**
Isa 6: 5 For I am a man of **u** lips,
        52:11 Touch no **u** thing!
La 1:17 Jerusalem has become an **u** thing.
Mt 15:11 that is what makes him '**u**.' "
Ac 10:14 never eaten anything impure or **u**."
Ro 14:14 that no food is **u** in itself.
2Co 6:17 Touch no **u** thing,

UNCLEANNESS [UNCLEAN]
Eze 36:29 I will save you from all your **u**.
Jn 18:28 avoid ceremonial **u** the Jews did not

UNCLOTHED*
2Co 5: 4 we do not wish to be **u** but

UNCONCERNED*
Eze 16:49 were arrogant, overfed and **u**;

UNCORRUPTIBLE (KJV)
See IMMORTAL

UNCOVER [UNCOVERED]
Ru 3: 4 Then go and **u** his feet and lie down.

UNCOVERED [UNCOVER]
Ge 9:21 he became drunk and lay **u**
Ru 3: 7 **u** his feet and lay down.
1Co 11: 5 with her head **u** dishonors her head
        11:13 to pray to God with her head **u**?
Heb 4:13 Everything is **u** and laid bare

UNCTION (KJV) See ANOINTING

UNDER
Ge 4:11 Now you are **u** a curse and driven
        24: 2 "Put your hand **u** my thigh.
        47:29 put your hand **u** my thigh
Ex 6: 7 from **u** the yoke of the Egyptians.
1Ki 4:25 each man **u** his own vine
Ps 8: 6 you put everything **u** his feet:
        91: 4 and **u** his wings you will find refuge;

95: 7 the flock **u** his care.
Pr 29:11 a wise man keeps himself **u** control.
Jer 3:13 foreign gods **u** every spreading tree,
Mic 4: 4 Every man will sit **u** his own vine
Mt 5:15 light a lamp and put it **u** a bowl.
 22:44 until I put your enemies **u** your feet.'
Lk 13:34 a hen gathers her chicks **u** her wings,
Jn 13: 3 Father had put all things **u** his power,
Ac 4:12 no other name **u** heaven given
Ro 6:14 because you are not **u** law,
1Co 9:21 God's law but am **u** Christ's law),
 15:27 he "has put everything **u** his feet."
Gal 4: 5 to redeem those **u** law,
Rev 6: 9 I saw **u** the altar the souls

UNDER THE SUN See SUN

UNDERGOES* [UNDERGOING]

Heb 12: 8 (and everyone **u** discipline),

UNDERGOING* [UNDERGOES]

1Pe 5: 9 are **u** the same kind of sufferings.

UNDERNEATH

Dt 33:27 and **u** are the everlasting arms.

UNDERSTAND [UNDERSTANDING, UNDERSTANDS, UNDERSTOOD]

Ge 11: 7 so they will not **u** each other."
Ne 8: 8 people could **u** what was being read.
Job 38: 4 Tell me, if you **u**.
 42: 3 Surely I spoke of things I did not **u**,
Ps 14: 2 to see if there are any who **u**,
 73:16 When I tried to **u** all this,
 119:27 Let me **u** the teaching of
 119:125 that I may **u** your statutes.
Pr 2: 5 then you will **u** the fear of the LORD
 2: 9 Then you will **u** what is right
 30:18 four that I do not **u**:
Ecc 7:25 to **u** the stupidity of wickedness and
 11: 5 so you cannot **u** the work of God,
Isa 1: 3 my people do not **u**."
 6:10 **u** with their hearts,
 44:18 They know nothing, they **u** nothing;
 52:15 they have not heard, they will **u**.
Jer 17: 9 Who can **u** it?
 31:19 after I came to **u**,
Da 1:17 And Daniel could **u** visions
 9:25 "Know and **u** this:
Hos 14: 9 He will **u** them.
Mt 13:15 **u** with their hearts and turn,
 24:15 let the reader **u**—
Mk 4:13 "Don't you **u** this parable?
Lk 24:45 so they could **u** the Scriptures.
Jn 13: 7 but later you will **u**."
Ac 8:30 "Do you **u** what you are reading?"
Ro 7:15 I do not **u** what I do.
 15:21 and those who have not heard will **u**.
1Co 2:12 we may **u** what God has freely given
 2:14 and he cannot **u** them,
 14:16 himself among those who do not **u**
Eph 5:17 but **u** what the Lord's will is.
Heb 11: 3 By faith we **u** that the universe was
2Pe 1:20 you must **u** that no prophecy
 3: 3 you must **u** that in the last days

3:16 some things that are hard to **u**,

UNDERSTANDING [UNDERSTAND]

Dt 4: 6 your wisdom and **u** to the nations,
1Ki 4:29 and a breadth of **u** as measureless as
Job 12:12 Does not long life bring **u?**
 28:12 Where does **u** dwell?
 28:28 and to shun evil is **u**.' "
 32: 8 of the Almighty, that gives him **u**.
 36:26 How great is God—beyond our **u!**
 37: 5 he does great things beyond our **u**.
Ps 49:20 A man who has riches without **u** is
 111:10 follow his precepts have good **u**.
 119:34 Give me **u**, and I will keep your law
 119:100 I have more **u** than the elders,
 119:104 I gain **u** from your precepts;
 119:130 it gives **u** to the simple.
 136: 5 who by his **u** made the heavens,
 147: 5 his **u** has no limit.
Pr 1: 6 for **u** proverbs and parables,
 2: 2 and applying your heart to **u**,
 2: 6 his mouth come knowledge and **u**.
 3: 5 and lean not on your own **u**;
 3:13 the man who gains **u**,
 4: 5 Get wisdom, get **u**;
 4: 7 Though it cost all you have, get **u**.
 7: 4 and call **u** your kinsman;
 8: 5 you who are foolish, gain **u**.
 9:10 and knowledge of the Holy One is **u**.
 10:23 but a man of **u** delights in wisdom.
 11:12 but a man of **u** holds his tongue.
 14:29 A patient man has great **u**,
 15:21 a man of **u** keeps a straight course.
 15:32 whoever heeds correction gains **u**.
 16:16 to choose **u** rather than silver!
 16:22 **U** is a fountain of life
 17:27 and a man of **u** is even-tempered.
 18: 2 A fool finds no pleasure in **u**
 19: 8 he who cherishes **u** prospers.
 20: 5 but a man of **u** draws them out.
 23:23 get wisdom, discipline and **u**.
Ecc 1:17 I applied myself to the **u** of wisdom,
Isa 6: 9 " 'Be ever hearing, but never **u;**
 11: 2 the Spirit of wisdom and of **u**,
 40:14 or showed him the path of **u?**
 40:28 and his **u** no one can fathom.
 56:11 They are shepherds who lack **u;**
Jer 3:15 with knowledge and **u**.
 10:12 stretched out the heavens by his **u**.
Da 1:17 God gave knowledge and **u** of all
 5:12 a keen mind and knowledge and **u**,
 10:12 that you set your mind to gain **u** and
Hos 4:11 which take away the **u**
Mk 4:12 and ever hearing but never **u;**
 12:33 all your **u** and with all your strength,
Lk 2:47 amazed at his **u** and his answers.
Ac 28:26 be ever hearing but never **u;**
Ro 10:19 by a nation that has no **u**."
2Co 6: 6 **u**, patience and kindness;
Eph 1: 8 lavished on us with all wisdom and **u**
Php 4: 7 which transcends all **u**,
Col 1: 9 through all spiritual wisdom and **u**.
 2: 2 the full riches of complete **u**,

Jas 3:13 Who is wise and **u** among you?
1Jn 5:20 of God has come and has given us **u,**

UNDERSTANDS [UNDERSTAND]

Dt 29: 4 a mind that **u** or eyes that see
1Ch 28: 9 **u** every motive behind the thoughts.
Job 28:23 God **u** the way to it
Jer 9:24 that he **u** and knows me,
Mt 13:23 the man who hears the word and **u** it.
Ro 3:11 there is no one who **u,**
1Ti 6: 4 he is conceited and **u** nothing.

UNDERSTOOD [UNDERSTAND]

Ne 8:12 because they now **u** the words
Ps 73:17 then I **u** their final destiny.
Isa 40:13 Who has **u** the mind of the LORD,
   40:21 not **u** since the earth was founded?
Da 9: 2 I, Daniel, **u** from the Scriptures,
Jn 1: 5 but the darkness has not **u** it.
Ro 1:20 being **u** from what has been made,

UNDERTAKEN

Lk 1: 1 Many have **u** to draw up an account

UNDESIRABLE*

Jos 24:15 serving the LORD seems **u** to you,

UNDISCIPLINED*

Pr 9:13 The woman Folly is loud; she is **u**

UNDIVIDED*

1Ch 12:33 to help David with **u** loyalty—
Ps 86:11 give me an **u** heart,
Eze 11:19 I will give them an **u** heart and put
1Co 7:35 in **u** devotion to the Lord.

UNDOING [UNDONE]

Pr 18: 7 A fool's mouth is his **u,**

UNDONE [UNDOING]

Lk 11:42 without leaving the former **u.**

UNDYING*

Eph 6:24 our Lord Jesus Christ with an **u** love.

UNEQUALED*

Mt 24:21 **u** from the beginning of the world
Mk 13:19 of distress **u** from the beginning,

UNFADING*

1Pe 3: 4 **u** beauty of a gentle and quiet spirit,

UNFAILING*

Ex 15:13 "In your **u** love you will lead
1Sa 20:14 But show me **u** kindness like that of
2Sa 22:51 he shows **u** kindness to his anointed,
Ps 6: 4 save me because of your **u** love.
   13: 5 But I trust in your **u** love;
   18:50 he shows **u** kindness to his anointed,
   21: 7 through the **u** love of the Most High
   31:16 save me in your **u** love.
   32:10 but the LORD's **u** love surrounds
   33: 5 the earth is full of his **u** love.
   33:18 on those whose hope is in his **u** love,
   33:22 May your **u** love rest upon us,

36: 7 How priceless is your **u** love!
44:26 redeem us because of your **u** love.
48: 9 O God, we meditate on your **u** love.
51: 1 O God, according to your **u** love,
52: 8 in God's **u** love for ever and ever.
77: 8 Has his **u** love vanished forever?
85: 7 Show us your **u** love, O LORD,
90:14 in the morning with your **u** love,
107: 8 thanks to the LORD for his **u** love
107:15 thanks to the LORD for his **u** love
107:21 thanks to the LORD for his **u** love
107:31 thanks to the LORD for his **u** love
119:41 May your **u** love come to me,
119:76 May your **u** love be my comfort,
130: 7 for with the LORD is **u** love and
143: 8 bring me word of your **u** love,
143:12 In your **u** love, silence my enemies;
147:11 who put their hope in his **u** love.
Pr 19:22 What a man desires is **u** love;
   20: 6 Many a man claims to have **u** love,
Isa 54:10 yet my **u** love for you will not
La 3:32 so great is his **u** love.
Hos 10:12 reap the fruit of **u** love,

UNFAILING LOVE See LOVE

UNFAITHFUL [UNFAITHFULNESS]

Lev 6: 2 is **u** to the LORD by deceiving his
Nu 5: 6 and so is **u** to the LORD,
   5:12 'If a man's wife goes astray and is **u**
1Ch 10:13 because he was **u** to the LORD;
Ezr 10: 2 "We have been **u** to our God
Pr 11: 6 but the **u** are trapped by evil desires.
   13: 2 but the **u** have a craving for violence.
   13:15 but the way of the **u** is hard.
   22:12 but he frustrates the words of the **u.**
   23:28 and multiplies the **u** among men.
   25:19 reliance on the **u** in times of trouble.
Jer 3:20 so you have been **u** to me,
Hos 5: 7 They are **u** to the LORD;

UNFAITHFULNESS [UNFAITHFUL]

Nu 14:33 for forty years, suffering for your **u,**
1Ch 9: 1 to Babylon because of their **u.**
Eze 18:24 Because of the **u** he is guilty of
Mt 5:32 except for marital **u,**
   19: 9 except for marital **u,**

UNFIT*

Tit 1:16 and **u** for doing anything good.

UNFOLDING*

Ps 119:130 The **u** of your words gives light;

UNFORGIVING*

2Ti 3: 3 **u,** slanderous, without self-control,

UNFORMED*

Ps 139:16 your eyes saw my **u** body.

UNFRIENDLY*

Pr 18: 1 An **u** man pursues selfish ends;

UNFRUITFUL

Mk 4:19 choke the word, making it **u.**

1Co 14:14 my spirit prays, but my mind is **u.**

UNGODLINESS* [UNGODLY]

Isa 32: 6 He practices **u** and spreads error
Jer 23:15 **u** has spread throughout the land."
Tit 2:12 It teaches us to say "No" to **u**

UNGODLY [UNGODLINESS]

Pr 11:31 how much more the **u** and the sinner!
Ro 5: 6 Christ died for the **u.**
1Ti 1: 9 the **u** and sinful,
2Ti 2:16 will become more and more **u.**
2Pe 2: 6 of what is going to happen to the **u;**
Jude 1:15 to convict all the **u** of all the **u** acts
they have done in the **u** way,

UNGRATEFUL*

Lk 6:35 he is kind to the **u** and wicked.
2Ti 3: 2 disobedient to their parents, **u,**

UNHARMED

Da 3:25 around in the fire, unbound and **u,**

UNHEARD-OF*

Eze 7: 5 An **u** disaster is coming.
Da 11:36 and will say **u** things

UNHOLY*

1Ti 1: 9 the **u** and irreligious;
2Ti 3: 2 to their parents, ungrateful, **u,**
Heb 10:29 who has treated as an **u** thing

UNINTENTIONALLY

Lev 4: 2 'When anyone sins **u** and does what
Nu 15:22 if you **u** fail to keep any of these
Dt 4:42 if he had **u** killed his neighbor

UNION [UNITE]

Zec 11:14 I broke my second staff called **U,**
Mt 1:25 But he had no **u** with her until

UNIT

1Co 12:12 The body is a **u,**

UNITE [REUNITED, UNION, UNITED, UNITES, UNITY]

1Co 6:15 the members of Christ and **u** them

UNITED [UNITE]

Ge 2:24 and mother and be **u** to his wife,
Mt 19: 5 and mother and be **u** to his wife,
Ro 6: 5 If we have been **u** with him like this
1Co 1:10 that you may be perfectly **u**
Eph 5:31 and mother and be **u** to his wife,
Php 2: 1 from being **u** with Christ,
Col 2: 2 be encouraged in heart and **u** in love,

UNITES* [UNITE]

1Co 6:16 who **u** himself with a prostitute
6:17 who **u** himself with the Lord

UNITY* [UNITE]

2Ch 30:12 on the people to give them **u** of mind
Ps 133: 1 when brothers live together in **u!**
Jn 17:23 May they be brought to complete **u**

Ro 15: 5 a spirit of **u** among yourselves as
Eph 4: 3 the **u** of the Spirit through the bond
4:13 until we all reach **u** in the faith and
Col 3:14 binds them all together in perfect **u.**

UNIVERSE*

1Co 4: 9 a spectacle to the whole **u,**
Eph 4:10 in order to fill the whole **u.)**
Php 2:15 in which you shine like stars in the **u**
Heb 1: 2 and through whom he made the **u.**
11: 3 the **u** was formed at God's command

UNJUST

Eze 18:25 O house of Israel: Is my way **u?**
Lk 18: 6 "Listen to what the **u** judge says.
Ro 3: 5 God is **u** in bringing his wrath on us?
9:14 Is God **u?** Not at all!
Heb 6:10 God is not **u;** he will not forget
1Pe 2:19 under the pain of **u** suffering

UNKNOWN

Ac 17:23 this inscription: TO AN U GOD.
17:23 what you worship as something **u**

UNLAWFUL

Mt 12: 2 Your disciples are doing what is **u** on
Ac 16:21 by advocating customs **u** for us

UNLEAVENED

Ex 12:17 "Celebrate the Feast of **U** Bread,
Dt 16:16 at the Feast of **U** Bread,
Mt 26:17 the first day of the Feast of **U** Bread,

THE FEAST OF UNLEAVENED BREAD
See FEAST

UNLESS

Ps 94:17 **U** the LORD had given me help,
127: 1 **U** the LORD builds the house,
La 5:22 **u** you have utterly rejected us
Lk 13: 3 **u** you repent, you too will all perish.
Jn 3: 3 **u** he is born again."
4:48 "**U** you people see miraculous signs
12:24 **u** a kernel of wheat falls to the
Ac 8:31 "**u** someone explains it to me?"
Rev 13:17 buy or sell **u** he had the mark,

UNLIKE

2Co 2:17 **U** so many, we do not peddle the
Heb 7:27 **U** the other high priests,

UNLIMITED*

1Ti 1:16 Jesus might display his **u** patience

UNLOVED*

Dt 21:17 the son of his **u** wife as the firstborn
Pr 30:23 an **u** woman who is married,

UNMARRIED

1Co 7: 8 Now to the **u** and the widows I say:
It is good for them to stay **u,**
7:32 **u** man is concerned about the Lord's

UNNATURAL*

Ro 1:26 exchanged natural relations for **u**

UNPLOWED*

Ex   23:11 the seventh year let the land lie **u**
Jer   4: 3 "Break up your **u** ground
Hos 10:12 and break up your **u** ground;

UNPRODUCTIVE

Tit   3:14 and not live **u** lives.
2Pe 1: 8 you from being ineffective and **u**

UNPROFITABLE*

Isa 30: 6 to that **u** nation,
Tit   3: 9 because these are **u** and useless.

UNPUNISHED

Ex   34: 7 Yet he does not leave the guilty **u;**
Nu   14:18 Yet he does not leave the guilty **u;**
Pr   6:29 no one who touches her will go **u.**
     11:21 The wicked will not go **u,**
     19: 5 A false witness will not go **u,**
     28:20 one eager to get rich will not go **u.**
Na   1: 3 the LORD will not leave the guilty **u.**
Ro   3:25 left the sins committed beforehand **u**

UNQUENCHABLE

Lk   3:17 burn up the chaff with **u** fire."

UNREPENTANT*

Ro   2: 5 stubbornness and your **u** heart,

UNRIGHTEOUS*

[UNRIGHTEOUSNESS]
Zep   3: 5 yet the **u** know no shame.
Mt   5:45 sends rain on the righteous and the **u.**
1Pe   3:18 the righteous for the **u,**
2Pe   2: 9 to hold the **u** for the day of judgment

UNRIGHTEOUSNESS

[UNRIGHTEOUS]
1Jn   1: 9 and purify us from all **u.**

UNSCHOOLED*

Ac   4:13 and realized that they were **u,**

UNSEARCHABLE

Ro   11:33 How **u** his judgments,
Eph   3: 8 to the Gentiles the **u** riches of Christ,

UNSEEN*

Mt   6: 6 pray to your Father, who is **u.**
      6:18 but only to your Father, who is **u;**
2Co   4:18 but on what is **u.**
      4:18 but what is **u** is eternal.

UNSETTLED*

1Th   3: 3 no one would be **u** by these trials.
2Th   2: 2 not to become easily **u** or alarmed

UNSHRUNK

Mt   9:16 a patch of **u** cloth on an old garment,

UNSPIRITUAL*

Ro   7:14 but I am **u,** sold as a slave to sin.
Col   2:18 and his **u** mind puffs him up
Jas   3:15 but is earthly, **u,** of the devil.

UNSTABLE*

Jas   1: 8 **u** in all he does.
2Pe   2:14 never stop sinning; they seduce the **u**
      3:16 which ignorant and **u** people distort,

UNSWERVINGLY*

Heb 10:23 Let us hold **u** to the hope we profess,

UNTHINKABLE*

Job 34:12 It is **u** that God would do wrong,

UNTIE

Mk   1: 7 not worthy to stoop down and **u.**
Lk   13:15 on the Sabbath **u** his ox or donkey

UNVEILED*

2Co   3:18 **u** faces all reflect the Lord's glory,

UNWASHED*

Mt   15:20 but eating with **u** hands does not
Mk   7: 2 that were "unclean," that is, **u.**

UNWHOLESOME*

Eph   4:29 Do not let any **u** talk come out

UNWISE*

Dt   32: 6 O foolish and **u** people?
Eph   5:15 not as **u** but as wise,

UNWORTHY*

Ge   32:10 I am **u** of all the kindness
Job 40: 4 "I am **u**—how can I reply to you?
Lk   17:10 should say, 'We are **u** servants;
1Co 11:27 the cup of the Lord in an **u** manner

UNYIELDING

Ex   7:14 "Pharaoh's heart is **u;**
Pr   18:19 An offended brother is more **u** than

UPHELD [UPHOLD]

Ps   9: 4 you have **u** my right and my cause;

UPHOLD [UPHELD, UPHOLDING,

UPHOLDS]
Ps   41:12 In my integrity you **u** me and set me
Isa 41:10 I will **u** you with my righteous
     42: 1 "Here is my servant, whom I **u,**
Ro   3:31 Rather, we **u** the law.

UPHOLDING* [UPHOLD]

Isa   9: 7 and **u** it with justice

UPHOLDS* [UPHOLD]

Ps   37:17 but the LORD **u** the righteous.
     37:24 for the LORD **u** him with his hand.
     63: 8 clings to you; your right hand **u** me.
    140:12 and **u** the cause of the needy.
    145:14 The LORD **u** all those who fall
    146: 7 He **u** the cause of the oppressed

UPLIFTED [LIFT]

Ex   6: 8 the land I swore with **u** hand to give
Ps 106:26 he swore to them with **u** hand

UPPER

Mk 14:15 He will show you a large **u** room,

UPRIGHT [UPRIGHTNESS]

Ge 37: 7 my sheaf rose and stood **u,**
Dt 32: 4 **u** and just is he.
Job 1: 1 This man was blameless and **u;**
 1: 8 he is blameless and **u,**
 2: 3 he is blameless and **u,**
 33: 3 My words come from an **u** heart;
Ps 7:10 who saves the **u** in heart.
 11: 7 **u** men will see his face.
 25: 8 Good and **u** is the LORD;
 33: 1 it is fitting for the **u** to praise him.
 64:10 let all the **u** in heart praise him!
 92:15 "The LORD is **u;**
 97:11 and joy on the **u** in heart.
 112: 4 in darkness light dawns for the **u,**
 119: 7 I will praise you with an **u** heart
Pr 2: 7 He holds victory in store for the **u,**
 2:21 For the **u** will live in the land,
 3:32 but takes the **u** into his confidence.
 11: 3 The integrity of the **u** guides them,
 14: 2 He whose walk is **u** fears
 15: 8 but the prayer of the **u** pleases him.
 21:29 an **u** man gives thought to his ways.
Isa 26: 7 of the righteous is level; O **u** One,
Mic 2: 7 do good to him whose ways are **u?**
Tit 1: 8 who is self-controlled, **u,**
 2:12 **u** and godly lives in this present age,

UPRIGHTNESS [UPRIGHT]

Ps 25:21 May integrity and **u** protect me,
 111: 8 done in faithfulness and **u.**

UPROOT [UPROOTED]

2Ch 7:20 then I will **u** Israel from my land,
Ecc 3: 2 a time to plant and a time to **u,**
Jer 1:10 and kingdoms to **u** and tear down,

UPROOTED [UPROOT]

Dt 28:63 be **u** from the land you are entering
Pr 10:30 The righteous will never be **u,**
Jer 18: 7 that a nation or kingdom is to be **u,**
 31:40 The city will never again be **u**
Lk 17: 6 'Be **u** and planted in the sea,'
Jude 1:12 without fruit and **u**—twice dead.

UPSET

Lk 10:41 and **u** about many things,

UPWARD

Ex 37: 9 cherubim had their wings spread **u,**
Eze 1:11 Their wings were spread out **u;**

UR

Ge 15: 7 the LORD, who brought you out of **U**
Ne 9: 7 and brought him out of **U** of the

URGE [URGED, URGENTLY, URGING]

Ru 1:16 "Don't **u** me to leave you or
Ro 12: 1 Therefore, I **u** you, brothers,
1Co 4:16 Therefore I **u** you to imitate me.
Jude 1: 3 and **u** you to contend for the faith

URGED [URGE]

Ge 19:15 the angels **u** Lot, saying, "Hurry!
Ex 12:33 The Egyptians **u** the people to hurry

URGENTLY [URGE]

Jnh 3: 8 Let everyone call **u** on God.

URGING [URGE]

Ru 1:18 she stopped **u** her.
1Th 2:12 and **u** you to live lives worthy

URIAH

 Hittite husband of Bathsheba, killed by David's
order (2Sa 11).

URIM

Ex 28:30 Also put the **U** and the Thummim in
1Sa 28: 6 not answer him by dreams or **U**
Ezr 2:63 a priest ministering with the **U**

USE [USED, USEFUL, USELESS, USES]

Lev 19:35 " 'Do not **u** dishonest standards
Jdg 2:22 I will **u** them to test Israel
Mt 7: 2 and with the measure you **u,**
Ro 12: 6 let him **u** it in proportion to his faith.
Gal 5:13 But do not **u** your freedom to indulge
1Ti 5:23 and **u** a little wine because
1Pe 4:10 Each one should **u** whatever gift

USED [USE]

Mt 22:19 the coin **u** for paying the tax."
Jn 10: 6 Jesus **u** this figure of speech,
1Co 9:15 But I have not **u** any of these rights.

USEFUL [USE]

Eph 4:28 but must work, doing something **u**
2Ti 2:21 **u** to the Master and prepared
 3:16 God-breathed and is **u** for teaching,
Phm 1:11 but now he has become **u** both to you

USELESS [USE]

1Sa 12:21 Do not turn away after **u** idols.
1Co 15:14 preaching is **u** and so is your faith.
Tit 3: 9 because these are unprofitable and **u.**
Phm 1:11 Formerly he was **u** to you,
Heb 7:18 because it was weak and **u**
Jas 2:20 that faith without deeds is **u?**

USES [USE]

1Ti 1: 8 the law is good if one **u** it properly.

USURY

Ne 5:10 But let the exacting of **u** stop!
Ps 15: 5 who lends his money without **u**
Eze 18: 8 He does not lend at **u** or

UTMOST

Job 34:36 Oh, that Job might be tested to the **u**

UTTER [UTTERED, UTTERLY, UTTERS]

Dt 23:23 Whatever your lips **u** you must
Ps 78: 2 I will **u** hidden things,
 115: 7 nor can they **u** a sound
Mt 13:35 I will **u** things hidden since
Rev 13: 5 to **u** proud words and blasphemies

UTTERED [UTTER]

Nu 23: 7 Then Balaam **u** his oracle:
Ps 89:34 or alter what my lips have **u.**

UTTERLY [UTTER]

Ps 119: 8 do not **u** forsake me.
Ecc   1: 2 "**U** meaningless!
SS   8: 7 it would be **u** scorned.
Ro   7:13 sin might become **u** sinful.

UTTERS* [UTTER]

Ps   37:30 of the righteous man **u** wisdom,
1Co 14: 2 he **u** mysteries with his spirit.

UZ

Job   1: 1 In the land of **U** there lived a man

UZZAH

2Sa   6: 6 **U** reached out and took hold of
1Ch 13: 9 **U** reached out his hand to steady

UZZIAH [AZARIAH]

Son of Amaziah; king of Judah also known as Azariah (2Ki 15:1-7; 1Ch 6:24; 2Ch 26). Struck with leprosy because of pride (2Ch 26:16-23).

V

VAIN

Lev 26:20 Your strength will be spent in **v,**
Ps   2: 1 and the peoples plot in **v?**
      33:17 A horse is a **v** hope for deliverance;
      73:13 in **v** have I kept my heart pure;
     127: 1 its builders labor in **v.**
Isa 65:23 not toil in **v** or bear children doomed
La   4:17 looking in **v** for help;
Eze   6:10 I did not threaten in **v**
Mt   15: 9 They worship me in **v;**
Ac   4:25 and the peoples plot in **v?**
1Co 15: 2 Otherwise, you have believed in **v.**
     15:58 labor in the Lord is not in **v.**
2Co   6: 1 not to receive God's grace in **v.**
Gal   2: 2 or had run my race in **v.**
Php   2: 3 out of selfish ambition or **v** conceit,

VALIANT

1Sa 10:26 **v** men whose hearts God had touched
     31:12 all their **v** men journeyed through

VALID

Jn   5:32 that his testimony about me is **v.**
      8:14 my own behalf, my testimony is **v,**

VALLEY [VALLEYS]

Jos   7:26 called the **V** of Achor ever since.
     10:12 O moon, over the **V** of Aijalon."
Jdg 16: 4 **V** of Sorek whose name was Delilah.
1Sa 17: 3 with the **v** between them.
2Ki 23:10 which was in the **V** of Ben Hinnom,
2Ch 33: 6 in the fire in the **V** of Ben Hinnom,
Ps   23: 4 through the **v** of the shadow of death,

Isa 22: 1 oracle concerning the **V** of Vision:
     40: 4 Every **v** shall be raised up,
Eze 37: 2 many bones on the floor of the **v,**
Hos   2:15 make the **V** of Achor a door of hope.
Joel 3:14 multitudes in the **v** of decision!
Lk   3: 5 Every **v** shall be filled in,

VALLEYS [VALLEY]

Dt   8: 7 with springs flowing in the **v**
SS   2: 1 I am a rose of Sharon, a lily of the **v.**

VALUABLE [VALUE]

Lk   12:24 much more **v** you are than birds!

VALUE [VALUABLE, VALUED]

Lev 27: 3 set the **v** of a male between the ages
1Ki 10:21 silver was considered of little **v**
Pr   10: 2 Ill-gotten treasures are of no **v,**
     16:13 they **v** a man who speaks the truth.
     31:11 in her and lacks nothing of **v.**
Mt   13:46 When he found one of great **v,**
Ro   3: 1 or what **v** is there in circumcision?
1Ti   4: 8 For physical training is of some **v,**
            but godliness has **v** for all things,
Heb   4: 2 the message they heard was of no **v**
     11:26 as of greater **v** than the treasures

VALUED [VALUE]

Lk   16:15 What is highly **v** among men is

VANISH [VANISHED, VANISHES]

Ps   37:20 they will **v—v** like smoke.

VANISHED [VANISH]

Ps   12: 1 the faithful have **v** from among men.
     77: 8 Has his unfailing love **v** forever?

VANISHES [VANISH]

Jas   4:14 appears for a little while and then **v.**

VANITIES, VANITY (KJV)

See BREATH, DECEIT, DELUSIONS, DESTRUCTION, DISHONEST, EMPTY, EVIL, FALSE, FALSEHOOD, FLEETING, FRUSTRATION, FUTILE, FUTILITY, LIES, MEANINGLESS, NO MEANING, WORTHLESS IDOLS

VARIOUS

Ge   1:11 according to their **v** kinds."
Jdg   2:12 and worshiped **v** gods of the peoples
Mk   1:34 Jesus healed many who had **v**
Heb   1: 1 at many times and in **v** ways,
1Pe   4:10 administering God's grace in its **v**

VASHTI*

Queen of Persia replaced by Esther (Est 1-2).

VAST

Ge   2: 1 completed in all their **v** array.
Dt   1:19 through all that **v** and dreadful desert
      8:15 through the **v** and dreadful desert,
Ps 139:17 How **v** is the sum of them!

VATS

Pr   3:10   and your **v** will brim over
Joel 2:24   the **v** will overflow with new wine

VEGETABLES

Pr 15:17   a meal of **v** where there is love than
Da   1:12   Give us nothing but **v** to eat
Ro 14: 2   whose faith is weak, eats only **v**.

VEGETATION

Ge   1:11   God said, "Let the land produce **v**:

VEIL [VEILED]

Ex 34:33   he put a **v** over his face.
La   3:65   Put a **v** over their hearts,
2Co 3:13   who would put a **v** over his face
      3:15   a **v** covers their hearts.

VEILED [VEIL]

2Co 4: 3   And even if our gospel is **v**,

VENGEANCE [AVENGE, AVENGED, AVENGER, AVENGES, AVENGING, REVENGE]

Ge   4:15   he will suffer **v** seven times over."
Nu 31: 3   and to carry out the LORD's **v**
Isa 34: 8   For the LORD has a day of **v**,
     61: 2   and the day of **v** of our God,
Jer 50:15   Since this is the **v** of the LORD,
Na   1: 2   LORD takes **v** on his foes

VENOM [VENOMOUS]

Dt 32:33   Their wine is the **v** of serpents,
Ps 58: 4   Their **v** is like the **v** of a snake,

VENOMOUS [VENOM]

Nu 21: 6   LORD sent **v** snakes among them;
Jer 8:17   I will send **v** snakes among you,

VENT

Pr 29:11   A fool gives full **v** to his anger,
La   4:11   LORD has given full **v** to his wrath;
Da 11:30   **v** his fury against the holy covenant.

VERDICT

1Ki 3:28   When all Israel heard the **v**
Jn   3:19   This is the **v**: Light has come into

VERSED*

Ezr 7: 6   He was a teacher well **v** in the Law

VERY

Ge   1:31   and it was **v** good.
     15: 1   your **v** great reward."
     17: 6   I will make you **v** fruitful;
Dt 30:14   No, the word is **v** near you;
Jos 23:11   So be **v** careful to love the LORD
1Ki 19:10   "I have been **v** zealous for the LORD
Ps 104: 1   O LORD my God, you are **v** great;
Mt   4: 8   devil took him to a **v** high mountain

VICTIM* [VICTIMS]

Ps 10:14   The **v** commits himself to you;
Hab 2: 7   Then you will become their **v**.

VICTIMS [VICTIM]

Pr   7:26   the **v** she has brought down;
Na   3: 1   full of plunder, never without **v**!

VICTOR'S* [VICTORY]

2Ti   2: 5   the **v** crown unless he competes

VICTORIES* [VICTORY]

2Sa 22:51   He gives his king great **v**;
Ps 18:50   He gives his king great **v**;
     21: 1   in the **v** you give!
     21: 5   the **v** you gave, his glory is great;
     44: 4   who decrees **v** for Jacob.

VICTORIOUS [VICTORY]

Ps 20: 5   We will shout for joy when you are **v**
Rev 15: 2   those who had been **v** over the beast

VICTORIOUSLY* [VICTORY]

Ps 45: 4   In your majesty ride forth **v**

VICTORY [VICTOR'S, VICTORIES, VICTORIOUS, VICTORIOUSLY]

Ex 32:18   replied: "It is not the sound of **v**,
2Sa 8: 6   The LORD gave David **v** wherever he
Ps 44: 6   my sword does not bring me **v**;
    60:12   With God we will gain the **v**,
   129: 2   they have not gained the **v** over me.
Pr   2: 7   He holds **v** in store for the upright,
    11:14   but many advisers make **v** sure.
    21:31   but **v** rests with the LORD.
    24: 6   and for **v** many advisers.
1Co 15:54   "Death has been swallowed up in **v**."
    15:57   He gives us the **v** through our Lord
1Jn 5: 4   the **v** that has overcome the world,

VIEW

Pr   5:21   man's ways are in full **v** of the LORD,
    17:24   discerning man keeps wisdom in **v**,
2Ti 4: 1   and in **v** of his appearing

VILE [VILEST]

2Ki 23:13   for Ashtoreth the **v** goddess
    23:13   for Chemosh the **v** god of Moab,
Ps 15: 4   who despises a **v** man
   101: 3   I will set before my eyes no **v** thing.
Eze 5:11   defiled my sanctuary with all your **v**
Rev 21: 8   the cowardly, the unbelieving, the **v**,

VILEST* [VILE]

1Ki 21:26   in the **v** manner by going after idols,
Hos 1: 2   the land is guilty of the **v** adultery

VILLAGE

Mt 10:11   "Whatever town or **v** you enter,
Mk   6: 6   went around teaching from **v** to **v**.

VINDICATE [VINDICATED, VINDICATION]

Ps 26: 1   **V** me, O LORD,
    35:24   **V** me in your righteousness,
    54: 1   **v** me by your might.
   135:14   For the LORD will **v** his people

VINDICATED [VINDICATE]

Job 13:18 I know I will be **v**.
Jer 51:10 " 'The LORD has **v** us;
1Ti   3:16 was **v** by the Spirit,

VINDICATION [VINDICATE]

Ps   24: 5 and **v** from God his Savior.
Isa 54:17 and this is their **v** from me,"

VINE [VINES, VINEYARD, VINEYARDS]

Ge   49:22 "Joseph is a fruitful **v**,
Dt   32:32 Their **v** comes from the **v** of Sodom
1Ki   4:25 under his own **v** and fig tree.
Ps   80: 8 You brought a **v** out of Egypt;
    128: 3 like a fruitful **v** within your house;
Isa 36:16 from his own **v** and fig tree
Jer   2:21 I had planted you like a choice **v**
Eze 17: 6 and became a low, spreading **v**.
Hos 10: 1 Israel was a spreading **v;**
Jnh   4: 6 Then the LORD God provided a **v**
Mk   14:25 not drink again of the fruit of the **v**
Jn   15: 1 "I am the true **v**,
Rev 14:18 clusters of grapes from the earth's **v**,

VINEGAR

Nu   6: 3 not drink **v** made from wine or
Pr   10:26 **v** to the teeth and smoke to the eyes,
Mk   15:36 filled a sponge with wine **v**,

VINES [VINE]

Dt   24:21 do not go over the **v** again.
Hab   3:17 and there are no grapes on the **v**,

VINEYARD [VINE]

Ge   9:20 proceeded to plant a **v**.
Dt   22: 9 not plant two kinds of seed in your **v;**
1Ki 21: 1 involving a **v** belonging to Naboth
Pr   31:16 out of her earnings she plants a **v**.
SS   1: 6 my own **v** I have neglected.
Isa   5: 1 for the one I love a song about his **v:**
     27: 2 "Sing about a fruitful **v:**
Mt   21:33 a landowner who planted a **v**.
1Co   9: 7 plants a **v** and does not eat of its

VINEYARDS [VINE]

Lev 25: 3 and for six years prune your **v**
SS   2:15 the little foxes that ruin the **v**,

VIOLATE [VIOLATED, VIOLATES, VIOLATION]

Lev 26:15 and so **v** my covenant,
Ps   89:31 if they **v** my decrees and fail

VIOLATED [VIOLATE]

Jos   7:11 has sinned; they have **v** my covenant,
Jdg   2:20 "Because this nation has **v**
Da   11:32 those who have **v** the covenant,

VIOLATION [VIOLATE]

Heb   2: 2 every **v** and disobedience received

VIOLENCE [VIOLENT]

Ge   6:11 in God's sight and was full of **v**.
Ps   7:16 his **v** comes down on his own head.

Isa 53: 9 though he had done no **v**,
     60:18 No longer will **v** be heard
Eze 22:26 Her priests do **v** to my law
     45: 9 Give up your **v** and oppression
Joel 3:19 of **v** done to the people of Judah,
Ob   1:10 of the **v** against your brother Jacob,
Jnh   3: 8 give up their evil ways and their **v**.
Hab   2:17 The **v** you have done to Lebanon
Zep   3: 4 the sanctuary and do **v** to the law.
Mal   2:16 hate a man's covering himself with **v**

VIOLENT [VIOLENCE]

2Sa 22: 3 from **v** men you save me.
Pr   3:31 Do not envy a **v** man or choose any
Eze 18:10 "Suppose he has a **v** son,
Mt   28: 2 There was a **v** earthquake.
1Ti   1:13 and a persecutor and a **v** man,
      3: 3 not **v** but gentle, not quarrelsome,
Tit   1: 7 not **v**, not pursuing dishonest gain.

VIPER [VIPER'S, VIPERS]

Pr   23:32 like a snake and poisons like a **v**.
Ac   28: 3 a **v**, driven out by the heat,

VIPER'S* [VIPER]

Isa 11: 8 child put his hand into the **v** nest.

VIPERS [VIPER]

Ps 140: 3 the poison of **v** is on their lips.
Lk   3: 7 "You brood of **v!**
Ro   3:13 "The poison of **v** is on their lips."

VIRGIN [VIRGINS]

Dt   22:15 proof that she was a **v** to
1Ki   1: 2 "Let us look for a young **v** to attend
Isa   7:14 The **v** will be with child
Jer 31:21 Return, O **V** Israel,
Mt   1:23 "The **v** will be with child
Lk   1:34 "since I am a **v?"**
1Co   7:28 if a **v** marries, she has not sinned.
2Co 11: 2 that I might present you as a pure **v**

VIRGINS [VIRGIN]

Mt   25: 1 be like ten **v** who took their lamps
1Co   7:25 Now about **v:** I have no command

VIRTUES*

Col   3:14 And over all these **v** put on love,

VISIBLE

Eph   5:13 exposed by the light becomes **v**,
Col   1:16 **v** and invisible, whether thrones
Heb 11: 3 was not made out of what was **v**.

VISION [VISIONS]

Ge   15: 1 of the LORD came to Abram in a **v:**
     46: 2 God spoke to Israel in a **v** at night
Nu   24: 4 who sees a **v** from the Almighty,
1Sa   3:15 He was afraid to tell Eli the **v**,
Ps   89:19 Once you spoke in a **v**
Isa 22: 1 oracle concerning the Valley of **V:**
Da   2:45 This is the meaning of the **v** of
      7: 2 "In my **v** at night I looked,
      8: 1 I, Daniel, had a **v**,
      8:26 but seal up the **v**,

9:24 to seal up **v** and prophecy
10: 7 was the only one who saw the **v;**
Zec 1: 8 During the night I had a **v—**
Lk 1:22 They realized he had seen a **v** in
Ac 9:10 The Lord called to him in a **v,**
10:17 about the meaning of the **v,**
16: 9 Paul had a **v** of a man of Macedonia
26:19 I was not disobedient to the **v**
Rev 9:17 I saw in my **v** looked like this:

VISIONS [VISION]

Nu 12: 6 I reveal myself to him in **v,**
1Sa 3: 1 there were not many **v.**
Isa 30:10 "Give us no more **v** of what is right!
Jer 23:16 They speak **v** from their own minds,
Eze 1: 1 and I saw **v** of God.
Da 1:17 And Daniel could understand **v**
Joel 2:28 your young men will see **v.**
Ac 2:17 your young men will see **v,**

VISIT [VISITS]

Mt 25:36 in prison and you came to **v** me.'

VISITS* [VISIT]

Mic 7: 4 the day God **v** you.
1Pe 2:12 and glorify God on the day he **v** us.

VOICE [VOICES]

Ex 19:19 and the **v** of God answered him.
Dt 4:33 the **v** of God speaking out of fire,
30:20 listen to his **v,** and hold fast to him.
1Sa 15:22 as in obeying the **v** of the LORD?
Job 40: 9 and can your **v** thunder like his?
Ps 19: 4 Their **v** goes out into all the earth,
27: 7 Hear my **v** when I call, O LORD;
29: 3 **v** of the LORD is over the waters;
66:19 and heard my **v** in prayer.
95: 7 Today, if you hear his **v,**
Pr 1:20 she raises her **v** in the public squares;
8: 1 not understanding raise her **v?**
Isa 30:21 your ears will hear a **v** behind you,
40: 3 A **v** of one calling:
Jer 31:15 "A **v** is heard in Ramah,
Eze 1:24 like the **v** of the Almighty,
Mt 2:18 "A **v** is heard in Ramah,
3:17 And a **v** from heaven said,
Mk 1: 3 "a **v** of one calling in the desert,
Jn 1:23 the **v** of one calling in the desert,
5:25 the dead will hear the **v** of the Son
10: 3 and the sheep listen to his **v.**
12:28 Then a **v** came from heaven,
Ro 10:18 Their **v** has gone out into all the earth
1Th 4:16 with the **v** of the archangel
Heb 3: 7 if you hear his **v,**
2Pe 1:17 God the Father when the **v** came
Rev 3:20 If anyone hears my **v** and opens

VOICE OF THE †LORD Ex 15:26; Dt 5:25;
18:16; 1Sa 15:22; Ps 29:3, 4, 4, 5, 7, 8, 9; Isa
30:31; Hag 1:12

VOICES [VOICE]

Nu 14: 1 raised their **v** and wept aloud.
Rev 10: 3 the **v** of the seven thunders spoke.
11:15 and there were loud **v** in heaven,

VOLUNTARILY [VOLUNTEERED]

1Co 9:17 If I preach **v,** I have a reward;

VOLUNTEERED [VOLUNTARILY]

1Ch 12:38 All these were fighting men who **v**
Ne 11: 2 the men who **v** to live in Jerusalem.

VOMIT [VOMITED]

Lev 18:28 it will **v** you out as it vomited out
Pr 26:11 As a dog returns to its **v,**
Isa 28: 8 All the tables are covered with **v**
2Pe 2:22 "A dog returns to its **v,"**

VOMITED [VOMIT]

Lev 18:25 and the land **v** out its inhabitants.
Jnh 2:10 and it **v** Jonah onto dry land.

VOW [VOWED, VOWS]

Ge 28:20 Then Jacob made a **v,** saying,
Nu 6: 2 a **v** of separation to the LORD as
21: 2 Israel made this **v** to the LORD:
30: 2 a **v** to the LORD or takes an oath
Dt 23:21 If you make a **v** to the LORD
Jdg 11:30 Jephthah made a **v** to the LORD:
1Sa 1:11 And she made a **v,** saying,
Ecc 5: 4 When you make a **v** to God,
5: 5 It is better not to **v** than to make a **v**
and not fulfill it.
Ac 18:18 because of a **v** he had taken.

VOWED [VOW]

Dt 12: 6 what you have **v** to give
Jdg 11:39 and he did to her as he had **v.**
Jnh 2: 9 What I have **v** I will make good.

VOWS [VOW]

Nu 6:21 of the Nazirite who **v** his offering to
30: 4 then all her **v** and every pledge
30: 5 none of her **v** or the pledges
Ps 22:25 who fear you will I fulfill my **v,**
50:14 fulfill your **v** to the Most High,
116:14 I will fulfill my **v** to the LORD in
Pr 20:25 and only later to consider his **v.**
Jnh 1:16 to the LORD and made **v** to him.

VULTURE [VULTURES]

Hab 1: 8 like a **v** swooping to devour;

VULTURES [VULTURE]

Mt 24:28 there the **v** will gather.

W

WADI

Nu 34: 5 the **W** of Egypt and end at the Sea.
2Ki 24: 7 the **W** of Egypt to the Euphrates

WAGE [WAGED, WAGES, WAGING]

Mic 3: 5 they prepare to **w** war against him.
2Co 10: 3 we do not **w** war as the world does.

WAGED [WAGE]
Jos 11:18 Joshua **w** war against all these kings

WAGES [WAGE]
Lev 19:13 back the **w** of a hired man overnight.
Pr   10:16 **w** of the righteous bring them life,
Mic   1: 7 as the **w** of prostitutes they will again
Mal   3: 5 who defraud laborers of their **w,**
Lk   10: 7 for the worker deserves his **w.**
Jn   6: 7 "Eight months' **w** would not
      12: 5 It was worth a year's **w."**
Ro   4: 4 his **w** are not credited to him as a gift
      6:23 For the **w** of sin is death,
1Ti   5:18 and "The worker deserves his **w."**
2Pe   2:15 who loved the **w** of wickedness.

WAGING [WAGE]
Da   7:21 horn was **w** war against the saints
Ro   7:23 **w** war against the law of my mind

WAIL [WAILED, WAILING]
Isa 13: 6 **W,** for the day of the LORD is near;
Mic   1: 8 Because of this I will weep and **w;**

WAILED [WAIL]
Nu 11:18 The LORD heard you when you **w,**

WAILING [WAIL]
Ex 12:30 and there was loud **w** in Egypt,
Nu 11: 4 and again the Israelites started **w**
Ps 30:11 You turned my **w** into dancing;

WAIST
2Ki   1: 8 and with a leather belt around his **w.**
2Ch 10:10 finger is thicker than my father's **w.**
Isa 11: 5 faithfulness the sash around his **w.**
Jer 13: 1 a linen belt and put it around your **w,**
Mt   3: 4 he had a leather belt around his **w.**
Jn   13: 4 and wrapped a towel around his **w.**
Eph 6:14 belt of truth buckled around your **w,**

WAIT [AWAIT, AWAITS, WAITED, WAITING, WAITS]
Ps 27:14 **W** for the LORD;
    33:20 We **w** in hope for the LORD;
    37:34 **W** for the LORD and keep his way.
  119:166 I **w** for your salvation, O LORD,
   130: 5 I **w** for the LORD, my soul waits,
Pr   1:18 lie in **w** for their own blood;
Isa 30:18 Blessed are all who **w** for him!
La   3:26 to **w** quietly for the salvation of
Hab 2: 3 Though it linger, **w** for it;
     3:16 Yet I will **w** patiently for the day
Ac   1: 4 **w** for the gift my Father promised,
Ro   8:23 as we **w** eagerly for our adoption
1Th 1:10 and to **w** for his Son from heaven,
Tit   2:13 while we **w** for the blessed hope—

WAITED [WAIT]
Ps 40: 1 I **w** patiently for the LORD;
Jnh   4: 5 and **w** to see what would happen to

WAITING [WAIT]
Heb 9:28 to bring salvation to those who are **w**

WAITS [WAIT]
Ps 130: 6 My soul **w** for the Lord more than
Da 12:12 the one who **w** for and reaches
Ro   8:19 The creation **w** in eager expectation

WAKE [AWAKE, AWAKEN, AWOKE, WAKENS, WOKE]
Isa 26:19 **w** up and shout for joy.
Ro 13:11 for you to **w** up from your slumber,
Eph 5:14 This is why it is said: **"W** up,
Rev   3: 2 **W** up! Strengthen what remains

WAKENS* [WAKE]
Isa 50: 4 He **w** me morning by morning,
    50: 4 **w** my ear to listen

WALK [WALKED, WALKING, WALKS]
Ge 17: 1 **w** before me and be blameless.
Lev 26:12 I will **w** among you and be your God
Dt   5:33 **W** in all the way that the LORD
     6: 7 and when you **w** along the road,
   10:12 to **w** in all his ways, to love him,
   11:19 and when you **w** along the road,
   11:22 to **w** in all his ways and to hold fast
   26:17 and that you will **w** in his ways,
   28: 9 your God and **w** in his ways.
Jos 22: 5 to **w** in all his ways,
1Ki   2: 3 God requires: **W** in his ways,
Ps   1: 1 Blessed is the man who does not **w**
    15: 2 He whose **w** is blameless
    23: 4 Even though I **w** through the valley
   84:11 from those whose **w** is blameless.
   89:15 who **w** in the light of your presence,
  115: 7 feet, but they cannot **w;**
  119:45 I will **w** about in freedom,
Pr   4:12 When you **w,** your steps will not
    6:22 When you **w,** they will guide you;
    9: 6 **w** in the way of understanding.
Isa   2: 3 so that we may **w** in his paths."
    2: 5 let us **w** in the light of the LORD.
   30:21 "This is the way; **w** in it."
   40:31 they will **w** and not be faint.
   43: 2 When you **w** through the fire,
   57: 2 Those who **w** uprightly enter
Jer   6:16 But you said, 'We will not **w** in it.'
Da   4:37 And those who **w** in pride he is able
Am   3: 3 Do two **w** together unless
Mic   4: 5 All the nations may **w** in the name
    6: 8 and to love mercy and to **w** humbly
Zec 10:12 and in his name they will **w,"**
Mk   2: 9 'Get up, take your mat and **w'?**
Jn   8:12 follows me will never **w** in darkness,
Ac   3: 8 to his feet and began to **w.**
1Jn   1: 6 with him yet **w** in the darkness,
    1: 7 But if we **w** in the light,
2Jn   1: 6 his command is that you **w** in love.
3Jn   1: 3 how you continue to **w** in the truth.
Rev 9:20 that cannot see or hear or **w.**
   21:24 The nations will **w** by its light,

WALKED [WALK]
Ge   5:24 Enoch **w** with God;
   24:40 'The LORD, before whom I have **w,**

Jos 14: 9 'The land on which your feet have **w**
Eze 16:47 You not only **w** in their ways
Mt 14:29 **w** on the water and came toward

WALKING [WALK]

Dt 8: 6 **w** in his ways and revering him.
1Ki 3: 3 his love for the Lord by **w**
Da 3:25 I see four men **w** around in the fire,
Mt 14:26 the disciples saw him **w** on the lake,
Ac 3: 8 **w** and jumping, and praising God.
2Jn 1: 4 of your children **w** in the truth,
3Jn 1: 4 that my children are **w** in the truth.

WALKS [WALK]

Pr 10: 9 The man of integrity **w** securely,
13:20 He who **w** with the wise grows wise,
28:26 but he who **w** in wisdom is kept safe.
Ecc 2:14 while the fool **w** in the darkness;
Isa 33:15 He who **w** righteously
Jn 11: 9 A man who **w** by day will not

WALL [WALLS]

Ex 14:22 with a **w** of water on their right and
Jos 2:15 lived in was part of the city **w.**
6:20 gave a loud shout, the **w** collapsed,
2Ki 25: 4 Then the city **w** was broken through,
Ne 1: 3 The **w** of Jerusalem is broken down,
2:17 let us rebuild the **w** of Jerusalem,
12:27 the dedication of the **w** of Jerusalem,
Da 5: 5 and wrote on the plaster of the **w,**
Zec 2: 5 I myself will be a **w** of fire around it,
Ac 9:25 a basket through an opening in the **w.**
2Co 11:33 in a basket from a window in the **w**
Eph 2:14 the dividing **w** of hostility,
Rev 21:12 high **w** with twelve gates,

WALLOWING

2Pe 2:22 goes back to her **w** in the mud."

WALLS [WALL]

Dt 1:28 with **w** up to the sky.
Ne 2:13 examining the **w** of Jerusalem,
Ps 51:18 build up the **w** of Jerusalem.
122: 7 May there be peace within your **w**
Pr 25:28 Like a city whose **w** are broken
Isa 26: 1 God makes salvation its **w**
54:12 and all your **w** of precious stones.
58:12 be called Repairer of Broken **W,**
60:18 but you will call your **w** Salvation
Jer 52:14 down all the **w** around Jerusalem.
Heb 11:30 By faith the **w** of Jericho fell,

WANDER [WANDERED, WANDERER, WANDERING]

Nu 32:13 he made them **w** in the desert
Jas 5:19 if one of you should **w** from the truth

WANDERED [WANDER]

1Ch 16:20 they **w** from nation to nation,
Ps 107: 4 Some **w** in desert wastelands,
Eze 34: 6 My sheep **w** over all the mountains
Mt 18:12 and go to look for the one that **w** off?
1Ti 6:10 for money, have **w** from the faith
2Ti 2:18 who have **w** away from the truth.

WANDERER [WANDER]

Ge 4:12 be a restless **w** on the earth."

WANDERING [WANDER]

Dt 26: 5 "My father was a **w** Aramean,

WANT [WANTED, WANTING, WANTS]

Lev 26: 5 and you will eat all the food you **w**
1Sa 8:19 "We **w** a king over us.
1Ki 3: 5 God said, "Ask for whatever you **w**
Ps 23: 1 I shall not be in **w.**
Mt 8:29 "What do you **w** with us,
19:21 "If you **w** to be perfect, go,
Lk 18:41 "Lord, I **w** to see," he replied.
19:14 don't **w** this man to be our king.'
Ro 7:15 For what I **w** to do I do not do,
13: 3 Do you **w** to be free from fear of
2Co 12:14 what I **w** is not your possessions
Gal 4:21 you who **w** to be under the law,
Php 3:10 I **w** to know Christ and the power
4:12 whether living in plenty or in **w.**

WANTED [WANT]

Ex 4:19 the men who **w** to kill you are dead."
Jnh 4: 8 He **w** to die, and said,
Mt 14: 5 Herod **w** to kill John,
21:31 of the two did what his father **w?"**
1Co 12:18 just as he **w** them to be.
Heb 6:17 God **w** to make the unchanging

WANTING [WANT]

Da 5:27 weighed on the scales and found **w.**
2Pe 3: 9 not **w** anyone to perish,

WANTS [WANT]

Mt 5:42 the one who **w** to borrow from you.
20:26 whoever **w** to become great
Mk 8:35 **w** to save his life will lose it,
10:43 whoever **w** to become great
Ro 9:18 on whom he **w** to have mercy,
1Ti 2: 4 who **w** all men to be saved and
2Ti 3:12 everyone who **w** to live a godly life
1Pe 5: 2 as God **w** you to be;

WAR [WARRIOR, WARS]

Ex 17:16 at **w** against the Amalekites from
32:17 the sound of **w** in the camp."
Jos 11:23 Then the land had rest from **w.**
1Sa 15:18 the Amalekites; make **w** on them
2Sa 11: 1 at the time when kings go off to **w,**
Ps 68:30 Scatter the nations who delight in **w.**
120: 7 they are for **w.**
144: 1 who trains my hands for **w,**
Ecc 3: 8 a time for **w** and a time for peace.
9:18 Wisdom is better than weapons of **w,**
Isa 2: 4 nor will they train for **w** anymore.
Da 7:21 waging **w** against the saints and
9:26 **W** will continue until the end,
Ro 7:23 **w** against the law of my mind
2Co 10: 3 we do not wage **w** as the world does.
1Pe 2:11 which **w** against your soul.
Rev 12: 7 And there was **w** in heaven.
17:14 They will make **w** against the Lamb,
19:11 With justice he judges and makes **w.**

WARM [LUKEWARM, WARMS]

Ecc 4:11 But how can one keep **w** alone?
Hag 1: 6 You put on clothes, but are not **w.**
Jas 2:16 keep **w** and well fed,"

WARMS [WARM]

Isa 44:15 some of it he takes and **w** himself,

WARN* [WARNED, WARNING, WARNINGS, WARNS]

Ex   19:21 and **w** the people so they do not
Nu   24:14 let me **w** you of what this people
1Sa   8: 9 but **w** them solemnly
1Ki   2:42 swear by the LORD and **w** you,
2Ch 19:10 **w** them not to sin against the LORD;
Ps   81: 8 O my people, and I will **w** you—
Jer 42:19 Be sure of this: I **w** you today
Eze   3:18 and you do not **w** him or speak out
      3:19 But if you do **w** the wicked man
      3:20 Since you did not **w** him,
      3:21 But if you do **w** the righteous man
     33: 3 the land and blows the trumpet to **w**
     33: 6 the trumpet to **w** the people
     33: 9 if you do **w** the wicked man to turn
Lk   16:28 Let him **w** them,
Ac   4:17 we must **w** these men to speak no
1Co   4:14 but to **w** you, as my dear children.
Gal   5:21 I **w** you, as I did before,
1Th   5:14 brothers, **w** those who are idle,
2Th   3:15 but **w** him as a brother.
2Ti   2:14 **W** them before God against
Tit   3:10 **W** a divisive person once,
      3:10 and then **w** him a second time.
Rev 22:18 I **w** everyone who hears the words of

WARNED [WARN]

2Ki 17:13 The LORD **w** Israel and Judah
Ne   9:29 "You **w** them to return to your law,
Ps   2:10 be **w,** you rulers of the earth.
     19:11 By them is your servant **w;**
Jer 18: 8 if that nation I **w** repents of its evil,
     22:21 I **w** you when you felt secure,
Mt   2:12 And having been **w** in a dream not
      2:22 Having been **w** in a dream,
      3: 7 Who **w** you to flee from
1Th   4: 6 we have already told you and **w** you.
Heb 11: 7 when **w** about things not yet seen,
     12:25 when they refused him who **w** them

WARNING [WARN]

Jer   6: 8 Take **w,** O Jerusalem,
Eze 33: 5 of the trumpet but did not take **w,**
1Ti   5:20 so that the others may take **w.**

WARNINGS [WARN]

1Co 10:11 and were written down as **w**

WARNS [WARN]

Heb 12:25 if we turn away from him who **w** us

WARRIOR [WAR]

Ex   15: 3 The LORD is a **w;**
1Ch 28: 3 you are a **w** and have shed blood.'

Pr   16:32 Better a patient man than a **w,**
Jer 20:11 LORD is with me like a mighty **w;**

WARS [WAR]

Nu   21:14 the Book of the **W** of the LORD
Ps   46: 9 He makes **w** cease to the ends of
Mt   24: 6 You will hear of **w** and rumors of,

WASH [WASHED, WASHING, WHITEWASH, WHITEWASHED]

Ex   40:31 used it to **w** their hands and feet.
2Ki   5:10 **w** yourself seven times in the Jordan,
Ps   51: 7 **w** me, and I will be whiter than snow
SS   8: 7 quench love; rivers cannot **w** it away.
Jer   4:14 the evil from your heart and
Lk   11:38 noticing that Jesus did not first **w**
Jn   9: 7 **"w** in the Pool of Siloam"
     13: 5 and began to **w** his disciples' feet,
Ac   22:16 be baptized and **w** your sins away,
Jas   4: 8 **W** your hands, you sinners,
Rev 22:14 Blessed are those who **w** their robes,

MUST WASH See MUST

WASHED [WASH]

Ps   73:13 in vain have I **w** my hands
Jn   9:11 I went and **w,** and then I could see."
1Co   6:11 But you were **w,** you were sanctified,
Heb 10:22 and having our bodies **w**
2Pe   2:22 "A sow that is **w** goes back
Rev   7:14 they have **w** their robes

WASHING [WASH]

Ex   30:18 with its bronze stand, for **w.**
2Ch   4: 6 to be used by the priests for **w.**
Jn   2: 6 used by the Jews for ceremonial **w,**
Eph   5:26 the **w** with water through the word,
1Ti   5:10 **w** the feet of the saints,
Tit   3: 5 through the **w** of rebirth and renewal

WASTE [WASTED, WASTING]

Isa 24:16 But I said, "I **w** away, I **w** away!
Jer   2:15 They have laid **w** his land;
Eze   4:17 and will **w** away because of their sin.
Mk   14: 4 "Why this **w** of perfume?

WASTED [WASTE]

Jn   6:12 Let nothing be **w."**

WASTELAND [LAND]

Ps   68: 7 when you marched through the **w,**
    106:14 in the **w** they put God to the test.
Isa 43:19 in the desert and streams in the **w.**

WASTELANDS [LAND]

Ps 107: 4 Some wandered in desert **w,**

WASTING [WASTE]

2Co   4:16 Though outwardly we are **w** away,

WATCH [WATCHED, WATCHER, WATCHES, WATCHFUL, WATCHING, WATCHMAN, WATCHMEN]

Ge   31:49 the LORD keep **w** between you

Dt	4:15	**w** yourselves very carefully,
Ps	39: 1	"I will **w** my ways
	59: 9	O my Strength, I **w** for you;
	90: 4	or like a **w** in the night.
	141: 3	keep **w** over the door of my lips.
Pr	4: 6	and she will **w** over you.
	6:22	they will **w** over you;
Jer	31:10	**w** over his flock like a shepherd.'
Mic	7: 7	for me, I **w** in hope for the LORD,
Mt	7:15	"**W** out for false prophets.
	24:42	"Therefore keep **w**,
	26:41	"**W** and pray so that you will not fall
Mk	13:35	"Therefore keep **w** because you do
Lk	2: 8	keeping **w** over their flocks at night.
Php	3: 2	**W** out for those dogs,
1Ti	4:16	**W** your life and doctrine closely.
Heb	13:17	They keep **w** over you
2Jn	1: 8	**W** out that you do not lose

WATCHED [WATCH]

| Mt | 26:16 | then on Judas **w** for an opportunity |

WATCHER* [WATCH]

| Job | 7:20 | O **w** of men? |

WATCHES* [WATCH]

Nu	19: 5	While he **w**, the heifer is to be
Job	24:15	The eye of the adulterer **w** for dusk;
Ps	1: 6	For the LORD **w** over the way of
	33:14	from his dwelling place he **w** all who
	63: 6	of you through the **w** of the night.
	119:148	My eyes stay open through the **w** of
	121: 3	he who **w** over you will not slumber;
	121: 4	he who **w** over Israel will neither
	121: 5	The LORD **w** over you—
	127: 1	Unless the LORD **w** over the city,
	145:20	The LORD **w** over all who love him,
	146: 9	The LORD **w** over the alien
Pr	31:27	She **w** over the affairs
Ecc	11: 4	Whoever **w** the wind will not plant;
La	2:19	as the **w** of the night begin;
	4:16	he no longer **w** over them.

WATCHFUL [WATCH]

| Col | 4: 2 | being **w** and thankful. |

WATCHING [WATCH]

Jer	1:12	for I am **w** to see that my word
	44:27	For I am **w** over them for harm,
Mk	15:40	women were **w** from a distance.
Lk	12:37	servants whose master finds them **w**

WATCHMAN [WATCH]

| Eze | 3:17 | I have made you a **w** for the house |
| | 33: 6 | but I will hold the **w** accountable |

WATCHMEN [WATCH]

Ps	130: 6	for the Lord more than **w** wait for
Isa	56:10	Israel's **w** are blind,
Mic	7: 4	The day of your **w** has come,

WATCHTOWER [TOWER]

| Isa | 21: 8 | my lord, I stand on the **w**; |

WATER [WATERED, WATERING, WATERS, WELL-WATERED]

Ge	1: 6	to separate **w** from **w**."
	1:20	Let the **w** teem with living creatures,
	7:18	ark floated on the surface of the **w**.
Ex	7:20	all the **w** was changed into blood.
	15:25	and the **w** became sweet.
	17: 1	but there was no **w** for the people
Nu	5:19	may this bitter **w** that brings a curse
	20: 2	there was no **w** for the community,
	21: 5	There is no **w**!
2Ki	2: 8	rolled it up and struck the **w** with it.
	6: 5	the iron axhead fell into the **w**.
Ps	1: 3	like a tree planted by streams of **w**,
	22:14	I am poured out like **w**,
	42: 1	As the deer pants for streams of **w**,
Pr	5:15	Drink **w** from your own cistern,
	9:17	"Stolen **w** is sweet;
	25:21	give him **w** to drink.
Isa	12: 3	With joy you will draw **w** from
	30:20	and the **w** of affliction,
	32: 2	of **w** in the desert and the shadow of
	49:10	and lead them beside springs of **w**.
Jer	2:13	the spring of living **w**,
	17: 8	be like a tree planted by the **w**
	31: 9	I will lead them beside streams of **w**
Eze	36:25	I will sprinkle clean **w** on you,
Zec	14: 8	On that day living **w** will flow out
Mt	14:29	on the **w** and came toward Jesus.
Mk	1: 8	I baptize you with **w**,
	9:41	a cup of **w** in my name because
Lk	5: 4	"Put out into deep **w**,
Jn	2: 9	the **w** that had been turned into wine.
	3: 5	unless he is born of **w** and the Spirit.
	4:10	he would have given you living **w**."
	7:38	streams of living **w** will flow from
	19:34	a sudden flow of blood and **w**.
Eph	5:26	cleansing her by the washing with **w**
Heb	10:22	our bodies washed with pure **w**.
Jas	3:11	fresh **w** and salt **w** flow from the same spring?
1Pe	3:21	and this **w** symbolizes baptism that
2Pe	2:17	These men are springs without **w**
1Jn	5: 6	the one who came by **w** and blood—
Rev	7:17	lead them to springs of living **w**.
	21: 6	from the spring of the **w** of life.
	22: 1	the river of the **w** of life,
	22:17	the free gift of the **w** of life.

WATERED [WATER]

| Ps | 104:16 | The trees of the LORD are well **w**, |
| 1Co | 3: 6 | I planted the seed, Apollos **w** it, |

WATERING [WATER]

| Ge | 2:10 | A river **w** the garden flowed |
| Isa | 55:10 | not return to it without **w** the earth |

WATERS [WATER]

Ge	1: 2	of God was hovering over the **w**.
	1:10	the gathered **w** he called "seas."
	7: 7	entered the ark to escape the **w** of
Ex	14:21	The **w** were divided,
Jos	4: 7	the **w** of the Jordan were cut off.

Ps 18:16 he drew me out of deep **w.**
23: 2 he leads me beside quiet **w,**
106:32 By the **w** of Meribah they angered
Ecc 11: 1 Cast your bread upon the **w,**
SS 8: 7 Many **w** cannot quench love;
Isa 11: 9 of the LORD as the **w** cover the sea.
43: 2 When you pass through the **w,**
55: 1 come to the **w;**
58:11 like a spring whose **w** never fail.
Hab 2:14 as the **w** cover the sea.
1Co 3: 7 nor he who **w** is anything,
Rev 8:11 A third of the **w** turned bitter,

WAVE [WAVES]
Ex 29:24 **w** them before the LORD as a **w** offering.
Lev 23:11 to **w** the sheaf before the LORD
Jas 1: 6 he who doubts is like a **w** of the sea,

WAVE OFFERING Ex 29:24, 26; 35:22;
38:24, 29; Lev 7:30; 8:27, 29; 9:21; 10:15; 14:12,
24; 23:15, 17, 20; Nu 6:20; 8:11, 13, 15, 21;
18:18

WAVER*
1Ki 18:21 "How long will you **w**
Ro 4:20 Yet he did not **w** through unbelief

WAVES [WAVE]
2Sa 22: 5 "The **w** of death swirled about me;
Ps 89: 9 when its **w** mount up, you still them.
Isa 57:20 whose **w** cast up mire and mud.
Mt 8:27 Even the winds and the **w** obey him!
Eph 4:14 tossed back and forth by the **w,**
Jude 1:13 They are wild **w** of the sea,

WAX
Ps 22:14 My heart has turned to **w;**
97: 5 melt like **w** before the LORD,

WAY [AWAY, WAYS]
Ge 3:24 to guard the **w** to the tree of life.
Ex 13:21 guide them on their **w** and by night
18:20 and show them the **w** to live
Dt 1:33 to show you the **w** you should go.
32: 6 Is this the **w** you repay the LORD,
Jos 23: 5 will drive them out of your **w.**
1Sa 12:23 the **w** that is good and right.
2Sa 7:19 Is this your usual **w** of dealing
22:31 "As for God, his **w** is perfect;
1Ki 8:23 continue wholeheartedly in your **w.**
8:36 Teach them the right **w** to live,
2Ch 6:27 Teach them the right **w** to live,
Job 23:10 But he knows the **w** that I take;
Ps 1: 1 or stand in the **w** of sinners
1: 6 For the LORD watches over the **w**
18:30 As for God, his **w** is perfect;
32: 8 teach you in the **w** you should go;
37: 5 Commit your **w** to the LORD;
86:11 Teach me your **w,** O LORD,
119: 9 a young man keep his **w** pure?
139:24 See if there is any offensive **w** in me,
139:24 and lead me in the **w** everlasting.
Pr 4:11 I guide you in the **w** of wisdom
12:15 The **w** of a fool seems right to him,

14:12 a **w** that seems right to a man,
16:17 who guards his **w** guards his life.
19: 2 nor to be hasty and miss the **w.**
22: 6 Train a child in the **w** he should go,
30:19 and the **w** of a man with a maiden.
Isa 30:21 saying, "This is the **w;** walk in it."
35: 8 be called the **W** of Holiness.
40: 3 prepare the **w** for the LORD;
48:17 directs you in the **w** you should go.
53: 6 each of us has turned to his own **w;**
55: 7 Let the wicked forsake his **w** and
Jer 5:31 and my people love it this **w.**
21: 8 I am setting before you the **w** of life and the **w** of death.
Mal 3: 1 who will prepare the **w** before me.
Mt 3: 3 'Prepare the **w** for the Lord,
5:12 for in the same **w** they persecuted
Lk 7:27 who will prepare your **w** before you.
Jn 14: 6 "I am the **w** and the truth and the life.
Ac 1:11 in the same **w** you have seen him go
9: 2 any there who belonged to the **W,**
19: 9 and publicly maligned the **W.**
22: 4 the followers of this **W** to their death
24:14 of our fathers as a follower of the **W,**
1Co 9:24 Run in such a **w** as to get the prize.
10:13 he will also provide a **w** out
12:31 I will show you the most excellent **w.**
14: 1 Follow the **w** of love
Col 1:10 and may please him in every **w:**
Tit 2:10 every **w** they will make the teaching
Heb 2:17 be made like his brothers in every **w,**
4:15 tempted in every **w,** just as we are—
9: 8 the **w** into the Most Holy Place had
10:20 by a new and living **w** opened for us
13:18 to live honorably in every **w.**
Jas 5:20 from the error of his **w** will save him
2Pe 2:21 for them not to have known the **w**

WAYS [WAY]
Ge 6:12 on earth had corrupted their **w.**
Ex 33:13 teach me your **w** so I may know you
Dt 10:12 to walk in all his **w,** to love him,
26:17 and that you will walk in his **w,**
30:16 to walk in his **w,**
32: 4 and all his **w** are just.
Jos 22: 5 to walk in all his **w,**
1Ki 8:58 to walk in all his **w** and to keep
2Ki 17:13 "Turn from your evil **w.**
2Ch 11:17 walking in the **w** of David and
Job 34:21 "His eyes are on the **w** of men;
Ps 25: 4 Show me your **w,** O LORD,
25:10 All the **w** of the LORD are loving
37: 7 not fret when men succeed in their **w**
51:13 I will teach transgressors your **w,**
77:13 Your **w,** O God, are holy.
119:59 I have considered my **w**
139: 3 familiar with all my **w.**
145:17 The LORD is righteous in all his **w**
Pr 2:12 Wisdom will save you from the **w**
3: 6 in all your **w** acknowledge him,
3:17 Her **w** are pleasant **w,**
4:26 and take only **w** that are firm.
5:21 a man's **w** are in full view of
6: 6 consider its **w** and be wise!

	7:25	Do not let your heart turn to her **w**
	16: 2	All a man's **w** seem innocent to him,
	16: 7	man's **w** are pleasing to the LORD,
	21: 2	All a man's **w** seem right to him,
Isa	2: 3	He will teach us his **w,**
	42:24	For they would not follow his **w;**
	55: 8	neither are your **w** my **w,**"
Jer	10: 2	not learn the **w** of the nations
	18:11	So turn from your evil **w,**
Eze	16:47	You not only walked in their **w**
	28:15	You were blameless in your **w**
	33: 8	speak out to dissuade him from his **w**
Da	4:37	and all his **w** are just.
Hos	14: 9	The **w** of the LORD are right;
Jnh	3:10	how they turned from their evil **w,**
Hag	1: 5	"Give careful thought to your **w.**
Lk	3: 5	the rough **w** smooth.
Ro	1:30	they invent **w** of doing evil;
1Co	13:11	I put childish **w** behind me.
Col	3: 7	You used to walk in these **w,**
Jas	3: 2	We all stumble in many **w,**
Rev	15: 3	Just and true are your **w,**

WAYWARD [WAYWARDNESS]

Pr	2:16	the **w** wife with her seductive words,
	23:27	and a **w** wife is a narrow well.

WAYWARDNESS* [WAYWARD]

Pr	1:32	the **w** of the simple will kill them,
Hos	14:4	"I will heal their **w**

WEAK [WEAKENED, WEAKER, WEAKLING, WEAKNESS, WEAKNESSES]

Jdg	16: 7	I'll become as **w** as any other man."
Ps	41: 1	who has regard for the **w;**
	72:13	He will take pity on the **w**
	82: 3	Defend the cause of the **w**
	82: 4	Rescue the **w** and needy;
Eze	34: 4	not strengthened the **w** or
Mt	26:41	is willing, but the body is **w.**"
Ac	20:35	of hard work we must help the **w,**
Ro	14: 1	Accept him whose faith is **w,**
	15: 1	to bear with the failings of the **w**
1Co	1:27	the **w** things of the world to shame
	8: 9	a stumbling block to the **w.**
	9:22	To the **w** I became **w,**
	11:30	That is why many among you are **w**
2Co	12:10	For when I am **w,** then I am strong.
Gal	4: 9	to those **w** and miserable principles?
1Th	5:14	help the **w,** be patient with everyone.
Heb	7:18	because it was **w** and useless
	12:12	your feeble arms and **w** knees.

WEAK-WILLED* [WILL]

Eze	16:30	" 'How **w** you are,
2Ti	3: 6	and gain control over **w** women,

WEAKENED [WEAK]

Ro	8: 3	in that it was **w** by the sinful nature,

WEAKER* [WEAK]

2Sa	3: 1	house of Saul grew **w** and **w.**
1Co	12:22	that seem to be **w** are indispensable,

1Pe	3: 7	with respect as the **w** partner

WEAKLING* [WEAK]

Joel	3:10	Let the **w** say, "I am strong!"

WEAKNESS* [WEAK]

La	1: 6	in **w** they have fled before
Ro	8:26	the Spirit helps us in our **w.**
1Co	1:25	and the **w** of God is stronger
	2: 3	I came to you in **w** and fear,
	15:43	it is sown in **w,** it is raised
2Co	11:30	boast of the things that show my **w.**
	12: 9	for my power is made perfect in **w."**
	13: 4	For to be sure, he was crucified in **w,**
Heb	5: 2	since he himself is subject to **w.**
	11:34	whose **w** was turned to strength;

WEAKNESSES* [WEAK]

2Co	12: 5	except about my **w.**
	12: 9	the more gladly about my **w,**
	12:10	for Christ's sake, I delight in **w,**
Heb	4:15	to sympathize with our **w,**

WEALTH [WEALTHY]

Dt	8:18	gives you the ability to produce **w,**
1Sa	2: 7	The LORD sends poverty and **w;**
2Ch	1:11	and you have not asked for **w,**
Ps	37:16	than the **w** of many wicked;
	39: 6	he heaps up **w,** not knowing who
	49: 6	those who trust in their **w** and boast
	49:10	and leave their **w** to others.
Pr	3: 9	Honor the LORD with your **w,**
	10: 4	but diligent hands bring **w.**
	10:22	The blessing of the LORD brings **w,**
	11: 4	**W** is worthless in the day of wrath,
	13: 7	yet has great **w.**
	13:22	but a sinner's **w** is stored up for
	15:16	than great **w** with turmoil.
	22: 4	and the fear of the LORD bring **w**
Ecc	5:10	whoever loves **w** is never satisfied
	5:13	**w** hoarded to the harm
SS	8: 7	give all the **w** of his house for love,
Ob	1:13	nor seize their **w** in the day
Mt	13:22	and the deceitfulness of **w** choke it,
Mk	10:22	because he had great **w.**
	12:44	They all gave out of their **w;**
Lk	15:13	and there squandered his **w**
	16:11	trustworthy in handling worldly **w,**
1Ti	6:17	nor to put their hope in **w,**
Jas	5: 2	Your **w** has rotted,
	5: 3	You have hoarded **w** in the last days.
Rev	3:17	say, 'I am rich; I have acquired **w**
	5:12	to receive power and **w** and wisdom

WEALTHY [WEALTH]

Ge	13: 2	Abram had become very **w**
Lk	19: 2	a chief tax collector and was **w.**

WEANED

Ps	131: 2	like a **w** child is my soul within me.

WEAPON [WEAPONS]

Ne	4:17	work with one hand and held a **w**
Isa	54:17	no **w** forged against you will prevail,

WEAPONS [WEAPON]

Ecc 9:18 Wisdom is better than **w** of war,
Isa 13: 5 the LORD and the **w** of his wrath—
Jn   18: 3 carrying torches, lanterns and **w.**
2Co   6: 7 with **w** of righteousness in
     10: 4 The **w** we fight with are not the **w** of

WEAR [WEARING, WORE, WORN]

Lev 19:19 not **w** clothing woven of two kinds
Dt   8: 4 not **w** out and your feet did not swell
     22: 5 woman must not **w** men's clothing,
             nor a man **w** women's clothing,
     29: 5 your clothes did not **w** out,
Ps 102:26 they will all **w** out like a garment.
Pr   23: 4 Do not **w** yourself out to get rich;
Isa 51: 6 the earth will **w** out like a garment
Mt   6:31 or 'What shall we **w?'**
Heb   1:11 they will all **w** out like a garment.
Rev   3:18 and white clothes to **w,**
     19: 8 clean, was given her to **w."**

WEARIED [WEARY]

Isa 43:22 you have not **w** yourselves for me,
     43:24 and **w** me with your offenses.
Mal   2:17 You have **w** the LORD

WEARIES* [WEARY]

Ecc 10:15 A fool's work **w** him;
     12:12 and much study **w** the body.

WEARING [WEAR]

Ge   37:23 the richly ornamented robe he was **w**
1Sa 18: 4 Jonathan took off the robe he was **w**
2Sa 13:18 She was **w** a richly ornamented robe,
1Ki 11:30 of the new cloak he was **w** and tore it
Jn   19: 5 When Jesus came out **w** the crown
             of thorns
Jas   2: 3 attention to the man **w** fine clothes
1Pe   3: 3 such as braided hair and the **w**
Rev   7: 9 They were **w** white robes

WEARY [WEARIED, WEARIES]

Ps   68: 9 you refreshed your **w** inheritance.
Isa   1:14 I am **w** of bearing them.
     40:28 He will not grow tired or **w,**
     40:31 they will run and not grow **w,**
     50: 4 to know the word that sustains the **w.**
Jer   9: 5 they **w** themselves with sinning.
Mt   11:28 all you who are **w** and burdened,
Gal   6: 9 Let us not become **w** in doing good,
Heb 12: 3 so that you will not grow **w**
Rev   2: 3 and have not grown **w.**

WEDDING

Ps   45: T A **w** song.
Mt   22: 2 a king who prepared a **w** banquet
     22:11 who was not wearing **w** clothes.
Rev 19: 7 For the **w** of the Lamb has come,

[BREAK] WEDLOCK (KJV)
See COMMIT ADULTERY

WEED* [WEEDS]

Mt   13:41 they will **w** out of his kingdom

WEEDS [WEED]

Mt   13:25 his enemy came and sowed **w** among

WEEK [WEEKS]

Mt   28: 1 at dawn on the first day of the **w,**
Lk   18:12 I fast twice a **w** and give
1Co 16: 2 On the first day of every **w,**

WEEKS [WEEK]

Ex   34:22 the Feast of **W** with the firstfruits of
Lev 23:15 count off seven full **w.**

WEEP [WEEPING, WEPT]

Ps   69:10 I **w** and fast, I must endure scorn;
Ecc   3: 4 a time to **w** and a time to laugh,
La   1:16 "This is why I **w**
Lk   6:21 Blessed are you who **w** now,
     23:28 do not **w** for me;

WEEPING [WEEP]

Ne   8: 9 For all the people had been **w**
Ps   6: 8 for the LORD has heard my **w.**
     30: 5 **w** may remain for a night,
    126: 6 He who goes out **w,**
Jer 31:15 Rachel **w** for her children
Mt   2:18 Rachel **w** for her children
      8:12 will be **w** and gnashing of teeth."
     13:42 will be **w** and gnashing of teeth.
     22:13 will be **w** and gnashing of teeth.'
     24:51 will be **w** and gnashing of teeth.
     25:30 will be **w** and gnashing of teeth.'

WEIGH [OUTWEIGHS, WEIGHED, WEIGHS, WEIGHTIER, WEIGHTS]

1Co 14:29 should **w** carefully what is said.

WEIGHED [WEIGH]

1Sa   2: 3 and by him deeds are **w.**
Job 28:15 nor can its price be **w** in silver.
Da   5:27 *Tekel:* You have been **w** on the
Lk   21:34 or your hearts will be **w** down

WEIGHS [WEIGH]

Pr   12:25 An anxious heart **w** a man down,
     15:28 heart of the righteous **w** its answers,
     21: 2 but the LORD **w** the heart.
     24:12 not he who **w** the heart perceive it?
Ecc   8: 6 a man's misery **w** heavily upon him.

WEIGHTIER* [WEIGH]

Jn   5:36 "I have testimony **w** than that

WEIGHTS [WEIGH]

Lev 19:36 Use honest scales and honest **w,**
Dt   25:13 Do not have two differing **w**
Pr   11: 1 but accurate **w** are his delight.
     20:23 The LORD detests differing **w,**

WELCOME [WELCOMED, WELCOMES]

Mt   10:14 not **w** you or listen to your words,
Mk   9:37 not **w** me but the one who sent me."
2Pe   1:11 a rich **w** into the eternal kingdom

2Jn 1:10 into your house or **w** him.
3Jn 1:10 he refuses to **w** the brothers.

WELCOMED [WELCOME]
Lk 10: 8 "When you enter a town and are **w**,

WELCOMES [WELCOME]
Mt 18: 5 "And whoever **w** a little child
2Jn 1:11 Anyone who **w** him shares

WELL [WELLED, WELLING, WELLS]
Ge 12:16 He treated Abram **w** for her sake,
Dt 5:16 that it may go **w** with you in the land
6: 3 to obey so that it may go **w**
12:28 so that it may always go **w** with you
2Ch 6: 8 you did **w** to have this in your heart.
Ps 109:21 deal **w** with me for your name's sake
Pr 5: 1 listen **w** to my words of insight,
5:15 running water from your own **w**.
23:27 and a wayward wife is a narrow **w**.
Isa 3:10 the righteous it will be **w** with them,
Mt 3:17 with him I am **w** pleased."
15:31 the crippled made **w**,
17: 5 with him I am **w** pleased.
25:21 "His master replied, '**W** done,
Lk 14: 5 that falls into a **w** on the Sabbath day
17:19 your faith has made you **w**."
Jn 4: 6 Jacob's **w** was there, and Jesus,
Ac 15:29 You will do **w** to avoid these things.
Eph 6: 3 "that it may go **w** with you and
Jas 5:15 in faith will make the sick person **w**;
2Pe 1:17 with him I am **w** pleased."
3Jn 1: 2 and that all may go **w** with you,

WELL-BEING
Ezr 6:10 pray for the **w** of the king and his
Ps 35:27 who delights in the **w** of his servant."

WELL-WATERED [WATER]
Isa 58:11 You will be like a **w** garden,
Jer 31:12 They will be like a **w** garden,

WELLED* [WELL]
2Co 8: 2 poverty **w** up in rich generosity.

WELLING* [WELL]
Jn 4:14 spring of water **w** up to eternal life."

WELLS [WELL]
Dt 6:11 **w** you did not dig,
Ne 9:25 **w** already dug, vineyards,
Isa 12: 3 water from the **w** of salvation.

WELLSPRING* [SPRING]
Pr 4:23 for it is the **w** of life.

WEPT [WEEP]
Nu 14: 1 raised their voices and **w** aloud.
Ezr 3:12 **w** aloud when they saw
Ps 137: 1 the rivers of Babylon we sat and **w**
Isa 38: 3 And Hezekiah **w** bitterly.
Lk 19:41 saw the city, he **w** over it
22:62 And he went outside and **w** bitterly.
Jn 11:35 Jesus **w**.
Rev 5: 4 I **w** and wept because no one

WEST [WESTERN]
Ge 13:14 and look north and south, east and **w**.
Ps 103:12 as far as the east is from the **w**,
107: 3 from east and **w**, from north and
Isa 43: 5 the east and gather you from the **w**.
Zec 14: 4 be split in two from east to **w**,

WESTERN [WEST]
Nu 34: 6 " 'Your **w** boundary will be the coast
Zec 14: 8 the eastern sea and half to the **w** sea,

WET
Lk 7:38 she began to **w** his feet with her tears

WHALE(S) (KJV) See CREATURES,
HUGE FISH, MONSTER

WHAT [WHATEVER]
Ge 3:15 woman, "**W** is this you have done?"
Ex 3:13 they ask me, '**W** is his name?'
Dt 10:12 **w** does the LORD your God ask of
30:11 Now **w** I am commanding you today
Mic 6: 8 showed you, O man, **w** is good. And
w does the LORD require of you?

WHATEVER [WHAT]
2Ch 1: 7 for **w** you want me to give you."
Ps 1: 3 **W** he does prospers.
135: 6 The LORD does **w** pleases him,
Mt 16:19 and **w** you loose on earth will
18:18 **w** you bind on earth will be bound
Mk 11:24 **w** you ask for in prayer,
Jn 14:13 I will do **w** you ask in my name,
15:16 the Father will give you **w** you ask
16:23 my Father will give you **w** you ask
Php 4: 8 **w** is true, **w** is noble, **w** is right,
1Jn 5:15 know that he hears us—**w** we ask—

WHEAT
Ex 34:22 with the firstfruits of the **w** harvest,
Mt 3:12 gathering his **w** into the barn
13:25 and sowed weeds among the **w**,
Lk 22:31 Satan has asked to sift you as **w**.
Jn 12:24 of **w** falls to the ground and dies,

WHEEL [WHEELS]
Eze 1:16 like a **w** intersecting a **w**.

WHEELS [WHEEL]
Ex 14:25 the **w** of their chariots come off so
Eze 1:16 appearance and structure of the **w**:
Da 7: 9 and its **w** were all ablaze.

WHENEVER
Dt 4: 7 near us **w** we pray to him?
1Co 11:26 For **w** you eat this bread
2Co 3:16 But **w** anyone turns to the Lord,
Jas 1: 2 **w** you face trials of many kinds,
1Jn 3:20 **w** our hearts condemn us.

WHERE [WHEREVER]
Ex 3: 5 **w** you are standing is holy ground."
Dt 11:24 Every place **w** you set your foot will
32:37 He will say: "Now **w** are their gods,
Job 28:12 **W** does understanding dwell?

	28:23	he alone knows **w** it dwells,
Ps	26: 8	I love the house **w** you live,
	42: 3	"**W** is your God?"
	121: 1	**w** does my help come from?
	139: 7	**W** can I go from your Spirit?
Hos	13:14	**w** are your plagues?
Mal	1: 6	**w** is the honor due me?
Mt	6:21	For **w** your treasure is,
	28: 6	Come and see the place **w** he lay.
1Co	15:55	**W**, O death, is your sting?"
Col	3: 1	**w** Christ is seated at the right hand
2Pe	3: 4	"**W** is this 'coming' he promised?"

WHEREVER [WHERE]

Jos	1: 7	that you may be successful **w** you go.
Mk	14: 9	**w** the gospel is preached throughout
Lk	9:57	"I will follow you **w** you go."
Rev	14: 4	They follow the Lamb **w** he goes.

WHETHER

Ro	14: 8	So, **w** we live or die,
1Co	12:13	into one body—**w** Jews or Greeks,
Php	4:12	**w** living in plenty or in want.
Col	3:17	whatever you do, **w** in word or deed,
1Jn	4: 1	but test the spirits to see **w** they are

WHILE

Ps	32: 6	pray to you **w** you may be found;
Isa	55: 6	Seek the LORD **w** he may be found;
	65:24	they are still speaking I will hear.
Da	9:21	**w** I was still in prayer,
Jn	12:35	Walk **w** you have the light,
	16:16	a little **w** you will see me no more,
Ro	5: 8	**W** we were still sinners,
2Co	5: 4	For **w** we are in this tent,
Tit	2:13	**w** we wait for the blessed hope—
1Pe	5:10	after you have suffered a little **w**,

WHIP [WHIPS]

Jn	2:15	So he made a **w** out of cords,

WHIPS [WHIP]

Jos	23:13	**w** on your backs and thorns

WHIRLWIND [WIND]

2Ki	2:11	and Elijah went up to heaven in a **w**.
Ps	77:18	Your thunder was heard in the **w**,
Hos	8: 7	"They sow the wind and reap the **w**.
Na	1: 3	His way is in the **w** and the storm,

WHISPER [WHISPERED]

1Ki	19:12	And after the fire came a gentle **w**.
Job	26:14	how faint the **w** we hear of him!
Ps	107:29	He stilled the storm to a **w**;

WHISPERED [WHISPER]

Mt	10:27	what is **w** in your ear,

WHITE [WHITER]

Isa	1:18	they shall be as **w** as snow;
Da	7: 9	the hair of his head was **w** like wool.
Zec	1: 8	brown and **w** horses.
	6: 3	the third **w**, and the fourth dappled—
Mt	5:36	for you cannot make even one hair **w**
	28: 3	and his clothes were **w** as snow.

Ac	1:10	dressed in **w** stood beside them.
Rev	1:14	His head and hair were **w** like wool,
	2:17	a **w** stone with a new name written
	3: 4	dressed in **w**, for they are worthy.
	6: 2	and there before me was a **w** horse!
	7:13	"These in **w** robes—
	14:14	and there before me was a **w** cloud,
	19:11	and there before me was a **w** horse,
	20:11	Then I saw a great **w** throne

WHITER [WHITE]

Ps	51: 7	and I will be **w** than snow.
Mk	9: 3	**w** than anyone in the world

WHITEWASH [WASH]

Eze	13:10	they cover it with **w**,
	22:28	Her prophets **w** these deeds for them

WHITEWASHED [WASH]

Mt	23:27	You are like **w** tombs,
Ac	23: 3	"God will strike you, you **w** wall!

WHOEVER

Mt	10:32	"**W** acknowledges me before men,
	12:50	does the will of my Father
Mk	3:29	But **w** blasphemes against
	4:25	**W** has will be given more;
	8:35	**w** wants to save his life will lose it,
	9:40	for **w** is not against us is for us.
Jn	3:36	**W** believes in the Son has eternal life
1Jn	4:16	**W** lives in love lives in God,
Rev	22:17	**W** is thirsty, let him come;

WHOLE [WHOLLY, WHOLEHEARTED, WHOLEHEARTEDLY]

Ge	11: 1	Now the **w** world had one language
	18:28	Will you destroy the **w** city because
Ex	12:47	The **w** community of Israel must
	19: 5	Although the **w** earth is mine,
Lev	16:17	the **w** community of Israel.
Nu	14:21	glory of the LORD fills the **w** earth,
	32:13	until the **w** generation of those
Dt	13:16	as a **w** burnt offering to the LORD
	19: 8	the **w** land he promised them,
Jos	2: 3	to spy out the **w** land."
1Sa	1:28	For his **w** life he will be given over
	17:46	the **w** world will know that there is
1Ki	10:24	The **w** world sought audience
2Ki	21: 8	and will keep the **w** Law
Ps	48: 2	the joy of the **w** earth.
	72:19	the **w** earth be filled with his glory.
Pr	4:22	and health to a man's **w** body.
	8:31	rejoicing in his **w** world
Ecc	12:13	for this is the **w** [duty] of man.
Isa	1: 5	your **w** heart afflicted.
	6: 3	the **w** earth is full of his glory."
	14:26	the plan determined for the **w** world;
La	2:15	the joy of the **w** earth?"
Eze	34: 6	They were scattered over the **w** earth
	37:11	these bones are the **w** house of Israel.
Da	2:35	and filled the **w** earth.
Zep	1:18	the **w** world will be consumed,
Zec	14: 9	LORD will be king over the **w** earth.
Mal	3:10	Bring the **w** tithe into the storehouse,

Mt   5:29 your **w** body to be thrown into hell.
      6:22 your **w** body will be full of light.
     16:26 be for a man if he gains the **w** world,
     24:14 be preached in the **w** world as
Mk   15:33 darkness came over the **w** land
Lk   21:35 who live on the face of the **w** earth.
Jn   12:19 the **w** world has gone after him!"
     13:10 his **w** body is clean.
     21:25 the **w** world would not have room for
Ac   17:26 that they should inhabit the **w** earth;
     20:27 to proclaim to you the **w** will of God.
Ro   1: 9 whom I serve with my **w** heart
      3:19 the **w** world held accountable to God
      8:22 that the **w** creation has been groaning
1Co   4: 9 a spectacle to the **w** universe,
      5: 6 works through the **w** batch of dough?
     12:17 If the **w** body were an eye,
Gal   3:22 that the **w** world is a prisoner of sin,
      5: 3 to obey the **w** law.
Eph   2:21 In him the **w** building is joined
      4:10 in order to fill the **w** universe.)
      4:13 to the **w** measure of the fullness
1Th   5:23 May your **w** spirit,
Tit   1:11 they are ruining **w** households
Jas   2:10 whoever keeps the **w** law and yet
1Jn   2: 2 but also for the sins of the **w** world.
      5:19 that the **w** world is under the control
Rev   3:10 going to come upon the **w** world
      6:12 the **w** moon turned blood red,
     12: 9 who leads the **w** world astray.
     13: 3 The **w** world was astonished

WHOLEHEARTED* [HEART, WHOLE]

2Ki 20: 3 faithfully and with **w** devotion
1Ch 28: 9 and serve him with **w** devotion and
     29:19 **w** devotion to keep your commands,
Isa 38: 3 faithfully and with **w** devotion

WHOLEHEARTEDLY* [HEART, WHOLE]

Nu   14:24 a different spirit and follows me **w**,
     32:11 not followed me **w**, not one of
     32:12 for they followed the LORD **w**.'
Dt   1:36 because he followed the LORD **w**."
Jos 14: 8 followed the LORD my God **w**.
     14: 9 the LORD my God **w**.'
     14:14 the God of Israel, **w**.
1Ki   8:23 with your servants who continue **w**
1Ch 29: 9 given freely and **w** to the LORD.
2Ch   6:14 with your servants who continue **w**
     15:15 the oath because they had sworn it **w**.
     19: 9 "You must serve faithfully and **w**
     25: 2 in the eyes of the LORD, but not **w**.
     31:21 he sought his God and worked **w**.
Ro   6:17 you **w** obeyed the form of teaching
Eph   6: 7 Serve **w**, as if you were serving

WHOLESOME*

2Ki   2:22 the water has remained **w** to this day,
2Pe   3: 1 to stimulate you to **w** thinking.

WHOLLY* [WHOLE]

Nu   3: 9 who are to be given **w** to him.
      8:16 who are to be given **w** to me.
1Ti   4:15 give yourself **w** to them,

WHORE(S) (KJV) See PROMISCUOUS, PROSTITUTE(S), PROSTITUTION, UNFAITHFUL

WHOREDOM (KJV) See ADULTERY, PROSTITUTION, UNFAITHFULNESS

WHY

Ge   4: 6 "**W** are you angry?
     12:19 **W** did you say, 'She is my sister,'
     32:29 "**W** do you ask my name?"
Jdg 13:18 replied, "**W** do you ask my name?
Job 24: 1 "**W** does the Almighty not set times
Ps   2: 1 **W** do the nations conspire
     10: 1 **W**, O LORD, do you stand far off?
     22: 1 my God, **w** have you forsaken me?
     42: 5 **W** are you downcast, O my soul?
     79:10 **W** should the nations say,
Isa   1: 5 **W** do you persist in rebellion?
     40:27 **W** do you say, O Jacob,
La   5:20 **W** do you forsake us so long?
Am   5:18 **W** do you long for the day of
Mt   9:11 "**W** does your teacher eat with
     17:19 "**W** couldn't we drive it out?"
     27:46 my God, **w** have you forsaken me?"
Mk   10:18 "**W** do you call me good?"
Ac   9: 4 Saul, Saul, **w** do you persecute me?"

WICK

Isa 42: 3 a smoldering **w** he will not snuff out.
Mt   12:20 a smoldering **w** he will not snuff out,

WICKED [OVERWICKED, WICKEDLY, WICKEDNESS]

Ge   13:13 the men of Sodom were **w**
     18:23 away the righteous with the **w?**
     39: 9 How then could I do such a **w** thing
Ex   23: 1 Do not help a **w** man by being
Nu   14:35 things to this whole **w** community,
Dt   15: 9 not to harbor this **w** thought:
Jdg 19:22 some of the **w** men of the city
1Sa   2:12 Eli's sons were **w** men;
     15:18 completely destroy those **w** people,
     25:17 a **w** man that no one can talk to him."
2Sa 13:12 Don't do this **w** thing.
2Ki 17:11 They did **w** things that provoked
2Ch   7:14 and turn from their **w** ways,
     19: 2 "Should you help the **w**
Ne   13:17 "What is this **w** thing you are doing
Job 15:20 the **w** man suffers torment,
     20:29 Such is the fate God allots the **w**,
     27:13 "Here is the fate God allots to the **w**,
Ps   1: 1 does not walk in the counsel of the **w**
      1: 5 the **w** will not stand in the judgment,
      7: 9 bring to an end the violence of the **w**
     10:13 Why does the **w** man revile God?
     11: 6 On the **w** he will rain fiery coals
     12: 8 The **w** freely strut about
     26: 5 and refuse to sit with the **w**.

WICKEDLY [WICKED]

WICKEDNESS [WICKED]

WIDE

WIDOW [WIDOW'S, WIDOWHOOD, WIDOWS, WIDOWS']

La	1: 1	How like a **w** is she,
Mk	12:19	the man must marry the **w**
Lk	2:37	was a **w** until she was eighty-four.
	18: 3	a **w** in that town who kept coming
	21: 3	"this poor **w** has put in more than all
1Ti	5: 4	if a **w** has children or grandchildren,
Rev	18: 7	'I sit as queen; I am not a **w**,

WIDOW'S [WIDOW]

Ge	38:14	she took off her **w** clothes,
Job	29:13	I made the **w** heart sing.
Pr	15:25	but he keeps the **w** boundaries intact.

WIDOWHOOD [WIDOW]

Isa	54: 4	no more the reproach of your **w**.

WIDOWS [WIDOW]

Dt	14:29	the fatherless and the **w** who live
Ps	68: 5	a defender of **w**,
Mal	3: 5	who oppress the **w** and the fatherless,
Lk	4:25	many **w** in Israel in Elijah's time,
Ac	6: 1	their **w** were being overlooked
1Co	7: 8	to the unmarried and the **w** I say:
1Ti	5: 3	to those **w** who are really in need.
Jas	1:27	and **w** in their distress

WIDOWS' [WIDOW]

Mk	12:40	They devour **w** houses and for

WIFE [WIVES, WIVES']

Ge	2:24	and mother and be united to his **w**,
	3:20	Adam named his **w** Eve,
	12:18	didn't you tell me she was your **w**?
	19:26	But Lot's **w** looked back,
	20:11	they will kill me because of my **w**.'
	24:67	she became his **w**, and he loved her;
Ex	20:17	not covet your neighbor's **w**,
Lev	18: 8	sexual relations with your father's **w**;
	20:10	adultery with another man's **w**—
Nu	5:12	'If a man's **w** goes astray
Dt	5:21	not covet your neighbor's **w**.
	21:15	the son of the **w** he does not love,
	24: 5	happiness to the **w** he has married.
Ru	4:13	Ruth and she became his **w**.
2Sa	12:10	and took the **w** of Uriah the Hittite to
Ps	128: 3	Your **w** will be like a fruitful vine
Pr	5:18	and may you rejoice in the **w**
	6:24	smooth tongue of the wayward **w**.
	12: 4	A **w** of noble character
	18:22	He who finds a **w** finds what is good
	19:13	and a quarrelsome **w** is
	19:14	but a prudent **w** is from the LORD.
	31:10	**w** of noble character who can find?
Ecc	9: 9	Enjoy life with your **w**,
Hos	1: 2	take to yourself an adulterous **w**
Mal	2:14	between you and the **w** of your youth
Mt	1:20	to take Mary home as your **w**,
	5:32	that anyone who divorces his **w**,
	19: 3	for a man to divorce his **w** for any
Mk	6:18	for you to have your brother's **w**."
	10: 2	for a man to divorce his **w**?"
	12:23	the resurrection whose **w** will she be,
Lk	17:32	Remember Lot's **w**!
	18:29	or **w** or brothers or parents

1Co	7: 2	each man should have his own **w**,
	7:11	a husband must not divorce his **w**.
	7:33	how he can please his **w**—
Eph	5:23	For the husband is the head of the **w**
	5:28	He who loves his **w** loves himself.
	5:33	each one of you also must love his **w**
	5:33	and the **w** must respect her husband.
1Ti	3: 2	the husband of but one **w**, temperate,
	3:12	be the husband of but one **w**
Tit	1: 6	the husband of but one **w**,
Rev	21: 9	the **w** of the Lamb."

WILD [WILDERNESS]

Ge	1:25	God made the **w** animals according
	8: 1	the **w** animals and the livestock
Ex	32:25	the people were running **w** and
Lev	26:22	I will send **w** animals against you,
Mk	1: 6	and he ate locusts and **w** honey.
	1:13	He was with the **w** animals,
Lk	15:13	squandered his wealth in **w** living.
Ro	11:17	and you, though a **w** olive shoot,
1Co	15:32	If I fought **w** beasts in Ephesus
Tit	1: 6	not open to the charge of being **w**
Jude	1:13	They are **w** waves of the sea,

WILDERNESS [WILD]

Isa	40: 3	in the **w** a highway for our God.

WILL [FREEWILL, WEAK-WILLED, WILLFUL, WILLFULLY, WILLING, WILLINGLY, WILLINGNESS]

Ex	18:15	people come to me to seek God's **w**.
Dt	10:10	It was not his **w** to destroy you.
	33:21	carried out the LORD's righteous **w**,
1Sa	2:25	for it was the LORD's **w** to put them
2Sa	7:21	your word and according to your **w**,
1Ch	13: 2	if it is the **w** of the LORD our God,
Ezr	7:18	accordance with the **w** of your God.
	10:11	God of your fathers, and do his **w**.
Ps	40: 8	I desire to do your **w**, O my God;
	103:21	you his servants who do his **w**.
	143:10	Teach me to do your **w**,
Isa	53:10	the LORD's **w** to crush him
Eze	12:25	the LORD will speak what I **w**,
Mt	6:10	your **w** be done on earth as it is in
	7:21	the **w** of my Father who is in heaven.
	10:29	apart from the **w** of your Father.
	26:39	Yet not as I **w**, but as you **w**."
Mk	3:35	Whoever does God's **w** is my brother
	14:36	Yet not what I **w**, but what you **w**."
Lk	22:42	yet not my **w**, but yours be done."
	23:25	and surrendered Jesus to their **w**.
Jn	1:13	of human decision or a husband's **w**,
	4:34	"is to do the **w** of him who sent me
	6:38	but to do the **w** of him who sent me.
	7:17	If anyone chooses to do God's **w**,
	9:31	to the godly man who does his **w**.
Ac	4:28	power and **w** had decided beforehand
	20:27	proclaim to you the whole **w** of God.
	21:14	"The Lord's **w** be done."
Ro	2:18	if you know his **w** and approve of
	9:19	For who resists his **w**?"

	12: 2	approve what God's **w** is—his good, pleasing and perfect **w**.
1Co	7:37	but has control over his own **w**,
Eph	1: 5	accordance with his pleasure and **w**
	1: 9	his **w** according to his good pleasure,
	1:11	conformity with the purpose of his **w**
	5:17	but understand what the Lord's **w** is.
	6: 6	doing the **w** of God from your heart.
Php	2:13	for it is God who works in you to **w**
Col	1: 9	fill you with the knowledge of his **w**
	4:12	may stand firm in all the **w** of God,
1Th	4: 3	It is God's **w** that you should be sanctified:
	5:18	for this is God's **w** for you in Christ
2Ti	2:26	has taken them captive to do his **w**.
Heb	2: 4	distributed according to his **w**.
	10: 7	I have come to do your **w**, O God.' "
	13:21	everything good for doing his **w**,
Jas	4:15	ought to say, "If it is the Lord's **w**,
1Pe	2:15	For it is God's **w** that by doing good
	3:17	It is better, if it is God's **w**, to suffer
	4: 2	but rather for the **w** of God.
	4:19	who suffer according to God's **w**
2Pe	1:21	never had its origin in the **w** of man,
1Jn	2:17	who does the **w** of God lives forever.
	5:14	if we ask anything according to his **w**
Rev	2:26	him who overcomes and does my **w**

WILLFUL [WILL]

| Ps | 19:13 | Keep your servant also from **w** sins; |

WILLFULLY* [WILL]

| Ps | 78:18 | They **w** put God to the test |

WILLING [WILL]

Ex	10:27	and he was not **w** to let them go.
	35: 5	Everyone who is **w** is to bring to
2Ki	8:19	LORD was not **w** to destroy Judah.
	24: 4	and the LORD was not **w** to forgive.
1Ch	28: 9	devotion and with a **w** mind,
	29: 5	who is **w** to consecrate himself today
Ps	51:12	and grant me a **w** spirit,
Da	3:28	were **w** to give up their lives
Mt	8: 3	"I am **w**," he said.
	18:14	not **w** that any of these little ones
	23: 4	but they themselves are not **w** to lift
	23:37	but you were not **w**.
	26:41	The spirit is **w**,
Lk	22:42	if you are **w**, take this cup from me;
Ro	12:16	but be **w** to associate with people
1Ti	6:18	and to be generous and **w** to share.
1Pe	5: 2	but because you are **w**,

WILLINGLY [WILL]

Jdg	5: 2	the people **w** offer themselves—
1Ch	29:17	in my people who are here have
La	3:33	For he does not **w** bring affliction

WILLINGNESS* [WILL]

| 2Co | 8:11 | so that your eager **w** to do it may |
| | 8:12 | For if the **w** is there, |

WIN [WINNING, WINS, WON]

| Pr | 3: 4 | Then you will **w** favor and |

Mt	23:15	to **w** a single convert,
1Co	9:19	to **w** as many as possible.
Gal	1:10	now trying to **w** the approval of men,
Php	3:14	on toward the goal to **w** the prize
1Th	4:12	that your daily life may **w** the respect

WIND [WINDS]

1Ki	19:11	but the LORD was not in the **w**.
Ps	1: 4	like chaff that the **w** blows away.
	18:10	he soared on the wings of the **w**.
	104: 3	and rides on the wings of the **w**.
Pr	11:29	on his family will inherit only **w**,
	30: 4	the **w** in the hollow of his hands?
Ecc	1:14	a chasing after the **w**.
	8: 8	No man has power over the **w**
Eze	5: 2	And scatter a third to the **w**.
Hos	8: 7	sow the **w** and reap the whirlwind.
Jnh	1: 4	the LORD sent a great **w** on the sea,
	4: 8	God provided a scorching east **w**,
Mk	4:41	the **w** and the waves obey him!"
Jn	3: 8	The **w** blows wherever it pleases.
Ac	2: 2	the blowing of a violent **w** came
Eph	4:14	and there by every **w** of teaching
Jas	1: 6	blown and tossed by the **w**.

WINDOW

Jos	2:21	And she tied the scarlet cord in the **w**
1Sa	19:12	Michal let David down through a **w**,
Ac	20: 9	Seated in a **w** was a young
2Co	11:33	in a basket from a **w** in the wall

WINDS [WIND]

Ps	104: 4	He makes **w** his messengers,
Mt	7:25	**w** blew and beat against that house;
	8:27	the **w** and the waves obey him!"
	24:31	gather his elect from the four **w**,
Heb	1: 7	"He makes his angels **w**,

WINE

Ge	9:21	When he drank some of its **w**,
	19:32	to drink **w** and then lie with him
Nu	6: 3	from **w** and other fermented drink
Dt	7:13	your grain, new **w** and oil—
Jdg	13: 4	Now see to it that you drink no **w**
1Sa	1:15	I have not been drinking **w** or beer;
Ne	13:12	new **w** and oil into the storerooms.
Ps	4: 7	when their grain and new **w** abound.
	75: 8	full of foaming **w** mixed with spices;
	104:15	**w** that gladdens the heart of man,
Pr	3:10	your vats will brim over with new **w**.
	9: 2	prepared her meat and mixed her **w**;
	20: 1	**W** is a mocker and beer a brawler;
	23:20	not join those who drink too much **w**
	23:31	Do not gaze at **w** when it is red,
	31: 4	not for kings to drink **w**,
	31: 6	**w** to those who are in anguish;
Ecc	2: 3	I tried cheering myself with **w**,
	9: 7	and drink your **w** with a joyful heart,
	10:19	and makes life merry,
SS	1: 2	your love is more delightful than **w**.
	7: 9	May the **w** go straight to my lover,
Isa	5:22	those who are heroes at drinking **w**
	28: 7	And these also stagger from **w**
	51:21	made drunk, but not with **w**.

	55:	1	buy **w** and milk without money
Da	1:	8	himself with the royal food and **w,**
Joel	2:	24	the vats will overflow with new **w**
	3:	18	the mountains will drip new **w,**
Am	2:	12	"But you made the Nazirites drink **w**
Mic	2:	11	'I will prophesy for you plenty of **w**
Mt	9:	17	pour new **w** into old wineskins.
	27:	34	There they offered Jesus **w** to drink,
Lk	23:	36	They offered him **w** vinegar
Jn	2:	3	When the **w** was gone,
	2:	9	water that had been turned into **w.**
Ac	2:	13	"They have had too much **w.**"
Ro	14:	21	to eat meat or drink **w**
Eph	5:	18	Do not get drunk on **w,**
1Ti	3:	8	sincere, not indulging in much **w,**
	5:	23	a little **w** because of your stomach
Rev	14:	8	the maddening **w** of her adulteries."
	14:	10	will drink of the **w** of God's fury,
	16:	19	gave her the cup filled with the **w**
	18:	3	the maddening **w** of her adulteries.

WINEBIBBER(S) (KJV)
See DRUNKARD(S)

WINEPRESS

Dt	15:	14	your threshing floor and your **w.**
Isa	63:	2	like those of one treading the **w?**
La	1:	15	In his **w** the Lord has trampled
Rev	14:	19	into the great **w** of God's wrath.
	19:	15	He treads the **w** of the fury of

WINESKINS

Job	32:	19	like new **w** ready to burst.
Mt	9:	17	No, they pour new wine into new **w,**

WING [WINGED, WINGS]

2Ch	3:	11	touched the **w** of the other cherub.
Da	9:	27	on a **w** [of the temple] he will set up

WINGED [WING]

Ge	1:	21	every **w** bird according to its kind.

WINGS [WING]

Ex	19:	4	and how I carried you on eagles' **w**
	37:	9	cherubim had their **w** spread upward,
Ru	2:	12	under whose **w** you have come
1Ki	8:	7	The cherubim spread their **w** over
Ps	17:	8	hide me in the shadow of your **w**
	91:	4	and under his **w** you will find refuge;
Isa	6:	2	each with six **w:**
	40:	31	They will soar on **w** like eagles;
Eze	1:	6	of them had four faces and four **w.**
	10:	21	Each had four faces and four **w,**
Zec	5:	9	They had **w** like those of a stork,
Mal	4:	2	will rise with healing in its **w.**
Lk	13:	34	a hen gathers her chicks under her **w,**
Rev	4:	8	of the four living creatures had six **w**

WINNING [WIN]

Ex	17:	11	the Israelites were **w,**

WINNOW [WINNOWING, WINNOWS]

Isa	41:	16	You will **w** them,
Jer	15:	7	I will **w** them with a winnowing fork

WINNOWING [WINNOW]

Mt	3:	12	His **w** fork is in his hand,

WINNOWS* [WINNOW]

Pr	20:	8	he **w** out all evil with his eyes.
	20:	26	A wise king **w** out the wicked;

WINS* [WIN]

Pr	11:	30	and he who **w** souls is wise.
	13:	15	Good understanding **w** favor,

WINTER

Ge	8:	22	cold and heat, summer and **w,**
Ps	74:	17	you made both summer and **w.**
Mk	13:	18	that this will not take place in **w,**

WIPE [WIPED]

Ge	7:	4	I will **w** from the face of the earth
Ex	32:	12	to **w** them off the face of the earth'?
Isa	25:	8	LORD will **w** away the tears from all
Rev	7:	17	And God will **w** away every tear
	21:	4	He will **w** every tear from their eyes.

WIPED [WIPE]

Ge	7:	23	on the face of the earth was **w** out;
Ps	119:	87	They almost **w** me from the earth,
Lk	7:	38	Then she **w** them with her hair,
Ac	3:	19	so that your sins may be **w** out,

WISDOM [WISE]

Ge	3:	6	and also desirable for gaining **w,**
Ex	28:	3	to whom I have given **w**
Dt	4:	6	for this will show your **w**
1Ki	4:	29	God gave Solomon **w**
	10:	6	achievements and your **w** is true.
2Ch	1:	10	Give me **w** and knowledge,
Job	9:	4	His **w** is profound, his power is vast.
	11:	6	for true **w** has two sides.
	12:	13	"To God belong **w** and power;
	28:	12	"But where can **w** be found?
	28:	28	'The fear of the Lord—that is **w,**
Ps	37:	30	mouth of the righteous man utters **w,**
	51:	6	you teach me **w** in the inmost place.
	111:	10	of the LORD is the beginning of **w;**
Pr	1:	7	but fools despise **w** and discipline.
	1:	20	**W** calls aloud in the street,
	2:	6	For the LORD gives **w,**
	3:	13	Blessed is the man who finds **w,**
	4:	5	Get **w,** get understanding;
	4:	7	**W** is supreme; therefore get **w.**
	8:	11	for **w** is more precious than rubies,
	9:	1	**W** has built her house;
	9:	10	of the LORD is the beginning of **w,**
	11:	2	but with humility comes **w.**
	13:	10	**w** is found in those who take advice.
	15:	33	fear of the LORD teaches a man **w,**
	19:	8	He who gets **w** loves his own soul;
	23:	23	Buy the truth and do not sell it; get **w**
	29:	3	A man who loves **w** brings joy
	29:	15	The rod of correction imparts **w,**
	31:	26	She speaks with **w,**
Ecc	1:	13	and to explore by **w** all that is done
	2:	3	my mind still guiding me with **w.**
	2:	13	I saw that **w** is better than folly,

7:12 **W** is a shelter as money is a shelter,
9:18 **W** is better than weapons of war,
10: 1 a little folly outweighs wisdom and honor.
Isa 11: 2 Spirit of **w** and of understanding,
28:29 in counsel and magnificent in **w**.
Jer 9:23 not the wise man boast of his **w** or
10:12 the world by his **w** and stretched out
Eze 28:12 full of **w** and perfect in beauty.
Da 2:14 Daniel spoke to him with **w** and tact.
5:14 intelligence and outstanding **w**.
Mic 6: 9 and to fear your name is **w**—
Mt 11:19 But **w** is proved right by her actions.
12:42 of the earth to listen to Solomon's **w**,
13:54 "Where did this man get this **w**
Lk 2:40 he was filled with **w**,
2:52 And Jesus grew in **w** and stature,
Ac 6: 3 to be full of the Spirit and **w**.
Ro 11:33 of the **w** and knowledge of God!
1Co 1:17 not with words of human **w**,
1:19 "I will destroy the **w** of the wise;
1:20 Has not God made foolish the **w** of
1:30 has become for us **w** from God—
2: 7 No, we speak of God's secret **w**,
3:19 For the **w** of this world is foolishness
12: 8 through the Spirit the message of **w**,
Eph 1:17 may give you the Spirit of **w** and
Col 1: 9 of his will through all spiritual **w**
1:28 and teaching everyone with all **w**,
2: 3 all the treasures of **w** and knowledge.
2:23 indeed have an appearance of **w**,
Jas 1: 5 If any of you lacks **w**,
3:13 in the humility that comes from **w**.
3:17 the **w** that comes from heaven is first
Rev 5:12 to receive power and wealth and **w**
7:12 and **w** and thanks and honor
13:18 This calls for **w**.
17: 9 "This calls for a mind with **w**.

WISE [OVERWISE, WISELY, WISDOM, WISER]

Ge 41:39 there is no one so discerning and **w**
Ex 7:11 then summoned **w** men and sorcerers
Dt 4: 6 a **w** and understanding people."
16:19 for a bribe blinds the eyes of the **w**
1Ki 3:12 give you a **w** and discerning heart,
Job 5:13 He catches the **w** in their craftiness,
32: 9 It is not only the old who are **w**,
Ps 2:10 Therefore, you kings, be **w**;
19: 7 making the simple.
94: 8 when will you become **w**?
107:43 Whoever is **w**, let him heed
Pr 3: 7 Do not be **w** in your own eyes;
6: 6 consider its ways and be **w**!
9: 9 Instruct a **w** man and he will be wiser
10: 1 A **w** son brings joy to his father,
10:19 but he who holds his tongue is **w**.
11:30 and he who wins souls is **w**.
13: 1 **w** son heeds his father's instruction,
13:20 He who walks with the **w** grows **w**,
16:23 A **w** man's heart guides his mouth,
17:28 a fool is thought **w** if he keeps silent,
23:15 My son, if your heart is **w**,
24: 5 A **w** man has great power,
26: 5 or he will be **w** in his own eyes.

29:11 **w** man keeps himself under control.
Ecc 2:14 The **w** man has eyes in his head,
7:19 Wisdom makes one **w** man more
9:17 The quiet words of the **w** are more to
12:11 The words of the **w** are like goads,
Isa 29:14 the wisdom of the **w** will perish,
Jer 8: 9 The **w** will be put to shame;
9:23 not the **w** man boast of his wisdom
Eze 28: 6 " 'Because you think you are **w**,
Da 2:21 He gives wisdom to the **w**
11:35 Some of the **w** will stumble,
12: 3 Those who are **w** will shine like
Mt 11:25 hidden these things from the **w**
25: 2 foolish and five were **w**.
Lk 12:42 then is the faithful and **w** manager,
Ro 1:22 Although they claimed to be **w**,
16:27 to the only **w** God be glory forever
1Co 1:19 "I will destroy the wisdom of the **w**;
1:26 of you were **w** by human standards;
3:18 a "fool" so that he may become **w**.
3:19 "He catches the **w** in their craftiness"
Eph 5:15 not as unwise but as **w**,
Col 4: 5 Be **w** in the way you act
2Ti 3:15 able to make you **w** for salvation
Jas 3:13 Who is **w** and understanding

WISELY [WISE]

Isa 52:13 See, my servant will act **w**;
Jer 23: 5 a King who will reign **w**

WISER [WISE]

1Ki 4:31 He was **w** than any other man,
Pr 9: 9 a wise man and he will be **w** still;
26:16 The sluggard is **w** in his own eyes
1Co 1:25 foolishness of God is **w** than man's

WISH [WISHED, WISHES]

Job 11: 5 Oh, how I **w** that God would speak,
Jn 15: 7 ask whatever you **w**,
Ro 9: 3 could **w** that I myself were cursed
Gal 4: 9 Do you **w** to be enslaved by them all
Rev 3:15 I **w** you were either one or the other!

WISHED [WISH]

Mt 17:12 have done to him everything they **w**.

WISHES [WISH]

Rev 22:17 whoever **w**, let him take the free gift

WITCH (KJV) See SORCERESS, SORCERY

WITCHCRAFT* [BEWITCHED]

Dt 18:10 interprets omens, engages in **w**,
2Ki 9:22 **w** of your mother Jezebel abound?"
2Ch 33: 6 practiced sorcery, divination and **w**,
Mic 5:12 I will destroy your **w**
Na 3: 4 prostitution and peoples by her **w**.
Gal 5:20 idolatry and **w**; hatred, discord,

WITH

I AM WITH YOU Ge 26:24; 28:15; Jos 3:7; 1Sa 14:7; 2Ki 10:15; Isa 41:10; 43:5; Jer 1:8, 19;

15:20; 30:11; 42:11; 46:28; Hag 1:13; 2:4; Mt 28:20; Jn 7:33; Ac 18:10; 1Co 5:3, 4; Gal 4:18

I WILL BE WITH YOU Ge 26:3; 31:3; Ex 3:12; Jos 1:5; Jdg 6:16; 1Ki 11:38; Isa 43:2; Jn 13:33

WITHER [WITHERED, WITHERS]

Ps   1: 3 in season and whose leaf does not **w**.
    37:19 In times of disaster they will not **w**;

WITHERED [WITHER]

Ge 41:23 seven other heads sprouted—**w** and
Zec 11:17 May his arm be completely **w**,
Mt 13: 6 and they **w** because they had no root.
    21:19 Immediately the tree **w**.

WITHERS [WITHER]

Ps 129: 6 which **w** before it can grow;
Isa 40: 7 The grass **w** and the flowers fall,
Jn   15: 6 a branch that is thrown away and **w**;
1Pe 1:24 the grass **w** and the flowers fall,

WITHHELD [WITHHOLD]

Ge 22:12 you have not **w** from me your son,
Ps 66:20 or **w** his love from me!
    77: 9 Has he in anger **w** his compassion?"
Hag 1:10 of you the heavens have **w** their dew

WITHHOLD [WITHHELD, WITHHOLDS]

Ne   9:20 not **w** your manna from their mouths,
Ps 40:11 Do not **w** your mercy from me,
    84:11 no good thing does he **w**
Pr 23:13 Do not **w** discipline from a child;

WITHHOLDS [WITHHOLD]

Dt 27:19 the man who **w** justice from the alien
Eze 18:17 He **w** his hand from sin

WITHIN

Ex   3: 2 in flames of fire from **w** a bush.
Ps 36: 1 An oracle is **w** my heart concerning
    40: 8 your law is **w** my heart."
    42: 5 Why so disturbed **w** me?
    46: 5 God is **w** her, she will not fall;
    51:10 and renew a steadfast spirit **w** me.
  122: 7 May there be peace **w** your walls
  142: 3 When my spirit grows faint **w** me,
Pr   2: 1 and store up my commands **w** you,
    4:21 keep them **w** your heart;
Zep 3: 5 The LORD **w** her is righteous;
    3:12 But I will leave **w** you the meek
Zec 2: 5 'and I will be its glory **w**.'
    12: 1 who forms the spirit of man **w** him,
Mt   6:23 If then the light **w** you is darkness,
Mk   7:21 For from **w**, out of men's hearts,
Jn   7:38 living water will flow from **w** him."
1Co 2:11 except the man's spirit **w** him?
Rev 11:19 and **w** his temple was seen the ark

WITHOUT

Ex 12:15 to eat bread made **w** yeast.
    34:28 and forty nights **w** eating bread
Lev 1: 3 he is to offer a male **w** defect.

Nu 27:17 not be like sheep **w** a shepherd."
2Ch 15: 3 long time Israel was **w** the true God,
    18:16 on the hills like sheep **w** a shepherd,
Ps 26: 1 trusted in the LORD **w** wavering.
    69: 4 Those who hate me **w** reason
Pr   6:27 Can a man scoop fire into his lap **w**
    9:13 is undisciplined and **w** knowledge.
    19: 2 not good to have zeal **w** knowledge,
Isa 13:14 like sheep **w** a shepherd,
    52: 3 and **w** money you will be redeemed."
    55: 1 Come, buy wine and milk **w** money
           and **w** cost.
Zec 14: 7 **w** daytime or nighttime—
Mt   9:36 like sheep **w** a shepherd.
    23:23 **w** neglecting the former.
Jn   3:34 for God gives the Spirit **w** limit.
    8: 7 "If any one of you is **w** sin,
Eph 2:12 **w** hope and **w** God in
Php 2:14 Do everything **w** complaining
Col 1:22 **w** blemish and free from accusation
Heb 4:15 just as we are—yet was **w** sin.
    9:22 and **w** the shedding of blood
Jas 2:18 Show me your faith **w** deeds,
1Pe 1:19 a lamb **w** blemish or defect.
Rev 21: 6 to drink **w** cost from the spring of

WITHSTAND

Jos 10: 8 one of them will be able to **w** you."
    23: 9 no one has been able to **w** you.
Na   1: 6 Who can **w** his indignation?

WITNESS [EYEWITNESSES, WITNESSES]

Ge 31:44 and let it serve as a **w** between us."
Nu 35:30 on the testimony of only one **w**.
Dt 19:15 One **w** is not enough to convict
Jos 22:27 it is to be a **w** between us and you
Jdg 11:10 "The LORD is our **w**;
1Sa 12: 5 "The LORD is **w** against you,
    20:42 LORD is **w** between you and me,
Job 16:19 Even now my **w** is in heaven;
Pr 12:17 A truthful **w** gives honest testimony,
           but a false **w** tells lies.
    14:25 A truthful **w** saves lives,
    19: 9 A false **w** will not go unpunished,
    21:28 A false **w** will perish,
Jn   1: 8 he came only as a **w** to the light.
Ro 2:15 their consciences also bearing **w**,
1Pe 5: 1 a **w** of Christ's sufferings
Rev 1: 5 who is the faithful **w**,
    2:13 my faithful **w**, who was put to death
    3:14 the faithful and true **w**,

WITNESSES [WITNESS]

Dt 17: 6 On the testimony of two or three **w**
    19:15 by the testimony of two or three **w**.
    30:19 I call heaven and earth as **w**
Jos 24:22 "You are **w** against yourselves
Ru   4:10 Today you are **w**!"
Ps 27:12 for false **w** rise up against me,
Isa 43:10 "You are my **w**," declares the LORD,
Mt 18:16 by the testimony of two or three **w**.'
    26:60 though many false **w** came forward.
Mk 14:63 "Why do we need any more **w**?"

Lk 21:13 This will result in your being **w**
Ac 1: 8 and you will be my **w** in Jerusalem,
    2:32 we are all **w** of the fact.
    6:13 They produced false **w**, who testified
Heb 12: 1 by such a great cloud of **w**,
Rev 11: 3 And I will give power to my two **w**,

WIVES [WIFE]

Ge   6:18 and your wife and your sons' **w**
Dt 17:17 He must not take many **w**,
    21:15 If a man has two **w**,
1Ki 11: 3 and his **w** led him astray.
1Ch 14: 3 In Jerusalem David took more **w**
Ezr 10:11 and from your foreign **w**."
Mt 19: 8 permitted you to divorce your **w**
Eph 5:22 **W**, submit to your husbands as to
     5:25 Husbands, love your **w**,
Col 3:18 **W**, submit to your husbands,
1Ti 3:11 their **w** are to be women worthy of
1Pe 3: 1 **W**, in the same way be submissive
     3: 1 by the behavior of their **w**,
     3: 7 considerate as you live with your **w**,

WIVES'* [WIFE]

1Ti 4: 7 with godless myths and old **w** tales;

WIZARD (KJV) See SPIRITIST

WOE [WOES]

Job 10:15 If I am guilty—**w** to me!
Pr 23:29 Who has **w**?
Isa 3:11 **W** to the wicked!
     5: 8 **W** to you who add house to house
     5:20 **W** to those who call evil good
     6: 5 "**W** to me!"
Jer 13:27 **W** to you, O Jerusalem!
    23: 1 "**W** to the shepherds who are
La   5:16 **W** to us, for we have sinned!
Hos 9:12 **W** to them when I turn away
Am   5:18 **W** to you who long for the day of
Na   3: 1 **W** to the city of blood, full of lies,
Hab 2:19 **W** to him who says to wood,
Zec 11:17 "**W** to the worthless shepherd,
Mt 18: 7 "**W** to the world because of the
    18: 7 **w** to the man through whom they
    23:13 "**W** to you, teachers of
    23:16 "**W** to you, blind guides!
Mk 14:21 But **w** to that man who betrays
Lk   6:24 "But **w** to you who are rich,
    11:42 "**W** to you Pharisees,
    11:52 "**W** to you experts in the law,
1Co 9:16 **W** to me if I do not preach
Jude 1:11 **W** to them!
Rev 8:13 **W** to the inhabitants of the earth,
    18:10 " '**W**! **W**, O great city, O Babylon,

WOES* [WOE]

Ps 32:10 Many are the **w** of the wicked,
Rev 9:12 The first woe is past; two other **w** are

WOKE [WAKE]

Ge 41: 7 Pharaoh **w** up; it had been a dream.
Mt   1:24 When Joseph **w** up,
    25: 7 "Then all the virgins **w** up

WOLF [WOLVES]

Isa 11: 6 The **w** will live with the lamb,
    65:25 **w** and the lamb will feed together,
Jn 10:12 So when he sees the **w** coming,

WOLVES [WOLF]

Eze 22:27 like **w** tearing their prey;
Zep 3: 3 her rulers are evening **w**,
Mt   7:15 but inwardly they are ferocious **w**.
    10:16 sending you out like sheep among **w**.
Ac 20:29 savage **w** will come in among you

WOMAN [WOMEN, WOMEN'S]

Ge   2:22 Then the LORD God made a **w** from
     2:23 called '**w**,' for she was taken out
     3: 6 **w** saw that the fruit of the tree—
     3:12 "The **w** you put here with me—
     3:15 enmity between you and the **w**,
     3:16 To the **w** he said,
    12:11 "I know what a beautiful **w** you are.
    20: 3 she is a married **w**."
    21:10 "Get rid of that slave **w** and her son,
Ex   3:22 Every **w** is to ask her neighbor
    21:10 If he marries another **w**,
    21:22 who are fighting hit a pregnant **w**
Lev 12: 2 'A **w** who becomes pregnant
    15:19 a **w** has her regular flow of blood,
    18:17 with both a **w** and her daughter.
    18:22 lie with a man as one lies with a **w**;
    20:13 lies with a man as one lies with a **w**,
Nu   5:29 a **w** goes astray and defiles herself
    30: 3 a young **w** still living in her father's
    30:10 a **w** living with her husband makes
Dt   4:16 whether formed like a man or a **w**,
    20: 7 Has anyone become pledged to a **w**
    21:11 a beautiful **w** and are attracted to her,
    22: 5 A **w** must not wear men's clothing,
    24: 1 a **w** who becomes displeasing to him
Jdg 4: 9 LORD will hand Sisera over to a **w**."
     9:54 'A **w** killed him.' "
    14: 2 "I have seen a Philistine **w**
    16: 4 love with a **w** in the Valley of Sorek
Ru   3:11 that you are a **w** of noble character.
1Sa 1:15 "I am a **w** who is deeply troubled.
    25: 3 an intelligent and beautiful **w**,
    28: 7 "Find me a **w** who is a medium,
2Sa 11: 2 From the roof he saw a **w** bathing.
    13:17 "Get this **w** out of here and bolt
    14: 2 and had a wise **w** brought from there.
    20:16 a wise **w** called from the city,
1Ki 3:18 this **w** also had a baby.
    17:24 Then the **w** said to Elijah,
2Ki 4: 8 And a well-to-do **w** was there,
     8: 1 to the **w** whose son he had restored
     9:34 "Take care of that cursed **w**," he said
Ezr 10:14 who has married a foreign **w**
Job 2:10 "You are talking like a foolish **w**.
    14: 1 "Man born of **w** is of few days
Ps 113: 9 He settles the barren **w** in her home
Pr   6:24 keeping you from the immoral **w**,
     9:13 The **w** Folly is loud;
    11:16 A kindhearted **w** gains respect,
    11:22 beautiful **w** who shows no discretion.

	14: 1	The wise **w** builds her house,
	30:23	an unloved **w** who is married,
	31:30	but a **w** who fears the LORD
Isa	54: 1	"Sing, O barren **w,**
Mt	5:28	looks at a **w** lustfully has already
	9:20	**w** who had been subject to bleeding
	15:22	A Canaanite **w** from that vicinity
	19: 9	marries another **w** commits adultery.
	26: 7	a **w** came to him with an alabaster jar
Mk	7:25	**w** whose little daughter was
Lk	7:37	a **w** who had lived a sinful life
	10:38	a **w** named Martha opened her home
	13:12	and said to her, **"W,** you are set free
	15: 8	"Or suppose a **w** has ten silver coins
Jn	2: 4	"Dear **w,** why do you involve me?"
	4: 7	a Samaritan **w** came to draw water,
	8: 4	**w** was caught in the act of adultery.
	19:26	he said to his mother, "Dear **w,**
	20:15	**"W,"** he said, "why are you crying?
Ac	9:40	Turning toward the dead **w,** he said,
	16:14	a **w** named Lydia,
	17:34	also a **w** named Damaris,
Ro	7: 2	a married **w** is bound to her husband
	16:12	another **w** who has worked very hard
1Co	7: 2	and each **w** her own husband.
	7:15	A believing man or **w** is not bound
	7:34	But a married **w** is concerned about
	7:39	A **w** is bound to her husband as long
	11: 3	and the head of the **w** is man,
	11: 6	If a **w** does not cover her head,
	11: 7	but the **w** is the glory of man.
Gal	4: 4	God sent his Son, born of a **w,**
	4:27	it is written: "Be glad, O barren **w,**
	4:30	"Get rid of the slave **w** and her son,
	4:31	we are not children of the slave **w,**
1Ti	2:11	A **w** should learn in quietness
	5:16	If any **w** who is a believer
Rev	2:20	You tolerate that **w** Jezebel,
	12: 1	a **w** clothed with the sun,
	12: 4	The dragon stood in front of the **w**
	12:13	pursued the **w** who had given birth
	17: 3	a **w** sitting on a scarlet beast
	17:18	The **w** you saw is the great city

WOMB

Ge	20:18	for the LORD had closed up every **w**
	25:23	"Two nations are in your **w,**
	29:31	he opened her **w,**
	30:22	to her and opened her **w.**
Ex	13: 2	The first offspring of every **w** among
Dt	7:13	He will bless the fruit of your **w,**
1Sa	1: 5	and the LORD had closed her **w.**
Job	1:21	"Naked I came from my mother's **w,**
Ps	22: 9	Yet you brought me out of the **w;**
	139:13	knit me together in my mother's **w.**
Pr	31: 2	O son of my **w,** O son of my vows,
Ecc	11: 5	the body is formed in a mother's **w,**
Jer	1: 5	in the **w** I knew you,
Lk	1:44	the baby in my **w** leaped for joy.
Jn	3: 4	a second time into his mother's **w** to
Ro	4:19	and that Sarah's **w** was also dead.

WOMEN [WOMAN]

Ge	4:19	Lamech married two **w,**

Nu	25: 1	sexual immorality with Moabite **w,**
Jdg	5:24	"Most blessed of **w** be Jael,
Ezr	10: 2	to our God by marrying foreign **w**
Ne	13:26	he was led into sin by foreign **w.**
SS	1: 8	most beautiful of **w,**
Isa	3:12	**w** rule over them.
Zec	5: 9	and there before me were two **w,**
Mt	11:11	Among those born of **w** there has
	24:41	Two **w** will be grinding at
	28: 5	The angel said to the **w,**
Mk	15:41	In Galilee these **w** had followed him
Lk	1:42	"Blessed are you among **w,**
	8: 2	and also some **w** who had been cured
	23:27	including **w** who mourned and
	23:55	The **w** who had come with Jesus
	24:11	But they did not believe the **w,**
Ac	1:14	the **w** and Mary the mother of Jesus,
	2:18	on my servants, both men and **w,**
	8:12	they were baptized, both men and **w.**
	16:13	to the **w** who had gathered there.
	17: 4	and not a few prominent **w.**
Ro	1:26	their **w** exchanged natural relations
	16:12	those **w** who work hard in the Lord.
1Co	14:34	**w** should remain silent in the
Gal	4:24	for the **w** represent two covenants.
Php	4: 3	help these **w** who have contended
1Ti	2: 9	I also want **w** to dress modestly,
	2:15	**w** will be saved through childbearing
	5: 2	older **w** as mothers, and younger **w** as sisters,
2Ti	3: 6	and gain control over weak-willed **w,**
Tit	2: 3	teach the older **w** to be reverent in
	2: 4	the younger **w** to love their husbands
Heb	11:35	**W** received back their dead,
1Pe	3: 5	For this is the way the holy **w** of the

WOMEN'S* [WOMAN]

Dt	22: 5	nor a man wear **w** clothing,
Rev	9: 8	Their hair was like **w** hair,

WON [WIN]

1Sa	19: 5	The LORD **w** a great victory
Est	2:15	And Esther **w** the favor
Ps	44: 3	It was not by their sword that they **w**
Mt	18:15	you have **w** your brother over.
1Pe	3: 1	they may be **w** over without words

WONDER [WONDERED, WONDERFUL, WONDERFULLY, WONDERING, WONDERS, WONDROUS]

Dt	13: 1	to you a miraculous sign or **w,**
Ps	17: 7	Show the **w** of your great love,
SS	1: 3	No **w** the maidens love you!
Isa	29:14	astound these people with **w** upon **w;**

WONDERED* [WONDER]

Lk	1:29	**w** what kind of greeting this might
	1:66	Everyone who heard this **w** about it,

WONDERFUL* [WONDER]

2Sa	1:26	Your love for me was **w,** more **w** than that of women.
1Ch	16: 9	tell of all his **w** acts.

Job 42: 3 things too **w** for me to know.
Ps 26: 7 and telling of all your **w** deeds.
    31:21 for he showed his **w** love to me
    75: 1 men tell of your **w** deeds.
    105: 2 tell of all his **w** acts.
    107: 8 his **w** deeds for men,
    107:15 his **w** deeds for men,
    107:21 his **w** deeds for men,
    107:24 his **w** deeds in the deep.
    107:31 his **w** deeds for men.
    119:18 that I may see **w** things in your law.
    119:129 Your statutes are **w**;
    131: 1 with great matters or things too **w**
    139: 6 Such knowledge is too **w** for me,
    139:14 your works are **w**,
    145: 5 and I will meditate on your **w** works.
Isa 9: 6 And he will be called **W** Counselor,
    28:29 **w** in counsel and magnificent
Mt 21:15 of the law saw the **w** things he did
Lk 13:17 delighted with all the **w** things he
1Pe 2: 9 out of darkness into his **w** light.

WONDERFULLY* [WONDER]

Ps 139:14 because I am fearfully and **w** made;

WONDERING [WONDER]

Ac 10:17 Peter was **w** about the meaning

WONDERS [WONDER]

Ex   3:20 with all the **w** that I will perform
    11:10 all these **w** before Pharaoh
    15:11 awesome in glory, working **w**?
Dt 10:21 great and awesome **w** you saw
2Sa 7:23 and to perform great and awesome **w**
1Ch 16:12 Remember the **w** he has done,
Job 37:14 stop and consider God's **w**.
Ps   9: 1 I will tell of all your **w**.
    65: 8 Those living far away fear your **w**;
    78:32 in spite of his **w**,
    89: 5 The heavens praise your **w**,
    119:27 then I will meditate on your **w**.
    136: 4 to him who alone does great **w**,
Da   4: 3 how mighty his **w**!
Joel 2:30 I will show **w** in the heavens and on
Jn   4:48 people see miraculous signs and **w**,"
Ac   2:11 the **w** of God in our own tongues!"
    2:19 I will show **w** in the heaven above
2Co 12:12 mark an apostle—signs, **w** and
2Th 2: 9 counterfeit miracles, signs and **w**,
Heb 2: 4 testified to it by signs, **w**

SIGNS AND WONDERS See SIGNS

WOOD [WOODEN, WOODS]

Ge   6:14 make yourself an ark of cypress **w**;
    22: 9 an altar there and arranged the **w**
Ex 15:25 the LORD showed him a piece of **w**.
    25:10 Have them make a chest of acacia **w**
    25:13 Then make poles of acacia **w**
    25:23 "Make a table of acacia **w**—
    26:15 "Make upright frames of acacia **w**
    27: 1 "Build an altar of acacia **w**,
Lev 14: 4 live clean birds and some cedar **w**,
Dt 28:64 gods of **w** and stone,
1Ki 6:32 olive **w** doors he carved cherubim,

    18:23 put it on the **w** but not set fire to it.
Isa 44:19 Shall I bow down to a block of **w**?"
    60:17 Instead of **w** I will bring you bronze,
Eze 20:32 who serve **w** and stone."
    37:16 take a stick of **w** and write on it,
Hos 4:12 and are answered by a stick of **w**.
Hab 2:19 Woe to him who says to **w**,
1Co 3:12 silver, costly stones, **w**, hay or straw,

WOODEN [WOOD]

Dt 16:21 Do not set up any **w** Asherah pole
Ne   8: 4 Ezra the scribe stood on a high **w**
Isa 48: 5 'My idols did them; my **w** image

WOODS [WOOD]

2Ki 2:24 Then two bears came out of the **w**

WOOL

Nu 19: 6 hyssop and scarlet **w** and throw them
Dt 18: 4 and the first **w** from the shearing
    22:11 of **w** and linen woven together.
Pr 31:13 She selects **w** and flax and works
Isa 1:18 they shall be like **w**.
Da   7: 9 the hair of his head was white like **w**.
Rev 1:14 His head and hair were white like **w**,

WORD [BYWORD, WORDS]

Ge 15: 1 the **w** of the LORD came to Abram
    37: 4 and could not speak a kind **w** to him.
Nu 30: 2 he must not break his **w**
Dt   8: 3 on bread alone but on every **w** that
    30:14 No, the **w** is very near you;
Jos 1:18 Whoever rebels against your **w**
1Sa 3: 1 the **w** of the LORD was rare;
2Sa 22:31 the **w** of the LORD is flawless.
1Ki 8:56 Not one **w** has failed of all
    17: 2 the **w** of the LORD came to Elijah:
1Ch 17: 3 the **w** of God came to Nathan,
2Ch 36:22 to fulfill the **w** of the LORD spoken
Ps 33: 4 the **w** of the LORD is right and true;
    56: 4 In God, whose **w** I praise,
    56:10 in the LORD, whose **w** I praise—
    107:20 He sent forth his **w** and healed them;
    119: 9 By living according to your **w**.
    119:11 I have hidden your **w** in my heart
    119:42 for I trust in your **w**.
    119:74 for I have put my hope in your **w**.
    119:89 Your **w**, O LORD, is eternal;
    119:105 Your **w** is a lamp to my feet and
    119:172 May my tongue sing of your **w**,
    139: 4 Before a **w** is on my tongue
Pr 12:25 but a kind **w** cheers him up.
    15: 1 but a harsh **w** stirs up anger.
    15:23 and how good is a timely **w**!
    25:11 A **w** aptly spoken is like apples
    30: 5 "Every **w** of God is flawless;
Isa 1:10 Hear the **w** of the LORD,
    40: 8 but the **w** of our God stands forever."
    55:11 so is my **w** that goes out
Jer 5:13 but wind and the **w** is not in them;
    23:29 "Is not my **w** like fire,"
Da   9: 2 to the **w** of the LORD given
Mt   4: 4 but on every **w** that comes from
    12:36 every careless **w** they have spoken.

15: 6 Thus you nullify the **w** of God for
Mk 4:14 The farmer sows the **w.**
Lk 1: 2 eyewitnesses and servants of the **w.**
Jn 1: 1 the beginning was the **W,** and the **W** was with God, and the **W** was God.
1:14 The **W** became flesh and made his
8:37 because you have no room for my **w.**
17:17 them by the truth; your **w** is truth.
Ac 4:31 with the Holy Spirit and spoke the **w**
6: 4 to prayer and the ministry of the **w."**
Ro 9: 6 not as though God's **w** had failed.
10: 8 "The **w** is near you;
2Co 2:17 not peddle the **w** of God for profit.
4: 2 nor do we distort the **w** of God.
Eph 6:17 which is the **w** of God.
Php 2:16 as you hold out the **w** of life—
Col 3:16 the **w** of Christ dwell in you richly
2Ti 2:15 and who correctly handles the **w**
Heb 1: 3 all things by his powerful **w.**
4:12 For the **w** of God is living and active.
6: 5 tasted the goodness of the **w** of God
Jas 1:21 and humbly accept the **w** planted
1:22 Do not merely listen to the **w,**
1Pe 1:23 the living and enduring **w** of God.
2Pe 1:19 And we have the **w** of the prophets
3: 5 by God's **w** the heavens existed and
1Jn 2: 5 But if anyone obeys his **w,**
Rev 3: 8 yet you have kept my **w** and have
12:11 the blood of the Lamb and by the **w**
19:13 and his name is the **W** of God.
20: 4 and because of the **w** of God.

WORD OF GOD 1Ki 12:22; 1Ch 17:3; Pr 30:5; Isa 40:8; Mt 15:6; Mk 7:13; Lk 3:2; 5:1; 8:11; 11:28; Jn 10:35; Ac 4:31; 6:2, 7; 8:14; 11:1; 12:24; 13:5, 7, 46; 17:13; 18:11; 1Co 14:36; 2Co 2:17; 4:2; Eph 6:17; Php 1:14; Col 1:25; 1Th 2:13, 13; 1Ti 4:5; Tit 2:5; Heb 4:12; 6:5; 13:7; 1Pe 1:23; 1Jn 2:14; Rev 1:2, 9; 6:9; 19:13; 20:4

WORD OF THE †LORD Ge 15:1, 4; Ex 9:20, 21; Nu 3:16, 51; Dt 5:5; 1Sa 3:1, 7; 15:10, 23, 26; 2Sa 7:4; 12:9; 22:31; 24:11; 1Ki 6:11; 12:24; 13:1, 2, 5, 9, 17, 18, 20, 21, 26, 26, 32; 15:29; 16:1, 7, 12, 34; 17:2, 8, 16, 24; 18:1, 31; 19:9; 20:35; 21:17, 28; 22:19, 38; 2Ki 1:17; 3:12; 4:44; 7:1; 9:26, 36; 10:17; 14:25; 15:12; 20:4, 16, 19; 23:16; 24:2; 1Ch 10:13; 15:15; 22:8; 2Ch 11:2; 12:7; 18:18; 29:15; 30:12; 34:21; 36:12, 21, 22; Ezr 1:1; Ps 18:30; 33:4, 6; 105:19; Isa 1:10; 2:3; 28:13, 14; 38:4; 39:5, 8; 66:5; Jer 1:2, 4, 11, 13; 2:1, 4, 31; 6:10; 7:2; 8:9; 9:20; 13:3, 8; 14:1; 16:1; 17:15, 20; 18:5; 19:3; 20:8; 21:11; 22:2, 29; 24:4; 25:3; 27:18; 28:12; 29:20, 30; 31:10; 32:6, 8, 26; 33:1, 19, 23; 34:12; 35:12; 36:27; 37:6; 39:15; 42:7; 43:8; 44:24, 26; 46:1; 47:1; 49:34; Eze 1:3; 3:16; 6:1; 7:1; 11:14; 12:1, 8, 17, 21, 26; 13:1, 2; 14:2, 12; 15:1; 16:1, 35; 17:1, 11; 18:1; 20:2, 45, 47; 21:1, 8, 18; 22:1, 17, 23; 23:1; 24:1, 15, 20; 25:1; 26:1; 27:1; 28:1, 11, 20; 29:1, 17; 30:1; 31:1; 32:1, 17; 33:1, 23; 34:1, 7, 9; 35:1; 36:1, 16; 37:4, 15; 38:1; Da 9:2; Hos 1:1; 4:1; Joel 1:1; Am 7:16; 8:12; Jnh 1:1; 3:1, 3; Mic 1:1; 4:2; Zep 1:1; 2:5; Hag 1:1, 3; 2:1, 10, 20;

Zec 1:1, 7; 4:6, 8; 6:9; 7:1, 4, 8; 8:1, 18; 9:1; 11:11; 12:1; Mal 1:1

WORD OF THE †LORD CAME Ge 15:1, 4; 1Sa 15:10; 2Sa 7:4; 1Ki 6:11; 13:20; 16:1, 7; 17:2, 8; 18:1; 19:9; 21:17, 28; 2Ki 20:4; 1Ch 22:8; 2Ch 11:2; 12:7; Isa 38:4; Jer 1:2, 4, 11, 13; 2:1; 13:3, 8; 16:1; 18:5; 24:4; 28:12; 29:30; 32:6, 26; 33:1, 19, 23; 34:12; 35:12; 36:27; 37:6; 39:15; 42:7; 43:8; Eze 1:3; 3:16; 6:1; 7:1; 11:14; 12:1, 8, 17, 21, 26; 13:1; 14:2, 12; 15:1; 16:1; 17:1, 11; 18:1; 20:2, 45; 21:1, 8, 18; 22:1, 17, 23; 23:1; 24:1, 15, 20; 25:1; 26:1; 27:1; 28:1, 11, 20; 29:1, 17; 30:1; 31:1; 32:1, 17; 33:1, 23; 34:1; 35:1; 36:16; 37:15; 38:1; Jnh 1:1; 3:1; Hag 1:1, 3; 2:1, 10, 20; Zec 1:1, 7; 4:8; 6:9; 7:1, 8

WORDS [WORD]

Ex 20: 1 And God spoke all these **w:**
24: 3 told the people all the LORD's **w**
34:28 on the tablets the **w** of the covenant
Dt 11:18 Fix these **w** of mine in your hearts
13: 3 not listen to the **w** of that prophet
18:19 If anyone does not listen to my **w**
31:24 finished writing in a book the **w**
32:45 Moses finished reciting all these **w**
32:47 They are not just idle **w** for you—
Jos 8:34 Joshua read all the **w** of the law—
2Sa 23: 1 These are the last **w** of David:
Ps 5: 1 Give ear to my **w,** O LORD,
12: 6 the **w** of the LORD are flawless,
19: 4 their **w** to the ends of the world.
19:14 May the **w** of my mouth and
49: 3 My mouth will speak **w** of wisdom;
64: 3 and aim their **w** like deadly arrows.
119:103 How sweet are your **w** to my taste,
119:130 The unfolding of your **w** gives light;
119:160 All your **w** are true;
Pr 2: 1 if you accept my **w** and store
2:16 wayward wife with her seductive **w,**
7:21 With persuasive **w** she led him astray
10:19 When **w** are many, sin is not absent,
12:18 Reckless **w** pierce like a sword,
16:24 Pleasant **w** are a honeycomb,
26:22 **w** of a gossip are like choice morsels
30: 6 Do not add to his **w,**
Ecc 5: 2 so let your **w** be few.
10:14 and the fool multiplies **w.**
12:11 The **w** of the wise are like goads,
Jer 15:16 When your **w** came, I ate them;
Da 9:12 You have fulfilled the **w** spoken
Hos 6: 5 I killed you with the **w** of my mouth;
Zec 1: 6 But did not my **w** and my decrees,
Mt 7:24 everyone who hears these **w**
12:37 by your **w** you will be condemned."
24:35 but my **w** will never pass away.
Mk 12:13 to Jesus to catch him in his **w.**
Lk 6:47 to me and hears my **w** and puts them
Jn 6:68 You have the **w** of eternal life.
15: 7 you remain in me and my **w** remain
Ac 2:40 With many other **w** he warned them;
Ro 8:26 with groans that **w** cannot express.
1Co 2:13 but in **w** taught by the Spirit,
14:19 five intelligible **w** to instruct others than ten thousand **w** in a tongue.

1Pe	3: 1	they may be won over without **w** by
1Jn	3:18	let us not love with **w** or tongue
Rev	1: 3	Blessed is the one who reads the **w**
	19: 9	"These are the true **w** of God."
	22: 6	"These **w** are trustworthy and true.
	22:19	And if anyone takes **w** away

WORE [WEAR]

Mk	1: 6	John **w** clothing made of camel's
Rev	9: 7	**w** something like crowns of gold,
	15: 6	**w** golden sashes around their chests.

WORK [HARDWORKING, WORKED, WORKER, WORKERS, WORKING, WORKMAN, WORKMANSHIP, WORKMEN, WORKS]

Ge	2: 2	seventh day he rested from all his **w.**
	2:15	in the Garden of Eden to **w** it
	4:12	When you **w** the ground,
Ex	20:10	On it you shall not do any **w,**
	23:12	"Six days do your **w,** but on the seventh day do not **w,**
	32:16	The tablets were the **w** of God;
	40:33	And so Moses finished the **w.**
Lev	25:40	**w** for you until the Year of Jubilee.
Nu	8:11	so that they may be ready to do the **w**
Dt	5:14	On it you shall not do any **w,**
	27:15	the **w** of the craftsman's hands—
1Ch	22:16	Now begin the **w,**
2Ch	2: 7	a man skilled to **w** in gold and silver,
	8:16	All Solomon's **w** was carried out,
Ezr	4: 5	They hired counselors to **w** against
	4:24	Thus the **w** on the house of God
	6: 7	with the **w** on this temple of God.
Ne	2:18	So they began this good **w.**
Job	1:10	You have blessed the **w** of his hands,
Ps	8: 3	the **w** of your fingers,
	19: 1	skies proclaim the **w** of his hands.
	90:17	establish the **w** of our hands.
Pr	14:23	All hard **w** brings a profit,
	21:25	because his hands refuse to **w.**
	31:17	She sets about her **w** vigorously;
Ecc	2:10	My heart took delight in all my **w,**
	2:24	and find satisfaction in his **w.**
	5:19	and be happy in his **w—**
	11: 5	you cannot understand the **w** of God,
Isa	2: 8	bow down to the **w** of their hands,
	64: 8	we are all the **w** of your hand.
Jer	48:10	lax in doing the LORD's **w!**
Mt	20: 1	in the morning to hire men to **w**
Lk	13:14	"There are six days for **w.**
Jn	5:17	"My Father is always at his **w**
	6:27	Do not **w** for food that spoils,
	6:29	"The **w** of God is this:
	9: 4	Night is coming, when no one can **w.**
	17: 4	by completing the **w** you gave me
Ac	13: 2	the **w** to which I have called them."
Ro	4: 5	not **w** but trusts God who justifies
	14:20	not destroy the **w** of God for the sake
	16:12	women who **w** hard in the Lord.
1Co	3:13	his **w** will be shown for what it is,
	4:12	We **w** hard with our own hands.
	12:11	the **w** of one and the same Spirit,

Eph	3:20	to his power that is at **w** within us,
	4:16	as each part does its **w.**
Php	1: 6	a good **w** in you will carry it on
	2:12	to **w** out your salvation with fear
Col	3:23	**w** at it with all your heart,
1Th	4:11	to mind your own business and to **w**
	5:12	respect those who **w** hard among you
2Th	2: 7	power of lawlessness is already at **w;**
	2: 9	with the **w** of Satan displayed
	3:10	"If a man will not **w,**
1Ti	5:17	those whose **w** is preaching and
2Ti	2:21	and prepared to do any good **w.**
	3:17	equipped for every good **w.**
Heb	4: 4	God rested from all his **w."**
	6:10	not forget your **w** and
	13:17	Obey them so that their **w** will be
1Pe	1:17	who judges each man's **w** impartially
1Jn	3: 8	to destroy the devil's **w.**
2Jn	1:11	shares in his wicked **w.**
3Jn	1: 8	that we may **w** together for the truth.
Rev	2: 2	your hard **w** and your perseverance.
	9:20	not repent of the **w** of their hands;

WORKED [WORK]

Ge	4: 2	Abel kept flocks, and Cain **w** the soil
	29:30	he **w** for Laban another seven years.
Ex	1:13	and **w** them ruthlessly.
Ps	98: 1	and his holy arm have **w** salvation
Isa	63: 5	so my own arm **w** salvation for me,
Jn	4:38	to reap what you have not **w** for.
1Co	15:10	No, I **w** harder than all of them—
2Th	3: 8	On the contrary, we **w** night and day,
2Jn	1: 8	that you do not lose what you have **w**

WORKER [WORK]

Ecc	3: 9	What does the **w** gain from his toil?
Lk	10: 7	for the **w** deserves his wages.
1Ti	5:18	and "The **w** deserves his wages."

WORKERS [WORK]

Mt	9:37	harvest is plentiful but the **w** are few.
Lk	10: 2	to send out **w** into his harvest field.
1Co	3: 9	For we are God's fellow **w;**
	12:28	third teachers, then **w** of miracles,

WORKING [WORK]

Ex	15:11	awesome in glory, **w** wonders?
Jn	5:17	and I, too, am **w."**
1Co	12: 6	There are different kinds of **w,**
Col	3:23	as **w** for the Lord, not for men,
Jas	2:22	faith and his actions were **w** together,

WORKMAN* [WORK, MAN]

2Ti	2:15	**w** who does not need to be ashamed
Rev	18:22	No **w** of any trade will ever be found

WORKMANSHIP* [WORK]

Eph	2:10	For we are God's **w,**

WORKMEN [WORK, MAN]

Ex	36: 8	among the **w** made the tabernacle
2Ki	12:14	it was paid to the **w,**
Ne	4:22	as guards by night and **w** by day."
2Co	11:13	are false apostles, deceitful **w,**

WORKS [WORK]

Dt   3:24   the deeds and mighty **w** you do?
  32: 4   He is the Rock, his **w** are perfect,
Ps   8: 6   You made him ruler over the **w**
  46: 8   Come and see the **w** of the LORD,
  66: 5   how awesome his **w** in man's behalf!
  92: 5   How great are your **w**, O LORD,
  103: 6   The LORD **w** righteousness
  138: 8   not abandon the **w** of your hands.
  145: 6   of the power of your awesome **w**,
Pr   8:22   brought me forth as the first of his **w**,
  31:31   and let her **w** bring her praise at
Ro   4: 6   credits righteousness apart from **w:**
  8:28   that in all things God **w** for the good
1Co   5: 6   Don't you know that a little yeast **w**
  12: 6   same God **w** all of them in all men.
Eph   1:11   who **w** out everything in conformity
  2: 9   not by **w**, so that no one can boast.
  2:10   created in Christ Jesus to do good **w**,
  4:12   to prepare God's people for **w**
Php   2:13   for it is God who **w** in you to will
Col   1:29   which so powerfully **w** in me.

WORLD [WORLDLY]

Ge   11: 1   Now the whole **w** had one language
  11: 9   the language of the whole **w**.
2Ki   5:15   no God in all the **w** except in Israel.
1Ch 16:30   The **w** is firmly established.
Ps   9: 8   He will judge the **w** in righteousness;
  19: 4   their words to the ends of the **w**.
  50:12   for the **w** is mine, and all that is in it.
  96:13   He will judge the **w** in righteousness
Pr   8:23   before the **w** began.
Isa 13:11   I will punish the **w** for its evil,
Zep   1:18   the whole **w** will be consumed,
Mt   4: 8   him all the kingdoms of the **w** and
  5:14   "You are the light of the **w**.
  16:26   be for a man if he gains the whole **w**,
Jn   1:10   the **w** did not recognize him.
  1:29   who takes away the sin of the **w!**
  3:16   "For God so loved the **w** that he
  3:17   but to save the **w** through him.
  8:12   he said, "I am the light of the **w**.
  9: 5   I am the light of the **w**."
  15:19   but I have chosen you out of the **w**.
  16:33   In this **w** you will have trouble.
  16:33   I have overcome the **w**."
  17: 5   glory I had with you before the **w**
  17:18   I have sent them into the **w**.
  18:36   "My kingdom is not of this **w**.
Ac 17:31   when he will judge the **w** with justice
Ro   3:19   whole **w** held accountable to God.
  5:12   as sin entered the **w** through one man
  10:18   their words to the ends of the **w**."
1Co   1:27   the foolish things of the **w** to shame
  3:19   the wisdom of this **w** is foolishness
  6: 2   that the saints will judge the **w?**
2Co   5:19   that God was reconciling the **w**
  10: 3   we do not wage war as the **w** does.
1Ti   1:15   Jesus came into the **w** to save sinners
  6: 7   For we brought nothing into the **w**,
Heb   1: 6   God brings his firstborn into the **w**,
  11: 7   By his faith he condemned the **w**

  11:38   the **w** was not worthy of them.
Jas   1:27   from being polluted by the **w.**
  4: 4   that friendship with the **w** is hatred
1Pe   1:20   chosen before the creation of the **w,**
  2:11   as aliens and strangers in the **w,**
1Jn   2: 2   but also for the sins of the whole **w**.
  2:15   not love the **w** or anything in the **w**.
  5: 4   the victory that has overcome the **w**,
Rev 11:15   "The kingdom of the **w** has become
  13: 8   slain from the creation of the **w**.

WORLDLY [WORLD]

Lk 16:11   trustworthy in handling **w** wealth,
1Co   3: 1   not address you as spiritual but as **w**
Tit   2:12   "No" to ungodliness and **w** passions,

WORM [WORMS]

Ps   22: 6   But I am a **w** and not a man,
Isa 41:14   Do not be afraid, O **w** Jacob,
Mk   9:48   where " 'their **w** does not die,

WORMS [WORM]

Ac 12:23   and he was eaten by **w** and died.

WORMWOOD*

Rev   8:11   the name of the star is **W**.

WORN [WEAR]

Ge 18:12   I am **w** out and my master is old,

WORRIED [WORRY]

Lk 10:41   are **w** and upset about many things,

WORRIES [WORRY]

Lk   8:14   they are choked by life's **w,**

WORRY [WORRIED, WORRIES, WORRYING]

Mt   6:25   I tell you, do not **w** about your life,
  6:34   Therefore do not **w** about tomorrow,
  10:19   do not **w** about what to say or how

WORRYING [WORRY]

Mt   6:27   of you by **w** can add a single hour

WORSE [WORST]

Mt 12:45   of that man is **w** than the first.
Jn   5:14   or something **w** may happen to you."
1Ti   5: 8   the faith and is **w** than an unbeliever.
2Pe   2:20   they are **w** off at the end than

WORSHIP [WORSHIPED, WORSHIPERS, WORSHIPING, WORSHIPS]

Ex   4:23   "Let my son go, so he may **w** me."
  20: 5   not bow down to them or **w** them;
  34:14   Do not **w** any other god,
Dt   12: 4   not **w** the LORD your God in their
Jos 22:27   that we will **w** the LORD
2Ki 17:37   Do not **w** other gods.
1Ch 16:29   **w** the LORD in the splendor
Ps   95: 6   Come, let us bow down in **w,**
  97: 7   All who **w** images are put to shame,
  100: 2   **W** the LORD with gladness;

Jer   23:27 forgot my name through Baal **w.**
Da   3:28 or **w** any god except their own God.
Jnh   1: 9 "I am a Hebrew and I **w** the LORD,
Zec 14:17 not go up to Jerusalem to **w** the King
Mt   2: 2 in the east and have come to **w** him."
       4: 9 "if you will bow down and **w** me."
Lk   4: 8 "It is written: '**W** the Lord your God
Jn   4:24 and his worshipers must **w** in spirit
Ro   12: 1 this is your spiritual act of **w.**
Heb 10: 1 perfect those who draw near to **w.**
Rev   4:10 **w** him who lives for ever and ever.
      13:12 and its inhabitants **w** the first beast,
      14: 7 **W** him who made the heavens,

WORSHIPED [WORSHIP]

Ex   12:27 Then the people bowed down and **w.**
Dt   29:26 and **w** other gods and bowed down
Jos   24: 2 beyond the River and **w** other gods.
2Ch 24:18 and **w** Asherah poles and idols.
      29:30 and bowed their heads and **w.**
Mt   28: 9 clasped his feet and **w** him.
Rev   5:14 and the elders fell down and **w.**
      13: 4 Men **w** the dragon because
      20: 4 had not **w** the beast or his image

WORSHIPERS [WORSHIP]

Jn   4:24 and his **w** must worship in spirit and

WORSHIPING [WORSHIP]

Jdg   2:19 other gods and serving and **w** them.
Ac   13: 2 While they were **w** the Lord
Rev   9:20 not stop **w** demons, and idols

WORSHIPS [WORSHIP]

Isa   44:15 But he also fashions a god and **w** it;

WORST [WORSE]

1Ti   1:16 the **w** of sinners,

WORTH [WORTHLESS, WORTHY]

Job   28:13 Man does not comprehend its **w;**
Pr   31:10 She is far more than rubies.
Mt   10:31 you are **w** more than many sparrows.
Jn   12: 5 It was **w** a year's wages."
Ro   8:18 not **w** comparing with the glory
1Pe   1: 7 your faith—of greater **w** than gold,
       3: 4 which is of great **w** in God's sight.

WORTHLESS [WORTH]

Ge   41:27 the seven **w** heads of grain scorched
Dt   32:21 and angered me with their **w** idols.
Ps   31: 6 I hate those who cling to **w** idols;
      60:11 for the help of man is **w.**
Pr   11: 4 Wealth is **w** in the day of wrath,
Jer   2: 5 They followed **w** idols and became
              w themselves.
Zec   11:17 "Woe to the **w** shepherd,
Mt   25:30 And throw that **w** servant outside,
Heb   6: 8 that produces thorns and thistles is **w**
Jas   1:26 and his religion is **w.**

WORTHY [WORTH]

1Ch 16:25 great is the LORD and most **w**
Ps   18: 3 who is **w** of praise,

145: 3 the LORD and most **w** of praise;
Pr   8: 6 Listen, for I have **w** things to say;
Mt   10:37 more than me is not **w** of me;
      10:38 and follow me is not **w** of me.
Lk   3:16 of whose sandals I am not **w** to untie.
      15:19 no longer **w** to be called your son;
Ro   16: 2 in the Lord in a way **w** of the saints
Eph   4: 1 I urge you to live a life **w** of
Php   1:27 a manner **w** of the gospel of Christ.
Col   1:10 that you may live a life **w** of the Lord
1Ti   3: 8 likewise, are to be men **w** of respect,
       3:11 are to be women **w** of respect,
Tit   2: 2 **w** of respect, self-controlled,
Heb   3: 3 Jesus has been found **w** of greater
      11:38 the world was not **w** of them.
3Jn   1: 6 on their way in a manner **w** of God.
Rev   3: 4 dressed in white, for they are **w.**
       4:11 "You are **w,** our Lord
       5: 2 "Who is **w** to break the seals
       5:12 "**W** is the Lamb, who was slain,

WOUND [WOUNDS]

Ex   21:25 **w** for **w,** bruise for bruise.
Jer   10:19 My **w** is incurable!
La   2:13 Your **w** is as deep as the sea.
1Co   8:12 and **w** their weak conscience,
Rev   13: 3 seemed to have had a fatal **w,**

WOUNDS [WOUND]

Job   5:18 For he **w,** but he also binds up;
Ps   147: 3 and binds up their **w.**
Pr   27: 6 **W** from a friend can be trusted,
Isa   53: 5 and by his **w** we are healed.
Zec   13: 6 'The **w** I was given at the house
1Pe   2:24 by his **w** you have been healed.

WOVEN

Ex   28: 4 a robe, a **w** tunic, a turban and a sash.
Jn   19:23 **w** in one piece from top to bottom.

WRAPPED [WRAPS]

Mk   15:46 took down the body, **w** it in the linen,
Lk   2: 7 She **w** him in cloths and placed him
Jn   13: 4 and **w** a towel around his waist.

WRAPS [WRAPPED]

Ps   104: 2 He **w** himself in light as with

WRATH

Nu   16:46 **W** has come out from the LORD;
Dt   32:22 For a fire has been kindled by my **w,**
2Sa   6: 8 the LORD's **w** had broken out
1Ch   27:24 **W** came on Israel on account
2Ch   36:16 the **w** of the LORD was aroused
Ps   2: 5 and terrifies them in his **w,**
       6: 1 or discipline me in your **w.**
      37: 8 Refrain from anger and turn from **w;**
      76:10 your **w** against men brings you praise
Pr   15: 1 A gentle answer turns away **w,**
Isa   13:13 at the **w** of the LORD Almighty,
      51:17 hand of the LORD the cup of his **w,**
Jer   6:11 But I am full of the **w** of the LORD,
      25:15 cup filled with the wine of my **w**
La   4:11 LORD has given full vent to his **w;**
Eze   5:13 when I have spent my **w** upon them,

20: 8 So I said I would pour out my **w**
Na   1: 2 on his foes and maintains his **w**
Zep 1:15 That day will be a day of **w,**
Mt   3: 7 you to flee from the coming **w?**
Jn   3:36 for God's **w** remains on him."
Ro   1:18 The **w** of God is being revealed
     2: 5 you are storing up **w** against
         yourself for the day of God's **w,**
     5: 9 be saved from God's **w** through him!
     9:22 What if God, choosing to show his **w**
     9:22 the objects of his **w—**
Eph 2: 3 we were by nature objects of **w.**
1Th 1:10 who rescues us from the coming **w.**
     5: 9 God did not appoint us to suffer **w**
Rev 6:17 the great day of their **w** has come,
    15: 1 with them God's **w** is completed.
    19:15 the fury of the **w** of God Almighty.

WRESTLED [WRESTLING]
Ge 32:24 and a man **w** with him till daybreak.

WRESTLING* [WRESTLED]
Col 4:12 He is always **w** in prayer for you,

WRETCHED
Ro   7:24 What a **w** man I am!
Rev 3:17 But you do not realize that you are **w**

WRINKLE*
Eph 5:27 without stain or **w** or any other

WRIST [WRISTS]
Ge 38:28 a scarlet thread and tied it on his **w**

WRISTS [WRIST]
Ac 12: 7 and the chains fell off Peter's **w.**

WRITE [WRITER, WRITES, WRITING, WRITTEN, WROTE]
Ex 17:14 **"W** this on a scroll as something to
    34:27 **"W** down these words,
Nu 17: 2 **W** the name of each man on his staff.
Dt   6: 9 **W** them on the doorframes of your
    10: 2 I will **w** on the tablets the words
    17:18 to **w** for himself on a scroll a copy
    27: 8 And you shall **w** very clearly all
Pr   3: 3 **w** them on the tablet of your heart.
     7: 3 **w** them on the tablet of your heart.
Jer 31:33 and **w** it on their hearts.
Lk   1: 3 to **w** an orderly account for you,
Jn   8: 6 But Jesus bent down and started to **w**
Heb 8:10 and **w** them on their hearts.
1Jn 2: 1 **w** this to you so that you will not sin.
Rev 1:19 **"W,** therefore, what you have seen,
     3:12 I will **w** on him the name of my God
    21: 5 Then he said, **"W** this down,

WRITER* [WRITE]
Ps 45: 1 my tongue is the pen of a skillful **w.**

WRITES [WRITE]
Dt 24: 1 and he **w** her a certificate of divorce,

WRITING [WRITE]
Ex 32:16 the **w** was the **w** of God,
Dt 31:24 After Moses finished **w** in a book
Da   5: 7 "Whoever reads this **w** and tells
1Co 14:37 am **w** to you is the Lord's command.
1Jn 2: 7 I am not **w** you a new command but
2Jn 1: 5 I am not **w** you a new command
Rev 5: 1 a scroll with **w** on both sides

WRITTEN [WRITE]
Ex 32:32 blot me out of the book you have **w."**
Dt 28:58 which are **w** in this book,
Jos 1: 8 be careful to do everything **w** in it.
    23: 6 to obey all that is **w** in the Book of
1Ki 2: 3 as **w** in the Law of Moses,
2Ki 23:21 it is **w** in this Book of the Covenant."
Ne   8:14 They found **w** in the Law,
Ps 40: 7 it is **w** about me in the scroll.
Pr 22:20 Have I not **w** thirty sayings for you,
Da 12: 1 name is found **w** in the book—
Mal 3:16 scroll of remembrance was **w**
Mt 26:24 Son of Man will go just as it is **w**
    27:37 the **w** charge against him:
Lk 10:20 that your names are **w** in heaven."
    24:44 **w** about me in the Law of Moses,
Jn 20:31 But these are that you may believe
    21:25 If every one of them were **w** down,
Ro   2:15 the requirements of the law are **w**
    15: 4 For everything that was **w** in the
         past was **w** to teach us,
1Co 4: 6 "Do not go beyond what is **w."**
    10:11 and were **w** down as warnings
2Co 3: 3 **w** not with ink but with the Spirit of
Col 2:14 the **w** code, with its regulations,
Heb 10: 7 it is **w** about me in the scroll—
    12:23 whose names are **w** in heaven.
Rev 2:17 a white stone with a new name **w**
    13: 8 not been **w** in the book
    14: 1 Father's name **w** on their foreheads.
    17: 5 This title was **w** on her forehead:
    19:12 a name **w** on him that no one knows
    20:15 not found **w** in the book of life,
    21:12 On the gates were **w** the names of
    21:27 names are **w** in the Lamb's book of

IT IS WRITTEN Jos 8:34; 10:13; 2Sa 1:18; 2Ki 23:21; Ne 8:15; 10:34; Ps 40:7; Da 9:13; Mt 4:4, 6, 10; 11:10; 21:13; 26:24, 31; Mk 1:2; 7:6; 9:13; 14:21, 27; Lk 2:23; 4:4, 8, 10, 17; 7:27; 19:46; 22:37; Jn 2:17; 6:31, 45; 8:17; 12:14; Ac 1:20; 13:33; 15:15; 23:5; Ro 1:17; 2:24; 3:4, 10; 4:17; 8:36; 9:13, 33; 10:15; 11:8, 26; 12:19; 14:11; 15:3, 9, 21; 1Co 1:19, 31; 2:9; 3:19; 9:9; 10:7; 14:21; 15:45; 2Co 4:13; 8:15; 9:9; Gal 3:10, 13; 4:22, 27; Heb 10:7; 1Pe 1:16

WRITTEN IN THE BOOK Jos 8:31, 34; 10:13; 23:6; 2Sa 1:18; 1Ki 11:41; 14:19, 29; 15:7, 23, 31; 16:5, 14, 20, 27; 22:39, 45; 2Ki 1:18; 8:23; 10:34; 12:19; 13:8, 12; 14:6, 15, 18, 28; 15:6, 11, 15, 21, 26, 31, 36; 16:19; 20:20; 21:17, 25; 22:16; 23:24, 28; 24:5; 2Ch 16:11; 25:26; 27:7; 28:26; 34:24; 35:12, 27; 36:8; Ezr 6:18; Est 10:2; Da 10:21; 12:1; Lk 3:4; Ac 1:20; 7:42; Gal 3:10; Rev 13:8; 17:8; 20:15

WRONG [WRONGDOER,
WRONGDOING, WRONGED, WRONGS]

Ex	23: 2	Do not follow the crowd in doing **w**.
Nu	5: 7	must make full restitution for his **w**,
Dt	32: 4	A faithful God who does no **w**,
1Ki	8:47	'We have sinned, we have done **w**,
Job	34:12	that God would do **w**,
Ps	5: 5	you hate all who do **w**.
	119:128	I hate every **w** path.
Isa	7:15	to reject the **w** and choose the right.
Da	9: 5	We have sinned and done **w**.
Hab	1:13	you cannot tolerate **w**.
Zep	3: 5	is righteous; he does no **w**.
	3:13	The remnant of Israel will do no **w**,
Lk	23:41	But this man has done nothing **w**."
Ac	23: 9	"We find nothing **w** with this man,"
Ro	13: 4	But if you do **w**, be afraid.
Gal	2:11	because he was clearly in the **w**.
Col	3:25	who does **w** will be repaid for his **w**,
1Th	5:15	that nobody pays back **w** for **w**,
Rev	22:11	him who does **w** continue to do **w**;

WRONGDOER⁺ [WRONG]

Ro	13: 4	to bring punishment on the **w**.

WRONGDOING [WRONG]

Job	1:22	did not sin by charging God with **w**.
1Jn	5:17	All **w** is sin,

WRONGED [WRONG]

Nu	5: 7	and give it all to the person he has **w**.
1Co	6: 7	Why not rather be **w**?

WRONGS [WRONG]

Ge	50:15	and pays us back for all the **w** we did
Pr	10:12	but love covers over all **w**.
1Co	13: 5	it keeps no record of **w**.

WROTE [WRITE]

Ex	24: 4	Moses then **w** down everything
	34:28	he **w** on the tablets the words of
Dt	10: 4	The LORD **w** on these tablets
2Ch	32:17	also **w** letters insulting the LORD,
Da	5: 5	The king watched the hand as it **w**.
Jn	1:45	and about whom the prophets also **w**
	5:46	for he **w** about me.
	8: 8	Again he stooped down and **w** on
Ac	1: 1	I **w** about all that Jesus began to do

X

XERXES

King of Persia (Ezr 4:6), husband of Esther. Deposed Vashti; replaced her with Esther (Est 1-2). Sealed Haman's edict to annihilate the Jews (Est 3). Received Esther without having called her (Est 5:1-8). Honored Mordecai (Est 6). Hanged Haman (Est 7). Issued edict allowing Jews to defend themselves (Est 8). Exalted Mordecai (Est 8:1-2, 15; 9:4; 10).

Y

YAHWEH See †LORD

YARN

Ex	25: 4	purple and scarlet **y** and fine linen;
2Ch	2: 7	and in purple, crimson and blue **y**,

YEAR [YEARS]

Ge	17:21	to you by this time next **y**."
Ex	23:14	"Three times a **y** you are to celebrate
	34:23	Three times a **y** all your men
Lev	16:34	Atonement is to be made once a **y**
	25: 4	in the seventh **y** the land is to have
	25:11	fiftieth **y** shall be a jubilee for you;
Nu	14:34	For forty years—one **y** for each of
Dt	1: 3	In the fortieth **y**,
1Sa	1: 3	**Y** after **y** this man went up
	7:16	From **y** to **y** he went on a circuit
1Ki	10:25	**Y** after **y**, everyone who came
2Ki	4:16	"About this time next **y**," Elisha said,
Ne	10:31	seventh **y** we will forgo working
Isa	6: 1	In the **y** that King Uzziah died,
	34: 8	a **y** of retribution, to uphold Zion's
	61: 2	the **y** of the LORD's favor and
	63: 4	the **y** of my redemption has come.
Zec	14:16	will go up **y** after **y** to worship
Lk	2:41	Every **y** his parents went
	13: 8	'leave it alone for one more **y**,
Jn	11:49	who was high priest that **y**, spoke up,
	18:13	the high priest that **y**.
Heb	9: 7	and that only once a **y**,
	10: 1	sacrifices repeated endlessly **y** after **y**

YEARNS⁺

Job	19:27	How my heart **y** within me!
Ps	84: 2	My soul **y**, even faints,
Isa	26: 9	My soul **y** for you in the night;
Jer	31:20	Therefore my heart **y** for him;

YEARS [YEAR]

Ge	1:14	to mark seasons and days and **y**,
	25: 8	an old man and full of **y**;
	35:29	old and full of **y**.
	41:26	The seven good cows are seven **y**,
	41:30	seven **y** of famine will follow them.
	47: 9	My **y** have been few and difficult,
Ex	12:40	lived in Egypt was 430 **y**.
	16:35	The Israelites ate manna forty **y**,
Lev	25: 8	" 'Count off seven sabbaths of **y**—
Nu	1: 3	the men in Israel twenty **y** old or
	14:34	For forty **y**—one year for each
Dt	2: 7	These forty **y** the LORD your God
	8: 4	not swell during these forty **y**.
2Sa	21: 1	a famine for three successive **y**;
2Ch	36:21	until the seventy **y** were completed
Ezr	5:11	the temple that was built many **y** ago,
Ne	9:21	For forty **y** you sustained them in
Job	36:26	number of his **y** is past finding out.
Ps	90: 4	a thousand **y** in your sight are like
	90:10	The length of our days is seventy **y**

	95:10	For forty **y** I was angry with
Pr	3: 2	they will prolong your life many **y**
	9:11	and **y** will be added to your life.
	10:27	but the **y** of the wicked are cut short.
Ecc	6: 6	even if he lives a thousand **y** twice
Jer	25:12	when the seventy **y** are fulfilled,
Da	9: 2	of Jerusalem would last seventy **y**.
Joel	2:25	for the **y** the locusts have eaten—
Mt	2:16	and its vicinity who were two **y** old
	9:20	been subject to bleeding for twelve **y**
Lk	3:23	Jesus himself was about thirty **y** old
	13:16	bound for eighteen long **y,**
Jn	2:20	"It has taken forty-six **y** to build
2Pe	3: 8	the Lord a day is like a thousand **y,**
	3: 8	and a thousand **y** are like a day.
Rev	20: 2	and bound him for a thousand **y.**

YEAST

Ex	12:15	to eat bread made without **y.**
	12:20	Eat nothing made with **y.**
Lev	2:11	not to burn any **y** or honey in
Mt	16: 6	"Be on your guard against the **y** of
1Co	5: 6	Don't you know that a little **y** works
Gal	5: 9	"A little **y** works through the whole

YES

Mt	5:37	Simply let your '**Y**' be '**Y**,'
2Co	1:17	"**Y, y**" and "No, no"?
	1:20	they are "**Y**" in Christ.
Jas	5:12	Let your "**Y**" be **y,** and your "No,"

YESTERDAY

| Heb | 13: 8 | Jesus Christ is the same **y** and today |

YET

Job	13:15	he slay me, **y** will I hope in him;
	19:26	**y** in my flesh I will see God;
Ps	42: 5	for I will **y** praise him,
Pr	30:24	**y** they are extremely wise:
	30:25	**y** they store up their food in
Ecc	1: 7	**y** the sea is never full.
Am	4: 6	**y** you have not returned to me,"
Hab	3:16	**Y** I will wait patiently for the day
Mal	1: 2	"**Y** I have loved Jacob,
Mt	6:26	**y** your heavenly Father feeds them.
Mk	8:36	**y** forfeit his soul?
Jn	2: 4	"My time has not **y** come."
	6:70	**Y** one of you is a devil!"
	7: 6	right time for me has not **y** come;
	7: 8	the right time has not **y** come."
	7:39	since Jesus had not **y** been glorified.
	8:20	because his time had not **y** come.
	20:29	not seen and **y** have believed."
Ro	8:10	**y** your spirit is alive because
	8:25	we hope for what we do not **y** have,
Heb	12: 4	you have not **y** resisted to the point
Rev	9:12	woe is past; two other woes are **y** to
	17:10	one is, the other has not **y** come;

YIELD [YIELDED, YIELDING]

Ge	4:12	it will no longer **y** its crops for you.
Lev	25:19	Then the land will **y** its fruit,
Pr	8:19	what I **y** surpasses choice silver.

YIELDED* [YIELD]

Ps	107:37	and planted vineyards that **y**
Isa	5: 2	but it **y** only bad fruit.
Lk	8: 8	It came up and **y** a crop,

YIELDING [YIELD]

| Rev | 22: 2 | **y** its fruit every month. |

YOKE [YOKED]

Ex	6: 6	from under the **y** of the Egyptians.
Dt	28:48	He will put an iron **y** on your neck
1Ki	12: 4	"Your father put a heavy **y** on us,
Mt	11:29	Take my **y** upon you and learn
	11:30	my **y** is easy and my burden is light."
Gal	5: 1	be burdened again by a **y** of slavery.

YOKED [YOKE]

Dt	22:10	with an ox and a donkey **y** together.
Ps	106:28	They **y** themselves to the Baal
2Co	6:14	not be **y** together with unbelievers.

YOUNG [YOUNGER, YOUNGEST, YOUTH, YOUTHS]

Ex	23:19	a **y** goat in its mother's milk.
Lev	1:14	he is to offer a dove or a **y** pigeon.
	5: 7	to bring two doves or two **y** pigeons
	14:22	and two doves or two **y** pigeons,
Nu	30: 3	a **y** woman still living in her father's
Dt	22: 6	do not take the mother with the **y.**
	32:25	**Y** men and **y** women will perish,
Ru	2: 5	"Whose **y** woman is that?"
1Sa	2:17	This sin of the **y** men was very great
2Ch	10:14	the advice of the **y** men
	36:17	spared neither **y** man nor **y** woman,
Ps	37:25	I was **y** and now I am old,
	78:63	Fire consumed their **y** men,
	119: 9	How can a **y** man keep his way pure?
Pr	7: 7	I noticed among the **y** men,
	20:29	The glory of **y** men is their strength,
Isa	11: 8	**y** child put his hand into the viper's
	40:11	that have **y.**
La	1:18	My **y** men and maidens have gone
Da	1: 4	**y** men without any physical defect,
	1:17	four **y** men God gave knowledge
Joel	2:28	your **y** men will see visions.
Mk	14:51	A **y** man, wearing nothing but
	16: 5	a **y** man dressed in a white robe
Lk	2:24	"a pair of doves or two **y** pigeons."
Ac	2:17	your **y** men will see visions,
	7:58	at the feet of a **y** man named Saul.
	20: 9	a **y** man named Eutychus,
1Ti	4:12	down on you because you are **y,**
Tit	2: 6	the **y** men to be self-controlled.
1Pe	5: 5	**Y** men, in the same way
1Jn	2:13	I write to you, **y** men,

YOUNGER [YOUNG]

Ge	19:35	**y** daughter went and lay with him.
	25:23	and the older will serve the **y.**"
	29:27	then we will give you the **y** one also,
Ro	9:12	"The older will serve the **y.**"
1Ti	5: 1	Treat **y** men as brothers,
	5:14	So I counsel **y** widows to marry,

Tit   2: 4 the **y** women to love their husbands

YOUNGEST [YOUNG]

Ge   9:24 found out what his **y** son had done
      42:20 you must bring your **y** brother to me,
Jos   6:26 cost of his **y** will he set up its gates."
1Sa 17:14 David was the **y.**
1Ki 16:34 at the cost of his **y** son Segub,
Lk   22:26 the greatest among you should be
             like the **y,**

YOUTH [YOUNG]

Nu   11:28 who had been Moses' aide since **y,**
1Sa 17:33 a fighting man from his **y."**
Ps   71: 5 my confidence since my **y.**
     103: 5 so that your **y** is renewed like
     144:12 Then our sons in their **y** will be
Pr   2:17 who has left the partner of her **y**
      5:18 in the wife of your **y.**
      7: 7 a **y** who lacked judgment.
Ecc   4:13 Better a poor but wise **y** than an old
      11:10 for **y** and vigor are meaningless.
      12: 1 your Creator in the days of your **y,**
Isa 65:20 a hundred will be thought a mere **y;**
Eze 16:60 with you in the days of your **y,**
Mal   2:14 between you and the wife of your **y,**
2Ti   2:22 Flee the evil desires of **y,**

YOUTHS [YOUNG]

2Ki   2:24 and mauled forty-two of the **y.**
Isa 40:30 Even **y** grow tired and weary,

Z

ZACCHAEUS

Lk   19: 2 A man was there by the name of **Z;**

ZACHARIAH, ZACHARIAS (KJV)

See ZECHARIAH

ZADOK [ZADOKITES]

2Sa 15:27 The king also said to **Z** the priest,
1Ki   1:26 But me your servant, and **Z** the priest
Ne   13:13 Shelemiah the priest, **Z** the scribe,

ZADOKITES* [ZADOK]

Eze 48:11 be for the consecrated priests, the **Z,**

ZALMON

Jdg   9:48 he and all his men went up Mount **Z.**
Ps   68:14 it was like snow fallen on **Z.**

ZALMUNNA

Jdg   8: 5 and I am still pursuing Zebah and **Z,**
Ps   83:11 all their princes like Zebah and **Z,**

ZAPHON

Jos 13:27 and **Z** with the rest of the realm
Ps   48: 2 Like the utmost heights of **Z** is
             Mount Zion,

ZAREPHATH

1Ki 17: 9 at once to **Z** of Sidon and stay there.
Lk   4:26 a widow in **Z** in the region of Sidon.

ZEAL [ZEALOUS, ZEALOUSLY]

Nu   25:11 in my **z** I did not put an end to them.
Dt   29:20 and **z** will burn against that man.
2Ki 10:16 "Come with me and see my **z** for
      19:31 The **z** of the LORD Almighty
Ps   69: 9 for **z** for your house consumes me,
     119139 My **z** wears me out,
Pr   19: 2 to have **z** without knowledge,
Isa 37:32 The **z** of the LORD Almighty will
      59:17 and wrapped himself in **z** as in
Eze   5:13 the LORD have spoken in my **z.**
Jn   2:17 "**Z** for your house will consume me.
Ro   10: 2 their **z** is not based on knowledge.
      12:11 Never be lacking in **z,**

ZEALOUS [ZEAL]

Nu   25:13 he was **z** for the honor of his God
1Ki 19:10 very **z** for the LORD God Almighty.
      19:14 very **z** for the LORD God Almighty.
Pr   23:17 be **z** for the fear of the LORD.
Eze 39:25 and I will be **z** for my holy name.
Ac   21:20 and all of them are **z** for the law.
Ro   10: 2 about them that they are **z** for God,
Gal   1:14 extremely **z** for the traditions
      4:17 Those people are **z** to win you over,
      4:18 It is fine to be **z,**

ZEALOUSLY* [ZEAL]

Ne   3:20 of Zabbai **z** repaired another section,

ZEBAH

Jdg   8: 5 I am still pursuing **Z** and Zalmunna,
Ps   83:11 all their princes like **Z** and Zalmunna

ZEBEDEE [ZEBEDEE'S]

Mt   4:21 James son of **Z** and his brother John.
      26:37 the two sons of **Z** along with him,
Mk   1:20 they left their father **Z** in the boat
      10:35 Then James and John, the sons of **Z,**
Lk   5:10 the sons of **Z,** Simon's partners.

ZEBEDEE'S* [ZEBEDEE]

Mt   20:20 Then the mother of **Z** sons came
      27:56 and the mother of **Z** sons.

ZEBOIIM

Dt   29:23 and Gomorrah, Admah and **Z,**
Hos 11: 8 How can I make you like **Z?**

ZEBUL

Jdg   9:30 When **Z** the governor of the city

ZEBULUN

Son of Jacob by Leah (Ge 30:20; 35:23; 1Ch 2:1). Tribe of blessed (Ge 49:13; Dt 33:18-19), numbered (Nu 1:31; 26:27), allotted land (Jos 19:10-16; Eze 48:26), failed to fully possess (Jdg 1:30), supported Deborah (Jdg 4:6-10; 5:14, 18), David (1Ch 12:33), 12,000 from (Rev 7:8).

ZECHARIAH

1. Son of Jeroboam II; king of Israel (2Ki 15:8-12).

2. Post-exilic prophet who encouraged rebuilding of temple (Ezr 5:1; 6:14; Zec 1:1).

ZEDEKIAH [MATTANIAH]

1. False prophet (1Ki 22:11-24; 2Ch 18:10-23).

2. Mattaniah, son of Josiah (1Ch 3:15), made king of Judah by Nebuchadnezzar (2Ki 24:17-25:7; 2Ch 36:10-14; Jer 37-39; 52:1-11).

ZEEB

Jdg   7:25 Midianite leaders, Oreb and **Z**.
Ps   83:11 Make their nobles like Oreb and **Z**,

ZELOPHEHAD [ZELOPHEHAD'S]

Nu 26:33 (**Z** son of Hepher had no sons;
Jos 17: 3 Now **Z** son of Hepher,

ZELOPHEHAD'S [ZELOPHEHAD]

Nu 36: 6 LORD commands for **Z** daughters:

ZEPHANIAH

Prophet; descendant of Hezekiah (Zep 1:1).

ZERUBBABEL

Descendant of David (1Ch 3:19; Mt 1:3). Led return from exile (Ezr 2:2; Ne 7:7). Governor of Israel; helped rebuild altar and temple (Ezr 3; Hag 1-2; Zec 4).

ZERUIAH [ZERUIAH'S]

2Sa   2:18 The three sons of **Z** were there:

ZERUIAH'S* [ZERUIAH]

1Ch   2:16 **Z** three sons were Abishai,

ZEUS

Ac 14:12 Barnabas they called **Z**,

ZIBA

2Sa   9: 2 servant of Saul's household named **Z**
        16: 1 beyond the summit, there was **Z**,
      19:26 But **Z** my servant betrayed me.

ZIKLAG

1Sa 27: 6 So on that day Achish gave him **Z**,
      30: 1 They had attacked **Z** and burned it,
      30:26 When David arrived in **Z**,

ZILPAH

Servant of Leah, mother of Jacob's sons Gad and Asher (Ge 30:9-12; 35:26; 46:16-18).

ZIMRI

King of Israel (1Ki 16:9-20).

ZIN

Nu 13:21 the land from the Desert of **Z**

ZION

2Sa   5: 7 David captured the fortress of **Z**,
2Ki 19:31 out of Mount **Z** a band of survivors.
Ps   2: 6 "I have installed my King on **Z**,
       9:11 to the LORD, enthroned in **Z**;

      14: 7 for Israel would come out of **Z**!
      48: 2 Mount **Z**, the city of the Great King.
      50: 2 From **Z**, perfect in beauty,
      65: 1 Praise awaits you, O God, in **Z**;
      74: 2 whom you redeemed—Mount **Z**.
      78:68 Mount **Z**, which he loved.
      87: 2 the LORD loves the gates of **Z** more
      87: 6 "This one was born in **Z**."
   102:13 and have compassion on **Z**,
   137: 3 "Sing us one of the songs of **Z**!"
SS   3:11 Come out, you daughters of **Z**,
Isa   1:27 **Z** will be redeemed with justice,
       2: 3 The law will go out from **Z**,
    14:32 "The LORD has established **Z**,
    28:16 I lay a stone in **Z**, a tested stone,
    40: 9 You who bring good tidings to **Z**,
    51: 3 The LORD will surely comfort **Z**
    51:11 They will enter **Z** with singing;
    52: 1 Awake, awake, O **Z**;
    52: 8 When the LORD returns to **Z**,
Jer 50: 5 They will ask the way to **Z**
La   2:13 O Virgin Daughter of **Z**?
Joel 2: 1 Blow the trumpet in **Z**;
     3:21 The LORD dwells in **Z**!
Am   1: 2 He said: "The LORD roars from **Z**
     6: 1 Woe to you who are complacent in **Z**
Mic 3:12 **Z** will be plowed like a field,
     4: 2 The law will go out from **Z**,
Zec 1:17 and the LORD will again comfort **Z**
     9: 9 Rejoice greatly, O Daughter of **Z**!
Mt 21: 5 "Say to the Daughter of **Z**,
Ro   9:33 in **Z** a stone that causes men
   11:26 "The deliverer will come from **Z**
Heb 12:22 But you have come to Mount **Z**,
1Pe   2: 6 I lay a stone in **Z**,
Rev 14: 1 standing on Mount **Z**,

ZIPH [ZIPHITES]

1Sa 23:14 and in the hills of the Desert of **Z**.

ZIPHITES* [ZIPH]

1Sa 23:19 The **Z** went up to Saul at Gibeah
    26: 1 The **Z** went to Saul at Gibeah
Ps   54: T the **Z** had gone to Saul and said,

ZIPPOR

Nu 22: 4 So Balak son of **Z**,

ZIPPORAH

Daughter of Reuel; wife of Moses (Ex 2:21-22; 4:20-26; 18:1-6).

ZITHER

Da   3: 7 **z**, lyre, harp and all kinds of music,

ZIV

1Ki   6: 1 in the month of **Z**, the second month,

ZOAN

Ps 78:43 his wonders in the region of **Z**.

ZOAR

Ge 19:22 (That is why the town was called **Z**.)
    19:30 Lot and his two daughters left **Z**

ZOBAH

1Sa 14:47 the kings of **Z,** and the Philistines.
1Ch 18: 3 David fought Hadadezer king of **Z,**

ZOPHAR*

One of Job's friends (Job 211; 11; 20; 42:9).

ZORAH

Jdg 13: 2 A certain man of **Z,** named Manoah,

ZOROBABEL (KJV)

See ZERUBBABEL

NUMERALS

40* [FORTY]

Eze   4: 6 I have assigned you **40** days,

42

Rev 11: 2 on the holy city for **42** months.

153*

Jn 21:11 It was full of large fish, **153,**

666*

1Ki 10:14 received yearly was **666** talents,
2Ch   9:13 received yearly was **666** talents,
Ezr   2:13 of Adonikam **666**
Rev 13:18 His number is **666.**

1,260*

Rev 11: 3 they will prophesy for **1,260** days,

12: 6 she might be taken care of for **1,260**

1,290*

Da 12:11 there will be **1,290** days.

1,335*

Da 12:12 and reaches the end of the **1,335**

12,000*

Rev   7: 5 From the tribe of Judah **12,000**
7: 5 from the tribe of Reuben **12,000,**
7: 5 from the tribe of Gad **12,000,**
7: 6 the tribe of Asher **12,000,**
7: 6 from the tribe of Naphtali **12,000,**
7: 6 from the tribe of Manasseh **12,000,**
7: 7 from the tribe of Simeon **12,000,**
7: 7 from the tribe of Levi **12,000,**
7: 7 from the tribe of Issachar **12,000,**
7: 8 the tribe of Zebulun **12,000,**
7: 8 from the tribe of Joseph **12,000,**
7: 8 from the tribe of Benjamin **12,000,**
21:16 found it to be **12,000** stadia in length,

144,000*

Rev   7: 4 of those who were sealed: **144,00**
14: 1 and with him **144,000**
14: 3 learn the song except the **144,000**

603,550*

Ex 38:26 a total of **603,550** men.
Nu   1:46 The total number was **603,550.**
2:32 by their divisions, number **603,550.**

Colophon

The New International Version database is copyrighted by
the International Bible Society of Colorado Springs, Colorado.

The Concordance was produced with original software created by Dennis Thomas
for an AST Bravo 486 running the Santa Cruz Operating System.
The phrase indexes were generated with WordCruncher 4.0
from the Electronic Text Corporation.

The NIV Compact Concordance was typeset by John R. Kohlenberger III,
using Xerox Ventura Publisher 3.0.

The database was edited and typeset on an AST Bravo 4/33 computer with a
Cornerstone XL single-page monitor. Page proofs were produced on an
NEC Silentwriter2 290 laser printer.

Final camera-ready pages were produced on a Linotype Linotronic P200
at the facilities of Multnomah Graphics in Portland, Oregon.

The NIV Compact Concordance was designed and edited
by John R. Kohlenberger III and Ed M. van der Maas.